The Sociology Project 3.0

Introducing the Sociological Imagination

From the New York University Department of Sociology

Jeff Manza

Richard Arum

Vivek Chibber

Troy Duster

Paula England

Thomas Ertman

Kathleen Gerson

Jeff Goodwin

Lynne Haney

Ruth Horowitz

Guillermina Jasso

Jennifer Jennings

Colin Jerolmack

Eric Klinenberg

Steven Lukes

Gerald Marwell

Harvey Molotch

Ann Morning

Caroline Persell

Patrick Sharkey

Iddo Tavory

Florencia Torche

Lawrence Wu

 Pearson

Content Management: Pamela Chirls/Holly Shufeldt
Content Production: Barbara Cappuccio/Rich Barnes
Product Management: Amber Mackey
Rights and Permissions: Ben Ferrini

Please contact https://support.pearson.com/getsupport/s/ with any queries on this content

Cover Image is Pearson Owned.

Library of Congress Cataloging-in-Publication Data
Names: Manza, Jeff, author.
Title: The sociology project : introducing the sociological imagination / Jeff Manza [and 21 others].
Description: 3.0. | NY, NY : Pearson, [2023] | Includes bibliographical references and index. | Summary: "Our aim is noting less than to reinvent the way we write introductory sociology texts. We envision an entirely new kind of introduction to the discipline, one that draws on the collective wisdom of a large, successful sociology department and its faculty to bring to our students and readers the real excitement of each of the main subfields of sociology"— Provided by publisher.
Identifiers: LCCN 2021047890 | ISBN 9780135685303 (paperback)
Subjects: LCSH: Sociology.
Classification: LCC HM585 .M3456 2022 | DDC 301—dc23/eng/20211216
LC record available at https://lccn.loc.gov/2021047890

10 2023

Access Code Card

ISBN-10: 0-13-568530-3
ISBN-13: 978-0-13-568530-3

Rental

ISBN-10: 0-13-645073-3
ISBN-13: 978-0-13-645073-3

Brief Contents

Contents

9 Markets and Organizations: The Sociology of Economic Life 210
Richard Arum and Jeff Manza

10 Culture, Media, and Communication 238
Eric Klinenberg with Matthew Wolfe

Part III Inequalities

11 Inequality and Poverty 264
Florencia Torche, Jeff Manza, and Richard Arum

12 Jobs, Occupations, and Professions: The Sociology of Work 296
Jeff Manza, Richard Arum, with Bhumika Chauhan

16 Families and Family Life   430
Kathleen Gerson

17 Sociology of Religion   460
Iddo Tavory and Gerald Marwell

18 Education   492
Caroline H. Persell and Jeff Manza

23 Population, Aging, and Social Demography 658
Lawrence L. Wu and Jeff Manza

24 Immigration 684
Guillermina Jasso and Jeff Manza

25 Globalization 712
Vivek Chibber and Jeff Manza, with Ned Crowley

Preface

In *The Structure of Scientific Revolutions*, his famous study of the history of science, Thomas Kuhn argued that introductory textbooks are inevitably the most backward part of any scientific field. He suggested that because they seek to appeal to the lowest common denominator to maximize their audience, they reproduce well-known but out-of-date ideas and findings far removed from the cutting edge of knowledge. Even worse, Kuhn argued, they provide beginning students an entirely misleading view of the discipline. When it comes to sociology textbooks, Kuhn's claim may be reinforced by the simple fact that sociology is such a wide-ranging discipline, with many rich subfields with their own bodies of scholarship and knowledge, that no one author (or small team of authors), however well-meaning and determined, can possibly attain mastery of the whole discipline (and adequately convey that knowledge to students).

We created this introductory text in the hopes of overcoming the problem Kuhn so famously identified. Our aim was nothing less than to reinvent the way we write introductory sociology texts, and at least one imitator has since appeared. We envision an entirely new kind of introduction to the discipline, one that draws on the collective wisdom of a large, successful sociology department and its faculty to bring to our students and readers the real excitement of each of the main subfields of sociology. Rather than reproducing what is said in existing textbooks, as so often happens, the chapters in this book are freshly updated by one or more faculty members (or in a couple of cases, by former faculty members who have moved to other universities) from the New York University Sociology Department who write and teach in the area and are at the cutting edge of their field. In this way, we seek to bring together the best of sociology as a discipline to meet the challenge of reaching our students.

At the center of this book is a set of tools for learning how to ask hard questions about the world around us. These tools are what we call, following C. Wright Mills, the "sociological imagination." In every chapter, we draw upon contemporary research findings, those of our colleagues and in some cases our own, to puzzle through how individuals are shaped by the contexts in which they live and act. We treat social norms, organizations, institutions, and global dynamics as a linked set of puzzles to explore. We identify the kinds of questions that sociological researchers are asking—and for students, learning how to ask such questions is a first step to thinking about the world in a sociological way. We introduce some ways of answering those questions, including the kinds of research,

data, and key findings we can use. We do not suggest that all of the answers are at hand, but we show how and in what ways sociologists and other social scientists struggle to answer them. If nothing else, we hope that our readers will take away from this book a determination to question things they observe every day in the social worlds they inhabit, and that they will also recognize that we can get closer to answering those questions with some sociological theories and insights.

We have entitled our text *The Sociology Project*, both to reflect our commitment to a collective agenda to understanding all of the different subfields of sociology as an evolving project and, as we move to version 3.0 in both print and digital format, because we want to signal to our readers our intention to continue to develop the book in future editions as sociology itself evolves. New findings, theories, and ideas are constantly being developed, and this iteration reflects those changes with a major overhaul of each chapter. Our book will continue to evolve as research develops in new directions, and we look forward to revising our ideas and questions as the evidence suggests we should. But perhaps most importantly, we think of this updated edition—*The Sociology Project 3.0*—as a dialogue with our readers, including both our students and our sociology colleagues around the country who use the text to introduce their students to sociology. We invite you to engage and challenge us where we come up short, tell us what we are doing wrong, and share ideas you have for the presentation of sociology as a field.

Jeff Manza for the NYU Sociology Department
New York City
July 2021

New to This Edition

This new edition of *The Sociology Project* (TSP) has been thoroughly revised and updated to integrate new analyses and discussions of important recent developments in American society. The text uses the example of the COVID-19 pandemic to uncover how and why social interaction is so important to us, and to show how the pandemic has revealed hidden inequalities and institutional dysfunction in America today. It also analyzes the recent national protests over racism, specifically as they relate to the Black Lives Matter movement and police brutality, as well as the #MeToo and environmental movements, and the growing prominence of right-wing militia groups (including those who participated in the attack on the U.S. Capitol seeking to overthrow the results of a democratic election in January 2021). These various movements and recent developments have raised important questions about how social processes and institutions work today. We expand our discussion of policing in reworked chapters on organizations, deviance, and criminal justice. We explore several new theories about systematic racism and White racial identity in the reworked chapter on "Race and Ethnicity" (now Chapter 13). We also added a completely new chapter on the sociology of American democracy (the latter addressing rising concerns about political polarization and the threats to democracy that sharpened in the Trump era and its immediate aftermath). We have also expanded coverage of markets, organizations, and work by creating two new chapters: Chapter 9, "Markets and Organizations: The Sociology of Economic Life," discusses the different types of capitalist economies and the new economic sociology, and contains dedicated sections on the sociology of organizations, while Chapter 12, "Jobs, Occupations, and Professions: The Sociology of Work," examines occupations (old and new), the nature of work and the labor process, and the future of the labor market. To give a greater sense of these changes and others, here is a brief summary of the updates to each chapter.

Part I The Sociological Enterprise

1. **The Sociological Imagination**

   In this chapter, we introduce the COVID-19 pandemic as a central example in considering what a sociological imagination can uncover and how sociology gives us a window on social inequalities and institutions.

2. **Social Theory**

   We have added Jane Addams as one of the founding figures of social theory (along with Marx, Durkheim, Weber, Simmel, and Du Bois) and further expanded our discussion of the immense contributions of W. E. B Du Bois. We also include new content on the theory of historical materialism according to Marx and contemporary neo-Marxists.

3. **Studying the Social World**

   We provide a new Big Question on "Big Data" and how to use new kinds of computational research methods for social research. We have also developed a new section on field experiments, which are a great tool for beginning students to conduct sociological research. Finally, we revised our discussion of survey research to incorporate new developments (another research tool that is possible for undergraduates to deploy).

Part II Building Blocks of Societies

4. **Social Interaction**

   This chapter presents updated and current examples throughout, particularly regarding COVID-19, to highlight the human need for interaction.

5. **Social Structure**

   Here, we provide expanded coverage of roles and role conflict, group identities, and social hierarchies, as well as a new and more extensive discussion of the concept of institutional fields and the concept of the institutional order.

6. **Environment and Society**

   We have moved this chapter earlier in the book to highlight the importance of the relationship between humans and the environment, particularly amidst the threat of global warming and climate change. We have also provided updated examples on environmental injustice and a discussion of the public/private paradox, as well as coverage of the role of human/animal contact as a contributing factor in the rise of new viral diseases (such as COVID-19).

7. **Deviance and Social Control**

   We have placed this chapter in a new, more primary location to stress the importance of social control as a core feature of society. We've extended our discussion of labeling theory; explored white-collar crime and corporate deviance in more detail, including a case study of Purdue Pharma, the manufacturer of Oxy-Contin; and added a new section on police deviance and the protections from sanction that police officers have long enjoyed.

8. **Power and Politics**

   While still retaining the core ideas from the previous edition and Steven Lukes's three dimensions of power, we've heavily revised and expanded this chapter to focus more systematically on how political systems still favor the interests of the powerful, while relocating the content on American democracy to the new Chapter 21.

9. **Markets and Organizations: The Sociology of Economic Life**

   This new chapter focuses on capitalist markets, the varieties of capitalism in the world today, and the sociological approach to studying economic markets, as well on organizations, their importance for social and economic life, and their relationship to the external environment.

10. **Culture, Media, and Communication**

    This chapter contains increased coverage and examples of ethnocentrism, cultural relativism, and ethnonationalist views that have become more central in the United States and around the world with the rise of right-wing populism. We also discuss the significance of social media in changing the nature of political communication, as exemplified by former president Donald Trump's use of Twitter and his overall communication strategy, and how this played a role in the assault on the U.S. Capitol in January 2021. In addition, the chapter examines the pressures and challenges on contemporary journalism and the news media and provides updated examples of the ways the Internet has created new opportunities and dangers for media and democracy.

Part III Inequalities

11. **Inequality and Poverty**

    We have significantly revised the historical treatment of inequality in this chapter, including new discussions of the rise of the welfare state and high-end inequality. We also present updated data on income inequality and reasons why economic inequality has increased in the United States in recent years, specifically related to earnings of college and non-college graduates, why the rich get richer, and the impact of globalization on the economy and employment. The chapter also contains new information on declining social mobility, factors that increase the likelihood of poverty, and more clearly describes individual versus structural sources of poverty than earlier additions.

12. **Jobs, Occupations, and Professions: The Sociology of Work**

    This is a new chapter dedicated to the sociology of work. It includes Big Questions on professional occupations, an extended discussion of the gig economy and self-employment, as well as new coverage on the nature of power in the workplace, the role of unions, what makes a good job, and the central challenges facing workers today.

13. **Race and Ethnicity**

    New and updated coverage and examples appear throughout, particularly regarding systemic racism, color-blind racism, and disparities in the treatment of people of color in the criminal justice system, as well in health care coverage and political participation. We also include a new section on the Black Lives Matter movement, White supremacism, and the future of race politics.

14. **Gender and Sexualities**

    Now entitled "Gender and Sexualities" (formerly "Gender and Sexuality") to highlight the recent trends toward more expansive understandings of sexual orientation, this chapter contains fresh examples, more current data on education, testing, and income gaps based on gender; discussion of nonbinary individuals, and a new section on the varieties of unwanted sexual encounters, such as rape and sexual harassment, and the rise of the #MeToo movement.

15. **Cities and Communities**

    In this chapter we have added a new Big Question on rural communities. We discuss the evolution and characteristics of rural communities, as well as the challenges of economic decline many are facing. We also provide updated sections on suburban patterns of settlement, urban poverty, and racial and ethnic segregation.

Part IV Core Institutions

16. **Families and Family Life**

    This chapter offers updated data and examples on the changing nature of families and the challenges of developing relationships and families.

17. **Sociology of Religion**

    NYU sociologist Iddo Tavory joins us this edition after the passing of the chapter's original author (Gerald Marwell), providing significant updates and examples of how we define religion, religion as a social institution, the role of theodicy, religious conversion, the varieties of new religious movements, the relationship between gender and religiosity in various major religions, and the classical sociological theory of secularization.

18. **Education**

    Significantly revised, this chapter has a new Big Question on higher education that discusses the challenges facing colleges today. It also presents new material on the early rise of educational systems in America, the concepts of active learning and human capital, income inequality and schooling, education and the elite, comparative differences in schooling around the world, the effects of homeschooling during the COVID-19 pandemic, and much more.

19. **Health and Medicine**

    This chapter contains a new opener on the COVID-19 pandemic, and a new Big Question on epidemics and society that reveals long-standing patterns of how societies respond to epidemics. We have also added a new section on the rise of the opioid epidemic. In addition, it presents new content on autism, the role of insurance in health care, and updated data and statistics throughout.

20. **Crime and Punishment**

    A new Big Question presents expanded coverage of the role of racism in the criminal justice system, incorporating recent data on police shootings and brutality. We've also added new sections on the decline of crime and content on social disorganization, revised sections on modern theories of crime and punishment, and updated material on incarceration rates in the United States and comparable countries.

21. **American Democracy and Political Life**

    This new chapter provides a sociological analysis of contemporary American politics and the consequences of aging political institutions anchored by a Constitution created in the eighteenth century. We cover the question of how "democratic" American political institutions really are, why voter turnout remains so low (in spite of the recent uptick in the Trump era), how and why some groups are attempting to restrict access to the ballot in various ways, the costs and consequences of political polarization, and how powerful groups are able to "get their way" in the making of government policies (considering, for example, the role of political money).

Part V Social Processes and Social Change

22. Social Movements and Revolutions

Several key changes can be found in this chapter. We include discussions of recent social movements and protest events: Black Lives Matter and the events on January 6, 2021, when hundreds of supporters of then-President Donald Trump stormed the U.S. Capitol in Washington, D.C., in attempt to overthrow the results of the 2020 election.

23. Population, Aging, and Social Demography

We provide updated statistics and data throughout this chapter, specifically on population growth and change as well as on rates of immigration.

24. Immigration

This chapter presents updated statistics on immigration and information on unauthorized immigrants and the effects of immigration on children, particularly regarding the stripping of DACA protections during the Trump presidency, as well as content on Americans' attitudes toward immigration.

25. Globalization

We've added new sections on the impact of globalization on social and cultural life and the globalization of ideas and politics across borders, specifically as it relates to the United Nations and recent developments with the European Union.

The Sociology Project 3.0 in Revel™

- Images, over 45 new videos, and interactive data visualizations are deeply integrated with core content.
- Integrated writing opportunities prompt students to engage their sociological imaginations and think critically about the research and theory presented to them.
- Assessment opportunities following every Big Question section and at the end of the chapter help students measure their understanding of key concepts before moving on.

Inspire engagement through active learning

Revel® improves results by empowering students to actively participate in learning. More than a digital textbook, Revel delivers an engaging blend of author content, media, and assessment.

With Revel, students read and practice in one continuous experience. Interactive content and assessments integrated throughout the narrative provide opportunities for students to explore and apply concepts. And Revel is mobile and user-friendly, so students can learn on the go—anytime, anywhere, on any device.

Learn more about Revel: www.pearsonhighered.com/revel/

Acknowledgments

Writing a textbook takes a village, as they say, and we have been blessed with a strong and committed team of colleagues, graduate students, and editors to pull the book together. Our first and most important debt is to our team at Pearson. Our initial advisors and editors, who threw themselves into a new and untested project with conviction and determination, were led by Dickson Musslewhite, then Vice President of Product Development; Brita Nordin, formerly Vice President–Courseware Content Development; and Billy Grieco, former Senior Portfolio Manager at Pearson. They embraced our project from the beginning, got it off the ground, and stayed in good spirits as we progressed, unevenly, toward completion and several revisions and development of the digital version of the text. We have had two brilliant development editors throughout this process who have been extraordinary colleagues to work with. Lisa McLellan did a masterful job wrestling the initial 23 different chapters written by different authors into a coherent whole. For this edition, Stephanie Ventura brought a new vision and editorial wizardry that has improved the text at every turn. The rest of our publishing team at Pearson also deserves our gratitude: Pamela Chirls, Holly Shufeldt, Barbara Cappuccio, and Amber Mackey. We are also thankful for the help of Marianne Peters-Riordan, project manager at Integra Software Services.

At NYU, we have a number of debts to acknowledge. Joe Juliano, formerly the Dean of Business Affairs at the College of Arts and Sciences, now the Vice Provost for Strategic Planning, connected us to Pearson through a personal relationship with Tim Bozik, then CEO of Pearson U.S. Higher Ed. Writing a textbook in the way that we did, with the full involvement of the faculty and many graduate students of the Sociology Department, including colleagues who have since left the department or retired, allowed us to draw on the great wealth of intellectual resources of a first-rate group of graduate and undergraduate students. As we've continued to update and revise, the team approach has continued to inform everything we do. For research and other assistance on this edition, we are especially grateful to Ned Crowley, Mario Soto, Sobha Gati, Charlotte Kahan, Ruby Bromberg, Glenys McGuire, and Helen Stec.

Pearson's Commitment to Diversity, Equity, and Inclusion

Pearson is dedicated to creating bias-free content that reflects the diversity, depth, and breadth of all learners' experiences. We embrace the many dimensions of diversity, including but not limited to race, ethnicity, gender, sex, sexual orientation, socioeconomic status, ability, age, and religious or political beliefs.

Education is a powerful force for equity and change in our world. It has the potential to deliver opportunities that improve lives and enable economic mobility. As we work with authors to create content for every product and service, we acknowledge our responsibility to demonstrate inclusivity and incorporate diverse scholarship so that everyone can achieve their potential through learning. As the world's leading learning company, we have a duty to help drive change and live up to our purpose to help more people create a better life for themselves and to create a better world.

Our ambition is to purposefully contribute to a world where:

- Everyone has an equitable and lifelong opportunity to succeed through learning.
- Our educational products and services are inclusive and represent the rich diversity of learners.
- Our educational content accurately reflects the histories and experiences of the learners we serve.
- Our educational content prompts deeper discussions with students and motivates them to expand their own learning (and worldview).

We are also committed to providing products that are fully accessible to all learners. As per Pearson's guidelines for accessible educational Web media, we test and retest the capabilities of our products against the highest standards for every release, following the WCAG guidelines in developing new products for copyright year 2022 and beyond. You can learn more about Pearson's commitment to accessibility at https://www.pearson.com/us/accessibility.html.

While we work hard to present unbiased, fully accessible content, we want to hear from you about any concerns or needs with this Pearson product so that we can investigate and address them.

- Please contact us with concerns about any potential bias at https://www.pearson.com/report-bias.html.
- For accessibility-related issues, such as using assistive technology with Pearson products, alternative text requests, or accessibility documentation, email the Pearson Disability Support team at disability.support@pearson.com.

Author's Note on Terminology

Jeff Manza

The terms and language we use to describe different groups in contemporary societies has always been controversial. Language can all too easily become a form of social oppression, especially when members of a more powerful group choose terms with negative connotations for subordinate or historically disadvantaged groups. In recent years, debates about appropriate terms has become especially heated, while at the very same time that terminology is shifting and unsettled.

For an introductory sociology textbook, many of the traditional terms long used to describe groups, especially in relation to race, ethnicity, gender, and sexuality, are being challenged and are evolving. Getting the language right is important—but not easy. As we complete revisions to this textbook in the spring of 2021, there are several unsettled and sometimes controversial new terms coming into use, as well as vigorous debates about what is and what is not appropriate. We have had to make choices that may not satisfy everyone. And it is possible that one or more of the choices we have made will appear out of date to some readers in a few years.

It's important to keep in mind that decisions on terminology often correlate to usage in sociological research findings, and this may not always correspond to emerging everyday practices. For example, consider gender. The man/woman binary is increasingly seen as out of date, yet much of the data we have to work with classifies all respondents as "men" or "women." An issue like the gender gap in pay—men earn about 20 percent more income than women—is a critically important and ongoing aspect of gender inequality, one that persists even in the face of laws that are supposed to eliminate it. To not discuss the extent of the gender gap in income between individuals who are coded in research studies or datasets as "men" and "women," would be sociological malpractice. But at the same time, those who reject the traditional gender binary (i.e., man versus woman) may feel as if we are writing them out of the picture. This is not our intention. Hopefully, future researchers will develop surveys and other data collections that gather information about nonbinary and trans people, and in a few years we will be better positioned to analyze the impact of a wider range of gender identities and inequalities. The same lesson applies to other terminological controversies. But for now, we would still insist that it is important to use the data we currently have to discuss group differences in income, wealth, education, politics, crime, and other topics, especially when we are examining historical trends where we simply don't have data that match contemporary or emerging terms and identities.

There are also choices we have made throughout the book that reflect deep and ongoing theoretical and political challenges, not just data limitations. Although the terms used to describe groups can create problems across many types of social identities, the most contested terms concern those for racial and ethnic groups, as well as gender identities and sexual orientation. Here are the most important of the choices we have made, and why we believe they are the best available options right now.

Race/ethnicity terms: As Ann Morning explains in Chapter 13, racial labels are social constructions, but because they are experienced as real in the world today, we should not shy away from using them for analytical purposes. She then notes that, generally speaking, race is based on (skin) color, while ethnicity is generally based on place of origin (of oneself or one's ancestors). For several decades, the term "African American" has been in wide circulation as a way of describing Black people, while the term "white" (in lower-case) has been applied to people of European ancestry (who historically were thought of as hyphenated Whites, like German-American, Polish-American, or Italian-American). The substitution of African American for Black reflected an ambition to remind people that, just as European-origin Whites have a shared ethnic background, so too do Black Americans have ethnic roots in Africa. The underlying vision of a post-racial society, in which people's backgrounds are thought of primarily in terms of where they are from (ethnicity), rather than their skin color, is an important but as yet unrealized dream. For one thing, although some writers bravely attempted to consistently refer to Whites as "European Americans," this usage did not catch on. In fact, in the decades following World War II, "white" increasingly became a generic, catch-all term for anyone with light skin no matter what their background. As the category grew to encompass around 90 percent of the American population circa 1950, most ethnic descriptors (such as "Italian" or "Irish") seemed to lose most of their meaning. Further, the term "African American," while still in wide use and preferred by many writers, implies a recent connection to a continent that is remote for many, whereas the term Black (or Black American) better captures the unique and tragic experience of oppression arising from slavery, Jim Crow, and the long history of stereotyping and discrimination targeted at Black people across American history. It recognizes a shared fate based on skin color, no matter where one's ancestors came from. The distinction is captured brilliantly by the actor, writer, and hip hop artist Donald Glover's character in the TV show *Atlanta,* when he is asked what part of Africa he is from. Glover replies, "I don't know. See, this spooky thing called slavery happened and my entire ethnic identity was erased."

So throughout the book, we will use the (capitalized) term Black. But this decision raises a different issue. Until recently, the term "white" was generally spelled with lower-case "w." This could imply that lower-case "white" people do not have a race, whereas Black people do. For sociologists, the implications of this are very problematic. For one thing, it makes the concept of White privilege altogether unclear. (How can you be racially privileged if you have no race?) In teaching introductory courses on

race, some sociologists will ask their White students when they first realized they were White, which is an unsettling question for some. In my own version of this exercise, I ask my students to anonymously describe (in writing) when they first came to think of themselves as the race that they do today (and what that race is). Many White students will respond that they don't think of themselves as White and/or offer some version of "I think of myself as a person, not a member of a race," or that they began to think of themselves as "White" only when they got to college. It is a remarkable privilege in a racially divided society that some groups can reach early adulthood without having to think about their race, while for others it is a central part of their identity. The asymmetry, then, between "Black" and "white," upon reflection, carries an important implication that sociologists should not ignore. As the historian Nell Irvin Painter has recently written, "No longer should white people be allowed the comfort of this racial invisibility; they should have to see themselves as raced. Being racialized makes white people squirm, so let's racialize them with that capital W." Throughout the book, when we are discussing White and Black people, we will use this parallel approach.

Turning to another complex issue in contemporary language on race/ethnicity, we have chosen to adopt the controversial term "Latinx" throughout the text, rather than either "Hispanic" or the more commonly used "Latino." The term Hispanic has largely fallen out of favor, in large part because today it evokes the colonial history of Spanish imperialism in Latin America. But more recently, feminists have challenged the use of the term "Latino" to describe a group, half of whose members are not men. One solution is "Latino/a," which many writers and sociologists have employed, but it is both clunky and, as members of the LGBTQ community have argued, just reinforces the binary character of gender identity (male/female). In the past decade or so, the term "Latinx" (with no "A" or "O") has come into greater use. It is controversial to use "Latinx" in the sense that most people tracing their roots to Latin America have not (yet) embraced it. (A recent survey by the Pew Research Center found in August 2020 that just 3 percent of people of Latin American origin use the term "Latinx" to describe themselves, and only a quarter had even heard of it.) Imposing a new term before it has been accepted by the group it is meant to describe is not ideal—and the long history of such impositions highlights the dangers. But we also believe that, from a sociological standpoint, a gender-neutral term is strongly preferred for research and analysis, without implying the assertion that it should be used as a self-description for anyone who finds it uncomfortable.

Next, we will follow the dominant current usage of the term "Asian American/Pacific Islander" to describe people who trace their roots to Asia or the Pacific Islands (the latter includes people from places located mostly in South Pacific, such as Samoa and American Samoa, Tahiti, any of the 600 islands that are part of the Federated States of Micronesia, Papua New Guinea, Fiji, and the other countries in the Melanesia region, as well as Native Hawaiians). The term "Asian American" emerged in the late 1960s to replace the older and heavily stereotyped term "Oriental" that was in common usage. Later, people from the Pacific Island regions pushed for a separate identification from those from the continent of Asia, arguing that their histories and national circumstances were very different. Sometimes a shorthand "Asian Pacific Islander" is used, but it is (at present) more common to use "Asian American/Pacific Islander" or its acronym (AAPI).

Finally, we continue to use the term "Native American" to refer to the groups that trace their origins to the period before Europeans began to settle in what is now the United States. This term has come under criticism for lumping together many different tribes under one umbrella that ignores their individual histories and cultures. In other countries in North America and South America, the more commonly used term is "Indigenous" people, and Canadians use the term "First Nations." We acknowledge the limits and concerns with the phrase "Native American," but it remains in wide use in the United States, and almost all existing datasets only identify all native peoples in one category, thus compelling us to follow conventional usage.

Gender/Sexuality Terms: Just as language relating to race and ethnicity is fraught with complications, so too are terms for gender identity and sexual orientation. As noted, in recent years the gender binary ("male/man/men" and "female/woman/women") has been challenged by transgender and nonbinary people as both denying them a gender identity and, less obviously, privileging people who are comfortable with their birth-assigned gender (for example, gender assignment based on their genitalia). Our solution to this particular issue is to avoid the general use of "he/him" or "she/her" when possible, except when referring to specific individuals. Instead, we try to use the more neutral term "they." This approach, although sometimes grammatically awkward, is becoming more widely adopted by sociologists and other writers, and we believe it is the correct approach moving forward.

Another important issue, which connects gender identities and sexual orientations, is the terms we use to describe the variety of nonconforming groups of people. Throughout the book, when we refer to people who are either sexual or gender nonconforming, we will use the term "Lesbian, Gay, Bisexual, Trans," or LGBT for short. Some have added "Q" to indicate "queer," creating an "LGBTQ" label. "Queer" is a term adopted by "nonbinary" people, that is, people who reject traditional gender and sexual thinking that divides everyone into "men" or "males" versus "women" or "females," and consider themselves to nonbinary. It is also a bold effort to reclaim what had once been a homophobic slur. However, it is important to note that "queer" continues to have a negative connotation in everyday language, and some in the LGBT community who seek full citizenship and equality reject its use as a descriptor. However, the growth of nonbinary gender identities and the continuing dominant use of "queer" as a descriptor for members of the group makes sense to use it whenever we are referring to all members of gender and sexual communities who are challenging either the heterosexual or gender binary norms.

When referring specifically to sexual orientation, we will use the phrases "same-sex" versus "different-sex" to describe gay and heterosexual couples, respectively. We use "same-sex marriage" to describe a marriage between a man and a man or a woman and a woman. We recognize the endless variety of intimate relationships, including those involving trans or nonbinary people, but we generally lack data to describe or analyze such relationships. This too will hopefully change in the future.

We hope these explanations both clarify our choices and signal our attentiveness to continuing controversies, as well as our desire to avoid offending any of our readers. We draw inspiration from New York University's campus in Abu Dhabi (NYUAD), in which students come from all over the world, with an incredible variety of backgrounds and identities. At NYUAD, constant contact with people from different cultures increases the possibility, or even the likelihood, of using a term that offends someone else. Students on campus have come to adopt a solution: Always assume the best intentions of people, so that the first time someone uses a term that another person finds offensive, avoid leaping to the conclusion that it was done with malicious intent. Often it is simply inadvertent, and most of the time a patient explanation of why some find it harmful is sufficient. It is only when people deliberately disregard such feedback and insist on continuing to use offensive language that we can reach the conclusion that it is being done in a way that is intended to harm. This approach, if widely adopted, would help to avoid many misunderstandings and tensions that currently surround these terms.

The Sociology Project 3.0

Chapter 1
The Sociological Imagination

by Jeff Manza, Lynne Haney, and Richard Arum

In early December 2019, a physician in Wuhan, China, named Li Wenliang reported that several of his patients were experiencing unexplained and severe respiratory problems. As similar reports began to accumulate in the area, the World Health Organization (WHO) was notified of a potential new health threat (although the Chinese government initially denied it). By early January 2020, Chinese scientists determined that the growing number of respiratory problems found in the people of Wuhan were caused by a new kind of coronavirus (a type of virus that is normally harmless, one of the main causes of the common cold). By the end of January 2020, the WHO had officially declared the outbreak of a new coronavirus and named it SARS-CoV-2. The illness that SARS-CoV-2 can cause in some people was called COVID-19. (The "19" refers to the year the virus was first identified, 2019.) Not long after, cases of COVID-19 began to appear around the world, in places as far apart as Iran, South Korea, and Italy. The first confirmed case in the United States was reported in mid-February 2020 (although it is likely there were earlier, undiagnosed cases). By March, the WHO had declared the coronavirus to be a global pandemic. By Fall 2021, deaths caused by COVID-19 in the United States had exceeded 700,000 even as the rollout of vaccines provided hope for an end to the pandemic.

The rapid spread of this new and highly contagious coronavirus (and the growing number of health problems and deaths associated with it) completely transformed everyday life. To try to limit its spread, governments across the world took drastic steps, ordering people to stay in their homes and shutting down all but the most essential of services. Following a period of quarantine, in which it was hoped that everyone carrying the virus would have recovered, governments began gradually reopening their economies but with strict limits and orders for people to wear masks in public (the one scientifically proven way to prevent the transmission of the virus from person to person). Although there were large differences in how successfully each country implemented these policies—with

the United States being one of the least successful—almost every country attempted some version of the same approach. The quarantines quickly led to a very sharp economic downturn and rising unemployment, the closures of schools and churches, and the disruption or complete elimination of public events such as sports, music concerts, theater and film viewings, funerals, and weddings.

The COVID-19 pandemic was miserable for everyone living through it. But it also provides an opportunity to learn important lessons about societies. COVID-19 reminded all of us how closely connected our lives are to others—human

My Sociological Imagination

JEFF MANZA

Mark Bussell

Growing up in the college town of Berkeley, California, my family was neither elite (my parents worked for the local university, but not as professors) nor unprivileged. I experienced the differences between these worlds, and in particular the inequalities they represented, as an endlessly fascinating puzzle. I was also always interested in politics and occasionally participated in political protests and movements. My intellectual interest in sociology began to develop while I was an undergraduate student because it provided a way of connecting my emerging concerns about inequality and injustice with a set of theories and ways of studying how those inequalities persist. Since then, I have been exploring how social inequalities influence political life. More recently, I have become interested in how public opinion does or does not shape government policies and how and when public attitudes can be manipulated or misused by political elites. I hope that my work can contribute, in some small way, to making American democracy more representative and egalitarian than it currently is.

Ringo Chiu/ZUMA Press, Inc./Alamy Stock Photo

Exceptionally long lines at food banks across America during the COVID-19 pandemic, as shown in these photos, highlighted how many families are living on the edge of not having enough to.eat and not having enough savings to survive when an economic downturn caused by the pandemic hit. In spite of being one of, if not the, richest country in the world, millions of Americans face the threat of food insecurity — and the pandemic highlighted the depths of this insecurity.

beings are, after all, social beings, and deprived of so many of the social anchors of daily life, we all suffer. To put it another way, our existence is always connected by our relationships to others. Our individual lives contain stories about **society**, which we can define in simple terms as a large group of people who live in the same area and participate in a common culture. **Sociology**—the study of societies and the social worlds that individuals inhabit within them—seeks to uncover and analyze the patterns that lie beneath the surface of our individual lives. We can better understand the full meaning of COVID-19 by applying a **sociological imagination** (that is, using sociological ideas to understand everyday life).

To see what a sociological imagination can do, let's look at some of the many lessons about society that the COVID-19 pandemic illuminated. First and foremost, the pandemic suggests how fragile our trust in each other—and the government officials and scientific experts guiding the response to the pandemic—can be. Most Americans followed the established scientific guidelines to maintain distance from others and wear masks in public. But many others refused to trust scientific expertise and government guidelines, putting other people at risk by not wearing masks or by attending social events with large numbers of people where the virus can spread.

To take another example, the pandemic highlighted many of the consequences of living in a society with a high degree of inequality that might have otherwise been largely hidden from view. For example, even though the coronavirus itself was an equal-opportunity microbe, seeking any human hosts it could find to take up residence, death rates from COVID-19 were much higher among the poor than the rich. Rich people could obtain much better care if infected, or flee to the safety of more remote locations to reduce their risk of exposure, than poor people and families. Further, poor people living in crowded cities or working in jobs deemed "essential" were exposed daily to the threat of infection. While middle-class and white-collar workers could work safely from their homes during the pandemic, essential workers were compelled to go to their workplaces and expose themselves to risk, many for low pay. Of the millions thrown out of work, poor and even many middle-class families with limited or no savings found themselves in a very vulnerable place. Lines at food pantries sometimes stretched for miles, and **food insecurity** (a condition of not knowing whether you or your family will have enough to eat) soared. In spite of all its wealth, the pandemic highlighted that in the United States, many families live right on the edge of catastrophe. Even something so taken for granted as having enough to eat is not guaranteed.

The COVID-19 pandemic also showed how racism and racial discrimination, so pervasive in American society and history, manifested itself and even took on new forms. Asian Americans were attacked in public as alleged perpetrators of the virus, and young Black men reported being harassed or viewed with suspicion when wearing masks

(that is, even when doing exactly what citizens were supposed to do). Black Americans also died from COVID-19 at rates almost three times that of White Americans, reflecting higher rates of exclusion from the health care system as well as greater exposure to the virus (at work or in the community).

We also learned many important lessons about family life and intimate relationships during the pandemic. Living in close quarters, without the normal release provided by school, work, churches, social activities and in-person time with friends, was very stressful. This was especially for couples and families residing in small apartments or houses. Separation and divorce rates rose, and rates of mental health problems shot up. Parents of all income levels faced hardships having to take care of their children around the clock while also trying to do their jobs, although here again those with resources could find solutions not available to most other families. Poor children suffered from significantly reduced learning during the pandemic, while children in middle class and richer families could count on better quality schools and other resources to reduce those losses. Older family members living in assisted living facilities—among the groups most vulnerable to COVID-19—were denied access to their children and family members, leaving many lonely and depressed.

The pandemic also shed new light on issues and defects of major social institutions that sociologists study very closely. For example, overcrowding and neglect of prisons turned them into places of viral spread and death. The American health care system revealed numerous problems and flaws during the pandemic. Despite the heroic work of frontline health care workers, the United States, which has 4 percent of the world's population, accounted for 20 percent of all global COVID-19 deaths before the arrival of vaccines. That such a rich nation, with a world-class scientific and medical research infrastructure, performed so poorly compared to other similar nations should raise an enormous red flag for every American to think about. How could this have happened?

Finally, a neglected but especially important aspect of the pandemic highlights our relationship with the natural world. Climate change threatens us, but because its full impact is likely a few decades away, many are prepared to ignore it. But COVID-19 didn't wait to reveal how our current approach to the natural world is deeply troubled. COVID-19 is what is known as a **zoonotic** disease, one which was caused by a virus that moved from animals to humans. The relentless destruction of natural habitats, for purposes such as mining, ranching, and the construction of ever more human settlements sprawling across the globe, is making it much easier for viruses to migrate from wild animals to humans. Public health experts have been raising concerns about this for a long time, and, in fact, there have been many other close calls with zoonotic diseases in recent years: the bird flu, swine flu, SARS (the first SARS coronavirus), Zika, Ebola, and West Nile virus. Although it appeared to be a unique, once-in-a-lifetime event, a global pandemic may actually have been long overdue. The 100-year respite from the last major pandemic to strike rich countries like the United States (the influenza virus of 1918–19) may prove, in the future, to have been an exceptionally long periord *without* an epidemic. Although no one wants to contemplate a similar pandemic, experts believe that if we do not reassess our relationship to the natural world, they are all but certain to recur.

These examples suggest to us some of the many ways in which studying sociology and developing a sociological imagination allows us to see beneath the surface of everyday life, to uncover and understand otherwise hidden features of our societies. It also gives us some tools to think about how we might change them. As we move through our investigation of societies and sociology, we'll find many examples. A central theme throughout the book is that everywhere we look, the unequal distribution of power and economic resources generates social inequalities that continue to divide us along economic, racial/ethnic, gender/sexuality, religious, and other lines.

The Big Questions

Each chapter in this book identifies a set of questions that have defined the research and teaching puzzles of that topic. These questions organize each chapter and provide a lens for exploring sociological thinking about the topics covered. In starting from questions, not answers, and puzzling together in the search for answers, you will learn to think sociologically. In this first chapter, we will explore the following questions:

1. **What is the sociological imagination, and why is it worth acquiring?** In this section, we introduce the concept of the sociological imagination and explore how it helps us learn to ask hard questions.

2. **What are social contexts, and why do they matter?** We introduce and explore the concept of social contexts. Sociology is fundamentally concerned with how individuals are shaped and influenced by their society. All of us are impacted by an array of social contexts. How do these contexts influence us and guide our behavior?

3. **Where did sociology come from, and how is it different from other social sciences?** Here we examine the social contexts in which sociology itself began to develop, and also explore the question of how sociology relates to the other social sciences.

Mark Bussell

BIG QUESTION 1.1 What Is the Sociological Imagination, and Why Is It Worth Acquiring?

THE SOCIOLOGICAL IMAGINATION

Since its inception, sociology has puzzled over how we are connected to each other and the broader societies in which we live. A **sociological imagination** is the capacity to think systematically about how things we experience as *personal* issues—for example, debt from student loans, competing demands from divorced parents, or an inability to form a rewarding romantic relationship, or living through the COVID-19 pandemic—are really *social* issues that are widely shared by others living in a similar time and place as us.

Fritz Goro/The LIFE Picture Collection/Shutterstock

The sociologist C. Wright Mills coined the phrase "the sociological imagination" in a 1959 book. Mills' own research and writings ranged widely across American society in the 1950s and early 1960s, before he died from a heart attack at the age of 45.

The sociologist C. Wright Mills (1916–1962), who coined the term in 1959, wrote that "the sociological imagination enables us to grasp history and biography and the relations between the two within society" (Mills 1959:6). To understand the world around us, and to begin to think in a deep way about how it works and how we might improve it, is to recognize the extent to which our individual lives are strongly shaped by where, when, and to whom we were born, and the range of experiences we have had as a child, as an adolescent, and later as an adult. At each stage, we are both individuals and members of social worlds. Our opportunities and potentials are always influenced by the inequalities and injustices we encounter, but understanding these requires that we think about them sociologically. In short, the sociological imagination helps us to ask hard questions and seek answers about the social worlds we inhabit. Used wisely, it will also provide tools to navigate those worlds more effectively in pursuit of the goals we have set for ourselves.

Looking at the Social World Through a Sociological Lens

1.1.1 Discuss how a sociological imagination helps to challenge stereotypes.

A sociological imagination challenges some very basic impulses all of us have. To simplify a complex world, we often take for granted that things around us are somehow inevitable or natural. Those who grew up in a social context where marriage is defined as a lifelong commitment between a man and a woman might be quick to conclude that such an arrangement was the way that intimate relationships were meant to be, that marriage is the "natural"

way for households to form. But if we look at different societies or our own over time, we will soon learn that marriage is only *sometimes* a lifetime commitment between a man and a woman, that many marriages will end in divorce, and that intimate relationships can last a lifetime *without* marriage. Further, intimate relationships may be between two men, or two women, or among varying romantic partners. Traditional ideas about appropriate marriage partners having similar racial, ethnic, or religious backgrounds are rapidly disappearing. Indeed, the new freedom in defining relationships is one of the major social changes of the last 50 years. A sociological imagination helps us to understand that there is no single or "natural" model of marriage or intimacy.

In a similar fashion, we are also often quick to identify differences across groups of people—men and women, rich and poor, Whites and other races, people of different religions—as inherent characteristics of the members of these groups. But this assumption—that "group" characteristics

America/Alamy Stock Photo

Many people assume that overweight people have caused their own weight problems by overeating and under-exercising. But sociologists studying obesity have pointed to many social factors that contribute to many people gaining weight. These factors include increasingly sedentary lifestyles centered on office jobs and leisure activities (such as watching TV or doing social media), the rise of the fast food industry, the increasing proportion of processed foods in the modern diet, and suburbanization and reliance on the automobile to get around instead of walking, among others.

apply to all members of the group or to any one individual—is always incorrect. No group contains members who are identical. Making faulty generalizations about individuals based on what we think we know about the groups they are members of is what is known as a **stereotype**. Yet it is very common. For instance, some people (and evidently many employers) think that older people are not as good workers as younger people. It *is* true that at some point, if we live long enough, we will become too old to perform jobs that we may have done for many years. But that does not mean that any specific person is incapable of doing a job because of their age. In fact, older workers may have wisdom and experience lacking in their younger colleagues.

A sociological imagination challenges such assumptions by raising questions about where stereotypes come from, what they are based on, and who stands to benefit from them. Sociology gives us tools to understand and think critically and creatively about everyday assumptions (such as stereotyped thinking) that others hold. It shows us that the things we often take for granted, or hear about in the media, are actually a lot more complicated than they appear. Seeing the social world in all its complexity is a challenge, but possessed of a sociological imagination we gain tools to be more active and effective participants in that world.

Engaging Our Sociological Imaginations: From Personal Puzzles to Sociological Questions

1.1.2 Explain the process for forming sociological questions.

Everyone possesses some elements of a sociological imagination. Sometimes we glide through life without thinking very hard about what is going on around us. But when we observe and reflect on the social worlds we experience, we are beginning to think sociologically. However, just observing the world around us does not necessarily mean we are fully engaging our sociological imaginations. It is only when we start to ask deeper and more meaningful questions about those worlds that our sociological imagination is fully active. *Our ability to ask hard questions, instead of just settling for easily available answers (or stereotypes), is the hallmark of a good sociological imagination.*

Where do sociological questions come from? Most professional sociologists, including many of the authors of this book, have had experiences in their lives, before they began doing sociological research, that ignited their sociological imaginations. For some it was triggered by a particular event, while for others it may have developed more slowly—a combination of things that inspired them to seek to develop this way of thinking. The short author biographies that appear at the beginning of each chapter give you some idea of the events that led the authors of this book to become sociologists. But you don't have to be a professional sociologist to develop your sociological imagination or ask sociological questions! One situation that often triggers our sociological imagination occurs when we see that something we have long taken for granted may be incorrect. That can happen at any moment, but when it does, and when we start to question our previous assumptions, we are taking the first step toward developing a sociological imagination.

Of course, we can also actively engage our sociological imaginations, rather than waiting for surprising puzzles or events (like COVID-19) to appear. One way is to think critically about "common sense." Common sense ideas are often very useful. For example, there are innumerable pearls of wisdom found in common sense *aphorisms*, short phrases stating a truth or opinion. Examples of aphorisms include "look before you leap," "a rising tide lifts all boats," "birds of a feather flock together," and so forth. We've all heard some of these phrases, and in many cases it is valuable to follow the wisdom they suggest. Standing at a busy intersection, we *should* look carefully before walking out in front of traffic. It is usually easier to make friends with someone when you have common interests. In such cases, common sense provides a useful guide to being human.

But if we look more closely, we quickly notice there is a problem. Almost every common sense aphorism only makes sense in some contexts, but not others (Watts 2011). In fact, most aphorisms have an equally plausible, but entirely opposite, aphorism. For example, compare "look before you leap" to "they who hesitate are lost." They provide the exact opposite advice! That is, in some situations, it is important to seize opportunities before they disappear, while in other cases careful diligence is recommended. So which is correct? They cannot both be right all of the time. The answer is that it depends on the context. We have to know *which* common sense rule to apply in which social context if we are to be competent at being human.

Once we start learning not to take stereotypes and common sense ideas for granted, we can begin to ask questions about the world we inhabit. But what are these questions? Reading this book will open up many issues and questions to think about. But for now, here are a few examples. Think about eating at a school cafeteria. Maybe you just want to enjoy your food and your friends. But if you look around, if your school is like most in America, you may notice that there are relatively few, if any, groups that include both Whites and Blacks. Or visit a bunch of churches; you will rarely find large numbers of Blacks and Whites worshipping together. Why is it that, many decades after major civil rights legislation has ended legal discrimination, school friendship networks and religious worship so rarely cross the racial divide?

Or think about the United States. Why is it that one of the richest countries in the world has so many people living in poverty—far more, in fact, than other wealthy countries? (Using the official definition of poverty developed by the U.S. government, about 10–15% of all American families are poor at any given time.) An assumption many people have is that, at some level, poor people are lazy and disinclined to work hard. Yet as we will explore in more detail later in the book, many poor people work long hours but make very little money, not enough to lift them and their children out of poverty. Further, there are never enough jobs for everyone who wants one, meaning that there will always be some people left without the opportunity to work.

Differences across regions highlights another way in which poverty is produced by factors beyond those at the individual level. No matter how hard someone works in a very poor country, it is extremely unlikely that they will rise into what people living in rich countries would consider a middle-class living standard. Here's a simple example. Even in a rich country like the United States, there is considerable variation in how rich and poor you are likely to be depending on where you live. Some places in America have very few families living in poverty, while others have very high rates of poverty. Why is poverty so unevenly distributed? (See Figure 1.1 to see how many families in different parts of the United States are living in poverty and eligible to receive food stamps [formally known as the "Supplemental Nutrition Assistance Program"]). You are more likely to be poor living in some places than others. There are many other puzzles about poverty that present themselves once we start questioning the belief that anyone who is poor brought their condition upon themselves.

Asking questions about things we have previously taken for granted is a great foundation for getting involved in making social change. Those who accept the world as it is, and don't question how and why it might be different, will never feel compelled to get involved in trying to improve things. But once we start asking hard questions and searching for answers, we transition from passive to active citizens. Of course, seeking change can be threatening to people in positions of power. Governments, in particular, do not like it when their citizens begin to ask questions about topics that officials would prefer to keep secret, such as secret military operations or corruption among leading government figures. Similarly, large corporations or other organizations also may not like it when their workers start to challenge management's authority rather than simply do what they are told. School administrators often do not like it when students, parents, or outside observers raise questions about the character and quality of student learning or teaching. Even challenging family members at the dinner table about their own stereotypes can lead to puzzled looks or strong words. Sociological knowledge challenges the status quo, and those who benefit from it may not enjoy such challenges.

Figure 1.1 Food Stamp Usage in the United States

Percent of Households Receiving Supplemental Nutritional Aid Program (SNAP) Benefits, 2019

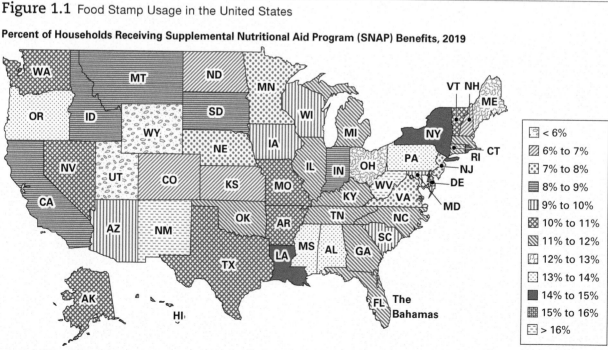

SOURCE: ACS 1-year estimates (2019) provided by SocialExplorer.com.

Sociological Questions: A Detailed Example

1.1.3 Identify the types of questions that sociologists are particularly well equipped to explore.

To get a better sense of how sociologists use questions to craft research projects, let's consider in more detail a recent research project undertaken by Richard Arum, one of the authors of this chapter (and a topic of interest to many of the readers of this book). Arum had taught at several universities around the country, and was puzzled by what he perceived to be the relatively modest amount of student learning that was actually going on at these universities. We usually take for granted that colleges and universities are places where teaching and learning are prioritized, but Arum, the sociologist, began to question this premise. To investigate how much learning is going on in higher education, he and a collaborator carried out a project following more than 2,000 young adults as they progressed through 24 diverse colleges and universities, and then as they left college to work, live with friends, move in with romantic partners, or return to live with their parents (Arum and Roksa 2011, 2014). The students in the study had quite different college experiences and fared very differently in terms of learning outcomes. Some of these students were in college settings where they were exposed to challenging coursework and successfully moved into well-paying jobs immediately following graduation. Yet many more students did not enjoy such fates. In fact, two years out of college, a full quarter of recent college graduates were back living at home with their parents or relatives.

Consider two of the students tracked in the project: Maria and Robert. Maria attended a highly selective, residential liberal arts college in a small Midwestern town. She had come to college with a high SAT score and three high school Advanced Placement course credits. In college, she quickly decided on becoming a social science major after taking a small first-year seminar with a sociologist who did her research on urban youth culture. She spent a semester of her junior year abroad in Europe, and during her semesters at college she reported that she met frequently with her instructors outside of class to discuss her work and that faculty at the school had high expectations for students like her. She also reported that her classmates—many of whom she had come to know well as the college had integrated her academic program with her residential dorm—were equally encouraging of her focus on academic work. On average, she estimated devoting 20 hours per week preparing for classes, many of which had significant reading and writing requirements in her social science major. When her performance on tasks that required critical

thinking, complex reasoning, and written communication was measured, her scores moved up dramatically from freshman to senior year. Two years out of college, she was living with a friend she had met in college and was working at a job where she made slightly more than $40,000 per year. Although she had assumed a great deal of student debt, she was on a path to adult success.

Contrast Maria's college experiences with Robert's. Robert attended a high school that was predominantly non-White before enrolling in a nonselective, large public university in his state that is known as something of a "party school." Like many of his classmates, he entered college without any Advanced Placement coursework completed, and he did not score particularly well on the SAT. In college, he reported rarely meeting with his instructors outside of class. When asked about whether faculty had high expectations for students like him, he reported that they largely did not. He muddled through coursework with passing grades but did not find his coursework either interesting or challenging. Instead, he found himself increasingly focused on socializing with his friends and earning spending money to support social activities outside of school. Like many of his peers, he studied about eight hours per week in college; when he did prepare for his classes, he often did so in group settings with his friends, who ended up often distracting him from really focusing on his work. During his senior year, when he was tested on the same tasks that Maria completed, there was no improvement in his performance—even after attending college for four years! Sadly, Robert was not alone. Arum and Roksa found that slightly more than a third of students in their study demonstrated no meaningful improvement on a test of general skills. And Robert was not rewarded in the labor market when he graduated in 2009. Two years after graduation, he was about $30,000 in debt, unemployed, and living back at home with his parents. About the only thing he had in common with Maria was a heavy debt load and a college degree.

Unfortunately, Maria's relatively smooth trajectory from college to well-paying job has not been true for most college graduates. Far more are struggling like Robert. The context has changed: 20 or 30 years ago, recent college graduates were finding more immediate opportunities in the labor market in jobs where their degree was required than in recent years. In the long run, having a college degree still pays off in much higher lifetime earnings, and eventually it is likely that Robert will be able to use his college degree to find his way but the context in which college graduates are entering the world of work is not as easy as it has been in the past. Many start out working at jobs that do not require a college degree and don't pay very well (see Figure 1.2).

How can we understand why Maria and Robert had such different college experiences and ended up on such different postcollege paths? There are many ways in

Figure 1.2 Employment Status of Recent College Graduates

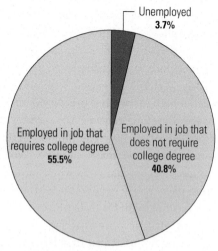

NOTE: Rates are from January 2020. Recent college graduates are those aged 22 to 27 with a bachelor's degree or higher.

SOURCE: Federal Reserve Bank of New York, "The Labor Market for Recent College Graduates," 2020. https://www.newyorkfed.org/research/college-labor-market/index.html

which the ideas and research of sociologists give us the tools to understand how Maria's and Robert's lives are unfolding the way they are. The common sense answer is simply that Maria just worked harder than Robert. And there appears to be some truth in that. But that is not likely the entire story. A sociological view of student experiences in high school and college poses a range of questions about how individuals (like Maria and Robert) and institutions interact in complex ways. For example, Maria's high school experience probably better trained her in how to study and helped her develop the discipline required to do well in her courses in college. Maria also seems to have gotten more support and mentoring along the way; perhaps this is just because she demanded it, but more likely her schools made it easier for her to find mentors and advisors, while Robert's high school failed in this critical mission. Instead of focusing on Maria's and Robert's individual differences, we might ask: How did Maria's educational background help prepare her for college, and how did Robert's handicap him?

There are also interesting questions we might ask from a societal perspective—after all, public high schools and colleges, and even private colleges, are subsidized by all taxpayers. Why is it that Robert (and others like him) are spending less time on their studies than students did a generation ago, but still earn passing grades? Have standards and expectations fallen across the board, and if so, why? Why do some schools become known as "party schools," and what are the consequences for students attending those schools? How has the nature of campus life changed in the past few decades? Are students more or less likely to join organizations or to interact with each other collectively

during their college years than at other points in their life? We could also ask these questions in a comparative context: Is the United States alone in these changes in higher education, or are there global shifts underway that are altering the meaning and experience of college across national borders?

As this example suggests, to fully grasp the meaning and outcomes of Maria's and Robert's college experiences using a sociological imagination, we need to take a step back and consider the contexts of their respective experiences. Rather than just patting Maria on the back while frowning on Robert for their respective college outcomes, we might think about the different ways in which they were each prepared to enter college. Sociological questions are concerned with a broad canvas of the modern world. They range widely from the basic units of human life—such as individuals' relationships with others—to the groups and organizations we are a part of, all the way up to a rapidly changing global economy that is impacting all of our social relationships.

As we move through the book, we will be introducing big questions concerning many of the most important topics sociologists are currently examining. But our first big point is this: Learning how to ask the important questions, and to think hard about how to probe for answers, is the heart of the sociological imagination.

The Endless Reach of the Sociological Imagination

1.1.4 Discuss the wide range of topics and areas of life that sociologists study.

Very few aspects of the social world *cannot* be studied sociologically. Consider a few of the different areas that some of the sociologists involved with *The Sociology Project* have examined in their own research:

- Harvey Molotch wrote a book about the sociology of the toilet, and another book about how common household products are first invented.

- Eric Klinenberg wrote a book on why so many people died in certain neighborhoods in Chicago during a heat wave in 1995.

- Ann Morning wrote a book about the social construction of racial classification schemes in biology and anthropology, showing how these schemes have changed numerous times and can never really be defined once and for all, even by so-called experts.

- Kathleen Gerson wrote a book about the conflicting relationship expectations of young men and women in the twenty-first century.

- Jeff Goodwin wrote a book about how and why revolutions occurred in some places, but not others.

- Steven Lukes wrote a book on how sociological ideas can better inform complex moral debates.

- Lynne Haney wrote a book exploring how mothers in prison raise small children while simultaneously serving time.

- Colin Jerolmack wrote a book about the relationship between humans and pigeons across the world.

- Paula England has written a number of papers on how the "hook-up" culture has changed the meaning and consequences of sexual activity among young adults.

- Jeff Manza wrote a book on how the rise of mass incarceration is undermining democratic elections in the United States.

We could mention many others. The point is that the reach of the sociological imagination is nearly endless and can be employed to explore almost any aspect of the human condition. But doing so requires a specific set of research tools and theoretical knowledge to begin seeking answers. In recent decades, methodological advances and the appearance of ever more information about human behavior (in the era of the internet and social media) has made it possible to study new topics or old topics in new ways. But there is one unifying theme. All of the questions sociologists ask build off a common starting point: How and in what ways do *social contexts* matter? We explore this in more detail in the next section.

Claudio Gallone/Avalon Licensing

| BIG QUESTION **1.2** | What Are Social Contexts, and Why Do They Matter? |

SOCIAL CONTEXTS: FROM INDIVIDUALS TO SOCIETIES

Sociology is fundamentally concerned with how individuals participate in, and are influenced by, the society in which they live. The stories of college students Maria and Robert provide one example. We refer to this influence of society on individuals as the **social context**. What do we mean when we refer to it?

One way of thinking about the diverse kinds of contexts individuals face is through the following thought experiment. Imagine being in the maternity ward of a large hospital, looking at a group of newborn babies (see the photo above). They are all helpless and adorable, with a full life ahead of them. In a perfect world, they would all have an equal opportunity to develop their many talents and abilities and succeed in life. In fact, we might look at those cute little creatures and think to ourselves, "Any one of these babies could one day be the president of the United States." But we also know that it is likely these babies will vary widely in their achievements and outcomes in life. Some will have a much easier path in life than others. Why?

At its core, the sociological imagination is the idea that individual lives unfold in contexts—in this case, social environments, including economic and cultural conditions, in which each of these infants will grow up and live. And those contexts are going to be very different for some babies than others. We don't know, looking at the babies in the cribs, which ones will have strong family support and encouragement growing up, or be able to attend good schools and afford to go to college, and if so, find mentors in college who can help guide them to a career pathway, or gain access to a good job and life opportunities as an adult. To be sure, if we did know something about the contexts in which each of these infants will grow up, we would be able to make much better-educated guesses about their prospects in life. So what are these contexts? We can immediately identify a variety of factors that are going to influence each baby's life:

- The child's immediate family (past and present), most importantly their parents' education level, wealth, and income

- The neighborhood and community the child will grow up in (and will live in as an adult)
- The education the child will get (including the quality of the schools they will attend)
- The types of organizations (churches, clubs, or groups) they will join or have access to
- The type of employment they will find

There are also other, broader contexts that each of these babies is born into that are important to keep in mind, such as

- the country and region they are born into (for example, a rich or poor country, a racist or sexist place or one that has taken measures to give everyone full citizenship), and
- the period of history into which they are born.

Each cute little baby will, in fact, enter social worlds that will have a huge impact on where they end up. Later in the book, we will explore each of these in more detail. For now, however, let's briefly consider some of these different contexts in more detail.

Families and Communities

1.2.1 Analyze how families and communities shape the social development of children.

We are born into families, and generations of sociological research have stressed the importance of family situations as a key to understanding how individuals develop. Our families shape who we are in a variety of ways: by giving us racial, ethnic, and religious identities; by teaching us the basic rules of society and how to behave in society or in particular social settings; by exposing us to certain networks of people; by providing the financial resources that our caregivers invest in our education and development, as well as the emotional and cognitive capacities they have developed in us through lifelong interactions; and (possibly) through the extent to which they are willing and able to help out later in life as we become adults and perhaps even attempt to raise a new generation of children of our own (such as helping buy cars or houses or pay for weddings).

This brings a second important context into view: the neighborhood and community in which we grow up. Living in a safe neighborhood with good schools, surrounded by families who encourage their children to do well and to be ambitious and confident, creates a different set of pathways than that experienced by a child living in an impoverished, high-crime neighborhood with poor schools. The latter environment can have many negative consequences, including not just obvious things like the continual risk of being a criminal victim and the lack of people who can provide positive role models and social networks helpful for finding jobs, but also more subtle

things like increased stress levels that come from living in such environments, as well as reduced sleep, elevated levels of anxiety, all of which have been shown to hinder school performance (Santiago et al. 2011).

For instance, New York University sociologist Pat Sharkey discovered a link between neighborhood violence and children's school performance (Sharkey 2010, 2019). He discovered that within the week following a homicide in their neighborhood, children in Chicago scored significantly lower on reading and vocabulary tests than they had in the week prior to the homicide. Among other things, Sharkey's research teaches us how violence can be absorbed by and transmitted through neighborhood contexts—and how children, who are perhaps the most vulnerable to such exposure, experience their effects at school as well as home. Aside from our collective interest in reducing violent crime, Sharkey's research also suggests we need to also think about the (usually hidden) consequences of neighborhood violence on innocent children.

Identities and Groups

1.2.2 Explain how our identities impact our opportunities in life.

Our **identities**—the conceptions we and others have about who we are and what groups or categories we are members of—provide another important type of social context in which individual lives unfold. We are born with certain physical attributes—most notably the color of our skin and our biological sex (although one or both may be ambiguous) and possibly a disability or an unusual physical characteristic (such as our height or weight). Our family also automatically imposes upon us other identities before we are old enough to play any role in choosing them ourselves, for example, religion, ethnicity, and the place or region we grow up in. As we move through life, we may be able to change some of these identities, and we often pick up new ones. Some identities are frozen; others can be shed or re-made over time.

However we acquire these identities, they are critical factors in predicting where we end up in life, the kinds of opportunities we have, and how the rest of the world views us. Some identities may be benign or neutral, and some may be positive or beneficial. Others may be a minor negative factor, while some can be a severe disadvantage that is difficult to overcome. For example, in virtually all societies that have ever been studied, men have more status and power than women; having the identity of "male" or "man" has historically conferred important advantages. Similarly, around the world today, members of dominant racial and ethnic groups have more opportunities and collect more rewards than members of other groups. Those living in the United States today may be especially aware of these divides and inequalities, but it is important to note that some version of them is found in virtually all societies. Yet just because they are universal does not mean we should accept or believe social hierarchies are fair and proper. Just because human societies almost always produce them, and those who benefit from them will struggle to maintain them, does not mean they are unchangeable.

Schools and Organizations

1.2.3 Discuss how the schools and organizations we participate in shape our lives and identities.

From the families we are raised in to the neighborhoods where we grow up, to the identities we have or adopt, the schools we attend and the organizations we join mark us in further important ways. Education is such an important element of our development into adulthood that it is hardly surprising that the quality and types of schools we attend will have a huge impact on our lives. What is more important is the ways in which the specific schools we attend convey a great deal about us to employers, friends and colleagues, and new people we meet.

The same thing is true of identities we form from the work we do and other organizational connections we forge: the churches, synagogues, or mosques we attend; the unions or professional associations we join as adults; how and where we volunteer; the clubs and civic or political groups in which we choose to participate in. All of these organizations provide potential contexts to gain important types of experience and insights, and/or find opportunities. Our membership in these organizations also associates us with a certain identity. Many may be positive associations, and some may even be more meaningful than other identities. There are, however, some organizations where membership can leave lasting negative marks that cannot easily be removed, such as becoming a prison inmate.

Getting involved in a church or other religious organization is one way in which people meet each other and form communities and social networks.

Social, Economic, and Historical Contexts

1.2.4 Analyze the ways in which the social and economic context we are born into shapes the opportunities available to us.

C. Wright Mills emphasized that the sociological imagination involves continual reflection on the connection between individual biography and historical context. What exactly does that mean? For one thing, the social, economic, and historical contexts we are born into matter enormously for what is possible for us to achieve and do. For example, a Black male born in the South in 1900 (during the era of Jim Crow, in which laws and opportunities in the South were explicitly designed to privilege Whites) faced a very different environment and very different opportunities than the same male born today, simply by virtue of the time and place he was alive. A child growing up in a working-class family in Detroit in the 1940s—when the automobile industry was booming and the city was home to a large number of well-paying working-class jobs—had a different set of economic opportunities than the same child growing up in contemporary Detroit (where in recent years the area has been hard hit by a devastating decline in manufacturing jobs, and unemployment among people without college degrees is very high). Women entering adulthood in the 1950s faced a different set of choices and cultural expectations than women entering adulthood since the gender revolution of the 1970s, when occupations and opportunities historically closed to women opened up and the ideal (if not always the reality) of egalitarian marriage began to develop. The historical contexts of our lives are often critical, and they change over time.

Finally, all of these contexts are influenced by a global environment. We live in an era where events in regions and countries around the world can influence us wherever we are located; in other words, what happens in one place can shape what happens in other places. For example, many types of jobs once done in the United States are now performed by workers in other countries, who will do those jobs for less pay. At the same time, individuals today have more opportunities than ever before to explore life in other places. Virtually every college has a study abroad program, where students can experience living elsewhere for a semester or a year. Individuals can also choose to move to another country and make a life there—there are some limits on this, but almost every country in the world has communities of immigrants, people who were raised in one country but now live in another. As jobs, ideas, and technology move around the globe at an unprecedented pace, it is increasingly clear that we are connected to people and places far away.

When people patiently stand in line, in an orderly fashion, they are obeying social norms that promote efficiency and fairness (i.e., "wait your turn"). Usually there is no authority figure who can enforce the norms; people just usually obey, and if they didn't, a chaotic situation would result.

Sociology as the Study of Social Contexts

1.2.5 Explain the distinction between social interaction and social structure.

Having introduced the critical idea of social contexts, we can now define sociology more fully and clearly: Sociology is the study of the diverse contexts within which individuals' lives unfold, how individuals navigate those contexts and, sometimes, when and how they contribute to changing them. More specifically, our social worlds have two central components: social interaction and social structure. **Social interaction** refers to the way people act together, including how they modify and alter their behavior in response to the presence of others. Social interaction is governed by a set of **norms**, which are the basic rules of society that help us know what is and is not appropriate to do in any situation. As we interact with others, we engage in a process of working within those rules and norms to try to present a pleasing version of ourselves to others. Examples include our social media and professional website profiles, our business cards, and the different ways we characterize ourselves in social settings when we meet new people or introduce ourselves to a group. For example, the authors of this chapter are sometimes sociologists, sometimes professors and teachers, sometimes parents, sometimes politically active citizens, and sometimes various other things depending on the situation. We always occupy the same body, but who exactly we are (or how we characterize ourselves) depends on our social contexts and how we or others characterize us.

The importance of the "social" part of social interaction becomes most clear to us when we violate societal rules of acceptable behavior (or when we imagine the social sanctions that would follow if we did violate the rules). Consider this example: What would happen if a student in a college classroom were to suddenly stand up on their desk and

Meeting other people involves a complicated set of social norms that can vary depending on cultural practices, the type of situation, and other factors. Handshaking is one way people commonly greet each other; however, there are different kinds of possible handshakes. We take social cues to know which handshake is appropriate.

shout profanities at the instructor or fellow students? Even if some students might occasionally feel like doing this, there are powerful constraints that discourage such action. Without anyone saying anything, it is understood that if we did this, our classmates might shun us; the instructor might lower our grade or, perhaps, call campus security to escort us out of the class. So even when we are annoyed or frustrated or bored in class, or in similar situations (like being in seemingly endless meetings or standing in long lines), we generally know to keep our true feelings to ourselves.

But even if you think there is no chance of any significant consequences, you still know when certain behaviors are regarded as wrong or inappropriate. How? Sociologists argue that we continually censor ourselves because of our concern for the social consequences of our action. We learn and absorb societal norms from our interactions with important others (such as parents, friends, teachers, ministers, or mentors). Knowing the norms, and rules for (if any) in any situation is important for avoiding embarrassment and acting appropriately in different contexts. Most of the time, we just want to "fit in" wherever we find ourselves, but in order to do so, we have to know what is expected of us.

Where do these norms and rules that govern social interaction come from, and why do they persist over time? Part of the reason is simply that people just do what is expected and, in the process, reinforce and reproduce those rules (or, sometimes, subtly begin to change them). But there is more to it than that. Sociologists use the concept of **social structure** to describe the many diverse ways in which the rules and norms of everyday life come together to form enduring patterns that shape and govern social interactions. Social structure, in this sense, lies in the background of every social interaction. Social structure is a messy but essential concept, one we explore in more detail in Chapter 5 and elsewhere throughout the book.

There are two critical components of social structure. First, every society has a complex set of roles and **social hierarchies**, the social positions that both define our relationships with each other, while also giving some individuals and groups higher status and more power than others. Whatever role or position we occupy in any interaction—student, child, parent, leader of a group, member of a group, and so on—our actions, and indeed our range of options for action, are impacted by the rules and powers that are associated with it. For example, the child is supposed to defer to the parent, the worker to the business owner, and the patient to the doctor.

The second aspect of social structure comprises the norms and **institutions** of society. The concept of institutions is one of the most difficult in the language of sociology, and we will encounter it repeatedly throughout the book, again, especially in Chapter 5. Institutions are longstanding and socially important practices (like marriage, families, education, and economic markets), and organizations that govern those practices. The simple point is this: Every society creates institutions that guide the development and behavior of all members of that society. These two aspects of social structure—roles/hierarchies and norms/institutions—provide the essential frameworks for almost everything we do in our daily lives, including our interactions with others. Although they are distinct, there is a critical point to

keep in mind, that we will return to throughout the book: Social structure and social interaction inform each other. It is through our social interactions that we reinforce (or occasionally challenge) norms and institutions, and those norms and institutions in turn shape and guide our interactions with others. We act, *and* we are acted upon.

In spite of their importance, social structures are rarely obvious to us unless we know where to look. Because they lie in the background of our experience, we may not necessarily notice our society's hierarchies and institutions. In many cases, social structures become most visible when they limit our freedom in some way. Sometimes the rules, customs, laws, and regulations of society can prevent us from doing something we otherwise might do if we were completely free of all social structures. Imagine if there were no laws or norms against cheating in college. At first, that might seem like a new kind of freedom has been granted. It's probably not too hard to guess that there would be vastly more cheating than there is today. But there are problems. Suddenly everyone's performance (cheaters as well as honest students) would quickly become suspect. Employers and graduate schools would have no good way of trusting students' grades. The value of college education might begin to erode. Sometimes, too much freedom can lead to unsatisfactory outcomes!

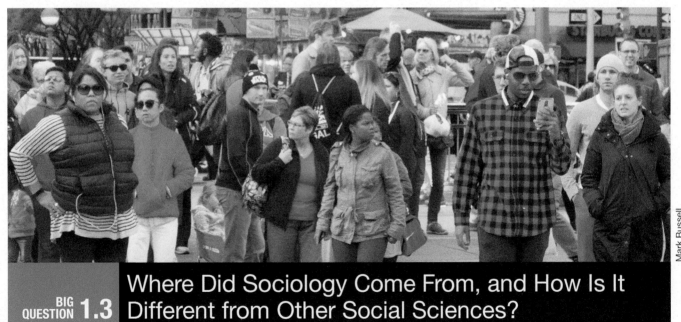

Mark Bussell

BIG QUESTION 1.3 Where Did Sociology Come From, and How Is It Different from Other Social Sciences?

THE SOCIOLOGY OF THE SOCIAL SCIENCES

We can apply the sociological imagination to study many topics, including even sociology itself! If we were to undertake the sociological study of sociology, we would need to ask questions such as the following: In what social contexts did sociology begin to develop? How does

sociology fit into, and relate to, the other social sciences? How is research conducted by sociologists different from research in other social sciences? Why and when is sociological knowledge thought to be valuable by ordinary people, people involved in trying to bring about social change, or even the people in positions of power who decide what kinds of knowledge should be obtained by citizens? And, of course, one last question that students (or their tuition-paying parents) would need to ask: What exactly can someone *do* with sociological knowledge? In this section, we explore these questions.

The Birth of Sociology

1.3.1 Discuss the origins of sociology as a discipline.

Scholars and ordinary people have puzzled about their social worlds for as long as humans have lived in settled communities. Early on, religious and philosophical thinkers dominated discussions about the social world, but most of their conversations focused on abstract debates (such as, "Is slavery wrong or immoral") and **anecdotes** (singular stories about incidents or people). Sociology, as well other social sciences, really began to develop when growing numbers of people started to turn from focusing on these abstract debates to wanting to know more systematically and more specifically about how things actually work in the real world. Perhaps if some of the religious and philosophical defenders of slavery in the nineteenth century had visited some slave plantations and interviewed enslaved people about their condition, or even better spent a few weeks living as a slave, rather than relying on anecdotes they received from other people, they might have been compelled to reach somewhat different conclusions about the morality of slavery. In other words, the desire to answer hard questions about the human experience with systematic information, or what is known as **data**, is at the center of the modern sociological enterprise.

The development of this new way of questioning and seeking answers to issues and problems of the modern world unfolded in fits and starts throughout the Middle Ages and into the nineteenth century, but the idea that the social world could be studied with rigor and scientific methods akin to those that had been applied to the natural world began to take hold from the 1880s onward. Key early thinkers who contributed ideas that were very influential in the development of sociology and social theory were at work long before that, (some of which are covered in more detail in Chapter 2) including Ibn Khaldūn (1332–1406), Adam Smith (1723–1790), Mary Wollstonecraft (1759–1797), Karl Marx (1818–1883), and Harriet Martineau (1802–1876). But these key thinkers would not have thought of themselves as sociologists (as there really was no such thing at the time). And in spite of their often extraordinary insights, they did not have access

to any of the kinds of data and other information available to modern social scientists to permit them to reach more careful conclusions.

The term *sociology* was first used by the French philosopher Auguste Comte (1798–1857), in 1839. Interestingly, Comte thought that sociology would eventually become the ultimate science of social life, with other disciplines contributing pieces of knowledge, while sociology would integrate those pieces into a coherent science of society. Comte envisioned that sociological science would entail both what he called "social statics" (the study of societies as they are) and "social dynamics" (the processes of social change) (Comte [1839–1853] 2009).

As the nineteenth century wore on, a variety of new ways of studying the social world began to emerge, just as Comte predicted. Between 1880 and 1910, the social sciences started to settle down into organized bodies of knowledge and develop distinctive disciplinary profiles. For sociology, this settling down first occurred in Europe—primarily in France and Germany, the latter of which had the best universities in the world at the time. Emile Durkheim (1858–1917) founded the first European sociology department at the University of Bordeaux in 1895, as well as the first major European journal of sociology (*L'Annee Sociologique*) in 1898. In Germany, a group of early sociologists—among them Max Weber (1864–1920)—created an influential journal called the *Archiv für Sozialwissenschaft und Sozialpolitik* (*Archives for Social Science*

The Chicago School of Sociology (based at the University of Chicago) developed many important ideas about society based on detailed studies in the city of Chicago (shown here in an image from the 1890s). It is apparent from this historic photo that the city faced problems related to overcrowding and sanitation during that time period. Such issues helped give impetus to the creation of sociology in the first place.

and Social Welfare), establishing an identity for sociology as a discipline in that country.

On the other side of the Atlantic, a distinctively American tradition of sociology also emerged around the same time, initially centered at the University of Chicago, where the first sociology department in America was founded in 1895. Frequently taking the city of Chicago as its laboratory, the so-called **Chicago School** intensively studied the problems of cities and the groups of people living in them, developing a body of knowledge that remains influential to this day.

It is worth noting that in both Europe and the United States, the early professional social scientists were almost all White men. Sociologists like W. E. B. Du Bois (1869–1963) and Jane Addams (1860–1935), although recognized both at the time and today for their genius and their social, intellectual, and political contributions, were not offered the kinds of academic appointments given to their White, male peers. Instead of just doing research, DuBois and Addams developed careers combining research and social activism. They, and a small handful of other pioneering sociologists, placed inequalities of race and gender squarely on the emerging agenda of sociology. The intellectual growth of the field in recent decades owes much to the recovery and expansion of the insights of a more diverse group of scholars.

By the 1920s, sociology had become an increasingly popular field of study for college students and was recognized for its distinctive way of understanding and researching social life. Sociology had emerged as one of the five major social sciences (alongside economics, political science, psychology, and anthropology). Today, as we noted earlier in the chapter, sociologists are engaged in the study of many key societal issues and controversies, working from universities as well as inside government agencies, in nonprofit and nongovernmental organizations, and in policy and political advocacy groups.

Sociology and the Industrial Revolution

1.3.2 Explain the roles of industrialization and urbanization in the development of sociology.

So far, our very brief sketch has focused on early sociological ideas and the thinkers who began to formulate them. While some key thinkers such as Marx, Durkheim, and Weber helped to create a new body of sociological knowledge, the existence of great thinkers and schools alone cannot explain what helps diverse ideas come together to create a disciplined body of knowledge. As with individual lives, so too does sociology have a "social context" that shaped its growth and development. Two critical developments spurred the social sciences in general and sociology in particular: the very rapid period of **industrialization** (the growth of factories

and large-scale goods production) and **urbanization** (the growth of cities) in the late nineteenth century in the United States, Europe, and elsewhere. This was a period when new technologies and innovations made possible the growth of large-scale manufacturing of consumer products, transforming economies based primarily in agriculture to those based in the manufacturing of goods. This period of urbanization was marked by growth in the proportion of the population living in urban areas and cities, which grew rapidly in size between 1850 and 1920 in both Europe and the United States. Figure 1.3 illustrates the growth of cities and surrounding metropolitan areas in the United States during this period. The new job opportunities in rapidly growing factories pulled people away from farms and rural communities and provided economic opportunities for wave after wave of immigrants from other countries who arrived in steadily increasing numbers from the 1870s until the early 1920s.

The social changes brought about by industrialization and urbanization were immense. The contexts of both individual lives as well as whole communities were changing rapidly. The exploding cities that developed in the United States and Europe from the middle of the nineteenth century onward were teeming with **social problems** that were markedly different from the agricultural economies of previous centuries. To begin with, these cities were rife with high levels of poverty. Even though incomes were rising, the cost of living was relatively high compared to the farms and small towns of the nineteenth century. The pace of home construction was always behind the rapidly growing demand, pushing up rents and forcing families to live in small spaces or double up with others. Food costs were also higher. Further, the early factories often had difficult working conditions, and in the United States few workers were organized into unions which could have provided some protections.

The upshot of this period of exceptional expansion of industry and cities was that urban life was viewed by many as troubled. Cities were dirty places—this was largely before public health and public sanitation measures

Figure 1.3 Growth of Urban Population in the United States

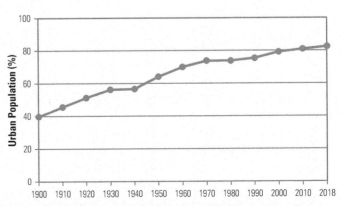

SOURCE: For years 1900–2010, Dicennial Census, U.S. Census Bureau. For year 2018, United Nations Population Division. data.worldbank.org.

A view of the Park Avenue Armory in New York City. Constructed in the late 19th century, it was used to provide private military training to young upper-class men (an enormous central hall inside the facility was used to practice drills), who were members of a privately-funded militia. It also served as a warehouse for military equipment in the event the militia had to go into battle. It was paid for by New York City's rich to provide protection in the event of an uprising by the city's poor. That anyone thought such measures were necessary highlights just how pervasive fears of social revolution were in a period of rapid social change.

had become widely implemented—and they were breeding grounds for disease, infant mortality, and early death. They were also places where crime and violence were much more common than in rural communities. Finally, and in a quite different vein, they were places where people could organize themselves to protest unpleasant conditions of life. Instead of tolerating misery alone on one's farm, now it was possible to meet and discuss problems with dozens or hundreds of people living in close proximity. These challenges threatened city rulers and economic elites, who even began creating their own private armies to repeal threats to their wealth.

In the face of these new conditions and challenges, sociology found its place as part of a broader effort to understand the sources of these emerging social challenges, and how they might be better addressed. Of course, sociology was not the only academic discipline to emerge from this period of social change; the other social sciences also appeared around the same time, in the late nineteenth and early twentieth centuries, and all were developing alongside another important context—the modern research university. Research universities were schools that began to develop graduate degree programs in many fields, including sociology. There, young scholars could be trained to do research, rather than figure it out on their own (as their nineteenth century predecessors generally had to). As noted, the most famous training ground for young sociologists was at the University of Chicago, but other significant

sociology PhD programs emerged by the 1910s and 1920s at a number of other universities.

Sociology's Siblings

1.3.3 Compare and contrast sociology with the other social sciences.

While all the social sciences were born from a similar impulse, to understand the emerging social worlds spawned by industrialization and urban growth, there was considerable disagreement over where to go from that common starting point. So how did sociology come to differ from other social sciences? What is the nature of the sibling rivalry between them? We would point to two fundamental distinctions:

1. Sociology's concepts and theories cover a wider range of topics than other disciplines—sociologists are rather "promiscuous" in what they study.

2. Sociology's explanations of how the external world shapes behaviors of individuals and social outcomes are broader than those of other disciplines, and encompass different units of analysis. Sociologists move *from individuals to groups to institutions to nation-states to global society*. Sociology is the social science discipline that is most concerned about how different parts of society link up to and mutually influence one another.

Of course, the danger of having such a broad spectrum of topics to study is that it can be hard to define the parameters of the field. The authors of this chapter are often asked this question: What exactly *is* sociology? Even professional sociologists struggle to give a short, simple answer. Sociologists don't define themselves according to a specific arena of life, unlike other social scientists. Political scientists are primarily concerned with topics that involve governments and the policies they produce. Economists are mainly concerned with individuals' economic behavior (microeconomics) and the performance of the national (or global) economy (macroeconomics). Psychologists are interested in understanding the workings of the human brain. Anthropologists claim special expertise in the practices of diverse cultures and how they vary across time and place.

Because sociology cannot be categorized by a specific subject matter, it often moves into areas that are the "home turf" of the other social sciences. As our name indicates, sociologists claim scientific expertise over those parts of life we call the "social," and in topics with social significance. But the "social" is a bit fuzzier of a topic and area of expertise than those studied by other disciplines. That is, most people can roughly grasp what a political scientist means when they study "government"—or what an economist does when researching "the economy." But sociologists often get perplexed looks when we say we study the "social world." It took one of our grandmothers 20 years to stop telling her friends that her granddaughter was a professor of "socialism" (rather than sociology). For her, this was a concrete way to make sense of the social and to translate it into something meaningful (and also a bit scary, as she was a staunch Republican!). So while sociologists' refusal to break up the world into small, narrow slices and proclaim expertise over them does cause confusion, most sociologists would have it no other way.

So how does the broad agenda of sociologists compare with other disciplines? Consider the difference between sociology and psychology. Psychology is centered on the study of the mind, the psyche, and the physical brain. Sociologists have much to learn from psychological findings, some of which we've already mentioned in this chapter (for example, psychologists invented the concept and have more deeply researched how and why humans so often rely on stereotypes). At the same time, sociologists part company with many traditional psychologists in insisting that individuals (and their minds and psyches) must also always be located in larger social contexts. For sociologists, it is not enough to explain individual behavior by simply understanding the intricacies of the psyche or the mental processes common to all humans. Because individuals are embedded in families and communities, as well as in cultural, economic, and political environments, sociologists view human behavior as caused by something more than just what individual brains tell us to do. To explain why individuals do what they do, in other words, social structures must also come into view.

A similar gap separates sociology from economics. Economists pride themselves on building and testing models of economic behavior using clear and simple assumptions about human nature. Their ideas, and the mathematical models of human behavior they develop, are often elegant and lead to clear predictions that can be tested by researchers. Sociologists, by contrast, tend to believe that for all of their impressive advances, economists sometimes miss important outcomes because they don't consider a wide enough range of factors and forces affecting human behavior. For example, when people engage in buying goods or services, they are not just influenced by getting the most value at a price they can afford. They are also influenced in their decisions by social norms, how much they trust the seller, fads or fashions that make the "value" of a good different than it might appear, and many other non-economic considerations. So while sociological theories tend to be messier and more difficult to

test than many economic theories, they can also produce a wider range of possible explanations that, when successful, can produce genuinely new understandings.

Sibling rivalry aside, most social scientists today end up drawing on the ideas and insights of other fields and disciplines as well as their own. After a century or so of building their own disciplines, bodies of knowledge, and professional associations, in recent years there has been a strong movement in the social sciences to blur the boundaries between the fields. **Interdisciplinary research**, as it is known, is an increasingly central part of learning about any topic in sociology or the social sciences. Few students and scholars in any social science would be foolish enough not to draw on ideas and research from neighboring social sciences. And sociology is perhaps the most likely to do this—it is unquestionably the most interdisciplinary of all the traditional social science disciplines. As a result, sociology has many subfields that reflect interdisciplinary connections: economic sociology, political sociology, social psychology, educational sociology, the sociology of public health, environmental sociology, and so forth. Depending on the question at hand, sociologists may need to know something about the research and theories developed by economists, political scientists, psychologists, or anthropologists (or sometimes more than one of these disciplines). Sociology also often draws on the work of historians—an area that is traditionally placed in the humanities but is increasingly closely related to the social sciences and sociology in particular. Although our main interest in this book is introducing you to sociological insights and approaches, we would certainly *not* want to leave the impression that sociology by itself has all the answers to all the questions that social scientists raise. It does not.

Sociology's Children

1.3.4 Identify some of the spin-off fields that originally started in sociology.

One interesting side note on the relationship between sociology and the other social sciences is the way in which sociology has helped to spawn a number of new areas of study. In most colleges today, there are a large number of spin-off majors and programs that largely began in sociology. This list includes such fields as criminology, gender studies, Black or African American studies, Latinx studies, LGBTQ studies, urban studies, rural studies, organizational or management studies, industrial relations or labor studies, demography, communication/media studies, and others. There was once a time when much of the research and scholarship on these topics was done within sociology. But for various reasons, these subfields eventually split off from sociology to become independent fields of study of their own (and develop their own bases of knowledge). It is, indeed, quite remarkable just how many spin-off academic disciplines originally started (at least in part) in sociology, a record of innovation and intellectual diversity of which sociologists can be proud. Even today, there are exciting new areas of study in sociology that may eventually grow into disciplines of their own. At its core, however, sociology will remain a foundational discipline for many of these interdisciplinary social sciences. And in this sense, learning the basics of sociology is an essential foundation for any one of these newer fields.

Conclusion: Looking Ahead

Our goal for this book is to provide our readers with the foundation for developing their own sociological imaginations. By understanding how individuals' lives are embedded in particular social contexts that are not always of their own choosing, as well as the role of social interaction and social structures, we hope that you will learn to appreciate how personal issues that individuals face are often larger societal problems. Our fondest hope is that our readers will go on to take other sociology courses. But even if this is your only experience with sociology, there are many take-away lessons for everyday life—learning how organizations work, how schools function, the tricks of social interaction, the cultural underpinning of inequality—that can arm readers with knowledge of the social world.

One of the unique aspects of *The Sociology Project* is that the authors of each of the chapters in this book are writing about the topics that they spend their lives researching and teaching. We believe that a collective approach to presenting the discipline of sociology provides a better way of unearthing and exciting our readers' sociological imaginations. In the course of thinking about (and teaching) the topics we are writing about, we have developed deep appreciation for the excitement of studying our respective topics that we hope to convey in the chapters that follow.

In order to create a unified text, we've taken a number of steps to make it easier to move from chapter to chapter. Each chapter opens with a puzzle or story about a sociological research project that highlights one or more of the key sociological problems that will be tackled in the chapter. Following this, each chapter identifies a set of big questions that have defined the research and teaching puzzles of the field. These questions organize what follows as the authors explore how sociological thinking about each question has developed. At all points, some basic facts and data are helpful to have in hand, but at the same time we want our readers to learn to think sociologically through learning how to ask hard questions, and where to look for answers.

In short, we want to stress that this book—and indeed sociology as a discipline—truly is a *project*: something we are collectively engaged in building and something for which there are relatively few completely settled answers. The problems confronted by sociologists are hard questions because there are so many things that influence individuals and group life. This is what makes sociology endlessly interesting and a sociological imagination very much worth acquiring.

The Big Questions Revisited 1

1.1 What Is the Sociological Imagination, and Why Is It Worth Acquiring? This section introduced the concept of the sociological imagination and explored how it helps us learn to ask hard questions.

The Sociological Imagination

Looking at the Social World Through a Sociological Lens

Learning Objective 1.1.1: Discuss how a sociological imagination helps to challenge stereotypes.

Engaging Our Sociological Imaginations: From Personal Puzzles to Sociological Questions

Learning Objective 1.1.2: Explain the process for forming sociological questions.

Sociological Questions: A Detailed Example

Learning Objective 1.1.3: Identify the types of questions that sociologists are particularly well equipped to explore.

The Endless Reach of the Sociological Imagination

Learning Objective 1.1.4: Discuss the wide range of topics and areas of life that sociologists study.

Key Terms

society (p. 4)   sociology (p. 4)   zoonotic (p. 4)
sociological imagination (p. 6)   stereotype (p. 6)

1.2 **What Are Social Contexts, and Why Do They Matter?** Sociology is fundamentally concerned with how we are influenced by society. All of us are situated in an array of social contexts. This section explored how these influence us and our behavior.

Social Contexts: From Individuals to Societies

Families and Communities
Learning Objective 1.2.1: Analyze how families and communities shape the social development of children.

Identities and Groups
Learning Objective 1.2.2: Explain how our identities impact our opportunities in life.

Schools and Organizations
Learning Objective 1.2.3: Discuss how the schools and organizations we participate in shape our lives and identities.

Social, Economic, and Historical Contexts
Learning Objective 1.2.4: Analyze the ways in which the social and economic context we are born into shapes the opportunities available to us.

Sociology as the Study of Social Contexts
Learning Objective 1.2.5: Explain the distinction between social interaction and social structure.

Key Terms
social context (p. 11) identity (p. 12) social interaction (p. 14) norm (p. 14) social structure (p. 14) social hierarchy (p. 15) institution (p. 15)

1.3 **Where Did Sociology Come From, and How Is It Different from Other Social Sciences?** This section examined the context in which sociology began to develop and explored the question of how sociology fits into, and relates to, the other social sciences.

The Sociology of the Social Sciences

The Birth of Sociology
Learning Objective 1.3.1: Discuss the origins of sociology as a discipline.

Sociology and the Industrial Revolution
Learning Objective 1.3.2: Explain the roles of industrialization and urbanization in the development of sociology.

Sociology's Siblings
Learning Objective 1.3.3: Compare and contrast sociology with the other social sciences.

Sociology's Children
Learning Objective 1.3.4: Identify some of the spin-off fields that originally started in sociology.

Key Terms
anecdote (p. 16) data (p. 16) Chicago School (p. 17) industrialization (p. 17) urbanization (p. 17) social problems (p. 17) interdisciplinary research (p. 19)

Chapter 2
Social Theory

by Jeff Manza, Thomas Ertman, Lynne Haney, and Steven Lukes

At the heart of the sociological imagination are the theories about society that give us tools to know what to look for and think about when we seek to understand the social world. The inspiration to develop ideas into social theories can come from a wide variety of sources. One of the authors of this chapter, Steven Lukes, recounts how he was motivated to think about some classical questions in social theory.

It was during a dinner conversation in Buenos Aires at the height of what was known as Argentina's "Dirty War" in the mid-1970s that I became motivated to think about morality and power. During this time thousands of people—among them trade unionists, journalists, and students—"disappeared" by orders of the Argentinean military government; that is, they were tortured and killed, often in clandestine detention centers, or in some cases simply dropped from planes into the sea. Powerful rulers and governments have resorted to torturing and killing their opponents as a way of holding on to power for centuries. When I voiced concern over what I then knew of these atrocities, my dinner companion— who was the local head of one of the world's leading news agencies—astonished me with his response. I should understand, he explained to me, that in Argentina a lower value was set on life than in Britain, from which I came.

My astonishment led me to a few questions with implications for approaching issues sociologically. In my simple disbelief of his factual claim, I first wondered on what evidence was it based? My second question was: What motivated him to make this sweeping claim? As a journalist, whose task was to give an unbiased account of the local scene to the world, he seemed to be drawing on personal impressions and stereotyping prejudices. Yet he also seemed to want to offer an impartial and comparative perspective to an overheated and ill-informed visitor.

While this is not, I hasten to say, a story about good journalism, it does raise the question of what corrective procedures sociology, as distinct from those of journalism, can bring to overcome bias and approach objectivity in marshaling evidence. That question is general, but it is especially intriguing where values are what is at issue, for we know that what people value is shaped by societal contexts and can vary from one context to another or one culture to another. While Argentineans surely have many

My Sociological Imagination

THOMAS ERTMAN

As an undergraduate I was passionate about both history and philosophy, but as graduation drew nearer, I wasn't sure how these interests could be reconciled. It was a history professor who suggested I might consider studying sociology because the field encompasses both social theory and historical sociology. I took his advice and quickly discovered that there is hardly an area of life, past or present, to which the sociological imagination cannot fruitfully apply itself. I myself have written and taught on the emergence of the state in the West; democracy and dictatorship in nineteenth- and twentieth-century Europe; the development of opera and ballet as art forms; and music, literature, and painting in France and Germany. The common thread that unites this research has been the inspiration I have derived from the classical social theorists, especially Max Weber. Although he died nearly a century ago, his writings remain as relevant as ever to our world.

Understanding the circumstances or conditions under which societies change is one of the three common themes that all of the major sociological theories have sought to address in one way or another.

Mark Bussell

Aduardo Di Baia, File/AP Images

Hebe de Bonafini, the head of Argentina's Mothers of Plaza de Mayo group, whose children disappeared during the dirty war of the 1970s, leads one of the marches in Buenos Aires's Plaza de Mayo in December 1979.

distinctive attitudes and customs, it was hard to imagine that caring less about their own lives was one of these. What can sociology contribute to assessing which values are variable and which are constant across contexts and cultures? We know, of course, that suicide bombers do sacrifice their lives, but to notice that is to raise the larger question of the power of ideology and the sociological task of identifying the conditions under which it can motivate individuals to such extreme behavior.

Moreover, it was striking that my journalist companion avoided all mention of power relations— understandably enough, for we were in a restaurant and could be overheard. The context in Argentina at that time was, of course, extreme: a context of terror and coercion, of censorship and self-censorship, where journalists and others bit their tongues and went along with the status quo. How do we ever know what part those in power play in shaping our values, beliefs, and preferences? Sometimes what is extreme can shed light on the normal and the routine. In Argentina, the impact of those in power on ordinary lives was all too visible, if unmentioned over dinner. But how is the sociologist to investigate the less overt and more hidden operations of power in normal times and places?

The memory of this striking conversation stayed with me and played an important role in turning my attention to social theories of morality and theories about the relationship between morality and power.

Lukes's inspiration to think about how social theory could contribute to both understanding individual and societal morality exemplifies the kinds of challenges that social theorists have taken on. By developing frameworks for understanding societies as a whole (or major components within it), leading social theories are a central part of the sociological imagination. In this chapter, we explore some of the most influential of these theories that have developed over the past 150 years.

The Big Questions

1. **What is social theory?** Social theories enable us to see the social world in different ways. In this section, we identify three common themes that all of the major sociological theories have sought to address.

2. **How did the early social theorists make sense of the world?** The foundations of modern sociology, and social theory as we know it today, can be traced to the writings of a handful of key thinkers working in the second half of the nineteenth century and the early twentieth century. In this section, we introduce the classical social theories of Karl Marx, Emile Durkheim, Max Weber, Georg Simmel, W. E. B. Du Bois, and Jane Addams.

3. **What innovations in social theory emerged in the mid-twentieth century?** After World War II, the interests of social theorists began to shift in new and unexpected directions, and leadership in the development of social theory and sociology as a whole passed from being located primarily in Europe to America. Here, we introduce the new directions in social theory that were embodied by functionalism, conflict theory, and symbolic interactionism.

4. **How has a new generation of social theory evolved?** Finally, we provide a brief sampling of some important new theories that have evolved since the 1960s. How have contemporary theorists built upon or transformed the work of classical and mid-twentieth century social theory?

Mark Bussell

BIG QUESTION 2.1 | What Is Social Theory?

SEEING THE SOCIAL WORLD THROUGH SOCIAL THEORY

Learning social theory is a little like putting on a pair of 3D glasses or night-vision goggles: *Theories*, like specialized glasses, enable us to see things in a different way. Theories guide, but they also provoke: They may encourage us to pay more attention to something we had ignored, ask new or unusual questions that we don't normally think about, or make arguments we so strongly disagree with that we are compelled to come up with a better approach. We don't necessarily need social theories to make observations about the world around us, but they help us know what to look for.

The ambitions of social theorists are considerable, often nothing less than developing a way of understanding how whole societies hold together and how they organize and impact the lives of the individuals who live within them. The best and most lasting social theories have changed the way we understand societies, and the relationships between individuals and groups within those societies, in fundamental ways. In this sense, social theory is central to the sociological imagination.

The Diversity of Social Theory

2.1.1 **Define social theory and the range of different social theories.**

Social theories are systematic ideas about the relationship between individuals and societies. To put it another way, they are analytical frameworks for understanding the social

Figure 2.1 Three Common Questions Examined by Social Theorists

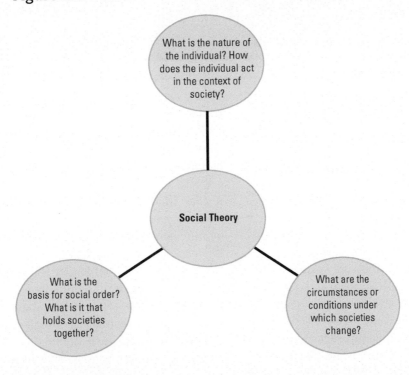

world. This definition is not, unfortunately, very helpful, because there is a wide variety of different kinds of social theories. Some can be very grand—seeking to explain universal features of all societies—while others are much more modest, applying only to a single topic that sociologists study, such as theories about race, gender, or religion.

Sociology is also somewhat unusual among the social sciences in having multiple and often competing social theories and theoretical traditions. The multiplicity of theoretical traditions can be confusing at first. While it does take some effort to sort out the competing ideas and how they relate to one another, we hope to show in this chapter that there are rewards to this effort as well. In spite of the abundance of competing theoretical traditions, there is also a great deal of dialogue among theorists and theoretical traditions, and most contemporary sociologists draw insights and inspiration from more than one theoretical tradition in their work. In this chapter, we will emphasize both the key distinctions and their vital connections as we introduce the most influential of the social theories that have appeared in the past 150 years.

There are three common themes that all of the major sociological theories have sought to address in one way or another, as illustrated in Figure 2.1 (see also Joas and Knobl 2009, p. 18).

Social theories must contend with each of these questions, and leading theorists have done so in varying ways. The first question—what is the nature of the individual?—raises the fundamental question of how to think about the relationship between individuals and the social world. Many of the themes raised in the first chapter reflect this puzzle. The second question—what is the basis for social order?—probes the question of what holds societies together. Despite all of the ways societies are riven with conflict, when we look back at the longer movement of history, what is most striking is how persistent common social practices and institutions actually are. Finally, the third question relates directly to the second: Societies and their major institutions may change only slowly, but change does happen. What are the conditions that make social change possible?

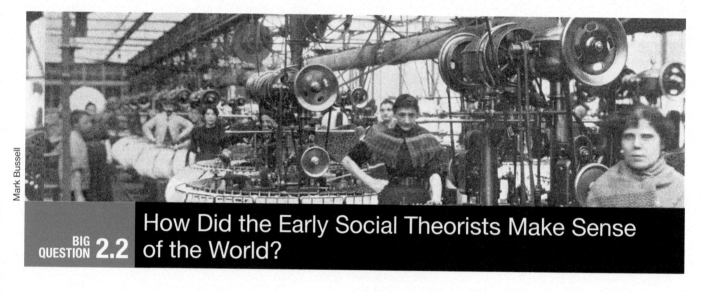

Mark Bussell

BIG QUESTION 2.2 How Did the Early Social Theorists Make Sense of the World?

CLASSICAL SOCIAL THEORY IN THE LATE NINETEENTH AND EARLY TWENTIETH CENTURIES

Some of the earliest theoretical ideas about society emerged hundreds of years ago and paved the way for the development of modern social theory. Islamic scholar Ibn Khaldun (1332–1406) was the first to use observation and history, rather than speculative moral or religious philosophy, in his attempts to develop a theory of societies. Eighteenth-century Scottish philosopher Adam Smith (1723–1790) developed theories of altruism and capitalism that framed later discussions of these topics. As noted in Chapter 1, French philosopher August Comte (1798–1857) was the first social theorist to explicitly use the term *sociology* as a distinct field of study. Comte is most well known

among sociologists for two things: (1) his landmark contributions to the rise of **positivism** (the claim that every valid idea should be able to be tested with evidence, including that of the social world), and (2) his view of the hierarchy of knowledge, or the idea that sociology plays a special role standing above the other social sciences and history. Comte's work became known to English readers via a very influential and heavily modified translation by nineteenth-century British social theorist and essayist Harriet Martineau (1802–1876), whose contributions to social theory were well-known to her contemporaries but largely forgotten until a quite recent rediscovery of her work. Martineau wrote widely about social institutions and, like Comte, emphasized that sociology (and careful sociological examination) could play an important role in moving the world toward a better societal order.

These were among the early thinkers who laid the groundwork, but the foundations of modern sociology, and of social theory as we know it today, can be traced to the writings of a handful of key thinkers working in the second half of the nineteenth century and the early twentieth century. They developed their ideas in a time of enormous change, characterized by four key transitions:

1. The change from an economy rooted in farming and agriculture to one based on industry and factory work (what is referred to as the *Industrial Revolution*)

2. The large-scale movement of people from rural areas to cities and from one country to another (urbanization and immigration)

3. The change of the predominant form of government from monarchies to democracies, organized as sovereign nation-states (many of the countries in Europe established their more-or-less permanent boundaries in this period)

4. Changes in the role of religion in society, with a decline in religious influence on public life as nonreligious ideas became increasingly important

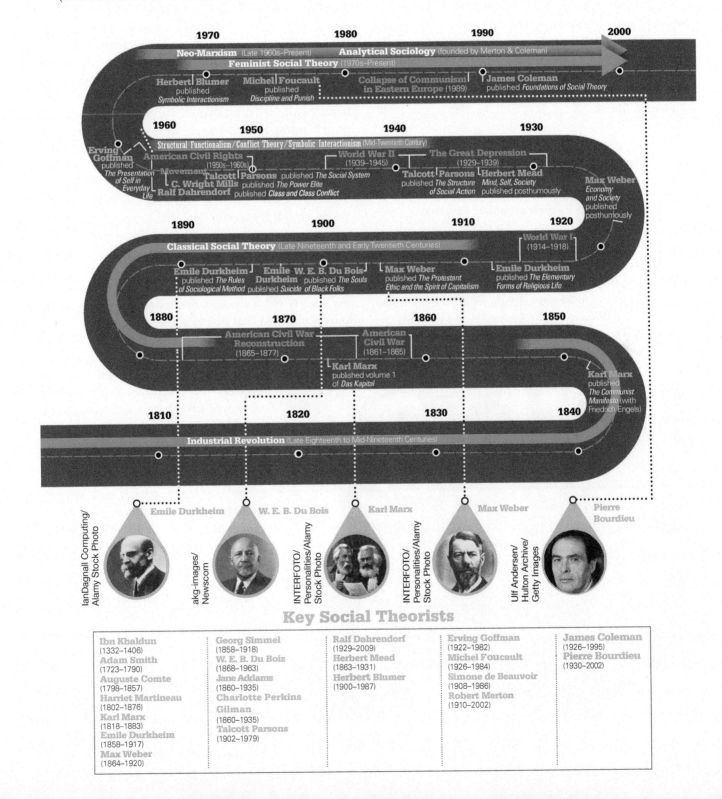

Key Social Theorists

Ibn Khaldun (1332–1406)	**Georg Simmel** (1858–1918)	**Ralf Dahrendorf** (1929–2009)	**Erving Goffman** (1922–1982)	**James Coleman** (1926–1995)
Adam Smith (1723–1790)	**W. E. B. Du Bois** (1868–1963)	**Herbert Mead** (1863–1931)	**Michel Foucault** (1926–1984)	**Pierre Bourdieu** (1930–2002)
Auguste Comte (1798–1857)	**Jane Addams** (1860–1935)	**Herbert Blumer** (1900–1987)	**Simone de Beauvoir** (1908–1986)	
Harriet Martineau (1802–1876)	**Charlotte Perkins Gilman** (1860–1935)		**Robert Merton** (1910–2002)	
Karl Marx (1818–1883)	**Talcott Parsons** (1902–1979)			
Emile Durkheim (1858–1917)				
Max Weber (1864–1920)				

These transitions unfolded slowly, and they were never complete either. Even today, people still farm, many live in rural areas, there are still many undemocratic governments (even monarchies), and religion still has an important influence. But already in the late nineteenth century, many thinkers and early social scientists were sensing that the world was changing, and social theory and the new discipline of sociology emerged in response to these transformations and the sense of crisis they evoked.

We begin our discussion of classical social theory with the writings of Karl Marx, who posed each of the three questions central to social theory in a way that many later theorists would debate and elaborate. We then turn to the writings of five other early thinkers who explored these central themes in ways that have lasting importance: Emile Durkheim, Max Weber, Georg Simmel, W. E. B. Du Bois, and Jane Addams.

Karl Marx (1818–1883)

2.2.1 Discuss why Marx believed that societies were so heavily shaped by their economic systems.

Karl Marx is most well known as a founding figure of the socialist movement. But his theoretical and sociological writings (often written in collaboration with his friend and lifelong intellectual collaborator Friedrich Engels [1820–1895]) also ignited great debate within the discipline of sociology, and many early sociologists and theorists developed their own thinking in critical reaction to Marx. The writings of Marx that have been the most influential for

later sociologists start from one key principle: the idea that the way humans produce the things they need to live is the essential foundation of any society. As a result, a society's economic system, and the relationships it creates between individuals and groups, is the defining feature of how that society works.

Because of the centrality of a society's economic system, Marx argued that human history is best understood through the history of different economic systems. In particular, he believed that a society's economic system largely determines what is possible in the realm of politics and culture, so if we want to understand why particular kinds of social or cultural ideas emerge, we should look to that society's economic system.

Why did Marx think that societies were so heavily shaped by their economic systems? His argument starts from the observation that all societies, except the simplest hunting and gathering societies, produce an economic surplus. That is, they collectively produce more goods than are required to meet their minimum physical needs *if* those goods were shared equally. But because it has never been the case that a society truly shares all goods equally, Marx believed that the starting point for the analysis of any society should be two questions about that inequality: First, who takes possession of this surplus? And second, by what means do they do so? Because control over the surplus gives some members of any society extra rewards not shared by everyone else, Marx suggested that in any society's economic system, tensions exist between groups that give rise to conflicts and in extreme cases social revolutions. He referred to the most important of these groups as **classes**, which he meant by those groups of people who share a similar set of economic interests.

In their most famous work, *The Communist Manifesto*, first published in 1848, Marx and Engels ([1848] 2011) divide the history of all societies from antiquity up to their own time into three distinctive **modes of production** that characterize the dominant economic system in a society and the classes that the economic system gives rise to: *ancient societies* based on slavery; *feudalism*, which was characterized by largely agrarian societies with a tiny group of landowners; and *capitalism*, economies organized around market-based exchange. Each of these modes of production consists of two parts—what Marx and Engels call the **forces of production**, or the technological and productive capacity of any society at a given point in time, and the **social relations of production**, which are the relationships

Karl Marx (1818–1865), left, with his lifelong collaborator, Friedrich Engels (1820–1895), on the right.

and inequalities between different kinds of people within the economy. The forces of production can be thought of as all of the different tools people use to make things, while the relations of production are how people are organized to carry out the tasks needed to produce those things.

Finally, Marx advanced the idea that this economic base exerts a strong influence on what he calls the societal "superstructure," by which he meant the combination of laws, cultural ideas, and political life that can be found in any society (Marx [1859] 1978). This theory is known as **historic materialism**, the idea that history moves in response to society's economic foundation, and the way we think and the possibilities for social and political action are inherently constrained by the economic world we live in. How can this be? How can the economic base influence people's ideas, the legal system, or the political system so directly? Don't we all have our own opinions that have nothing to do with the economy? Marx's idea was that human minds, cultural products, and the legal and political system are always closely tied to the time and place we live in. In other words, individuals form their consciousness from their social context. In the sixteenth century, when agriculture was the dominant form of production, no one would have had the tools to envision what life in the nineteenth or twentieth centuries would become (and all the inventions that would irrevocably change human lives, such as planes, cars, and televisions). Even today, we can barely glimpse a future in which artificial intelligence may enable machines to perform human tasks—although it is true that science fiction does try. The legal system is also a reflection of its time and place; the law continually changes as societies evolve and new questions and problems come before courts or legislatures. No sixteenth-century court of law would have faced the question of whether Google has a de facto monopoly on internet searches. Social change

driven by economic change prompts other changes in the law, politics, and a society's culture. In Figure 2.2, we have diagrammed Marx's model of society, starting with the two elements of the mode of production (the forces and relations of production) on the bottom, with an arrow showing the influence of the economic base on what he calls the "superstructure."

As noted, because of the overall importance of the economy in society, Marx thought that the mode of production would largely determine the superstructure, shown on the top of the figure. What Marx meant by superstructure were all of the laws, cultural and intellectual ideas, and political system. In other words, the mode of production would shape or even determine what kinds of laws and government systems were possible at any one point in time, as well as the kinds of ideas that people have about politics and society (Marx [1859] 1978).

Marx's analysis of the capitalist mode of production in his magnum opus, *Das Kapital* (Marx [1867] 1976) is the starting point for his most systematic analysis of modern (capitalist) societies, as Marx rightly anticipated that capitalism would soon become the dominant economic system around the world. At the heart of capitalist societies, Marx believed, lies the central conflict between members of two classes: the **bourgeoisie**, who possess special resources called **capital**—money or other assets that can be used for business investments—and everyone else. Possession of capital is the critical dividing line between the bourgeoisie, who can use their capital to hire other people to work for them, and the working class, or **proletariat**. Because members of the proletariat own no capital, Marx noted that they must seek paid employment in order to meet their basic needs. Marx also acknowledged that other social groups such as shopkeepers, craftsmen, and farmers occupied a space between elite capitalists and workers. However, because larger enterprises can produce more cheaply than smaller ones, Marx predicted that these intermediate groups would shrink as small producers were driven into bankruptcy and forced to join the ranks of the proletariat. Modern capitalist societies, he thought, would increasingly be polarized between a very small bourgeoisie and an increasingly large working class.

While any mode of production can sustain itself for an extended period, even centuries, Marx thought that eventually every mode of production becomes stagnant and falls into crisis, and when this happens a social revolution is likely to occur, leading to the establishment of a new mode of production. In order

Figure 2.2 Marx's Model of Society: Components of a Mode of Production

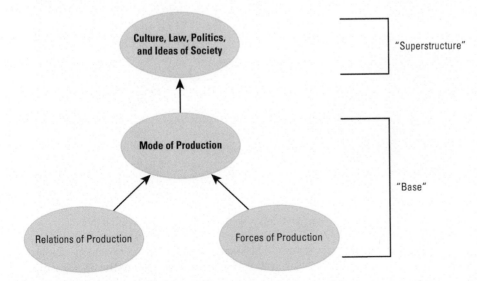

for capitalism to arise, Marx argued that all of the heredi-tary privileges of landlords, including rules that allowed them to control the lives of agricultural workers, had to be destroyed. This revolutionary change was brought about, according to Marx, by a rising class of capitalists who de-manded economic freedoms that did not exist under feu-dalism. Eventually, just as capitalists overthrew feudalism to create a new and dynamic economic system, Marx thought that the proletariat would create a revolution that would overthrow capitalism in favor of a **socialist society**, in which the productive forces of society are owned by ev-eryone (not by individual business owners). They would be motivated to do so, Marx thought, because over time capitalists, in order to maintain or increase their profit, would be driven to push down the wages of workers until those workers would finally revolt. This theory is known as the theory of **class struggle**, and it is based on the idea that classes of people who are treated so differently by the economic system are inevitably going to be in conflict with one another.

The world in which we live today, especially after the collapse of communism in the Soviet Union and most other communist countries since 1989, seems far removed from what Marx envisioned. If anything, capitalism seems more entrenched than ever. But capitalism has also changed in ways that Marx (and Engels) did not antici-pate in their writings in the nineteenth century. Capitalist societies, especially in the wealthier parts of the world, have developed large government-funded and -operated social programs such as social security, unemployment insurance, free or low-cost health insurance, and educa-tional systems designed to reduce poverty and inequal-ity even in the context of thriving capitalist economies. These economic systems have grown far more diverse, and proven far more versatile, than Marx envisioned. Marx also under-estimated the willingness of capital-ists to pay workers decent wages, especially when they need to recruit workers with valuable skills or in or-der to keep workers satisfied. Instead of things getting steadily worse for workers, living standards have steadily risen from the nineteenth century onward.

Yet in two respects Marx's model of society and social change seems very relevant today. First, the German thinker was an early theorist of what we now call **globalization**: the idea that economies and societies are in-terconnected in ways such that what happens in one place impacts what

happens in another. He and Engels anticipated the spread of the capitalist economy to the entire world in the late 1840s, a revolutionary idea at the time, and one that proved remarkably insightful in light of later develop-ments. And the analytical tools of his social theory do provide one way of understanding the role of economic exchange in fostering globalization. Second, the failure of socialism in places like Russia and Eastern Europe, which would seem to contradict Marx's assumptions, can actually be viewed as conforming very well to what Marx himself predicted. One of Marx's most fundamen-tal claims is that only capitalism is capable of building up the tremendous productive capacity needed to make socialism and communism work. Socialist leaders such as Lenin and Mao (in Russia and China respectively) attempted to skip this crucial stage of development by moving from a feudal mode of production directly to so-cialism (that is, they tried to skip over the stage of capi-talism altogether). This proved to be impossible, and in responding to these failures later rulers in these countries eventually resorted to reintroducing capitalism (as Marx might well have predicted). The resulting expansion of economic activity that the turn to capitalism has created more recently, especially in China which has had some of the fastest growth rates in the world, has been impres-sive. If he were alive today, rather than seeing the failure of communism as the failure of his idea of history, Marx might well argue that the true socialist revolution still lies in the future for countries like Russia and China, but only after they go through a long period of capitalist growth and development.

A factory in Zhejiang, China. Marx and Engels would not have been surprised that the Chinese economy has grown rapidly after the introduction of free-market capitalism since the late 1970s. However, they probably would be surprised that Marxism remains the official ideology of the Chinese government, in spite of its embrace of capitalist reforms!

Lou Linwei/Alamy Stock Photo

Emile Durkheim (1858–1917)

2.2.2 Analyze Emile Durkheim's theory of what holds societies together.

The French sociologist Emile Durkheim is properly regarded as one of the founding figures of the discipline of sociology. Like Marx, Durkheim sought to try to understand the changes taking place around him during a period of extraordinary growth and change in the late nineteenth and early twentieth centuries. Durkheim wondered how societies would continue to function in the face of these changes. Durkheim believed that the sociologist was responsible for answering these questions, almost like a doctor treating a patient—the sociologist's patient was society, and the sickness that needed to be cured was the various forms of social disorder that rapid industrialization was producing. Durkheim's contributions were many, but we will focus on three: his development of the concept of the social fact, his analysis of the roots of social solidarity, and his analysis of religion as a force in modern life.

In *The Rules of Sociological Method* (Durkheim [1895] 1982), Durkheim made a case for the need for sociology by comparing it to the sciences of biology and physics. He argued that just like biology or physics, sociology examines a force in the world that is objective and exists independently of our ability to control it. For example, just as gravity is a force that exists external to us and is not made by

Many ordinary rituals appear to us as completely natural, yet they are the result of societal forces. Marriage, for example, is both expected and valued in most societies. Durkheim called ideas about the importance of rituals such as marriage as one of the many "social facts" that most members of a society learn and take for granted.

us, so too do social forces exist objectively in the world. We cannot defy gravity (at least not easily), but we also cannot usually defy what Durkheim referred to as **social facts**—those regularities and rules of everyday life that every human community has. Shortly after Durkheim defined the social fact, sociologists and other social scientists began to refer to them as **social forces** rather than social facts. The term *social forces* connotes something broader than what Durkheim originally meant by *social fact*, but the two are closely related. Social facts, or social forces, are "social" in the sense that they arise from human action at some point in the past, and they are "facts" (or "forces") in the sense that we are born into a world where there are many rules and customs (sometimes written down, but often not) that we are obliged to obey if we are to fit in to our community and successfully interact with others.

How do these social forces work? In asking this question, Durkheim was on to something that would become the foundation of nearly all social theories that would follow: Human behavior is not natural but learned; in other words, we are trained, or socialized, to act the ways that we do. And for Durkheim, one of the key things involved is the **socialization** process, the way we are taught to behave in society (and all of the different situations we encounter). Among the most important of all social forces that act upon us are *norms* (see Chapter 1). Durkheim noted that one of the ways that we know norms exist is what happens when we violate them and we receive some kind of sanction for our misstep.

Emile Durkheim (1858–1917). In the early twentieth century, Durkheim was the most famous sociologist in the world, and his contributions to the development of sociology as a social science are central.

The idea that social forces are important for their influence on individual behavior was put to the test in Durkheim's next book, *Suicide* (Durkheim [1897] 1997), which was not only a classic demonstration of the power of sociological analysis but also a landmark in the integration of social theory and empirical research. At first glance, the act of ending one's own life appears to be the most private act imaginable, rooted in the unique details of an individual's personal life or psyche. Yet by stepping back and carefully analyzing the statistics on who commits suicide—such as variations in the suicide rate between countries, or annual and regional fluctuations of suicides within the same country—Durkheim concluded that the probability that a certain number of people will kill themselves at a given time and place is in fact very much influenced by social factors (such as religious beliefs, marital status, the country you live in, whether or not a war is being fought, and an individual's educational level).

Durkheim's insights about social forces impacting the likelihood of suicide will not help us to explain, let alone accept, a suicide committed by a friend or family member. But they do underline in striking fashion a broader truth, namely that we as individuals are embedded in a larger social world, and our likelihood of committing suicide is not entirely random.

Related to the question of the impact of social forces is one of the critical questions that occupied Durkheim throughout his career: What is it that holds societies together? This is the problem of what Durkheim called **social solidarity** (Durkheim [1890] 1997). In particular, he wondered where the shared morals and connections between individuals come from; how it is that social facts get established in the first place. Durkheim drew a contrast between two distinct forms of social solidarity—mechanical and organic solidarity—each of which is connected with different kinds of shared morals reflecting the different kinds of societies in which they arise. **Mechanical solidarity** is the dominant form of solidarity in what Durkheim called "primitive" societies, which are built around extended families or clans connected in tribes, such as the Iroquois or the Apache. They are characterized by a very minimal **division of labor** (or specialization of tasks), with an economic system consisting primarily of hunting and gathering or simple agriculture. By contrast, modern societies are characterized by **organic solidarity**, in which a very extensive division of labor and mutual dependence among people can be found.

How, according to Durkheim, did we move from a world of simple, "mechanical" societies (represented for Durkheim in tribal communities in which responsibility for tasks was shared) to those of today, characterized

Emile Durkheim's ideas about tribal societies (where he thought there was little room for individuality) contrasted with modern societies where diversity and social complexity is common. Both types of societies face the problem of creating social solidarity, but Durkheim argued they do it in very different ways.

by a division of labor involving people who do lots of different things and may have little in common with one another? Durkheim argued that premodern societies were held together because people were engaged in much of the same or similar activities and therefore shared a worldview. Modern societies, Durkheim wrote, resemble the ways in which a living organism operates, where specialized organs work together to hold the whole together. As the populations of simpler societies expanded outward and then, running up against natural or human barriers, became denser in cities, competition for survival among their members increased. One particularly successful response to this situation proved to be specialization: Individuals could acquire skills as carpenters, stonemasons, or blacksmiths and make a living doing it.

So what exactly holds modern (organic) societies together? Durkheim eventually came to advance the idea that modern societies, characterized by growing diversity and complexity, still require some widely shared, sacred beliefs to hold people together. What kinds of beliefs could achieve this level of acceptance? Durkheim suggested a surprising answer: that the key to the forms of solidarity in modern societies lies in the fact that these societies guarantee individuals a measure of freedom that primitive societies did not. He even characterized this as the "cult of the individual." By this, Durkheim meant that in modern societies, we are freer to express our individual tastes, preferences, and interests because society does not seek to make everyone conform to the same set of beliefs about morality, and we perceive these individual rights as so central that they become sacred (and embedded in social institutions and the law).

As he continued to reflect on the nature of social solidarity, Durkheim developed a profound and original theory of the role religion has played in both primitive and modern societies. From his investigations, Durkheim developed a particular definition of religion as centering on the **sacred**—those objects, places, and symbols that are set apart from daily life and elicit awe and reverence, sustained by myths and rituals. The sacred for Durkheim did not require reference to the supernatural. While many sacred objects (such as the Bible or Koran) or practices (Christmas) make reference to God, there are many other things that are sacred that do not. For example, for many Americans burning or desecrating the American flag is to violate a sacred (but not religious) object. Durkheim's idea that it is social forces that create our sense of what is sacred opens the door to a whole new way of understanding religion. If religion is not the creation of God or some other supernatural force, it must inevitably be a human creation. But why is religion so common in all societies? And how, when, and why do humans come to create and recreate these sacred practices? Durkheim's answer relates back to his general interest in social solidarity: Religion helps to knit groups of people or whole societies together. It provides individuals with a common set of beliefs and makes both individuals and societies stronger.

Max Weber (1864–1920)

2.2.3 Discuss Max Weber's contributions to our understanding of motivations for behavior, legitimacy and authority, and status groups and social closure.

The German sociologist Max Weber's contributions to the development of our understanding of modern societies were varied, complex, and important in ways that sociologists continually rediscover. His range of knowledge was so vast—in his writings he explored the history and societies of many major civilizations and religious traditions of the world, as well as such technical topics as agricultural production and prices in Prussia—that it is perhaps not surprising that his lasting contributions to

Max Weber (1864–1920). Weber's intellectual career was slowed by periods of depression, but his outpouring of work covering such a wide range of topics, usually guided by research about multiple countries and historical periods, established how wide-ranging sociological theory and research could be.

social theory addressed several important issues. We will focus on three: his writings on the motives of individual behavior, the forms of legitimate authority, and his concept of the status group and the seemingly universal process of how groups seek to monopolize opportunities for their members.

One of Weber's foundational contributions was to consider the role of individual action and behavior as a foundation for social order. Whereas Marx focused on material conditions and Durkheim on morality and social forces, Weber argued that there is something else we need to consider when we study societies: the motivations that guide individual behavior—in other words, the reasons we behave the way that we do. This is especially important for understanding human societies because Weber believed those motivations have changed over time.

Weber's analysis of motives stands in sharp contrast to Durkheim's emphasis on social facts, which are characterized by their objectivity and by being external to the individual. Weber argued that in order to

Figure 2.3 Weber's Typology of Motives for Action

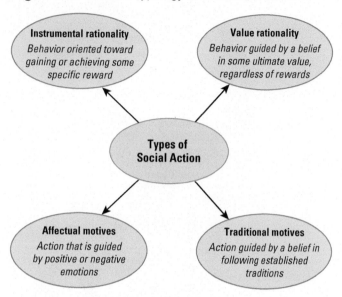

understand the motivations for behavior, we need to not just look at the social environment but also get inside people's heads and figure out how they interpret and give meaning to the world around them. In this way, Weber introduced a whole new dimension to the work of sociologists: interpretation of individual action. In *Economy and Society*, published shortly after his death, Weber writes that "Sociology is a science concerning itself with the interpretative understanding of social action" (Weber [1922] 1978, p.4). This approach is known as **interpretive sociology**, a translation form of the German word *verstehen*, which means understanding.

Weber went on to develop a typology of different kinds of social action, each differentiated by the motivations (or rationales) that guide them, as Figure 2.3 illustrates.

We can understand more concretely Weber's ideas about the different motives of action in terms of a specific example. Let's consider the different reasons a student might choose to attend a class while they are in college. The instrumental reasons are pretty straightforward: A student attends class because her goal is to graduate from college, perhaps in the hopes of finding a good career and making more money than she otherwise would. Coming to class will increase her chances of getting good grades, which will lead her to graduate with a strong GPA, which will enable her to land a good job, which may enable her to make a good income. In contrast, another student could come to class guided by value-rational principles, in which case he attends class because he believes in the value of education for its own

sake, without thinking about any instrumental or self-interested outcomes it might provide him. Another student might come to class guided by emotions, for example a fear that missing a class even when attendance is not required is just disrespectful or will be sanctioned by the instructor. In this case, we would say his behavior expressed an affectual orientation. And finally, yet another student attends class because that is what her parents and grandparents did, and going to school is what she has been doing since kindergarten. It is, in other words, a tradition for which she doesn't think about any alternative.

In his most famous work, *The Protestant Ethic and the Spirit of Capitalism* (Weber [1904] 2008), Weber applied his concern with individual motivations for behavior to advance a startling theory about why capitalism appeared earlier and grew faster in some parts of the world than in others. He argued that the influence of certain religious movements—notably Protestantism—seemed to be closely connected to those places that had the earliest and most successful capitalist economies. In particular, he argued that the

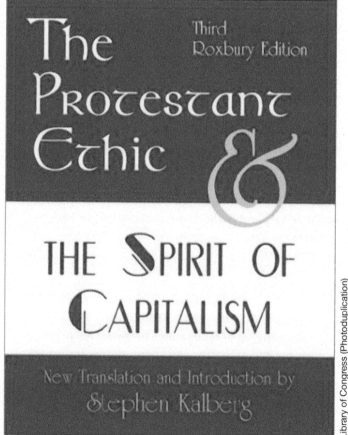

In his influential book *The Protestant Ethic and The Spirit of Capitalism*, Max Weber observed that Protestantism seemed to be closely aligned to the most successful capitalist economies. Weber argued that devout Protestants believed that hard work and economic success meant that you were in God's good graces. He theorized that this was the reason that capitalism grew faster in some parts of the world than in others.

appearance of strict forms of Protestantism fundamentally altered market behavior in places where they were most numerous (first in Britain, America, the Netherlands, and parts of Germany and Switzerland, and later elsewhere) because these early strict Protestants believed that it was a sign that you were in God's good graces if you became economically successful. This encouraged Protestants to work in a highly disciplined, methodical manner, and then save and reinvest whatever they earned (as opposed to consuming it). Weber believed that this gave strict Protestants an advantage over market participants from other religious groups in Europe (most notably Catholics). Eventually, the success of the strict Protestants encouraged others to assume the work habits and investment practices if they were to survive in the marketplace. By the eighteenth century, then, a new set of distinctly modern behavior norms ("the spirit of modern capitalism") had emerged out of what had been the religious attitudes ("the Protestant ethic") of a small minority.

A second major contribution to sociology developed in Weber's work concerns how and why people respect hierarchies and obey orders. Weber made a famous distinction between power and authority. He defines **power** as a person's ability to achieve his or her objective even if someone else wants to try to prevent it. An example of this would be when a ruler gets people to submit to his will and follow his orders by compelling them to do so through force or the threat of force. However, Weber argues that this is the exception; you can't always get your way by using force. There are far more cases where governments (or even our superiors) invoke what Weber called **authority**: the capacity to get people to do things because they think that they should abide by the commands of people above them.

Where does authority come from? Most of the time people tend to voluntarily obey orders—that is, they accept the authority of their rulers. But why? Weber explored the sources of authority by developing a theory of why and how leaders gain what he called **legitimacy**. When authority figures have legitimacy, we obey them not because of the threat of force but because we believe obeying their orders is the right thing to do. And in this way, Weber argues, the most successful political regimes are those that are able to legitimize their rule. As with Weber's basic proposition that behavior is guided by how people interpret the world and give meaning to it, he argues that voluntary obedience to authority comes as a result of people interpreting the ruler to have legitimacy.

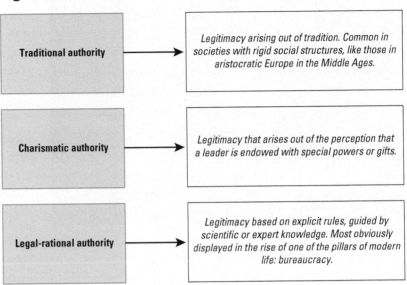

Figure 2.4 Three Types of Legitimate Domination

Traditional authority → *Legitimacy arising out of tradition. Common in societies with rigid social structures, like those in aristocratic Europe in the Middle Ages.*

Charismatic authority → *Legitimacy that arises out of the perception that a leader is endowed with special powers or gifts.*

Legal-rational authority → *Legitimacy based on explicit rules, guided by scientific or expert knowledge. Most obviously displayed in the rise of one of the pillars of modern life: bureaucracy.*

Weber distinguishes between different kinds of legitimacy, each connected to different interpretations of why one should voluntarily obey the ruler. Figure 2.4 illustrates these three distinct types of legitimate domination, which Weber called traditional, charismatic, and legal-rational.

Authority based on tradition is when the system of ruling authority is simply taken for granted because "that is the way things are done." Monarchies are classic examples; when the king or queen dies, the oldest son typically inherits the throne. Monarchies and other traditional systems of authority may seem permanent, but we know from history that kingdoms do not last forever. So how can change ever come to traditional societies, for example, those that are structured around extended families and rigid status hierarchies, and have rulers who have virtually unlimited power? Weber was especially fascinated by the role played by key individual leaders whom he saw as having **charisma**. The term *charisma* is derived from a Greek word meaning "gift of grace." Weber introduced the term into modern language to account for special cases in which unique individuals have appeared who claim special powers or gifts that their followers believe to be true. Most famously, these have been revolutionary religious figures—the Hebrew prophets, Jesus, Mohammed, Buddha—but the idea of charisma can also apply to modern social and political leaders as well (for example, Gandhi, Martin Luther King Jr., Adolf Hitler, or perhaps even Donald Trump). If such figures are to attract a following, they must demonstrate their special powers through extraordinary deeds that appear to be like miracles. Belief in a leader's charisma in turn inspires people to reject the status quo and join a new community of disciples. In this way a charismatic figure possesses the power, according to Weber, to break

Charismatic leader? Donald Trump's 2016 presidential campaign exhibited many of the characteristics of charisma identified by Max Weber. Trump repeatedly proclaimed that he possessed certain special skills and gifts that make him uniquely able to "Make America Great Again."

through the constraints of traditional authority to create new forms of legitimate domination built upon personal charisma. This authority is potentially revolutionary because the charismatic leader who calls into question traditional norms and rules proposes to replace them with new moral guidelines revealed to the leader by a higher (perhaps godly) power.

Finally, a third major contribution to social theory and sociology in Weber's writings was an important and influential theory of what he called **status groups**, groups of people with similar kinds of attributes or identities such as those based on religion, ethnicity, or race. Recall that Karl Marx had argued that classes and class conflict arising out of the economic system of any society were the central source of tension (and ultimately revolution) in any society. Weber acknowledged that economic class conflict was sometimes important, but conflicts between religious groups or racial and ethnic groups were often just as important or even more so. In contrast to economic classes, Weber emphasized that status groups are based on communities of members that share a common identity that can arise from many different sources. We all have various potential groups we could identify with; for example, depending on the families we are born into (and the religion and race or ethnicity our families confer upon us) or identities we develop as we get older (such as our occupation, our education, our sexuality, or communities we may voluntarily join like a neighborhood association or a feminist activist group). But which of these statuses become a source of our conscious thoughts and actions depend in part on which are organized into communities of similar people. An individual may be a Catholic, gay, a woman, able bodied,

from California, with parents born in Mexico; they may aspire to be an actor, become a volleyball player, and be a fan of Beyoncé. Which of those possible identities becomes a source of status-group membership depends in part on which distinctive communities or organizations are capable of influencing people to actively identify with them.

Status groups based on one's religion, sexual orientation, gender, race, ethnicity, and disability status have all shown to be meaningful factors in access to jobs or other kinds of opportunities; in limiting what job you can aspire to, who you can date or marry, and where you can live; and in whether you can gain membership in desired social clubs or groups. Status-group struggles, Weber argued, have been an important aspect of every society's **stratification system**, that is, all of the major forms of inequality between groups that persist over time. Weber did not deny that conflict between classes could be important, but he thought that Marx's emphasis on class struggle as the motor force of history neglected many other ways in which group competition and conflict influence the process of historical change.

Weber not only advanced a broader conception of group conflict and struggle than Marx, but he also introduced an important concept for understanding *how* groups seek to gain advantage over other groups: by systematically excluding nonmembers from gaining access to opportunities (or, to put it another way, groups try to monopolize opportunities for their own members). He called this process **social closure**, a term that captures the various ways that groups seek to close off access to opportunities by other groups. Closure is, in short, the process by which groups seek to monopolize opportunities or rewards. Social closure can be formalized in law (such as in the American South after the Civil War, under the Jim Crow system, or the system of *apartheid* in South Africa, where Blacks were often legally prevented from attending the same schools, using certain public facilities, marrying Whites, or living in the same neighborhoods as Whites). But closure need not be written into law; it can also occur in less formal ways. For example, limited opportunities for women and minorities to enter the ranks of top management in large corporations persisted long after civil rights laws were changed to give everyone equal opportunity. How? One way is that companies can change hiring and promotion policies in subtle ways to favor White men, thereby maintaining a kind of corporate culture in which women or minorities are often disadvantaged (Kantor 1977; Dobbin 2011).

Georg Simmel (1858–1918)

2.2.4 **Explain how Georg Simmel's insights on social circles and social distance help us understand how individuals and groups relate to one another.**

The German sociologist Georg Simmel was a contemporary and colleague of Max Weber, and he shared an interest (with Weber) in the study of groups. The social theory he pioneered, however, departed from Weber's to build upon a key set of insights about the nature of social order: Any individual stands at the intersection point of overlapping social circles. Societies, Simmel argued, are built from the group up through these social circles (Simmel 1964).

This insight is perhaps, at first, not surprising: Our group memberships are in many ways defining features of our lives. For example, we belong to a particular family; have groups of friends or colleagues at school or in the workplace; may also belong to a religious community, a neighborhood association, a sports club, or a political group; and have groups of friends or acquaintances because of shared passions or hobbies. For Simmel, however, a key aspect of the rise of modern societies from early types of human communities was the widening of the social circles to which we could become members. Whereas in earlier times membership in a single social

Georg Simmel (1858–1918). Simmel's study of social circles laid the foundation for the study of social networks, a thriving field of social research in the twenty-first century.

circle—like that centered on a local Catholic parish—might have dominated or dictated many other aspects of an individual's life, by the beginning of the twentieth century individuals had much greater freedom. They were able to choose their friends and acquaintances across different spheres of life, independently of one another, forming an intricate web of relationships, as he called them. If Simmel were alive today, of course, he would have marveled at the ways that this expansion of the range of possible social circles has increased through social media (which make almost an infinite number of possibilities available to us).

In developing a theory of how individuals fit into social circles, Simmel provided a key concept for sociology—the idea of **social distance**, which is a way of describing the importance of how close or distant the individuals in groups, or groups themselves, are from one another. Simmel famously redefined the everyday understanding of a "stranger" as someone who is a member of a group but never accepted as a full member (and can be contrasted with "insiders" who are fully part of the group, or in the "inner circle," as well as complete non-members) (Simmel [1908] 1971). We are all familiar with strangers (in Simmel's terms) in our own circles—people who are part of a group but often excluded or not invited to fully participate in group activities. Indeed, most of us have probably had the experience at one time or another of being a stranger in a group where we aspired to be an insider, undoubtedly an awkward and difficult position to be in (but a sociologically important one to understand). Simmel's insights about social distance raised larger questions about the nature of relationships between individuals and within or between groups. Social distance describes the quality of the relationships between people, and later sociologists developed measures of the degree of closeness or distance that individuals and groups feel toward one another.

What are the implications of these insights? On the one hand, it means that as adults we enjoy an unprecedented degree of latitude in shaping our social relations according to common interests, views, and preferences. While as recently as a few decades ago members of many ethnic and religious groups came under great pressure from their families and communities to avoid close relationships with those from outside of their group, this is much less the case today (as witnessed by rising rates of intermarriage across ethnic, religious, and even national lines in both North America and Western Europe). On the other hand, the number and diversity of social circles to which greater freedom of choice permits us to belong also leads to conflicts, not only over how best to spend our time but also over values and norms of behavior attached to particular circles that may not be compatible with one another. Thus the young corporate lawyer might have to decide, for example, whether to stay late every night at the office like other coworkers or violate this unwritten expectation of long working hours and leave earlier in order to spend more time with their partner or family (as time with one's family is also highly valued). Or we may find that the attitudes expressed by our work colleagues or the language they use violates our religious or political beliefs, and that we therefore must choose whether to give short shrift to these beliefs or speak up and object, thereby risking alienating those with whom we spend many hours daily. At any point, such conflicts may give rise to feelings of social distance or turn a potential insider into a "stranger."

Simmel noted that the way we see ourselves, and which social groups we most value, is not necessarily the same way as others see us. While our family members and closest friends may be aware of all of the overlapping social groups to which we belong, and even which of those group memberships are most important to us, outsiders or passing acquaintances will most often focus on one of our multiple identities—our nationality, race, ethnic background, religion, regional origin, or place of residence—and assume it to be primary (drawing conclusions about us based on what they hold to be "average" or "common" traits of persons with those characteristics).

Simmel's work also began to bring insights from mathematics into the study of the social world, using ideas imported from geometry (and geometric space) to characterize the relationships among individuals. Simmel's insights about the formal properties of groups provided the foundation for the rise of **network analysis**, the study of how individuals are connected to other individuals and the consequences of those connections. Although the full value of these insights was not immediately clear to Simmel's contemporaries, later sociologists recognized them as a useful foundation for developing new ways of understanding society. For example, how do new ideas become popular? Often, it is through **social networks**, people (including strangers) who are tied together in ways they don't typically notice. See Figure 2.5 for a simple example of a fictional social network using some of the characters from the popular television show *The Walking Dead*. The lines in the figure show how the

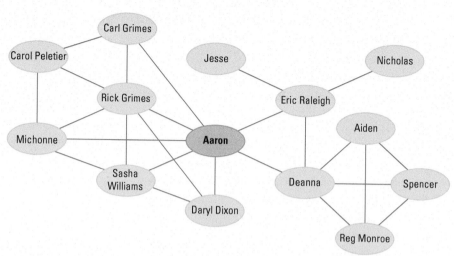

Figure 2.5 An Example of a Social Network Using Characters from the Television Show *The Walking Dead*

ties between individuals connect them to others, with Aaron indirectly connecting several different groups together through his relationships.

To see more vividly how social networks work, consider how rumors spread: One person may tell a close friend a secret, and if the friend tells another person (who may be completely unknown to the first person), it can begin a remarkable chain of action that can spread the secret far and wide (perhaps to the complete embarrassment of the first person). While many rumors may be harmless, the same kinds of chains of interactions can spread information about a protest, whether or not a movie is any good, or how to cheat on your taxes and get away with it. With the use of mathematical tools, social network analysts have been able to generalize Simmel's insights into a wide range of different applications, from health behaviors to fads to patterns of housing segregation. It is a foundational contribution to analyzing how societies work.

W. E. B. Du Bois (1868–1963)

2.2.5 **Explain W. E. B. Du Bois's views of the diverse ways in which racism influences the lives of Black Americans and how racism produces a double consciousness.**

W. E. B. Du Bois's long and varied career as a social scientist, historian, journalist, essayist, and political activist was extraordinary in many ways. Among his many political activities, he was one of the founders of the National Association for the Advancement of Colored People (NAACP), and for decades his editorship of the premier intellectual magazine aimed at Black Americans—called *The Crisis*—provided a platform to intervene in the many

W. E. B. Du Bois (1868–1963). Du Bois's long and diverse career as a scholar, writer, political and anti-racist activist, has few parallels. Denied the elite academic post he so richly deserved, Du Bois developed his scholarship, especially after World War I, in dialogue with real-world events, history, and the social movements of his time. He was doing for decades what today we call *public sociology*.

debates and issues of the time. Du Bois's race, however, prevented him from attaining the prestigious academic post to which his scholarship would have normally entitled him (Morris 2015). His overriding concern as a sociologist and social theorist was the problem of race and racial inequality in American society, although his theoretical writings contained powerful insights that were (and are) relevant to all disadvantaged groups and had implications for the study of group conflict everywhere.

The dominant theories about race in Du Bois's time claimed that European Whites and Blacks descending from Africa were biologically endowed differently, especially in terms of intelligence, capacity for hard work, and ability to respect the law and be good citizens. These theories stressed that there were deep-seated genetic reasons why European Whites were superior to Blacks and that the poverty and inequality Blacks experienced were the result of these innate differences. If racial differences were rooted in biological differences, then it hardly mattered whether American society gave Blacks equal opportunity, as they would be fundamentally incapable of taking advantage of those opportunities. Du Bois rejected these assertions,

arguing across his 60-year career that racial inequality was not rooted in biological differences but rather manufactured by American society. He developed a substantial body of research as well as new theoretical ideas about how **racism**—the assumption that members of a racial group are inherently inferior to other races—prevented Blacks from achieving at the same level as Whites. At every turn, throughout his career, Du Bois had to challenge the entrenched view of White superiority, which denied that racism mattered.

How did racism play this role, according to Du Bois? In his first major book, a study of the Black community in Philadelphia in the late 1890s, Du Bois showed that every aspect of the lives of Black Americans was shaped by the limited opportunities they were afforded (Du Bois [1899] 1995). Du Bois carried out an intensive data-collection effort, employing multiple and often innovative methods in the study. These included the use of statistical data about the neighborhoods where Philadelphia's Black population lived, what kinds of jobs they held, and how they were divided along economic lines. Du Bois supplemented this statistical portrait with interviews on a house-to-house basis, where he explored the social conditions of life in the Black community beyond what statistical data could show. For example, he explored how the Black poor survived on low incomes, how marriages and families were organized and functioning, and how relatively privileged Blacks viewed poor Blacks. The latter analysis gave rise to a concern about what Du Bois viewed as the failure of Black "elites" to help poor Blacks and "uplift the race," as Du Bois famously put it in a later essay (Du Bois [1903] 2008).

The role of racism in American life, and how it impacted Black Americans, was dissected in a different way in Du Bois's most famous and influential work, *The Souls of Black Folks* (Du Bois [1903] 1997). Here, in a collection of essays and studies that are still widely read today, Du Bois presented more fully his view that stereotypes about Blacks as lazy, unintelligent, or prone to crime were in fact the result of their place in American society. In the more sociological parts of the book, Du Bois argued that a lack of educational opportunities, not innate intelligence, produced the appearance of lower intelligence among Blacks. Lack of economic opportunity, by contrast, made it appear that Blacks did not work as hard as Whites (a myth all the more ridiculous in the face of the backbreaking work of many Southern Blacks involved in agricultural or domestic labor). And he noted that because of poverty and racial segregation, Blacks tended to be concentrated in poor communities where crime rates naturally tended to be higher. In short, Du Bois argued, the social structure of American society was the cause of the appearance of inferiority in the Black community.

Du Bois's most famous concept in *Souls*, however, was a theory of how racism and social structure impact individual Blacks, producing in them what he called a kind of "double consciousness." Because of their marginalization from the mainstream of American life, Du Bois argued that, unlike White Americans, Blacks lived multiple lives, one as a Black person and one as an American. Further, because Black Americans saw themselves as devalued in the eyes of White Americans, they suffered from having to view themselves in this way through the eyes of others. In a famous passage, Du Bois defined this double consciousness as

> a world which yields him no true self-consciousness, but only lets him see himself through the revelation of the other world. It is a peculiar sensation, this double-consciousness, this sense of always looking at one's self through the eyes of others, of measuring one's soul by the tape of a world that looks on in amused contempt and pity. One ever feels his two-ness—an American, a Negro; two warring souls, two thoughts, two unreconciled strivings; two warring ideals in one dark body, whose dogged strength alone keeps it from being torn asunder (Du Bois [1903] 1997, p. 6).

The idea of multiple selves suggested a novel way in which social structure imposes psychological costs on Blacks, and it proved to be an idea that later social scientists applied to many other disadvantaged groups.

Du Bois's writings on social structure also examined the larger context of American politics and race relations. His most important book in this vein was his study of the tragedy of the post–Civil War Reconstruction in the South (Du Bois 1935). In contrast to the standard historical accounts of the time, which claimed the Reconstruction governments run by Blacks were corrupt and incompetent, Du Bois argued that the Reconstruction governments

struggled against virulent White violence and obstructionism at every turn in their efforts to build a new political system in the South in which Blacks and poor Whites would be able to participate. Dismissed at the time, later scholarship on Reconstruction has confirmed many of the insights of Du Bois's original historical account.

Jane Addams (1860–1935)

2.2.6 Analyze the relevance of Jane Addams's ideas of sympathetic knowledge and social ethics for addressing social problems today.

Similar to Karl Marx and W. E. B. Du Bois, Jane Addams's career mixed activism and scholarship. Most known for establishing Hull House in Chicago, one of the first and most famous of the **settlement houses** of the early twentieth century, Addams is primarily thought of as a social worker who developed ideas about how to address social problems from her practical experiences. But she was also a significant writer and thinker who made a number of important contributions.

Hull House opened in an old, rundown mansion in the Near West Side neighborhood of Chicago in 1889. It was designed to provide services and support for the poor, immigrant communities in the neighborhoods surrounding it, but it quickly became a gathering place for reformers and intellectuals who were interested in providing these individuals with tools for building better lives. Reformers and activists branched out from doing neighborhood improvement projects (such as building parks, getting public health programs off the ground, and establishing adult education programs and libraries) to advocating reform policies. By the 1920s, Addams's work at Hull House was internationally renowned, earning her the Nobel Peace Prize in 1931.

Despite her success with Hull House, Addams considered herself first and foremost a sociologist of societal problems, especially those involving women and people of color. She was a founding member of the American Sociological Society in 1905 and long maintained ties with the famous Sociology Department at the University of Chicago. Addams thought that sociological insights could be applied and developed to solve social problems, but she rejected most kinds of academic writing and scholarship in favor of engagement with a broader public. She also became involved tirelessly in a large number of social and political campaigns throughout her life: women's suffrage, civil rights for minorities (Addams worked with Du Bois in building the NAACP), birth control (a very controversial idea at the time), equal opportunity for women, peace and anti-war activity, and unions and workers' rights (among other things, she helped establish unions for women workers). In her writings, she even challenged many of the negative stereotypes about adolescents and young people. She also took up topics that male sociologists of the time paid no attention to, such as

Du Bois's view of the "double consciousness" of Black Americans was continually reinforced by the practice of segregation, especially in the American South, which prevented Blacks from participating in the mainstream of American life.

Jane Addams (1860–1935). Like Du Bois, Addams was one of the first "public sociologists," a leading intellectual and social theorist who put her ideas into practice through the establishment of the Hull House, and an active participant in prominent public debates.

prostitution and pornography and how they exploit women (poor and immigrant women, in particular).

In Addams's popular and scholarly writings—she authored a dozen books and some 500 articles—she argued for a conception of democracy and the idea that a good society would emphasize the importance of helping everyone develop what she called **sympathetic knowledge** about other people and ways of life through contact and experience. Rather than rely on abstract knowledge of people we don't know, Addams urged that we create avenues to connect with one another. Only in this way, she believed, could people trying to improve the lives of the poor actually achieve their goals.

In her most important work on democracy, she argued that true democracy required more than just holding regular elections. Citizens need to have some understanding of "social ethics," by which she meant that citizens had an obligation to try to understand each other (even those who are very different from one another). In other words, Addams felt strongly that informed democratic participation was fostered in situations where citizens seek what unites them, not what divides them. (If she were alive in 2020, she would have been very worried about the health of American democracy!)

Addams wrote many other sociological and philosophical works, but a lot of her key ideas and insights can be found in the book on her experiences at Hull House, entitled *Twenty Years at Hull House* (Addams 1910), which was widely read at the time and remains a sociological classic. In the book, she describes her own process of acquiring sympathetic knowledge, admitting to many mistakes along the way. (For example, she came to realize the original fine furnishings of the Hull House mansion were unfamiliar and uncomfortable for the poor immigrants who attended events or classes, so she eventually switched them out for more modest alternatives.) Addams also came to recognize the importance of not trying to speak for others, but rather to provide them with platforms to identify their problems and come up with their own solutions. Finally, she advocated for an expansive democratic citizenship, where women and Blacks would be able to participate in government in areas such as voting. Like Du Bois, Addams's remarkable life is a testament to the possibilities of combining scholarship and social and political activism in challenging the social problems of her age.

What Innovations in Social Theory Emerged in the Mid-Twentieth Century?

BIG QUESTION **2.3**

NEW DIRECTIONS IN SOCIAL THEORY, 1937–1965

While the classical tradition in social theory is represented in the writings of Marx, Durkheim, Weber, and Simmel,

and the public sociology tradition is seen in the works of Du Bois and Addams, the interests of social theorists began to shift in new and unexpected directions from the late 1930s onward. Leadership in the development of social theory and sociology as a whole passed from being primarily located in Europe—even the Americans Du Bois and Addams had both been educated in Germany and were influenced by European social theorists—to America. Part of the reason for this shift was due to the spread of fascism across Europe. Fascist governments viewed the questioning nature of sociology as a threat, and made it virtually impossible to do sociological research in several countries. At the same time, new American leadership in the discipline emerged, in particular in the widely read and debated work of the Harvard social theorist Talcott Parsons (1902–1979). Parsons's effort to develop a *functionalist* theory of society sought to explain key aspects of social life by examining the *functions* they serve for society as a whole. Parsons's work was greeted with enthusiasm in some quarters but also spawned enormous controversy in others. Like Marx in the classical period, his theories served as a major source of critical reflection and theoretical debate for other theorists in this era (and to come). This period, which we can date from approximately 1937 (when Parsons published one of the most important books in the history of sociological theory, a two-volume study of mostly European social theorists entitled *The Structure of Social Action* (Parsons [1937] 1967) to the mid-1960s, saw both the elaboration of the functionalist model of society and the development of several key alternatives to Parsons's functionalist theory—most importantly conflict theory and symbolic interaction. In this section, we briefly discuss each of these new theoretical traditions and some of their key insights.

Structural Functionalism

2.3.1 **Discuss the roles that norms, values, and institutions play in society, according to the theory of structural functionalism.**

Parsons's functionalist theory of society represented a grand attempt to provide a unified theory for all of sociology, a theory that could apply to all human societies (even if the details vary, he thought there were common patterns that were universal). Parsons argued that the key elements of any society were organized around the broader (and often hidden) needs of the society as a whole (for example, Parsons 1951; Parsons and Smelser 1956). For example, all societies have some kind of religion, functionalists have argued, because religion serves many useful purposes: Religious ideas and doctrines give societies a shared moral code to live by, they help people explain the unexplainable, and they encourage social solidarity between people. At different times in history, religion may play different roles, but the reason it persists is because societies find it useful. Parsons eventually came

to describe this theory of society as **structural functionalism**, that is, a theory of society in which individuals, groups, and the institutions of any society are guided by an overarching social system.

According to structural functionalism, the social system contains powerful norms, values, and institutions—enduring practices of society and the organizations that manage those practices. Within the social system, individuals take on certain *roles*, such as "student" or "teacher," or "worker" or "boss," throughout life, and while in those roles they tend to act a certain way (to follow an appropriate script, like an actor). The structural functionalist theory emphasizes that norms, values, and institutions arise and persist because they prove to be good ways of maintaining social order.

While Parsons spent an enormous amount of time elaborating this framework in his later writings, examining specific norms, values, roles, and institutions, there are three critical ideas of structural functionalism to remember: (1) enduring features of society can ultimately be explained in terms of their "functional" purpose—societies develop religion, for example, as a way of creating common values or accounting for things that cannot be explained without reference to a supernatural being; (2) individuals are heavily shaped and constrained by the social system in which they are living; and (3) conflicts are minimized by the social system as individuals learn (or "know") and more or less accept their "place."

What about social change? How do societies change over time? In the structural functionalist view, social change is something that generally happens gradually, as norms and institutions adapt to meet new challenges. In contrast to the way Karl Marx envisioned social change happening through revolutionary class struggles, Parsons and his collaborators believed that social change happens much like the theory of evolution in biology. Evolutionary biology has demonstrated that animal species adapt over time through a process of **natural selection**, where advantageous traits are selected over traits that are not, generation by generation. Parsons saw this metaphor as useful for understanding how a society as a whole (and its component parts) evolve as well. Things that work well become permanent, and those features of any society that are "dysfunctional" are slowly weeded out. As an illustration of a dysfunctional practice that eventually disappeared, consider this example: For much of human history, when an enemy was captured during wartime they were likely to be tortured (for information or simply because they were the enemy). Eventually, however, societies came to recognize that torturing your enemies meant that your own fighters would be tortured when captured. It would, seemingly, be better for everyone if no one used torture. Over time, enough people around the world came to understand that a no-torture rule in war-time was an improvement, and today using torture on foreign combatants is a strong violation of international law.

Structural functionalism seemed to provide a way of integrating the diverse elements of any society into a single, coherent theory. It seemed like it could account for everything. But, as many critics pointed out, it did so only by ignoring many important aspects of contemporary societies that did not seem to fit the theory. We now will move on to consider two of the most important streams of criticism of Parsons and structural functionalism that emerged in the 1950s in the next two sections.

Conflict Theory

2.3.2 Discuss how conflict theory attempted to explain social inequalities.

One of the major objections to functionalist social theory was that it seemed to suggest that societies are largely conflict-free, self-regulating places in which all of the different parts of society serve important functions and fit together more or less harmoniously. Structural functionalist theory, in its most extreme form, did indeed seem to suggest that the order-imposing elements of society (such as religion) were vastly more powerful than the conflict-generating elements, such as those arising out of the inequalities between groups that Marx, Weber, Du Bois, and Addams had seen as central to all societies. Parsons and other functionalists, by contrast, argued that these classical social theorists tended to exaggerate the role of conflict, especially insofar as social change was concerned.

A number of social theorists in the late 1950s and in the 1960s vigorously disagreed with Parsons, and they proposed an alternative to functionalist social theory that came to be known as **conflict theory**. Conflict theory traces its roots to Marx and Weber, and it attempts to synthesize elements of each thinker's work into a new theory of society. One of the founding figures of conflict theory, German sociologist Ralf Dahrendorf (1929–2009), who did much of his most important work while living and teaching in Great Britain, argued that while Marx's view of social change based on class struggle was outdated, it was nevertheless true that many types of economic conflict still exist in the modern world and are critical components of social life (Dahrendorf 1959). Some of these conflicts had been channeled into the relationship between unions and employers, for example, while others

took place over the policies of governments, such as the taxes that corporations and rich individuals have to pay, or policies that would help poor or low-income individuals and families live better lives. Dahrendorf also argued that noneconomic conflicts, such as over who has the authority to make decisions within organizations, are an often hidden but important type of conflict. The problem with Parsons's functionalist approach, for Dahrendorf and other conflict theorists, was that it neglected the critical importance of conflicts in society, thereby presenting an unrealistic image of society that exaggerated consensus and social harmony.

The most popular and influential work in the conflict theory tradition was that of C. Wright Mills (1918–1962), who wrote a series of books on class and power that argued that America in the 1950s was governed by a "power elite" that strove to protect its privileges and dominated the making of government policy (Mills 1956). (It was Mills who invented the concept of the **sociological imagination** as a way of describing the mission of the discipline of sociology, as we discussed in Chapter 1.) For Mills, the power elite consisted of the top ranks of the leading political, economic, and military institutions in American society, and this power elite was able to exclude ordinary citizens from exerting much influence over government policies. Mills viewed the classical notion of democracy—rule by the people—as a fiction in the context of the power wielded by those at the top.

Conflict theory evolved in the 1960s to become, for a time, the principal home for those sociologists seeking new ways of thinking about inequality and social injustice. The popularity of conflict theory stemmed in large part from the growing sense that functionalist theory did not seem to provide a very good way of explaining why inequalities exist within society, or at its extreme even seemed to some to justify those inequalities as functional for societies. For example, in one famous essay first published in 1945, functionalist social theorists argued that economic inequality was a necessary component of society in order to encourage the most talented individuals to pursue careers that would be the most useful for society as a whole (Davis and Moore 1945). The authors of this paper argued that no one would undergo the long training period necessary to become a physician, for example, unless doctors received more pay than jobs not requiring such training. Because societies need well-trained doctors, it is necessary to provide the financial incentives to ensure an adequate supply of such people in the medical field.

By contrast, conflict theory placed these social and economic inequalities under the microscope, noting that inequalities of wealth and power are not natural outcomes but rather their privileges persist because powerful individuals and groups go to great lengths to protect them. For example, some employers treat their workers poorly or may use legal or illegal means to prevent workers from organizing unions. Professions that claim to serve the public interest have developed many ways to enhance their incomes and prevent their clients from challenging them. Physicians (a profession we don't normally think of as exploiting others) created organizations like the American Medical Association that have worked very hard to ensure that the supply of doctors is limited by law to those who complete a licensed medical school. By holding down competition, physicians are able to receive higher fees than they otherwise might.

Why does this particular cake have special meaning? Symbolic interactionists highlight the importance of the symbolic meanings we attach to objects, gestures, and conversations, which might otherwise seem like ordinary events. A cake is not always just a cake!

Conflict theorists argued that inequality inevitably produces tensions between groups and individuals over who gets what. People who feel oppressed (whether via sexism, racism, economic wealth, or other forms of inequality) will eventually begin to struggle against those who take advantage of them. Sometimes these struggles happen informally (such as when workers may refuse to give their bosses their best effort), while other times they are more open (such as when a union declares a strike). In highlighting the importance of inequality as a form of social conflict and struggle, conflict theory sought to revive some of the classical concerns of Marx and Weber, in particular in their respective writings on class and status-group inequality. But conflict theory never became a full-fledged system of social thought, as some of its early thinkers had thought it might. Having reminded sociologists that societies do not always function smoothly and without conflict, it was not always clear where conflict theory could go next. While conflict is unquestionably an important component of social life, a theory of conflict proved too vague to be the basis for a new social theory.

Symbolic Interactionism

2.3.3 Analyze how everyday social interaction lies at the heart of understanding society, according to symbolic interactionism.

Another critical response to functionalism that emerged in the 1950s and 1960s was known as **symbolic interactionism**, a theory of society that focuses on how people interact with one another and the role that symbols play in those interactions. While Talcott Parsons and his followers saw individuals and individual action as heavily shaped by society and its constituent parts, symbolic interactionism turns this idea on its head, arguing that social order starts from individuals and the meanings they give to objects, events, and relationships with others. Its founding theorists were two scholars who taught at the University of Chicago—philosopher George Herbert Mead (1863–1931) and Herbert Blumer (1900–1987), a sociologist and student of Mead's (see Blumer 1969; Mead 1934).

Symbolic interactionists argue that understanding everyday social interaction—including basic things such as people eating together, being in a classroom together, or greeting each other on the street—lies at the heart of understanding society, as it is through such interactions that both individual identities and societies are formed. In this way, while most sociological theories (including all of the theories we have discussed so far) focus on big-picture topics like economy, religion, politics, or society more generally, symbolic interactionism zooms in to focus on everyday human behavior and the ways in which we interact with one another as the building blocks of society.

Why study everyday behavior? What could such everyday things as people eating together possibly tell us about society? The answer, according to symbolic interactionists, is that what distinguishes humans from other species is that in our everyday interactions we interpret and give meaning to objects, activities, and people in ways that animal species do not. Mead famously argued that what distinguishes humans from animals and defines what it is to be a social being is that we are both *subjects* who act in the world as well as *objects* who exist in the world and are interpreted and defined by others. To explain this, Mead divided identities into two parts, what he called the "I" and the "Me." The Me represents the objective dimension of the self—that which is interpreted by others—while the I represents the subjective dimension of the self—in other words, that part of our self-understanding that interprets how others see us and that decides how to act based on how our actions will appear to others. In these ways, symbolic interactionists argue that our sense of self comes directly from the evaluations of others. In his later writings on symbolic interaction, Mead's student Blumer distinguished three types of objects that can be the subject of interpretation: physical objects (a table, a tree), social objects (people), and abstract objects (ideas).

Digital Vision/Getty Images

How we "present" ourselves to others is an important aspect of how everyday life is performed. The influential interactionist Erving Goffman (1922–1982) compared getting ready to go out in the world as analogous to actors in a play getting ready to go on stage.

The symbolic interactionists challenged social theorists to pay more attention to the centrality of everyday acts in creating the conditions for social order. But how, a conflict theorist of this era might ask, do the powerful inequalities and distinct social roles that characterize societies impact interaction? Symbolic interactionists were very aware of this issue, noting that the evaluations and opinions of *some* people count more to us than others, depending on the relationship. But in each case, our behavior is shaped by the opinions others have of us, and when we decide how to behave we consider the values of these others, giving greater deference to those with more power. In this way, inequalities penetrate our everyday interactions.

If our sense of self is determined by the opinions others have of us, and we all want others to have good opinions of us, it makes sense that we will try to behave in a way that will lead others to interpret us in a positive way. This idea forms the basis of a classical work by Erving Goffman, who, more than any other sociologist, popularized interactionist ideas. In *The Presentation of Self in Everyday Life* (Goffman 1959), Goffman employs the famous Shakespearian quote that "all the world's a stage" to compare social life to theater, arguing that our behaviors are similar to the performances of actors. Like actors, we play roles, follow scripts, and have our performances evaluated by an audience (in this case, other people with whom we interact with in our day-to-day lives). In this "dramaturgical" approach to social life, Goffman argues that we are constantly seeking to influence how people interpret our behaviors by strategically acting in certain ways to achieve a desired interpretation from others. Consider, for example, going on a job interview. We want the person who is interviewing us to think that we are organized, careful, hardworking, and conscientious. How might we give off these impressions? On the one hand there are things we can say about ourselves, but there are also nonverbal cues that we give off, as well as the way that we carry ourselves, which may signal these qualities. So we may wear a suit instead of the jeans we are more comfortable in, we sit up on the chair instead of slouching, we comb our hair in a conservative way instead of letting it go wild, and so on. In such ways, Goffman says we engage in **impression management**—strategically organizing how we present ourselves in order to influence how others see us. In our internet profiles, we are inevitably involved in one kind of impression management.

BIG QUESTION 2.4 How Has a New Generation of Social Theory Evolved?

SOCIAL THEORY SINCE THE TURBULENT 1960s

Sociology and the leading social theories underwent an enormous transition in the 1960s and the early 1970s as social movements around the world demanded, and sometimes won, important types of social change (Sica and Turner 2005). This was, after all, the era of the civil rights movement, the feminist movement, the environmental movement, the anti–Vietnam War movement, and the beginnings of the gay and lesbian rights movement, among others. In this vortex of social and political change, traditional ways of understanding society, including some of those that had only recently been popular, were thrown into question. The dominant position of functionalism was dislodged by the late 1960s, and functionalism came to be widely (although not always accurately) dismissed as a theory that justified the inequalities of the existing social order. Conflict theory disappeared as well, replaced by other critical theories of inequality that emerged (or reemerged) in this period. Symbolic interactionism, in contrast to the other midcentury traditions, did remain vibrant, and some of the key insights of symbolic interactionists were incorporated into leading contemporary social theories, but in general interactionism retreated to a small corner of sociology.

In the wake of the social changes brought about during the 1960s, a new generation of social theories and theorists appeared on the scene. Some had an explicit desire to connect to social movements of the times, while others sought, in different ways, to build upon aspects of the classical and midcentury traditions to develop new insights about the relationship between individuals and society, the nature of social order, and the conditions of social change. In this section, we can only provide a brief sampling of some of the most important of these theories, but we hope to indicate some of the main strands of contemporary social theory.

The Revival of Marxism

2.4.1 Discuss neo-Marxist ideas about the capitalist state, social classes, and globalization.

The older theoretical tradition of Marxism underwent a significant revival in the 1960s and afterward. A new generation of Marxist social theorists sought to update Marxism for the late twentieth century, taking into account the fact that history had not—at least up until then—worked out the way Marx and Engels had predicted it would, which demanded explanation. One central focus of what is known as **neo-Marxism** was to expand upon Marx's original ideas about politics to develop a theory of the **capitalist state**—that is, the governing institutions of a capitalist society. Neo-Marxists developed new understandings of how and why governments in capitalist societies ultimately make policies in the interests of the capitalist class, but at the same time they also began to investigate the conditions under which governments and powerful economic groups had to make concessions to the working class in order to stave off revolutionary challenges. For example, capitalist governments could establish social programs such as pensions for the elderly (what is known as Social Security in the United States), unemployment insurance, health insurance, and free or low-cost public education—programs that provide some benefits to poor and working class people—while simultaneously ensuring that capitalist firms remain profitable and the capitalist economy as a whole is able to grow.

It was abundantly clear by the early 1970s that the establishment of such government programs, as well as the class compromises employers made after World War II, dramatically improved the lives of ordinary people and even helped to save capitalism from its own worst tendencies (i.e., the tendency to fall into economic crisis). The benefits these programs provided were seen by neo-Marxists as key to persuading the working class that it did not need socialism (Poulantzas 1978). At the same time, however, neo-Marxists insisted that such concessions could not go on forever; at some point, their costs would become too great for capitalist economies or governments to bear. This "fiscal crisis" would ultimately open the door to the possibility of a new kind of socialist revolution (or at least make it one possible outcome among other alternatives) (O'Connor 1973).

In addition to rethinking the classical Marxist theory of the state, neo-Marxist scholars also developed a much more elaborate understanding of the nature of social classes and the class structure within capitalist societies. Marx's two-class model—a small dominant class and a large subordinate class—clearly did not fit modern capitalist societies very well. By the middle of the twentieth century, it was obvious that the growth of a large middle class made up of professionals (such as doctors, lawyers, engineers, and teachers) and business and sales managers (who worked for large companies, but did not own them) bore little resemblance to the classical proletariat that Marx envisioned. The "embarrassment of the middle classes," as neo-Marxist theorist Erik Olin Wright (1985) put it, required a new body of theory about how modern societies are divided. Wright's effort to solve this problem argued that just as the ownership of a business is an "asset" that can be used to generate greater economic rewards (for example, when you hire people to work for you), so too are credentials (like a law degree) and supervisorial positions (in an organization) (Wright 1985, 1997). Possession of any of these assets, Wright argued, would generate surplus incomes that blur the classical two-dimensional division of classes based on ownership of capital, as illustrated in Figure 2.6.

Neo-Marxist social theorists were also among the first to revive the study of capitalism as a global economic order. Immanuel Wallerstein's (1974, 2011) work on what he called the **capitalist world system** represents one widely debated example, while Robert Brenner's (2006) analysis of the global crisis of capitalism provided an alternative view. For Wallerstein, capitalism is an economic system that exists not just *within* countries but also in the economic relationships *between* countries (where rich countries are able to exploit poor countries, just as rich capitalists can be seen as exploiting workers). Wallerstein and other neo-Marxists anticipated the rise of globalization long before social scientists in other theoretical traditions began to pay attention to an increasingly global world and how the economic inequalities between countries were reproduced over time. Other

Figure 2.6 A New Understanding of Social Classes in Capitalist Societies

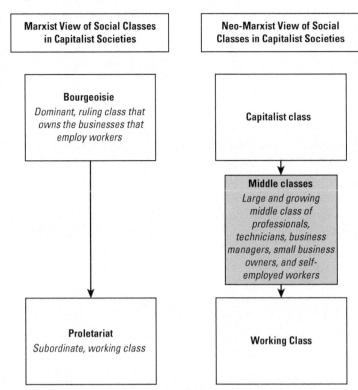

Karl Marx and many of his nineteenth and early twentieth century followers thought the industrial revolution, and the creation of ever-larger factories owned by a tiny bourgeoisie and worked by an ever-growing working class was the future of capitalism. But over time, many societies like the United States saw those large factories fall into disuse (as has this one in Bridgeport, CT). Workers today are much more likely to be employed in offices than factories, requiring new thinking about the concept of class.

neo-Marxist contributions have highlighted inherent crisis tendencies arising from unstable features of global capitalism, particularly those in the financial sector (Brenner 2006). The global financial crisis of 2007–08 and the economic decline brought about by COVID-19 in 2020 are reminders that, for all its tools, the capitalist state cannot prevent economic crises from arising, and *perhaps* some day one of these crises will topple the entire system.

Feminist Social Theory

2.4.2 Analyze the role of intersectionality in theories of gender inequality.

One important limitation of neo-Marxism was that its focus on class relations and class power tended to downplay other types of inequalities. Just as Weber and Du Bois made important contributions to sociology by emphasizing the importance of status-group conflicts and racism, so too did a new generation of social theorists seek to invigorate a sociological understanding of inequalities beyond just those rooted in social class. One such alternative was the emergence of **feminist social theory** in the 1970s. Feminist social theory placed gender and gender inequality at the center of its theoretical lens and challenged many of the assumptions of classical social theory for its male-centered biases.

An early and influential thinker in the development of feminist social theory was the French philosopher and writer Simone de Beauvoir (1908–1986). While Beauvoir wrote on a range of issues, from ethics and philosophy to politics, it was her work on sex and gender that made the most direct contributions to social theory. In her classic book *The Second Sex* (Beauvoir 1952), she offers an analysis of what has come to be known as **patriarchy**—the idea that societies are set up to ensure that women are systematically controlled (and devalued). For Beauvoir, women were not born to be subordinate, but they are made to seem different and distinct from, and inferior to, men. In Beauvoir's own words, "One is not born but becomes a woman." This idea was central to the distinction that later feminists made between **sex**, which is a biological characteristic, and **gender**, which is the social meaning attached to being a "man" or a "woman" (and more recently, trans and nonbinary gender identities). Simone de Beauvoir was thus one of the first theorists to insist that gender and femininity are **social constructions**—that is, societies *create* gender categories, which are not natural outcomes of biological differences–and these gendered categories are translated into enduring inequalities between men and women.

As contemporary feminist theory grew in the 1970s, it built upon and extended Beauvoir's early insights in a variety of ways. Feminist theorists share a commitment to understanding how and why the social world is designed as it is for men and women. It is possible, however, to discern three key approaches to social theory. The first approach arose as early feminist scholars began to see the social world from the perspective of women, leading them to theorize **sex differences**, or the different ways the world worked for men and women. These early works often began by making the point that most social theories had ignored women and were thus based on male realms of experience. Therefore, feminist social theorists set out to include women as the subjects of theoretical analysis. The result was often quite transformative. For instance, the sociologist Dorothy Smith (b. 1926) showed how the basis of sociology changed when women were put at the center of the analysis. From a woman's perspective, Smith argues we see how the social sciences had systematically neglected important aspects of the experiences of women, demonstrating a male-centered bias (Smith 1974). For example, if we define "labor" as only involving paid work out of the household, we ignore another kind of labor (housework and caring for others) that was historically performed by women. Echoing this, other feminist theorists analyzed how sociological inquiry would have to change if it took women's lives seriously—from rethinking its notions of the individual to expanding its areas of inquiry to include the private sphere (such as the role of power in families).

Early feminist theorists not only rethought particular scholarly fields, they also revised theoretical traditions that crossed disciplines. One of the most important was that of **psychoanalysis** (the study of the conscious and unconscious individual mind and its influence on individual behavior), which was quite important to some early feminist theorists who wanted to understand how men and women formed their senses of self. Most traditional theories of the individual in psychological and psychoanalytic theory were based exclusively on male experience. When women were brought into focus, however, those models had to change. It was argued that since women tended to develop their selves in relation to others, through their attachments and ability to care, they inevitably had different sources of identity. This insight was most famously elaborated on by the sociologist Nancy Chodorow (b. 1944), who traced the

Although progress has been made toward breaking professional gender stereotypes, the continuing segregation of men and women into different types of jobs, and the lower pay received by women than men working in the same job, suggests one way in which the power of gender stereotypes persists in modern societies.

psychological basis of sex differences to the structure of the family. Drawing on psychoanalysis, Chodorow (1978) theorized that the sexual division of labor in the family, where women were primarily responsible for childrearing, created distinct development pathways for boys and girls. Thus, sex differences were rooted deep inside our heads, in our unconscious desires and emotional attachments.

Throughout the 1970s and 1980s, most feminist theorists were searching for *the* cause of gender inequality. Far too often, though, this made their theories seem somewhat simplified—as if gender inequality comes from a single fixed aspect of societies or individuals (or the relationships between individuals). Similarly, they frequently lumped all women together, ignoring critical differences among them. In the process, they tended to highlight issues of concern to privileged women, such as the social isolation of middle-class housewives or the exclusion of some women from paid labor. But these were not the concerns of all women. Later feminist theorists have paid special attention to the ways in which gender is experienced differently by different women (Collins 1990).

From these critiques a second feminist approach to theory emerged, one that shifted from explaining sexual inequality in general to making the very existence of gender something that needed to be examined and challenged. This feminist approach explores how the categories of male and female emerge and shape social life. For instance, feminists have explored gender dynamics in different institutions (for example, families, schools, workplaces, churches). Others have looked at how gender "gets performed" in these social settings. So while sociologists of gender might study the division of labor in the family or at work, theorists of gender might seek to *explain* why work is divided up in gendered ways across different public and private arenas—and why we interact the way we do as women and men (Connell 1987; West and Zimmerman 1987).

Even more recently, a distinctive third approach has emerged in which feminist theorists have moved away from looking at gender on its own to considering it alongside other social hierarchies. This third type of feminist theory allows for social life to be understood in more fluid, interconnected, and variable terms. The most influential social theorist working in this vein has been Patricia Hill Collins (b.1948), who has argued that the oppression Black women have historically experienced requires a broader social theory of how race, class, and gender intersect to produce complex forms of inequality and injustice (Collins 1990). Here the emphasis is on how relationships between men and women are formed in relation to multiple types of social inequalities such as race, class, sexuality, and religion. The social world is stratified in all these ways. So when gender is constructed or performed, it is done so along with these other categories. For example, the implications of gender inequality in families are very different for upper-middle-class women who can afford high-quality childcare for their children and housekeepers to clean their houses than for poor women who have far fewer choices.

This theoretical approach thus highlights the interlocking nature of inequality, or what has come to be known as **intersectionality**—a focus on the linkages among disadvantaged groups. The key innovation is to look at the way inequalities are experienced together. The experience of gender, in other words, is different for poor or rich women, White or women of color, and so forth (Crenshaw 1991; McCall 2005; Choo and Ferree 2010).

Michel Foucault and the Problem of Power

2.4.3 Explain Foucault's theory of how power operates in society.

If recent feminist social theorists call our attention to the multiple and overlapping forms of oppression, the writings of the French social theorist Michel Foucault (1926–1984) sought to uncover how power works in all of its many manifestations. Foucault did not fit into any of the usual disciplinary boundaries: He was a philosopher and an intellectual historian, although his writings had many implications for social theory. He wrote books on topics such as prisons and asylums and the history of madness, and a multivolume study on the history of sexuality. In contrast to the standard way of thinking about power as something that some people have (for example, those in the government or military, the ruling class, the authority figures in important institutions) and others do not (for example, the working class, the poor, minorities), Foucault says that power is everywhere, operating in hidden as well as open forms.

Foucault was particularly interested in the role of "discipline" across societies—both how we try to discipline ourselves and how others (and institutions) try to discipline us. Foucault was interested in the ways in which institutions such as schools, prisons, mental institutions, sports teams, and others train (or retrain) individuals to conform in certain ways (including not just their minds but also their bodies). Foucault famously suggested in his book *Discipline and Punish* (1977) that we live in a "disciplinary society," using imagery from a proposed model prison designed by social philosopher Jeremy Bentham called the Panopticon. Placed at the center of the prison, the Panopticon is a visual tower that allows for continuous surveillance of all the inmates, with the goal of "inducing in the inmates a state of permanent and conscious visibility that assures the automatic functioning of power." Foucault argued that whole societies are constructed in similar ways. He argued we are all subjected to a disciplining power that we can't see but that is all around us.

In modern society, then, Foucault believed that discipline is both a major characteristic and function of power. However, power should not be thought of as something imposed on us from above. Foucault argued that what makes it even more difficult to confront is that everyone

The French social theorist Michel Foucault emphasized the role of architecture (such as a version of the famous Panopticon designed by Jeremy Bentham in the eighteenth century) and technology in enabling specific forms of surveillance and control. By the 21st century, the constant collection of information about each of us is very well-known. Our movements and actions are continually tracked by media companies, schools, banks, credit card companies, security cameras, and, of course, government agencies. Social media companies have in recent years made immense profits by selling the information we voluntarily give them to advertisers. Government agencies have also routinely been able to gain access to even out "private" social media. It is almost impossible today to remain completely "off the grid" — our digital fingerprints are everywhere, and they can be used in all kinds of ways that we may not approve of. In this way, Foucalt's view of power and surveillance is even more relevant today than when he wrote about it in the 1970s.

disciplines everyone else—from friends who make fun of each other for acting in particular ways to processes through which we discipline our own behaviors by internalizing norms in society. For example, almost everyone in America these days seems to either be on a diet or think they should lose weight, or fears that if they do not discipline their eating habits they will gain weight. When we come to feel guilty about certain things and monitor our own behavior, as most of us do with respect to things like diet and exercise, we are doing something that Foucault says is the hallmark of modern power: We become, in short, our own police agents, monitoring our own behaviors.

Foucault's radical reimaging of power, surveillance, and discipline challenges us to think about societies in a new way. These are indeed exciting ideas that have inspired many interesting and important studies by social scientists. But more recently, a growing number of social theorists have criticized Foucault's ideas. These critics have noted that if power is "everywhere," it becomes such a vague and slippery concept that it is difficult to study in a scientific way.

Pierre Bourdieu: A New Approach to Theorizing Social Inequality

2.4.4 Discuss how Bourdieu redefined classes and the nature of class differences.

Michel Foucault's French colleague, sociologist Pierre Bourdieu (1930–2002), took a very different approach to understanding power and inequality. Bourdieu's insights and theoretical arguments were a direct outgrowth of his own experiences in a life marked by climbing up the French social ladder from humble origins. His social theory attempted to analyze the ways in which individuals behave in the context of class differences of which

they are largely unaware. In many ways, Bourdieu's focus on class follows the work of other social theorists, especially Karl Marx, who also argued that understanding classes and class conflict was the key to understanding society. However, Bourdieu breaks with Marxist and later neo-Marxist theories of class by reconceptualizing how sociologists think about classes and the nature of class differences. Whereas Marx and other sociologists usually define classes as groups of people who share the same position within the structure of the economy (as either workers or owners of the means of production, or in terms of quantitative measures such as income), Bourdieu enlarges the definition of class to include multiple dimensions, including how people think and act in the world, and the kinds of knowledge and sophistication they display. In this way, Bourdieu's work combined insights from interactionists about how individuals interact with one another with theories (like Marx's) of how inequalities in economic resources influence the choices and opportunities available to all of us as individuals.

At the core of Bourdieu's analysis of class and society are the everyday actions that people perform. From how we carry ourselves when talking to people, to the different kinds of music or food that we like, to the different ways we interact with authority figures, Bourdieu argued that people act differently in the world depending upon their class location. Bourdieu says that these differences emerge from the fact that each individual has what he calls a **habitus** (a term based on the Latin word for a "habit"). Our individual habitus develops from birth to adulthood, and it is what causes us to act in certain ways in certain situations where we display our class of being. Different people have different kinds of habituses, depending on their upbringing and education. In this way, the habitus is not something we are born with but rather a set of habits that are deeply rooted in the experiences we have growing up. Bourdieu argues that because of their different upbringings, members of different classes tend to have different habituses, and this is one of the key differences between members of different classes.

To illustrate and document these class-based differences in taste and dispositions, Bourdieu turned to studying culture, specifically to the consumption patterns of members of different classes. In one of his most famous books, *Distinction: A Social Critique of the Judgment of Taste* (Bourdieu [1979] 1984), Bourdieu interviewed a cross-section of French society about their tastes and preferences regarding a range of cultural products, from music to art to literature. What Bourdieu found is that people from different economic classes express different cultural tastes, and that one of the markers of belonging to one or another class is precisely that it influences the tastes and preferences of individual members of those classes regarding cultural objects. Importantly, Bourdieu argued that when we express our preference for one or another cultural object, such as one genre of music over another, we are at once indicating that we belong to one group while defining ourselves in opposition to another.

Building off of his recognition that people in society compete to define their tastes and preferences as better than others, Bourdieu argued that groups in society fight over not just economic resources but also cultural resources. Bourdieu expanded Marx's idea of capital (recall that Marx used the term "capital" to describe any resource that can be invested to generate monetary returns) to include not just economic capital but also other kinds of capital. Most famously, he introduced the idea of **cultural capital,** the stock of cultural knowledge and sophistication each person possesses. For example, our ability to be able to talk intelligently about art, films, literature or world events suggests the amount of cultural capital we have. Importantly, although people with high economic capital often have high cultural capital, the two do not directly overlap. Bourdieu argued that a person's position in the social hierarchy cannot be reduced to simply the amount of economic capital they have but must take into account a combination of economic and cultural capital.

Bourdieu found the extended notion of capital so useful for understanding inequality that he argued that a full understanding of the social position of any individual also required examining the role of other kinds of capital, most notably what he called **social capital** (resources based on who you know and can call upon for help when you need it) and **symbolic capital** (your reputation). Social capital refers to a person's connections, such as the people they know from their membership in groups or organizations, their friends and acquaintances, and other people they can call on for help when needed. Durable networks of friends remain valuable throughout someone's life. For instance, one may benefit from a job referral from a friendship first formed in college. Symbolic capital consists of how a

Similar to Marx, Bourdieu recognized the importance of monetary and material capital in social hierarchies. However, Bourdieu argued that other forms of capital—such as how culturally sophisticated you are, or who you know—also determine one's social class. Meeting someone for the first time is one important setting in which our cultural capital is immediately on display, and being judged.

person or group is judged by a particular community, often in reference to someone's accomplishments. Professionals are judged by other professionals in the same field and can be accorded more or less prestige depending on how they are accorded by their peers. War veterans generally receive social honor by virtue of having served their country. An actor or musician may not have had much commercial success, but if they are well regarded by the people in their industry they will accumulate symbolic capital (for example, an actor who appears in small, well-reviewed independent films may have more symbolic capital than a more famous actor who appears in Hollywood blockbusters that don't require as much skill to perform). Reputations can also be negative—if your peers come to think you are incompetent, your symbolic capital will quickly disappear.

In short, Bourdieu saw the different forms of capital as providing different pathways into the class system. Someone who has a lot of economic capital may be able to get away with a lack of symbolic capital (a poor reputation may not matter too much if you are rich) whereas someone who has a lot of cultural capital or social capital may be able to rise up in the class system even if they are not particularly wealthy.

Analytical Sociology

2.4.5 Discuss the relationship between the individual and society for analytical sociologists.

Pierre Bourdieu's rich theories of inequality highlight how social theory can provide useful insights by paying renewed attention to individual behavior and interaction. His insights have influenced a new generation of social theorists who have sought to develop what are known as **middle-range theories**—or theories that make specific, researchable propositions about particular aspects of society that consciously connect social structure with individual action. Under the loose umbrella of **analytical sociology**, these sociologists and social theorists have argued that the problem with many existing approaches in both classical and midcentury social theory was that they failed to pay adequate attention to the ways in which individual actions and motivations provide the foundation for how societies operate and how they change. At the center of analytical sociology is the idea that sociologists must simultaneously study the relationship between the "macro" aspects of societies (for example, institutions, organizations, the economy) and the "micro" aspects of how and why individuals make the choices that they do. Analytical sociologists define their approach to linking the micro and the macro as **structural individualism**, a theory that starts from the idea that societies rest on the choices and actions that individuals make, individually and together, even though these choices and the actions that follow from them are always constrained by society as a whole.

Robert Merton (1910–2002) and James Coleman (1926–1995) are regarded as two of the founding figures of analytical sociology (Hedstrom and Udehn 2009). Merton was an American sociologist who attended Harvard on scholarship, where Talcott Parsons was one of his teachers. But despite this pedigree, Merton largely rejected the ambitions of structural functionalism to build what he called **middle-range theory** (Merton 1957). Merton invented some of the most famous concepts in all of sociology, for example, the **self-fulfilling prophecy** (the idea that if you start to think or predict something will happen, it becomes more likely to actually happen than if you had not) and the **unanticipated consequences of social action** (the idea that the outcomes of any action we undertake may well be unanticipated, as for example when we get a dog for companionship but soon make new human friends we meet at the dog park). Merton was a much-admired sociologist during his career, and his insights have gained in importance in recent years as a new generation of sociologists has sought to elaborate on some of his central ideas.

From the standpoint of social theory, one especially important idea that Merton proposed was that good theories should neither be aimed at such a high level of generality that they leave out important details (as examples, he specifically pointed to Marx's theory of history based on class struggle or Parsons's structural functionalist theory of societies), nor be so specific to a particular situation that they have no general implications. In other words, when theories are too grand, they are impossible to really test. For example, it would be difficult to design research to prove or disprove that religion is "functional" for societies, as Parsons proposed. In contrast, I may have a theory about why one park in my neighborhood is popular with families while another is a popular place to sell drugs, and my "theory" could be studied (so in that sense, it solves the problem of overly grand theories). But whatever theory I come up with will probably not be able to say very much else about parks,

drugs, or communities outside my neighborhood. The middle range stands between the two, looking for the general in specific contexts and always based in part on the actions of individuals. What does this mean in practice?

James Coleman's contributions to analytical sociology grew out of these kinds of questions. Coleman spent much of his career developing mathematical models of social life, applying insights from economics about how individuals are motivated to act on what they take to be their interests and goals. In his major theoretical study, Coleman (1990) argues for the importance of requiring micro (or individual) explanations in any sociological research project. To exemplify what he means, Coleman gives an example of how an individual-level explanation works using Weber's *The Protestant Ethic and the Spirit of Capitalism*. Recall Weber's famous thesis—that capitalism developed in countries and regions where Protestantism was strongest. It can be simply diagrammed as follows:

Strong Protestantism → Early Capitalist Development.

This implies that all we need to know is where Protestantism was strong, capitalism developed earlier. But Coleman argues that what Weber actually did, and what makes *The Protestant Ethic* such a great book, is something much more than this, as displayed in Figure 2.7 (based on Coleman 1990). Versions of this diagram have been called the "Coleman Boat" (or sometimes the "Coleman Bathtub"). The logic of the diagram is that for a theory like Weber's to work, it has to be able to specify *how* the macro (in this case, how the presence or absence of Protestantism) influenced the micro (in this case, the values and behaviors of individuals—with Protestants more likely than non-Protestants, Weber thought, to behave in ways that would help capitalism flourish) to produce a new (macro) outcome (the rise of capitalism).

The upshot of this powerful insight is that we need to build social theories at least partially from the ground up, always paying attention to individuals, their motivations and likely behavior, as well as the larger social forces at work. In this focus, they share certain impulses with some of the theorists we have discussed up to this point, for example, with the symbolic interactionists and their focus on the importance of individuals' interactions with others.

Figure 2.7 Coleman's Boat

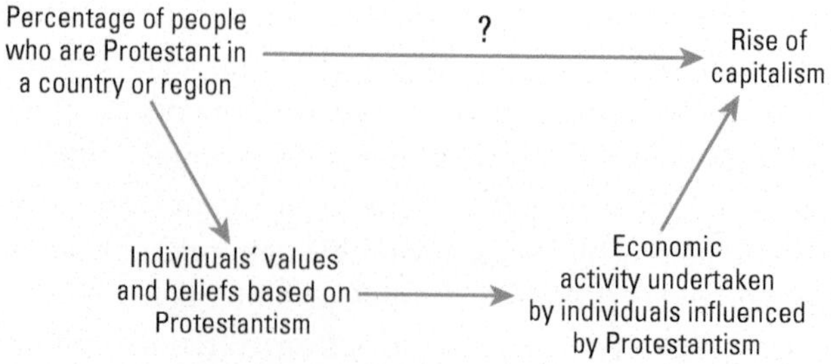

SOURCE: Based on Coleman (1990).

Figure 2.8 Structural Individualism

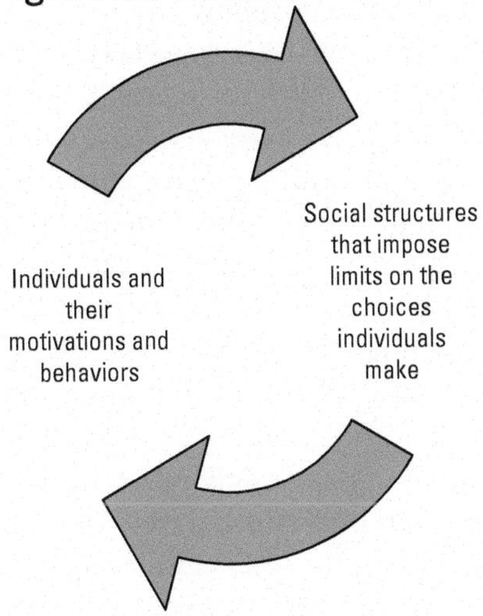

Individuals and their motivations and behaviors

Social structures that impose limits on the choices individuals make

analytical sociologists, these mechanisms are the "cogs and wheels" of social life (Bearman and Hedstrom 2009).

What are these "cogs and wheels"? One of the most important connections between the micro and the macro occurs through social networks (building upon ideas first introduced by Georg Simmel in the early part of the twentieth century). Analytical sociologists have argued that social networks are important for many reasons; we often learn valuable information about educational or employment opportunities, find new lovers, and learn new ideas or even gossip through our social networks. Networks also provide the backbone of not-so-beneficial dynamics—for example, transmittable diseases flow through networks. The basic idea about the power of social networks has been demonstrated with the growth of social media, and "networking" is now widely understood as an important strategy for building a career or a good life. Indeed, one of the most important but hidden benefits of going to college is that you will make friends and acquaintances who will (hopefully) become part of your social network!

Analytical sociology is very much in the process of development, and full assessment of its theoretical contributions must await further developments and applications. One of the most important questions that analytical sociologists have yet to take up in a serious way is the implications of their emphasis on individual actions in relation to the classical sociological ideas about class, power, the state, and globalization. In other words, the micro side of social life (the factors that motivate individual beliefs and actions) has been far better worked out than the link upward to the macro aspects of societies. In this way, the challenge of constructing adequate social theories that can provide suitable ways of connecting individuals and societies remains to be solved.

But they go beyond these earlier theorists in various ways. Perhaps most importantly, analytical sociology has made a considerable effort to absorb and import ideas from the discipline of psychology to understand how and why individuals think and act the way they do. Ideas about how the mind works in social situations are one of the hallmarks of analytical sociology. But analytical sociologists do not stop there. There are always two sides to the relationship: individuals and their motivations and behaviors, and social structures that impose limits on the choices individuals can make. Most importantly, this is a *dynamic* relationship (one informs the other in an endless cycle), as illustrated in Figure 2.8.

How does this dynamic cycle work? Analytical sociologists are keen to identify the key **mechanisms** (that is, the processes through which one thing causes something else) that make the connection between individuals and social structures happen. In the words of two of the leading

Conclusion: Social Theory and the Sociological Imagination

We started from three central themes that have motivated social theorists over the past 150 years:

1. What is the nature of the individual (who are we?), and how do individuals act in the context of society?
2. What is the basis for social order?
3. What are the conditions under which societies change?

We can now see that there is no single approach that can answer these questions once and for all. This might be viewed as a source of frustration—who wouldn't want to just "know" the answer to these questions?—but it can also be a source of fruitful thought and puzzle. Put another way, the fact that individuals, societies, and social change appear differently depending on which theoretical lens you put on underscores the endless complexity of the social world.

Does this mean that we cannot choose among theories? How is it that someone—say a young sociologist—decides that one theory is better than another? To answer that question, it is important first to understand the history of social theory and how it is different from the history of theories in related disciplines. Unlike theories in the natural sciences, for example, where "old" theories are discarded as "new" theories arise, social theories have tended to layer new ideas on top of older ideas. Classical theoretical ideas continue to inform the development of new social theories. As a result, there has been a steady accumulation of more and more theory over time, as new theories pile on top of old ones. What is a new student to do?

One way of approaching this is to think about the ways that each of the major theories we have described in this chapter approaches answers to the three central questions. Here, there are clearly important differences, and these different starting points nevertheless still leave a couple of possibilities for choosing among social theories. On the one hand, it may be that different theories can be useful depending on what questions we are focused on. In this way, we can think of different social theories as akin to different kinds of maps. Consider the differences in Google Maps between the "map view," the "earth view," and the "satellite view." Each provides a different way of looking at a single address or location. The same analogy works for old-fashioned printed maps: We use one kind of map to help navigate the streets of one city or in driving from one place to another, a different kind of map when hiking in the mountains, and a globe when trying to locate an unfamiliar country. Each kind of map provides useful orientation for some things but not others.

But all social theories cannot be equally valid for every question we might want to examine. We have tried to point out some of the shortcomings of various theories in this chapter. In these situations, where two theories are completely incompatible on some key point of interest, a sociologist must think about how to weigh their relative merits and shortcomings. Some possible questions in such comparisons could be as follows: Which theory is more consistent with what we believe we know or, to put it another way, "the facts"? Which theory helps us ask more interesting or important questions? Which theory fits better with our own political views (or perhaps even better, which forces us to challenge those views)? In some cases, the best way to make use of different theories is to synthesize them, taking ideas from different theorists and seeing how they do (or don't) fit together.

However we come to choose the theory or theories we identify with most closely, all of the major social theories we have explored in this chapter provide insights into the social world and its constituent parts. And social theories are very much part of the sociological imagination: Understanding how and why social theorists have puzzled over the questions they have underscores why sociology exists in the first place. As social theory continues to evolve and develop in the twenty-first century, we can be sure that new theoretical traditions (or revivals of older traditions) will appear to further challenge the sociological imagination.

The Big Questions Revisited 2

2.1 **What Is Social Theory?** Social theories enable us to see the social world in different ways. In this section, we identified three common themes that all major sociological theories have sought to address.

Seeing the Social World Through Social Theory

The Diversity of Social Theory
Learning Objective 2.1.1: Define social theory and the range of different social theories.

Key Terms
social theory (p. 25)

2.2 **How Did the Early Social Theorists Make Sense of the World?** The foundations of modern sociology, and social theory as we know it today, can be traced to the writings of a handful of key thinkers working in the second half of the nineteenth and early twentieth centuries. In this section, we introduced you to Karl Marx, Emile Durkheim, Max Weber, Georg Simmel, W. E. B. Du Bois, and Jane Addams.

Classical Social Theory in the Late Nineteenth and Early Twentieth Centuries

Karl Marx (1818–1883)
Learning Objective 2.2.1: Discuss why Marx believed that societies were so heavily shaped by their economic systems.

Emile Durkheim (1858–1917)
Learning Objective 2.2.2: Analyze Emile Durkheim's theory of what holds societies together.

Max Weber (1864–1920)
Learning Objective 2.2.3: Discuss Max Weber's contributions to our understanding of motivations for behavior, legitimacy and authority, and status groups and social closure.

Georg Simmel (1858–1918)
Learning Objective 2.2.4: Explain how Georg Simmel's insights on social circles and social distance help us understand how individuals and groups relate to one another.

W. E. B. Du Bois (1868–1963)
Learning Objective 2.2.5: Explain W. E. B. Du Bois's views of the diverse ways in which racism influences the lives of Black Americans and how racism produces a double consciousness.

Jane Addams (1860–1935)
Learning Objective 2.2.6: Analyze the relevance of Jane Addams's ideas of sympathetic knowledge and social ethics for addressing social problems today.

Key Terms

positivism (p. 26)   class (p. 28)   modes of production (p. 28)   forces of production (p. 28) social relations of production (p. 29)   historic materialism (p. 29)   bourgeoisie (p. 29) capital (p. 29)   proletariat (p. 29)   socialist society (p. 30)   class struggle (p. 30)   globalization (p. 30)   social facts (p. 31)   social forces (p. 31)   socialization (p. 31)   social solidarity (p. 32)   mechanical solidarity (p. 32) division of labor (p. 32)   organic solidarity (p. 32)   sacred (p. 33)   interpretive sociology (p. 34)   power (p. 35)   authority (p. 35)   legitimacy (p. 35)   charisma (p. 35)   status group (p. 36)   stratification system (p. 36)   social closure (p. 36)   social distance (p. 37)   network analysis (p. 38)   social networks (p. 38) racism (p. 39)   settlement houses (p. 40) sympathetic knowledge (p. 41)

2.3   **What Innovations in Social Theory Emerged in the Mid-Twentieth Century?** After World War II, the interests of social theorists began to shift in new and unexpected directions, and leadership in the development of social theory and sociology as a whole passed from being located primarily in Europe to America. In this section, we explored the new directions in social theory that were embodied by functionalism, conflict theory, and symbolic interactionism.

New Directions in Social Theory, 1937–1965

Structural Functionalism

Learning Objective 2.3.1: Discuss the roles that norms, values, and institutions play in society, according to the theory of structural functionalism.

Conflict Theory

Learning Objective 2.3.2: Discuss how conflict theory attempted to explain social inequalities.

Symbolic Interactionism

Learning Objective 2.3.3: Analyze how everyday social interaction lies at the heart of understanding society, according to symbolic interactionism.

Key Terms

structural functionalism (p. 42)   natural selection (p. 42)   conflict theory (p. 43)   sociological imagination (p. 43)   symbolic interactionism (p. 44)   impression management (p. 45)

2.4   **How Has a New Generation of Social Theory Evolved?** The chapter concluded with a brief sampling of some important theories that have evolved since the 1960s and examined an emerging theory known as analytical sociology.

Social Theory Since the Turbulent 1960s

The Revival of Marxism

Learning Objective 2.4.1: Discuss neo-Marxist ideas about the capitalist state, social classes, and globalization.

Feminist Social Theory

Learning Objective 2.4.2: Analyze the role of intersectionality in theories of gender inequality.

Michel Foucault and the Problem of Power

Learning Objective 2.4.3: Explain Foucault's theory of how power operates in society.

Pierre Bourdieu: A New Approach to Theorizing Social Inequality

Learning Objective 2.4.4: Discuss how Bourdieu redefined classes and the nature of class differences.

Analytical Sociology

Learning Objective 2.4.5: Discuss the relationship between the individual and society for analytical sociologists.

Key Terms

neo-Marxism (p. 46)   capitalist state (p. 46)   capitalist world system (p. 47) feminist social theory (p. 48)   patriarchy (p. 48)   sex (p. 48)   gender (p. 48)   social constructions (p. 48)   sex differences (p. 48) psychoanalysis (p. 48)   intersectionality (p. 49)   habitus (p. 50)   cultural capital (p. 51) social capital (p. 51)   symbolic capital (p. 51) middle-range theory (p. 51)   analytical sociology (p. 52)   structural individualism (p. 52)   self-fulfilling prophecy (p. 52) unanticipated consequences of social action (p. 52)   mechanism (p. 53)

Chapter 3
Studying the Social World

by Lynne Haney, Jeff Manza, and Ned Crowley

Most of us have a clear idea about what prisons look like: located in a far-off locale, enclosed by wire fencing and concrete watchtowers, and filled with scary-looking men spending their days in tiny cells. When the first author of this chapter (Lynne Haney) entered her first prison, located in a large, dilapidated mansion on an inner-city street in northern California in 1992, as a young researcher eager to understand how women were "socialized" by the criminal justice system, a very different image confronted her. The "inmates" were young women, all official wards of the state of California, who had been sent to this prison to serve their time with their children. In place of small, dark prison cells were nicely decorated bedrooms; in place of the prison mess hall was an open, well-stocked kitchen; and in place of the barren prison recreation room was a cozy living room. Then there was daily life. It was comprised not of big, burly men sitting in cells but of small children running around, chased by their mothers. The only fights she ever saw were between hungry, sleepy kids and their exasperated mothers—over what the kids should eat or when they should go to bed—hardly the stuff of movies or TV shows such as *Prison Break, OZ,* or even *Orange Is the New Black.*

One of the most common mistakes young researchers make is to assume that our own research insights are shared by others. Haney made just such a mistake in this prison study—while she had been shocked by the existence of "mommy/baby" prisons, other sociologists had been writing about them for years. And whereas she was unnerved by even the idea of small children being raised in prison, other researchers seemed optimistic about the practice. These other researchers often insisted that one way to end the pains of incarceration and to stop the familial cycle of imprisonment was to keep women and children together—even if it meant bringing kids to prison. Of all these studies, the most seemingly definitive was a statistical study by the California Department of Corrections. It tracked rearrest records of thousands of women who had done time in these prisons and found they had slightly

lower repeat arrest rates than those who had served time in traditional facilities. Although the effects were small, researchers found mommy/baby prisons to be a success—and a real alternative to traditional incarceration.

My Sociological Imagination

LYNNE HANEY

Sometimes I think I was born with a sociological imagination—although that would be thoroughly unsociological of me to say. I grew up in the California Bay Area in the 1970s, when the feminist, civil rights, and gay rights movements were at their peak—and all kinds of identities and relationships were being questioned. As a result, thinking sociologically seemed to be in the air; everyone was asking the big questions about why the world was the way it was. But then the context changed and morphed into the 1980s of Ronald Reagan and social conservatism (as well as bad hair and bad fashion). And much of the social and cultural questioning I grew up with began to wane as more rigid and limiting assumptions about the world and our places within it became acceptable. This shift left me wondering how people come to accept or reject received wisdom: Was it just a matter of who had the power and resources to impress their version of reality on others? Or was there some way to discern fact from fiction, myth from reality? It was around this time that I discovered social science research. As a young college student, sociology appealed to me because it seemed to offer the empirical tools to resolve many political and social conflicts. It offered the possibility that not everything was relative, a matter of opinion, or open to ideological debate. In this way, although I've had a sociological imagination for a long time, it was not until I learned to conduct social research that I could use my imagination productively—as a way of teaching myself and others how to learn from and be surprised by the social world.

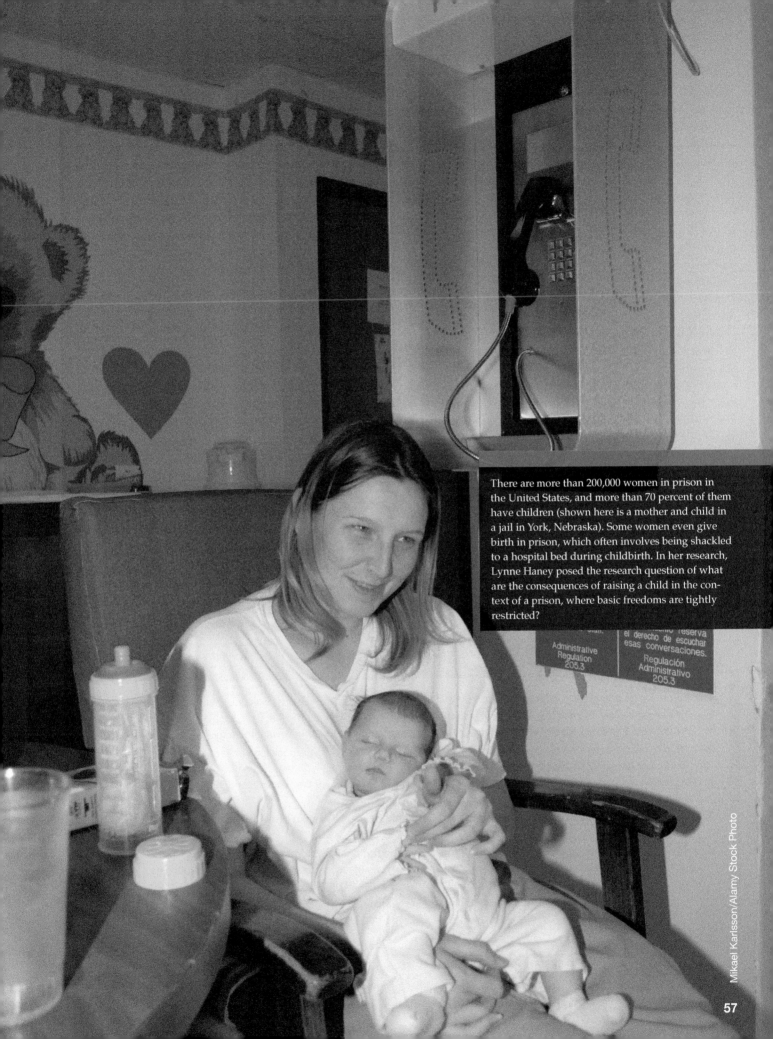

There are more than 200,000 women in prison in the United States, and more than 70 percent of them have children (shown here is a mother and child in a jail in York, Nebraska). Some women even give birth in prison, which often involves being shackled to a hospital bed during childbirth. In her research, Lynne Haney posed the research question of what are the consequences of raising a child in the context of a prison, where basic freedoms are tightly restricted?

57

All of this left Haney wondering: Perhaps raising children in prison wasn't such a bad idea. So she returned to prison to do a more extensive study. This time, she chose her sample carefully, locating her research in the state's model facility and joining its prison life. This is what **ethnographers**—researchers who enter the everyday lives of those they study in hopes of understanding how people navigate and give meaning to their worlds—do in their research. For more than three years, Haney observed as hundreds of women and children passed through the prison's steel doors. She went to group sessions, attended mothering classes, taught inmates creative writing, and went to staff meetings. By the end of the research, Haney was so integrated that the staff had given her keys to the prison!

Yet the more integrated into prison life she got, the more convinced she became that these were brutal, punishing places—but not in the way one might expect. The children, whom she thought would suffer most from the loss of freedom, seemed okay. With three meals a day, good childcare and education, health care, and other kids to play with, they were surviving life in prison fairly well. It was their mothers who were suffering. They suffered from a prison environment that stripped them of all parental power—how could they gain any maternal authority when they were ordered around, told where to go and what to do? They suffered from the loss of privacy—how could they parent when unsupervised, one-on-one time with children was

not even allowed? In the end, some women became extremely anxious about their mothering; others simply collapsed under the pressure. But no one experienced the hope and optimism promised in other research accounts.

So were other researchers wrong? Not necessarily. Although they studied similar criminal justice facilities, they had different research questions, used different research methods, and collected different kinds of **data**—the facts and information used in research. Other researchers were interested in examining whether serving time with kids made it less likely for women to reoffend, so it made sense for them to track rearrest data and interview women who had reoffended. Had Haney been interested in this, she might have used a similar approach to her research. But she wasn't. Her research questions revolved around how the women and children did time together—the practice of mothering behind bars and its implications for the mother/child bond. For this, ethnographic observation made the most sense because it gave her access to the data she needed to answer her research questions. All of this led her to paint a very different picture of these prisons and to draw very different conclusions about their possibilities and limitations.

Doing social research—whether on prisons or any other aspect of society you may want to study—raises many difficult challenges. In this chapter, we will explore those challenges and how researchers try to overcome them.

The Big Questions

1. **Where do sociological questions come from?** We begin with the basic stages of sociological research, discussing the issues that often come up as researchers practice sociology for the first time, such as how sociologists turn their research interests into workable questions and how we know what to study.

2. **What is the best method to research different sociological questions?** Once sociologists have a working research question, they need to decide the best way to go about answering it. In this section, we examine the different types of methods that sociologists use in their research and discuss the process for determining which method is best for particular research questions.

3. **What challenges do sociologists face when collecting data?** Here, we explore some of the practical issues and challenges that surface during data collection.

4. **How do sociologists make use of "big data" and new computational methods for social research?** The internet and communication technology have opened up new lines of research for sociologists. We introduce the concept of "big data" and some emerging new techniques for analyzing it.

5. **How do sociologists make sense of their findings?** Finally, we consider how sociologists make sure their findings are reliable and trustworthy and how they decide what kind of general claims to draw from their research.

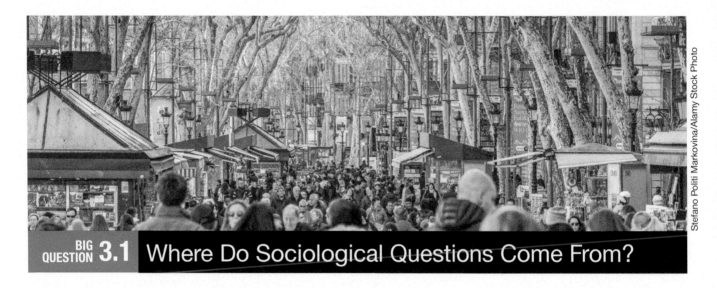

BIG QUESTION 3.1 Where Do Sociological Questions Come From?

THE BUILDING BLOCKS OF SOCIOLOGICAL RESEARCH

Sociology and the social sciences are built upon the discoveries made by doing research on a topic. How do sociologists begin a research project? What prompts them to think something is worth studying? Our **sociological imaginations**, the way we take into account how our individual lives are impacted by social contexts, are at the center of what prompts us to ask particular kinds of questions about the world. All sociological research shares a series of basic building blocks—ways of asking questions that arise from our sociological imaginations and our approach to concrete problems of doing research, such as collecting and analyzing data and drawing conclusions from our investigations. Good research is attentive to the particular issues that arise at all stages of the research process—with the specific research method reflective of the specific research question being asked in a study. The order here is critical: Sociologists first decide what they want to ask, and then they figure out the best tools and methods that can help answer those questions.

Crafting Good Research Questions from Important Topics

3.1.1 Identify the six issues sociologists should consider to determine a research question's merit and feasibility.

Few of us are ever at a loss for good topics to study. If you've found your way to a sociology course, chances are there is at least one thing about society you feel strongly about—if not many more. The challenge is not usually to find an interesting topic to investigate. The hard part is carving out a researchable question from that topic. Most often, this involves narrowing and focusing. It often will involve breaking the topic down into several parts and deciding which ones can be studied. It is a hard lesson to learn, but not all questions we are interested in can be studied.

There is no recipe for turning an interesting topic into a good research question. In general, good questions are both feasible and relevant. Feasible questions are those that can be studied given the limits of our time and resources. Feasible questions also lead us to think more specifically about a topic and to turn our ideas about that topic into a working **hypothesis**, which is the tentative prediction we have about what we are going to discover before we begin the research. A research question is relevant when it has the potential to tell us something about the world that we don't already know. For this reason, conducting a careful review of existing research on a topic before formulating a research question is essential. This helps not only to narrow down interests to questions, but also to know whether the ground to be covered is already charted territory. There is nothing worse than thinking you have an original sociological question, only to discover late in the research process that others have already asked it—and have published articles and books about it. On the other hand, just because someone else has done research on a topic or question you are interested in does not mean you can't re-examine it, especially if you think there is something about the earlier work that is unsatisfactory or if you have an idea for a new angle on the topic.

Although there is no easy-to-follow recipe for turning a research topic into a question, there are at least six questions sociologists should ask about a potential research question to determine its merit and feasibility (see Table 3.1).

Table 3.1 What Six Questions Should a Sociologist Ask to Determine Merit and Feasibility of a Research Question?

Question 1	**Do I already know the answer?**	Research focuses on questions for which we don't have answers. The point of social research is to ponder and then dig for information; it's not to confirm what we already know (or think we know).
Question 1: Example	What might not be known about divorce?	We know from decades of research that close to half of all marriages in America will end in divorce. Rather than studying what's already known—how many marriages split up—focus on an aspect that we know far less about, such as why do some divorced people remarry while others choose not to.
Question 2	**Is my question researchable?**	Your question must be one that can actually be answered. Not even the best social researcher can answer "What is the meaning of life?" or when world peace will finally happen. Instead, ask questions that can be addressed with data that are accessible to you.
Question 2: Example	What is the source(s) of the conflict between Country X and Country Y?	Although most of us might want to know how we could stop all wars, the kind of data that might answer such a broad general question do not exist. A sociologist would be better off examining specific wars or conflicts and looking for the causes of the conflict and thinking about how that conflict may help us understand future conflicts.
Question 3	**Is my question clear?**	A clear research question uses well-defined concepts. State the question simply to ensure anyone can understand it. In particular, make any hidden assumptions explicit. Such assumptions can be definitional, including terms or concepts we draw on without being clear about their meanings.
Question 3: Example	How are children's career aspirations shaped by their parents' social class?	Concepts like "social class" have several possible definitions that are debated in sociology. A clearer question would choose one specific dimension of social class, like education or occupation. This question also reveals an assumption: We can't take for granted that parents' characteristics affect their children's aspirations. Whether and how there may be a relationship is exactly what needs to be researched.
Question 4	**Does my question have a connection to social scientific scholarship?**	Decide what to research (and what questions to ask) after you are familiar with what others have already discovered. This helps you avoid repeating what has already been done, uncover specific debates about the topic, learn from the methods and approaches that other researchers have used, and discover questions or issues that previous researchers have ignored.
Question 4: Clarification	Do I know enough about the latest research on my topic?	While sociologists don't have to read everything before they form their research question, they need to have at least a general idea about the debates in the area of the proposed research, as well as the concepts and frameworks that structure those debates.
Question 5	**Does my question balance the general and the specific?**	Good research questions should not be so broad that they can't be grasped in a meaningful way. Yet at the same time, good research questions should not be so narrow and specific that their findings, however carefully done, may appeal only to us or to a very small group of people like us.
Question 5: Example	How are recent immigrants with professional degrees affected when they take service-sector jobs?	A student researcher is interested in how students who recently emigrated from Thailand to a specific Bronx neighborhood make sense of their parents' work in service-sector jobs. This question could be too narrowly focused on this student's own experience, however, so she needs to step back and reformulate it. She might ask: How does downward mobility affect recent immigrants?
Question 6	**Do I care about the answer?**	Sociologists aren't in the business of producing knowledge that no one cares about. If we don't care about our research, chances are that others won't either. Of course, caring about our subject should not lead us to sacrifice the integrity of our research and put advocacy before science.
Question 6: Clarification	Can I be very engaged in what I'm researching, yet remain objective?	The goal is to maintain a critical distance from what we study while remaining passionate about and committed to the questions we ask. Being a researcher is a different role from being an advocate, even if the results of our research eventually help to inform social change.

How Do We Know What to Study

3.1.2 Identify key factors that shape sociologists' choices about what to research.

If you ask practicing sociologists why they study what they study, you will likely get a response about all of the scholarly debates that motivate them. Such explanations are surely accurate. But probe a little deeper and other influences may also come to the surface. There are endless scholarly debates and topics for sociologists to choose to study. So why do we gravitate toward some topics or questions as opposed to others? For many, the pull is personal: We find ourselves asking sociological questions that have personal significance. That significance may be direct—as when a sociologist researches something he or she has experienced first hand, like racial inequality, religious discrimination, divorce, or educational stratification. Indeed, many sociologists have looked to their biographies to enhance their sociological imaginations and used those imaginations to inform their research agendas. But personal influences can also be more indirect, as when a sociologist forms a research interest by observing others' experiences.

For others, the pull to certain sociological questions may be less personal and more political. For instance,

Figure 3.1 What Influences Social Research?

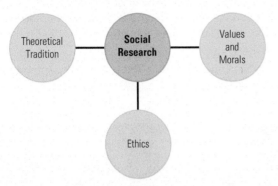

many sociologists are interested in questions of power and privilege because of their understandings of the causes of social inequality and because of their sense that research and knowledge can help point to better policies to address that inequality. Others grew up in periods of intense social and civil unrest, which left them with an understanding of the importance of collective mobilization and an interest in studying how and when it emerges. It is not by chance that the study of social movements really took off in the 1970s, when the antiwar, civil rights, and feminist movements were at their peak, or that sociological interest in the environment has surged in recent years as more political and media attention has been devoted to issues of climate change and environmental racism.

Indeed, there are many factors that shape sociologists' choices about what to research. In this section, we will explore three key influences, as Figure 3.1 illustrates.

Values—or the belief systems that shape sociologists' own views of and perspectives on the world we study—play a critical role in shaping the questions sociologists find interesting and intriguing about the social world. To say that our values influence our research questions is not, however, the same as saying that they determine our findings. Like all scientists, sociologists must remain open to all kinds of answers to our research questions—especially those we may not like. That said, the values we bring to our research clearly motivate us to work on specific themes. For instance, if a sociologist values the democratic process, she might orient her research to examining questions about the factors enhancing or inhibiting democracy in specific organizations or countries. Or if a sociologist places high value on equality of opportunity, he might be most intrigued by research questions that focus on the policies enacted by different societies that attempt to level the playing field and give everyone an equal chance at success.

Second, sociologists typically choose to focus their research based on the **theoretical traditions** that they use to make sense of the world. There is a wide range of different theories that guide sociologists—depending on which tradition sociologists find most compelling—to ask some questions but not others (see Chapter 2 for an introduction to leading theoretical traditions). Theories are lenses through

which we see the world, and the theory that guides a particular sociologist's research will have an important impact.

For instance, many sociologists working in the tradition of nineteenth-century German theorist Max Weber see the social world as comprised of status groups; those sociologists influenced by work of nineteenth-century social and political theorist Karl Marx would be more likely to see the divisions based on social classes. And whereas a Marxian sociologist might search the world for examples of revolution, a researcher working in the tradition of twentieth-century social theorist Michel Foucault might set out to document everyday forms of power. Theoretical traditions thus play a critical role in shaping the questions sociologists find interesting and intriguing about the social world.

This leads to a final area of influence on social research: the **code of ethics**—a set of guidelines that outline what is considered moral and acceptable behavior—that all scientists share (although each discipline has its own version). This code is especially important when the objects of investigation are real people, as they usually are for sociologists. Perhaps even more than those working in the natural sciences, social scientists (and medical and health researchers, who are also conducting research on humans) must commit to protecting those we study and to not doing them any harm. Among other things, this requires us to disclose our identity as researchers and to obtain **informed consent** from our subjects by making their participation voluntary and based on a full understanding of possible risks and benefits involved. We also maintain confidentiality, guaranteeing that we will not reveal the true identities of our subjects. These commitments then shape the kind of questions sociologists can ask in our research. While we could dream up all sorts of questions we'd love to be able to research, we must consider the ethics involved in exploring them.

So while a sociologist might want to ask why people acquiesce to authority and commit violence—as social psychologist Stanley Milgram did in a classic early 1960s study that pretended to have his subjects administer electric shocks to others when ordered to do so—this might be considered harmful and detrimental for research subjects today. Or if a sociologist wanted to study the experience of prison—as Philip Zimbardo and Craig Haney did in their early 1970s Stanford Prison Experiment (which is the subject of a 2015 movie by that title) that turned young students into guards and prisoners—this would most likely be considered out of bounds and dangerous for participants today.

Of course, researchers are not always aware when their questions could jeopardize their subjects' well-being. When both the Milgram and the Zimbardo–Haney studies were conducted, the researchers did not anticipate how much harm their studies would inflict on participants. Moreover, what constitutes harm can and has changed over time—in both of these cases, researchers worked within the acceptable protocols of their universities at the time. Today, to help researchers foresee any potential dangers and to safeguard the ethical standards of their work, **institutional review boards (IRBs)** operate at most universities and are required at all universities that receive research funds from the federal government. These boards review researchers' proposals before any work can begin in order to assess the potential for harm to study participants. They also evaluate whether ethical procedures will be in place and followed by researchers.

Needless to say, such reviews have influenced the questions sociologists ask. Consciously and unconsciously, sociologists end up steering themselves away from those areas they know will encounter problems in these boards, like the electroshock studies of authority and simulated prison experiments mentioned earlier. Today, less risky approaches to studying those questions would be required.

OtmarW/Shutterstock

BIG QUESTION 3.2 What Is the Best Method to Research Different Sociological Questions?

SOCIOLOGICAL RESEARCH METHODS AND CHALLENGES

Once we have worked through all of these questions and have at least a working version of a research question, we need to decide on the best way to go about researching it. This implies deciding on a research method and a research design. This is the "who, what, where, when, and how" stage of the research process. Researchers decide what to focus on; how many people, places, or things will be included in the study; where to locate the project in terms of both time and place; and when to conduct the research and for how long. In this section, we consider these issues in more detail.

Getting Started

3.2.1 Discuss how sociologists operationalize their research questions and distinguish between independent and dependent variables.

Answering these "who, what, where, when, and how" questions will help researchers to **operationalize** their research, that is, specify the operations and techniques that will be used to examine the concepts that are the focus of the study. And it's when we decide how to measure our **variables**—those factors, attributes, or phenomena to be studied. Most commonly, researchers seek to separate the **independent**

variable(s) from the **dependent variable(s)**. Independent variables are those factors we think influence or cause a particular outcome, the dependent variable. No variable is always an independent or dependent variable; it will depend on the study. For example, if you want to predict how much income people with college degrees earn, income is the dependent variable. But if you want to predict which people vote for the Democratic or Republican Party, income may be one of the independent variables you select.

When we say there is a relationship between an independent and a dependent variable, what we mean is that we expect that when the independent variable changes, the dependent variable will change as well. For example, existing sociological research leads us to expect that, for most people, most of the time, finishing college or getting more years of schooling or training will increase their income. Increasing the independent variable (years of schooling) should cause the dependent variable (income) to increase. Or, as we know from both personal experience and long-established medical research, if you start to consume more calories, you will gain weight. In these examples, education and calorie consumption are the independent variables, and income and weight are the dependent variables. Figure 3.2 shows another example of a research hypothesis concerning crime.

Being clear about what factors are causing what—that is, what independent variables you think are causing the

Figure 3.2 A Hypothesis About Crime, with Independent and Dependent Variables

outcome(s) you are interested in—is central to beginning any research project. Indeed, that is what developing a hypothesis that can be put to the test is all about. In most cases, sociologists start from an intuition or from their review of previous research about what independent variables may be causing an outcome they are interested in studying.

Unfortunately, examples like the impact of getting more education or consuming more calories are much easier to study than most research hypotheses that sociologists actually consider, and even those seemingly simple examples may have more complexity than you might think at first glance. For example, if athletes in heavy training begin consuming more healthy calories as part of a program to expand their lean muscle mass, they may actually lose weight. In the real world, there are usually many possible independent variables, and those variables may influence each other as well as the dependent variable. For example, in the case of crime, we know that crime rates tend to be higher in neighborhoods with more concentrated poverty and lower levels of educational attainment. But on that basis alone we cannot say for certain that crime is caused by either poverty or low levels of education, especially because each of these independent variables could affect the other. Living in a neighborhood with greater poverty might inhibit a person's educational attainment, and less education could correspond with lower wages and more poverty, so it is not obvious which (if either) of these factors is the fundamental cause of crime. Clearly, there are a number of variables to account for, and these may interact with each other in complex ways. The more sophisticated our research becomes, the more we will have to take into account multiple variables and how they influence each other as well as the dependent variable.

The Classical Scientific Method of Research

3.2.2 **Identify the steps of the classical scientific method, and explain why sociologists might take a looser approach to research.**

The logic underlying any research, from beginning to end, can vary. But sociologists and other scientists try, as much as possible, to remain true to the classic steps of the **scientific method**, which are detailed in Table 3.2.

It is important to be familiar with the steps of the scientific method, but it is also important to note that in the real world of research, a somewhat looser approach to the

process of discovery is often necessary. Sociologists may cover each of the steps in the classical scientific method, but sometimes in a slightly different order, depending on the research project and how it develops. For example, sociologists sometimes begin research with a hunch based on observation or experience rather than a traditional hypothesis derived from earlier research, and it is only after working with data that hypotheses begin to emerge. Further, there are some research questions that are impossible to organize neatly into a set of relationships between variables. In that case, sociologists may opt to remain more flexible about what they are looking for, allowing the people they observe and interview to help define key issues and problems. Or they may begin by collecting information on several issues until they decide which they want to focus on. All of these examples suggest that in the real world of research, sociologists and other social scientists will go back and forth between the steps of the classical scientific method. They will return to their questions for refinement and specification once the research is underway. Knowing the steps of the classical method of scientific research is important, but at the same time good researchers should continually reflect on what they are doing and change course when they sense it is necessary. It might be nice if research could be conducted like following a recipe, but it is usually much more complicated.

Table 3.2 What Are the Steps of the Scientific Method?

Step 1: Formulate a research hypothesis	Formulate research questions and hypotheses based on previous scholarship.
Step 2: Predict the relationship between the independent and dependent variables	Identify the variables that are key to the hypothesis and predict relationships among those variables (with one or more independent variables predicted to influence a dependent variable).
Step 3: Find existing data or collect new data	Identify a source of data that you can use to test the hypothesis. If no existing data can be found, you must collect your own data on each of the variables.
Step 4: Analyze data	Once the data are collected, begin analyzing the data to determine if the relationship researchers hypothesized between the key variables held up.
Step 5: Draw conclusions	Finally, draw empirical and conceptual generalizations from the data and write up the results.

Quantitative versus Qualitative Research Methods

3.2.3 Compare and contrast quantitative versus qualitative research methods.

There are two broad types of research employed by sociologists: quantitative research and qualitative research. While both types of research are subject to similar rules about research design, they are in many ways different from one another. At the heart of the difference between the two types of research methods is the kind of data they rely upon to draw conclusions. **Quantitative research** relies upon data that are statistical in nature, for example, data that come from the census or other government surveys, or polls or surveys conducted by social scientists, or any kind of information that can put into numerical form (such as, "How many times does the typical police officer in a city stop a White male versus a Black male?"). Quantitative research takes raw data that come in a numerical form and uses it to analyze how one or more independent variables are related to a dependent variable which is also measured numerically.

Qualitative research, by contrast, relies on detailed interviews with informants, direct observations, historical records, or even pictures as data. Qualitative research typically involves the analysis of large amounts of textual material by a researcher, whereas quantitative research involves the use of statistical methods to examine the numerical data used in the study. To complicate matters further, some researchers use evidence that is both qualitative and quantitative; they employ what is known as **mixed-method research**. In such studies, the researcher (or research team) hopes to gain different insights into a question by combining numerical and textual evidence. Sociology is somewhat unique within the social sciences in that it encompasses a wide range of research methods, and many studies employ more than one approach.

How do we know what method is best suited for a particular study? The starting point is to think about what kind of evidence is needed to answer the question we have posed. Can the question be answered by surveying large numbers of people and comparing the responses of different groups? Or it is best addressed by talking directly to a subset of these people in more depth and for a longer period of time? Or is it best addressed by observing them and watching them interact in their day-to-day lives, or in a laboratory? Or can the question be captured by looking at similar or different groups of people in other times and places? The decision about which method should be used must always be based on the research question—methods are means to an end, not an end themselves.

Just as the choice of a research question should lead to a specific research method, the choice of a method implies specific research challenges. To provide a concrete sense of this as well as a feel for what each of the main sociological methods actually involves in practice, in this section we discuss one of the main issues confronting sociologists using each method—including examples of how they grappled with it. For example, how do interviewers choose who to interview? And how do ethnographers select a particular research setting—especially if they are interested in generalizing their findings to other times and places?

Survey and In-Depth Interview Methods and the Challenges of Design

3.2.4 Identify the key strengths and weaknesses of survey and interview methods.

Data gathered from interviews are a basic and widely used type of sociological research. They come in many shapes and sizes: surveys, in-depth interviews, and more.

Carrying out a survey can be done in person, on the telephone, or increasingly on the internet. Here a researcher conducts an in-person survey and records the respondent's answers. In-person surveys are the highest quality possible, but they are very expensive to conduct. Telephone surveys are cheaper, but the rise of the cell phone and the disappearance of landlines have created obstacles to obtaining representative samples on the phone. Today, a growing number of researchers are looking to internet surveys as the best way of gathering data.

SURVEYS

The most common type of interview is the **survey**, which is a questionnaire that asks standardized questions of representative groups of people. These questions can be asked in person, on the phone, by mail, or, increasingly, on the Internet. (Surveys are also sometimes called *polls*, although the term "poll" usually refers to surveys conducted by media or political organizations with less rigorous methods than academic or government surveys.) Because surveys can be used to collect information about any aspect of social life of interest to the investigator, including information about such topics as jobs, family life, health, education, wealth and income, and religious and political attitudes and values, it is hardly surprising that surveys have been widely used since the 1930s to answer many different kinds of research questions.

In a typical survey, all of the respondents are asked identical questions, and they are generally required to choose among the answers provided to them. These are called "closed-ended" questions. For example, a researcher might ask their respondents "Which of the following best describes your job?" and then follow up with a list of categories for them to choose from, such as "Manager," "Professional," "Clerical Support Worker," and so forth. But there are also other kinds of surveys that include some "open-ended" questions, in which interviewees provide answers to questions in their own words. For example, you might ask someone, "What kind of job do you do?" and then have the respondent describe their job in their own words. Closed-ended questions are easier to work with. There are far fewer possible responses to consider, whereas an open-ended question requires more effort to translate responses into a workable number of categories akin to the closed-ended question. Because of this, most surveys rely on closed-ended questions.

Surveys are very good at generating data about an entire population. The most famous survey in the United States and most other countries is the periodic national **Census** of the entire population. The U.S. Census is a closed-ended survey, mandated by the U.S. Constitution, that has been conducted every 10 years since 1790. It provides a comprehensive profile of the population of the United States. The Census and other government surveys are essential research tools for many social science questions. For example, if you want to know how many children the average family has, how many Americans are of Mexican descent, or what the population of small town is, Census data can provide the answer. The Census is unique in that it attempts to gather responses from every single household unit in the United States (and, as a result, costs billions of dollars to collect). In addition to its cost, the Census is very limited—by law—in the kinds of information it can collect; it is not allowed to ask questions about politics, religion, or about any opinions. It is essentially focused on gathering basic information about each household, useful for a limited range of research questions.

Agencies of the federal government, such as the Bureau of Labor Statistics (BLS), also carry out important regular national surveys, although they include only a small subset of all households. Every month, the BLS conducts a survey known as the Current Population Survey (CPS), which interviews all of the adults in about 50,000 households, so somewhere around 90,000 to 100,000 individuals are interviewed in all. It is the primary source of information about ongoing trends in employment and unemployment, as well as family trends in the social life of cities and communities, and many other things. Each household stays in the survey for 3 years, so it gathers data on individuals and families over a period of time; for example, the CPS gathers information not just about how many people are unemployed, but how long workers remain unemployed. Another very important large-scale survey of special interest to sociologists is the American Community Survey (ACS), which is conducted by the Census Bureau. The ACS is collected continuously over the course of the year and contacts 3.5 million households annually (or approximately 290,000 a month) to gather additional information about families, households, jobs, income, and other important information that both social scientists and policymakers use.

Large government-run surveys are valuable for many research questions. But social scientists often want to know much more than the relatively limited and basic information available in them. For example, sociologists are interested in information about people's attitudes and opinions, political affiliations, group memberships, their mental health, religion and religious values, or many other issues not included in any government survey. To gather this kind of data, more specialized surveys are needed. Some of the most useful of these researcher-driven surveys are those that are carried out by large groups of investigators on a regular basis, such as the **General Social Survey (GSS)**, a survey created and fielded by sociologists every year since 1972 (or every other year since 1994) that contains questions about both an individual's background and a wide range of topics. Two other ongoing surveys that are of great value to sociologists are the **Panel Study of Income Dynamics (PSID)**, a survey conducted biennially since 1968 that re-interviews members of several thousand families and their children about topics such as employment, income, wealth, expenditures, health, marriage, childbearing, and child development, and the **American National Election Study (ANES)**, a biennial survey of political attitudes and voting conducted in every national election year since 1948. These surveys are valuable for historical reasons, as they allow researchers to investigate social, demographic, and political trends over long historical periods by comparing answers to the same questions over decades (for example, the ANES started in 1948). All three of these surveys are funded by the National Science Foundation (NSF), one of the major government agencies supporting scientific research.

LIMITATIONS OF SURVEYS

Surveys can be very good at generating data about an entire population, assuming that the group of people included in the survey are representative of the larger population being studied (or what is known as the **sample**). We will discuss the problems of how to draw a good sample later in the chapter—it is a challenge that all sociological research faces—but for now it is also important to note that almost all surveys involve interviewing a subset of a population (often a very small group) to generalize about an entire population. When survey researchers (or pollsters) try to estimate who will win the next election, their sample may include only 500 or 1,000 people to represent the entire voting population of the United States (somewhere around 240 million people). Because it is not possible to interview everyone, every survey will have a **margin of error**; the smaller the sample, the larger the margin of error. In the case of election polling, most polls will declare, in the fine print, that they have a margin of error of "+/− 3%" or "+/− 4%." A margin of error of +/−3% means that the reported result of the poll could be anywhere from 3 percentage points above or below the estimated value. But as long as the people chosen to participate are selected in a way that gives the entire population of eligible voters an equal chance of being selected, even a small sample can produce a result that should approximate the final vote most of the time.

Surveys are often expensive and time consuming to conduct. Designing a survey takes skill and practice, and much time and effort can be wasted if the survey is not well designed from the beginning (and sometimes it is difficult to know this until you actually start the research). For most beginning researchers, it may be best to start with publicly available surveys rather than try to conduct your own survey. But if you want to do research on a specific group that you know how to contact, such as the students at your university, it is possible to design and implement your own survey.

IN-DEPTH INTERVIEWS

Surveys have many uses, but sometimes they are not enough for certain research questions. For example, they typically constrain the kinds of answers that can be given (as in surveys relying on closed-ended questions) and they don't allow those being interviewed to elaborate or explain their answers. For many research questions, that is not necessarily a limitation, but if you want to know *why* people think or act the way they do, or how and what people *feel* about various situations or events, the limitations of the survey format can become overwhelming. In many instances, a different kind of interview, known as the **in-depth interview**, provides a better research tool. In-depth interviews are extended conversations with a much smaller number of respondents, capable of getting deeper and richer answers to the questions posed. There are two broad approaches to an in-depth interview: **semi-structured interviews** (in which the questions asked follow a systematic order, prepared ahead of time) versus those that employ more **open-ended interviews** (where the researcher employs a looser format of questions, allowing the subject to tell their story in their own way with the interviewer guiding them more loosely and often improvising depending on what the subject is saying). As a sociological method, the in-depth interview's main strength is its ability to allow researchers to understand *how* people make sense of their worlds and *why* they make the decisions that they do, and to provide information about the *context* of some action that a short survey probably would not be able to cover.

What is required to do successful in-depth interviews? Perhaps the most important issue is to decide whom to interview. A researcher will want to select respondents carefully, depending on the research question. In all cases, it is important to do enough interviews to gather data from the full range of people being studied. Second, the researcher has to know enough about the subject of the interview in order to ask effective questions and to know when to follow up on an answer. But most importantly, an interviewer needs to establish trust with their interview subjects so they will feel comfortable answering questions that can be sensitive. Learning how to develop the trust of interviewees is an important skill for all in-depth interviewers to seek to master.

LIMITATIONS OF SURVEYS AND IN-DEPTH INTERVIEWS

Although both surveys and in-depth interviews gather data from the answers provided by an interviewee, these methods have important differences. A survey is typically shorter, often lasting only 20–25 minutes (although the GSS and ANES surveys take about 90 minutes to complete, an unusually long survey). By contrast, in-depth interviews tend to last much longer than typical surveys (and can in some cases stretch for 3-4 hours). The length of in-depth interviews, and the time and costs needed to transcribe and analyze them, however, means that studies based on in-depth interviews will have far fewer cases than surveys. But it is important even with in-depth interviews to interview enough people to gather the information needed to answer your research question. To that end, the researcher is relying on a small number of interviews to develop information related to the research question. But if you only interview people on one side of an issue, you might get a very distorted view. For example, let's say you were interested in studying why some police officers use unnecessary force against unarmed people who are suspected of committing a crime. You might reach the conclusion that police brutality is a myth, that it is often necessary to treat suspects with force. If you only interviewed victims of police brutality, you might reach the conclusion that all or most police officers are violent in their administration of justice. A better approach might be to interview both police officers and victims in relation to specific incidents, where you might find there is much more complexity to the situation than interviewing only one or the other group would show. The most difficult problems that arise in typical in-depth interview studies, however, are that interview subjects are not always reliable: They may be embarrassed about a sensitive subject, they may conceal attitudes they worry are not socially acceptable to say. For example, interviewees may not want to express racist or sexist attitudes to an interviewer. Further, they may not recall past events or behaviors accurately, or they may simply not understand the question itself and give incomplete or misleading answers as a result. Sometimes even the best interviewer cannot get accurate or informative responses; some interview subjects are simply unreliable. In that case, the researcher needs to treat the information very carefully and perhaps not use it at all.

Ethnographic Methods and the Challenge of Developing Generalizable Knowledge

3.2.5 Explain why the main strength of ethnography is also its central weakness.

If people don't always do what they say—or can't tell an interviewer what they really think and how they actually behave in different settings—what is a researcher to do? Overcoming this problem is one reason why direct-observation research—known as **ethnography**—has long been a prominent and widely used method for conducting sociological research (Jerolmack and Khan 2014). Ethnographers get inside the worlds they study, up close, sometimes even as direct participants alongside the people they are studying. Critical to doing ethnographic research is the decision about where to locate these observations—that is, in what "site" they think the phenomenon they are interested in can be found. Then, once "in the field," ethnographers need to decide who, where, and what to observe. Ethnographic researchers are always asking themselves if they should include different kinds of observations, or if they should expand the kind of people and interactions they are focusing on. And because their work is typically centered in one place, a major challenge arises as researchers try to make sense of their data and figure out whether and how their research applies to contexts other than the one they studied.

Ethnographic research was pioneered by anthropologists, who traditionally carried out their research in foreign environments to understand different cultural practices and social norms, initially because they considered non-Western places as examples of "pre-modern" societies. Sociological ethnographies, by contrast, typically involve research set in contemporary communities or organizations. Almost any social setting can be the subject of ethnographic research. Families, neighborhoods, factories and workplaces, schools, government offices, Wall Street financial firms, sports clubs, churches, social movements, and many other places and organizations have been the subject of prominent ethnographic research. For instance, one ethnographic study examined how the "party culture" in universities impacts students' overall college experience and their future pathways (Armstrong and Hamilton 2013). These sociologists spent a year living on a dormitory floor at a Midwestern university, getting to know each of the 53 students living on the floor and following them through their college careers and then into post-college life. Through this deep immersion in the lives of a handful of college students, the authors were able to observe aspects of the lives of these students that may not have surfaced during a survey or in-depth interview.

Ethnographic research can be viewed as a continuum (Luker 2010). On the one end are studies undertaken in contexts researchers are fairly familiar with, whether from their own experience or previous research. They can, before starting their research, focus on questions that are clearly defined, such as an ethnographer who goes out to study how men interact in a local barbershop in Philadelphia or an ethnographer who studies how women negotiate the dynamics of power and beauty in local nail salons in New York City (see image below). On the other end is total immersion in another culture or subculture for long periods of time, such as an ethnographer who heads off to the African country Rwanda, which experienced a brutal civil war in the mid-1990s, to study a post-conflict society; or an American ethnographer who is not Muslim observing the religious practices of Muslim women in Eastern Europe. Most ethnographic work in sociology falls somewhere in

Some ethnographers immerse themselves deep into the culture or subculture they are studying. Others observe people in contexts they are familiar with, such as ethnographer Miliann Kang of the University of Massachusetts, who studied how people interact in a nail salon (Kang 2010).

Dragon Images/Shutterstock

the middle, with researchers documenting the patterns, processes, and practices of everyday life, some of which may be familiar and other aspects seem unfamiliar.

The strength of ethnographic research is that it can produce some of the richest, most nuanced accounts of social life. Done well, ethnography transports us to places and spaces we don't normally have access to, from the inside of prison cells to the dealings of street gangs to the struggles of homeless heroin addicts to the careers of sex workers. It can provide **thick descriptions** of the people living in those spaces—that is, rich and detailed descriptions of the ways they make sense of their lives, from the perspective of those people themselves. And it is the ideal method to use for getting at the point where words and actions collide, and often diverge. Instead of taking people's words at face value, ethnographers are able to link them to the way people act, a connection that frequently leads to fascinating examples of inconsistency—which can themselves tell us an enormous amount about social life.

LIMITATIONS OF ETHNOGRAPHIC RESEARCH

The irony of ethnographic research is that it's main strength can also be its central weakness. In the process of producing thick descriptions of interesting aspects of social life, ethnographers may encounter difficulty generalizing their findings beyond the scope of their specific field site. Ethnographers can find it hard, if not impossible, to claim that their case is truly representative of a larger trend or issue. They can find it hard, if not impossible, to move beyond the places and everyday lives they are embedded in and to analyze them in terms that would seem foreign to those lives. And they can find it hard, if not impossible, to reach broader conclusions from the small, local contexts ethnographers tend to research. All of this can leave ethnographers wary of using their work to engage in the larger theoretical and conceptual debates of sociology.

Of course, the ability of ethnographers to provide very detailed accounts of local settings is not considered a weakness by everyone. In fact, some embrace and celebrate this aspect of ethnographic work. Clifford Geertz (1973), the famous anthropologist who came up with the term *thick description* to describe what ethnographers do, saw it as an asset of the method—a way for social scientists to render what he called an "understanding of understanding." More recently, there are some ethnographic studies whose goal is simply to offer new and different descriptions of social life. One of the best and most prominent examples of this is an ethnographic account of book vendors and magazine sellers on the streets of New York City, a study by a sociologist Mitchell Duneier that provided a *tour de force* of detail and insight into what everyday life on the street looks and feels like for these people: the indignities they suffer, the ways they interact with the community and each other, how they attempt to protect their sense of self and dignity, and the strategies they use to maintain a "moral order" on the street

(Duneier 1999). And while no one can read this study and not learn an enormous amount about how those in this situation live and survive, there is not much in the way of explanation or theory in the account. There is not even very much about what others have found in studies of similar topics. In fact, Duneier almost explicitly rejects using theory even to organize his account, opting instead to divide up his story according to the different types of men on the street and the different labor they engage in. Hence, ethnographies in this tradition are so engaging and so captivating that they reveal the power of good thick description. Yet they can also leave readers without a sense of what these people's lives tell us about broader sociological concepts and theory.

There are, however, other ethnographic traditions and approaches. There are ethnographers who try to move beyond descriptive accounts of specific locales to connect their ethnographic insights to larger sociological debates and theoretical questions. For instance, sociologist Michael Burawoy has argued that ethnography can be used to engage general, theoretical questions. To do this, he has developed the **extended case method**, a way of doing ethnography that emphasizes its contribution to social theory (Burawoy 2009). A simple diagram of how this method works can be seen in Figure 3.3.

As Burawoy points out, an ethnographic site need not be representative of a large social process to extend the reach of theory. It need not cover lots of randomly sampled cases to contribute to social theory. Instead, he insists that ethnographers can and should be theoretically focused from the start of their research: When they head out into the field, ethnographers should go prepared with concepts and theories to organize their research and focus their attention. Because the real world is almost always more complex than our theories of it, an ethnographer's job is to revise social theory in light of what they observed in that world. So rather than striving for thick description, these ethnographic accounts aim to test, challenge, and improve sociological theories.

Figure 3.3 The Extended Case Method

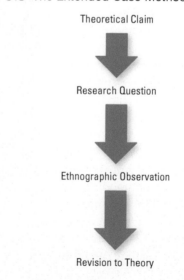

Theoretical Claim

Research Question

Ethnographic Observation

Revision to Theory

Field Experiments

3.2.6 Discuss the advantages of field experiments.

Ethnography is not the only way sociologists can conduct their research in real-world settings. *Field experiments* are another. Sociologists and other social scientists are ultimately interested in establishing whether and how an independent variable affects a dependent variable. To be confident that the relationship between cause and effect is real, researchers try to minimize any other factors that might influence the relationship between independent and dependent variables. Unfortunately, however, this often proves very difficult in practice, because social behavior is hard to predict and social outcomes can have many possible causes.

For example, let's say we want to know whether gender discrimination in the sciences can explain why fewer women than men pursue PhDs in science, technology, engineering and math fields (the so-called STEM fields). If we want to really test the discrimination thesis, we have to try to include all of those other factors (and perhaps some we haven't thought of) in our study. For example, perhaps fewer women receive bachelor's degrees in related disciplines; they are less likely to apply to graduate degrees than men; they are less likely to be admitted to graduate programs; they are less likely to find a (mostly male) faculty mentor to guide them; family issues such as pregnancy and childbirth impact their completion of the PhD degree; or perhaps male scientists may have gotten more encouragement from their families, friends, and professors and other adult mentors, to go for the PhD. There are statistical techniques to control for different factors, but no matter how sophisticated the analysis, there still will be a lot of uncertainty about the results.

One response to this situation would be to conduct randomized experiments in a controlled environment, like a laboratory. But in the real world, we can scarcely conduct controlled experiments the way researchers can in laboratories. However, there is an alternative: Sociologists can bring experiments out of the laboratory and into the field, to see how people actually behave. **Field experiments** apply methods of experimental design within a naturally occurring social context (Baldassarri and Abascal 2017). To do so, researchers assign subjects to different experimental conditions or groups. Some subjects are assigned to a group that is exposed to the independent variable of interest (this is known as the **treatment group**) while the other group is not (the **control group**). Randomization means that subjects' assignment to either the treatment or control group is not related to any other potential variable. In other words, each participant in the experiment is equally likely to end up in the treatment or control group. This means that only a single independent variable is being tested, while everything else is held constant.

Here's a relatively simple example, continuing on our discussion of whether gender discrimination, or something else, explains why fewer females have STEM PhDs. In order to test whether gender discrimination is a cause for the lower share of women with PhDs in STEM fields, our field experiment will need to isolate the effect of gender while controlling for all other potential explanations that we mentioned above. One experiment might test whether PhD-granting programs are more likely to admit male applicants compared to equally qualified female applicants. In our experiment, we could construct identical (but fictitious) resumes for some prospective male and female scientists, changing only their names to signal their gender (using names that are strongly associated with men or women, respectively). We would then submit our fictitious resumes to PhD programs, randomly selecting which programs would receive the resume from our fictitious woman applicant (the treatment group in this experiment) and which would receive our fictitious man's resume. Finally, we would record the outcomes of all of these applications to determine which of our two applicants was more successful, the man or the woman. In this experiment, the only factor that would be different between the applicants is the gender, allowing us to reach conclusions based on how the PhD programs respond. If the graduate programs receiving the fictitious applications from equally qualified men and women, and still admit men at a higher rate, we would have solid grounds for concluding that the only possible explanation would be discrimination against women.

Several researchers have used variants of this approach to test for discrimination (Bertrand and Duflo 2017). One example can be seen in the Visible Hand experiment (Doleac and Stein 2013). Here, an advertisement to sell an Apple iPod (a popular device before the introduction of the Apple iPhone, which stored and played only music) appeared on Craigslist, which allowed photos of the device to be displayed in the ad. The researchers used photos of a White hand holding the iPod in some images, a Black hand holding the iPod in others, and finally a White hand with several tattoos (to see if buyers also discriminated among White sellers with and without the tattoo). The accompanying image (see next page) shows the different hands used in the study. Results showed that White sellers (as signified by the photo) received significantly higher offers and fewer questions about handling the money than the White tattooed hand, with the Black hand receiving the lowest offers and lowest degree of trust about the exchange.

Taking experiments into the field offers some advantages. For one thing, because the experiments are conducted in actual social environments, we have more confidence that the results are not driven by something peculiar or artificial, as might be the case in a laboratory setting. Field experiments involve a kind of deception that allows the researcher to uncover behaviors that people would otherwise be reluctant to reveal to a scientist. Employers usually say that they never discriminate based on race, for example, but many of them will show bias in a field experiment where they are presented with

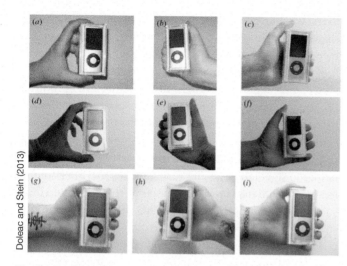

Doleac and Stein (2013)

These were the actual images used in the Visible Hand experiment. They accompanied text advertising the product for sale on Craigslist in ads placed around the country, but each ad showed only one of the hands to see how it impacted the responses the researchers received.

identical resumes from Black and White applicants (Pager and Quillian 2005). So, field experiments can bring to light discriminatory behavior. And last, field experiments can allow researchers to study groups of people outside the reach of a laboratory. Rather than constructing a sample from whomever responds to an advertisement, researchers can recruit people less often studied using experimental methods.

LIMITATIONS OF FIELD EXPERIMENTS

Field experiments can be developed and conducted by anyone, including undergraduate sociology students (Gashol 2018). (Designing a simple field experiment is a great way to do your first data collection.) However, researchers must always strive to protect their subjects. As noted, some field experiments involve minor deceptions. For example, in the Visible Hand experiment, potential buyers did not actually get to buy the product they were interested in (after replying, they were told in a follow-up communication that it had been sold to someone else). Generally, in the interests of scientific knowledge, approval to conduct field experiments has been granted by Institutional Review Boards (necessary for any published research), but in all cases the researcher (not just the IRB) should make certain that the design of the experiment isn't going to harm anyone in any significant way.

Another important thing to keep in mind is that field experiments deal with producing generalizable knowledge based on results, similar to ethnography. Just as with ethnography, we have to ask whether the results of an experiment in one place means we would find the same thing somewhere else? Field experiments are most valuable when they have been repeated many times in many places. But for an individual researcher, this isn't very helpful. One way to contribute to general knowledge is to apply a version of the extended case method, where well-designed experiments test specific previously established theoretical ideas.

Matching the Question with a Method

3.2.7 **Explain why choosing the right research method to study motivations and behavior is a complex process.**

So far, we've explored several of the most prominent methods used by sociological researchers. But how do we know what method is the best to use? Sometimes the choice is obvious: When a research question centers on patterns of behavior among large groups of people, survey methods are usually the best bet. When the question is about the thought processes that lead people to have certain opinions or engage in certain behaviors, those questions more often will benefit from in-depth interviews. But if the question has more to do with how people actually interact as opposed to how they *say* they interact, then ethnographic observation is often the way to go. Field experiments are also viable when we are trying to see how people behave in the real world, while limiting the complicating effects of intervening variables.

In some cases, the decision about which research method to employ is less obvious. Indeed, many studies go wrong precisely by choosing the wrong method to study the problem: They ask a good, clear research question grounded in the existing scholarship, but they end up collecting data that don't help them answer it. For example, whenever Lynne Haney (this chapter's first author) teaches a research methods course, she often has students wanting to study gender differences in romantic relationships in their research paper for the class. Usually, they want to know something about how men and women behave differently in their relationships—whether men are more distant and withdrawn (from Mars) and women are more open and connected (from Venus). And usually these students start off planning to use interview methods, largely because those seem most familiar to them.

Then they inevitably encounter problems with the question/method choice: First and foremost, asking interview questions about motivations rarely gets at actual behavior. What people say about what they do in relationships may have nothing to do with how they really act in them. For instance, research shows that, when interviewed, married men almost always overestimate how much housework they do, while married women exhibit the opposite reporting error, claiming to do less housework than they actually do. And this is not because either group is being consciously deceptive. We all have powerful scripts we tell ourselves about how and why we act like we do, especially when it comes to emotionally laden things like romantic relationships. So while interviews are often a great way to capture those scripts and opinions, they are not the best way to learn about what men and women actually do in their relationships—much less the invisible influences that shape those behaviors.

The reverse problem can also surface—that is, when a researcher wants to study individuals' opinions about something and tries to do so by observing behavior. Over the years, Haney has had many students interested in knowing what young people think about interracial dating. Their hypothesis is usually that attitudes toward interracial dating have changed, and thus they want to test their hunch. So they propose observing women and men as they date. Haney has had students propose to do ethnographic work in college parties, campus groups and clubs, and bars (if they are 21, of course)—all with the intention of observing young people's dating interactions to see if they approve or disapprove of interracial romantic relationships and encounters.

What's the problem with this? Quite simply, looking at behavior doesn't allow them to say much about opinions or motivation. People are complicated—they often act in ways that are inconsistent with their ideas and opinions. This is especially true when it comes to dating and sexuality, since we often have powerful beliefs about what we should and should not be doing—beliefs that can shape what we are able

to admit to actually doing. Let's say these students saw people of different races talking and flirting. Would that tell them anything reliable about their views of interracial dating? Not really. Just like we can't assume that opinions lead clearly to behavior, there's a danger in reading motivation from actions.

Hence, choosing a research method is a complicated and complex process; it requires considerable thought, and some experience through trial and error also helps. It requires good logic and analytical skills to foresee what kind of evidence is needed to answer a research question. But it also requires an honest assessment of what kind of person the researcher is. Extremely shy sociologists (they do exist) are perhaps best advised not to carry out in-depth, face-to-face interviews. Socially awkward sociologists (they exist, too) would perhaps not make the best ethnographers because that method requires lots of social interaction and rapport building. And those researchers who are allergic to math might want to stay clear of statistical work with large surveys and data sets.

Mike Goldwater/Alamy Stock Photo

What Challenges Do Sociologists Face When Collecting Data?

THE CHALLENGE OF DATA COLLECTION

Once our questions are defined and narrowed and our research method is selected, sociologists begin collecting

data. We search for evidence that helps to answer the question. It is the stage when researchers must deal with the nuts and bolts of research. That may sound dull, but it is also when sociologists sometimes discover new things about the social world. Of course, the process of discovery looks different depending on the research method being used. Sociologists who rely on survey data must either conduct those surveys or work with data already collected in large data sets (such as the census, the GSS, or other existing surveys available to researchers). Other sociologists recruit respondents and conduct in-depth interviews with them. Still others set off to work and live among those being studied for participant observation. In this section, we will explore in more detail some of the challenges all of these methods of research face.

Sampling Issues

3.3.1 Explain sampling issues that sociologists grapple with when they begin their research.

One of the most critical problems all sociologists face, regardless of the method they use, is the problem of how to construct a proper **sample** of people to study. Sampling is the process of identifying the subjects a researcher will study. Why not just study everyone or everything that could possibly be relevant for your project? The short answer is that researchers almost never have the time and resources to study everybody and everything we might be interested in knowing about. Only the federal government, spending billions of dollars to carry out the Census every 10 years, can conduct a survey of all Americans—and even the Census misses some people despite all of their efforts. So, inevitably, we must make choices: What groups will be examined? Which settings will be observed? Which smaller group of people will be interviewed in depth? What factor(s) are chosen for a field experiment, and how will it be tested?

A valid sample is one in which the subjects (or documents) chosen should be representative of the entire population the researcher is interested in studying. That population could be students at a college, lawyers in California, immigrants to the United States from China, or all people living in the United States (including students, lawyers, pilots, and Chinese immigrants). Whatever the population of interest, the findings on the smaller group should be similar to what we would expect to find if we magically had the time and resources to study everyone in the group. Whether or not a sample is representative of the entire population a researcher is interested in is a critical issue that can undermine the value of an otherwise carefully designed research project. To put it another way, imagine a chef only tastes the broth of the soup at the top but not the rest of the soup. They would get a very misleading impression of the entire pot of soup. So too with sampling. Researchers need to make sure that they "taste" from the entire bowl, so to speak, even as they use a single tablespoon to represent the entire pot (so they will stir the soup before testing, thereby insuring they are sampling equally from the entire soup, not just the top). The social sciences are very different from the natural sciences (or soup), where research "subjects" do not have the ability to refuse to participate! There are no magical ways to draw the perfect sample, but fortunately there are some basic rules that have been established by decades of research that can guide us.

To understand the general importance of sampling, it might help to start with a famous failure that helped teach researchers a great deal. In 1936, the then very popular magazine *The Literary Digest* carried out a poll to predict the presidential election that year (in which the incumbent, Democrat Franklin Roosevelt, ran for reelection against Republican Alf Landon, the governor of Kansas). The magazine sent out "ballots" to two large

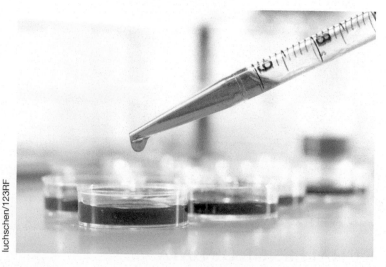

A doctor who takes only a single test tube of our blood to test for a whole range of possible problems is drawing a sample of all of the blood in our body. But the doctor does not face the challenge of sociologists who must acquire information not from one person but an entire population (or a smaller group that is a representation of the entire population) being studied.

groups for which it could obtain contact information: car owners and people who had telephones. Ten million ballots in all were sent out, and 2.4 million were returned. The results predicted a huge victory for Governor Landon. The *Digest* pronounced with great fanfare and publicity that Landon would win the election with 57 percent of the vote and 370 electoral votes. On election day, however, Roosevelt crushed Landon, winning more than 60 percent of the popular vote and 523 electoral votes, while Landon won just two states and received a grand total of just 8 electoral votes.

The resulting embarrassment contributed to putting *The Literary Digest* out of business. But how could the opinions of 2.4 million *Digest* readers (out of a population of approximately 125 million) have been so wrong? There were a number of problems with the sampling method used by the magazine. Most significantly, they used a list of car owners and people with telephones to mail out the survey. But in 1936, in the middle of the Great Depression, people who owned cars and had telephones in their homes were, on average, much more affluent than other Americans. These more affluent voters tended to prefer Landon, the Republican candidate, while the (far more numerous) poor and working class voters, who were much less likely to own a car or have a phone in their home at that time, generally sided with Roosevelt, the Democratic incumbent. The sample of Americans included in the *Digest* poll was not representative of voters in general, and thus the vote intentions of lower class Americans were underestimated.

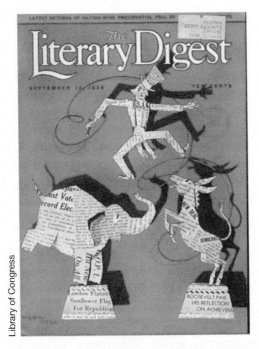

Library of Congress

In 1936, *The Literary Digest* conducted a poll that predicted a landslide win for Kansas Governor Alf Landon against the incumbent, President Franklin Roosevelt. The magazine made several critical errors when selecting their sample, and the embarrassing error ultimately put *The Literary Digest* out of business.

Today, survey researchers (and pollsters) can usually predict the results of presidential elections fairly closely (at least within a few percentage points) by interviewing as few as several hundred or a thousand people. How do they achieve this? Instead of drawing their sample of people to interview from a skewed list (like *The Literary Digest*'s use of car and telephone registry records), they are careful to draw a **representative sample** in which each member of population has an equal likelihood of being contacted. As a result, this small subset can, like the chef testing the soup, approximate the entire population. In fact, a well-drawn sample of as few as 1,000 people can produce a reasonable approximation of a very large population (even the entire population of the United States—over 330 million people).

Modern polls and surveys cover an enormous range of issues in American society; however, in order to conduct a valid survey or poll, a variety of steps are needed. In general, the key to drawing a good sample is to use some type of what is known as **random sampling**, in which each subject is selected entirely by random. For example, if a researcher conveniently has a list of the entire population they want to sample, taking every third name (or fifth, or hundredth, or some other randomly chosen but systematically sampled number) would produce a truly random sample. Unfortunately, most of the time, researchers don't have access to a list of everyone in their population, and cannot generate a simple random sample so easily. In that case, social scientists use more sophisticated methods for securing a sample that approximates a truly random one. One approach is to have a computer randomly dial phone numbers so that everyone who has a phone is equally likely to be contacted (since a phone is something that virtually all adult Americans have). But in recent years, because of spam calls, many people now refuse to answer a number they don't recognize. And those who do pick up are increasingly quite different than the rest of the population. So that approach, relied on for decades by pollsters, is no longer considered very reliable.

In addition to imperfect samples, another problem arises from the fact that some kinds of people who are asked to do an interview are more likely to agree to participate than others. A common solution to both of these problems is for researchers to employ statistical adjustments known as **weighting**, in which they attempt to make sure that the characteristics of their sample reflect those of the total population they are studying (if known). They do this by giving individuals from groups underrepresented in the sample a slightly higher "weight"—that is, their answers to each question are given slightly more value than those of groups that are sampled in the right proportion. Here is an example: If a sociologist is interested in understanding how college students juggle going to school while holding a job, and about 57 percent of college students are female (as is currently the case in the

United States), this gender disparity should be reflected in the sample. If, however, the survey, when finished, included interviews with respondents who were evenly split between men and women, the researcher has undersampled women (relative to their share of the college population). Because it is entirely possible that male students respond differently than female students, our results can be biased by the sample if we want to produce results for all students. One way to adjust for this is to give a little extra weight to the responses of each of the women who did respond. On the surface, this may seem unwise or even unfair. Why should any respondent's answers be given more weight than anyone else's? But if we are worried about our sample being representative of the population we are trying to study (in this case, *all* college students), we get closer to the true population by using statistical weighting to adjust the sample to be more representative of the population of college students.

When it comes to doing in-depth interviews, the problem of constructing a sample gets more complicated. Clearly, no one researcher, or even a large team of researchers, can complete long interviews with enough respondents so that anyone in an entire large population (such as all Americans) has an equal probability of being selected. But that does not mean that in-depth interviewers can just talk to a few people and get valid results. If a researcher is studying a small population, for example, women advertising executives in New York City, a few dozen interviews may be enough to be confident that you've talked to a wide enough range of subjects. If the study is of a larger group, say all women executives in the United States, it would be essential to be able to identify subjects from different industries and different regions, and far more interviews would be necessary.

Decisions about choosing a sample and recruiting subjects affect virtually all sociological research, not just surveys and in-depth interviews. In particular, the issues of **access** and resources are always critical. If planning an original survey, do we have access to the resources necessary to contact a sufficiently large group of people who will be representative of the entire population? If we are conducting in-depth interviews, can we locate and persuade enough subjects to participate? Or if we are doing ethnographic research, can we get access and permission to study in settings that encapsulate the processes we are most interested in? Sociologists can dream up the perfect population or setting from which to address our research questions, but that population and setting might be completely inaccessible to us. This is why so few studies are done about the very rich and powerful—it is often impossible to get them to agree to give researchers unfettered access to their lives.

Thus, sociologists work with what we can get. For survey researchers, this might mean settling for a data collection that only approximates the target population or includes only those survey questions that can be asked in a relatively short amount of time (to hold down the costs of the survey). For an ethnographer, it might mean working in a setting where some, but not all, of the processes they hoped to analyze are at play.

Issues of Reliability and Validity

3.3.2 Compare and contrast reliability and validity and explain their importance in sociological research.

When collecting data, all sociologists, regardless of the specific method they use, tend to obsess over issues related to the reliability and validity of the information they gather. While these two concepts are related, sociologists tend to think of them in distinct ways. When sociologists talk about the **reliability** of a research result, they want to know whether, if they used the same measurement technique in a second study, they would end up with similar results. If the results can indeed be **replicated**—that is, the same results can be found by more than one researcher—we say that the results are reliable. However, reliability does not necessarily mean that the measurement correctly reflects what the researcher is trying to uncover. One can get the same measurement again and again, but the results might not mean what the researcher thinks they mean. For instance, if most White Americans do not want to appear to be racist, they may consistently provide favorable answers to survey questions about topics such as their willingness to send their children to schools with a high percentage of Black children. But in practice, they may choose to move to largely all-White suburbs. In such a case, the results from the survey question are reliable, but there is something wrong. They are not actually measuring what many White American parents are really doing. The concept of **validity** captures this—namely, whether the measurement a researcher is using is actually accurate. If the measurement reflects what the researcher is hoping to understand about the social world, we say the results are valid.

The Complications of Causality

3.3.3 Explain why the ability to make causal inferences is so important yet challenging for sociologists.

One of the biggest worries for sociologists is their ability to make causal arguments (that is, to explain *why* some outcomes occurred). The concept of **causality** is central to sociological research. Sociologists interested in understanding the world or informing social policy often want to go beyond simply documenting that two social phenomenon appear together—in other words, that they "co-vary" with each other. This is what known as a **correlation**. An obvious example of this is the relationship between income and education—they are correlated in that higher income is associated with higher education. Put another way, those who are better educated tend to be more affluent. These social attributes vary together; a change in one is linked to a change in the other. But how are they linked? What is actually causing the higher incomes received by those with more education? To answer this, sociologists often need to know if it is likely that one thing is caused by another. That's what **causal inference** is all about. In other words, researchers ultimately want to know what causes what. And it's not easily done. Figure 3.4 displays a classical example of why something that appears to be caused by something else can be false.

To illustrate the challenges of establishing causality, let's look at one area of research that not only has been a prominent focus of sociological attention but also is familiar to all twenty-first-century students: educational achievement as measured by standardized test scores. Sociologists have long sought to understand variation in student test scores and why some groups of students do better on these tests than other seemingly equally well-qualified students.

While schools and the U.S. government began widely using test scores to assess individuals and schools early in the twentieth century, the most important contributions of sociologists were made in the past half century. With the Civil Rights Act of 1964, Congress explicitly required the government to "conduct a survey and make a report to the president and Congress, within two years of the enactment of this title, concerning the lack of availability of equal educational opportunities for individuals by reason of race, color, religion or national origin in public educational institutions at all levels in the United States." A prominent sociologist, James Coleman, was put in charge of the effort. Researchers in the fall of 1965 collected and processed 639,650 surveys and, remarkably, by the summer of 1966 completed and distributed a report of approximately 1,000 pages, which came to be known as the Coleman Report (Coleman et al. [1966] 1974).

Coleman and his associates had collected data on student test scores. Based on this information, they explored how student background and school characteristics were related to test score performance.

At the time, many individuals assumed that differences in test score results were likely the product of inequalities in school resources—that is, many members of Congress and the public worried that Black students were often placed in schools with inadequate science labs, libraries, and other resources that inhibited their academic achievement. If you looked simply at test score results in poor or wealthy schools, you would find just that pattern. Test scores were higher in schools with more resources.

However, the analysis in the Coleman Report demonstrated that this relationship between school resources and student test scores was largely a **spurious**

Figure 3.4 Correlation, but Not Causation

Does the number of countries in the world cause global warming? If we look at the increase in the number of countries recognized by the United Nations, and the world's average temperature, we would see both going up, as shown in the two figures. We could easily think there is a relationship (for example, each country contributes something to global warming, so if there are more countries it is likely there is more global warming). However, what appears to be related at first glance is entirely false. No scientist believes that the fact that the world has more recognized countries than before is a cause of global warming; we have just divided up the world's people into more countries. Instead, climate scientists point to the increase in emissions as the cause of global warming.

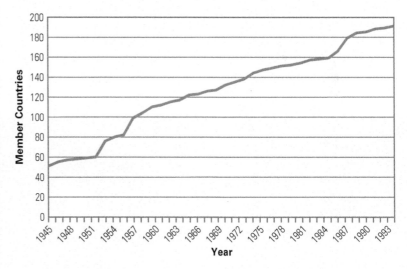

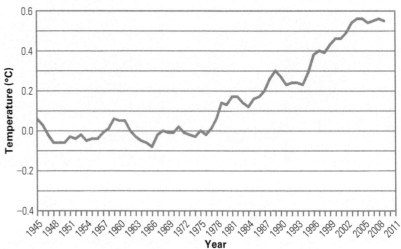

SOURCE: About.com (2009); GISS/NASA (2012).

relationship. When two factors seem to move in the same direction but both are themselves caused by something else (that is, a third factor), sociologists refer to the apparent relationship between the first two factors as a spurious. Coleman and his colleagues showed that such was exactly the case with the relationship between educational resources and student test scores. Specifically, Coleman demonstrated that while it looked like one caused the other, in fact other factors — namely, the parents' education, levels of the children attending different schools, as well as other factors such as the racial composition of schools — were behind the relationship. The report implied that if you wanted to reduce racial inequality in student outcomes, equalizing funding would not do much. Instead, you would have to better integrate U.S. public schools so that the school peers of the typical Black student more closely resembled those of the typical White student.

The Coleman Report, however, was based on data with a serious limitation: They were **cross-sectional**—that is, they were all collected at one point in time. How could one hope to get at what caused what, when both things examined were being measured simultaneously? By 1980, Coleman and other social scientists had convinced the government that what was needed was **longitudinal data**, which are collected over a long period of time, to address these questions more productively. A new data collection was undertaken, starting with the sample of 10th graders that were interviewed every two years as they grew older. With students followed over time, sociologists were able to measure how much individual test scores improved between 10th and 12th grade, and then how students did in college (for those who continued their schooling).

This change in methods allowed researchers to more accurately identify the effects of school on student academic achievement. Rather than trying simply to compare test scores between students from differing social backgrounds, as had been done in the Coleman Report, social scientists were now able to see how much test scores changed over time in different school settings. In analyzing these new longitudinal data, Coleman and his colleagues found that students in Catholic schools learned more than similar students in public schools (Coleman and Hoffer 1987). Coleman thought this was most likely due to better discipline in Catholic schools that emerged from the fact that parents and students in these schools were part of closely knit social communities with shared agreements on appropriate student behavior. Whereas findings from the original Coleman Report were used to support busing students for racial integration, this new set of findings was used by many to argue in favor of school vouchers, which are government-issued certificates parents can use to send their children to private schools instead of the public schools they were zoned for. This is a controversy that continues right up to today.

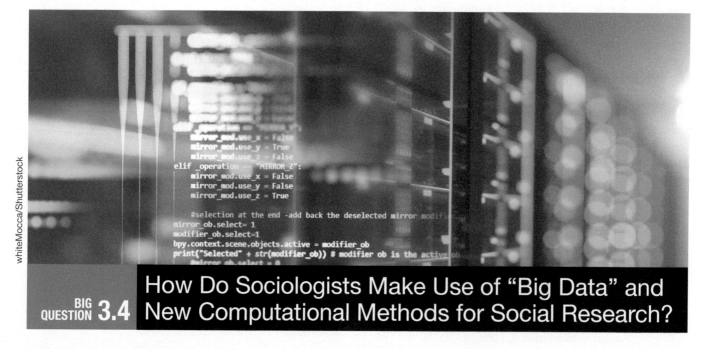

whiteMocca/Shutterstock

BIG QUESTION 3.4 How Do Sociologists Make Use of "Big Data" and New Computational Methods for Social Research?

THE RISE OF BIG DATA

The rapid evolution of computers and digital technology over the last half-century has created new forms of data about human behavior at unprecedented scales. **Big data** have emerged as more and more aspects of our everyday life leave behind a digital trace (whether we realize it or not). We generate digital information about everything from our tastes in music to our preferences for romantic partners to our political beliefs. We call this kind of data "big" data because it involves a huge amount of information about entire populations. Although getting a precise number is impossible, it would be difficult to overstate the sheer volume of data created through people's use of information and communication technology. Recent estimates suggest that users of the internet create, on average, 2.5 *billion* gigabytes of data *every day* (Holmes 2017). To give some sense of comparison, scholars in 1997 estimated that all of the books, videos, compact discs, photos, and maps in the vast collection of the Library of Congress was equivalent to about 3 *million* gigabytes (Lesk 1997). And the amount of data in existence is expected to grow at an increasing rate. The incredible volume and diversity of information we generate, store, and share has ushered in what many call an "age of big data" (Lohr 2012), offering social scientists some potentially remarkable new opportunities for research. But what makes big data different from traditional sources of data studied by social scientists, and what kinds of social scientific questions can big data help us answer?

How Is Big Data Defined and Where Does It Come From?

3.4.1 Explain the distinguishing features of big data.

The most essential—and obvious—distinguishing feature of big data is its *volume*. A data set is generally considered big data when the quantity of information it contains far exceeds what humans can process without the assistance of modern computing power. To see how data volume matters for research, let's compare a traditional approach to studying what kinds of issues are important to people today. In some of the traditional approaches discussed earlier in the chapter, a researcher might conduct in-depth interviews with a few dozen people or conduct a survey with 1,000 respondents. Such studies would yield information about what a number of respondents seem to care about. But a big data approach might instead take advantage of the vast stream of data from major social media platforms. With its 500 million new Tweets every day, Twitter provides a real-time look at political discussion on a large scale. Using automated and algorithmic software—in concert with Twitter's application programming interface (API)—researchers can rapidly download, organize, and analyze millions of Tweets.

While big data are distinctive for their sheer volume, most experts point out that they are not simply more of the same old data social scientists have long used. Big data are also novel for their velocity and variety (along with volume, these features form the "three Vs" [Holmes 2017; Laney 2001; Monroe 2013]; see Table 3.3). *Velocity* refers to the frequency with which the data are generated. Traditional forms of social science data, such as in-depth interviews, surveys, or ethnographic observations, can take months if not years to collect. And due to the cost associated with data collection, repeat observations or new waves of data gathering happen only at lengthy intervals. For example, the General Social Survey, one of the most important nationally representative surveys of Americans, is fielded once every two years, and the data are released some months after they are collected. Big data, on the other hand, are generated continuously and stored in real time. As individuals post on social media platforms, move about the physical world with GPS trackers on their mobile phones, and shop at online retailers, they are (often unwittingly) generating huge quantities of data that are simultaneously captured and stored by the service provider, which may be a commercial business, a government agency, or even a private person who owns the server that hosts the website.

Because big data are generated every time individuals interact with some digital technology, they come in a wider *variety* of formats and structures than traditional social science data. Big data can come in the form of unstructured text (from, say, a collection of thousands of blog posts), a network of interactions among millions of individuals (as is the case with private messages among users of a dating website), or even as pictures and video (such as media on Instagram or YouTube). The companies that run these platforms often restrict researchers' access to information about specific individuals, but there are a variety of ways that researchers can "harvest" data that is publicly available.

Most big data that can be obtained from digital platforms also include **metadata**. Metadata are data about data, such as the time of day a message was sent, the location at which a picture was taken, the age of a social media user's account, or even the sort of device used to create the data. Information like this allows researchers to explore patterns in big data across a number of dimensions like time and place. For example, consider SMS text messages that you send and receive on your mobile phone. The primary data contained in a text message is textual, but each message is also described by metadata such as the time and date it was sent, the phone numbers of the sender and recipient, and even the mobile phone service each person uses.

Table 3.3 The Three V's of Big Data

Volume: The quantity of data is too great to collect, store, manipulate, and analyze using traditional computer and statistical methods.

Velocity: Big data are generated continuously as people use information and communication technology and are stored in real time (that is, as they are produced).

Variety: Big data can come in many formats and structures, which may or may not be conducive to traditional social science research techniques. Besides numerical information, big data may include, for example, images and video, as well as unstructured posting by unidentifiable people (or even bots).

While online behavior has been the most common source of big data, the ever-increasing spread of digital technologies across all aspects of life is generating information about behavior offline as well. For example, an increasing number of objects outside of the web are connected to the internet. Though we may not realize it, we are constantly generating data through our interaction with this **internet of things**, the variety of devices all around us that gather and transmit data, such as our smartphones, smart watches, and a growing array of "smart" home appliances like televisions, speakers, and even thermostats. For example, anytime you use the "maps" application on your smartphone, you transmit data about your location to the service provider (such as Google). Service providers can compile these data to uncover aggregate trends in movement, and they can use this information to learn about your individual behaviors. Companies can use your personalized location data to send you traffic alerts, recommend restaurants near your home, or show you customer reviews for nearby dry cleaners, among many other things.

Although most technology under the broad rubric of the internet of things has been for commercial or industrial purposes, we are also beginning to see its application toward more public-minded or research goals. For example, "smart city" technologies integrate digital and electromagnetic sensors, wireless data transmission, and automation into ordinary features of the built environment like street lamps, garbage bins, and parking meters. Social scientists are beginning to use data from smart city technologies to understand social behavior in urban environments. For example, researchers have used air quality sensors built into streetlights and park benches to measure pollution in real time. And by linking air quality data to tracking data from mobile phones, researchers can pinpoint exactly where and when urban dwellers are exposed to pollution "hot spots" (Nyhan et al. 2016).

Another illustration of the possibilities—and potential risks—presented by these sources of big data can be found during the COVID-19 pandemic. Public health officials in cities around the world have rolled out applications for mobile phones

that can track the movements of people, and when someone becomes infected those with whom they may have come into contact can be warned (Ferretti et al. 2020). This gives public health and other government officials real-time data on how well people are abiding by stay-at-home rules (see Figure 3.5). Some cities have even used pedestrian sensors built into smart streetlights to detect changes in foot traffic to see if people are observing (or disobeying) stay-at-home orders (Urban Observatory 2020). Although this kind of monitoring of individual movements can serve an important public health function, the same technologies could be used by an authoritarian government determined to crush opposition to identify people who participate in a protest event, and later arrest or harass them into silence.

Analyzing Big Data

3.4.2 Identify how social scientists analyze big data.

The explosion of these new sources of data has allowed social scientists to ask new questions as well as revisit old puzzles. The "three V's" (volume, velocity, and variety) of big data push the boundaries of conventional social

Figure 3.5 Google Location Mobility Trends for the State of New York, March to June 2020

The trends documented here show that after about March 12, 2020, people in New York were much less likely to go to work, ride public transit, and do either retail (non-grocery) shopping or recreation. It shows us what date marked the arrival of the COVID-19 pandemic in New York, as measured by where people were spending their time (around March 14, when people suddenly began altering their behavior in response to the pandemic). Where were they? At their residence. At first, even grocery/pharmacy shopping declined, before returning to near normal. Other activities were slower to recover. The state of New York was hit hard by COVID-19 in the early phase of the pandemic (March–June 2020), so perhaps it is not so surprising that people were staying home.

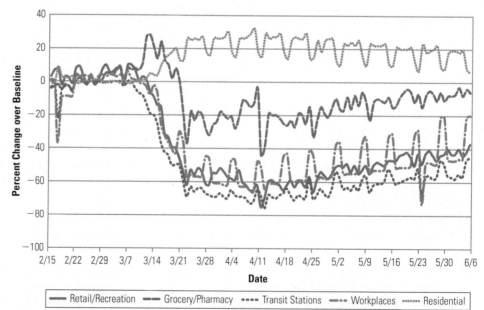

NOTE: Values are percent change in visits to select locations according to Google Location Service tracking for the dates February 15 to June 7, 2020, as compared to the median value from the five-week period January 3–February 6, 2020.
SOURCE: Data from Google Location Services

science research methods. Fortunately, the advent of big data has coincided with rapid advancements in the power and affordability of computers, wider fluency with computer programming languages, and more interdisciplinary exchange between social scientists and computer scientists. This interchange has been a boon for the growth of **computational social science**, a new subfield that combines big data with algorithmic methods to answer social scientific questions.

Algorithm is an imposing word, but it simply means a set of rules used in a decision-making process. Our brains are the original algorithmic machines; we "input" sensory data like smells and sights, process these data according to some (often fuzzy) rules, and "output" a decision. For example, if you have ever been suspicious about a carton of milk in the back of your refrigerator, you might have checked the expiration date, given it a sniff, or visually inspected its texture. Based on these data, you calculate whether the milk has spoiled and, depending on your personal tolerance and alternatives, you decide whether to use it or toss it out. Computer algorithms work in much the same way: Using features of the data and some rules, a computer algorithm can sort data into categories, detect clusters of similar data points, and even make predictions about future data. One of the simplest computer algorithms we use every day (perhaps without knowing it) is for the purpose of spam e-mail detection. Your e-mail program "reads" every e-mail you receive and makes a guess as to whether it is spam according to a number of variables, including who sent it and what the e-mail says. E-mails from suspicious senders and those that include combinations of words like "Click here to win a million dollars" get classified as spam. These are known as **classification algorithms**, and they are widely used in social science research. For example, scholars of political discourse use precisely this kind of algorithm to detect hate speech on social media (MacAvaney et al. 2019). By "training" an algorithm to classify social media posts that contain racial and ethnic epithets as hate speech, researchers are able to process far more data than if they were coding every post by hand. However, no algorithm is perfect; The lack of human oversight means that some posts are liable to be misclassified (which is also why your spam filter will sometimes wrongly catch an innocent e-mail or let a particularly deceptive spam message through). For example, algorithms are not good at picking up on sarcasm or understanding nuance. Thus, while computational methods can allow us to exploit big data, they come with trade-offs and potential risks.

One important risk concerns the use of **predictive algorithms**. These algorithms use information about past events to estimate the probability of some future event. Your credit score, for example, is based on a predictive algorithm that uses information about you to calculate the risk that you will default on your debt. In social science, these kinds of algorithms have been used to predict a wide variety of outcomes, including individuals' risk of suicide or the likelihood that armed conflict will break out in a country (Walsh, Ribiero, and Franklin 2017; Salganik et al. 2019). Despite their varied applications, all of these algorithms are based on similar principles. Researchers use data about the past to estimate which factors appear most likely to cause a particular outcome in the future.

In spite of, or perhaps because of, their wide applicability, predictive algorithms have spurred controversy. For example, many people feel that their credit score is a number that doesn't reflect who "they" are (and if the score is low, it can have real consequences for getting a loan, an apartment, or even a job). A growing concern of many critics is the use of predictive algorithms in the criminal justice system. A number of **risk assessment algorithms** purport to predict the chances that an individual will commit a crime in the future, and some courts use these risk assessments to inform sentencing and parole decisions (Harcourt 2006; Barry-Jester et al. 2015). The ethical question here is whether applying a standard approach to all convicted criminals will unjustly punish some people more than necessary. For example, young people are more likely to commit crimes; should a young person convicted of one crime receive a longer sentence because the *average* young person is more likely than the average older person to commit other crimes?

Another interesting example of the use of predictive algorithms arises in case of admissions to selective universities, as well as the allocation of scholarships and grants based on merit. College admissions officers can (and usually do) calculate a score for each application based on data such as standardized test scores, grade-point averages, the high school attended, and even the number of extracurricular activities a student is involved with. They hope these scores can predict a student's chance of succeeding at their college, and, to an extent, such admissions formulae have some validity. However, many things about individual college applicants are impossible to quantify. For example, how would an algorithm predicting students' future academic success account for differences in individuals' economic circumstances, family backgrounds, or learning styles? These are often left out, even though sociologists know they are very important.

One of the most useful current applications of computational methods can be seen in the study of media and communication. Compared with traditional mass media like newspapers and television, online media are virtually free to produce and distribute, allowing more numerous and diverse voices to participate in the public sphere and creating unprecedented opportunities for interaction.

Sociologists are interested in using this new media environment to study a wide variety of social phenomena, everything from political beliefs to consumers tastes to cultural creativity. One of the most important developments for social research has been the explosion of research using what is known as **text-as-data** approaches. This refers to the possibility that texts can be analyzed as systematically as other kinds of data, and in this way we can find underlying patterns that researchers might miss if they just read the words on the page.

Enthusiasm for big data research applications in the social sciences is currently very high, and it is likely new findings will emerge as research progresses. But it is always important to keep in mind that the rules for doing research that emerged long ago still apply. That very basic point can sometimes get lost in the quest for unexplored data sources.

Monty Rakusen/Getty Images

BIG QUESTION **3.5** How Do Sociologists Make Sense of Their Findings?

ANALYZING DATA AND REACHING CONCLUSIONS

With our questions asked and data collected, sociologists are finally in the position to make sense of what we have found. This stage of the research process is called **data analysis**—when we interpret the information we've collected and look for patterns in it. Some sociologists wait until this stage before they do any analytical work. Those who work with survey data, for instance, rarely stop midway to analyze a partial sample of their subjects. Instead, they tend to wait until all the data are in to begin analyzing them and drawing conclusions from them. Yet with other methods, it is essential that analysis occurs while the data are being gathered, so that the researcher is, in a sense, going back and forth between collecting data and thinking about what it means and whether different kinds of data need to be gathered. For ethnographers—especially those who spend years in the field—it would be a disaster to wait until all observations are made before analyzing them. Facing hundreds of pages of unanalyzed field notes would overwhelm even the most experienced researcher. In this section, we examine some of the issues that commonly occur when sociologists try to make sense of their data.

How Do the Puzzle Pieces Fit Together?

3.5.1 Identify the goal of data analysis and describe the process sociologists use to interpret research.

Whichever logic a sociologist uses, the goal of data analysis is the same: to figure out how the pieces of the empirical puzzle fit together. Indeed, we can think about data as pieces of a larger puzzle—and the job of the researcher is to put them together into patterns and make research conclusions. But for anyone who has struggled with a thousand-piece puzzle, it is clear that the process of making it whole can be very difficult. Sociologists have many strategies to aid them here. First, in most projects researchers engage in some form of **data coding**—that is, organizing the data according to key categories and concepts. Transforming raw data into a usable format is a key part of beginning to analyze that data. For instance, those doing statistical analysis must first put their data into a form that is suitable for analysis by standardizing the raw data, usually by assigning numbers to them, and also looking for obvious errors, a process known as "cleaning" the data.

Because interviewers and ethnographers collect their own data, they must do their own coding. In the past, this would have been done by hand; fortunately, a variety of software packages are now available that make it infinitely easier to work with most kinds of qualitative data. Still, even with computer-assisted data analysis there is much to be done. On the one hand, a specific code has to be used to classify a specific piece of data. Those codes then become the mechanism through which the data are sorted, systematized, and arranged. It is the way data are categorized across cases. Figuring out an appropriate coding scheme is a critical step to finding what is in those thousands of documents or pages of interview transcripts.

Once the data are coded, sociologists usually do more analytical work before making research conclusions. This work involves making sense of the data and breaking them down to see emergent patterns. For those who think visually, **data displays** can be a useful way to go about this. These are visual images that represent the data they are, in other words, summaries of what has been found. Such displays include diagrams, flowcharts, typologies, tables, and matrices. Even if these visuals never make it into the final research product, their importance lies in the process of constructing them and in drawing out the connections being made across the data as well as the patterns that still need to be fleshed out.

For those who tend to think verbally, **research memos** can serve a similar purpose. These are extended versions of research notes, usually organized analytically, that allow researchers to work through their findings and the evidence they have to support them, as well as to make sure the analytical forest is not lost amid all the trees of data.

What Do Our Conclusions Tell Us About the Social World?

3.5.2 Explain how sociologists use generalization to draw conclusions from their research.

In the end, the goal of all research is to reach reliable and valid conclusions. In the final step of any project, sociologists have to go back to the research question they began with and figure out how the empirical patterns that we uncovered help to answer it. Put another way, they strive to make general claims about the issues posed by the research question. Yet **generalization** is a tricky thing in much sociological research. On the one hand, sociologists don't want to limit their conclusions only to the specific sample of people, places, or things they studied directly; they also want to form conclusions from those samples to say something overall about broad social patterns. But in doing this, they need to make sure they don't overextend their claims; they must be careful that the conclusions they draw from the data are reliable and valid.

So sociologists proceed with caution as they turn to writing up their results. All researchers would love to have "proven" some new hypothesis or finding that will change the way we think about the world. Some have conducted their research in a way that allows them to claim **empirical generalizability**—they apply conclusions from their findings beyond its immediate context (as when we conduct a survey with a few hundred people with a representative sample of an entire society). Other sociologists who do not work with representative samples cannot make those kind of empirical claims. But they can apply conclusions from their findings to larger sociological processes explored in other studies. In this way, they can still claim **theoretical generalizability**—that is, that the results of their study relate to broader theoretical puzzles, and contribute to advancing our understanding. To use one sociologist's phrasing, they "bump up a level of generality" to bring their findings to bear on a broader concept or theory (Luker 2010). Whatever level a sociologist decides to generalize to, we all strive to address the "big questions" in the social sciences—questions that we will outline and discuss throughout this text.

Conclusion: Thinking Critically about Research

It is certainly true that reading about research is a lot less fun than actually doing it. But understanding how research is done, and the challenges of each of the major research methods, should not only help you to think about *how* to do a research study, but also make critical thinking about sociological research easier. Whether the research is on

the family, culture, race and ethnicity, religion, power and politics, or the environment, understanding the methodological issues guiding the research reported is always the same: What was the research question? Was the method used appropriate for addressing the question? Were the data collected systematically? Were the findings reliable and trustworthy? And what's the larger take-away from the work? What does it teach us about the larger world we live in?

Being able to read and critically review other scholars' research is an important step, but it is generally easier to be critical of other research than it is to be of our own. Ultimately, then, the goal of studying research methods is to prepare us for doing our own studies. And we hope that you will join the army of sociologists mapping the contours of the social world.

The Big Questions Revisited 3

3.1 Where Do Sociological Questions Come From?
We began the chapter with the basic stages of sociological research, discussing the issues that often come up as researchers practice sociology for the first time, such as how sociologists turn their research interests into workable questions and how we know what to study.

The Building Blocks of Sociological Research

Crafting Good Research Questions from Important Topics
Learning Objective 3.1.1: Identify the six issues sociologists should consider to determine a research question's merit and feasibility.

How Do We Know What to Study?
Learning Objective 3.1.2: Identify key factors that shape sociologists' choices about what to research.

Key Terms
ethnographers (p. 58)   data (p. 58)   sociological imaginations (p. 59)   hypothesis (p. 59)   value (p. 61)   theoretical traditions (p. 61)   code of ethics (p. 61)   informed consent (p. 61)   institutional review boards (IRBs) (p. 62)

3.2 What Is the Best Method to Research Different Sociological Questions? Once sociologists have a working research question, they need to decide the best way to go about answering it. This section examined the different types of methods that sociologists use in their research and discussed the process for determining which method and design is best.

Sociological Research Methods and Challenges

Getting Started
Learning Objective 3.2.1: Discuss how sociologists operationalize their research questions and distinguish between independent and dependent variables.

The Classical Scientific Method of Research
Learning Objective 3.2.2: Identify the steps of the classical scientific method, and explain why sociologists might take a looser approach to research.

Quantitative Versus Qualitative Research Methods
Learning Objective 3.2.3: Compare and contrast quantitative versus qualitative research methods.

Survey and In-depth Interview Methods and the Challenges of Design
Learning Objective 3.2.4: Identify the key strengths and weaknesses of survey and interview methods.

Ethnographic Methods and the Challenge of Developing Generalizable Knowledge
Learning Objective 3.2.5: Explain why the main strength of ethnography is also its central weakness.

Field Experiments
Learning Objective 3.2.6: Discuss the advantages of field experiments.

Matching the Question with a Method
Learning Objective 3.2.7: Explain why choosing the right research method to study motivations and behavior is a complex process.

Key Terms
operationalize (p. 62)   variable (p. 62)   independent variable (p. 62)   dependent variable (p. 62)   scientific method (p. 63)   quantitative research (p. 64)   qualitative research (p. 64)   mixed-method research (p. 64)   survey (p. 64)   census (p. 65)   General Social Survey (GSS) (p. 65)   Panel Study of Income Dynamics (PSID) (p. 65)   American National Election Study (ANES) (p. 65)   margin of error (p. 66)   in-depth interview (p. 66)   semi-structured interview (p. 66)   open-ended interview (p. 66)   ethnography (p. 67)   thick description (p. 68)   extended case method (p. 68)   field experiments (p. 69)   treatment group (p. 69)   control group (p. 69).

3.3 **What Challenges Do Sociologists Face When Collecting Data?** This section explored some of the practical issues and challenges that surface during data collection.

The Challenge of Data Collection

Sampling Issues

Learning Objective 3.3.1: Explain sampling issues that sociologists grapple with when they begin their research.

Issues of Reliability and Validity

Learning Objective 3.3.2: Compare and contrast reliability and validity and explain their importance in sociological research.

The Complications of Causality

Learning Objective 3.3.3: Explain why the ability to make causal inferences is so important yet challenging for sociologists.

Key Terms

sample (p. 72)   representative sample (p. 73)
random sample (p. 73)   weighting (p. 73)
access (p. 74)   reliability (p. 74)   replicated
(p. 74)   validity (p. 74)   causality (p. 74)
correlation (p. 75)   causal inference (p. 75)
spurious relationship (p. 76)   cross-
sectional (p. 76)   longitudinal data (p. 76)

3.4 **How Do Sociologists Make Use of "Big Data" and New Computational Methods for Social Research?** The internet and communication technology opened up new lines of research for sociologists. This section introduced the concept of "big data" and some innovative techniques for analyzing it.

The Rise of Big Data

How Is Big Data Defined and Where Does It Come From?

Learning Objective 3.4.1: Explain the distinguishing features of big data.

Analyzing Big Data

Learning Objective 3.4.2: Identify how social scientists analyze big data.

Key Terms

big data (p. 77)   metadata (p. 78)   internet of
things (p. 78)   computational social science
(p. 79)   algorithm (p. 79)   classification algorithms
(p. 79)   predictive algorithms (p. 79)   risk assessment algorithms (p. 79)   text-as-data (p. 80)

3.5 **How Do Sociologists Make Sense of Their Findings?** This section considered how sociologists make sure their findings are reliable and trustworthy and how they decide what kind of general claims to draw from their research.

Analyzing Data and Reaching Conclusions

How Do the Puzzle Pieces Fit Together?

Learning Objective 3.5.1: Identify the goal of data analysis and describe the process sociologists use to interpret research.

What Do Our Conclusions Tell Us About the Social World?

Learning Objective 3.5.2: Explain how sociologists use generalization to draw conclusions from their research.

Key Terms

data analysis (p. 80)   data coding (p. 81)   data
display (p. 81)   research memo (p. 81)   generalization (p. 81)   empirical generalizability
(p. 81)   theoretical generalizability (p. 81)

Chapter 4
Social Interaction

by Harvey Molotch

The public restroom might be the last place you would expect to learn about the ways people interact with others. We spend our days carefully managing how we present ourselves and interact with others in all different kinds of social situations. But nowhere is the presence of others felt more strongly than in a public restroom, making it an interesting place to learn about social interaction. What happens in the public restroom provides clues about how we achieve and safeguard our own identity, always in ways appropriate to the context we are in. The intense controversy over transgender bathrooms, as a growing number of places have established the rights of transgender and nonbinary people to use the bathroom that best fits their gender identity, is an important example of the stakes in getting things right. And maybe this justifies, even invites, bringing it up as an academic topic.

The specific restroom predicament is that we humans need to eliminate our own body waste, but that process is somewhat animalistic. It conflicts with our efforts to show ourselves as civilized. We must do it, but unlike other creatures in the animal kingdom, our culture intervenes to shape what it means to perform this so-called natural act. We notice who is present and where and how they look—at themselves and at us. We manage in tiny, moment-by-moment ways what others see and hear, looking inward and outward at the same time. A casual touch or accidental bump registers immediately, just as we acutely pick up on gestures, sounds, and movements.

Among the reasons the stakes are so high is that, in sociologist Erving Goffman's famous terms, the bathroom is part of our "backstage" where we set up our "presentation of self" (Goffman 1959). More usually, we are in the privacy of our own home when we do these core personal activities. In contrast, the public restroom is not private. So besides avoiding the usual public embarrassments—slipping on the floor, crying out loud, wearing mismatched socks—we take on other worries of giving away something so private: There should be no suspicious soiling or water splash

on our clothes. Indeed there should be no evidence at all of where we've been or what we've done. And while on task inside the restroom, we must carefully monitor what we expose and to exactly whom. To mess up in any of these regards would risk spoiling our identity, maybe implying we were not decent or competent in other regards as well.

One way we avoid such perceptions is through our specific cultural knowledge of what to do and when. This includes smoothly working the hardware and equipment at hand: sinks, toilets, toilet paper, and stall doors, as well as

My Sociological Imagination

HARVEY MOLOTCH

I came to sociology through a college professor of philosophy who thought that a book by a sociologist, C. Wright Mills, called *The Sociological Imagination*, contained profound social and ethical lessons. I read Mills and absorbed the idea that meaningful community cannot happen when some people have so little power compared to others. The solution, as Mills advocates, is for people to link up with others to see their problems as common ones, caused by the same types of external forces. Particularly in regard to cities (which became a focus of my own research), I learned how business groups, mostly based in real estate, dominate urban agendas and promote projects regardless of their social and environmental impacts—"growth machines," I called them. I came to wonder why so many people went along, even when the results were so counter to their own interests. I've always been interested in physical things, like buildings and sewer lines, and more recently in the apparatus used in security, like at airport gates. This combines my interest in cities and their stuff with my abiding fascination with ordinary goods of daily life—toasters and toilets, for example.

While it may seem an unusual place for sociological research, we can actually learn a lot by studying social interaction in any public space, even restrooms.

the social aspect. We ordinarily do not fumble with doorknobs or shout approval at the sound of another person's defecation. We follow the rule of respecting separate rooms for women and men without being told by a police officer to do so. Men choose a urinal, if available, not adjacent to one being used by a stranger.

But imagine the problems for visitors from a part of the world where things are different. In other countries, people may squat over an opening—in fact a superior arrangement both in sanitary and physiological terms compared to the chair-sit of the Western world. They may cleanse themselves not with toilet paper but by using water piped into the stall that they can spray at fouled body parts. Women and men may share facilities by using them at different *times* instead of having different *places*. And what a contrast all of it is with the practices in the Roman Empire, where citizens did their business with as many as 80 to 90 individuals sitting adjacent along a room's perimeter, open to one another and apparently speaking about issues of the day. Speaking for myself, I would be culturally lost and quite disturbed to be so exposed.

Besides worry about germs, something common among modern restroom users, there is concern about social contamination. So the very presence of the wrong kind of person, one imagined as inappropriate for social interaction, is a pollutant. In India, this means avoiding persons of the lowest caste (whose role is, among other lowly tasks, cleaning toilets); in countries like the United States, those who appear unkempt or disorderly may generate worries about being too close by. Some people will not enter a restroom with a homeless person inside and avoid sharing one with any of those too far below their own social standing. And it is for similar reasons that some people fight so hard to resist letting the "wrong" kind of person into a bathroom if transgender people are allowed options.

Our behavior in public restrooms is heavily influenced by gender in other ways. In their respective restrooms, men and women behave differently, much beyond constraints imposed by biological variation. Men, for example, virtually never have conversation from stall to stall (women apparently do so on occasion) and converse only in very constrained ways at the urinals. They take pains to keep their eyes straight ahead, never looking at the exposed anatomy of another man *and not looking like they are trying not to look* at another man's anatomy. Yet women are more at ease. They report that restrooms are where they go to chat. It is where, they sometimes say, they learned as girls how to groom themselves, hold their bodies, use menstrual products, and adjust their clothes—with pals and relatives fussing around them with help and suggestions (Suarez 2008). Whether male or female, in choosing the "right" room to go in and then engaging in practices appropriate to that room, users reinforce their unique identity as a particular kind of person, namely a man or woman, and one

who grooms him or herself and handles the presence of others in a specific way. All these longstanding differences are threatened when communities establish nongendered bathrooms, which anyone can use.

As the example of the public restroom suggests, our actions are guided by the watchful judgments of those who matter to us, even strangers. This chapter examines how we can each be distinctive individuals yet subject to the influence of others. How can there be, sociologists ask, both individual identity yet also conformity? And just how does all this get accomplished in human interaction? The answers, as it turns out, come not from thinking of "individual" and "society" as opposite or even separate things at all. Instead, an individual and their society influence one another continuously through history and constantly from moment to moment. It happens—and this is a fundamental starting point for understanding human beings—through how we interact and how we think. Here is the key: We introspect, and we do it with the help of other people.

Mark Bussell

For as long as societies have had bathrooms, they have been separated by gender. However, this traditional division was increasingly uncomfortable for some as gender non-conformity is growing. In response, governments and some corporations are beginning to create non-gendered bathrooms, such as this "all-gender" bathroom in a building in New York City. Note that the sign also indicates that traditionally gendered bathrooms are available for anyone who would be uncomfortable in a non-gendered bathroom, exemplifying how the public restroom continues to be a place of societal controversy.

The Big Questions

1. **How do we develop a sense of self?** Each one of us has a unique identity. But is this sense of self a single thing, or is it a process of interaction? In this section, we examine how we know ourselves through the reflections of ourselves that mirror back others' opinions of us—the "looking glass" of others.

2. **How do we make sense of our worlds?** Human beings have specific methods for demonstrating competence as interacting members of society. In this section, we explore how the sociological field of ethnomethodology examines these methods.

3. **What challenges do we face as we move from one social context to another?** The social self is not fixed but is always changing, which can sometimes bring challenges. Here we examine what happens when individuals experience role conflict and how informal rules and our keen awareness guide our behavior. We also look at how and why people conform and what consequences conformity has on how people live together.

Mark Bussell

BIG QUESTION 4.1 How Do We Develop a Sense of Self?

THE SOCIAL SELF

We have the ability to think not just about objects before us, like a banana or a building, but about our very selves. Not even smart and sensitive French poodles can do that. Like other nonhumans, dogs are driven by instinct rather than introspection, which is why they pee all over town even when they will get the same amount of food and love by going only once or twice and only in one spot. The remarkable human capacity for consciousness of *self* becomes the vehicle through which we take our actions, interpreting and evaluating everything that comes our way, including other people.

The social self is the only kind of self there can be: *The self is not a thing, but a process of interaction.* This important school of thought in sociology, based in the thinking of the early twentieth-century philosopher George Herbert Mead, is called *symbolic interaction,* or just interactionism, and it guides ideas for this chapter. Central to this line of thinking is the idea that an individual's personality, preferences,

ideas, and so forth are constructed and shaped by communication with both others and his or her self. It is why isolation of the kind we experienced during the COVID-19 pandemic was so disorienting and difficult.

The Looking-Glass Self

4.1.1 Explain how the opinions and judgments of others shape our identities.

The concept of the **self**—that is, one's own identity and social position, as made and reformulated through interaction—is so basic that if it becomes too hard to achieve, even physicality becomes problematic. For example, we know from studies of orphanages that babies have a hard time surviving biologically without social stimuli. In a classic 1945 study, the psychoanalyst René Spitz compared the babies and small children in an orphanage versus those in a nursery for the children of incarcerated mothers. Caring professionals staffed both facilities, which were clean, warm environments where the babies received good medical attention and nutritious food. But there were differences. In the nursery (but not the orphanage), the infants could see everything and each other right through the bars of their cribs. They could see the bustle of attendants and visitors going about their business all around them. The biggest medical problem in the nursery was the common cold, and the infants were otherwise healthy and happy.

Meanwhile, in the orphanage, the babies were separated from the staff most of the time and only had human contact when being fed or changed. They lived in cubicles, making it impossible to see each other, and their cribs had solid sides so they could not even see out of them. The result, wrote Spitz, was that "each baby lies in solitary confinement up to the time he is able to stand up in his bed" (Spitz 1945). Unlike the nursery, the orphanage infants suffered emotionally and physically. They became progressively more withdrawn and more susceptible to hosts of chronic maladies as they grew. Forty percent actually died within two years of Spitz's first observations. He concluded that the poor emotional and physical health of the orphanage babies was caused by a lack of social contact with others. When the orphanage switched cribs and caregivers started interacting with children, mortality sharply declined.

Adults do not fare much better in solitary confinement. In U.S. prisons, it is common to discipline inmates by sending them "to the hole" for weeks, months, and even years for breaking rules. In windowless cells, prisoners' food may be delivered through a slot in the door, and if they are allowed visitors at all, these may be restricted to videoconference. In what psychologist Craig Haney dubbed the supermax prison, inmates are typically confined to their cell for 23 hours a day and effectively denied contact with other humans. Without real social contact, prisoners' mental health falls apart. The minds of some begin to grind to a halt with confusion, lethargy, and inability to concentrate. The minds of others go wild with hallucinations, paranoia, and intense anxiety. That's why, in search of basic social contact, some may resort to tapping on the pipes and air ducts running through their cells just to be acknowledged by someone else who might tap back (Haney 2003). Or they commit suicide.

Although life during the COVID-19 pandemic was not nearly so extreme, there was substantial evidence of rising mental health problems that were partly associated with the social isolation the pandemic induced. One study by the Centers for Disease Control and Prevention showed major increases in levels of depression, increased drug and alcohol abuse, and evidence of traumatic stress (Czeisler et al. 2020). When the CDC carried out the survey used for the report, in June 2020, 40 percent of Americans overall had at least one new mental health issue arise during the pandemic, with 11 percent of Americans reporting contemplating suicide. The same survey showed an astonishing 26 percent (more than 1 in 4) of young people aged 18–24 were thinking about

Thinkstock Images/Getty Images

Deprived of social interaction, prisoners fare poorly in solitary confinement. Human rights organizations and United Nations officials have argued that long-term solitary confinement is a form of torture. In the United States, such confinement is all too common; in 2020, it was reported that the state of Texas alone had 1,300 inmates who had been in solitary confinement for more than five years (Hart and Cabera 2020).

suicide. Lacking regular social contact, with schools mostly closed in the spring of 2020 (and with most summer camps and many schools still closed in the fall of that year), children and adolescents were at a heightened risk of suffering from mental health problems.

So where does this need for social contact come from that looms so large and can be a matter of life or death itself? We really only know ourselves—even that we exist—through the eyes of other people. The actions that we take, the expressions that we use, and the gestures we give enlist evaluations from those around us. Those others tell us, not necessarily with explicit words, what we are, and we interpret their evaluations as representing our being. It starts, of course, with our parents or other caregivers who can't help but notice our early babbling and silly movements. Their smiles and frowns become the stuff that gives us an early sense that we even exist. From then on feedback comes about what *type* of person we are, including how good or bad.

The judgments accumulate throughout our lives as we gather playmates, siblings, friends, teachers (sometimes psychiatrists and police)—a stream of judges and judgments that fill in our sense of our own being. Are we clever? Pretty? Short or tall? Nice or selfish? We are, in effect, asking all these things all the time, and others are providing the answers. We know ourselves through the "looking glass" of others that mirror back to us the impressions we create. The term **looking-glass self** was coined by sociologist Charles Horton Cooley in 1902 to emphasize the extent to which our own self-understandings depend on how others view us. It was a profound insight. Interaction makes our world go round.

Looking for approval becomes truly motivating. If there is a fundamental human instinct, this is it. Because we want to belong and make connections with others, we try to anticipate what will be made of what we do. We have the ability to, in the lingo of sociology, "take the role of the other." This gives us the tool to conform to others' expectations because we can imagine how they will receive what we do or say. And those others shape their behaviors in light of their expectations of how we will receive them. It becomes a complicated system of interactions across a wildly complicated array of people in direct and indirect communication. This is a key setting, sociologically speaking, where conscience and guilt come from. We don't want to let others down. We really do want to satisfy their expectations for us because that is also the way to create a positive sense of one's own being and to socially belong and be connected in positive ways with others. Even if it is only indirect contact through things we have read, seen on television, or picked up on social media, we take note and gain some understanding of what we need to do to please and fit into social behavior expected by others.

Significant Others, Reference Groups, and Generalized Others

4.1.2 Compare and contrast the roles that significant others, reference groups, and generalized others play in guiding our behavior and in shaping our sense of self.

We know that we are motivated by the approval of others, but do all *others* matter to us equally? Sociologists try to determine how other people, by virtue of their social location, do or do not matter to us. We take some people and types of people more seriously than others, which is evident in the ways we defer to them and seek their approval.

At the individual level, sociologists, following in the footsteps of George Herbert Mead, use the term **significant other** to denote individuals close enough to us to have a strong capacity to motivate our behavior. Everyone has more than one significant other in the sociological sense. The concept might be confusing at first, because in everyday usage today a "significant other" refers to the person we are in an intimate relationship with, and that person is undoubtedly important. But from the standpoint of the people who have

a strong influence on us, the interactionist term significant other might also include our parents and other close relatives, siblings, and even very close friends. In fact, one or more of these "other" significant others might have more influence on us than our romantic partner.

Sometimes individuals have a more or less similar level of significance because of their common membership in a relevant social category. Doctors are alert to the opinions of other doctors. They are not as dependent for their sense of self on the viewpoints of say, the custodial staff. College students are likely more interested in the opinions of their fellow students than those they once knew who left high school without going on to higher education. In figuring out how we are doing, we *reference* others whose social positions and preferences makes them especially relevant to our own sense of worth. Sociologists call these groups that influence us our **reference groups**. Each of us has our own set of these groups, and we tend to stick with our reference groups in part because, once we are in, we spend our time doing things that people like us do alongside other people who do them. We model our behavior on such individuals, and sometimes there are particular individuals in the group who may function as **role models**. They have disproportionate influence as we imitate how they move, dress, and carry out life.

We are each associated with a number of reference groups, even at the same time. For many of us this is made vivid through online social networking sites: We are located in webs of groups that are themselves clustered around commonalities of age, taste, or status. Others we know share some of the same linkages; our list of groups and their list have high overlap. Those we friend, they friend. Clubs we join, they join. Their influence on us is likely to be particularly strong compared to, say, an acquaintance who hardly knows anyone else we know or does any of the things we do. While we may of course develop bonds to such outsiders, sociologists who study social networks found that these relationships tend to be few in number and dissolve more quickly than with those in groups having multiple links into our own social circles and interests (McPherson, Smith-Lovin, and Cook 2001). Birds of a feather do stick together and keep at it; if they go off, it is an unstable departure.

Some of our ties are far more general than our immediate social networks, whether face to face or electronic. Grounded in the larger cultures in which each of us participates, people have a sense of what everyone knows to be appropriate as proper behavior. For example, in the United States no one goes about her or his business in public while naked. Wearing clothes is so commonly understood that there generally does not need to be a rule about it; it's just taken for granted. Also, Americans do not eat dogs or insects (although people in other societies do). We all know these things and risk making a severely bad impression if we betray them. Sociologists call this social control

The generalized other is social control exercised by commonsense understandings of what is appropriate in a specific time and place.

Buccina Studios/Getty Images

exercised by commonsense understandings of what is appropriate in a specific time and place the **generalized other**. We walk around with all kinds of unspoken knowledge of do's and don'ts without much understanding or need to consult where we got them. We just do it. Virtually all the significant others do it, all the role models do it, and the reference groups do, too.

Life's a Stage

4.1.3 Discuss how we differ in the ways we present ourselves to others.

We are always, in a sense, on stage—performing the self in the spotlight of others. We need approval not just as some kind of bonus for a nicer life. We need it to *be*. The show must go on, and the show is our life.

Evidence of how carefully we consider which parts of ourselves to share can be found by examining the stuff we carry around each day. Ethnographer Christena Nippert-Eng (2010) likened our wallets and purses to toolkits for managing the multiple faces we show to others. Business cards, if we have them, are meant for just about anyone we might meet. They are props on our most public stage. But more personal things in the same wallet, such as a drug prescription, may be kept secret from our closest friends yet shared with any random employee of a pharmacy. While we all conduct life through these multiple faces, Nippert-Eng found different people think differently about what they are willing to share. Some would be horrified

to let others see the receipts in their wallets, but others do not worry about what these slips of paper might reveal. We think differently from one another about what aspects of our identities we are willing to show, and exactly how.

While we all share the fact that we live as if on stage, we are not all the same. A geneticist might think we are each unique because of our biological codes, but a sociologist views each of us as different because no one has had the same set of social interactions. Each of us bounces, searches, lurches, and passes through particular settings, interacting with a different array of individuals and expectations throughout the day. There are overlaps for sure, especially among those with common origins and similarities of gender, class, or ethnicity, but never in a way that creates identical individuals.

It also follows that we are always changing. Because the process never stops and our circumstances keep shifting, we constantly alter our identity over time, even if only in tiny ways, even from minute to minute or hour to hour. Sometimes we are simply American; sometimes we are Irish American or Korean American. Sometimes we identify ourselves by our occupation ("I am a lawyer"), other times by hobbies or passions ("I am an activist" or "I am a Giants fan"). As we act in the world and the world responds to us, we become different selves—including how "good" or "bad" we take ourselves to be and in just what ways. Note that we may also think of our identity in terms of personality traits (such as "I am shy," "I am smart," "I am generous," and so forth), but for sociology it is always our social identities that are the key to understanding the importance of identity.

Mark Bussell

BIG QUESTION 4.2   How Do We Make Sense of Our Worlds?

THE PEOPLE'S METHODOLOGY

We know that social interaction forms the individual. But then what? What underlies the capacity to make this happen? At the most basic level: How do individuals demonstrate competence as interacting members of society? How do we show that we are safe to be around and capable of sharing in social life? Some sociologists, influenced by interactionism but branching out in some new directions from it, study this problem with precise observations and experiments. It turns out that human beings have specific methods for interacting with others, and people all over the world, regardless of culture or historical moment, use these same methods. That at least is the perspective of the influential sociologist Harold Garfinkel, the inventor of a sociological subfield he called **ethnomethodology**—the study of people's methods.

Context, Context, Context

4.2.1 Explain how context gives meaning to words and situations.

What do those methods look like? One of them—a kind of master method—is that people persistently and intensively take context into account. So even a word that may seem straightforward, such as *kill*, gets its meaning from context. When we hear a phrase like "I'll kill you," it matters whether it is a child tickling her brother, a teenager whose sister ruined her new sweater, or an interrogator in a secret prison. The participants in "I'll kill you" draw on context to figure out what it really means at the particular moment. The setting doesn't just adjust the meaning of the word *kill*; it can radically alter it—teasing a laughing child

versus threatening an arch nemesis, for example. There is no freestanding meaning; people always construct meaning by drawing on social context.

There are other methods that follow from taking context into account, like not demanding that people provide complete responses to the questions we ask them. Instead, drawing on context, we have a sense of how much there should be and let it go at that. Otherwise, those answers could go on infinitely. So when we ask people "How are you?" we ordinarily don't want to know their body temperature (unless, of course, they have a fever, or as in the COVID-19 pandemic when body temperature became a screen for possible infection). We often just want a simple "fine" or "okay." Of course, what is or is not the appropriate answer varies by who is asking and under what circumstances: Our grandmother or a close friend we haven't talked to in a while might really want to know how we're getting along. It all depends, and in pretty exact ways, on who is doing the asking, who is doing the answering, their relationship, and the specific occasion. And we generally understand this and act accordingly; it is our method.

Conversational Precision

4.2.2 Explain how conversation patterns can demonstrate social competence.

We can see people's methods in action in a conversation—any conversation. Without being fully aware that they do so, people fit each utterance in a precise way to the ongoing flow of what the other is saying. Sociologists who study such ordinary talk learn exactly how turn taking, the fundamental basis of conversation, can occur, and how people use careful tactics to allow it to happen.

We notice the slightest forward nod of the head as signaling that somebody wants a turn—and we often defer to it by becoming silent ourselves. We pick up on silence. It only takes three-tenths of a second before a conversationalist notices that nothing is happening and thus there is an opportunity to come in, like the way a jazz performer can "feel" a signal to come in on a beat—or take that three-tenths of a second of silence to notice that something *is* happening. UCLA sociologist Emanuel Schegloff learned that even very brief silences are in fact information (Schegloff 1996). So if you ask somebody on a date, if the answer is going to be "yes," the yes happens immediately—within a split second of the request or even overlapping the end of it. But if the answer is going to be "no," the answer comes with a delay, indeed *through* the delay. A tiny silence serves notice of the bad news that's coming. Or the "no" can be detected in little words and utterances that sort of waste time, like "uh" or "well" or "gee" or even a string of all of them—a turn-down in process.

Here is an actual example to get the full effect (it might be helpful to read it aloud with someone else) (from Davidson 1984):

EDNA: Wanna come down and have a bite of lunch with me? I got some beer and stuff.

NANCY: Well, you're real sweet, hon. Uhm. Let—I have—

EDNA (coming in on Nancy's "Let"): Or do you have something else t—

NANCY (coming in at the middle of Edna's "else"): No, I have … to, uh, call … Bob's mother.

One of the nice things about saying "no" in convoluted ways is that the questioner can reframe the request, maybe adding something like "or do you have something else to…" (as Edna does). Often, saying no in a roundabout way takes some of the sting out of rejection. We do this for each other all the time. This method, and many others like it, helps us build a sense of safety and solidarity even when we can't agree to one another's requests. We help each other "save face," as we sometimes say, and retain a more positive sense of self. And it can only happen because of the remarkable capacity we have for sensing the very small moves we all make. Even when we argue with others, we tend to maintain these types of "practical ethics." It builds a sense of safety and solidarity with other human beings even when we can't agree on the substance.

People take turns because simultaneous talk is almost impossible to maintain (try it with a friend and you'll see). Somebody has to bow out, and they almost always do so within seconds of the start of an overlap. Sociologists refer to this kind of response to conversation disruption as a *repair*, a way one of the speakers helpfully acts to safeguard

the interaction (Schegloff 2000). It turns out we are all active in doing such repairs, but some of us are more ready to do it than others.

Sociologists have discovered some patterns to who gives in. Allowing of course for some frequent exceptions, men, quite counter to the stereotype of being "strong and silent," interrupt women more than the reverse. Should both be speaking simultaneously, it is the women who most often relent. Doctors interrupt patients more than patients interrupt doctors—except when the doctor is a woman; then the pattern becomes more equal (West 1984). Adults interrupt children more than children interrupt adults, something that goes against the common assumptions (certainly that of parents) (West and Zimmerman 1977).

So the process is not necessarily democratic. Besides the gender and age difference, bosses—it will not be surprising to learn—show their power in talk, something employees may pick up on in sensing their employer has "talked down" to them. Conversational inequalities, precisely because of the subtleties involved, are sometimes hard to notice or at least describe by those taking part. But they are important not just because being interrupted, for example, is insulting. When someone lacks access to a conversational turn, they miss the opportunity for their opinions to count. They have less capacity to help create the reality that they and others live by.

Consider the following conversation between the journalist George Stephanopoulos and then-presidential candidate Donald Trump. Their exchange is not simply a conversation about whether thousands of Muslims were cheering in New Jersey after the terrorist attacks on September 11, 2001; by interrupting each other, each participant in the conversation is jockeying for the power to control the direction and content of the conversation.

GEORGE: You've never come up with a video of those thousands of people cheering in New Jersey on 9/11.

DONALD: Oh, there were plenty of people cheering, believe me. And I've come up with plenty … People were celebrating all over the world, and I think it's disgusting.

GEORGE: There were people celebrating in the West Bank. There were not people celebrating in Jersey as far as any evidence we have seen, but I do want to move on—Those comments—

DONALD: (coming in on George's "on") Of course there were, George. There were articles written about it.… Don't tell me that. There were people celebrating. When the World Trade Center was coming down there were people celebrating, George.

GEORGE: (coming in on Donald's "When the") Well, there was nothing—Let's, let's, let's—Let's move on.

Emotion

4.2.3 Discuss how individuals manipulate emotion in social interaction.

Another method people use in social interaction is emotion. Emotions are not, as the stereotype might imply, utterly beyond our control. Sometimes we speak of emotions as "outbursts"—laughs and cries that break out contrary to anyone's intentions. But for sociologists, emotions are also performances we arrange for specific purposes, although the specific content of the display varies by context.

Who should cry differs from society to society. In some cultures and some situations, people who fail to cry are thought to be inappropriate; they "should" do so at the death of a loved one. Certainly, they should not laugh on such an occasion, although in some settings of the world (New Orleans or Bali), it can be appropriate to *dance* at funerals. At football (what Americans call soccer) matches in Europe and South America, disorderly mayhem and interpersonal belligerence occur with some frequency; in the United States such behavior is much less frequent. Yet rates of some violent crimes in the United States, including "crimes of passion," are higher than in most parts of the world. Somehow there are conventions of time and place for exhibiting aggression and emotional breakdown toward others.

At a more micro level, sociologists studying fights and conflict notice how contestants carefully fit their threats and gestures into a script of calls and countercalls that all parties understand ("oh yeah," "says who?"). The sociologist Randall Collins calls such strings of events "interaction ritual chains." By looking systematically at confrontations among people on the street or in other settings, Collins saw how seldom individuals come to blows. This is because, in the great majority of instances, the participants know their own bluster and rant, as well as that of their opponent, is theatrical. And besides, most people have no idea how to fight physically; we are afraid of one another. So we look for ways to end the argument without resorting to violence—and socially talented as we all are, we find them. People only *appear* to be out of control (Collins 2008).

Bursts of laughter alongside others are, as UCLA ethnographer Jack Katz argues, also displays of how context affects emotion and its display. By studying families looking at each other in funhouse mirrors, Katz discovered that unlike conversation, where turn taking is the rule, in laughter everyone can get in on the action all at once. Others may invite us into laughter with a chuckle, but when we all laugh together, we laugh also in collective agreement that something warrants abandoning our façades of emotional reserve. Together, our laughter affirms one another's emotion, our togetherness in feeling that emotion, and that it is safe to express that emotion with loud yelps and unconventional bodily movement (Katz 1999). In contrast to conversation turn taking, it would be considered odd, even disruptive, to hold off one's laugh until the prior laugher was finished.

One way to understand the social nature of emotion is to study how audiences interact with those who perform on stage. We excite each other. Appreciating a performance with others of like mind and spirit is *rousing*. After going to a concert, we sometimes remark not just about the performer but also about the audience. And indeed performers acknowledge that they feed off the audience in front of them just as the audience feeds off the performer. It becomes a cycle of mutual reinforcement.

Again, people fit their response to the conditions at hand. One does not hoot and holler at a Catholic Mass, and one does not remain somber and still at a rock concert. To do either would be an offense not just to those on the stage but also to one's compatriots in the audience. We need each other to build a common experience, and the greater the mutual appreciation, the greater the show. We like it when someone knows how to rouse us in the crowd. There is a "collective effervescence," as Emile Durkheim ([1912] 2001) famously called it in 1912, when audience members egg each other on. If nothing like this happens, it is

Hiroko Tanaka/Alamy Stock Photo

Societies differ in the way individuals express emotion, and the role of emotion in different settings will also vary. An interesting sociological question regarding emotions is, "What specific occasions call out particular ways of expressing emotion, and why?"

disappointing. The crowd, it will be said, was "dead." As in a frequent sociological dynamic, people change the situation that changes them.

The British sociologist Max Atkinson (1984) studied a version of all of this in a very precise way. Atkinson recorded speeches being made by British politicians at party rallies, paying close attention, split second by split second, to what the speakers were doing and how their audiences responded. Using a decibel meter, he measured the volume of audience applause and how long each round of applause lasted, including the clapping interruptions during the speech itself. Atkinson learned that applause happens in bursts, quickly rising to a crescendo in about one second before gently leveling off (see Figure 4.1).

We all know the embarrassment of applauding alone—of not knowing, for example, that a symphony has a series of movements and that one should wait until the end of the last one before clapping. Regular symphony goers learn the ropes and avoid the stigma. But in other situations, such as being at a political speech, knowing when to let loose can be more ambiguous.

So Atkinson learned that the talented speechmaker provides audience members with cues that tell when to applaud—moments when they can presume others will be applauding with them. As one example, Atkinson learned that effective orators speak in threes—"of the people, by the people, for the people." When these are aligned with the right kind of intonations, audience members will respond appropriately and clap at just the right moment and together. Sometimes we say people who can generate such a response are charismatic. We think that there is some trait deep within them that causes others to respond with obedience or enthusiasm—as if they have magic or some kind of spiritual gift not found in ordinary human beings. In reality, Atkinson argues, good orators have simply mastered the art of knowing what people need to act together. The art of

working a crowd is a social skill that can be very effective at parties, at meetings, or anywhere interaction occurs. We all, with one degree of success or another, "work the crowd," and the crowd indeed wants to be worked.

Another way that performers try to connect to their audience is by selecting the appropriate type of speech, or speech code, for a particular audience. Some audiences prefer a fancy or intellectual speech, other audiences may appreciate a more casual and down-to-earth speech. Many audiences enjoy moments when the speaker identifies in some way with them, for example, by speaking their language. Former President Bill Clinton, who was born and raised in Arkansas, would use a Southern accent when speaking to audiences in the South. Having developed that accent growing up, Clinton could pull it off effortlessly. But when Hillary Clinton, who was raised in Illinois, attempted the same trick, it backfired (Dowling 2007). Audiences could tell she wasn't really one of them, even though she had lived in Arkansas for many years when her husband was governor of that state. America's two most recent former presidents, Barack Obama and Donald Trump, were both masters at using codes to connect with their audiences.

Self-Presentation in a Digital Age

4.2.4 Analyze the impact of digital communication technologies and social media on our methods of self-presentation.

We strive to use the same techniques as communication moves to other media. Social media of course change some of the details of the patterns of interaction, but these patterns have many of the same features. When we fret over our social media profiles or about the information that comes up when people search our names, or when we arrange and rearrange the details of our online identities, we are manipulating our presentation of self in ways that Goffman would immediately recognize. Based on others' responses (or lack thereof) we alter our presentation accordingly. How many people "like" us (or our postings) provides immediate feedback in the social media environment. We can see, in this e-version, once again how much people yearn for the approval of others and work social media to bring it about.

This goes on even as we figure out some rudimentary ways of compensating for a lack of face-to-face interaction. Sociologists studying a group of other researchers communicating mostly by e-mail found, indeed, the participants often got confused about one another's meanings (Menchik and Tian 2008). They didn't catch each other's tone and spent a great deal of time clarifying how

---

Figure 4.1 Applauding Together

Using a decibel meter and sound recordings, sociologist Max Atkinson found that applause for a speech by a skilled politician started very fast (reaching its full crescendo in about a second) and remained level for about 5.5 seconds before trailing off fairly fast. This suggests how strongly people work to coordinate their applause with one another, careful to start clapping at the "right" time and careful to stop when it seems others are stopping.

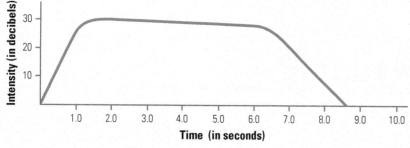

Time (in seconds)

SOURCE: Atkinson 1984.

they intended their words to be heard. One round of e-mails got particularly heated when one of the participants seemed to imply another had engaged in plagiaristic behavior (a very critical allegation for these academics), giving rise to offense. The person who sent that e-mail then wrote to all:

> I wrote "I think it would appear plagiaristic" (though I failed to put the word 'plagiaristic' in quotes as I had intended). A careful reading of this, I believe, is that I am not absolutely certain and I am not calling Victor a plagiarist as he seems to imply . . . .

Other kinds of communication via social media can have similar issues. For example, if you don't carefully spell out your disapproval of a controversial video you've shared, your followers might get the impression that you actually approve of it. Similarly, text messages and the 280-character limit on Twitter encourage short but sometimes misleading forms of communication.

To combat this possible miscommunication, people often incorporate little signs to clarify how they want their words to be understood. Sometimes, this means words in all capital letters to show emphasis or quotation marks to show some qualification; other times it means adding one of a countless number of emojis, or perhaps just a smiley face. People might sign off by saying what city they are in as a signal that they are traveling (so maybe were less available), in a different time zone, busy with something unusual, or about to get on a plane. Social media users are creative in figuring out ways to adjust to the technology, increasing their clarity and lessening the likelihood of being misunderstood (Menchik and Tian 2008). As we see, changes in how we communicate stimulate new ways to send social signals. But they are not a complete substitute for the real person-to-person thing and indeed show us what we are missing when we make the switch from being there to relying on media technology. Indeed, much e-mail involves making arrangements for face-to-face interaction, especially when matters become emotionally or logistically complex.

Interaction in Public

4.2.5 Identify some of the methods we use when interacting in public.

Another set of special conditions comes about when people are interacting not with people they know but in public spaces among strangers. This alters our interaction strategies

somewhat: We become wary about dealing with those with whom we may lack prior experience and whose intentions are less routinely known to us. The public restroom is extreme in the careful monitoring that goes on, but we use the same basic techniques most everywhere in public places. For example, in dealing with strangers pretty much anywhere, we glance at faces, but only for a fleeting moment. To do otherwise implies we have some special business with them or may even be attracted to them. If that is not plausible, we may be perceived as a threat or as weird or mentally-ill. So in Goffman's terms, the parties solve the problem by mutually "dimming the lights" as their paths cross. They engage in **civil inattention**— ignoring each other to an appropriate degree although noticing that the other is present. In this way, dozens and dozens, maybe even hundreds and hundreds on city streets and crowded campus walks, see and hear each other without being a needless bother or stirring up anxiety. According to one of the great social theorists, the German sociologist Georg Simmel, *inattention*, especially in dense places, is precisely what makes social life in large cities possible (Simmel 1950).

The next time you enter an empty bus or movie theater, or another place where strangers sit together, you are likely to see civil inattention in action. As people search for a seat, they look at the empty chairs, not the faces of others already sitting. Everyone may be drawn toward a particular region of the space, like the middle rows of the theater, but as more people file in one at a time or in groups, they are likely to take seats that are not directly next to strangers. If they did, it would be considered odd—almost as bad as a

It is not always rude to ignore someone. If you see a friend, it might be rude to not say hello. But it might also be rude to start talking to random strangers. Civil inattention in a public setting like public transportation where we may be surrounded by strangers is common and appropriate.

Randy Duchaine/Alamy Stock Photo

man choosing the adjacent urinal when others are available. The person the newcomer sat next to might be alarmed. So without any sign we are paying any attention to those around us, we navigate to a place where others have a bit of space from us, and we from them. But when there are not so many open spaces, the seats next to strangers become fair game. Even then, however, we usually do not pay obvious attention to those strangers right next to us.

Sometimes our public performances are imperfect—but we have remedies. One famous and simple method is to just say, "oops." Goffman made a big deal out of *oops*. By blurting out this one syllable, not even really a word at all, one can signal that all is okay, the world is functioning in a more or less reasonable way, and that you have not gone out of role or out of your mind (Goffman 1978).

But just as there are rude interrupters, sometimes people are not very nice in how they deploy their demeanor, and it is not due to being clumsy or socially unskilled. Individuals may deliberately not avert their glance. Schoolyard bullies may stare down their victims as a form of intimidation. If a stranger sits next to you on an empty bus and proceeds to stare at your face, all the right alarms go off because something is going very wrong. Ethnographer Mitchell Duneier and I analyzed troubles that happen between street people and those they bother with requests for small change or call out to for other reasons. Most of us know the experience of being asked for money by strangers or being approached by someone promoting some political cause looking for a signature and perhaps a donation. Often those who ask do not observe the fine points of conversation. They approach us even when we do not signal we want to talk. In that regard, they pay us no mind. They may blurt out their request and do not seem to register the fact we are not showing any interest. They do not modify their question to avoid us having to give a flat-out "no." They may force the issue and require us to be rude. And that is something people do not like to do to one another. We are upset precisely because we are forced to behave in an uncivil way.

These issues are especially acute for women in public spaces (Nielsen 2004). Duneier and I noticed these problems in particular with women passersbys, who faced frequent catcalls as men on the street routinely remarked on their bodies and how they looked, and tried to entangle them with questions. Duneier recorded one such set of interactions in New York in the year 1999, between a man named Mudrick and a woman passerby:

MUDRICK: Hey pretty. (8/10ths of a second go by)

WOMAN (flatly): Hi, how you doin.

MUDRICK (coming in on "doin"): You alright? (2.2 seconds go by)

MUDRICK: You look very nice, you know. I like how you have your hair pinned. (8/10ths of a second go by)

MUDRICK: You married?

WOMAN: Yeah.

MUDRICK: Huh?

WOMAN: Yeah.

MUDRICK (interrupting): Where the rings at?

WOMAN: I have it home.

MUDRICK: Y' have it home?

WOMAN: Yeah.

MUDRICK: Can I get your name?

MUDRICK: My name is Mudrick, what's yours?

We see here the tactics at work that many of us find so difficult. Timing is everything. The woman responds to Mudrick's initial greeting, but only after what is, in conversational terms, a lengthy silence of nearly a second. And her "how you doin" is said as a statement, not a question. Both are signs that she wants the conversation to stop there. Mudrick ignores the signals as he delivers a follow-up attempt at further conversation (line 3) before she even finishes her response. The woman does not respond as more than two seconds pass—an eternity. Mudrick tries again with another compliment, followed by yet another barrage of questions. The woman gives some responses, but each of her responses signals a desire to end the conversation. Mudrick is still asking questions as the woman walks away.

When people pay a compliment or ask a question, they almost always get a response, and get one pretty quickly if they have a willing conversation partner. But people may signal they don't want to talk through pauses and nonresponses, what conversation analysts call *disaffiliative gestures*. Mudrick not only ignores those signals the woman gives, he ups the ante with even more intrusive questions. The woman's disaffiliative gestures escalate until she does something rude by not responding at all to repeated questions—just as she was a bit rude in the first place by not really taking up Mudrick's efforts to converse.

The way Mudrick forces the woman to be really rude by ignoring her signals to end the conversation is what Duneier and I called *interactional vandalism* (Duneier and Molotch 1999). An offense takes place, but one that is very subtle. When it happens to us we are aware of a problem, but without the kind of painstaking sociological observations carried out by Duneier, it is hard to pin down. We see from the start that Mudrick does not count for much to the woman, and this had something to do with the bad footing on which the whole thing began. If it had been the mayor of New York or a movie star being abrupt, she might have gone along even if she was spoken to in the same way. This tells us that besides the intricacies of conversational technique, people put up with more from others depending on the kinds of statuses in play and how individual identities are socially categorized, with unhoused people way down on the totem pole.

Mark Bussell

SHIFTS AND DILEMMAS

Our social selves are always set up for potential change as we move from one social location to another. And as we move between these social contexts, we sometimes encounter difficulties in deciding how to act.

Status and Role Change

4.3.1 Identify the causes of role conflict.

One type of challenge comes from the fact that we enter into different life statuses as we age or just change our life situation. A **status** is a distinct social category that is set off from others and has associated with it a set of expected behaviors and roles for individuals to assume. Each of the status changes brings different types of groups, and the expectations they have for us, into play. So in terms of educational status, we move from elementary school to being high school and then college students; on the personal front, we become girlfriends or boyfriends, husbands or wives, parents, business managers, professionals, or employees (of course, many of these statuses overlap). Of interest to sociologists is that these different statuses each come with a set of roles *others* expect us to perform. Think of a menu of statuses, each with text accompanying societal expectations.

So the readers of this book are mostly students, and students are supposed to fulfill certain expectations, or **roles**, as students: respect the teacher, show up for class, keep hands to one's self while sitting in the classroom, complete assigned papers, and take exams. Because students do generally conform, life in the college classroom is pretty stable and looks a lot different from a mosh pit. And so it goes: What is appropriate for a funeral director differs from that for a lawyer, for a teenager from that for

a husband, for a restaurant chef compared to a physician. If the doctor really made us the chicken soup she suggests we drink, we would find it to be creepy.

Sometimes we will experience **role conflict**—fulfilling the expectations of one of our roles conflicts with meeting the expectations of another. Most of us have experienced this

ESB Basic/Shutterstock

The student role may come into conflict with other roles, such as fulfilling the expectations of a friend or romantic partner. As a student, we want to fulfill our teachers' expectation that we keep up with assignments and prepare for tests and get good grades. But if our best friend is having a crisis and needs our help, or if a romantic partner wants to blow off homework and chill for the evening, which role are we supposed to fulfill?

uncomfortable situation when our role as son or daughter conflicts with fulfilling the expectations of a friend. As a son or daughter, we want to fulfill our parents' expectation that we come home for a grandmother's birthday, but our best friend needs our help during a move to a new apartment. We are damned if we do and damned if we don't.

Inconsistent demands arise in many different situations because of the variety of reference groups exerting influence on us. For example, it may be important for certain types of working-class youths to satisfy peer-group expectations that are not consistent with those of school authorities. Sociologists who study delinquency, for example, have found exactly this kind of conformity dilemma. A teenager's peers may encourage kinds of behavior frowned upon by the adults, leaving the teen in a complicated situation of trying to fulfill two different roles. If the teen chooses to engage in delinquent behavior, it is not that she or he is a nonconformist; rather, they are conforming to the norms of one group that is devalued by another (those with authority).

Labeling

4.3.2 Explain how a self-fulfilling prophecy can influence label formation.

However similar people are in the fact that they conform, they are made different depending on others' opinions of the groups with which they identify. Sociologists have long been concerned with people regarded as a problem by dominant members of society, often referred to as **deviants** by those who make the rules and express opinions about behaviors they find troubling. According to the sociological school of thought called labeling theory, so-called deviants come about because there is a person or group that can serve as the object of the label "deviant" and an individual or institution that can apply the label and make it stick. Sociologists long ago stopped believing it was useful to think of people like criminals or most of the mentally-ill as essentially different from others. Indeed, it was once common to regard people like divorced women and gay and lesbian individuals as deviant, even criminal or diseased in the case of gays and lesbians. We no longer think this way, at least in the United States, and we understand these labels to have been conventions of their time and place but not as corresponding to the nature of the individuals involved.

One consequence of being labeled (no matter whether it makes sense or doesn't), some versions of the theory say, is that the individuals so identified in fact change their conduct and embrace the very behavior that led them into the deviant category in the first place. So the kid who is told he is no good links up with others told the same thing.

Whatever their common bonds before, they now at least share a label—presto, a gang. Their networks may start to overlap, especially if they are put in the same detention centers or programs. The boys provide mutual social support and clear the way for, even value, the disapproved behavior. Just as the nice kids evolve into virtual saints, so it is that others fulfill the expectations of delinquents, rebels, or bad girls (Chambliss 1973). This is an example of what the sociologist Robert Merton identified as a **self-fulfilling prophecy** (Merton 1948). Something becomes true because people say it is true.

Sociologist Thomas Scheff studied how this works in a psychiatric facility. Some people fight against the label of "crazy" but may face an uphill battle as everyone around them pressures them to accept it (Scheff 1999). Their diagnosis, after all, rests on a whole set of labeling institutions, largely held to be legitimate, of doctors, nurses, and the institution. The patients often learn, according to Scheff, that the best route to being released from treatment is to acknowledge the judgments of others that they are mentally-ill. People in prison due to a sex crime conviction may face the same pressure to conform in order to complete the therapy programs that are often a condition of release. Insisting on one's innocence, even if true, will simply prolong the period of incarceration (Kaden 1998).

But quite apart from the labeling process, people inside a mental institution may indeed be about as normal as anyone else. To test this idea, psychologist David Rosenhan sent his research assistants, all with no history of mental health issues, to present themselves to different psychiatric hospitals and tell a single lie: that they were hearing voices in their heads. The people on duty diagnosed all of them as having psychiatric disorders and admitted them to the hospital. Once in the hospital, the undercover assistants told everyone, doctors and nurses included, that they had no more symptoms and continued acting normally. Some of the researchers were held for months (this was true research commitment!), and none were released by the hospital until they agreed that they, indeed, had a mental illness (Rosenhan 1973). Sometimes even our freedom depends on agreeing to the labels placed on us.

The Rosenhan study—published under the title "Being Sane in Insane Places"—did lead to some reform, and many took to heart the dangerous power of labeling in psychiatric (and other) institutions. In an example of how social research can lead to policy change, it (along with the writings of Scheff and some by Goffman) became part of the deinstitutionalization movement that led to the closing of many psychiatric hospitals and their replacement (alas, often not fulfilled) by community-based treatment facilities.

Rule Use

4.3.3 Identify the role of informal rules in social interaction.

Even for those of us not in mental institutions, we are surrounded by organizations we have to answer to, and they all have their rules. These rules often are explicit (such as laws or institutional regulations), but they can also be informal and include norms and expectations for individual behaviors. We must enact our various statuses and roles within the businesses, government agencies, and schools where we make our living, buy our stuff, and get our housing. In doing so, we also have some tricky maneuvering to do.

Consider, for example, the way we understand and deal with rules that are supposed to determine how we relate to each other. Let's get back to *kill*. The Bible is explicit: Don't do it. The law says the same. But only a jerk would reprimand somebody who swats a mosquito or shoots a rattlesnake about to bite a baby. We might have to kill the person getting ready to throw a bomb in a theater. If we are on active duty in the military, it is not acceptable to denounce someone (at least someone on your side) who is prepared to kill others. Most people believe that killing Adolf Hitler to halt the Holocaust and end World War II would have been justified. So even this most important of rules requires human interpretation. And that is just what happens, whether in everyday life or in a large-scale organization: interpretation, interpretation, interpretation.

Here's an example quite common to ordinary life, one that we witness all the time in places like restaurants or the Department of Motor Vehicles: "first come, first served." But if a huge celebrity like Taylor Swift or LeBron James wants some service, any competent receptionist would not make them wait in line before being served. And this revision is not limited to celebrities. Sociologist Don Zimmerman studied how receptionists handled clients in a welfare agency, finding that they continuously modified the "first come, first served" rule in order to keep the overall operation running smoothly (Zimmerman 1970). If there were screaming children, they and their parents were taken ahead of others to curtail the deafening noise that would inhibit anyone from getting work done. If somebody came in who was visibly ill, disorderly, or injured, they got early attention, even if it was to call in help from the outside, like police or an ambulance.

Similarly, although there may be no official rule that instructs the doctors in busy emergency rooms to make intoxicated patients wait longer for care (even risking their lives), they will likely give preference to a more innocent individual, for example, an older person hit by a car or a suffering child (Sudnow 1967). Each of us judges the context and uses the amazing human capacity to scan organizational and individual needs to come up with the appropriate behavior by bending the rules. Sometimes we invoke what sociologists have called informal rules that exist alongside the official ones, notions like "respect the needs of children," perhaps. We may use some informal rules to explain to others (or even to ourselves) after the fact that we "really" were not breaking a rule, just following a different one. For example, as I learned in researching the New York subways, the train conductors and other workers explain they rarely report suspicious packages to their supervisors, as they are supposed to do, because that would slow down the system, and that, in turn, would defeat the more informal rule that it is their job to keep the trains running on time.

What really makes us competent members of society is not so much knowing all the rules (formal or informal) but rather knowing what to do on particular occasions given what is expected of us. We don't so much follow rules as use them to make what we did appear both to ourselves and to others as a rational and appropriate action. We act to maintain the normalness of the world so we can all move forward. It's kind of like saying "oops" so people will know things are pretty much OK.

There are people who seem unable to function in this way; they have trouble taking context into account. They insist on "going by the book." When we meet them in real life, they strike us as silly or severely incompetent. We have all come across such extremely annoying people. They seem to lack proper discretion. Garfinkel referred to such individuals as "judgmental dopes" (Bernie Weiner's attribution work). This makes them difficult as coworkers, as neighbors, or even as friends. They may literally live in communities, but they are more like ants in the anthill than humans who interpret and know, as we often say, "it all depends."

On occasions when people do follow the rules in literal ways, everything can easily get screwed up. For example, to cause disruptions, labor unions sometimes call on the rank and file to "work to rule." It is a call to go by the book—exactly. This means not taking the kind of shortcuts that allow the work to actually get done. It is a good union tactic because the only response for employers is to insist workers go back to their old ways of *not* strictly following procedures, an awkward stance for management to take. In one study of an Idaho sawmill, an employee in a work-to-rule action left a fire burning in an expensive piece of machinery and walked away to make it to a "mandatory" safety meeting on time (Richardson 2009). After the protest period, workers returned to the ordinary ways of working, acknowledging that a fire was a good exception to the "mandatory" requirement, to get it all done.

Conformity Experiments

4.3.4 Explain what makes people conform and how conformity impacts how we live together.

Just how people conform to their social circumstance has fundamental consequences for how people live together. Social scientists sometimes set up laboratory experiments to see how people interact under one condition or another, in particular the way they do or do not go along with social pressure. It is almost like a laboratory for rats, except that the experimenter watches people instead of some other kind of animal. Unlike with watching other animals, we get to see how the special human capacities for social awareness enable manipulation, conformity, and sometimes also resistance. The stakes can be high.

What does it take, an experimenter asks, to get people to give an obviously wrong answer to an easy and factual question? Not much, as it turns out. A social psychologist named Solomon Asch, in a classic midcentury study, presented individuals with a line drawn on a card and asked them to choose among three lines drawn on another card the one that matched it most closely in length (see Figure 4.2). It was pretty simple to do because one of the lines indeed matched perfectly. Asch staged groups of five to seven people to make the call. But except for one person in each group, the participants were, in fact working with the experimenter. Only one individual in each group was naïve. After a few warm-up runs, where everyone provided the same correct response, the clued-in participants gave consistently wrong answers. Conformity started happening, with naïve subjects (127 males participated) agreeing

to a wrong answer *37 percent of the time.* Three-quarters of them conformed at least once, 5 percent conformed every time, but about 25 percent never did (Asch 1955). So there we have it: Group pressures can change people's behaviors or thoughts in many—but not all—instances.

In various versions of this experiment, some conducted by other researchers following in Asch's footsteps, it was possible to change the specific conditions to see what causes conformity to rise or fall. One striking finding is that a single ally strongly influences results. If the experiment permitted one person to join the naïve subject in reporting an accurate result, the impact of a majority opinion to the contrary lost much of its power. This implies the importance of people having even just one other person in support. It is much easier to "go against the world" if you have a companion, whether it is a companion in love, or crime, or truth.

These kinds of experiments have their critics. Real life might be different, say the skeptics. And we do not know if those taking part in the experiment really believed that the group was right, only that they *reported* wrong answers to the experimenter. Even so, saying things you don't believe is also conforming and has effects: If nobody says the emperor has no clothes, it makes it easier for the emperor to continue to rule even though he is naked—or to use a more dramatic example, if no one says anything when a dictator decides to use police and military power to kill large numbers of citizens, the killing will go on and on. And the experimental results, it could be argued, are especially impressive given that the research subjects had no good reason to lie other than the pressure to conform. In real life, we really are trying to gain other people's favor.

We may not want to go against significant others and reference group members who could fire us from our jobs, flunk us in our courses, or put us in prison. Generally speaking, people will go along to get along when nothing is at stake. This also helps to explain why they do so even when there are strong reasons for compromising the truth.

An even more severe lesson from the social science laboratory is that when conditions are right, people—ordinary people—will harm other ordinary people, perhaps even kill them. Inspired by concerns about major real-life situations, the Yale social psychologist Stanley Milgram (1963) wanted to learn the conditions that might cause otherwise respectable individuals to harm one another, merely because they were asked to do so. Milgram conducted his experiments in the post–World War II period when the Holocaust was fresh in people's minds. Some were speculating that the Germans blindly followed Hitler because of some

Figure 4.2 The Asch Conformity Experiment

Solomon Asch showed groups of research subjects two cards like these. He asked them to match the line on card 1 with one of the same size on card 2. Asch's research collaborators were secretly mixed in with the research subjects and sometimes agreed that the wrong lines matched. Asch found that the naïve subjects went along with the research collaborators and sometimes agreed that the wrong lines matched. Asch found that the naïve subjects went along with the research collaborators about one-third of the time, and approximately 75 percent conformed to the research collaborators' wrong answer at least once.

 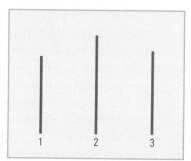

SOURCE: Asch (1955).

peculiar attribute of the German personality, or at least particular patterns distinct to German culture. Repeated in various settings besides the original version at Yale University, Milgram's so-called obedience studies revealed the Germans who followed orders in World War II to be not so special in these regards.

In his experiments, Milgram (1963) induced his subjects (sometimes college undergraduates) to deliver what they thought were painful, even fatal, electrical shocks to a stranger who had given a wrong answer in what they were told was some kind of learning training. In fact no such learning training was taking place; the whole thing was just a ruse to see how much harm subjects would deliver when instructed to do so. Even with the "learner" (who actually was an employee of the professor) letting out painful screams and the experimenter indicating the learner had a heart condition, over 60 percent of subjects eventually delivered, three times in a row, the last-stage shock of 450 volts. The learner went silent to imply there was in fact a fatal dose, but the shocking continued after that point in all these cases (Blass 1999).

In real life, of course, much violence occurs only in indirect ways. Legislators say it's okay to bomb another country, assassinate another person, or close a health clinic down—without ever getting close to the bodies or being on the scene. Those situations, like the extreme case of the Nazis, do not involve direct aggression but only indirect bureaucratic action. Many conclude from the Milgram results that it could happen here and in our own time.

Another famous study followed up on the problem of obedience a few years later. Twenty-four Stanford undergraduate men were recruited by Professor Philip Zimbardo to live in a mock prison. They were randomly assigned roles either as prisoners or guards. Psychologists had selected them out of a total of 75 volunteers because they were deemed the most psychologically stable and healthy. In many cases, the guards became intensely sadistic, humiliating their prisoners, forcing them to go naked, and limiting their capacities to urinate or defecate. Early on, the prisoners rebelled but then, after their rebellion failed, submitted to gross abuse. Several had emotional breakdowns, and about a third were judged to have had strongly negative psychological effects. Despite the fact that it was all make believe, the prisoners became radically dependent on their guards' attitude toward them. Some became supplicants, weeping and trembling in the face of those on whom they bestowed authority.

The consequences of the experiment were so intense that Zimbardo had to shut it down after only the sixth day of what was supposed to be a two-week run. Five students had quit rather than go through with even the six days. It became apparent that Zimbardo was risking the mental health and perhaps long-term well-being of others. That people would so readily accept a social role and so fervently conform to the expectations surrounding it provides sobering information about how far people will go to conform to their role set, with perhaps catastrophic consequence.

We can start to understand how face-to-face interactional systems can build up group loyalties, which can follow along ethnic, racial, or national lines. Unlike among the Stanford students, these demarcations are not randomly assigned, and as is the case with race, for example, individuals have little choice in how they start the process. People really are born into particular groups and have to deal with how others react to those identities.

A person can act out to satisfy their reference group, and this can put them in opposition to other people's groups. People link up and cast others away as deviant or different in some lesser or dangerous way. But like fish that live in the same school and never even get out of the water, sometimes they do not know that another world is possible—where people have different beliefs and judgments that, in their context, make sense. Our deviance is their normal and vice versa. Other people's ways of life, if known at all, are inferior or maybe even evil—in part just because they are different. Those who belong to groups at the top of the structure have special capacity to demean and punish those below, whether within their same community or in societies farther afield.

Courtesy Wikipedia/ZUMA Press/Newscom

The United States military extensively employed torture tactics against prisoners during the war in Iraq from 2003 onward. Psychologist Philip Zimbardo, who conducted the Stanford Prison Experiment, was later to note, in connection with U.S. guards' especially sadistic treatment of Iraqi prisoners at a detention facility, known as Abu Ghraib, that his experiments were only too relevant to real life and the extremes to which otherwise normal people will go if supported by role expectations and the right (that is, wrong) kind of social context (Zimbardo 2007).

Conclusion: What We Know and What We Don't Know

Interactionism provides us the tools for understanding the social self. To understand what an individual is, it introduces the presence of others. For each of us, those relevant others differ, and this helps create uniqueness. At the same time, these unique individuals must gain approval from at least some people and groups to have a positive sense of self and to be able to function in the world. To achieve these ends, people have all sorts of artful techniques to know exactly what to do and under what conditions. We read contexts, we use exacting precision as we converse, and we play our emotions to fit the conditions at hand. We do not simply obey rules but creatively interpret them to make them work for ourselves and the organizations that, for better or worse, we come to serve.

This creates not only distinctiveness but also conformity. At the individual level we can be challenged to conform to inconsistent demands coming from opposing parties. It can mean trouble for whole groups who get labeled as deviant because of the relevant others and reference groups that shape their identity and destiny. At the macro level, terrible danger can arise when people conform in ways that create harm and havoc on a mass scale (as the Milgram and Zimbardo experiments vividly demonstrate). Building a society that gives people a sense of their own dignity while at the same time doing the least harm to others is a huge challenge. Many of the important dramas of world history reveal instances when we did not get it right.

Sociology still has some explaining to do; while we have concepts that explain the overall order, we have trouble with the exceptions. So although most people conform to society's laws and accepted codes, some are renegades. One-fourth of Asch's subjects would not conform; five of Zimbardo's dropped out. In the Milgram experiment, not only were there people who would refrain from giving the fatal shock (about one-third), there was a scattering of subjects who walked out early on. Given how much people usually conform to the social circumstances at hand, we do not have a strong explanation for those who do not go with the flow. We don't know why some Germans risked their lives to hide Jewish families from the Nazis nor, at a different part of the moral spectrum, what mix of social factors could produce an individual who would terrorize strangers at a shopping mall or students on a college campus.

These kinds of puzzles are especially acute in understanding behavior during the COVID-19 pandemic. Why is it that most people wear masks in public, but some do not? In societies where mask wearing was universal, rates of infection were very low, and life could be close to normal, even before a vaccine appeared. In these societies, conformity was very high. In other countries and regions, however, mask wearing was not universal, and over and over we found that it only takes a few unmasked people to start spreading the virus that causes COVID-19 in a community.

Nor do we have a firm understanding of why some individuals, of whatever background and circumstance, seem more interactionally creative or effective than others. These people can work a room, work an audience, and work their lives in ways that overwhelm others of similar sociological location. Labels, especially negative ones, may come their way, but they do not often stick. Maybe having such strengths could enable people to lead social and political movements as well as more satisfying personal lives. If we could find ways to "bottle it," maybe working with like-minded scholars from psychology, we could conceivably encourage, through child-rearing and education, more of these people into being.

The Big Questions Revisited 4

4.1 How Do We Develop a Sense of Self? Each one of us has a unique identity. But is this sense of self a single thing, or is it a process of interaction? In this section, we explored how we know ourselves through the reflections of ourselves that mirror back from others' opinions of us—the "looking glass" of others.

The Social Self

The Looking-Glass Self

Learning Objective 4.1.1: Explain how the opinions and judgments of others shape our identities.

Significant Others, Reference Groups, and Generalized Others

Learning Objective 4.1.2: Compare and contrast the roles that significant others, reference groups, and generalized others play in guiding our behavior and in shaping our sense of self.

Life's a Stage

Learning Objective 4.1.3: Discuss how we differ in the ways we present ourselves to others.

Key Terms

self (p. 87)   looking-glass self (p. 89)
significant other (p. 89)   reference group
(p. 89)   role model (p. 89)   generalized other
(p. 90)

4.2 How Do We Make Sense of Our Worlds? We all have specific methods for demonstrating competence as interacting members of society. In this section, we explored how the sociological field of ethnomethodology examines these methods.

People's Methodology

Context, Context, Context

Learning Objective 4.2.1: Explain how context gives meaning to words and situations.

Conversational Precision

Learning Objective 4.2.2: Explain how conversation patterns can demonstrate social competence.

Emotion

Learning Objective 4.2.3: Discuss how individuals manipulate emotion in social interaction.

Self-Presentation in a Digital Age

Learning Objective 4.2.4: Analyze the impact of digital communication technologies and social media on our methods of self-presentation.

Interaction in Public

Learning Objective 4.2.5: Identify some of the methods we use when interacting in public.

Key Terms

ethnomethodology (p. 91)   civil inattention
(p. 95)

4.3 What Challenges Do We Face as We Move from One Social Context to Another? The social self is not fixed but is always changing, which can sometimes bring challenges. This section examined what happens when we experience role conflict and how informal rules and our keen awareness guide our behavior. We also looked at how and why people conform and what consequences conformity has on how people live together.

Shifts and Dilemmas

Status and Role Change

Learning Objective 4.3.1: Identify the causes of role conflict.

Labeling

Learning Objective 4.3.2: Explain how a self-fulfilling prophecy can influence label formation.

Rule Use

Learning Objective 4.3.3: Identify the role of informal rules in social interaction.

Conformity Experiments

Learning Objective 4.3.4: Explain what makes people conform and how conformity impacts how we live together.

Key Terms

status (p. 97)   role (p. 97)   role conflict
(p. 97)   deviant (p. 98)   self-fulfilling prophecy
(p. 98)

Chapter 5
Social Structure

by Jeff Manza

Inge Deutschkron was born in 1922 and grew up in a socially mixed neighborhood in Berlin, Germany. Her father, Dr. Martin Deutschkron, belonged to a high-status group in Germany because he held a doctoral degree and taught at an elite secondary school. Despite his social standing, Inge's father was a socialist, believing that modern society should be far more egalitarian than capitalism normally allows. Martin and his wife sympathized with unions and labored tirelessly for the German Social Democratic Party, a moderate left-wing party.

In January 1933, Adolf Hitler's Nazis came to power in Germany. Shortly thereafter, Inge's father was dismissed from his teaching position as an enemy of the Nazi regime for his political views. But there were worse things to come for the family. On March 31, 1933, Inge's mother sat the 10-year-old down and revealed to her something she could barely comprehend: The country's new rulers considered her Jewish, and she could expect to be persecuted for this. This news came as a surprise to the young girl as religion had played no part whatsoever in her upbringing. Yet for the Nazi government, Jewishness was a matter of "racial" identity that one is born with and could not escape. Because Inge's grandparents were Jewish, she was considered Jewish as well. It had nothing to do with how she felt as an individual; despite her upbringing in a nonreligious household, the Nazi government viewed her as a member of an alien people locked in an eternal struggle with German "Aryans." Although her father managed to flee in 1939 to England, Inge and her mother remained trapped in Berlin, threatened after 1941—like all other people classified as Jewish—with deportation to concentration camps and a near-certain death (6 million Jews in all died in the camps). With the help of a network of sympathetic fellow citizens, however, she and her mother miraculously survived underground in Berlin—the heart of Hitler's Third Reich—until the end of the war. In February 1945, they took advantage of the destruction and occupation of many cities in Germany to pass themselves off as refugees who had lost their identity papers. Yet even this return to a "legal" German identity nearly proved fatal when Russian soldiers reached greater Berlin in April 1945 and could only see Inge and her mother as members of a hated nationality (German). Only after they could produce documents attesting to their Jewishness were they granted the status of "victims of fascism."

My Sociological Imagination

JEFF MANZA

Growing up in the college town of Berkeley, California, my family was neither elite (my parents worked for the local university, but not as professors) nor unprivileged. I experienced the differences between these various worlds, and in particular the inequalities they represented, as an endlessly fascinating puzzle. I was also always interested in politics and occasionally participated in political protests and movements. My intellectual interest in sociology began to develop while I was an undergraduate student because it provided a way of connecting my emerging concerns about inequality and injustice with a set of theories and ways of studying how those inequalities persist. Since then, I have been exploring how social inequalities influence political life. More recently I have become interested in how public opinion does or does not shape government policies and how and when public attitudes can be manipulated or misused by political elites. I hope that my work can contribute, in some small way, to making American democracy more representative and egalitarian than it currently is.

Mark Bussell

Jewish children waiting for lunch in the Lodz ghetto in Poland, 1942. Because of the German government's attempt during World War II to kill all Jews in Europe in what is known as the Holocaust, it is likely that most of these children later died in concentration camps. Some came from families that had no direct involvement with the Jewish faith, but even having Jewish grandparents could be enough to be sent to the camps.

Born in 1922, Inge Deutschkron and her mother of Jewish ancestry miraculously survived living underground in Berlin at the heart of Hitler's Third Reich until the end of the war.

The remarkable story of how Inge Deutschkron survived the Holocaust, described in her best-selling memoir (Deutschkron 1989), illustrates in a particularly graphic way how social forces outside the control of individuals can shape lives and fates in dramatic ways. The way Inge's family members were forced to see themselves, and were seen by others, was determined by social and political factors entirely beyond their control (in this case, the Nazi government's imposition of a system of racial classification that turned the secular Deutschkron family into Jews). For many in Nazi-occupied Europe in the 1940s (not only Jews but also Roma people, gays and lesbians, communists, disabled people, and eventually anyone who disagreed with or protested the Nazi government), social classification proved to be a matter of life and death.

In most times and places, people have not been subjected to arbitrary racial laws or the whims and extreme injustices of a dictatorial state like the victims of the National Socialism era in Germany. But in many other ways, the system of social classification found in any society exerts powerful influences over individuals. A contemporary example in the United States is the way in which unauthorized (or "illegal") immigrants are treated, compared to legal immigrants. The lives of two otherwise very similar immigrants can have dramatically different consequences depending on their legal status. In effect, forces beyond the control of individuals set limits on our choices and opportunities, enable and motivate us to do some things and not others, and make some outcomes much more likely than others. Social structures, of which classification systems are one important component, are often mysterious and hard to see. We don't normally think about all of the social forces that shape our lives. But they are truly very powerful, enduring, and slow to change. As we will explore in this chapter, understanding human life requires us to consider the impact of social structure on the lives of individuals.

The Big Questions

1. **What is social structure?** Why do sociologists reject the view that the world is simply made up of a collection of individuals? In this section, we introduce the concept of social structure. Although social structures are normally hidden from view, they are essential to making social life possible. The key elements of social structure (roles and hierarchies, and norms and institutions) are introduced.

2. **How do roles and social hierarchies shape our life chances?** The social structure of any society consists of a wide range of different roles and social divisions, or hierarchies, between groups. In this section, we will explore where these various roles and social hierarchies come from and why they matter.

3. **How do norms and institutions influence social life?** A society's social structure also contains an elaborate set of norms and institutions. In this section, we will explore some of the central aspects of norms and institutions and why they influence our behavior.

4. **How do social structures influence our daily lives and social interactions?** Where do the identities and roles that are so important for social interaction come from? How do changes in social structure influence social interaction? Does acknowledging the existence of social structure mean we have limited free will?

5. **Why are social structures slow to change?** What are the forces that make social structures endure? Why is change such a slow process?

Mark Bussell

SOCIAL STRUCTURE AS THE CONTEXT OF HUMAN ACTION

Social structure is a concept that is fundamental to the entire way sociologists understand social life. But not everyone agrees that such a thing as social structure does, in fact, exist. The former British prime minister Margaret Thatcher once famously declared that "There is no such thing as society." By this, she meant that the concept of "society" (as used in everyday conversations) and "social structure" (the more precise concept used in the research and writings of social scientists) are a myth, a vague idea that could be used as a way of making excuses for poor behavior or disappointing outcomes for individuals. Thatcher instead wished to promote the idea that individuals are always entirely responsible for their own behaviors, successes, and failures in life. While sociologists do agree that individuals have room to shape their own destiny, they would fundamentally disagree with Thatcher that individuals are not heavily influenced by social structures they encounter and interact with as they go about their daily routines.

The Architecture of Social Structures

5.1.1 Explain how social structure can be thought of in architectural terms.

Let's start with a straightforward example of how social structure impacts individual lives. If you are born into a poor family, it is much more likely that you will be poor as an adult than if you are born into a rich family. Why? Margaret Thatcher's answer is that it comes down to the personalities and actions of each individual: The rich child who becomes a rich adult has made himself that way by simply working harder and/or taking advantage of opportunities better than the poor child/adult. Success, however we measure, is the result of individual initiative. For sociologists, however, the answer is always more complicated. There are, in addition to individual initiative, many external influences that also are likely to contribute to helping the rich child become a rich adult, and make it much more difficult for the poor child to become a rich adult. Rich children are far more likely to have opportunities for intellectual growth (such as having parents who value education, travel to foreign countries to learn about other cultures, attending very good private schools, or having tutors and other forms of special help along the way). They are more likely to meet or know people who will help them find their place in the world (like private school counselors who help place students in the best possible college or university, or family friends who may help in landing a great job or building a career). The poor child, by contrast, typically enjoys far fewer or even none of these critical resources. While the Thatcher theory provides an individual explanation, sociologists adopt a "structural" explanation to explain such adult outcomes.

What exactly is **social structure?** As we saw in Chapter 1, sociologists use the concept of social structure to describe the diverse ways in which the rules and norms of everyday life become enduring patterns that shape and govern social interactions. The sociological definition of social structure attempts to capture the many different elements of society that have power over us, that exist separately and independently from individuals while playing a role in influencing both our individual actions and the nature and outcomes of social interactions between individuals and groups. In the example above, the rich child benefits from their place in the social structure, while the poor child suffers. Because of these social structures, the odds of adult success are dramatically higher for the rich child.

The elements of social structures starts from the norms governing the interactions between people, such as between friends, fellow students or colleagues at work, or lovers. And it extends all the way up to the global environment in which governments make decisions about war and peace. Social structures are *all* of the elements of society that provide the regular patterns that we can all count on, or anticipate, in our daily lives. They provide the background foundation of daily life.

Like anything that is often hidden from view, it is often only when social structures are *absent* that their importance becomes clear. We've all seen movies and TV shows or read novels about situations where social structures completely break down—for example, in the aftermath of a nuclear war when only a few strangers have survived, or in horror films where zombie-like creatures have taken over the world. In fictional accounts such as these, individuals or characters have to make do without the order normally provided by social structure. Dramatic fictional renderings like these play off a very real idea: that underneath everyday social life is a foundation that makes social order possible.

One of the most important points about any structure, physical or social, is that if it is correctly designed, it will endure over time, even as other things change around it. A building provides a good example of how physical structures work, and helps us think about social structures as well. A tall, old building will have many different occupants over the years, each doing different things (and living very different lives). But, unless

the building meets the wrecking ball, it will continue to exist even as all of its occupants change or even if its exterior or interior is modified. This is also true of social structures. Social structures, like the hidden framing of a building, may evolve over time, but usually only slowly and within narrow limits (see photo on previous page). The human beings of any society will be replaced by new people when they die off, but the social structures governing their lives and those who follow will likely remain in place. Social and historical changes do occur—sometimes even revolutions that can bring about seemingly big changes in society—but most of the time changes to social structures happen slowly and modestly. The very persistence of social structures—and their durability—is an important part of what gives them their power. We will explore this idea in more detail later in the chapter.

Key Components of Social Structure

5.1.2 Identify the two key components of social structure.

Although the concept of social structure is a bit challenging to define, we all know about the existence of social structures in one way or another, once we start thinking about them. Poor people "know" that the world is stacked against them, and the rich "know" they have a lot of advantages (even if they sometimes prefer to think that isn't true). College students "know" that if they complete their degree they will have better life opportunities than if they flunk out. We all "know" we are supposed to show respect to our teachers, doctors, judges, ministers, and the president of the country. And we are all at least somewhat attuned to the ways social structures are slowly changing—just think about the types of jobs and careers that will be opening up in the future versus the kinds of jobs and careers that were common 50 or 100 years ago. You would have to be blissfully unaware of what is going on in the economy right now not to know that the job market is changing in various ways, and that change in the economic structure of modern societies will have a considerable impact on everyone.

As a general starting point, it is helpful to distinguish two main components of social structure, as illustrated in Figure 5.1. Both of these components, individually and in combination, make up the essential core of what sociologists mean when they refer to social structure. To get a better grasp on them, we will discuss each component separately in the next two sections, before exploring how they are connected in their impact on daily life and social interaction. Our central overriding point

When social structures break down, social order is threatened. A powerful example of this was during Hurricane Katrina in 2005, when New Orleans was flooded and the people who couldn't get out of the city—most of whom were poor—were left to fend for themselves for several days until help finally arrived.

Figure 5.1 Key Components of Social Structure

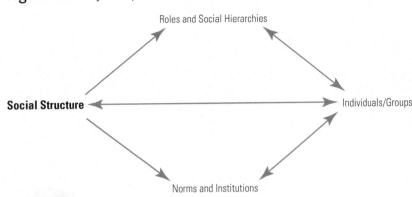

Roles and Social Hierarchies

Social Structure ⟷ Individuals/Groups

Norms and Institutions

in Figure 5.1 is that all of us, as individuals, are subject to the powers of roles/hierarchies and norms/institutions of the society we live in. At the same time, however, by acting in accordance with the social structures of the society we are living in, we help to maintain their stability. On the other hand, when individuals or groups we are a part of challenge them in some way, the possibility of change can emerge.

Rafael Ben-Ari/Alamy Stock Photo

BIG QUESTION 5.2 How Do Roles and Social Hierarchies Shape Our Life Chances?

THE FIRST DIMENSION OF SOCIAL STRUCTURE: ROLES AND SOCIAL HIERARCHIES

Roles and social hierarchies are critical components of a society's social structure. They define who we are, as well as provide the foundation for the power of some over others. Let's look at how they shape our lives.

Roles

5.2.1 Identify individual roles and role conflicts that exist.

Every human society contains within it a complex set of social positions. Sociologists use the term **role** to describe the rules and expectations that are associated with different positions. Every role we can think of—child/parent, doctor, sorority member, garbage collector, director, assistant to the director, priest, counselor, roommate, subcontractor, chairperson, sports fan, subway rider, teammate, United States Senator, and on and on—has a distinct set of expectations and rules associated with it.

The body of sociological work on how roles shape human behavior is known as **role theory**. The classical metaphor is that when we take on a role, we are like an actor in a play. As the sociologist Erving Goffman explained in his influential writings in the 1950s (described in more detail in Chapters 2 and 4), we are expected to perform these roles in a certain way. We do have some flexibility in exactly how we perform the role (just as different actors playing the same role will do it somewhat differently), but we are also heavily constrained in what we can (and must) do while in the role because of its script.

We are almost always in a role of one kind or another, and no matter how insignificant they may appear, they may entail important responsibilities—not just to ourselves, but to others as well. For example, our responsibilities on a city street depend on whether we are a pedestrian, a driver, or a traffic cop. There are norms and rules that apply to each role.

There is a pathway through life that defines the kinds of roles we are likely to have. At birth, our only role is that of an infant. We lie there, sleep, eat, poop, and occasionally cry or make cute faces. Life is pretty simple. There are no responsibilities or expectations in this state (although parents may get frustrated by loud crying, especially at night, but they also know that a newborn has no control over their emotions and just needs comforting). But once we reach a certain age, that all changes. We begin to take on multiple roles. We even switch from one role to another throughout a single day. For example, when we wake up, we may be either parent or child. When we leave for the day, we assume the role of "driver" if we drive a car, or "rider" if we use public transportation, or "bike rider" if we use a bicycle. When we get to our destination, let's say school or work, we then take on other roles (student, teacher, worker, boss, and so forth). It may be that most of these different roles are entirely compatible with one another. But sometimes they may come in conflict with one another. Consider a teenage parent, struggling to finish high school and take care of an infant. Or think about the relationship between working and being a parent. In situations like that, we can talk about the experience as a type of **role conflict**, in which the responsibilities of one role conflict with the responsibilities of another.

In the process of moving from one life stage to another, we are expected to alter our behavior to fit new roles. Sociologists call this process the **life course**. For example, as a person shifts from toddler to kindergartener to high school student to college student to graduate student to lawyer to elected politician to retiree to resident in an assisted living facility, they are expected to behave differently at each stage, and the process of adapting to

these different roles is what marks the passage through the life course. In the workplace, for example, it is not uncommon to notice that when someone you work closely with is promoted into a supervisorial or managerial role, their behavior changes. You might have once thought of this person as a good friend at work, someone you could share your secrets with and complain to about other coworkers and the boss. But once the coworker is promoted, suddenly they begin to treat you differently, and they may no longer be available to hang out and share confidences. They may even start to give you directions, which you may resent. Their behavior in both cases is guided by the role they are in.

While some roles—like being a driver or a pedestrian—may not have clear differences of status built in, many other roles do, including gaining the responsibilities of a supervisor or manager. Roles come with varying amounts of power and privilege; not all roles are equal. In this way, they contribute in important ways to what we call **social hierarchies**, that is, significant and enduring societal positions ordered from high to low, that grant some individuals and groups higher status and more power than others. But roles are only one of the forces that produce hierarchical, unequal, social relationships.

Group Identities and Social Hierarchies

5.2.2 Explain how group identities are formed and their relationship to social hierarchies.

Every society in the world contains multiple types of groups, and they are typically organized in a hierarchical fashion when they overlap. They are "hierarchical" in the sense that one group is typically accorded more status, opportunities, power, or authority than others. But before we try to understand why groups almost always form hierarchies, we first need to understand how social groups get created in the first place. The process can be found in very early human societies and can start from very simple premises (Heider 1958; Schwartz 2010). Consider this chain of relationships:

-A friend of my friend is my friend

-A friend of my enemy is my enemy

-An enemy of my enemy is my friend

-An enemy of my friend is my enemy

These statements should all make intuitive sense. Someone introduces one friend to another, and they become friends. That happens all the time. When a friend of ours talks about another friend of theirs we don't know in a positive way, we too will naturally be inclined to think well of that person. The reverse is also likely to be true; we may not automatically dislike someone just because a friend of ours dislikes that person, but it certainly isn't going to help. Finally, a common enemy is frequently a source of unexpected new relationships. A famous global example is during World War II, when the Western democratic capitalist countries overcame their hostility to communism to become close allies with the Soviet Union in order to fight together against the menace of German fascism. For a brief period of time, Soviet communists went from "enemy" to a vitally important "friend."

But even though it is a very simple chain of relationships, out of them social groups and ultimately social hierarchies and inequalities emerge. How does such an important outcome derive from such a simple starting point? As individuals begin to form groups with their friends' friends (or even their enemy's enemies), they also typically begin to establish ways of marking themselves off from others. They often establish group names, symbols and rituals, and decide what ideas are supposed to be important for group members (or, to put it another way, they

There is plenty of evidence that White men continue to dominate the most desired positions in American society. This is a source of racial and gender conflict in the workplace, and one that impacts the lives of all women and people of color who seek entrance, for example, into top managerial positions in large corporations. But many White men would object to the notion that they are consciously trying to make sure that only White men get ahead. It is an interesting feature of social hierarchies that the most powerful groups do not always have to acknowledge their privilege or even formally maintain a status group identity. One of the privileges of the very powerful is that they can deny that they are even a group at all, even as they somehow manage to protect and maintain their privileges against challenging groups.

begin to establish the group's shared values). Being a member of a group often carries with it the expectation that you will act in certain ways, and hold certain beliefs and attitudes. So if you are a "Russian," a "Christian," a union member, a dentist, or a member of the LGBTQ community, you will be aware of certain expectations that being a member of one of these groups entails. The influential German sociologist Max Weber introduced the concept of the **status group** early in the twentieth century to describe the process by which groups of individuals who share characteristics or attributes come together to protect and promote members of the group. Members of status groups come to think of themselves as "friends" or allies, and they typically find a common interest in promoting and helping each other (Weber 1922 [1978]). And one way they can do that is by denigrating other groups, which are all too easily characterized as less good or even as "enemies." Status groups are fully established whenever group members start to share a common identity with each other, but also a sense of who the opposing groups are.

The formation of group identities is also helped along by the ways that the human brain is constantly trying to simplify complex information that exists in the world around us. In this way, there is an important bridge between sociology and psychology. Sociologists have borrowed heavily from psychological research to understand why the existence of groups is so consistent in every society in the world. One leg of the answer comes from psychology. The investigation of how our thought processes connect to groups begins with the basic, long-standing evidence that to reduce the complexity of the world around us, our brains employ simple categories to organize our worlds (DiMaggio 1997; Strauss and Quinn 1998; Vaisey 2009). These categories are known as **schemas**. Schemas help us in every complicated setting, not just when it comes to individuals and groups. We all develop schemas to help us cut through the vast amount of information that we encounter every day. Because schemas are natural processes everyone's brain produces, they allow us to do a lot of stuff every day without having to think through everything we are confronted with. They are, in other words, shortcuts that we rely on most of the time (Kahneman 2011). If we did not have schemas to help us make decisions, but instead had to constantly think carefully about every single thing we did, life would quickly become overwhelming. For example, when we get up in the morning and make coffee or grab some cereal, we do not have to always think through and inspect all of the components of the machine we use to make coffee, or whether we should grab a spoon, a knife, a fork or find a special kind of bowl for eating breakfast cereal. We can just do those things without a lot of thought. We use our "gut." This allows us to focus deeper thought on what we think is important.

So while schemas are essential to how we live and navigate the world, when it comes to social groups, they encourage us to rely on simplifications about others based on whatever information we may know about an individual or a group. For example, someone's appearance can lead us to categorize them and think we know them. Like consuming cereal with a spoon, if we don't force ourselves to pause and think more deeply, we automatically reach for the quickest available ideas about the members of a group when we see someone who belongs to that group. The dark side of this process is that it is all too easy for those categories to become invested with prejudice of one kind or another (Stagnor et al. 1992; Massey 2005). We will consider the implications of those simplifications in the next section.

Power and Privilege in Social Hierarchies

5.2.3 Discuss the roles that power and privilege play in social hierarchies.

Social hierarchies arise and persist in any situation in which members of one group are able to use their possession of some *asset* or *attribute* as a basis for claiming special advantages over others (or other groups) who do not possess it (Tajfel 1979). An example might be something individuals are born with, like their skin color or sex. It might be a situation they are born into but can potentially change in adulthood, such as membership in a particular religious denomination. Or it could be something they attain later in life, such as an educational credential or business achievement. Hierarchies can be based on almost any way that people divide themselves into groups or categories.

Social hierarchies, then, establish relations of **power**—the ability to influence the behavior of others—and **privilege**—the ability or right to have special access to opportunities or claims on rewards. Dominant groups within any hierarchy will seek to monopolize opportunities and control rewards or at least prevent its existing privileges from eroding. This was a key extension of Weber's classical ideas about status groups. The process by which groups try to monopolize access to opportunities and rewards by limiting their availability to other groups was what Weber and his followers (Parkin 1979) have called **social closure**. Social closure is a nearly universal pattern of power maintenance.

Subordinate groups within a hierarchy face inferior status and more limited opportunities via social closure. The most common way in which privilege is denied to subordinates is through **discrimination**, in which a dominant group uses either legal or informal means to control opportunities and reduce or eliminate challenges from subordinate groups. Legal means of exclusion are blunt and powerful. The rules of social hierarchies become most visible and have their biggest impact when they are explicit and clear to everyone and when the sanctions for violating them are most clear. Consider this example. Imagine it's the 1950s and you're somewhere in the South, let's say Alabama. And let's say you are Black. And you need to go to the bathroom or find a restaurant. Your choices are limited. And they are limited because of certain features of the social structure—in this case, race and racism—that are in place. Other laws that were common in Southern states limited your right to attend the schools of your choosing, marry who you wanted, or compete for jobs on equal terms with White workers.

But when hierarchies are organized by laws and rules which blatantly violate fundamental ideas about equality in modern democratic societies, they are subject to challenge and often cannot be sustained. Challenges have come both from **social movements**—organized groups engaged in collective efforts aimed to bring about some kind of change, like those of the civil rights movement, the women's movement, the LGBTQ movement, and disability rights groups—as well as through legal challenges drawing upon the law to enforce equal treatment. In the past century, subordinate groups have won countless battles to overturn forms of discrimination

History is filled with examples of the power imbalance within social structure. It can be seen in the capacity of the powerful to influence the behavior of others, including establishing laws that will exclude subordinate groups and reproduce the power inequality. Pictured here are segregated public restrooms, photographed in 1965 at a gas station in rural South Carolina.

Bruce Roberts/Science Source

written into laws or rules, and have in many cases established that in the eyes of the law they must be treated the same as more powerful groups.

However, just because explicit legal restrictions on subordinate groups disappear does not mean that social hierarchies and the inequalities associated with them suddenly cease to exist. Dominant groups can still assert their power through a variety of informal means that do not rely on formal laws. What are these informal processes? One of the most important is the maintenance of negative **stereotypes** about subordinate groups. Stereotypes are false or exaggerated generalizations about a subordinate group that are applied to all members of the group. The stereotyping of subordinate groups is a nearly universal aspect of any social hierarchy. (In Chapters 13 and 14, we will examine racial, ethnic and gender stereotypes—among the most widely studied—in more detail.)

Why do stereotypes exert such a powerful hold on us? In the previous section, we described how the human brain draws on simplified schemas to get by. The power of stereotypes draws on these simplifications. Examples of classic negative stereotypes include that some groups are lazy, unintelligent, prone to criminal activity, or better suited for caring work than high-paying professional employment, have bad attitudes, or lack ambition. Any of these stereotypes, if widely held by members of the dominant group and others in society, can promote continuing discrimination against members of subordinate groups *even if* formal legal equality is achieved. For example, laws can be passed that require employers to consider all applicants for jobs equally. But if employers hold negative stereotypes about subordinate groups, research suggests that they will consistently favor members of the dominant group in making decisions about whom to hire or promote. One way to examine this is to look at differences in outcomes, say income, by members of different groups working in the same occupation. When we do this, we can begin to see how informal means of discrimination against subordinate groups persist. Figure 5.2 shows the difference in wages of men and women, and Whites and Blacks, who are working full-time in the same occupation.

By studying the wage differences within the same occupation, we can see how even those women and Blacks who attain the same occupation as men and Whites, respectively, can *still* be denied access to the most attractive or well-paying opportunities for workers in that occupation. What this tells us is that prejudice and stereotyping continue to operate *even when formal barriers to entry crack open*. Social hierarchies that generate inequality are remarkably difficult to dislodge. Powerful groups rarely give up their advantages easily.

Population Size and Social Hierarchies

5.2.4 **Explain the impact that population size has on the ways in which groups within a social hierarchy relate to one another.**

Social hierarchies are strongly influenced by the relative size of competing groups, especially when one group begins to grow in size relative to others. It is often—but not always—the case that larger groups are likely to be more powerful within a social hierarchy than smaller groups.

Figure 5.2 Inequality in Income by Gender and Race within the Same Occupation

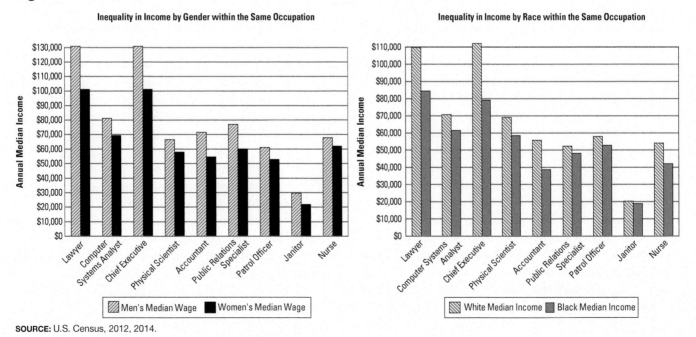

SOURCE: U.S. Census, 2012, 2014.

Powerful groups usually have more members, more resources, more votes, and even, if necessary, can more plausibly threaten weaker groups with force and violence should conflicts intensify. Religious and ethnic minorities have often been overwhelmed by larger groups, and throughout history that has sometimes involved considerable violence. The history of religion is littered with examples of violence used to suppress minority religions. Ethnic groups have often resorted to war as well, in fights over who gets to control what territory, or even who gets to live there (with victorious ethnic groups sometimes forcing members of the losing ethnic group to leave, an especially nasty process known as "ethnic cleansing").

The size of the groups making up a social hierarchy, however, can change over time. And such changes can threaten the status quo (and can make powerful groups anxious). We'll look at some examples shortly, but the general pattern is that because key social groups are often competing for desired positions and opportunities, the sense of competition between groups can change as one group gets larger relative to another. For example, when a subordinate racial or ethnic group becomes more numerous in a particular community, members of a dominant group may begin to feel more threatened than before (Blumer 1958; Blalock 1967; Olzak 1992).

One of the most common ways in which the size of social groups change over time is the result of **migration**, the process by which individuals and families move from one region or country to another. When the migration of people into a new place begins, most people will hardly notice their presence. But as the new migrants grow in size relative to the existing population, and begin to compete for jobs and other opportunities, their presence can threaten those who have long been there. The previously dominant group may not like the newcomers. They may begin to explicitly seek to exclude newcomers from opportunities by heightening stereotypes and other forms of active discrimination, or even by using violence, as noted.

The threats arising from foreign immigration—and the hostile responses of groups already in the United States—has been a recurring theme throughout American history. There have been two especially significant waves of immigration into the country that have fundamentally altered the population mix. This first wave peaked between 1880 and 1910, at which time the predominant flow of immigrants were from Europe, especially Southern and Eastern Europe. The second major wave of immigration began in 1965, when the U.S. adopted a much less restrictive policy toward immigration. During the more recent period, the largest flow of immigrants has been from Mexico and other Latin American countries and Asia (especially China, Vietnam, Thailand, and India). In Chapter 24 (on immigration), we describe these different eras of immigration and the hostile responses they provoked in much greater detail.

Another important internal population shift in American history that gave rise to immense and sometimes deadly conflcit was the **Great Migration**, the movement of large numbers of Blacks from the South to Northern cities from the 1910s through the 1950s. The Great Migration involved millions of Black families moving to the North in search of better opportunities for jobs and education for their children. In 1900, there were only a couple hundred thousand Blacks who were born in the South and had migrated out of the region in their lifetimes; by 1980, there were more than 4 million (Tolnay 2003). In the process, they changed the racial composition of the cities where they moved: Chicago, Detroit, St. Louis, New York, Washington, D.C., Pittsburgh, Cleveland, and many others. As the population composition of these cities shifted, tensions and racial conflicts developed, often leading to explosions of violence. A particularly deadly case occurred in Tulsa in 1921, when Blacks resisted a White mob attempting to lynch a young Black man. In response, a group of heavily armed Whites, aided by local officials, proceeded to destroy what was known as the "Black Wall Street," a thriving commercial district, and hundreds of nearby homes. Airplanes were used to drop bombs against helpless people on the ground, leaving somewhere between 200 and 300 dead and over 10,000 homeless (Hirsch 2014). This tragedy is memorialized in the opening scenes of the HBO show *The Watchmen*. Populations can shift and change, but powerful groups typically fight to hold on to their privileges.

Economic Change and Social Hierarchies

5.2.5 Describe how economic changes can impact individual lives.

Social hierarchies are often related, not surprisingly, to economic opportunities. Individuals and families need an income to survive, and the vast majority gain that income from a job. This simple fact calls attention to the enormous importance of the economy in the lives of individuals, and a crucial way in which social structures matter. When large-scale economic changes occur, they can have a major impact on both individuals and their families and also on whole communities. Let's explore in more detail.

Economies, especially in the period since the Industrial Revolution, do not stand still. They are in constant motion for many reasons, but especially because of new technologies and inventions, new types of consumer demands, and sometimes the discovery of new kinds of raw materials or ways of producing goods. These changes create a constant process of creation and destruction of jobs and sometimes entire industries. As these changes unfold, they can propel some people forward but severely harm the lives of others. This pattern—some benefitting, others losing out—has been a continual feature of economic change. For sociologists, studying the societal consequences of these shifts is a central preoccupation.

Three critical long-term economic trends have unsettled social lives over the past 150 years. The first of these developments was the decline in agricultural production and employment and the rise of manufacturing jobs— a process that begins with the Industrial Revolution. For most of the nineteenth century, a majority of Americans worked on small farms that either they or someone else owned (including the vast majority of the Black population before and after the Civil War). An additional large group of workers had jobs related to agriculture, such as providing farmers with supplies or transporting and selling farm products in cities. Today, with enormous advances in the technology of farming, just 3 percent of Americans work on farms, but that tiny group produces far more food than ever before. This decline in agricultural employment can be found in all rich countries around the world, and today it is occurring in many developing countries as well. This shift, whenever it happens, is typically devastating for small farmers and the rural communities where farming was once dominant.

So where did all of the farmers go? The short answer is that the enormous growth of manufacturing provided new opportunities for them or their children, as well as millions of new immigrants who came to America and settled in the booming late-nineteenth and early-twentieth century cities where factories were located. Manufacturing jobs were the primary source of employment growth in the American economy between the end of the Civil War and the 1960s. If the typical American worker in 1850 was a farmer, in 1950 they worked in a factory or another job supporting manufacturing. Employment in manufacturing skyrocketed in the late nineteenth century, and entire communities were built around large factories and sometimes a single dominant manufacturing industry. During this period, rapid **urbanization** took place, as the populations of American cities underwent enormous growth. One of the most famous and successful of the industrial centers dominated by manufacturing was the concentration of the automobile industry in Detroit, but there were many others as well (for example, steel in Pittsburgh, Pennsylvania, and Gary, Indiana; meatpacking in Chicago; rubber in Akron, Ohio; grain milling in Buffalo, New York; and transportation hubs for manufacturing companies in places like New Orleans, Louisiana). All of these cities and regions prospered, as demand for manufactured products grew both in America and increasingly around the world.

But beginning in the late 1950s, employment in manufacturing began a steep and seemingly irreversible decline, as Figure 5.3 shows. Today, only around 8 percent of all workers are employed in manufacturing. While the causes of the decline in manufacturing jobs in recent decades have been widely debated, one key factor that all analysts agree on is that major technological advances both displaced human workers *and* made it possible for manufacturing companies to efficiently produce in countries where wages were far lower than in the United States, such as China. Most of the consumer goods we buy today are produced outside the United States.

The downward sloping line in Figure 5.3 represents a tremendous change in the lives of millions of people. What has replaced those manufacturing jobs? The third critical long-term economic trend that has transformed the United States and other societies around the world in recent decades has been the dramatic rise in employment in **white-collar jobs**, knowledge-based occupations, a dynamic that accelerated in the second half of

Figure 5.3 Percentage of American Workers in Manufacturing Employment, 1890–2020

Percent of all Nonfarm Workers Employed in Manufacturing, 1890–2020

SOURCE: For 1910 data: Bureau of Labor Statistics, U.S. Department of Labor, The Economics Daily, Employment by industry, 1910 and 2015, available at https://www.bls.gov/opub/ted/2016/employment-by-industry-1910-and-2015.htm. For annual data for 1939–2020:U.S. Bureau of Labor Statistics, All Employees, Manufacturing [MANEMP] and All Employees, Nonfarm [PAYEMS], retrieved from FRED, Federal Reserve Bank of St. Louis; https://fred.stlouisfed.org/series/MANEMP.

the twentieth century and continues today. The new jobs that have been created since the 1970s have primarily been in the so-called "service sector," a term used to describe a wide range of industries that include finance, real estate, professional and personal service of all kinds (ranging from expensive lawyers and doctors to child- and elder-care workers), sales jobs of one kind or another, and new occupations in computers and information technology (including IT professionals, repair technicians, and software and hardware developers). For workers without college degrees, the new jobs that are available often pay less than the manufacturing jobs of the past. Rapidly growing jobs such as service and maintenance work, call-center work, janitorial services, personal and household service work, paperwork clerks, fast-food restaurant work, and others may have grown in number but tend to pay relatively low wages and have few opportunities for advancement. That said, the overall mix of new jobs involves less physical toil and higher levels of education than 50 years ago (Wright and Dwyer 2003). Social scientists often describe the current economy as a **post-industrial economy**, signifying the decline of manufacturing employment and the rise of white-collar work. Increasingly, there has been a rise in both good jobs and bad jobs, with fewer jobs in the middle, especially for those without college degrees. Many people are being left behind in the post-industrial economy.

The consequences of these economic changes are beyond the ability of individuals to control. Being in the right place at the right time can mean a very satisfying life, but if you are caught on the wrong side of economic change, and your knowledge and skills become obsolete, you may experience downward mobility that you cannot stop. For example, someone born in a working-class community in 1940, growing up with the expectation of working in a factory, could expect to find a decent job in their late teens or early 20s (say around 1960). But 20 to 25 years later, in middle age, those factory jobs were rapidly disappearing. Millions of factory workers lost employment in this period and struggled to find similar paying jobs, and young people entering the labor market without college degrees struggled to find jobs similar to those of their parents. It's not hard to see how painful these shifts were. If you were in your 40s and 50s and had spent a lifetime acquiring the knowledge to be a skilled factory worker, and suddenly there were no jobs for someone with your skills, what could you do?

Cities and communities dependent on manufacturing jobs have been hit very hard. Nowhere is this more extreme than in the case of Detroit, Michigan, as noted, once the home of the auto industry. Today the city of Detroit has only a handful of automobile manufacturing jobs left. While a new economy based on service-sector work has grown, it remains very small in comparison to what it once was, and many people whose lives were built on working in the auto factories are simply unable to transition into these different jobs that require different skills. Once an emblem of economic strength, Detroit now symbolizes the impact of the changing economic system.

The decline of manufacturing jobs, in places like Detroit and elsewhere, has meant that higher education is an increasingly important source of quality employment and income. The gap between college-educated workers and those with a high school degree or less has risen significantly in recent decades (Hout 2012). When manufacturing employment was abundant, a high school education was frequently adequate to find a job that paid a good income. Today, an individual with only a high school education is at a severe disadvantage in competition for better-paying jobs in the service-sector economy, where knowledge and credentials are increasingly important. Just as during the transition from farming to manufacturing, economic changes have rendered one type of skill set less valuable than other skills; in this case knowledge acquired through education is increasingly critical (Goldin and Katz 2008).

Brian Synder/Reuters/Alamy Stock Photo

Youngstown, Ohio, is one of the many cities in the Northeast and Midwest that have been devastated by the closure of factories that once employed millions of workers. Shown here are some of the many abandoned factories in the city.

BIG QUESTION 5.3 How Do Norms and Institutions Influence Social Life?

THE SECOND DIMENSION OF SOCIAL STRUCTURE: THE POWER OF NORMS AND INSTITUTIONS

The second major dimension of social structure is rooted in the norms and institutions that influence social interaction and human behavior. Social norms shape the way we interact with one another by providing a complex set of rules we are supposed to know and follow—in other words, they are scripts for everyday action. Norms also guide the behavior of groups and entire organizations. Institutions emerge when societies turn norms into enduring customs of social life. Central societal institutions include families, schools, religion, health care, criminal justice, the economic system, and the government. These vital institutions regulate and enforce the rules, norms, and customs in every field of human activity. They are, just as roles and social hiearchies, foundational building blocks of any society.

Norms and Rules

5.3.1 Distinguish between social norms and formal rules of behavior.

As the unwritten rules of society, norms tell us what is and is not appropriate to do in any situation, and provide guidance for selecting courses of action. In this way, norms are related to formal rules of behavior, like laws and written guidelines, even though norms are generally not written down anywhere. Rules are more formal, explicit guidelines for behavior. Norms, by contrast, are somewhat more ambiguous (although written rules are often ambiguous as well). Norms are things we just know, whereas rules are things we may have to refer to a rulebook, handbook, or legal code to find. Sometimes the distinction between the two is fuzzy. For example, drivers are required to stop and wait for pedestrians to cross inside a crosswalk. If the pedestrian is outside the crosswalk, however, the formal rules are ambiguous (the driver is responsible for avoiding an accident, but the pedestrian is responsible for not walking across the street in front of a car). Social norms come into play here—it would be polite for the driver to wave the pedestrian across.

Norms and formal rules and laws are important, but they are not always followed (including rules that are attached to criminal sanctions if violated). Indeed, it is only the saint among us who has never committed a single act that could be considered a norm violation or even, perhaps, criminal. Much of the time we can get away with petty violations of rules and norms. But not always. There are considerable risks of sanction if someone in a position of authority chooses to enforce norms or rules that we've violated.

Norms and rules are one critical way in which social structures gain power over us as individuals. We seem to be free to do what we want in most situations, except that there are usually clear norms and/or rules that guide or tell us what we should be doing (and how we should be doing it). We usually don't know where those norms or rules come from, they are just there. The great French sociologist Emile Durkheim called them "social facts," by which he meant those parts of society that are independent of individuals but exert a force over us. We are powerless in part because no one individual can change the norms or rules very quickly, even ones that are irrational or harmful.

Where Do Formal Rules Come From?

5.3.2 Describe the tragedy of the commons and the origin of rules.

Norms harden and become more mandatory when they become formal rules. It is not easy to trace the origin of all of the formal rules that societies establish. For many types of everyday interactions, norms seem to be enough. But rules are a universal feature of every known society, so they must have some purpose. And this raises an important question: why do human beings accept the existence of most rules, at least most of the time?

A classic sociological answer to the puzzle is that formal rules help solve problems that might exist in their absence. Norms can be vague. Rules are more specific. A major contribution to understanding the origins of rules in human societies is what is known as the **tragedy of the commons**, a theoretical analysis of a problem in which the absence of agreed-upon rules can make everyone worse off (see Chapter 6). The concept was popularized in an essay by the ecologist Garrett Hardin in 1968, and that essay remains one of the most cited social science papers ever written. Hardin drew upon an example from medieval England, in which open spaces were used by cattle herders to graze their cattle for free in these shared spaces (which were known as the "commons"). As long as the numbers of cattle were low enough so that each cow had enough to eat, and everyone followed norms of not over-grazing the land, everything was fine. But because the use of the commons was free and unregulated by any rules, a problem would arise if some herders brought too many cattle to use the same commons. Perhaps some norms operated successfully in some places that kept the Commons healthy. But in other cases, over-grazing could ruin the Commons for everyone (hence the "tragedy"). To resolve this kind of problem, neighbors had to impose rules on themselves so that no one herder would cause overuse of the commons.

The great insight from this essay is that establishing and enforcing formal rules can, in many situations, make everyone better off. Human societies have, over-time, developed countless rules that attempt to prevent the actions of some to harm the interests of all (Ostrom 1990). Let's consider a more modern example. People all over the world want the freedom to buy whatever kind of car they want, to be able to use it whenever they want. Yet gas and diesel-powered cars are making an immense contribution to causing climate change. If everyone stopped driving, or switched to an electric car, we would get much closer to preventing future global warming catastrophes. Even using more energy efficient cars helps (i.e., cars that get better gas mileage). But just like the herders on the Commons over-grazing their cattle, absent some rules many people will still drive whatever car they want and leave it to others to reduce their auto emissions. So governments across the world have stepped in to require cars that reduce emissions, and eventually all car companies will be selling electric vehicles only (that's still a ways off in the future, but it is inevitably going to happen). As these kinds of rules are imposed, they have the potential to make everyone better off by reducing the risks of environmental crises.

Or here's an even newer example involving cars. In most places, the freedom to drive as much as you want is more or less harmless. But in extremely crowded cities, the lack of rules can produce exceptional traffic congestion at rush hour, or even throughout the day. No one enjoys sitting in traffic, but congestion wastes not just time but can also increase costs for businesses that rely on shipping goods in one way or another, make it difficult to get school children to schools or home on time, and can slow public buses to a crawl. The creation of mass transportation systems – cars, buses, trains – is one way of getting people out of cars. But that hasn't been enough to halt congestion in the world's most crowded cities, so several newer solutions are being developed around the world. One is known as "congestion pricing," where drivers pay a fee to be able to drive in the most crowded centers of large cities (this strategy is being used in several European countries, and has been proposed for New York City as well). You can imagine how, if cattle herders had to pay even a significant fee for grazing more than their fair share of cattle on common land, they might not have been as likely to over-use it. An even more extreme approach can be found in Hong Kong, the most densely populated city in the world. There, the local government has devised an alternate-day rule system, in which each car is allowed to drive in the city center only on certain days (and drivers who use their car on the wrong day will get an expensive ticket). Where once it was nearly impossible to get anywhere, today Hong Kong's central business district is often relatively free of the traffic jams.

Institutions and the Patterning of Social Life

5.3.3 Explain the process of institutionalization and identify examples of common practices that have been institutionalized.

While norms and rules are powerful, they become truly significant when they come to be incorporated into one or more of the major institutions in society. Institutions emerge whenever groups of people begin to try to formalize something that members were already doing informally—an important norm, rule, or common practice in society already. This process of **institutionalization** is complex, and institutions come into existence only very slowly. It may take decades or even centuries for institutions to fully take shape. But once they do become established, they will play a critical role in the life of all of the members of any society.

Human societies build and maintain institutions for many reasons, but most importantly to try to ensure that things are done a certain way, and that there is continuity to this over time. Institutionalization is always accompanied by the establishment of **organizations** that are designed to enforce or execute the now formalized norms and rules. Organizations are groups of people acting together in pursuit of some common goal, and they provide the day to day contexts in which individuals actually engage with institutions. It is easy to confuse organizations and institutions, and everyday language often doesn't help. For example, we often refer to an individual college or university as "institutions," even though the institution of education is much broader than any single school (no matter how big or seemingly powerful). We will learn more about organizations in Chapter 9. The key point for now is to understand that organizations operate within institutions, and every institution will have many organizations associated with it. Think of the institutions of modern market economies: a single institution (the market economy) consisting of countless organizations (commonly called businesses) jousting with each other for customers and profits.

This may all seem a bit abstract, so let's consider a couple of historical examples of the institutionalization process. Consider first the case of religion. For vast stretches of human history, people would gaze at the sky and wonder what it all meant. At different moments in different places, however, some people began to develop more systematic ways of thinking about the wonders of nature and the place of human beings in the world. They began to develop ideas and theories about how the world began and the possibility of a higher being that might have created it. Eventually, in many places in many different ways, people and communities began to create ideas about gods and supernatural forces, perhaps to explain things that otherwise seemed inexplicable. At some further point, human societies began erecting sacred places, where religion and religious rituals could be enacted (the forerunners of today's churches, mosques, and temples). As these ideas and rituals passed from one generation to the next, certain people began to take on the task of creating more regular forms of religious practice. As the followers of these leaders became more numerous, they began to create organizations to help them manage the workload. These religious organizations created the materials necessary for the institutionalization of religion. Canonical religious texts (that is, sacred writings) began to appear

within each of these religious traditions, instructing their ministers and ordinary followers on what to believe and how to behave. Eventually, special schools were created to spread religious teachings more widely. Elaborate rituals reinforced the importance of religious ideas for followers to apply in their lives. Today, we can see the fruits of the institutionalization of religion in the fact that many of those rituals and doctrines are so similar to what they were many hundreds of years ago.

Another example of the process of institutionalization can be seen in education. Teaching and learning have existed from the very beginning of human civilization. Parents taught their children as best they could to do whatever was necessary to survive, for example, how to hunt, gather food that was safe to eat, or grow their own food. Even small nomadic tribes and the very earliest human settlements developed ways of passing knowledge from one generation to the next; these included, before written texts, stories, songs, legends, and above all else, practice. At some point, humans got the idea that learning could be facilitated by bringing children together in groups rather than every family teaching each child individually. This grouping of children together encouraged the formation of the first schools. As schools appeared, some people began to argue that schools should teach a concrete **curriculum**, that is, a sequence of topics that made it easier for learners to progress. Eventually, the curriculum started to be written down, and courses making up a program of study in a school or school system developed.

For many centuries, all but the most basic education was reserved for privileged children (and often just boys). Many of the earliest schools, and especially colleges, were founded by religious orders wanting to train future religious leaders. But the institutionalization of education gradually moved beyond religious instruction and spread outward to encompass more and more children, and eventually all of them. In the United States, this process of expanding education to everyone took place in the late nineteenth and early twentieth centuries.

The rise of mass, universal, and mostly free schooling, is found today almost everywhere in the world, although in very poor countries there are still significant numbers of children who receive little formal schooling. Critical to the evolution of education, as with religion, were the organizations—schools, colleges, and universities—that were created to implement education. Once the idea of a formal systematic curriculum took hold, and children and young adults began learning in a systematic way from one generation to the next, education had reached its modern, fully institutionalized form. The subject matter of the teaching shifted over time, and new subjects were adopted into the curriculum, but in the United States and many other countries, the educational system looks fairly similar to the way it did 100 years ago.

Johnston, Frances Benjamin, 1864-1952. Washington, D.C., school survey

The importance of teaching children is nearly universal, but education became institution-alized as soon as the first schools appeared and a formal and systematic curriculum was established that would be taught to children from one generation to the next. Although the curriculum evolves every year, the modern classroom and many of the core subjects that are taught share many features with this early classroom in Washington, D.C.

The Institutional Order

5.3.4 Explain the importance of laws and government in establishing the institutional order in society.

The **institutional order**—all of the major institutions of any society—extends far beyond religion and education. Many of the chapters in *The Sociology Project* explore one major institution in more detail: the economy, families, politics, criminal justice, health, even global institutions. But before we begin, we need to make a few further clarifications. Each major societal institution contains within it what sociologists call the **institutional field**. This is because, like religion and education, every major institution has multiple groups and organizations that are all operating (and sometimes competing) with one another within the confines of the institution. So we use the term "institution" to refer to entire domain of human activity that it governs, and we refer to all of the groups and organizations that operate within that domain as the "institutional field."

Each institutional field has its own rules and logics for the groups that operate within them. So in the case of health, for example, the institutional field consists of many groups and organizations. Groups that represent doctors and nurses, the unions that organize hospital workers, all of the companies that market and sell medical products, all of the insurance companies that provide health insurance, the hospitals and clinics that provide care, the pharmaceutical companies and research

scientists who invent medications, vaccines, and other treatment solutions, patient advocacy groups, hospice care facilities (end-of-life), mental health and dementia care facilities, and others are all part of the health insitutional field. One institution (health), but many players and organizations within the institutional field of health.

Each major societal institution is partially independent of others. What goes on in, for example, health care is largely separate and independent from what is happening in criminal justice. But there can, and frequently is, some overlap. In the case of health and criminal justice, for example, there have long been people within the medical field who provide health care and mental health services in prisons. The overlapping relationship between the two institutional fields intensified when the COVID-19 pandemic struck in 2020. While the healthcare system was directly impacted by the sudden need to treat millions of infected patients, and many organizations within the field turned their attention to that crisis, at the same time new health-related issues arose in criminal justice as well. Because the virus that causes COVID-19 spreads most easily in confined indoor spaces, prisons became hotbeds of infection, which matters not only for inmates and prison staff but also the community (prison staff can carry the virus from prison to community). To control the spread of the virus outside of prisons, health organizations were brought in to work with criminal justice officials to devise strategies to try to reduce the threat. There are many ways in which this kind of interaction between societal institutions (and the organizations and groups within their institutional fields) occurs routinely.

Institutions, and all of the organizations and groups active within the institutional field each have their own primary domain, but there are two institutions that have special powers: law and government. Both the legal system and governments stand above the other institutions of society in the sense that they have the power to force institutional change. Other institutions do not have that power. Health officials cannot order prison officials to release enough inmates so that each prisoner could have a cell to themselves, even though that would have greatly helped to reduce viral spread. Prison officials cannot order hospitals to open new treatment facilities in prisons to improve care to inmates who become infected. Only governments and the legal system have that kind of authority.

The power of legal and government institutions to change the lives of individuals is easy to see when we think about dramatic cases like Hitler's Nazi government in Germany in the 1930s and 1940s, under which Inge Deutschkron lived and was forced by Nazi law to have only one legal identity—that of a Jew. Brutal dictatorships often literally choose who gets to live and who must die. Joseph Stalin, the dictator of the Soviet Union at the same time that Hitler ruled Germany, was famously said to have as his bedtime reading a list of Communist Party members marked for possible death; he would go through the list and mark off those who were to be executed and those who were to be sent to prisons in the outer reaches of the Soviet Union or left alone (Khlevniuk 2008).

Life and death examples are extreme, but all modern states have enormously significant powers that at times seem to have few limits. Governments make policies that help determine things like the wealth and income gap between individuals, how many people will be allowed to live in poverty, and how much damage to the natural environment will be allowed. In deciding important cases, courts of law can reach into any institutional field and create or apply rules that the participants in that institutional field would not do on their own. The recent struggle over the institution of the family is a good example. While the Supreme Court decided in *Obergefell* v. *Hodges* (2015) that it is unconstitutional for any state to deny marriage to same-sex couples, this decision came only at the end of a decades-long struggle by same sex couples to claim the same rights as different sex couples.

Table 5.1 Key Institutional Concepts

Institutions: The structured and enduring practices of human life that are built around well-established rules and norms.

Institutional order: The set of core institutions (such as families, economy, religion, law and government, health/medical, education, criminal justice, and others) found in every society. In contemporary societies, the institutions of law and government are the most important of these institutions in that they can regulate or change other institutions. Over time, the importance of a society's institutions can change; at one point in human history religious leaders exerted considerable power over governments, but that is much less common today.

Organizations: Groups of people who are pursuing common goals within the context of an institutional field. Organizations typically compete with one another, to varying degrees, to shape and influence the institutional field. Businesses are a common type of organization; They compete with one another for profit within a society's economic system.

Institutional field: Within any institution, all of the organizations and groups that are active in shaping or implementing institutional rules and norms. Within the institution field of education, that list would include teachers and teacher unions, individual schools, colleges, and universities, school administrators, superintendents, college and university administrators, local school boards, PTAs or other active parents' groups, schools of education that train teachers and conduct research on education, specialized government organizations concerned with education (in the federal government, the Department of Education and its branches), nonprofit organizations that seek to shape educational policies, and many others.

During the course of countless protests and legal challenges, the conception of what is required for marriage began to change. There is a very good reason why governments and courts of law are so important for the overall social structure of any society (see Table 5.1 for a summary of the core institutional concepts).

Institutional Change

5.3.5 Discuss how institutional change occurs.

Although very powerful in providing an organizational framework for the social world, it is important to keep in mind that institutions are ultimately the creations of human beings, and as such they can be, and sometimes are, reformed or reinvented over time. When institutions undergo significant change, it may come either from above (especially when government or courts of law compel institutions to change) or from below (when individuals, groups, or social movements demand it). For example, because twenty-first century institutions all claim to be designed to provide equality for everyone, every lingering examples of institutional inequality can be the source of conflict and pressure for change. For example, for much of human history, the law and practice of marriage often provided definite advantages to men. For instance, until the latter part of the nineteenth century, married women could not own property in their own name in most parts of the United States. Sexual violence against women, especially if it occurred inside a marriage, was rarely, if ever, treated as criminal by courts of law as rape; it wasn't until 1993 that all 50 states in America had established laws recognizing the possibility of marital rape. Today, marriage and divorce laws in the United States are far more egalitarian than they used to be. Although that is not the case in all countries around the world, pressures everywhere to give women equality in marriage is growing.

The privileged position of law and government institutions in producing institutional change is the other major pathway that change happens, and a key to understanding any society's institutional order. When a new president and Congress are elected, they may decide to pass laws that force institutions to change in some way. Courts of law can do the same thing, by deciding an important case and requiring institutional change. For this reason, many of the efforts that groups and organizations make to change institutions are typically directed *both* inside a particular institutional field (in the case of same-sex marriage, for example, efforts to redefine how we think about the family) *and* through law and government (activists sought both legal and political sources of change to require the recognition of same-sex marriages).

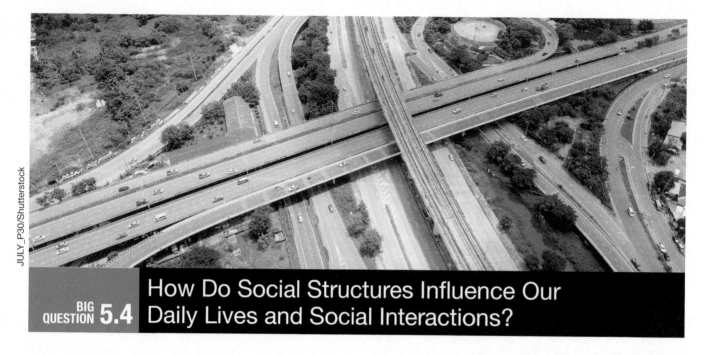

JULY_P30/Shutterstock

THE CONTEXT OF SOCIAL INTERACTION

One of the important questions to consider about social structures is exactly how they penetrate into our thoughts, actions, and interactions with others. How do we acquire knowledge of the powers of social structure? Why, when, and how do social structures shape our daily lives? In this section, we consider some of these issues.

Socialization

5.4.1 Discuss how socialization contributes to the creation of roles and norms.

If roles, hierarchies, norms, and institutions are so important in shaping our identities and social interactions, how do we learn about them? The short answer is through the lessons we receive from parents, teachers and mentors, as well as our own participation in various roles, organizations, and institutional settings. By being exposed to the power of social hierarchies throughout our lives, we learn about and (usually) are compelled to adapt to the basic norms and rules of the society we live in. By participating in organizations, we learn about how institutions work. All college students would probably agree that they know more about the system of higher education *after* they've been in college a couple of years than before they started. We learn as we go along.

At the heart of the transmission of ideas about the importance of conformity in our participation in social life is what is known as socialization. **Socialization** is the process through which we learn how we are expected to behave in society or in particular social settings. It is how we come to understand the expectations and norms of our groups. Throughout our lives, we are constantly being socialized to behave in certain ways (or to not behave

in others). The process begins in families, where parents attempt to teach their children a wide range of different rules and norms and more generally how to apply them. We also learn by practicing; the first time we attempt to do something the "right" way, we may mess it up, but eventually we should get the hang of it. Our parents play key roles early on in teaching us how to do things, beginning right at birth. When an infant sitting in a high chair picks up their food and throws it on the ground and is greeted with a stern "no" from their parents, they are receiving an early message about the importance of being neat and handling food appropriately.

Socialization continues at every stage of the life course and involves learning from many different people, groups, and organizations. Children play games, and these games sometimes involve role playing of one kind or another where children "practice" being adults (Corsaro and Eder 1990). Psychologists who study child development find that these games are vital because they teach children the importance of subscribing to an assigned role, even if only for the purposes of the game at hand. As they get older, children move from play to structured learning environments. Here, among other things, they learn about rules and the need to conform to rules in places like daycares, schools, and the various group activities (including sports) they participate in. As children grow up and begin to organize their own relationships with other children, they have to learn things like how to get along and interact with others. As they move through school, they learn how to do things that will be rewarded—like how to take a test or how to write a paper—and their success in mastering these activities goes a long way toward determining their outcomes in life.

Learning and adapting to new situations and contexts is something everyone has to do throughout their lives; socialization is a never-ending process. Taking a new job, participating in a new activity or hobby, making new friends and entering a new circle of people, or joining a new kind of organization all require the acquisition of new skills and ways of handling ourselves. As we take on new roles, we have to learn new guidelines and rules. There is a saying that "you can't teach an old dog new tricks"; however accurate it may be for dogs, it doesn't apply to humans very well. We continue learning and adapting to new situations until the end of our lives. For example, older people who move into an assisted living facility learn to follow the rules of their new home fairly quickly, even though they have previously lived independently.

Socialization works in large part because the human mind is capable of learning and remembering immensely complicated rules. A simple, but nearly universal, example of how individuals adapt to new situations occurs when we learn how to drive. Driving is not at all the simple process many think it is—cognitive psychologists have shown that learning to drive is mentally challenging in many ways—but it is a skill that almost everyone can eventually master with enough practice. Driving requires us to learn a large set of rules and to be able to apply them in making split-second decisions where mistakes can have large consequences. Our ability to learn those rules and apply them correctly (at least most of the time) is critical to what makes car travel as (relatively) safe as it is.

Learning how to be a parent is one especially complicated role many people take on. Reading a book on parenting or having a nurse at the hospital provide a few instructions on how to breastfeed your child and change their diaper can only help so much. Parents learn how to care for their children by practicing and talking to other parents as well as teachers, counselors, and perhaps their own parents. While what it means to be a "good" parent is widely debated, almost all parents do many caring and good things for their children and try the best they can within the limits of their resources.

Social Structure and Social Interaction

5.4.2 Discuss how social structure exerts influence over our interactions with others.

We are now in a position to examine the multiple ways in which social structure exerts influence over our interactions with others. Through socialization and daily practice, we absorb the rules and norms associated with social structure. As we discussed earlier in the chapter, when we take on new roles, we adapt to the expectations of those roles. We learn about hierarchies and appropriate deference to people in positions of authority. We also learn biases and stereotypes about different groups, and if we are not careful (and do not exercise our sociological imaginations) we will come to adopt those stereotypes, which may subsequently guide (in subtle or explicit ways) our behavior toward others. In the course of conforming to the rules and norms imposed by social structure in our interactions, we make a small contribution toward reproducing social structure!

In Chapter 4, we discussed a number of different examples of how our daily interactions with others are shaped by norms and social rules. But the influence of social structure does not stop there. What happens when we consider interactions within and between organizations? Most organized group activities are governed by internal and external rules of various kinds that shape what they

do. Consider American professional football. There is a set of rules that governs play; these rules are established by the governing body of the sport (the National Football League, in this case), which can be thought of as playing a similar role to a society's government. Within the rules established and enforced by the NFL, teams (organizations) select players and coaches, and coaches (leaders) have developed a small number of different ways to organize play. On the field, a football team consists of different players assigned different responsibilities based on the positions that they play and the plan designed by their coaches. There's the quarterback, the wide receivers, the running backs, the linebackers, the cornerbacks, and so forth. Each of these players, as a result of the position he occupies and the team he plays for, has a specific *role* to play. That is, each of them is expected to do certain things: If you're the quarterback, you had better throw the ball accurately (and not to the other team!), and if you're a wide receiver, you'd better catch the ball when it comes to you. To be sure, individual players have different ways to perform their job, and variation in how well they succeed is what determines which players are "great" and others less so, but the jobs and tasks they perform are still all conducted within the broader rules associated with a particular role.

Social Structure and Individual Free Will

5.4.3 Discuss the relative impact of social structure versus individual choice.

We've seen that social structures are powerful. Indeed, when social scientists write about the powers of social structures, it

American football provides a good example of how social structures guide our interactions with others. On the field and off, each member of the team as well as the coaches have specific roles to play, all of which are governed by the rules of the sport.

have some choices about what we can do, about how we behave and what course of action we might take. And, surely, things can change as a result of human action. New laws are passed, old institutions adopt new rules (and old once are replaced). Social hierarchies change shape as new identities emerge or old privileges are revoked.

Plenty of everyday examples from our own lives make the same point. For example, we can readily observe that two people will often behave very differently even when they find themselves in the same situation. This will be true even if they live in the same society and face the same rules and norms governing their behavior. Take two people who hear someone cry out for help: One may intervene, while another may simply ignore it. Take two investment bankers facing a shortfall in a large investment fund: One may try to raise more money from other investors, the other may illegally move funds from other accounts to cover the losses. A huge body of research makes this point over and over again: People are not robots. They will respond in different and occasionally unpredictable ways, depending on the choices and opportunities confronting them. Such examples and evidence from experiments suggest that people do indeed have some significant measure of individual choice. Philosophers of free will can rest easy; the sociological account of social structure does not mean that all individual choice is irrelevant!

may appear as if they are *too* powerful, with individuals almost becoming robots who fulfill roles and act according to scripts handed down to them. Social structures create positions that are filled by people who are entirely replaceable by other individuals, and have little control over the worlds they inhabit. It can almost seem as if individuals, have no free will of their own, no capacity to choose how to act. If this were the case, society would just reproduce itself in the same shape over and over, and nothing would ever change. But we know from our own experiences that this is not true. Of course we

BIG QUESTION 5.5 Why Are Social Structures Slow to Change?

THE ENDURANCE OF SOCIAL STRUCTURES

Earlier in the chapter, we noted that institutions are human creations, and they can evolve and change. So too can societies alter social hierarchies to prevent discrimination

and injustices in which one group is given preferential treatment. Social change is important and essential. But it doesn't happen very often. One of the hallmark features of social structures is their endurance. People come and go, but roles/social hierarchies and norms/institutions continue to operate more or less as they always have. The authors of this book, professors at a particular university (New York University), all know that eventually they will retire and be replaced; this will happen at all other colleges and universities. And it is very likely these universities will continue to exist more or less as they do today, even as new people with new ideas come along. This raises an important question: Why are social structures so persistent? Or to put it more bluntly, why do those parts of the social structure that many people come to think are unfair persist for long periods of time? There are a number of answers to these questions that we will explore in this section, beginning with the process known as path dependency.

Path Dependency

5.5.1 Explain how past outcomes impact present choices.

Social structures persist in part because earlier developments and institutionalization make it much easier for individuals to work within them than to try to rip them apart. This process is commonly known as **path dependency**, or more specifically, the ways in which outcomes of the past impact actors and organizations in the present, making some choices or outcomes logical and others illogical. A classical example of this is the QWERTY keyboard. Nobody in their right mind today would invent an English-language keyboard laid out the way the keys are, with many of the most commonly used letters placed in hard-to-reach locations. Yet attempts to replace the QWERTY keyboard have always failed. Why? One answer is simply that in order to use any keyboard, more or less everyone learns to navigate the QWERTY layout. Switching to a better-designed and more efficient keyboard layout, like the system designed by August Dvorak in 1936 (see the photos), will be initially time consuming and costly, and even if you were willing to master the other keyboard, every time you use a friend's computer or any device like a smartphone that

has a QWERTY layout, you will have to unlearn your new keystrokes and go back to the QWERTY. And if you practice enough on the new machine, your fingers will develop a different kind of muscle memory that will make it hard to go back and forth. So instead of switching to a new keyboard, we struggle with the one we are used to.

Path dependency, as the QWERTY example suggests, rests on the simple idea that any path, once adopted, is extraordinarily difficult to reverse (Pierson 2000). In other words, what has happened in the past sets limits on what is possible today or in the future. Path dependency is a historical process, one that is closely tied up with how and why particular norms and institutions come to be established, and, once established, are difficult to change. Studying the development of many institutions over long historical periods suggests a rough model that is displayed in Figure 5.4. For long periods of time, there may be many different ways of doing things, and no one approach is dominant. Indeed, in the early phase of the development of any component part of the social structure, a disorganized and seemingly random process of human interaction may exist. Almost anything goes. It takes time for norms and institutions to take root and develop. But at some critical point, things begin to change, often in response to a single key event that establishes a new norm, rule, or way of doing things, and institutions may emerge to organize and maintain it. This phase is sometimes described as the "critical juncture," in that the range of possible actions begins to narrow. Finally, as more and more people and groups get used to doing things a certain way, a third phase can emerge, known as the "lock-in." From that point on, changes will be sharply limited by the rules, norms, and institutions that are now firmly in place and difficult to dislodge. Figure 5.4 provides a hypothetical visual image of how path dependency develops, as the wide range of possibilities in Phase 1 declines, narrows in the second phase, and then finally "locks in" in the third phase.

A new typewriter keyboard layout devised by August Dvorak in the 1930s. Although its layout is much more efficient and easier to use (once mastered) than the standard QWERTY keyboard—for English writers, it places 70 percent of the most commonly used letters in the main row, versus 32 percent of the standard keyboard—very few people use it today. It's an example of what sociologists call path dependency, the idea that once something becomes established as a standard, it is very hard to change it.

The history of the U.S. Constitution provides a dramatic example of how path dependence works. In colonial history, people in small towns experimented with different ways of organizing democracy and establishing rules for governing themselves. There were only a few examples from other places the early colonists could draw on, so they made up the rules as they went along, and the process was pretty messy at first (Phase I). After the successful conclusion of the Revolutionary War against the British, and one failed attempt at a national constitution (the Articles of Confederation), a group of leaders from the various colonies began to draft a new constitution, which was completed in 1787 and ratified by the 13 colonies in 1789 (Dahl 2003). This "critical juncture," or narrowing phase (Phase II), put in place a single constitutional system that became the "law of the land." The Constitution as it was initially drafted was in many ways a remarkable document, envisioning an entirely new form of democratic government that was quite different from anything that had existed previously around the world. But it was also filled with ideas that later were rejected (such as various clauses that assumed slavery would continue forever) and has been amended many times.

In recent decades, formal amendments have been rare (there have been no new amendments passed since 1971). The U.S. Supreme Court serves as the ultimate arbiter of the Constitution, applying and adjusting as new cases and challenges arise, but always justifying its decisions within the framework of the original document (Phase III). Legal and political disagreements over the Constitution mean that there is always room for interpretation, but at the same time the Constitution prevents, or makes very difficult, dramatic departures from established legal practice. For example, the Constitution sets up institutions of democracy that make it very hard for more than two political parties to win seats in Congress. Unlike later innovations in democracy developed in other countries, where the seats are divided up among parties based on the percentage of votes each party receives at each election, U.S. elections for Congress take place in either districts (House

elections) or in individual states (Senate elections). Each district or state elects the person who gets the most votes. This makes it difficult for a small party trying to build up support by getting a small percentage of the votes and seats and then more over time, as is possible in most other democracies that award seats on a proportional basis. In fact, dozens and dozens of third parties have tried and failed to break the stranglehold of the two major parties (the Democratic and Republican parties) since the Civil War (Rosenstone, et al. 1996). It would hardly be controversial to say that we are now seemingly locked in to a two-party system, and have been, with but one big exception (the rise of the Republican Party in the 1850s). Almost everyone agrees that more political competition and additional parties would be valuable, but Americans are saddled with political institutions that make it exceptionally difficult for that happen.

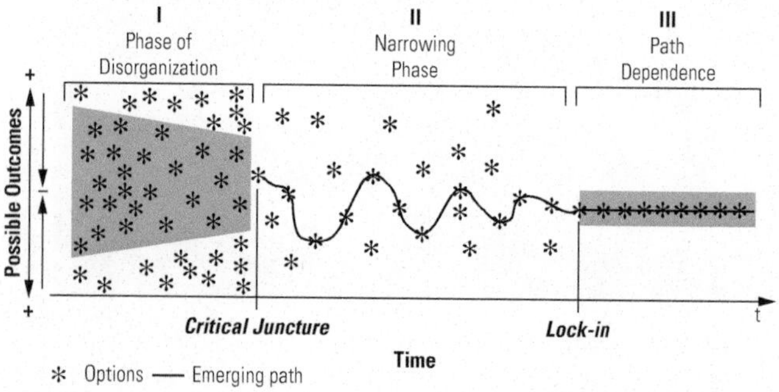

How Social Structures Persist

5.5.2 Analyze the power of path-dependent processes.

The idea of path dependence is important, but we need to develop an understanding of why it is so powerful. What are the processes and mechanics of path dependence? Social structures tend to persist over time for a number of concrete reasons. An important place to start is with individuals: We all play a role in reproducing social structure through our everyday actions that conform to existing norms, expectations, and institutional rules. When we obey the commands of hierarchy without challenging it, we tacitly accept it as reality and inadvertently help to maintain it. We don't realize it unless we think about it, but by simply following the scripts and rules that social structure provides in our daily actions and interactions, we are helping to reproduce social structure. When we stand in line without cutting, we are confirming norms of "waiting your turn." When we refer to someone as "Dr. Ramirez" rather than "Ms. Ramirez," we are confirming the special status of "Dr. Ramirez" and the institutions that have conferred status and title.

Another reason social structures persist is political: Once a particular element of social structure comes to be established, be it either roles/hierarchies or norms/institutions, it may generate its own **interest groups**, that is, organizations established to promote the concerns of groups or businesses that are related to a particular institutional arena. These interest groups will fight to protect and extend existing social arrangements when they are viewed as beneficial to their members. The fact that both the Democratic and Republican Parties have fought to prevent changing the Constitution to a different electoral system that might make it easier for smaller parties to be competitive is one example of this. However much the two major parties may disagree with one another, they can

Figure 5.4 Path Dependency

* Options —— Emerging path

We follow both social scripts and explicit rules when we go through airport security. The scripts, such as waiting your turn in line, go way back. But the rules of travel have changed in the United States and many other countries around the world since the 9/11 terrorist attacks.

agree on one thing: Let's not make it easy for any new parties to take our place. We've also already discussed how this works in the maintenance of social hierarchies, where members of a dominant group have strong incentives to organize themselves to maintain their privileges.

Similar dynamics exist in many organizations and institutions. For example, organizations create jobs, and the workers in those jobs have incentives to try to maintain the organization. Proposals to cut the budgets for any of the organizations in an institutional field—such as schools, the military, prisons, and so forth—are routinely met with strong opposition from those who have jobs and currently draw an income from one of those organizations. Similarly, even people who do not work for an organization but benefit from it in some way will often resist any changes

to it. Not just police officers will oppose cuts to the police force; citizens who fear an increase in crime can easily be mobilized to fight police budget cuts as well. The slogan "defund the police" (which is really a call to redirect some anti-crime spending away from law enforcement to other kinds of crime prevention spending) is deeply unpopular because it challenges both the jobs of police officers *and* public perceptions about how to stop crime. When a local church is threatened with closure, both the members of the church as well as the clergy who might lose their positions are likely to rally in support.

Finally, and perhaps most importantly, social structures also persist simply because there is often broad public support for existing roles/hierarchies and norms/institutions, or fear of the consequences of dramatic change. We are frequently more comfortable living within the worlds we know and trying to make them better in small ways, rather than opting for something radically new. The expression "you are better off with the devil you know than the one you don't" is the commonsense version of this idea, and it expresses a powerful reality that social psychologists have called "risk aversion" (Kahneman 2011). Of course, not everyone feels completely averse to change all the time, and under extreme or unusual conditions, large numbers of people can and sometimes do opt to try to tear down parts of the social structure rather than reform it. But most of the time, however often we might complain about it, we tend to accept the status quo or try to reform in small ways the parts that are not working rather than trying to tear it down.

Conclusion: Social Structure and the Complexity of Social Change

Social structures are everywhere around us, and they matter deeply. Writing about the social and political upheavals in France in the middle of the nineteenth century, Karl Marx opened a famous little book he wrote on French politics by declaring that "Men make their own history, but not under circumstances of their own choosing." Setting aside the sexist language (typical for Marx's day), few clearer expressions of the importance of social structures can be found.

When he wrote that sentence, Marx was thinking about nineteenth-century France, but his idea really applies

to all of us. Our ability to act, and the choices we make, are always limited by the circumstances in which we find ourselves. We noted in the chapter's introduction that Inge Deutschkron would not have been Jewish but for the rise of Adolf Hitler and the Nazi government's racial laws. She did not become Jewish because she suddenly discovered religion. Rather, she was forced to completely alter her life and her self-understanding and identity because of an arbitrary and external decision imposed upon her. There are many similar, if less dramatic, examples all around us. We will begin to notice these sources of constraint once we understand the deep logic of social structures. Throughout our lives, we are continually making choices shaped by the existing roles and hierarchies, on the one hand, and existing norms and institutions on the other. We are never completely free of the constraints of social structure.

Fortunately, social structures that are in conflict with emerging societal realities or the needs of ordinary people can change, even if the pace of change may be very slow. If we go back far enough and study social structures historically, we will find many examples of how hierarchies and institutions have changed more dramatically over time. Throughout the rest of this book, we will consider important changes to social structure in different areas of social life. For example, in Chapter 13, we will discuss in much more detail how the racial hierarchy has proved permeable and has shifted over time. In Chapter 14, we will consider a variety of ways in which gender and sexuality have shifted over time, becoming somewhat more egalitarian between men and women and, in a process which is ongoing, more accepting of gays and lesbians and nontraditional forms of sexual and social intimacy. In other chapters, we will look at how the market economy has changed in dramatic ways since the nineteenth century (Chapter 9), as well as how schools (Chapter 18), religious

institutions (Chapter 17), immigration (Chapter 24), health care (Chapter 19), and criminal justice (Chapter 20) have all evolved in important ways over time.

For now, however, we can note one very important general point. Behind many of the most important changes to social structure are politics: subordinate groups demanding fairer or more equitable treatment and institutions responding to demands of their members to respond to changes that occur elsewhere in society. The powerful usually can protect their interests in maintaining the status quo, but sometimes subordinate groups win changes. In particular, when subordinate groups organize themselves into *social movements,* a topic we treat in detail in Chapter 22, they are in a better position to challenge hierarchies in various ways.

Understanding social structures is central to the larger project of the sociological imagination. Sociologists pay so much attention to trying to understand the different elements of social structure, and where and why they limit the possibilities for improving the human condition, out of a recognition that only by understanding these underlying structures can we develop appropriate understandings and make meaningful progress in addressing the pressing social problems of society.

The Big Questions Revisited 5

5.1 **What Is Social Structure?** Why do sociologists reject the view that the world is simply made up of a collection of individuals? In this section, we introduced the concept of social structure and explored how it is very much like the structure of a tall building—normally hidden from view, but essential to what is possible to build. The key elements of social structure (roles and hierarchies, and norms and institutions) were introduced.

Social Structure as the Context of Human Action

The Architecture of Social Structure
Learning Objective 5.1.1: Explain how social structure can be thought of in architectural terms.

Key Components of Social Structure
Learning Objective 5.1.2: Identify the two key components of social structure.

Key Term
social structure (p. 107)

5.2 **How Do Roles and Social Hierarchies Shape Our Life Chances?** The social structure of any society consists of a wide range of different roles and social divisions, or hierarchies, between groups. In this section, we explored where these various roles and social hierarchies come from and why they matter.

The First Dimension of Social Structure: Roles and Social Hierarchies

Roles
Learning Objective 5.2.1: Identify individual roles and role conflicts that exist.

Group Identities
Learning Objective 5.2.2: Explain how group identities are formed and their relationship to social hierarchies.

Power and Privilege in Social Hierarchies
Learning Objective 5.2.3: Discuss the roles that power and privilege play in social hierarchies.

Population Size and Social Hierarchies
Learning Objective 5.2.4: Explain the impact that

population size has on the ways in which groups within a social hierarchy relate to one another.

Economic Change and Social Hierarchies

Learning Objective 5.2.5: Describe how economic changes can impact individual lives.

Key Terms
role (p. 109)   role theory (p. 109)   role conflict (p. 110)   life course (p. 110)   social hierarchies (p. 110)   status group (p. 111)   schemas (p. 111)   power (p. 112)   privilege (p. 112)   social closure (p. 112)   discrimination (p. 112)   social movement (p. 112)   stereotypes (p. 113)   migration (p. 114)   Great Migration (p. 114)   urbanization (p. 115)   white-collar jobs (p. 115)   post-industrial economy (p. 116)

5.3   How Do Norms and Institutions Influence Social Life? A society's social structure also contains an elaborate set of norms and institutions. This section explored some of the central aspects of norms and institutions and why they influence our behavior.

The Second Dimension of Social Structure: The Powers of Norms and Institutions

Norms and Rules

Learning Objective 5.3.1: Distinguish between social norms and formal rules of behavior.

Where Do Formal Rules Come From?

Learning Objective 5.3.2: Describe the tragedy of the commons and the origin of rules.

Institutions and the Patterning of Social Life

Learning Objective 5.3.3: Explain the process of institutionalization and identify examples of common practices that have been institutionalized.

The Institutional Order

Learning Objective 5.3.4: Explain the importance of laws and government in establishing the institutional order in society.

Institutional Change

Learning Objective 5.3.5: Discuss how institutional change occurs.

Key Terms
tragedy of the commons (p. 118)   institutionalization (p. 119)   organizations (p. 119)   curriculum (p. 119)   institutional order (p. 120)   institutional fields (p. 120)

5.4   How Do Social Structures Influence Our Daily Lives and Social Interactions? Where do the identities and roles that are so important for social interaction come from? How do changes in social structure influence social interaction? Does acknowledging the existence of social structure mean we have limited free will?

The Context of Social Interaction

Socialization

Learning Objective 5.4.1: Discuss how socialization contributes to the creation of roles and norms.

Social Structure and Social Interaction

Learning Objective 5.4.2: Discuss how social structure exerts influence over our interactions with others.

Social Structure and Individual Free Will

Learning Objective 5.4.3: Discuss the relative impact of social structure versus individual choice.

Key Term
socialization (p. 122)

5.5   Why Are Social Structures Slow to Change? Why and how do social structures change? In this section, we explored the forces that hold societies and social structures together and why change in social structure is relatively slow.

The Endurance of Social Structures

Path Dependency

Learning Objective 5.5.1: Explain how past outcomes impact present choices.

How Social Structures Persist

Learning Objective 5.5.2: Analyze the power of path-dependent processes.

Key Terms
path dependency (p. 125)   interest groups (p. 127)

Chapter 6
Environment and Society

by Colin Jerolmack

In the remote and rugged region of northwestern Alaska, on a small island separated from the coast by five miles of choppy Arctic waters, lies the village of Shishmaref. While roughly 600 indigenous Inupiat inhabitants enjoy some of the conveniences of modern living, such as television and snowmobiles, many maintain a traditional lifestyle in which they obtain the necessities of life through hunting, fishing, and bartering. For centuries, the Inupiat of Shishmaref and the mainland have developed and relied on a vast stock of knowledge about animal migration patterns, ocean currents, and seasonal variations in ice thickness in order to persevere in such an unforgiving climate. However, in recent years their environment has changed in rapid and threatening ways. Since 1979, more than 30 percent of the polar ice cap has melted as a result of rising global temperatures, and scientists project that summer Arctic sea ice could disappear entirely by 2030. The Inupiat fear that their livelihoods, their villages, and their culture will vanish along with the glaciers.

These days, the sea surrounding Shishmaref freezes later and thaws earlier than ever before. With the decrease in sea ice, which forms a protective barrier around the island, Shishmaref has become vulnerable to storm surges. Large waves eat away 10 miles of the coast every year and literally pull houses out to sea. Lacking the resources to fortify the island perimeter, villagers voted in 2016 to abandon their homes and relocate to the mainland. Many residents worry about the loss of their community and way of life, and the state government worries about who will pay the estimated $200 million cost of building a new village and moving all the residents.

Several years ago, I traveled to northwestern Alaska to study the consequences of climate change for indigenous people. My guide was Caleb Pungowiyi, a resident of the town of Kotzebue and a senior advisor to Oceana, a nonprofit ocean conservation organization. Caleb did not need to look at the annual reports on sea ice retreat to determine

that exceptional global warming is occurring—he could look to his backyard. Hunting expeditions, and travel in general, have been curtailed because snowmobiles are falling through ice that once was rock solid. Hotter, drier summers are leading to a rash of brush fires. Permafrost—the eternally frozen earth under the tundra that holds the landscape together—is melting, leading to coastal erosion, landslides, and sinkholes that are destabilizing towns and swallowing up houses. As animals such as caribou and

My Sociological Imagination

COLIN JEROLMACK

As a beginning graduate student interested in city life, I spent a lot of time wandering around the streets of New York City's Greenwich Village. I was particularly drawn to neighborhood parks that were undergoing renovations because the process of deciding how to redesign the parks afforded a window into how community members used, imagined, and complained about their public spaces. I was surprised to learn that many civic associations and park users complained about pigeons, whose feces made park benches unusable and posed a potential disease threat. However, in observing public behavior, I saw that pigeon feeding was a popular activity among park visitors. I realized that urban wildlife impacted how people interpreted and experienced their public spaces, for better and for worse. Over time, I became fascinated by the ways the natural environment shaped city life, and I came to see that people's responses to urban wildlife revealed how they draw boundaries between environment and society. Because of the humble pigeon, I developed a passion for environmental sociology without even leaving the metropolis.

The coast of northwestern Alaska is crumbling into the sea as global warming melts the frozen earth that glues the landscape together. Shown here, a home destroyed by beach erosion tips over in the Alaskan village of Shishmaref.

bearded seals adjust their migration and mating habits in response to warming temperatures, hunting becomes a less reliable means of securing food.

Given the high cost of groceries that must be flown in from Anchorage and the lack of steady jobs, indigenous Alaskans are caught in a double bind: Their traditional lifestyle may soon cease to be viable, but there are few feasible alternatives. The future of this region likely holds many more scenarios like Shishmaref—impoverished and politically marginalized communities forced to abandon their ancestral homes and many of their customs in the face of global warming.

Though the evidence for climate change may not yet be as obvious for most Americans, in the extreme conditions of the Arctic the signs of global warming are clearly recognizable. While scientists compile records to demonstrate that the changes occurring in Alaska and elsewhere are unprecedented, the Inupiat already know this to be true because of the unprecedented challenges they face on a daily basis as they struggle to secure their existence.

Sociology is usually thought of as the study of what Emile Durkheim, one of the founders of sociology, called "social facts." However, we have come to understand in the twenty-first century that it is impossible to understand and explain social life without accounting for humans' relationship to the natural world. The plight of indigenous Alaskans makes apparent the ways that society simultaneously shapes and is shaped by the physical environment. While their traditional lifestyle and culture were forged as adaptations to their natural world, the contemporary environmental crisis that threatens to overwhelm the Inupiat has social origins. There is now a consensus in mainstream environmental science that much of the global warming we are witnessing is the result of burning fossil fuels. Environmental problems, then, have both societal causes and social consequences. There is another sense in which the predicament of the Inupiat is emblematic of environment–society relations: People of color and the poor have historically suffered the most from environmental degradation. The costs of environmental problems are unevenly distributed, reflecting and reproducing social inequality.

The Big Questions

1. **How does social life relate to the natural environment?** Environmental sociologists study the *interaction* between environmental facts and social facts and emphasize their interdependency (Freudenberg and Gramling 1989). Every society consumes and transforms the natural environment to satisfy its needs and desires, yet every society must also adapt to its physical surroundings and confront natural limits. And while there is an objective natural world "out there," how we interpret and interact with it is always influenced by cultural, political, and economic processes.

2. **How has human activity harmed the environment?** The most pressing environmental problems of our time—such as deforestation, water pollution, and global warming—are the results of human activities. Finding solutions to these problems will require collective social action, and making those solutions equitable may prove to be the biggest challenge of all.

3. **How do environmental factors impact inequality?** Consider the devastating natural disaster Hurricane Katrina, which overwhelmed New Orleans's levees in 2005, killing 2,000 people and displacing more than 1 million. As the storm menaced the Gulf Coast, wealthier residents were able to evacuate because they had automobiles and the finances to pay for hotel rooms. The poorest residents—many of whom were Black—did not have the means to get out and became stranded in their homes as the water rose. As a result, they were disproportionately represented in the storm's death toll. When sociologists examine environmental catastrophes like Katrina, they ask: How does the structure of society shape the effects of these natural events?

4. **How can we create more sustainable societies?** As the global population expands and environmental degradation worsens, it seems that there are simply not enough natural resources for every human being on Earth to use as much oil and electricity, and dispose of as much waste, as citizens of wealthy nations currently do. How can members of rich countries be convinced to adopt more sustainable lifestyles? And how can we enact international environmental regulations yet still help developing countries increase their standard of living through industry?

Accent Alaska.com/Alamy Stock Photo

BIG QUESTION 6.1 How Does Social Life Relate to the Natural Environment?

UNDERSTANDING ENVIRONMENT-SOCIETY RELATIONS

Many social transformations have accompanied the transition of societies from traditional to modern forms: Capitalism supplanted feudalism, people migrated from small villages to large cities, the division of labor intensified, close-knit communities gave way to mass societies characterized by impersonal and contractual ties, and so on. Yet as societies went through these dramatic social changes, their relationship to the physical environment was also rapidly transformed. In fact, many social theorists have concluded that the transition of societies from traditional to modern forms was, to a large degree, driven by the development of technology that enabled the greater exploitation of natural resources.

Classical sociologists writing more than 100 years ago, like Karl Marx and Max Weber, considered resource scarcity and environmental degradation to be important natural constraints on how societies could develop. More than a half-century before the coining of the term "global warming," Weber presciently observed in 1920 that all societies must learn how to adapt to "climatic changes" (quoted in Foster and Holleman 2012, p. 630). Although in the intervening period the environment–society relationship received reduced attention, since the 1990s environmental sociologists have been doing important research on that relationship. This sociological scholarship has seen the economy–society relationship as dynamic and interdependent, and they have sought to understand how it varies over time and across social contexts, as well as how

climate change and other environmental issues are changing social life today, and will continue to do so in the future.

Traditional Societies

6.1.1 Explain how a society's environment contributes to the cultural and religious traditions it develops.

The term *primitive*, though sometimes considered to have a negative meaning, can be usefully employed to think about how traditional societies typically interacted with their environment. *Primitive* evokes the image of preindustrial societies in which people live close to the land, build simple homes out of natural materials, rely on their feet for transportation, hunt and gather, make only superficial changes to the environment, and consider nature to be sacred.

The field of anthropology was born over a century ago out of the study of these societies. As Western powers colonized far-flung regions of Africa and Latin America, they encountered people who lived much like the hypothetical "primitive" society described above. Anthropologists lived among these strangers in order to understand their cultures and lifestyles. Here were people, it seemed, virtually untouched by the forces of modernization. And here were societies characterized by a lack of control over, and a dependence on, nature. These environment–society relations structured their cultural and religious systems.

The anthropologist Bronislaw Malinowski (1948) spent the years surrounding World War I observing native culture in the Trobriand Islands of the Western Pacific. He noticed that the islanders performed elaborate ceremonial rites before they set out on fishing expeditions in the ocean, but that such rituals were entirely absent from their fishing trips in the lagoon. The reason for this difference was simple. Fish were plentiful in the lagoon, and the waters were calm. Thus, islanders could predict that fishing would be safe and produce a high yield. The yields from ocean fishing were far less predictable, and such trips could be treacherous. Facing a situation that was out of their control, they resorted to magic to try to bring a sense of order and predictability to the natural world. This finding seemed to explain many of the systems of magic that anthropologists found in traditional cultures, and it helped explain the relative absence of these systems in modern societies, which tame nature through the application of science.

Social scientists noted another common feature of traditional societies—they often attributed spiritual significance to nature. Emile Durkheim, another of the founders of sociology, produced one of the most well-known explanations of "primitive" religion based on his study of Native tribes in Australia. He noted that these tribes were organized into clans based on spiritual rather than blood kinship, with each clan adopting a particular plant or animal—called a totem—as the symbol of the clan. Clans considered their totem plants or animals to be sacred, and so killing and consuming them was generally taboo. Clans inscribed ceremonial objects with the emblem of their totem, which made these objects sacred as well. This belief system, called **totemism**, was common among many indigenous groups—including Native Americans.

Durkheim realized that it was only once plants or animals became a symbol of the clan that they were elevated to the status of sacred. He took this as evidence that the Native tribes did not actually consider nature to be divine. Rather, the totem was sacred because it stood for the clan. Durkheim did not think that the Native tribes were as different from modern societies as they first appeared. Every society has its sacred objects and rituals that help bring together its members as a community. Americans, for instance, salute the flag and play the national anthem before sporting or other events. "Primitive" people chose animals and plants as their sacred objects, Durkheim believed, simply because their lifestyles were intimately connected to nature (Durkheim 1915).

Modern Societies

6.1.2 Discuss the ways in which modern societies gained more control over their environment and developed stratified social structures.

As natural forces came to be more understandable and predictable through the accumulation of scientific knowledge, the environment became a safer, more useful, and more urban place. Humans ceased to be the playthings of nature, applying technology to exert greater control over their surroundings. The first step in this process was the agricultural revolution. Through animal and plant domestication and the invention of the plow, tangled forests gave way to manicured fields. Irrigation channels reduced humans' dependency on rainfall. Permanent settlements sprang up, trade intensified, and roads were developed.

The next great technological leap was the Industrial Revolution, ushered in by the discovery of the process of "coking" coal and the invention of the steam engine. While the Industrial Revolution gave rise to modern capitalism, it was—as Karl Marx and Friedrich Engels ([1846] 1977) observed—founded on the "subjection of nature's forces to man." Entire forests (and animal habitats) were destroyed for their lumber, mountains were leveled to expose coal seams, holes were punched deep into the Earth's surface to extract oil, rivers were dammed and rerouted, fields were smothered in cement, and smokestacks blackened daylight skies. Animals were captured on an unprecedented scale to serve as involuntary laborers, or killed to satiate a growing desire for cheap meat or simply because they came to be viewed as pests (Dietz and York 2015).

We have used technology to alter our environment in seemingly miraculous ways. Projects such as the diversion of the Colorado River westward through almost 300 miles of tunnels, dams, and aqueducts made possible the transformation

In Papua New Guinea, indigenous societies were traditionally organized into clans that each adopted a particular animal as the sacred symbol—or totem—of the group. We can find traces of totemism in modern societies as well, such as when sports teams use an animal as their mascot and group name.

Deco/Alamy Stock Photo

of a bone-dry desert into the expansive metropolis of Los Angeles; the city of Chicago even succeeded in permanently reversing the directional flow of its river so that sewage and industrial toxins were carried away from the city. The capacity to alter nature to enhance the Industrial Revolution hastened urbanization (the movement of people into cities). Cities became the centers of industry, and the advent of trains and highways allowed people to fill in the countryside with sprawling suburbs.

In *The Communist Manifesto*, Marx and Engels argued that "the whole internal structure" of a society, including the "nature of individuals," was dependent on the extent to which its members could harness technology to transform natural resources into social goods (Marx and Engels [1848] 2011, p. 161) (2011:161). The lack of productive technology of early hunter–gatherer societies, they believed, kept the social structure of these groups very simple. There was little division of labor—perhaps just one chief who had authority over everyone else—because almost all of the members of a tribe had to busy themselves with looking for food sources. Because everybody performed the same tasks, there was little individuality. Once humans began to transform vast stretches of forests into fields through agriculture, a more complex social structure could develop. Eventually, with enhancements in productivity, a division of labor emerged because it only took a fraction of a society's members to produce enough food for everyone. Other members could be enlisted to produce tools or serve as warriors. An elite class also began to take shape as those who owned the agricultural food surpluses—and the land—could translate these resources into economic power.

As societies moved from agriculture to the production of goods, made possible on a grand scale by fossil fuels and the technological advances of the Industrial Revolution, their social structure became even more stratified. A sophisticated division of labor emerged as peasants migrated to cities to work for a wage, and factory owners maximized efficiency by dividing up the job of a single skilled artisan into discrete tasks that could be carried out by a team of relatively unskilled workers.

Marx and Engels's thesis leaves us with a puzzle: Why did some societies develop more quickly than others? Why, for example, did the Industrial Revolution take place in western Europe and not southern Africa? The influential geographer Jared Diamond argues that global inequalities emerged in prehistoric times and are rooted in differences in people's environments—namely, geographic differences in the availability of naturally occurring food sources (Diamond 1997).

Diamond provides a compelling illustration of his thesis in New Zealand. A thousand years ago, the favorable climate of present-day New Zealand enabled a group of Polynesian settlers known as the Maori to develop a thriving agricultural society. At one point, a group of Maori moved to the Chatham Islands. For hundreds of years, this society—which became known as the Moriori—remained isolated from the Maori on the mainland. But because the Chatham Islands did not support the tropical crops that the Moriori brought with them, they reverted back to the hunting-and-gathering lifestyle of their preagricultural ancestors. Because natural resources were so scarce, the Moriori remained a small society with little division of labor. Meanwhile, the Maori continued to improve their agricultural technology so that they could support many people. Population density and resource abundance spawned a division of labor: a stratum (or segment of society) of craft- and tool-making specialists, a group of political leaders, and a warrior class. Over time, the Maori invaded and conquered other societies and acquired new technologies from them, such as guns. Everything came around full circle in 1835, when the Maori arrived in the Chatham Islands with axes, guns, and other weapons. Finding a tiny, peaceable society with simple technology and a rudimentary political system, the Maori slaughtered and enslaved the Moriori with ease.

Though cut from the same cloth, in the intervening centuries the Maori and Moriori developed in different directions based on adaptations to their environment. Diamond contends that the societies around the globe that developed the fastest were those graced with an abundance of plants and animals that could be readily domesticated. Many parts of Europe and Asia (particularly western Asia in the region known as the Fertile Crescent) naturally possessed many of the large mammals that could be domesticated—horses, pigs, cows, and sheep—as well as many of the cereals and grains that became the backbone of agriculture, such as wheat. As these societies flourished and modernized, they settled new places, conquered the locals, and brought their technology, animals, and crops with them. This is the modern history of the Americas, whose relatively resource-deprived and preindustrial indigenous societies met their demise at the hands of technologically advanced invaders from Europe.

Our society is now a long way from the world of rain dances and enchanted forests. As the German sociologist Max Weber famously observed one hundred years ago, the cold, hard rationality of science and economics drained the natural world of magic and mysticism. Modern societies primarily view the environment as a source of natural resources. And their success at taming and exploiting it encourages cultural attitudes of humans as separate from, and superior to, the natural world—a belief called **anthropocentrism** (literally, "man in the middle"). In an influential essay, pioneering environmental sociologists William Catton and Riley Dunlap (1980) lamented that the field of sociology itself is rife with anthropocentrism. For the most part, the discipline has "systematically cordoned off the realm of the social from that of the biophysical" (Foster and Holleman 2012, p. 1626). A common presumption is that humans in technologically advanced societies are exempt from environmental influences. That premise was always false: Nature has played a major role in shaping every society. But in a climate-changed world, this reality is becoming impossible to ignore. NYU sociologist Eric Klinenberg and his colleagues (2020, p. 651) argue that "all manner of subfields" in sociology, from race and ethnicity to politics to cities, will soon be forced to "grapple with climate concerns."

The Environment–Society Dialogue

6.1.3 Explain determinism and social constructivism and the ways in which environment both guides and constrains social life.

Marx, Engels, and Diamond are sometimes labeled **determinists** because their theories imply that a society's environment, or the technology that it has developed to exploit its environment, determines everything else—from its social structure to individuals' thoughts. But it is perhaps more appropriate to say that they view material conditions as the most fruitful *starting point* for understanding the development of society. Marx and Engels's conception of social change is in fact rooted in the assumption that there is a reciprocal relationship between environmental and social conditions. The transition from an agricultural to a capitalistic mode of production, for example, was realized through social revolutions that reorganized society around commodity production.

Though most scholars reject the argument that the environment is the most important determinant of social structure, the notion that the environment guides and constrains social life has become an important part of recent sociological thought, as it was early in sociology's history. For example, in the early 1900s an influential group of sociologists at the University of Chicago turned to **ecology**—the branch of science that studies the relationship between organisms and their environment—to explain the physical and social organization of modern cities. They examined how natural landscape features like rivers served as both resources and barriers that dictated where industries were placed and how city streets were laid out. Further, these Chicago sociologists saw the city as the "natural habitat of civilized man," in which various sections of the city were akin to ecological niches (Park and Burgess 1925, p. 2). Human behavior, they believed, could be largely understood as social adaptations to a particular urban area: Ethnic and neighborhood conflict was rooted in competition for scarce resources, such as jobs, and deviance was largely a product of living in derelict slums—not individual pathology.

Today, urban sociologists continue to explore the ways that the built environment shapes behavior and social outcomes, such as important recent studies on the effect that one's neighborhood – and it's enviornmental conditions – have on their chances for upward mobility in life. And environmental sociologists continue to explore how natural resources shape community life, such as my own recent study of how the extraction of shale gas in central Pennsylvania is creating social conflict and degrading communal resources (Jerolmack 2021). Beliefs, values, and ideas also play an important role in guiding environment–society relations. For instance, there is evidence that the Europeans who settled the Americas committed wanton environmental destruction, slaughtering wildlife and burning forests in excess of their material needs, because they viewed the untamed wilderness as alien and literally God-forsaken. They aimed to reproduce the "civilized" pastoral landscapes of their beloved European countryside (Taylor 1998).

Complementing the urban-focused subfield of human ecology, **rural sociology** emerged in the first half of the twentieth century. Some of the early work by rural sociologists focused on understanding how social groups living outside of cities and employed mostly in agriculture had lives that were structured and constrained by natural resources and the landscape. Before modern technology enabled farmers to adjust better to changing environmental conditions, farmers and entire farm communities were often at the mercy of nature. Their livelihoods depended on adequate rain and predictable temperatures; when these varied in unpredictable ways, entire crops could be destroyed, threatening financial ruin.

Why do different people interpret the environment differently? The value a person places on the environment often depends on their position in society. Take the Amazon rainforest. The multinational lumber company sees a profitable commodity to be harvested, environmentalists see a priceless natural sanctuary to be left untouched, and the few remaining indigenous communities see a home that enables their physical and spiritual well-being. The profit-seekers' orientation encourages them to cut down the forest, while the preservationists' orientation encourages them to protect it against any human incursion. Where do these differing orientations come from? The answer, many sociologists argue, can be found by studying the social contexts in which environment–society interactions are embedded. Research shows, for example, that people's socioeconomic status and political orientation strongly condition whether or not they believe scientific claims about climate change or whether they consider human-induced ecological disruptions to be a problem at all (Taylor and Buttel 1992). More specifically, conservatives are far more likely than liberals to support environmentally destructive land uses and minimize the risks associated with them, and to deny that human activity contributes to climate change (Jacques et al. 2008; Mayer 2017).

To get a handle on how social contexts shape people's interactions with the environment, sociologist Rik Scarce documented the conflict that erupted over the reintroduction of the gray wolf into Yellowstone Park. In sociological terms, he was interested in the **social construction** of the environment—the process by which the natural world was interpreted and made meaningful to people who lived in the vicinity of the park. In an era that celebrates the restoration of ecosystems to their original state, the return of once-endangered gray wolves was a feel-good story to many people. But Scarce found that local farmers had a different view. One concern was economic: Wolves would eat their livestock. But their animosity toward the wolves ran deeper. For years, farmers felt that their community was slowly being undermined by the growing presence of wealthy neighbors who valued the area only for its wilderness and did not involve themselves in local life. This feeling led farmers to interpret the reintroduction of gray wolves as a misguided effort by "outsiders" to impose their will on the local community (Scarce 2005).

People's attitudes toward ecological restoration in Yellowstone were patterned by their social position in society, revealing how our relationships with nature reflect who we are and what we value (Greider and Garkovich 1994; Farrell 2015). We interact with the environment, then, not just in a material sense—but also in a profoundly social sense (Bell 1994).

through-my-lens/Getty Images

Environmentalists rejoiced at the reintroduction of the endangered gray wolf to Yellowstone Park, but many local farmers viewed the event as a threat to their community and lifestyle. Competing interests and power shape the way people interpret nature and the relationship of humans to the natural world.

Tyler Olson/Shutterstock

BIG QUESTION 6.2 How Has Human Activity Harmed the Environment?

CONTEMPORARY ENVIRONMENTAL PROBLEMS

If our relationships with nature reflect who we are, then it may be time to take a long, hard look in the mirror. In

pursuit of material comfort and profit, individuals and corporations have irreparably damaged the oceans and surface of the Earth and destabilized its natural equilibrium. The end of the last ice age more than 10,000 years ago ushered in an era of natural global warming known as the Holocene. But in just 200 years, we have sped up the process of global warming so much, and altered the Earth's topography and chemistry so dramatically, that we seem to have pushed the Earth into a new geologic era. Fittingly, geologists propose to call this era Anthropocene (Zalasiewicz et al. 2010). Given the social and economic origins of so many contemporary environmental problems, it is appropriate that sociologists are increasingly turning their attention to an area of study that was once thought to be the exclusive domain of the natural sciences. As a recent review of research in this area observes, "sociologists have made important contributions to our knowledge of the human drivers of contemporary climate change" (Dietz et al. 2020, p. 135).

Global Warming

6.2.1 Identify the variety of environmental transformations caused by climate change.

In 1958, the chemist Charles David Keeling began monitoring the levels of carbon dioxide (CO_2) in the atmosphere. The results were startling. Each year evidenced a greater concentration of CO_2 than the last, and the escalation corresponded with global increases in the burning of **fossil fuels**, which are energy sources such as coal, oil, and natural gas that are made of fossils that decomposed over millions of years under high pressure. Though the concentration of atmospheric CO_2 held steady for thousands of years, over the last 50 years it has increased by 20 percent. CO_2 emissions can linger in the atmosphere for a century and produce what is called the **greenhouse effect** by allowing the sun's heat to pass through to the Earth's surface while stopping it from spreading back into space. As a result, the Earth's average temperature continues to rise. This is called **global warming**, and there is now wide agreement in the mainstream scientific community that human activity is the primary culprit.

Climatologist Michael Mann and his colleagues have demonstrated that global temperatures were more or less constant over the past 1,000 years and that the spike in global temperatures over the past half-century maps onto the spike in atmospheric CO_2. The Intergovernmental Panel on Climate Change estimates that Earth's global surface temperature increased about 1.5°F over the twentieth century, and it estimates an increase of 7.2°F this century. While some skeptics point to the occasional April snowstorm or an unusually harsh winter as evidence that global warming is not happening, such an argument confuses short-term weather events with long-term climate trends. The long-term warming trend is unmistakable, and it is unequal to anything human history has witnessed. Figure 6.1

illustrates how CO_2 rates have risen significantly since 1960 and how temperatures remained relatively constant until they climbed noticeably starting in 1900.

While a growing number of automobiles, planes, and factories are producing ever-greater carbon emissions, deforestation is crippling the Earth's natural ability to absorb CO_2. Sea ice in the Arctic is melting so quickly that it may only be a few decades until the Arctic Sea is devoid of ice in the summer; and the thickness of wintertime sea ice may thin from 12 feet to less than 3 feet (Kolbert 2007). Because the ocean absorbs more heat than ice (which deflects light), sea ice retreat hastens the warming of the ocean, which in turn speeds up the melting of the ice floating on its surface. As a result of melting mountain-top glaciers, and because water expands as it warms, the sea level is rising. The small island nation of the Maldives, whose highest point is only 6 feet above sea level, is already contending with the effects of sea level rise. The ocean is advancing over the rims of its islands and may eventually cover them entirely. The nation's president held an underwater cabinet meeting to draw attention to its plight, and he even considered purchasing land in other countries in case the entire nation is forced to abandon its homeland.

The sea level is predicted to rise anywhere from several inches to several feet this century, depending on the extent to which nations act to limit carbon emissions. Assuming a "business-as-usual" scenario, meaning that companies and industries are allowed to continue environmentally harmful production practices in the pursuit of profit maximization, millions of people could be displaced, and some coastal cities like New Orleans and Miami might need to be abandoned, while many others would have to build massive and highly expensive levees. Global warming also means that millions of farmable acres around the world may become arid and useless. While this would directly threaten critical food sources, it would also alter the Earth's ecosystems so dramatically that many plant and animal species would be unable to adapt. While polar bears have become the face of animal endangerment due to global warming, scientists predict that as many as 20 to 50 percent of all animal species may become extinct over the next 100 years because of rising temperatures (Kolbert 2007). Of course, some species would thrive in warmer weather—for example, we can expect mosquitoes to expand their habitat, introducing malaria to new locales.

The notion of global warming does not fully capture the complexity of how carbon emissions impact the Earth's climate. Global warming upsets the balance of ecosystems to such a degree that they become destabilized. Some regions of the planet may even become temporarily

Figure 6.1 Rising Rates of Atmospheric CO$_2$ and Global Temperatures

Although the level of atmospheric CO$_2$ concentration—measured in parts per million (ppm)—fluctuates by season, the overall trend has been upward for many decades in a row. Notice the dramatic increase in average temperature, starting around 1900 in the graph on the right.

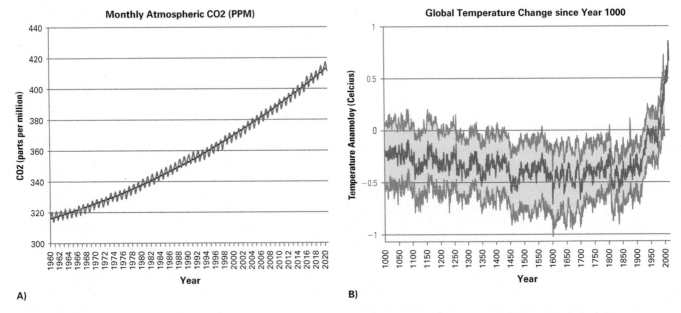

A)

B)

SOURCE: (A) Data from National Oceanic and Atmospheric Administration's (NOAA) Earth System Research Laboratory (ESRL) Global Monitoring Laboratory. Retrieved from: https://www.esrl.noaa.gov/gmd/dv/data/; (B) Ensemble median and intervals from PAGES2k Consortium 2019. "Consistent multidecadal variability in global temperature reconstructions and simulations over the Common Era." *Nature Geoscience, 12*, 643–649. https://doi.org/10.1038/s41561-019-0400-0. Note that in (B), temperatures are indexed to the period 1850–1900.

cooler because of the disruption of oceanic and atmospheric circulation. And climatologists predict that extreme weather events, from heat waves to hurricanes to floods, will likely occur with greater frequency. For example, we can expect more extremely hot and dry summers like the West Coast of the U.S. endured in 2020, when some of the largest wildfires on record burned millions of acres from Washington state to southern California and

forced hundreds of thousands of residents to evacuate. We may also see so-called "hundred-year storms" (that is, storms of such magnitude that they are expected to happen only once a century) like Hurricane Katrina (which struck the Gulf Coast in 2005) or Hurricane Sandy (which struck the New York/New Jersey area in 2011) happening several times in a decade as tropical storms are able to gather greater force from the additional heat and evaporation given off by warming oceans. Such storms can cause immense damage and displace tens of thousands of people, and cost immense sums to rebuild.

Because of the complex variety of environmental changes that warming temperatures are producing, a growing number of scientists prefer to use the term **climate change** instead of *global warming*. Climate change better captures the diverse ways in which the natural environment is changing in response to human behavior. NYU sociologist Eric Klinenberg prefers the term *climate crisis*, which "captures the condition of urgency and

The island nation of Maldives in the Indian Ocean (shown here) is threatened with extinction from rising ocean tides caused by climate change.

danger engendered by a heated world" (Klinenberg et al. 2020, p. 650). Whatever name one chooses, the changes that societies are producing in our environment through carbon emissions pose the single greatest hazard to both our ecosystems and humanity. Putting the brakes on global warming has been called the most important task of this century—and beyond.

Natural Resource Depletion

6.2.2 Discuss how the rapid depletion of major natural resources—oil, coal, forests, living species, and water—-affects all forms of life.

On April 20, 2010, a British Petroleum offshore drilling operation known as the Deepwater Horizon exploded off the coast of Louisiana. The explosion killed 11 workers and spewed more than 50,000 barrels of petroleum *per day* into the Gulf of Mexico for three months. The petroleum created an 80-square-mile "kill zone" in the ocean where virtually all sea life was destroyed. Black tar washed up on the coast, injuring wildlife and scaring off vacationers. Gulf Coast fishermen were out of work for months.

The United States is the world's leading consumer of oil, burning through about 19 million barrels every day (India, whose population is about four times larger than that of the United States, consumes about 4.5 million barrels per day). Of that amount, about 70 percent is used to power its automobile-centered transportation system (U.S. Energy Information Administration 2019). No one knows how long the world's supply of "black gold" will

last, though many experts predict a time frame of several generations, not centuries. Despite this forecast, wealthy countries have been slow to move away from their dependency on oil. In fact, most have sought to increase domestic oil production and invest in new techniques of oil extraction, such as hydraulic fracturing ("fracking"), to reduce their reliance on imports from the Middle East and Russia. Drilling rigs move further and further offshore and dig deeper and deeper, sometimes in dangerous ways (as we saw dramatically in the Deepwater Horizon explosion). And industry is setting its sights on protected natural areas like the Arctic National Wildlife Refuge in Alaska because of their potential caches of oil.

Ever since the Industrial Revolution, humanity's energy requirements have escalated exponentially. And the most valuable sources of energy, like petroleum, come from deep underground or within mountains. As highlighted in Figure 6.2, oil, coal, and natural gas—which are nonrenewable resources, meaning that there is a limited supply that cannot be replaced—currently provide about 85 percent of the energy consumed around the world (Rapier 2020).

The Industrial Revolution was built on coal, which released plumes of black smoke into the sky as it fired everything from steam engines to the furnaces that melted iron. Today, coal combustion still generates a quarter of the electricity consumed by Americans and is the world's greatest—and dirtiest–source of electricity (U.S. Energy Information Administration 2020). Though coal combustion is a leading source of air pollution and global warming, it is attractive because coal reserves are widely dispersed around the globe. This means that many countries do not need to rely on imports because they can extract it domestically.

Perhaps the most environmentally harmful form of resource depletion is deforestation. Tropical rainforests provide a natural habitat for two-thirds of all species on the planet, including many plants that are used in medicine, and play a crucial role in capturing CO_2 and converting it into oxygen. Though forests are often cut down to produce paper and lumber, most deforestation is a result of farming. As the global demand for beef continues to grow, firms and individual ranchers are eager to burn down stands of trees and replace them with pastures where cattle can graze or to plant fields of soy beans, which are grown to feed cattle (see Figure 6.3).

Petty Officer 3rd Class Tom Atkeson/U.S. Coast Guard/Tribune News Service via Getty Images

The explosion of the Deepwater Horizon drilling rig in the Gulf of Mexico symbolizes the environmental and human costs of our continuing dependency on oil and other fossil fuels.

Figure 6.2 Global Energy Sources (Quadrillion BTU)

This figure presents the absolute level of energy produced at a global level by each source in 2005, 2010, 2015, and 2020, and projections for the next few decades.

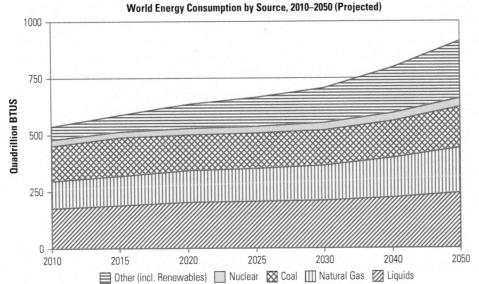

World Energy Consumption by Source, 2010–2050 (Projected)

Legend: Other (incl. Renewables) ■ Nuclear ⊠ Coal ⫴ Natural Gas ⫽ Liquids

SOURCE: U.S. Energy Information Administration. *International Energy Outlook*, 2019.

A Greenpeace report attributes 80 percent of deforestation in the Brazilian Amazon to cattle ranching, and the United Nations estimates that, through the slashing and burning of CO_2-absorbing trees, meat production contributes more to global warming than either car tailpipes or industrial smokestacks (Greenpeace 2009). Deforested areas also suffer greatly from soil erosion, sometimes degenerating into desert-like landscapes. Ecologists estimate that deforestation is causing the extinction of as many as 50,000 plant and animal species every year (137 species per day), and they predict that the rainforests, which once covered 14 percent of the Earth's land surface, may be entirely gone by the end of this century unless major restrictions are put in place and enforced (Kolbert 2007).

Habitat fragmentation and the clearing of forests for ranching, mining, and human settlements is also enabling diseases that circulate in wild animals to spill into human populations. Most of the pandemics that have spread across the globe over the past quarter-century, from AIDs to the so-called bird flu (H5N1), Ebola, and COVID-19, originated in animals. To prevent pathogens like COVID-19 from jumping the species boundary, we must stop creating the conditions that foster novel encounters between human and animal populations. This would require reversing habitat and biodiversity loss and reducing the mass confinement and consumption of animals. The World Health Organization warned at the end of 2020 that while the COVID-19 "pandemic has been very severe . . . it is not necessarily the big one" (Berger 2020).

Animal and plant species also face extinction because we consume them faster than they can reproduce. A dramatic example is the collapse of the cod fishing industry. Cod were once so numerous off the eastern coast of Canada that explorers reported catching them with baskets. Over the course of the twentieth century, massive mechanized trawlers replaced small fishing boats. The sea filled up with gigantic nets that scraped the bottom of the ocean floor. Profits soared as trawlers worked around the clock, processing and freezing the fish below deck. At their peak in 1968, trawlers hauled in 800,000 tons of cod in a year. But by the early 1990s, cod were so overfished that their entire population was estimated to be just 1 percent of what it had been 30 years before. A complete ban on cod fishing was implemented in 1992, leading to the loss of as many as 40,000 jobs. To this day, however, the cod population has not rebounded. Though

Figure 6.3 Total Cattle Herd Size and Deforestation in Amazon

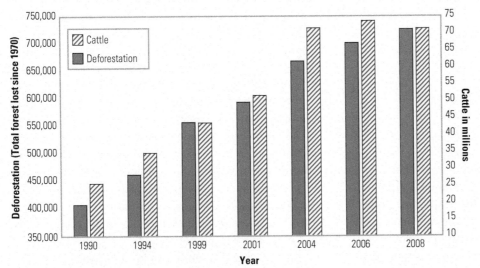

SOURCE: Figure based on data from Greenpeace, 2009.

the fishing industry now places restrictive quotas on the amount of a given species that can be caught, the number of marine species threatened by "factory fishing" steadily increases (*E Magazine* 2001).

Water is one of the most precious natural resources and may be the one most taken for granted in developed countries. Though global access to clean water has increased dramatically over the past several decades, many experts worry that supply will not keep pace with demand. Around the world, the amount of water held in *aquifers*—naturally occurring underground wells—is declining. The Ogallalla aquifer, which is tucked beneath parts of eight states in the American Midwest and which supplies almost a third of the groundwater used for irrigation in the United States, is currently only regenerating 10 percent of the amount of water that is taken out each year. The typical American uses more than 80 gallons of tap water each day and pays pennies. But anticipated future water shortages may very well make water the most valuable natural resource of the next century.

Natural resource depletion is not a unique problem of the modern era. Historians point to Easter Island as evidence. It appears that the small island off the coast of Chile was the site of a thriving society between the 1200s and the 1600s. However, extensive deforestation led to soil erosion and the extinction of many species of edible plants and animals. By the 1800s, the civilization collapsed amid famine and warfare over scarce resources. In today's global economy, societies need not be self-sufficient because they can import goods. But we should not overlook the lesson of Easter Island. Geographer Jared Diamond writes that the rate and scale of global resource depletion and population expansion is slowly nudging our entire planet toward collapse (Diamond 1995). This outcome can be avoided, but doing so will likely require an unusual way of thinking: making decisions about resource consumption based not primarily on what is profitable or convenient for us but on what will benefit future generations.

Solid and Chemical Waste

6.2.3 Discuss how attitudes toward waste and modes of waste removal threaten our health and environment.

While natural resource depletion can be thought of as an input crisis, the world faces an output crisis that is just as serious. Though the production of some amount of waste is unavoidable, wealthy countries like the United States create such an excess of garbage that they have been labeled "throwaway societies." Much of this is about convenience: Disposable razors, diapers, and cups mean that we do not have to sharpen blades, clean messy cloth diapers, or walk around with our own beverage containers. But all those plastic bags, Styrofoam peanuts, and wrappers add up.

Despite the slogan of "reduce, reuse, recycle," the amount of trash that each American produces in a day nearly doubled between 1960 and 2013 (from about 2.5 pounds to almost 4.5 pounds). This equals 250 million tons of solid waste per year. To this annual figure must be added the nearly *8 billion* tons of industrial waste generated by American businesses and the untold amounts of hazardous waste—from paint can lids to spent nuclear fuel—that require special collection and storage methods (Environmental Protection Agency 2020). Figure 6.4 (next page) shows these trends from 1960 to 2018. It also prompts the question: What is our garbage trying to tell us about the "throwaway society" lifestyles we currently enjoy?

In 1960, virtually no one thought about recycling, yet today most people know about the concept. Towns and cities (and most companies) encourage recycling by providing waste disposal bins, and state and federal laws require many kinds of recycling as well. Or take the increase in paper waste. Americans increasingly prefer to read and consume digital versions of newspapers, magazines, and books rather than hard copies. In workplaces, people rely mostly on digital forms of communication, including e-mail and websites. Yet, despite the awareness and increased recycling and digital practices, we are generating more unrecycled waste than ever! Part of the problem is that the recycling industry is still not very effective at converting waste products into a reusable form; the Environmental Protection Agency estimates that in 2017, only 32% of all recycled materials were actually being recycled successfully, and recycling itself requires massive energy inputs (Environmental Protection Agency 2020, 2021).

Why are Americans producing so much more trash today than they did 50 years ago? Given that elaborate packaging helps producers sell commodities and that most consumers pay a flat fee for garbage removal regardless of how much they throw out, both buyers and sellers have little incentive to be more conscientious about waste. In addition, many products—from pens to toasters to cars—are increasingly designed to provide a limited amount of use before they need to be replaced—a phenomenon that has been dubbed **planned obsolescence**. This allows producers to make more money. Consumers generally accept it because these less durable products are cheaper, and it is easier (at least in the short run) to buy a new one than to get the old one fixed. But those old pens, toasters, and cars have to go somewhere. Apple products like the iPhone are a good example—every few years minor improvements and new software compel many of us to ditch a perfectly usable older model for a new one.

Changes in the amount and kind of waste produced also reflect technological innovations. As shown in

Figure 6.4 What Our Garbage Says About Us

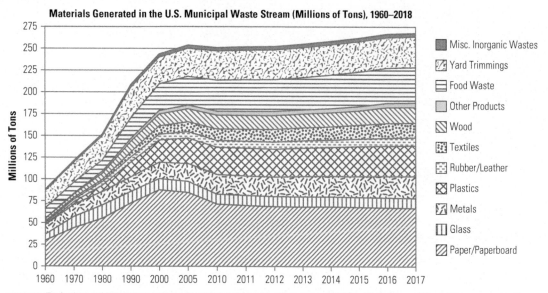

Materials Generated in the U.S. Municipal Waste Stream (Millions of Tons), 1960–2018

Legend:
- Misc. Inorganic Wastes
- Yard Trimmings
- Food Waste
- Other Products
- Wood
- Textiles
- Rubber/Leather
- Plastics
- Metals
- Glass
- Paper/Paperboard

SOURCE: Environmental Protection Agency, *Sustainable Materials Management (SMM) - Materials and Waste Management in the United States Key Facts and Figures*, 2017.

Figure 6.4, plastic, for instance, comprises over 125 million tons of consumer waste. Yet it was not produced on a mass scale in the 1960s. The rise of consumer electronics and computers and related hardware—typically expected to have a lifecycle of three years or less—has produced yet more garbage. Many plastic products are not currently being recycled (only about 8% of plastic waste, according to the EPA), because it is easily contaminated and can usually only be recycled one time (as opposed to paper, which can be recycled 6-7 times before it is too degraded to use).

Where does all of this waste go, when it is not recycled, and what are the consequences? Most of our unrecycled waste is simply dumped into massive holes and covered over. Though it may be out of sight and out of mind, much of our trash (like that old TV) will linger in landfills for centuries. The problem is that these landfills keep filling up, and nobody wants a trash heap in their backyard. New York City ran out of landfill space in the early 2000s and had to pay hundreds of millions of dollars per year to ship its trash to cash-strapped regions of Pennsylvania and Virginia, where poorer residents now *do* live with trash heaps in their backyard.

Landfills are also toxic stews where battery fluid mingles with mercury, and household cleaners and other industrial hazards slowly leach into the surrounding earth and groundwater. In 1953, the Hooker Chemical Company covered over a giant chemical dump known as Love Canal and sold it to the city of Niagara Falls, New York, for a dollar. Convinced that the hazardous waste was safely sealed below ground, the city built a school on the site and oversaw the construction of about 100 nearby homes. It took 25 years for residents to realize there was a problem. After a period of heavy rain in 1978, rusted metal drums filled with carcinogenic waste broke through the surface of people's backyards, puddles of oozing toxins choked trees and plants to death, and children playing outside returned home with chemical burns. The number of area miscarriages, birth defects, and cancer cases skyrocketed. While the Love Canal tragedy led to more stringent federal regulations of toxic waste disposal, there are still thousands of sites in the United States where toxic waste has been improperly disposed (Szasz and Meuser 1997).

Convenience has its consequences. But the full cost of all of the industrial waste and throwaway products and packaging that sustain modern lifestyles and corporate profits is not reflected in their sticker price. Though efficient waste management systems seem to make rubbish disappear, the environment pays the penalty. As Love Canal indicates, the cost may also be borne by people's bodies. This is especially true in poor countries, where erratic trash collection and the lack of proper facilities for the disposal of toxins means waste may spread disease as it festers in the streets.

Air and Water Pollution

6.2.4 Discuss the impact human consumption has on air and water supplies.

The freeways of Los Angeles were designed to whisk commuters across the sprawling city at speeds of 55 miles per hour. These days, however, the average rush hour speed on Los Angeles freeways may be 5 or 10 miles per hour, and "rush hour" now means a time window as wide as 5:00 to 10:00 AM and 3:00 to 7:00 PM. The average Los Angeles resident spends almost five days a year sitting in traffic. Yet even as those millions of cars sit idle on congested freeways, they continue to pollute the air. Los Angeles is

Tailpipe emissions from automobiles harm the atmosphere—and our lungs. This image captures traffic in Los Angeles, California, one of the places with the most miles travelled by car per person in the world. In the twentieth century, many American cities, like Los Angeles, were developed in a sprawl-like pattern in which the automobile was intended to be the way that people got around. Designing alternative methods of transportation in the twenty-first century is critical.

legendary for its **smog**, a smoky haze produced when tailpipe emissions that linger in the atmosphere chemically react with the sunlight. Although the number of smog days has declined significantly in recent years, Los Angeles continues to endure "smog alerts," where schools are closed and residents are warned to stay inside because of poor air quality. Smog can burn the lungs and irritate the eyes and nose, and it has been known to aggravate asthma, bronchitis, and other respiratory illnesses.

Toxic air pollution is as much a product of smokestacks as tailpipes. In one year, a single coal-based electrical plant pumps tens of thousands of tons of noxious gases into the atmosphere. These include nitrogen oxide and sulfur dioxide, which react with water molecules in the air to create acid that returns to earth when it rains. So-called **acid rain** has been shown to kill plant life and marine animals. Industrial pollutants have also severely depleted the atmosphere's ozone layer, which shields the Earth's surface from the sun's ultraviolet radiation. UV rays are harmful to a number of plant and animal species and have been linked to cancer and cataracts in humans. The toxins most responsible for ozone depletion are chlorofluorocarbons (CFCs), which until recently were commonly found in aerosol sprays and liquid coolants.

No one can avoid inhaling microscopic pollutants produced from the combustion of fossil fuels. Their effects can mimic those of cigarette smoke, and it is estimated that 50,000 Americans die each year from cardiopulmonary diseases linked to breathing in toxic particles (Dollemore 2008). In October 2010, it was estimated that almost 600 residents of Hong Kong had died since the beginning of the year because of air pollution. Over the same nine-month period, experts also attributed a staggering 4.63 million doctor visits and 45,000 hospitalizations to poor air quality caused by coal-burning plants and automobiles (Bryskine 2010). Though city air quality is improving somewhat in developed societies as a result of cleaner technologies, it is worsening in developing countries that must rely on cheaper, dirtier methods to produce energy. Mexico City's smog is so thick that the nearby mountains are often shrouded in brown haze. Clean air and healthy lungs are luxuries it can't afford.

Clean, potable water is another luxury that many people in developing countries cannot afford. Over half the world's rural population still lacks access to clean water, leading desperate people to rely on polluted sources—including sewage—to supply their cooking, bathing, and drinking needs. Exposure to contaminated water causes tens of thousands of deaths each year worldwide from preventable diseases such as dysentery and cholera—diseases that Americans have not had to worry about for many years.

The United States, however, is hardly immune from concerns about water quality. Aside from acid rain, contamination of rivers, streams, and aquifers from agriculture and industry is common. Cow manure, which is often filled with infectious agents such as *E. coli*, regularly enters waterways as runoff after a rainstorm. Agricultural runoff, which can also include chemical agents from synthetic fertilizers, is the single biggest source of water pollution in the United States. Despite this fact, farm waste for the most part is not regulated under federal laws. When it comes to industry, a *New York Times* investigation found thousands of instances where companies openly flouted the Clean Water Act but were never punished. In one case, the drinking water in a West Virginia town was contaminated with lead, manganese, and nickel because coal companies purposely injected over 2 billion gallons of toxic sludge into the ground over a period of five years. Residents who continued using the stained yellow drinking water suffered from severe rashes, rotting teeth, miscarriages, and kidney and bladder diseases. The problem of chemical wastes being discharged into drinking water goes beyond the coal industry, encompassing natural gas extraction ("fracking"), dry cleaners, gas stations, and sewage treatment plants (Duhigg 2009).

Pollution is cheap. Consumers want inexpensive goods and sources of energy, and producers operate in a cutthroat environment where they must keep down costs to be competitive. Unless firm, enforceable limits are placed on the amount of air and water pollutants that businesses can generate, or unless businesses are given financial incentives for adopting "greener" (or more environmentally friendly) practices, we should expect pollution to worsen.

philipus/Alamy Stock Photo

BIG QUESTION 6.3 How Do Environmental Factors Impact Inequality?

It is unlikely that most producers and consumers will voluntarily discontinue "business as usual" and pay the higher cost of sustainability.

THE ENVIRONMENTAL MOVEMENT AND SOCIAL INEQUALITY

In response to the unfolding ecological crisis, a powerful social movement has emerged over the last half-century that challenges "business as usual." The movement has made notable gains in remedying some of the damage wrought by society on the environment. But socially produced environmental problems have also led to new environmental issues. And not everyone suffers equally: The wealthiest people tend to reap most of the benefits and suffer few of the costs of environmental problems. One of the most vital contributions that sociologists have made to the study of environmental problems is an understanding of how they are linked to social inequality.

The Environmental Movement

6.3.1 Identify early preservationist figures and movements that have contributed to environmental awareness.

As early as the 1800s, there were those who sensed something tragic about the destruction of natural landscapes in the face of urbanization. None may be more famous than the philosopher Henry David Thoreau. His 1854 book *Walden* documented a two-year experiment in which he built and lived in a cottage on the wooded outskirts of Boston. Living simply and close to the land, he wrote, rejuvenated the spirit and reawakened the senses. A

rallying cry against the social ills of the city, *Walden* framed the discourse for future generations of **preservationists** (Brulle 1996)—those who believe the environment has intrinsic value and should be maintained in as pristine a state as possible. The leading figure of early efforts to preserve the countryside and wilderness was John Muir, who successfully petitioned U.S. president Theodore Roosevelt—an avid outdoorsman—to set aside the Yosemite area as a protected national park in 1906. Among Muir's many other lasting legacies was founding the Sierra Club, which to this day is the most influential environmental protection group in the United States. A firm believer in preserving nature in pristine form, Muir rejected the utilitarian view of **conservationists**—who argue that the point of environmental protection ought to be to responsibly manage natural resources so that they are available for commercial use by future generations.

It took until the second half of the twentieth century for environmental problems to begin to be seen as dire threats to humanity. There may have been no greater wakeup call than Rachel Carson's best-selling 1962 book *Silent Spring*. The book's title referred to an imagined future where songbirds could no longer be heard because they had all been killed by pesticides like DDT. Carson blamed the government for allowing the use of toxins without knowing the long-term consequences, and she compared pesticides to nuclear fallout. "Can anyone believe," Carson pleaded, "it is possible to lay down such a barrage of poisons on the surface of the earth without making it unfit for all life?" (Carson 1962, p.8).

Silent Spring directly led to the ban on the use of DDT in the United States. But, perhaps more fundamentally, the book led Americans to question their faith in better living through chemistry. Carson argued that science had been hijacked by the titans of industry, who were driven by short-term profit, and that there was little reason to

Over a century ago, the preservationist John Muir gave U.S. president Theodore Roosevelt a tour of Yosemite in an attempt to convince him to use the powers of the federal government to protect the area's natural beauty. Protecting natural environments from development is an important issue that comes up over and over in the struggle between business interests and environmental preservation.

assume chemical producers cared about public safety. She also challenged society's anthropocentrism, contending that humans are only one component of a fragile ecosystem that, if further degraded, could undermine the foundations of mankind's existence. Grassroots movements began to spring up across the country, advocating for stronger government regulation of the chemical industry.

Before the decade of the 1960s ended, and amid the emergence of the civil rights movement, several catastrophes brought the environmental movement to a head. In 1969 alone, a massive oil spill off the coast of California killed thousands of marine animals and blackened the shoreline of Santa Barbara, while Cleveland's Cuyahoga River actually caught on fire because the surface of its brown, oozing, toxic water was covered in oil. These events sparked tremendous public outrage, resulting in the first Earth Day the following year and in a string of significant political victories for the environmental movement. Most notably, the Nixon administration—which was generally on the side of "big business" and thus viewed environmentalism as a threat to productivity and profit—bowed to this unprecedented groundswell of popular protest by creating the Environmental Protection Agency (EPA) and signing the Clean Water Act into law. Meanwhile, best-selling books like Paul Ehrlich's *The Population Bomb* (Ehrlich 1968)

sounded alarm bells about the potential collapse of societies as an exploding global population pressed up against the limits of finite natural resources (see Chapter 23 for more details). Though new technologies demonstrated that humans could extend natural limits (for example, genetically altering plants to increase crop yields), and the world's population did not expand in the way Ehrlich predicted, it is nevertheless clear that technology is not a cure-all as the scope of environmental risks kept increasing.

Despite growing public concern about our planet's health, efforts to enact environmentally friendly policies are routinely thwarted by political alliances between private businesses and some conservative lawmakers, many of whom voice skepticism about scientific claims regarding environmental problems or contend that "going green" will harm the economy (Dunlap and McCright 2011). President George W. Bush, for instance, memorably refused to sign the Kyoto Protocol, an international pledge to cut carbon emissions, in 2001 because he said that it was not clear that global warming was caused by people and that the pact would result in a loss of productivity and jobs. Fifteen years later, President Donald Trump, a known "climate denialist," pulled the United States out of the Paris Accord—the first agreement to combat climate change adopted by all 193 United Nations member states (discussed in more detail later in the chapter)—for similar reasons. What's more, companies engaged in fracking, a process by which oil and natural gas are extracted from shale rock by the injection of millions of gallons of water and sand laced with toxic chemicals into the ground, were long able to avoid submitting to more stringent environmental regulations and having to disclose the contents of what they pump into the earth (which they argue is a trade secret) by maintaining close ties with business-friendly governors of the states where they drill.

Environmental Justice

6.3.2 Discuss environmental racism and what progress is being made to ensure equal protection for all people.

In the summer of 1978, a trucking company illegally dumped 31,000 gallons of used transformer oil along hundreds of miles of roads in Warren County, North Carolina. The location was no accident: This was the poorest county in the state, and 65 percent of its residents were Black. Adding insult to injury, the state decided to place a hazardous waste landfill in the area that would store the used oil and also serve as a repository for toxins from other counties. Rather than accept their fate, locals fought back. As a group, they lobbied against the proposal, filed a civil lawsuit, and were arrested for staging protests. The language and strategies they employed helped shape an emerging social movement (Szasz and Meuser 1997).

Bettman/Getty Images

The 1969 Cuyahoga River Fire in Cleveland was one of the most shocking examples of the mistreatment of natural resources. The fire was caused by years of dumping chemicals and other debris into the river. Ironically, the river had caught fire once before, in 1952, but it was the 1969 fire that inspired the environmental movement of the late 1960s and 1970s that demanded reforms aimed at air and water pollution.

While the environmental movement of the 1960s and 1970s advocated for the preservation of natural areas and for increased federal regulations to protect air and water, many people of color and people in poverty felt that the movement did not address the problems that affected them. Their concerns were grounded in the disproportionate number of hazardous waste facilities that were placed in their communities and in the higher rates of asthma and other environment-induced illnesses that they had

to endure. A 1987 report issued by the United Church of Christ found, based on a comparison of ZIP Codes across the United States, that race was the most significant predictor of living close to a hazardous waste facility (for example, garbage incinerator, sewage treatment plant). As shown in Figure 6.5, the higher the concentration of people of color in a particular ZIP Code, the greater the number of hazardous waste facilities it contained (Commission for Racial Justice 1987).

The report's findings echoed the pioneering research of sociologist Robert Bullard, who showed that 21 of Houston's 25 garbage dumps and incinerators were located in Black neighborhoods even though Blacks comprised only 25 percent of the city's population (Bullard 1983). The disproportionate share of environmental hazards has been labeled as **environmental racism** by Bullard and other sociologists (Bullard 1990). Though "environmental racism" suggests conscious discrimination against people of color, it is often the case that polluting industries choose the path of least resistance, placing facilities where land is cheaper and where residents are not politically organized (Brulle and Pellow 2006). Such decisions often seem to be based on economics rather than race, but the enduring association between poverty and race in the United States means that the areas where environmental hazards are clustered usually have the highest concentration of people of color. In the past, discriminatory housing practices forced minorities to live in undesirable

Figure 6.5 Household Proximity to Hazardous Waste Sites by Race

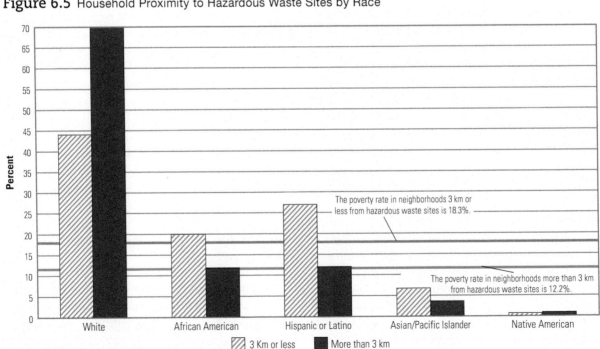

The poverty rate in neighborhoods 3 km or less from hazardous waste sites is 18.3%.

The poverty rate in neighborhoods more than 3 km from hazardous waste sites is 12.2%.

3 Km or less   More than 3 km

SOURCE: Bullard, Mohai, Saha, and Wright, 2007.

neighborhoods with greater levels of pollution; today, those with low incomes simply cannot afford to move to cleaner, healthier places.

New York University's Institute for Environmental Medicine looked at the link between air pollution and health in the South Bronx, historically one of the poorest neighborhoods in New York City, and in the 1970s and 1980s one of the poorest in the country. Home to many poor and working-class people of color, the South Bronx also hosts over a dozen waste-transfer stations, a sewage-treatment plant, and miles of congested expressways. It has one of the highest hospitalization rates for asthma among children in New York. By placing air-monitoring devices in students' backpacks, the NYU researchers found that children in the South Bronx were exposed to unhealthy levels of air pollution from car exhaust on a regular basis. They also saw that the students exhibited symptoms of asthma, such as wheezing, during the times when the amount of air pollution was highest (Fernandez 2006). This and other studies show that people in the poorest neighborhoods, many of which are occupied by people of color, often do not breathe the same air or drink the same water as their wealthier counterparts (Szasz and Meuser 1997).

One of the most tragic recent examples of environmental racism occurred in Flint, Michigan. Located 70 miles north of Detroit, Flint is a very poor city of about 100,000 people (about 40 percent of its residents live below the poverty line), most of whom are Black. State and local government officials, looking for a way to cut costs, began getting public water from the Flint River in 2014. The river had not been used as source of water for city residents since the 1960s due to its polluted character, but government officials claimed it was now in good enough shape to provide drinking water for Flint residents. Shortly after the city began drawing water from the new source, however, residents began complaining about the taste of the water and said they were getting sick. No action took place for months, as government officials claimed there were no problems with the water. But eventually, investigations found high levels of fecal matter and lead in the water, both of which are extremely harmful to humans. There are special worries about children exposed to the contaminated water. An independent panel investigating the Flint water catastrophe concluded that the episode showed a complete disregard for the poor that led the panel to "the inescapable conclusion that this is a case of environmental injustice" (Bosman 2016).

To address what they perceive as environmental racism or classism, poor and minority communities have organized grassroots political campaigns and sued polluters in court. The goal is **environmental justice**, conceived of as the achievement of equal protection from environmental hazards for all people, regardless of race, class, gender, or geography. To put it another way, environmental justice requires that harms are spread out so that each person has the same risk as everyone else. Environmental justice also entails giving community members a voice in shaping decisions that affect their environment and their health.

Sociologists Robert Brulle and David Pellow identify two major strands of the environmental justice movement that emerged in the 1980s. The antitoxics movement was based primarily in White working-class communities and drew its inspiration from the local response to the Love Canal catastrophe. Fueled by concern for her children and her neighbors, a resident named Lois Gibbs turned her neighborhood homeowner's association into a citizen action group. She also helped forge a national coalition of community organizations facing similar environmental threats. These groups shared information, organized protests, filed class-action lawsuits against polluters, and helped make the nation aware of the extent to which factories and industry were poisoning the communities around them.

Around the same time, people of color who were inspired by the Warren County landfill protests began forming a movement that tackled similar issues, such as the location of hazardous waste facilities and illegal dumping. What made their movement unique was its framing and strategies. People of color explicitly defined local environmental problems as a violation of their civil rights, and many of them adopted the civil disobedience tactics of the 1960s, such as staging massive protests and occupying the offices of politicians and polluting companies (Brulle and Pellow 2006).

Environmental justice groups have achieved some notable gains, such as shutting down dangerous incinerators and landfills and convincing the EPA to create an Office of Environmental Justice (Brulle and Pellow 2006). In one landmark case, Navajo Indians in New Mexico—who were unwittingly exposed to harmful levels of radiation for decades by mining companies that extracted uranium on behalf of the U.S. military—helped propel the passage of a law in 1990 that requires the government to compensate people who have suffered from nuclear bomb testing and uranium mining. Increasingly, environmental justice movements are cropping up in developing countries, where they challenge the business-as-usual tradeoff of pollution for profit and attempt to hold wealthy countries accountable for local environmental problems caused by global warming.

The Social Dimension of Natural Disasters

6.3.3 Explain the reasons some groups are more adversely affected by natural disasters than other groups.

In July 1995, the residents of Chicago experienced one of the city's most severe heat waves. In just one week, more than 500 people died as a direct result of the heat. Medical workers were so overwhelmed that they had to store the corpses in refrigerated meat-packing trucks until they could perform autopsies. Were these deaths the unavoidable consequence of natural events? While the mayor, and for the most part the media, framed them this way, NYU sociologist Eric Klinenberg (the author of Chapter 10 of this book) argued that the massive loss of life was in fact a "structurally determined catastrophe" that could mostly have been prevented. The heat wave did not take lives at random. Rather, Klinenberg discovered that vulnerability was concentrated in "the low-income, older people, African-American, and more violent regions of the metropolis" (Klinenberg 1999, p.230). Poor neighborhoods were underserved by municipal agencies that could have reached out to social isolates and people without air conditioners, and their local hospitals were overwhelmed and understaffed. Klinenberg also argued that the city had allowed poor neighborhoods to become so deteriorated and dangerous that residents feared leaving their homes even as the temperatures rose to dangerous levels. As a result, they quietly and anonymously perished.

While sociologists do not deny the destructive power of natural disasters such as floods, earthquakes, and heat waves, they analyze the ways in which the outcomes of such events—such as who lives and who dies, who evacuates and who remains—are patterned by social forces. In the wake of Hurricane Katrina in 2005, one of the most devastating hurricanes ever to hit the United States, most of the desperate faces of those stranded on their roofs or packed into the temporary shelter of New Orleans's Convention Center were poor people of color. Despite these compelling scenes, politicians and media pundits hotly debated whether or not poor people of color disproportionately suffered from the storm. Sociologists played a key role in offering evidence of social disparities and revealing government neglect of the vulnerable.

Research on the consequences of Hurricane Katrina has found that Blacks, along with older people, were much more likely to die than would be expected given their presence in the population, and deaths in particular were concentrated in New Orleans's Black communities (Sharkey 2007). A panel of social scientists convened by the Social Science Research Council (SSRC) showed that many of the people who stayed behind lacked the necessary means to evacuate, most notably a car and money for a hotel. The SSRC panel also documented the major role that governmental disorganization and miscommunication played in hindering assistance to vulnerable residents. The Federal Emergency Management Agency (FEMA), for instance, failed to coordinate evacuation plans with local officials and neglected to give the go-ahead to the U.S. military to begin airdrops of food and water rations (Social Science Research Council 2006).

Socially patterned differences in vulnerability are even more pronounced on a global scale, as revealed by the earthquake that rocked poverty-stricken Haiti in 2010. Lacking the money to erect reinforced buildings, Haitians had little choice but to inhabit structures that crumbled under the force of the 7.0-magnitude quake, killing more than 100,000 people and leaving more than 1 million homeless. The substandard quality of the nation's infrastructure, from roads to hospitals, also contributed to the high number of casualties. Poverty, in the face of natural disasters, is often deadly.

Global Environmental Inequality

6.3.4 Identify the connection between global environmental responsibility and global environmental equality.

In 1984, more than 40 tons of highly toxic gas escaped from a pesticide plant in Bhopal, India, and killed nearly 10,000 people who lived in a nearby slum. In the subsequent 20 years, as many as 20,000 premature deaths resulted from lingering bodily effects of exposure. The factory belonged to the Union Carbide Company, an American chemical producer lured to India by its lower environmental standards and lax rule enforcement. Though Union Carbide denied responsibility, the facility was operating with "safety equipment and procedures far below the standards found in its sister plant" in West Virginia (Broughton 2005, p.2).

People made homeless by Hurricane Katrina, which struck the Louisiana Gulf Coast in September of 2005, sleeping on the floor of the New Orleans convention center. The hurricane destroyed tens of thousands of houses and 1,800 people lost their lives. The city of New Orleans was at the center of the storm, and many of the levees that normally protect the city from flooding failed, leading to the destruction of entire areas of the city. Rich and middle class residents of the city were able to get out before the storm hit, but poorer people, lacking transportation and resources to flee, were left behind to bear the brunt of the storm. For many, it would take years to rebuild their lives.

In the global economy, production and consumption are usually disconnected. If we look at the labels on our clothing or the packaging of our electronics, we will likely see that they were made in China or another country where companies can pay workers lower wages than in the United States—and where companies can pollute more. In this way, wealthy countries benefit from cheap industrial and consumer goods while developing countries bear the environmental and health risks.

More and more sociologists are reconnecting the points of production and consumption and documenting the environmental suffering that the developing world endures to prop up Western lifestyles. In one study, ethnographers analyzed an impoverished shantytown in Argentina surrounded by an immense petrochemical compound (Auyero and Swistun 2009). The village's 5,000 residents suffered from convulsions, rashes, psychological problems, bloody noses, and constant headaches—all of which are linked to ingesting lead and other toxic industrial chemicals. The source of much of the pollution was Shell Oil, an American subsidiary of a Dutch multinational company that used the facility to carry out the dirty process of refining crude oil so that it is ready for global consumption and industrial use.

Despite overwhelming evidence, the researchers found that residents remained unsure about the causes of their illnesses and rarely mobilized against Shell. This was because Shell, as a powerful and wealthy company, was able to manipulate how residents perceived and responded to contamination. Many of the locals worked for Shell, and Shell also ran a town health clinic and performed its own environmental tests. Because residents could not afford independent doctors or consultants, their main source of information about illness and exposure came from biased Shell representatives, and locals faced losing their jobs if they protested. Their enduring suffering is one of the hidden social costs of the world's refined oil (Auyero and Swistun 2009).

The greatest environmental problem the world faces today—climate change—may also be the greatest source of environmental inequality. While rich nations have, by far, contributed the most to climate change, poor countries disproportionately suffer from its effects. For those who must make a living off the land, small changes can have huge impacts on their ability to subsist. A report issued by Columbia University researchers concluded that by 2008 climate change had already forced as many as 50 million people, almost all of them living in the least developed countries, to migrate to new areas in order to secure a livelihood. Given the dismal forecast of continued deforestation, melting glaciers, rising sea levels, and an increase in the frequency and intensity of extreme weather events, we can expect hundreds of millions of worldwide "environmental refugees" by the year 2050 (Cooperative for Assistance and Relief Everywhere 2008).

Mark Bussell

BIG QUESTION 6.4 Can We Create More Sustainable Societies?

CONSUMPTION, PRODUCTION, AND SUSTAINABILITY

Some experts believe the global population is growing so rapidly that in several generations, the Earth may no longer be able to support everyone. The problem is not merely numbers, for if we were all hunter–gatherers we would consume far fewer resources and produce much less waste. According to biologist Paul Ehrlich, the impact of a given group of people on the environment is a function of the size of its population multiplied by its degree of affluence and its level of technology. For example, wealthy, developed countries tend to use an exponentially greater amount of natural resources *per person* than poor, less developed countries.

Americans comprise only 5 percent of the world's population but consume about 17 percent of the world's energy. A single American consumes as much energy as dozens of people in developing countries. Understandably, most people in poor countries would like to enjoy the same kind of material comforts that wealthy nations take for granted. But something has to give. Even though new technologies enable us to stretch Earth's natural limits, ecologists believe we will eventually hit the wall.

Here are some examples. Innovations in food production are increasingly predicted to lag behind population increases in many parts of the world, especially as climate change makes agriculture more difficult in many places. Rising levels of air and water pollution are damaging our habitat's ability to sustain. Despite the fact that current consumption and pollution patterns are already unsustainable, the world's energy demand in 2050 is predicted to be 50 percent greater than it was in 2018. Almost three-quarters of that increase will likely come from dirty, nonrenewable fossil fuels (U.S. Energy Information Administration 2020). As depicted in Figure 6.6, scientists project that the global carbon emissions of developed Organisation for Economic Co-operation and Development (OECD) countries will modestly increase by 2040, but among less developed countries, global carbon emissions are projected to increase by more than 30 percent.

Ecologists argue that, to avoid impending environmental and social crises, societies must work toward a model of **sustainability**, which refers to development and consumption that satisfies a society's current needs without imperiling the ability of future generations to do the same. Achieving long-term sustainability in the face of surging global production of waste and carbon dioxide emissions is, perhaps, the single most pressing social problem of the future.

The Tragedy of the Commons

6.4.1 Compare the advantages and disadvantages of self-regulation and political regulation of environmental resources.

A key principle of economics is that competition among commodity producers trying to capture a greater share of the market leads to lower prices for consumers. Many economists point to this as evidence that a free market self-regulates and produces optimal collective

Figure 6.6 World Energy-Related Carbon Dioxide Emissions, 2010–2050

The vertical axis indicates the carbon dioxide emissions, measured in million metric tons. The figure shows how the world's total emission of CO_2 is expected to increase steadily over the next three decades. However, developing countries will experience a much larger increase of carbon dioxide emissions compared to the developed OECD countries.

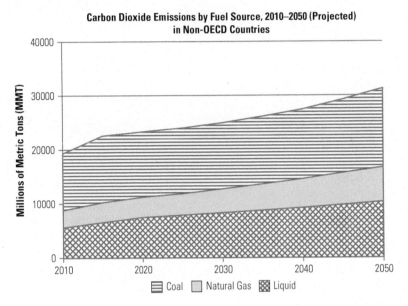

Carbon Dioxide Emissions by Fuel Source, 2010–2050 (Projected) in Non-OECD Countries

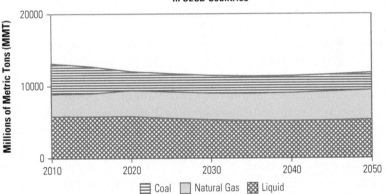

Carbon Dioxide Emissions by Fuel Source, 2010–2050 (Projected) in OECD Countries

SOURCE: U.S. Energy Information Administration, 2019.

outcomes. But in the influential article "The Tragedy of the Commons," ecologist Garrett Hardin (1968) contended that the opposite is often true: Each individual acting in their own self-interest will, in the long run, bring ruin to everyone.

Imagine a shared pasture (the "commons"), Hardin wrote, where herders graze cows. Because they earn a living from their cows, all herders have an interest in maximizing the number of cows they have grazing in the pasture. The herder who adds a cow to the pasture reaps all the benefits from that cow, but the negative impacts on the pasture created by overgrazing (when too many cattle are added) eventually harms all herders. But in the short term, each herder will want to keep adding cows to increase their profit—until

Shepherds and their flock of Anatolia sheep grazing on a Zagros Mountain pasture in Turkey. The theory of Tragedy of the Commons grew out of an analysis of overgrazing of shared lands in the English countryside.

finally the pasture is entirely overgrazed and everyone loses. The freedom of each herder to pursue their interests produces collective devastation.

Hardin's analogy of the commons highlights the tension between short-term and long-term rewards, and between individual and collective interest. Economists rightly point out that businesses will adopt more sustainable practices if and when there is a market for them. But ecologists, pointing to societies that collapsed in the past, argue that preventing future environmental calamity requires making sacrifices today. As discussed earlier, the cod-fishing industry went bust because each trawler sought to maximize its own haul of fish without regard for future generations. And global warming threatens us all because it is in the short-term economic interest of people, firms, and nations to continue business-as-usual practices rather than pay the cost of going green. The lesson is that we cannot expect the majority of people to regulate themselves as long as the negative consequences of their actions (1) will not be apparent until far in the future or (2) fall on other people.

Many of the actions we take that contribute to harming the planet, like driving a car or eating meat, are considered *private* choices. The problem is that, when summed with countless others' individual acts, these choices have *public* consequences—sea-level rise, wildfires, droughts, and hurricanes—that make it harder for other people, and future generations, to survive and thrive. In my latest book (Jerolmack 2021), I call this the **public/private paradox** and argue that, to the extent that our "freedom" to pursue unsustainable lifestyles erodes others' right to enjoy clean air, water, and finite natural resources, personal actions should be regulated in the name of equality and democracy.

In order to promote environmentally friendly behavior, we would need to restrict the amount of a particular resource that a single entity can use (for example, through permits or quotas), enact economic sanctions that punish polluters (taxes or fines), and create economic incentives that reward sustainable practices (tax breaks). The idea, again, is to replace self-regulation with political regulation. Our entire planet is our "commons." If we continue to eschew regulation and foul our own nest, future generations may find it uninhabitable.

Unlike what Hardin's thesis may suggest, however, we are not all equally responsible for climate change and environmental degradation. Environmental sociologist William Freudenberg (2008) argued that just a small number of elite economic actors are disproportionately responsible for the majority of ecological destruction; in effect, they divert finite shared resources for their own private benefit while saddling the public with pollution. Indeed, just 100 companies, many of them petroleum firms, are responsible for over 70 percent of the world's greenhouse gas emissions. While everyone should do all they can to minimize their impact on the environment, this striking statistic suggests that policies targeting the elite group of corporate "super polluters" would produce the greatest benefits for the planet.

The Treadmill of Production

6.4.2 Explain how economic systems focused on competition and expansion can contribute to serious environmental issues.

A number of sociologists argue that uncontrolled destruction of the environment is not simply the result of the failure of collective organization, but rather an essential feature of the contemporary economic system. Sociologist Allan Schnaiberg forcefully advanced this perspective through his concept of the "treadmill of production." While one of the principles of ecology is balance and a tendency toward equilibrium, such as when a forest fire clears out the underbrush so that new trees can grow, the pursuit of profit tends toward disequilibrium. The basis of capitalism is continued economic expansion—measured in profits, market shares, gross domestic product, and so on. Producers, laborers, and governments all share an interest in growing the economy by increasing production and consumption. Doing so, of course, entails the consumption of more energy and the production of more pollution. Thus, economic expansion increases wealth, but at the expense of the environment. Schnaiberg argued that the treadmill of production helps ensure business's profits by externalizing the environmental costs of their activities to the poor and the powerless, meaning that economic growth also increases environmental inequality (Schnaiberg 1980).

Economic growth is driven by competition. While competition among producers leads to technological innovation and lower prices, it can also discourage sustainable business practices. Why should one producer voluntarily pay the higher cost of adopting cleaner technology if she does not have to? This would decrease her profits, and if she raised prices to reflect her higher cost of doing business, consumers would go elsewhere.

There is an important place, then, for regulations that might apply to everyone. However, businesses faced with costly environmental laws may simply move their facilities to regions that have fewer restrictions. Similarly, countries or states sometimes loosen environmental regulations to lure businesses away from other regions. These two dynamics set in motion a "race to the bottom," whereby companies and governments conspire to remove or avoid environmental protections that harm profit. The toxic effects of the race to the bottom are evident from the Bhopal gas leak in India to the smog-choked skies of Beijing.

The implication of the treadmill-of-production idea is that achieving environmental sustainability will likely require a major restructuring of the economy away from a materials-intensive growth model. And the lesson of the race-to-the-bottom phenomenon is that political remedies will have to be harmonized across regions so that polluters do not pick up and move somewhere else when new regulations are put in place. These are tall orders, but some important steps have already been taken in this direction.

Toward Sustainability

6.4.3 Discuss ways in which technology, politics, and lifestyle changes can contribute to environmental protection and sustainability.

While technological innovation will most likely play a central role in helping societies reduce their impact on the environment, it is no magical solution. Reining in pollution on the scale and timetable needed to head off an ecological crisis will also require that governments take a more active role in regulating pollution and steering the economy away from the treadmill of production. Last but not least, sustainability requires civic engagement. While the notion of the throwaway society points to the unsustainability of contemporary lifestyles, it implies that everyday citizens can vote for sustainability at the ballot box and with their wallets by changing their patterns of consumption.

Technology will have a major role to play in making societies more sustainable. Recall that roughly 85 percent of the world's energy comes from fossil fuels. Because fossil fuels are nonrenewable, and because their combustion is the leading source of global warming, transitioning to **renewable energy** sources capable of being replaced by natural ecological cycles such as wind, sunlight, and water would have major environmental benefits. This is already happening. Solar panels and wind turbines have taken their place alongside hydroelectric dams as viable and important sources of "green energy." In 2019, U.S. annual energy consumption from renewables surpassed coal consumption for the first time since 1885. Despite this promising sign, over 80 percent of the energy consumed by Americans was still derived from nonrenewable resources (U.S. Energy Information Administration 2020). We can expect, however, that the decades ahead will see an enormous increase in renewable energy production. Almost every source of green energy can now compete on cost with fossil fuels. And a recent policy study found that America could produce 90 percent of its electricity from carbon-free sources by 2035 without increasing wholesale power costs (Goldman School of Public Policy 2020). Nuclear power, which does not produce greenhouse gases, could also

havana1234/Fotolia

The toxic consequences of avoiding environmental protections for fear that they will harm profits can be seen clearly in the smog-filled skies of Beijing, the capital of China and home to over 20 million people.

play a role in lowering emissions. But concerns about its safety, especially after the meltdown of the Fukushima Daiichi nuclear reactors following a tsunami off the coast of Japan in 2011, have led environmentally conscious countries like Germany to turn away from nuclear power.

As more people around the world pursue middle-class lifestyles, the demand for automobiles escalates. Unless we develop cars that do not rely on oil, any gains made in reducing carbon emissions through wind, solar, or nuclear power could be cancelled out by tailpipe emissions. The development of hybrid vehicles has been an important step in reducing carbon emissions, and their popularity shows that there is a market for "green" cars. Hybrids are powered by gasoline combustion, like traditional vehicles, yet they also draw energy from batteries. By using less gas, hybrids can produce significantly lower carbon emissions. However, hybrids still pollute. A number of manufacturers aim to create alternative fuel vehicles that do not emit any carbon.

One promising path to this objective is the electric vehicle (EV), which draws all of its energy from batteries. Rather than filling up at a gas station, the driver plugs the EV into an electrical outlet. EVs have actually been around for decades but have only recently begun to be mass produced. But several technological obstacles remain that turn off many car buyers: Most EVs can travel less than half the distance of gas-powered vehicles before they need to refuel, and it can take hours to fully recharge an EV. However, some automobile manufacturers have recently managed to make attractive and relatively affordable EVs that can travel over 300 miles before needing to recharge. Tesla Motors, a California-based company that only makes EVs, has also constructed a network of "superchargers" across America and Europe that can take as little as 30 minutes to charge EV batteries. Given the strides made over the past decade, there is reason to believe that EVs will eventually be competitive with gas-powered vehicles. Most of the major car companies now have EVs in development, and as production increases, the price of these vehicles should fall. However, for EVs to truly be green, the electricity that powers them must come from clean and renewable resources rather than coal or oil. For example, many of Tesla's refueling stations are powered by large solar panels above the station, and more and more homeowners are installing solar panels on their rooftops, making it possible to power their cars with energy from the sun. In 2021, President Joe Biden proposed using federal government funds to build a nationwide network of solar-powered refueling stations as part of the nation's basic infrastructure.

Politics has played an important part in promoting the development of green technology; but many environmentalists are pushing governments to assume a larger role in moving societies toward sustainability. While the American government offers tax rebates to businesses that adopt green technology, environmentalists seek much stronger federal legislation that would place a legal limit on carbon emissions. But some efforts have been blocked by the courts; for example, in 2016, the Supreme Court overturned a presidential executive order made by Barack Obama that required power plants to cut their carbon emissions. The case exemplifies the complexities of getting all branches of government behind laws and regulations that would cut emissions.

In the absence of federal regulations, some regions, states, and cities are creating climate action plans themselves. States in the northeastern United States and Canada, for instance, set a target to reduce the region's total carbon emissions to 10 percent below 1990 levels by 2020, and most reached that goal. And New York City aims to reduce its citywide carbon emissions to 80 percent below 2005 levels by 2050. One way to reduce regional carbon emissions is to limit suburban sprawl. Because cities cluster people and the businesses that serve them within a self-contained area where many errands can be done on foot, bike, train, or bus, urban living is a surprisingly green lifestyle. The state of Oregon has long recognized this—since the 1970s, it has enforced land-use laws that concentrate residential and commercial growth in urban areas.

One method for achieving carbon reduction goals that requires less intrusive regulation is through what is known as the **cap-and-trade program**. The idea is that governments set a limit on the total amount of carbon emissions that are allowable (the cap) and then sell permits to businesses that entitle them to a designated amount of emissions. If firms need to emit more than their permit allows, they must purchase pollution credits from other firms that are emitting less than their permit entitles them to (the trade). Such a system ensures a reduction in the total amount of carbon emitted into the atmosphere, rewards firms that move toward clean technology, and makes dirty firms pay for their pollution. The European Union was an early adopter of a trading program for greenhouse gases.

To prevent a race to the bottom, in which firms move their operations to regions that have not implemented limits on greenhouse gas emissions, it is now clear that global agreements between nations are essential. Only if countries work together to reduce the global carbon footprint can the overall level of emissions around the world be cut (and ultimately, what matters for climate change is not how much one region or country emits, but how much the entire world is emitting).

Though achieving global agreements is difficult, the world has begun to take steps in this direction.

A promising historical precedent was established in 1987, when countries from around the world gathered in Montreal to tackle the threat of ozone depletion. Acknowledging that the primary source of the so-called ozone hole over Antarctica came from aerosol sprays and liquid coolants containing CFCs, 196 countries eventually signed on to an agreement to phase out the production of these pollutants by 2000. Under guidance from the United Nations, wealthy nations set aside a special fund to help developing countries meet the phase-out requirements. Dubbed the Montreal Protocol, the CFC phase-out agreement is usually considered the most successful international environmental treaty of all time. Figure 6.7 shows the dramatic decline in CFC production after this landmark agreement.

Though curbing carbon emissions is more complicated, the Montreal Protocol is a useful example of how it could be done. Other important efforts have been made, most notably the 1997 Kyoto Protocol and the 2015 Paris Accord. Under the Kyoto Protocol, industrialized nations committed to reducing greenhouse gas emissions by an average of 5 percent below 1990 levels by 2012, set aside a fund to aid developing countries in adapting green technologies, and laid the foundation for an international cap-and-trade agreement. However, Kyoto highlighted the tension between environmental and business interests. The United States, at the time the world's largest polluter, refused to ratify the agreement because it would hamper economic growth. Meanwhile, environmentalists argued that the 5 percent carbon emissions goal was far too meager to prevent dangerous levels of global warming.

In December 2015, following several years of negotiations under the auspices of the United Nations, representatives from 195 countries signed an agreement in Paris (known as the Paris Accord) which pledges countries to adopt policies to reduce their emissions toward an overall goal of limiting the increase in global temperatures to 2 degrees Celsius. Prior to the agreement, Chinese president Xi Jinping and American president Barack Obama signed a landmark climate pact in November 2014, in which China pledged, for the first time, to cap its greenhouse gas emissions by 2030, and the United States promised to reduce its greenhouse gas emissions well below previous commitments. Given that the two countries account for 45 percent of the world's greenhouse gas emissions, that agreement helped to re-energize international climate talks leading to the Paris Accord.

In spite of the major commitments made by the countries signing the Paris Accord, the agreement lacks any binding enforcement mechanism to ensure that countries live up to their commitments. The agreement relies, instead, on a kind of "name and shame" approach, where countries that fail to live up to the general goals will be criticized by the global community. Still, voluntary compliance is often uneven and does not guarantee anything. It may prove necessary in the future to adopt legally binding agreements. Especially problematic, as noted earlier, was President Trump's decision in 2017 to withdraw the United States from the Accord, although his successor in the White House, Joe Biden, restored America's commitment to the Paris goals.

Economics and politics are arguably the biggest arenas where changes are necessary in order to move toward sustainability. However, environmentalists stress that small changes to one's lifestyle can also have a major impact. California alone uses over 15 billion disposable plastic bags every year—600 bags every second. (Californians Against Waste 2011). These bags are made from petroleum, a nonrenewable resource, and their production releases toxins into the air. Essentially nonbiodegradable, after one use plastic bags usually wind up in a landfill or become litter that fouls the land and waterways and chokes unsuspecting animals. To avoid this waste, many people are turning to reusable bags made out of durable materials like canvas. Similarly, consumers concerned about the waste produced by billions of paper cups and Styrofoam containers are switching to travel mugs and reusable food containers. Public campaigns against bottled water highlight the large amount of waste—1.5 million tons annually—that this convenience produces and the strain it places on precious resources (in most parts of the developed world, tap water is perfectly safe to drink) (Baskind 2010).

Figure 6.7 Levels of CFC Production Before and After the Montreal Protocol (1987)

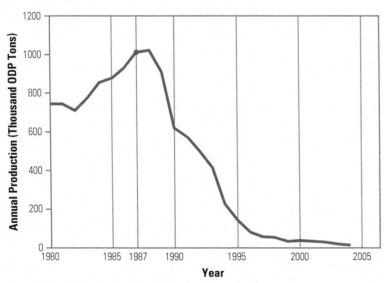

SOURCE: European FluoroCarbons Technical Committee, 2012.

Mark Bussell

Many cities have created designated bike lines to make biking a more appealing and safer option for commuters and residents.

Businesses respond when consumers demand green alternatives. Because of consumer anxiety about the toxic chemicals that wind up in the ground and water as a result of conventional farming practices, organic produce is now widely available in supermarkets and even in Walmart. And in part because of growing anxieties about the environmental footprint of beef and other meat sources (as well as increased concerns over animal welfare), more people are adopting vegetarian and vegan lifestyles; a massive new market in plant-based meat alternatives has emerged, including burgers that look, taste, and even bleed like beef. Also, in many parts of the country, consumers can tell their electric company that they would like part or all of their energy to come from renewable resources. Given the added cost, not everyone can afford to make these choices, but more and more consumers are deciding that the benefits are worth it.

Another lifestyle choice that has major implications for sustainability is transportation. While there is always room for improvement, cities like New York and Portland have taken great strides to make walking, biking, and public transportation more attractive by adding bike and bus lanes and extending service hours and regional service.

But old habits die hard. As I look out my office window in Manhattan, a sea of cars (especially yellow cabs!) chokes the six-lane road. Large SUVs containing a single occupant idle for minutes at a time, and tailpipe exhaust fills the air above them. Meanwhile, a few cyclists zip by, regularly beating cars to the same destination, but the nearby bike lanes remain underutilized. Many of those automobile commuters will fight traffic for an hour or more to get to their homes in Long Island or New Jersey, even though a commuter train makes the same journey in less time.

Certainly, many Americans seem to have no choice but to drive most of the time—particularly if they live outside of urban areas or even in cities lacking good public transit. Green transportation advocates recognize this reality. Rather than expecting people to ditch their cars, they urge people to be more selective about when and how they use them. Can they carpool? Is the train a viable option? Considering one's alternatives for a particular trip or daily commute, rather than simply making one's car the default choice, will contribute to reducing greenhouse gas emissions; and, if enough people begin to make these changes, the cumulative impact will be significant.

Depending on where you live and how much money you have, certain sustainable practices may not be an option for you. But everyone can take steps to learn more about the wider ecological impacts of their lifestyle and then decide what environmentally friendly changes are possible or attractive to them. One easy way to do this is to calculate your carbon footprint. A number of websites will estimate the amount of carbon emissions that you or your household are responsible for each year based on information you provide about transportation choices, electricity usage, and so on. After computing your carbon footprint and comparing it to the national and global average, the websites offer tips on how you can take steps to reduce your environmental impact (check out www.nature.org/greenliving/carboncalculator/).

Civic engagement in the form of voting and activism may be the single biggest way that all of us can contribute to making the world a greener place. A Swedish

Daniel Bockwoldt/dpa picture alliance/Alamy Stock Photo

Swedish teenager Greta Thunberg (shown here holding up a sign that says "School Strike for Climate") helped galvanize millions of high school students around the world to protest climate change and demand that government authorities accelerate their efforts to respond to the climate crisis. Thunberg and other youthful protesters have rightly pointed out that it is their generation that faces the greatest risks from inaction, so their elders in positions of power should listen!

teenager, Greta Thunberg, helped inspire a global youth climate strike that has contributed to reframing climate change as an existential threat to humanity (see image left). In the U.S., grassroots environmental protest movements like Sunrise and others have successfully fought against the construction of fossil fuel infrastructure such as natural gas pipelines. Although many conservative politicians still resist environmental protection efforts, there is now strong bipartisan support, especially among younger people, for enacting environmentally friendly regulations. Environmental policies that seemed farfetched only a few years ago, such as a carbon tax or the phasing out of fossil fuels, are now being seriously considered in Washington, D.C., and many state capitols, in large part as a response to the demands of younger people.

Conclusion: Linking Environmental and Social Facts

Any comprehensive analysis of society must account how humans interact with the environment, especially in the midst of the ongoing climate crisis. Studying the ways in which environment and society are enmeshed fosters dialogue between the natural and the social sciences, helping us see how the "natural" is always linked to the social. Because the ways we interact with our environment—whether we seek to protect or destroy it—are based on our interpretations of it, solving environmental problems will require acknowledging, and reconciling, disparate environmental worldviews.

Environmental sociologists make it clear that solving environmental problems will require significant social change, not just new technology. But is the pursuit of profit incompatible with sustainable development? Certainly, history has shown that capitalism leads to environmental degradation. However, the last several decades have also witnessed the emergence of green technologies and innovative environmental policies such as cap-and-trade programs for carbon emissions. While there is still a long way to go, societies are nonetheless making strides toward sustainability without sacrificing their gross domestic product. This has led a number of scholars to argue that economic growth *can* be adapted to sustainable goals. As society's preference for environmentally friendly products and industries escalates, so goes the argument, firms will compete for market shares by producing green

commodities and technologies. Can we leave it to the economy to produce sustainability? Would this alleviate environmental inequality or exacerbate it?

Sociologists agree a correlation exists between socioeconomic status and environmental risk. But what, exactly, is the nature of this relationship? While some studies clearly show that poor people of color are more likely to live near toxic waste facilities, this reveals a correlation but not causation. We are left wondering: Did companies discriminate by locating the facility there, or is it simply the case that both the residents and the firm settled in an area because it was affordable? Also, given that the majority of those in poverty are non-White, sociologists are often unable to determine whether it is race or class that plays the most important role in determining environmental risk.

How do we define and measure environmental risk? Even if we find that a poor neighborhood has higher rates of asthma than the surrounding areas, for instance, how can we actually demonstrate that the increased rate is because of nearby smokestacks and not other factors such as diet or exercise? At this point, we do not have enough data, or the right instruments, to precisely map the connections among geography, socioeconomic status, and risk. Gaining the ability to do so is crucial because environmental justice will only be achieved if we can reveal the mechanisms of injustice.

The Big Questions Revisited 6

6.1 **How Does Social Life Relate to the Natural Environment?** In this section, we explored how every society consumes and transforms the natural environment to satisfy its needs and desires while also adapting to its physical surroundings and confronting natural limits.

Understanding Environment–Society Relations

Traditional Societies

Learning Objective 6.1.1: Explain how a society's environment contributes to the cultural and religious traditions it develops.

Modern Societies

Learning Objective 6.1.2: Discuss the ways in which modern societies gained more control over their environment and developed stratified social structures.

The Environment–Society Dialogue

Learning Objective 6.1.3: Explain determinism and social constructivism and the ways in which environment both guides and constrains social life.

Key Terms

totemism (p. 134)   anthropocentrism (p. 134)
determinist (p. 134)   ecology (p. 134)
rural sociology (p. 134)   social construction
(of the environment) (p. 134)

6.2 **How Has Human Activity Harmed the Environment?** The most pressing environmental problems of our time—such as deforestation, water pollution, and global warming—are the result of human activities. This section described contemporary environmental problems and discussed how they are caused by industrial production and consumption.

Contemporary Environmental Problems

Global Warming

Learning Objective 6.2.1: Identify the variety of environmental transformations caused by climate change.

Natural Resource Depletion

Learning Objective 6.2.2: Discuss how the rapid depletion of major natural resources—oil, coal, forests, living species, and water—affects all forms of life.

Solid and Chemical Waste

Learning Objective 6.2.3: Discuss how attitudes toward waste and modes of waste removal threaten our health and environment.

Air and Water Pollution

Learning Objective 6.2.4: Discuss the impact human consumption has on air and water supplies.

Key Terms

fossil fuels (p. 138)   greenhouse effect (p. 138)
global warming (p. 138)   climate change (p. 139)
planned obsolescence (p. 142)   smog (p. 144)
acid rain (p. 144)

6.3 **How Do Environmental Factors Impact Inequality?** This section explored how sociologists examine environmental catastrophes, such as Hurricane Katrina, and how the structure of society shapes the effects of these environmental hazards.

The Environmental Movement and Social Inequality

The Environmental Movement

Learning Objective 6.3.1: Identify early preservationist figures and movements that have contributed to environmental awareness.

Environmental Justice

Learning Objective 6.3.2: Discuss environmental racism and what progress is being made to ensure equal protection for all people.

The Social Dimension of Natural Disasters

Learning Objective 6.3.3: Explain the reasons some groups are more adversely affected by natural disasters than other groups.

Global Environmental Inequality

Learning Objective 6.3.4: Identify the connection between global environmental responsibility and global environmental equality.

Key Terms

preservationist (p. 145)   conservationist (p. 145)
environmental racism (p. 147)   environmental
justice (p. 148)

6.4   **Can We Create More Sustainable Societies?** In this section, we discussed the social, political, and economic obstacles to adopting sustainable lifestyles in developed and developing countries, and we explored the ways in which we might be able to overcome these obstacles.

Consumption, Production, and Sustainability

The Tragedy of the Commons

Learning Objective 6.4.1: Compare the advantages and disadvantages of self-regulation and political regulation of environmental resources.

The Treadmill of Production

Learning Objective 6.4.2: Explain how economic systems focused on competition and expansion can contribute to serious environmental issues.

Toward Sustainability

Learning Objective 6.4.3: Discuss ways in which technology, politics, and lifestyle changes can contribute to environmental protection and sustainability.

Key Terms

sustainability (p. 151)   public/private paradox (p. 152)   renewable energy (p. 153)   cap-and-trade program (p. 154)

Chapter 7
Deviance and Social Control

By Troy Duster and Jeff Manza

Why do some kinds of behavior violate societal rules while other similar behaviors do not? How is it that *deviant* behavior is defined as such, and violators are sanctioned? We don't ordinarily observe the process by which deviance is defined until we notice what happens when someone tries to challenge those rules. Consider the universally accepted norm of wearing clothes. In the fall of 1992 at the University of California, Berkeley, a tall, thin, angular 20-year-old undergraduate began coming to his classes wearing only his key chain. Known as "Naked Guy," Andrew Martinez quickly achieved local and later national and international fame. At that time, neither the campus nor the city of Berkeley had any rules or regulations requiring people to wear clothes (Zengerle 2006). Long known for their progressive political traditions, Berkeley citizens and elected officials grappled with the novel question of whether Martinez should have the right to not wear clothes.

For several weeks, Martinez continued to walk the streets of the city and campus and attend his classes completely in the nude. Naked Guy sightings became events, and Martinez became a local celebrity. Even when he showed up at a party fully clothed in the middle of winter, students were thrilled to see him (Richards 2006). Defending his actions in a local newspaper and elsewhere, Martinez suggested that in his view clothing was oppressive. He claimed that "[w]hen I walk around nude, I am acting how I think it is reasonable to act, not how middle-class values tell me I should act. I am refusing to hide my dissent in normalcy, even though it is very easy to do so." With a local theater troupe (the X-Plicit Players), he even helped to organize a "nude-in," which succeeded in getting two dozen sympathizers to participate.

While many people simply ignored him, some students and residents complained to campus administrators and the local police. Soon thereafter, campus officials decided enough was enough and Martinez was suspended from the campus, but he continued to appear naked in public,

My Sociological Imagination

TROY DUSTER

The first 16 years of my life were spent in a low-income, racially segregated neighborhood on Chicago's South Side. It was a period in the United States in which racial segregation was taken for granted at barber shops, bowling alleys, swimming pools, and many public accommodations—even in the urban North. Frank Wong, the son of a Chinese restaurant owner in the area, was the only student in my high school who was not Black. Then, at age 17, I crossed town to attend Northwestern University, where I was one of only seven Blacks on a campus of over 7,000 Whites. Anthropologists call it "culture shock" when the deep assumptions about what is normal are disrupted by new circumstances, whether by travel to a foreign country or by being thrust into an unfamiliar social world where previously held assumptions have little or no relevance. For me, sociology provided a handle on my situation, a way to understand why and how people explain away their privilege as if it were an individual accomplishment. I watched with the astonishment of the outsider how people from wealthy families concluded unreflectively that the way the world was ordered was natural and right. Of course, many poor people also see the way the world is organized as normal, so that was no surprise. But it was the attempt to explain the "why" that caught my attention, intrigued and stoked my intellectual curiosity, and brought me into sociology.

Cyclists ride naked for the World Naked Bike Ride.
Deliberately engaging in acts of public deviance is
one way to force both the authorities and ordinary
people to think about the boundaries of acceptable
behavior.

Jason M. Grow/KRT/Newscom

The Naked Guy of Berkeley, Andrew Martinez, attending a class at the University of California, Berkeley in 1992.

even attending a City Council meeting unclothed to plead his case. But it was to no avail—the council passed a measure banning public nudity and shortly thereafter began arresting Martinez whenever he appeared naked in public. Eventually, Martinez disappeared from public life, and the controversy he had created quickly disappeared from the news.

The story of the naked guy may seem like an "only in Berkeley" story—a strange and easily forgotten episode. Yet, it actually raises a number of profound questions. For starters, why exactly do we have to wear clothes? Who decided that clothes are a necessary part of our everyday appearance? Further, why do governments, in this case the Berkeley city government, assume the authority—in the name of the public—to arrest and punish someone simply for refusing to wear clothes? It's not likely to become a leading civil rights cause anytime soon, but once we ask ourselves why covering our bodies is an obligation, we open up a whole series of questions that go to the heart of how society exerts its force over individuals and with what consequences. That is the subject of this chapter.

The Big Questions

1. **What is deviance?** To understand deviance, we first need to ask the question, "What is normal?" We explore the origins of deviant behavior by examining the role of groups and group boundaries in the creation of social norms. We also explore the distinction between statistical and social deviance and introduce the concept of stigma.

2. **How is social control imposed on society?** Next, we examine how and where social control is developed. Social control involves how societies regulate and sanction behavior in such a way that it encourages conformity and discourages deviance from the norms. These range from basic socialization processes to social approval and disapproval, all the way to the criminal justice system (where the most serious violations are handled).

3. **How is moral behavior defined and regulated?** Societies have long tried to dictate and control individuals' behavior and morality, which highlights a special kind of deviance. We explore two moral crusades (alcohol and morphine misuse in the United States) to highlight the process of defining normal behavior and why certain kinds of behavior come to be labeled deviant or even criminal. We then look at some contemporary moral crusades and consider the future of moral regulation.

4. **How do power and inequality impact deviance?** Insights into deviant behavior come from studying the social and economic positions, cultural practices, and attendant political power of dominant groups. In this section, we explore the relationship between deviance and power.

archna nautiyal/Shutterstock

BIG QUESTION 7.1   What Is Deviance?

DEVIANCE AND THE GROUP

Before we can consider what is deviant, we first need to ask the question, "What is normal?" And this question in turn raises a prior question: "Who decides what is normal and therefore what is deviant?" To explore these questions, we begin with the most fundamental building block of normality and deviance: the group.

Groups and Group Boundaries

7.1.1 Identify how groups distinguish themselves.

From small groups like families and sports teams to larger ones like neighborhoods, organizations, and even entire nations, individuals belong to groups. Sociologists define a **social group** as a collection of people who interact with one another and who have a shared sense of belonging. One such group is the family. Most humans across the globe are born into families that impose fundamental rules such as when and how to eat food and whom to obey. In *Civilization and Its Discontents*, Sigmund Freud (1961 [1930]) pointed out that all cultures impose on their young some very strict rules about the most basic of needs (for example, at an early age, the child is told to stop "playing with your food!"), which sets up the first great conflict between individual and society. Freud saw this as one of the first lessons of dominance and social control—and, in turn, among the first lessons about the futility of rebellion. Anyone who has reared a child understands Freud's idea as a metaphor for what happens throughout life. Just as the child ultimately gives up and gives over to the behavioral rules established by others, so too must we consent to group rules and norms if we are to fit in. And here we come to the first axiom in the study of deviance and control: This early struggle is first and foremost about the

parents' notion of normality and only secondarily about the child. Deviance and control always constitute a paired relationship, and even in this earliest of all subsequent pairings, it is the more powerful member of the group (the parents) that determines what is normal and thus what is deviant for other group members (children).

Throughout our lives, groups outside the family exert similar pressures to conform. Much of the time, our consent to these pressures is voluntary. How do groups achieve this power? One way is through *positive affirmations*—or claims—that groups use to establish boundaries. An infinite variety of markings, behaviors, and attributes are possible. Examples range from cutting three lines across the forehead (common among the Nuer people of Sudan) to pledging fraternity or sorority X versus Y (common in U.S. colleges). Some groups in society—such as many street gangs—may wear certain kinds of clothing and/or have tattoos and body piercings. Others may develop a specific code of speech and/or behavior. Such positive affirmations signal who is in the group and who is out. But merely being a compliant member in good standing of a group is not the whole story; the *negative affirmations* of group membership—what we aren't allowed to do if we are to retain membership—constitute the other side of group influence. Both are important, and we need to examine them in more detail.

All groups set markers at their boundaries. Beginning with our earliest group—our family—we quickly learn who is and who is not in the group. While groups are often defined through objective criteria such as having a shared language or the same job, the identity of the group is more importantly tied to the way group members define themselves and are defined by others. In high school, students may refer to those who seem to study too hard as "nerds" and the ones who play sports as "jocks." These are not innocent labels but include value judgments. The ideas and values about who the group members are, what sociologists call **symbolic boundaries**, really give a group its identity (Lamont and Molnar 2002).

One way to think about symbolic boundaries is to consider the role of space and how different spaces are defined. When you enter a church, for example, you are not simply crossing a physical boundary between the church doors and the outside world but also a symbolic boundary between a religious space and a secular one. The very meaning of the space is different, as is how we are supposed to behave in it. Immigration—the process of moving from one country to another—provides another good example of how physical and symbolic boundaries work to define groups. Countries often mark boundaries by establishing physical borders, such as on the U.S.–Mexico border. Such borders signal that we are moving from a territory belonging to one group to a territory belonging to another.

However, boundaries differentiate not only physical space but also symbolic space. Just because immigrants cross from Mexico into the United States does not mean they have become American. On the contrary, as the conflict over immigration in the United States shows, people use a whole range of symbolic boundaries to differentiate those who are considered true "Americans" from those who are not. These symbolic boundaries involve setting up differences between our ideas of "us" and "them," including ideas about who Mexicans are and why they may be considered different than Americans.

Group boundaries are a key aspect of understanding deviance because of the role groups play in defining and setting limits of acceptable behavior. We have powerful incentives to do as the group demands if we want to be part of the group. Being part of a group means behaving within the boundaries of the community. As long as we abide by these rules, we can expect to enjoy the benefits of group membership, which may include status and honor, the friendship of other group members, and access to special opportunities or rewards. Groups often police their boundaries to prevent outsiders (especially unwanted outsiders) from entering. Symbolic and physical boundaries are set up with the explicit purpose of keeping outsiders out, and the crossing of such boundaries by group members can be considered an act of deviance. Consider again the example of immigration: "Illegal immigration" is defined as the unauthorized crossing of a boundary. In this way, deviance takes place both when someone moves outside the boundaries he or she is expected to live in and when he or she enters another group's space.

What are the benefits of maintaining and marking boundaries and restricting access to outsiders? Some groups, like political parties, gain status when they have as many members as possible. In this case, there will be few, if any, barriers to membership—for example, anyone can decide to call themselves a Republican or a Democrat. The more the merrier. Some political parties, especially in other political systems, require you to fill out a membership card and perhaps pay some dues, although again usually almost anyone is welcome, even if there is a formal process of joining. Political parties are unusual groups in that their status derives from having as many members as possible. For many other kinds of groups, however, limiting membership as a way of maintaining the status of the group is essential. If just anyone can join, membership will be devalued. The most prestigious groups are usually very exclusive. Think of an expensive suburb—the cost of housing can be very high, partly because that suburb will typically prevent cheap apartments from being constructed. In this way, the value of houses is not diminished by having less affluent people living in the neighborhood (and residents of expensive suburbs will often fight hard to prevent any such construction). A fancy country club, an honorary association (where only the "best" are selected as members), or a professional sports league raise the value of membership by holding down the number of slots available to others.

In addition to rules for what members *must* do, all groups also have rules for what members must *not* do. The set of excluded behaviors, or prohibitions, is the key ingredient of deviant behavior: It is the behavior that violates the group consensus of what *we must not do*. Any couple that has dated or married across sharply defined group boundaries (Blacks and Whites, Chinese and Koreans, same-sex couples, Hindus and Muslims, and others) has likely experienced expressions of disapproval from other group members (perhaps including one's own family). The major religions of the world have many explicit rules believers must follow. For instance, the Christian commandments forbid murder, adultery, and theft. The Koran forbids these three and alcohol consumption. Such prohibitions empower authorities to punish those group members who deviate, with the punishment of ostracism for violators serving as the ultimate way groups maintain boundaries.

Explicit rules banning certain kinds of behaviors are often written down. The oldest known written set of laws in human history is the Hammurabi code. It originated in the ancient city of Babylon, around 1780 BCE. Most known for the famous justice maxim of "an eye for an eye," the Hammurabi code also included a specific set of punishments that aimed to best fit specific deviant acts. Since the time of the Hammurabi code, as groups and societies began to prescribe punishments for specific acts, they have revealed in the process much about what they truly value. For example, during the early and middle parts of the nineteenth century, governing bodies in the western region of the United States sometimes imposed the death penalty for horse thieves, while a conviction for murder could be punishable by just a few years in prison. This speaks loudly to what was most valued by those with the power to decide punishment at that time.

Sentences and punishments, when they appear whimsical or irrational, raise questions about the legitimacy of the group or society making the rules. Indeed, in the late eighteenth and early nineteenth centuries, as the first prisons and criminal justice systems began to appear in Western societies, their credibility was often undermined by the arbitrary manner in which punishments for crimes were determined and given out. Some thieves were hanged for stealing cloth worth very little, while rapists and murderers could serve as little as a few months in prison. Moreover, for the same crime, one person could get 20 years of imprisonment while another served only a few weeks.

Numerous social theorists, essayists, historians, and moral philosophers observed, lamented, analyzed, and commented on how the chaotically uneven punishments undermined the legitimacy of the government's use of its punitive powers. Some eighteenth- and nineteenth-century philosophers began to argue that it was imperative to find a way to "make the punishment fit the crime," implicitly criticizing the arbitrary character of medieval systems of justice. The first major reform of the penal codes was inspired by this situation, and codification finally occurred in the mid-nineteenth century and swept through most Western societies. The most important influence on the reform movement in punishment was a book published in 1764 by Italian social theorist Cesare Beccaria. Simply titled *On Crimes and Punishments*, Beccaria set forth a theory of how and why justice should be meted out to the perpetrator. His main concern was that the citizenry had a sense that the criminal justice system was fair. A key element was the open, transparent, and public nature of laws and the corresponding transparency of the punishment attached to criminal activity. This left room for the possible fluidity of the severity of punishment (attached to a specific crime) if there was a public outcry about the unfairness—an issue that remains heavily debated today in extreme cases. For example, a man was sentenced to 50 years to life for stealing a few DVDs for his children at Christmas (one was reported to be *Snow White*); this was his "third strike" under California's three-strike criminal justice law in which anyone receiving a third felony conviction would be sent to prison for a long mandatory sentence, no matter what the third offense was (Cannon 2005).

Statistical versus Social Deviance

7.1.2 Discuss how statistical deviance differs from social deviance.

As we think further about the nature of deviance, it is important to make a distinction between frequent and

rare behaviors and whether or not those behaviors violate written or unwritten rules. Rare behaviors can be "deviant" in the sense that they are uncommon but not necessarily deviant in the sociological sense. Consider the following example: In a high school class, one or more students may choose to wear a baseball cap, a scarf, or a beret during class. In this case, wearing head coverings could be defined as **statistically deviant** (most students do not wear head coverings during class), but it would not be defined as **socially deviant** (behavior that violates societal rules)—at least not in most classrooms and schools in the United States. To be sure, if one or two of those students chose to take off their clothes and get naked, it would quickly become socially deviant (as the case of Andrew Martinez suggests in the chapter opener). In schools that require students to wear uniforms, those who are out of uniform are socially deviant and can expect to be sanctioned. But unless there is an explicit dress code, students usually can get away with dressing the way they please. Those who wear unusual clothing may stand out from others, but they are not violating any societal or school rules.

The distinction between statistical deviance and social deviance is important because what is considered deviant (or even criminal) has little to do with how common it is. We might think that being socially deviant means doing something most people don't do, and likewise that acting "normal" means doing what most people do. But that is simply not always the case. Take

In 1989, the French government banned the wearing of headscarves known as the hijab worn by Muslim women in public schools. The policy was said to be designed to prevent the display of religious symbols in public places and underscore France's secular values. The law created an international controversy, and the government soon announced that it was up to individual school administrators to decide whether to enforce it. Later, however, in 2011 the French government took a further step in the same direction by banning the wearing of full-face coverings, known as the niqab or the burqa, in any public place. These laws transfer what might be statistical deviance (Muslims are a small minority of the population in France) into social deviance.

smoking marijuana or committing adultery. Many adult Americans have tried cannabis products at some point in their lives, which is still a criminal act in a majority of states in the U.S. and countries around the world (although many states and countries are now moving toward legalization). Yet most people who have smoked a joint or taken an edible cannabis product would probably not think of themselves as criminals. Similarly, adultery is statistically very common in the United States, with some estimates suggesting that more than 20 percent of married persons have committed adultery at some point during their marriage. Adultery is no longer a criminal act in the United States, but despite so many spouses cheating on each other, it is still considered deviant (except in "open" marriages). It violates a social norm about marriage and crosses boundaries of acceptable behavior for a married partner.

When thinking about social deviance, then, it is important to distinguish between deviant behavior and deviant persons. Just because someone engages in some form of behavior that others in the group or society would label as deviant does not mean that the person will be so characterized. Indeed, in the normal course of life, each of us will transgress some rule, and when large numbers of people start disregarding the same rule, the typical response is to **normalize** the deviant behavior—that is, to recast the behavior into a frame that rescues the person as "normal" even as the behavior is deemed deviant.

Social Norms: The Unstated Rules of Everyday Life

7.1.3 Define the term *social norm*.

Contemporary societies like the United States have vast legal systems and criminal codes that specify criminal or illegal activity in far greater detail than our forebears could have envisioned. When the explicit, written rules of the criminal code are violated, we have names for the so-called deviants—ranging from murderer to thief, from arsonist to rapist. Yet a vital aspect of social control is the enforcement of the unstated, unwritten, and nonarticulated rules—what sociologists call **norms**. Every society, even those with elaborate written rules and criminal codes, inevitably has an enormous number of *unwritten* rules of behavior that must be mastered to avoid appearing deviant. French sociologist Emile Durkheim, writing more than a century ago about such matters, called this "the unstated terms of the social contract" (Durkheim [1890] 1997). Durkheim was referring

to the fact that rules of behavior do not need to be written to require conformity. For example, when you enter an almost empty auditorium, and only one other person is seated, "everyone knows" that unless that person is a friend, the seats on either side are off limits. The norm is that we do not sit next to strangers unless there is no alternative seat available (and to be safe, if there is only one other person in the auditorium, you should probably choose a different row to sit in).

Norms, then, are basic rules of society that help us know what is and what is not appropriate to do in any given situation (see Chapters 4 and 5 for other discussions of the importance of norms). At a very basic level, these unstated rules tell us a lot about the nature and character of our society. One of those unwritten rules is the "norm of engagement." Nowhere is it written, but North Americans have a near universal understanding that they must always be engaged with some object or person (Goffman 1963). If you doubt this is true, try the following experiment: In the presence of those who know you (family, friends, or people at work), sit for several minutes and do nothing. Have no object in your hand (no book or magazine, smartphone, iPad, or other object) and have no music or television playing to provide a possible object of your attention. Just sit there. Within a few minutes, you will experience what happens when the norm of engagement is violated: Those around you will start to become uncomfortable and wonder what is wrong with you. Should you persist long enough in this comatose state, at some point your family or friends will start to worry that perhaps some kind of mental disturbance is occurring.

It is not easy to trace where such unwritten rules of behavior come from. In contrast to written rules and laws, which have a history that can be traced by researchers using historical records, legal case law, and other written sources, the origins of norms are more obscure and often impossible to uncover. One idea is that they have their roots in societal processes where the desires and preferences of powerful groups get extended throughout an entire society. The norm of engagement that sociologist Erving Goffman analyzed likely has its roots in fears of idleness ("an idle mind is the devil's workshop") and is perhaps also linked to the idea that we should always use our time productively in some fashion. The norm of personal space may have its roots in larger ideas about personal privacy and "private property" (which space can become yours once it is claimed). But whatever the precise origin of these norms, we can be sure that they grew out of a social process of defining what is normal in light of other ideas about proper behavior.

Images-USA/Alamy Stock Photo

BIG QUESTION 7.2 How Is Social Control Imposed on Society?

SOCIAL CONTROL AND SOCIAL ORDER

As we have seen so far, society imposes rules about normal and deviant behavior, most definitively by establishing criminal laws and criminal codes, which deliver the final word about what is deviant behavior when the prison door slams shut. When some kinds of deviance become crimes, they pass into the realm of the *institutions of social control*—such as the police, criminal courts, and prisons and jails—that are all around us. For early sociologists, like Emile Durkheim, the question of how societies control deviant behavior was a central puzzle: What is it that prevents societies from dissolving into chaos? What holds them together (Durkheim [1890] 1997; for an early and influential American sociologist asking similar questions, see Ross [1901] 2009)? And one key answer was through **social control**. In Chapter 4 and Chapter 5, we discussed how contemporary sociologists view the problem of social control through the lens of social interaction and social structure.

In this section, we examine how social control—the societal regulation of behavior to encourage conformity to and discourage deviance from the norms—is taught to beginners, enforced through everyday actions, and how it extends all the way up to the institutions of criminal justice in cases of certain kinds of behaviors that are not only deviant, but considered criminal.

Socialization: Learning the Rules of the Game

7.2.1 Explain how acceptable behavior is learned through socialization.

The heart of the process whereby individuals learn what is and is not acceptable is known as **socialization**. All of the new social contexts in which we find ourselves as we move through life will require undergoing some type of socialization to learn the appropriate rules and how to avoid engaging in deviant behavior (see Chapter 5 for further details). A newborn infant knows nothing about societal rules of any kind. Infants want immediate gratification of needs, and they will not hesitate to scream or cry when those needs are not met. But infants are more or less happily indulged, as their adult caregivers recognize that they are not yet capable of other ways of expressing themselves. If older children were to scream or cry every time they did not get what they want, however, they would sooner or later suffer some significant negative responses from the adults around them. "Use your words," parents might say to a 2-year-old, and heard often enough, eventually the child learns to use words to express needs or preferences. But an older child who continues to scream and cry and refuses to use words to express needs would eventually be referred for some kind of therapy to figure out why they cannot master basic rules of human communication.

The process of socialization starts in infancy and extends throughout life. We've already noted how groups—ranging from families to friends, clubs, religious groups, sports teams, fraternities and sororities, racial and ethnic groups, and so forth—maintain rules that members must follow. But how do new members learn these rules? The short answer is through socialization. Each time we become a member of a new group, we have to learn the ways of the group and what is and is not acceptable for group members. Imitating others is a critical way in which newcomers learn how to behave. If there is someone available to teach a new member the rules—a social role known as *mentor*—the process can be considerably eased, particularly when it comes to the subtleties of appropriate behavior that may not be easily learned through simple imitation. For example, many of the things

New sorority (of fraternity) members, such as those pictured here, will learn the norms and rules of the organization through a process of socialization. Thereafter, they will be expected to follow the customs of the group.

we need to know upon joining a sports team for the first time can be learned through imitation—just do what the other players do. But some important things may not be obvious to the novice. On the football team, putting on the uniform, running out on the field, celebrating successful play, listening to the coach's instructions, and many other things can be learned simply by doing what everyone else does until they become habit. But there are less obvious things that someone such as a coach or another player will have to tell the new player so he doesn't make a mistake. For example, not tipping off a play to the other team involves subtle cues and body language that can be learned but often must be taught.

Socialization into "normal" behavior is necessary throughout life, and not just when we enter new groups. Most of the time, we don't even realize we are undergoing socialization. We absorb rules about acceptable or unacceptable behavior without consciously thinking about it. We probably do not notice the moment where we go from novice to competent (if not expert) performer. But avoiding mistakes and doing what is expected in all of the settings around us is one of the most powerful ways in which the process of "being human" is achieved.

Sanctions and Rewards for Conformity and Resistance

7.2.2 Analyze ways in which societies exert social control through positive and negative sanctions.

A key dimension of social control occurs through the **sanctions**, or punishments, that groups and societies establish to enforce norms. Sanctions serve to enforce the lessons of socialization and are applied to socially deviant behavior. At the extreme, sanctions against deviance include punishments of various kinds, all the way up to imprisonment or even the death penalty. But sanctions are not the only way social control is promoted. We often follow rules and norms not just because we are worried about punishment, but also because we may seek rewards that good behavior provides. Positive rewards might include things like praise, awards, and salary raises. Doing what the boss wants, no matter how irrational it may be, is generally a better way of getting a raise or moving up in a company, whereas challenging the boss—even if entirely warranted—can put an employee at risk.

Sociologists distinguish between two types of sanctions and rewards: formal and informal. *Formal sanctions* are used to enforce norms that are written down and may be enforced by a group of people who have been given the power to do so, such as parking supervisors, school principals, human resource professionals, or police officers. *Formal rewards*, by contrast, are designed to bestow something concrete to a person who has conformed to the group rules and norms especially well. These kinds of formal rewards or sanctions often become part of a performance record such as a report card, written citation, or year-end evaluation at the workplace.

On the other hand, *informal sanctions* include all of the ways in which we express disapproval without invoking some kind of written rule. This might include such things as insults or simply giving someone a dirty look. Similarly, *informal rewards* include things like giving people compliments of one kind or another. The fact that such informal sanctions and rewards are not generally part of any written record is important. If a teacher compliments you on your work, that is nice, but you really want to see that positive evaluation expressed as a higher grade. Similarly, most employees would be much happier with raises and promotions than verbal compliments from their boss (even if the compliments are nice).

The process of conforming to norms is not always so simple as just following the rules. Although deviance usually elicits a negative response, it can sometimes paradoxically result in a positive response. Think of the cool "bad boy" or "bad girl" at the high school you attended (every high school has such figures). In defying the school's authority and rules, they gained a higher status than their more conformist peers. Or think of the classic (mythical) example of Robin Hood. As the story goes, Robin Hood was a thief, and societies generally treat robbery as a deviant act that deserves punishment. However, Robin Hood's act of stealing from the very rich and giving the money to the destitute poor is more typically viewed as heroic. Or, consider the strategic visions of Mahatma Gandhi and Martin Luther King Jr. In promoting the use of **civil disobedience** (nonviolent protests) to challenge unjust laws, Gandhi and King today are heroic figures for refusing to bend to the will of an oppressive authority and inspiring major social change with the independence movement in India and the civil rights movement in the United States, respectively.

By contrast, conformist behavior can in some cases result in negative responses or perceptions. Consider for example people who do whatever it takes to please others and get their approval. In school (or work settings), these conformists may be ridiculed by other students (or co-workers) as the teacher's (or employer's) "pet," while at the same time they may be rewarded by their teacher (although if their conformity is too obvious, it can become grating even for the teacher or boss). We have all kinds of nasty names for people who are too conformist in their behavior. In the extreme case, simply following the orders of Adolf Hitler and the Nazi government during World War II is today not only regarded as inappropriate, but criminal. The government officials who ran the concentration camps where the Holocaust was carried out—millions of innocent people were killed because of their religion or political beliefs—were, as they all said at their trials after the war, just doing what they were told to do by their superiors. They were, in short, conforming to the rules. But the acts they engaged in were so heinous that conformity is generally not regarded as an appropriate defense. In fact, the social deviants of Nazi Germany—the groups that resisted Hitler and the Nazi Party, and in many cases lost their lives—are now considered the heroes of that period. In all of these situations, it is not so simple as saying that following rules and norms entails approval while not following social norms means disapproval. Knowing how to strike the right balance reflects a full understanding of the written and unwritten rules.

The ambiguities between deviance and conformity have created pressures to expand the definition of deviance to cover all possible types of behaviors and contingencies, even though this is ultimately a hopeless effort. This endless expansion of rules was a point that German social theorist Max Weber noted early in the twentieth century, calling the rise of ever greater formality the "iron cage" of modern society. As societies have become ever more complex, there has been a shift away from emphasis on informal means of social control toward more formal means. We are all subject to a much longer list of formal rules than our ancestors a couple of hundred years ago would recognize. Bureaucracies grow for many reasons, but one important one is simply to fairly administer the growing system of rules that humans constantly create. A good example of this today can be seen in the case of the enforcement of sexual assault and harassment rules on college campuses. Behavior that once might have been dismissed is now subject to careful review and sanctioning by administrators tasked with identifying and punishing assault and harassment on college campuses (Hirsch and Kahn 2020).

Social Stigma and the Marking of Deviance

7.2.3 Explain how a social stigma can serve as a sanction for deviant behavior.

One of the most vicious ways in which societies impose sanctions on individuals who engage in some deviant acts is through what is known as a **stigma**, the labelling of individuals as defective in some way and the tendencies for others to read the individual accordingly. Social theorist Erving Goffman (1961) wrote elegantly and persuasively about the ways in which stigma creates a *spoiled identity* for anyone who has one. This spoiled identity is often difficult or impossible to erase (especially in the era of social media). There are many forms of stigma, but what they all have in common is that they impose a negative identity or credential on someone that others will recognize. Some types of stigma are related to physical characteristics, not behavior. A disfigurement, a disability, or skin color are all examples of physical characteristics that can be stigmatizing for an individual. However, other kinds of stigma can arise from some past deviant behavior that attaches to an individual and influences the way others see her or him.

How does stigma arising from deviant behavior become visible? Gossip and information can spread among communities and social networks. But sometimes stigma is announced. Perhaps the most famous literary example related to deviant behavior can be seen in Nathaniel Hawthorne's 1850 historical novel *The Scarlet Letter*. Set in puritan Boston in the mid-seventeenth century, the protagonist of the story, Hester Prynne, is forced to wear a scarlet letter "A" on her clothing to constantly remind everyone in the community of her deviant behavior. (Prynne had committed adultery and became pregnant outside of marriage, a significant violation of prevailing social norms in puritan society.) In this dramatic example, Prynne's stigma is made visible in a way she cannot escape. Another famous example was the identification of Jews in Germany and later in

Nazi-controlled areas of Europe during World War II. All Jews were forced to wear a yellow star of David to identify their Jewish identity and mark their stigma for all to see.

Although in the United States today we do not require people with stigmas to wear identifying marks, there are important ways in which an individual's past deviant behavior may be marked and made visible for others to see. The most dramatic example of this happens when someone acquires a **criminal record**, a formal written report of an individual's illegal actions. The criminal record may be created by the police during an investigation of a crime or following an arrest, and, if a conviction is entered, the record will often become permanent. Once it is entered, a criminal record will potentially influence many other parts of an individual's life. For example, many employers will be reluctant to hire someone with a criminal record. Finding an apartment to rent or even a partner to date can be negatively impacted by the existence of a criminal record, even if the offense was long ago or for a minor offense. The issue of criminal records and their importance for individuals has increased in recent decades. Prior to the rise of the Internet, an individual's criminal record was often buried in written records that would be hard for anyone to search and typically only a trained investigator could access. Today, in most states, criminal records are easily accessible via an Internet search (see Jacobs 2014).

Another important way in which the Internet has made it harder to remove a stigma for past deviant behavior is media coverage. Anything covered in the media—traditional or social—that is discoverable through an Internet search can become a stigma. Scandals or negative publicity are no longer short-term events that will be forgotten but are now potentially something that will stay with an individual for life. Erving Goffman would have marveled at this new social capacity to publicly display a spoiled identity. The significance of this kind of stigma is so great that there are companies that offer services (for a significant fee) to try to remove, or "scrub," negative information from the Internet.

Identifying Criminal Deviance

7.2.4 Analyze the differences between social and criminal deviance.

Many forms of social deviance are handled as internal matters by groups and organizations, and authority figures within these groups will impose sanctions or provide rewards for good behavior. But some socially deviant behaviors are so problematic that they are not left in private hands for appropriate societal response. These forms of deviance, which we generally think of as criminal deviance, are handled by criminal justice institutions. The **criminal justice system** includes criminal law (in the United States, the federal government, all 50 states, and county and local governments have their own criminal codes), formal authorities who administer these laws (such as police forces that identify and apprehend offenders, lawyers, judges, and court systems through which offenders are evaluated and assigned sentences when a conviction is obtained), and the jails and prisons where offenders may be sentenced to serve time (as well as the corrections officials such as probation and parole officers who supervise convicted offenders not sent to jail or prison). Compared to what existed 200 years ago, the vast expansion of criminal justice institutions is a remarkable and important development, making possible a much wider and harsher range of sanctions for deviant behavior.

The question of what kinds of behaviors come to be viewed as criminal is complicated. One important source is the role of the powerful in defining what is criminally deviant, a topic we treat in the next section. But for now, we can get a better sense of the difference between social and criminal deviance by exploring a punishment pyramid developed by criminologist John Hagan (1994). He proposes a three-dimensional model that distinguishes among deviant acts as a way of separating those treated as "criminal" and among the "criminal" acts treated with more or less severity by a society. See his representation of this idea in Figure 7.1.

Figure 7.1 Hagan's Punishment Pyramid

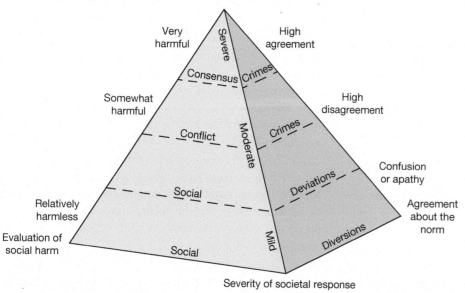

Severity of societal response

SOURCE: Hagan 1994.

The three legs in Hagan's pyramid takes into account (1) many kinds of socially deviant behaviors for which the harm is widely viewed as minimal (picking your nose in public) and (2) potentially deviant behaviors for which there is not consistent agreement about the underlying social norm (for example, smoking marijuana or premarital sex). In cases where an act is regarded as socially harmful and for which there is widespread agreement about the violation of an underlying norm, the offender is much more likely to face a sanction through the criminal justice system.

How is the punishment of deviant behavior in the criminal justice system different from other kinds of sanctions? One way is to note that the dominant purposes of punishment in the criminal justice system go beyond simply preventing future crimes, although that is certainly one of the reasons for criminal punishment. Societies also employ criminal sanctions as a form of simple vengeance, resting on the idea that a criminal deviant should suffer in ways comparable to the victim. The other major purpose of punishment relates specifically to the idea that removing criminal deviants from society and sending them to prison will prevent them from committing further offenses (at least for some period of time), and/or provide a context for helping offenders to stop committing further crimes through therapy, education, and job training (see Chapter 19 for more on the purposes of criminal punishment).

BIG QUESTION 7.3 How Is Moral Behavior Defined and Regulated?

Coombs Images/Alamy Stock Photo

THE PROBLEM OF MORAL REGULATION

At the center of the societal struggle over what is and what is not deviance is a provocative question: What is morality and appropriately moral behavior? At all times and places, societies struggle with questions of **moral behavior**—that is, which types of behaviors will be considered good and right (*moral*) versus those that are bad and wrong (*immoral*). Some common examples in contemporary America include debates over whether or not drug use or same-sex relationships are compatible with social understandings of morality. What is considered immoral behavior is constantly at issue because in any society, different groups will inevitably have different views and understandings. When societies attempt to outlaw certain kinds of previously common and widespread behavior across society, it is invariably a highly controversial process. How do moral and immoral behaviors come to be defined, and how does the definition of moral behavior change over time? How and why does society attempt to control and police the moral behavior of individuals—and with what consequences?

Interested versus Disinterested Punishment

7.3.1 Distinguish between interested and disinterested punishment.

A useful place to start is to note a classical distinction between what has been called *interested punishment* versus *disinterested punishment* (Ranulf 1938). This distinction refers to two different kinds of reasons for creating rules for moral behavior and systems of punishment for their violation: (1) those that arise out of a desire to protect wealth and private property versus (2) those that attempt to direct and control the behavior of individuals for the common good. Because there is an existing distribution of wealth and power in any society, the most privileged groups and classes have a strong and direct interest in maintaining their wealth and social and political domination. To be sure, we all have an interest in having our private property protected, but for holders of great wealth, the stakes are much higher. Laws against theft and fraud originated in the desire of the powerful to protect their wealth and privilege without having to maintain private security forces. These laws eventually filtered down into ordinary criminal law rules against theft of all kinds. Transgressors, insurgents, and rebels who threatened the private property of wealth-holders could expect firm punishment, and it was a short step from there to generalizing these types of punishment to protect everyone's property. The biblical commandment "thou shalt not steal" is entirely consistent with the interests of wealth-holders, but provides benefits for ordinary people as well.

On the other hand, many rules and laws have nothing to do with the distribution of wealth. These laws relate to behaviors, such as tobacco use, alcohol and drug consumption, gambling, and prostitution, and can even include such behavior as the way one dresses, engages in demonstrative behavior in public places, or has same-sex liaisons (all of which have at one time or another been the subject of societal rules and even criminal laws). These kinds of rules and laws are designed not to protect property but rather to control the morals and social behavior of people. But in order for proposals for specific kinds of moral regulation to prevail, they had to find broad popular support. Most moral crusades have included public information campaigns designed to demonize individuals engaged in behavior that the crusaders consider immoral.

Keeping the two kinds of punishments in mind is important. But they are not necessarily always independent. Throughout American history, right up to the present, the effort to control morality among certain lower-status groups—people of color, poor people, immigrants, and others—has been closely connected to the interests of the powerful in maintaining social order (Beisel 1997). Moral reformers targeting the poor may have had good motives, believing that encouraging good behavior on the part of the poor will make them better workers and citizens. But in attempting to bring about these outcomes, moral reformers have frequently contributed to stigmatizing poor people and creating negative images in the public mind about the poor. In the next section, we consider a classic example.

An Example: The Temperance Movement as a Moral Crusade

7.3.2 Analyze the history of alcohol use and how it relates to definitions of normal and deviant.

How do moral and immoral behaviors get defined? How do they evolve over time? How do these behaviors relate (or not) to group interests? To help answer these

questions, it is useful to study some historical examples. Perhaps the most famous case in American history was the long campaign against alcohol. Once upon a time, at the beginning of the nation and for its first few decades, people drank so much alcohol that one historian suggested that the United States could appropriately be called the "Alcoholic Republic" (Rorabaugh 1979). In the early eighteenth century, Americans drank five gallons of alcohol per capita every year. By 1830, per capita consumption had gone up even further, to seven gallons. That is the equivalent of nearly two bottles of 80-proof hard liquor per drinking adult per week—even factoring in low drinkers and nondrinkers (Okrent 2010, p.8). (To give a sense of the magnitude of this consumption, today Americans consume about two gallons per capita; in the 1830s, the average person was drinking 3.5 times as much alcohol as today!) So how did the United States go from being a nation soaked in alcohol to the only rich democratic country ever to enact a constitutional amendment banning the consumption of alcohol during the period known as **Prohibition** (1920–1933)?

Up until the middle of the nineteenth century, while it was common for a man to down several swigs of hard liquor every single day, it was typically done in the home, not in taverns, saloons, public bars, or in the streets. As more and more people moved from rural farms to cities, with industrialization and the massive influx of European immigrants in the last half of the century, all of that changed. The new immigrants were often concentrated in the poorest sections of cities in the industrializing North. The older generation of Americans—mainly from northern and western Europe—felt threatened by what they perceived as a change in "American values" and traditions. More specifically, the movement for the prohibition of alcohol was a crusade to reestablish the traditional values that the upper-middle classes believed were slipping away (Gusfield 1963). It was, in short, the late-nineteenth-century version of "Make America Great Again."

Still, it is remarkable that we could go from a nation in which a pint of liquor a day was normal to a period of constitutionally mandated prohibition. How did this happen—and more importantly, why? The story begins in a small town in Ohio in 1873, when a small group of middle-class White women entered a saloon, sunk to their knees, and prayed for the souls of the owners that they might stop serving alcohol. While this is often cited as the launch of what is known as the Temperance Movement ("temperance" in this period meant moderation, not abstinence), historians note that there had been strong and insistent calls for moderation of alcohol consumption for much of the previous three decades. No single factor explains the success of the movement to rid the nation of alcohol, but there is a consensus that the new

The most prominent group calling for the prohibition of alcohol in the nineteenth century was the Women's Christian Temperance Union, although they found many allies who found reasons to support anti-alcohol laws.

immigrants—"the infidel foreign population," as one historian has described them—became the increasingly public face of alcohol excess. Eighty percent of licensed saloons were owned by first-generation Americans, and they "set at once to selling liquor... to Italians, Greeks, Lithuanians, Poles—all the rough and hairy tribes," as one of the muckrakers of the Progressive Era put it (all quotes from Okrent 2010, p. 26).

The small group of women who prayed at the Ohio saloons in December 1873 would be the initial spark that eventually became the Women's Christian Temperance Union (WCTU). Within three months of that first pray-in, the spark ignited the closing of taverns in more than 75 communities. In the next few decades, this small group had remarkable successes in getting school boards across the nation to insert new instructional materials denouncing alcohol as an evil then getting legislation passed at both local and state levels outlawing the sale of alcohol. Jurisdictions soon came to be known as either "dry" (no alcohol sales permitted) or "wet." A good part of the movement's effectiveness came from the fact that the most determined advocates and leaders were primarily, if not exclusively, the wives of the most successful upper-middle-class professionals; their husbands were bankers, doctors, lawyers, or very successful business owners. During the peak of its power in the first decade of the twentieth century, the membership in the WCTU was overwhelmingly drawn from the ranks of the most privileged groups in American society. In 1919, advocates of prohibition succeeded in getting a constitutional

amendment passed that made alcohol consumption illegal anywhere in the United States (the Eighteenth Amendment to the Constitution).

Yet, less than two decades later, the pendulum swung back with ferocity. Millions of Americans refused to stop drinking, creating a campaign of mass civil disobedience that undermined the legitimacy of the new constitutional amendment. In the face of continued widespread drinking, attempts to enforce the ban on liquor proved exceptionally difficult, often met with local resistance when done by federal agents. The symbolic act that broke the back of Prohibition occurred when then-New York governor Franklin Delano Roosevelt, shortly before he became president, raised a glass of liquor at a public event, signaling yet another shift in the constitution of the moral center when it came to alcohol. Prohibition was repealed soon thereafter, and the consumption of alcohol today is permitted with relatively few restrictions (for example, bans on drinking under the age of 21, or laws against driving or operating machinery while under the influence of alcohol are among the few major restrictions).

The Campaign against Opium

7.3.3 Analyze the history of opium use and how it compares to the campaign against alcohol.

While the alcohol crusade was one major example of a moral crusade that successfully, if only temporarily, turned everyday behavior into deviant behavior, a very different morality play of normality and deviance was being staged in relation to another mind-altering substance, opium (and its two derivatives, morphine and heroin), during the same time period. The similarities and differences between these two campaigns can tell us much about what factors influence the construction of deviance.

Opium has been around for thousands of years, but morphine was not discovered and developed until the first decade of the nineteenth century. It took 50 years before it became the most effective painkiller in medical history—in large measure owing to the invention of the hypodermic needle in 1857. This occured just in time for the Civil War.

The toll of human suffering during the Civil War was monstrous, not just in terms of the huge proportion of the U.S. population that was killed during the War, but also those who suffered maiming injuries and debilitating health consequences. In this context, morphine was introduced, fast becoming the preferred drug for dealing with pain of all kinds. When the war ended, ex-soldiers often returned home with strong habits. While injections of morphine relieved many sources of pain, a new pathway into the blood came from ingesting the drug as a soothing syrup. For just a few pennies, one could purchase the product at the local pharmacy. Drug prescriptions were not part of the U.S. regulatory system until 1914, so anyone, of any age, could purchase bottles of this syrup, with a morphine content as high as 10 to 14 percent. There was no Food and Drug Administration until the dawn of the twentieth century. Thus, there were no requirements to label ingredients, much less disclose proportionality of contents.

Here we come to the most fascinating feature of the "tale of two drugs" (alcohol versus morphine). Between the end of the Civil War and 1904, records from pharmacies indicate that the heaviest usage of morphine was by middle-class, middle-aged White women (Terry and Pellens 1970). This was the same four-decade period in which alcohol producers and distributors were demonized and alcohol consumers were characterized harshly by those seeking to demonize alcohol. Yet during this very same period, morphine use was characterized primarily as a medical problem. Rather than being labeled as social deviants, middle-class morphine consumers were the objects of sympathy—as people in need of help. Morphine producers and distributors were not vilified; they were mainly ignored and did not register as a problem of any moral character, certainly not that of a transgression of the moral order. Treatment, not punishment, was the order of the day.

But that began to change. Up until the first decade of the twentieth century, anyone could walk into a pharmacy and purchase morphine or heroin without a prescription. New York State was the first to break with this practice, with the passage of the Boyle Act of 1904. The New York State legislation (and the federal law modeled on it

a decade later in 1914, known as the Harrison Act) was originally intended as a step toward enhancing the power of medical doctors by requiring prescriptions for the first time. However, when it came to opiates, these laws had the opposite effect. Physicians were suddenly confronted with scores of "patients" waiting for their prescriptions while regular patients were crowded out of waiting rooms. The response was to simply prescribe *en masse*—signing many prescriptions and having an assistant distribute them to those who had waited in the long lines (Duster 1970). The federal government strenuously objected to this practice and took several physicians to court to stop it. In 1916, the Supreme Court sided with the government position, ruling in *Webb* v. *U.S.* that prescriptions must be individually prescribed and based on an individualized medical assessment. This ruling suddenly criminalized the practice of *en masse* prescriptions, sent several newly created law violators to prison, and scared the medical profession away from the treatment of opiate users.

Within a few years, a black market in the production and distribution of the opiates was created, and opiate addicts were suddenly portrayed as morally reprehensible, not simply the victims of physiological dependency. In the short space of two decades, morphine and heroin addicts were transformed in the public eye—no longer as middle-class, middle-aged, White female victims of a health and medical problem but as working-class, male, youthful criminals, and increasingly "of color." Legal prescriptions for opioids were now limited to the treatment of pain.

It is one of the least appreciated ironies of American history that just when the pressure to end Prohibition peaked in the early 1930s, laws and media coverage emerged that sought to demonize what had previously been *normal* opiate use. These two juxtaposed stories offer a good example of the structural forces that shape who gets to be normal and who gets labeled as deviant. The important element to note in this story is that the pharmacology of the drugs did not change. Rather, it was the pattern of consumption that changed, and *that* changed everything about what was determined to be deviant behavior and who could be categorized as engaging in immoral, deviant behavior.

By the late 1930s, alcohol had shifted from the metaphorical "demon rum" (the evil inherent in the mind-altering substance) to a substance that some could gracefully handle (the casual social drinker) and some could not (the problem drinker). In sharp contrast, morphine, heroin, and opium had shifted from medical analgesics that victimized

In the second half of the nineteenth century, morphine was advertised as a soothing syrup to help manage the pain caused by teething in young children.

Stock Montage/Getty Images

unwitting middle-class citizens (in the late nineteenth century) to drugs that drove the unfit to willful, licentious thrill-seeking. (Criminal sanctions against the sale and consumption of opioid products rose even further in the era of the war on drugs, as discussed in the next section). Again, nothing about the pharmaceutical product had changed, but those perceived as the primary consumers had been dramatically transformed into morally reprehensible deviants in just three decades.

Our story takes a final turn in recent years. The rising **opioid epidemic** across America, in which growing numbers of mostly White users have overdosed and/or died from opioids (increasing from under 5,000 in 2000 to over 63,000 by 2019; see Katz et al. 2020), has led to renewed sympathy for addicts and calls to build treatment centers to help addicts recover (rather than sending them to prison.) Once again, this reflects a shift in the societal understanding of a pharmaceutical product, not the product itself.

Recent Moral Crusades

7.3.4 Discuss how the crusade against drug use and same-sex relationships has implications for the future of moral crusades.

The attempt to regulate morality remains very much part of contemporary American society. One important example, which has parallels to the campaigns against alcohol and morphine, can be seen in the **war on drugs**. Launched by President Ronald Reagan in 1985 (although President Richard Nixon before him also briefly launched a "war on drugs" in the early 1970s, as had some state-level politicians, notably Governor Nelson Rockefeller in New York), Reagan's war on drugs was widely embraced by government officials across the country. The initiative involved significantly increasing surveillance of and criminal penalties for the sale, possession, and consumption of nonprescription drugs. At its peak in the early 2000s, America's jails and prisons were filled with hundreds of thousands of drug offenders, with millions more under criminal justice supervision on probation or parole, all in the name of social order. (The criminalization of drugs was a significant contributor to the rise of *mass incarceration*, a set of topics we will explore in more detail in Chapter 20.) The reasons for the vast increase in the criminalization of drugs since the 1980s are

Figure 7.2 Percent Drug Use by Race, Aged 12 or Older, 2019

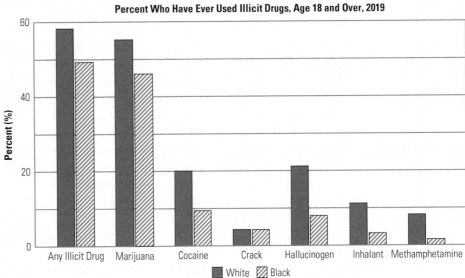

SOURCE: National Survey on Drug Use and Health, 2020. https://www.samhsa.gov/data/report/2019-nsduh-detailed-tables

complicated, but certain facts are indisputable. The groups serving time for criminal drug activity are not representative of the population actually using drugs. Numerous studies show that far more poor people and far more Black people are arrested and convicted than White, middle-class, and affluent people (Tonry 2012). Yet, as Figure 7.2 makes clear, Whites consume, on average, more drugs than Blacks in the United States. Whites are more likely to consume "popular" drugs such as marijuana, ecstasy, OxyContin, and cocaine. Blacks consume slightly higher amounts of crack cocaine and LSD, but the difference is slim. For example, a 2011 survey from the Substance Abuse and Mental Health Services Administration showed that twice as many Whites as Blacks or Latinxs had used cocaine in any form (SAMHSA 2011). Yet the middle-class White college student experimenting with illegal drugs or the suburban couple or business executive who enjoys occasionally getting high is drastically less likely to face criminal charges than poor people or people of color (Alexander 2010).

In recent years, many state governments have begun pulling back from criminalizing drug use, and the war on drugs has abated for the time being. This pullback has been large enough to level off the total number of jail and prison inmates after four decades of steady increases. It does not, however, rule out the possibility that future politicians will start new "wars" on drugs. But for now, at least, drug criminalization is widely seen by liberals and conservatives as a failure.

Another important failed moral crusade in recent decades in America was an effort to punish gays and lesbians on the basis of their sexual orientation. For centuries, same-sex relationships were largely practiced "in the closet," although gays and lesbians were subject to arrest or harassment wherever they were discovered. Gay bars were continually subjected to police raids, but the practice of homosexuality remained sufficiently invisible under the radar of public consciousness that few explicit campaigns or formal legal sanctions against homosexuality needed to be launched. All that changed in August 1969 when patrons of a gay bar in New York's Greenwich Village—the Stonewall Inn—fought back as police raided the bar. After three days of riots and growing protests in support of the Stonewall patrons, the movement for gay liberation and freedom (now referred to as the LGBT movement, including bisexuals and trans people) was born. From that moment forward, the LGBT movement has demanded, and increasingly won, full citizenship rights, as explicit laws against same-sex relationships have mostly disappeared. In addition, same-sex preference is no longer plausibly regarded as deviant for most Americans.

But this did not happen without a terrific fight, one that continues to this day. Opponents of same-sex relationships sought—with varying degrees of success—to follow in the footsteps of earlier moral crusades to use the legal system to repress those relationships and/or to restrict the rights of gays and lesbians at every opportunity. In the 1970s, the campaign against same-sex relationships peaked. During this period, a number of states and local governments across America passed laws restricting the employment rights of LGBTQ people, for example, to prevent them from teaching in public schools or working at childcare centers or other public institutions. The military enforced an affirmative ban against openly gay and transgender soldiers for decades (only fully repealed by President Barack Obama in 2009). The AIDS epidemic, beginning in 1981, provided another context for attacking gays and lesbians. HIV/AIDS was initially cast as a "gay disease," even though many thousands of heterosexuals were also diagnosed as HIV-positive.

The moral crusade against same-sex relationships was vigorously pursued by anti-gay activists but ultimately did not succeed in either making same-sex unions illegal or successfully ostracizing gays. Increasing numbers of gays and lesbians in public life began to acknowledge their sexual orientation, with Massachusetts congressmen Gerry Stubbs and Barney Frank openly acknowledging they were gay in the early 1980s. Slowly, it became possible for gays to affirm their sexual orientation

without fear of punishment or sanction by employers, family members, or friends. The individual ritual of "coming out of the closet," as gays and lesbians openly acknowledged their sexuality, became so common that today virtually all Americans have at least one gay family member or friend. In 2003, the Supreme Court acknowledged (in *Lawrence v. Texas*, 539 U.S. 558) the shift in public attitudes and societal trends by overturning a 1985 ruling that had allowed the states to keep anti-gay laws on the books. Later, the struggle over same-sex relationships shifted to a long-fought and often bitter campaign over the rights of gays and lesbians to marry (which was finally established by the Supreme Court in *Obergefell v. Hodges* [2015]). It now appears that the long effort to criminalize same-sex relationships has come to an end, although informal prejudice and discrimination and acts of violence against LGBTQ people remains significant. One of the largest mass shootings in American history occurred in June 2016 at a gay nightclub called Pulse in Orlando, Florida, when a gunman killed 49 people and injured 53 others in a horrific hate crime. Since 2013, the FBI has been recording hate crimes against members of the LGBTQ community, and although these data are flawed in various ways (many people don't report crimes to local police, and local police may not record violent acts as hate crimes), there does appear to be evidence of rising levels of anti-LGBTQ violence in recent years (Hauck 2019).

The apparent failure of the crusade against same-sex relationships, in spite of the Orlando shooting and continuing acts of violence directed against LGBTQ individuals, indicates that there is an uncertain future for such crusades (and the effort to legislate morality). Growing

In June 2016, an anti-gay gunman armed with assault rifles entered a popular LGBTQ nightclub called Pulse in Orlando, Florida, and opened fire, killing 49 people and injuring dozens more in the most vicious act of hate against the LGBTQ community to date.

Paul Hennessy/Alamy Stock Photo

numbers of younger and middle-aged Americans, regardless of their political or religious views, favor lifestyle freedom over laws and regulations telling people what they can and cannot do (for example, Baker 2005). Increasingly, the line seems to be drawn at the point of behavior that threatens to harm others: Drinking is fine, but driving a car while drunk is now subject to major criminal penalties that have dramatically increased in recent years. The growing campaign to legalize cannabis—with many states moving toward outright legalization—exemplifies the changing dynamics of moral regulation. It is increasingly difficult for opponents of marijuana to persuade citizens that it makes sense to allow alcohol consumption (which can be at least as problematic in many ways for both individuals and society) while still outlawing cannabis. At the same time, harsh penalties against the sale or possession of other drugs remain on the books and are widely enforced by the police, so it is important to note that some forms of moral regulation in relation to drug use continues even where cannabis is legal. Attempts to regulate the behavior of the poor, immigrants, and other disadvantaged groups are not likely to completely disappear any time soon.

It is easy to conclude that the moral campaigns of the past were misguided. Most people want as much freedom as they can have. But another, even more recent

moral crusade—the campaign encouraging people to wear masks to reduce the spread of COVID-19—suggests a different set of issues. As COVID-19 spread across the globe in 2020, experts in infectious disease and related scientific fields were unified on one critical point: To stop the spread of the new coronavirus, citizens would need to wear masks in public. Wearing a mask became, for a large majority of Americans, an ethical responsibility. As Anthony Fauci, the government's leading authority put it, "It's sort of respect for another person and have that other person respect you. You wear a mask, they wear a mask, you protect each other" (quoted in Hider 2020). But not all Americans accepted either the scientific wisdom or the ethnical imperative to protect others. At the top of the government, President Donald Trump refused to wear a mask and used his vast audience on Twitter to make fun of people wearing masks, including his 2020 presidential opponent, Joe Biden. Images of maskless gatherings became common, horrifying those who accepted the scientific consensus. Because the virus can spread without universal protection, it continued to flourish producing over 700,000 deaths in the United States by October 2021. The idea that we all have an obligation to protect others by always wearing a mask proved to be an unsuccessful moral and scientific campaign, leading to considerable unnecessary loss of life.

Gregory Smith/Corbis Historical/Getty Images

BIG QUESTION 7.4 How Do Power and Inequality Impact Deviance?

CRIME, DEVIANCE, AND POWER

Much of the discussion in the chapter so far has pointed to one important conclusion: What is considered deviant, or criminal, is often quite arbitrary. We've noted that what is and is not deviant is not always an obvious or natural thing, but rather the result of the conscious

decisions and actions of specific groups and individuals. But who are these groups and individuals? And more specifically, what is the connection between economic and political power, on the one hand, and the definition of deviant behavior? Recall that our first experience with the idea of normality and its boundaries (deviance) is from the small social group into which we are born, almost universally the family or kinship unit. The small and relatively homogeneous group is our first encounter with who gets to define normality (starting with our parents); however, as we grow up and encounter other groups, stronger and more compelling forces determine *which* group's view of normality will prevail in society as a whole. Foremost among these forces is the notion that power, whether hidden or direct, plays a central role (see Chapter 8). In the historical example of how alcohol and opioids traded places as the symbols of normal and deviant behavior, for example, the advocates with greater access to political power had much more influence over the establishment of relevant laws. It was only when powerful groups sought to criminalize alcohol and opiates that those campaigns succeeded (and once some elites like Roosevelt and others turned against Prohibition, it was reversed). An important example of how deviance is defined by those with more power which has recently become a matter of intense national controversy in the United States: the ways in which police officers are generally protected from being charged with crimes in the course of duty. Police violence against unarmed or non-threatening citizens, particularly Black men, has been going on for as long as there have been police. For most of this history, these actions were not documented in ways that could raise questions about police behavior. More recently, however, citzens carrying cellphones with video cameras, as well as requirements in most jurisdictions that police wear video cameras, have documented what had previously been hidden from view. But for the most part, officers engaging in unnecessary violence have been cleared of any wrong-doing for the same actions that would lead to very long prison sentences for ordinary citizens.

In this section, we turn our attention to other important struggles over defining deviance in which the role of economic and political power in shaping punishment becomes explicit.

Labeling Deviance and Crime

7.4.1 Discuss how labeling theory explains deviance.

In the 1960s, in an effort to understand the processes through which deviance is defined, some sociologists began doing systematic research in contexts where deviant, criminal, and abnormal behavior were defined by individuals in positions of authority. When they did so, wherever they looked, they found plenty of evidence of arbitrariness, and/or bias in terms of racism, sexism, and other social inequalities, in who was labelled deviant. Here are a few examples. One line of research involved riding around in police cars to closely observe what police officers actually do. These studies produced the important finding that cops overlook a lot of things that could be considered violations of the law, while other equally minor acts could meet with immediate arrest (Bittner 1967; Cicourel 1967). Other researchers studied district attorneys and public defenders, noting how often cases were dismissed and how they were dismissed. For example, lawyers on both sides would work together to get minor guilty pleas from certain suspects but not others (Sudnow 1965). Sociologists studied intake decisions at psychiatric facilities, where some types of psychological disorders are ignored and others are subjected to long stays (Goffman 1959). This body of sociological research on how deviance gets defined and applied in different ways has been repeatedly confirmed in later studies.

One of the more interesting of the new theories that emerged out of this research challenged the idea that there are real and objective differences in behavior that is normal versus what is deviant. Most sociologists today argue that the *process* by which a behavior comes to be defined as deviant is critical to understanding what actually causes it. In other words, instead of focusing on the behavior of individuals, sociologists argue that we need to look at how the behavior came to be defined as deviant. Deviant behavior is, at least in part, "caused" by the process through which a behavior comes to be labeled as deviant.

These ideas are associated with a radical rethinking of the theory of deviance in the 1960s, in particular the idea that many kinds of behaviors are deviant solely because they are labeled as such. **Labeling theory** proponents argue that defining deviance is not an objective process, but rather happens when powerful groups are able to create and impose the definition they want. An action that may be considered normal at one point becomes defined as deviant at another point, even though the act itself may not change (recall our earlier examples of alcohol and morphine prohibition). In this way, a basic premise of labeling theory is that social control does not simply respond to deviance; it *constitutes* deviance. So, to understand deviance, we need to focus on how social control actively makes certain behaviors unacceptable. Think about deviance not as a momentary act (when someone snorts cocaine or drives through a red light) but as a *process*. In other words, look at how a behavior *becomes* deviant. Who gets to define the situation, and what criteria do they use? (We'll discuss labeling theory again in Chapter 20 in relation to the criminal justice system).

The lessons of labeling can be seen in a recent controversy in New York City over the police department's use of "stop-and-frisk" tactics, whereby police officers are free to detain anyone they think might be carrying a weapon or posing a threat to the police officer. Almost 700,000 people were frisked in 2011, and well over 80 percent of those were either Black or Latinx. Although young Black and Latinx males between the ages of 14 and 24 make up just 4.7 percent of New York's population, they received 42 percent of all stops. With the election of a new mayor and appointment of a new police chief, in recent years there have been some changes, but the disparities in use of stop-and-frisk tactics continues to be an issue. What's more is that in the vast majority of cases, the police did not find guns or other weapons, but rather a small amount of marijuana or other drugs (New York Civil Liberties Union 2011; Kohler-Hausmann 2014). More than 50,000 people were arrested for simple cannabis possession in New York in 2010 and 2011, and more than 45,000 in 2014, in most cases resulting from a stop-and-frisk event in which a police officer found not a gun but a cannabis product in someone's pocket. Because so many of the people being stopped are young men of color, it is hardly surprising to learn that a disproportionate number of people sanctioned for cannabis possession, and in some case being put into correctional supervision, are young Black and Latinx men. When a group is intensively policed in the way that young minority men were being investigated in New York City, their deviance—even if it is minor—is much more likely to be uncovered. (After a high-profile lawsuit uncovered this racial bias, the New York City police reduced their stops by over 90% by 2019).

Corporate Deviance

7.4.2 Explain why corporate deviance is rarely punished as crime.

Deviant behavior on "the street" by ordinary people, especially young people, is often met with formal punishment. But what about white-collar deviance, or more specifically, the crimes of the economically powerful? In general, it is all too often a simple truth that there is one standard of punishment for the poor and another standard for the rich. It is also often the case that high-level corporate executives can take actions that would be considerable criminal in many contexts, but are not punished as such when they are wearing their corporate hats (Barak 2017; Reiman and Leighton 2020). The full story here is more complicated than this: It is true that if caught, the corporations may face financial penalties, often in very large amounts, for the illegal activity of their executives (Diskant 2008). But the general point still holds; corporate offenders and individual corporate officers are often fined far less than the true societal costs of their crimes, and it is very rare that top corporate executives are ever sent to prison. We can best see how these disparities work by considering two examples: (1) the

handling of the U.S. banking and financial crisis of 2008, which arose from the illegal peddling of certain types of loans, which would throw the entire American and global economy into a severe recession, costing millions of jobs and income; and (2) the case of large pharmaceutical companies' marketing of pain killers—here we will focus on the case of Purdue Pharmaceuticals and its marketing and sale of the most widely used opioid drug OxyContin, which has been responsible for tens of thousands of deaths.

To understand the banking crisis more fully, and how and why so many banks and other financial corporations were able to take actions that generated billions of dollars in profits while causing millions of homeowners to lose their homes, we need to briefly investigate the historical background. After the banking collapse during the Great Depression of the 1930s, new laws and regulations were put in place to prevent bank failures. Banks were limited in the kinds of risky investments they could make. While many in the banking world objected to these constraints, for decades they served to reduce the risk of financial crisis. But beginning in the 1980s, as memories of the Great Depression faded, powerful banking interests persuaded Congress to begin loosening the rules and allowing them to take on more risk in the search for higher profits. For example, in 1982, Congress voted to deregulate the savings and loan (S&L) industry. Risky investments by S&Ls ensued almost immediately, and within a decade, some had gotten rich while scores of these institutions failed. As a direct consequence, taxpayers were slapped with a bill of $124 billion to bail out the failed S&Ls. But that was only the beginning.

In the 1990s, the growing movement to tear down banking and financial regulations had reached a fever pitch. Congress and President Bill Clinton, at the urging of the financial industry, undid many of the remaining restrictions on financial organizations dating back to the 1930s. In this increasingly "anything goes" environment, financial companies aggressively pursued new avenues of profit. One of these, which would ultimately trigger the development of the financial crisis, was the mass marketing of new home mortgage products, known as *subprime loans*, to consumers who had little hope of repaying them. Preying on the desire of most Americans to own their own home, the subprime loans typically had a low initial "teaser" rate, but the fine print revealed that they would eventually jump to a much higher rate. Many of the people taking out these loans did not understand the risk they were accepting, and laws that once might have protected them had been eliminated.

There are many elements to this story, more than we can fully convey here, as the levels of fraud throughout the home mortgage industry were breathtakingly pervasive and widespread. One key point was that the banks and loan companies making the subprime loans discovered that they were able to make handsome profits reselling the loans to other investors, who then assumed all of the risk. So they soon began giving out loans to virtually anyone they could find who would sign the paperwork. The secondary institutions (other banks, insurance companies, and investment firms) who bought up the subprime loans were continually assured they were safe. At this level, far removed from the original loan, the new loan holders could not understand, nor were fully informed, about the risks they were accepting.

The crisis began to unfold in 2007, when the American economy went into recession, unemployment started to rise, and home prices began to decline at the same time that many subprime loans were reset to their higher rate. Large numbers of subprime borrowers began defaulting on their loans. As a result, the repackaged loans went into default, and in short order the entire financial sector faced a severe crisis that would ultimately require the federal government to provide many billions of dollars to keep the big banks from going out of business. The phrase "too big to fail" came to be applied to large banks that had taken on these risky loans. Although all other businesses in America go bankrupt when they make poor decisions, in this case the risks to all of American society if large banks were allowed to fail was too great to let happen. The federal government's bailout of the banks kept them in business, but the full cost of the financial crisis of 2007 and 2008 is still being felt today. Unemployment rates shot up after the crisis began, and the American economy performed very poorly by historical standards for many years thereafter.

By effectively lobbying Congress to overturn regulations of financial institutions and energy production, powerful corporate actors enabled the redefinition of what would constitute normality, deviance, and criminality. By their own admission in congressional testimony, many bank and financial executives admitted to routinely practicing deception in withholding vital information from their own clients in relation to mortgage and subprime loans and in the sale of financial products related to those loans. Goldman Sachs, the most famous financial firm in the world, paid $50 million in fines and faced many embarrassing revelations about its executives' behavior and treatment of their clients during the crisis. In late 2011, the CBS television news journal *60 Minutes* aired a two-part segment in which two whistleblowers testified as to just how routine and systematic fraudulent mortgage loan practices had indeed become "normal." These mid-level managers had explicitly warned their senior managers, only to be ignored, then offered monetary settlements to remain silent about what they knew, and then fired for not cooperating with the cover-up.

Now let's consider a second, especially poignant and contemporary example. Anyone caught selling illegal drugs on the street is subject to significant punishment; if you are caught selling large amounts of such drugs, you may be at risk of a very long prison sentence. But what happens when large corporations create, produce, and market these drugs? Our final case, still being sorted out in 2021, involves a company called Purdue Pharma, based in Stamford, Connecticut. A family-owned company founded in the late nineteenth century, its primary line of business in recent decades has been the production and sale of opioid painkillers. In 1996, the company released a new drug called OxyContin. The company claimed that the drug could be used safely and was nonaddictive and that there would be no effects once a patient stopped taking it. Within one year of its release, however, the company was informed in multiple ways about problems with the product (Chakradhar and Ross 2019). In particular, patients experienced withdrawal symptoms when they attempted to stop using it, and many stayed on it long after they should have. Further, the chemical high that users experienced led many people to seek excessive amounts of the drug, or they began to share it with friends who also became addicted. As the word got around, a massive underground market for Oxyies, as they were known on the street, began to develop. But Purdue did nothing to stop this. In fact, it did just the opposite: The company aggressively marketed the drug in part by providing special benefits to doctors who wrote large numbers of prescriptions. One such doctor, known as the "Candyman," proscribed enormous doses of OxyContin to his patients, and Purdue regularly interacted with this doctor (meeting him over 300 times to take him out to expensive meals to encourage yet more prescriptions and sales). The owners of the firm—the Sackler family, especially the group of family members who served on the company's board of directors—were fully notified of these and many other issues with the drug, and some of them actively helped devise marketing strategies to overcome any objections that might arise.

For a few years, the issues with OxyContin and its role in the opioid epidemic did not make the news, even as drug abuse clinics were being overrun with Oxy addicts. The company saw sales and profits go through the roof, as did the other producers of opioid pain medication. External consultants came up with new plans to "turbocharge sales." The company's marketing to doctors continued to falsely emphasize that the drug was safe. As noted earlier in the chapter, there were tens of thousands of deaths from opioid overdoses in the 2010s, many involving Oxy, and a far higher number of lives wrecked from long-term opioid addiction that did not cause death. In one of the most sickening revelations, in 2017 a marketing consultant proposed to the company that they pay drugstore chains like CVS a rebate of about $15,000 for each overdose that could be connected to prescriptions filled at the chain (Bogdanich and Forsythe 2020). It was a kind of hush money payment to keep the profits rolling in.

By the mid-2010s, however, the growing epidemic of opioid overdoses put a spotlight on the producers of these medications and their role in convincing doctors to prescribe it. Eventually, producing firms faced lawsuits and had to pay large fines. Purdue Pharma is not solely responsible for the opioid epidemic that caused so much harm to so many individuals. There were other legal manufacturers of opioid pain medications, as well as underground producers making and selling heroin products on the street. But Purdue's efforts to maximize sales of Oxy was deeply troubling. As a large corporation, a number of courts have concluded, they had a legal obligation to not mislead physicians and users about the safety of their product. That they were knowingly and aggressively marketing a toxic drug as safe and nonaddictive for years helped accelerate the crisis. Yet no responsible executive has been criminally charged.

The actions of many in the financial sector in the 2000s and of Purdue Pharma from 1996 to the present were clearly fraudulent and in violation of federal and state laws. The amount of money illegally obtained in each case was in the billions, and (in Purdue's case) the direct cause of thousands of unnecessary deaths, but the criminal justice system had (and has) chosen not to punish almost anyone for these crimes. The executives involved could, of course, afford to hire an army of top lawyers as well lobby Congress and state legislatures to adopt a hands-off approach. In the subprime case, only one banker—a mid-level Credit Suisse executive named Kareem Serageldin—received a prison sentence (in this case, 30 months for lying about the value of his bank's securities; Eisinger 2014). Fines were imposed, but often in amounts that are trivial given the billions of dollars that were lost. For example, one of the most aggressive offenders in the subprime scandal was Angelo Mozilo, president and CEO of Countrywide Financial, one of the companies that led the way in issuing and profiting from subprime loans. Despite making about $500 million while at Countrywide, Mozilo not only did not go to prison; he ended up settling the case against him by paying a fine of $47.5 million (a fraction of the wealth he accumulated during the subprime era). Similarly, the Sackler family has been allowed to keep billions of dollars in profits even as they face seemingly large fines over their role in marketing OxyContin. Although the precise details are not yet known, it now appears that they will retain approximately $7 billion of the more than $10 billion of stock they sold once lawsuits against the company were filed and government agencies began investigating its marketing and distribution.

Contrast this with the rough treatment of low-level drug dealers we mentioned earlier. Such examples dramatically highlight the frequently light treatment of white-collar crime compared to other kinds of crime, and, in doing so, they raise two critical points. First, the kinds of deviant behaviors that get punished, and the severity of the punishment, are often linked in part to who is the perpetrator. Second, we are reminded again that what counts as deviant behavior or a punishable crime is in large part shaped by the overall distribution of power. Deviance in the streets faces one standard, while deviance in corporate suites faces a different, much more lax standard.

State Deviance, Terrorism, and War Crimes

7.4.3 Describe governmental deviance and why powerful countries can avoid being charged with criminal acts during wartime.

So far, we have considered deviance as acts of individuals or corporations. But this is too limiting. In fact, there are ways in which governments can engage in deviant behavior, and many of the same ideas about what gets defined as "normal" versus "deviant" will

REUTERS/Kevin Lamarque/Files

Countrywide Financial Corporation CEO Angelo Mozilo testifying before Congress about his firm's promotion of subprime mortgages. Countrywide was one of the leaders of the subprime lending industry, ultimately writing hundreds of thousands of such loans that failed, causing billions of dollars in losses.

apply. Let's consider the possibility of what we might call government or **state deviance**, that is, policy and actions carried out by governments and government employees in their official capacities. Some recent examples arise in the context of the long-running **war on terror**—the effort of the American government since the attacks on the World Trade Center in New York and the Pentagon on September 11, 2001, to find, capture, or kill those individuals and groups suspected of plotting terrorist actions. In recent years, few topics have received more attention than **terrorism**—the use of violence to achieve some political objective. No one defends terrorism. Anyone who uses force to kill innocent people is a murderer. Extreme examples, such as the televised beheading of journalists or other innocent people shock our conscience. But if we consider each human life as equally valuable and sacred, it is sometimes hard to say who the real terrorists are. For example, in the name of fighting terrorism, leading U.S. government officials and military leaders have sought to radically change long-held interpretations of its obligations under international law and widely accepted views about human rights in the modern world.

Studying deviance can help us better understand how power influences what we understand terrorism to actually be. Let's first ask the question: What is terrorism? To appreciate how the modern understanding of terrorism developed, it is important to first explore the concept of the "theater of war." Five hundred years ago, European armies were composed of men who designated the battlefield as the sole appropriate arena of conflict. Much like contemporary prize-fighters who are limited to the ring, boxing gloves, and rounds set off by agreed-upon parameters, these battlefields delimited the legitimate landscape for the war. While there were skirmishes that leaked off the battlefield, the arena of conflict was established by this limited notion of an agreed-upon terrain.

In the theater of war, generals deploy troops, have soldiers dig trenches, and take hills to capture the high ground. But what of situations in which one army so outnumbers another, or is so much better equipped, that there is no real contest? Do generals really want to go into battle when their numbers are one-tenth that of their enemy? The answer is no, at least not on a straightforward battlefield encounter where their inferiority inevitably lead to doom. Instead, strategy enters the formula, and tactics evolve. In the case of the European armies half a millennium ago, methods such as cutting armies off at passes and starving them by destroying supply lines began to enter the theater of war as legitimate strategies. That is, before opponents ever got to some place called the field of battle, it was legitimate to intercept and harass them, to use decoys, and even to send false signals, among other tactics. "All is fair in love and war" goes the saying, which made sense (at least for war) once armies began fighting their opponents

using a variety of tactics, not all of which were limited to the theater of war.

It is only a matter of degree to shift away from grand strategy on or around the battlefield, to the cunning of ambush (before the "battle"), to the next major development. **Guerrilla warfare** happens when a fighting force hides from its enemy and carries out targeted raids designed to wear down its numerically superior opponent. So long as European nations were doing battle with each other, the notion of a theater or arena of battle was more or less agreed on as to the terms of action and ultimate settlement. However, in the colonial period, European powers had to battle people who were to face them with inferior arms and employing different rules of the game. Their inferior arms meant that Europeans could slaughter thousands of natives at will. That slaughter was never called terrorism. Yet one may ask, what greater terror is there than to be enslaved on one's own land by a people who have contempt for your culture and your way of living?

More important to this line of argument, however, is that the colonized would later employ tactics that would shift the very meaning of war. Now, rather than regular soldiers conducting a battle in designated uniforms, increasingly *the people* themselves might be the enemy. In some ways, the Americans started it during the Revolutionary War. The British Redcoats, marching in formation, were fair game for the locals. They could devise clever ways of attacking an initially superior enemy. Later, other colonized people around the world would further blur this distinction. Women could and did carry muskets and fire them. Children could be used as runners. In guerrilla war, any actor in the occupied territory could be a soldier in disguise.

Imagine what might have happened if England had won the American War of Independence. Aside from the obvious result that the United States would have remained an English colony, there is little doubt that George Washington, John Adams, Thomas Jefferson, and scores of others that history today regards as heroes of the American Revolution would have been hung as traitors, or "terrorists" (Paul 2009). In fact, in 1779, at a particularly bleak moment in the war, Jefferson abandoned his Virginia home and "headed for the hills" just to escape such a likely fate (Gordon-Reed 2008, p. 136). And had the British prevailed, those colonists who sided with the British would have been anointed heroes. Of course, because the American revolutionaries did win the war, Washington, Adams, and Jefferson are our heroes; those who sided with the British were branded traitors, and some were put to death.

Seen from this angle, the emergence of terrorism in the contemporary world is a progression from the battlefield to the strategic ploys of generals to avoid the battlefield, to guerrilla warfare, and finally to terrorism. If we are to understand terrorism, we must try to penetrate the social and political situation of the perpetrators of terrorist acts. On the surface, the most powerful nations clearly dominate the weaker nations, and the United States has by far the strongest military in the world. In the theater of war, a weak nation would no more do battle with a strong nation than a middle weight would get into the boxing ring with a heavyweight. But outside the ring, the middle weight, even the lightweight, can offset the greater strength of the heavyweight, by using different rules of engagement. And, indeed, outside the theater of war, the guerrilla warrior begins to equalize matters by finding ways to make the fight fairer.

Let's move forward in time to the post–9/11 era. Americans have heard a great deal about the attacks on 9/11 and the continuing threat of a terrorist attack from Al Qaeda and other organizations such as the Islamic State in Iraq and Syria (ISIS) since then. The government and the media have stoked fears about the possibility of further attacks on American citizens. And several dramatic videos of the beheading of American citizens by terrorist groups in foreign countries have added to that fear. Much of this fear is wildly exaggerated. The most careful estimates, and using a generous definition of terrorism to avoid undercounting, show that a grand total of 141 people have been killed by terrorist attacks in the United States since 9/11 (Kurzman 2021). Of those, 49 were killed in one attack alone, at a nightclub in Orlando, Florida in 2015, noted earlier in the chapter. Murder by Islamic terrorists overall have accounted for about 1 out of every 2,000 murders in the United States since 9/11. More people die from an accident in their bathtub, by being hit by lightning, falling off a ladder or down a flight of stairs, in a single year than from terrorism. To say that Islamic terrorism is a threat to Americans' lives is simply not an accurate reflection of that risk.

Yet, the United States has carried out an immensely costly war on terror for the last two decades. While we hear a lot about alleged terror plots, we learn far less about aspects of the war on terror where the U.S. government has sanctioned and employed tactics such as kidnapping and torturing suspected terrorists, using drone autonomous aircraft strikes to attack housing complexes occupied by suspected terrorists (as well as children and adults not involved in any terrorist activity), and even assuming the right to kill without trial people accused of membership in terrorist organizations (Brooks and Manza 2013, chap. 1).

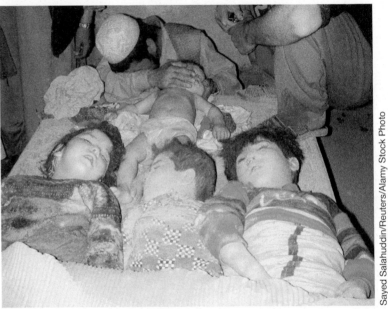

These images show the bombing of the World Trade Center, September 11, 2001, (top) and the bodies of innocent children killed by an American drone strike in Afghanistan, which residents say claimed 150 lives (bottom). Why is one of these attacks considered terrorism and the other not?

The question is, why is it considered terrorism when ISIS or Al Qaeda or an individual kills innocent Americans in the name of Islam, but *not* terrorism when the U.S. government engages in actions that lead to the deaths of innocent civilians? We even have a new name for what the United States has been engaged in since 9/11: **counterterrorism**. The term is informative. America's enemies engage in terrorism, while the U.S. government practices counterterrorism. And the latter has been far more deadly.

The counterterrorist actions of the U.S. government have included the use of tactics such as drone strikes on other countries' territories that have killed thousands of innocent non-combatants, torture, the kidnapping and detention without trial of suspected terrorists enemies, and in some cases even their execution without trial. The U.S. government has even killed, without arrest or trial, two American citizens suspected of being involved in terrorist activity while living outside the United States. However, in the two decades since 9/11, a single powerful metaphor dominated much of the thinking of government officials (and one that exerted considerable influence within the media and broader public). The metaphor was that of a "ticking time bomb," the idea that additional terrorist plots and attacks were imminent and, in order to foil them, immediate and unconditional action was both necessary and justified. For many years, the U.S. government was also engaged in a program of rounding up many people suspected of being involved in terrorist activity and taking them to hidden locations where they could be subjected to "enhanced interrogation" techniques, otherwise known as torture, in the hopes of gathering intelligence. We know now—as a result of important journalistic revelations—that many of the interrogation techniques used by agents of the Central Intelligence Agency (CIA) and special military units defied long-held interpretations of the international human rights protections codified in the **Geneva Conventions**, a series of international agreements about the fair treatment of

prisoners of war. (For some of the most important of these accounts, see Hersh 2005; Mayer 2008; Lichtblau 2008). We also know, from these same sources, that many of the people subjected to torture had little or no connection to any terrorist or terrorist activity.

The techniques of torture used in these investigations, especially from 2002 to 2005, are important to learn about if we are to fully grasp what state deviance may look like. They included sleep and sensory deprivation, isolation, and repeated beatings as well as humiliation, forcible administration of drugs, and (most famously and brutally) "waterboarding," a technique that simulates the sensation of drowning. Evidence of these top secret interrogations was uncovered and revealed over an extended period of time, and the full story of America's use of torture has not yet been written. But the first unambiguous evidence of torture came with the release of photographs of inmate abuse at the Abu Ghraib prison in April 2004, reported by *New Yorker* reporter Seymour Hersh and broadcast in a special *60 Minutes* report. An official military review of treatment of inmates at Abu Ghraib rebuked the prison's commanding officers. Interviews with prison officials and military investigators, as well as evidence shown in the photos that were released (and more graphically in photos not released for public viewing), documented gross mistreatment of inmates. This included evidence that inmates had been raped and sodomized, physically and deliberately injured, urinated on, and subjected to attacks by guard dogs. At least one inmate was killed, and many others suffered serious injuries.

The initial response of the U.S. military to the abuses at Abu Ghraib was to place blame on lower level military personnel and their immediate supervisors, implying these were random, unauthorized occurrences (Hersh 2005). This theory – which is sometimes known as the "bad apples" theory, that is a few wayward soldiers did it not their supervising officers – is the most common way to defend state deviance. Whatever the particulars of the chain of command at the Abu Ghraib prison, later evidence suggested that the systematic use of torture was quite widespread and sanctioned by officials at the very top of the U.S. government (including then-Vice President Dick Cheney, who has openly and repeatedly defended the use of torture in later interviews since leaving office in 2009). Abu Ghraib was only one of a number of sites where torture was employed, but it is the one we know the most about. Some of the other unknown sites were called "black sites," foreign prisons operated by the CIA or the American military (or sometimes the military or secret police of friendly nations) in which individuals accused of terrorist activities could be interrogated outside the reach of any legal authority. Secret prisons were located in countries such as Poland, Romania, and Lithuania, and other facilities have been identified in Africa and the Middle East. The existence of black sites was initially denied by the government, but in September 2006, President George W. Bush

Staff Sgt. Ivan Fredericks

The torture of detainees at a prison operated by the U.S. military at Abu Ghraib in Iraq highlights how institutional cultures like those in the military can encourage individual army officers to engage in horrific acts of violence without perceiving themselves to be in violation of the law.

was finally forced to publicly acknowledge their existence. In addition to the use of black sites, suspects have sometimes been turned over to foreign governments known for their use of torture and other aggressive techniques of interrogation and punishment (Mayer 2008).

As the strongest military power in the world, perhaps the United States government feels it does not have to play by the same rules as everyone else. It can, and does, refuse to participate in international legal proceedings that have been brought against high government officials involved in planning and sanctioning many of these violations of international law. In more recent years, the U.S. government has halted some of the violations of international law in the war on terror, but others have continued or even increased in recent years. For example, the American military has continued to widely use autonomous drone planes in places like Afghanistan, Pakistan, and Yemen to attempt to kill suspected terrorists. These strikes—which involve sending U.S. planes into countries where the governments have repeatedly demanded they not fly—have killed an estimated 1,700 innocent people as of 2019, including 400 children (Muchina and Merryman-Lotze 2019). Imagine if the Canadian or Mexican government repeatedly sent airplanes into the United States to kill Americans it said were involved in terrorism, and lots of obviously innocent people like children were being killed in those attacks. Would Americans not view that as mass murder and demand that the people responsible for the attacks be held criminally liable?

Police Deviance and the Concept of Qualified Immunity

7.4.4 Explain the relationship between police deviance and qualified immunity.

One of the more remarkable examples of the role of power in defining what constitutes socially improper behavior can be seen in the behavior of some police officers on the job. Police officers who engage in violent mistreatment of people in their custody, disproportionately people of color, are rarely charged with crimes or disciplined on the job (Nelson 2001; Butler 2017). They also benefit from the legal doctrine of **qualified immunity** that protects police officers from being held accountable for many of their actions when on the job. Three law professors (Capers et al. 2020) have recently bluntly summarized the current state of affairs as follows:

> Police officers enjoy almost complete immunity from civil suits in federal court. They can shoot someone, taser someone, choke someone, or press their knee into someone's neck until they can't breathe. They can brutalize peaceful protesters. And yet, in large part because of the court-made rule of qualified immunity, officers rarely face liability.

Most states have adopted further protections for police officers, and the unwillingness of courts, state governments and local police departments to hold their officers accountable for actions which, if done by anyone else, would surely result in arrest and punishment or large financial settlement remains one of the unique features of the American criminal justice system.

However, in response to national outrage over the 2020 killing of George Floyd in Minneapolis at the hands of police, a surprising thing happened. This horrific incident involved four police officers, one of whom pressed his knee into Floyd's neck for nearly nine minutes, cutting off his breathing, refusing to let up even as Floyd gasped "I can't breathe," while the other three officers watched and did nothing to save the dying man. In this case, all of the police officers were immediately fired, and the officer directly responsible for Floyd's death was charged with (and later convicted of) murder. Because it was all captured on video, it was impossible for the officers to assert that the unarmed Floyd presented a direct threat to them. And in April 2021, the officer (Derek Chauvin) was found guilty. But in the vast majority of cases, especially when there is no eyewitness video, nothing happens. (We discuss this in more detail in Chapter 20.) For example, a very similar police killing in Minneapolis a few years before Floyd's death, in which a man named David Smith died in police custody from asphyxiation caused by physical force by a police officer, has gone entirely unpunished to this day (Satija 2020). Countless other examples can be found.

Why are police officers granted the freedom to "shoot, choke, or press their knee into someone until they can't breathe?" As with state terrorism, this is an important issue for the theory of social deviance. It is also an example of how which powerful actors—in this case, the heads of police departments, local mayors, and state and federal politicians—get to define what is deviance. All have strong incentives to avoid publicizing the actions of rank-and-file police. Police officers are trained by their department before they are put out into the field, meaning that their behavior on the job reflects their superiors (and the politicians who ostensibly oversee police departments). When civilians sue police departments or individual officers, they frequently encounter courts that invoke varieties of qualified immunity or simply trust officer accounts over those of plaintiffs who have suffered an injury.

The vast majority of officers do the best they can on the job, and do not routinely engage in violence. And police officers are at some risk in the performance of their jobs. In a typical year, around 40 to 50 police officers will be killed in the line of duty (out of a total of nearly 700,000 officers in the entire United States) (Sullivan et al. 2019). Yet when compared to over 1,000 people killed each year by police officers, not to mention many thousands of cases of mistreatment of suspects, it is hard not to conclude that what would be considered deviant or criminal in any other arena of life is allowable. Most officers who use excessive force will not lose their jobs. The concept of qualified immunity has given those police who willingly engage in unnecessary violence further protections from being sued. The clear message is that if a police officer does it, it isn't wrong.

It should now be clear that the central insights from the sociological study of deviance do not come from attempts to explain the personal characteristics, attributes, or pathologies of pirates or terrorists, of alcohol runners or drug cartel operatives, of predatory loan sharks peddling subprime loans or of CIA agents torturing suspected terrorists. Rather, insights into such deviant behavior come from studying the social and economic positions of those who define and label deviance and crime and how they can shape those definitions to suit their own purposes. As we've mentioned, the answer to the question of how and why some kinds of behaviors are punished while other, seemingly similar, ones are not comes from the explicit values articulated by those in power.

Conclusion: Deviance and the Sociological Imagination

The sociological study of deviance raises powerful questions for the sociological imagination, and in many ways studying what is normal and what is deviant is to take a microscope to all of a society in its full complexity. We have explored a number of these puzzles in this chapter. For example, understanding how and why certain kinds of actions come to be labeled and punished for being socially deviant in one context while other similar or worse actions in another do not is an enduring issue in all human societies. There are no obvious answers, but as we explore more deeply we do find one important pattern that recurs no matter what the particular form of deviance: Those individuals and groups with power have a special capacity to define or impose particular definitions of deviance and to turn those definitions into written laws and forms of punishment (or avoid having those same laws applied to them). Defining deviance downward—when the powerful define ordinary behavior of the weak as deviant—is a common pattern that the study of deviance reveals.

One of the challenges of the sociological imagination is the need to look beneath the surface of social life to uncover the normally hidden forms of inequality and injustice in the world around us. In no arena of social life is this more apparent than in the case of deviance and punishment. Once we begin to scrutinize what is "normal" and what is "deviant," a new way of looking at the world presents itself.

The Big Questions Revisited 7

7.1 **What Is Deviance?** In order to understand deviance, we first need to ask the question, "What is normal?" This section explored the origins of deviant behavior by examining the role of groups and group boundaries in the creation of social norms. We also examined the distinction between statistical and social deviance.

Deviance and the Group

Groups and Group Boundaries

Learning Objective 7.1.1: Identify how groups distinguish themselves.

Statistical versus Social Deviance

Learning Objective 7.1.2: Discuss how statistical deviance differs from social deviance.

Social Norms: The Unstated Rules of Everyday Life

Learning Objective 7.1.3: Define the term social norm.

Key Terms

social group (p. 163)   symbolic boundary (p. 164)   statistically deviant (p. 165)   socially deviant (p. 165)   normalize (p. 166)   norm (p. 165)

7.2 **How Is Social Control Imposed on Society?** This section examined how and where social control—the ways societies regulate and sanction behavior in such a way that it encourages conformity and discourages deviance from the norms—is developed.

Social Control and Social Order

Socialization: Learning the Rules of the Game

Learning Objective 7.2.1: Explain how acceptable behavior is learned through socialization.

Sanctions and Rewards for Conformity and Resistance

Learning Objective 7.2.2: Analyze ways in which societies exert social control through positive and negative sanctions.

Social Stigma and the Marking of Deviance

Learning Objective 7.2.3: Explain how a social stigma can serve as a sanction for deviant behavior.

Identifying Criminal Deviance

Learning Objective 7.2.4: Analyze the differences between social and criminal deviance.

Key Terms

social control (p. 167)   socialization
(p. 167)   sanction (p. 168)   civil disobedience
(p. 169)   stigma (p. 169)   criminal record
(p. 170)   criminal justice system (p. 170)

7.3   **How Is Morality Defined and Regulated by Societies?** Societies have long tried to dictate and control individuals' behavior and morality. In this section, we explored two moral crusades in the United States to highlight how the process of defining normal behavior is achieved and how certain kinds of behavior come to be labeled deviant or even criminal. We then examined some contemporary moral crusades and considered the future of moral regulation.

The Problem of Moral Regulation

Interested versus Disinterested Punishment

Learning Objective 7.3.1: Distinguish between interested and disinterested punishment.

An Example: The Temperance Movement as a Moral Crusade

Learning Objective 7.3.2: Analyze the history of alcohol use and how it relates to definitions of normal and deviant.

The Campaign Against Opium

Learning Objective 7.3.3: Analyze the history of opium use and how it compares to the campaign against alcohol.

Recent Moral Crusades

Learning Objective 7.3.4: Discuss how the crusade against drug use and same-sex relationships has implications for the future of moral crusades.

Key Terms

moral behavior (p. 171)   Prohibition (p. 172)
opioid epidemic (p. 175)   war on drugs (p. 175)

7.4   **How Do Power and Inequality Impact Deviance?** Insights into deviant behavior come from studying the social and economic positions, cultural practices, and attendant political power of dominant groups. In this section, we explored the relationship between deviance and power.

Crime, Deviance, and Power

Labeling Deviance and Crime

Learning Objective 7.4.1: Discuss how labeling theory explains deviance.

Corporate Deviance

Learning Objective 7.4.2: Explain why corporate deviance is rarely punished as crime.

State Deviance, Terrorism, and War Crimes

Learning Objective 7.4.3: Describe governmental deviance and why powerful countries can avoid being charged with criminal acts during wartime.

Police Deviance and the Concept of Qualified Immunity

Learning Objective 7.4.4: Explain the relationship between police deviance and qualified immunity.

Key Terms

labeling theory (p. 178)   state deviance
(p. 187)   war on terror (p. 182)   terrorism
(p. 182)   guerrilla warfare (p. 182)   counter-terrorism (p. 183)   Geneva Conventions
(p. 184)   qualified immunity (p. 185)

Chapter 8
Power and Politics

by Steven Lukes and Jeff Manza

The decade of the 1960s is famous today as a period of protest and turmoil all around the world. In the United States, protests against the Vietnam War were rapidly growing and other kinds of social movements were also sprouting up, especially on college campuses. One particularly dramatic set of protests took place at Columbia University in New York City in April 1968. Student rebels, demanding a variety of changes in the governance of the tradition-bound Ivy League campus, had taken over the office of University President Grayson Kirk. After occupying the office for several days, police officers stormed President Kirk's office and forced the students out. Here is how one observer described the scene:

One and a half hours after the president's suite had been cleared of student demonstrators, Grayson Kirk stood in the center of his private office looking at the blankets, cigarette butts and orange peels that covered his rug. Turning to A.M. Rosenthal of the New York Times *and several other reporters who had come into the office with him he murmured, "My God how could human beings do a thing like this?" It was the only time, Truman [Kirk's dean] recalled later, that he had ever seen the President break down. Kirk's windows were crisscrossed with tape and on one hung a large sign reading "Join Us." His lampshades were torn, his carpet was spotted, his furniture was displaced and scratched. But the most evident and disturbing aspect of the scene was not the minor damage inflicted by the students. The everything-in-its-place décor to which Kirk had grown accustomed was now in disarray—disarray that was the result of the transformation of an office into the living quarters of 150 students during the past six days. (Goffman 1971, p. 288)*

Commenting on this report, the famous sociologist Erving Goffman wrote:

The sociological question, of course, is not how could it be that human beings would do a thing like this, but rather how is it that human beings do this sort of thing so rarely? How come persons in authority have been so overwhelmingly successful in conning those beneath them into keeping the hell out of their offices? (Goffman 1971, p. 288, cited in Lemert 1997, pp. 133–34)

Goffman's astute observation highlights a critical question for the sociologist studying power and politics: Why is it that, in most times and places, people accept injustice and learn to live with it? Why don't the vastly larger number of poor and middle class people demand a greater share of societal wealth held by the very rich? In recent years, police brutality and the killing of unarmed people has prompted major protests across America, but police brutality has been an issue for people of color for as long as we have had police. Why now? The protest era of the 1960s also included important challenges to police brutality, but then mass protests over policing largely disappeared for

My Sociological Imagination

STEVEN LUKES

My first book was about the life and ideas of Emile Durkheim, one of the founders of the sociological tradition, whose classic works raise large questions about how to understand what "social" means and why the explanations typical of economics and psychology, at the level of individuals and their interactions, will always be inadequate. They also, however, leave other questions unaddressed: They largely neglect power relations, class, and other social conflicts within societies. My subsequent work has addressed both sets of questions, with books on individualism, power and Marxism. I started to think sociologically about morals when still an undergraduate student: Where our moral judgments come from, if not from our social context, and why they should apply beyond it, are questions I continue to pursue. And reading Durkheim's great book on religion led me to ask to what extent our religious, scientific, and even logical thought is socially shaped.

In Parliament Square, London, a protestor is detained by police following clashes during student demonstrations over the proposal to triple university tuition fees. Why are protests like this one so unusual?

Ben Stansall/AFP/ Getty Images

189

decades. As a consequence, the explosion of nationwide protests in 2020 led by the Black Lives Matter movement seemed to many observers surprising, when perhaps we should have asked the opposite question: Why did it take so long for those groups that have been suffering to rise up in mass protest?

In this chapter, we will explore these questions by examining power and its larger political underpinnings. Power is a complex idea, and one that we have introduced in our discussion of social structure and the institutional order of society earlier in the book (see Chapter 5). We have already noted there that the most powerful institutions are those of the state (a concept which we will more carefully define later in the chapter, but one which covers the institutions of government, the legal system, and the military and police). This is because state institutions have the capacity to force change in all other societal institutions. In a sense, it stands above and shapes everything below it. For this reason, an examination of who has power in state institutions becomes central to understanding how social order is advanced and maintained. To do this, we will examine power from the ground up, from individuals and groups, all the way to the pinnacle of power in the modern state.

We have one critical guiding principle to keep in mind. We are often not fully aware of the impact of power on us, and sometimes we are not even aware of its operation at all. Sometimes we can be mistaken about the causes of what afflicts us, and we may see power at work when it is not, attributing our misfortunes to conspiracies of one sort or another. One huge task for the sociologist studying power is to shed light on how power works, especially in relation to the central institutions of power in the halls of the government. For example, what are its typical *mechanisms*, or modes of operation? Why do we sometimes go along with relationships or support government policies that work against our interests? Does power influence our compliance, and, if so, how is our compliance secured? And where does power lie? Who has power? Are we looking for individuals, or groups, or impersonal institutions? Are the answers to such questions always obvious to us? As we will see, power is most effective when it is least observable to participants and observers alike. And if that is so, then the task facing the sociologist of power is all the more daunting – but important!

Associated Press

The late 1960s were a rare moment in which protests all over the world challenged those in power. Here, student rebels assist each other in climbing up into the offices of Columbia University President Grayson Kirk at the Columbia campus in New York City, April 24, 1968.

The Big Questions

1. **What are the distinct forms of power?** In this section, we explore three dimensions of power, using a sociological lens to examine not only the most visible ways in which power is expressed but also its more subtle forms.

2. **What is the state, and how does it distribute power in a society?** Here, we examine the institutions of power, which sociologists refer to as the state. We explore how and why states matter in the distribution of power.

3. **Why does the capitalist state normally protect the interests of the economically powerful?** In this section we examine why states in capitalist societies over the world typically adopt policies that favor the interests of the powerful. In doing so, we will study two broad theories related to capitalist societies.

Robert Munro/Alamy Stock Photo

BIG QUESTION 8.1 What Are the Distinct Forms of Power?

THE THREE DIMENSIONS OF POWER

Power in the most general sense simply means the capacity to bring about some outcome; in other words, either to affect changes, or to prevent changes from occurring. In social and political contexts, the effects of power will be those that are significant to people's lives. When these effects of power negatively affect someone's interests, we can speak of power being held or exercised *over* them. In such cases, the sociologist's quest is to try to reveal what this involves. There are also other ways of identifying social and political power, for instance, as *collective* power to achieve shared goals (as when people cooperate to promote a cause or a campaign) or as *positive* power, where power serves others' interests (as, ideally, parents, teachers, doctors, philanthropists, and social workers are supposed to do).

In the first part of this chapter, we will focus on what is involved in having and exercising power, and then we will turn to an analysis of how power over others is facilitated in the political institutions of the state. Since the publication of the classic work *Power* by the first author of this chapter (Steven Lukes) nearly 50 years ago (Lukes 1974),

it has become widely accepted that power contains three distinct dimensions, as Table 8.1 illustrates. The first of these dimensions—the one-dimensional view—involves situations where we can see power at work when one party prevails in a conflict. A second dimension of power involves the ways in which those with power prevent or deflect challenges

Table 8.1 The Three Dimensions of Power

	First Dimension	Second Dimension	Third Dimension
Power of A over B	A has superior resources and wins open conflicts.	A constructs or benefits from barriers that prevent B from challenging A's position or even raising a challenge in the first place.	A influences B to support or think the way A does, even when it is not in B's interests to do so.
Powerlessness of B versus A	B has few resources to win open conflicts.	B fails to get its challenge to A to be taken seriously, or B is so frustrated by lack of power that B fails to issue a challenge to A.	B comes to believe in A's ideas, even when it is not in B's interests to do so.

SOURCE: Gaventa, 1980.

to their authority from arising in the first place. Finally, a third dimension occurs when those with power are able to convince those without that the views of those with power are correct and should be accepted or assumed to be correct. In this case, power may appear completely invisible. In the rest of this section, we will elaborate on each dimension of power.

The One-Dimensional View of Power

8.1.1 Identify who has power in the one-dimensional view.

The most straightforward situation where we can see power at work is one where there is a conflict between two or more individuals or groups, and one of them prevails. Let's call the more powerful individual or group "A" and the less powerful individual or group "B." There are countless examples of power at work in this observable form, involving conflict over an issue or issues for which the participants have interests that are in contention. The conflict can be interpersonal—between lovers or within families—or it can occur within or between organizations. It can even exist between countries.

A bully in the schoolyard, a mugger in the street, a landlord versus a tenant, a struggle between employers and unions over wages, a group of people rising up against a dictatorship, a country locked in civil war or at war with other countries—all of these involve power in a directly visible form. Usually one side has much more power than the others. But sometimes, the balance of power can shift, and the usually powerless actor can gain and sometimes even exercise power. In some cases, the power of the powerful is illegitimate (such as the bully or the mugger), sometimes it is legitimate (the landlord's rent might be legal and fair), and sometimes (as for example in a war within or between countries) what is right and wrong itself may be what is at issue (that is, whoever wins a war gets to write its history and declare "right" and "wrong").

Power is often exercised just by following the "rules of the game." For example, when companies compete for market share in selling some good or service, they are playing by the rules of the economic game. When a group of legislators wins a vote, they are using the rules to compete (and win) in the political game. But in other cases, those who win may do so not by *following* the rules of the game but rather by *manipulating* them in some way. Using threats or bribes to get what you want are examples of how someone or some group can gain power by breaking the rules.

When citizens protest, governments can call out police or military forces to contain or shut down the protests. It is one way in which in the first dimension of power, the authorities almost always have the upper-hand. Escalating the conflict by having the police or military attack protestors, however, can backfire; it may anger protestors and bring other people out in the streets to join the protests, thereby escalating the conflict.

Nikolas Georgiou/Alamy Stock Photo

But exercising power by breaking the rules of the game is an uncertain undertaking. For example, when threats of violence escalate into the actual use of force, it means that the threat itself has failed. The use of force often signifies weakness. For instance, when governments headed by dictators face social rebellions, as we saw in some of the Arab Spring protests in the Middle East in 2011, they often use military force to try to stop the protests. This may stop or slow down the protests, but in many cases these governments will eventually fall if protests continue to grow in spite of attempts to stop them. Indeed, using force over and over is rarely sustainable over the long haul. If the more powerful A must use force against the less powerful B, A has not succeeded in getting B to comply, but only to temporarily give in. If that situation persists, A's control over B is likely to become tenuous at some point (as B figures out a way to increase its capacity to fight back).

The Two-Dimensional View of Power

8.1.2 Explain the role of agenda setting in the second dimension of power.

Treating power as a one-dimensional process focused only on outcomes when there is visible conflict ignores the fascinating puzzle of why some important issues or ideas never come up for discussion or debate in decision-making arenas. We can define a second dimension of power in which a power holder (A) prevents a subordinate group or individual (B) from raising issues that would challenge A's power. Power in this second dimension refers to the ability of some actors to prevent others from ever getting alternative ideas proposed or considered in the first place. This process, like one-dimensional power, is present at all levels of social life, from interpersonal relationships to international relations between countries. *It is the power to decide what gets decided.*

At the heart of the second dimension of power is the process of **agenda setting**—the act of consciously or unconsciously averting the challenge of potential issues the more powerful actor would rather avoid. The ability to control or set the agenda is a critical resource of power, whether we are talking about family relationships, a small or large business organization, a church or a sports team, in Congress or even the United Nations. When power is exercised through agenda control, the grievances of excluded or marginal groups can be denied a hearing.

There are a variety of ways agenda control can be achieved, the most common being the literal manipulation of agendas through the control of procedures, thereby affecting what gets discussed and decided. For example, if a city council does not want to respond to a citizen's complaints that streets are not being cleared of snow fast enough, the council may avoid holding hearings to prevent giving more publicity to the issue (and giving larger numbers of people a platform to complain). The council could invite citizens to submit written reports about their concerns, which then could be safely filed away and ignored. Or the council could schedule hearings on the matter for the summer, long after the problems with winter snow are forgotten.

This second dimension of power requires us to stretch our understanding of what issues are important where power may be at stake: They are not *just* those that are the subject of open conflict but *also* those that are prevented from becoming the subject of challenge. Small children might prefer that more of the family budget be spent on candy than vegetables or that more (or less) time be spent with relatives, but parents typically do not let small children have much say over what kinds of foods the family buys or how many times the children visit the relatives. In this way, the parents control the agenda for discussion without the child even necessarily being aware of it. The same kind of dynamic arises in politics. Researchers have long puzzled over why some topics are the focus of intense discussion and debate, while other equally or even more important topics are ignored (Best 2008). Why do some issues become widely discussed social problems, while other equally or more pressing issues do not?

As we have discussed elsewhere in the text, economic, racial, and gender/sexual inequalities have always been a part of the American experience. But only rarely, and typically under fierce pressure from social movements, do those issues begin to get "on the agenda"—to be covered extensively by the media, to get new laws proposed, and to become part of everyday conversations. Even when such movements arise, however, they often only succeed in temporarily altering the agenda. Consider, for example, the relative lack of attention to issues surrounding the persistence of poverty and rising inequality versus the enormous amount of attention given to the health and well-being of big business, banks and Wall Street, and corporate profits. Every major newspaper in America has a section devoted to business, covering the comings and goings of business executives, the profitability (or lack thereof) of various local and national companies, and the ups and downs of the stock market. But there is no comparable coverage devoted to the daily struggle of those living in poverty or to the insecurity faced by millions of American families or to the trials and tribulations of the groups that try to represent the interests of the poor.

In the fall of 2011, the social movement Occupy Wall Street (known as "Occupy") exploded in New York City and then spread around the world (Gould-Wartofsky 2015). It spurred considerable attention to issues of rising inequality on the part of the media and politicians, but once the movement faded in 2012, the topic was largely pushed off the policy agenda. In 2017, in fact, the U.S. Congress actually cut taxes on the largest corporations and richest individuals, doing the exact opposite of what was being demanded by the Occupy movement – and exacerbating already large inequalities by giving the largest benefits to the richest people (and corporations).

A more recent example—the case of racial injustices involving the use of force by police officers against Blacks—highlights significant ways in which agenda control can help the powerful prevent change. At the peak of the Civil Rights movement of the 1960s, racial injustices in policing briefly received a good amount of attention, as noted in the chapter introduction. Indeed, the most important original motivation for the formation of the Black Panthers in Oakland, California was to reduce police violence (the group originally called itself the Black Panther Party for Self-Defense)—"policing the police" (Bloom and Martin 2016). But in the decades since the heyday of the Civil Rights movement, a wave of "law and order" policies *expanded* the powers of the police and led to a massive increase in imprisonment of Blacks (see Chapter 20). In 2020, in the face of yet another killing of an unarmed Black person (a man named George Floyd in Minneapolis, Minnesota), activists from the Black Lives Matter (BLM) movement and other groups mobilized nationwide protests that demanded officials address problems related to racism in the criminal justice system and the police, creating a second moment of discussion (Joseph 2020).

Yet whether the mass protests over police practices that have occurred across the United States will prompt greater attention to the problem remains to be seen. History strongly suggests that the most likely outcome will be similar to the results of previous protests against police brutality. Police departments will promise to reform and train their officers better. Local governments and mayors may fire their police chief and bring in someone new who promises to make big changes. Congress may get involved, passing legislation that provides local police forces with money to better train their officers and make them more careful in using violence to subdue a suspect. But if the past is any indicator, none of this will have any real impact; as (one recent study calls it, "the mirage of police reform" comes and goes and nothing really changes (Worden and McLean 2017)).

The case of police reform illuminates another kind of agenda control via complex **bureaucracies** (a kind of large organization in which there are multiple levels of authority and a large number of rules and regulations that have to be followed). Leaders of bureaucracies can truthfully say to protestors that "I am doing the best I can, but there are a lot of steps involved; it's not as simple as you think." Since only people inside the bureaucracy really know the truth, they often very easily hide behind the claim that changes are being made, without anything fundamentally changing. The German sociologist Max Weber described the rule of bureaucracies as imposing an "iron cage" in which the appearance of rules and order in the name of efficiency have the effect of making it difficult for ordinary people to change things. Student protestors at college campuses across the world have often had this experience, in which their protests will lead to a meeting with the university president or another senior administrator, who will appear sympathetic and promise to make some changes, and then nothing really gets done.

The study of agenda setting has paid special attention to the mass media (such as television, newspapers, talk radio, and the major online news sites) as playing an especially crucial role where the second dimension of power operates. When the media give a large amount of attention to a particular issue, it becomes much more likely that it will receive attention by politicians and policymakers. The fact that coverage of big business is so pronounced is perhaps unsurprising once we observe that most important media outlets are themselves owned by corporate entities or conglomerates (see Chapter 10 for details). The search for profit in the news media is also a critical factor determining what we read or watch. Much of the focus of the media today is driven by editors' perceptions of what sells—that is, what citizens are most interested in reading about. For example, there is an old saying that "if it bleeds, it leads." Sensational stories about murders and other violent crimes have always generated a lot of attention. The celebrity in trouble with the law, or celebrity couples falling in and out of love or marriage, can be sure to provoke especially intense coverage, with only the names changing from year to year. By contrast, the media usually pay much less attention to challenges to the status quo and seldom provide opportunities for these challengers to reach other like-minded people.

Francis Specker/Alamy Stock Photo

News stories about celebrities like Kayne West (shown here) always generate intense fascination in the media (both traditional and social media). A good question to ask is, why do these types of news reports get so much more attention and coverage than reports about poverty, injustice, or inequality?

The Three-Dimensional View of Power

8.1.3 Discuss the various ways in which the workings of power can be hidden.

The first and second dimensions of power are important, but they do not exhaust the possibilities. Seeing power three-dimensionally involves understanding the various ways in which its workings can be hidden from the view of those subject to it and perhaps even from those who possess power. A third dimension of power operates when a powerful actor can persuade a weaker actor to adopt beliefs or behaviors that serve the interests of the powerful. Power can, in some cases, result from the *anticipation* by others of what they believe the powerful would do if they were not to comply with their interests.

Research on power has demonstrated that in many contexts people will defer to, or are even attracted toward, those with power. The power of wealth, privilege, and **status**—the prestige accorded to certain individuals and to important social or economic positions—is often at work without the powerful having to lift a finger to exercise it or even being conscious of its impact or its reach. Many of us will behave differently in the presence of powerful or famous people than with others. When the chief executive of a large company visits the office, or when a celebrity walks into a restaurant, people tend to make extra efforts to try to ensure their happiness and please them. In this way, these powerful people do not even need to assert their authority to secure respect or obedience on the part of others.

But the third dimension is operative not just in situations of deference. The most effective—and potentially the sneakiest—use of power is to prevent conflict from arising in the first place by persuading B that whatever A wants is in B's best interests. Powerholders may attempt to gain consent to their power by shaping the perceptions and beliefs of the powerless. Where the powerful are in the business of preserving and protecting the status quo, the effects of such power are to encourage people to accept their role in the existing order of things—perhaps because they cannot imagine any alternative, or they see it as impossible to change, or they see it as divinely ordained and beneficial. All of these reasons have been invoked to encourage ordinary people to accept the rule of monarchs or dictators. But just because people don't actively protest against a dictator or king does not prove that their apparent consent is not the outcome of power. To assume that the absence of a grievance is the same thing as genuine consensus rules out the possibility of manipulation in how people think.

The powerful are often in a position to prevent change by exploiting their power to shape perceptions and get people to accept as true all kinds of mythical and simplistic versions of reality. Those in power may do this by playing not only on their followers' fears, prejudices, and limited information but also on the many ways in which people are susceptible to biased and/or faulty reasoning. In the most extreme form, such as propaganda issued by a dictator's government, the attempt at persuasion is open and direct. But persuasion can be more subtle and need not be deliberately engaged in, and it can coexist with power in the first and second dimensions.

The third dimension is important because it enables us to consider the possibility that power over others is not always simply a matter of being able to prevail over them when conflicts of interest occur, or even to set the agenda of what such conflicts are about. It can *also* consist of being able to secure the dependence, allegiance, or compliance of others. The third dimension of power, in other words, reveals itself when the powerless embrace the interests of the powerful as their own. Let's take a famous example. Charles Wilson, then president of General Motors (GM), testified before Congress in 1953 that "what is good for General Motors is good for America." All Americans benefit, in other words, from policies that make GM more profitable. What Wilson had in mind when he made this statement was that when GM is profitable, it will hire more workers and generate more business for the subcontractors who supply GM

General Motors President Charles Wilson testifying before Congress in the early 1950s. Wilson's famous statement that "what is good for General Motors is good for America" unintentionally captured an important sociological lesson. Wilson probably did not think of himself as a sociologist, but the claim that the health and well-being of powerful business organizations is central to societal well-being reminds us of why corporations have the power they do - and also calls attention to the risks inherent in allowing them to do anything that makes them more profitable.

with parts used in the manufacture of automobiles. But GM—or any large corporation—does not exist only to provide jobs for Americans; its main objective is to maximize its profits and payouts to its shareholders. In order to maximize those profits, GM has an interest in trying to keep the wages it pays its workers as low as possible, to have minimal regulations applied to its products, to try to pay as little in corporate taxes as it can, to not have to spend large sums to reduce the pollution its cars cause, to reduce competition from public transportation, and so forth. None of these things are in the general interests of all Americans, or even necessarily of all GM employees.

Throughout this section, we have suggested that a sociological understanding of power compels us to examine not only the most visible ways in which power is expressed, but also its more subtle forms. Power is sometimes revealed in open conflict. But more often it reflects the ability of a power holder to keep challenges from arising in the first place, or even the capacity of a power holder to convince subordinate groups that it is in their interests to support the existing arrangement. When power is hidden from our view, the only way to find it is to dig beneath the surface and consider that not all is necessarily as it seems!

Mark Bussell

THE INSTITUTIONS OF POWER

Power in all of its forms can be expressed in any setting in a multitude of ways. A parent, a teacher, a small business owner, or a religious leader may all have some kinds of power, but power is consequential on a grand scale when the government is involved. Governments make laws, spend large sums of money on a huge number of areas, tax individuals and companies, and prepare for (and sometimes go to) war. Large government bureaucracies define policies and procedures and issue and administer regulations that are to be adhered to by others. Courts and legal institutions interpret and enforce laws and government policies (and sometimes find those policies unconstitutional). Taken as a whole, these institutions are supposed to make our lives better, but they also have a huge impact on the overall distribution of power in any society and often favor some groups over others. If we are to study power in all its forms, then, we have to develop an understanding of the central political institutions and how they operate. That is the task of this section.

What Is the State?

8.2.1 Define the state and explain how it regulates the economy.

Sociologists use the term **the state** (as noted in Chapter 5) to refer to all of the formal and enduring political institutions of any society. In the United States, these include the three branches of government (the executive, legislative, and judicial branches) as well as all of the bureaucracies

that support the work of each branch. Other government institutions at lower levels of administration—such as local governments or intermediate regional governments (like the "state" government in California or Texas, or regional governments such as those in the provinces in Canada)—can also be considered part of the "state," but we will focus on national political institutions.

It is important to note that the state is not simply just an elected government, like the elected officials who comprise the executive branch, or even the executive branch and legislative branch together. Although elected officials are certainly key parts of the state during the time they hold office, the state also includes the legal system (and the courts that enforce the law), as well as the military and those permanent bureaucracies that will remain in place regardless of who is the head of the current government. In the United States, for example, a new president appoints a few thousand senior administrators and staff upon taking office, but the entire federal government employs over 3 million people. Most of these employees remain in office no matter who is president. Similarly, judges are often appointed for long terms or for life and are not dependent on who holds elected office. When the president leaves office and a new Congress and president are elected, those permanent bureaucracies will continue doing what they were before the change in elected government. This is one reason why bringing about change in national politics—regardless of which major party is in office—is often difficult to achieve.

What are the powers of the state? First and foremost, as noted, the state controls a nation's military and it, not the public, decides when to go to war against an enemy. One of the central reasons the modern state came into existence in the first place was to raise a military that would be capable of protecting a nation's territory. There is a famous statement by sociologist Charles Tilly that captures this idea: "war made the state, and the state made war" (Tilly 1975, p. 42). To effectively field the increasingly large and expensive armies, however, states had to develop a system of taxation to raise revenues as well convince young men that they should serve and risk their lives in war. As a result, the ruling monarch had to establish the branches of the state that could go around and collect money, as well as people to serve in armies and navies, an undertaking that changed the nature of political institutions in a fundamental way (Ertman 1997). In the contemporary world, preparation for war, rather than actual fighting against foreign nations, continues to be a central purpose of the state (Brooks 2016).

The next major role of the state involves a nation's economy. For economic markets to function properly and at maximal efficiency, states have to provide a wide range of legal guarantees and rules and have the capacity to enforce those rules when they are violated. For example, market exchanges rely on contracts between buyers and sellers. A contract exists when one person agrees to provide certain goods or services at a certain price and the other person agrees to pay that price. As long as both parties do what they promise, the terms of the contract are fulfilled, and everyone is more or less satisfied. But what happens when one party fails to do what it promises? It is ultimately state institutions—sometimes the courts or government agencies—that provide the necessary assurance that if one party fails to live up to its contractual commitments, it will be penalized. For most individuals and business organizations, however, the critical backing provided by the state provides confidence and trust that a stranger will do what they promise (and makes contractual exchange possible).

The role of the state in the economy has grown over time to include a wide range of other supports that help make both the economy and society work. One vitally important thing states do is accomplished through **regulation**, rules that can promote fairness and protect the public good, and if well-designed support economic growth as well. For example, state agencies regulate economic markets to try to create a level playing field for all participants and to prevent large companies from making false claims that confuse consumers or harm innocent third parties. Here are some examples of important regulatory policies designed to protect citizens from being harmed by economic actors that all modern states have some version of:

Mark Bussell

Laws and regulations exist to prevent companies from falsely advertising their products, such as labeling nonorganic food products organic. If companies were free to make any claims they wanted, consumers would have the burden of separating what is true from what is false—and in many cases would have no way to tell the difference.

- Laws and policies that prevent large corporations from taking advantage of their size to cut special deals with suppliers or using their size to drive competitors out of business and create uncompetitive monopolies (for example, in the 1990s when Microsoft Corporation provided low-priced operating software for new computers but then made it very difficult for consumers to run non-Microsoft programs).

- Laws preventing stock market traders from using insider knowledge to unfairly profit (for example, laws preventing employees at a company who know of a new product that will increase the value of the firm's stock from using that knowledge to buy up the company's stock in advance of the new product's release and later sell at a profit).

- Laws and regulations that prevent firms from making false advertising claims about their products (for example, not allowing a food manufacturer to call nonorganic food products organic – see image above).

- Laws and regulations that require companies to meet minimal standards in terms of safety for workers and consumers (for example, laws barring a clothing manufacturer from making clothes that might catch on fire).

- Laws and regulations that make companies or individuals compensate innocent third parties when their actions cause harm (for example, if a company's factory creates pollution that damages the health of families living near the factory).

These examples are just some of the many ways that modern states try to solve some of the problems and limitations of a market economy through regulation. In each of these cases, one can argue that the regulations are in the general interests of the broad public—by making sure that there is competition between firms or by protecting consumers and innocent third parties. These policies also give individuals who want to start a business a reasonable expectation that if the goods or services they provide are of high enough quality, they will be able to compete against existing businesses on fair terms. Some critics believe that excessive regulation is harmful, and it is certainly possible for states to over-reach. But *without* extensive regulation, economic activity as we know it would be impossible.

The state also provides much-needed infrastructure for the economy to work. The state funds and operates most of the schools where future workers learn to read, write, and think (about 90 percent of all U.S. children, for example, attend public schools). It builds and maintains the roads, bridges, and trains that businesses use to transport goods to markets or workers use to get to their jobs – what is known as infrastructure. It regulates the banking system, prints and controls the supply of money, and sets interest rates in order to try to produce stable economic growth. It builds and operates the airports and regulates the skies so

that planes do not crash into each other. It funds scientific research that can lead to innovations in the future. (Many people are surprised to learn, for example, that it was a U.S. government research lab that invented the Internet (see Block and Keller 2011).) It maintains numerous public health programs that we take for granted, such as providing clean drinking water and proper sewage disposal, without which millions of people would die every year.

States all over the world also have, since the late nineteenth century, developed a set of programs known collectively as the **welfare state**. We can think of the welfare state as a "state within the state," a bundle of programs designed to provide individuals and families with both greater opportunities and access to basic necessities of life. Some of the permanently established programs in the U.S. (and virtually all other rich and many developing countries) include Social Security (pensions for people over 65), Medicare (health insurance program for people over 65), unemployment insurance, disability insurance, and income support programs for poor families.

Finally, it is states that step in when a crisis hits. For example, during the COVID-19 pandemic, states provided active measures to prevent a global economic collapse. In the United States, the federal government provided $2.3 trillion in 2020 to help businesses and unemployed workers survive (an amount equivalent to almost one-tenth of the entire American economy), and later provided another $1.9 trillion in 2021 to help families and the economy recover from the huge losses they suffered. It was the federal government that provided the huge investments in the development of vaccines that speeded up their introduction faster than anyone thought possible. Only states have the immense resources needed to intervene on a large enough scale to reduce the harms of an economic crisis and manage economies and societies back to a better place. Indeed, the list of things that states do that make possible so many other beneficial activities is so long that it is virtually impossible to imagine a modern economy—or society—without it.

Why States Matter in the Distribution of Power and Wealth

8.2.2 Explain how the state influences who gets what government services.

The policies and programs adopted and maintained by the state are hugely important in many different ways. But they can be designed in ways that help some people more than others. Policies could, for example, be designed to ensure that poor families receive a greater share of the economic pie, or, by contrast, they can be designed to allow the rich to maintain or even increase their share of wealth. These policies, known as **tax and transfer policies**, are especially important for the distribution of income and wealth. All governments must tax their citizens to pay for government services, but whether the rich will pay a higher share than the poor varies widely across countries and over time. And whether the social spending programs of the welfare state will significantly reduce or even eliminate poverty can also vary widely, depending on how much and in what forms states develop welfare state programs (Kenworthy 2020).

Taken as a whole, *who gets what* is determined in very significant ways by the policies of the governmental agencies. There are many specific examples of how states impact who gets what in any society. Here are a few examples:

- States set or alter the rules of the game within which individuals and groups contest each other for power: Policies can favor big business, small business, farmers, or workers and unions, but not everyone all at the same time. For example, states decide whether or not employers have to take special precautions to ensure their workplace is safe, or whether water in areas that don't get much rain will go to farmers or to urban areas, or whether workers will have an easy or hard time organizing a union.

- States allocate a huge amount of resources and income through various kinds of welfare state spending programs, as noted earlier. These social policies reduce poverty and bolster living standards for poor families. The rise of the welfare state in the twentieth century represented an important step toward using state power in the interests of everyone, not just the rich.

- States decide who bears the burdens of paying for all government spending programs, primarily through their tax policies (for example, should tax burdens be equal for everyone, or should the rich pay a higher percentage, and/or should large companies be taxed on the profits they earn or allowed to avoid most taxes?)

- States have the power to decide life-and-death matters such as who has to fight wars. For example, will privileged people be able to avoid service? States also decide whether the death penalty is legal (and whether the government is allowed to kill) and, if so, which kinds of people will be subject to the penalty. Other life-defining public policies include whether or not food and health care should be provided to those who cannot afford to pay for it themselves. Should those who are truly destitute be given the means to survive or not?

In each of these policy areas, states make choices that impact the distribution of power across the entire society. In many important ways, states provide the institutional backdrop for market economies to function and directly or indirectly ensure that investments can be made profitably, as noted earlier. And sometimes states will directly intervene on behalf of the powerful, especially in periods of political conflict and stress. But states are not simply tools of the ruling classes of a society. States also sometimes make policy decisions, as we will see, that can empower the poor and help the disadvantaged obtain a greater share of the benefits of economic growth.

Bill Chizek Photography/Alamy Stock Photo

BIG QUESTION 8.3 Why Does the Capitalist State Normally Protect the Interests of the Economically Powerful?

PROTECTING THE POWERFUL

In this section, we will examine some general reasons why states often adopt policies in the interests of the powerful. Or more specifically, how and why do states tend to adjust their policies to support the interests of powerful

businesses over ordinary people? In particular, when it comes to the most important arenas of state policy, economically powerful actors have usually—not always, but usually—been able to get what they want. The dominant economic system around the world—*capitalism*—builds in a number of tools that facilitate the power of the strongest economic actors. Sociologists sometimes refer to the state as the "capitalist state," to highlight the importance of the capitalist economic system in shaping and constraining state policies.

Social scientists who have studied the question of why capitalist economic elites have enhanced power over others have proposed two broad sets of answers. The first view is what is known as the **structural power of business** (Lindblom 1977; Block 1987; Bernhagen and Brauninger 2005).

The basic idea is that states in capitalist societies are normally compelled to focus on making policies that will keep the economy growing and healthy (and avoiding policies that might serve other goals—for example, policies to reduce carbon emissions and fight climate change). It often does not serve governments well to propose policies that are disliked by leading businesses.

The second view focuses on political elites and how they are selected into positions of power in the capitalist state. This **power elite** thesis starts from the simple observation that the people promoted into positions of power have been groomed and selected for those roles by people already in power. Political decision makers are thus already predisposed to favor the interests of the group that put them there in the first place. In this way, there tends to be an endless cycle of reproduction of elite interests.

At the outset of this discussion, we want to underscore two critical points. First, these two theories are not incompatible with one another—we think that both contain important insights and can supplement each other to provide a fuller picture of power and politics in capitalist societies. Second, in spite of all of the ways that people who benefit from the status quo may seek to prevent significant changes from occurring, change does sometimes happen (as discussed in Chapter 5 and later in this section). Like all institutions, political institutions evolve over time and what seems impossible at one point in time can become government policy or law the next. Key to these changes is the existence of a democratic political system, which enables social movements to arise and the opinions and preferences of ordinary people to (sometimes) influence the behavior of politicians and government officials (see Chapter 22). We will explore in more detail these two broad theories of power in the rest of this section. Our discussion here is about the political power of business that is common to all capitalist countries; in Chapter 21 we provide a more detailed examination of how these factors operate in the unique political system of the United States.

The Structural Power of Business

8.3.1 Explain why all governments want business organizations to be successful, and why this reflects a structural power in capitalist societies.

In order to grasp the idea that large, powerful businesses have built-in structural power, we need to briefly review how **capitalism**, the dominant economic system around the world, creates a particular set of incentives that are universal to all states in capitalist society (see Chapter 9 for a comprehensive discussion). The term *capitalism* has been defined in different ways by social scientists, but common to all definitions is the idea that the predominant form of economic activity—buying, producing, selling, investing—is done through markets. Further, capitalism is an economic system based on private property, in which those who have resources are able to hire other people to work for them. The creation of ever larger business organizations first began to arise when those with wealth were able to take advantage of technological advances that made possible ever bigger factories and workplaces, and they figured out how to use their **capital** (wealth that can be used to invest in pursuit of profit) to generate income. Today, because of the heavy concentration of wealth in the hands of a small number of individuals and enormous corporations, the decisions these entities make can have an immense impact on the health of a nation's economy (Piketty 2014; Dayen 2020).

The general health of the economy is of central importance to everyone. We all are impacted by the state of our national economy in one way or another. In survey after survey, respondents will inevitably choose having a healthy economy as their most important national concern, however the question is worded (brief exceptions arise in special periods of crisis, such as we saw with the rise of COVID-19). A famous slogan in politics, originally designed to discipline candidates for office about voters' central concerns, is this: "It's the economy, stupid." This slogan underscores the idea that voters want to know elected officials will work hard to adopt policies that will keep the economy healthy. Citizens care about the economy because they know through experience that a healthy economy means that jobs are plentiful, and it is possible to get raises or move to better-paying jobs. In downturns, by contrast, employers lay off workers, pay freezes are common, and those who keep their jobs are often tasked with doing more with less.

Once in office, government officials are also centrally concerned with economic growth. This is true both for democratic governments (where regular elections provide opportunities for citizens to remove government officials from office) and for authoritarian governments that want to try to prevent revolts from happening. Government leaders, beginning with the head of state, know that a strong, growing economy will make people more enthusiastic about the overall performance of the government. They also know that the opposite is true (a bad economy leads to unhappy citizens). Further, a healthy economy means that governments can collect more tax revenue to pay for whatever programs they want. Taxes are typically paid by both individuals (primarily income taxes plus sales taxes) and businesses (taxes on profits). When unemployment is very low and everyone who wants a job has one, there are more individual taxpayers paying taxes. When businesses are profitable, they too will pay more in taxes. The upshot of both of these critical motivations is a single, universal, and virtually inarguable point: Governments have extremely strong motivations to make the economy as successful as they can.

Given that universally accepted conclusion, the question becomes: What policies are essential to maintaining a healthy economy? Politicians and policymakers know there is no special sauce, no secret ingredient, that always works. (If there was, it would certainly be much easier to be a successful politician or government leader!) But there are a few universally understood factors that are of central importance. For a capitalist economy to grow and thrive, businesses and investors (and the banks that loan them money) have to continually make investments in technology, facilities, hiring and training of workers, and many other basic areas to sustain their business. And in a global economic system, a government wants to ensure that investors and corporations make those investments in their own country, not in a foreign country.

So what makes business leaders decide to make these investments? The key point is this: Business owners and managers have to be confident that they will be able to make a profit (or at the very least, break even, or keep losses to a reasonable amount in the short term, in anticipation of an eventual turnaround). If they lose confidence in their ability to make a profit from their investments, they can (1) choose to simply keep their cash and wait for a better investment environment (known as hoarding), or (2) they can use their capital to make investments in other countries. If businesses choose not to invest, inevitably there are fewer jobs, which in turn means fewer workers who have the income to buy products and keep the economy going. This is exactly what happens in **economic recessions**, which have periodically occurred throughout the history of capitalism. (A severe recession, such as what happened in the 1930s, is called a **depression**.) In recessions, a downward spiral occurs; as unemployment rises, there are fewer customers to buy products and services, which triggers further layoffs as businesses reduce their investments in anticipation of reduced market activity.

Economic recessions and depressions can have multiple causes, but maintaining the confidence of business leaders is essential to avoid accidentally creating one or to making an existing downturn worse (Block 1977; Lindblom 1977; Young et al. 2018). The structural power theory holds that whatever the preferences of elected governments are when they assume office (for example, whether a liberal Democrat or a conservative

Republican), there are powerful and ongoing incentives to make sure that big businesses have the confidence and security they need to want to make investments that will create jobs and produce economic growth. In an era where there are high levels of economic trade and investments being made in other countries, maintaining a healthy business environment at home is especially important to discourage companies from moving abroad, or alternatively, to encourage foreign companies to invest at home. A newly elected government has to take these issues into consideration.

To see why this is true, we can look to historical examples. Throughout the twentieth century, there have been a number of governments elected to power that have made proposals that are very strongly disliked by business leaders, and those governments have faced an immediate backlash in the form of a **capital strike**. A capital strike is analogous to a worker strike, except it involves investors and businesses refusing to invest (instead of workers refusing to work). Three well-known examples of capital strikes occurred after the election of socialists Salvador Allende in Chile in 1970 and Francois Mitterand in France in 1981 and in Sweden in the 1970s when the ruling Social Democratic Party decided to support a radical plan to slowly transfer stock ownership in business from their owners to firm workers.

In Chile, shortly after Allende's election, a mobilized business community drove the economy into a severe recession, helping pave the way for conservative opponents of Allende (including the military), with an assist from the United States' Central Intelligence Agency, to overthrow Allende in 1973 (Miliband 2014). In France, before the newly elected socialist government's most radical proposals could even be adopted, a massive withdrawal of investment and business opposition to the government's plans forced the government to retreat (Short 2014). In the late 1970s, when a leading member of the Swedish ruling Social Democratic Party, Rudolf Meidner proposed a plan in which firm profits would be taxed to pay for shares in the company, and those shares would in turn be distributed equally to all of the workers of the firm (thereby eventually creating worker-owned firms). This plan was met with bitter opposition from Swedish business, and eventually watered down and killed (Gowan and Viktorsson 2017).

Even the very moderate administration of Democratic President Barack Obama (2009–2019) faced important challenges from the business community (Young et al. 2018). For example, the then-Speaker of the House of Representatives, John Boehner, declared in response to Obama Administration policies, that *"Job creators are essentially on strike* [emphasis added]. The problem is not confusion about [Obama's] policies... the problem is the policies"* (quoted in Young et al. 2018, p. 10).

Horacio Villalobos/Corbis Historical/Getty Images

The aftermath of the bombing of the Presidential Palace in Santiago, Chile in September 1973. The Chilean military, at the behest of leading businesses and the United States government, forcibly removed the democratically elected President Salvador Allende from office in Chile. The socialist policies advocated by Allende and his supporters were deeply threatening to powerful interests. The National Security Advisor of the United States, Henry Kissinger, famously declared that "I don't see why we need to stand by and watch a country go communist due to the irresponsibility of its people. The issues are much too important for the Chilean voters to be left to decide for themselves." So the CIA helped Chilean military officials carry out a coup against Allende, and Chile would not hold another democratic election until 1990.

Banks and financial firms play a special role in reinforcing the structural power of business in capitalist societies, and leaders of these groups have especially strong influence (in the U.S., they are often called "Wall Street," the famous street in New York City where many leading firms were once located). The availability of loans from banks is a critical source of capital for business firms, as well as necessary for families to buy homes or to make other large purchases. The stock market is also an important indicator of how financial leaders feel about the economy and government policies. When the leaders of the financial sector lose confidence in the direction of the economy, they may stop or reduce lending and sell-off stocks, which can bring on a recession. Everyone loses. The health of the stock market is also important for many reasons, not only for the very rich who own stocks, but for ordinary people whose pensions or retirement saving are often based on the value of stocks. The financial crisis of 2008 highlights both of these points: (1) It showed how important finance is for a healthy economy; when banks suddenly stopped lending in September 2008, the American economy entered a long and protracted slump; (2) It also showed how politically important "Wall Street"

interests were, for example, when Congress and the Obama Administration decided to pursue a strategy of bolstering the largest banks, which were "too big to fail," while allowing homeowners all across America to lose their homes (Sorkin 2010).

The Power Elite

8.3.2 Describe who are members of the power elite, and why they are able to influence government policy.

The second major theory for why states tend to promote the interests of the powerful focuses on the relative political power of different groups in the political system, which often provides more affluent individuals and corporations privileged access to government officials (Domhoff 2006; Winters 2011; Drutman 2015). The notion of the importance of the politically powerful elite was made famous in the 1950s by C. Wright Mills (1956), thus launching a tradition of political analysis that continues to this day. Who are the members of this elite? They are the subset group of people who reach top positions in business, politics, the media, and other major institutions and who have gone through a process of *socialization* that begins in childhood. Many (but not all) elites are born into established upper-class families who typically have a multi-generational history of involvement in elite organizations and schools. Elites tend to have had common schooling experiences (at the top prep schools and private universities), they are members of elite clubs (where they mingle with each other), they have close friendships and even marriage ties with each other, and they develop and maintain social relationships with other elites as they build their careers (Kahn 2012). Not all powerful people have elite backgrounds, and not all elites will choose to enter positions of power. The group of people who have truly elite backgrounds and attributes are perhaps no more than 1 or 2 percent of the population, and yet they are vastly overrepresented in positions of influence and power, in and out of government (Domhoff 2013).

Members of the power elite are thought to be "groomed" for power as they pass through each stage of the socialization process. This does not mean that they all agree; quite the contrary, differences of opinion exist, but always within a fairly narrow range (Mills 1956; Domhoff 2013). The group is neither liberal nor conservative, but rather tends to favor moderate solutions to social problems that draw in both liberal and conservative ideas. Many elites can be, or are, quite supportive of LGBTQ rights and gender and racial equality, opposed to excessive policing and mass incarceration, and in favor of taking steps to try to reduce climate change. When it comes to poverty and inequality, they tend to favor a single solution: education. They often will support high levels of spending on public education and policy initiatives (such as charter schools) to improve the quality of schooling. On these issues, the power elite has been moving to more liberal positions, just as the rest of the public has (Baldassarri and Park 2020).

The power elite also shares certain policy and political ideas which are not at all liberal. It is strongly supportive of the global economy, including immigration across borders and free trade between nations. *Globalization* is almost universally favored by elites, who themselves typically travel extensively and probably have business or personal interests in many parts of the world (see Chapter 25 for more information on globalization). Globalization is often opposed, in different ways and to different degrees, by many liberals and conservatives. This opposition highlights one of the many ways in which former President Donald Trump was sharply at odds with traditional elites, reflecting the fact that in spite of his wealth Trump was never a fullfledged member of the power elite (Kranish and Fisher 2017; Trump 2020).

Former presidents Barack Obama and George W. Bush (a Democrat and a Republican, respectively) provide interesting case studies of elites who obtained the pinnacle of power. Both went to private preparatory schools and Ivy League colleges (and both received graduate degrees from Harvard). Their political careers were sponsored by older elites, who in a sense "selected" them from all of the many others who aspired to positions in power. Both of them can be considered moderates in the context of their more liberal Democratic Party (Obama) or more conservative Republican Party (Bush). In this sense, they stand for acceptable liberal and acceptable conservative positions within the power elite.

Let's consider Obama's trajectory in more detail (as it may seem more surprising to characterize him as a member of the power elite). Despite being raised by a single mother who was not wealthy, he won a variety of scholarships and was educated at Punahou High School in Hawaii (an elite prep school), Columbia University (for his BA) and Harvard Law School, as noted. In these elite educational settings, Obama made contacts and developed a style of interaction that made other elites comfortable, as the many biographies on his life confirm (e.g. Remnick 2010). He also developed and maintained close ties with a number of affluent and influential Chicago families, and those networks eased his way into politics and helped him raise the huge sums needed to be elected to the U.S. Senate, which he achieved in 2004, and the presidency in 2008. While in the White House, Obama took a variety of actions favored by elites. He promoted international trade and tried to balance the federal budget (failing, but not for a lack of trying; he was willing to make major cuts to government spending to achieve that oft-sought elite goal). In response to growing public demands for more equality, he proposed very slight increases in taxes on the wealthiest Americans, which slightly reduced inequality without making any other significant or threatening changes. He promoted policies either favored by most elites, or acceptable to them, and actively resisted calls from within his own party to promote more radical solutions to addressing climate change and other environmental issues. Obama also made no effort to use his presidency to help unions. His most important policy initiative—his national health reform measure (the Affordable Care Act, known as Obamacare)—did extend coverage to more Americans, but it also kept in place private insurance companies and did not challenge huge corporate profits in the health care sector, which in fact were higher when he left office than ever before (Rosenthal 2016).

If we analyzed the pathways to Congress, we would also find many members with elite backgrounds as well (Carnes 2012). But not all presidents and members of Congress come from elite backgrounds. Neither of the two most recent U.S. presidents – Donald Trump or Joe Biden – would qualify as true elites, although Trump came from a very wealthy but not upper-class background (his father was a real estate developer who successfully built apartments for middle class people in the outer boroughs of New York City). Trump did attend the University of Pennsylvania's Wharton School of Business, but he never was involved in the kinds of policy groups and clubs that elites seeking to enter politics generally participate in. Instead, Trump was a self-styled outsider, interested in making money however he could; prior to his run for president in 2015, he had sold everything from steaks to wine to deodorant to water bottles to vitamins to a fake Trump University scam (Tyler 2018), as well as being on a TV show, owning golf courses, and selling his famous name to real estate developers around the world who would put it on buildings (Kranish and Fisher 2017). Biden's background was fairly ordinary in many respects. His father was a used-car salesman and he attended public schools and the University of Delaware (for his BA) and Syracuse Law School before entering politics at a very young age (Biden was elected to the Senate at age 29 in 1972, beginning his life-long national political career).

Why do power elite theorists believe that a small group of elites are said to be so powerful? Since large corporations and rich individuals have more resources to influence political life than do other groups representing working-class and middle-class people, they are often more successful in getting what they want out of government (Hacker and Pierson 2010; Gilens 2012). Rich individuals and corporations can also use their financial resources not only try to influence elections and election outcomes, but also to build connections to individual politicians in the expectation that when they need a favor, it will be done. Some of the largest donors in the American political system give generously to politicians in both major parties, suggesting influence seeking rather than politically motivated giving (Heerwig 2018). As a result of all of these tactics, corporate executives and rich individuals are also far more likely to have access to politicians than are poor or middle-class people.

All of this is important. But elite theories emphasize the ways in which members of this group also shape the less visible forms of political power. It is on the second dimension of power—the agenda-setting mechanism of influence—that elites often have their greatest influence. For example, elites often develop career pathways that involve going back and forth between government appointments, elected office, and then service for private corporations or consulting firms. A particularly interesting example of this is the way in which members of the U.S. Congress and top congressional staff members frequently leave their less well-paid political jobs to go work for organizations known as lobbies, which work to try to get Congress to pass laws that serve their interests

or to get government bureaucrats to take a benign view of the corporations. Former members of Congress can earn millions of dollars working as lobbyists once their time in Congress is finished. This system is called the **revolving door**. It once was not particularly common; one estimate is that in 1950 only 3 percent of the members of Congress who left office went to work for lobbyists, whereas today it is closer to 50 percent (Leibovich 2013). The inevitably clubby relationship between current members of Congress and their former congressional friends who are now trying to convince them to support policies benefiting the corporations the latter now work for raises many critical questions about privileged access (Drutman 2015). Another revolving door occurs between government officials who regulate banks and other financial organizations and the credit ratings agencies that evaluate risk of those investments and the financial companies being evaluated and regulated (Bond and Glode 2014). One study showed that employees at credit ratings agencies gave significantly higher ratings to the firm they later joined (Cornaggia et al. 2016).

The revolving door is one of the clearest ways in which elite influence can operate. After a period of public service, in Congress or a government agency, many of these very same people go to work for companies that have important business before Congress or their former government agency. This is potentially problematic in two ways. First, their time in public service may be impacted by them looking for a lucrative job in the private sector. Second, they carry with them both knowledge of how to bend the rules in favor of their new employer and/or the capacity to call on friends still in public service for help when needed. While it's not certain from his time in the White House what exactly Donald Trump meant when he campaigned for president and talked about his goal of "draining the swamp," the revolving door between government and business would certainly qualify as one very swampy place.

Another important agenda-setting activity that elites perform to shape government policy in their favored direction is through the creation and funding of **policy planning organizations** (Domhoff 2013). These organizations, the most important of which tend to be based in Washington, D.C., or New York, include **think tanks** (research organizations that bring researchers together to develop policy proposals; see Rich 2004; Medvetz 2012), **foundations** (organizations, often established upon the death of an ultra-rich individual, which funds both research and policy programs; see Dowie 2001; Reich 2019), and **policy advocacy organizations** (which try to get policy ideas enacted into law; see Baumgartner et al. 2009; Peschek 1987). There are think tanks, foundations, and policy advocacy groups of all kinds, but the most powerful and influential, with the biggest budgets and greatest access to the media and policymakers, overwhelmingly tend to be created, funded, and participated in by members of the power elite and the large corporations they are involved with. Some of these organizations tend to be more liberal, others more conservative, but almost all of them are within a range of opinion that excludes more radical ideas on either the political left or political right. Among the most important of each type in policy and political debates in recent decades are listed in Table 8.2.

So far, we've focused mainly on elites at the national level. But at the very top of the elite group are the most influential figures in the world of corporate management, finance, and banking, who operate on a global, not national, scale. In the twenty-first century, these individuals and their multinational firms are finding that having connections with multiple governments and leaders around the world is especially valuable. Members of this small but especially prestigious group meet at regular events, the most famous of which is in an annual meeting in Davos, Switzerland, where they network with each other and with the many government officials who are invited to speak (Freeland 2006; Rothkopf 2008). From these connections arise appointments on the corporate boards of directors of multinational firms, in national and international commissions and organizations, to key positions in government (especially in foreign policy and diplomacy), and opportunities to write for prestigious newspapers and magazines. The top business consulting firms, such as McKinsey or Bain, often play important roles in connecting international businesses and governments together.

The global elite has played a significant role in enhancing trade and trade agreements between nations and in building up international organizations like the European Union, international commissions, and global nonprofit organizations. In recent years, however, the work of the global elite has come under fire. A group of politicians around the world known as **populists**, including Donald Trump, have effectively attacked these global elites, arguing that they are "out of touch" with ordinary people. Populism is a kind of political movement that claims to be "of the people" and the nation against elites and foreigners, although it can take varying forms in different national contexts. In one of the most significant manifestations of the rise of populism to date, in 2016 the United Kingdom voted to leave the European Union (EU) (what is known as **Brexit**). Many of the supporters of Brexit successfully used stereotypes and images of a European global elite adopting policies that are not in the interests of ordinary UK citizens (Evans and Menon 2017).

Connections Between the Theories

8.3.3 Discuss the connections between the structural power of business theory and power elite theory.

For decades, social scientists have treated the structural power of business and power elite theories as distinctive, alternative theories, and they have debated which one is superior. In recent years, however, it has become

Table 8.2 Leading Think Tanks, Foundations, and Policy Advocacy Organizations

Think Tanks	Foundations	Policy Advocacy Organizations
American Enterprise Institute	Gates Foundation	Chamber of Commerce
Brookings Institute	Howard Hughes Institute	National Association of Manufacturing
Cato Institute	Kaiser Family	Council on Foreign Relations
Heritage Institute	Lilly Endowment	Business Council
Rand Corporation	Robert Wood Johnson	Business Roundtable
Center for American Progress	Ford	Committee for Economic Development
Center for Strategic and International Studies	J. Paul Getty Trust	Conference Board
Urban Institute	William and Flora Hewlitt	Trilateral Commission
Aspen Institute	Kellogg	Committee for a Responsible Federal Budget
Hoover Institute	Packard	American Civil Liberties Union
Manhattan Institute for Policy Research	John D. and Catherine T. MacArthur	National Association to Advance Colored People
Open Society Institute	Rockefeller	American Israel Political Action Committee
Freedom House	Carnegie	Sierra Club
New America Foundation	Scaife	National Association of Realtors
Commonwealth Fund	Bloomberg	American Medical Association

Bill Gates, the founder of Microsoft and one of the richest people in the world, is also one of the most iconic members of the global elite. An active participant in the World Economic Forum, which sponsors the annual Davos gathering, Gates also regularly offers his opinion on political questions in the U.S. and across the globe. The Bill & Melinda Gates Foundation (named after him and his ex-wife) has assets of over $50 billion and uses those funds to support public health and education initiatives around the world that Gates believes are important. Former President Donald Trump, one of the recent group of populist political leaders around the world, has routinely denounced global elites such as Gates, and often tells his supporters that "elites" like Gates are harming their well-being.

clear that they need not be viewed as entirely in conflict. It is true that the theories propose different processes through which power is exercised in capitalist societies. But as the largest companies have gotten bigger and bigger (Dayen 2020), so has their ability to influence politics directly or indirectly—through structural power (indirectly) or by the influence their executives and their government service (directly). For example, does the elite Wall Street investment bank Goldman Sachs have influence because of the importance of keeping the financial system healthy or because so many Goldman Sachs executives have served important positions in the White House? Both are likely important. Most sociologists today agree the power of the largest business interests remains as secure as ever, precisely because they can utilize both indirect and direct power.

Another factor that links these theories together is that they both focus on how the most powerful political groups can (usually) exercise power in the more subtle second and third dimensions of power. We rarely think about how elites populate our institutions. For example, there are virtually no ordinary working people who run for Congress, much less win (Carnes 2018). We don't usually consider the premise that a healthy economy is a top priority. But there may be good reasons to ask questions about whether growth without attention to climate change or economic inequality deserves greater consideration.

The Powerful Do Not Always Get Their Way

8.3.4 Analyze some of the conditions under which the less powerful sometimes can prevail.

Taken together, the two theories of power tend to suggest that policy will always favor the powerful. But we know that cannot be right. Sometimes, governments do adopt policies that are against the wishes of the powerful, and the powerless get at least some of what they want instead (Piven and Cloward 1997). In the 1930s, for example, a wide range of new government programs was adopted that included the Social Security system (eventually creating pensions for all Americans over 65), unemployment insurance, mammoth job creation programs, increased regulation of business, and increased taxes on the rich. These programs, part of Franklin D. Roosevelt's New Deal, were bitterly resisted by many wealthy Americans and leading business interests at the time. But protests by millions of ordinary people as well as workers organizing unions compelled the federal government to adopt new policies that sought to aid poor people in a variety of ways. Similarly, in the 1960s, the federal government created both Medicare (health insurance for everyone over 65) and Medicaid (health insurance for the poor), adopted civil rights legislation that gave women and minorities new rights and opportunities

The civil rights movement pushing for the integration of schools in the 1960s helped change the context of political power in America and brought about an end to the Jim Crow system in the South.

Elections can also sometimes be the harbinger of significant change. From the late nineteenth century to the 1930s, political parties of the left—usually known as Socialist or Social Democratic—gained enough votes to gain power across much of Europe, and they used that power to establish large welfare states, as noted, against the wishes of big businesses and most of the rich (who had to pay higher taxes to pay for the new social programs). The extension of the right to vote to all citizens made it possible for these parties to win elections. In the United States, the Democratic Party in the 1930s played a similar role. These parties established, through elections, that people did support more equality and government programs that help those in need. Right-wing parties have also sometimes won power through elections. The most famous example of this was Adolf Hitler's rise to power in Germany in the 1930s, as his National Socialist Party (Nazi) rose from a tiny party winning few votes to the largest party in Germany by the early 1930s. Across the globe in recent years we have witnessed frequently surprising elections of right-wing populist leaders in countries like India, Turkey, Hungry, the Philippines, Brazil, Mexico, and the United States (with the election of Donald Trump). These politicians, as noted earlier in the chapter, explicitly oppose the global orientations of the power elite. They have also brought racial and ethnic divisions back into political life in a way that the traditional power elite has opposed. For example, businesses enjoy having immigrant workers available to hire at low wages, while right-wing populists rail against immigration. The wave of elections that have brought populists to power has shaken up longstanding political parties and national political systems in a variety of ways, although it is less clear how different or effective these populist politicians are in office. As of the early 2020s, it's not yet clear whether populist leaders will establish lasting change through democratic elections, but it is certainly possible that some will. More worrisome is the possibility that populists in office will seek to undermine democratic institutions, as the fascists did in the 1930s.

to compete on a more equal footing with White men, and significantly increased spending on welfare state programs, as noted earlier. The civil rights legislation was largely prompted by the massive civil rights movement of the 1950s and 1960s. These examples suggest that it is hardly the case that the powerful always win.

Periods of dramatic change like this are, however, relatively rare. It is much harder for people without significant resources to exert influence and win power. What conditions help usually powerless people make gains? Many of the most significant reform moments occur when ordinary people organize mass social movements (see Chapter 22). If there is one thing that both the 1930s and 1960s had in common, it is that in both eras large social movements of poor people (especially unions and the unemployed in the 1930s, and the civil rights and anti-war movements of the 1960s) changed the context of political power. Thinking in terms of the three dimensions of power gives us a more systematic understanding. Mass social movements help to make political conflicts more even, or can even tilt toward the underdog, in terms of the open conflict that we see in the first dimension of power. Large dramatic protests that are sustained over a significant period of time can force politicians and the media to reorient the agenda of topics that are being considered. On the third dimension, social movements can sometimes change people's minds and cause them to reassess positions that they had previously taken for granted.

Conclusion: The Many Faces of Power

Power is a central force in any society, and it is the source of many of the greatest disparities and injustices in the world. In this chapter, we have argued that the key to understanding power is to not limit ourselves to situations where it is most obvious. Those with power may be challenged, and they have to prevail in those challenges to retain their power. But much of the time, power is exercised in more subtle ways. The three-dimensional view of power calls attention to critical ways in which the powerful maintain influence and control without having to directly assert their authority.

When the study of power extends to the world of politics—where many of the most important uses of power occur—sociologists can apply our general understanding of power to analyze the various ways in which power is exerted and maintained. As with power in everyday life, proceeding from what is clearly observable to what is normally hidden is the key to developing a broader understanding of states and political systems. In other words, sociologists contribute something distinctive to the study of political life by suggesting that elections and the conflicts between political parties and politicians that capture the attention of the media are not the *only* processes we should keep our eye on. To get at these less obvious forms of power—agenda control and persuasion of those without power to adopt the views of the powerful—requires considerable digging and investigation. Once we learn to think about power and politics on all three dimensions, and seek out its manifestations, we begin to develop a different way of thinking about political life.

Because power and power relations are such a pervasive aspect of social life, the study of power has to be considered a central task for all of sociology (and one that is important for all citizens to ask questions about). We have mostly drawn on examples from national politics in the United States, but power and the power elite can be studied at lower levels of societies or in other countries and historical periods. In our towns and cities, workplaces and other organizations, or even in our own families, power can be analyzed in terms of the three dimensions and how they reinforce one another. And, as we have insisted throughout *The Sociolgly Project*, asking unexpected questions and developing an analysis is always the precursor to effective change.

The Big Questions Revisited 8

8.1 What are the distinct forms of power? In this section, we examined the three dimensions of power, using a sociological lens to examine not only the most visible ways in which power is expressed but also its more subtle forms.

The Three Dimensions of Power

The One-Dimensional View of Power
Learning Objective 8.1.1: Identify who has power in the one-dimensional view.

The Two-Dimensional View of Power
Learning Objective 8.1.2: Explain the role of agenda setting in the second dimension of power.

The Three-Dimensional View of Power
Learning Objective 8.1.3: Discuss the various ways in which the workings of power can be hidden.

Key Terms
power (p. 200)   agenda setting (p. 193)
bureaucracies (p. 194)   status (p. 194)

8.2 What Is the State, and How Does It Distribute Power in a Society? In this section, we examined what the institutions of power (the state) actually do. We also explored why states matter in the distribution of power.

The Institutions of Power

What Is the State?
Learning Objective 8.2.1: Define the state and explain how it regulates the economy.

Why States Matter in the Distribution of Power and Wealth
Learning Objective 8.2.2: Explain how the state influences who gets what government services.

Key Terms
the state (p. 196)   regulation (p. 197)   welfare state (p. 198)   tax and transfer policies (p. 198)

8.3 Why Does the Capitalist State Protect the Interests of the Economically Powerful? In this section we examined why states all over the world have adopted policies in favor of the powerful. We studied two broad theories related to capitalist societies.

Protecting the Powerful

The Structural Power of Business

Learning Objective 8.3.1: Explain why all governments want business organizations to be successful, and why this reflects a structural power in capitalist societies.

The Power Elite

Learning Objective 8.3.2: Describe who are members of the power elite, and why they are able to influence government policy.

Connections Between the Theories

Learning Objective 8.3.3: Discuss the connections between the structural power of business theory and power elite theory.

The Powerful Do Not Always Get Their Way

Learning Objective 8.3.4: Analyze some of the conditions under which the less powerful sometimes can prevail.

Key Terms
structural power of business (p. 200)
power elite (p. 200)   capitalism (p. 200)
capital (p. 200)   economic recession (p. 201)
depression (p. 201)   capital strike (p. 201)
revolving door (p. 204)   policy planning
organizations (p. 204)   think tanks (p. 204)
foundations (p. 204)   policy advocacy
organizations (p. 204)   populists (p. 205)
Brexit (p. 205)

Chapter 9

Markets and Organizations: The Sociology of Economic Life

by Richard Arum and Jeff Manza

In September 2008, the world's leading financial organizations—the large banks and investment funds that provide the capital and loans needed for businesses to operate—suddenly froze and came shockingly close to a complete collapse. It all happened for the deceptively simple reason that too many Americans were defaulting on their home loans. Those defaults helped create a severe economic recession that started in America and quickly spread around the world. Unemployment shot up (reaching 10 percent in the United States in 2009), the stock market crashed over the next six months (with stock prices falling by nearly 50 percent), houses lost a third of their value, and bankruptcies and home foreclosures rose dramatically. Even after the recession ended in 2010, the economic recovery that followed was very slow, and many families and workers took years to regain what they lost.

How did the 2008 financial crisis happen, and what are the sociological lessons about organizational and market failures it teaches us? The answers are complex and are still being debated by social scientists. But several things are clear. Most large banks and investment funds had, by the late 1990s, collectively latched on to what seemed like a remarkably profitable idea: to take the ordinary loans made to home buyers, package a large number of them together into what came to be called a mortgage-backed security (MBS), and then sell these securities to another bank, which would assume the risk for the loans in each MBS they acquired.

At first it seemed like there was virtually no risk, and the more loans a bank could issue, the more MBS they could sell, and the more profit they could earn. Soon, everyone in the industry began to move in the same direction (Fligstein 2021). To increase the number of loans, banks began issuing a kind of loan known in the industry as a *subprime* loan—a loan to a borrower who did not qualify for a regular loan. These loans were "packaged" with good loans and resold to

someone else for a profit. Because subprime loans were riskier, banks charged those less affluent buyers higher interest rates in anticipation that more of them would fail to make their payments. How did this work? Say that you wanted to buy a house around the year 2003, but you didn't have enough income and money saved for a down payment to qualify for a regular loan. In the past, you would not have been able to buy that house until your economic situation

My Sociological Imagination

RICHARD ARUM

Although I grew up in the suburbs of New York, I had an unusual background as my father was a sports promoter, and cultural icons and civil rights heroes such as Muhammad Ali spent time in our home. This early personal exposure shaped who I was and the choices I made as an adult. In the years following, I received a teaching certificate from Harvard University and subsequently worked as a teacher in a segregated public high school in Oakland, California. In that institutional setting, in order to make sense of the dysfunction of the school as an organization as well as the impact that the school was having on the lives of the students, I increasingly was drawn to asking sociological questions of the world. To move beyond simply asking these questions, I enrolled at the University of California–Berkeley with the goal of developing sociological tools and skills to better understand the problems around schooling in America. For me, developing a sociological imagination was an attempt to develop a set of analytical competencies to participate actively in policy discussions that could substantively improve the outcomes of youth.

Bankers at Lehman Brothers on the day the bank went out of business in September 2008. What are the sociological lessons of a major event like the financial crisis of 2008?

improved. The vast expansion of the subprime loan market, however, meant that it was now very likely that one or more banks would offer you one of these subprime loans (and then package and sell the loans to other banks).

All was good until early 2007. All across the United States, people were marveling at stories about how much money their neighbors were getting for selling their homes. With all these new home loans and home buyers, and the ease with which anyone could get a loan, housing prices rose faster between 1998 and 2006 than ever before or since (Shiller 2012). It wouldn't last. Unfortunately, but not surprisingly, many of the subprime borrowers found they couldn't afford to make the payments required by their loans. This was especially true when the interest rates on the loans went up (many had a low initial interest rate but increased after a couple of years). As these subprime loans failed, the trillions of dollars invested in MBS were at risk as borrowers could not make their payments. Once enough of them stopped, the entire financial sector, heavily invested in real estate, was now in deep trouble. Many major banks and investment firms went bankrupt. Housing prices crashed, and millions of families abandoned homes that were now worth less than they paid for them. Eventually, the federal government had to step in and inject billions of dollars to keep the largest banks from failing, to prevent the economic crisis from getting much worse.

How did market institutions and the large organizations with billions of dollars at stake fail on such a large scale? The central overriding contribution of the sociological imagination, as we have suggested throughout this book, is to always look at how social forces shape and impact human behavior. We can't find the right answer without examining the ways in which economic markets, and the individuals who engage in buying and selling for profit, are heavily influenced by the social worlds they are a part of. One central contribution of the sociological approach is to examine how those banks that were behind the MBS system were operating in an organizational environment in which companies almost always tend to imitate each other. What one does, others do (DiMaggio and Powell 1983; Fligstein 2021). There was intense pressure on individual bankers and banking executives to participate in the rapidly growing MBS market, despite whatever misgivings they might have had. Loan officers, who were professionally trained to carefully evaluate potential buyers, learned to simply look the other way and process as many loans as possible. Everyone was doing the same thing—and how could everyone be wrong?

In this chapter, we will explore a variety of ways in which economic market institutions are shaped by social forces that can alter the behavior of individuals and companies. In some cases, like the financial crisis of 2008, these forces can nudge market participants in ways that can be socially destructive. But other social forces can be seen in a more beneficial way. For example, as we will see, human beings are not only selfish; they also care about other people and their communities. As a result, they will often do things that are not in their self-interest to help others (think of why people give money to charities or businesses that don't cheat their customers even when they could get away with it). Other social forces are not always harmful or beneficial but important for understanding how market institutions work. For example, we buy things from people we know or who have been recommended to us by friends, even if that means paying higher prices. We do so because humans operate in social networks that influence our behavior far more than we know.

The Big Questions

1. **What are capitalist markets?** In capitalist societies like the United States, market institutions are a core part of the social structure of society. In this section, we introduce and define a sociological conception of capitalism and its economic markets. We explain the rise of capitalism and the pervasiveness of markets in modern societies.

2. **What are the varieties of capitalism in the world today?** In this section, we first examine how and why the economic system in communist countries failed to survive as a viable alternative to capitalism. We then explore the large differences in capitalist economies around the world today, focusing on three different historical varieties of capitalism: laissez-faire, liberal market capitalism, and social democratic market capitalism.

3. **What is the sociological approach to the study of economic markets?** Economic markets are strongly influenced by social processes such as norms, power, trust, and social networks. The human actors who participate in these markets are also influenced by psychological factors. In this section, we examine how noneconomic social influences shape what happens in economic markets, as well as introduce the contributions of behavioral economics.

4. **Why are organizations important for social and economic life?** To gain a deeper understanding of how modern economies work—and ultimately how social forces influence the economy as a whole—sociologists place considerable importance on analyzing the organizations that exist within markets.

5. **What is the relationship between organizations and their external environment?** The ecological framework of organizational sociology challenges whether organizations actually adapt to their environment or whether the organizations that survive do so because they were uniquely suited to the environment from the start. In this section, we explore the relationship between organizations and their environment.

Business/Alamy Stock Photo

BIG QUESTION 9.1 What Are Capitalist Markets?

THE CREATION AND FUNCTIONING OF CAPITALIST MARKETS

To understand how contemporary economic institutions function, we need to begin with an introduction to the dominant economic system around the world today, what is known as **capitalism**. The term "capitalism" has been defined in different ways by social scientists, but common to all definitions is the idea that the predominant form of economic activity—buying, producing, selling, investing—is done through **markets** in which all people in a society are participants in at least one way. Capitalism is an economic system based on private property, in which those who have resources are able to hire other people to work for them. The creation of the large **firms** (organizations that seek profit)—typical of twenty-first century capitalism—first began to arise when those with wealth were able to take advantage of technological advances that made possible ever bigger factories and workplaces and figured out how to use their **capital** (wealth that can be used to invest in pursuit of profit) to generate income. The people who own capital are called **entrepreneurs** when they invest that capital in business enterprises of one kind or another. In this section, we will explore how capitalist markets came to dominate the world's economy.

The Rise of Capitalism

9.1.1 Explain the factors that gave rise to capitalism and economic growth.

Markets have existed in some basic form in various parts of the world for centuries. Ordinary people traded one thing for another from the very earliest human settlements. There were ancient bazaars (also known as souks) along trade routes in Asia and the Middle East for thousands of years. As towns and cities grew in size around the world, they became places where people could come to buy or sell goods. Beginning in

the late Middle Ages, the buying and selling of rare goods found or produced in one part of the world and consumed in another represented a step toward the first global markets, although only a few wealthy people and early companies could participate in these activities (Erikson 2016).

Despite the existence of markets in which those with money or goods to trade could participate, the predominant type of economic system in the world before the nineteenth century was not capitalism as we understand it today. Slave and feudal societies were economic systems in which large groups of people were unfree and could not participate in economic markets. Slave societies were most common in the New World and persisted until the late nineteenth century. The economic system known as **feudalism** took a variety of forms around the world but had in common with slavery two things: the unfreedom of most of the people who worked the land, and wealth from land-ownership was the primary form of wealth. The vast majority of the population, known as **serfs**, were legally bound to their landlords and obligated to work for them. Any society characterized by a significant percentage of the population being unfree and not able to participate freely in economic markets should not be considered capitalist.

The **Industrial Revolution**—the rapid increase in the production of manufactured goods with the development of factories and the enhanced use of technology—was driven by the rise of capitalism (and the ability of people to invest in factories and find and hire workers to work in them) while also enabling capitalism to spread around the globe (as the rapidly increased production of goods led to a search for new markets to sell them). The Industrial Revolution began in the late eighteenth century in England and spread to Western Europe and the United States in the first half of the nineteenth century. At the same time, capitalism began to take off as well. Early entrepreneurs with funds to invest took advantage of some of the

An example of a factory in West Yorkshire, England using some of the technologies that drove the Industrial Revolution.

opportunities to convert their wealth into capital. Many used their new wealth to invest in new companies created by other people (for example, through the stock market). This in turn made resources available for investment, which made it possible for people to borrow money to launch new businesses.

There was also a closely related spinoff effect of the changing value of land and the growth of factories: Both factors pushed growing numbers of people to move from farms and rural areas into cities in search of work. As a consequence, the size of many cities grew rapidly. Take Chicago: In 1840, there were only 4,000 people living in the city; by 1860, the population rose to 112,172; by 1880, it was 503,185; by 1900, 1.7 million, and 1920, 2.7 million. The incredible growth of cities like Chicago created remarkable new opportunities for people with things to sell. Suddenly there were increasing numbers of people living in one place, all of whom needed housing, food, clothing, and goods and services. Unlike farm families who could make much of what they needed, living in cities meant that almost everything had to purchased with money. Entrepreneurs emerged quickly to fill those needs at a profit.

Second, from the late eighteenth to the early twentieth centuries, many remarkable advances in technology led to new opportunities to engage in profitable, market-oriented production. From the spinning jenny in 1764 to the internal combustion engine in the 1850s–1880s, innovations during this period were unprecedented in human history (Gordon 2016). In a short time, these advances led to the invention of the automobile, the airplane, indoor plumbing, the skyscraper, the telegraph, the telephone, refrigerators, plastics for a wide range of applications, and many other new products (see Table 9.1 for a summary of the most important technological developments of the industrial revolution).

earliest innovations of the Industrial Revolution and began to develop the manufacturing industries that eventually revolutionized the world economy. Meanwhile, the growth of market capitalism gave inventors and creative people opportunities and incentives to earn profits for their efforts. In other words, the emergence and growth of capitalism and the Industrial Revolution were symbiotic: Each made the other possible, and each enhanced the growth of the other.

The rise of capitalism in the context of the Industrial Revolution was driven by four specific factors (Wood 2002; Appleby 2010; Piketty 2014). The first was the rapid increase in the value of land. The new factories needed land, and it was easier to build on former farmland near population centers or close to natural resources. This caused the value of land to soar, encouraging landlords to sell their land to investors wanting to build factories, as well as housing for the workers employed in their factories (Piketty 2014, chpts. 3–4). Flush with cash, many former landlords took advantage of

Table 9.1 Some of the Major Technological Advances in the Industrial Revolution (1760–1900)

Invention	Why It Was Important
1. Spinning Jenny (1764)	Major increase in the speed with which workers could transform wool into cloth. The spinning mule, introduced a few years later, made further improvements.
2. Steam Engine (1775)	Allowed trains, ships, and industrial engines to be much more efficient, facilitating transportation and factory production.
3. Cotton Gin (1794)	Separated seeds from cotton, which previously had to be done by hand, making cotton production vastly more efficient and profitable.
4. Cement (1824)	A critical building material that enabled cheap production of large structures.
5. Bessemer Process for Steel (1856)	An invention that allowed for the removal of waste products from raw iron to create steel products more efficiently.
6. Electricity and Its Applications (1780s–1880s)	The critical power source that allowed for massive leaps in efficiency. Thomas Edison is often credited with the crucial breakthrough in 1879, although he built on the contributions of others over the previous century.
7. Internal Combustion Engine (1850s–80s)	Critical to making electricity useful, enabled the production of energy from raw materials (such as coal, gas, and oil). The foundation for the invention of the automobile.

Farming was practiced essentially the same way for centuries. But beginning in the nineteenth century, the rapid appearance of a wide range of new farm tools and technologies made it possible for farms to become much more efficient and produce far more output than before. The two images displayed here capture some of the differences in farming of the past versus today.

It is also worth noting that alongside advances that enabled the growth of manufacturing, there were parallel improvements in agricultural production. After centuries of limited change, the introduction of new machines to assist farming meant that fewer workers were needed to work the land, and that larger farms (where machinery could be used more effectively) became more profitable than smaller farms. This set in motion the long, slow decline in farming as a type of employment (even as ever more food was being produced). It also led many former farm workers to migrate to cities to find employment (Appleby 2010, chpt. 3). Others shifted to work in the rapidly growing extractive industries such as coal mining (the critical source of energy to run early factories). It is estimated that nearly 1 in 10 English workers in 1900 worked in coal mines alone (Pomeranz 2000).

The third critical factor in the rise of capitalism was the improved ability to trade across long distances (Wood 2002). Most notably, in the eighteenth century, ships became increasingly more durable and could travel faster between destinations, and in the nineteenth century, the development of the steam engine made train travel (and the shipment of goods) vastly less expensive. As noted, the internal combustion engine allowed for the development of cars and trucks, the latter of which was especially useful for the movement of goods over shorter distances. The upshot was that goods produced in one place could be acquired and then resold, sometimes at an immense profit, in a location where those goods were scarce or in high demand. And at each stage, profits could be made, creating a role for traders, bankers, and lawyers in the process. For example, in the United States, a key wealth-generating commodity was cotton, which was largely produced under the slave system in the South before the Civil War, and on large plantations after that. Cotton was sold to buyers in Europe at such great profit that it helped to stimulate the growth of many of other industries—especially transportation (trains and ships) and banking, insurance, and finance. These industries, in turn, helped create the conditions for the rapid expansion of capitalism in America after the Civil War (Beckert 2015).

Finally, there were critical legal and political changes that transformed the feudal system across Europe and North America and supported the rise of capitalism. From the late eighteenth century onward, governments and courts of law gradually assumed responsibility for (1) protecting private property and wealth, and (2) regulating and enforcing contracts made between market participants (or punishing noncompliance). Both of these kinds of legal and political protections for economic markets helped convince people that investing money could be done safely (that is, that they would not be ripped off), and that their private property and wealth would be protected from thieves. The new legal system also freed working people from the legal constraints that allowed them to sell their labor to the highest bidder. Serfs and enslaved people were eventually legally freed of their obligations to their landlords, and by the late nineteenth century all across Europe and the Americas everyone was able to work for pay. The freeing up of all of these workers made it increasingly possible for those with capital to find and hire workers at wages low enough to produce profits.

Capitalist economies in Europe and North America grew so fast that they generated both immense wealth for the rich but also rapidly rising living standards for everyone (Gordon 2016). In the nineteenth century, growing national wealth also allowed European countries to seize territory all over the world—the process known as colonialism—and spread Capitalism across the globe. But the people who were being colonized, especially in Africa, South America, and Asia, were not able to enjoy the same benefits as the citizens and elites of colonizing countries. To this day, we see slower economic growth in many former colonies in Africa and, to a lesser extent, Asia. But even there, living standards have been rising as more and more countries develop their own capitalist economies.

Jeff Manza

Poor countries undergoing rapid industrialization are often caught between traditional poverty and the trappings of new wealth. This is a street scene from Accra, Ghana, in January 2017.

The Pervasiveness of Capitalist Markets Today

9.1.2 Discuss the pervasiveness of markets in modern societies.

So what exactly are markets, the foundation of capitalism? The answer may seem intuitive—one of those "you know it when you see it" kind of things, but on closer inspection it is a bit more complicated. To be sure, in the simplest way markets involve buying and selling. The neighborhood "flea market" or yard sale, where people sell stuff to others, are a simple approximation. The stock market is a special type of market, for example, one we all hear a lot about. But there are also a lot of markets that appear more ambiguous. Consider the case of online dating sites. Are those also a market? Certainly, there are "buyers" (people who respond to ads) and "sellers" (those who put up profiles seeking dates). But no money changes hands (at least between users—there are many online dating sites that charge fees to use). Or consider the annual cultural festival Burning Man, held in the Nevada desert (see the

accompanying photo). Once you have purchased your ticket and travelled to the festival, there are both formal and informal rules against the exchange of any currency, and all goods and services are exchanged through a barter economy only. Do markets operate there? We can answer the question by noting that market activity can apply in many arenas of social life, but only those markets in which the exchange is **monetized** (that is, it involves an exchange that has a monetary price attached to it) can be said to be a capitalist market. So Burning Man and online dating sites are markets with exchanges going on, but they are not a *capitalist* market.

Sociologists who study capitalist markets have noted that in recent decades, these markets have increasingly been penetrating more areas of social life. Almost everything seems to be for sale these days. Let's look at some examples. Families at all income levels hire others to do things for them: To take care of their children, to prepare their meals (at home or at restaurants), to clean their houses, or to take care of their yards. They also use doctors and psychologists for physical and mental health and pay for lessons or sports teams for their children. They hire people to fix or renovate their houses or buy a new one, plan weddings and funerals, invest their money. Even relatively poor families use some of

Brad Horn/AP Images

Pictured here is the Burning Man festival in the Nevada desert. The absence of currency exchange at the festival does not mean that markets are not operating, but they are not capitalist markets in which the exchanges that take place have the goal of allowing one or both sides to earn profits.

The ability of people to find markets for their services is endless. In a large city like New York, dog walking—taking other people's dogs for a walk once or twice a day when they are at work—is one example of the many different jobs people find to earn some income.

these same services, if less expensive versions, and with much less frequency. For more affluent people, sociologist Arlie Hochschild (2012) has analyzed even more dramatic examples of the "outsourcing" of our own individual lives: There are specialists who help us find lovers, "nameologists" who help choose a name for children, and "life coaches" who will help us discover our "true self," or even help us to figure out what it is we "really" want out of life. All for a fee.

BIG QUESTION 9.2 What Are the Varieties of Capitalism in the World Today?

ALTERNATIVES TO CAPITALISM

The central ideas behind the rise of capitalism—that it was an economic system in which people were free to participate as they were able (as buyers, sellers, or workers) and keep the fruits of their efforts—was closely associated with rapid economic growth in the nineteenth and early twentieth centuries. In principle, everyone should be better off with such freedoms (Friedman 1962). *However*, there is also a darker side to capitalism. It has also been associated with high levels of poverty, inequality, and insecurity for many, sometimes most, individuals and families. As a consequence, from the beginning of its ascent in the nineteenth century, a wide range of reformers and radicals have sought ways to challenge the capitalist societies they were observing and experiencing. For some, this led to a

search for an alternative, noncapitalist economic system. Karl Marx is but one of many thinkers who believed that only by getting rid of capitalism could everyone flourish. And for a period of time in the twentieth century, there was a distinct alternative to capitalism that emerged in formerly communist countries such as Russia, China, and a number of countries in Eastern Europe. Many others, however, sought efforts to reform capitalism rather than replace it. This has led to several different *varieties of capitalism* around the world, each reflecting distinct ways of organizing who does what and who gets what. In this section, we consider the rise and fall of the major alternative to capitalism (communism), a contrast that enables us to better understand capitalism itself. We will then examine the major varieties of capitalism that exist today.

The Rise and Fall of Communist Economies and Societies

9.2.1 Describe why communist economies failed to compete with capitalism.

The most historically significant alternative to capitalism was **communism**, a social, economic, and political system built around government-based planning of economic activity, and a political system in which a single political party (the Communist Party) is allowed to exist and control government policy. The undemocratic, authoritarian aspects of communist societies, and the role of citizens demanding basic freedoms in the downfall of communism in Eastern Europe, are very well known. Less widely discussed are how the economic systems of communist societies actually worked. We will refer to them as **state socialist economies**, or SSEs, for short. Here, the term "state" emphasizes the central role of government officials in making major economic decisions, as opposed to letting the market guide economic activity in capitalist societies, while "socialist" reflects their roots in the socialist tradition from Marx onward ("communism" was Marx's term for a future utopian society that socialism would create). At one time, SSEs were thought by many social scientists to be a viable alternative to capitalism. Around 1970, approximately a third of the world's people lived in a society with an SSE. However, SSEs have largely disappeared since 1989, holding on today by its fingernails in the very poor country of North Korea and to some extent in Cuba (which is also in the midst of a very slow transition toward capitalism). China maintains a communist political system, but since the late 1970s it has become a fully capitalist (and rapidly growing) economy. Even though they have largely disappeared, because SSEs were unique it is quite valuable to have some understanding of how they were organized, how they were different than capitalist economies and why they failed.

The early roots of the SSE can be traced to Russia, where a self-declared communist society was established after the second Russian Revolution in October 1917 (the revolutionaries, known as Bolsheviks, took control of the government and renamed the entire Russian Empire the Soviet Union in the early 1920s). After World War II, several other countries came to be ruled by communist parties and built their own SSEs (in Eastern Europe and in China, when the Chinese Communist Party won a civil war in 1949 and took control of the government). All of these communist governments proclaimed that they were building economies organized without markets, and took active measures to prevent individuals from gaining enough wealth to start businesses. In SSEs, government officials decided, or planned, what would be produced and in what quantities, and how they would be distributed. They were all based on the principle of radical equality: That all labor should be respected and rewarded equally (at least in principle), and that all citizens and families should be provided with the necessities of life via government-run programs.

Communist economic systems—the SSEs—failed to achieve many of their goals and over time became increasingly stagnant, especially by comparison with the leading capitalist countries. Why did SSEs ultimately fail? For one thing, fearing a military challenge from richer capitalist countries, the Soviet Union and its allies invested enormous resources into building their own military forces to compete with richer countries. In addition, they placed a high priority on the development of large-scale or "heavy" manufacturing industries like steel and extractive industries (such as coal, oil, minerals, and other raw materials needed for manufacturing), thinking that this was the key to long-term economic growth. Consumer goods, like shoes, jeans, automobiles, and color televisions, were always in short supply. This was a constant source of frustration to consumers, who often had to stand in long lines, known as queues, to obtain basic goods when they were available (as seen in the accompanying photo).

Bettmann/Getty Images

Consumers waiting in long lines, known as "queuing," in central Moscow under communism in the 1980s. The shortages of many goods and food products were a constant problem for state socialist economies.

SSEs also suffered from being disconnected from the global economy. International companies had little or no interest in making investments in communist countries (nor would they even have been allowed to, if they did). Further, because of the hostile relationship between capitalist and state socialist countries, there were few opportunities to develop beneficial economic trades with the nonsocialist world. Industries that might have developed, such as tourism, were largely blocked by fears that foreigners might stir up unrest (and communist governments did not want their citizens to learn about the higher standards of living in the much richer West).

Another critical set of problems was that SSEs produced relatively few incentives for individuals to work hard or for organizations to do anything above meeting their assigned production levels as set by the central plan; there was no reason to improve upon the plan, in terms of either quality or quantity, as no additional profits could be earned. Over time, this combination proved debilitating. Government slogans and prizes failed to get workers to raise their productivity. Workers and managers often found that petty theft was an easier way to get ahead. Corruption was rampant and built into the system in ways that made it exceptionally difficult to identify and prevent. Organizational managers became experts at requesting more raw materials than they needed in order use their surplus to barter for other materials, or to create monetary benefits for themselves and/or their workers by selling those raw materials to another organization. This created imbalances and shortages throughout the system, which central planners simply could not fully understand (Kornai [1992] provides a comprehensive guide to understanding the failure of the SSEs).

Perhaps most disappointingly for its strongest supporters, state socialism even failed to achieve equality (Bergson 1984). Different wages were paid to different types of workers, depending on how important the government viewed their job and how hard it was to find people to do it. Privilege also reemerged in the form of special rewards and benefits for the members of the ruling parties and others whom these governments favored. Although the level of inequality under SSEs was far lower than in capitalism, its sacred commitment to equality did not prove viable. By the late 1980s, the problems of organizational dysfunction, combined with growing demands for political freedom, led to communism's downfall (with most of Eastern Europe

One of the symbolic capstones of the end of communism in Eastern Europe occurred when the Berlin Wall (which symbolically divided communist East Berlin from capitalist and democratic West Berlin) came down, beginning on November 9, 1989, after months of protests across the region.

overthrowing communism in 1989, and its final collapse in the Soviet Union occurring in 1991).

Varieties of Capitalist Market Economies

9.2.2 Describe the main features of three different varieties of capitalist economies.

Having survived the challenge from communism, capitalism is the dominant economic system in the world today. Yet that does not mean all capitalist countries and economies are identical. In fact, just the opposite is true. Several different **varieties of capitalism** have emerged in the past 150 years (Hall and Soskice 2000; Pontusson 2006; Kenworthy 2020). Three broad types can be identified: Laissez-faire market capitalism, liberal market capitalism, and social democratic market capitalism. No one country or economic system has ever *exactly* fit any of the three types of capitalism, but in the nineteenth century many market economies were of the first type, and most contemporary capitalist economies fall comfortably into one of the latter two types. Let's briefly examine each one.

Laissez-faire capitalism refers to an economic system in which individuals and firms are free to do what they want, or make whatever agreements they want, without oversight by third parties or the government. "Laissez-faire" is a French term that literally translates to "let go," or more loosely to "leave it alone." In this type of capitalism, the government plays little or no role in regulating economic markets, or taxing the income generated by market activity. So if the owner of a factory pollutes the air in the community, or contaminates the groundwater that the community drinks, or wants to hire children to work in their factory, there is no place in a truly laissez-faire system for the government to be involved in preventing such practices (say, for example, by establishing environmental rules or child labor laws). Of course, many advocates of laissez-faire capitalism recognize that there are probably some limits that need to be placed on economic actors, most importantly the principle that they should not be able to harm third parties (Friedman 1962).

As capitalism first developed, there were indeed relatively few rules or limits imposed by governments. It is more or less accepted that the European and American capitalist economies in the nineteenth century were mostly characterized by the laissez-faire ideal, especially England. Today a laissez-faire approach continues to be promoted by thinkers known as **libertarians**, who argue that modern economies would benefit from eliminating virtually all forms of government interference and going back to a mid-nineteenth century economic system (Hayek 1944; Nozick 1974).

However, history suggests that truly laissez-faire market capitalism has never lasted very long, as market participants, whether buyers, sellers, employers, workers, or local communities, eventually began to demand government intervention in the form of rules and regulations to create a level and secure playing field. Consumers don't like being cheated or being sold unsafe products. Workers want to work in safe environments for a fair (or living) wage. Business owners don't like competitors who lie or cheat to get ahead. The recognition that only governments and the legal system could police the excess of unregulated capitalism grew as a consequence. And in recent decades, as we've become increasingly aware of the major threats from environmental damage caused by endless economic growth, the realization that market capitalism was not always healthy for the entire earth has prompted even more intervention (and will almost certainly increase in the future as the climate crisis worsens).

Although libertarians would disagree, the real question today is not whether governments need to regulate economic activity, but what *kinds* of rules and regulations are most effective, and *how much* government involvement in the economy is advisable. This brings us to the two major contemporary types of capitalist market economies we find around the world today. The first of these is what is known as **liberal market economies**, or LMEs. Among the rich countries, the United States is probably the country that best represents the LME model. The central principle of an LME approach is that markets should be as free as possible, but governments should assume responsibility for regulating abuses (against consumers, against workers, against firms) as well as to ensure some level of income

protection for certain groups of people who cannot support themselves through market activity due to factors such as old age (older workers are supplied pensions), disability (people with disabilities are given benefits to support themselves), and unemployment (people who have been laid off are given temporary support). LME systems, as they have evolved in the last 100 years, have often included considerable emphasis on education (to equip individuals with the knowledge they need to participate in the market).

At the heart of what distinguishes all modern capitalist societies from the laissez-faire model are the bundle of social programs known as the **welfare state**. The welfare state (see Chapter 8 for more details) is the term social scientists use to describe all government-run programs that provide benefits for citizens, such as health insurance, old age pensions, unemployment insurance, education, and antipoverty programs. In LMEs, the total size of the welfare state programs are smaller than in other modern capitalist societies. LMEs are also generally hostile to **unions** (collective organizations of workers who band together to seek better pay and working conditions). The rules of the LMC economies are, in that sense, more favorable to employers. Reducing poverty is a relatively low priority in LMCs; able-bodied poor people are expected to work their own way out of poverty rather than being given generous help.

Social democratic market economies—SMEs for short—are quite different from liberal market economies. **Social democracy** is a political and intellectual movement that arose in the late nineteenth century in Western Europe. It merges some of the ideas in the socialist/communist tradition about the importance of equality, with the laissez-faire idea that capitalist markets are efficient and should not be eliminated (as happened in the Soviet Union). Many countries in western and northern Europe, especially in Scandinavia, have SMEs. In these economies, there are very substantial rules and regulations that govern what firms and large private corporations can do, and how they treat their workers and customers. Most SMEs have strong unions that help protect workers and fight for a higher share of company profits. SMEs also have larger and more generous welfare states that provide individuals and families with secure lifelong benefits: These include free health insurance, generous retirement pensions, free college tuition, generous unemployment benefits combined with free or low-cost job training or retraining programs (Kenworthy 2020). These benefits are guaranteed for all citizens, and everyone pays somewhat higher taxes to fund these services.

One question that often gets asked is this: Are LMEs more efficient and better at achieving economic growth than SMEs? Don't the higher tax rates in SMEs undermine economic growth? The short answer to the question, based on decades of research, is a resounding no. In fact, economic

Table 9.2 Three Types of Capitalist Economic Systems

Type of Economic System	Government Regulation of the Market?	Societal Responsibility for Ensuring Minimal Standard of Living	Examples
Laissez-Faire	Little or None	Little or none (everyone fends for the themselves)	England in mid-nineteenth century
Liberal Market Capitalism (LMC)	Moderate: Rules designed to prevent injury or unfair (or corrupt) activity; laws that try to prevent discrimination and give everyone opportunity	Moderate: Social programs for older or disabled workers and some support for children; everyone else must earn a living via the market. Modest programs to help some but not all people get housing and health care	Contemporary United States
Social Democratic Capitalism (SDC)	High: All of the rules and regulations of the LMC plus laws protecting unions; more extensive job training or retraining	High: "Cradle to Grave" programs that attempt to eliminate all poverty and ensure that everyone has adequate food, housing, clothing, and access to health care	Contemporary Northern European Countries (Sweden, Norway, Germany)

growth has been about as high, or even higher, in SME countries than in LME ones in recent decades. This is particularly true if we focus on median incomes rather than average incomes. The U.S., the world's largest LME, looks good if we consider growth in average incomes. But averages are inflated by super high earners. People in the middle have seen very little growth in recent decades (Piketty and Saez 2018). By contrast, median incomes in most SME countries have risen in parallel with economic growth. It is a reasonable conclusion that SMEs have managed to balance economic growth and equality much better than LMEs (Kenworthy 2020). LMEs are better for rich people, but for everyone else SMEs have many advantages.

To summarize the differences between these three types of capitalism, we've identified their central features in Table 9.2 above.

Mark Bussell

BIG QUESTION 9.3 What Is the Sociological Approach to the Study of Economic Markets?

SOCIAL INFLUENCES ON ECONOMIC MARKETS

Over the past 150 years, the discipline of economics has developed many powerful theories and tools for understanding and studying market behavior. At the core of classical economic ideas is the notion that everyone is better off by buying and selling in markets, and that people who participate in markets make decisions based on their unique capacity to figure out what is best for them (as either buyers or sellers). To learn more about why, you'll have to take an economics class! But, as we will see in this section, there are some critically important ways in which factors other than our desire to make ourselves better off are important factors shaping market behavior. These *noneconomic* factors, specifically psychological ones (the ways our brain works, and can be tricked) but also sociological forces (such as power, norms, trust, social networks, and altruism) are also important for understanding how markets work and why people make the economic decisions that they do. We start this section by reviewing a powerful line of thinking that psychologists have launched that focuses on how individual brains make decisions in market contexts. This will set the stage for the rest of this section, in which we describe what sociologists have contributed to understanding markets and economic life more generally.

Psychology and the Rise of Behavioral Economics

9.3.1 Describe psychological findings that have impacted the way we view economic behavior.

Theories about economic behavior based on psychological research on how our brains process information have led to a new branch in the field called **behavioral economics**. Behavioral economics blends psychology and economics into a new way of understanding markets and economic life. Many of its core ideas are also important for **economic sociology**, so in this section let's consider a few basic premises.

Why is it important to understand how our brains work when we engage in markets? Psychologists have shown literally dozens of ways in which human beings—both the buyers and the sellers who together make markets—are not always capable of acting in predictable and rational ways. To take just one example, consider how scarcity, or the appearance of scarcity, changes our behavior. Study after study shows that people are consistently willing to pay more to buy a consumer product or service if they think it is scarce and hard to obtain (whether it really is or not). Some researchers believe that scarcity has this effect because way back in the evolution of the human species, when scarcity was a universal problem, our brains may have adapted to learn to grab what we needed. Whether such theories are right or not, it is certainly the case that a sense of scarcity impacts how we think and behave (Huijsmans et al. 2019). There are many examples in which businesses have taken advantage of this type of irrationality. Bright flashing lights that say "Limited Supply Only" or "Only One Left" are trying to trick consumers into activating their sense of scarcity.

Another famous psychological finding concerns what is known as **loss aversion** (the idea that individuals place greater value on keeping what they have as opposed to giving something up to get something new

[Tversky and Kahneman 1992]). In other words, people are willing to pay more to avoid a loss for no other reason besides the fact that they already have the item in question. Clever parents can use this insight to trick their children into good behavior: Instead of giving them an allowance when the child does their chores, a better method is giving the child the reward first then taking it away if the child fails to do their chores. The wish to not lose the allowance they already received will be a stronger motivator than just paying the allowance every week and hoping for the best (as most parents do). Or consider that for centuries, the private insurance industry has benefitted from the fact that people are willing to pay to insure themselves or their families against a loss, no matter how remote the possibility might be. Most people tend to buy more homeowner's insurance than they would if they actually calculated the true risks they are facing. As with scarcity, we can see how people don't always think rationally or calculate the benefits and losses of losing or gaining something.

Scarcity and loss aversion are only two of dozens of findings that psychologists have uncovered about how the human brain works and how people reason. The key point in the work of psychologists who study marketplace behavior is that we often use simplistic ideas to make complex decisions, and we can be easily convinced to do faulty things that are not in our self-interest. These insights have been so widely influential that one of the leaders in the field, the psychologist Daniel Kahneman, won the Nobel Prize in economics in 2002, and one of his collaborators, economist Richard Thaler, received the Nobel in 2017 (Lewis 2016); for two books that summarize their thinking, see Kahneman (2011) and Thaler (2015).

Sean Gallup/Getty Images

Daniel Kahneman, a psychologist whose research with the late Amos Tuersky led to the creation of behavioral economics.

Economic Sociology: An Introduction

9.3.2 Define the concept of embeddedness.

Behavioral economics starts from the study of individuals and how their brains work, moving on to consider how market contexts influence our mental states. Sociologists, as readers know by now, do not start from the standpoint of individuals (or their psychological states) per se but rather the *social* contexts in which our mental states evolve and operate. If we had to summarize the core ideas of sociologists who study the economy, it would probably not surprise you that they believe that markets are heavily shaped and influenced by the patterns and rules of social interaction and social structures, and the inequalities they create. Sociologists argue that instead of pursuing their self-interest, individuals will often take into account the feelings and needs of others or worry about how selfish they appear to others. Because of the power disparities inherent in societies divided by social hierarchies, markets do not operate as institutions that are blind to the social world, nor are they equally fair to all who enter them. In particular, information is not shared equally to all, but rather some insiders have more knowledge than others and can take advantage of that knowledge to pursue profitable action.

The single term that captures the range of sociological insights into the workings of economic markets is **embeddedness**: It doesn't really roll off the tongue, but embeddedness captures the idea that the individuals and firms doing things in those markets (such as buying, selling, and producing) are also embedded in their society and its social influences. As one of the key figures in the development of contemporary economic sociology put it, embeddedness is "the intersection of economic with noneconomic aspects of society" (Granovetter 2017, 15). In particular, while we may often be self-interested, we can *also* be influenced by a broad category of social sentiments known as **altruism**, or our concerns for others. In short, we care not only about ourselves but also about others (Bowles 2017). We are also influenced by others around us and sometimes do irrational things. We care about how others feel about us, about our reputation, so we try to avoid being cheap or noticeably cheating others. In other words, sociologists add to the psychological study of individual thinking processes with the broader social forces that also shape those thinking processes. This idea is central to all of sociology, and it has important implications when we apply it to economic markets and the activity of individuals in those markets.

Now that we've introduced two basic concepts of economic sociology, let's consider more specific applications to the study of capitalist markets.

Norms and Economic Behavior

9.3.3 Explain how norms influence economic markets.

One of the most powerful social forces impacting our behavior, including when we participate in economic markets, are social **norms**. We discussed the importance of norms in Chapters 4 and 5, as factors guiding our actions in many different settings. As we noted, many of the rules that govern market behavior, like all arenas of human interaction, are not formal, written, or even explicit; rather, they are informal, absorbed into our everyday consciousness in ways that we take for granted and don't normally notice (or until we take a sociology class!). For example, without norms about how market interactions are supposed to operate, it would be very difficult for successful exchanges to occur. These informal rules are as much a part of the market as the formal rules, and participating in a market requires knowing both sets. We all are familiar with the dating market, where unspoken rules have to be mastered. Those rules include how and when to express interest in someone else, how quickly to respond to someone else's expressed interest in us, as well as how to express appropriate levels of enthusiasm (not too much, not too little – there is a fine line that is tricky to get right). Or to take another example, the knowledge of how to bargain for the best deal with someone else in a market situation (let's say with an employer when you are negotiating a salary) is not that different. An experienced employer may know those rules better than a young prospective employee and offer less pay as a result. But if you master the basics of the art

Bastian/Agencja Fotograficzna Caro/Alamy Stock Photo

Most of the time, we buy things from stores or companies we know, and the price is marked and can be easily compared to other similar products or stores. But what about when we are shopping at a flea market, a farmer's market, or a garage sale? At the Grand Bazaar in Istanbul, Turkey (shown above), a vast informal marketplace that is one of the world's largest gatherings of buyers and sellers, where almost anything is for sale, there are many complicated rituals between buyers and sellers as they attempt to negotiate what they want.

of negotiation, you will likely get a better result. But you need to know what the norms of negotiating are to be most effective.

Norms are important for economic behavior because they may cause individuals to act in ways that are not consistent with always maximizing their self-interest (as classical economic theory would have it). Let's say you are selling your old car. Someone approaches you to possibly buy the car. You want to get as much money as you can for it. When the prospective buyer asks some questions about the car, you will certainly want to talk about its virtues, but you also know there are strong norms against lying about its condition. You might be especially ruthless and tell the buyer the car is in perfect condition, but if you do, you risk the shame that comes from being discovered having deliberately misled someone. Perhaps the buyer will take the car to a professional mechanic who will readily identify your exaggerations and you will feel foolish. Or perhaps even worse, the buyer will naively agree to pay your price based on what you have told them, in which case you know that your lies tricked the (naive) buyer. Most likely, you will feel it was improper to lie and you will feel guilty and ashamed afterward.

An interesting test of how norms can override self-interest comes from a laboratory experiment called the **ultimatum game**. It was first created by a group of German economists in the early 1980s (Güth et al. 1982) and has been modified and tested numerous times around the world since then. How does it work? In the ultimatum game experiment, player A is given an amount of money and is instructed to make an offer to share some of it with player B, and if player B accepts the offer, they both keep their share. If B rejects the offer, neither A nor B get anything. For example, player A is given $10, makes an offer to player B of $1, and player B accepts the offer. As a result, A walks away with $9 and B gets $1. In the standard version of the ultimatum game, players A and B don't know each other, and don't have a chance to communicate about the offer to each other.

When versions of this game have been performed on countless laboratory participants, including many college students and all over the world, the results strongly suggest that people aren't motivated solely or primarily by selfishness. Instead, norms of fairness and equality seem to be far more important. The typical offer among college students when they are player A is at or just below $5 (or 50 percent of whatever amount is at stake in the game). Similarly, player B typically insists close to half of the amount (or $5 in our example), and frequently rejects offers significantly below that (Camerer 2003, chpt. 2; Sanfey et al. 2003). Whether playing the A or B role, most college students offer and/or accept offers around the middle. They act more like altruists, choosing to share a significant amount of this "free" money (as player A) or expecting to receive a "fair" offer and will reject free money if it is less than what they think is fair (as player B). These results were echoed in experiments around the world, such as in small tribal communities in Africa, Asia, and South America (Heinrich et al. 2004). There, the median offer was 41 percent of the total (or $4.10 in a $10 experiment), and the vast majority of the offers in most cases were accepted. The only plausible conclusion that can be reached from these experiments is that even in radically different cultures and societies, individuals are far more influenced by altruism and not just focused on their own self-interest.

Power

9.3.4 Explain how power influences markets.

Capitalist markets should, in principle, treat every participant the same. Those who favor a laissez-faire approach make this argument all the time: Free markets give every individual and/or business idea a chance to succeed. Yet a close study of how markets actually work, in the real world with real human beings and all of their social and psychological dispositions, suggests something different: That those with power and resources are able to tilt market processes to their benefit. The notion that the powerful benefit in institutions like economic markets gave rise to the oft-quoted concept of sociologist Robert Merton (1973, 20) called "the Matthew Effect"—the idea that those who are already privileged are likely to become even more so over time, while those who are not are much less likely to achieve success. Merton called it the Matthew Effect because of a biblical passage in the Christian Gospel attributed to Matthew that reads in part, "For to every one who has will more be given, and he will have abundance; but from him who has not, even what he has will be taken away" [Matthew 25:29]. The concept was originally developed by Merton to explain why famous scientists get more credit for work done jointly with junior scientists and graduate students, but it is also highly applicable to capitalist markets. For example, large retailers like Amazon or Walmart can compel suppliers to charge them lower prices than a small neighborhood store can. This in turn allows those companies to charge lower prices to consumers than the neighborhood store, which can put it out of business.

Another example of the Matthew effect in action can be seen in the ways that an individual or company with funds to invest can hire other people to work for them (and create profits). Karl Marx's basic observation is that the possession (or lack thereof) of capital changes how people approach the world of work. Employers have lots of power over their employees once they are hired—they can promote them, raise their pay, fire them, cut their pay, give them a pleasant schedule, or have them laboring long into the night. Employees can resist—they can organize a union or work as slowly as possible—but it is always from a position of dependence and weakness.

Walmart is the largest retail chain in the world (shown on the left is a typical Walmart store, this one in Utah). As a result, it has enough buying power to get better deals than smaller companies. Many of the latter will ultimately be put out of business because they lack the power that Walmart has.

We also know that certain occupations, like law and medicine, have privileged legal status that limits the amount of competition in the market and allows them to charge high fees. Why? In Chapter 12, we will describe the unique nature of professional occupations. The high fees professionals can charge are, in part, because only they can do certain kinds of work. For example, if you need legal representation, you are compelled to use a lawyer. Anyone who has not passed the "bar"—the test to become a lawyer—cannot practice law. The range of occupations with partial protections from normal market competition is fairly large—as much as 20 percent or more of the workforce, depending on which occupations we include. These occupations represent a major kind of power that operates in markets (Weeden and Grusky 2012).

One of the most important ways in which power operates in economic markets is through access to loans and credit. Many college students already know how important access to finance is because of the loans that help pay for their college education. If you are fortunate, most of your loans will be heavily subsidized by the federal government (such as through the Stafford loan program). But imagine if you—or other students you know—couldn't borrow any money to pay for college. For many students, if they had to pay the full cost of their education with cash on hand, it would be much more difficult to complete college. It is difficult for most families or students on their own to pay for college entirely out of savings, or for students to earn enough money working while also attending college. These educational loans are provided in the expectation that (1) graduates will be able to pay them off, and (2) they help to create a more educated, productive society. The student loan program is an unusual example of a government policy that creates equal access to credit for everyone.

In most credit markets, however, access to credit is much more unevenly distributed, and it is the already wealthy who are in the best position to be able to effectively use the financial system. Banks like to loan money to customers who already have assets they can use as "collateral" on a loan. They also give their richest customers many great deals not available to everyone else: No fees, higher interest rates on money deposited in the bank, and lower interest rates on money they loan them. And the final kicker is that the more an individual or a firm can borrow, the larger the profits they have the potential of attaining. In this way, the Matthew Effect kicks in—the more an individual or a firm has, the more they can borrow to make new investments which will return even higher profits and/or an accumulation of wealth, if managed wisely. No matter how savvy a poor or middle-class borrower might be, they will have a much harder time financing a business or obtaining an investment loan. And when they do, they are likely to pay higher interest (as we saw in the opening to this chapter in relation to the subprime housing mortgage market).

Another important example of the role of power is in economic markets that the poor are charged far more for basic banking services than middle-class people. Almost 7 percent of American families do not have a bank account at all, mostly because they either cannot afford the fees and/or cannot keep the minimum amount necessary to maintain an open account (Federal Deposit Insurance Corporation 2017). As a result, they often must rely on check cashing companies to cash checks (in exchange for high fees), and many will also periodically use the services of payday loan companies. A payday loan is a small loan given to someone who can demonstrate they have a job and can pay back the loan in the near future. Payday loan companies charge astronomical interest rates, taking advantage of the desperation of borrowers who need access to immediate cash. A recent survey of average interest rates on payday loans in different parts of the United States found the annual interest rate to be as high as 661 percent in Texas, 652 percent in Nevada, 521 percent in Mississippi, and 460% in California (Center for Responsible Lending 2019). Lacking market power, the poor often pay more for the same services as rich people.

Trust

9.3.5 Discuss why trust is important for economic exchange.

When we go to a restaurant, we trust that the kitchen staff is regularly washing their hands and keeping the kitchen clean, even though we probably don't see them actually doing either. When a parent hires a babysitter, they trust that the sitter will take proper care of their child and not harm them in any way. When we get in our car, we trust that the other drivers will follow the rules of the road, at least enough so that we can get safely to our destination. **Trust**, "the belief that another person with whom you might interact will not cause you harm even though he or she may be in a position to do so" (Granovetter 2017, 58), is important in many, many ways. If trust between citizens breaks down, and people become more suspicious and distrustful of each other, they may no longer be willing or able to work together to collectively solve social problems in a democratic way (Putnam 1993; Tilly 2007). Americans' trust in the political system and in the goodwill of people who are members of a different political party is at a very low point in the early 2020s, and everyone agrees this is a huge problem (see Chapter 21 for more details). Problems of trust also arise in war: Learning to trust one's fellow soldiers is something that all military forces seek to instill (Ricks 1997).

In many similar ways, trust is also critical for economic markets to function with maximal efficiency (Arrow 1974). When trust is high, people can operate with more confidence and certainty. For example, when you trust a company you are doing business with, you can focus on the nature of the transaction, not worry if they will try to cheat you or that they will go bankrupt and cost you money. In large, anonymous workplaces, like factories or big office-based firms, workers may need to trust each other to perform their jobs most effectively. When you are part of a work team, for example, you need to know that you can trust other members to complete their share of the work. Employers must be able to trust that their employees will not steal from them or sabotage the firm's products and that they will put in an honest work effort.

But the issue of trust has become complicated in modern times. People no longer rely on their trusted neighborhood stores for their shopping. The rise of big department stores and online retailers has changed the landscape. The workers at the large "box stores" like Walmart are largely anonymous (although most big stores require their workers wear a name badge, as if that implies more personalized service). Unlike your local butcher or hardware store, they have no incentive to get to know you and treat you well so you will want to come back again. In addition, as some companies have grown to enormous size (Walmart and Amazon each employ over a million workers), the distance between management and workers has also increased. Top managers in the largest firms may not know a single ordinary worker in the company. Finally, the growth of economic trade and investment across national boundaries means that companies are increasingly doing business with strangers in other countries.

So how do trust issues get solved to allow markets to operate? One way that sociologists have identified is the establishment of name recognition and the idea that products sold anywhere by the same company will be of the same quality. This process was famously described as the **McDonaldization** of society by the social theorist George Ritzer (1993). Ritzer argued that in the modern world people are more likely to choose name brands they feel they can trust, so rather than trying something new they default to the product that they know. Why? Have you ever visited a part of the world where you didn't like the local coffee, but stumbled upon a Starbucks—and whether you normally get coffee at Starbucks or not, you feel like you know what you will get? Or if you are grabbing a meal at the airport, do you gravitate toward chains whose names are familiar to you (like McDonald's)? If so, those are quite common choices people make. We will often (not always, but often) go for what seems familiar. For this reason, large companies pour immense resources into marketing themselves to consumers, so that buyers will remember (and hopefully trust) the name of the brand when they shop. Ritzer's theory of McDonaldization suggests that in the future everything will be standardized, like a McDonald's restaurant, threatening variety and innovation. That might not ever happen, but the power of companies we trust to be the "same" everywhere is indeed a powerful trend.

A variety of helpful tools have also been invented in recent years to try to compel trustworthy behavior. The growing reach of legal courts and governments into supervising economic markets reflects, in part, an attempt to reinforce trust among market participants. They do this through both regulation and enforcement. For example, if person A rents an apartment to person B, and B fails to pay the rent or damages the apartment, A has recourse of using local courts and police to evict B. But it works both ways; Landlord A also has obligations to maintain the apartment in livable conditions and cannot arbitrarily evict B during the terms of the lease (Glendon 1982). In this way, both A and B are much better protected from untrustworthy behavior on the part of the other. Having the legal protections afforded by the courts does not mean that landlords and tenants don't often have conflicts, or that landlords can't find other ways to rip off their tenants, or that tenants can't skip out without paying all the rent that's due, but at least both parties have a greater basis for trusting each other, knowing that there is oversight from the legal system. There are also a wide variety of legal regulations that seek to prevent untrustworthy behavior before it happens (or punish it when it does). For example, a common rule prohibits what is known as "insider trading."

One of the more famous people who was caught using insider knowledge to profit at other people's expense was Martha Stewart, a popular TV personality who had a long-running show called *Martha Stewart Living* on homemaking ideas. Shown in this photo is her departure from prison. Stewart's nickname while incarcerated was M-Didi.

This is when a person who has special knowledge about a company, such as information about the company's strategy or if the company is going to be sold soon, is not legally permitted to trade that company's stock using the "insider" information. This rule exists to help create an equal playing field among market participants, most of whom would not have this kind of inside knowledge; if insiders were allowed to freely act on the special knowledge they have, they would be able to make super profits at the expense of others.

Social Networks

9.3.6 Explain how social networks influence markets.

Norms, power, trust—when it comes to how markets work, these social forces are often activated by **social networks**. Networks, in turn, are especially important for how economic action takes place. As we've discussed, rather than operating solely as isolated individuals who make decisions completely on their own, we are all embedded in social networks that exert great influence over us and our behavior in economic markets. To put it another way, we live in social worlds, and the connectivity between people is an important part of how market exchange happens.

Today, the term *social network* is widely associated with technological platforms that connect individuals and facilitate the exchange of information and, increasingly, goods and services (Snapchat, Instagram, Facebook, TikTok, and a myriad of other social media

sites). When sociologists talk about social networks, however, they are interested in a much broader set of social relationships: the ties between people, either through family/kinship relationships or through relationships involving friends, colleagues, classmates, or even friends of friends. People who study markets through the lens of networks tend to argue in a similar fashion—that economic activities, including market activities, are often built on kinship and friendship, and trust and goodwill, initially between people who know each other. Markets often need these social ties to establish the levels of trust that are necessary to carry out economic exchanges. For example, word of mouth about a business is extremely important for building and maintaining a business; no matter how much advertising a business might do, most will benefit far more from their existing customers referring their friends. In addition, sociologists who have studied banks and loan-making have found that, while we might expect that a person or a business would search for the lowest interest rate when borrowing money, many businesses, in fact, prefer to stay with the bank that they know, even if they have to pay a bit more (Uzzi 1999). There may be good reasons for maintaining such a relationship. Having a good history of

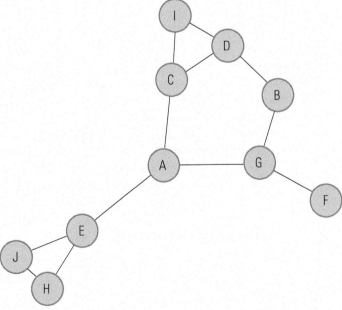

A visual representation of a social network, with the letters representing individuals. In this case, person A connects two groups of people who otherwise might be strangers, making it possible for information or ideas to spread to everyone in the network. In other words, A's position makes it possible for persons E, J, and H to learn or hear about the same things as persons C and G, even though they may never have met.

repayment may provide a certain level of wiggle room for a business or individual from their banker when it comes time to negotiate the terms of a new or more complicated loan or if the customer is having temporary issues making the payments on a loan.

Social networks have proven especially important for the ways they spread information related to markets. One famous example of how connections matter for economic outcomes can be found in a very influential line of work established by Mark Granovetter in the 1970s, showing that someone's chances of getting a job are highly influenced by who they know (Granovetter 1973). Studying how people found jobs in the Boston area in the early 1970s, Granovetter interestingly discovered that it wasn't someone's primary connections (the people whom one knows personally) but rather second-degree connections—friends of friends—who were most helpful for securing new jobs. Later research found mixed results for this specific argument (Mouw 2003). But the general point that Granovetter was making—that hiring often does not simply involve an employer choosing from among the best available applicant, but rather that referrals and recommendations from friends and acquaintances play a vitally important role as well—remains central to how we understand the hiring process (Beaman 2016).

Related, social networks potentially matter a great deal for how individual careers develop, either inside a company or when moving from one job to another. Managers inside companies may promote the "best" people on staff, but how do they decide who that is? In part, they often think the people they consider friends, or enjoy being around, are the people most qualified for promotion. Or, perhaps more likely,

they will hire or promote someone who has been recommended to them by someone they trust. And moving from one job to another, or finding opportunities, is often facilitated by whom you meet in your current job. As people move to new companies and become involved in hiring, they often look to former colleagues and people they know as potential hires. In many professional and managerial occupations, paid intermediaries known as "head hunters" or executive search firms help companies identify and recruit top employees from other firms (or help individuals seeking such positions find them). In this way, the search firm creates networks that companies (or individuals) may not have found on their own.

Understanding your own social network and thinking about the people who have had the biggest impact on your life so far (and how you may or may not have helped them) is a very useful exercise. Writing it down may also help you recognize individuals who may be able to help you in the future. It may also highlight the role you play in your network. Do you know some social **connectors** (individuals who introduce people from different social networks who might not otherwise know each other?) Are you a person who brings people together? (To learn more about your own social network, complete the following activity.)

Markets and Discrimination

9.3.7 **Explain why markets don't treat everyone the same.**

Social structures include norms and institutions but also social hierarchies. How do markets relate to those hierarchies? Can economic markets be truly blind, in the sense that everyone is treated the same? This is an interesting

---

Figure 9.1 Mapping Your Social Network

What kind of social networker are you? By identifying the most important people in your life (not including your family or lifelong friends), you can determine what type of network you currently have and see how your "networking practices" are working. For college students doing this exercise, it may be best to focus on friendship networks (as your future professional network may not have many entries). On a separate piece of paper, draw the three columns. In the left-hand column, fill in the names of the most important contacts in your network—people you rely on for the exchange of private information, advice, creative inspiration, or fun. In the second column, identify how you met this person—who introduced you (or did you introduce yourself?). In the column on the right, identify people you have introduced that friend to, and the people the friend has introduced you to. Are you a "super-connector" who introduces a lot of people to each other? Do you have one (or more) super-connectors in your own network, who introduces you to many people?

Name of contact	Who introduced you to contact?	Who have you introduced you to contact?	Who has contact introduced you to?

SOURCE: This exercise was originally developed by Uzzi and Dunlop 2005 and is slightly modified here by the authors.

question to ponder, in large part because two Nobel Prize winning economists, Milton Friedman and Gary Becker, both famously argue in classic works that in the long run, capitalist markets will weed out companies that discriminate against any group. The reason, they suggest, is that buyers and sellers look for the best quality product at the lowest price they can afford. They don't care who is selling it to them. Further, Friedman and Becker argue, employers have very strong reasons to want to hire the best workers, irrespective of their race, gender, religion, or any other attribute. And employers who do discriminate against some groups will lose out on talented people they could have hired and be stuck with less effective employees who fit their biases. The discriminating firm will suffer a cost for its choice to discriminate. By contrast, the open-minded firms that *do* hire these workers will outcompete the discriminating firms, with the latter eventually going out of business. In principle, then, markets could serve as the great equalizer. Both Friedman and Becker therefore opposed most kinds of civil rights laws that required employers to hire without discrimination (Friedman 1962; Becker 1976).

Sociologists have strongly disagreed with these theoretical propositions and done extensive research to disprove them. When studying how actual employers operating in markets behave, as opposed to how they should behave in theory, research finds that people's biases do impact their market choices. From decades of studies, we know that employers do not treat all potential job applicants simply on the basis of merit; they also look at demographic characteristics such as age, gender, race, and ethnicity. Employers can be truly open-minded in the way predicted by Friedman and Becker, and some are, but far too many employers still are biased against certain kinds of workers and have been shown to discriminate in experiments in which identically qualified applicants apply. White employers are less likely to hire a person of color with an identical resume to a White applicant (Pager, et al. 2009). A large number of studies find similar results (Bertrand and Duflo 2017).

These biases extend to other kinds of economic transactions. For example, Whites are less likely to purchase identical products from a Black person than a White person. As described in Chapter 3, in an experiment on Craigslist, two economists found that White buyers were less trusting and less willing to pay as much to a seller who was identified as Black by virtue of an image displaying the object for sale (in this case, an Apple iPod; see Doleac and Stein 2010). White cab drivers are less likely to pick up a Black rider than a White rider (Gambetta and Hamill 2005). Whites are also much less willing to travel to Black neighborhoods to go to restaurants than Blacks are willing to go to restaurants in mostly White neighborhoods, making it more difficult for restaurants in Black neighborhoods to compete (Moore 2016).

Kevin Frayer/Getty Images

BIG QUESTION 9.4   Why Are Organizations Important for Social and Economic Life?

ORGANIZATIONS IN THE MODERN WORLD

We live in the age of markets, but these markets are not typically just made up of a bunch of individuals selling goods to other people. Rather, contemporary markets contain within them a variety of organizations, large and small, that shape the boundaries of most markets. In almost everything we do, we encounter an organization, and an almost endless array of organizations impact our daily lives—day care centers, schools, churches, businesses, hospitals, and government. Virtually every market has a set of key organizations that operate within it in both competitive and noncompetitive ways. To gain a deeper understanding of how markets and modern economies work—and ultimately how social forces influence the economy as a whole—sociologists have placed considerable importance on analyzing how organizations work.

What exactly is an **organization**? It can be defined as a group engaged in a specific activity that has an identifiable purpose or goal and an enduring form of association independent of the people involved in it at any one moment. If we break this definition down a bit, the key points are (1) an organization has to be more than just a collection of individuals doing the same thing. For example, a group of friends going fishing is not an organization, but a company that farms fish and sells them to supermarkets is; (2) the organization is not dependent on who the current members are, and will persist over time even as new people come. For example, the New York Yankees baseball team is an organization, with new players replacing old ones all the time, whereas a group of friends who regularly meet to play softball but stop when some of the players move away or don't have time anymore is not.

Given this admittedly broad definition, it is no surprise that there are many different types. Organizations can be huge (such as the U.S. Army, Walmart) or as small as three or four people. Some are organized around the pursuit of economic goals (firms), spiritual goals (religious organizations), leisure or athletic goals (sports teams), altruistic goals (voluntary or nonprofit groups), advocacy goals (organizations that try to influence government policy), political goals (organizations that try to influence elections or start social movements), or student goals (student organizations). In spite of the vast differences in the size and purpose of the organizations found around the world, sociological research over the past few decades has found that they have many things in common. In this section, we discuss several of these well-established common features.

One clarifying point at the outset: A common confusion many people have is between organizations and institutions. Organizations often exhibit many of the same features of institutions: They are enduring forms of social organization, they have strong norms that shape the behavior of the individuals who become involved in them, and they are typically slow to change. But the term "institution" is much broader. The Catholic Church is an organization, but religion (which includes all denominations) is properly known as the institution. Mississippi State University is an organization, while education is the institution. Institutions usually have multiple organizations that engage in activities that fall under a single institutional umbrella.

The Formation and Features of Organizations

9.4.1 Explain how organizations form.

Organizations are human constructions. They come into being whenever a group of people decide to create a more formal structure to pursue some common objective. Almost every organization has a name (although there are some secret organizations that try to avoid naming themselves to remain invisible to outsiders—the Mafia is one example; see Catino 2019) and a distinct culture. In many cases, members work to incorporate their values into the thinking of new members. An organization, like any society, will develop its own norms that members are expected to follow. For example, what kinds of clothing are appropriate in the organizational space? What kinds of speech do people use when in the organization and how is it different than the way people talk to family, friends, or out on the street? What kind of knowledge is everyone in the firm expected to know? Long-established organizations may have their own rituals that will seem strange to outsiders but perfectly understandable to insiders.

One central pattern within most organizations of a certain size is the creation of what is known as **bureaucracy**. Not all organizations necessarily have formal bureaucracies, but as soon as they get big enough to create written rules and establish defined roles for organization of members, the beginnings of a bureaucracy are present, and the bigger a company or organization gets the more likely it will become more bureaucratic. Creating a set of written rules is an important way of clarifying how the group is going to carry out whatever tasks they have assigned and how decisions are to be made. Once a bureaucratic form emerges, people can join and leave the organization, but the organization itself persists because it has established operating principles and procedures that do not rely on particular individuals to maintain it. In these cases, the organization has now become more than the sum of all of the individuals within it.

To see how this works, let's consider the very well-known case of Apple Computer, maker of MacIntosh computers, iPhones, and other popular consumer devices (Linzmayer 2004; Isaacson 2011; Dormehl 2013). The computer industry is particularly interesting as it has long prided itself on avoiding bureaucracy and maintaining an innovative "start-up" culture. Although the story of Apple is frequently presented as a story about the brilliant business acumen of CEO Steve Jobs (the visionary who combined a fascination with both technology and design with a willingness to explore new products), Apple is also a surprisingly typical story of an organization that evolved over time from a small organization created by a couple of individuals to a larger bureaucratic firm. Founded in a garage in Palo Alto, California, in 1977 by two young computer enthusiasts, Steve Jobs and Steve Wozniak, Apple produced the first commercially successful personal desktop computer (The Apple II) in 1977, and in 1984 launched the Macintosh computer, which became one of the company's staple products. Few individuals in the history of American business are so closely tied to the success of their company as Steve Jobs and Apple; Henry Ford and his automobile company is one, but there aren't many other figures in business history so highly thought of as Jobs (as shown by best-selling books and Hollywood movies about this life).

But Apple survived after Jobs' death in 2011, as well as during the period between 1985 and 1997 when he left the company after being fired by Apple's board of directors over sharp disagreements about the company's direction. The company survived during its ups and downs in the 1980s and 1990s, before the introduction of its breakthrough products in the 2000s, such as the iPod, the iPhone, and the iPad. That survival, and its huge successes after 2000 hinged in large part on the creation of an organizational structure that could survive and function even without its leader. In the history of the company, Jobs always played a key role as an inventor and innovator, and perhaps if Jobs had not returned to Apple, it would have remained a much smaller company, or even gone out of business. But it was never just his company. It survived and persisted because it became a bureaucratic organization that could control its costs, workforce, and marketing operations. It was never solely dependent on any one figure, even someone as important as Steve Jobs, although we love to admire the heroic single genius.

The Downside of Bureaucracy

9.4.2 Identify the benefits and limitations of bureaucratic processes and regulations.

While the process of bureaucratization can provide strength, coherence, and stability for an organization, it can also create barriers to effective decision making. We have a number of shorthand expressions for these problems: Bureaucracies, as we all have heard, are allegedly full of "red tape," are "inefficient," "bloated," and ineffective. Calling someone a "bureaucrat" can often be an insult. Let's probe these issues a bit further.

To ensure stability and predictably, organizations often come to rely strongly on rules and regulations. The sociologist Max Weber, observing the German civil-service sector in the early twentieth century, provided the first comprehensive analysis of bureaucratic organizations (Weber [1922] 1978). The move of any organization toward a bureaucratic form, Weber thought, was a necessary response to the complexities of modern large-scale markets and big governments. An organization that embraced

bureaucratic means was attempting to find ways to allocate resources and make decisions more efficiently than it otherwise would. The hallmark of a bureaucracy, according to Weber, was the existence of formal procedures and rules, which are supposed to ensure both consistency (the same problem or task is addressed the same way each time) and accountability (individuals in the bureaucracy are accountable to those above them). Bureaucracy, Weber thought, was an inevitable feature of the modern world. Yet Weber also saw many negative aspects of bureaucracies. While undertaken with efficiency as the end goal, the bureaucratic form of organization also creates stifling routines and boring jobs, makes it more difficult for individuals within a bureaucratic organization to be creative and innovative, and can make it more difficult for an entire organization to respond to changes in the environment in which it operates.

Weber's theory of bureaucracy emphasized three central features. First, bureaucracies establish positions of authority that are hierarchically organized—that is, the higher up you go in a bureaucracy, the more authority is vested in that position. Bureaucracies are hierarchically organized so that there is a chain of command, and everyone working in the bureaucracy is responsible to the office above him or her. (Even the president or CEO of an organization is typically responsible to an outside board of some kind.) Second, written rules define the scope and responsibility of each position within a bureaucratic organization. Each employee is expected to perform those (and only those) roles. Third, while organizations may have volunteers, they are only properly considered bureaucratic when the decision-making officers of the organization are full-time, salaried positions.

Weber's classical theory captured many of the key features of the bureaucratic organizations that were growing rapidly in the late nineteenth and early twentieth centuries. But Weber missed a few things. In particular, he focused on the formal aspects of bureaucratic organizations but did not analyze the informal aspects of how bureaucracies actually work. Later critics and researchers who studied many organizations in both the for-profit and not-for-profit sectors noted just how often bureaucratic organizations deviate from their formal rules. Rules are routinely broken or ignored and often can only prescribe what someone does in an actual job in a vague way. Bosses are only sometimes able to effectively supervise their subordinates. Bureaucratic officials are also self-interested in ways that Weber's model did not anticipate. For example, bureaucrats often seek to increase the amount of resources available to their unit, whether or not that is the wisest use of the entire organization's resources. Having a bigger budget under their control provides many benefits, even if the money might have been better spent somewhere else in the organization.

In the real world, then, bureaucracies are often messy places where rules and regulations are difficult to define and implement. Organizational decision making seldom follows a clear path. **Loose coupling** is one way many managers within bureaucratic organizations try to disentangle themselves and their unit from irrational rules and regulations or to implement those rules in creative ways that make sense. In sociological terms, loose coupling decentralizes decision making and permits multiple approaches within the same bureaucratic organization to emerge. Loose coupling is evident in many different organizational environments. It has both positive and negative elements. It can be valuable because it provides organizations with the flexibility to maneuver as challenges arise. For example, a few years ago, the New York City Department of Education mandated that schools adopt a zero-tolerance policy for student possession of cell phones on campus. The district policies required that all student cell phones be confiscated and held until parents were notified and came to school to pick up what had been defined as contraband. Administrators and teachers in many schools, however, understood that while the intention of the policy was perhaps laudable, attempts at implementation would at best be laughable. In many schools, students had cell phones with the full support of their parents, who used these devices to keep in touch with them. Confiscating phones of the entire student body and summoning a mob of irate parents would not have been an effective practice.

But loose coupling has downsides. For example, it can't go so far as to allow principals and schools the freedom to disregard federal rules requiring standardized testing, without putting federal funding in jeopardy. More generally, too much loose coupling within an organization can mean that overall objectives can never be properly implemented or that individual units will tend to be in conflict and competition with each other. But large bureaucratic organizations need some room for loose coupling to avoid the worst consequences of bureaucratic inefficiencies or one-sided rules that don't fit in some cases. The key is to find the right balance, which is never easy and can change in a short period of time.

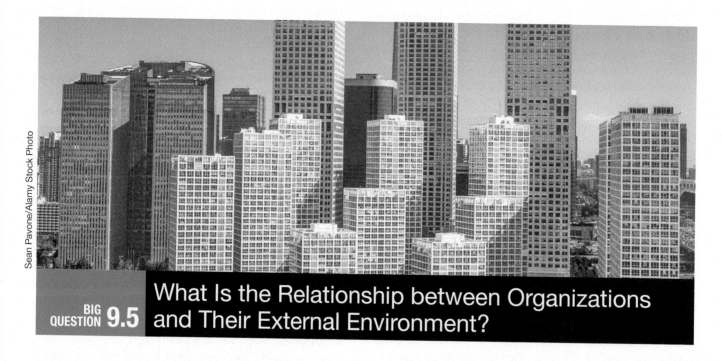

Sean Pavone/Alamy Stock Photo

BIG QUESTION 9.5 What Is the Relationship between Organizations and Their External Environment?

ORGANIZATIONS AND THEIR ENVIRONMENTS

The sociological imagination, as we have discussed throughout this book, urges us to look at the social contexts in which individuals and groups—and now organizations—interact. Like individuals and groups, organizations operate in the context of a larger environment, in this case consisting of other competing firms, government policies and legal requirements, and sometimes unions. And in an increasingly global world, organizations also face pressures (but may also have opportunities) that may arise from developments happening a long way from their headquarters. Just as individuals are affected by their environments, so too are organizations.

To better understand this, it may be useful to start with an analogy about nature. Every animal, plant, or other organism lives within a particular natural environment. Evolutionary theory teaches us that the environment influences not only the life and death of any organism, but also the ways in which the organism changes across generations. Like organisms, organizations depend on their surroundings to provide resources necessary for survival. Whereas an animal might depend on its environment to provide food and water, an organization depends on it for economic, social, and political resources. Without these resources the organization will perish. This ecological metaphor is useful for understanding how organizations work; in fact, social scientists use the term **organizational ecology** to refer to the study of the ways in which organizations survive (or fail) in their environment. In this section, we consider some classical ideas about organizations and their environments that have grown from this analogy.

Organizational Structure

9.5.1 Discuss how an organization's structure and niche may contribute to its success or its failure.

An ecological approach to understanding organizational structure raises these questions: Do successful organizations continually adapt to the environments in which they operate? Or do they survive because they were uniquely suited to the environment from the start? Either way, organizations must have features that are suitable for their environment if they are to stay alive and prosper. Large organizations do sometimes go out of business or shrink and change dramatically. Generally, the organizations that survive and thrive over time have created an internal culture that is a good match to their environment, one that makes it possible to change as the external environment evolves (Hannan and Freeman 1989). But many organizations have developed internal cultures that resist change, perhaps because their bureaucratic rules are too rigid. Strong resistance to change is referred to as **structural inertia**, and it can be terminal if the environment dramatically changes and the absence of adaptation leads to organizational mortality.

It is not hard to see why structural inertia occurs. An organization that is successful early in its history has little reason to change. As the expression goes, "Why fix what isn't broken?" But structural inertia may also prevent the organization from adapting needed changes at some point. How would this happen? Though structural inertia is necessary, once it is set in place it is difficult to change. Think of the famous story of the *Titanic*, a luxury cruise ship that tragically sank in the Atlantic in April 1912. The first of its kind when built, the ship's massive size made it famous, but its size also contributed to its inertia, thereby rendering it unable to avoid hitting an iceberg. As organizations become successful, they can become like the *Titanic*—the very things that won them success may actually make them eventually fail. The history of business organizations is littered with once successful firms that are now bankrupt because they could not adapt to oncoming challenges despite their initial success.

How do organizations survive in the face of competition? Although situations can be unique, the most common way that an organization competes is to successfully identify and fulfill a **niche** (a distinct segment of a market or social process) for which the organization's services or products are in demand. A niche might provide high-end (expensive) products or services to a small group willing to pay very high prices for the "best," cheap goods and services to a larger group, or a good or service that no one else is currently providing. The car company Tesla provides one example. Tesla only makes battery powered cars, even though in 2020, only a handful (about 5 percent) of new cars sold are battery powered. The company doesn't try to compete in the vast market for gasoline-powered cars. Their "niche" is attempting to build the most attractive luxury and mass-market battery-powered cars. Though there will still be competition from similar organizations (the other major auto manufacturers are also trying to build battery-powered cars), an organization that is effective at identifying and servicing a unique niche will often do well, at least as long as that niche exists. (In 10 or 20 years, *all* new cars are expected to be battery powered, at which point Tesla's unique niche will disappear and they will be in competition with much bigger auto manufacturers.)

The competition to control a niche is easiest to imagine among for-profit organizations, but we can even see the same thing if we look at nonprofit organizations. Take, for example, higher education. All of the organizations in higher education (such as New York University, the University of California–Berkeley, Miami Dade College, or the for-profit University of Phoenix) attempt to create for themselves a unique niche that appeals to certain kinds of students. By identifying a particular market of students that the institution can serve, a school limits the amount of competition it must face to survive in its environment. Think of the difference between a state university and an expensive private university. While the state university has institutional competition in the form of other state universities, its identification as a public institution partly funded by the state government gives it a mission (to educate the future leaders of the state) and a special niche as a state university. A state university does not necessarily need to compete with private colleges for the same students; students interested in or able to afford private colleges are likely to be somewhat different from their peers who chose state schools during their college application process. A larger state school, for example, may have many more majors than a private college or very specific programs (let's say in veterinary medicine) that a small private school is unlikely to have.

Organizational Similarity

9.5.2 Explain organizational isomorphism and identify the differences among three types: Coercive, normative, and mimetic.

While organizations compete, one of the most well-established sociological findings about organizations is that over time successful organizations in the same institutional field will tend to look a lot like each other. In spite of the endless array of organizations in the modern world, there are many common features among organizations doing similar things that make them easy to recognize or understand. For example, consider high schools. There are obvious differences between public and private high schools, between affluent suburban schools and impoverished urban ones, or between high schools that have a large percentage of immigrant students versus those that do not. Despite these differences, almost all of these schools are organized in a very similar way. They all have principals who administer the school, they offer the same core subjects, they have more or less the same kinds of sports teams and physical education systems, they organize the day into periods where students move from class to class and work with different teachers, and so forth. Experimental schools vary some of these dimensions but rarely depart too far.

Why are there so many similarities in the ways organizations (like high schools) operate? Let us begin with a concrete example. The 1990 Americans with Disabilities Act (ADA) was a landmark piece of legislation that declared that those citizens with disabilities should have the same access to physical spaces, such as buildings and bathrooms, as their nondisabled peers. The ADA includes a set of rules for the physical buildings in which organizations operate. These rules and regulations mandate that certain facilities in every commercial and public-service building be accessible to all individuals, including those who are challenged with a mobility disability. Organizations then have to modify their physical structures to comply with these rules. Modification of a

building by adding additional wheelchair ramps, elevators, handicap-accessible bathrooms, and the like, however, is very expensive and time consuming, and the likelihood of being caught for failing to comply is low. But researchers have found that most large organizations make a serious effort to comply. Why?

There are several reasons an organization might comply with the demands of increasing accessibility, all of which are related to a sociological concept called **organizational isomorphism**. Isomorphism refers to the process whereby organizations in the same field tend to become increasingly similar to each other over time (DiMaggio and Powell 1983). Isomorphism is a complicated word and concept—definitely hard to pronounce (eye-so-more-fizzum)—but it is an important and valuable one to try to grasp and remember. The phenomenon of isomorphism has been found repeatedly in research across a wide range of organizations and industries. So why might organizations in the same field, market, or industry become more similar over time? The most straightforward way this occurs is when organizations are pressured to comply with certain legal regulations or requirements (such as the ADA's requirements that all buildings must provide wheelchair access). When applied to all organizations in the field, **coercive isomorphism** occurs. In this case, these organizations are compelled to take the same actions to avoid facing consequences that might include being sued by a customer or fined by a government agency.

But compulsion is hardly the only way isomorphism occurs. There are two other reasons an organization might adopt similar behaviors or policies.

Approaches to meeting requirements for disability access can take many forms, but over time organizations developed similar approaches to meeting the legal requirements. This is the process of organizational isomorphism in action.

gyn9037/Shutterstock

Imagine that an organization, in response to the ADA, must make a significant investment in making physical building changes. While these expenses may be considerable, the damage that could be done to the organization's legitimacy by *not* complying might be even greater. Imagine if protestors in wheelchairs began picketing in front of the organization's headquarters because it refused to provide access for disabled persons. That would clearly not be a good thing for the organization's reputation.

By contrast, if an organization moves quickly to promote equal access it may be able to advertise itself as especially fair, sensitive, and responsive (and perhaps even imply that its competitors are not). In recent years, many companies have voluntarily adopted "green" practices and asserted they are environmentally sensitive organizations. Employers within the organization often have expectations—learned in schools or from professional associations—about what the organization should do. Responding to these kinds of (positive or negative) expectations is what is known as **normative isomorphism**: The organization is responding to pressures that are exerted on its legitimacy. Here, the word *normative* indicates the general feelings or expectations of the people that the organization serves (for example, employees and customers or clients). Failing to attend to those expectations and needs of its supporters, the organization would fail to address the normative environment in which it lives and, thus, would potentially lose its legitimacy within that environment.

Now let us assume the organization feels pressure both legally and from wanting to allow disabled attendees entrance to their building (or avoid appearing insensitive). Then what? How does it know which type of modifications would be appropriate to build? Facing this uncertainty, it might look at what other organizations are doing and then do something similar. In this way, the company is engaging in what is known as **mimetic isomorphism**, which means it literally imitates or mimes the practices of other organizations. The phrase that organizational insiders often use to capture this process of imitation is "best practices." By making itself look like all the others, that is, by adopting the best practices in the industry, the organization and its leaders do not attract negative attention. So the practice of keeping an eye on competitors to see how they do things is an example of mimetic isomorphism.

Conclusion: The Sociological Approach to the Economy

Economic markets are fundamental institutions in the modern world. After the collapse of communism, virtually all societies today rely on markets to distribute goods, services, income, and wealth, and in one form or another are capitalist economies. These markets, as we have seen, are pervasive.

The subfield of economic sociology has contributed to the study of the economy in several ways. Most importantly, it amends the assumption that human behavior is driven by self-interest. In fact, people often follow societal norms much more than would be expected if monetary gain were a key motivating factor. People can also be altruistic at times: Indeed, helping others and avoiding the appearance of cheating are critical motivations guiding even economic action. These same social dynamics impact large organizations as well.

One of the most significant implications of the sociological analysis of capitalism is that markets need rules and regulations to operate successfully. The ideals of laissez-faire and free markets are powerful, but when we closely examine *how* markets work, we see the importance of regulatory institutions (including the state and its legal system), as well as societal norms and values that inform the economic action in markets by individuals. We also see that economic markets do not always treat everyone the same. Social hierarchies can be exacerbated by market functioning. The Matthew Effect is a powerful metaphor for understanding how capitalist markets tend to overreward those who already have advantages.

The most important actors in economic markets, of course, are the large organizations that use their existing advantages to limit competition and receive elevated profits. We've seen how these companies develop bureaucratic forms of organization and tend to imitate each other. Yet organizational niches provide opportunities for new kinds of organizations to emerge. Social media companies like Apple, Google, Amazon, Facebook, and Alibaba are good examples that new organizations can arise. Change does happen. This does not mean that all of the insights of organizational theory we have discussed in this chapter are going out the window. Quite the contrary: The pressures to emulate one another—what sociologists call isomorphism—appear to be driving some of the ongoing changes in organizational forms we have observed. For example, when one company or organization figures out how to cut its costs or implement a new style of workplace organization, other firms study that change and may implement it as well.

The Big Questions Revisited 9

9.1 What Are Capitalist Markets? In capitalist societies like the United States, market institutions are a core part of the social structure of society. In this section, we introduced and defined a sociological conception of capitalism and its economic markets. We explained the rise of capitalism and the pervasiveness of markets in modern societies.

The Creation and Functioning of Capitalist Markets

The Rise of Capitalism

Learning Objective 9.1.1: Explain the factors that gave rise to capitalism and economic growth.

The Pervasiveness of Capitalist Markets Today

Learning Objective 9.1.2: Discuss the pervasiveness of markets in modern societies.

Key Terms

capitalism (p. 213)   markets (p. 213)   firms (p. 213)   capital (p. 213)   entrepreneurs (p. 213)   feudalism (p. 213)   serfs (p. 213) Industrial Revolution (p. 213)   monetized (p. 216)

9.2 What Are the Varieties of Capitalism in the World Today? In this section, we first examined how and why the economic system in communist countries failed to survive as a viable alternative to capitalism. We then explored the large differences in capitalist economies around the world today, focusing on three different historical varieties of capitalism: Laissez-faire, liberal market capitalism, and social democratic market capitalism.

Alternatives to Capitalism

The Rise and Fall of Communist Economies

Learning Objective 9.2.1: Describe why communist economies failed to compete with capitalism.

Varieties of Capitalist Market Economies

Learning Objective 9.2.2: Describe the main features of three different varieties of capitalist economies.

Key Terms

communism (p. 218)   state socialist economies (p. 218)   varieties of capitalism (p. 219)   laissez-faire capitalism (p. 219)   libertarians (p. 220) liberal market economies (p. 220)   welfare state (p. 220)   unions (p. 220)   social democratic market capitalist economies (p. 220)   Social Democracy (p. 220)

9.3 What is the Sociological Approach to the Study of Economic Markets? Economic markets are strongly influenced by social processes such as norms, power, trust, and social networks. The human actors who participate in these markets are also influenced by psychological factors. In this section we examined how noneconomic social influences shape what happens in economic markets, as well as introduced the contributions of behavioral economics.

Social Influences on Economic Markets

Psychology and the Rise of Behavioral Economics

Learning Objective 9.3.1: Describe psychological findings that have impacted the way we view economic behavior.

Economic Sociology: An Introduction

Learning Objective 9.3.2: Define the concept of embeddedness.

Norms and Economic Behavior

Learning Objective 9.3.3: Explain how norms influence economic markets.

Power

Learning Objective 9.3.4: Explain how power influences markets.

Trust

Learning Objective 9.3.5: Discuss why trust is important for economic exchange.

Social Networks

Learning Objective 9.3.6: Explain how social networks influence markets.

Markets and Discrimination

Learning Objective 9.3.7: Explain why markets don't treat everyone the same.

Key Terms

behavioral economics (p. 222)   economic sociology (p. 222)   loss aversion (p. 222)   embeddedness (p. 223)   altruism (p. 223)   norms (p. 223)   ultimatum game (p. 224)   trust (p. 226)   McDonaldization (p. 226)   social networks (p. 227)   connectors (p. 238)

9.4 Why Are Organizations Important for Social and Economic Life? To gain a deeper understanding of how modern economies work—and ultimately how social forces influence the economy as a whole—sociologists place considerable importance on analyzing the organizations that exist within markets, a topic explored in this section.

Organizations in the Modern World

The Formation and Features of Organizations

Learning Objective 9.4.1: Explain how organizations form.

The Downside of Bureaucracy

Learning Objective 9.4.2: Identify the benefits and limitations of bureaucratic processes and regulations.

Key Terms

organization (p. 230)   bureaucracy (p. 230)   loose coupling (p. 232)

9.5   What Is the Relationship between Organizations and Their External Environment? The ecological framework of organizational sociology challenges whether organizations actually adapt to their environment or whether the organizations that survive do so because they were uniquely suited to the environment from the start. In this section, we explored the relationship between organizations and their environment.

Organizations and their Environments

Organizational Structure

Learning Objective 9.5.1: Discuss how an organization's structure and niche may contribute to its success or its failure.

Organizational Similarity

Learning Objective 9.5.2: Explain organizational isomorphism, and identify the differences among three types: Coercive, normative, and mimetic.

Key Terms

organizational ecology (p. 233)   structural inertia (p. 233)   niche (p. 233)   organizational isomorphism (p. 234)   coercive isomorphism (p. 235)   normative isomorphism (p. 235)   mimetic isomorphism (p. 235)

Chapter 10
Culture, Media, and Communication

by Eric Klinenberg with Matthew Wolfe*

In 2004, a 19-year-old Harvard undergraduate named Mark Zuckerberg created a website designed to help students at his university connect with each other. This new social website, which he called The Facebook—later shortened to just Facebook—was unexpectedly popular. Within a year, it had a million users. Within a decade, it had a billion. In Facebook's wake, other social media platforms, such as Twitter, LinkedIn, Instagram, TikTok, Reddit, and YouTube, emerged, each of which offer unique features and attract different types of users. Teenagers, for example, currently favor the video-sharing site TikTok, while middle-aged professionals congregate on the employment service LinkedIn. But what all these social media sites have in common is that they allow individuals to link to and communicate with "friends" or followers. More importantly, they provide users with a means of creating or joining new communities. Through these networks, individuals become tied together.

The founders of Facebook and Twitter probably didn't realize that the ideas behind the sites they built drew upon some very basic sociological insights about how **social networks** (the ties between people, groups, and organizations) work; human beings are not simply individuals with a few close friends and family members who randomly bump into strangers in the course of their daily lives. Rather, we all are part of normally hidden social networks, in which we know people who know other people we don't know but who have much in common with us (interests, backgrounds, and areas of expertise). For instance, information about new job opportunities is something that has always been shared by people in otherwise hidden social circles, but now social media sites are making those networks visible.

The rise of social media also represents a radical transformation in how information is produced and consumed. In the past, the only way to speak to a large audience or publish a message was to use an expensive form of *mass communication*, like a radio station, a television network,

My Sociological Imagination

ERIC KLINENBERG

I grew up in the center of Chicago, and my interest in the sociology of culture and cities grew out of my experiences there. I lived in a bohemian but rapidly gentrifying neighborhood called Old Town, a place that was long famous for its vibrant street life and for its blues clubs, jazz bars, cafés, and counterculture scenes. Chicago is a segregated city, and Old Town is wedged between two of the city's most affluent areas, the Gold Coast and Lincoln Park, and Cabrini Green, a housing project (recently demolished) where most of the residents were Black and poor. I was always puzzled by this arrangement, and trying to understand it as a child was the beginning of my sociology career.

My research examines cities, culture, climate, and communications. My first book, *Heat Wave: A Social Autopsy of Disaster in Chicago*, explores two questions: Why did so many people die during a short heat spell in 1995? And why was this disastrous event so easy to deny, overlook, and forget? My second book, *Fighting for Air: The Battle to Control America's Media*, examines how media consolidation has affected newspapers, radio stations, television news, and the internet and tracks the emergence of the global media reform movement. My third book, *Going Solo: The Extraordinary Rise and Surprising Appeal of Living Alone*, analyzes the incredible social experiment in solo living that began in the 1950s and is now ubiquitous in developed nations throughout the world. I then teamed up with comedian Aziz Ansari to investigate how sex and dating have been changed by the rise of social media and online dating apps, publishing our findings in the bestselling *Modern Romance*. In my most recent book, *Palaces for the People: How Social Infrastructure Can Help Fight Inequality, Polarization, and the Decline of Civic Life*, I argue that, in our fractured time, we can help rebuild democratic values and mutual trust by investing in shared spaces, such as libraries, childcare centers, churches, and parks, where individuals from different backgrounds meet and form important connections.

---

*An earlier version of this chapter was co-authored by David Wachsmuth.

The rise of social media has profoundly changed the way people communicate. The central sociological question is how, if at all, is it impacting social interaction and social structure.

or a newspaper. With the internet, the costs of producing and distributing information was drastically reduced. Suddenly, for no more than the cost of a phone or a laptop, *anyone* could, in theory, show *anything* they could write, film, or record to *everyone*. No longer would the gatekeepers of mass communication decide which facts and opinions deserved to enter the world. This shift also changes how we think about ourselves and participate in society. We are no longer just members of an audience; now, we are all potential speakers and publishers. Yet, while social media is supposedly designed to "bring the world closer together," as Facebook has described in its mission statement, critics charge that the technology has also created new kinds of political and social fractures.

The consequences of social media's rise for culture and civil society are staggering and raise a number of questions that sociologists have only begun to answer. How, for example, has new technology changed the form, content, and character of friendships and groups? How has online dating changed the nature of intimate relationships? How has technology changed the way work is organized, how employment is found, and what kinds of jobs are likely to be available in the future? New technologies are helping governments spy on their citizens much more intensively than before, but the ability of whistleblowers to leak information about the measures taken by governments to spy on citizens also appears to be on the rise; what does this mean for democratic rights? And governments are not the only ones acting in this way: Universities and employers are increasingly reading social media produced by prospective students or job applicants to evaluate them beyond traditional means. Today, our "digital footprint" forms a part of who we are in a way that would have been completely unimaginable a couple of decades ago.

In this chapter, we will look at how these transformations of communication and culture are changing the way we live our lives. One important aspect of the sociological study of culture involves studying people's daily routines and practices. Another involves examining the values, social norms, and collective beliefs that make some behaviors acceptable and others suspect. Fortunately, the search for this kind of information is as rewarding as its discovery, which explains why the sociology of culture is one of the fastest-growing parts of the field today.

The Big Questions

1. **What is culture?** When sociologists talk about culture, they refer to a shared system of beliefs and knowledge, more commonly called a system of meaning and symbols; a set of values, beliefs, and practices; and shared forms of communication.

2. **How does culture shape our collective identity?** Cultural practices both reflect and define group identities, whether the group is a small subculture or a nation.

3. **How do our cultural practices relate to class and status?** People's cultural habits help define and reproduce the boundaries between high status and low status, upper class and lower class.

4. **Who produces culture, and why?** The cultural field is the place for creativity and meaning making. But it is also a battlefield: Who controls the media and popular culture, and what messages they communicate, are central to how social life is organized and how power operates.

5. **What is the relationship between media and democracy?** The media are arguably the most important form of cultural production in our society. The news is vital to democracy, and new ways of participating in the media are changing how democracy works.

Sebastian Kahnert/dpa-Zentralbild/ZB/dpa/Alamy Stock Photo

BIG QUESTION 10.1 What Is Culture?

THE MANY MEANINGS OF CULTURE

The latest song by Beyoncé, a performance of the opera, the places we choose to go on vacation, our assumptions about monogamy, a viral meme on TikTok: These are all examples of culture. People use the word *culture* to refer to all sorts of things, from art to traditions to individual learned behavior. In everyday language, culture is often a synonym for art or artistic activities, as indicated by the expression "getting some culture," or a synonym for refined taste, as when we call a person "cultured." These are certainly two of the ways that sociologists use the word, but there are a number of others. In fact, as one writer puts it, "culture is one of the two or three most complicated words in the English language" (Williams 1976, p. 87).

The modern Western history of the concept of culture begins with the rise of world travel in the eighteenth and nineteenth centuries, when merchants from Europe came into contact with non-Europeans for the first time. These merchants were struck not only by the physical differences between themselves and the non-Europeans but also by the differences in how they behaved. This included everything from how they dressed to the way their families were organized. In an attempt to make sense of these differences, scientists in the nineteenth century connected the physical differences with the behavioral differences, arguing that people's biology—and particularly their race—determined how their societies were organized.

Toward the end of the nineteenth century, anthropologists began to criticize this idea and instead argued that it was not race that was responsible for these differences but something else—something that was not hereditary but rather learned, something that was not natural and biological but rather socially produced. That something was culture. These days, the argument that the differences

between groups of people are more than just biological, and that we learn how to behave, seems obvious. But at the time, it was an important discovery.

From this early research came some basic conclusions about culture. First, culture is a shared characteristic of groups, not individuals. Second, culture is a way of understanding differences *between* groups as well as similarities *within* groups. Last, culture is an aspect of social life that is different from nature or biology. Indeed, what makes culture a social phenomenon is precisely that it is not natural. While it's difficult in practice to draw a line between nature and culture, sociologists now recognize that certain biological things about humans are relatively constant throughout history (for example, everyone gets hungry), while cultural things are not (for example, the kind of food we eat and how we eat it).

Defining Culture

10.1.1 Define culture from a sociological perspective.

In the early twentieth century, sociologists and anthropologists generally defined culture as the entire way of life of a people. If we were transported back to ancient Rome, what kinds of things would we need to fit in? We would certainly need language and information about art, customs, and traditions. But we would also need all sorts of material objects, including clothing, tools, and a place to live. This was all considered part of a society's culture: both material and nonmaterial aspects.

Today, when sociologists talk about **culture**, they are usually referring to three things: A shared system of beliefs and knowledge, more commonly called a system of meaning and symbols; a set of values, beliefs, and practices; and shared forms of communication (Sewell 2005). We will explore each of these components of culture in the next three sections.

Culture as a System of Meaning and Symbols

10.1.2 Explain how a group's symbols can be considered its culture and give examples of collective symbols of contemporary U.S. culture.

Every society is full of **symbols** that communicate an idea while being distinct from the idea itself. Some are straightforward: For example, in contemporary American society, a red heart implies love and a green traffic light tells us that we are allowed to drive. Other symbols are less obvious: When a car commercial shows a car driving off-road at high speeds, it is likely that the advertiser is trying to make us think about freedom and excitement and associate those ideas with the car. A national flag might have a number of different meanings for different people. Symbols, whether simple or complex, are things that communicate implicit meaning about an idea. Taken together, a group's symbols are an important part of its culture.

We can analyze and interpret collective symbols to learn about particular cultures. The anthropologist Clifford Geertz demonstrated the idea that culture is a system of collective meaning by analyzing a Balinese cockfight in 1950s Indonesia (Geertz 1972). Cockfights—boxing matches between roosters—were outlawed by the national government but were still important events in local communities. Multiple pairs of birds fought over the course of an afternoon, and hundreds of residents watched, cheered, and placed bets. Geertz studied the cockfight the way a student of literature might study a novel, as an object full of symbols needing to be interpreted. For example, Geertz found that participants in the cockfights often gambled far more money than seemed to be rational from an economic

perspective. He concluded that the betting wasn't just about winning or losing money; it was a way of indicating and reworking status hierarchies (those who bet aggressively and were successful were simultaneously securing and displaying high status in the eyes of other participants). The cockfights allowed the Balinese to collectively interpret their own status hierarchies: "A story they tell themselves about themselves" (Geertz 1972, p. 28).

Symbols always exist in specific social contexts—a green traffic light would be mysterious to someone raised in a society without cars, for example, while most of us would find the rituals of a Balinese cockfight equally mysterious. For this reason, studying symbols helps us understand things about society that are not often discussed, such as distinctions of honor, inequality, and competition. For instance, if Geertz had asked them directly, the Balinese cockfighters would not have told him that betting was more a status issue than a financial one. That was something that he could only perceive through careful observation of a place where he had moved and a group that he had gotten to know well. This research method, based on lengthy and intimate observation of a group, is called *ethnography* (see Chapter 3 for more details).

How could we use Geertz's insights to interpret the collective symbols of the contemporary United States? In the place of a cockfight, we could study the Super Bowl—the most-watched cultural event in the country, which features familiar rituals and symbols such as betting on the outcome, Super Bowl parties with friends and family, an elaborate halftime show, and blockbuster television ads. But collective symbols don't have to be massive spectacles to be meaningful. Nowadays we might focus on different cultural events, such as trending video clips on YouTube, which would uncover a different America. From vlogs to comedy skits to impassioned monologues, sites such as YouTube and TikTok display our new collective symbols by allowing people to share and interpret culture together (Burgess and Green 2009).

Culture as a Set of Values, Beliefs, and Practices

10.1.3 Describe how our values and beliefs influence how we live our lives.

Consider again the Super Bowl. The rituals we described above are more than cultural symbols; they also demonstrate common **values**—judgments

Ian Trower/Alamy Stock Photo

The collective rituals we display in our cultural events, such as this cockfight in modern Indonesia, can demonstrate shared values. What cultural events could reveal shared American values?

about what is intrinsically important or meaningful, such as patriotism, competitiveness, and consumerism. But how does such collective meaning and its expression help to shape our social behavior? Is culture just a set of values and beliefs, or does it actually influence how we live our lives? In other words, how is culture actually practiced? The answer is that culture influences the kinds of decisions we make in our lives, whether or not we are aware of it.

The influential work of French sociologist Pierre Bourdieu developed an analysis of how culture works in this way. Bourdieu argued that we all develop certain sets of assumptions about the world and our place in it: Our tastes, preferences, and skills. We also develop habits—what Bourdieu called **habitus**—in the course of growing up and socializing with others that become so routine we don't even realize we are following them (Bourdieu 1992).

Bourdieu's concept of habitus helps explain how our future choices and opinions are always guided by our past experiences. Someone raised in a wealthy family on Park Avenue on the Upper East Side of Manhattan will have no trouble fitting in at a fancy dinner party but perhaps quite a bit of trouble fitting in on a farm, while someone raised on a farm will have the opposite experience. But people are exposed to all sorts of different cultural systems and forms of meaning, after all. So how is it that we choose to act one way at one time and a different way at another? One way to answer this question is to think of culture as a **tool kit**—a set of ideas and skills that we learn through the

cultural environment we live in and apply to practical situations in our own lives (Swidler 1986).

If a friend introduces us to someone, how do we behave? If we're single and interested in the person romantically, we'll draw on one set of cultural tools we've developed; if we're in a relationship and just trying to be polite, we'll draw on a different set of tools. Just as a car mechanic has a box of tools at their disposal for fixing a variety of problems, people have a kind of tool kit of behaviors and opinions that they apply to different situations they find themselves in. Some people will have better tools for certain situations, and some people will have better tools for others. What's more, even though people immersed in the same cultural environments will tend to have similar cultural tools in their tool kit, they probably will have quite different levels of expertise and familiarity with the tools. So two people who hang out in similar social circles might have the same basic set of conversational tools in their cultural tool kits, but the one who keeps to himself will be less comfortable using them than the one who frequently chats with people they don't know very well.

One sociologist studying love in contemporary America found that the two most important cultural tools are the idea of love as a voluntary choice and the idea of love as creating a set of commitments to another person (Swidler 2003). Most Americans have both of these tools, or ways of understanding love, available to them. But their personal backgrounds will affect which one they tend to rely on and which one they are more

George Doyle/Getty Images

Jovan Vidaakovic/Alamy Stock Photo

The way we eat is an example of the kind of habitus we develop. Think about how people in Western societies hold a fork and a knife. Some people hold a fork upside down in the left hand, with the tines facing downward. Others hold a fork in the right hand and use the tines in a scooping fashion, or use the fork to cut the food. These styles of using a fork and knife express class distinctions in something as basic as eating food. In China, by contrast, there are no class differences in how chopsticks are used, only in the quality of the chopsticks themselves.

competent with. Our own past experiences with love might make us leery of thinking of it in terms of commitment, so this will change how we navigate future romantic encounters. Or we may not have had much experience with commitment, such that when we try to use that cultural tool we don't do a good job of it. From this perspective, culture does not just establish differences in how we interpret the world and give it meaning but rather influences what kinds of strategies and actions are practically available to us.

Culture as a Form of Communication

10.1.4 Explain the ways in which culture is a form of communication.

Both culture as a system of meaning and symbols and culture as values, beliefs, and practices describe forms of *communication,* which is the sharing of meaningful information between people. One important way this occurs is through language. **Language** refers to any comprehensive system of words or symbols representing concepts, and it does not necessarily need to be spoken, as the hundreds of different sign languages in use around the world suggest. Culture and language are closely related. The ancient Greeks called the supposedly uncultured peoples they encountered "barbarians," which literally means people who babble—who have no language.

Researchers have disagreed over the years as to the importance of language for culture. At a basic level, language is a **cultural universal**, a cultural trait common to all humans: As far as we know, all human societies throughout history have used language to communicate with each other. Some linguists have even argued that language is the fundamental building block of thought—that if we don't have a word for something, we literally can't think it. The implication of this view is that a group's language is directly responsible for many of its cultural symbols and practices. A simple example is the distinction between two different words for "you" in French: An informal *tu* and a more formal *vous*. English used to have a similar distinction (*thou* versus *you*), but it died out over time. As a result, English speakers place less emphasis on formality in their communication with each other and hence in their group culture. But just because people speak the same language does not mean they share the same culture. Canadians and Americans both speak English, but of course there are many cultural differences between (and within) the two countries. Now most linguists and cultural sociologists believe that language *influences* culture without completely determining it. So while English no longer has an informal *you* and a formal *you*, this doesn't mean that all our conversations are informal. Instead, we have developed different ways of communicating those concepts, such as the frequent use in the South of *ma'am* and *sir* when speaking to an elder.

Communication can occur between individuals, or it can occur at large within society—what is normally called **mass communication**. In recent history, mass communication has occurred primarily through the mass media: Television, radio, and newspapers. At their peak, tens of millions of Americans watched the same nightly news broadcasts, and millions read the same daily newspaper in large metropolitan areas. To be sure, even prior to the emergence of the mass media, meaning was still communicated on a large scale, just not quite as large or as quickly; the Balinese cockfight could be considered a form of mass communication at a smaller scale, for example, as could a minister giving a sermon to a large congregation.

As the chapter opener illustrates, the internet has emerged as the main medium for mass communication today. People increasingly access traditional media sources online via newspaper websites or streaming video platforms such as Hulu and YouTube. In so doing, they also transform formerly passive media consumption (as represented by a printed newspaper or television news) into something they can participate in by writing comments, reposting stories, and blogging. Old media and new media now blur together (Jenkins 2006). But the internet has also created a whole new set of communication possibilities only loosely tied to previous forms of mass communication, most notably through messaging and platforms like Twitter.

Social media have altered the way children, adults, and (increasingly) older people engage with each other, both online and in person and at distances near and far. They have changed the ways corporations as well as anticorporate activists operate, the ways that charitable organizations raise funds (especially after a catastrophe), the ways that political officials campaign and govern, and the ways that social movements organize. They have affected the ways we get, and sometimes even make, news and entertainment. Cultural sociologists are curious about how and to what extent social media have transformed everyday life for people at different ages and in different places, as well as about how the rising use of social media will affect our interest in other kinds of media, from newspapers to telephones and radios to books.

The social theorist Manuel Castells argues that we are participating in a new form of internet-centered communication that he calls **mass self-communication** because it can potentially reach a global audience, but its content is often self-generated and self-directed (Castells 2009, p. 58). Everyone can create their own social media

Amy Sussman/KCA2021/Getty Images

One of the biggest TikTok stars in 2020 was Charli D'Amelio, a 16-year-old from Norwalk, Connecticut, who began making and posting dance videos filmed on her phone on TikTok in May 2019. Within months, she gained millions of followers and signed marketing deals with a number of corporations, developed her own line of clothing, and appeared in the Super Bowl halftime show in 2020. She and her family also launched their own reality TV show for the Hulu streaming service.

products. There have even been many examples of breakout social media stars who, starting with homemade videos posted on social media sites like YouTube or TikTok, have become international celebrities. At "collab" houses, like the Hype House in Los Angeles, some of the most successful practitioners live together and make and post new videos to be viewed by audiences numbering in the millions. In other words, the internet offers both the large-scale and ever-present nature of the mass media while also providing a platform for the creation of individualized content of interpersonal communication. The use of social media has exploded over the past decade, such that it now exceeds the reach of traditional media outlets among young people.

How are the internet and mass self-communication changing cultural systems and practices? If the constant flow of communications, information, and entertainment online makes it difficult to focus, does this also mean that our work and our relationships will suffer? Will our accumulation of Instagram followers be offset by a loss in deep friendships, or does connecting through social media make us more likely to spend time with others offline? Will our ideas become more superficial because we'll lack the attention span necessary to develop them? Will we lose interest in certain cultural genres—traditional news reporting, literary novels, nonfiction books—in favor of others—news briefs, pulp fiction, video games—that either require less of our minds or deliver more immediate rewards?

It's hard to know for sure: When it comes to information and communication, the last few decades have probably been the most rapid period of transformation in history. And access to technology is creating new types of divisions of haves and have-nots, in the form of the social, economic, and cultural gap between those with and without effective access to information technology, known as the **digital divide**. In the early days of the internet, this was the divide between those who were connected and those who were not, or between those with high-speed access and those in the slow lane. While there are households without high-speed internet access, more recently the divide has come to be understood as between those with the education and media literacy to navigate around the more innovative and independent sites and those who mainly visit the big commercial sites (Klinenberg 2007). There is also a clear age divide, with younger "digital natives" growing up in the age of the internet versus older "digital immigrants" who have to try to keep up with the changes (Palfrey and Gasser 2008).

As computers and the internet become more important to everyday life around the world, understanding the causes and effects of the digital divide will be one of the most important tasks for sociologists of culture and communication.

Mark Bussell

BIG QUESTION 10.2 How Does Culture Shape Our Collective Identity?

CULTURE AND GROUP IDENTITY

We all think of ourselves as belonging to numerous different groups. Some of these groups are relatively easy to define—for example, nationality or religion—but others are less clear. Are football fans a group? What about university students? If so, how can we tell? More fundamentally, what makes up group identity, and how do sociologists study it? It turns out that culture is central to group identity—both in defining a group and in maintaining it. Some scholars even suggest that we should only use the word *culture* to refer to differences and similarities that form the basis for groups coming together or clashing with each other (Appadurai 1996, p. 13).

Mainstream Culture, Subcultures, and Countercultures

10.2.1 Discuss the role culture plays in establishing group style, and explain what distinguishes a subculture from the mainstream.

In the absence of clear ways to define where one cultural group ends and another begins, we need to take our cues from shared behaviors. One way of thinking about identity in cultural terms is through the concept of **group style**, or the set of norms and practices that distinguishes one group from another (Eliasoph and Lichterman 2003). Different groups have different **norms**, or shared assumptions about correct behavior. And because most of us belong to multiple groups, we learn to adopt the right style for the right occasion. Adopting the right style is not always a simple matter, though—think of how difficult it would be to fit in if we were suddenly transported to a different time or place. Group style is thus a way for people to communicate

belonging (or not belonging). According to this account of identity formation, culture is a practice of communication.

Mainstream culture—the most widely shared systems of meaning and cultural tool kits in a society—is expressed in the activities and norms of many groups. The Chamber of Commerce, established religious groups, alumni associations, sports teams, civic organizations, and many other such groups accept and embrace the mainstream culture in one or another aspect of their activities. But some groups deliberately set themselves off from mainstream culture. Contemporary sociologists refer to such groups as **subcultures**, or relatively small groups of people whose affiliation is based on shared beliefs, preferences, and practices that exist under the mainstream (literally *sub*cultures) and distinguish them from the mainstream. Examples might include bodybuilders, online gamers, skateboarders, and cosplayers. Sociologist Claude Fischer (1975) claimed that subcultures are most likely to emerge in cities, where—unlike in small towns and traditional villages—the large, concentrated population allows many such groups to flourish. Some subcultures may have a clearly articulated sense of common purpose or definition, while others may be only loosely connected by mutual interests. Social media has done a remarkable job of allowing individuals to find peers who share common interests and experiences that they are unable to find in their offline lives. From trans teens to "bronies" to people suffering unusual medical ailments, platforms like Facebook, Reddit, and Twitter have served as the umbrellas under which countless new communities and identities can grow and thrive, creating abundant new sources of support and intimacy.

While subcultures often exist in harmony with mainstream culture—there's nothing socially threatening about rock climbers, for example—cultural-studies scholars have argued that some subcultures express differences in political

Countercultural groups such as punks use their appearance and behaviors to deliberately set themselves off from mainstream culture, as these individuals do at a May Day demonstration in Trafalgar Square in London.

and economic power and that setting ourselves apart from the cultural mainstream is often an act of "resistance through rituals" (Hall and Jefferson 1975). This type of subculture is usually called a **counterculture**—a group whose ideas, attitudes, and behaviors are in direct conflict with mainstream culture and who actively contest the dominant cultural practices in the societies of which they are a part. Some recent or current countercultural groups include antigovernment militias, the Tea Party, the Black Lives Matter movement, and the hippies of the 1960s. The fervent supporters of Donald Trump, especially in organizing a "Stop the Steal" campaign after the 2020 election, could also be considered a countercultural group in their challenge to democratic elections and standard vote-counting procedures.

Sociologists consider culture an arena of struggle, that is, competing ways of thinking, acting, and believing are always in competition with one other. It could also be the case that mainstream cultures, subcultures, and countercultures are unequally ranked and seek to reap the rewards that come from gaining cultural influence (Clarke et al. 1975, p. 11).

Is There a Dominant Culture in the United States Today?

10.2.2 Discuss the concept of "culture wars," and explain the importance of practicing cultural relativism in the multicultural United States.

It only makes sense to speak of subcultures and countercultures when there is a dominant mainstream culture that they can challenge. In some times and places, it may be clear that there is a single, dominant mainstream culture. In other places, it is less clear. We can reasonably ask, is there a single dominant culture in the United States in the twenty-first century?

The Italian revolutionary and Marxist theorist Antonio Gramsci famously argued in the 1930s that the dominant economic classes in any society attempt to maintain their power by encouraging certain moral and cultural understandings that are favorable to them. The process by which powerful groups gain legitimacy and hold power based on establishing or reinforcing widely shared beliefs about what is right or wrong, proper or improper, valuable or not, is called **hegemony**. When these views become taken for granted, they can help to reinforce the dominant group's authority. For example, in America today, it's common sense to think that people should work to earn enough money to live, that those who work harder or better will get ahead, and that people who choose not to work should only be entitled to the bare minimum of financial support. But such commonsense notions could easily be said to serve the interests of wealthy business owners, who need to find hard workers for their businesses to succeed. Gramsci argued that movements seeking to radically transform a society needed not just to win political power but to overthrow cultural hegemony—to fight common sense with good sense. Culture, in other words, is not just entertainment; it's an arena of perpetual conflict.

In the early 1990s, the sociologist James Hunter argued that the main battle lines of American electoral politics were shifting from economic questions to moral questions and that conflicts over family and religious values were so intense as to constitute **culture wars** (Hunter 1991). Hunter claimed that Americans tended to line up on one of two sides on many "hot-button" issues such as abortion, guns, gay rights, and the role of religion. He labeled these two camps "progressive" and "orthodox." Being socially progressive or orthodox, sometimes called "conservative," didn't necessarily correspond to social class or political affiliation—though those who identified with orthodox cultural issues tended to vote for Republicans, while progressives tended to align with Democrats—but instead to a person's definition of right and wrong. In the last three decades, new fronts of the culture war have opened, with battles including such issues as climate change; the Black Lives Matter movement; the inclusion of women and people of color in television, movies, and video games; transgender rights; monuments of Confederate soldiers and slave owners; NFL players kneeling during the National Anthem; and getting vaccinated—or the explicit refusal to do so—during the COVID-19 pandemic.

Former President Donald Trump did much to intensify the divisions of the culture wars relating to racial and ethnic diversity. He took loud and very determined positions about who is appropriately thought of as American,

Mark Bussell

A recent protest against abortion and euthanasia in Washington, D.C. The battle over abortion has been raging in the United States and around the world for many decades. Most countries have now adopted the right of any woman to have an abortion, even in majority Catholic countries like Ireland, in which 66 percent of voters in a 2018 referendum voted to repeal abortion restrictions.

emphasizing Christianity, patriotism, and the belief that Americans are superior to other peoples. He often used very derogatory terms when talking about immigrants and people of color. He characterizes his ideological opponents as both dangerous and anti-American. As a political leader engaging in the culture wars, Trump sought to reinforce a narrow definition of American cultural identity—with "real" Americans limited, in effect, to those who supported his policies. The "Make America Great Again" slogan harkened back to a time when the United States had fewer immigrants, such as in the 1950s. Trump's power in the culture wars is evidenced by the fact that even after he left the presidency, there are large numbers of Americans who continue to believe and promote his message.

Trump's vision about the virtues of an American culture similar to the one he grew up in the 1950s is at odds with a very different way of describing the contemporary group-identity landscape of the United States: Multiculturalism. **Multiculturalism** refers to beliefs or policies promoting the equal accommodation of different ethnic or cultural groups within a society. Societies with large immigrant populations, such as the United States, will contain people of different cultural backgrounds, creating new and varied types of cultural ideas. Indeed, in a country where 40 percent of Americans are non-White and about a quarter of the population are either first or second generation immigrants, it is increasingly complicated to define what exactly it means to be American today. From a sociological perspective, this makes it increasingly difficult to identify what, exactly, is the mainstream culture. Even the English language is hardly universal in American households

(about 30 percent of Americans do not speak English in their homes). To see this, explore just how multilingual the United States is in Figure 10.1.

For some observers, the current challenge of multiculturalism will eventually go away, as immigrant groups assimilate into the mainstream. Historically, the standard metaphor for this process was the *melting pot*, the idea that although immigrants come from all sorts of diverse cultural backgrounds, they will eventually become assimilated into American society until they become, at some point, genuinely American. The history of White immigrant groups from Europe in the late nineteenth and early twentieth centuries seems to confirm this idea (Jacobson 1998). But the melting pot idea is a controversial one today; it is often seen as an example of **ethnocentrism**—an inability to understand or accept cultural practices different from one's own. It also has never been clear whether Black Americans are allowed to "melt" into the mainstream (Coates 2015). More generally, the question may become whether the "mainstream" will itself become more accepting and diverse, or more exclusionary and hostile to new groups.

The problem with ethnocentrism is that it encourages us to make incorrect assumptions about others on the basis of our own experience—the classical issue of stereotyped thinking. If Clifford Geertz had observed the Balinese cockfight from an ethnocentric point of view, he simply would have concluded that many Balinese made risky and irresponsible bets, or he might have focused on the issue of animal rights and the harms of cockfighting to the cocks used in the fights. Or imagine if we went to a Chinese restaurant and concluded that the owners must not have heard about forks and knives because they brought us chopsticks. Although we have all been raised in specific cultural contexts that will influence our thinking in unacknowledged ways—and so we can never escape ethnocentrism entirely—these kinds of assumptions make it difficult to understand other cultures with any kind of depth. We will misinterpret shared meanings or fail to grasp what is important in a given situation.

For this reason, **cultural relativism**—evaluating cultural meanings and practices in their own social contexts—is central to the sociological imagination (Lukes 2008). For example, Geertz didn't try to discover the cultural significance of the Balinese cockfight in general, but rather its significance *for the Balinese*. When we travel to foreign lands, we will have a much more enriching experience trying to understand what we observe if we try not to compare it to

Figure 10.1 The Multilingual United States

America has always had a history of multilingualism, and with every new wave of immigration the linguistic diversity of the United States continues to grow. This map shows the wide variance in the percentage of Americans who spoke a language other than English at home in 2019. In some parts of the U.S., over one-third of households do not speak English at home.

Americans Who Do Not Speak English at Home

200 mi

SOURCE: American Community Survey, 2019.

our own world but rather try to understand it on its own terms. In fact, we will often learn far more new things from travelling and experiencing new cultures if we are open to the possibility that embedded within strange or unusual foreign traditions are things that our own cultural traditions might benefit from. From a global perspective, no one culture can ever be truly universal. Thus, cultural relativism is the opposite of ethnocentrism.

The issues raised by ethnocentrism and cultural relativism are often complicated in ways that require us to think more deeply if we are to apply a sociological imagination. For example, consider the question of **female genital cutting**, the practice of altering female genitalia. It is routinely denounced by journalists and activists in rich Western countries (the famous writer Alice Walker is one outspoken critic; see Walker and Parmar 1993). The United Nations estimated in 2016 that 200 million women had undergone the procedure, primarily in Africa, the Middle East, and parts of Asia, and usually at a young age (UNICEF 2016). The practice has a complicated history and purpose, but everywhere it is rooted in gender inequality and ideas about female sexuality. It is an example of a local practice that, through Western eyes, seems at first glance utterly and unquestionably oppressive, it is also one that—like the Balinese cockfight—can be viewed very differently in the local contexts where it has long been practiced (James and Robertson 2002; Wade 2012).

How can sociological research and theories provide insights that go beyond denouncing genital cutting from a Western perspective? For one thing, sociologists and other scientists can assess, through systematic empirical research, whether the practice is in fact safe for the women subjected to it (typically before the age of 5), as its proponents claim. That is a researchable question that could shed new light on the practice. Sociologists can also examine the role of power and compulsion in the practice; although some women may voluntarily accept the procedure, others clearly do not. Understanding the role of compulsion and violence may provide an alternative way of thinking about the practice (and its local reception). But above all else, a sociological approach should also consider the possibility that we can only fully understand the persistence of genital cutting if we first grasp the "moral background" of the communities in which it is practiced, and the meanings and purposes it serves (Abend 2014). Doing so can provide a much richer and more complex portrait (Wade 2012).

National Cultures

10.2.3 Explain what produces and reproduces national cultures and what effects they have.

Even in the era of globalization, the most important group identity in the modern world is surely the nation. The entire world is divided into nation-states, and most people are citizens or subjects of a single one of them. So it is not surprising that **national culture**, the set of shared cultural practices and beliefs within a given nation-state, is an important principle for sociology. Are there differences between cultural norms, assumptions, and identities between different nations? If so, what are they, what produces and reproduces them, and what effects do they have? These are the questions that sociologists try to answer about national cultures.

Today, it seems obvious that the world should be divided into nations and that people should think of themselves in these terms: I'm American and you're Canadian, she's British and they are Chinese. But it wasn't always so. The rise of **nationalism**—the fact that people think of themselves as inherently members of a nation and often take pride in that identity—is a relatively recent phenomena in world history. National communities only became possible with the mass production of books and newspapers written in local languages for simultaneous mass consumption by an increasingly literate public (Anderson 1991). When French people read French newspapers and German people read German newspapers, they not only learn what's happening in their respective countries, they also confirm their membership in a shared national culture. Even today, when newspaper readership is on the decline, other forms of shared media consumption follow the same pattern. A study of the geography of Twitter, for example, found that people's sources of news and information are generally national and unilingual—although in theory our experience of Twitter could be truly global, in practice it is likely to reinforce our sense of belonging to a certain nation (Takhteyev, et al. 2012).

A rising form of nationalism, one that combines a narrow definition of national identity with anti-immigrant sentiment, has created a new realm of cultural conflict. People holding **ethnonationalist** views believe that only a limited number of people can rightfully claim membership in a country—generally those who are native born or who are members of the dominant race, religion, or ethnicity (Bonikowski 2017). Ethnonationalism has been a feature of many emerging far-right movements in Western countries, including those supporting Donald Trump in the United States, Marine Le Pen in France, and Geert Wilders in the Netherlands, as well as the Brexit movement in the United Kingdom. These movements draw much of their support by employing a form of politics called **populism**, in which ordinary people are venerated and corrupt "elites" are vilified. While many politicians praise ordinary people and criticize elites, populists take this a step farther, claiming that they *alone* can represent the interests of "the people" (Müller 2016). Moreover, under right-wing populism,

only some people get to consider themselves a member of "the people," with other groups deemed unworthy of political representation. In right-wing populist movements, the "people" are never *all* the people.

When we examine national cultures around the world, we quickly realize that the situation in the United States is hardly unique. While it is true that citizens of any country will likely share many commonalities with each other, there are inevitably diverse influences and cultural traditions present almost everywhere in the world. At one extreme, consider a country like Indonesia, composed of 13,000 islands and home to over 700 languages. With the notable exception of some separatist regions at the periphery, Indonesians generally are able to imagine themselves to be a single national community. And importantly, they view their community as limited, as one among many. A national community is not like a religious community, whose practitioners may hope to convert the entire world to their faith. Indonesians, for example, don't want to make all Italians into Indonesians.

In contemporary life, cultural sociologists generally take nations for granted, the same way we all do, and many of them study the differences between national cultures: What makes the people of one nation different from another, and what are the implications of the differences? Before we turn to a discussion of the complexities, examine the data in Figure 10.2 about the large differences between people of different nations on some basic cultural attitudes.

To take one of the most widely believed differences as an example, Americans are thought to be more individualistic than people in other countries. Compared to people in other rich countries, Americans are more likely to believe that individuals should take care of themselves rather than look to the government to support them (Brooks and Manza 2007). But the importance of individualism is complicated. Consider the cultural shift in which more and more people choose to live by themselves. In spite of their apparent individualism, Americans are actually far less likely to live alone than are residents of apparently less individualistic nations, such as Sweden, Norway, Finland, and Denmark, (Klinenberg 2012). Why might this be? It can't be because of genetics or different types of human nature: There isn't anything fundamentally different about people in these countries. It turns out that a combination of different factors—including economic prosperity, the rising status of women, the communications revolution, mass urbanization, and the longevity revolution—all influence whether people want to and are able to live alone, not just the degree to which people have individualist views.

Indeed, many important social, political, economic, and cultural institutions are organized along national

Figure 10.2 Measures of Differences Between Nations

As these graphs illustrate, there are notable differences between people of different nations on some basic cultural attitudes.

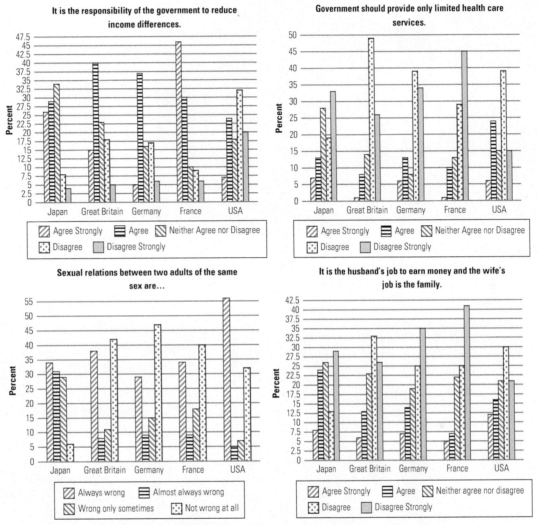

SOURCE: Author's analysis of International Social Survey Programme (ISSP) data.

lines, and these have systematic effects on the way people live their lives and the kinds of attitudes and worldviews they develop. These different worldviews can in turn have a big impact on other features of national life. In the United States, CEOs are paid extremely well, earning on average around 300 times more than the average worker at their company. Yet, in Japan, CEOs are paid far less, earning only one-ninth the salary of their U.S. counterparts (Kubota 2019). Researchers have struggled to explain this enormous and persistent difference between the two countries on the basis of economic considerations alone. Instead, it is likely that there are cultural factors at work (such as the different willingness of Japanese and American workers and citizens to accept income disparities; see Pan and Zhou 2018).

One important area of research is early childhood, because it is when we are children that many of our cultural assumptions are formed. There is a wonderful documentary made by the filmmaker Thomas Balmes called *Babies*, which shows remarkable differences in how the parents from four different societies raise their children (see also Druckerman [2013] for a comparison of French and American styles of raising a baby). One study of preschools in Japan, China, and the United States found very different roles that preschools play in forming cultural identities in these three countries (Tobin et al. 1989). By recording classroom activities and then discussing the videos with teachers and parents, the researchers found that U.S. preschools put heavy emphasis on creativity and respect for the children as individuals. In China, which used to restrict married couples to only a single child, the emphasis was on instilling order and discipline in the children, an approach that is understandable in the context of a society where

Preschools follow very different educational approaches in different countries. In this photo, Chinese preschoolers go on a field trip in Shanghai holding on to a group rope with their teachers.

"little emperors" are often seen as spoiled by their parents and grandparents. In Japan, meanwhile, educators left children to their own devices to a much greater degree than in the other two cases, forcing them to learn to get along respectfully with others.

These might seem like stereotypes, but that's exactly the point. If there are durable differences in cultural norms between different countries, we would expect to find evidence of them in institutions such as preschool. As the authors of the preschool study indicate, preschool both *reflects* national culture—because teachers and parents are influenced by certain ideas and try to pass them along—and helps *reproduce* it—because children inherit these same ideas.

BIG QUESTION 10.3 How Do Our Cultural Practices Relate to Class and Status?

CLASS, STATUS, AND CULTURE

How do we know whether people are wealthy or powerful? We can't see their bank accounts or tax returns. The chances are, however, that we can make an educated guess because of cultural signs: The way they dress, how they speak, the sports they play, the music they like, the kinds of things they like to do—in short, their **taste** and cultural preferences. Although we normally think about social class in mainly economic terms, taste—and culture

more broadly—plays a crucial role in setting and maintaining class distinctions.

Cultural Capital

10.3.1 **Define cultural capital and discuss ways American elites have become cultural omnivores.**

Contrary to popular belief that it is the land of opportunity for all, the United States is an intensely class-bound society. Someone who is born into the working class is very likely to stay working class for their entire life, and the same is true for someone born into the upper class. One way of understanding why that is the case is to think about the kinds of resources people can bring to bear in their lives. One kind of resource is money and other economic assets; another is social connections and networks of friends and acquaintances. Sociologist Pierre Bourdieu referred to these as *economic capital* and *social capital*, respectively. He also suggested a third type of resource important for determining class position: In addition to the money we have and the people we know, our success in life is also influenced by our **cultural capital**. This is our education, tastes, and cultural knowledge and our ability to display sophistication (or a lack thereof) in our speech, manners, and other everyday acts. Bourdieu argued that our cultural capital, as much as our wealth or connections, confers on us higher or lower status in the eyes of others (Bourdieu 1984).

We use our cultural capital all the time in interactions with others and often don't even realize we are doing so. Others size us up the moment we open our mouths and start offering opinions or thoughts about the world around us. Bourdieu did not consider public or over-the-top displays of status symbols to be an important form of cultural capital; instead, he emphasized the various ways that people display taste in everyday life. Being able to discuss why you enjoy the films of German director Werner Herzog, for example, signals to others that you have sophisticated taste in movies. Taste also implies distaste; if the person you are talking to doesn't know who Herzog is, perhaps you will have negative judgments about their own tastes and status. Even if you don't *consciously* judge other people on their tastes, the chances are that tastes will influence the kinds of people you want to spend time with or avoid. Tastes, therefore, help maintain status boundaries between different groups (Holt 1997).

Cultural capital requires scarcity: Cultural experiences that everyone can share cannot serve as the basis for status distinctions. Before the Swedish home-products company IKEA began to sell its inexpensive furniture, the aesthetic it applied (Scandinavian modernism) was considered a sign of high status. But because the middle class can afford IKEA furniture and shops there extensively, this aesthetic is no longer an embodiment of significant cultural capital. The issue is not money but difficulty: In order to provide a basis for signaling distinction, high-status cultural consumption must not be easy to participate in, and if it becomes easy it will stop being high status.

How does this notion of cultural capital apply to contemporary life in the United States? In his study of cultural capital in France, Bourdieu emphasized that upper-class groups tend to appreciate high culture and arts in ways that ordinary working people cannot appreciate. But the United States has a more pervasive mass culture than many other countries, one in which people of many different classes may listen to similar music or enjoy similar kinds of music or television. Recent research has suggested that American elites are less snobbish than those in other countries and are increasingly behaving as **cultural omnivores** who demonstrate their high status through a broad range of cultural consumption, including low-status culture. Highly educated Americans today are more likely than average to consume not only high culture but popular culture as well. It is a sign of distinction to have wide-ranging tastes, such as an appreciation for sports and modern dance, hip-hop as well as classical music, and so forth (Peterson and Kern 1996; Kahn 2009). In fact, a person who only knows about high-cultural stuff is at risk of being dismissed as a snob or seen as someone who is hopelessly out of touch.

Cultural capital is only valuable if it is rare or hard to obtain. Now that the middle class can easily buy modernist furniture at IKEA, that kind of furniture is no longer an important status symbol in and of itself. We now have new divisions, by brand. IKEA could be considered low-brow modern, while the more exclusive and expensive furniture sold by Herman Miller or expensive Italian design studios is considered high-brow modern.

Zhuravlev Andrey/Shutterstock

The idea of the cultural omnivore can be used to help us understand how elites sometimes pick and choose among the popular cultural forms they enjoy. For example, some cultural elites show a fondness for country music (a low-status genre more associated with the working class), but the type of country music elites generally enjoy is not the commercial country of Miranda Lambert or Jason Aldean but rather more "alternative" country acts such as Wilco or classic country such as Johnny Cash and Patsy Cline (Holt 1997). In the 1960s, some cultural analysts saw television as creating a new kind of mass culture, in which everyone was watching the same shows (Wilensky 1964). Yet this was actually a very unusual period, in which there were only three national television networks to watch. Once cable television arrived, and later digital streaming services, people started watching different shows (with networks like HBO attracting a more affluent group of viewers than the over-the-air broadcast channels like ABC, CBS, NBC, and FOX).

How Culture Reproduces Class

10.3.2 Analyze how money and culture reproduce status over the long term.

An important topic for sociologists concerned with power and inequality is the process that causes class boundaries and distinctions to be maintained over time, known as **class reproduction**. There are lots of reasons why some people are rich and others poor, but how do those boundaries get maintained in the short term as well as over the longer term? Bourdieu's theory of cultural capital examines how, in countless everyday interactions, we remind ourselves and others about our relative statuses, and this helps to ensure that our status differences persist. But what explains class and status reproduction over the long term and across generations? For example, why are middle-class children likely to grow up into middle-class adults and working-class children likely to grow up into working-class adults?

One obvious answer is money: Wealthier families will have an easier time affording private schools, ACT or SAT preparation courses, college tuition, and personal tutors, for example, and they also will likely leave sizable inheritances to their children. But money only explains part of the story: Sociologists have shown that people make meaningful choices about how to live that are limited but not solely determined by their economic circumstances. The question of how and why we make the choices we do is what culture helps to explain.

For example, in one famous study, the sociologist and ethnographer Paul Willis (1977) followed a set of boys from working-class homes in a British industrial town in the 1970s. They frequently behaved badly in school, were rebellious, and didn't seem to care much about their futures. A standard opinion at the time was that such cases were simply people failing to make the right choices to get ahead in life. But Willis found it was quite the opposite: The boys' apparently unproductive behavior in school was in fact their way of adapting to their class circumstances. The same attitudes that got them in trouble with their teachers turned out to serve them very well in factory work a few years later, where standing up to authority and not working hard on command helped workers gain collective leverage against their bosses. The rebellious boys were learning how to be working-class men.

A more recent study by sociologist Annette Lareau compared middle-class and working-class families in the United States to see how different class positions affect parents' approaches to childrearing and what the implications of the differences are for children's futures. During the study, it became clear that there were two quite different approaches. Middle-class parents followed an approach of what Lareau called *concerted cultivation*, actively fostering their child's talents and intervening on their behalf, thereby instilling a sense of entitlement. Working-class parents, by contrast, followed an approach of *accomplishment of natural growth*, caring for their children but leaving them to fend for themselves socially in a variety of settings (Lareau 2003). The middle-class children's sense of entitlement will make it more likely that they push to succeed socioeconomically when they are older, while the reverse is true of the working-class children, making it more likely that as they get older these children will stay in the class they were born into.

The implication of both of these classical studies is that class is reproduced not only through the money you (or your family) have but through the culture you learn and practice growing up.

Allan Baxter/Getty Images

BIG QUESTION 10.4 Who Produces Culture, and Why?

THE CONDITIONS OF CULTURAL PRODUCTION

In 1845, Karl Marx and Friedrich Engels argued that the people who have the most wealth and power in a society generally also have the greatest ability to produce and distribute their own ideas and culture (Marx and Engels [1845] 1972). In nineteenth-century Europe, these people were capitalists, such as factory owners and bankers, who valued their rights to own private property and their freedom to run their businesses as they saw fit. By using their influence with newspaper owners, politicians, and some intellectuals, they were able to make liberty and freedom the dominant ideas of the age.

Marx and Engels's argument suggests that cultural production is a historical phenomenon. Ideas and fashions don't just change randomly over time; they respond to other changes in a society's political and economic circumstances. At the same time, in the nineteenth century it was much more difficult to spread ideas than it is today. Printing presses were expensive, and much of the population was illiterate. Today, with the internet and social media, do powerful people and classes still have control over the production of culture? Does Gramsci's notion of hegemony adequately characterize the cultural environment of the twenty-first century? Sociologists of culture are paying increasingly careful attention to the changing *conditions of cultural production*: Who controls the production of ideas in society, and to what ends?

The Public Sphere

10.4.1 Analyze how the concept of the public sphere explains how culture is produced in society.

A basic premise of public life in a democracy such as the United States is that everyone is allowed to participate in the discussions, debates, and elections that decide who shall govern. In theory, everyone over 18 can vote, can run for public office (usually if a person is over 25, or 35 to run for president), or can start a political organization to try to convince other people of their point of view. This vision of equal participation in political life is a powerful one, and it centers on the idea that there exists what German sociologist Jurgen Habermas described as the **public sphere** (Habermas [1962] 1989). According to Habermas, when private citizens assemble in groups (wherever that might be) to confer about matters of general interest, they are engaging in critical activities for democratic life. In an ideal public sphere, citizens set aside their own interests, as well as their wealth and status, and meet as equals to collectively debate and generate ideas about how to govern collectively. And individuals have influence only because of the power and value of their ideas.

In eighteenth-century Europe, when the public sphere began to emerge, it was centered in a range of institutions such as newspapers, pubs, social clubs, and coffee shops—in short, any location where people could gather and discuss the news of the day. The public sphere stood apart from the state and offered citizens a way to criticize and influence the government, which was a novel idea in an age of absolute monarchies. In modern welfare states such as the United States, the public sphere is where different social groups organize to become political actors and compete for influence. Lobbying groups like the National Rifle Association, which generally promotes the expansion of gun ownership; social movements like the Tea Party, which sought to lower taxes and reduce government spending; Fight for $15, which has called for an increase in the minimum wage; Black Lives Matter, which has been working to end structural racism and reform the criminal justice system—these are examples of groups that have prominent voices in today's public sphere. An important way they compete is by trying to shape public opinion through the production of ideas, for example, in newspapers, on television, and with advertising. In contemporary society such as the United States, the public sphere today is increasingly becoming organized online, and in particular through social media.

However appealing the image of the ideal public sphere may be, in practice public participation is massively unequal. Many people choose not to have any interest in politics or to vote in elections. Further, it is very hard to attract an audience for your ideas if you don't have a fair amount of money backing you. For example, the previously mentioned Tea Party movement, which emerged in 2009 and has generally sought to lower taxes and reduce government spending, received many millions of dollars in funding from a small number of wealthy conservatives. The Black Lives Matter movement, which formed in 2013 and promotes racial justice, has relied on much smaller amounts of money, generally from small donations. As a result, the Tea Party was able to spend more money on advertising and promotion, on bankrolling their preferred political candidates, and on other activities that gave its members influence in the public sphere. (The movement was largely abandoned by Republicans with the election of Donald Trump, who, while lowering taxes, pushed the government's deficit to an all-time high. Trump was actually not initially supported by many Tea Party groups for this reason.) Meanwhile, for many years, Black Lives Matter activists struggled to be heard; only with the national outcry over the murder of George Floyd in Minneapolis in the spring of 2020 did BLM protests gain national media attention (see chapter 22 for more details). In general, sociologists argue that the same things that give some people power over others in private life—such as race, gender, class, and education—will give some people more influence in the public sphere (Fraser 1992).

Another problem with the ideal image of the public sphere is that there has never been one overarching public sphere; rather, various social groups—and subcultures—have frequently constituted their own **counterpublics**, alternative public spheres through which they produce and circulate their own values, beliefs, and ideas. The unions produced one kind of counterpublic in the first half of the twentieth century, and the networks of Black churches that formed the backbone of the civil rights movement and the bars and clubs where the gay liberation movement began are all examples of American counterpublics over the years.

Fragmented publics do not necessarily need to be subordinate, either: The concept can apply to any subculture. For instance, the users of social networking sites such as Twitter or Instagram can be understood as constituting what researchers sometimes refer to as a **networked public**, or online public sphere. Networked publics attract participation from teenagers in particular because of things they offer that face-to-face public settings cannot. Social networking allows for persistence (on many social networking sites we can browse through posts and message histories years after they were initially posted), searchability (we can seek out other people with similar interests and connect with existing friends regardless of geographical proximity), replicability (it is hard to distinguish the "original" from the "copy" when copy-and-paste is ubiquitous), and invisible audiences (much of our activity on social networks is potentially being observed by people we don't know, and perhaps at totally different times), and these features make networked publics distinct public spheres (Boyd 2008). Regardless of whether there is one public sphere or many, the concept of the networked public forces us to think broadly about how ideas and culture are produced and how people participate in that production.

The Culture Industry versus Cultural Democracy

10.4.2 Compare and contrast the cultural industry and the cultural democracy perspectives.

Who controls popular culture today, and who benefits from it? Is it the corporations that produce it at a profit, or the public who consumes it, shares it, and enjoys it? If record labels, movie studios, and advertising agencies heavily push the latest songs and movies on us, when we enjoy them are we dupes or are we exercising cultural free will? Sociologists have been largely split on these questions between two perspectives: One that sees popular culture as an industry and one that sees popular culture as a democratic arena—a cultural public sphere.

Writing after World War II, the German sociologist and philosopher Theodor Adorno argued that the popular culture that dominates the public sphere encourages a passive, conservative public. He was referring to popular music, movies, and other types of mass culture, all of which he labeled the **culture industry** (Horkheimer and Adorno [1947] 2002). His chief complaint was that popular culture encourages audiences to passively consume what they are watching, reading, or listening to rather than participating or engaging creatively with the work. The kind of culture that the culture industry produces is standardized and commoditized, and does not challenge the status quo; at the end of the day, it is advertising rather than art.

Other sociologists have argued that Adorno's critique of popular culture (along with others like it) was too pessimistic. They instead believe that popular culture provides an arena through which we all debate the meaning of the good life and the conditions for attaining it—an explicitly cultural version of Habermas's public sphere. One response, for example, to Adorno's claim that most people passively receive the culture that is offered to them is that popular culture is user driven. Cultural producers want to attract an audience, so they tailor their art to reflect popular preferences (Gans 1999). Movie studios wouldn't keep releasing the same kind of movies if people didn't want to watch them, and when people vote with their time and money by choosing not to watch a certain kind of movie, studios will stop making that kind of movie. According to this perspective, popular culture is an element of *cultural democracy*. In the cultural marketplace, lots of different tastes—including those of subcultures, such as hip-hop, that elites disapprove of—are accommodated. Different cultural styles exist "because they satisfy the needs and wishes of some people, even if they dissatisfy those of other people" (Gans 1999, p. 91).

The Medium Is the Message

10.4.3 Discuss the ways in which communication changes with the form or medium.

Debates over whether popular culture is an industry, a democracy, or something else focus not only on the content of popular culture but just as often on its form. If the same content is broadcast on cable TV and on Twitter, will it communicate the same thing? The answer from communications theory is that it won't. As the media theorist Marshall McLuhan famously declared, the medium is the message (McLuhan 1964). By this, McLuhan meant that different media encourage different ways of communicating, of organizing power, and of centralizing or decentralizing social activity.

Compare listening to a news bulletin on the radio with reading the same news on a website. There are some obvious differences: For example, when we hear the news on the radio, we hear only what the announcer says, while on a website we have the opportunity to follow hyperlinks and look up unfamiliar things on Wikipedia. In this respect, the web offers a richer experience than the radio. But there are some other differences that may not be as obvious. On the radio, we can't follow hyperlinks, but we also have a harder time skimming the material the way we can on a website. Radio dominates one of our senses—hearing—and prompts us to devote most of our attention to receiving and processing the information we are hearing. A website, by contrast, provides us with a more ambiguous sensory experience. There might be sound and video on the webpage, but there might be just text. We might be listening to music in the background, or we might have an instant messaging window open simultaneously. Reading news on a website requires more of our direct engagement than listening to the radio does. Different forms of communication can thus provide very different experiences even when communicating the exact same content.

Cultural production in the United States is increasingly occurring online. But an arguably greater transition was from the age of typography to the *age of television* (Postman 1985). From the sixteenth century until midway through the twentieth century, discussions of public issues in the West were primarily based in the written word and in this sense biased toward careful and considered thought. Personal communication, for example, largely occurred via letters, which took a long time to write and be delivered, encouraging people to thoughtfully consider what they wanted to say. Similarly, large-scale communication occurred through books and pamphlets, which also encouraged thoughtfulness. Beginning in the 1950s, however, public communication increasingly shifted toward television. TV became the primary way in which people got their news about the world. According to some communications scholars, this age of television led to a decline in the quality of public discourse. How much of what we see on the news has any actual relevance for our lives in the sense that it will cause us to make different decisions? Endless reporting of distant natural disasters, for example, is irrelevant to our daily lives, and this helps promote a loop of impotence because we become used to passively receiving information without expecting to be able to act on it in any meaningful way. What's more, the information we receive through television tends to arrive in a series of short, disconnected sound bites, which make it difficult for us to put them in any coherent context. Ultimately, the bias of television as a medium is toward stimulation and entertainment, possibly at the expense of understanding.

We no longer live in the age of television. Things have changed dramatically since the 1980s, when the internet only existed in a few scientific and government laboratories, and no one had cell phones. Our media consumption habits have changed as well. Today, no single medium of communication dominates the way television did for most of the second half of the twentieth century. One particularly striking change in media consumption is the increase in cultural multitasking—for example, when you watch TV, how often are you also checking Instagram, browsing the internet, or texting with a friend? The contemporary media environment is a "torrent": a nonstop flow of information that we rarely if ever disengage from. The torrent doesn't so much command our active attention as it forms a sensory background for our lives (Gitlin 2007). As we all live our lives in an increasingly online and interconnected fashion, just how cultural production continues to change in the years ahead will be a crucial question for both sociologists and the public at large.

Social media has also changed the nature of political communication, perhaps exemplified most clearly by former President Donald Trump's extraordinarily successful use of Twitter. As a presidential candidate and while in office, Trump tweeted constantly, allowing him to bypass the filter of traditional media outlets and communicate directly to voters, while also building and maintaining a direct connection with his supporters. Stylistically, the tweets—short, pugnacious, and occasionally vulgar—set him apart from other American politicians, who have traditionally favored communicating in long, formal speeches. Yet, Trump's social media rhetoric also often pushed the boundaries of political decorum. On numerous occasions, Trump used Twitter to make false and misleading statements, many of them targeting ethnic and racial minority group members, to disparage individuals, leading to their harassment—in 2018, for example, he insulted the leader of a steelworker's union in Indianapolis, Indiana, after which the man received numerous threatening phone calls—as well as to occasionally re-tweet violent, far-right videos to his followers. Long after the 2020 presidential election was settled (and he lost), Trump used Twitter to tell his followers that he really won the election and that the election results were fraudulent.

Mark Bussell

BIG QUESTION 10.5 What Is the Relationship between Media and Democracy?

MEDIA AND DEMOCRACY: A CHANGING LANDSCAPE

It has long been obvious that how the news is presented is vital to how citizens develop their social and political views about the world. In this sense, the news media are a key element of the larger impact of culture in society. Writing nearly 100 years ago, the famous journalist Walter Lippmann was skeptical of the media's ability to provide the public with the information necessary for a democracy. He argued that "news and truth are not the same thing." Democracy requires truth, but the news can only describe and discuss events from day to day. Lippmann believed democracy required a collective intelligence, which could only be had with extensive social organization, and that here the press could only play a small part, although a necessary one (Lippmann 1922, p. 358). The media are arguably the most important form of cultural production in our society, and if we want to understand the broader impact of culture in society, it is important to consider how the media relate to democracy (a topic we broached in the previous section when we introduced the concept of the public sphere). In this section, we consider that relationship.

Making the News: The Media as a Cultural System

10.5.1 Explain the role the media play in making the news.

Journalism—the production and dissemination of information of general public interest—is above all else a form of cultural communication. But sociologists of the media are in broad agreement that the news does a lot more than just pass along facts to the public. By deciding what to cover and how to cover it, journalists don't simply report on the news, they actually help to create and change it (Schudson 2003, p. 11).

How does the news have this kind of power, and is it a good thing? There are plenty of concerns about the power of the media. Common leftist critiques suggest that the mass media support corporate power, militarism, and the interests of the wealthiest. Common conservative critiques suggest that the media make the culture more liberal and spread feminism, environmentalism, and the acceptance of same-sex relationships and the LGBTQ community. Political insiders on all sides believe the media exert a kind of **agenda-setting** power—that is, the ability of media executives to choose what is important enough to be considered "news"—that can change the course of political events.

The problem with these debates is that it is difficult to prove that the media actually have this influence. There are anecdotes on both sides. For example, one famous example of apparent media influence was during the Vietnam War. Up until 1968, TV news coverage was favorable to the war, sanitizing violence and especially U.S. casualties. That changed in 1968, most famously with CBS news anchor Walter Cronkite's February on-air editorial calling for negotiations with the Viet Cong (the North Vietnamese forces battling the U.S.). It is widely believed that media criticism of the war prompted a turning point in galvanizing opposition to the war. An example of the opposite situation occurred in the aftermath of the terrorist attacks of 9/11, when relentless media coverage of the bombings led to overwhelming public support for going to war against the perceived perpetrators, in Afghanistan and later in Iraq (even though there was no evidence that the Iraqi government had any involvement). These examples suggest that when it comes to even the most important decisions the government makes—those concerning wars—the media may exert considerable influence. Yet these are relatively rare examples in which there was a one-sided flow of information (for or against a war). In most cases, the news media are either less focused or provide more ambiguous coverage.

Dramatic examples like 9/11 and the Vietnam War also neglect the fact that people get their information about the world not just from what they hear in the media but also from talking to other people, from the views expressed in groups they may be a member of (including their churches), and from ideas they may have learned in school or through their own personal experiences. Because the media are so visible and audible, they are sometimes presumed to be important forces in society. But if the public doesn't passively receive whatever the media tell it, how do the media have their influence? According to media scholar Michael Schudson, the media act as a cultural system: They set the context for making events in the world intelligible. They do this by helping construct a community and a public conversation. Regardless of our opinions on a given issue, when we hear about it in the news we are more likely to treat it as an event of importance. This is why public relations experts say, "There's no such thing as bad press." The news amplifies issues and makes them publicly legitimate.

Pressures on Contemporary Journalism and News Media

10.5.2 Identify trends in the U.S. media landscape that have put commercial pressure on journalism.

One of the premises of the free press in a democracy is that citizens will be exposed to a variety of perspectives and sources of information in order to participate meaningfully in public life. Journalists covering stories and uncovering corruption are central to the flow of information to the people. More Americans now get their news from social media. Indeed, with the ceaseless flood of tweets, Instagram posts, and Facebook updates, it can feel like we get *more* news than ever. Yet increasing pressures on news journalism may serve to actually limit the kinds of information Americans receive. In addition, there are growing threats to the journalism profession that are making its critical role uncertain in the future.

Historically, journalists were employed by traditional media outlets. But revenues for many of these outlets have dropped precipitously, as fewer people subscribe to print magazines and newspapers or watch television news programs. Businesses are spending less money on print and television news advertisements than in the past. Today, tech companies command a high proportion of online advertising fees.

In recent years, more and more local radio stations, TV stations, and newspapers have also been bought up by large corporations. The politically conservative Sinclair Broadcast Group, for example, now owns almost 300 local TV stations in 89 different markets, while Tribune Publishing owns one of every five daily newspapers. Many of these corporations, looking for a higher return on their investment, have cut costs through layoffs. Between 2008 and 2019, the number of newsroom employees—including reporters, editors, and photographers—dropped by approximately half. While online news sites, like *Buzzfeed* and *Vox*, have grown, there are still fewer people reporting the news now than there was 20 years ago, especially when it comes to local news. And many online sites have struggled to raise enough revenue from online ads to stay viable. This means fewer journalists are available to act as the public watchdog of government and to hold the powerful accountable. How can you know what's happening in Washington—or City Hall—unless there's a reporter there to pay attention? The decline of local news reporting has been an especially important source of decline in news information available to citizens. In many communities, there are few or no professional journalists covering stories.

Another important source of pressure on journalism that has emerged in recent years is the idea, held by many supporters of former President Donald Trump, that professional journalists are producing "fake news." (We'll discuss the consequences of the spread of fake news in more detail in the next section.) Presidents and political leaders everywhere have always complained about the press, but former President Trump took this animus to worrisome new heights. According to one analysis, while Trump was president, 1 in 10 of his tweets insulted or criticized journalists, specific news organizations, or the media as a whole (Sugars 2019). He frequently accused reporters of falsifying information, labeling journalists as "the enemy of the people" (recycling a popular phrase from Communist Russia and China). This rhetorical assault appears to be taking a toll. By 2018, more than half of Americans said they had lost faith in the media. If journalists are to continue providing a check on the powerful in the future, that loss of confidence will need to be restored.

Media, Democracy, and the Internet

10.5.3 Discuss the ways the internet has created new opportunities and dangers for the free media and for democracy.

The notion that the press is vital to democracy is an old one. Thomas Jefferson, for instance, famously said that "Were it left to me to decide whether we should have a government without newspapers, or newspapers without a government, I should not hesitate a moment to prefer the latter." Almost all scholars who study politics and democracy believe that the media are necessary to provide a forum for debate (to help constitute the public sphere, in other words), to give a voice to public opinion, to serve as citizens' eyes and ears in politics, and to serve as a public watchdog over government and business (Graber 2003).

When social media first emerged, there was hope that, by unleashing new kinds of information and bringing more people into the public sphere, it would help create societies that were more open, participatory, and fair. These hopes received a boost with the 2011 Arab Spring uprising in the Middle East. Crucial to those protests' initial success was the use of social networking sites, particularly Facebook and Twitter, which helped activists mobilize supporters, coordinate their actions, and publish up-to-the-minute news on demonstrations against the authoritarian governments. Not only were people receiving information that those in power would prefer they not, but they were using it to organize and petition for expanded rights. Yet the dream of social media ushering in a new era of democracy soon dimmed. Many authoritarian governments quickly figured out that they, too, could make use of social media to surveil and track protestors, spread disinformation, and crack down on dissent (Tufecki 2018).

In a broader sense, social media as a source of news and information has come to be viewed much more ambivalently than it was at first. Just as social media has enormous power to spread truth, it has an unparalleled ability to spread misinformation. Social media has comparatively few restrictions on what users can publish. This has led to the proliferation of completely false stories—headlines or articles that resemble news stories but are designed to make people angry or change their opinion about something. There is even some evidence that fake stories are written and deliberately spread by software tools known as bots (Guglielmi 2020). In some cases, these made-up

stories have been spread by foreign governments attempting to manipulate American political life.

Unfortunately, many people are unable to tell the difference between a false and real news report. By highlighting sensational (or false) claims, fake stories can sometimes spread more easily than genuine ones! One analysis, for example, found that the most popular fake stories about the 2016 election received more shares and comments than the most popular stories from legacy media organizations like the *Washington Post* and the *New York Times* (Silverman 2016). In addition, a study by researchers at MIT of rumors on Twitter found that false rumors tended to reach far more people than true ones (Vosoughi et al. 2018). Allowing untruths to proliferate without interference has serious implications for democracy. Not only does it leave citizens ignorant, but it also gives political parties and governments new tools to shape public attitudes. As noted, authoritarian governments can employ the platforms to discredit their opposition and disseminate dangerous propaganda, including in other countries. In the worst cases, governments have used disinformation to sway elections, at home and abroad, or to demonize minority groups. Myanmar's military, for example, used hundreds of fake accounts on Facebook to systematically spread false rumors and incite hatred of the Muslim Rohingya ethnic group, leading to thousands of its members being raped, killed, and exiled through forced migration (Mozur 2018).

Social media's special propensity to spread misinformation is vividly illustrated by the growing popularity of conspiracy theories. "Conspiracy theories" are attempts to explain the causes of significant social and political events by pinning responsibility on a set of malevolent actors, working in secret (Douglas et al. 2019). Most of these theories have little basis in fact and involve significant leaps in logic. (This is not to say that *conspiracies* themselves cannot exist: Indeed, throughout history, groups have frequently plotted in secret to commit illegal or harmful acts. The distinction between conspiracy and conspiracy theories, however, is that the latter is inherently speculative and lacks a solid grounding in evidence.) Social media has allowed a number of conspiracy theories, many originating on the far right, to flourish. These include "Pizzagate," in which prominent Democrats were rumored to be abusing children in the basement of a Washington, D.C., pizza parlor, and QAnon, an elaborate, constantly evolving theory that describes President Trump's efforts to foil a plot by members of the "deep state" to control American politics. Among QAnon's many baseless conspiracies are those alleging that Trump was engaged in battle with a secret cabal of blood-drinking pedophiles (LaFrance 2020). (QAnon's posts have been reliably reported in a 2021 HBO documentary to have been authored by Ron Watkins, an American conspiracy theorist living in Japan with no known connections to the American government, who used Q posts to drive traffic to a now defunct website called 8kun.)

These issues became especially important in the aftermath of the armed assault on the U.S. Capitol by a group of supporters of Donald Trump. The backstory to this incident is that following his loss of the 2020 election to Joe Biden, Trump sought to cast doubt on the election, asserting with no credible evidence that the election had been marred by fraud and that he was its true winner. Dozens of legal challenges were rejected, and Democratic and Republican state officials alike rejected claims of fraud. However, while the mainstream news outlets carefully refuted his claims, Trump, using social media, spread a fictitious account of a "rigged" election. He asserted that thousands of ballots were cast by dead people and that millions of votes were discarded (Trump lost the popular vote by over 7 million votes). To many of his most devoted followers on social media, Trump's false claims were persuasive. Soon, one-third of Americans, including more than 70 percent of Republicans, said they did not believe the election had been fair (Montanaro 2020).

Two months later, on January 6, 2021, Trump, having exhausted a number of legal attempts to overturn the election, attended a protest in Washington, D.C., initially organized by his supporters, with a number of groups planning in advance to bring guns to the rally. In his speech to the group, Trump repeated his lies about the election result and encouraged the thousands-strong crowd to march to the Capitol building, where Congress was convening to certify the election results. What followed led both to the President's impeachment—his second—and to a furious debate about the regulation of speech in the age of digital media. At Trump's behest, thousands of his followers stormed the Capitol, and hundreds pushed their way past security, sending members of Congress to seek shelter, as some members of the mob threatened them and then-Vice President Mike Pence (who was overseeing the count). The mob occupied the building for several hours, ransacking offices and streaming images of their raid on the internet (Leatherby et al. 2021). Five people died in the violence, including one protestor shot by law enforcement and one police officer hit in the head by a fire extinguisher.

In the wake of the insurrection, several large tech companies took steps to limit the ability of Trump and members of the far right to use their services. The social media networks Facebook, Instagram, and YouTube all indefinitely suspended Trump, with Twitter—on which Trump had, in the four years of his presidency, posted over 26,000 times—banning him for life. Facebook deleted pages promoting false theories of election fraud, while Twitter deleted 70,000 accounts linked to QAnon. Around the same time, Google and Apple both removed Parler, a social media platform favored by conservatives, from their app store, claiming it represented a public safety risk. Shortly after, Amazon booted the company from its cloud hosting service, taking it offline.

These events stood as the logical culmination of several overlapping trends that had been in ascendance for over a decade: The growing power of social media as a political organizing tool; the medium's vexing potential to quickly spread consequential falsehoods; and the unprecedented influence that Big Tech companies, as *de facto* regulators and gatekeepers of online discourse, had come to wield within the public sphere. It also created something of a paradox with regard to free speech and the preservation of democracy. Many conservatives, including Trump, alleged that the social media networks were, with their bans, engaging in political censorship (Klas 2021). The charge has some merit to be sure. But others countered that the companies, offering a private service, had no obligation to provide a forum to anyone. Further, the use of their platforms to spread knowingly false information should not be regarded as "free speech" but rather as a public menace. It is important to note that the decision to suspend Trump and those challenging the election—enacted, in effect, to uphold the rule of law—was made not by the government but by private, extraordinarily wealthy corporations. By the end of 2020, Apple was the third most valuable company in the world, and Google's parent company Alphabet was the fifth most valuable. What did it mean that tech companies had become so omnipotent that they – not the government or courts of law - were now responsible for safeguarding the democratic process, despite having little public accountability themselves?

The 2020 election and its aftermath also raised a broader, trickier question, about what *should* be OK to say on social media. The right to free speech in the United States, guaranteed in the First Amendment to the Constitution, has never been an absolute right. A century ago, Supreme Court Justice Oliver Wendell Holmes famously wrote that the protection of free speech did not extend to a someone "falsely shouting fire in a theatre and causing a panic"—which is to say, speech that is both dangerous and false (Volokh 2015). But what exactly counts as dangerous or false isn't always obvious. And tech companies can set different limits on speech than the courts. The questions are complex. If we were to re-imagine social media, what would we want it to look like? What speech would be allowed and what forbidden? And, more importantly, to whom—to what company, entity, or individual— would we want to grant the awesome duty to choose?

There is a final, important issue related to social media and democracy that sociologists and other researchers are studying closely. If one of the premises of the free press in a democracy is that citizens will be exposed to a variety of perspectives and sources of information in order to participate meaningfully in public life (as mentioned in the previous section), the ability of social media websites to help us *limit* our exposure to other views is worrisome. There is growing evidence that instead of using social media to find new viewpoints, growing numbers of people are likely to receive news and opinions within ideological "echo chambers" that seem to confirm their previously held views (Sunstein 2009; Bakshy et al. 2015). This tendency is reinforced by the design of social networks and search engines, which often filter the content visible to individual users using sophisticated algorithms, making guesses about what the user will enjoy based on what they've seen in the past. This can limit individuals'

exposure to alternative opinions (Pariser 2011), reinforce their existing biases (Noble 2018), and, potentially, lead them to take on more extreme political positions (Roose 2019). If you appear to search engines to be a liberal, you will get liberal news fed to you, and vice versa if you are a conservative. This situation has likely helped increase the country's political polarization, and has made it increasingly difficult for social and political debates to start from a common, shared set of "facts." While the assault on the Capitol may be a unique event, the possibility of future conflicts arising from these underlying divides remains all too real.

Conclusion: The Complex Future of Culture in the Age of Social Media

It is the nature of culture that it is constantly evolving. The collective meaning and shared rituals of the Balinese cockfight from 50 years ago would probably be scarcely recognizable to most contemporary Indonesians, and no doubt popular culture products in the United States today will seem equally strange to Americans in 50 or 100 years. What would be truly shocking, in fact, is if culture stayed the same.

But even if we accept that culture is constantly changing, it is fair to say that the current moment is one of especially dramatic cultural transformation. The rise of the internet and the global flow of cultural products it permits is a genuinely new and important development that is changing many cultural processes before our eyes. Many of the most pressing questions for the sociological study of culture in coming years will likely be concerned with the implications of the internet and other new forms of interconnectivity that social media in all its forms has begun to

deliver. Even as we become aware of the harms associated with it, almost of all of us are too addicted to give it up. In fact, social media is designed to be habit-forming, and like cigarettes, once you're hooked it is very difficult to get off.

We shouldn't make the mistake, though, of assuming that the increasing prominence of the internet in society means that all of our important cultural questions will relate to social media. The persistence of offline forms of cultural life—old-fashioned town halls, organized meetings where ideas and information are exchanged through oral discussion, live performances of all kinds, not to mention the survival of traditional print media, films, and books—will continue to be important. One of the most pressing questions will be whether or not societies can find ways to harness the best of the new cultural forms while not destroying the best parts of the older, or more traditional, ways in which people have practiced and produced culture.

The Big Questions Revisited 10

10.1 What Is Culture? This section explored how sociologists talk about culture as a shared system of meaning and symbols; a set of values, beliefs, and practices; and shared forms of communication.

The Many Meanings of Culture

Defining Culture

Learning Objective 10.1.1: Define culture from a sociological perspective.

Culture as a System of Meaning and Symbols

Learning Objective 10.1.2: Explain how a group's symbols can be considered its culture, and give examples of collective symbols of contemporary U.S. culture.

Culture as a Set of Values, Beliefs, and Practices

Learning Objective 10.1.3: Describe how our values and beliefs influence how we live our lives.

Culture as a Form of Communication

Learning Objective 10.1.4: Explain the ways in which culture is a form of communication.

Key Terms
social networks (p. 238)   culture (p. 241)
symbol (p. 242)   value (p. 242)   habitus
(p. 243)   tool kit (p. 243)   language
(p. 244)   cultural universal (p. 244)   mass
communication (p. 244)   digital divide (p. 245)

10.2 How Does Culture Shape Our Collective Identity? This section explored how cultural practices both reflect and define group identities, whether the group is a small subculture or a nation.

Culture and Group Identity

Mainstream Culture, Subcultures, and Countercultures

Learning Objective 10.2.1: Discuss the role culture plays in establishing group style, and explain what distinguishes a subculture from the mainstream.

Is There a Dominant Culture in the United States Today?

Learning Objective 10.2.2: Discuss the concept of "culture wars," and explain the importance of practicing cultural relativism in the multicultural United States.

National Cultures

Learning Objective 10.2.3: Explain what produces and reproduces national cultures and what effects they have.

Key Terms

group style (p. 246)   mainstream culture (p. 246)   subculture (p. 246)   counterculture (p. 247)   hegemony (p. 247)   culture wars (p. 247)   multiculturalism (p. 248)   ethnocentrism (p. 248)   cultural relativism (p. 258)   female genital cutting (p. 249)   national culture (p. 250)   nationalism (p. 250)   ethno-nationalist (p. 250)   populism (p. 250)

10.3 How Do Our Cultural Practices Relate to Class and Status? In this section, we discussed how people's cultural habits help define and reproduce the boundaries between high status and low status, upper class and lower class.

Class, Status, and Culture

Cultural Capital

Learning Objective 10.3.1: Define cultural capital, and discuss ways American elites have become cultural omnivores.

How Culture Reproduces Class

Learning Objective 10.3.2: Analyze how money and culture reproduce status over the long term.

Key Terms

taste (p. 253)   cultural capital (p. 253)   cultural omnivore (p. 253)   class reproduction (p. 254)

10.4 Who Produces Culture, and Why? The cultural field is the place for creativity and meaning making. But it is also a battlefield. In this section, we explored who controls the media and popular culture and what messages they communicate.

The Conditions of Cultural Production

The Public Sphere

Learning Objective 10.4.1: Analyze how the concept of the public sphere explains how culture is produced in society.

The Culture Industry versus Cultural Democracy

Learning Objective 10.4.2: Compare and contrast the cultural industry and the cultural democracy perspectives.

The Medium Is the Message

Learning Objective 10.4.3: Discuss the ways in which communication changes with the form or medium.

Key Terms

public sphere (p. 255)   counterpublic (p. 256)   networked public (p. 256)   culture industry (p. 256)

10.5 What Is the Relationship between Media and Democracy? The media are arguably the most important form of cultural production in our society. This section examined the media's relationship to democracy and the new ways in which it is changing how democracy works.

Media and Democracy: A Changing Landscape

Making the News: The Media as a Cultural System

Learning Objective 10.5.1: Explain the role the media play in making the news.

Pressures on Contemporary Journalism and News Media

Learning Objective 10.5.2: Identify trends in the U.S. media landscape that have put commercial pressure on journalism.

Media, Democracy, and the Internet

Learning Objective 10.5.3: Discuss the ways the internet has created new opportunities and dangers for the free media and for democracy.

Key Term

journalism (p. 258)   agenda setting (p. 258)

Chapter 11
Inequality and Poverty

by Florencia Torche, Jeff Manza, and Richard Arum

How does growing up poor impact children? We would like to think that all children have an equal chance to succeed in life. How true is this? This is a question that social scientists have been especially interested in examining in recent years. Despite the levels of wealth and economic productivity that capitalist societies such as the United States have achieved, many families continue to live in poverty, in some cases lacking the resources to meet their everyday needs. And evidence is accumulating that children are especially harmed by poverty, sometimes in subtle and hidden ways. One of these ways is that the stress of a mother's poverty may be toxic to her child even *before* birth. Until recently, researchers believed that the fetus was fully isolated from its environment by the placenta, which would shield it from any damaging exposures. We now know that this is not the case. Researchers have confirmed, for example, that alcohol, tobacco, and drug use during pregnancy can affect the fetus. But what about the stresses caused by poverty? Is it possible that the stress faced by mothers living in poverty can affect the fetus, just like smoking or drug use? If so, it would suggest that the impact of poverty goes well beyond the lack of material resources.

The ideal research project to study the impact of stress during pregnancy would involve assembling a group of pregnant women and giving stress to half of them selected at random (treatment group) while not giving stress to the other half (control group). Of course, for ethical reasons, this sort of experiment is not possible. But in 2005, a massive earthquake in Chile provided an alternative strategy to assess the impact of stress. Because the earthquake came unannounced, and because it affected some Chilean cities but left others untouched, it created a kind of natural experiment similar to what might have happened if we had assigned only some pregnant mothers to have added stress. In other words, those women who happened to live in the earthquake were, like poor mothers everywhere,

exposed to extra stress during their pregnancy, while others who happened to live in areas far away from the earthquake served as the control group for the study. By comparing these two groups of pregnant women, one of the authors of this chapter (Florencia Torche) was able to measure the effect of stress separate from other factors usually associated with it.

The findings were striking. Babies exposed to the earthquake in the first trimester of gestation were far more

My Sociological Imagination

FLORENCIA TORCHE

I grew up in Chile, one of the most unequal countries in the world. Growing up, I could "breathe" inequality not only in the economic disparities between the poor and the rich but also in the wide gaps between cities and the countryside, the economic segregation or schools and neighborhoods, and the way people of different classes related to each other—when they did—as if they were citizens of different worlds. As a child, I took inequality for granted. As a college student, I gained the tools to understand that high inequality is not "natural." Rather, it exists and persists because of specific policies and institutions—and it can also be changed through policies and institutions. My research became a way to systematically understand how inequality is reproduced across generations—that is, how advantages and disadvantages are transmitted from parents to children, and the role that education and marriage can play in shaping inequality. Many of my studies use cross-country comparisons to examine how institutions shape inequality. My most recent research elucidates how the context individuals live in shapes their life chances early in life—as early as in the prenatal period.

High levels of inequality, such as that found in the United States, can produce examples of wealth and poverty in close proximity to one another. A question often asked is why is there so much poverty in a country as rich as the United States. A sociological answer focuses on the structural conditions that enable (or limit) high levels of inequality and poverty.

Jenny Matthews/Alamy Stock Photo

Poverty can impact a child even before they are born, if the mother carrying the child faces high levels of stress and insecurity.

likely to be born preterm and at a low birth weight, two conditions that have been shown to have very serious consequences. Babies born preterm require much more medical attention and are at a higher risk of dying in the first year of life and of experiencing health, developmental, and cognitive problems later on if they survive. And this is only an extreme impact; other, less obvious negative consequences of being exposed to stress can be found among a much larger group of babies in the study.

Why did the earthquake affect the chances of being born preterm? The most likely explanation is that the acute stress elicited by the earthquake has an effect on the placenta.

Basically, stress sends a message to the fetus that says, "the outside world is not too safe, so you should get out as soon as possible," which sets a biological clock for early delivery. Because premature birth predicts developmental problems later on, this study strongly suggests that being exposed to a stressful environment due to poverty even before birth may have a negative effect on a child's outcomes. Given strong evidence that poor mothers have more stressful pregnancies, this leads to a very troubling conclusion: Even before they are born, poor children are much more likely to be exposed to stress that impacts their development in the womb, and that stress is very damaging and will have life-long impacts. This is, as we will see, just one of the many ways in which poverty and inequality have negative consequences for individuals and society as a whole.

This research suggests but one of the many complex ways in which inequalities in any society can hide as well as more obvious consequences. A widely shared value in all modern democratic societies is the idea of "equality of opportunity," which means that everyone, regardless of the resources of the families they are born into, has an equal chance at succeeding in life. But the fact that poverty handicaps children from conception and results in cumulative disadvantages as they grow up raises serious questions about the ability of these societies to achieve full equality of opportunity. In this chapter, we will examine why inequality exists, how it is maintained over time, and what the consequences of inequality are for society.

The Big Questions

1. **What is inequality?** We know that some people simply have more than others. But why? Has the enormous gap between rich and poor always existed? What is the sociological concept of class, and does it help us understand inequality? We examine all of this in the first section of the chapter.

2. **Why is America so unequal?** Inequality in the United States today is about as high as it has ever been since we started measuring it in the early twentieth century, and poverty rates have remained persistently high. How does the United States compare with other developed countries most similar to it? And does the United States have more people living in poverty than other countries? Why is America so unequal?

3. **Do we all have an equal opportunity to succeed in life?** Social mobility, which refers to the movement of individuals from their family's social position to their social position in adulthood, is one of the most important topics in the study of inequality. Inequality of opportunity arises whenever some individuals or groups have privileged access to better jobs and/or schools by virtue of the family they were born into. In this section, we examine how social mobility is measured, why countries differ in opportunity, how the United States compares to other countries, and the relationship between education and mobility.

4. **How much poverty exists in the United States and around the world?** Poverty is a complicated concept. Beyond a minimum of resources to ensure subsistence, it is difficult to define our "basic" needs. In this section, we examine two ways of viewing poverty and how much poverty exists in the United States and in other countries around the world. We will also look closely at the problem of childhood poverty.

Jeff Manza

INEQUALITY: AN INTRODUCTION

Few social issues in the United States have generated more public and political discussion in recent years than rising economic inequality. Inequalities in any society—in whatever form they take—can have both obvious and more hidden consequences. One of the most obvious consequences in recent decades is that many workers have seen their wages stagnate while the very richest households, especially those in the top 1 percent of the population, have seen their income and wealth soar. Inequality is also closely related to poverty. In highly unequal societies like the United States, despite immense overall wealth it is still common to find many families living in poverty, struggling to maintain a roof over their heads and put food on the table. But inequality impacts not just individuals, but societies as a whole. For example, it can change the nature of democracy when the wealthiest individuals and corporations use their resources to influence the political process to get favorable outcomes. And inequality threatens one of the most cherished values in American society: The idea of "equality of opportunity," or what is sometimes called the "American Dream," in which everyone, regardless of the resources of the families they are born into, has an equal chance to succeed. In this section, we introduce the concept of inequality.

A Brief History of Inequality

11.1.1 Define inequality and explain how the form and level of inequality has varied throughout history.

Some people have more than others. **Inequality**—the unequal distribution of valued goods and opportunities—is a feature of virtually all known human societies. But throughout history, the form and level of inequality have varied widely. Hunting and gathering societies, for example, typically shared their limited food supplies and resources among all members of the tribe, although the tribe's "Big Man" might claim more than his share, laying the foundation for societal inequalities. A Big Man is someone who, whether because of physical strength or cunning, is able to hoard desirable goods and accumulate more status and power within the tribe or community (Flannery and Marcus 2012). Big Men developed ways of showing off their wealth to establish their higher status within the tribe, for example, by building bigger huts or shelters, displaying jewelry or other special goods at ceremonies, or being able to take in multiple wives. But these differences were modest compared to later human societies. The great nineteenth century theorist of inequality, Karl Marx, referred to these early societies as "primitive communism," in the sense that survival required community members to work together and share whatever they had.

As more settled agricultural communities began to form around 12,000 years ago, larger inequalities began to emerge. In particular, the establishment of **slavery** was an important landmark. A slave system facilitates the creation of wealth for the slave owners, which enslaved people do not share, and creates a divide between humans living in the same vicinity. This was true in the slave societies of the ancient world, such as ancient Egypt, where enslaved people were employed to build monuments to rulers, and famously in ancient Athens and the Roman Empire (where large percentages of the entire population were enslaved people). Slavery persisted throughout history (and indeed, still exists today in small pockets of the world), most often in societies or places where agriculture is the primary type of economic activity.

While slavery produces an extreme form of inequality, two other important types of inequality developed throughout the world prior to the advent of capitalism in the eighteenth and nineteenth centuries. One historical source of wealth accumulation involved traders who acquired desired goods in one place and sold them at a profit in another. The most successful of the merchants were able to become rich by buying and selling goods, building lavish homes for themselves and their families (and their many servants). A major impetus to trade as a source of wealth came from the rise of **colonialism**, the conquering and control of foriegn lands by the rich countries of Western Europe. As armies and governments began to develop and expand their influence around the globe, they seized valuable goods and resources from captured territories, enabling rulers and their favored supporters to become wealthy.

But the most common and important source of inequality prior to the Industrial Revolution arose from land ownership under a system known as **feudalism**. Feudalism refers to an economic system based on agriculture in which those who own land (landlords) are entitled to receive the products of the laborers, or **serfs**, who in turn are legally obligated to work the land. The largely agrarian settlements and societies of the Middle Ages were places where a handful of landlords were able to accumulate sometimes considerable fortunes (as we can see today in the grand castles that have survived from that era). Their ownership of large swaths of land permitted them to lease it out to serfs, who typically became indebted to the landowner and obligated to continue working the land (and those obligations would carry over to their children).

Looking at the big picture, for most of human history the vast majority of people lived harsh, difficult lives. Most died very young by contemporary standards (life expectancy at birth in Medieval England was about 30 years; today it is around 80 years or more in the United States and similar rich countries). In the absence of other data, life expectancy is a good measure of the quality of living conditions (Deaton 2013), and for many centuries it barely changed. Further, there were also no significant numbers of people in "middle" classes – however we define it – as in today's societies.

The system of inequality as it has evolved over the past 200 years has developed in new directions. The Industrial Revolution, which begins in the late eighteenth and early nineteenth centuries, allowed for rapid and sustained economic growth (see Chapter 9 for more details). In the 130 years between 1820 and 1950, average incomes in Western Europe increased nearly four times. And in just the 50 years between 1950 and 2000, they increased an additional four times over. Even more rapid growth was achieved in the United States, which had become the richest country in the world by the early 1900s (Gordon 2016). Although the gains were never evenly distributed, all groups of Americans saw steady and extraordinary gains. Farmers benefited from new technologies that vastly increased farm output and made living on a farm much easier. Workers saw their wages rise, sometimes the result of being organized into unions that were able to demand higher wages from their employers. Innovations in ideas and technology opened up many brand new ways of earning a living, including the rise of new professional occupations that paid very good wages.

These trends were also reinforced by the massive growth of government programs designed to provide everyone with some degree of protection from the worst ravages of poverty, including a living wage in retirement; support for poor families, disabled people, and the unemployed; as well as the rise of government-sponsored health care, universal educational opportunities, and many other programs. These types of programs and benefits, known collectively as the **welfare state** (as noted elsewhere in the text), have bolstered living standards of the non-rich, and for a long period of time the rich were taxed at higher rates to support these programs, which helped to moderate inequality, especially in the decades after World War II.

North Wind Picture Archives/Alamy Stock Photo

As this drawing suggests, under feudalism, landlords often built large homes (or even castles) and could afford many servants and other luxuries, while generations of serfs who worked their land barely had enough to survive.

But in recent decades, especially in the United States, living standards for most types of people have stopped increasing as much as they did from 1820-1980. One reason for this is that most of the benefits of the gains of economic growth have been enjoyed by those at the top of the income ladder. There are many reasons why this has happened, as we will explore later in the chapter. Especially significant has been the process by which the very wealthiest individuals and families have been able to use their surplus income and wealth to acquire even more wealth, pulling away from everyone else in the process (Piketty 2014). Social scientists use the term **high-end inequality** to describe such a society. Today, high-end inequality characterizes both the United States and many other countries across the globe that are also seeing similar patterns.

If we look globally, it is beyond doubt that those individuals and families who enjoy extraordinary wealth are richer than at any point in human history. *Forbes* magazine studies the richest people in the world and estimates their wealth on an ongoing basis. Topping their list in the winter of 2020 was Amazon founder Jeff Bezos, who was estimated to have a net worth of $197 billion, followed by Elon Musk (Tesla cars) at $184 billion, Bill Gates (Microsoft) at $129 billion, Mark Zuckerberg (Facebook) at $98 billion, Larry Page and Sergey Brin (Google) at around $90 billion, famed American investor Warren Buffet at $89 billion, Larry Ellison (founder of the software firm Oracle) at an estimated $89 billion, and France's Bernard Arnault (luxury fashion and marketing) at $76 billion. Clearly, the richest individuals collectively control an enormous share of the world's wealth (Winters 2011). One key report by a leading team of wealth investigators (Lawson et al. 2019) notes these astonishing findings:

- The bottom 50 percent of the world's population (3.8 billion people) has the same total wealth as approximately the 23 richest people in the world. Imagine a tug of war game, with 23 people on one side and 3.8 billion on the other—the two sides are equally matched in terms of wealth.

- As of 2015, the world's richest 1 percent own more than the bottom 99 percent combined (Oxfam 2016).

- Over half of all the wealth in the world is controlled by the top 1 percent of the world's population. The bottom 99 percent of the world's population shares less than 50 percent of all wealth.

- The number of millionaires around the world is predicted to increase by 46 percent over the next five years to a total of 49.3 million adults. However, despite this dramatic increase, the total number of millionaires will only account for 0.7 percent of the world's adult population.

In the early decades of the twenty-first century, we find that the great promise of the middle decades of the twentieth century—in which all groups participated in the benefits of economic growth—has faded.

Measures of Economic Inequality: Wealth and Income

11.1.2 Compare and contrast income and wealth as measures of economic inequality.

To better understand these trends in inequality, we need to clarify the specific ways in which societies are unequal. Social scientists have focused most of their attention on two critical measures of inequality: Income and wealth. These are fundamentally different measures, and it is important to understand the difference. **Income** refers to the receipt of money or goods over a particular accounting period (such as hourly, weekly, monthly, or yearly). There are multiple possible sources of income: Earned income from a regular job, income received from investments or ownership of income-generating properties or businesses, income transfers from the government (such as Social Security), income received from family or friends (inheritances or gifts), and income from illegal or "underground" earnings (such as from crime or informal and untaxed work or business activity). Most people, before retirement age, receive most or all of their income from their primary job, but some have multiple sources of income.

We can also consider other measures of well-being, and it is good to be aware of these. The most important of these measures would be **consumption** (how much an individual or family actually consumes in a month or a year, which may not directly correspond to their income if they are able to borrow money), health and well-being, and opportunity (a concept we discuss in much more detail later in the chapter). But most of the focus of research and policymaking debates center on income and wealth, so that will be our focus in the rest of this chapter.

Wealth, which refers to the net value of the assets (that is, assets minus debts) owned by individuals or family, is an alternative measure of household resources. The most commonly owned wealth asset is real estate (in most cases, a home). Approximately two-thirds of Americans own the primary residence in which they live. Because homes tend to increase in value over time, home ownership has historically been the primary way that families with modest incomes can accumulate wealth (by buying a house and living in it for many years while it appreciates in value). A smaller subset of the population owns **net financial assets (NFA)**. These include the total value of savings, investments, retirement accounts, and other convertible assets (less outstanding debts). While most families have savings accounts, far fewer have NFAs that are substantial.

The median American family (the individual or family exactly in the middle) had NFAs (not counting the value of their home) of approximately $30,000 in 2019, but many families have little or no financial assets, including savings for retirement (Brandon 2012; Bricker et al. 2014).

Overall, we find that wealth differences between individuals and groups are far larger than income differences (Keister 2006). Figure 11.1 illustrates the trends in recent decades (adjusted for inflation). The top figure shows three different lines: (1) the top line is the *average* household wealth for the bottom 90 percent of households (so the wealth of a family at 90th percentile is averaged with a family at the 10th percentile); (2) the middle line shows median wealth (that is, the wealth of the household in the middle, with equal numbers of households above and below) – most of this wealth is in the form of home ownership; and (3) the lowest line shows families at the 37th percentile (with approximately two-thirds of households

Figure 11.1 Wealth Inequality: Bottom 90% (Top Panel) and Top 1% (Bottom Panel)

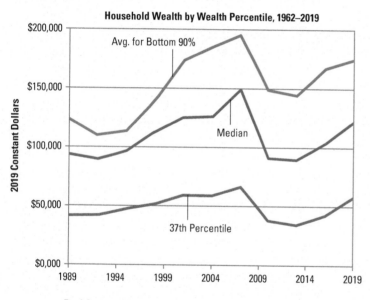

Household Wealth by Wealth Percentile, 1962–2019

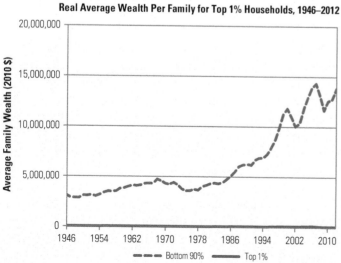

Real Average Wealth Per Family for Top 1% Households, 1946–2012

SOURCE: Zucman and Saez, 2016.

above and one-third below). Although the average and median households have seen their wealth grow modestly over time—especially the average household, which has seen about $50,000 in growth since the late 1980s, versus $30,000 in the middle—households below the median have seen virtually no change. Contrast those trends with those of the rich shown in the bottom figure, which shows trends in total household wealth in the United States for the wealthiest one percent of households. To properly understand these figures, note that the top figure (for the bottom 90%) is in thousands of dollars, and the bottom figure (for the top 1%) is shown in *millions*. Wealth at the top has increased dramatically, rising over $10 million for rich household since the late 1970s.

The Sociological Concept of Class

11.1.3 Define class and identify what constitutes a social class.

The system of inequality today does not, of course, consist only of the rich and everyone else; sociologists have developed a variety of tools for understanding inequality across the entire range of income and wealth. In most countries, and indeed all of the developed countries most similar to the United States, there is a large **middle class**. If we think just about income, in this middle class are people working for a wide range of businesses in mostly professional, technical, or managerial jobs, or are small business owners running modestly successful businesses. Those who have manual jobs, such as skilled factory workers, can also earn incomes that put them in the middle class, although that is much less common in recent decades. Middle-class people and their families enjoy enough income to allow them to buy homes, cars, and the latest in consumer and technological gadgets. They also have some savings and retirement accounts to help cushion them in the event of illness and when they retire.

But the concept of "middle class" that many people talk about is rather vague. How exactly do sociologists conceptualize what is meant by the middle class, and more specifically, what do they mean by class? Sociologists use the term **class** in general to identify groups of people in similar social and economic positions. Classes are groups, not individuals. And it only makes sense to think about classes in relation to each other. Using the concept of class to understand some of the broad patterns of inequality in American society can be useful beyond what we can learn by studying individuals and families.

What makes up a class? There is disagreement about how to define classes, and sociologists disagree about how many different classes there are. But most agree that classes are made up of people sharing a similar economic situation who (1) have conflicting economic interests with other classes (for example, workers want more pay while business owners want to hold down workers' pay to increase profits), (2) share similar **life chances** (that is, members of the same class are likely to have similar incomes and opportunities as they move through life), (3) have similar attitudes, and (4) have the potential, at least, to engage in collective action (such as when workers organize a union).

Class analysis is the sociological study of how, when, and to what extent classes exist along these four dimensions in any society at any point in time, and how these classes have changed over-time. Classes become more visible when there are sharp differences between them on some key political controversy or in periods of sharp economic grievances. This is most vivid in a situation where revolutionary change is in the air, and large numbers of people—unified by membership in lower classes—demand a more equal distribution of economic goods and opportunities. But revolutions and other types of collective action by entire classes are relatively rare. What about everyday life?

Karl Marx and Friedrich Engels introduced the concept of class in their many economic and political writings in the nineteenth century (most famously in *The Communist Manifesto* in 1848). Marx's concept of class built on the idea that as a result of its economic system, every society has a single, critical division between two classes (one dominant, one subordinate), based on their economic position. Under feudalism, as we have already seen, those two classes would be landowners and serfs. Marx and Engels thought that in capitalist societies the most important class distinction was between business owners (or what they called the **bourgeoisie**) and workers who do jobs for pay (a group they referred to as the **proletariat**). Other classes could exist, but they were of minor (and declining) importance.

But since Marx and Engels developed the first conception of classes and class divisions in the nineteenth century, it

One way in which social class becomes visible is when comparing consumer behavior. Certain products serve as status symbols that reflect one's social standing. Members of higher social classes, for example, are able to buy luxury products, such as expensive or exclusive cars and fashion items, that mark them as different from everyone else.

Bart78/Shutterstock

Jules Selmes/Pearson Education Ltd.

has become clear that more was to be done for the concept of class to provide a meaningful description of contemporary capitalist societies. Various middle-class groupings—such as business managers, professionals, and those who are self-employed—are not usefully lumped together with factory workers, sales workers, or the baristas at Starbucks. Any sophisticated theory of class in American (or any other modern) society will need to attend to the groups in the middle.

But to ask the question "what is middle about the middle classes?" (Wright 1986) is to raise a whole host of problems for the concept of class. It is usually not too hard to identify the groups at the very top and the very bottom, but identifying the middle layers and defining their boundaries is more difficult. There have been three broad solutions to this problem. The first solution is to distinguish classes based on income. Those with high incomes belong in one class, those with incomes near the median are in the middle class, and those with low incomes are in the lower classes. Simple, right? But the problem with using income to define classes is that there are no clear-cut boundaries between classes. Do we really think, for example, that having an annual income of $79,000 places a person in the middle class, while an income of $80,000 places another person in the upper class? Further, sociologists have argued that more important than the amount of income is the *source* of income. *How* people earn gives us a better way of predicting how people will behave, who their friends are, and what kinds of opinions they may hold. For example, a part-time college instructor who is completing their PhD may have the same *current* income as the janitor who cleans up their office at the end of the day. But in the process of earning an advanced degree, and possessing a very different set of knowledge and skill than the janitor, the college instructor is likely to have very different friends, ideas about what is just and fair, and perhaps most importantly have the potential to earn far more income over a lifetime than the janitor. The sociological concept of class attempts to capture these varying life chances in dividing society into class locations, so most sociologists conclude that income alone is not the best way to think of what we mean by classes.

A second approach to class that some analysts employ is to utilize more information about individuals, such as education, income, and current occupation, to assign them to a class location. Using this approach, researchers can construct a score for each individual's **socioeconomic status (SES)**. The basic premise of the SES approach is that by combining a number of different attributes of any individual, we can properly place him or her in relation to others and assign him or her to a class. While different weights can be assigned to each, one basic decision rule is that someone scoring high on all three dimensions (income, education, occupation) is "high SES," someone scoring low on all three is "low SES," and everyone else is somewhere in the middle (or "middle SES").

SES is useful for many purposes, and generally does a better job than simple income measures to distinguish among people for research purposes. But a key aspect of class theory is that members of the same class should have the potential to act together to try to improve their lot in life in some way. People in the same SES location are not ever likely to act together on that basis. Have you ever seen someone holding a sign at a protest saying "low SES people of the world unite"? Probably not!

A third approach to class, and the one favored by a majority of sociologists, is to focus on occupation in adulthood. This approach views the place of each individual in the economic system as crucial, and their primary occupation provides one way of measuring that (Weeden and Grusky 2014). Unlike income or SES, there are many examples of occupational groups having similar political views and acting together to push for higher wages or to change government policies (for example, in unions or professional associations like the American Bar Association or the American Medical Association, and for business owners there is the Chamber of Commerce and other business associations). Most of the occupation-based approaches divide different occupations into a small group of distinct classes that have similar kinds of life chances, organizations, and (less often) social and political viewpoints. The most popular of these schemes is that of sociologists Robert Erikson and John Goldthorpe (Erikson and Goldthorpe 1992), who have identified seven core classes displayed (in a slightly simplified way) in Table 11.1. The Erikson–Goldthorpe scheme makes distinctions between those individuals who own their own businesses (or are self-employed) and those who work for someone else. Among those who are employed, distinctions are made between those who have jobs that either entail supervising others or require employer trust (what they call "the salariat") and those that do not; between those involving manual work or not; and, among manual workers, those that require special skills and training versus those that do not. Table 11.1 shows some of the representative types of occupations falling into each category.

Table 11.1 The Erikson–Goldthorpe Class Scheme

Salariat/Service Class: Professionals, managers, and administrators; higher grade technicians; supervisors of nonmanual workers

Routine Nonmanual Workers: Nonsupervisorial employees in administration and commerce positions; sales workers; secretaries, clerks, and other rank-and-file white-collar workers

Petty Bourgeoisie/Self-Employed: Business owners (other than farm), self-employed workers and consultants, artisans

Farm Owners: Farmers and ranchers (landowners)

Skilled Workers and Supervisors: Skilled manual workers, supervisors of manual workers (foremen), lower grade technicians/repairmen

Nonskilled Workers: Semi- and unskilled manual workers

Farm Laborers: Farm and ranch employees

SOURCE: Erikson and Goldthorpe, 1992, slightly modified by the authors.

BIG QUESTION 11.2 Why Is America So Unequal?

UNEQUAL AMERICA IN COMPARATIVE PERSPECTIVE

Today, economic inequality in the United States is almost as high as it has ever been, at least since good data about incomes became available in the early twentieth century. Inequality is also, as we shall see, higher in the United States than in any other similar rich, democratic country (although there are less developed countries that have even more inequality). And in spite of its enormous overall wealth, the United States has more people living in poverty than most other similar countries. More inequality, more poverty. These two facts are of critical importance for understanding the United States, requiring us to think hard about how and why America is so unequal. These lessons apply, of course, to other countries as well, even if their levels of inequality are not as high as they currently are in the United States.

Trends in Income Inequality in the United States and Around the World

11.2.1 Discuss trends in income inequality and compare inequality in the United States to other countries around the world.

Let's start with an analysis of inequality trends in the United States to get a handle on what is going on. When did inequality start increasing? Is this a new trend, or has inequality always been high? One method that researchers have used to measure long-term trends in inequality is to examine the share of total national income that goes to different groups in the country. In a perfectly **egalitarian** (equal) society, the income share of each family (or household)

is the same. Inequality rises when the difference between households goes up.

In the last couple of decades, researchers have been able to examine tax returns as a source of information about income in order to measure income inequality in the United States. Tax return data go back to 1917, soon after the federal income tax was established permanently by the 16th Amendment. Because virtually every adult or married couple has to file a tax return, it is possible to track the incomes of all U.S. households or taxable units (individuals or couples), over a long historical time period. The pioneering and important work of economists Thomas Piketty and Emmanuel Saez has led the way in uncovering those trends (see, for example, Piketty and Saez 2014). What does their analysis show? Figures 11.2 and 11.3 highlight

Figure 11.2 Share of Total National Income for Top 10% of Families, 1917–2017

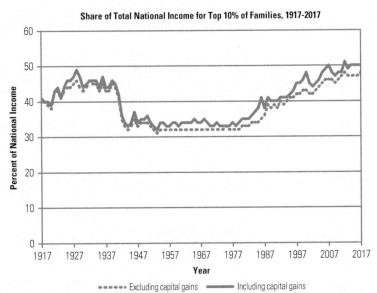

SOURCE: World Inequality Database. Retrieved from: https://wid.world/data/.

some important results on the trends in income inequality and its consequences.

Figure 11.2 shows the long-run trend in the share of national income received by the top 10 percent of households since 1917 (in other words, the percentage of all income earned in a single year that went to the top 10 percent of households). In the figure, we separate earned income only—the black line—versus income plus financial investments—the red line (with the latter being closer to a household's total income). There are two periods in which the top 10 percent reach or exceed 50 percent of all income: In the late 1920s, right before the stock market crash of 1929; and the period since 2007. But notice the long period from 1940 to 1980, when the top 10 percent of households received only about one-third of the national income. It may be hard to imagine exactly how enormous that difference is, but think of this way: If in 2017, the top 10 percent of households had received 33 percent of all income, instead of the approximately 50 percent they did get, it would mean that 17 percent of all national income in the United States could be redistributed to the bottom 90 percent. If we could magically do that, in an economy that in 2017 generated approximately $20 trillion in income, taking 17 percent of all income away from the 10 percent and transferring to the bottom 90 percent would have meant about every single person in the bottom 90% would have received a check for over $6000!

However, the story is more complicated than a focus on the top 10 percent of households would tell us. In fact, one of the critical findings of the Piketty and Saez research team has been that the income share of the wealthiest groups has always been higher than their population share, but *how much more* has changed considerably over time. One way to see this is to separate out the top 1 percent from everyone else in the top 10 percent. In Figure 11.3, we show trends in the percentage of all income received by different segments of the top 10 percent. The top 1 percent (this is the grey region) received about 20 percent of income in 2017. Interestingly, most of that increase at the top is going to the people and families at the very, very top (Winters 2011; Piketty 2014). So those lucky families at the 0.995 percentile—the top one-half of the top 1 percent—have done much better than those merely at the 0.990 percentile—the bottom half of the top 1 percent.

What about everyone else? The bottom panel of Figure 11.3 shows all households by income quintiles (that is, households representing each quintile: 0–20, 20–40, 40–60, 60–80, and 80–99, with the top 1 percent identified separately). In 1980, the income share of the top 1 percent was 11 percent, and today it is around 20 percent. When people at the very top *double* their share of income, there is correspondingly less income for everyone else. In the bottom quintile, the poorest 20 percent have seen very little change—they've received 4 to 5 percent of all income every year. So it isn't exactly true that as the rich get richer, the poor have gotten poorer. However, the middle four income groups (20–40, 40–60, and 60–80, and 80–99th percentiles) have all experienced a declining share of all income.

Figure 11.3 Share of Income Received by Income Groups, 1967–2017

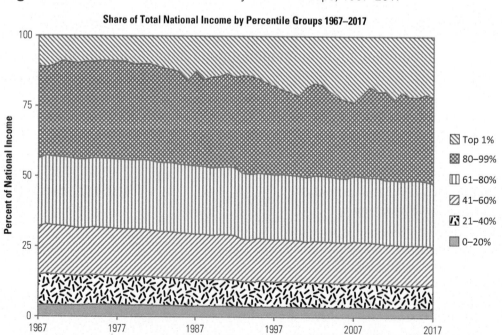

Share of Total National Income by Percentile Groups 1967–2017

SOURCE: World Inequality Database. Retrieved from: https://wid.world/data/

Figure 11.4 Income Inequality around the World

Developed by the Italian statistician and sociologist, Corrado Gini, the Gini Index is the most commonly used measure of overall income inequality. The Index ranges from 0 to 1, where 1 indicates complete inequality (one family gets all the income, and all other families get nothing). The larger the Gini, the more inequality.

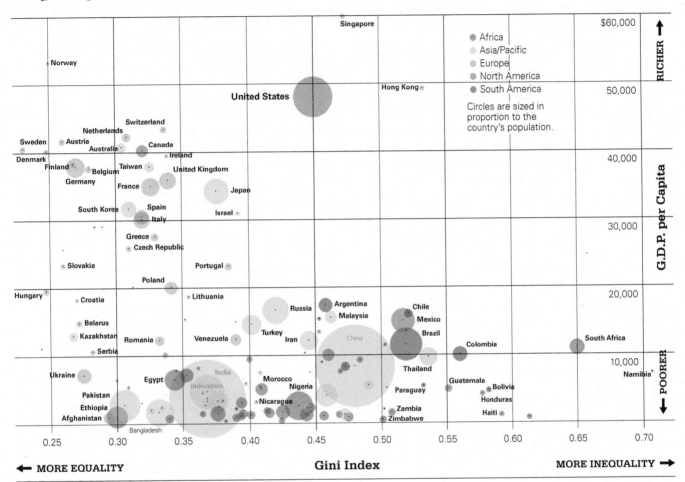

SOURCE: C.I.A. World Fact Book, 2012.

How different is the level of income inequality in the United States compared to other countries around the world? See Figure 11.4 for one way of depicting these differences. The circles in the graph represent the size of different countries. Thus, China is really big, Hong Kong is very small, and the U.S. is among the largest circles displayed.

What this figure shows is that overall, the level of inequality in the United States is approximately twice that of Sweden (a very egalitarian country) and about one-third higher than most other European countries. This is instructive, in that these are countries that have similar levels of economic development to the United States as well as similar educational systems and democratic political institutions. The United States is the most unequal country of the developed world, and the difference with other countries is, in most cases, very substantial. Indeed, to find countries with *more* inequality, we would have to

include in the comparison group a couple of countries in Latin America and Africa that have extremely high levels of inequality (South Africa and Namibia are the most inegalitarian countries in the world, while many countries in Central and South America have high levels of inequality).

Why Did Inequality Increase?

11.2.2 Identify factors explaining why economic inequality in the United States has increased since the 1960s.

What factors explain the increase in economic inequality over the last decades? The increase in inequality is not limited to the United States, but rather is happening in many other countries too, just not as quickly as in the United States (Piketty 2014). The fact that inequality has also risen in most advanced industrial countries suggests that at least some of these factors are shared across the industrialized world. On the other hand, the fact that inequality is higher and has risen faster in the United States than in other countries suggests that something else is going on in the United States.

Researchers are hard at work trying to address the question of why inequality has been growing, and the theories that have been advanced are still being debated. We do know that several factors have played a role. In this section, we focus on four: (1) Technology, (2) the decline of manufacturing, (3) globalization, and (4) government policies—the most important of the U.S.-specific developments.

One possible explanation for rising inequality focuses on how technology—especially the growth and development of computing—has impacted society. From the 1970s onward, the United States and other rich countries have experienced major technological advancements. There was a time not so long ago when nobody used computers and when face-to-face meetings or typed letters instead of e-mail and smartphones were the norm for communication.

Technology matters for inequality because it complements or even upgrades some jobs, while displacing others. In other words, the impact is uneven, and in that way can widen inequality. For example, changes in computer technologies have dramatically reduced the need for bank tellers (an occupation that requires middle-level skills), with ATMs as well as online access to your banking records allowing a bank's customers to make most routine financial transactions themselves. At the same time, these improvements in computer technology have increased the need for a new type of banker: Financial analysts, who usually have an MBA or at least a BA. In general, technology complements jobs that require higher levels of education—especially a college degree or more—while it tends to replace jobs with middle and lower levels of education. As a result, having a college degree or more pays off more than ever before—the so-called **college wage premium**—whereas people with less than a college degree have seen their earnings decline or have increasing trouble finding good jobs.

To see this, let's examine the expected lifetime earnings difference between a college graduate and a high school graduate. The average college graduate today can expect a lifetime premium of around $900,000 over their high school graduate counterpart. If they go on to graduate school, that difference grows to over $1.5 million (Tamborini, Kim, and Sakamoto 2015). Figure 11.5 shows the gap by displaying differences in average weekly earnings for different education groups. A quick way to read this graph is to notice how much closer together the lines representing different educational groups were in 1979 than in 2019. Among full-time workers, a person with a college degree earned about $350 a week more than someone with just a high school degree. By 2019, the gap had reached $650 a week, an increase of 86 percent (and a $650 gap is just for one week; multiplied over an entire career, it will grow into an enormous sum). The increase is even larger for workers without a high school degree, and it also grows for people who start college but do not finish with a BA.

Why is the college wage premium rising? This is where technology has come into play. As the kinds of technology used in all types of jobs become ever more sophisticated, workers need more years of education to do these jobs effectively. Further, what has happened in the United States in the last few decades is that higher education has not expanded at the pace required by technological change (see Chapter 18 on education for further details). As a result, people who have a college degree have become scarcer relative to the needs of the economy, and because of their relative scarcity they have been receiving higher salaries. As two economic historians have put it, a dynamic economy is characterized by a "race between education and technology" (Goldin and Katz 2010). If technology advances faster

Figure 11.5 College Wage Premium Over Time

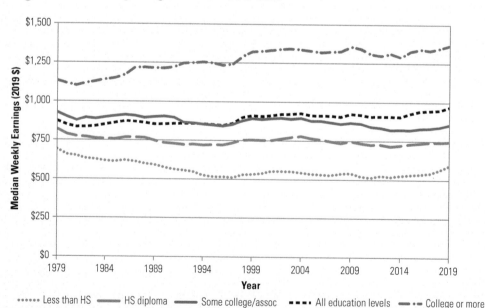

..... Less than HS ⸻ HS diploma ⸻ Some college/assoc ▪▪▪▪ All education levels ⸻▪⸻ College or more

NOTE: Includes only full-time workers over age 25. Adjusted for inflation using the Bureau of Labor Statistics' (BLS) Consumer Price Index Research Series.

SOURCE: Calculations based on weekly and hourly earnings data from the Current Population Survey, Table 5. Retrieved from https://www.bls.gov/cps/cpswktabs.htm.

than the educational system can produce trained workers, then the educational premium increases. This, some researchers argue, is what has happened in the United States since the 1980s.

A second set of factors contributing to inequality concerns the changing mix of jobs and opportunities in the late twentieth and early twenty-first centuries. Developed countries like the United States have undergone a steady decline in industrial or manufacturing jobs. This process, known as **deindustrialization**, has had a number of important consequences. In 1950, almost 40 percent of all jobs were in industry and manufacturing, and wages for experienced manufacturing workers were relatively high. Today, only 10 percent of jobs are in manufacturing, and the constant threat of manufacturing jobs moving to other countries has helped hold down wages for many of the manufacturing jobs that are left.

The loss of jobs in manufacturing has meant replacing what were once good paying jobs for workers without college degrees, with jobs in newer industries that provide less certain prospects. Many of the industries that have been growing pay less, offer fewer benefits such as health care and pensions, and are more likely to be part-time for workers without college degrees. For example, food preparation workers, security guards, childcare workers, customer service representatives, health care aides, and cashiers are typically paid lower wages, certainly compared to the mostly unionized factory jobs of 50 or 75 years ago. And it is the latter type of jobs that are growing fastest.

Why have manufacturing jobs disappeared so rapidly in the United States and other rich countries? The heart of the answer is not that there is less manufacturing being done in the world, but rather that it is increasingly being done in regions of the globe where workers will accept lower wages and companies can make higher profits by producing goods there. At the center of this important development is the process of **globalization**, in which there is a growing permeability of national borders and the increase in flows of goods, services, and even people across national borders (see Chapter 25 for more details about globalization). One of the most important aspects of globalization is the increasing *trade* between countries, which results in cheaper imported goods from these countries and, as noted, often allows companies to relocate manufacturing jobs in other countries, a process called **offshoring**. Because developing countries can often manufacture products at lower cost than in richer countries, trade can depress the wages of low-skill domestic workers who produce these goods. In many well-documented cases, these lower costs are often the result of **sweatshop** conditions, workplaces that are characterized by extremely low wages and poor or unsafe working conditions and that in some cases even employ children. Not surprisingly, products being manufactured under such conditions are controversial, and there have been numerous boycotts when they have come to public attention.

Related to globalization is another important development: Changes in the way the economy, firms, and employment relations are organized that have taken place since the 1970s. In the post–World War II decades, most companies attempted to provide their employees with long-term job stability and the possibility of promotions from within. Since the 1970s, this system of lifetime employment has slowly disappeared. Based on a desire to cut costs and increase profits, firms increasingly sought to squeeze their workers and make terms of employment more flexible and easier to replace workers. More jobs became temporary, part-time, and less secure in various ways (see Chapter 12 for more information about these changes in the nature of work). One of the major reasons that companies have been able to restructure the terms of employment for many workers is that unions are playing much less of a role than in earlier decades. Union membership has plummeted from a peak of about 35 percent of all workers in the 1950s to just a little over 10 percent today. Unions help workers win higher wages and benefits, and perhaps most importantly, compel employers to share more of the firm's profits with their workforce (Fantasia and Voss 2004; Western and Rosenfeld 2011; Rosenfeld 2014). But when unions disappear, many employers do not have to share as much of their earning with their workers. By one estimate, in 1947, 67 percent of corporate income was paid to workers; by 2018, the percentage was down to 56 percent (McKinsey Global Institute 2019). That may not sound like much, but it represents a huge shift in the distribution of earnings away from workers.

The cumulative impact of economic restructuring and union decline can be seen most clearly in the flattening out of wages for workers in the middle and lower half of the American economy. Figure 11.6 (next page) illustrates the grim details. The critical takeaway from this figure is that employers are getting more work output without having to pay their workers more to get it.

Finally, we can look to government policies as a contributing factor to inequality. So far we have focused on economic changes in driving the overall pattern of income inequality, but the pattern is also very much the result of government policies. The most important of these policies are (1) policies related to taxes (that is, the amount of taxes everyone has to pay on their incomes), and (2) the minimum wage (the lowest wage an employer is allowed to pay).

Taxes have a big impact on the overall level of inequality in a society because of their impact on high earners (and also because the revenue raised by taxes can be used to pay for government programs that support the poor, older people, or people with disabilities, and other disadvantaged individuals and families). A **progressive tax system** is one in which tax rates are higher on richer people than poorer people, with the idea being that it is fairer to ask those who can afford to pay more to do so. Many tax systems around

Figure 11.6 Average Hourly Wage and Productivity, 1947–2018

The vertical axis in this graph indicates the percent change in productivity and hourly wage relative to 1947. Productivity is a measure of the economic output per worker per hour. It has been measured by the federal government's Department of Labor for the same way since 1947, making it possible to compare over time. The graph shows that, after nearly two decades of simultaneous growth of productivity and wages, wages have stagnated since the 1970s, reflecting the restructuring of American firms. However, productivity kept rising and, as indicated in the graph, the average worker was far more productive in 2018 than the same worker would have been in 1970. What does this say about income inequality? It means that workers, on average, receive a smaller share of their average economic output than four decades ago.

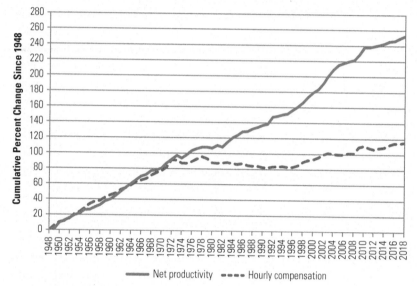

SOURCE: Economic Policy Institute, 2020.

the world, including in the United States, are progressive. Some have argued that if tax rates on the rich are high enough, they will constrain their incomes (why try to earn more if you are going to give most of it back in the form of taxes?). Of course, it is never that simple; because the tax code contains a large number of deductions and exemptions, the actual rate paid by high earners (who typically employ a small army of tax lawyers and consultants to reduce their tax burdens) is always lower than the official rate. Still, the federal income tax rates paid by the highest-earning Americans have fallen dramatically over time, from over 90 percent to 37 percent today. To see this evolution, explore Figure 11.7.

Figure 11.7 shows the official rates, not the rates that people actually pay. It is important to note that the tax rate does not fully apply to many high earners, who are able to shield much of their earnings from some or even all taxation. For example, as the cache of leaked financial documents known as the Panama Papers vividly illustrated in 2016, wealthy people all over the world make use of offshore accounts in order to conceal large sums of money and avoid paying taxes (Zucman 2015). Other rich people simply take advantage of loopholes in the tax code of their home country to hold down their rate of tax. For example, in the United States, high-income tax payers pay a significantly lower rate of tax on income that qualifies as "capital gains," and tax advisors are skilled at helping many wealthy people shift much of their income into the form of capital gains, or to take advantage of other kinds of tax breaks.

How much does the legal avoidance of taxes by the rich matter? A couple of examples should help us understand why the issue is so pressing. In a famous article in the *New York Times*, Warren Buffet, one of the richest people in the world, stated that after his accountants are done with his taxes, he pays a lower share of his income in taxes than his secretary does (Buffett 2011). Former President Donald Trump, who claims to be worth many billions of dollars and lives a well-publicized lavish lifestyle with multiple million-dollar residences, paid *no taxes* at all in 10 of the previous 15 years, and just $75,000 in 2017 and 2018 (Buettner, Craig, and McIntire 2020).

The primary reason Trump was able to avoid taxes is because he was legally allowed to report huge business losses, raising the question of how he could simultaneously be losing so much money and yet be visibly living an expensive lifestyle?

Is Trump unusual in his ability to avoid taxes? Not really. In a stunning recent finding, two economists

Figure 11.7 Top Marginal Tax Rates, 1960–2021

The top marginal tax rate refers to the rate that applies to the wealthiest taxpayers.

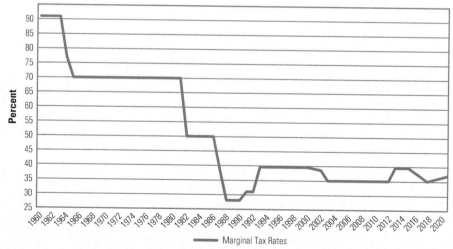

SOURCE: Tax Foundation, 2015, and author's update.

One of Donald Trump's many residences. In spite of his wealth, Trump managed to avoid paying federal income taxes in 10 of the last 15 years. The ability of many rich people to avoid or minimize their taxes through sophisticated accounting methods and employing an army of tax lawyers means that everyone else must pay higher taxes to make up the difference.

concluded that the percentage of federal income tax paid by the highest 400 Americans (at 23 percent) was *lower* than the average rate paid by the bottom 50 percent of households in 2018 (24 percent) (Saez and Zucman 2019). If the idea that the rich should pay a bit more than everyone else is widely shared – and every poll or survey ever conducted will show that it is (e.g. McCall 2013) – the United States is a long ways away from that goal today.

The flip side of the reduced taxes paid by the rich is the declining value of the **minimum wage**—the lowest amount an employer can legally pay a worker. The

federal government has chosen not to raise the minimum wage to keep up with inflation, so the lowest paid workers make much less now than they did in earlier times. While the minimum wage grew steadily between the 1940s and the late 1960s, it has changed very little for most of the period from the 1980s onward (see Figure 11.8). Prices kept rising, but the minimum wage did not. So after adjusting for inflation, the real (inflation-adjusted—the black line) value of the federal minimum wage dropped from about $10.79 in 1968, to $9 an hour in 1978 in inflation-adjusted dollars, to a value that was between $6 and $8 an hour since 1990 (once adjusted for inflation). It is important to note that cities and states have the right to set their own minimum wage, and in the last few years a number of states (30 in all) have established minimums that are higher than the federal minimum (shown in the red line, currently $7.25 an hour). About half the states currently have adopted a higher minimum for workers in their state, with 19 states having established a $10/hour minimum. But in half the states, $7.25 to $8.00 is still the minimum wage.

What are the consequences of minimum wage policy on inequality? The stereotypical portrait of the minimum-wage earner is a teenager working part-time. In fact, in recent years about 70 percent of minimum-wage earners are adults, many of whom are women and/or people of color. Even if the minimum wage affects only a small proportion of the working population (about 5 to 6 percent of all workers currently make the minimum wage), it does matter for inequality because it affects the well-being of families at the bottom of the income distribution *and* because many workers are paid just over the minimum wage (so when it does not go up, those workers are not likely to see any increases either). Increasing the minimum wage motivates employers to increase the wages of other workers who are at or just above the minimum if they want to keep those workers happy. For this reason, proposals to dramatically increase the minimum wage—to $15 per hour, as proposed by the social movement called the "Fight for 15"—have been strongly opposed by many corporate executives.

Who Are the 1 Percent?

11.2.3 Describe who comprises the "1 percent" in America.

Most people would rather be rich than poor. But how rich is too rich? In the fall of 2011, a social movement initially calling itself Occupy Wall Street exploded on the scene, first in New

Figure 11.8 The Declining Value of Minimum Wage, 1938–2018

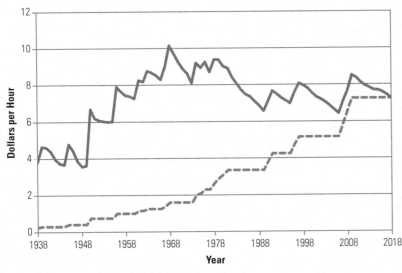

- - - Nominal Min. Wage (Current $) ——— Real Min. Wage (2018 $)

SOURCE: Economic Policy Institute, 2019.

York City and later across America and in other countries around the world. The movement highlighted the disparity between what it called the "1 percent"—that is, individuals and families in the top 1 percent of income and/or wealth—and everyone else (the "99 percent"). In 2019, a household would have had to earn around $539,000 to join the lower rungs of membership in the top 1 percent. To reach the top half of the top 1 percent, however, you would have needed to earn over $800,000 a year.

So who are the people at the very top, the so-called 1 percenters? Do they work, or did they inherit their money? For those who work, what kinds of jobs do they have? How different are the group of people in the entire top 1 percent, as opposed to the top 0.1 percent (or the top tenth of the top 1 percent, who in 2019 would have needed to earn $1.5 million to reach that rarified threshold)? Three economists have studied this question, using data from tax returns (Bakija, Cole, and Heim 2012; see Table 11.2). Perhaps somewhat surprisingly, only 6 percent (of the top 0.1 percent; it is 7 percent if we look at the entire top 1 percent) are not working. So the vast majority of high earners do have jobs, as opposed to living off inheritances and/or investments (although many combine working income with income from investments of various sorts). Two occupations stand out: Executives and high-level managers (41 percent of the top 0.1 percent and 30 percent of the top 1 percent), finance (18 percent of the top 0.1 percent and 13 percent of the top 1 percent), and then a scattering of high earners in many different occupations, including law, medicine, real estate, arts, media and sports, and entrepreneurs (business owners). The growth in pay received by top company executives has received a great deal of attention and discussion in recent years, and for good reason. In 1965, the average top executive made about 20 times as much as the average-paid worker at a large company; in 1978, it was 30:1. In other words, top executives were paid a lot more than the typical worker at these companies, but the gap was a small fraction of what it is today. In 2014, the average top executive made 204 times as much as the average worker in the same company (Hodgson 2015).

Looking at Table 11.2, several other interesting observations stand out. For one thing, the differences in the occupations between the top 1 percent and 0.1 percent are interesting to note; as we move downward to look at the entire top 1 percent, we see some occupations like those in the medical field (mostly doctors) increasing dramatically (from 4.4 percent of the top 0.1 percent to fully 15 percent of the top 1 percent). There are also a scattering of new occupational fields that appear, such as blue-collar workers and government employees. It may be surprising to see people working in these occupations earning extremely high incomes, but keep in mind that very, very few blue-collar or government employees earn incomes that put them in the top 1 percent, and even in jobs such as these there are only a handful of people with very specialized skills or abilities that enable them to earn very high pay.

Table 11.2 Occupations of the Top 1% and Top 0.1% of Income Earners

This table shows the occupations reported on the tax returns of the highest earning Americans, in the top 0.1 percent and the top 1 percent. Executives and financial professionals are more common at the very top (almost 60 percent) than in the less rarefied and larger group in the top 1 percent, where physicians, lawyers, computer/math/engineering, and skilled sales professionals are more highly represented.

	Top 0.1%	Top 1%
Executives, managers, supervisors (nonfinance)	40.8%	30.0%
Financial professions	18.4	13.2
Not working	6.3	7.4
Lawyers	6.2	7.7
Real estate	4.7	3.9
Medical	4.4	14.4
Entrepreneur	3.6	2.8
Arts, media, sports	3.1	1.7
Computer, math, engineering, technical	3.0	4.2
Business operations	2.2	2.8
Skilled sales (except finance or real estate)	1.9	3.7
Professors and scientists	1.1	1.8
Farmers and ranchers	1.0	0.8

SOURCE: Bakija, Cole, and Heim, 2012.

Bob Ebbesen/Alamy Stock Photo

BIG QUESTION 11.3 Do We All Have an Equal Opportunity to Succeed in Life?

INEQUALITY, EDUCATION, AND SOCIAL MOBILITY

So far, we have discussed inequality in terms of income and wealth. But this is only part of the story. One important type of inequality is **inequality of opportunity**, which refers to the ways in which opportunities for children and young adults to maximize their potential may be very unequal. Equality of opportunity would exist in a world where all children have similar chances to succeed in life, regardless of whether they were born to wealthy or poor families. If everyone, regardless of their social background, has similar chances of success in life as an adult, we could say that opportunities are truly equally distributed, and only merit and hard work are rewarded. If, in contrast, an individual's chances to do well in life depend on the advantages (or disadvantages) of the family and circumstances they were born into, then we can say opportunity is unequally distributed. This is one of the most important topics in the study of inequality, and we will explore it in this section.

Measuring Opportunity: The Concept of Social Mobility

11.3.1 Define social mobility and describe how inequality of opportunity is measured.

While most Americans accept some degree of inequality in outcomes as an inherent feature of a capitalist economy, there is broad support in the United States today for the ideal of equality of opportunity. Most of us believe very strongly, for example, that children should have the

opportunity to flourish even if they are born into families with limited resources. This idea is part of what is known as the American Dream, and it is one of the most cherished aspects of life in United States. Politicians and social theorists have also sometimes called for equality of opportunity on the grounds that it benefits society: If poor children have no chance to succeed in life, their talent and potential contributions will be lost, and this is inefficient for the society as a whole.

But do we have something approximating equality of opportunity? Measuring opportunity in any society is not a simple research question. Whereas we can measure other kinds of inequalities—income, wealth, consumption, even well-being—in relatively straightforward ways (even if the details are complicated!), there is no one obvious way of determining how much opportunity individuals really have. The solution that social scientists have settled on is to examine what is known as **social mobility**, or more specifically, the pattern of intergenerational inheritance in a society. Social mobility is a measure of the extent to which parents and their children have similar or different social and economic positions in adulthood. A high-mobility society is one where there is relatively little connection between parents' and children's place in life. By contrast, when there is a relatively close connection between parents and their children's positions when children reach adulthood, social mobility is low. A high-mobility society approximates the ideal of equality of opportunity; in such a society, where a child ends up in life is determined largely through her or his own achievements. An immobile society, by contrast, is one where your chances are largely determined at birth; in extreme cases, immobility creates a **caste society**, one in which the advantages or disadvantages of birth determine fully your social position (such as was traditionally the case in India, where being born into a lower caste traditionally meant no chance to move into a higher caste).

In other words, in a perfectly mobile society, parents' resources would be completely irrelevant for children's outcomes; that is, everyone would have the same chances of succeeding in life regardless of their family background. In a perfectly immobile society, however, chances of success would be entirely determined by parental resources. Children of poor parents would grow up to be poor, while children of rich parents would grow up to be rich. In the real world, all societies fall somewhere in between these two extremes. To study where different societies fall, we ask the question: To what extent do family resources (that is, who your parents are) determine how well you will do in life?

Accounts of individual social mobility often focus on effort and ability. Stories about upward mobility usually highlight exceptional individuals who overcame massive difficulties and experience upward mobility—the "rags to riches" story—and, less frequently, individuals who decline in spite of the many opportunities they had and experience downward mobility. Countless movies and novels have portrayed either of these situations. These anecdotal cases often highlight the extent to which individual upward and downward mobility can be linked to specific individual attributes: Hard work overcoming disadvantage, drug abuse offsetting privilege, and so forth. But these individual stories can

Christopher Victorio/The Photo Access/Alamy Images

Oprah Winfrey is an example of a "rags to riches" upward mobility story. Born into poverty in rural Mississippi to a teenage single mother and raised in an impoverished neighborhood in Milwaukee, she overcame severe adversity to become a billionaire television host, media mogul, and philanthropist. Winfrey's story is so exceptional that it is difficult to draw any lessons from it. But it does prompt the question: What would it take for biographies like hers to be more common in the United States?

mislead us about the general patterns that we can observe across different societies that suggest that mobility is not simply an attribute of individuals and their successes or failures. We explore this in more detail in the next section.

Social Mobility in Comparative Perspective

11.3.2 Compare and contrast chances for social mobility in the United States to other countries.

One way in which social scientists measure social mobility in different societies is by identifying the strength of the **association**—that is, the relationship between two factors, or **variables**, that change together—between parents' social standing (which could be measured based on income, occupation, or other measures of social standing) and their children's outcomes on the same variables as adults. An association of zero means that there is literally no connection whatsoever between parents' income and children's income (or parents' and children's occupation, or education). Thinking about income, for example, if parents' income does not make any difference to how small or large their children's income will be, we can say that a situation of *perfect mobility* exists. An association of one, in turn, means that parents' income fully determines children's income. In that situation, which is one of perfect **immobility**, if your parents have an income that is, say, 50 percent higher than the average income, you too as an adult will have an income 50 percent higher than the average. In other words, you wouldn't go up or down—you'd end up exactly where your parents were.

As noted in the previous section, all societies fall somewhere in between perfect mobility and perfect immobility. The question for researchers is to estimate how close a country is to either side. Figure 11.9 displays one important and well-regarded analysis of the association of parents' and adult children's earnings in the United States versus other advanced industrial countries for which we have comparable data. As the figure suggests, the chances of mobility vary substantially across countries. Countries such as the United Kingdom, Italy, and the United States have relatively high intergenerational association, that is, less social mobility. At the other extreme, Nordic countries such as Denmark, Norway, and Finland have much weaker associations between parents' and children's income, indicating higher chances of mobility. For example, the intergenerational association in Norway is 0.18. That means that, on average, Norwegian parents pass on 18 percent of their economic advantage (or disadvantage) to their kids. For example, a Norwegian parent who earns $100,000 more than the

Figure 11.9 Intergenerational Association of Earnings in the United States and Other Advanced Industrial Countries

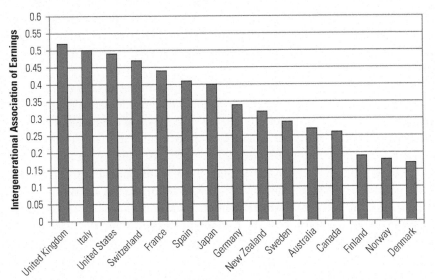

SOURCE: Based on data from Corak, 2013.

mean income for all Norwegians will, on average, have kids who will earn $18,000 more than that same mean as an adult.

Figure 11.9 reveals some troubling evidence about the state of social mobility in America. The intergenerational association of 0.49 in the United States means that if your earnings are $100,000 higher than average, then your kids can expect to make $49,000 more than average (of course these are averages; there will be a lot of variation from one family to the next). That is vastly more than in Norway and many other countries. What this means is that your success (or difficulties) in life is much more closely related to your parents in the United States than it is in many other countries. There are other rich countries, however, that also have lower rates of social mobility similar to the United States. Nevertheless, it is often said that America is "exceptional" for having high rates of social mobility. That idea should be rejected. Many children will *not* be able to live as well as their parents as wages and income have not gone up (as noted earlier).

To get a closer look, we can examine individual families (i.e., parents and their children). A team of social scientists led by the economist Raj Chetty did just that. They examined the patterns of social mobility using (confidential) tax data, the same kind of data used by Thomas Piketty and his colleagues we described above. They were able to see how much

parents made at age 34, and how much their children earned when they reached 34. For each year, they took a sample of tax returns of parents, and then 34 years later, matching the Social Security numbers, identified the tax return of all the children in the family. The results of this exercise are shown in Figure 11.10. Chetty and his colleagues found that a child born in 1940 had more than a 90 percent chance of earning more than their parents did (in 1974, when they were 34). That 9 in 10 children earned more than their parents is extraordinary evidence of societal-wide upward mobility. However, in 1985, the last year the researchers examined, a child had only a 50 percent chance of earning more (in 2009, when they were 34) than their parents did at age 34 in 1985.

Measuring social mobility through the association of earnings between parents and their adult children in the developing world is more challenging because good quality data on both parents and adult children are scarcer. But we do have some high-quality research on a number of countries in Latin America. Based on the best available estimates, the intergenerational association is much higher in countries such as Brazil, Chile, or Mexico than in very rich countries, reaching values between 0.5 and 0.6. This means that, on average, parents pass along more than half of their economic advantage (or disadvantage) to their children (Torche 2014).

Figure 11.10 Declining Social Mobility, Birth Cohorts 1940–1985

This figure displays the percentage of children earning more than their parents at age 34. The first year of the graph shows the percent chance that a child born in 1940 to parents aged 34 would have more income than their parents when they reached 34 (in 1974). The last birth cohort, born in 1985, were measured in 2009 when they were 34.

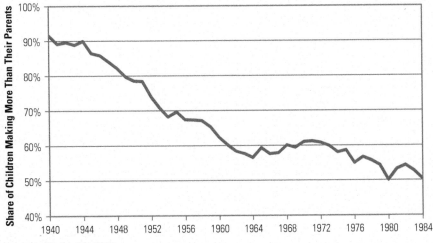

SOURCE: Chetty et al. 2017.

Factors Influencing Mobility

11.3.3 Identify factors that affect how much social mobility exists in a society.

What specific factors affect how much social mobility exists in a society? This is also not an easy question, as researchers have found that there are a large number of different factors that influence social mobility. For example, the amount of mobility will depend on what goes on inside families, as well as the process of slotting individuals into jobs (that is, the process by which employers hire individual workers, known as the **labor market**). In a context where good jobs are expanding, upward mobility is more likely than in a society where good jobs are declining. Perhaps most importantly, however, the policies that governments adopt are very important, especially in relation to the education system. And these factors also overlap.

Families matter because parents play a large role in shaping how much education and other social and intellectual assets children acquire, and it is education and other assets that will largely determine children's incomes. If a society's education system is very limited, no matter what kinds of efforts parents make to encourage their children to learn, it may not lead to better educational outcomes. Labor markets—the way workers are hired and promoted—matter because it is in the labor market that education pays off in economic terms. Government policies matter because government regulates both labor markets and educational systems. Governments decide whether and to what extent disadvantaged children should get compensatory assistance (such as the Head Start Program, which provides education and health services to low-income children and their families), which may help them overcome disadvantages associated with their family background. Governments also decide how equal schools are in rich and poor areas and how much support students receive for going to college.

These four factors—families, education, labor markets, and government policies—are all highly correlated with the level of inequality children face when they are growing up. High inequality of opportunity usually means that advantaged families can invest much more than disadvantaged families in their children's education and that the quality of schools that wealthy children attend will be much better than schools serving poor children. High inequality is also closely related to a high payoff of having a college degree

(in fact, as we discussed, there is a growing college wage premium in the United States). And high inequality is related to the role of the government. If the government has a weak system of policies to compensate for the disadvantages that poor children face, these children will have much less opportunity to succeed as adults (thus reinforcing inequality).

As mentioned, social scientists have shown that the overall level of inequality of conditions in a country is indeed typically related to the level of intergenerational mobility (or equality of opportunity) in that country. Again, higher inequality overall is associated with lower mobility. Figure 11.11 plots the level of inequality when children were growing up in each country in the y axis (the vertical axis) against the intergenerational earnings association in the x axis (the horizontal axis). We can see here, too, that countries with higher levels of inequality display stronger intergenerational associations between parents' income and children's earnings. In contrast, mobility is much higher in low-inequality countries.

Figure 11.11 suggests a clear relationship between inequality and mobility, although it is not perfect (the dots move from the lower left to upper right, but there is a lot of variation). Despite the apparent connection, we cannot jump to the conclusion that high inequality *causes* low mobility. The reason is that there may be other factors that produce both inequality of conditions and low intergenerational mobility. The figure, however, does suggest that a society's overall level of inequality plays an important role and helps to explain the differences in mobility between countries. Researchers are continuing to study this question.

Figure 11.11 Relationship Between Income Inequality and Mobility in Selected Countries, Around Year 2013

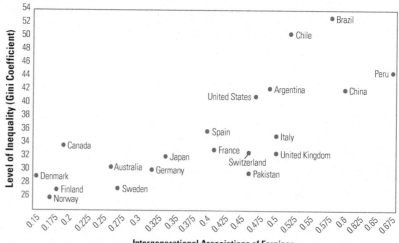

SOURCE: Corak, 2013; should be Corak, 2013.

Education and Social Mobility

11.3.4 Discuss the relationship between education and social mobility.

For many decades, sociologists have emphasized the critical role of education in understanding social mobility. In all complex societies, privileged, high-status positions by definition are scarce—that is, after all, what makes them valued. In modern times, these privileged positions in general are rarely directly inherited by children of the upper class, but rather through the education system. Upper-class parents are (almost always) unable to directly transfer privileged occupational positions to their children; a doctor or lawyer cannot simply pass on the family business to their child unless the child can get into and through medical school or law school. Instead, these parents invest for decades in their children's education in the hopes that similar occupational opportunities will be conferred indirectly.

To understand this important insight into how education and social inequality are linked, it is worth reviewing how sociologists have emphasized different aspects of this relationship over the past century. Education has a dual character with respect to attaining privileged, high-status positions. On the one hand, education systems can function to challenge other traditional forms of allocating privileged positions in society. In traditional societies, for example, occupations are often simply passed on from parent to child. If a father was an agricultural laborer, his sons would also likely be agricultural laborers. The establishment and spread of public education broke down these traditional forms of occupational inheritance and substituted a new way of deciding who will get what. Educational systems do this through what are known as principles of **meritocracy**, a system where rewards and positions are distributed by ability, not social background or personal connections.

Education systems, however, can also be used to maintain and preserve privileged access to scarce positions if families with more resources are able to invest in more or better education for their children, for example, by moving to a better neighborhood or paying for private school or private tutoring. Furthermore, educational systems produce credentials, and groups can use these credentials to separate those with privilege from those without. In modern societies, high-status positions increasingly require educational credentials. It no longer matters how good you are at a particular thing, for example, teaching or healing people. Without the proper educational certificate, you are typically denied access to privileged jobs such as being a doctor or university professor.

Sociologists recognize that schools play a fundamental role in society, not simply by training individuals for employment but also by working to select those who will be granted access to more desirable occupations. To the extent that schools facilitate the movement of talented individuals from lower social origins to privileged occupations, sociologists consider the society "open" rather than "closed." When individuals from disadvantaged socioeconomic backgrounds attain privileged occupational positions with associated higher social rewards (such as status, prestige, and income), social mobility has occurred. Sociologists have repeatedly demonstrated that schools play a critical role in either blocking or facilitating social mobility.

In recent decades, however, there is growing evidence that affluent American parents with enough resources are "hoarding" the opportunities that the educational system provides (Reeves 2017). Parents with enough income can provide their children with far greater learning opportunities outside of school, and also make sure their children attend better schools (private or public, the latter by moving to communities with top-rated public schools or finding the best option within large urban districts). They also pay for such things as test preparation courses and private tutoring, to give their children a further leg up on everyone else. This process starts in childhood, when parents enroll their children in a variety of activities and take them on foreign trips that cultivate both knowledge and skills that will be rewarded in the educational system (Lareau 2002). We'll explore these issues more fully in Chapter 18 (on education), but the key point is that there is only so much educational systems can do to give children equal opportunity in a very unequal society like the United States.

anek.soowannaphoom/Shutterstock

The children of relatively wealthy families consistently perform better on standardized tests. To understand why wealthy children score better, it is important to examine the structural conditions of their educational experiences. Wealthy families tend to live in school districts with more educational resources and have access to far more opportunities for enrichment—such as tutoring—than do poor families. Poor families can still help their children, but it requires far greater investment of time and limited resources than for richer families.

MATTRAVEL/Alamy Stock Photo

LIFE AT THE BOTTOM: THE PROBLEM OF POVERTY

So far, we've focused largely on inequality and the implications it has for social mobility. In this section, we turn to an analysis of poverty. Defining who is poor is not straightforward. In the simplest of terms, poverty is a condition that involves the inability to afford basic needs such as food, clothing, shelter, and health care. But beyond a minimum of resources to ensure subsistence, it is difficult to define what those basic needs are. Adam Smith, the eighteenth-century Scottish philosopher, wrote the following in the classic 1776 book *The Wealth of Nations*:

> *A linen shirt is, strictly speaking, not a necessary of life.... The Greeks and Romans lived, I suppose, very comfortably though they had no linen. But in the present times, through the greater part of Europe, a creditable day-labourer will be ashamed to appear in public without a linen shirt, the want of which would be supposed to denote that disgraceful degree of poverty which, it is presumed, nobody can well fall into without extreme bad conduct.* (Smith [1776] 1976, p. 466)

Today, it may be the case that having a cell phone that can connect to the Internet and social media is every bit as necessary as having a linen shirt was in the late eighteenth century, when Smith was writing. Yet for most of human history, no one had such devices, even the richest of people. What about a car? It is entirely possible to argue that, given the importance of transportation, especially in rural areas or places where mass transit options are limited, a car is fairly essential to life in the twenty-first century (even too essential, perhaps, given problems of climate change). So we could reasonably argue

that access to information and communication as well as a reliable means of transportation are crucial for finding a job, going to school, or just living an ordinary life in the twenty-first century. These are things that even the richest person in the world in the late nineteenth century could only dream about!

Poverty researchers face a sharp challenge in defining what it means to live in poverty, as well as analyzing the societal conditions that cause it. In this section, we will explore these questions.

Different Measures of Poverty

11.4.1 Distinguish between absolute and relative measures of poverty.

The official method in which the federal government measures poverty in the United States is by setting an income threshold—the minimum income necessary to afford basic necessities. This threshold is called the **poverty line**. But how is that minimum income determined? The story is a fascinating one, with major implications for how we understand and discuss poverty. The official poverty line was defined for the first time in the mid-1960s as part of a major government effort to reduce the amount of poverty in the United States (what came to be known as the War on Poverty). The task was assigned to an obscure official in the Social Security Administration named Mollie Orshansky in 1963, and her formula, once established, has simply been updated each year to take inflation into account. Orshansky started from the observation that, at the time, the typical American family spent about one-third of its income on food. By calculating what she thought was the cost of a nutritionally minimally adequate diet and

Table 11.3 Poverty Line for Various Household Types

U.S. Census Bureau Poverty Thresholds, 2020	
Size of Family Unit	Poverty Threshold
One person (unrelated individual) Under age 65	12,760
Two people	17,240
Three people	21,720
Four people	26,200
Five people	30,680
Six people	35,160
Seven people	39,640
Eight people	44,120

SOURCE: U.S. Department of Health and Human Services.

then multiplying by three, a family (or individual) would have an adequate amount to live on (and not be in poverty). Her design allowed her definition of poverty to vary by family size, and to adjust each year for changes in the cost of living. In 2020, for example, the poverty line for a family of four was $26,200. So families of four people with an income less than $26,200 were considered poor. The poverty line for a person living alone, however, was $12,760. Using the official definition of poverty, in 2013, about 15 percent of Americans lived in poverty (more than 45 million people, out of a total population of approximately 313 million), although by 2019 it had fallen to about 10 percent (after years of continuous economic growth poverty rates during the COVID-19 pandemic rose again). Table 11.3 summarizes the poverty line for various household types as of 2020.

The official measure of poverty, designed by Orshansky in the early 1960s, has not been significantly altered since then. Many criticisms have been raised about it: For example, it accounts for some kinds of income that poor people may receive, like food stamps, but does not take into account taxes they pay or adjust for differences in cost of living across states or cities. The cost of food has fallen relative to the cost of other necessary things such as housing, so basing an overall family budget anchored to the cost of food is problematic. Almost all poverty researchers believe that we are underestimating the size of the poverty population.

What are some alternative ways of measuring poverty? The official definition of poverty used by the American government is a measure of **absolute poverty**, which attempts to define the minimum amount of income necessary to meet basic needs but does not adjust for changes in living standards, the latter being an important shortcoming. The official measure also doesn't give us any way to think about poverty as something other than a bundle of things needed to live, and rather as a way to think

about how people are deprived in ways that make it difficult for them to participate in everyday life. The examples discussed above about a car and a cellphone can make it hard for a poor person to connect with others in addition to the implications for finding and maintaining employment or taking care of children.

In response to concerns about absolute poverty measures, many European governments and most social scientists today have instead adopted an alternative measure of poverty known as **relative poverty**, which attempts to capture changes in living standards to define who is poor. Relative poverty is most commonly defined as those families with incomes below 50 percent of the median income (as noted, the median is the midpoint of the income distribution in the country, with half of the population above and half below). The median income serves as a benchmark of what is common or typical in a society, and the idea is that all families and individuals with incomes 50 percent below the median are sufficiently disadvantaged in comparison with other members of society to be considered poor. For example, the U.S. median household income for a family of four is currently around $70,000. A family of four with an income below $35,000, then, would be considered relatively poor, even if they are not absolutely poor (that threshold is $26,200). Using a relative measure of poverty, several million more families and individuals would be considered poor in the United States than by using the official definition.

Poverty in the United States: Who Are the Poor?

11.4.2 Identify factors that increase the likelihood of poverty.

Figure 11.12 (next page) plots the proportion of people living in poverty in the United States since 1959, based on the official government definition described in the previous section (keep in mind that the trends over-time can be shown using any definition of poverty, as long as it used consistantly). As we can see, the proportion of poor people declined sharply over the 1960s, but there has been little improvement since the early 1970s. In fact, poverty increased after the recessions of the early 1970s, early 1990s, and early 2000s, when the economy worsened and unemployment increased. In 2019, however, before the arrival of the COVID pandemic, the proportion of people in poverty (using the official measure) was 10.5 percent, the lowest it had ever been. The low poverty rate was the result of nine years of steady economic growth with no economic recessions. If past trends are any indication, it is extremely likely that the overall poverty rate will increase when the economy slows down, as it did with the arrival of the COVID-19 pandemic.

Figure 11.12 Poverty Trends in the United States, 1959–2019

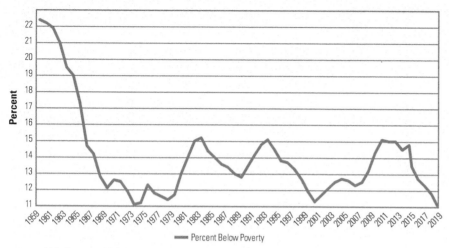

SOURCE: U.S. Census, Table B-1.

What causes individuals or families to fall into poverty? Even though the individuals and families living in poverty are diverse, a number of factors increase the likelihood that someone will be poor. Among these, the most important are education, employment status, minority status, age, and family structure. Education matters because, as we have discussed, schooling is an important determinant of the skills that people can sell in the market in exchange for a wage. Having less than a high school diploma puts anyone at higher risk of poverty. Employment status and type of job are basically the outcome of education and other skills and assets. Having and maintaining a job that pays wages higher than the poverty line will keep anyone out of poverty. But there have never been enough jobs for all who want and need one, and even full-time jobs at the federal minimum wage are not enough to lift a family out of poverty. So those who either do not have jobs or have very low-paying ones will be poor. Race and ethnicity also matters in the United States. Blacks, Latinxs, and Native Americans are much more likely to live in poverty than Whites. However, it is also important to note that the largest numbers of poor people are White. For example, in 2014 there were 19.6 million Whites, 9.6 million Blacks, and 13.1 million Latinxs living in poverty. Finally, family structure also matters. Families in which there is a single parent—usually a female—are much more likely to be poor. This phenomenon has been called the *feminization of poverty*, and it highlights the difficulties of complementing the roles of primary caregiver and provider on a single income.

One widespread belief about the poor is that most do not have jobs. This is not true. In fact, most of the people living in poverty engage in the labor market at least some of the time. About two-thirds of families living below the poverty line have at least one working family member, and over half of these workers are working full-time (Stevens and Pihl 2016). These statistics highlight the fact that many poor people in the United States are engaged in the labor market. They are known as the **working poor**, people who cannot make enough income to be free from poverty even if, as many do, they work part or full-time jobs. How can this be? Many jobs simply do not pay enough to lift people working in them above the poverty line. For example, according to the Bureau of Labor Statistics for 2015, a food preparation worker earned $9.70 an hour, and a home health aide made $11.54 an hour. If these workers worked 40 hours a week for 48 weeks a year, they made, respectively, $18,624 and $20,237 a year, which was well below the 2015 poverty line of $24,300 for a family of four. But this is not all. For the working poor, poverty is not just about low income. Low-paying jobs are often unstable, and many people working in these jobs work on a temporary or part-time basis. Such jobs are not secure enough to save money to rely on for an illness, an unexpected large expense, or to plan for the future. Even those families that are usually above the poverty line may be very vulnerable to economic and family circumstances. A recession, a divorce or spousal abandonment, or a severe illness can change the picture for families living close to the poverty line in ways for which middle-class families have more of a cushion. Most poor families have very little in the way of savings to fall back upon in the event of any crisis. They live, in short, at the edge of insecurity.

Two broad sets of explanations—individual and structural—have informed the debate over poverty. Those who favor the individual-level perspective believe that to understand poverty, we have to look to those traits of individuals and families (such as their values or work ethic) that help them achieve success or lead them to failure. The central assumption of those who take an individualist perspective on poverty is that there are always enough opportunities for individuals to find a good job and a chance to get ahead, but not everyone is able and willing to do so. If the poor are "trapped" in poverty, it is because they have not developed the right set of attributes to seize the opportunities that are all around them. In their discussions of poverty in recent years, those who take the individualist perspective often emphasize two factors: (1) The role of governmental policies in discouraging the poor from working, and (2)

Mark Bussell

Sitting in a coffee shop to pass the time is one way unemployed people get through the day. There are never enough jobs for everyone who wants one. There will, as a result, always be people without work.

the importance of the decline in two-parent (generally male–female) families (we don't yet have data on same-sex family trends)—and in particular the rising percentage of births outside of the context of marriage—for their contributions to weakening the commitment to hard work among the poor. According to this view, the problem with government assistance as a solution to poverty, in whatever form it takes, is that it does not require recipients to earn it, thereby encouraging the very behaviors that cause poverty in the first place. The solution to ending poverty, therefore, lies in helping individuals change their behavior (Sowell 2016).

The structural approach to poverty, in contrast, focuses on how opportunities and resources are distributed across the population, giving some people a better chance to succeed in life than others. A structuralist would begin by pointing to all of the social and economic forces that impact our lives and argue that these forces are the primary explanations for poverty. Structuralists also point to many reasons why some people are just not able to take advantage of whatever opportunities there may be for them. There are the disabled and those with mental health problems. There are people who struggle with drug addiction or alcoholism. There are people living in small towns or rural areas that lack jobs and economic opportunity. Trying to force people with these kinds of problems or issues into jobs (which may not exist) is not necessarily going to solve their individual problems or make society better off.

Almost all sociologists think about poverty from a structuralist perspective. Rather than trying to explain why one person is poor, sociologists ask, why are so many people poor? A good metaphor for thinking about the structural sources of poverty is the child's game of musical chairs. In the game, the number of chairs is always one less than the number of players. The game begins when some music is played, and when it stops, the players scramble to get a chair. One is always left out; the game is designed to have a loser in each round (the game continues, removing one player and chair until there is only one player left). Just as the game of musical chairs always leaves someone out, so too do capitalist economies. Rather than trying to "solve" the problems of the losing player, perhaps societies need to examine how to provide an extra chair for the loser.

Poverty in International Comparative Perspective

11.4.3 Compare and contrast the level of poverty in the United States to similar countries.

Is the level of poverty in the United States comparable to other advanced industrial countries? On the one hand, all of the rich countries have experienced similar economic trends in terms of deindustrialization and economic restructuring, which suggests they are likely to have levels of poverty that should be broadly similar. But on the other hand, America's policies toward poverty reduction are quite different than the policies of other countries in Western Europe, Canada, or Australia. The United States spends less to directly alleviate poverty through welfare programs than any other wealthy country, although the United States does spend a lot on education relative to other countries which is sometimes viewed as an anti-poverty program (Garfinkel, Rainwater, and Smeeding 2010).

Comparing poverty levels across countries is no easy task. It requires a common measure of income, a common poverty line, and a way to make currency similar across nations. Comparing the effectiveness of government anti-poverty programs is also very challenging. One important ongoing comparative study by poverty researchers has undertaken this task (Gornick and Smeeding 2018). In order to compare poverty, the researchers distinguish between "market" income (what is received just from earnings), and "disposable" or usable income (what families have to spend after taking taxes and government programs

Figure 11.13 Pre- and Post-Transfer Poverty Rates in Select Advanced Industrial Countries

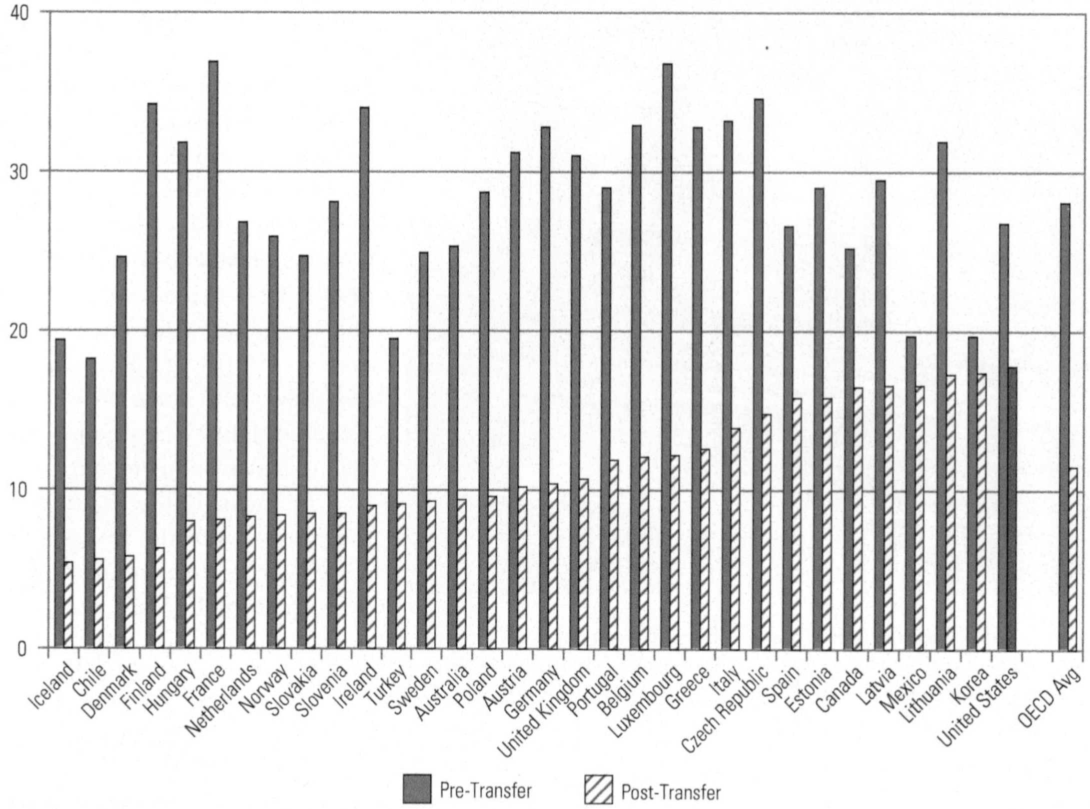

SOURCE: Organization for Economic Cooperation and Development (OECD) Income Distribution Database. Retrieved from: https://stats.oecd.org/Index.aspx?DataSetCode=IDD#.

into account, which can significantly alter their household incomes). Taking everything into account, the answer of how the United States compares to other countries is somewhat complicated, but in terms of disposable (usable) income poverty, after all taxes and government programs are taken into account, is higher in the United States than in other rich countries, and more than twice as high as in many of those countries. Figure 11.13 shows the comparison across select countries in 2016.

What is interesting to note in this figure is that the poverty rate based just on market incomes would be slightly *lower* in the United States than several other countries, but because the U.S. government does much less to help poor families than other countries, the percentage of poor families declines only from about 27 percent to 18 percent. In the average OECD country in this database, the rate of poverty before taxes and transfers is very similar to the U.S., but the average country has a poverty after taxes and transfers of just 12 percent. In some countries, the decline is even greater. In France, for example, it goes from 37 percent to just 8 percent). The U.S. could do much more to relieve the burdens of poverty if it followed the approaches of other countries most similar to it.

Poverty and Children

11.4.4 Explain the impact of growing up in poverty on children.

A particularly important concern that social scientists and government officials have about poverty is how it impacts children. Why is childhood poverty a powerful predictor of poverty in adulthood? Childhood poverty creates a vicious cycle that reproduces disadvantage across generations. This is an especially important problem in the United States. In recent and typical years, using the official poverty rate measure, somewhere around 13 to 15 percent of adults and over 20 percent of children live in poverty. (Note that these rates were both lower in 2019, the last year we have full data for. In 2021, Congress passed a major expansion of support provided to poor families with children, known as The American Families Plan, that provides income and other benefits sufficient to lift over half of all poor children out of poverty. However, other children will remain trapped below the poverty line, and even many of those lifted above it will still be very insecure.

That about one in five children have been growing up in poverty in recent decades is worrisome for many reasons. Lack of basic nutrients, shelter, immunization,

Stephanie Keith/Getty Images

People waiting in line at a food bank during the COVID-19 pandemic in Brooklyn, New York. The problem of food scarcity for so many individuals and families during the pandemic highlighted how much economic insecurity so many people live with.

and access to health care is detrimental to children's development. When extra money prevents hunger, homelessness, or buying medical care and other necessities, it can make a huge difference in the lives of children. But in the United States, unfortunately, most poor families struggle to meet these basic material needs and often do not receive enough help from the government to give their children all of the basic necessities of life. **Food insecurity**, a concept that refers to any family that cannot provide adequate food for each member every day, is an especially important aspect of poverty, one that any person who has experienced for any length of time will never forget. During the COVID-19 pandemic, in spite of the federal government's increased support for food programs, millions of additional families and children did not have enough to eat (Bauer 2020). Exceptionally long lines at food banks that provided food to the hungry were a common site across the country.

But the detrimental consequences of poverty are not limited to cases of extreme deprivation. As researchers in the social and biological sciences have shown, living in poverty or near poverty an important source of stress, and stress is extremely bad for children (as we also noted in the introduction). Poverty is not just about the inability to afford things. Poverty is also usually associated with exposure to environmental toxins, neighborhood violence and insecurity, anxiety about making ends meet, difficulties in accessing institutional services such as health care or schools, and many other stressors. Poverty and its attendant stressors can shape the neurobiology of the developing child in powerful ways, which

may compromise cognitive development and concentration, thus affecting school attainment. This is a direct effect of poverty on the child. Poverty is stressful for parents too, and it may affect the investments of time and resources that parents make in children, as well as parents' interactions with children. This is an indirect effect of poverty on children—stress takes a toll on parents, which in turn will affect children's learning and development.

Homelessness

11.4.5 Discuss the problem of homelessness in the United States and identify some contributing factors.

One of the most extreme consequences of poverty for any individual or family is to fall into **homelessness**, literally the lack of permanent shelter to live in. Homelessness is a significant social problem in many parts of the world, including the United States. Individuals and families can become temporarily homeless for any number of specific reasons, including wars and violent conflicts that can in some cases create millions of refugees (as the world saw recently in Syria due to the very violent civil war there). But under more normal circumstances, the nearly universal cause of homeless is that of extreme poverty (although other problems such as mental illness or personal disasters are also significant). Most people who become homeless will not remain so indefinitely, but even brief periods of homelessness can be devastating. A smaller proportion will remain homeless for a longer period of time, in some cases for years. Life on the streets or in homeless shelters can be dangerous, and not having a regular address makes many aspects of daily life difficult.

The problem of homelessness in America grew considerably in the 1980s, when the closing down of mental hospitals, decline of social programs for the poor, destruction of low-cost housing in urban areas (especially single-room occupancy hotels), and rise in unemployment among high-risk groups combined to increase the number of people without regular residences (Jencks 1995). While a variety of government programs have reduced the size of the homeless population since the early 1990s, the problem has hardly been eliminated. As noted elsewhere, the cost of renting an apartment in urban areas has been rising much faster than the rate of inflation or the ability of incomes to keep up, creating a growing number of families at risk of eviction and homelessness in cities across America (Desmond 2016). In order to prevent mass homelessness

Mark Bussell

Homelessness has been a persistent condition of extreme poverty in America. Shown here is a homeless encampment under a bridge in Washington, D.C., in 2016, just a few blocks from the famous Watergate Hotel. Unlike most other similar countries, the U.S. does not provide long-term shelter for its poorest citizens.

during COVID-19, for the first time ever the federal government temporarily banned evictions (although the moratorium was lifted in 2021).

The most rigorous estimate of the homeless population in the United States is the annual survey conducted by the U.S. Department of Housing and Urban Development (HUD), using innovative methods of locating the homeless. HUD estimated that on a single night in January 2010, there were about 650,000 people who were not housed. Of this total, about 400,000 lived in shelters, and the remainder were unsheltered out on the street (U.S. HUD 2010). HUD also estimated that about 1.6 million people were homeless at some point during the previous 12 months. In 2020, the homeless population had reduced slightly to 580,466 on the night of the annual survey (results for 2021 have not yet been released but most experts are certain the homeless population increased during the COVID-19 pandemic). But even these figures do not capture the full extent of the problem. There are millions of people who are living doubled up, temporarily or indefinitely, with family or friends. Attempts to estimate this more inclusive population produce much higher estimates of the total homeless population; one study in the 1990s estimated that 14 percent of all Americans have at some point in their lives been homeless, if we include being forced to double up because of an inability to afford a place to live. A more recent study found a lower rate (about 6 percent), but higher levels among Blacks and Latinxs (Link et al. 1994; Fusaro, Levy, and Shaefer 2018).

Although homelessness is most common among single men, the lack of a regular dwelling creates especially significant hardships for families with children and is yet another example of how poverty impacts the innocent young. Using a broader definition of homelessness that includes doubling up with family or friends, it has been estimated that some 1.5 million children experience homelessness in the United States at some point during a given year, a number that is particularly disturbing given the strong evidence of high levels of stress and dislocation that eviction and homelessness cause for children (Bussuk et al. 2011; Desmond 2016).

Conclusion: Should We Be Concerned About Excessive Inequality?

As we conclude our survey of inequality, it's natural to ask this question: To what extent does inequality matter? The simplest answer to this question is the most straightforward: Higher levels of inequality mean that the poor have fewer resources to acquire needed goods and services than they would in more egalitarian countries. At the same time, the lives of middle-class families have stopped improving as they did for much of the twentieth century while the very richest individuals and families have received most of the benefits of economic growth in recent decades. This is a vitally important fact in its own right. The further down the income distribution you look, the more difficult it becomes for families to meet basic needs, and for the past 35 years there have been very few improvements in living standards for most American families. The fact that the rich are absorbing a larger share of the total income being produced in the United States and many other countries makes it difficult for families to address those needs or to envision a brighter future for themselves or their children. Finally, higher levels of societal inequality are associated with higher rates of poverty.

But beyond the consequences of rising inequality for household well-being and shared prosperity, what else can be said? We've discussed in this chapter how economic inequalities are related to child development, education, and social mobility into adulthood, but are there other consequences? A few issues are worth paying attention to. One is political. Every adult citizen has one and only one vote, but there are other ways to influence political outcomes that can enable those with money to exert influence. Perhaps the most important of these is by donating money to candidates for political office, which has increased dramatically in recent decades. As rising wealth at the top makes it easier for affluent individuals to "invest" in the political system, this may be harmful to the country as a whole: The interests and concerns of the rich are not necessarily the same as those for everyone else.

Another issue to consider is the fact that societies with high levels of overall economic inequality have appeared, in a number of studies, to have poor societal health, while societies that are more equal consistently seem to have better health. The main reasons researchers have suggested to explain this finding are that rich people are in a better position to purchase much *more* health care than they otherwise would, potentially squeezing out poorer people who are less likely to have coverage, and further that the stress associated with poverty or low income causes additional health problems (Wilkinson 2006).

Another more subtle consequence is that inequality may change our preferences and desires in ways that are unhealthy. In particular, the desire to keep up with the rich when it comes to consumption may be pushing us to consume more stuff than we really need. To the extent that people look up to those who have more than they do, they will never feel completely satisfied with the possessions they do own, and will want more. This has become a problem because many American families are taking on ever-higher levels of debt to try to acquire such goods. With the United States being a world leader in levels of household debt, many social scientists have noted the precariousness of this situation for the American national economy (Sullivan, Warren, and Westbrook 2001). "Luxury fever" also impacts subjective well-being—we are never fully satisfied with what we have when we hear or read about the lives of the rich (Frank 1999). Even though the United States has a higher average income than virtually all other countries in the world, international surveys show that Americans are not as satisfied as we would expect. High levels of income inequality are a likely culprit (Oishi, Kesebir, and Diener 2011).

Inequality is always going to be with us, but the *amount* of inequality that a society allows is not set in stone. As we have seen throughout this chapter, governments *can* choose to adopt policies that can reduce the amount of income and wealth controlled at the very top, and they *can* choose to adopt policies that will reduce the number of people living in poverty. Upon entering the White House, U.S. President Joe Biden made a series of dramatic proposals that would indeed significantly reduce the long-term poverty rate if they were enacted, although fierce opposition to such programs makes their liklihood of passage remote. Many very successful and rich countries have made those choices. But the United States has not. America has high levels of poverty and inequality, and government policies of recent decades have done little to ensure that the benefits of economic growth are shared more equitably among the entire population.

The Big Questions Revisited 11

11.1 What Is Inequality? In this section, we explored the history of inequality and the ways societies and thinkers have typically justified inequality. We also discussed the sociological concept of class.

Inequality: An Introduction

A Brief History of Inequality

Learning Objective 11.1.1: Define inequality and explain how the form and level of inequality has varied throughout history.

Measures of Economic Inequality: Wealth and Income

Learning Objective 11.1.2: Compare and contrast income and wealth as measures of economic inequality.

The Sociological Concept of Class

Learning Objective 11.1.3: Define class and identify what constitutes a social class.

Key Terms

inequality (p. 267)   slavery (p. 267)   colonialism (p. 268)   feudalism (p. 268)   serf (p. 268)   welfare state (p. 268)   high-end inequality (p. 269)   income (p. 269)   consumption (p. 269)   wealth (p. 269)   net financial assets (NFA) (p. 269)   middle class (p. 270)   class (p. 270)   life chances (p. 271)   class analysis (p. 271)   bourgeoisie (p. 271)   proletariat (p. 271)   socioeconomic status (SES) (p. 272)

11.2 Why Is America So Unequal? Inequality in the United States today is about as high as it has ever been since we started measuring, and poverty rates have remained persistently high. In this section, we compared the United States with other similar developed countries and asked why America is so unequal.

Unequal America in Comparative Perspective

Trends in Income Inequality in the United States and Around the World

Learning Objective 11.2.1: Discuss trends in income inequality and compare inequality in

the United States to other countries around the world.

Why Did Inequality Increase?

Learning Objective 11.2.2: Identify factors explaining why economic inequality in the United States has increased since the 1960s.

Who Are the One Percent?

Learning Objective 11.2.3: Describe who comprises the "one percent" in America.

Key Terms

egalitarian (p. 273)   college wage premium (p. 276)   deindustrialization (p. 277)   globalization (p. 277)   offshoring (p. 277)   sweatshop (p. 277)   progressive tax system (p. 277)   minimum wage (p. 279)

11.3 Do We All Have an Equal Opportunity to Succeed in Life? Social mobility is one of the most important topics in the study of inequality. In this section we examined how social mobility is measured, why countries differ in opportunity, how the United States compares to other countries, and the relationship between education and mobility.

Inequality, Education, and Social Mobility

Measuring Opportunity: The Concept of Social Mobility

Learning Objective 11.3.1: Define social mobility and describe how inequality of opportunity is measured.

Social Mobility in Comparative Perspective

Learning Objective 11.3.2: Compare and contrast chances for social mobility in the United States to other countries.

Factors Influencing Mobility

Learning Objective 11.3.3: Identify factors that affect how much social mobility exists in a society.

Education and Social Mobility

Learning Objective 11.3.4: Discuss the relationship between education and social mobility.

Key Terms

inequality of opportunity (p. 281)   social mobility (p. 281)   caste society (p. 281) association (p. 282)   variables (p. 282) immobility (p. 282)   labor markets (p. 284) meritocracy (p. 285)

11.4 How Much Poverty Exists in the United States and Around the World? Poverty is a complicated concept. Beyond a minimum of resources to ensure subsistence, it is difficult to define what our "basic" needs are. In this section, we examined two ways of viewing poverty and just how much poverty exists in the United States and in other countries around the world. We also looked closely at the problem of childhood poverty.

Life at the Bottom: The Problem of Poverty

Different Measures of Poverty

Learning Objective 11.4.1: Distinguish between absolute and relative measures of poverty.

Poverty in the United States: Who Are the Poor?

Learning Objective 11.4.2: Identify factors that increase the likelihood of poverty.

Poverty in International Comparative Perspective

Learning Objective 11.4.3: Compare and contrast the level of poverty in the United States to similar countries.

Poverty and Children

Learning Objective 11.4.4: Explain the impact of growing up in poverty on children.

Homelessness

Learning Objective 11.4.5: Discuss the problem of homelessness in the United States and identify some contributing factors.

Key Terms

poverty line (p. 286)   absolute poverty (p. 287) relative poverty (p. 287)   working poor (p. 288) food insecurity (p. 291)   homelessness (p. 291)

Chapter 12

Jobs, Occupations, and Professions: The Sociology of Work

by Jeff Manza, Richard Arum, with Bhumika Chauhan*

What if machines could perform the routine tasks that humans currently do? A growing number of researchers and thinkers believe that large-scale automation may be only a couple of decades away. Thousands of start-up companies around the world, as well as technological giants like Google, are investing heavily in designing such machines. The backbone is what is known as **artificial intelligence (AI)**, which refers to development of hardware (such as robots) and software with human-like intelligence. The field of AI research has been around since the 1950s, drawing insights from many different scientific fields (including sociology). For much of its history, AI struggled against the basic challenge of trying to capture the extraordinary capacities of the human brain and coming up short. It took decades, but in 1997 a computer defeated the world's reigning chess champion, which had been one long-standing goal of AI advocates and represented a remarkable demonstration of AI's potential (Greenemeir 2017). Since then, some extraordinary advances in AI research and real-world applications have begun to suggest the possibility of a world in which machines could begin displacing human labor on a mass scale.

Technology has been replacing humans for centuries, but up until now, labor-saving technologies have appeared at a slower pace than new jobs have been created. What is likely to be different in the future is a scenario in which AI researchers and technology firms solve their most difficult problems in a short window of time, allowing employers in many industries to replace large numbers of workers all at once, before other kinds of jobs get

created. Such breakthroughs could have unprecedented consequences on the availability of jobs, and we are just on the cusp of seeing these transitions come to fruition. To take just one example, consider the self-driving vehicle.

My Sociological Imagination

RICHARD ARUM

Although I grew up in the suburbs of New York, I had an unusual background as my father was a sports promoter, and cultural icons and civil rights heroes such as Muhammad Ali spent time in our home. This early personal exposure shaped who I was and the choices I made as an adult. In the years following, I received a teaching certificate from Harvard University and subsequently worked as a teacher in a segregated public high school in Oakland, California. In that institutional setting, in order to make sense of the dysfunction of the school as an organization as well as the impact that the school was having on the lives of the students, I increasingly was drawn to asking sociological questions of the world. To move beyond simply asking these questions, I enrolled at the University of California–Berkeley with the goal of developing sociological tools and skills to better understand the problems around schooling in America. For me, developing a sociological imagination was an attempt to develop a set of analytical competencies to participate actively in policy discussions that could substantively improve the outcomes of youth.

---

*Dirk Wittveen, Michael McCarthy, and Owen Whooley also contributed to this chapter.

Work is central to our lives, and in the twenty-first century many changes in the patterns of employment are creating challenges for everyone. For example, major changes in the technology of work, with the relentless rise of automation and artificial intelligence, has already led to the displacement of workers in many fields such as construction, manufacturing, and mining and is moving into office and professional employment as well.

Mark Bussell

297

Several companies are currently (as of 2021) in the process of road-testing driverless cars and trucks. There are many challenges that self-driving vehicles must overcome. In particular, they have to be able to anticipate every possible thing human drivers and pedestrians do if they are to avoid causing accidents. They have to properly interpret every signal and learn how to drive through snow and bad weather conditions. But let's say that someday soon these obstacles are overcome, as most experts believe they will. What next? There are millions of people who make a living driving vehicles, such as truck drivers, cab drivers, bus drivers, limo drivers, uber drivers, and ambulance drivers. Self-driving vehicles would make it much cheaper for companies to save on wages and, perhaps, earn greater profits with far fewer workers. Companies would eventually purchase a fleet of those vehicles to replace all of the buses, cabs, and trucks currently operated by humans. Even cities and local governments would be compelled to replace public bus drivers with cheaper automated buses that do not require salaries, health and retirement benefits, sick days, and other costs associated with human drivers. This is just one example of the way in which the jobs of millions of people could be lost in a relatively short span of time. Automation already is leading to the displacement of workers in many other industrial sectors such as manufacturing, mining, construction, service and repair, and numerous routine white-collar jobs. While higher skilled professional jobs are not likely to be completely replaced, the more routine aspects of these jobs can be automated, making it possible for fewer lawyers, surgeons, or architects to produce the same volume of work (Susskind 2020).

Projections of massive future job losses due to AI can be scary to think about. The phrase "job apocalypse" has come into use to describe a jobless future. How big could the displacement be? The global consulting firm McKinsey produced a detailed analysis of 2,000 different jobs across the global economy and for each examined how much of the job was replaceable by AI (McKinsey Global Institute 2017). They concluded that in the next 15 years, somewhere between 400 and 800 million jobs in the world might be displaced by machines, with up to 54 million in the United States (out of a current full-time workforce of 130 million). Job losses on that scale would leave millions of people unemployed and without easy prospects for the future. A new kind of divide, between those with jobs and those without, would likely emerge, with a huge jobless population stuck without realistic prospects of work.

It is important to be cautious when projecting into the future, and there is a long history of overestimating the capacity of technology to displace workers (the first protests against technology in the workplace were the famous "Luddites" of England, who destroyed machines that threatened their jobs as early as the 1810s). And to be sure, in the past technological enhancements have always led to the creation of new kinds of jobs. That will also happen in the future. For example, some displaced drivers might be needed to service a fleet of self-driving vehicles, while others might find work monitoring and adjusting online platforms that move cars and trucks wherever they are needed. But it is also entirely possible, perhaps even likely, that these kinds of new jobs will absorb only a fraction of displaced workers. The future may not be like the past.

A sociological imagination raises many questions and provides some important insights into how an impending automation revolution might play out. In particular, we need to explore the nature of work and how jobs are organized. In this chapter, we develop that investigation.

Phillip Bond/Alamy Stock Photo

Self-driving cars (such as Google's, shown here) could potentially displace millions of workers who have jobs that involve driving.

The Big Questions

1. **What is the division of labor in modern societies?** In this section, we introduce the classical sociological idea of the division of labor and provide an overview of the kinds of jobs that can be found in the United States. We also trace how jobs in the U.S. have changed over time.

2. **What is the labor process?** Here, we explore how work is organized in the United States by introducing the concept of the labor process and exploring how power is embedded in workplace relationships. How do employers maintain control over their employees? How do workers resist employer's efforts to control them?

3. **What is the difference between good jobs, regular jobs, and bad jobs?** The kinds of jobs we have are important to us as individuals for our sense of self. A "good" job for one person may not be such a good fit for someone else. In this section, we examine what constitutes a rewarding job in America. Then, we explore precarious work, in which workers are entirely interchangeable and jobs are highly insecure. In recent years, the economies of rich countries like the United States have seen a significant increase in precarious jobs. We also discuss migrant and immigrant workers as well as the effects of unemployment.

4. **What are professional occupations, and why are they distinct?** There is one set of occupations that has succeeded in establishing and maintaining a significant degree of control and protection for their members: the professions. These occupations now make up somewhere around 20 percent or more of the workforce in rich countries. How did professional occupations become established, and why have they been able to resist change?

5. **What are the central challenges facing workers in the twenty-first century?** As the nature of work and the labor market evolves, there are important issues and challenges that confront workers in the twenty-first century. Some of these issues have been around for a long time, and others are taking on new forms. In this section, we focus on issues in the United States such as long work hours, challenges to young workers (especially those without college degrees), and age discrimination.

INTERFOTO/History/Alamy Stock Photo

BIG QUESTION 12.1   What Is the Division of Labor in Modern Societies?

THE DIVISION OF LABOR AND THE LABOR MARKET

All societies have a **division of labor**, in which some people do some things and other people do other things. Imagine you were dropped down in a strange place and asked to figure out what kind of society you were observing. Two things you might want to know would be: What kinds of work do people do in this place? And how is that work organized and rewarded? Hunting-and-gathering and agrarian societies of past and present are defined by the basic fact that most individuals are engaged in a wide range of the activities needed for survival. There is, in some sense, a relatively simple division of labor: Only a few different types of jobs need to be performed at any one time. By contrast, contemporary societies like the

United States are defined by an immensely complicated division of labor, in which there are hundreds of different kinds of jobs in a bewildering array of organizational settings.

Social scientists use the term **labor market** to describe the process through which workers and employers find each other. The term *market* captures the role of both employers (who offer jobs) and workers (who offer their labor). The simplest example of how a labor market works would be in the case of employers looking for workers to fill jobs that require no special skills (or skills that can be learned by anyone in a few hours or days). Think of jobs like cashier, fast-food worker or day laborer. Employers offering such jobs can consider almost anyone physically and mentally able to show up to do the work, and they will pay the lowest possible wage they can while still being able to attract the workers they need (in many cases, the legal minimum wage or perhaps just a bit above it).

But there is no singular labor market. Distinctive **occupations** that require special training or educational credentials—and which individuals may perform over an entire career—have labor markets in which employers do not look at all possible individuals seeking work, but only those with the requisite skills and training to do the job. If those skills are in short supply, workers usually have more leverage than in the case of non-skilled jobs and may be able to bargain for higher wages. In the case of professional labor markets, employers may search nationally or even internationally for the best candidates. Some labor markets are truly international—perhaps most famously in professional sports, where a top football (or soccer, as it is called in the United States) player can have a career that involves playing for many different teams in different countries at different points in time, and because top players are always in short supply, the player/employee can bargain aggressively for a high salary.

Throughout the rest of the chapter, we will use *labor market* when talking about the current mix of jobs that people work to earn their living. It is a term that is less broad than the division of labor, however, which includes both paid and unpaid work. For example, housework or caring for a child or older family member is a critical part of any society's division of labor, and we can use the phrase division of labor in the family to describe how couples divide up the labor of their household. But whatever arrangements are made, they are not formally compensated work as such. The distinction between paid and unpaid labor marks the difference between the labor market and the entire division of labor. When families hire other people to clean or maintain a physical shelter or care for family members (such as nurses, in-home aids, assisted living facility workers, and so forth), however, those jobs (which are paid) are part of the labor market. In this section, we will explore the evolution of the division of labor and describe the contemporary labor market from a sociological perspective.

The Historical Evolution of the Division of Labor

12.1.1 Describe changes in the division of labor over time.

Humans began to produce their own food by domesticating plants and animals around 10,000 years ago. This made it much easier for people to settle in one place. Gradual improvements in agriculture, especially related to the production of grain products, allowed for populations to grow. The introduction and expanded use of tools and animals in agricultural production enabled further development. Eventually, human communities based on an agricultural foundation spread, and agricultural practices expanded and took on diverse forms depending upon land and climate. For example, grassy regions allowed for pastoral animal breeding systems, while temperate and tropical forests allowed for slash-and-burn cultivation that exists even today. Farm families took care of almost all of their own needs (building their own house, making their own clothes, and so forth). Innovations in farming, such as cross-breeding, use of flood plains or other methods of irrigation, wet-rice cultivation, and many others helped move human societies beyond subsistence farming into surplus farming (that is, farmers could grow more food than they and their families needed, and they could sell the extra product). As this happened, farm families could afford to pay for goods and services to people not working on farms (such as shoemakers, clothing manufacturers, construction workers who would build shelters and houses, and so forth). In this way, the first truly modern type of division of labor began to emerge.

It is at the intersection of more complex agricultural systems and the ability to produce a surplus for sale that the division of labor truly took shape. Having lots of children was an advantage for increasing the number of farmhands, but taking care of them and raising them encouraged specialization within families (and in the nineteenth century, the rise of public schooling spurred a major increase in the specialization of the tasks involved in raising a child). In addition, the very same technological advances that created surplus farming generated new kinds of specialization. The new tools had to be made and serviced by someone, so some people began to specialize in toolmaking. Tools required raw materials: Metals, wood, and so forth. Someone had to acquire that. So mining, logging, and other "extractive" jobs were created.

The division of labor from farming to other new kinds of activities also spread because humans wanted more than just enough food to eat, and once they began to have the means to acquire new things, they would. As noted, from very early human agricultural settlements onward, the production of clothing, household goods, and rudimentary luxury items that could be exchanged for other goods took place alongside routine agricultural work. Most of these items and ventures were at first produced inside homes. But as human settlements expanded into larger towns and cities, opportunities for specializing in the production of goods for trading, or even specializing in trade itself as a merchant, began to emerge. The dedicated **craftsman**, a worker who develops detailed and specialized knowledge of how to make or fix things, began to appear. These craftsmen typically operated small workshops, with one or more apprentices or assistants, and sold their products in local markets frequented by the community. Trade in produced goods grew, particularly as enhancements in shipping eased the movement of goods between communities and eventually into far-flung trading centers.

Over time, as increasing numbers of people moved to more populated areas, some towns and cities began to develop new industries and professions such as law and banking that helped facilitate trade. The discovery of the New World—the Americas—further opened up trade opportunities of goods produced by enslaved people imported from Africa. But it was the rise of the **Industrial Revolution**—the introduction of large-scale production of goods and products for mass markets—that dramatically changed the nature of work and the division of labor. The Industrial Revolution gave birth to the factory, a central place where large numbers of workers were grouped together. The first factories appeared in the late eighteenth and early nineteenth centuries in the most developed countries in Europe, notably England, and they used relatively simple technology. Much of the work had to be done by skilled craftspeople; each individual was capable of producing a finished product more or less on their own. In this way, the first factories were really more like collective workshops that brought together several craftspeople under one roof but did not really alter how a product was made.

But during this period, technology advanced very rapidly (see Chapter 9 for more details). Factories grew in size, and they began to require more sophisticated forms of management and control over workers employed therein. Further, as Adam Smith famously predicted in 1776, jobs in the emerging factories were increasingly subdivided into different areas. A new kind of division of labor arose, in which **specialization** within enterprises grew. No longer did all of the workers in a single factory more or less do the same thing. Instead, some did one task, while others did other tasks, and no single worker produced a finished product alone. Rapid economic growth spurred the expansion of many new kinds of work and the range of occupations available continued to rise right up to the present. Large office settings mimicked the early factories, except that instead of entering a factory, workers entered an office building.

In the long history of the division of labor, the role of unpaid labor is important to recognize and include in our overall understanding. For most of human history, housework and **caring work** (such as raising children or taking care of sick or aging family members or close friends) has been performed within families and by women, not as paid work. Richer families have always been able to hire people to clean and maintain their estates, take care of their children, and prepare their meals, whereas less affluent families could not afford such help. Since the late nineteenth century, however, more of this work is performed outside the home, and at costs that most families can afford to one degree or another. This includes the expansion of childcare facilities and nursery schools, assisted living facilities for aging adults, and restaurants and grocery stores that prepare meals for families to be either eaten onsite (restaurants) or taken home. These are all examples of how the division of labor has changed: What once was done by families (and women within those families) for themselves is now much less likely to be done without relying on help from others (Thistle 2006).

The Evolving Labor Market

12.1.2 Discuss the kinds of jobs people do today.

The evolution from farming to manufacturing represented a critical transition in human history. Since humans had primarily been farming for centuries, the shift to a manufacturing economy was relatively swift. Yet it did not last long. Beginning as early as the 1920s, but especially in the decades after World War II, the numbers of workers engaged in manufacturing and associated industries (like mining) were surpassed by the rapid growth of a new set of industries: Professional services, business management, education, sales, finance, real estate, and government. Beginning in the 1970s, the computer industry and associated spin-offs became another growth area. Historically these kinds of jobs have been referred to as **white-collar jobs**, in the sense that (male) workers would wear white shirts and ties to work. Manufacturing jobs were called **blue-collar jobs** to refer to the typical clothing worn at work by (male) workers. The pattern of change, especially from the 1960s onward, was pretty remarkable: In each of these professional industries, ever greater numbers of workers were hired each year, while the numbers of workers employed in manufacturing began to decline in almost all countries similar to the United States.

The contrast between the era of manufacturing and the era of white-collar employment is shown in Figure 12.1. The mix of industries employing large numbers of workers is, not surprisingly, very different when comparing 1910 and 2015. Manufacturing jobs were 32 percent of the total

Figure 12.1 Employment by Industry in 1910 and 2015

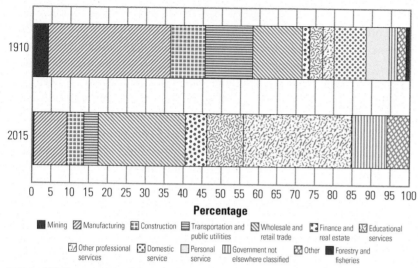

SOURCE: U.S. Bureau of Labor Statistics, 2016, available at https://www.bls.gov/opub/ted/2016/employment-by-industry-1910-and-2015.htm.

of non-farm jobs in 1910, whereas today they are less than 9 percent. Almost 10 percent of jobs in 1910 were in mining, while today they are only a small fraction. Construction has fallen by half (9 percent to 4.5 percent), though it has held up much better than manufacturing. Domestic and personal services performed inside the household (such as household maids, cooks, nannies, and personal servants) combined were almost 15 percent of the workforce in 1910 but are just 1 percent today (again, many of these jobs are still done but are now outside the home, such as at childcare centers, assisted living facilities, or in restaurants and fast food establishments). On the other hand, professional services—this includes both professionals and the people who assist them—have shot up from 3 percent to 29 percent. And smaller changes can be seen in finance and real estate, which nearly tripled from 2 percent to 6 percent. What the Bureau of Labor Statistics (BLS) calls "wholesale and retail trade" (this includes all kinds of workers involved in selling things) has grown from 13 percent to 23 percent.

The visual depiction in Figure 12.1 provides a broad view of the contemporary labor market. But what kinds of jobs are people actually doing inside these various industries? Figure 12.2 provides a different view of these trends, based on the occupations reported to the U.S. Census Bureau between 1900 and 2019. The graph shows how employment in farming collapsed, going from about one-third of total employment in 1900 to just 2 percent at the end of the twentieth century. The skilled and nonskilled manual labor has declined

dramatically over the course of the twentieth century, with skilled manual workers making up 15 percent of the workforce in 1940 but just 9 percent today. The less-skilled manual worker category has also declined, although many of the workers in less-skilled jobs today are not working in factories but rather doing things like janitorial services. Both skilled and less-skilled categories include construction, which has not declined as much. Professionals have shot up from about 5 percent in 1900 to about 23 percent by 2019. White-collar clerical and sales workers, as well as business managers of all kinds, have also increased dramatically since 1900.

In the face of these trends, some sociologists began describing the emergence of a **post-industrial society** (for example, Touraine 1971; Bell 1973). The idea was that in countries like the United States in the late twentieth and early twenty-first centuries, economic growth would increasingly be generated not in the production of goods as in industrial societies, but rather by knowledge and professional expertise applied in white-collar industries. The post-industrial theorists were partially right. As discussed, employment has continued to rise in non-manufacturing jobs, while technology has steadily displaced certain kinds of factory-based jobs. But at the same time, employment in low-paid and low-skill jobs—such as store clerks and cashiers, janitors and other maintenance workers, fast-food and other restaurant workers, baristas, farm laborers, and in-home aides and attendants—has also continued growing. These often highly insecure jobs are as

Figure 12.2 Changes in the Types of Jobs Held by Workers Over the Course of the Twentieth Century

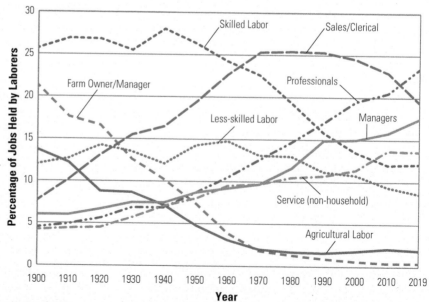

SOURCE: IPUMS.

much a part of the post-industrial economy today as are the white-collar jobs (a topic we'll cover later in the chapter).

An interesting recent development that has gotten a lot of attention is the rise of what is known as the **gig economy**. Companies like Uber and Lyft (ride services), TaskRabbit (home repair services), Seamless and DoorDash (food delivery services), Care (babysitting services), Instacart (grocery delivery services), Airbnb (apartment/house rentals) and similar firms facilitate matching workers and consumers via Internet platforms. Proponents have extolled the unique ability of these firms to provide flexible employment to those who sign up to work for them, allowing people to work whenever they want and as much or as little as they want. Some have seen these companies as "disruptors" with the ability to replace many kinds of traditional jobs, stating that the on-demand nature of these jobs makes it easier for companies to avoid hiring workers with benefits on payrolls (Mizhari 2018).

Yet there is nothing really new about these kinds of jobs; people have done informal work for a day or a few hours in exchange for money or some other type of compensation for centuries. **Day laborers**, for instance, have worked as farm and construction workers, cleaners, and dockworkers since the rise of the modern economic system. Terms like "hobo" or "vagrant" came to be used for these casual workers in the early nineteenth century, as rather than keeping a year-round residence they would move to where work became available at different times of the year. Instances of casual wage work can even be found in texts from ancient Babylon and Greece, as well as ancient India and China (van der Linden 2008; Hofmeester and van der Linden 2017).

In the twentieth century, long before the appearance of companies like Uber, temporary work was facilitated by companies known as **temp agencies**. These firms specialized in placing workers in temporary jobs. Companies would contract with a temp agency to replace workers who might be out sick or suddenly quit. But the temporary worker would not normally be hired permanently, filling in only as long as needed. The history of temp agencies reveals considerable exploitation of these workers, who often took temp work as a last resort (Hatton 2011).

While the use of temporary labor has a long history, it has become increasingly common in recent years. The gig economy has supplemented existing sources of temporary work to generate an important space in the modern labor market. If we include all workers doing gig work or temporary work, the U.S. Department of Labor estimates that it would include about 14 percent—about one in six—of the American workforce. We will dig deeper into these forms of employment later in the chapter, but for now we will just note that wages and working conditions for most workers doing contingent work are below those of regular workers, often significantly so (Ravenelle 2019; Schor

2020). Claims or assertions that the gig economy is a path to a golden future for workers are, to put it mildly, quite an overstatement.

The Changing Character of Self-Employment

12.1.3 Explain why self-employment is popular and how it is changing.

When we think about companies in the United States, names like Walmart, Google, Apple, or Chevron come to mind. But of the nearly 6 million companies in the United States with employees, just over 5 million are small businesses owned and operated by someone who employs fewer than 20 people, and many are sole-operated businesses with no employees at all. Most of us know family members or friends who work for themselves. And entrepreneurship and self-employment are aligned with many Americans' hopes and dreams: To tell an employer to "take this job and shove it," to "be one's own boss"; to build something from scratch that you own is widely appealing. Yet while many people do start businesses or work for themselves at some point, most do not last in this status for long. Most start-up businesses typically fail within the first few years.

A few years ago, as part of a larger research project, one of the authors of this chapter (Arum, with co-author Josipa Roksa) asked college students about their entrepreneurial aspirations during their senior year of college, and then he and his team followed up with this nationally representative group of students after graduation. During their senior year, 5 percent of students reported that they planned to own their own businesses within two years of completing college, while 36 percent of respondents reported that they aspired to be entrepreneurs at some point in their lives.

Although in the year or two after graduation only 2 percent of graduates in Arum and Roksa's study actually ended up fully immersed in self-employment, it turns out that the students' estimate of being self-employed at one point in their lives is not far from what we would expect from national data. About 20 percent of people have been self-employed by the time they are in their early thirties, and more than 30 percent have been self-employed by the time they are in their early fifties (Arum and Roksa 2014).

The character of self-employment has changed dramatically in recent decades. While self-employment had been in decline in most developed economies throughout the twentieth century, and many social scientists believed that it was likely to disappear altogether in the face of markets increasingly dominated by large companies, self-employment surprised many social scientists by beginning to grow again in the last quarter of the twentieth century and continuing into the twenty-first. When we look closely, we find an additional surprise. Traditional self-employment—an activity dominated by small shopkeepers, restauranteurs, and craftsmen—is still declining. But new forms of self-employment emerged to replace it. In particular, two types of self-employment are growing: Professional freelancers (including consultants, artists, designers, and writers, who value independence and flexible job hours) and low-income, marginal, informal forms of self-employment, such as in-home childcare or day labor. Although professional and unskilled forms of self-employment are increasing for both men and women in most settings, it is interesting to see the extent to which rich countries differ on how much self-employment currently exists, as shown in Figure 12.3.

Why is this occurring? The forms of self-employment that are growing are related to a larger restructuring of the American economy (see Chapter 9), in which companies are increasingly **outsourcing** work to self-employed people, both professionals and people with relatively few skills. Stable organizations and individual careers inside those organizations that were so common in the middle of the twentieth century are becoming increasingly less common, but oftentimes workers can take the skills and experience they learned working for someone else to go work for themselves. Typically, this outsourcing can save money; instead of the employer having to pay for an employee's benefits and Social Security taxes, and providing them with office space, a self-employed person covers all of those expenses themselves. In this, the rise of outsourcing is parallel to the gig economy.

Some self-employed individuals may hire other workers (for example, a shop owner with one to two employees or a larger, but still small, business owner with 10 or 20 employees), but most work alone. Self-employment is found among those without a college degree as well as those with a college degree (Hipple and Hammond 2016). In terms of income, the median annual income for self-employed workers was $32,020 in 2016 (Torpey and Roberts 2018). However, averages can mislead. Self-employed dentists, lawyers, accountants, and personal financial wealth management consultants can earn well over $100,000 annually, while a day laborer who works when jobs are available may make less than $10,0000 a year.

At the higher end of the income spectrum, many workers may prefer the flexibility of self-employment or independent contracting and find it liberating. The phrase many of these individuals use to describe their work is **freelancing**, in which people are able to work with multiple clients, control their own work hours, and select among different challenges and opportunities they may be offered. However, at the same time, even well-paid freelancers lack the security that comes with a regular paycheck, and that can often create anxiety when work is slow. ("Where is my next job coming from?" is a common lament.) At the lower end of the income spectrum, many "self-employed" workers do not have much flexibility and often are on-call as needed (akin to gig economy workers).

Jobs and Earnings

12.1.4 Analyze how much different jobs pay.

We've now covered a variety of ways of understanding the division of labor and changes in the mix of jobs over time. A question that everyone naturally wants to know is this: How much do different jobs pay? Are you thinking about a career in which people are well-paid or not? In Table 12.1, we've gathered data from the federal government's Bureau of Labor Statistics on incomes for 100 of the most common jobs and displayed two ways of measuring how much those jobs pay. The first statistic is the average pay for all full-time workers in that job. The second statistic is the median pay—the pay going to the worker in that occupation at the mid-point, or 50th percentile—to full-time workers in the job. The two statistics are often nearly identical, but in some higher paying jobs the highest earners earn significantly more than everyone else, which pushes up the average but not the median. The greater the gap between the two, the larger the difference between the higher paid and lower paid workers in that job. To take an example, notice that the average pay of lawyers is $143,200, but the median lawyer is paid just $120,670. This means that there are a

Figure 12.3 Rates of Self-Employment in Selected Countries

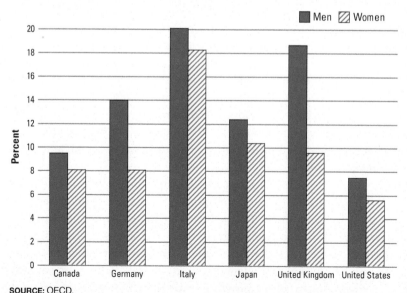

SOURCE: OECD.

Table 12.1 Pay in 2019 for the 100 Job Titles with the Most Workers

Rank (no. of Workers)	Occupation	Mean Annual Wage	Median Annual Wage
1	Laborers and Material Movers	$30,570	$28,130
2	Retail Salespersons	$29,360	$25,250
3	Fast Food and Counter Workers	$23,250	$22,740
4	Cashiers	$24,400	$23,660
5	Secretaries and Administrative Assistants	$43,410	$39,850
6	Drivers/Truck Drivers	$42,170	$40,310
7	Home Health and Personal Care Aides	$26,440	$25,280
8	Building Cleaning Workers	$29,080	$26,370
9	Registered Nurses	$77,460	$73,300
10	Office Clerks, General	$36,360	$34,040
11	Customer Service Representatives	$37,320	$34,710
12	Waiters and Waitresses	$26,800	$22,890
13	Cooks	$27,550	$26,360
14	General and Operations Managers	$123,030	$100,780
15	Elementary and Middle School Teachers	$63,820	$59,670
16	Software and Web Developers	$106,980	$102,330
17	Wholesale Sales Representatives	$75,180	$63,000
18	Health Care Support Workers	$36,910	$35,630
19	Nursing Assistants/Orderlies/Psychiatric Aides	$30,790	$29,680
20	Bookkeeping, Accounting, and Auditing Clerks	$42,960	$41,230
21	Supervisors of Office Workers	$60,130	$56,620
22	Teaching Assistants	$30,280	$28,210
23	Supervisors of Sales Workers	$52,900	$44,250
24	Maintenance and Repair Workers	$41,960	$39,080
25	Assemblers and Fabricators	$34,800	$32,350
26	Accountants and Auditors	$79,520	$71,550
27	Supervisors of Food Preparation and Serving Workers	$39,140	$34,830
28	Security Guards	$33,080	$29,710
29	Secondary School Teachers	$65,850	$61,660
30	Receptionists and Information Clerks	$31,250	$30,050
31	Sales Representatives, Services	$66,760	$56,130
32	Construction Laborers	$41,730	$36,860
33	Grounds Maintenance Workers	$33,100	$30,890
34	Passenger Vehicle Drivers	$35,790	$33,300
35	Food Preparation Workers	$25,820	$24,800
36	Computer Support Specialists	$59,290	$54,760
37	Auto Mechanics	$45,150	$40,812
38	Health Technicians	$37,800	$35,610
39	Counselors	$53,120	$48,780
40	Miscellaneous Production Workers	$33,980	$31,070
41	Carpenters	$52,850	$48,330
42	Computer and Information Analysts	$97,570	$92,360
43	Management Analysts	$95,560	$85,260
44	Therapists	$80,850	$78,790
45	Human Resources Workers	$68,200	$62,440
46	Social Service Workers	$43,810	$39,100
47	Shipping and Inventory Clerks	$36,030	$34,190
48	Licensed Vocational Nurses	$48,500	$47,480
49	Electricians	$60,370	$56,180
50	Recreation/Fitness Workers	$36,830	$30,490

(continued)

Rank (no. of Workers)	Occupation	Mean Annual Wage	Median Annual Wage
51	Social Workers	$54,190	$50,470
52	Marketing Analysts	$71,570	$63,790
53	Lawyers	$143,200	$120,670
54	Police Officers	$67,620	$63,240
55	Rental Clerks	$33,610	$29,860
56	Marketing and Sales Managers	$144,660	$130,700
57	Financial Managers	$147,530	$129,890
58	Bartenders	$28,000	$23,680
59	Network Administrators	$96,380	$91,390
60	Supervisors of Production Workers	$65,220	$61,310
61	Industrial Truck Operators	$37,930	$36,200
62	Supervisors of Construction Workers	$71,440	$66,210
63	Substitute Teachers	$32,460	$28,790
64	Inspectors and Testers	$43,000	$39,140
65	Childcare Workers	$25,510	$24,230
66	Preschool/Kindergarten Teachers	$40,370	$34,630
67	Designers	$51,490	$44,400
68	Postal Service Workers	$51,740	$52,060
69	Dishwashers	$24,410	$23,970
70	Education Administrators	$98,270	$91,130
71	Industrial Repair and Maintenance Workers	$54,640	$52,860
72	Supervisors of Mechanics and Repairers	$70,550	$67,460
73	Special Education Teachers	$65,230	$61,040
74	Plumbers and Pipefitters	$58,570	$53,900
75	Cafeteria Attendants	$25,020	$23,470
76	Billing and Posting Clerks	$40,620	$38,740
77	Transportation Supervisors	$57,850	$55,040
78	Construction Equipment Operators	$53,370	$48,160
79	Welders	$44,800	$42,100
80	Correctional Officers	$50,210	$45,300
81	Bank Tellers	$31,660	$31,230
82	Financial Services Sales Agents	$93,090	$62,270
83	Computer Systems Managers	$156,390	$146,360
84	Engineering Technicians	$62,130	$59,620
85	Restaurant Hosts	$24,010	$23,090
86	Protective Service Workers	$32,070	$28,660
87	Buyers and Purchasing Agents	$69,680	$64,380
88	Insurance Sales Agents	$67,780	$50,940
89	Hairdressers	$31,710	$26,270
90	Health Services Managers	$115,160	$100,980
91	Miscellaneous Computer Occupations	$92,410	$88,550
92	Machine Operators	$33,590	$30,990
93	Machinists	$46,120	$44,420
94	Production and Expediting Clerks	$50,640	$48,260
95	Entertainment Attendants	$25,090	$23,550
96	Agricultural Workers	$28,510	$25,820
97	Butchers	$30,920	$29,520
98	Installation, Maintenance, and Repair Workers	$41,310	$37,250
99	HVAC Mechanics and Installers	$51,420	$48,730
100	Credit Counselors	$73,750	$61,090

SOURCE: U.S. Bureau of Labor Statistics.

lot of lawyers earning much more than $120,000 a year (in fact, a few partners at large law firms can earn $1 million a year or more).

What are we to make of the different pay associated with different jobs? Two things stand out. First, some of the highest-paying and lowest-paying job titles are among the largest 100 job titles in America, and if we were to examine the fastest growing jobs, that would be true as well. By contrast, many of the job titles with pay in the middle are declining (and many are not on this list). This reflects the process of the *bifurcation* of the labor market, in which the best and worst jobs have been expanding.

Second, of these 100 largest jobs, the best paying tend to require advanced educational credentials, involve the supervision of other workers, or both. We've noted in other chapters that there is an increasing wage premium going to college-educated workers compared to those without. Or to put it another way, generally speaking we find higher pay in occupations that require a college degree than those that do not.

Joe Raedle/Getty Images

BIG QUESTION 12.2 What Is the Labor Process?

THE SOCIAL ORGANIZATION OF WORK

In the previous section, we considered the types of jobs that people do and how that has changed over time. Now we need to turn our sociological imagination to consider issues of power and control in the world of work. The **labor process** is the term that sociologists have developed to describe how jobs are organized and controlled by managers and bosses from above. The study of the labor process attempts to open up the workplace by examining how workers actually do their jobs, how managers and supervisors direct them, and how the relationships between the two unfold.

The Labor Process: An Introduction

12.2.1 Describe the main features of the labor process.

With the rise of large-scale factories in the eighteenth and nineteenth centuries came numerous commentaries and prescriptions about how work should be organized from manufacturers, engineers, and scientists. The Scottish philosopher and economist Adam Smith wrote extensively about the benefits of a highly detailed work organization.

Industrial engineers of the time were tasked with designing work processes to improve productivity. One such influential figure was Frederick Winslow Taylor (1856–1915), whose principles of **scientific management** gave expression to, and inspired, modern managerial organization of the labor process. Taylor sought to make the labor process more efficient by closely studying each minute movement of workers, thus effectively wresting the knowledge of the production process from workers and putting it in the hands of supervisors.

Many early sociological researchers followed Taylor's lead and attempted to understand why some workplaces were more productive than others. In the famous **Hawthorne studies** from the 1920s and 1930s, Harvard industrial psychologist Elton Mayo and his associates conducted a variety of experiments with different teams of workers. The studies aimed to identify what factors might induce workers to produce more output in the same amount of time. While Taylor dealt with technical aspects, Mayo and his associates focused on various social aspects of the workplace. Among other things, the researchers found that cooperation between workers was especially important for increasing productivity. Workers were more productive when their work was organized in such a way that they had to work together, not just follow orders (Thompson 1983).

Later studies in industrial sociology focused on the ways in which working in factories could be deeply dissatisfying to workers doing repetitive tasks day after day (Blauner 1964). Like earlier findings, these works also emphasized reform of management styles and social reorganization of the workplace to improve efficiency, but they also considered the question of how changes impacted workers' satisfaction. However, the 1974 publication of *Labor and Monopoly Capital* by labor activist and writer Harry Braverman marked an important shift. This widely discussed and famous study argued that to maximize profits, capitalist firms and their managers were continually driven to reduce their employees' ability to control what they do on the job. Braverman, at one time an industrial worker himself, levelled a powerful critique of industrial sociologists, claiming that much of their analysis and reforms were rather superficial and concerned with making things more tolerable for the workers. Instead, he brought the focus back to Frederick Taylor and what "scientific management" was about. Scientific management, Braverman argued, is premised on the idea that managers need to figure out how to understand and control what the workers under them are doing. Instead of allowing workers to decide how something should be done, or done differently, managers should decide for them and keep workers focused on precise, increasingly fragmented tasks. The pinnacle of scientific management is the well-developed assembly line system of production, in which every task a worker must perform is completely scripted and usually paced by a machine. Henry Ford, the founder of the Ford automobile company in Detroit, was among the first to fully implement such a design early in the twentieth century. His assembly line was copied all over the world.

The typical factory or workplace Braverman described was one in which workers faced a steady process of **deskilling**, in which jobs were made ever simpler, and workers became more interchangeable. The ultimate form of deskilling is **automation**, when a machine performs a task that once was completed by a worker. In this way, management seeks to block or prevent workers from having the upper hand because the worker (rather than management), knows how to "get the job done." While it seems like an engineer just trying to improve efficiency, the point Braverman is making is that this very process disempowers the worker and takes away their ability to control they way they work. And, since workers increasingly no longer have special skills, they are more easily replaceable (by another worker or by a machine), they might think twice before asking for a wage increase or considering going on strike.

To see Braverman's theory in action, let's take as an example the craft of shoemaking. Prior to the development

The assembly line system, in which every task a worker must perform is completely scripted, helped to usher in the era of labor market specialization. Pictured here are female factory workers putting lids on bottles at a medical company in Brighton, England, in the 1950s.

Allan Cash Picture Library/Alamy Stock Photo

of capitalism, Braverman argued, a shoe was typically made in its entirety by a craftsman known as a cordwainer (that is, a shoemaker). A single person would make the pair from start to finish. These handmade shoes were built to last, but they were expensive as even a master craftsman could produce only a few pairs of shoes a week. In order to mass produce shoes in a more efficient way, shoe companies and their managers had to study and break down each step in the process used by a master craftsman, and assign each of these steps to a different person on a factory assembly line (today usually in a place like China or Vietnam). Most of these modern factory workers probably do not know how to make the shoe in its entirety (including how to make the raw materials). Their individual tasks at work were heavily routinized and fairly easy to learn (contrast that with the years of training required to learn how to make quality footwear from scratch). The workers in such a factory are thus easily replaceable, and had a weak position to resist what management wanted as a result. Moreover, these workers (unlike craftsmen) had no trade secrets or unique knowledge to back their claims about how much time it would take to perform their task. In fact, if the pace of their work were controlled by a mechanized assembly line, management can increase the pace of work to increase production, while paying the workers the same wage.

Braverman's thesis generated an enormous amount of debate about the extent of deskilling in modern workplaces. Many later sociologists have found that technology has had a more complex pattern than Braverman's argument suggested. While some jobs clearly were being deskilled, there were also *new* types of jobs that required *more* skills and education than the jobs they replaced (for example, knowledge about computers that direct robots). The **skill-biased technological change** (SBTC) hypothesis argues that technological changes since the 1970s increased demand for high-skill workers and the wages they could command (Levy and Murnane 1992; Katz and Murphy 1992; Autor et al. 1998). Indeed, if we look at the overall pattern of job growth over time within the United States (as we saw in the previous section of the chapter), it does seem clear that there has been a long-term shift toward jobs that require *more* skill and *more* education, not less—one reason the income differences between college graduates and those without college degrees has been growing in recent years (Goldin and Katz 2010).

Alongside the shift toward more education and more skill in jobs have been changes in the design of the workplace. Both factories and offices are increasingly designed to encourage workers to move around and collaborate in teams. Many organizations have eliminated offices with closed doors in favor of an open floorplan. Probably the most famous examples of these kinds of business organizations are the large tech firms. If you go into the headquarters of Google or Facebook, you will not find a set of rows or workstations, but rather very large open spaces with desks and couches and small meeting spaces everywhere. No one is "assigned" to a desk, but rather people grab whatever location looks comfortable to them. Even in traditional industries like auto manufacturing, the newfound emphasis on flexibility is filtering in. Team work, the rotation of job tasks among workers, as well

as worker–management cooperation, is now increasingly common.

This naturally leads to the question of whether Scientific Management—the close monitoring and control of the workplace by the employer—is a thing of the past. It is not. Even as firms adopt more flexible workplaces, they continue to closely monitor their employees. For example, having workers use laptops or smartphones provided by the employer allows the company to literally monitor everything the employee does, from the total amount of time each worker is "on task" all the way down to individual keystrokes they type on their computer. Firms can also use technology in factories or warehouses to monitor workers' movements more precisely than ever before. It is a level of surveillance that Fredrick Taylor could only dream about. Indeed, some analysts have even described the emerging workplace representing the rise of *surveillance capitalism* (Zuboff 2019).

The COVID-19 pandemic introduced a startling change into modern workplaces, by keeping most white-collar workers at home. Working from home—known as **telecommuting**—may be desirable in some respects, but it comes with important disadvantages for both workers and employers. Being at home makes it easier to mix work and family duties, but it takes workers away from their peers and coworkers. Many people find some of their most rewarding relationships at work, and those relationships are severely diminished when working from home (no matter how many Zoom meetings they are on). Working from home also means that the worker absorbs the costs of maintaining their office space, transferring expenses once covered by the employer to the workers. There may also be a tendency for workers to allow work time to bleed into family or personal time: Whereas when a worker leaves the office or job site, the day is usually done, but when working from home there is no such formal departure and work may come in during off-hours. On balance, however, from the prospective of most workers, the growth of telecommuting options (perhaps mixing some days in the office with some days at home) can be viewed in as having some distinct advantages.

There are also costs for employers that arise from telecommuting. For one thing, employers often find that maintaining a strong workplace culture and sense of common purpose among workers is more difficult when those workers are scattered. But the cost factor should

Assembly line workers, such as those in this shoe factory, are often relatively easy to replace because their tasks are routinized and easy for a replacement worker to learn.

ADEK BERRY/AFP/Getty Images

not be ignored. In many white-collar industries, employers are actively seeking ways to reduce their expensive office spaces (which cost not only rent but also "overhead" such as furniture, heating, cooling, lightening, janitorial services, and security services). How far employers will go in having their workers telecommute remains to be seen, but because of the financial savings it offers, it is certain that it will be increasingly common in the future.

Sources of Power and Control in the Workplace: Workers versus Employers

12.2.2 Describe contexts in which workers have power.

Firms in a capitalist market economy, like that in the United States, can organize work in a variety of different ways, but workers may have different ideas about how best to get the work done. When there are conflicts, the winner of each battle depends on the balance of forces and the sources of power each group can leverage. Employers have a lot of advantages. In general, jobs only exist to the extent that employers make investments that create work and (they hope) profits. The workplace itself, and the tools needed to get things done are (usually) the private property of the employer. In some industries, the threat of moving jobs to other countries or regions can be a significant source of power of employers over their workers.

What about workers? Are they helpless? No. There are two broad ways in which workers can potentially leverage power over their employers (Wright 2000). The first is when workers have skills that are in short supply. Skilled or knowledgeable workers are in a position to walk away from one job and know they can find another. But most workers do not have that particular luxury. The second source of power is one that all workers can potentially benefit from. It is the formation of collective organizations of workers, such as unions, or when workers act together (such as in a strike).

The role of government laws and regulations also plays an important role. Government policies can, in some cases, be an important tool for workers. For example, some countries have adopted laws that make it easier for employees to create unions and provide strong protections for all workers (whether in a union or not). Other countries – like the United States -- make it harder for workers to form unions and give employers a freer hand to determine how work is organized (Rosenfeld 2014).

Historically, the most important source of workers' power was when they formed unions. What do unions do? Unions create a way for workers to negotiate more effectively with their employers, instead of having each worker negotiate for themself. Unions also help monitor working conditions and ensure that employers abide by agreements with workers or government regulations. Unions negotiate contracts called **collective bargaining agreements** with employers that give both sides—employers and workers—a set of guidelines that govern the workplace. Where unions and management have built bonds of trust with each other, they can often work together over long stretches of time.

How common are unionized workplaces? The answer is that unions were once very powerful, but in the United States and many other countries around the world they have been in sharp decline for the past 50 years or so. In the U.S., unionization rates reached their peak in the 1950s, when about 35 percent of the workforce was organized into unions. At that time, even companies without unions often followed unionized workplaces in terms of pay and benefits for workers. Today, that is not the case. Just slightly over 10 percent of the American workforce belongs to a union. Today, America has the weakest private sector unions of any advanced economy; while unions are still common in many government agencies and nonprofit organizations (like universities and hospitals), only about 1 in 16 workers in a private sector job is in a union (U.S. Bureau of Labor Statistics 2020). In the public sector, where the "employer" is the government, unions are much more common (33 percent of all government workers are members of unions). However, a 2018 Supreme Court ruling (*Janus* v. *AFSCME*) extended the very same anti-union rules to cover public sector employment, so in the future of public unions may also begin to decline.

Chicago hotel workers on strike in 2018. When unions can threaten an employer with a strike that shuts down the business, they have more power over their working conditions. The decline of unions and the ability of workers to strike has shifted the balance of power in the workplace towards employers.

Todd Bannor/Alamy Stock Photo

What are the causes of the general decline in unionization in the U.S.? It's often thought that unions are unpopular, but this is not true; survey after survey shows that majorities of Americans support unions and/or wish they had a union in their own workplace. Since 1936, the Gallup polling company has periodically asked Americans a simple question: "Do you approve or disapprove of unions?" In 1936, 72 percent of Americans supported unions, and 65 percent do so today (Brenan 2020). Although attitudes have fluctuated (hitting a low point of 48 percent in support in 2008), consistently strong majorities have almost always approved of unions for as long as they have been asked about them (see Figure 12.4).

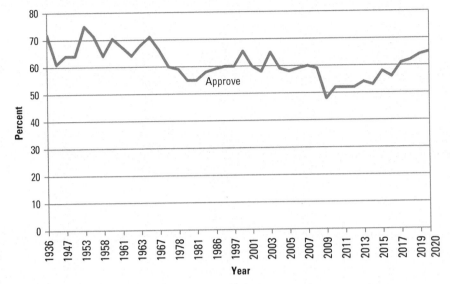

Figure 12.4 Americans' Approval of Labor Unions, 1936–2020

SOURCE: Brenan, 2020.

So if it is not because people don't want unions, what is the reason for their decline? Employers' militant stances against unions have probably been the most important factor; beginning the 1970s, American employers vigorously resisted unions with considerable success (Rosenfeld 2014). In doing so, they were able to rely on many important changes to the laws that govern the right of workers to organize unions, making it much harder for union organizing drives to succeed (Greenhouse 2019). Unlike many other countries, where workers can establish a union once a majority of workers have signed union cards, unions are only certified in the U.S. after long election campaigns in which employers are free to do whatever they can to convince their workers not to join a union. For example, employers can threaten to move jobs to another location or out of the country, leaving the workers with nothing even if they succeed in getting a union in place. Another reason for union decline is that employment in manufacturing industries that were once mostly or completely unionized has declined, while employment has grown in historically nonunionized sectors of the economy (for example, services and white-collar occupations). Walmart, Starbucks, McDonald's: All of these large companies are union-free. Further, for a variety of reasons, it has historically been more difficult to organize white-collar workers into unions (so most white-collar workers do not have a union). Finally, some internal critics in the labor movement have argued that the largest American unions have not been sufficiently aggressive in waging effective membership campaigns, even though the legal environment makes success difficult (McAlevey 2014). Some combination of all of these factors is at work.

The decline of unions has had many effects. Scholars studying declining wages and rising income inequality in the US have attributed a significant share of that trend to the drop in unionization rates (Western and Rosenfeld 2011; Kristal and Cohen 2016). To put this another way, the decline of unions has meant that a smaller share of corporate income is being paid to workers, with more going to shareholders and owners instead. Unions also play an important role in organizing workers politically, and in making policy proposals to Congress and state legislatures to protect workers' rights (McAlevey 2020). We do know that unions provide important protections and benefits to workers, and their steady decline has benefitted employers in how they treat their workers (Rosenfeld 2019).

Some of the same benefits that unions can win for workers can also be achieved through government regulations. For example, governments can regulate how many hours workers can be required to work, how much pay workers must get for overtime, under what conditions a

Fast food workers at a rally in Detroit, Michigan in 2021 demanding a $15 an hour minimum wage.

Jim West/Alamy Stock Photo

worker can be fired, whether a worker can be forced to work an extra shift, that workplaces and jobs be safe, and what the minimum wage should be. Some countries with particularly weak unions (such as France and Japan) achieve some of the same results as countries with strong unions (like Sweden or Germany) because of strong government regulations. The United States, by comparison with most other countries, has both weak unions *and* fewer government protections than workers in Europe or Canada (Pontusson 2005). America does have a minimum wage, rules about overtime pay, and rules about fair treatment of employees in the hiring and firing process, but on the whole, U.S. employers face far fewer workplace regulations than most other countries. Even those rules that do exist can often be (and are) ignored by many employers (Kalleberg 2011).

One way to think about how unions and workplace regulations potentially complement each other is to visualize it in a 2 × 2 figure. In any country, unions can be strong or weak, and government protections of workers can be either strong or weak. Workers can potentially be protected by their union, by regulations, or by both. Figure 12.5 provides an approximate grouping of countries. Canada is like the United States in having

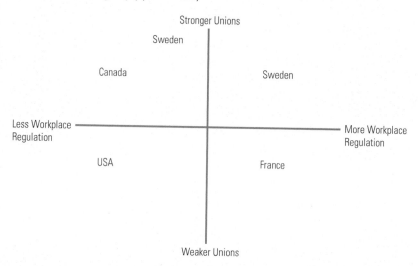

Figure 12.5 Cross-National Comparison of Workplace Regulation and Union Strength (Approximate)

relatively limited government regulation of the workplace, but Canada has significantly stronger unions than the United States. Sweden and some other Nordic countries have been moving toward fewer workplace regulations, combined with extremely strong unions and generous unemployment benefits. France has weaker unions, like the United States, but much stronger workplace regulations. Germany is an example of a country that has moderately strong unions and very strong workplace protections.

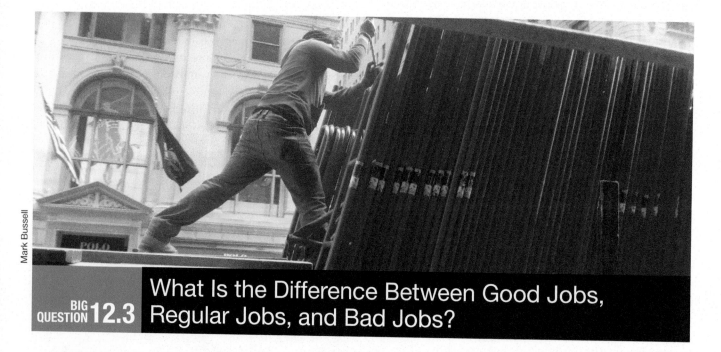

Mark Bussell

BIG QUESTION 12.3 What Is the Difference Between Good Jobs, Regular Jobs, and Bad Jobs?

WORK IN CONTEMPORARY AMERICA

Work is a huge part of the lives of most adults. Getting up every morning (or night, depending on the job) and going

to work gives our lives structure and meaning. Mastering a set of complex tasks and acquiring the experience and knowledge to know what to do when problems arise becomes an important part of our identity. Friendships are often formed at work or with others in our field, and it is often at work where people have many of their most significant conversations with nonfamily members about life and politics. Many people even meet romantic partners through work.

None of this should seem very surprising. People with full-time jobs spend about a third or more of their waking hours at work, so its importance is evident simply in the time commitment involved. But the critical role work plays can also be seen in a large body of research about what happens to people when they lose their jobs and are unemployed for an extended period of time. Symptoms such as depression, anxiety, increased consumption of alcohol and drugs, tensions in marriages or with a romantic partner, and, above all, dramatically increased levels of stress (which is in turn associated with a wide range of poor health outcomes) are common among those who are out of work. Indeed, being unable to find work can literally kill; mortality rates among people who have been out of work for long periods of time increase significantly (Tapia Granados et al. 2014).

What makes for satisfying employment may seem simple to define, yet we have no clear consensus about how to identify "bad," "good," or even "great" jobs. The amount of pay is, of course, one fairly universal metric (the higher paying the job, the better, at least for most people). Yet even income received from a job may not be enough. Many workers even in well-paying jobs may feel that their work is not making a meaningful contribution to the world, and that if it were eliminated no one would be any worse off (30 to 40 percent of European workers in surveys have reported these feelings; see Graeber 2018).

Beyond income, there is even less of a consensus. Consider this question: If the pay were identical, would you prefer driving a truck, processing insurance claims, or installing cable or Internet services? Would you rather spend your life as a company manager, a lawyer, or a dentist? It's clear that what is a good job for one person may not be so great for someone else. That said, there are *some* features of jobs that make them more or less attractive to anyone who might work in them. In this section we consider some of these issues. We also discuss the world of what is known as *precarious work*, jobs that have lowpay and are highly insecure.

Work Satisfaction

12.3.1 Explain the key factors that contribute to job satisfaction in most workplaces.

What makes a job satisfying or "good?" Sociologists who have studied this question find that aside from pay, several things stand out: **autonomy** (How much does this job allow me to control my activities versus being constantly told what to do?); **discretion** (How much does my employer trust me?); **status** (Do people admire and respect me because I do this job, or do they look down their noses at me?); **fringe benefits** (Does the job offer health insurance, retirement benefits, vacation pay, and sick pay?), the level of skill and the importance of the credentials required by the job (Am I using my skill set and continually building on it, or am I working well below my ability?); and, finally, job security (How likely will I be able to stay employed in this job?) (cf. Kalleberg 2011).

The level of autonomy and discretion (or trust) in a job is important. Having an employer's trust (handling secrets and not being monitored or supervised closely by anyone) is often associated with having greater responsibilities and higher pay. By contrast, in very low-trust workplaces where actions are tightly controlled and monitored, employees rate satisfaction lower. Cameras may monitor workers' every move, and supervisors may determine when workers can take breaks or even go to the bathroom. Those in low-trust office environments typically have their access to the Internet closely monitored, severely limited, or completely blocked. In high-trust positions (such as management positions or those requiring advanced degrees and certification to practice), people work without much or sometimes without any direct supervision. They may be trusted with important responsibilities and company secrets. They are generally able to control the pace of their work efforts. They can go online and read the newspaper or the sports page or plan their evening activities when they choose (although, as we noted earlier, technology has made it easier for employers to monitor the work even of higher level employees).

The status or amount of **prestige**, as sociologists call it, attached to a job affects satisfaction as well (Hodge 1981). Imagine you are at a party with a lot of people you don't know. One of the first questions someone might ask is, "What do you do?" Whatever answer you give will tell the other person a bit about how you spend your days, but it will also signal your status. If your answer is "Supreme Court Justice," you can be quite certain that you will impress your new acquaintance. If your answer is "cashier," they will be considerably less impressed. When you work in an occupation with a high degree of prestige, it likely will make you feel good about your work—or at least make you feel that other people respect what you do for a living. Sociologists have studied this insight, asking two questions: (1) how much prestige do different occupations have, measured in surveys in which respondents are asked to rate a range of occupations (specific questions used vary—some ask about the "general standing" of jobs, while others ask about their "social usefulness" or

Table 12.2 Occupational Prestige Scores

The following are the highest and lowest occupations tested in the General Social Survey (Scored 1–8, based on survey respondents' average rating).

Highest-Rated Occupations:		Lowest-Rated Occupations:	
Surgeon	7.7	Fortune Teller	2.6
Physician	7.6	Shoeshiner	2.6
Astronaut	7.4	Attendant in an Ice-Skating Rink	2.6
Nuclear Scientist	7.3	Cotton Picker	2.5
Mayor of a Large City	7.2	Envelope Stuffer	2.5
University or College President	7.1	Telephone Solicitor	2.5
Obstetrician/Gynaecologist	7.0	Parking Lot Attendant	2.4
University or College Professor	6.9	Table Clearer in a Restaurant	2.3
Aeronautical Engineer	6.9	Panhandler	2.1
Biologist	6.9	Street Corner Drug Dealer	1.9

SOURCE: Smith and Son (2014).

"desirability")? (2) what factors explain why some occupations have more prestige than others? Table 12.2 summarizes the results of a 2012 survey of occupational prestige that was part of that year's General Social Survey. Here, we've listed the 10 highest and 10 lowest occupations that were considered in the survey.

The possession of supervisory authority and the amount of skill required in a job are often key components differentiating jobs. For example, having one or more subordinates to supervise is frequently associated with making a job more attractive, though some find it stressful or unpleasant to supervise others. Having supervisory authority does usually mean higher pay. In many situations, supervisors can delegate selected tasks to other workers, so they can concentrate on more desirable or challenging work tasks. The skill level of a job is an important part of what provides security and ultimately more pay. Some jobs can be learned in a matter of hours or days. Operating a cash register or making a hamburger at a fast-food restaurant are skills that workers can master easily and quickly. As a consequence, an employee in such a job is easily replaceable. By contrast, jobs that require long apprenticeships or educational credentials—such as plumber, accountant, or doctor—are far more difficult to achieve, providing a stronger foundation for job security and claims for increased pay. The same job can, however, be associated with big disparities depending on context. For example, compare a partner at a Wall Street law firm versus a self-employed lawyer who defends mostly low-income or even unwaged clients. Both attorneys may share law degrees, yet their paychecks probably look very different.

Finally, it is hard to feel secure in a job when one does not know whether it will still be there in six months or a year. Relatively few jobs provide exceptionally high security; these tend to be government jobs, teaching jobs (college professors may even possess tenure, the granting of

which provides protection against being fired for almost any reason), and many experienced and in-demand professions. The vast majority of jobs, however, provide considerably less security. Small businesses frequently fail, and medium and large firms can also go out of business or lay off large numbers of workers when business declines. During the COVID-19 pandemic, millions of workers were laid off and job insecurity was especially high, although insecurity was already rising prior to the pandemic.

Precarious Work

12.3.2 Describe the features of precarious work, and explain why it has become more prevalent.

By 2010, one in five employees in the United States worked part-time (up from 13 percent in 1968). Do this many people want to work part-time? Some surely do, but most part-timers report that they would prefer to work full time. Part-time jobs typically provide little security, pay low wages, do not provide health or retirement benefits, and in some cases put workers on erratic schedules. It's one thing for a college student to pick up a few hours at a nearby mall to help defray some of the costs of attending school, but something altogether different for an adult struggling to survive with only part-time work or having to stitch together two or three part-time jobs to make ends meet.

Alongside the high numbers of part-time workers, there is another category of highly insecure work that has been growing in recent decades, known as **informal work**, which refers to jobs that are outside the scope of labor laws and government regulations and in which workers are frequently paid in cash and "off the books" (Venkatesh 2009). Informal workers are truly on their own, and have few protections that regular workers gain from government laws. They also are not part of the social security system, so they are not receiving benefits towards retirement or for a disability.

The rise of part-time and informal work is not just happening in the United States; it can be found across the globe over the past few decades. In Italy, some labor activists created a new phrase—*il precariato*, or in English translation, the **precariat**—to describe the workers in these jobs (the term combines Karl Marx's "proletariat" with "precarious"). Whether or not there is a distinct category of people who are permanently in this condition, the kinds of jobs it refers to are called **precarious work** by sociologists. This kind of work is "employment that is uncertain, unpredictable, and risky from the view of the worker" (Kalleberg 2011). Not surprisingly, Blacks, Latinxs, immigrants, and women are much more likely than Whites and men to be in such jobs (Kalleberg, et al. 2000).

Precarious jobs are hardly a new development. Around the world, precarious jobs have always existed on the margins of the economy, especially in developing countries but also in the rich countries of Europe and North America. Yet for most of the second half of the twentieth century, precarious work was limited in the rich countries and was even declining in some rapidly developing countries. Between the end of World War II and the 1980s, almost all workers in rich countries could find stable full-time jobs (Moody 1997). The rise of precariousness accelerated only in the period since then. Even in developing countries like India and China, where precarious or informal work has always been common, there has been a decline in regular, secure jobs in recent decades, *even* as these countries have seen spectacular economic growth (Zhao 2013; Lee 2019).

Precarious work is truly what are often called dead-end jobs, which may provide income but no other benefits and do not lead toward a stable employment or a career. There is no single definition of precarious work, but any job that has several of the following features would qualify:

- Low wages (at or near minimum wage, or below)
- Part-time or temporary employment (including day labor)
- No permanent work schedule (shifting hours, depending on employer's needs)
- Informality (such as the lack of a work contract specifying the terms of employment)
- Home-based work (for example, childcare done at a private residence, or small-scale production of goods that are then sold by someone else)
- No realistic chance for a promotion
- No realistic avenue to appeal arbitrary treatment by a supervisor, unsafe work conditions, or failure to be paid in a timely fashion
- May be paid in cash

A United Nations agency based in Geneva, Switzerland, called the International Labour Organization (ILO), has been studying trends in precarious work around the world for the last couple of decades and provides the best available information about the prevalence of these jobs. The ILO estimates that in the very poorest countries around the world, particularly in Africa, as much as 70 to 80 percent of jobs are precarious. The figure is 51 percent for South and Central America, and 65 percent in Asia (excluding the developed countries—Japan, South Korea, Taiwan, and Singapore). In the developing countries in these regions, a large percentage of the workforce makes a living peddling goods or services on the street, with little or no chance to accumulate any wealth or save for the future or a child's education (ILO 2015). In China, informal jobs are estimated to be around 60 percent of all urban employment, largely performed by people migrating from rural areas, living in cheap, dilapidated housing (Huang 2009).

Precarious work is common among the self-employed in poor countries, but there are also many large factories engaged in **sweatshop manufacturing**. The low-wage jobs found in these factory settings typically involve working conditions that do not meet regular health and safety standards. For instance, in India, firms with fewer than 10 employees are not subject to the state's labor regulations, and over 90 percent of all jobs are either via self-employment or with small employers (Breman 2013). And regular and precarious jobs only *seem* to be entirely separate; many regular firms subcontract to firms using cheap precarious labor to lower their costs (Agarwala 2009).

In rich countries, the situation is not nearly so bleak. Precarious jobs make up a much smaller fraction of total employment, and however bad those jobs are, they generally pay higher wages than those in very poor countries. Nevertheless, there is worrisome evidence that precarious work is becoming more common. The ILO estimates that in the European Union countries and in OECD respectively, between 8 and 9 percent of jobs were precarious in 1985, and those numbers jumped to about 12 to 15 percent in 2007. In the United States, given what we know about the economy overall, it is likely that the percentage of workers in precarious jobs is toward the higher end of this estimate, although it was not included in the ILO study.

What is it like to work in a precarious job? A group of seven social scientists produced the first systematic national survey of precarious work in 2009 (Bernhardt et al. 2009). The researchers interviewed 4,387 low-wage workers in precarious jobs in Chicago, Los Angeles, and New York City. They made special efforts to locate and interview workers who might be missed by conventional surveys, such as undocumented immigrants. The study found that fully 26 percent of the workers were paid less than the minimum wage, and that 76 percent of workers who logged more than 40 hours of work in a week did not receive overtime pay. The average pay for full-time workers in these industries was $17,616, but the authors also found that the average worker was cheated out of $2,634 in earnings from unpaid overtime, or not being paid the full amount they were owed. These workers also reported numerous unsafe conditions and a lack of compliance with federal and state laws regarding worker health and safety.

Working "Off the Books": The Underground Economy

12.3.3 Describe the main features of work in the underground economy.

A subset of precarious jobs are those in the so-called **underground economy**. This refers to all economic transactions and jobs, legal or illegal, that are completely "off the books," in the sense that all payments are in cash (that is, not traceable) and nothing is reported to the government. It is as if these transactions never happened. Prominent examples of jobs in the underground economy can be found in criminal organizations (money laundering, trafficking, the large-scale distribution of drugs, or prostitution), but it also includes anyone or any company that operates without an official address or license and is able to mask what they do to avoid taxes and regulations. This might include nannies whose employers don't pay Social Security or other taxes as required, non-union construction jobs, cash-based small businesses (restaurants and bars are common offenders), or even those selling stolen goods (what is known as "fencing"). Put simply, those who cannot find full-time or regular employment may, out of desperation, turn to ways of earning an income that pays them under the table.

Although the underground economy is often thought of as mysterious and unknowable, social scientists have developed a variety of methods for attempting to study it. It is estimated that about 10 percent of America's entire GDP is off the books, and some tentative evidence shows that it is growing over time (Schneider and Enste 2000; Goldstene 2015). The existence of a large underground economy is a complex societal issue. It is socially harmful in a variety of ways. For one thing, employers who cheat the rules harm other businesses. The former gain an unfair advantage when they don't pay taxes, and they don't have to treat their workers with dignity or respect (much less provide health insurance or any other benefits). If these employers go into debt, they can just shut down and move on, leaving their creditors with no way to make up their losses. Most underground economy jobs pay poorly, and employers regularly cheat their employees. Hustling to make ends meet in the underground economy can also be dangerous, insecure, and overall a poor substitute for a regular job. If the activity is against the law, there is the further risk of arrest and possible prison.

Some of the most detailed findings on the underground economy can be found in the research of the sociologist Sudhir Venkatesh (2009, 2014). He has argued that legitimate and illicit economic activities are often closely connected to one another, and the latter is a key part of the fabric of poor urban neighborhoods in many large cities. In his research, he has examined a variety of economic relationships—from prostitutes and drugs dealers to back-alley auto mechanics and petty smugglers—in a ghetto in South Chicago and more recently in New York City. In one investigation of the economic lives of drug dealers in Chicago, Venkatesh and economist Steven Leavitt (Leavitt and Venkatesh 2000) found that—in contrast to the more glamorous images sometimes portrayed in film or television—working for a large drug gang is not a good way to make much money. They discovered that entry-level street drug dealers often make less than minimum wage, while working long hours in dangerous conditions with no other benefits; only much higher up in the organization are people making significant amounts of money. But even for the higher level participants, there is a catch. Almost everyone eventually who stays in the drug trade long enough ends up either dead or in prison. But much of Venkatesh's research has focused on less dangerous and more ordinary kinds of "hustles" that people rely on to get by. One of the interesting lessons of his and other work on poor communities is that the level of entrepreneurship and hard work required to survive when regular, secure employment is not available, is substantial and important to recognize (see also Edin and Lein 1997).

Migrant and Undocumented Workers

12.3.4 Explain why migrant and immigrant workers are attractive to some U.S. employers.

The American labor force consists not just of U.S. "citizens" holding jobs, but also of a large number of migrant and immigrant workers. **Migrant workers** are individuals born in another country who move to the United States and seasonal workers who come to the United States for a specific job and then return home. **Immigrant workers** work in the country they moved to and plan to settle there. Not all immigrants come searching for work, of course. Many relocate to a different country as refugees fleeing from war, violence, climate disasters, or other threats to life. Regardless of their motivation, the inflow of people to a country can have an effect on the existing population and on work. In 2019, out of a total of 163 million workers, 28.4 million (17.4 percent) were foreign born (U.S. Bureau of Labor Statistics 2020).

Unless they have permanent residence (a green card), many immigrant workers typically lack the social protections that permanent residents and full citizens have, such as eligibility for unemployment benefits. They also must rely on their employer for health insurance, as they are not eligible for regular government programs like Medicaid or Medicare. The situation is even more difficult for **undocumented immigrants**, who have not established any legal residence in the United States (see Chapter 24 for more information about immigration). They have the least amount of bargaining power and often find themselves in the most precarious and exploitative jobs. Because they do not have work authorization or legal documentation to be in the U.S., these workers essentially lack all of the rights that other workers enjoy, and they cannot easily make employers live up to their promises. This constant grayness is a source of stress, magnified by the threat of being sent back home (Menjívar 2006).

In the U.S., undocumented immigrants are most typically employed in agricultural and service sector jobs, where it is difficult to find enough Americans willing to do them. These include meatpacking, cleaning and maid services, and some kinds of construction jobs. These are often low-wage, subcontracted, non-union jobs. In the worst-case scenario, many undocumented workers will not be paid the full amounts they are owed and can be compelled to work under appalling conditions. Two sociologists tried to estimate the disadvantages associated with being undocumented. They compared available wages of Mexican migrants to their undocumented counterparts and found that undocumented workers earned 20 percent less than legal immigrants regardless of their

sex or education (Massey and Gentsch 2014). Other studies also found that wages increased when workers moved out of undocumented status, even when their education and occupations did not change (Rivera-Batis 1999). These differences in wages allude to the possible discrimination and exploitation that undocumented workers face.

When Jobs Disappear: The Impact of Long-Term Unemployment

12.3.5 Describe the effects long-term unemployment can have on individuals, families, and communities.

Work, as we've noted, is important to the lives of individuals in adulthood. But what happens when it is lost? Changes in the economy in recent decades have significantly increased the percentage of workers who are unemployed for long periods of time. As noted at the beginning of this section, being unemployed for an extended period—six months or more—can have many negative consequences. For instance, in a study conducted among individuals who have never experienced mental health issues, researchers found that joblessness significantly increases psychological distress among the long-term unemployed (Diette et al. 2012). Job losers are, on average, more likely to suffer from lower general health and depression symptoms after taking into account many other characteristics (Burgard, Brand, and House 2007). These factors can form obstacles for re-employment. Even if previously long-term unemployed workers return to the labor market, they are significantly more likely to lose their job again, compared to others (Krueger et al. 2014).

Not surprisingly, long-term unemployment also affects the well-being of the people surrounding the jobless individual. For example, a recent study by the Urban Institute (2014) found a strong association between job loss and destabilizing changes in family arrangement in subsequent months. These signs of instability were found in both two-parent and single-parent families, and affected both parents' and children's personal and emotional relationships. A long bout of unemployment can also strain marriages and relationships. There is also evidence that children who experience the unemployment of their parents are on average more likely to suffer in terms of mental health and even academic performance can suffer. The loss of income may impact many things a family normally pays for, especially if the family doesn't have a significant savings account to draw on. In a worst-case scenario,

Protests by immigrant groups and their supporters, such as the march shown here in New York City, have demanded better and fairer treatment of all types of immigrant workers.

Mark Bussell

falling behind on house payments or being unable to afford medical care can lead to homelessness or bankruptcy.

Moreover, entire communities experiencing economic decline (and higher shares of long-term unemployment) are impacted by these trends. This is most obvious in places where manufacturing jobs were the primary source of employment. Beginning in the late 1960s and accelerating in the 1980s and beyond, many once-vibrant cities that relied on manufacturing jobs have suffered severe declines as unemployment rates shot up, as mentioned earlier. These were often communities once built around large factories and sometimes a single dominant manufacturing industry. The most famous of these industrial centers dominated by manufacturing was the concentration of the automobile industry in Detroit, Michigan, but there were also many others (for example, steel in Pittsburgh, Pennsylvania, and Gary, Indiana; meatpacking in Chicago, Illinois; rubber in Akron, Ohio; grain milling in Buffalo, New York; and transportation hubs for manufacturing companies in places like New Orleans, Louisiana). All of these cities and regions prospered as demand for manufactured products grew both in America and around the world, and all suffered profound declines as those industries closed and jobs disappeared.

In places that have experienced economic decline, a variety of common social problems have increased in severity. When long-term unemployment becomes a way of life for many people, social ills such as crime and violence may increase. Lacking other opportunities, young people in these areas in particular are more likely to engage in criminal activity, and rates of violence typically go up (in recent years, for example, the larger cities and surrounding regions with the highest murder rates are virtually all places where severe losses of manufacturing jobs have occurred and recovery has been slow: St. Louis, Baltimore, Detroit, New Orleans, Cleveland and other Northeast Ohio communities, Newark, Kansas City, Buffalo, Chicago and others; see Asher 2017). As the taxes paid by the industries and workers they once employed disappear, local governments lack the resources to maintain high-quality schools and public services, which can exacerbate other problems and lead to new forms of unemployment. High rates of long-term unemployment in a community often contribute to a cycle of decline that is very difficult to reverse.

Dmitry Serebryakov/TASS/Alamy Stock Photo

BIG QUESTION 12.4 What Are Professional Occupations, and Why Are They Distinct?

PROFESSIONS: A UNIQUE OCCUPATIONAL NICHE

Some of the most privileged and unique contemporary occupations are known as **professions**. These are knowledge-based occupations that limit competition in their field by establishing licensing rules that prevent uncertified individuals or groups from doing the same work. In most cases, professional occupations have gained this privileged status by convincing governments to sanction and enforce rules that they have created. In fact, in many cases, governments allow members of the profession to regulate themselves, marking a big departure from the rules of free markets. As one study has put it, professional occupations "spin knowledge into gold" (Derber, et al. 1992).

In this section, we will examine professional occupations, identify some common features among them, and distinguish professions from semiprofessional occupations, which have some but not all features of traditional professional occupations. To dig a bit deeper, we then present a case study of one of the canonical professional occupations – that of physicians. As we will see, physicians gained the power and prestige they hold today after a long and difficult struggle against competing groups that sought to shape the health care system. Although not all professions are as robustly organized and sanctioned by the government as physicians, understanding how they won professional status highlights the pathways that other professions have followed.

Professions Defined

12.4.1 Describe what qualifies as a profession.

Professions refer to a small group of knowledge-based occupations that have some unique features. **Professionalization** is the process by which these occupations come to be recognized by government officials and/or the public as possessing a kind of expertise that can only be self-regulated and which is protected from competition from nonmembers. In other words, only members of the profession have the expertise to evaluate other members (Friedson 2001). Professional occupations are thus granted a high degree of control over their work. Different professions—such as law, engineering, architecture, accounting, and dentistry—vary in how and to what degree they are organized and in how successful they are in obtaining control over their work, but they all have unique powers that no other kinds of jobs enjoy. Professionals (individual members of a profession) are typically organized into professional associations (like the American Medical Association for physicians, the American Bar Association for lawyers, or even the American Sociological Association for sociologists) that carry out a number of tasks such as (1) determining the standards for specialized training and education and requiring all practitioners to have obtained the relevant degrees, or **credentials**, to become a member of the profession; (2) controlling membership through licensing by the government; and (3) reestablishing and maintaining professional norms through a **code of ethics** that all members of the profession are supposed to abide by. (In Chapter 3, we described the code of ethics that professional sociologists are bound to comply with in their research.)

Because professions limit competition from other sources, they are not subject to the pressures of capitalist markets to the same degree as nonprofessional occupations, as noted (Derber et al. 1992; Weeden and Grusky 2013). The German sociologist Max Weber introduced the idea of social closure to describe how groups seek to monopolize opportunities and rewards for themselves and limit competition from members of other groups (see Chapters 2 and 5 for further discussion of Weber's theory). Professions are classical examples: They seek to establish a monopoly over their area of practice, and then find ways to eliminate competition. Those occupations that succeed in this have achieved closure: Non-lawyers cannot represent clients in court; non-physicians are not allowed to perform surgery; non-engineers cannot sign legally binding documents assuring that a proposed newly designed structure is safe and can be built; and so forth. If you need one of those things, you will inevitably need a professional to do it.

Professional occupations are generally among the most high-paying and privileged of all occupations, but not all elite occupations are professions. For example, business executives and business managers may have similar backgrounds to professionals, but their careers are ultimately tied to the profitability of the firms they work for and/or to their own ability to generate profits for their firms. They are, in this sense, more "exposed" to the market than professionals, who don't really have the same kind of pressures. While professionals compete with each other to some extent, the total number of professionals is limited so there is usually plenty of work to go around for everyone in the field. Professionals may make mistakes, and a few may even lose their license to practice, but this is very rare and usually involves very high-level malfeasance of some kind, or repeated incompetence. Managers and executives, by contrast, enjoy none of the kinds of protections that being in a profession provides. In addition, there is no single body of knowledge that someone must master to work for a business—the MBA is a much looser requirement than a law or medical degree, for example, and many top business executives never even receive one. (There are multiple routes to the executive suite, and while an MBA may be useful, it is not required.) There is also no required "code of ethics" for executives and managers to follow.

Business executives often have the resources and power to *hire* professionals to work for them—indeed, many professionals earn most or all of their income working on projects that come from business executives—so it is not the case that professionals have more "power" or status than business executives. And top business executives often earn far more money than professionals. Both of these facts highlight that becoming the chief executive officer (CEO) of a large corporation enables far more privileges and resources than even the most famous of lawyers, doctors, or engineers. But professionals have a kind of job security that most business executives do not. The typical (median) CEO tenure (that is, the amount of time they will keep their job) at the largest American companies is just five years (Marcec 2018). CEOs and other executives come and go all the time, whereas the market for professional services tends to remain very stable over time. Once a professional has established themselves in their field, it is likely that they can continue to practice in that profession for the rest of their working life. Managers and executives working for businesses, however, can be replaced at any time, and in recent years many senior executives find themselves being pushed out in their 50s or 60s in favor of younger, cheaper executives. Professionals, by contrast, can and often do maintain their practices as long as they want—into their 70s or even 80s.

Professional Knowledge Jurisdictions

12.4.2 Explain why it is important for professions to monopolize relevant knowledge.

As we've noted, one of the most important ways that professions establish and enforce their control over certain kinds of work is through establishing a distinctive expertise about their area of practice (Abbott 1988). Over time, the knowledge base they create to speak to each other becomes increasingly hard for outsiders to comprehend. If you've ever read a legal contract drafted by a lawyer, you will readily understand what we mean: the contract will be filled with jargon that only other lawyers can grasp. Professional expertise is often a combination of real scientific advances *and* specialized language that only insiders know. Expert knowledge requires mastery of both, typically achieved in a special graduate school program that provides certification.

The sociologist Andrew Abbott (1988) has described this as a **knowledge jurisdiction**, an area of professional practice in which members of the profession develop new advances and ideas, generally in the guise of science or theoretical knowledge. The connection between education and professional practice is especially important

in this regard. It is often academic researchers in professional fields (such as professors of law, architecture, and medicine) who both train young people going into the field and do much of the basic research that will further enhance the knowledge base and the prestige of the profession.

The idea of knowledge jurisdiction may seem complicated, but it's really pretty straightforward. If you have a broken arm, you would probably go see a physician who specializes in the treatment of broken bones (an orthopedist). If you need to build or renovate a house, you would probably consult an architect to draft plans, and perhaps consult a structural engineer to make sure the house won't fall down. If you need advice about where to invest some money, most likely you will want to consult with a financial professional, someone who will have specialized knowledge in the various investment options that might be available. Why would you choose someone, no matter how smart they may be, to advise you on something important that they are not expert in? In that sense, we live in an age of expertise. In each of these and many other kinds of problems people face, getting the benefit of the knowledge held by experts is usually the best way to go.

What are the major professional occupations that have succeeded in gaining control over their own destiny in this way? We've noted some of them already, but Table 12.3 lists the major professional occupations in two broad tiers, distinguishing those that have achieved the greatest degree of professional control over the entire occupation (Tier 1) from those have only partially succeeded in establishing their professional status (Tier 2). We must remember that these categories may vary over time, and some occupations will have Tier 1 status in the U.S. but not elsewhere. The second tier includes some high-status occupations (for example, business consultants) as well as some lower-status professional occupations, most notably nurses and teachers. The latter group are sometimes considered **semiprofessions**, in that they have some but not all of the powers of traditional professional occupations. There are also occupations like business consultants and financial analysts that have very minimal (finance) or no (consultant) formal credentials required to practice. Anyone can do these jobs, but only *if* clients will take you seriously and want to employ you. Some of the Tier 2 occupations have found that organizing themselves into unions has provided a better pathway to making claims for higher rewards and income than professions. For example, nurses, musicians, actors, and journalists all have unions that represent a large percentage of workers in those

Valerii Honcharuk/Alamy Stock Photo

Psychotherapy is an example of a professional occupation that did not exist prior to the twentieth century, but which has grown immensely in the past 100 years.

Table 12.3 Major Professional and Semiprofessional Occupations

Tier 1: Classic Professional Occupations
Actuaries
Accountant
Architect
Dentist
Economist
Engineer
Epidemiologists and Public Health Experts
Financial Advisor
Investment Banker
Mathematical and Computer Scientists
Nurse
Optometrist
Physician
Scientist
Social Worker
Surveyors
University Professors
Veterinarians

Tier 2: Professional Occupations Without Full Licensure or Professional Status
Actors
Advertising
Air Traffic Controllers
Community College or Adjunct College Instructors
Artists
Theater, Music and Film Directors and Producers
Chiropractors
Clergy/Religious Leaders
Consultants*
Computer and Software Technicians
Data Analysts
Editors
Elementary and Secondary School Teachers
Health Technicians
Hotel Managers
Journalists
Librarians
Medical Technicians
Musicians
Occupational and Physical Therapists
Public Relations Specialists
Urban Planners

SOURCE: U.S. Bureau of Labor Statistics.

*Members of Tier 1 professional occupations may serve as consultants based on their professional knowledge. However, there is no general certification process to work as a consultant, and many consultants are not members of any Tier 1 profession, so they are placed in Tier 2.

occupations. Unions can sometimes achieve some of the same results as professions—limiting access to opportunities for nonmembers—but they can only do so if they are well organized and their internal rules are acceptable to the firms or individuals that hire their members. In the United States, in recent years the decline of unions (discussed earlier in this chapter) has made it challenging to provide those benefits for their members.

An Example of Professionalization: The Rise of the Medical Profession

12.4.3 Analyze how the rise of the medical profession exemplifies the professionalization process.

In the previous section, we noted that professions come into existence by establishing that their members are the only ones qualified to do certain things, and that they develop a body of knowledge that outsiders cannot easily understand. But this process of professionalization entails multiple steps (Larson 1977). To better understand, let's consider a classic example that has been widely explored by sociologists: How the medical profession, dominated by licensed physicians, gained control over health care in the nineteenth and early twentieth centuries.

In a country like the United States, when we get sick we will almost certainly go see a physician, or a medical doctor. (A small subset of people may choose non-Western healing practitioners.) Physicians and medical care have been around for centuries, but for most of its early years, the practice of medicine was of limited value to patients, and indeed some widely used healing practices actually made people sicker. During the eighteenth century, most health care was provided by local doctors with little training, although community folk healers and religious leaders also participated (the latter combining health and spiritual concerns). These early doctors learned their trade in a kind of apprentice system, akin to the way a plumber or carpenter learns. Haphazard training, coupled with the undeveloped state of medical science and therapies, made practicing medicine a low-prestige occupation.

Throughout much of the nineteenth century there was intense competition among a diverse array of medical sects and folk practitioners, all vying to control medical treatment and to become successful in the medical market. One prominent form of alternative medicine, known as **homeopathy**, used infinitesimal doses of medicines and potions to treat disease and presented a particularly strong challenge to practitioners of regular medicine. In response to rising competition from homeopaths and others, physicians formed the American Medical Association (AMA) in 1847. The AMA had the express goal of combating "quackery" in all its forms. Yet, despite its best efforts, the AMA was ineffective in its early decades in stopping the competition. Indeed, alternative approaches grew steadily in popularity and provided a considerable threat.

Nineteenth-century medicine looked different than it does today. First, doctoring took place primarily in the

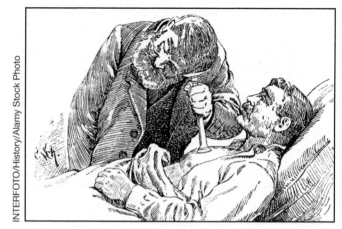
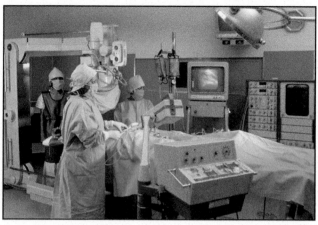

Professional occupations can evolve over time, as shown here by the contrast between nineteenth-century medical care and that of a modern hospital. The success of the medical profession built from major advances in medical science that could be used to treat patients. But it also needed enough political power to eliminate its rivals during the professionalization phase.

home, not in complex organizations like hospitals. Indeed, nineteenth-century hospitals were modest institutions focused more on charity and social welfare than on medical treatment, and they primarily served the poor. Hospitals were widely (and rightly at the time) viewed by the middle- and upper-classes as bastions of illness and neglect. Second, lacking sophisticated diagnostic testing and technologies, doctors depended on the external symptoms and self-reports of the patient when determining both diagnosis and treatment. Third, when making their assessments, doctors eschewed complex theories and instead adopted a pragmatic and particularistic approach, catering treatment to the individual patient as best they could.

Medical care remained in this disorganized and undeveloped state—with little regulation, negligible education, and scant research—until the end of the nineteenth century. A common misconception is that the health and well-being of the country improved largely because of innovations in medical science. The idea that science triumphed over ignorance and disease is a compelling one, but it does not tell the whole story. For one thing, historians and social scientists have shown that much of the decline in mortality prior to the 1920s resulted from the severe decline in death by infectious diseases—like cholera, typhoid, and smallpox—that periodically created epidemics (like COVID-19 in recent times) in the mid-nineteenth century. The eradication of these diseases was mostly attributable to improved sanitary conditions and better **public health**—basic sanitary policies aimed at cleaning up the environment and reducing the spread of disease through measures such as street cleaning, garbage removal, and provision of clean water supplies. The public health movement was an alliance between concerned elites, reform-minded politicians, and some civic-minded physicians (including some pioneering women physicians). It emerged in response to the filthy conditions of urban centers plagued by overcrowding and developed a number of important social interventions in health that go beyond the treatment of individuals.

If the rise of the medical profession cannot be attributed simply to advances in medical science, how did physicians, a group mocked and ridiculed for much of the nineteenth century for being incompetent, emerge from the early decades of the twentieth century as among the most powerful professionals in the United States? How did physicians, acting through the AMA and the local state medical associations they created, secure nearly complete control over the practice of medicine? The AMA's brilliant insight was to limit the influence of alternative approaches to medical care. They did this through public education campaigns, political lobbying, and internal policing of its members to ensure they were not collaborating with homeopathic groups or other competing sects (Starr 1982). Beginning in the late nineteenth century, state governments also granted professional licenses to physicians to practice medicine and establish rules that only those who had been granted a license could practice. The AMA convinced state medical boards to restrict who could call themselves a physician by requiring a degree from an approved medical school and the passing of an examination (Haller 1981; Horowitz 2013). This eventually gave physicians a legal monopoly over the practice of medicine. Because physicians and the AMA controlled the licensing of medical schools, they could prevent unapproved schools from popping up and creating competition. In short, the pathway to professionalization for physicians was first organizational (with the creation of the AMA). Once that process was complete, homeopaths and other groups found it very difficult to compete against licensed physicians and found their own practices limited to a small number of areas.

Alongside all of these efforts, there were a number of major scientific breakthroughs in the late nineteenth century; the development of germ theory, vaccines against disease, and innovations in surgery eventually created a firm scientific basis for the professional authority of physicians. By the early twentieth century, as medical education became substantially more rigorous, physicians began to help many sick patients. Treatment shifted from the home bedside to hospitals, increasingly large bureaucratic organizations that applied the latest medical technology. Diagnosis no longer depended primarily on patient testimony but rather on laboratory tests. Thus came the "golden age of American medicine" by which doctors as professionals achieved autonomy and control over all aspects of medicine and were considered the unquestioned authorities of all things pertaining to health and illness.

In more recent years, there have been important challenges and limits to the professional power of physicians. As the cost of medical care has risen dramatically in the United States (now consuming almost one-fifth of the entire American economy; see Chapter 19 for more details), pressures to contain costs and focus medical treatment in more efficient ways has become a central challenge. In particular, government health insurance programs—Medicare

for people over 65 (about 18 percent of all Americans) and Medicaid for poor families and individuals under 65 (covering an additional 19 percent)—have, through their rules and regulations, changed professional practice in important ways. Further, private health insurance companies, which cover about two-thirds of all Americans, have also set limits on what they will cover and imposed oversight over the decisions of individual physicians in many ways. In both of these situations, the professional autonomy of physicians has been squeezed, in the sense that doctors cannot simply order all of the tests and procedures they think are best for their patients. And most physicians abhor all of the paperwork and time spent meeting the requirements of either public or private health insurance. It's a very complex set of rules and regulations that show how even the most powerful of professions can face limits (Field 2006).

BIG QUESTION 12.5 What Are the Central Challenges Facing Workers in the Twenty-First Century?

CORE PROBLEMS FACING WORKERS TODAY

As we've discussed throughout the chapter, the world of work in the twenty-first century is changing in many important ways. These changes are especially visible when we compare American workers with those of their European, Australian, and Canadian counterparts. We immediately notice that Americans are working longer hours and are receiving fewer vacations than those in countries that are most like the United States. Further, young workers are facing greater difficulties in transitioning from school to career employment, and older workers are increasingly struggling to keep their jobs.

Long Hours

12.5.1 Compare and contrast Americans' working hours with workers in similar countries.

American workers on average work longer hours and take fewer paid vacations than workers in other countries. We are, as one journalist recently put it, "the most overworked developed nation in the world" (Miller 2017). This hasn't always been the case. In 1970, hours worked per person were similar in Western Europe and the United States (some studies even found that Europeans worked more hours than workers in the United States at that time). Today, however, the average full-time worker in America works several hundred hours more than the average number of hours worked per year by full-time workers in other similar countries (see Figure 12.6). A careful and conservative recent estimate finds that American workers are averaging about 258 hours a year, or almost 25 percent more time, at work than the typical European worker (Bick et al. 2016). Other studies find even larger gaps, depending on the measures and data they rely on; a gap of 400 hours is not uncommon (for example, Prescott 2004; Alesina et al. 2005). However we measure it, the difference can be thought of as approximately six to seven extra weeks of work a year, or two extra hours of work a day.

Why do Americans work longer hours than those in other similar countries? The biggest single factor is that workers in other rich countries around the world have seen the number of days they work and/or the number of hours they work each day fall significantly in recent decades, while American workers have not enjoyed any measurable decline in working hours. In many European countries, the typical work day is 7 or 7.5 hours, shorter than the 8-hour standard found in most full-time jobs in the United States. Workers in many European countries also typically receive more time off for meals and/or breaks during the day than American workers. In many countries, lunch time is taken more seriously as a full break from work than it is by many Americans (who may eat their lunch while continuing to work—something unheard of for most Europeans). As technology and other changes enable each worker to become more productive, Europeans have steadily reduced the amount of time they spend at work. By contrast, Americans are continuing to work just as hard as before, in spite of the increases in worker productivity. In some occupations, work time has actually increased in recent decades, especially in jobs where people use computers and can perform tasks at home as well as in their workplace.

Another key factor is vacation time. Most countries *require* employers to grant their employers several weeks of paid vacation every year, and many also require employers to pay their workers on public holidays. For example, European countries like Germany, France, Italy, Spain, and Portugal all require employers to give their workers at least a month of paid vacation and holidays in some combination (Hess 2013). Even many poorer countries give employees paid days off. Mexico requires employers to give workers at least 12 days of paid vacation a year (5 days of holiday, 7 legal holidays). Brazil gives workers 30 paid days off; China provides 16; Egypt mandates 28; and Hungary gives workers 33 paid days off. Figure 12.7 displays a range of countries and their paid holiday laws. These minimums do not preclude employers from offering workers even more time off; many do exactly that. The United States stands out for not requiring any employer to provide workers with *any* paid days off. A majority of U.S. employers do voluntarily offer paid vacation days to their workers (77 percent of all workers, according to the Bureau of Labor Statistics), with wide variation in how many paid holidays workers are provided (Van Giezen 2013). Still, the fact that these days are voluntary and not required by law tends to reduce the amount of vacation days workers receive, and about a quarter of all workers do not get any paid time off at all.

Longer working hours in America also reflect a noticeable increase in hours worked by three different kinds of workers: Those with higher levels of education, those in self-employment, and those working extensive overtime (often not by choice) in their primary job or in some cases taking on second jobs, typically for people with less education and/or in lower-paying jobs. High-earning Americans often work long hours, either by choice or because they are in jobs where the expectation of hard work and long hours has become standard (Conley 2008). These workers at the top of the labor market are either receiving significantly greater compensation relative to the average worker or can aspire (especially if they are younger) to a big payoff down the road (Bell and Freeman 1994). The fact that incomes are far more unequal in the United States than other countries means there is a bigger payoff for those who reach the top 10 percent or 5 percent or (especially) the top 1 percent. Rising levels of self-employment, as we noted earlier, is often associated with working long hours. When you are the boss, especially if you are running a small business, long working hours are often quite common. That may also be

Figure 12.6 Average Hours Worked in a Calendar Year by Full-Time Workers

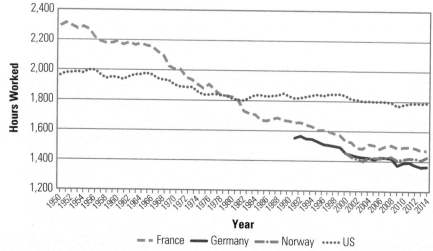

SOURCE: OECD, 2016.

Figure 12.7 Paid Vacation and Paid Holidays Around the World

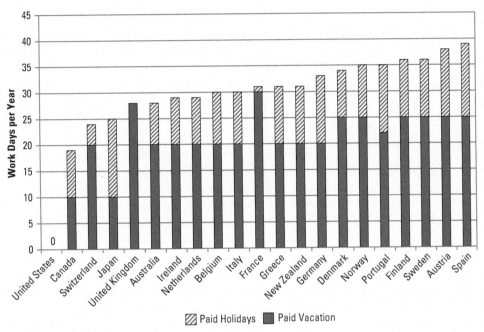

SOURCE: Maye 2019.

reach the middle class. For the most part, this reward of the American educational system no longer extends to high school graduates. If one hopes to reach middle-class status, chances are they will need a college diploma. This raises two sets of questions about younger workers:

1. What about the vast majority—around two-thirds—who will not attain a college degree (and even more worrisome, almost 15 percent of recent cohorts don't even finish high school by their early 20s)?
2. Will the promise of stable jobs and successful careers still hold in the future even for college graduates?

by choice—self-employed people may hope to grow their business into a successful venture that will eventually provide a good income.

Finally, the percentage of Americans in working-class jobs who work overtime is much higher than in other countries, and about 5 percent of workers also hold a second job. Mandatory overtime can be required by employers in most states, and employers can also threaten workers' jobs if they refuse to work overtime. This has long been an issue in the United States, and there is some evidence that it has gotten more common in recent years (Jorgensen and Golden 2002; Scheiber 2016). Employers are required to pay workers higher wages when they work more than a 40-hour week, and the extra pay can be desirable in many cases; however, workers who are regularly asked to work overtime may find it difficult or unwanted. Further, many American workers are given a salary to do a job, and they may be expected to put in longer than normal hours with no extra compensation. Overall, about one-quarter of employees report regularly working more than 40 hours a week (U.S. Bureau of Labor Statistics 2017).

Young Workers Entering the Labor Force

12.5.2 Explain why the transition from school to work has become more challenging for young workers.

The transition from school to work also looks quite different today than it did for previous generations. For most of the twentieth century, a high school diploma or any post-secondary qualification provided a decent opportunity to

For the first group, those who haven't gone to or finished college, and even more so for those who don't graduate from high school, the American economy is simply not producing enough good jobs at the point of entry, and advancement is often slow and marked by potential bouts of unemployment. One way to see this is to look at trends in the youth employment rate, that is, the rate for job-seeking members of the civil labor force between ages 16 (the earliest age in which many states allow children to stop attending school) and 24. Unemployment among young workers is typically around double the unemployment rate of the rest of older workers. Figure 12.8 compares the unemployment rate of younger workers and everyone else in the labor force. In recent recessions, such as in the early 1980s and in the period between 2008 and 2011, almost one in five young workers were unable to find jobs.

Although some of the increase of youth unemployment in recent years can be attributed to the recession in 2007–09 and the slow recovery that followed, there are many reasons to worry that it will continue to be an important problem in the future. The Organization of Economic Cooperation and Development (OECD), a 34-country group of the richest nations in the world, estimates that across their member countries, more than 15 percent of individuals under age 24 are not engaged in education, employment, or training. There is, it appears, a growing gap that exists between the preparations of (young) job candidates and optimal job skills of vacancies, and this is happening in most of the rich, developed countries around the world.

At the individual level, such a mismatch is almost inevitable when starting a job. Young people who have just

Figure 12.8 Unemployment Among Youth Aged 16–24, 1948–2020

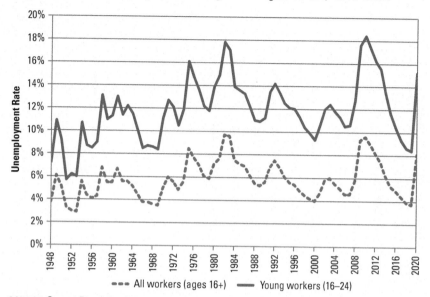

SOURCE: Current Population Survey. Retrieved from: https://www.bls.gov/cps/demographics.htm#age.

finished their educations are particularly vulnerable to labor market mismatch because they have limited skills and work experience to rely on when looking for their first job. New hires rarely have the skills and experience that employers require, so on-the-job training is always needed. Yet in the United States and many other OECD countries, employers increasingly do not want to pay the costs of such training. In many countries, the government steps in with skills training (known as **vocational education**) for beginning workers. But in the United States, this is much less common, and mostly takes place in community colleges or for-profit colleges that do not always provide the skills young workers need. The federal government provides very limited funds for vocational education, and state and local governments often do not have the resources to provide young workers with the training they need either. Other countries do better. Germany's education-to-work system contains vocational, professional, and academic programs that are closely tied to apprenticeships and internships offered by employers. It has therefore been relatively successful at guiding young people from school to the labor market, holding down youth unemployment. Other countries, especially in Northern Europe, have similar models to the German approach. In the United States, limited training opportunities leave young people to mostly fend for themselves.

Youth unemployment matters because the effects of missing out on training and experience accumulate quickly during the early phases of a career. Young mismatched workers are often forced into job trajectories with limited opportunities to develop skills and to move up the occupational ladder, simply because they need a job. An extended period in young adulthood in insecure and low-skilled precarious jobs may be necessary to pay bills, but it does

nothing to help someone move closer to stable long-term employment. This is also an issue for young people who are sent to prison, who then often find it difficult to find a job when they get out (Western 2006; Pager 2007).

Not every new worker is equally vulnerable. College-educated young workers have far better chances in comparison to lesser educated groups. In 2015, for example, recent college graduates faced an unemployment rate of 7.2 percent (and an underemployment rate of 14.9 percent, that is in part-time or temporary work plus unemployment), compared to an unemployment rate of 19.5 percent and an underemployment rate of 37 percent for those the same age without a college degree. But even here there is a paradox: Part of the increasingly high unemployment of the non-college educated is because college graduates are often employed in jobs that might be taken by less-educated workers. The phenomenon of college graduates working for car rental companies, as clerks in drug or retail stores, as waiters in restaurants, and other such jobs that do not require a college education is becoming increasingly common (Arum and Roksa 2014). Eventually, however, the vast majority of these recent college-educated workers will move into better jobs, but in the meantime, they are taking jobs away from less-educated young people while they wait for better opportunities to open up.

In short, it is simply taking much longer, a decade or more, for young workers to find their way into career employment. In the 1950s and 1960s, workers without college degrees could find long-term employment in factories or other jobs in their late teens or early 20s; by the late 1990s, it was taking the same group another decade, into their late 20s or early 30s, to find long-term employment (Bernhardt et al. 2001). Eventually, most workers do find their way into long-term stable employment, but it is taking longer and longer for that to happen, disrupting lives and families along the way.

Older Workers and Age Discrimination

12.5.3 Identify the three primary contributors to challenges facing older workers.

Most rich countries, including the United States, have pushed back the expected age of retirement, and assume workers will continue to be employed until they reach their mid- to late-60s. In the United States, the minimum

Robert Kneschke/Alamy Stock Photo

Many studies find that older workers are just as productive as their younger peers, yet often face discrimination in looking for jobs or in the workplace.

age at which workers will receive full Social Security benefits has risen to 67, with a significant bonus if you keep working until age 70. Yet as workers get older, many will face challenges in keeping their jobs and careers. Three main factors contribute to the problems faced by older workers: (1) Prejudice from employers, (2) physical limitations on their ability to do demanding physical labor for those in blue-collar jobs that require such effort, and (3) in some cases, competition from younger workers who will accept lower pay. Because many workers were not able to save enough for their retirement, the need to continue working into old age is essential for many. The plight of older workers is one that deserves careful attention in any discussion of problems of work and careers.

The problem of age discrimination, or **ageism**, as it is known, has much in common with other kinds of discrimination we explore in other chapters (for example, see Chapter 13 on racial discrimination and Chapter 14 on gender discrimination), but it receives far less attention (Applewhite 2016). Arising out of prejudice (the application of stereotypes about an entire group to individual members of that group), many older workers find it harder to keep their jobs or especially to find a new job if they are

unemployed. Older workers may be perceived by their coworkers as less able to work hard, less physically durable, or less mentally acute than younger people. Most research on these types of prejudices have shown them to be ungrounded—in particular, older workers often have experience and perspectives that may help to make up for any other limitations—but prejudices survive regardless of the facts (Nelson 2002).

In very physically demanding jobs—for example, in construction, agriculture, mining, and some kinds of manufacturing—older workers can reach a point where they are no longer able to perform the job, but still need to work in order to earn a living. For these workers, the problem becomes a potential mismatch between skills and available opportunities. Consider a construction worker who has been building houses and office buildings for 35 years, but by age 55 or 60 may be physically worn down from years of toil. The skills acquired working in construction may not easily translate into taking a less physically demanding office job, and retraining opportunities are often limited at this age. Further, this worker may face additional hurdles from prospective employers who may prefer to hire younger people for such a job.

The third main source of age-related employment issues arises most typically in careers or jobs that provide increased pay with seniority, especially where competition from younger workers may lead employers to prefer the latter. This is especially true for business executives and professionals, where pay can vary substantially over the course of a career and senior employees can command significantly higher salaries than less experienced workers. The risk of losing one's position—and the fear and anxiety that provokes—and not being able to regain it is a very painful experience. For older workers, losing a job can be much more damaging than for younger workers.

Conclusion: Work in the Twenty-First Century

The world of work is changing. For much of the second half of the twentieth century, most workers in rich countries like the United States enjoyed some measure of job security and opportunity within the firms they worked. But things began to change, as we have described in this chapter. Today, young people entering the labor market can an-

ticipate the possibility of having to change jobs every few years and the possibility of going through periods without work. Rising insecurity for individual workers and their families is likely to be one of the most pressing social issues in the near future. Precarious employment—and even working in the underground economy—have been growing sources of work for people squeezed out of the regular labor market. The decline of unions as organizations to promote and protect workers may be permanent, although that is not certain. The possibility of significant job displacement from the implementation of artificial intelligence, although not yet a reality, poses the threat of even more disruption.

It remains to be seen how the COVID-19 pandemic will change the work landscape in the next few years, as large numbers of individuals have been laid off or forced to work from home. Will the latter become more common? If so, it will be an ironic return to the work–family arrangements of previous centuries where work and family life took place under the same roof, such as in agrarian communities. For some people and families, working from home will offer new forms of flexibility, but it will strip the workplace of the social and cultural benefits of having different people work together in the same place and at the same time. A return to the past of this sort, if it happens on a large scale, will have positive and negative aspects, but it will unquestionably change the nature of working as most people have known it for the past 150 years.

Sociologists studying work and employment in the twenty-first century will continue to try to understand how individual workers' lives are impacted by the wide range of different social processes that are shaping the labor market. It's an interesting challenge for everyone to ponder, because almost all of us are, or will be in the future, in the labor force. And our work will shape the rest of our lives in many ways.

The Big Questions Revisited 12

12.1 What Is the Division of Labor in Modern Societies? In this section, we introduced the classical sociological idea of the division of labor and provided an overview of the kinds of jobs that can be found in the United States. We also traced how jobs in the U.S. have changed over time.

The Division of Labor and the Labor Market

The Historical Evolution of the Division of Labor

Learning Objective 12.1.1: Describe changes in the division of labor over time.

The Evolving Labor Market

Learning Objective 12.1.2: Discuss the kids of jobs people do today.

The Changing Character of Self-Employment

Learning Objective 12.1.3: Explain why self-employment is popular and how it is changing.

Jobs and Earnings

Learning Objective 12.1.4: Analyze how much different jobs pay.

Key Terms
artificial intelligence (p. 296)   division of labor (p. 299)   labor market (p. 300)   occupations (p. 300)   craftsman (p. 301)   Industrial Revolution (p. 301)   specialization (p. 301)   caring work (p. 301)   white-collar jobs (p. 301)   blue-collar jobs (p. 301)   post-industrial society (p. 302)   gig economy (p. 303)   day laborers (p. 303)   temp agencies (p. 303)   outsourcing (p. 304)   freelancing (p. 304)

12.2 What Is the Labor Process? In this section, we explored how work is organized in the United States by introducing the concept of the labor process and exploring how power is embedded in workplace relationships. We analyzed how employers maintain control over their employees, and how workers resist employer's efforts to control them.

The Social Organization of Work

The Labor Process: An Introduction

Learning Objective 12.2.1: Describe the main features of the labor process.

Sources of Power and Control in the Workplace: Workers versus Employers

Learning Objective 12.2.2: Describe contexts in which workers have power.

Key Terms
labor process (p. 307)   scientific management (p. 307)   Hawthorne studies (p. 307)   deskilling (p. 308)   automation (p. 308)   skill-biased technical change (p. 309)   telecommuting (p. 309)   collective bargaining agreements (p. 310)

12.3 What Is the Difference between Good Jobs, Regular Jobs, and Bad Jobs? Here, we examined what constitutes a rewarding job in America. We then explored precarious work, in which workers are entirely interchangeable and jobs are highly insecure. In recent years, the economies of rich countries like the United States have seen a significant increase in precarious jobs. We also discussed migrant and immigrant workers as well as the effects of unemployment.

Work in Contemporary America

Work Satisfaction

Learning Objective 12.3.1: Explain the key factors that contribute to job satisfaction in most workplaces.

Precarious Work

Learning Objective 12.3.2: Describe the features of precarious work, and explain why it has become more prevalent.

Working "Off the Books": The Underground Economy

Learning Objective 12.3.3: Describe the main features of work in the underground economy.

Migrant and Undocumented Workers

Learning Objective 12.3.4: Explain why migrant and immigrant workers are attractive to some U.S. employers.

When Jobs Disappear: The Impact of Long-Term Unemployment

Learning Objective 12.3.5: Describe the effects long-term unemployment can have on individuals, families, and communities.

Key Terms

autonomy (p. 313)   discretion (p. 313)   status (p. 313)   fringe benefits (p. 313)   prestige (p. 313)   informal work (p. 314)   precariat (p. 315)   precarious work (p. 315)   sweatshop manufacturing (p. 315)   underground economy (p. 316)   migrant workers (p. 316)   immigrant workers (p. 316)   undocumented immigrants (p. 317)

12.4 **What Are Professional Occupations, and Why Are They Distinct?** There is one set of occupations that has succeeded in establishing and maintaining a significant degree of control and protection for their members: The professions. We discussed how professional occupations became established, and why have they been able to resist change.

Professions: A Unique Occupational Niche

Professions Defined

Learning Objective 12.4.1: Describe what qualifies as a profession.

Professional Knowledge Jurisdictions

Learning Objective 12.4.2: Explain why it is important for professions to monopolize relevant knowledge.

An Example of Professionalization: The Rise of the Medical Profession

Learning Objective 12.4.3: Analyze how the rise of the medical profession exemplifies the professionalization process.

Key Terms

professions (p. 319)   professionalization (p. 319)   credentials (p. 319)   code of ethics (p. 319)   knowledge jurisdiction (p. 320)   semi-professions (p. 320)   homeopathy (p. 321)   public health (p. 322)

12.5 **What Are the Central Challenges Facing Workers in the Twenty-First Century?** As the nature of work and the labor market evolves, there are important issues and challenges that confront workers in the twenty-first century. In this section, we focused on issues in the United States such as long work hours, challenges to young workers (especially those without college degrees), and age discrimination.

Core Problems Facing Workers Today

Long Hours

Learning Objective 12.5.1: Compare and contrast Americans' working hours with workers in similar countries.

Young Workers Entering the Labor Force

Learning Objective 12.5.2: Explain why the transition from school to work has become more challenging for young workers.

Older Workers and Age Discrimination

Learning Objective 12.5.3: Identify the three primary contributors to challenges facing older workers.

Key Terms

vocational education (p. 326)   ageism (p. 327)

Chapter 13
Race and Ethnicity

by Ann Morning and Jeff Manza, with Ned Crowley

What exactly is race? Does biology play a role in it? What about culture? Is it something that people invented, or has it always been part of the human experience? The study of race and ethnicity has long been central to American sociology and has also featured prominently in other fields, such as anthropology, psychology, and biology. But in spite of this longstanding scholarly attention, we have yet to come up with widely agreed-upon definitions of *race* and *ethnicity*. Even experts struggle to precisely define what they mean when they invoke the concept of race.

The primary author of this chapter, Ann Morning, describes research she undertook as a graduate student on changing understandings of the meaning of race.

About 15 years ago, I traveled around the northeastern United States to interview anthropology and biology professors about how they understood the concept of race. What I found surprised me because it ran counter to what many of my graduate school professors had told me—that social and natural scientists today all agree that race is a human invention without any basis in biological characteristics. When I actually spoke with anthropologists and biologists, though, it immediately became clear that their views on race varied a great deal and hardly reflected the consensus that my graduate school advisors presumed.

One of the discoveries that intrigued me the most was the way they used me—*or more specifically, my physical appearance—to back up their views. In several instances, the professor I was interviewing would say something about* my *race in order to support his or her definition of the term in general. What struck me most, though, was that even with the same "data" at hand—namely, me and my physical features— these academics came up with wildly different interpretations of race.*

In one of my very first interviews, a cultural anthropologist at a large urban public university asked me how I identified myself in racial terms. It's a question I'm used to because with my African, European, Asian, and American Indian ancestry, people are often curious about my background. The anthropologist's reaction was to use me as evidence that race does not really have any biological underpinning. "You're a perfect walking example of why [race] doesn't work," he concluded. "I just wonder, looking at you," he went on, "how anybody could maintain that there are these hard and fast races. . . ."

A few weeks later, a biology professor at a state university explained to me how race might come up in

My Sociological Imagination

ANN MORNING

My sociological imagination developed from my experiences growing up with people from many different cultural backgrounds. I was raised in Harlem, the famous Black neighborhood in New York City. But even though my home community was very ethnically homogeneous at the time (it isn't anymore), I was exposed every day to people from all over the globe because I studied at the United Nations International School. The contrast between those two worlds really got me curious about how social environments shape our thinking. As a sociologist today, my research focuses precisely on how people from different social backgrounds think differently about some of the things that seem most natural or objective to us, like racial identities or scientific knowledge. My research connecting these areas was published in my first book, *The Nature of Race: How Scientists Think and Teach about Human Difference* (Morning 2011), and I am continuing my research on these topics.

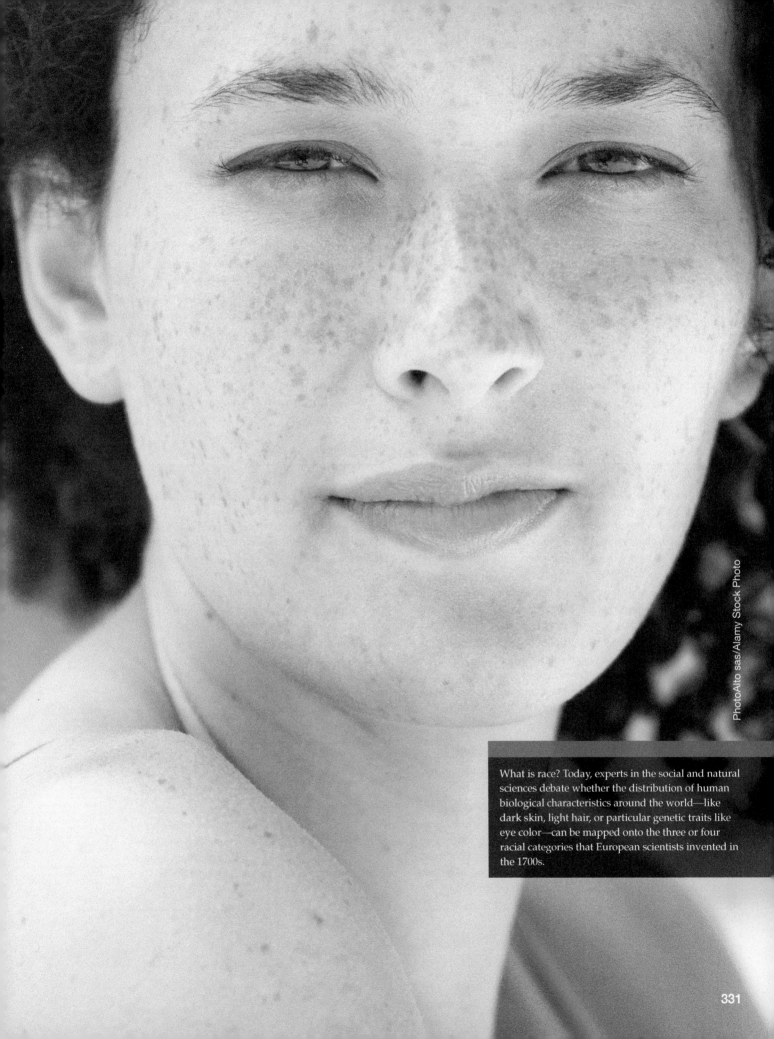

What is race? Today, experts in the social and natural sciences debate whether the distribution of human biological characteristics around the world—like dark skin, light hair, or particular genetic traits like eye color—can be mapped onto the three or four racial categories that European scientists invented in the 1700s.

PhotoAlto sas/Alamy Stock Photo

a lecture on genetics. Skin color, he suggested, "could be used as an example of quantitative genetics . . . the general thought is that, by and large, although there are some environmental influences, there are four sets of genes which determine skin color." Peering over his glasses at me, he mused, "I take a look at you, and you might have—don't be offended—you have, if there are four . . . that means there are eight genes, and I would say you have three or four Black genes and four or five White genes . . . just on skin color." In contrast to the cultural anthropologist who felt that my appearance disproved the existence of races, this biologist thought I was a textbook example of how race is rooted in DNA.

Finally, one rainy afternoon a physical anthropologist at an Ivy League university gave me a tour of his large laboratory, pointing out various human skeletons and the traits he argued reflected their racial heritage. Soon our talk turned to the uncertainty involved in determining race from skeletal remains. "Environments have changed enormously," the anthropologist

explained. "There's been more intermixing." Then he turned to me and said, "I mean, if you give me your skull and so forth, and I look at your nasal aperture, I'm not going to have a clue that you have any Black ancestry." But then he corrected himself: "Now I might, given your teeth, because they're large."

As these anecdotes drawn from Morning's research suggest, contemporary scientists' ideas about race—and what it has to do with biology, society, or anything else—span a wide spectrum. A cultural anthropologist who thought it was impossible to identify clear-cut races (and thus that they do not exist) disagrees sharply with the biologist who thought that race could easily be traced back to an individual's genetic profile. These encounters sum up a fundamental characteristic of today's scientific perspectives on human difference: Even thoughtful and highly trained specialists, working with the same data, have yet to reach a consensus on the basic question of what race is. So it is hardly surprising that everyone else struggles with these issues as well.

The Big Questions

1. **What is the difference between race and ethnicity?** More often than not, the words *race* and *ethnicity* get used interchangeably, as if they mean the same thing. And indeed they have more than a passing resemblance. But sociologists make clear distinctions between race and ethnicity and use the two terms to describe different kinds of categories and identities.

2. **Is race real?** If there's one thing academics agree on, it is that race is real. Where they part ways is on the question of whether race is anchored in deep-seated physical differences between individuals or is an invention not determined by human biology but nonetheless is "real" because it has an unmistakable impact on daily life.

3. **What is racism?** In classroom discussions of race and ethnicity, students often preface their comments with phrases like "I don't know if I should say this, but..." or "I'm not sure what the right term for this group is, but..." Concern about the "political correctness" of our ideas, speech, and behavior is a prominent feature of both public and private conversations on race today. Sociologists have thought a lot about prejudice and discrimination, providing ample food for thought on racism in the contemporary United States.

4. **Do race and ethnicity matter anymore?** Has America finally become a "color-blind" society, as so many have hoped and some have declared? Is it fair to say the United States has entered a "postracial" era, especially in view of the fact that the country twice elected a Black president (Barack Obama)? Sociological research suggests that while it may not be too soon to talk about a "postethnic" era, race is still closely linked to socioeconomic inequality.

5. **How are race and ethnicity changing in the twenty-first century?** Today, the face of America is very different from what it was 200 years ago. Immigrants come from a wider range of countries than ever before, people are more likely to marry partners from a different racial background, and changing attitudes have led more and more people to identify themselves as multiracial. These and other demographic changes will certainly have an impact on the nation's racial and ethnic makeup, on its patterns of socioeconomic inequality, and on its inhabitants' attitudes and beliefs about race and ethnicity.

R. Gino Santa Maria/Fotolia

What Is the Difference Between Race and Ethnicity?

UNDERSTANDING RACE AND ETHNICITY

Sociologists share fairly precise understandings of both race and ethnicity. Yet the sociological distinction between the two terms runs counter to everyday practice, where *race* and *ethnicity* are often used as synonyms for each other. People from all walks of life—journalists, teachers, doctors, advertisers, and politicians—routinely use the two terms interchangeably.

Why do we often tend to treat race and ethnicity as the same thing in everyday conversations? Sometimes the term *ethnicity* is seen as a polite replacement for *race*—a way to avoid using a term associated with racism and racial inequality. For example, the federal government's designation of the category "Hispanic" as an "ethnic group" on the Census was an attempt to do that, yet most Americans seem to view them as simply another racial group, akin to Blacks and Whites. The introduction of the ethnic term "African American" to refer to Black people, was a similar attempt.

But the bigger confusion between race and ethnicity is in part due to the fact that, at their core, the two concepts have a great deal in common. Both are systems for classifying human beings into groups based on shared ancestry. The crucial distinction between them lies in the different kinds of characteristics that are used to assign people to ethnic or racial groups.

Sociological Definitions of Race and Ethnicity

13.1.1 Compare and contrast contemporary sociologists' and Max Weber's definitions of race and ethnicity.

Max Weber (1864–1920), one of sociology's founding figures, was also one of the first sociologists to define ethnicity

and race. Weber described ethnic groups as "those human groups that entertain a subjective belief in their common descent," spelling out that "it does not matter whether or not an objective blood relationship exists" (Weber [1922] 1978, p. 389, 385). The most striking aspect of Weber's definition is that the key ingredient for ethnic membership is *belief* in shared descent. The subjective dimension of ethnicity became a central fixture of later sociologists' thinking.

Weber did not portray race as equally subjective, however. Instead, like most scholars of his era, he felt that races stemmed from "common inherited and inheritable traits that actually derive from common descent." This view of race is called **essentialism**; that is, it presumes an individual's identity depends on fundamental and innate characteristics that are deep-seated, inherited, and unchangeable. These traits are thought to be part of people's "essence," their very being. Whereas Weber observed that many different characteristics or experiences could serve to indicate who belonged to which ethnic group—including physical resemblance, historical memories, and common cultural practices—he believed that physical makeup alone determines an individual's race. In a nutshell, for Weber, ethnicity is based on people's cultural practices, and race is based on their biological traits.

Not all early sociologists held an essentialist view of race. Across many books and essays examining racial oppression in America, W. E. B. Du Bois (1868–1963) challenged the view that distinctive traits had a biological component common to all Blacks, and that those traits could be determined by examining how Blacks in America lived and worked. Du Bois argued that the racism so prevalent in American society in the late nineteenth and early twentieth centuries had made it nearly impossible for Blacks to obtain the same kinds of jobs or success in the way that Whites could aspire to. High unemployment among Blacks did not mean that they were lazy or lacked ambition, but rather that they lacked access to decent jobs. Heavy policing of Black neighborhoods meant more arrests, which seemed to confirm higher rates of criminality as opposed to what groups and what neighborhoods the police chose to persecute. In other words, the refusal of most White employers to hire Blacks or of the police to treat Whites and Blacks equally created the very "facts" used to affirm stereotypes that Whites commonly held.

While contemporary sociologists share Weber's view of ethnicity, most reject his definition of race in favor of the position Du Bois advocated. Sociologists today believe racial identification is as subjective a process as ethnic classification. The major difference between race and ethnicity lies in the ways in which racial group boundaries are drawn. In other words, we look for different clues or signs when we think about people's ethnicity as compared to their race.

Why exactly do contemporary sociologists reject Weber's description of race as based solely on inherited physical traits? The difference in viewpoints is subtle but meaningful. In a sense, today's sociologists have taken to heart Weber's message about the subjectivity of group definitions and have come to believe that even our perceptions of biological similarity are subjective. So our racial classifications are based not on some objective measure of physical resemblances (as Weber claimed) but rather on our beliefs and socially influenced perceptions of which kinds of people are biologically similar and which are different.

A useful illustration comes from the United States' **one-drop rule**, a custom that became enshrined in many state laws around the turn of the nineteenth century. According to this longstanding method of identifying a person's race, someone with one Black grandparent and three White grandparents is a Black person because their "drop of Black blood" means they somehow have more in common with Blacks than with Whites. This is the same reasoning that leads us to label former President Obama as Black even though his mother was White. Clearly, there is no natural biological rule that makes him more Black than White. Instead, there are social rules—cultural customs—that determine how we classify people by race and even how we "see" race.

In this chapter, we define **ethnicity** as a system for classifying people who are believed to share common descent based on perceived cultural similarities. We define **race** as a system for classifying people who are believed to share common descent based on perceived innate physical similarities. Framing the two concepts in this way makes clear how much they have in common, but it also highlights the fundamental difference between them. Following convention, we use color terms to describe Blacks and Whites, and ethnic-geographic terms for Asian American/Pacific Islanders (AAPI), Latinx Americans, and Native Americans. We will use the phrase "people of color" when referring to the entire non-White population.

Key Distinctions Between Race and Ethnicity

13.1.2 Discuss key distinctions between race and ethnicity.

Contemporary sociologists have written extensively on the similarities and differences between the concepts of race and ethnicity. One of the first things researchers identified is that in any given place, the notions of race and ethnicity may not be equally important for people (Cornell and Hartmann 2007). In the United States, race has historically mattered much more than ethnicity. For most of the nation's history, being White was a necessary requirement in order to enjoy the full benefits of citizenship. Not only did Whiteness protect one from enslavement in the antebellum period (1789–1860), but even after the Civil War, it opened access to the voting booth, better jobs, schools and hospitals, and more affluent neighborhoods. Until 1952, only White immigrants could become U.S. citizens, and it was not until 1967 that non-Whites were allowed to marry Whites in all 50 states.

Although ethnic groups of European descent such as Irish, Italian, and Jewish Americans have faced considerable discrimination, their exclusion was not written into U.S. law to the same extent as race-based barriers. Not surprisingly, then, racial differentials in key socioeconomic outcomes—like income, wealth, and educational attainment—are usually much wider today than comparable gaps between ethnic groups. In other words, being White rather than Black makes a bigger difference than being Swedish rather than Polish, or Jamaican rather than Haitian—and that has been true throughout most of the nation's history.

Another key difference is that racial categories tend to be imposed on individuals or groups by others, while ethnic labels are more likely to be chosen for themselves by the individuals or groups concerned. This contrast can be described as external versus internal classification. The concept of race gained much of its power and reach from Europeans' imperial encounters with Africans, Asians, indigenous Americans, and others, beginning in the fifteenth century. Prior to that, Western medieval societies were divided by religion (that is, Christians versus non-Christians), and going back even farther, the ancient Greeks distinguished between themselves and "barbaric" people. But a color-coded hierarchy of race as we understand it today did not yet exist in the Western imagination. Instead, it was not until European explorers, armies, clergy, and settlers sought to dominate people across the globe that the race idea formed. Europeans came to believe the differences they observed in appearance and behavior between themselves and others could be explained by intrinsic, racial characteristics. Equally importantly, they were persuaded that races fell along a hierarchy in which they occupied the top rung, so European domination and colonization of others was only natural. Beliefs about racial difference then grew out of a context of conquest, exploitation, and enslavement and were further cultivated to justify power inequalities.

A similar modern example can be seen in the creation of the "Hispanic" category to characterize people from many different countries in Central and South America. Although the U.S. government considers Latinx to be an ethnic and not a racial group, they have effectively been "racialized" into being considered by many to be a race comparable to Whites or Blacks. Yet the very notion of a Latinx race—or even a Latinx ethnicity—is a very recent one, stemming from the federal government's attempts in the 1960s and 1970s to develop a set of official racial classifications (Graham 2002). Before then, it was not obvious that people from Central America, like Mexicans and Guatemalans, had much to do with people from the Caribbean, like Cubans and Dominicans, let alone with people from South America, like Peruvians and Argentines. So, although they did not choose or invent the label for themselves, people with origins in any of these places now find themselves in a society in which, regardless of how they prefer to identify themselves, they are labeled by the government, other institutions, and other people as Latinx. Among people so labeled, the term Latino or Latina is increasingly converted to a non-gendered form "Latinx," and that is the term we will use in the rest of the chapter and in the entire book, as noted previously (see also the Note on Terminology for more information).

Distinguishing Racial and Ethnic Labels

13.1.3 Distinguish racial labels from ethnic ones.

So how can we tell just which groups are ethnic and which are racial? Any list or taxonomy depends entirely on time and place. In Ann Morning's research on censuses conducted around the world (Morning 2008), she discovered that the official racial and ethnic categories used by different countries to classify their populations vary widely. In Guatemala, ethnic groups on the census included "Garifuna" and "Ladino" people; in Bulgaria, the main categories were "Bulgarian," "Turkish," and "Gypsies." The New Zealand census classified people as "New Zealand European," "Maori," "Samoan," "Tongan," "Chinese," and "Indian" (among others), while Sri Lanka recognized ethnic groups like

"Sinhalese," "Sri Lanka Tamil," "Indian Tamil," "Sri Lanka Moor," "Burgher," "Malay," "Sri Lanka Chetty," and "Bharatha."

Despite immense local variation, in the U.S. and around the world, there is a rule of thumb we can use to distinguish racial labels from ethnic ones. Race is anchored in color terms—like "Black" and "White"—that denote vast, often continental groupings that include millions if not billions of people. "Black" might refer to most people from Africa or the Caribbean, and "White" to most of the natives of Europe, Australia, Canada, Japan, and Israel. Even if they are not frequently used today, color terms like "red," "yellow," and "brown" refer to similarly large-scale groups: Indigenous (or native) American, Asian (or AAPI), and Latinx people.

In contrast, ethnic groups tend to be much smaller in size and associated with local, national, or regional geography rather than with continents. It is not surprising, then, that different countries recognize startlingly different sets of ethnicities; they are concerned with groups that differentiate themselves within national borders.

Sometimes these ethnic groups are considered native to the area, like Hopi or Navajo people in the United States; other times they are recognized to be descended from immigrants, like Korean Americans, German Americans, and Cuban Americans. Yet often the historical distinction between native and migrant is murky. When the United States annexed large swaths of Mexican territory in the nineteenth century, many people went overnight from being residents of Mexico to becoming residents of the United States. Were these Mexican Americans then an immigrant or a native ethnic group?

Why are Native Americans, such as these Hopi Indians, regarded as a distinct ethnic group in the United States, even though their ancestors were native to the area? The question of why Native Americans are not simply "Americans" and later arriving groups are defined by an extended ethnic definition remains a puzzle.

Julien McRoberts Danita Delimont Photography/Newscom

BIG QUESTION 13.2 Is Race Real?

THE SOCIAL CONSTRUCTION OF RACE

Sociologists often describe race as a **social construct**, or a social phenomenon invented by human beings and shaped by the social forces present in the time and place of its creation. The idea of *invention* often leads people to assume that something socially constructed is not real. But since when are inventions not real? Thomas Edison invented the light bulb, but it is real. Steve Jobs and Apple invented the iPhone, and it is real. Similarly, the belief that human beings come in four or five colors or flavors called "races" is invented—but as long as people and governments act as if these ways of characterizing people are meaningful, they are real. Or, to put it differently, races are real—but they are not biological. They are real social groupings that have real effects on people's lives. The **constructivist** view of race used by sociologists today—that is, the argument that racial categories are social creations, not biological facts—can be contrasted with the essentialist view of race, which asserts that enduring differences between races are rooted in biological sources and do not change from one generation to the next.

Race and Society

13.2.1 Explain how changing American definitions of who counts as White supports the constructivist view of race.

To say that race is socially constructed means several things. First is the idea that race is a classification system that is invented, created by human beings, and therefore artificial rather than something natural or biological. Second is the perspective that it is *socially* created—not the work of a single individual but rather the product of

masses of people who form a society. In that sense, race is a lot like language: No single person invented English, or Spanish, or Korean, but languages are real social phenomena that millions of unnamed people have shaped. Third, the social foundation of race implies that as societies change, so do their ideas about race. Many sociologists, historians, and anthropologists have investigated just how societal factors—such as economic conditions and organization, shifts in cultural values, or political upheavals—-influence beliefs about race.

One puzzle that has fascinated researchers is how Americans' ideas about who is White have changed over time. Many people whom we consider to be White today would not have been classified as such more than a century ago. Americans of Irish, Italian, Jewish, and other European ancestries were routinely excluded from the White category. The historian Matthew Frye Jacobson (1998) argues that the massive wave of European immigration to the United States over the period of roughly 1880 to 1920 had a major impact on who was considered White. If Whiteness had seemed self-evident at the founding of the Republic, when the European-origin population was largely of English descent (though with German, Irish, Scottish, Dutch, and French members as well), its boundaries were much less clear when immigrants began arriving from places like Poland, Italy, Greece, Hungary, and Russia in the late nineteenth century. As a result, politicians, scientists, and everyday people started to view the newcomers as members of separate races, distinct from—and inferior to—"true" Whites, who were of northwestern European origin.

So why do we consider Polish Americans and Greek Americans today to be White? Or, in the memorable phrase of one anthropologist, "How did Jews become white folks?" (Sacks 1994). Paradoxically, because

The Feast of San Gennaro is annual Italian American festival held in New York City's Little Italy neighborhood since 1926. Festivals like this one allow groups to express their heritage to the larger community.

prejudice against these "non-White" Europeans became so great, Congress passed a law—the 1924 Immigration Act—that severely limited the numbers of people allowed to emigrate to the United States from Southern and Eastern Europe. The sharp downturn in European immigration that followed meant that over the following generations, fewer and fewer Americans of European descent were immigrants who spoke foreign languages and practiced unfamiliar customs, while more and more were native-born, English-speaking U.S. citizens who embraced American cultural forms, from music and dress to sports and food.

In other words, southern and eastern Europeans underwent cultural **assimilation**, a process by which immigrants come to be incorporated into their new society by taking on the cultural tastes and the practices of that society. Part of the process of becoming American for these immigrant groups was being quietly folded into the White population. For example, the first-generation Pole had a second-generation Polish American son, who might simply have a third-generation American daughter.

Changing American definitions of who counts as White lend powerful support to the constructivist view of race. If race were simply a matter of our physical makeup, the boundaries of the White category would not have shifted so dramatically over the last 200 years; people's bodily characteristics have not changed over that time. What changed instead were Americans' beliefs about who belonged to what race as they went about constructing and reconstructing race categories.

Race and Biology

13.2.2 Analyze the arguments against a biological determination of race.

The hardest thing for most people to accept about the constructivist perspective on race is that it seems to contradict what they see with their very own eyes. How can anybody claim that race is not a biological fact, when we can easily "see" race? Every day we come across people whom we can immediately identify in racial terms, for example, as White or Asian.

The simple answer is this: We can easily spot surface physical differences between people. But the ways in which we then assign people to racial groups is purely a matter of **socialization**—that is, of having been trained (consciously or not) to pick out particular bodily characteristics and then associate them with particular groups.

Consider a very simple example. Pretend you are in a laboratory with a researcher who puts three colored blocks in front of you—red, yellow, and blue—and asks you to divide them into two groups. You might decide that red and yellow go together, while blue remains its own category, or perhaps you might choose to group red and blue together, leaving yellow on its own. There is no obvious similarity here, no clear-cut grouping of which two colors go together. But if every time you make a choice, the researcher corrects you by putting the yellow and blue blocks together and leaving the red apart, you will learn very quickly that the colors yellow and blue fit together. From that point forward, you will easily be able to classify yellow and blue—but not red—as part of the same group, even when you're asked to sort toy cars or beach balls instead of blocks. Matching items to groups based on color will become an automatic reaction you don't even have to think about; after a while, it will seem natural that yellow and blue go together, but not red.

Race works the same way. We grow up learning to look for certain pieces of information about a person's body (notably skin color, hair color, hair texture, and eye color and shape), while disregarding other things, like height, weight, ear shape, and hand size, to come up with an idea of which race they belong to. And, today at least, we're usually right: The race we think the person belongs to is in fact the race with which he or she identifies. But that does not mean that our racial classification of others, and their racial identification of themselves, is based on some innate racial characteristics they possess and that we simply observe. Instead, it's more like a situation in which, instead of blocks, we have yellow-colored, blue-colored, and red-colored people, and we've all been trained to think of the yellow and blue people as being in a different racial category than the red ones. In other words, both the observers and the observed share exactly the same mental rules of who belongs to what race. But that does not mean there is anything natural or necessary about blues and yellows being matched together, or about reds being held apart. Human beings vary in their surface (and other) biological traits as we move around the world. And we are very good at spotting physical differences between the members of our species.

We can generally see physical differences between Norwegians and Italians, Italians and Nigerians, Nigerians and Ethiopians, Ethiopians and Indians, and Indians and Koreans. We can even sometimes see physical differences between siblings (and in some South American countries, a brother and a sister with different physical features can even be considered belonging to different race groups)! But in the United States and in most places around the world, we don't generally consider those differences to indicate that a brother and sister are members of different races. Similarly, we may or may not consider the physical differences we notice between different groups around the world to reflect racial differences. For example, we can see surface differences between Norwegians and Nigerians and Koreans, and indeed we usually consider them to be members of different races. In these examples, racial difference maps onto observable physical difference. But in other cases, like the comparisons of Norwegians to Italians, or Nigerians to Ethiopians, or Indians to Koreans, we see physical differences between them but still classify them as members of the same racial group. Despite their distinctive surface characteristics, in the United States today Norwegians and Italians are considered to be racially White, Nigerians and Ethiopians Black, and Indians and Koreans, Asian. It is not biology that dictates that Indians and Koreans are members of the same race while Ethiopians are not, but rather socially created and widespread rules for grouping people.

In the last few decades, some scientists have argued that even if surface physical features are not a reliable indicator of race, patterns in our **DNA** (the material that carries genetic information) reveal the existence of human racial groups. This assumption underpins criminal forensic experts' analysis of DNA evidence (extracted from crime scene specimens like blood or saliva) to try to guess a perpetrator's race. It is also behind the new pastime of genetic genealogy, where several companies such as Ancestry.com and 23andMe analyze, for a fee, anyone's DNA to estimate the racial and ethnic makeup of their family tree. The companies promise, depending on the test you select, to trace your family tree back at least five to seven generations, and in some cases as much as 150,000 years.

But just as in the case of sorting blue and red blocks, racial analysis of DNA starts with socially constructed rules for assigning individuals to racial groups, and depending on what criteria are used can produce widely varying results. Before categorizing a customer's DNA sample, (or a criminal suspect, as DNA has in recent years become a staple of criminal investigations), scientists have to decide which characteristics of the DNA will be indicative of which kind of racial ancestry. And to do that, they have to come up with a list of which race(s) they believe are out there, and then sample individuals from those assumed races to find out what kinds of genetic characteristics they typically have. In the United States, genetic genealogy firms generally try to identify European, African, or East Asian ancestry. In the United Kingdom, where much of this forensic technology was developed, the categories of interest are "Caucasians, Afro-Caribbeans, and Asians from the Indian subcontinent" (Evett et al. 1996, p. 398). In both cases, scientists divide humankind into racial categories that are familiar, given their society's histories. But this technology could be used with any kind of geography-based grouping—even a simple division of human beings into "red" and "blue" races. Once two or more categories have been created, and individuals have been selected to provide representative DNA for each of those categories, then it is simply a matter of working through a statistical algorithm for assessing how similar the particular customer's (or suspect's) gene variants are to those typically found within the "red" or "blue" sample. Crucially, the genetic genealogy companies' estimates can never be disproved or properly assessed: If you are informed that your ancestry is 30 percent African, 40 percent Asian, and 30 percent European, what independent and reliable data can you use to verify—or challenge–this statement? In fact, sociologists have begun to study how individuals make sense of surprising genetic ancestry test results, from White supremacists who are told they they have non-White ancestry (Panofsky and Donovan 2019) to others who are pleased to discover their family trees are more mixed than they ever expected (Roth and Ivemark 2018).

For many people, the constructivist view of race is hard to truly grasp because it flies in the face of what we think we see and know. Its basic premise is that even though we may *think* race is grounded in human biology, it isn't really—it just claims to be.

Race and Place

13.2.3 Discuss how race is understood differently around the world.

The strongest evidence for the sociological view that race is socially constructed comes from a comparative (or cross-national) perspective. Depending on location, the *race concept*—people's beliefs about race, including their notions of which groups are races and who belongs to which race—has emerged in different forms at different times, or perhaps not at all. Because Western scholars have focused less on societies outside Europe and North America, the study of race thinking elsewhere is still in its infancy. But the research that has been done in this area offers some fascinating insights on how race can be imagined differently across the globe.

Researchers sometimes ask how we can explain the noticeable variations in the way people around the world think about race. One study of West Africa found that local racial groupings like Black, White, and Red had little to do with individuals' surface physical appearances but instead were based on whether individuals were believed to have noble ancestry, which in this context meant Arab heritage (Hall 2011). Similarly, Brazilians do not link physical appearance to racial group the same way Americans do; in Brazil, dozens of racial labels exist to classify people based on very specific combinations of skin color, hair color, hair texture, facial features, and so forth. As a result, full siblings can be of different races in Brazil, a situation that is unthinkable by American standards (see the photograph below).

Scholars have noted that while contemporary Americans attribute racial differences to genes, people elsewhere (and at different times) have thought of racial difference as residing in the blood, or the mind, or the soul (Nelkin and Lindee 1995). What causes the race concept to take on such different forms? Researchers have concentrated on two types of explanations for such variations in race thinking. The first is that as the Western race concept spread across the globe in the wake of imperial conquest, it blended with local traditional beliefs and prejudices to create many new versions of race (Dikötter 2008). For example, South Koreans' ideas of race today reflect historical Korean and Japanese color preferences, Confucian beliefs about groups' proper places, a mixture of ideas brought by U.S. military personnel stationed there since the mid-twentieth century, and longstanding images of Korea as being a nation based on shared blood (Kim 2008).

The second approach for explaining local variants of race tends to focus on demographic, economic, and political factors. Why, for example, have Americans traditionally classified people with White and Black ancestry as Black, while Australians thought that mixture between Whites and Aboriginal people resulted in White, and not Native descendants? A key difference lies in the economic roles that European settlers expected Blacks and Aboriginal Australians to play. Because Black enslaved persons in the United States were a source of free labor, it was in White Americans' best interest to increase their numbers, and the one-drop rule of treating mixed-race people as Black was one way to add to the Black population. In contrast, for White Australians, Aboriginal people represented a source of free land, but to successfully occupy that land, they had to empty it of Aborigines. For the European settler community in Australia, then, it was preferable to erase the Aboriginal population by absorbing it into the White one—or by removing it and concentrating it on undesirable lands (Wolfe 2001). Again, there is nothing natural or inevitable about the way human beings have created racial categories; the conventions and classifications we come up with are reflections of the social, economic, and political worlds we live in.

In Brazil, race labels are meant to give more specific details about people's appearance in terms of facial traits, skin color, eye color, hair color, and hair texture. This focus on physical appearance means that a person's race depends on how they look as much as if not more so than on their ancestry. As a result, even full siblings can be considered to be of different races in Brazil. Members of this Brazilian family may not be regarded as all belonging to the same race.

HOMER Sykes/Alamy Stock Photo

Heather Coit/Associated Press

CONTEMPORARY RACISM

Americans use the word *racist* or *racism* to describe an astonishingly long list of things. In addition to labeling individual people as racist because of things they say or do, we also talk about ideas, speeches, sermons, movies, songs, books, policies, laws, and even political parties as being racist. Whether something or someone is racist is often the subject of heated debate. Are laws making unauthorized immigration into the United States a crime racist? Are sports mascots and team names representing American Indians racist (most of which have been changed in recent years)? Is it racist to oppose affirmative action policies? Such controversies stem in part from the lack of an explicit, widely shared notion of what racism is.

How Do Sociologists Define Racism and Discrimination?

13.3.1 Discuss the roles of prejudice, stereotyping, and discrimination in the sociological definition of racism.

For sociologists, the term **racism** has generally included two phenomena: *Prejudice* and *discrimination*. The influential historian Ibram X. Kendi (2019, p. 17–18) defines racism this way: "Racism is the marriage of racist policies and racist ideas that produces and normalizes racial inequalities." Kendi's definition usefully notes that government or corporate policies can play a significant role, creating legacies that perpetuate racist practices. An important element of racist ideas is **prejudice**, or negative beliefs, feelings, or attitudes held about entire groups. They are often broadly applied and based on subjective and often inaccurate information. Prejudices involve prejudgments of individuals based on **stereotypes**, which are simplified generalizations about a group. These blanket images are hard to change because, as psychologists have

shown, we tend to look for and remember information that seems to confirm our stereotypes while ignoring or dismissing information that does not support them.

Discrimination differs from prejudice in that it involves actions rather than beliefs. It includes any behavior that harms individuals or puts them at a disadvantage on the basis of their group membership. Discrimination maintains and reinforces social hierarchy by keeping subordinate groups from advancing. This can vary in degrees of severity. The mildest form of racial discrimination is the use of negative words or phrases in reference to a particular group. While names or phrases may be hurtful or even work toward perpetuating stereotypes, they usually do not impact people's life chances directly. A more extreme type of discrimination involves placing limits on people's opportunities based on their racial group. This involves preventing specific racial groups from equally accessing schools, employment, housing, and other institutions that are part of membership and participation in society. At its most extreme, discrimination can take the form of violence against an individual or members of a racial group. From the Civil War on, for many decades, **lynching** was an act of violence used primarily to intimidate, punish, and terrorize Blacks in the South. Many other societies, such as South Africa, Rwanda, and Bosnia, have also experienced violent forms of racially and ethnically charged discrimination, including **genocide**, which is the deliberate and systematic killing of a category of people.

Acts or patterns of racial or ethnic discrimination can be classified as individual or as institutional and structural. **Individual discrimination** is an action carried out by an individual or small group that harms one or more individuals based on their group membership. An employer refusing to hire Blacks, a landlord who does not rent apartments to Mexican Americans, or a group of teenagers who paint swastikas on a Jewish synagogue are all examples of individual-level discrimination. In these cases, individuals or small groups take purposeful actions to negatively affect members of specific racial or ethnic groups.

Discrimination may not always be intentional, however. Recent psychological research suggests that our behaviors are influenced by many kinds of **implicit (or "unconscious") prejudice**, involving stereotypes that can be activated in our minds without our being aware of them (Greenwald and Banaji 1995). Even people who consciously reject racial stereotypes may nonetheless be influenced by them. Psychologists have discovered this through various research studies, the most well-known of which is the Implicit Association Test, which you can take for yourself at http://projectimplicit.net. This test has repeatedly shown that when given a task to complete, people are generally slowed down if it involves recognizing nonstereotypical associations (such as matching the words "black" and "pleasant") and can usually speed up when required to make stereotypical matches (such as "white" and "pleasant"). Although negative implicit bias is widespread—nearly 85 percent of Whites taking the test are estimated to have some degree of unconscious racial prejudice—research suggests it can be reduced through introspection and positive exposure to the target group, in much the same way that thought exercises and habituation can help people control powerful emotions like fear and anger. In fact, implicit prejudice may be to emotion what explicit (or conscious) prejudice is to thought (Quillian 2006). Implicit bias seems to come into play when it is difficult for individuals to regulate themselves (for example, in split-second decisions or through their body language), whereas explicit prejudices may have a greater impact on deliberate or premeditated actions (like a speech). Recent tragedies where police officers have killed Black men, women, or children raise distressing questions about how important implicit prejudices may be.

People are not the only actors who may discriminate, however. Sociologists maintain that institutions can also be discriminatory. **Institutional (or structural) discrimination** occurs when the actions or policies of organizations or social institutions exclude, disadvantage, or harm members of particular groups. Jim Crow—a system of laws and social norms that governed interactions between Blacks and Whites in the American South in the early twentieth century—represented an institutionalized system of discrimination. Schools, housing, transportation, and public facilities all formally engaged in discriminatory practices by keeping Blacks and Whites separate and in grossly unequal facilities. South Africa's system of apartheid is another example of this institutional form of discrimination where Whites were able to secure their social position by excluding non-Whites from the majority of institutions.

As in the case of individual discrimination, institutional discrimination may or may not be intentional. An example of intentional institutional discrimination is the United States' 1790 naturalization law, which explicitly stipulated that only White immigrants could become citizens. An example of discrimination that may, or may not, have been intentionally racist is the federal government's sentencing guidelines, first adopted in the 1980s, that penalized individuals in possession of crack cocaine 100 times more heavily than those who possessed powder cocaine (even though they are essentially identical substances). Although the guidelines did not explicitly refer to race—and so did not appear to be intentionally discriminatory—the fact that powder cocaine was used disproportionately by Whites and crack by Blacks meant that the latter group was more likely than Whites to face the heavier penalties dictated by the sentencing guidelines. (Congress has recently reduced, but not eliminated entirely, the cocaine disparity.) As this example suggests, it is not always easy to determine whether institutional discrimination is intentional or not. Even though the guidelines did not overtly base criminal sentences on race, they may well have been adopted because they were likely to have a disproportionately harsh impact on Black offenders. Or they may have been adopted out of genuine (if incorrect) concerns that the crack form of cocaine was causing more harm (whether that was true or not does not mean that many lawmakers could have believed it to be true).

The difficulty of determining when an institution or organization has consciously intended to discriminate has led to an important, and controversial, precedent in the U.S. legal system that it is not always necessary to prove negative intentions in order to arrive at a finding of discrimination. Instead, statistical evidence of biased patterns, what is known legally as the "disparate impact" of an institution's or organization's policies—for example, that an employer's hiring or wage-setting procedures lead to worse outcomes for some groups than others—may suffice to demonstrate discrimination in the courtroom, regardless of whether intentionality can be ascertained. Most sociologists would agree that organizations are discriminatory if the ultimate impact of their actions is to exacerbate inequality, regardless of whether or not that was the original intention behind them.

The full reach of racial discrimination is best grasped by understanding it as a complex, multi-layered process. Sociologists have described the broad array of discriminatory practices as **systemic racism** (Bonilla-Silva 1996; Reskin 2012), where discrimination in one realm can reinforce or produce discrimination in another. In this sense, racial discrimination can be thought of as a *system* that will not disappear simply by addressing one arena in which it exists. For example, if federal and state governments made sustained efforts to ensure that Black and White people were treated identically by the police and criminal courts, so that the only difference was the amount of crime members of each group commit, we might pat ourselves on the back and think that finally we've overcome racism in the criminal justice system. But we've learned that because of employer discrimination and housing segregation Black people are more likely to suffer from poverty and to live in urban neighborhoods where job opportunities are lower. Crime is higher among all groups who are poor or lack opportunities for legal economic activity (Lofstrom and Raphael 2016). Even if police officers are reformed such that they treat Blacks and Whites the same, they will continue to patrol high-poverty neighborhoods with higher crime rates, which almost inevitably means that Black people will be arrested at higher rates simply because there are more police around to observe behavior that might be illegal. The problem doesn't stop there. A Black defendant may be more likely to be convicted for the same behavior as a White defendant, if White jurors are prejudiced and more likely to find the Black defendants guilty. These examples highlight how interconnected racial discrimination is and why it is so difficult to address it in one arena. For example, highly selective colleges can adopt affirmative action programs to try to diversify their student body and faculty, but there are so many other ways in which race impacts educational opportunity that such policies alone—however important they are within higher education—cannot fix the problem of racial inequality in education.

The concept of systemic racism also calls attention to issues of **intersectionality**, which we can define as the overlapping character of inequalities (Choo and Ferree 2010; Collins 1990; Crenshaw 1991). We are all more than just the racial and ethnic group we identify with, or are categorized as a member of by others. Inequalities based on class, income, education, religion, gender, sexuality, appearance, disability, even height or appearance are also important sources of inequality (and social identity). And these inequalities can reinforce each other in ways that magnify their impact. Consider a couple of examples. White men will benefit from their Whiteness and their gender, but if they are also well-educated and raised in an upper-class family that provides them with some wealth assets, the benefits of their Whiteness are magnified. On the other hand, a White man who is gay, has a physical disability, and is born into poverty in a declining rural town with relatively few job opportunities will receive fewer benefits from his race and gender. Conversely, a Black woman with a college degree will likely experience greater discrimination (on the basis of her gender) than her twin brother with the same degree (although the brother might be disadvantaged relative to her in encounters with the police). And a Black woman who is a practicing Muslim, is born into poverty, and has few opportunities to complete her education is likely to experience multiple forms of discrimination that magnify the cost of being Black in a society with high levels of prejudice or disadvantage associated with each of their characteristics. It is often difficult for researchers to disentangle which factor is most relevant, or how each factor interacts with others to produce unequal outcomes, but a fuller understanding of discrimination demands we develop tools to see racism in relation to other social hierarchies.

Why Does Racism Occur?

13.3.2 Explain how people can be socialized into racism.

Some of the earliest research on prejudice and discrimination was conducted by psychologists, who saw racism as an expression of particular personality disorders. Yet such psychological approaches to prejudice came to be criticized for overlooking the social contexts that give shape to the beliefs and behaviors that underlie racism. Moreover, because these early theories treated racism as if it were an abnormal and thus unusual condition, they did not square with the fact that historically, large numbers of Americans have held prejudices and acted in a discriminatory fashion. To put it another way, when large numbers of people in a particular time and place express similar views about a racial or ethnic group, it is hard to ascribe those views to individual personality disorders.

Accordingly, sociologists have sought to develop theories of racism that pay attention to the role of social rules and guides to behavior that vary across social contexts. These theories consider the type of situations where norms are in place that could encourage or give rise to prejudicial beliefs or discriminatory acts. Through socialization, people learn the norms that operate in an environment or society at large. Research has shown that even very young children absorb racial prejudices and act on them—for example, when choosing play partners (Van Ausdale and Feagin 2001). In addition, many studies find that even in integrated schools, middle and high school children voluntarily segregate along racial and/or ethnic lines (Lewis 2003; Kao et al. 2019). For that matter, one sociologist has shown that even blind people—who cannot see the visual cues like skin color that we rely on to identify a person's race—nonetheless learn from their sighted family and friends to make distinctions between members of different races (Obasogie 2014). Far from being "color-blind," they are often taught to look down on and avoid people of other races, even when it means refusing valuable assistance or rewarding friendships. In short, people learn from those around them to think and act in a racist fashion—they are socialized into racism.

The challenge remains, however, to explain why racism comes to permeate a given society in the first place. Sociologists have responded to this challenge by highlighting the connection between racism and power. Whether we think of the origins of racial thinking in contexts of imperialism and slavery or in more contemporary manifestations like the official racial segregation of schools until the 1950s (and widespread unofficial segregation since), it is evident that racist exclusions and handicaps both reflect and perpetuate imbalances in the amount of power that different groups hold. Race-based hierarchies do not occur by chance but rather are the product of human efforts to acquire and preserve social privileges. In other words, we can ascribe racism to groups' sustained efforts, conscious and unconscious, to shore up their own status in society.

Does Racism and Racial Discrimination Still Exist in the United States?

13.3.3 Analyze evidence that racial prejudice and discrimination still exist in the United States.

Researchers have used a wide variety of methods to gauge the extent of racial prejudice and discrimination in the post–civil rights era. Surveys today show relatively min-iscule levels of support in the United States for Jim Crow–era measures such as racial segregation in public facilities or transportation. Very few people today will tell a pollster or survey researcher that they believe Whites and Blacks should not be allowed to marry or should attend completely segregated schools. Such views, sometimes called "old-fashioned racism," hold much less popular support than they once did. Take a look at Figure 13.1 to see how White opinions on specific topics have changed over time. Whites have become more likely to support racial equality or racial integration (with the percentage of Whites favoring living in a neighborhood that is half Black changing the least).

The kinds of attitudes reflected in Figure 13.1 are not, however, a sure-fire indicator of declining prejudices. An optimistic interpretation of survey findings is that Whites have become less prejudiced toward Blacks over time. A more pessimistic interpretation, however, is that Whites

have simply become less likely to admit to racial prejudice, but their true sentiments have not changed much over time (Kinder and Sanders 1996). Evidence can be found for both propositions. On some questions, White Americans who may have abandoned the old-fashioned racism of a previous generation still harbor negative stereotypes about Blacks and other minorities. For example, when asked in 2018, "Do you think differences [in jobs, income, and hous-ing between Whites and Blacks] are because most African Americans just don't have the motivation or will power to pull themselves out of poverty?," 40 percent of White Americans surveyed agreed with the statement. The atti-tudes displayed in Figure 13.2 display questions that ask *why* racial inequality persists or whether the government should do anything about it. These questions show that Whites' attitudes have changed much less, in some cases not at all, or only very recently. Whether these shifts will continue is an open question.

Figure 13.1 Post-Civil Rights Era Attitudes on Racial Segregation and Integration

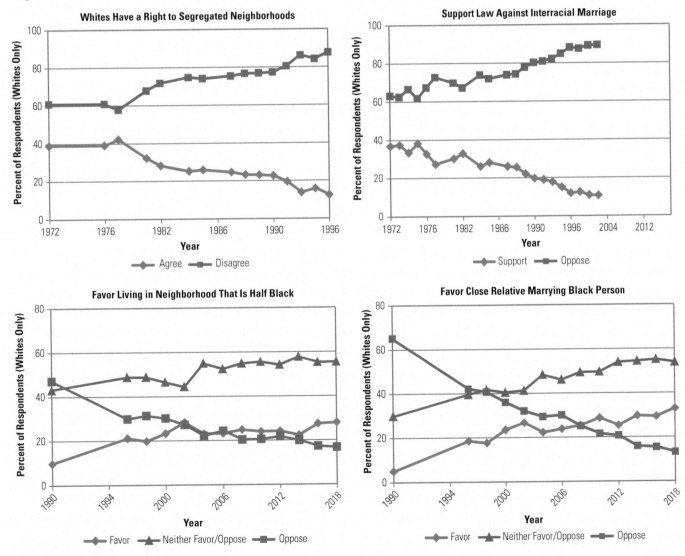

NOTE: Figures include White respondents only.
SOURCE: General Social Survey.

Figure 13.2 Post-Civil Rights Era Attitudes on the Causes of Racial Inequality

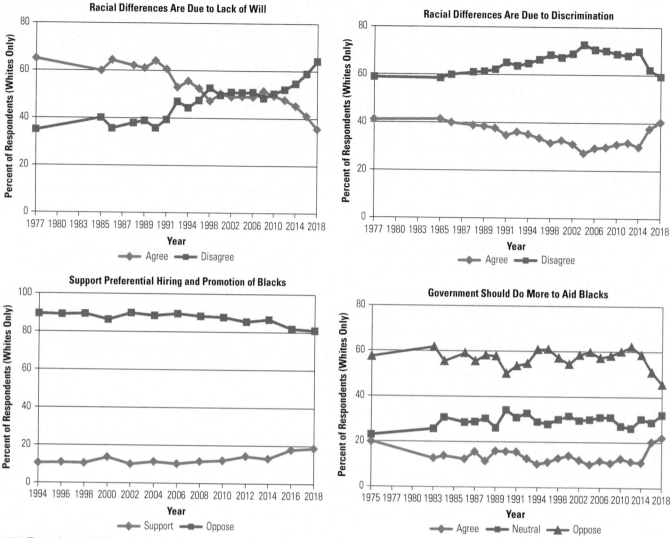

NOTE: Figures include White respondents only.
SOURCE: General Social Survey.

Survey research findings like these are valuable for studying changes over time in the racial attitudes of different groups. But they are also limited, in that they ask the same kinds of questions even as society changes. This is deliberate, as researchers can't do comparisons of attitudes over time if we change the wording of questions, but this also means that researchers are limited to the existing items if they want to study attitude change. Another way to explore how Americans think about race is to analyze everyday conversations, or how people talk about race. Through long, in-depth interviews, many studies have found ample evidence that Whites in particular often try to avoid openly discussing race and that they frequently use "color-blind" rhetoric that downplays the possibility of racism still playing a role in American life (Frankenberg 1993; Bonilla-Silva 2002). In his influential book *Racism Without Racists*, sociologist Eduardo Bonilla-Silva has argued that in modern-day America, White people mostly hold views that he describes as **color-blind racism**. By this, he means that most Whites believe themselves to be racially tolerant, to reject prejudice, and believe

everyone should be treated the same based on their merits. And they may respond in similar ways to researchers conducting a survey. But according to Bonilla-Silva, color-blind racism exists whenever people explain racial inequality by denying the role of race or minimizing its significance. Bonilla-Silva identifies a variety of widely held beliefs that are said to support such conclusions: That civil rights legislation in the 1960s or other government measures have fixed the basic problems of race in the past, that everyone now has an equal chance to succeed, and that the successes of once-disadvantaged European ethnic groups prove this. Individuals may also harbor doubts about whether certain groups are as hardworking or determined as others, although that is not required for color-blind racism. Or they may attribute persisting racial disadvantages to economic factors and conclude that the real problem lies in economic inequality, so that if we reduced class inequality, racial differences would decline.

A different but related set of ideas has recently become widely discussed with the publication of a best-selling book entitled *White Fragility* by diversity consultant Robin

DiAngelo. DiAngelo has run diversity workshops for 20 years at corporations and other large organizations, and in her book she draws on these experiences to offer an explanation for the staying power of White racism. In her experience, Whites are uncomfortable whenever they are asked to reflect on the role of racial advantage in shaping where they end up in life, and often angrily reject the very idea of White privilege. Even just discussing the problem of racism, DiAngelo claims, is perceived by many Whites as threatening to them. Their frequent reactions—of dismissing or refusing to engage with the reality of contemporary racial inequality—close off opportunities to address this fundamental schism in American society.

Why do racial attitudes so easily morph into new forms that can help reinforce prejudice and discrimination? The writer and art historian Teju Cole once tweeted, "If the books, websites, television and films you spend time on value White life above all others, you probably do too." Cole's thought-provoking tweet draws a link between mass media and racial prejudice; indeed, social scientists routinely point to mass media portrayals of racial groups as evidence of the persistence of racial prejudice. These portrayals are often based on stereotypes in which people of color are presented in roles defined by negative or demeaning characteristics. Studies of newspapers, television programming, and movies as well as the Internet use a research method called content analysis that looks for patterns in presence and meaning in order to study how racial groups appear in the media. For example, Gilens (1999) finds that the mass media overrepresent Blacks among welfare recipients. At the time of his study, Black people were 28 percent of welfare recipients but 60 percent of the individuals appearing in news media photos representing welfare recipients. Newer research has found that since the 1980s, media representation of racial groups has become somewhat more diverse and positive, with minority groups taking on more positive representations. But significant media biases still exist in many areas. For example, in coverage of crime, Blacks are still significantly overrepresented, reinforcing the idea that crime is a problem disproportionately caused by Black people (Entman and Rojecki 2001; Sun 2018). Another example comes from media coverage of the COVID-19 pandemic that has been linked to a rise in anti-Asian hate crimes (Gover et al. 2020).

So there is evidence that racially biased attitudes still exist, even as they have changed over-time. But does this mean that racial discrimination still exists? It is not easy to measure discrimination in an era in which blatantly biased behavior is widely frowned upon and, in many instances, legally prohibited. In fact, in some social settings, expression of racial prejudice has even become a form of deviance, or to put it more bluntly, "politically incorrect". So how can we really know if discrimination is still real? To get at it, sociologists have to study discrimination using indirect, unobtrusive, or anonymous measures. For example, employers are not likely to admit to interviewers that they

practice racial discrimination—and they may not even be aware of it. To adequately explore discrimination, social scientists often try to observe behavior through two principal strategies: Experiments and ethnographies.

One experimental study of discrimination that has garnered a lot of attention is the work of sociologist Devah Pager and her colleagues (Pager 2003, 2007; Pager et al. 2010). She tested the influence of a criminal record on the employment prospects of Black and White job applicants. Employing matched pairs of two Black and two White college students pretending to apply for entry-level jobs at 350 companies, Pager showed that the negative effects of a criminal record are 40 percent greater for Black job applicants than for White job applicants. Considering the disproportionate number of Black men who have been incarcerated, this bias disadvantages a large segment of the Black applicant pool. The study was also remarkable for showing that White applicants *with a criminal record* were more likely to be considered for a job than Black applicants without one. Pager (2007, p. 91) concluded, "Being Black in America today is just about the same as having a felony conviction in terms of one's chances of finding a job." In other work, Pager and Quillian (2005) showed that even employers whom the researchers knew were discriminating in their hiring practices, when asked in a seemingly anonymous survey, said that they treated all applicants and workers equally. (To see what this kind of research involves, there is a short documentary using an audit design to test for everyday racism, using hidden cameras to show what happens to matched White and Black testers, made by the ABC show *Primetime Live* in the early 1990s entitled "True Colors" which is readily available on YouTube. It presents striking examples of how Whites and Blacks are sometimes treated differently when shopping, buying a car, trying to rent an apartment, or applying for a job. "True Colors" remains highly relevant today, and is very much worth viewing.)

Another widely noted experiment involved creating fictitious résumés of both high and low quality and then randomly assigning some résumés either a stereotypically White name (like "Emily" or "Greg") or a stereotypically Black one (like "Lakisha" or "Jamal"). The researchers sent out these fake résumés in response to more than 1,300 sales, administrative support, clerical, and customer service job listings found in *The Boston Globe* or *Chicago Tribune* Sunday newspapers. Their results showed that when controlling for applicant quality and neighborhood, résumés with "White names" received 50 percent more follow-up phone calls than résumés with "Black names." Moreover, an increase in the quality of the applicant did not reduce this difference. In fact, the study showed that the disadvantage of a "Black name" increased as the quality of the résumé increased (Bertrand and Mullainathan 2004). Like the Pager study, this experiment makes a strong case that racial discrimination plays a significant role in employment in the United States today. Indeed, since the appearance of those landmark studies 15 years ago, there have been numerous studies using field experiments of this sort. A field experiment examining racial discrimination is one in which researchers use experiments in real-world settings (see Chapter 3 for more detail on field experiments). While some experiments find stronger evidence of prejudice and discrimination than others, most well-designed field experiments have found significant evidence of discrimination in most domains researchers have studied (Bertrand and Duflo 2017; Neumark 2018).

A different approach to investigating racial discrimination is to study it through close observation over an extended period of time, as NYU sociologist Deirdre Royster (2003) did in a study of 25 Black and 25 White working-class men going through the same job training program. Comparing the two groups, Royster debunked the idea that the job market is a meritocratic and fair arena where the most qualified candidates are the first to be hired. In contrast, Royster found that employment was determined by social networks that led to personal referrals and recommendations among the White blue-collar community. Not only were Black blue-collar workers disadvantaged by the absence of connections to owners, managers, or supervisors that were integral for White workers in finding employment, but the White blue-collar community erroneously perceived Blacks as having an advantage through affirmative action policies and practices. This myth of "reverse racism" meant that White workers were often unwilling to make recommendations or referrals for Black workers. Although the advent of affirmative action policies has been used to claim reverse discrimination, sociological research maintains that discrimination against racial minorities, specifically Black applicants, remains a significant explanation for racial stratification in employment.

In the next section of the chapter, we will examine in more detail some of the ways in which racial and ethnic divisions still matter in the twenty-first century.

JIM West/Alamy Stock Photo

BIG QUESTION 13.4 Do Race and Ethnicity Matter Anymore?

THE IMPACT OF RACE AND ETHNICITY TODAY

Given the widespread prejudice and discrimination that social scientists continue to document today, how much of an impact does it have? The passage of the Civil Rights Act of 1964 and the Voting Rights Act of 1965—landmark pieces of legislation that legally prohibited discrimination—are often thought of as the culmination of the civil rights movement, marking the end of the long and arduous struggle to secure the civil and political rights of people of color (and women). Many Americans, as the concept of color-blind racism suggests, point to the passage of these laws as the moment when race and ethnicity began to shrink to insignificance in the United States. But the massive protests against police brutality in encounters with Black men that occurred in 2020 have reminded us that, unfortunately, prejudice and discrimination are not a thing of the past.

So how, exactly, does race and ethnicity continue to be a barrier to success in the twenty-first century? Sociologists have taken this question seriously. In addition to developing experimental, survey, and ethnographic studies of contemporary racism, researchers have long studied difference in outcomes between racial and ethnic groups. According to almost any measure they have explored, a clear racial hierarchy emerges, with Whites (and sometimes Asian Americans/Pacific Islanders [AAPI]) on top, and Latinxs, Blacks, and Native Americans on the bottom. To see how much race and ethnicity matter in the contemporary United States, we need a statistical snapshot of how different groups live today. The evidence we provide here is limited to a few important domains, but enough to highlight some of the most critical examples.

Figure 13.3 Median Household Income by Race, 1967–2019

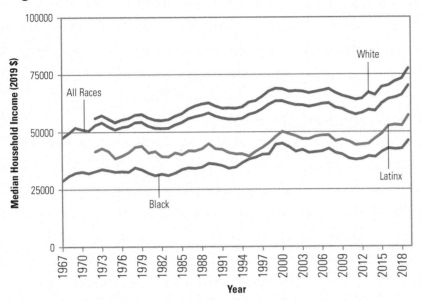

SOURCE: Current Population Survey, Annual Social and Economic Supplement: Historical Household Income Tables. Author's tabulations

Disparities in Income, Wealth, Employment, and Poverty

13.4.1 Discuss racial disparities in income, wealth, employment, and poverty.

When examining a broad range of economic outcomes, it is important to start with one key point: As the era of Jim Crow ended in the South and equal employment opportunity laws were put into place, racial and ethnic minorities made important gains. Yet despite those gains, sociologists and economists have documented persistent gaps in family income between White and non-White households for the last 50 years (see Figure 13.3). In fact, the income gap between Whites and Blacks and Latinxs has barely changed, although all three groups have seen increases. Asian Americans have been the highest earning group in recent years for which data is available.

It is true, however, that since the 1960s, a stable base of middle-class Black and Latinx families has emerged. As rates of college completion grow among these groups (see the next section), the racial gap in income shrinks, although it does not entirely disappear (Conley 1999; Emmons & Rickets 2016). Even within the college-educated middle class, there is still a broad disparity between Whites and Black and Latinx families. For example, Black graduates of the most prestigious universities in America gain less than White graduates of the same university. One study found that the value of a Harvard or Stanford degree for a Black person is equivalent to a degree from the University of California at Riverside or the University of North Carolina–Greensboro for a White graduate (Gaddis 2015).

Although a substantial income gap remains among Whites, Blacks, and Latinxs, it is important to note that Whites are not at the top of the income hierarchy in the United States. Asian Americans/ Pacific Islanders have the highest median household income among the major racial and ethnic groups in the United States. AAPI have also seen the sharpest income gains of any group. However, we should be cautious with our interpretation of these data. Because these data are not separated by country of origin or specific Asian ethnicity, they hide the fact that Asian families tend to fall at both ends of the income spectrum. For example, some Asians who trace their origins to places such as Bangladesh, Hmong and Nepal are at the bottom of the income hierarchy, while other AAPI groups, such as Indian, Filipino, and Japanese Americans, are at the top of the racial income hierarchy (López, Ruiz, & Patten 2017).

Household income figures can be slightly misleading because they do not take into account the number of people in a household whose income contributes to the total, and there are more multigenerational Asian families than any other group. Further, AAPI families also have tended to cluster geographically on the two coasts, where both average incomes and the cost of living are higher. In fact, when one compares Whites and AAPI who live in the same place, work in the same field, and have a similar level of education, Whites earn more (Kim and Sakamoto 2010). In short, we need to be cautious when interpreting summary statistics like median household income, because such statistics might actually conceal important details about why one group's average income appears to be higher than another's.

In addition to looking at income differences by group, we also need to examine poverty rates. Black and Latinx families are more likely than White families to fall below the poverty line. In 2019, at the point at which poverty rates were the lowest they have ever been (the result of nearly a decade of sustained economic growth), about 18 percent of all Black and Latinx families were living in poverty, compared to just 7 percent of White families. (Poverty rates rose for all groups following the onset of the COVID-19 pandemic.) For most of the period since 1959, the gap in poverty rates by race were even higher, at about 3:1 (in which the Black and Latinx poverty rate has fluctuated between 25 and 30 percent of all families, while the White poverty rate generally has been below 10 percent; see Creamer 2020). Since the election of President Barack Obama in 2008, the gap has declined to about 2:1, the lowest it has ever been (see Figure 13.4). AAPI families have poverty rates similar to Whites.

Sociologists have also focused attention on a much larger racial gap between racial and ethnic groups: Household wealth. **Wealth** refers to the sum of all owned

Figure 13.4 Family Poverty Rate by Race and Ethnicity, 1959–2019

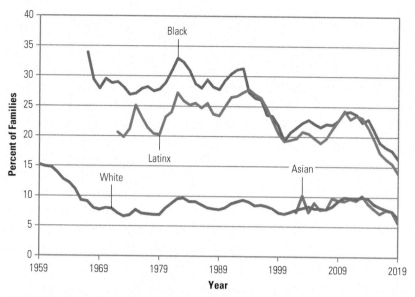

SOURCE: U.S. Census Bureau. Historical Income & Poverty Tables; Table 4. Poverty Status of Families by Type of Family, Presence of Related Children, Race, and Hispanic Origin: 1959 to 2019.

assets (such as a house, if owned; savings and checking accounts; and financial assets such as stocks and retirement accounts) minus the sum of all debts (such as mortgages, auto loans, and credit card debt). Despite changing demographic trends, the racial/ethnic gap in wealth remains a persistent feature of socioeconomic inequality in the United States, reflecting generations of discrimination and disadvantage faced by non-White families.

We show the persisting wealth gap in Figure 13.5. This highlights an area in which progress toward equality has been very limited, and one that is central to current patterns of racial inequality. If we compare White families and Black

families with the same *income*, the White family has (on average) seven times more wealth assets than the Black family (Conley 1999). How can this be? The accumulation of wealth, much more than current income, depends heavily on intergenerational transfers between parents and children (such as gifts, informal loans, and inheritances). In this way, it is rooted in historical patterns, especially in relation to home ownership (the most important type of wealth accumulation). Because Black families have experienced multiple generations of exclusion from home ownership or the ability to purchase homes in neighborhoods where home values rise the fastest, they have been unable to build up a base of assets to pass on from generation to generation (Massey and Denton 1993; Oliver and Shapiro 1997; Brown et al. 2003). Black families that are able to purchase a home are more likely than any other racial group to live in a segregated neighborhood, which diminishes property values and home equity, and they are more likely to receive unfavorable terms on their home mortgage than are comparable Whites (Brown et al. 2003, p. 14). One study finds that a comparable home in a White versus a Black neighborhood will be worth on average 23 percent, or about $48,000 more (Perry et al. 2018). As a result, the net worth of Black families persistently lags behind the net worth of White families. The situation is similar for Latinx families.

Finally, if we turn to trends in employment, we find some areas of progress because of increased opportunities since the passage of the Civil Rights Act of 1964 (which legally prohibited discrimination in the labor market). People of color have been able to move into middle- and upper-middle-class occupations from which they were previously excluded (Landry and Marsh 2011; Claytor 2020). However, many of these middle-class occupations are concentrated in the government sector, such as primary and secondary education, social work, and public administration, which tend not to pay as well as comparable jobs in the private sector. This concentration in the public sector is largely because antidiscrimination laws were more easily enforced in public bureaucracies than in the private sector (Brown et al. 2003). A smaller proportion of Blacks were able to move into upper-middle-class occupations such as law, medicine, and executive and managerial positions. Despite

Figure 13.5 Racial Wealth Gap in the United States

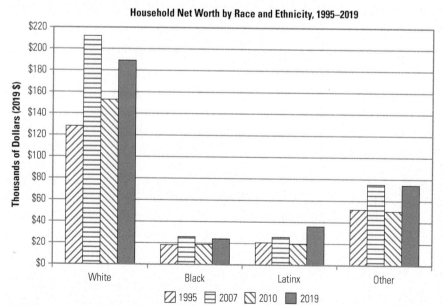

SOURCE: Survey of Consumer Finance.

these gains, Blacks remain underrepresented in professional and managerial positions and overrepresented in the lower-wage service sector. Moreover, they still earn only about 85 percent of the income of Whites in similar professions (Landry and Marsh 2011, p. 385).

Despite the upward mobility experienced by some Blacks since the civil rights era, overall they continue to lag far behind Whites in one key dimension of inequality: Unemployment rates. In 2020, before the onset of COVID-19 and the economic downturn it created, the unemployment rate for Blacks was 6.3 percent, twice the rate for Whites (3 percent; Latinx workers had a 4.8 percent unemployment rate and Asian Americans just 2.8 percent) (U.S. Bureau of Labor Statistics 2020). In early 2021, as the full impact of COVID-19 on the economy was felt, all groups had significantly higher unemployment rates, but once again the White unemployment rate was close to half the rate for Blacks (6 percent and 10 percent, respectively); Latinxs were again in the middle (at 9 percent). This pattern of much higher unemployment rates for Blacks and Latinxs is true no matter what year or economic period we check. The Black–White unemployment gap has been a durable feature of racial inequality since the 1960s. In fact, the unemployment rate for Blacks has been consistently roughly double that of Whites in the 50 years since the civil rights movement (DeSilver 2013). It is, as one economist has put it, "built into the labor market" no matter what the overall societal level of unemployment is (Ajilore 2020).

Disparities in Education

13.4.2 Describe patterns of educational attainment for minority groups over the last 30 years.

As Figure 13.6 shows, Black Americans have experienced substantial gains in educational attainment over the last three

decades. Between 1980 and 2020, Blacks' rates of high school completion have risen by over one-third and rates of college completion have more than doubled, while high school dropout rates have shrunk by nearly half. Similarly, Latinx students have experienced patterns of improved educational attainment since 1980. Between 1980 and 2020, rates of high school completion have risen substantially for Latinxs, rates of college completion have doubled, and high school dropout rates in 2020 are half of what they were in 1980.

However, many of the educational gains made by Blacks and Latinxs during this period were paralleled by gains among Whites and AAPI. So, although Blacks and Latinxs have made a great deal of progress over the last three decades, the gap between Whites and AAPI on one hand, and Blacks and especially Latinxs on the other, remains very high. AAPI have the highest rates of educational attainment of any racial group in the country, and rates of college completion are nearly triple those of Blacks and quadruple those of Latinxs.

Why has the education gap persisted, or, to put it another way, why haven't Black and Latinx children achieved at rates closer to that of Whites and AAPI? One key is that education is linked to family resources, and, as noted in the previous section, White and AAPI households generally have higher incomes and more wealth than Latinx and Black ones. Strikingly, Black and Latinx families where parents have college educations produce children who achieve in schools at levels similar to their White and AAPI peers (Espenshade and Radford 2009). Another important point that has been emphasized by many researchers is that because of segregated patterns of housing, Black and Latinx children tend to be concentrated in urban areas where the quality of schools is below that of the middle-class or affluent suburbs where many White children go to school (Pattillo-McCoy 1999; Quillian 2014). It is not just the quality of schools that may hold children

---

Figure 13.6 Gains in Educational Attainment

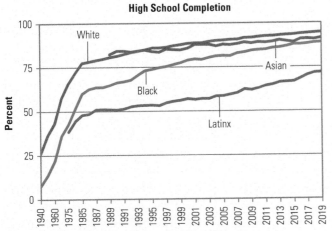

SOURCE: National Center for Education Statistics, 2019.

back; people of color are also more likely to be living in neighborhoods where rates of violence are high, creating stresses and anxieties that children in more affluent neighborhoods do not experience (Sharkey 2013). In spite of these disadvantages, however, the gap between Black and White students has narrowed in recent years. The larger trend, which we discuss in more detail in Chapter 18, is that the class gap in educational attainment is increasing, even as the racial gap is declining (Reardon 2011).

Residential Segregation

13.4.3 Describe persistent patterns of residential segregation in the United States.

Despite the fact that the Civil Rights Act of 1968 outlawed discrimination in housing markets, Blacks continue to be the most residentially segregated group in the United States (Massey and Denton 1993; Sharkey 2008). In addition to being spatially isolated, Black families are also more likely to live in low-income neighborhoods over successive generations than any other racial group. More than half of all Black families live in the poorest neighborhoods in the United States and have done so over multiple generations since the 1970s (Sharkey 2008, p. 933). Black children who grew up in poor neighborhoods in the 1970s were more likely than any other group of children to remain in those poor neighborhoods as adults. Even children in middle-class Black families are far more likely to live in close proximity to a poor neighborhood than middle-class White children (Pattillo-McCoy 1999). Sociologists have extensively documented the consequences of residential segregation. Beyond limiting the ability of Black families to accumulate wealth via home ownership (as we noted), there is considerable evidence that growing up in poor, racially segregated neighborhoods—or **ghettos**—severely truncates children's life chances. Residents of ghetto neighborhoods are much more likely to attend low-quality schools and be exposed to crime and violence, and are less likely to have access to economic opportunities and employment networks (Sharkey 2008; Quillian 2014). Sociologists have also shown that residents of segregated urban neighborhoods have less political influence than residents of more racially diverse suburban neighborhoods (Trounstine 2018). They also have been subjected to much higher rates of scrutiny by the police, leading to situations in which people of color are arrested at much higher rates than they otherwise would (Soss and Weaver 2017). Perhaps above all else, racial segregation in housing means that Americans of different racial backgrounds are less likely to have significant contact with each other, reducing the likelihood of minimizing racial stereotypes about members of other groups.).

Disparities in the Criminal Justice System

13.4.4 Identify sociological explanations for high rates of incarceration of people of color, especially men.

The large disparities in the treatment of people of color in the criminal justice system have become the subject of a mass social movement—Black Lives Matter (BLM)—in recent years. The initial spur for the creation of BLM was the excessive use of force by the police against people of color, and the greatest outrages were the killing of unarmed people, although racial inequalities in the criminal justice system are much more extensive than just police brutality. In an era in which citizens carry cellphones with cameras, and most police are supposed to carry cameras on their uniforms, video evidence of police violence is increasingly available, shedding light on distressing actions previously hidden from view (and often covered up in police reports). Police killings in Ferguson, Missouri; Chicago, Illinois; Brooklyn, New York; Baltimore, Maryland; and Louisville, Kentucky, triggered local and some national protests, but it was the video footage of the May 2020 killing of George Floyd in Minneapolis that provoked universal outrage and led to nationwide and even international protests that continued for months. Unfortunately, these tragic deaths are far from random accidents. In recent years, news organizations and public interest groups have begun the process of gathering information about every police killing, and the results have been shocking. Overall, about 900 to 1000 people are killed by police officers each year in the United States (compared to five or fewer in most European countries), about one every 10 hours (Karabel 2017). Some people argue that the police are constantly under threat, but the data do not support this claim. For example, in 2019, police killed 1,004 people, while only 48 police officers were killed in the line of duty (Federal Bureau of Investigation 2020). The police are virtually never prosecuted for unnecessary killings, even though in a typical year and in at least 20 percent of the cases the victims are unarmed and a majority do not have a gun but may wield some other weapon. Between 2005 and 2015, only 54 officers faced any criminal charges, as prosecutors rarely charge officers (a case usually has to be extreme), and even then, only about a third of those cases result in a conviction (Kindy and Kelly 2015).

We also see enormous racial disparities in terms of rates of arrest, conviction, and imprisonment. The phenomenon known **mass incarceration** (the very high levels of imprisonment found among certain groups) has been the subject of much public discussion and debate in recent years. America sends more people to prison than any other similar country in the world. On any given day in America, more than 2 million adults are serving time behind bars, accounting for a quarter of all prison and jail inmates worldwide (Liptak

Figure 13.7 Police Shooting Deaths From 2015 to 2020, Total Deaths and Rate Per Million Population

Although twice as many Whites than Blacks were killed by police in this time-frame, Blacks were killed at more than 2.4 times the rate of Whites (13 per million for Whites versus 32 per million for Blacks), and Latinxs at almost double the rate (24 per million versus 13 per million for Whites).

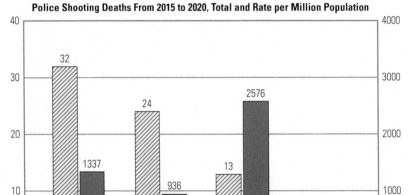

Police Shooting Deaths From 2015 to 2020, Total and Rate per Million Population

SOURCE: *The Washington Post* Police Shootings Database (https://github.com/washingtonpost/data-police-shootings).

2008). However, as shown in Figure 13.8, incarceration is not evenly distributed across the population. As of 2020, Black men account for 34 percent of the (male) prison population, while accounting for only about 12 percent of all men; Latinx men were 17 percent of the male population and 21 percent of inmates. (Black men were nearly five times more likely to be incarcerated than White men and more than twice as likely as Latinx men.)

Figure 13.8 Incarceration Rates per 100,000 People by Race and Gender in 2018

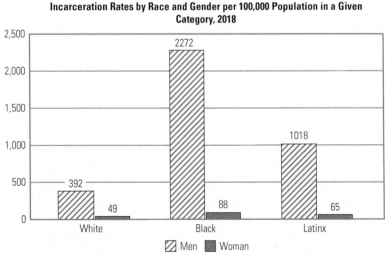

Incarceration Rates by Race and Gender per 100,000 Population in a Given Category, 2018

SOURCE: Bureau of Justice Statistics.

Young Black men without a college degree are especially likely to be incarcerated. Among Black men who finish high school but do not attend college, nearly one in three will serve time in prison. Of those who drop out of high school, 60 percent will be incarcerated at some point in their lives (Western 2006). For this group, incarceration has become a common life event, more likely than college attendance or military service. Sociologists estimate that a third of adult Black men have a felony conviction on their record. When misdemeanor convictions and arrests are taken into account, about half of all Black men have a criminal record (Shannon et al. 2017).

Why are rates of criminal conviction so high among Blacks? Some—but by no means all—of the disparity is due to the fact that Black Americans commit more crimes on average than Whites or Latinx people, although that depends on how we construe "crimes" (Sampson and Lauritsen 1997). Once we control for education and income, rates of criminal activity are similar for different racial groups (with Latinxs having a slightly lower rate than Whites). But crimes committed by all groups have fallen dramatically since the early 1970s, while the rate of imprisonment and criminal conviction has increased (Western 2006). In other words, even though fewer crimes are being committed, Blacks are far more likely to be sent to prison today than in 1970. One important reason for this has been the so-called war on drugs (introduced in Chapter 7), in which, despite the fact that there are few significant racial differences in drug consumption, Blacks are far more likely than Whites to be sent to prison for drug use (Alexander 2010; Tonry 2012). We explore issues relating to racial differences in crime and punishment much more extensively in Chapter 20.

Disparities in Health and Health Care Coverage

13.4.5 Explain racial and ethnic disparities in indicators related to health.

Racial inequality is not just reflected in socioeconomic indicators such as income, wealth, and education; there are also large disparities in a variety of other indicators of basic well-being, particularly those related to health. Figure 13.9 highlights some of the differences in health-related indicators for various groups.

Figure 13.9 Health Indicators by Race and Ethnicity

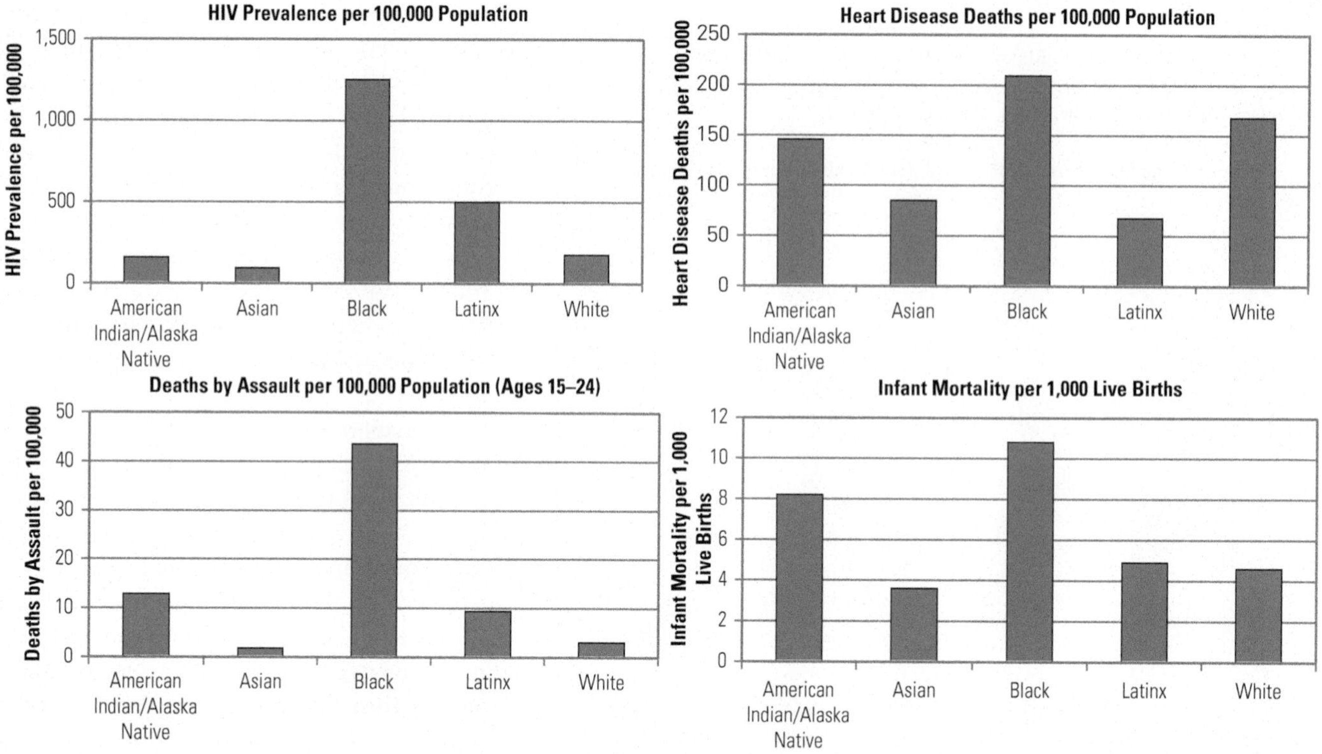

NOTE: In this figure, "AIAN" stands for American Indian/Alaska Native. Heart disease mortality rates are age adjusted for all groups except Latinxs. Assault mortality rates are for people aged 15 to 24.

SOURCE: Centers for Disease Control and Prevention National Center for Health Statistics WONDER Database.

Why is there such a big gap in health well-being? Some of these disparities in health are related to differences in health care coverage. Blacks and Latinxs lack health insurance or access to a regular source of health care to much greater extent than Whites. As a result, Blacks and Latinxs are far more likely than Whites to rely on emergency clinics as their usual source of health care. Even when Blacks and Whites go to the same hospitals for the same treatment, a recent study finds evidence that many hospitals segregate them into treatment by different quality "care teams," with Whites getting better care in hospitals where racial segregation is higher (Hollingsworth et al. 2021).

There are also important group differences that arise from basic living conditions and situations, which can be magnified by residential segregation. For example, the combination of lower household incomes and housing segregation has meant that it is far more likely that Blacks and Latinxs live in higher poverty, and higher crime neighborhoods (Sharkey 2013). The resulting stresses from such factors accumulate over a lifetime, and can be very damaging to an individual's health and well-being. People of color are also more likely to be exposed to environmentally harmful conditions (see Chapter 6 for more details about environmental inequalities by race and ethnicity).

The coming of the COVID-19 pandemic has highlighted just how large the disparities in health care coverage between Whites and people of color are. Prior to the arrival of vaccines, Blacks were more than twice as likely to die of COVID-19 than Whites, while Latinx people had 50 percent higher death rates (see Figure 13.10). These tragic and excessive deaths have occurred even though research has found *higher levels* of mask wearing among Black and Latinx people than among Whites (Sanchez and Vargas 2020). Several factors are probably at work here. Black and Latinx workers are far more likely to work in "essential industries" in which workers are often more exposed to the virus; as noted, higher rates of poverty are found among Black and Latinx people, leading to both reduced access to high-quality health care and greater numbers of untreated chronic health problems, which makes dying from COVID-19 more likely once the virus is contracted; and, again, a greater number of these individuals live in urban residences and crowded housing where the virus has more opportunity to spread (Scientific American 2020). As we've noted throughout the book, COVID-19 reveals patterns that might otherwise have been less visible. These very large differences in mortality during the panedmic remind us how health and well-being are so unequal across racial and ethnic groups.

Figure 13.10 COVID-19 Deaths per 100,000 People by Race and Ethnicity (as of October 2020)

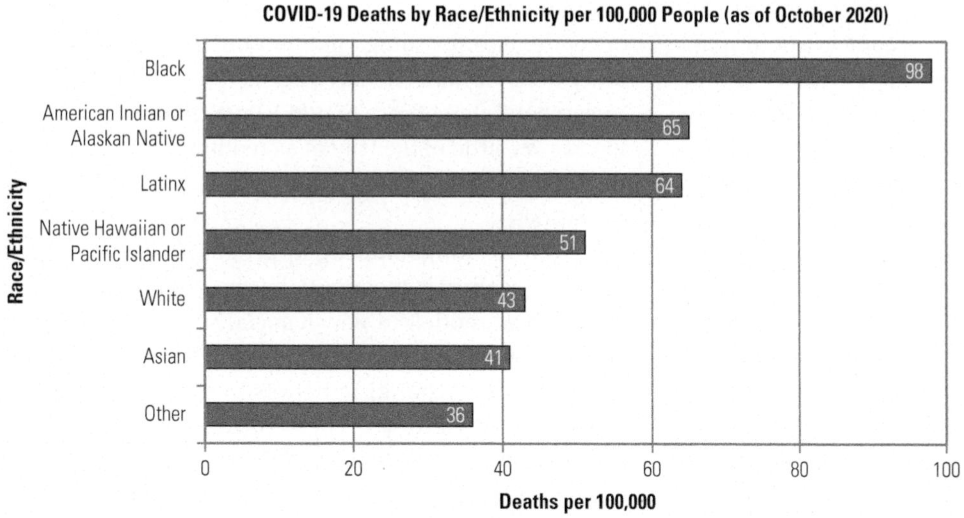

COVID-19 Deaths by Race/Ethnicity per 100,000 People (as of October 2020)

Race/Ethnicity	Deaths per 100,000
Black	98
American Indian or Alaskan Native	65
Latinx	64
Native Hawaiian or Pacific Islander	51
White	43
Asian	41
Other	36

SOURCE: COVID Racial Tracker (https://covidtracking.com/race).

Disparities in Political Participation and Representation

13.4.6 Discuss racial differences in political participation and representation.

There is a long history of political inequality in the United States. Prior to the Civil War (1861–65), Blacks were barred from voting in all but six states in the North and had no rights of any kind in the southern slave states (except for the small numbers of free Blacks, but even they had no political rights). At the end of the war in 1865, the federal government introduced a set of initiatives known as **Reconstruction**, which included, most importantly, an attempt to enforce full political equality on the former slave states. For roughly a decade, in most parts of the South, most Blacks were able to vote, and a number of Blacks were elected to local, state, and federal offices (including two members of the U.S. Senate and 14 to the House of Representatives). After the end of Reconstruction in 1877, however, the advent of Jim Crow disenfranchising measures largely prevented Blacks from participating in politics (as either voters or candidates) in most southern states, and few Black or Latinx officials were elected anywhere in the country prior to the 1960s. Outside the South, Blacks gained the legal right to vote from the 15th Amendment in 1870, although other ways of limiting their participation in political life persisted into the 1930s and even beyond.

Since the passage of the Civil Rights Act of 1964 and the Voting Rights Act of 1965, Blacks and other people of color have finally gained the full legal right to participate in all elections without any formal restrictions.

Since the 1960s, there has been significant progress in political representation, as measured by election to office or rates of voting. Differences in rates of participation in elections have narrowed dramatically between Whites and Blacks, and the number of Black and Latinx, and AAPI populations, winning elections and holding office at all levels of government has grown dramatically. In 2015, nearly 9 percent of elected officials in state legislatures nationwide were Black, up from only 2 percent in 1971 (Kurtz 2015). AAPI and Latinx Americans have also seen far more candidates winning elections across the country in recent years. People of color have become increasingly prominent in national politics, such as Barack Obama, U.S. president from 2008 to 2016, and Kamala Harris, the first woman of color to become vice-president in 2021. As of 2021, there were 56 Black members of Congress, about 10 percent of the total, but just three Black senators out of 100 (Tim Scott, R–SC, Corey Booker, D–NJ, and Raphael Warnock, D–GA). At the state and local levels, particularly in cities and towns that have Black majorities or large Black populations, Blacks regularly hold office and exert political influence. The Latinx community has also been gaining political influence and representation, with 46 Latinx members of the House and five senators (Bob Menendez, D–NJ, Marco Rubio R–FL, Ted Cruz R–TX, and Catherine Masto D–NV) (Congressional Research Service 2020). Increasing numbers of AAPI and a smaller but growing number of Native Americans have also won seats around the country.

However, turnout rates in elections among Latinx voters and Native Americans are well below those of Whites and Blacks, in part because many Latinxs who have full legal residence status have not yet become U.S. citizens. But even among eligible Latinxs, voter turnout has lagged (Fraga 2018; Leighley 2001). As is the case with Blacks, it has been in those parts of the country where Latinxs are most numerous that Latinx politicians have tended to win elections. As the proportion of Latinx and AAPI people continues to grow, many analysts are predicting dramatic changes in the future political makeup of the country (Fraga et al. 2011).

Despite the gains in political participation that resulted from the civil rights movement, people of color still face obstacles in exercising their voting rights (see Chapter 21 for more details). The Voting Rights Act has been significantly altered in recent years to make it more difficult to challenge legislative district boundaries that may be drawn to reduce representation for people of color. The most important development was a Supreme Court ruling in *Shelby County v. Holder* (2013), which eliminated requirements that states that had historically discriminated must have their election laws and boundaries evaluated prior to holding an election. Another important development in recent decades has been the denial of voting rights of convicted felons, and in some states this ban continues even after the sentence is entirely completed (Manza and Uggen 2006). The expansion of punishment in the era of mass incarceration, and the racial disparities in the system, have reduced access to the political system. Even more troubling, in recent elections some campaigns and political organizations have used threats or intimidation that largely targeted minority voters (Piven et al. 2009). An important set of developments has been recent efforts to pass state laws making voting more difficult (for example, by requiring voter IDs). Someone without a car or any other government-issued identification may have to purchase one prior to voting in the states that are adopting ID requirements. Here again, because people of color are more likely to be poorer than Whites and may not have proper ID, voting eligibility is reduced.

How Do We Explain the Privileges of Being White?

13.4.7 **Discuss how sociologists account for White privilege on various dimensions of social and economic status.**

Thus far, we have documented a wide variety of ways in which people of color continue to be disadvantaged in the United States today. These persisting gaps have been described as some of the costs of being a person of color or, alternatively, the privilege of being White. How can we account for this **White privilege?**

A century ago, American scholars embraced essentialist explanations that attributed non-Whites' poorer health outcomes to their natural physical inferiority or that tied group differences in income levels to their inborn intellectual capacity. Sociologists today dismiss such biological explanations of racial disparities for several reasons. For one thing, they do not consider races to be biologically determined groupings but rather socially invented ones. For another, biologists claim that a trait like intelligence—if

it were rooted in a person's DNA—would not be distributed across the human species following the same pattern as supposedly racial traits like skin color. And, finally, attempts to measure and distinguish racial capacities or tendencies for things like intelligence, criminality, or other behavioral traits have been so obviously biased by researchers' stereotypes of non-Whites that they have provided very little in the way of a credible empirical basis on which to build essentialist theories of racial socioeconomic disparities.

Another longstanding approach to explaining racial socioeconomic inequality has been sometimes called the cultural model, in which social scientists attempt to explain racial socioeconomic inequality by attributing distinct and unchanging beliefs, norms, and values to separate racial groups. These fixed, cultural attributes supposedly drive their members to certain behaviors that are advantageous or disadvantageous in the labor market, in school, or elsewhere in social life. In this view, groups that fare well have "good" cultural traits, while groups faring poorly do not. Today, however, most social scientists reject this rather simplistic view of culture. Instead, they argue, as W.E.B. Du Bois did 100 years ago, that cultural attitudes and ideas develop in response to the social context in which individuals and groups are found. In other words, culture may contribute to racial stratification not because it involves an unchanging set of values that group members are destined to hold, but because it is largely a response to the structural obstacles certain racial groups face in pursuing the American dream of upward mobility.

So how do sociologists explain White privilege? They point to opportunities and constraints that result from the social context in which American society places people of color at a disadvantage. This context arises from history, continuing forms of discrimination, and the legacies of limited opportunity that they have created. These conditions have a self-reproducing character, so that what happens in one generation influences another.

One issue that sometimes arises in discussions about racial and ethnic differences is why Blacks, Latinxs, and Native Americans have not achieved the same socioeconomic status as other racial and ethnic groups. Here it is important to consider the many different ways in which racial groups have "arrived" in the United States. Native Americans were at first forcibly excluded, then segregated in reservations; Africans were kidnapped and brought against their will to perform slave labor; and Mexican Americans and other Latinx populations were originally incorporated through U.S. territorial conquest. And although voluntary immigration has historically fed the growth of both the Asian and European American populations, it is worth noting that the former faced an array of immigration, residential, and administrative restrictions that the latter did not (although in the wave of immigration since 1965, those barriers have largely been removed). The particular social, economic, and political climate a group encounters when it arrives in the United States influences its initial status and potential path.

Racial inequalities created by formal and informal discrimination in the past continue to shape the stratification we see today—this is the idea of systemic racial inequality that we mentioned earlier. For example, historical legal and informal prohibitions against residential integration isolated racial minorities into poor neighborhoods that lack access to quality public education, sufficient employment opportunities, and community infrastructure such as hospitals, libraries, or even grocery stores that are taken for granted in White neighborhoods. In very poor neighborhoods there is also, but not always, a lack of well-functioning nonprofit organizations and public institutions like job training centers that can help provide young people with opportunities (Sharkey et al. 2017). Taken together, these factors can have a large cumulative impact.

Finally, we have already seen that many researchers, across different disciplines and using a wide array of techniques, have come to the conclusion that racial discrimination is alive and well in the United States. It may take the form of employment discrimination, where workers are treated differently by race when hiring, promotion, or firing decisions take place; it may show up in the housing market, when a person's race influences which neighborhoods or homes brokers and real estate agents show them. Discrimination can be subtle or it can be blatant, and it can be intentional or unintentional. Whenever it materializes, however, it contributes to the racial inequality that has been a feature of U.S. society from its very beginnings.

What about Affirmative Action?

13.4.8 Analyze the debate surrounding affirmative action as a tool in the fight against racial inequality.

Racial inequality has been an enduring characteristic of United States history. For most of the nation's history, White political elites expected and actively promoted White privilege. Moreover, Whites felt it was natural and even desirable for Whites to occupy the top economic, political, and social rungs until very recently. For at least the first 150 years of the nation's existence, White supremacy was effectively the law of the land, ensuring through both formal policies and informal practices that Whites had unrivaled access to the best

jobs, housing arrangements, education, and public facilities, among other things.

Large numbers of White Americans have only recently accepted the idea that such racial stratification is unfair and undesirable. The civil rights movement, largely a phenomenon of the 1950s through the 1970s, was at the heart of this sea change. Thanks to its strategy of organizing large-scale, peaceful protests and securing the support of federal courts in key legal battles, U.S. laws were rewritten or introduced to prohibit the favoritism toward Whites that earlier laws had protected.

Civil rights–era laws—most notably the Civil Rights Act of 1964 and the 1965 Voting Rights Act—largely embraced a principle of color blindness, forbidding the use or consideration of race in varied contexts, like employment. However, a tool developed later in the fight against racial inequality is grounded instead in a color-conscious approach: The policy of **affirmative action**. First deployed by Republican President Richard Nixon in the late 1960s (in a policy initiative that was designed

Demonstrators support affirmative action

to ensure that minority-owned businesses would have equal opportunities to compete for government contracts with more established White-owned firms), affirmative action refers to those policies that require organizations or institutions to "actively" consider individuals' race or gender when making important decisions. (Although affirmative action sought to address *both* racial and gender inequality, its gender measures have been much less controversial than its race component—and thus much more successful and far-reaching.) The examples of affirmative action that have drawn the most attention in the United States are those for college admissions and employment.

Affirmative action in relation to race and ethnicity is hotly debated, in part because it involves opinions on a whole series of issues that people don't often stop to tease apart. First, a person's view of affirmative action will depend on whether they believe racial inequality exists in the United States today. Second, even if they do think so, they may believe its causes cannot be addressed by social policy. If racial inequality simply reflects the biological and behavioral capacities of each race, there may be little public policy can do about it. If instead, however, they believe that racial inequalities exist, but they do not believe that governmental policies or laws should interfere with "private" markets, they may not think race-based affirmative action is a good approach. And finally, even if they think race-based affirmative action is the way to go, they may be unsure of how exactly to implement it. Should all institutions and organizations be required to implement it? (Currently very few are obligated by law to do so.) Should it take into account the races that people identify themselves with or the races that other people ascribe to them? And should it call for "hard" affirmative action—for example, numerical quotas or points—or "soft" affirmative action, like race-targeted recruitment of potential employees from underrepresented groups or scholarships for minority students?

In summary, affirmative action is a complex set of policies whose subtleties are often lost in raucous public debate. In recent years, the debate over affirmative action has shifted toward concerns about achieving diversity by advancing historically underrepresented minorities (URMs) in organizations. Diversity exists when a range of different people are found in an organization, in both leadership and subordinate roles. For example, women make up half the population, so one might ask whether half of the managers of an organization are women. The same issue applies to race and ethnicity: Are groups that were historically excluded from colleges, government offices, and other positions represented in numbers comparable to their share of the local (or national) population?

Diversity proponents argue that it has a variety of important benefits, and thus provides a much firmer basis for affirmative action policies. When it comes to selective colleges, the premise of diversity among both students and faculty is that it will be valuable for all students—who will be entering a more diverse twenty-first century world and workforce—to interact with a wider range of other students and faculty than they would in the absence of affirmative action. When it comes to government jobs, having a workforce that is representative of the community it serves is both fairer but also likely to encourage government officials to develop sensitivity to all groups in the community. This has long been thought to be especially important for police forces, but they often still remain far Whiter than the communities they serve (Ashkenas and Park 2015). In many large cities—including New York, Chicago, Houston, St. Louis, Dallas, Los Angeles, and San Francisco—White officers are at least 15 percent more numerous than they are in the city's population, and in some cases much more. The disparity in many suburban areas that are becoming more diverse is often much more extreme. For example, in the 2014 police slaying of an unarmed Black man named Michael Brown in Ferguson, Missouri, which led to protests in that community and around the country, the police were a massive 55 percent more White than the community (see Chapter 20 for more details).

After centuries of racial privilege for Whites, Americans remain torn about whether we can eliminate racial stratification simply through formal, or legal, color blindness. As President Lyndon B. Johnson famously put it in 1965: "You do not take a man who for years has been hobbled by chains, liberate him, bring him to the starting line of a race, saying, 'you are free to compete with all the others,' and still justly believe you have been completely fair." Sociologists have described this difference as a difference between support for the *principle* of equality and support for *implementation of policies* that might help create more equality. Yet the attempt to do so through affirmative action programs has frequently led to counterclaims that it is unfair to make young Whites today pay for the sins of earlier generations. In this framing, the claim is sometimes made that affirmative action is "reverse racism." The mixture of policy, morality, and race has made affirmative action a deeply controversial program ever since it was first introduced.

BIG QUESTION 13.5 How Are Race and Ethnicity Changing in the Twenty-First Century?

RACE AND ETHNICITY IN THE FUTURE

"Interracial," "multiracial," "postracial"—is the United States on its way to becoming any of these? One thing is clear: The face of America has changed a great deal since the nation's founding over 200 years ago. At that time, the former colony contained for the most part people from only three regions of the world: Northern Europe (especially England, Ireland, and the Netherlands), the enslaved population from West Africa, and indigenous people. The first U.S. Census, in 1790, did not classify any races other than those covering these origins; official categories for Asians were almost a century away and for Latinxs closer to two centuries. Yet by 2010, the most common ethnic ancestries among Americans were no longer limited to longstanding English or Black communities. Instead, the descendants of later European arrivals like Germans, Italians, and Poles are now among the most numerous in the nation, and "Mexican" ranks sixth on the list of the most common ancestries Americans report (Brittingham and de la Cruz 2004).

Changes in demographic makeup, however, are only part of the story of how race and ethnicity are changing in our lifetimes. In this section, we will not only explore the factors behind transformations in the nation's population composition but also investigate how racial and ethnic stratification, identities, classifications, and conceptions are rapidly changing. In all these areas, we will take a look backward in time to see what trends have brought us to the present and to consider the predictions that social scientists make about the future.

A Changing Population

13.5.1 Discuss changes in attitudes toward interracial unions and multiracial people in the United States.

In its November 18, 1993 issue, *TIME* magazine put on its cover a beautiful young woman who smiled at readers over the title, "The New Face of America." Her tawny skin, light brown eyes, and chestnut hair gave no clue to her ethnic origins. And no wonder: The image was not a picture of a real person but rather a morphed composition assembled from photographs of dozens of individuals from a wide array of ancestries. According to *TIME*, the morphed face was "15% Anglo-Saxon, 17.5% Middle Eastern, 17.5% African, 7.5% Asian, 35% Southern European and 7.5% Hispanic." Its purpose was to illustrate "How Immigrants Are Shaping the World's First Multicultural Society."

Although the United States is far from being the first multicultural society, the exaggeration is consistent with the story that many Americans tell themselves about how the country has changed over the last two centuries. As the *TIME* magazine headline suggests, it is a narrative about a nation whose growing tolerance leads to greater immigration and interracial mixture over time.

What this account overlooks is that the United States has always been a multiracial—not to mention multicultural—society. From its earliest beginnings as a collection of English colonies, racial intermixture was common. As far back as the 1630s and 1640s, colonial records attest to interracial sexual unions and mixed-race offspring (Williamson 1980). As the enslavement of Africans continued over the next two centuries, interracial mixing—notably

Stephen Barnes/UK/Alamy Stock Photo

Meghan Markle, a (former) member of the British royal family, is of Black and European descent. A former actress, she has described her "ethnic ambiguity" as both a challenge and an opportunity in competing for acting roles. Markle is one of a long list of twenty-first century celebrities—such as Nicki Minaj, Jessica Alba, Naomi Campbell, Dwayne Johnson, Vanessa Hudgens, Tiger Woods, Mariah Carey, and Ne-Yo—with multiracial and/or multiethnic ancestry.

through the coercion of Black female enslaved persons by White male slaveholders—was so widespread that by 1915, the U.S. Census Bureau estimated that three-quarters of the Black population had some non-Black ancestry (U.S. Census Bureau 1918). Similarly, Latinx people are largely of mixed European, Native American, and African descent. Yet we do not usually include Latinxs and Black people in our picture of multiracial America because their mixed ancestry is old, dating back to the eras of slavery and colonial conquest. Instead, we prefer to think of multiracialism as something new, linked to the contemporary era in which individuals have had new freedom to enter voluntarily into interracial relationships. The artificiality of this picture of multiracial America is sharply conveyed by the writer Danzy Senna's comment on the *TIME* magazine photomorphed image: "Of course, anyone could see that women just like the

computer face they had created did exist in Puerto Rico, Latin America, and Spanish Harlem."

Although neither interracial unions nor multiracial people are new in the United States, what *has* changed is our attitudes toward them. It was not until 1967 that the Supreme Court struck down all state laws banning interracial marriage. In the late 1990s, the federal government revised its official racial classifications to permit individuals to identify with more than one race. Both decisions signaled a sea change in Americans' willingness to recognize and even accept new ways of thinking about race. Yet for those with multiracial backgrounds, the experience of having to explain to others "what" they are in racial terms when they do not fit the major racial categories often remains a constant challenge (DaCosta 2007). Here is how Meghan Markle described the issues she faces in this regard: "'What are you?' A question I get asked every week of my life, often every day. 'Well,' I say, as I begin the verbal dance I know all too well. 'I'm an actress, a writer, the Editor-in-Chief of my lifestyle brand The Tig, a pretty good cook and a firm believer in handwritten notes.' A mouthful, yes, but one that I feel paints a pretty solid picture of who I am. But here's what happens: They smile and nod politely, maybe even chuckle, before getting to their point, 'Right, but what are you? Where are your parents from?' I knew it was coming, I always do. While I could say Pennsylvania and Ohio, and continue this proverbial two-step, I instead give them what they're after: 'My dad is Caucasian, and my mom is African American. I'm half Black and half White'" (Elle Magazine 2016).

These policy shifts are mirrored in both public attitudes and behaviors. For example, in the last 40 years, the percentage of newlyweds married to someone of a different race or ethnicity has more than doubled: Less than 7 percent of the individuals who married in 1980 had a spouse of another race or ethnicity, but by 2010, more than 15 percent did. More than a third of U.S. adults now say they have an immediate family member or close relative who is married to someone of a different race (Wang 2012).

National statistics also show an increase in the mixed-race population. From 2000, when the U.S. Census first counted multiracial people, to 2010, the number of people identified with more than one race rose from fewer than 7 million to more than 9 million, or nearly 3 percent of the total population (Humes, Jones, and Ramirez 2011). When the 2020 Census is released, it is certain to show further increases. (See p. 359 for the race questions used on the 2020 Census.)

These statistics, however, have several limitations. Figures on interracial marriages do not include people who live together or have other intimate relationships. Additionally, Census counts of mixed-race people exclude

Figure 13.11 Race Questions on the 2020 Census

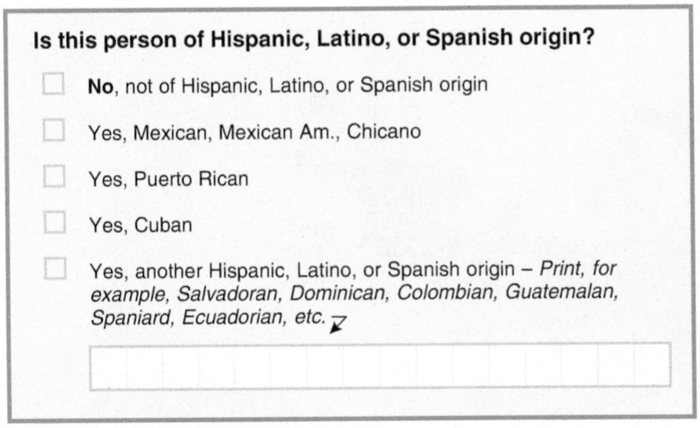

Is this person of Hispanic, Latino, or Spanish origin?

☐ **No**, not of Hispanic, Latino, or Spanish origin

☐ Yes, Mexican, Mexican Am., Chicano

☐ Yes, Puerto Rican

☐ Yes, Cuban

☐ Yes, another Hispanic, Latino, or Spanish origin – *Print, for example, Salvadoran, Dominican, Colombian, Guatemalan, Spaniard, Ecuadorian, etc.* ↘

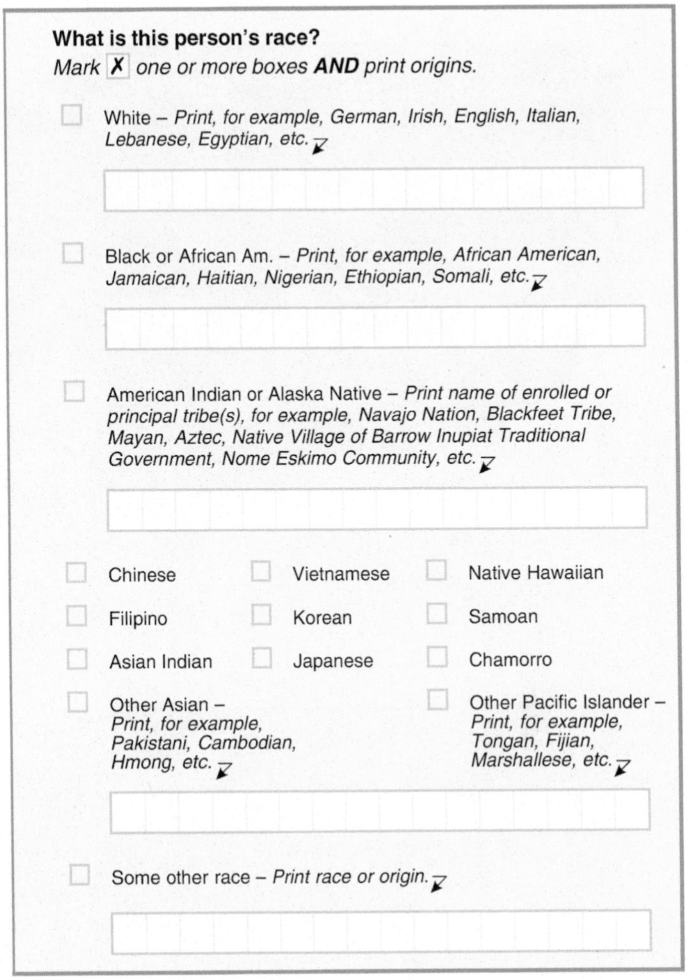

What is this person's race?
Mark ☒ *one or more boxes **AND** print origins.*

☐ White – *Print, for example, German, Irish, English, Italian, Lebanese, Egyptian, etc.* ↘

☐ Black or African Am. – *Print, for example, African American, Jamaican, Haitian, Nigerian, Ethiopian, Somali, etc.* ↘

☐ American Indian or Alaska Native – *Print name of enrolled or principal tribe(s), for example, Navajo Nation, Blackfeet Tribe, Mayan, Aztec, Native Village of Barrow Inupiat Traditional Government, Nome Eskimo Community, etc.* ↘

☐ Chinese ☐ Vietnamese ☐ Native Hawaiian

☐ Filipino ☐ Korean ☐ Samoan

☐ Asian Indian ☐ Japanese ☐ Chamorro

☐ Other Asian – *Print, for example, Pakistani, Cambodian, Hmong, etc.* ↘

☐ Other Pacific Islander – *Print, for example, Tongan, Fijian, Marshallese, etc.* ↘

☐ Some other race – *Print race or origin.* ↘

This image shows an extract form of the "race" questions on the 2020 U.S. Census that was mailed to every household. There are 14 checkboxes to choose from, in addition to a "Some Other Race" option. A separate, prior question asked people to indicate whether or not they were of Hispanic (Latinx) origin. There are several aspects of these questions that are controversial. For one thing, people are not given the opportunity to choose "more than one race" – although respondents are allowed to write it in. People who consider themselves multiracial have no direct way to say that. Most people end up choosing one of the main categories, even if it is only a partial fit; Latinx respondents in particular may think of themselves as neither "White" nor "Black," but feel they have to select one or the other. Whites, Blacks, and Indigenous people (still called "American Indian" on the 2020 form) and some other ethnic groups are identified (such as Chinese or Samoan), while others must choose a broader "other" category. Arab Americans and other people from the Middle East are strongly encouraged to select "White," even though many people from that region of the world do not feel that matches their identity or how they are treated living in the United States. The social construction of race in any census questionnaire will always be contentious; as we have noted throughout the chapter, there is no unambiguous or natural way to divide up populations into racial and ethnic groups that everyone would agree on. But in 2020 the U.S. Census fell short in ways that hopefully will be avoided in the future.

SOURCE: U.S. Census Bureau

large numbers of people who have multiracial ancestry—like most Blacks and Latinxs—but who are not aware of, or choose not to report, their mixed background. Sociologists estimate that if these people were counted as mixed-race in official statistics, nearly one-fifth of the U.S. population would be considered multiracial (Morning and Saperstein 2018). These and other shortcomings make it difficult to compare the numbers of interracial unions and multiracial people today to those in the past. However, the statistics that are available do point to an upward trend underway for both, and even though rates of interracial marriage remain far below those of within-group marriage, over time the percentage of people with one or more non-White or multiracial grandparent is likely to become a numerical majority (Kaufman 2019).

Immigration is the other major demographic trend reshaping the racial and ethnic makeup of the United States. Here there is no question that the twenty-first century is very different from the nineteenth century (when most immigrants came from European countries). Take a look at the maps in Figure 13.12 to see how Whites have

declined as a percentage of the population of each state since 1900. The increasingly darker shades of the 2018 map reveal that almost every state has a lower percentage of Whites than it did a century ago; the only exceptions are a few southern states where the Great Migration led to a significant decline in the Black population (and hence, Whites became a larger share of the population). In 1965, immigration reform made it significantly easier for people from other countries to enter the United States, and the resulting waves of immigration from Latin America, the Caribbean, and Asia have left their mark on the nation's demographic composition (Kritz and Gurak 2004). The top countries sending immigrants in recent years to the United States have been Mexico, China, Cuba, India, the Philippines, Vietnam, the Dominican Republic, and El Salvador (Walters and Trevelyan 2011; Budiman 2020). For example, while in 1970 people of Latinx descent were a little over 4 percent of the population, by 2014 they were 17 percent, and that percentage is projected to rise to almost 25 percent by 2040 and perhaps as much as 31 percent by 2060, according to Census Bureau projections. Although not quite

Figure 13.12 Becoming a Majority–Minority Nation: Whites as a Percent of State Population in 1900 (top panel) and 2018 (bottom panel)

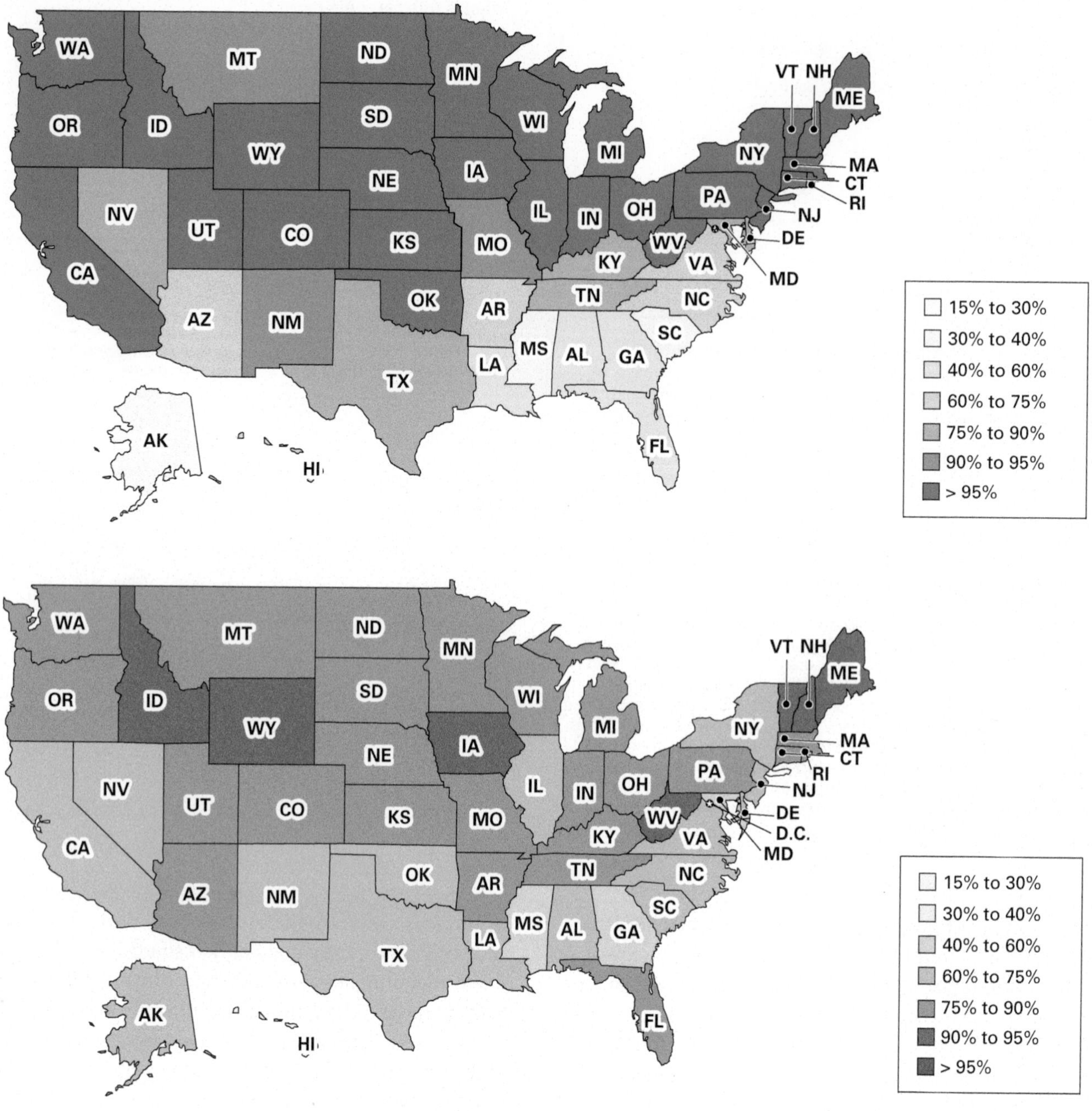

Legend (top panel):
- 15% to 30%
- 30% to 40%
- 40% to 60%
- 60% to 75%
- 75% to 90%
- 90% to 95%
- > 95%

Legend (bottom panel):
- 15% to 30%
- 30% to 40%
- 40% to 60%
- 60% to 75%
- 75% to 90%
- 90% to 95%
- > 95%

SOURCE: 1900 Census and 2018 ACS 5-year estimates provided by Social Explorer.

so dramatic, the rising proportion of AAPI people is also significant; from less than 1 percent in 1970 to 4.7 percent today, and by 2040 AAPI are expected to make up over 7 percent of the total population. The White population in the United States, meanwhile, has declined from 83.5 percent in 1970 to 63.7 percent in 2010, and is projected to fall below 50 percent by 2045.

These estimates of the American population are, of course, based on many assumptions—about fertility (birth rates), mortality (death rates), and whether immigrants will continue to choose to move to, and remain

and raise families, in the United States—so they may not prove exactly accurate. For example, they presume the continuation of trends that have been underway for decades now: The decrease in the White population and stability in the Black and Native American ones, compared to dynamic growth among both Latinx and Asian American populations. However, another factor may play a role in ways that are difficult to anticipate now—namely, the choices that people will make about how to identify themselves in racial and ethnic terms and the options they are given for doing so. We explore that issue in the next section.

Changing Classification and Identity

13.5.2 Explain how the U.S. Census has adapted to the evolving shifts in how Americans identify themselves.

The twentieth century saw several major shifts in how Americans identified themselves—and were identified by others—in terms of race and ethnicity. And, in fact, the official government racial and ethnic categories on the Census have changed with almost every Census (or 10 years) throughout American history (Lee 1993). The only group that has consistently been named on the Census is White; everything else was added later, anywhere from the eighteenth to the twentieth century. Will the next 100 years usher in another round of momentous change in the ways Americans classify by race and ethnicity?

As we have seen, perhaps the most significant change in recent years has been the federal government's shift in 1997 to allow people to identify themselves with more than one race when filling out the Census or other official documents. Although government policies are not a direct reflection of how everyday people think about racial and ethnic categories, the emergence of grassroots organizations for mixed-race people in recent decades suggests that Americans have grown increasingly accepting of the idea that a person might belong to more than one race (Williams 2006; DaCosta 2007).

A change that has yet to take place but that seems likely in the future is the inclusion of "Hispanic/Latino" (or "Hispanic/Latinx") as a race on government forms. At present, the U.S. government considers Latinx to constitute an ethnic group and so does not include it in the Census race question. In the wider society, however, the terms *Hispanic* and *Latino* tend to be used as if they were akin to races: Journalists, politicians, academics, and everyday people use phrases like "Blacks, Whites, and Latinos," suggesting that Hispanics/Latinxs are seen as a racial group like "Whites" and "Blacks." Moreover, the current lack of a "Hispanic or Latinx" category on the Census creates problems for people who would rather identify themselves using those terms instead of being forced to choose among options like "White," "Black," and "American Indian or Alaska Native." As a result, large numbers of Latinx people select "some other race."

Changing Stratification

13.5.3 Analyze the impact of modern demographic and social changes on racial inequality in the United States.

Immigration inflows that are more diverse than ever, rising rates of interracial marriage, and new openness to multiracial identities—what impact will these demographic and social changes have on racial inequality in the United States? Some observers believe they all point the way to a more racially inclusive and egalitarian society. Consider, for example, some newspaper headlines: "A New Generation Is Leading the Way: What Young People of Mixed Race Can Tell Us about the Future of Our Children" (Jackson Nakazawa 2003) or "The New Face of America: Blended Races Making a True Melting Pot" (Puente and Kasindorf 1999). The basic idea is that demographic trends reveal a new openness to bridging historical racial divides, and therefore that race is growing less significant as a factor in social, political, and economic life.

A closer look suggests that while race may be becoming less important for some groups, it remains a powerful barrier for others. The question, as sociologists Jennifer Lee and Frank Bean (2004, p. 221) put it, is "whether racial boundaries are fading for all groups or whether America's newcomers are simply crossing over the color line rather than helping to eradicate it." It is important to note, for example, that although the rate of interracial marriage overall has grown considerably in recent years, Asian and Latinx newlyweds are more likely than Blacks to have spouses of a different race (Wang 2012). In addition,

The growing demographic diversity of the United States suggests that it will become more and more common for Americans to share workplaces, schools, families, and social settings with people of different races. Interracial married couples, like the one shown here, are slowly becoming more common and are likely to continue to increase as a percentage of all marriages in the future.

ADDICTIVE STOCK CREATIVES/Alamy Stock Photo

individuals of mixed-race ancestry are more likely to identify themselves (or be identified) as multiracial if they have Asian ancestry but to be assigned to a single race—Black—if they have African ancestry (Gullickson and Morning 2011). The one-drop rule on Blackness that we discussed earlier has survived into the twenty-first century.

As we have seen, race is also still associated with pronounced differences in socioeconomic status, with Blacks, Latinxs, and Native Americans generally worse off than Whites and Asians. These kinds of findings have led some scholars to conclude that the color line is hardly disappearing from American life; it is simply shifting from one that separated Whites from non-Whites to one that distinguishes Blacks from non-Blacks. In this scenario, more groups, perhaps including all multiracial people, may be considered "White," while a few dark-skinned groups will remain barred from "White" status. In other words, we may have a new "beige majority" (Lind 1995) where Whites, most Asians, light-skinned Latinxs, and mixed-race people can lead lives relatively free of racial discrimination, while darker Latinxs, some Asians, Native Americans, and Blacks remain stigmatized by color (Gans 1999).

Other sociologists take a more optimistic view. Over the next 20 years, the post–World War II "baby boom" generation, born between 1946 and 1966, will gradually retire from the workforce. They will be replaced by a younger cohort that has a much smaller percentage of Whites, thus placing larger shares of non-Whites in the relatively good jobs that the baby boomers held. Sociologist Richard Alba (2009, 2020) foresees an inevitable transfer of opportunities for a comfortable middle-class life from Whites to people of color with minimal conflict. The historical dominance of Whites over opportunities will inevitably fall, simply because of the new demographic reality that is rapidly emerging in the twenty-first century. Alba stresses that this is not a foregone conclusion; for example, he calls on the nation to invest more wisely in education for historically disadvantaged groups in order to better prepare the future workforce. His vision, however, reminds us that race and ethnicity—both as ideas and as structuring social forces—have never been static and that even as short a time span as a quarter century may bring about striking changes.

Black Lives Matter, White Supremacism, and the Future of Race Politics

13.5.4 Analyze the two visions of America's racial and ethnic future.

In 1903, W.E.B. Du Bois wrote an essay entitled "The Problem of the Century," in which he famously declared, "The problem of the Twentieth Century is the problem of the color-line" (Du Bois 1903 [1989], p. 35). What about the twenty-first century? In recent years, struggles over the racial and ethnic future of America have become especially intense. The rise of the Black Lives Matter (BLM) movement, which we discussed earlier in this chapter (and more extensively in Chapters 20 and 22, on criminal justice and social movements, respectively), has forced the country, yet again, to address issues of racial inequality. The BLM movement, carrying on in the footsteps of the civil rights movement of the 1950s and 1960s, is demanding that the country make good on its promises of justice and equality for all. Just as in the 1960s, growing numbers of (mostly) young Americans of all races have embraced the BLM protests and agenda, and millions participated in nationwide protests in 2020.

Yet if the rise of BLM suggests the possibility of one direction for the American future, the growing prominence of White supremacist groups represents another. **White supremacism** is the belief that White people are superior to people of all other races, and that it is natural and appropriate for Whites to control institutions of power, like the government, large corporations, courts of law, the police, and the military. White supremacism has been around as long as people have thought of themselves as "White"; indeed, it gave rise to the system of racial classification we use today. It is different from what we described as White privilege earlier in the chapter, in that White supremacists believe that Whites *should* be privileged even as they may feel that White dominance is slipping away.

Many historians have noted that White supremacism was a core, taken-for-granted set of beliefs in the early American Republic (Parkinson 2016), co-existing alongside other classical beliefs that combined to create the U.S. Constitution and its incorporation of liberal, Republican, and pro-slavery ideals under one umbrella whose legacy continues to the present (Smith 1997). The Jim Crow system in the American South rested on ideas about White supremacy. The Ku Klux Klan, which peaked in the 1870s and again in the 1920s, was perhaps the most famous group promoting White supremacy, but there have been many others, past and present (Klinkner and Smith 1999; Gordon 2016; McVeigh and Estep 2020). In the nineteenth and twentieth centuries, White supremacism increasingly became tied to American nationalism and to the idea that America was a "White Christian" nation that should compete with European countries to control foreign lands. In the twentieth century, the concept of "America First" appeared and reappeared several times, for example, in the form of the neo-Nazi movement in the late 1930s and early 1940s. Most recently, it was brought back into common use by former President Donald Trump and many of his supporters (Churchwell 2018). There are many reasons why Trump rose to power, but chief among them was his ability to persuade White voters that they were losing control of "their" country, and that they needed a president who would restore the old way of life and "make America great again" (Sides, et al. 2018a; Kaufman 2019; Fording and Shram 2020). In countless examples, Trump's statements and political appeals employed explicitly racist and anti-immigrant rhetoric. More recently, White supremacists were among those leading the assault on the U.S. Capitol On January 6 2021, where several thousand supporters of former President Donald Trump halted the counting of electoral votes that would make Joe Biden the next president. These domestic terrorists tried to reverse the results of the election by force, placing the flag of the old Southern Confederacy squarely in the Capitol rotunda. It was the most significant expression of White supremacy in many decades.

Both the Black Lives Matter movement and White supremacism are rooted in some of the oldest social and political traditions in the United States, so their rising prominence today has set the stage for what seems to be an epic battle for American hearts and minds. White supremacy clashes, inevitably, with the ideals of freedom, democracy, and the notion that "all men are created equal," as the Declaration of Independence proclaims. Most Americans firmly support these ideals and would angrily reject being called White supremacists themselves. Yet many are also reluctant to support the full agenda of the Black Lives Matter movement. Some are perhaps uncomfortable with the protests that spread so quickly in 2020, while others may support the principles of the BLM movement but are simply unsure about what should be done. It is clear that the social, legal, and political changes that would be required to eradicate racism and racial inequality are

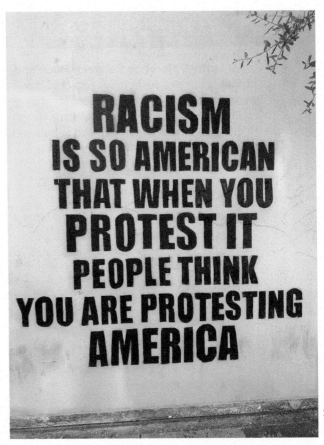

A protest billboard posted in the Wynwood neighborhood in Miami, Florida in 2020. It brilliantly captures a deep insight about the problem of race in American social and political history.

perhaps a long ways off. But as journalist Elizabeth Dias (2020) reminded us on the eve of the 2020 presidential election, "The state of the soul of the nation has often been tied to the country's oppression of Black people."

Conclusion: Developing a Sociological Imagination on Race and Ethnicity

In trying to uncover the cultural and structural forces that shape our lives, even when we are not aware of them, sociologists often come up with answers that are not intuitive because they go against the grain of common sense. The study of race is a good example. It is an everyday term for Americans and one that we usually think is a straightforward descriptor of people's physical characteristics. What sociology tells us, though, is that there are no such simple, obvious groupings of human beings based on bodily traits and that labels like "Black" and "White" tell us more about the way societies choose to classify people than they do about the individuals who get assigned to these categories.

In this area, as in so many others, developing a sociological imagination means looking beyond widespread beliefs that are too often taken for granted.

It is certain that political controversies over racial inequality, immigration, and Whites' declining share of the population will recur, over and over, in the years to come. Sociological theories and ideas will be at the center of those debates. In thinking about these issues, a sociological imagination also compels us to not settle for simple answers but to try to understand the roots of these inevitable contests, and how America might better connect its values to its treatment of people of color.

The Big Questions Revisited 13

13.1 What Is the Difference Between Race and Ethnicity? In this section, we explored how the words *race* and *ethnicity* often are used interchangeably, as if they mean the same thing. Sociologists make clear distinctions between race and ethnicity and use the two terms to describe different kinds of categories and identities.

Understanding Race and Ethnicity

Sociological Definitions of Race and Ethnicity

Learning Objective 13.1.1: Compare and contrast contemporary sociologists' and Max Weber's definitions of race and ethnicity.

Key Distinctions Between Race and Ethnicity

Learning Objective 13.1.2: Discuss key distinctions between race and ethnicity.

Distinguishing Racial and Ethnic Labels

Learning Objective 13.1.3: Distinguish racial labels from ethnic ones.

Key Terms

essentialism (p. 333)   one-drop rule (p. 334)   ethnicity (p. 334)   race (p. 334)

13.2 Is Race Real? In this section, we analyzed the question of whether race is anchored in deep-seated physical differences between individuals or is an invention that is not determined by human biology but which nonetheless is "real" because it has an unmistakable impact on daily life.

The Social Construction of Race

Race and Society

Learning Objective 13.2.1: Explain how changing American definitions of who counts as White supports the constructivist view of race.

Race and Biology

Learning Objective 13.2.2: Analyze the arguments against a biological determination of race.

Race and Place

Learning Objective 13.2.3: Discuss how race is understood differently around the world.

Key Terms

social construct (p. 336)   constructivist (p. 336)   assimilation (p. 337)   DNA (p. 338)

13.3 What Is Racism? In this section, we examined how political correctness of our ideas, speech, and behavior is a prominent feature of both public and private conversations on race today. Sociologists have thought a lot about prejudice and discrimination, providing ample food for thought on racism in the contemporary United States.

Contemporary Racism

How Do Sociologists Define Racism and Discrimination?

Learning Objective 13.3.1: Discuss the roles of prejudice, stereotyping, and discrimination in the sociological definition of racism.

Why Does Racism Occur?

Learning Objective 13.3.2: Explain how people can be socialized into racism.

Does Racism and Racial Discrimination Still Exist in the United States?

Learning Objective 13.3.3: Analyze evidence that racial prejudice and discrimination still exist in the United States.

Key Terms

racism (p. 340)   prejudice (p. 340)   stereotype (p. 340)   discrimination (p. 340)   lynching (p. 340)   genocide (p. 342)   individual discrimination (p. 340)   implicit (or "unconscious") prejudice (p. 341)   institutional (or structural) discrimination (p. 341)   systemic racism (p. 341)   intersectionality (p. 342)   color-blind racism (p. 344)

13.4 Do Race and Ethnicity Matter Anymore? In this section, we explored whether America has become a "color-blind" society or has reached a "postethnic" era. Sociological research suggests, however, that race is still closely linked to socioeconomic inequality.

The Impact of Race and Ethnicity Today

Disparities in Income, Wealth, Employment, and Poverty

Learning Objective 13.4.1: Discuss racial disparities in income, wealth, employment, and poverty.

Disparities in Education

Learning Objective 13.4.2: Describe patterns of educational attainment for minority groups over the last 30 years.

Residential Segregation

Learning Objective 13.4.3: Describe persistent patterns of residential segregation in the United States.

Disparities in the Criminal Justice System

Learning Objective 13.4.4: Identify sociological explanations for high rates of incarceration of people of color, especially men.

Disparities in Health and Health Care Coverage

Learning Objective 13.4.5: Explain racial and ethnic disparities in indicators related to health.

Disparities in Political Participation and Representation

Learning Objective 13.4.6: Discuss racial differences in political participation and representation.

How Do We Explain the Privileges of Being White?

Learning Objective 13.4.7: Discuss how sociologists account for White privilege on various dimensions of social and economic status.

What about Affirmative Action?

Learning Objective 13.4.8: Analyze the debate surrounding affirmative action as a tool in the fight against racial inequality.

Key Terms

ghetto (p. 350)   mass incarceration (p. 352)   Reconstruction (p. 353)   White privilege (p. 356)   affirmative action (p. 355)

13.5 How Are Race and Ethnicity Changing in the Twenty-First Century? Today, the face of America is very different from what it was 200 years ago. Immigrants come from a wider range of countries than ever before, people are more likely to marry partners from a different racial background, and changing attitudes have led more and more people to identify themselves as multiracial. These and other demographic changes will certainly have an impact on the nation's racial and ethnic makeup, on its patterns of socioeconomic inequality, and on its inhabitants' attitudes and beliefs about race and ethnicity.

Race and Ethnicity in the Future

A Changing Population

Learning Objective 13.5.1: Discuss changes in attitudes toward interracial unions and multiracial people in the United States.

Changing Classification and Identity

Learning Objective 13.5.2: Explain how the U.S. Census has adapted to the evolving shifts in how Americans identify themselves.

Changing Stratification

Learning Objective 13.5.3: Analyze the impact of modern demographic and social changes on racial inequality in the United States.

Black Lives Matter, White Supremacism, and the Future of Race Politics

Learning Objective 13.5.4: Analyze the two visions of America's racial and ethnic future.

Key Term

White supremacism (p. 363)

Chapter 14
Gender and Sexualities

by Paula England and Jeff Manza

In the summer of 2021, women held CEO positions at 30 of the largest 500 American companies (Catalyst 2021). Women have headed companies like Yahoo, PepsiCo, Xerox, and Hewlett Packard, achievements few dreamed possible just decades earlier. These women, and many of today's women leaders in other fields, exude confidence and assertiveness. Naturally, we would assume these qualities would extend from a woman's professional life to her personal life, but do they?

Can a woman be a strong leader, communicator, and innovator at work but also feel like asking a man on a date is inappropriate because of her gender? A few years ago, I was conducting research on sex and relationships among college students. During one of my interviews, I met Janine, a graduate student studying for her master's in business administration (MBA). As we spoke about dating, relationships, and sex, she expressed her preference for traditional dating rather than "hooking up." Janine took great pride in waiting for men to ask her on dates. Her reasoning for never asking men on dates was that she believed men wouldn't see her as "relationship material" if she did. What a paradox, I thought—a woman who feels absolutely entitled and confident about scaling upper management, which was off-limits to women a few decades ago, but who wouldn't even consider asking a man on a date. Clearly, some things have changed and others have stayed the same!

In this chapter, we will consider patterns and change in gender and sexualities. The term **gender**, as used by sociologists, refers to the way in which social forces structure how being seen as male or female affects what is expected of you, how you are treated, what opportunities you have, and the results for individual women and men. We will also examine how sociologists study sexualities, a topic closely related to gender. Our discussion of sexualities will include relationships between men and women, as well as between same-sex partners. In addition to consensual sex, we will consider unwanted sex and sexual attention, including sexual assault and sexual harassment. We will also consider individuals who reject the gender binary and want to be neither male nor female, masculine nor feminine.

My Sociological Imagination

PAULA ENGLAND

My mother didn't have enough money to go to college and never considered a career after she married at age 19 and became a stay-at-home mom to four children. Later, when I was grown, she claimed she was lucky to be able to stay at home with her kids. But she also talked about feeling underappreciated by my dad. Gender inequalities often made her feel "less than." Dad had the education, not her, and she often felt that principals, doctors, and community leaders didn't respect "just a housewife," even though she saw importance in what she was doing. I became fascinated by sociology, seeing it as a way to understand social causes of human suffering. I wondered how much my mother's suffering would have been lessened had the gender regime been different. My early research focused on why some occupations are filled mostly with men and others mostly with women, why women earn less than men, and why mothers earn less than women without children. These topics interested me because I wanted to understand the social forces that hold women back. Later, I began to study the increasing trend toward young couples having unplanned pregnancies followed by births outside of marriage. Recently I conducted a study of relationships and sex among college students, trying to understand how the sexual revolution intersects with the gender revolution.

Ideas about gender and sexuality are often closely linked to cultural expectations. As pressures for gender equality and societal openness to gender and sexual freedoms grows, longstanding and widely held beliefs are forced to change, creating cultural conflicts that are all around us.

367

The Big Questions

From the early writings of the founding sociologists over a century ago until about 1970, not many sociologists studied gender or sexuality. These topics were seen as more in the realm of nature than society. But since about 1970, sociologists have used their methods and approaches to study these topics. In this chapter, we will examine how sociologists answer the following big questions about gender and sexuality:

1. **Where do gender differences come from?** In this section, we will explore gender differences and examine their origins, with a focus on what sociologists have shown.

2. **How have the lives of women and men changed in the last 50 years?** Women's lives have changed so much in the last 50 years that we often call the changes a gender revolution. Here, we explore some of these changes as well as how they have affected men's lives.

3. **How are our sex lives shaped by biology and society?** There is no question that sexual attractions and behavior are affected by biology, but, as we will see in this section, they are also strongly affected by social construction.

4. **How has sexual behavior changed in the last 50 years?** Sexual behavior of young unmarried adults has changed substantially over the last several decades, but what about the extent to which sexual and relational behavior is affected by gender norms and inequalities and societal reactions to nonconsensual sex? In this section, we will explore sexual behavior and its link to gender.

hotgranny/Stockimo/Alamy Stock Photo

BIG QUESTION 14.1 Where Do Gender Differences Come From?

GENDER DIFFERENCES

All around us, we see differences between the way men and women (or boys and girls) dress, the activities they engage in, and what they say they want. More boys than girls play certain sports, more girls than boys play with dolls, many college majors and occupations contain either mostly men or mostly women, and more women than men are stay-at-home parents.

But sometimes we exaggerate the size of these differences. Take, for example, the common belief that males score higher than females on standardized math tests. One way

to quantify this is by computing the difference between the average (also called the *mean*) male and female score. In 2019 data on the mathematics part of the SAT Reasoning Test many students take to apply to college, men's average score, on a scale from 200 to 800, was 537, and women's was 519, a difference of 18 points. (The SAT is very similar to the ACT; most readers of this book have taken one or the other.) Another way sociologists examine the gender difference is to plot the whole distribution of scores for each sex, showing the percentages for men and women at each score. Figure 14.1 shows both the male and female means and the whole male

Figure 14.1 Men's and Women's Mean Scores and Distributions on the 2019 Math SAT Test

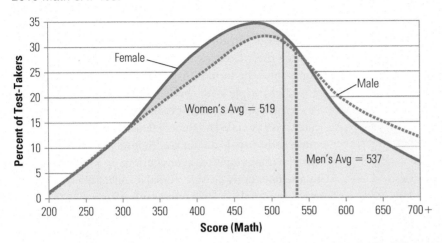

NOTE: Source of data on percent of men and women in various score ranges provided by The College Board, 2019. Data smoothed by Paula England to approximate density distributions.

and female distributions for the 2019 Math SAT test. Each of the two curves has a large bulge in the middle, which tells you that more people score in the middle of the distribution than at either extreme. The male mean (or average) is a bit higher than the female mean. But the figures also show how much the two distributions overlap, and that the mean difference looks rather small compared to the amount of overlap. Thus, even on a characteristic where one sex has a higher average, there will be many members of the sex with the higher average who are below the average of the sex with the lower average. This point is critical to keep in mind so as not to exaggerate gender differences.

In the rest of this section, we will explore some of the main factors affecting gender identities and inequalities.

Small differences between boys and girls on standardized tests are dwarfed by differences *among* boys and girls. This raises an important question: Why do we often pay so much attention to differences between genders, as opposed to focusing on differences *within* gender categories?

Sex versus Gender: The Social Construction of Gender

14.1.1 Distinguish the concepts of sex and gender, and explain how gender is socially constructed.

When women and men differ, what shapes these differences? Many people believe that sex differences in behavior and preferences are "natural," caused by biological differences such as differences in hormones, anatomy, or brain structure. There is some truth to this. A person's **sex** is a biological matter. Humans group into two sexes, where males and females differ in anatomy, chromosomes, and average levels of certain hormones.

But it is also true that men and women overlap on many of these characteristics, and some people, called **intersex individuals**, are born with some typical anatomical characteristics of both men and women. Despite this overlap, babies are routinely assigned to one sex category at birth based on their genitals.

One example of a biological influence is the evidence that testosterone, a hormone present in both women and men but generally in much greater amounts in men, encourages some kinds of aggressive or dominance-seeking behavior. This suggests that the higher levels of aggressive behavior that we see in men, on average, are caused in part by the fact that men have higher testosterone than women.

Yet causation is not just one-way, from hormone to behavior; changes in the social environment can also change testosterone levels. For example, one study showed that men's testosterone levels increase before a competitive athletic event, and those of the winners stay elevated afterward, while the testosterone levels of the losers drop afterward (Mazur and Booth 1998). Another biologically based difference is that only women can breastfeed infants. But men participate much more in infant care in some societies than others, showing that social contexts also have an effect.

When sociologists talk about gender, they focus on the ways that social forces create differences between men's and women's behavior, preferences, treatment, and opportunities. While biology clearly creates some differences between men and

Fathers of the Aka tribe in West Africa spend more time in close contact with their infant children than in almost any other society. Wide variation in a father's involvement in child rearing highlights one of the many ways in which societies can play a role in influencing gender differences.

women's behavior and preferences, research in sociology has shown that social arrangements have powerful effects on these differences. The entire system of social processes that create and sustain gender differences and gender inequality is often referred to as the **social construction of gender**. Societies have a broad gender system that includes the workings of small groups and large institutions (Risman 2004, 2018). In small groups, what people are expected to do and rewarded for doing depends on the sex category they are assumed to be in based on looking at them. At the same time, institutions like schools, churches, corporations, and governments set up policies or rules that affect women and men differently. To the extent that men have more power than women in politics, the economy, and the family, the gender system is called **patriarchy**.

One interesting group of people challenges many of our assumptions about sex and gender and how they go together. **Transgender** (or trans) individuals are those who were assigned one sex category at birth, based on the usual anatomical criteria, but feel strongly they belong in another gender category. Individuals may transition from male to female, becoming transwomen, from female to male, becoming transmen, or from either

sex category to being **nonbinary**, reflecting that they see themselves as neither male nor female. Transitions may occur in childhood (Meadow 2018) or in adulthood. Some transgender individuals take hormones and/or undergo surgery as part of their transition; others change their clothing or behavior but not their bodies. Sometimes the term transgender is also used to refer to a group of people who challenge the common notion that sex or gender are each binaries—having only the two categories of male and female. These nonbinary or gender-queer individuals do not see themselves as either male or female; they may dress conventionally male while being in a female body or vice versa, or reject the need to look male or female in dress and style altogether (McKenna and Kessler 2006; Risman 2018). Because of the intolerance by many toward those who challenge the cultural belief that one's sex or gender is something fundamental and unchanging, transgender people are often subjected to ridicule and even violence.

Gender Socialization

14.1.2 Describe the process of gender socialization.

One way that gender is socially constructed is through **socialization**, a concept we explored in more detail in Chapter 5. Socialization is the means by which members of a society are taught its norms and practices. Some of what gets taught is conventions about gender—what boys should do differently than girls or women differently than men.

Parents are important agents of gender socialization. Many parents dress boys and girls differently, decorate their rooms differently, have different aspirations for them, and give them different toys. Parents' socialization practices have changed in that girls are now encouraged to take

Parents are powerful agents of gender socialization. Many parents dress boys and girls differently, for example. In so doing, perhaps without thinking about it, they are reinforcing the idea that boys and girls are different.

part in a broader range of activities than in the past. For example, many parents now encourage their girls to play sports and give them what used to be thought of as boys' toys, such as Lego and racing cars. But not many parents have started to give their boys dolls. Studies show that fathers—more than mothers—are particularly discouraging of boys doing anything they see as feminine, like playing with dolls or ballet dancing. Peer groups are also agents of socialization. Male peer groups often ostracize boys who are not seen as stereotypically masculine enough and ridicule boys believed to be gay (whether they are or not) (Pascoe 2007).

Another important agent of socialization is the mass media—popular music, movies, television shows, Internet sites, and advertisements. Most of us see and hear hundreds of media messages every day. In movies and television, women portrayed in romantic roles are almost always young and thin and look like models. In contrast, men can be cast in a romantic role even if they are older and heavy. Ads typically show women rather than men doing housework. Men are seen in powerful roles in the economy, politics, and athletics. Some of this simply reflects the current social reality, but women and men are portrayed in a narrower range of roles in the media than they take in real life (Holtzman 2000).

Socialization does not only affect children but continues through adulthood as those around us continue to affect us, we continue to see and hear media images, and we are affected by major institutions such as religion and government.

Gender Differences Vary by Setting and Time

14.1.3 Explain how gender differences vary by setting and time.

There are two main reasons why we know that many of the typical differences we observe between women and men are, at least in part, socially constructed. First, these gender differences vary between different social settings—that is, between different cultures and even between different situations within one society. Second, gender arrangements have changed over time. For example, the proportion of married women with young children who hold paid jobs has increased dramatically. If biology were driving all the differences between men and women, we would not expect things to vary by the social setting or change over time.

One example of gender changing between different social settings is that women and men conform more closely to norms of masculinity or femininity when they are aware of being watched. Look at the data from one

revealing study: One research team discovered this in a study in which they asked college students to play a video game in which they first defended and then attacked by dropping bombs. The number of bombs a student dropped in the video game was taken as a measure of aggressive behavior. The researchers were interested in whether there were gender differences in aggression because most people think of men as more aggressive than women, and some past studies have found this sex difference (Hyde 1984, 2005). But how much of that difference is just a matter of people doing what others expect of them rather than enduring differences in preferences? To find out, the researchers randomly assigned half of the students who had agreed to be in their study into each of two groups. As long as a truly random process is used, this guarantees that the two groups should be just about equivalent on anything before the treatment. In this **random-assignment experiment**, participants in one group were led to believe that their actions during the video game would be monitored by the researcher. The other group received a different treatment; they were given the impression that no one would be monitoring their games. Among this second group, men did not drop any more bombs than women. In the first group, the group that believed they were being watched, men dropped significantly more bombs than women (Lightdale and Prentice 1994).

As Figure 14.2 illustrates, the researchers concluded that gender-stereotypical behavior is more likely to happen when people believe that they are being watched. Of course, people are being watched by others in a good

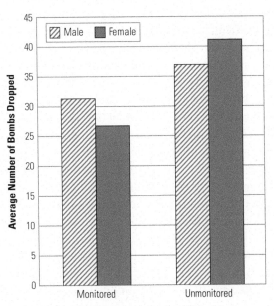

Figure 14.2 Gender Differences in Aggression in Monitored and Unmonitored Conditions.

SOURCE: Data from Lightdale and Prentice, 1994.

deal of their life—in school, at home with family, at work, at social gatherings, or out on the street. This suggests that some of how women and men act results from trying to live up to what they think others expect from someone of their sex. Apparently this social pressure, even with no rewards or punishments, has an effect. Although this study only focused on aggression, you can imagine all sorts of other gender differences that social expectations might affect.

The Impact of Stereotypes

14.1.4 Discuss the role of stereotypes in constructing social expectations of gender.

Some social expectations are based on **stereotypes**, beliefs about a group that are often untrue or exaggerated as a description of the group. These beliefs are then applied to individual members of the group, for whom they may not be true at all. Educators worry about the stereotype that girls and women perform worse in math because math is so crucial for many technical majors and careers. Men do better on the math SAT test, on average, as we saw in Figure 14.1. But a recent review of many studies found that most other standardized math tests show only small gender differences, with the average differences virtually disappearing on most tests but the SAT since the 1990s (Hyde et al. 2008). Despite the lower average scored by girls on some standardized tests, when they take math classes in high school or college, girls average higher grades than boys, mainly because they study more (Dee 2007; DiPrete and Buchmann 2013).

Researchers have wondered if exposure to the stereotype that men perform better at math helps to produce the very reality it claims to merely describe. To find out, one researcher randomly assigned male and female college students to two groups—one in which they were told that men perform better on a particular test, on average, and one in which they were told that there is no gender difference on the test. Then participants were asked to assess their own skills on a scale. In the group that had been told that men perform better, women assessed themselves lower on the scale than men did, but this difference was smaller in the group told there is no gender difference (Correll 2004). In another study, researchers had women take math tests like those on the GRE, an exam often required for application to graduate school. Before taking the test, half the women were randomly assigned to read an essay saying that scientists had found genetic differences explaining gender differences in math performance, while the other half were told that any gender differences on math tests arise from differences in what men and women have experienced.

The study found that women did worse on the math test when they had been told gender differences on math tests are genetically determined (Dar-Nimrod and Heine 2006; see Spencer, Steele, and Quinn 1999 for a similar finding in earlier research). In these studies, we see that what people hear from others about whether their sex is better at something affects their confidence and even their actual performance. Stereotypes, whether true, untrue, or exaggerated, will tend to produce the very difference they claim is true, even if the difference didn't exist before.

Social context can also determine how "macho" men act. A team of sociologists showed this in an experiment in which male and female college student participants were randomly assigned to two groups. First, the students were given a gender identity survey. Then they were given feedback on whether their answers to the survey showed them to be more feminine or masculine. But, in fact, what they were told about their scores on the survey was made up. Men randomly assigned to the group having their gender identity threatened were told they were somewhat feminine; the others were told they were masculine. Similarly, a group of women was randomly assigned to have their gender identity threatened by telling them they were somewhat masculine, with the others told they were feminine. See Figure 14.3 for the results of this intriguing study. What was interesting was the effect on men of being told they were feminine rather than masculine. When the participants were given a second survey, compared to the men told they were masculine, these men expressed more negative views of same-sex relationships more favorable views of strong groups dominating weak groups, more support for the Iraq War, and more favorable views of SUVs (Willer et al. 2013). In contrast, women's attitudes on the second survey weren't significantly different for those who were told they were feminine and masculine. The authors concluded that men desire to appear masculine, and if they have reason to think others doubt their masculinity, they redouble their efforts to engage in behavior culturally coded as masculine. Women seem to be less worried about how feminine they appear, reflecting less social pressure on women to act feminine than on men to act masculine.

These studies do not necessarily prove that biological influences have no impact on gender differences. But, because the studies show that gender differences fluctuate depending on the social situation, we can be sure that some of the differences we observe come from social forces. In addition, the fact that gender inequality has changed over time is further evidence that gender is at least partly socially determined and that biology does not completely dictate destiny. Next, we will examine these changes.

Figure 14.3 Effect of Gender Identity Threat on Men's and Women's Reported Attitudes

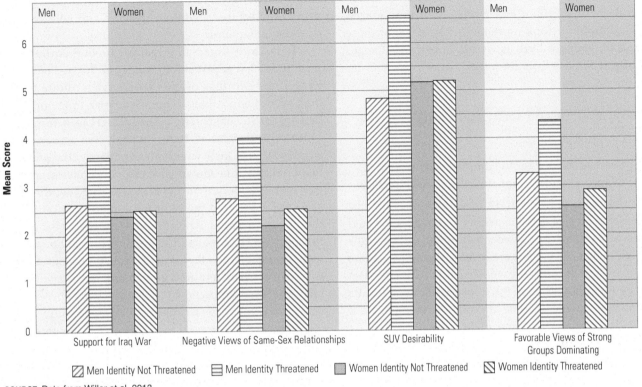

SOURCE: Data from Willer et al. 2013.
NOTE: All differences between the "threatened" and "not threatened" conditions are statistically significant for men. None are significant for women.

How Have the Lives of Women and Men Changed in the Last 50 Years?

BIG QUESTION 14.2

THE GENDER REVOLUTION

Women's lives have changed so much in the last 50 years that we often call the changes a gender revolution. Most of these changes consist of ways in which girls and women have taken on activities and roles previously limited mostly to boys or men. More girls than ever are playing on sports teams, more young women hold offices in student government than previously, more women than men now get college degrees, women's employment has increased, some women have moved into traditionally male professions, women hold some elected offices in state legislatures and Congress, and the first woman vice president, Kamala Harris, was elected in 2020, women are on the Supreme Court, and many women retain their birth-given last name when they marry. In this section, we look more closely at a few of these changes in women's lives as well as how these changes have affected men's lives since the 1970s.

Rising Women's Employment and Education

14.2.1 Discuss reasons for the dramatic increase in women's employment and education since 1970.

Of all the changes in the lives of women over the last 50 years, the biggest is the increase of women in the paid workforce. Even married women with small children now hold jobs outside the home at high rates. Figure 14.4 shows the percentage of men and women in the United States who were employed from 1970 forward among adults 25 to 54 years of age. (People are counted as employed if they held a paying job any time in the last week.)

Men's employment declined somewhat in the last 50 years. Women's employment rose dramatically between 1970 and 2000 to over 70 percent and then plateaued, with little increase since then. While women's employment is still lower than men's (between 80 and 90 percent of men are employed), the two groups have converged substantially; however, the convergence has stalled since 2000 (see Figure 14.4).

The two main reasons that women's employment increased were economic. First, as wages in most jobs increased during the 1960s and 1970s, so did the incentive for women—or couples—to decide in favor of a woman working for pay (Bergmann 1986). In addition, the economy changed to include a higher share of jobs in service work (jobs like secretary, receptionist, nurse, and store clerk), which had always employed many women. As

the demand for service workers rose, more opportunities became available for women (Oppenheimer 1970). One result of this growth of women's employment is that many families that include a husband and wife are now dual-earner families.

Today men's median wages are no higher than they were in 1970, if adjusted for changes in the cost of living. In fact, the earnings of men who have no more than a high school education—who often work in factories, as drivers, or in construction—have decreased (England, Levine, and Mishel 2020), which has encouraged employment of their wives. Men in managerial and professional jobs (like lawyer and engineer) have seen their pay increase more than the cost of living, yet the typically well-educated wives of these men have increased their employment dramatically as well (Juhn and Murphy 1997). Laws against sex discrimination made it more possible for well-educated women to achieve high-level careers. The **feminist movement** encouraged these laws and their enforcement, which in turn encouraged many women to have a career as well as a family.

To that end, men used to receive college degrees more than women, but since the early 1980s, more women than men have earned college degrees. If we go back to 1950, women received only 24 percent of the bachelor's degrees granted (Digest of Education Statistics 2016, Table 318.10). As Figure 14.5 shows, in 1970, women got 43 percent of the degrees. Given that there are approximately the same number of women as men, if men and women were equally likely to get degrees, then we would expect 50 percent of degrees to go to women. That parity was achieved by 1983, as the figure shows, and then women's percent of degrees continued to rise until the early 2000s, after which it stabilized at approximately 57 percent. Thus, for more than 30 years, more American women than men have gotten college degrees. Women are now a slight majority of those getting doctorates as well (England et al. 2020). If we look just at Black Americans, women are an even higher percent of graduates (McDaniel et al. 2011). And, interestingly, the trend toward more women than men getting college degrees is not found only in the United States; similar trends are occurring in many countries around the world (DiPrete and Buchmann 2013).

That more women than men obtain a college degree reflects a few facts. Girls generally like school better, study a bit harder, and get higher grades in elementary and high school. Also, fewer of them have discipline problems in school, and fewer are involved in crime (Steffensmeier and Allan 1996; DiPrete and Buchmann 2013). But, on average, boys have been more involved in crime and have received slightly lower grades than girls for decades, so these

Figure 14.4 Percent of U.S. Men and Women Employed, 1970–2018

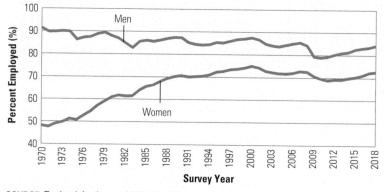

SOURCE: England, Levine, and Mishel, 2020.

NOTE: Percentages pertain to women and men, aged 25 to 54, employed in the last week.

Figure 14.5 Percent of All Baccalaureate Degrees Going to Women, 1970–2015

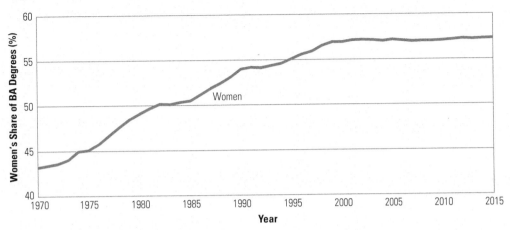

SOURCE: Computed by Paula England from data in England et al. 2020, Figure 3.

facts cannot explain the dramatic shift. Researchers are still trying to figure out why the gender gap favoring college degrees for men has reversed to one favoring college degrees for women. They suspect that even though girls were performing better in high school, parents prioritized paying for sons to attend college in the era when most women became full-time homemakers. Today, both young men and women plan to work for pay during much of their future lives, so now girls doing as well as their brothers are just as likely to go to college, and if they are doing better, they are more likely to complete college (DiPrete and Buchmann 2013).

Change in Women's Jobs and in the Pay Gap

14.2.2 Describe occupational sex segregation and discuss factors affecting the gender pay gap.

In the past, many women worked in traditionally female occupations such as maid, secretary, nurse, or teacher. But since about 1970, an increased number of women have entered traditionally male fields, becoming managers, lawyers, doctors, engineers, or professors, and more women have enlisted in the military. Sociologists measure **occupational sex segregation** with an index that ranges from 100 for complete segregation (all occupations are either 100 percent male or 100 percent female) to 0 for complete integration (each occupation has the same percentage of females as the paid workforce as a whole). Using this measure, occupational sex segregation declined in every decade since 1970, but while declines continue, the pace has slowed in recent decades (England et al. 2020).

Women with college and graduate degrees have entered traditionally male occupations much more frequently than women graduating only from high school. In the United States, as well as most countries, male jobs not requiring a college degree—such as carpenter, welder, electrician, or truck driver—have seen only small numbers of women join their ranks. In less affluent, developing nations, college women are even more likely to choose traditionally male majors like natural science and engineering than they are in the United States (Charles and Bradley 2009).

Despite some integration, jobs remain quite sex segregated. This is partly because socialization still encourages young men and women to aspire to different jobs. Another

pryzmat/Shutterstock

In the last 50 years, occupational segregation has declined significantly. Many of the professional schools in fields such as law and medicine are seeing that half or more of their recent graduates are women, and in some of these fields women are between one-third to one-half of all members of the workforce. One profession—engineering, shown here—has also seen more women in the field, although it still remains a largely male-dominated occupation. (As of 2019, only 13 percent of all licensed engineers nationally were women.)

Figure 14.6 Women's Median Wage as a Percent of Men's, 1970–2018

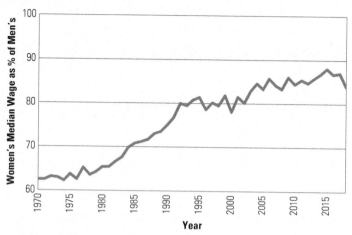

NOTE: The ratio is of women's to men's median hourly wages among full-time working women and men, aged 25 to 54, employed in the last week.
SOURCE: England et al. 2020.

factor is hiring discrimination. Although it has been illegal to refuse to hire people for a job because of their race or sex since the Civil Rights Act was passed in 1964, the law has not entirely ended discrimination.

Women's earnings have also increased relative to men's. Figure 14.6 shows the median women's earnings as a percent of the median men's earnings for each year. (The median for either sex is the level where half the people of that sex are below it and half are above.) The figures include only those who worked full-time the whole year. Women earned about 60 to 65 percent of what men earned in the 1970s. In the 1980s there was a dramatic shift upward in this ratio to about 75 percent by 1990. Since then further equalization has occurred so that women earn between 80 and 85 percent of what men earn. But the graph makes clear that progress has slowed, and that women's earnings relative to men's were no higher in 2018 than around 2005.

Why do women still earn less than men? A number of explanations have been proposed, starting with the simple fact that some employers still pay women less than men in the same job. This has been strictly illegal since the passage of the Equal Pay Act in 1963, unless the difference is based on seniority, performance, or some factor other than sex itself. But it sometimes happens. Because of cultural messages that women should be modest while men should promote themselves, women may negotiate less strongly for pay (Babcock and Laschever 2003). Other times, employers simply offer women less. Another explanation is that employers pay people more when they have more years of experience, and women are more likely than men to have dropped out for a time to take care of children.

Another key factor in the pay gap is that women are concentrated in lower paying occupations. Some of this is because women choose occupations—for example, those

helping other people—that pay less than other jobs requiring the same amount of education. This may reflect different socialization by gender. Another part of the concentration of women in lower paying jobs is that, as mentioned earlier, some employers discriminate against women when hiring in higher paying jobs, leaving the women no choice but to seek lower paying jobs (Reskin 2000).

Additionally, employers often set lower pay rates in jobs filled mostly by women than in different jobs requiring the same amount of education but filled mostly by men (England 1992; Levanon, England, and Allison 2009). For example, administrative assistants (mostly women) in some organizations earn less than assembly workers on the factory line or janitors (mostly men) even though the administrative assistants need more education and as much (though different kinds of) skill.

Why do employers fail to pay mostly female jobs as much as comparably demanding yet different male jobs? Research that I conducted some time ago convinced me that employers often do this out of a biased perception that whatever is done by women must be easier and not as important for the company. Often the bias is unconscious, but many researchers see it as a form of discrimination. While this is not recognized as illegal discrimination in U.S. federal law (England 1992), it is in some other nations. If an employer won't hire someone into a particular job because she is female, or pays a woman less than a man in the same job when their seniority and performance are equal, the employer is violating U.S. law. But American laws do not cover setting lower pay levels in particular jobs because they are filled largely with women, even though there is evidence that employers do this.

Another type of discrimination some women face is discrimination based on motherhood, although in most cases this is illegal. One study investigated this type of discrimination by sending fake résumés to real job ads. Two identical résumés were developed that showed the same credentials and experience except that, in the section of the résumé where many people list their hobbies or community activities, one résumé said the woman was an officer in the Parent–Teacher Association (revealing that she is a mother), while the other résumé said the woman was an officer in some other community club. Just this difference resulted in a significant difference in how many calls for interviews were received. Interestingly, the same manipulation to fake men's resumes showed no fatherhood penalty (Correll et al. 2007).

Some of these factors in the gender pay gap are also factors in why the pay gap is smaller than before. Women's employment has become more continuous, with more women staying employed when they have small children, so the average woman's years of job experience are now closer to those of the average man. Because salaries tend to increase with more years of experience, this convergence between women's and men's years of experience has reduced the pay gap among those employed. However, as we saw in Figure 14.4, women's employment is no longer increasing, so this progress in the experience gap may be stalled as well. As more women than ever have chosen traditionally male, high-paying fields, such as law, medicine, and management, this has increased women's pay relative to men's. Also, enforcement of antidiscrimination law has reduced employer discrimination. All these factors have contributed to the reduction of the gender pay gap. But progress toward gender equality in employment, occupations, and pay has slowed down since the 1990s or early 2000s (England et al. 2020). Figure 14.6 shows the trend toward equality in pay. It shows the ratio of women's median pay to men's median earnings. The ratio moved up much faster in the 1980s than it has in any decade since, although some progress has continued fairly steadily. Interestingly, in the 1990s attitudes about gender, which had become more egalitarian among both men and women in the 1970s and 1980s, reversed and moved in a more conservative direction, but have resumed movement in an egalitarian direction since 2006 (Cotter et al. 2014).

The Impact on Men

14.2.3 Discuss the impact of the gender revolution on men's roles.

The gender revolution has also impacted men's and boys' lives. Since the 1970s, married men began spending substantially more time with their children and doing a bit more housework. In this way, their roles expanded to take on some traditionally female activities, parallel to the way more women moved into traditionally male activities. But what is striking is how asymmetric these changes were. Men moved much less into what had been women's arenas than vice versa. In fact, probably the larger change for boys and men was not taking on formerly female activities, but how all the movement of girls and women onto what had been their turf impacted them. Let's look at how these changes affected men's lives.

We saw that women's employment increased dramatically, especially from the 1960s to about 2000. As this happened, men's attitudes, like women's, became more accepting of female employment (Cotter et al. 2011). But men didn't move in large numbers into being full-time homemakers; we saw in Figure 14.4 that most men are still employed. Indeed, norms of masculinity seem relatively unchanged in insisting that married men are supposed to have a job—so much so that when men aren't employed, couples more often divorce (Sayer et al. 2011; Killewald 2016). Even if norms had shifted to make men's employment more optional,

Employed fathers spend more time caring for their children than they did 50 years ago, but so do employed mothers, and women's hours of paid work have increased much more than men's hours in household work. Why do men's roles seem to be more resistant to change than women's?

it would have been impractical for most couples, as the wives entering employment typically didn't make as much money as their husbands, so families would have taken a reduction in pay if men quit their jobs.

Many advocates of work–family balance and gender equality have hoped that more couples could have each partner employed half the time while they share child-rearing and household work relatively equally. Surveys show that many young adults would like this arrangement if they could have it without penalty to their careers (Pedulla and Thébaud 2015). But that is very difficult to do without financial sacrifice in the U.S. economy. In all countries in the European Union, the law requires that employers pay part-time workers the same amount per hour as full-time workers in the same job. But in the United States, employers do not have that constraint, and part-time jobs typically pay substantially less per hour than the same job done a full 40 (or more) hours per week. Thus, few couples could move from one full-time earner to each partner working half-time without a loss in income. For all these reasons, the biggest change for men as a result of women's increased employment was not that more men started staying home or working part-time but that many of them got used to being part of a two-earner couple. The obvious benefit of this for men is that they share in the increased earnings that result. But it also means that women are more able to support themselves and more apt to leave unhappy marriages (Sayer et al. 2011).

With more women working for pay, women also don't have as much time for housework, so we might expect that women would look to men to do more housework and childcare than before. Employed fathers increased the time they spent caring for children substantially, but so did mothers (Bianchi et al. 2006). Men's housework on average did increase, but only by a small amount. See Figure 14.7 for evidence on this, drawing from surveys asking people how much housework they did on a recent day, excluding time in childcare. It shows that between 1965 and 1995, on average, married women decreased their housework by about 2.5 hours per day. This was mainly because more of them took jobs. But married men increased their housework by only a little more than 1 hour a day. Since then, as the figure shows there has been little change in either men's or women's housework and, thus, little change in the gender gap whereby women do approximately an hour a day more housework than men. The gender division of household work and paid work in couples is an example of how women have entered traditionally male spheres (for example, employment) more than men have taken on traditionally female activities (for example, housework).

As more women chose traditionally male fields of study in college, and careers previously filled mostly by men, very few men decided in favor of traditionally female majors, like elementary education, and only a trickle of men moved into occupations filled mostly with women. Thus, the desegregation of occupations and fields of study was a largely one-way street, with women moving into traditionally male fields while few men entered traditionally female fields (England 2010).

Men didn't enter female-dominated occupations in large numbers for several reasons. One is that these occupations, as we discussed earlier, often pay less than male-dominated occupations—even when you compare jobs requiring the same amount of skill or education. Second, as boys, their socialization often encouraged "guy" hobbies and activities more consistent with jobs such as athletic coach or engineer than preschool teacher or fashion designer. In addition, the social stigma of doing anything that makes a male seem feminine is much greater than any parallel stigma of females engaging in male-identified activities. It has long been a feature of our culture that males are ridiculed for doing anything seen as feminine. Thus, men risk both lowering their income and being stigmatized if they undertake activities and jobs thought of as feminine. Some still do so because of a real sense of calling in a caring profession or because some unusual life circumstance brought them into a nontraditional role. While they may earn less than if they chose a more male-dominated field, just as women do, research shows that men are not treated worse than women within the female jobs but, if anything, tend to be welcomed and rise to the top of these fields (Budig 2002).

In sum, the large changes in gender roles of the last 50 years have moved men into what had been female realms much less than they have moved women into previously male-dominated activities. It has been less appealing for men to enter traditionally female activities such as childcare, homemaking, and female occupations because they often pay less than traditionally male occupations, if at all, and such moves are much more stigmatized than women taking on male roles. Of course, the changes in girls' and women's lives have created changes for boys and men. Boys have had to get used to girls competing with them more openly in school, and men find women competing for the same types of jobs they have. Men have gotten used to employed wives, and most now accept women's employment.

At the same time that all this has happened, since about 1973, earnings have become much more unequal among men. Earnings for men at the top have increased enormously, while those of men at the very bottom have decreased, and those of men in the middle class have stagnated (Eckstein and Nagypal 2004; Gordon and Dew-Becker 2007; Autor et al. 2008; England et al. 2020). (These figures are after adjusting for changes in the cost of living.) As global

Figure 14.7 Husbands' and Wives' Average Daily Housework Hours, 1965–2019

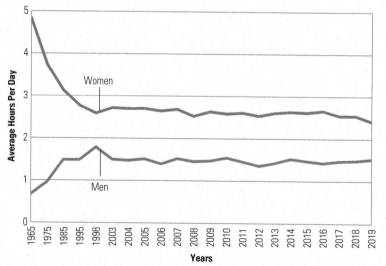

SOURCE: Averages pertain to married women and men, aged 25 to 64. For 1965–2003, Bianchi et al. 2012. For later years, Paula England's computations from American Time Use Survey.

competition has increased, few employers provide secure employment for life. Whole industries have moved largely overseas, taking away many good-paying, skilled manual jobs in U.S. factories. Thus, for most men, it is increasingly difficult to count on being able to hold a job steadily, to earn more than their fathers, and to earn more as they get older—all features of the American Dream. Yet

there is still a strong norm that suggests men are responsible to be breadwinners in families, even as acceptance has grown for women also sharing this role. Men are still judged—in a way that women are not—by their earnings, even as changes in the U.S. economy have made it more difficult for many men to do this and as they face increasing competition from women who have equal education.

Ingolf Pompe/Image Professionals GmbH/Alamy Stock Photo

BIG QUESTION 14.3 How Are Our Sex Lives Shaped by Biology and Society?

SEXUALITIES

We've already examined many aspects of men's and women's lives, but we've so far ignored one key area: Sex. We often think of sex as an entirely natural, biological matter, not socially constructed at all. It seems biological because nonhuman animals as well as humans have sex, and the age at which we are interested in sex is affected by hormones. There is no question that sexual attractions and behavior are affected by biology, but, as we'll consider in this section, they are also strongly affected by social construction (Gagnon and Simon 1973).

For example, social norms regulate fine details about what appearances are seen as sexually appealing or disgusting. In China prior to 1920, many upper-class girls' feet were bound, a painful process that stunted their growth; men evidently found tiny feet sexually alluring (Mackie 1996). Today's notion that thin women are the most beautiful would mystify people in many cultures, where such women would be seen as unhealthy and not sexy at all! In Mauritania, a country in West Africa where among some groups plumpness is considered beauty, many young girls are force-fed to become fat enough to attract a mate (Waterlow 2013).

Societies also put many restrictions on sex. In some societies, sex with same-sex partners is illegal and punishable by prison time (Ottosson 2010), while, by contrast, the right to same-sex marriage is protected by law in the

Chris Hammond Photography/Alamy Stock Photo

In the "Long Neck" tribe in Northern Thailand, women are seen as more beautiful if they have long necks, and some take drastic measures to achieve this beauty. Most societies strongly encourage women to take steps to alter their bodies in some way.

United States and in some countries around in the world. Having sex and bearing children outside the context of marriage have been stigmatized in some historical periods, and still are today in some nations, but they are extremely common in other societies. In this section, we will explore these and other social influences on sexualities.

Sexual Orientation and Identities

14.3.1 Discuss the influence of biology and society on sexual orientation.

The term **sexual orientation** refers to whether individuals are attracted to different-sex partners, partners of their same sex, or both. Today, when talking about the identities that sometimes correspond with these orientations, we generally distinguish three groups: *Heterosexuals*, gay men and lesbians (although sometimes the term *gay* is also used to describe either men or women), and *bisexuals*. But not everyone fits neatly into one of these three categories. One researcher writing decades ago suggested a continuum exists from homosexual to heterosexual and that people could be various places along this scale (Kinsey et al. [1948] 1998; Kinsey et al. [1953] 1998; Sell 1997). A recent study followed women who, at the beginning of the study, identified as something other than heterosexual. The study found that about two-thirds of these women shifted the sexual orientation they identified with over 10 years. They moved in all directions between identifying with the labels *lesbian, bisexual,* and *heterosexual,* and even preferring no label (Diamond 2008). Also, this study and others have shown that behavior (who one has sex with), attraction (the sex(es) or gender(s) one is attracted to), and identity (for example, bisexual, or heterosexual) are not always consistent (Brown and England 2016; Diamond 2008).

An interesting question is where our sexual orientation comes from. As with other aspects of sex, there is evidence that both biology and society have their effects. Evidence that genetics affect sexual orientation comes from research on twins and other siblings. Researchers asked samples of gay men or lesbians, some of whom were twins, about the sexual orientation of their siblings. They compared how often same-sex siblings—including identical twins, fraternal twins, and adoptive siblings—of gay or lesbian individuals were also homosexual. Siblings differ in their degree of genetic relatedness—with identical twins having identical genes, fraternal twins being as related as nontwin siblings, and adoptive siblings being the least genetically similar. The researchers found that a higher percentage of the identical twins of gay men were also gay, compared to a lower percentage of the fraternal twins of gay brothers and an even lower percentage of the adoptive brothers of gay men. A similar pattern was found for women (Bailey and Pillard 1991; Bailey et al. 1993, 2000). On the one hand, the study proves that genes don't entirely determine sexual orientation

because even among identical twins, when one is gay or lesbian, most of the time the other is not. Because identical twins are genetically identical, if they don't have the same sexual orientation, something else from their experiences must explain their differences (Stein 2001). On the other hand, the study shows that there is some influence of genes on sexual orientation as the finding is that siblings who are more genetically related are more similar in sexual orientation than siblings who are less genetically related.

Sexual Behavior

14.3.2 Discuss the impact of biology and society on sexual behavior.

How do biology and society affect other aspects of our sexual behavior? A big debate in this area is whether men like casual sex more than women, and, if so, if this is because of some biological difference or is a result of social influences (Schmitt 2003). Evolutionary theories say that this is a gender difference that we would expect to have evolved millennia ago. According to these theories, in any population, variation in genes occurs at random. Some of the randomly occurring new genes lead to things that enhance survival, others hurt survival, and still others are neutral. Over many thousands of years, the genes that enhance survival will be more represented in the population because the people (or other animals) with these genes are more likely to survive long enough to reproduce, and their descendants will carry those genes. If there are sex-specific genes, then genes that helped women to produce offspring that survive will be carried in women today, while genes that helped men produce offspring that survive will be carried in men today. Because a woman carries a fetus for nine months, her number of surviving children will not be enhanced much by frequent sex with multiple partners. But this is different for males, who could potentially impregnate many women in the nine-month period it takes a woman to gestate one child. Thus, any combination of genes that encouraged frequent, casual sex would increase men's number of offspring and the representation of this combination of genes in the future gene pool. But it probably would not increase women's. According to one evolutionary theory, this is why evolution led to more preference for casual sex among men (Buss 1994).

Even if evolution is one factor in why men seek casual sex more than women, sociologists also point to a social factor. Our culture features a **double standard of sexuality** (Crawford and Popp 2003; England, Shafer, and Fogarty 2008; Kreager and Staff 2009; England and Bearak 2014). This is the tendency to judge women more harshly than men for having casual sex. One piece of evidence that a double standard is in play is that we have many more pejorative terms to refer to women who we think have sex too casually—terms like *slut* or *whore*—than we have for

Frilet Patrick/Hemis/Alamy Stock Photo

Nightclubs and college parties generally feature women showing more skin than men. This has been true for decades. Why?

men doing the same thing. Many men engage in the same behavior, but we are less likely to call them similar names. There are some terms like this to refer to men (such as *man whore* or *player*), but they are less consistently negative. Indeed, within male peer culture, being a player is often a positive source of status. Recognizing the double standard, sociologists point out that women are more motivated than men to avoid casual sex because it does greater damage to their reputations. It is not entirely a matter of a biologically dictated lack of interest.

One way that we know biology has some relevance to sex is that among youth of the same age, those who are experiencing puberty and have the associated increases in certain hormones are more likely to have sexual fantasies and engage in sexual behavior. But the same study that shows this also shows that social factors are relevant. For example, youth brought up in religious households that discourage early sex are less likely to engage in such behavior (Udry 1988). Further evidence of social influences on sex is the fact that the prevalence of sex before marriage has changed quite drastically in most modern societies, as we'll discuss later.

LGBTQ Discrimination

14.3.3 Identify the biases that lesbian, gay, bisexual, transgender, and questioning (LGBTQ) individuals encounter.

Sociologists use the term *minority* to refer to groups that are relatively small in number. For example, in the United States, Blacks, Latinxs, and Asians are racial or ethnic minorities, and Jews and Muslims are religious minorities. Similarly, LGBTQ individuals are sexual minorities. In terms of gender, people who have a gender identity that is the same as the one they were assigned at birth, those who are **cisgender**, are the dominant group, while those who have a gender identity that is different from the one they were assigned, those who are transgender people are minorities. In terms of sexualities, heterosexuals comprise the dominant group, meaning that lesbians, gays, and those who are bisexual are minorities.

To examine one example of what it means to be a member of a sexual minority group, consider the situation of a hypothetical 17-year-old named Noah, who has just recently begun to identify himself as gay. If Noah is typical of the young American gay men interviewed in one study, he was first aware of attractions to other males at age 8, first knew the meaning of the term *homosexual* at age 10, first applied the term *homosexual* to his own attractions at age 13, and first had sexual contact with another male at 14, yet he didn't think of himself as gay until age 17, won't tell any of his friends he is gay until age 18, and won't tell his family until age 19 (Savin-Williams 1998). Why the secrecy and the delay in squaring one's identity with one's urges? The answer lies in the messages about sexual orientation that one gets from social experiences growing up. This is called **heteronormativity**, a situation where the culture and institutions send the message that heterosexuality is the norm.

To see what heteronormativity is like, consider all the experiences our hypothetical young man is likely to have had growing up. Noah listens to rock music, and most of the songs are about sex or romance between women and men. The plots of most television shows or movies feature romances or sexual escapades between women and men. In his high school, bias against gays abounds (Pascoe 2007). His male friends frequently insult each other with the pejorative term for gay men, and another common put-down is, "You're so gay!" Noah was never on the receiving end of these insults, and he doesn't want to be, either; that's one reason he doesn't want to tell people at his high school that he is gay. He also hears friends say, "No homo" jokingly when they are touching each other. At his family's church, nothing is said pro or con about gay people, but his friend who belongs to a more conservative church says that, at his church, the preacher talks about the evils of being gay from the pulpit. Noah reads that same-sex marriage is now legal in the United States, but the only weddings he or his parents have been to involve a man marrying a woman. He has never met a married couple consisting of two men. He certainly can't imagine gaining popularity, and figures he might invite ridicule if he asks a boy to his senior prom. It is little wonder that Noah gets the impression that his same-sex attractions are something to hide. His experience is typical of many young people growing up gay, lesbian, or bisexual. You can see from Noah's example some of the difficulties of growing up as a member of a sexual minority in a heteronormative environment.

But some members of the LGBTQ community experience even worse things. Those who show affection for someone of the same sex are often ridiculed by youth peer groups, regardless of whether they appear masculine or feminine. Some employers refuse to hire those they think are gay or fire people upon discovering it (Tilcsik 2011; Mishel 2016). Such discrimination, even if completely open, does not violate any federal law; discrimination in employment based on race, religion, sex, or national origin is illegal, but discrimination based on sexual orientation is not prohibited by U.S. federal law, although some states and cities now have such laws. In renting or selling housing, it is illegal to discriminate based on race according to federal law, but, again, there is no federal protection if someone won't rent to gay people, although some states and cities have such protections. Surveys indicate nearly half of people in the LGBTQ community report that they experienced some kind of discrimination in housing or employment based on sexual orientation, about 40 percent report being threatened with violence, and about 80 percent say they have been verbally harassed because of their sexual orientation. Terms used for any of these kinds of bias directed at a person because of their sexual orientation are **heterosexism** or **homophobia**; these terms are often used interchangeably. Probably as a result of these various forms of ridicule and harassment, gay and lesbian youth are two to three times as likely to commit suicide as heterosexual youth (O'Brien 2000). If one dresses or looks in a way that social norms see as more appropriate for the other sex, one may be stigmatized and sometimes even visited with violence in school or on the street, whether or not one is actually gay or lesbian.

Despite this grim picture of what a young person growing up as a member of a sexual minority has to face, the scene has changed substantially over the last few decades, due in part to a social movement for gay rights (Armstrong 2002) and to a change in public opinion toward more tolerance of sexual diversity. The gay rights movement has sought to make gay, lesbian, bisexual, and transgender people appear as individual human beings

rather than as negative stereotypes, to support legislation against various sorts of discrimination based on sexual orientation, and to get rid of legislation that explicitly forbids sexuality or marriage between those of the same sex.

Many things have changed in a way more friendly to the lives of LGBTQ people. The U.S. military dropped its ban on service by gay and lesbian people in 2011. Most colleges and universities have LGBTQ centers providing services and a place to socialize. Many cities also have such centers. Some high schools have gay/straight alliance groups. Newspapers and magazines are directed at the LGBTQ community. There are neighborhoods, sometimes called "gayborhoods," with high concentrations of LGBTQ people living in one area of some large cities. Some gay college and professional athletes have "come out"; in 2013, veteran NBA player Jason Collins announced he was gay, and in 2014 Michael Sam was the first openly gay football player to be drafted by an NFL team. Finally, in the world of beauty pageants, 2016 marked the first year an openly lesbian Miss America contestant competed.

Mark Bussell

The struggle over bathroom freedoms has become especially heated in recent years. In some places such as New York City, by law all bathrooms are supposed to be gender neutral, although many private establishments continue to maintain gendered bathrooms. In the example above, an attempt to accommodate everyone means the creation of three types of bathrooms: Men's, women's, and gender neutral ("all-gender"). To even ask the question of why bathrooms are gendered in the first place is to raise profound questions about gender and society.

Yet these changes have brought about a strong backlash. Some groups oppose public acceptance of gay lifestyles because they challenge their members' ideas of gender and family. Some opposition stems from religious teachings that same-sex relationships is wrong. Other religions practice tolerance of same-sex love and sex. These conflicting views have coalesced in recent political controversies over same-sex marriage. In 1993, a state court in Hawaii said that the state law limiting marriage to unions of one man and one woman was unconstitutional unless the state could show some compelling reason for it. Political mobilization against this ruling led to passage of an amendment to Hawaii's state constitution stating that the legislature could limit marriage to male–female couples. Opponents of gay marriage, afraid that other states would get rid of their restrictions of marriage to male–female couples, lobbied Congress to pass a law stating that states prohibiting gay marriage would not have to recognize the gay marriages allowed in other states. (Prior to this most states had recognized marriages contracted in other states, so that, for example, a couple married in California who moved to Oregon would be considered married in Oregon as well.) In 1996, Congress adopted the federal

Defense of Marriage Act (DOMA). It said that for purposes of any federal benefits that hinge on marriage, marriage refers only to the legal union of one man with one woman. Under this law, for example, partners in a lesbian or gay male marriage do not have the same right to pass property from one to the other upon death without paying any federal estate tax, a right enshrined in federal law for married couples. In 2013, the U.S. Supreme Court ruled in *U.S.* v. *Windsor* that DOMA violated the U.S. Constitution; this ruling means that same-sex spouses are entitled to the same federal benefits as heterosexual spouses, such as exemption from the federal estate tax if one spouse dies and leaves money to the other.

Massachusetts was the first U.S. state to legalize same-sex marriage, in 2004. A few other states followed between 2004 and 2012, but during that period even more states passed state versions of something like DOMA prohibiting same-sex marriage. Other states provided an option of domestic partnerships for same-sex couples that had some of the benefits of marriage. However, shortly after the *U.S.* v. *Windsor* case was decided, many lower courts started to overturn prohibitions on same-sex marriage so that by 2014, 30 of the

50 states permitted same-sex marriage. Then, in the following year, the United States Supreme Court ruled in *Obergefell* v. *Hodges* that the Fourteenth Amendment to the United States Constitution guarantees the right to marry to same-sex couples, wherever they might reside within the United States. Outside the United States, the Netherlands became the first country to allow same-sex marriage in 2001, and since then Belgium, Canada, Spain, South Africa, Norway, Sweden, Portugal, Iceland, Argentina, Denmark, Brazil, France, Uruguay, New Zealand, England, Wales, and Luxembourg have followed suit. Among the most recent countries are Germany (2017), Australia (2017), Austria (2019), Iceland (2020), Taiwan (2019), and Costa Rice (2020).

In the United States, attitudes toward same-sex marriage are clearly changing. As Figure 14.8 shows, there has been a massive increase in support for same-sex marriage since 1988. In fact, this issue has seen faster change in attitudes than almost any social issue in recent history (Rosenfeld 2021).

mauritius images GmbH/Alamy Stock Photo

The annual gay pride parades in June, now generally known as Pride (to be more inclusive), are held in most cities in the United States and around the world in late June every year. This event, which commemorates the struggle against a police crackdown in 1969 at New York's Stonewall Inn, has become an important part of the struggle for sexual equality.

Figure 14.8 Percent Agreeing That Same-Sex Marriage Should Be Legal, 1988–2018

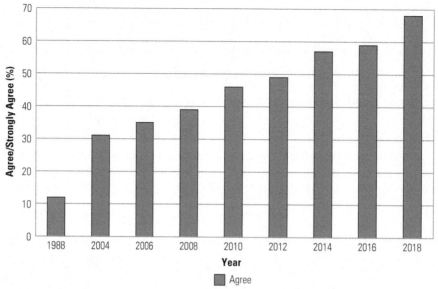

NOTE: The question read, "Should homosexuals have the right to marry one another?" Percents are those who agree or strongly agree. Percents calculated using GSS default weight for all years.
SOURCE: Paula England's calculations from General Social Surveys, various years.

BIG QUESTION 14.4 How Has Sexual Behavior Changed in the Last 50 Years?

THE SEXUAL REVOLUTION AND BEYOND

Over the last 50 years, sexual behavior of young unmarried adults has changed substantially. There has been some, but much less, change in the practices of married couples. In this section, we will explore changes regarding sex and childbearing outside the context of marriage. We will also explore persisting gender inequality in heterosexual relationships, and attempts to lessen sexual assault and sexual harassment.

Sex Outside of Marriage

14.4.1 Discuss how attitudes and behaviors involving sex outside of marriage in relationships, and casual sex outside of exclusive relationships have changed over the last 50 years.

To look at changes in sexual behavior, it is best to rely on data from surveys based on **probability samples**. This method of drawing a sample to survey from the U.S. population ensures that everyone has an equal probability of

Figure 14.9 Percent of Women Who Had Sex Before Marriage by Birth Cohort

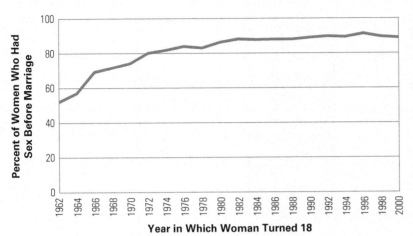

SOURCE: Wu et al. 2020.

being in the sample, so we can be confident it is representative of the population. Surveys using probability samples have asked Americans about the age at which they first had (penile/vaginal) intercourse as well as the age they first married, if they have. These surveys paint a picture of a substantial increase in the proportion of Americans having sex outside the context of marriage. Figure 14.9 classifies women by the year in which they turned 18, and shows that if you go back to those turning 18 in 1962, only slightly more than half of women ever had intercourse before marriage. But this percent rose steadily during what we sometimes call the "sexual revolution." Among those turning 18 in 1990 or more recently, approximately 90 percent had sex before marriage. In most groups, sex before marriage has become acceptable. In some religiously conservative groups (Christian, Jewish, or Muslim), however, young people are taught to avoid sex outside of marriage, and some even take virginity pledges. For the most part, though, studies show that a teen's religious denomination doesn't have much effect on whether he or she has sex. Instead, more religious youth, from almost any denomination or faith tradition, tend to start having sex later, but, still, many have sex before marriage (Regnerus 2007).

What do parents think about their own children having sex? It depends on what country you live in. One study compared attitudes of American and Dutch middle-class parents by interviewing parents of 16-year-olds in both nations. The researcher asked parents how they would feel about their son or daughter having a girlfriend or boyfriend sleep overnight in the family's home. Almost all Dutch parents said this was okay. They thought sex should be in a relationship with a nice person and saw sex as a natural and appropriate progression of a relationship. They preferred to have their teen child have sex at home in a safe, comfortable place. They wanted to talk to their child about using protection from sexually transmitted

infections (STIs) and pregnancy. In answer to the same question, almost all the American parents said they were vehemently against their child having sex. They expressed concern that kids who have sex are driven by "raging hormones," not making considered decisions. They saw teen sex as the outcome of a "battle of the sexes" rather than envisioning a caring relationship among the teens. Even if they knew that sex was common and their own child might be doing it, most didn't want to approve of it in their own home (Schalet 2011).

American parents may hope that their children don't have sex while still in high school, but at least half of them do have first intercourse that early, as Figure 14.10 shows. The median age at first intercourse is somewhere between the 17th and 18th birthday, about the end of high school. Only 11 percent of girls and 16 pecent of boys have intercourse by age 15, but over 50 percent have done so by age 18 and 75 percent by age 20. It is also worth noticing, however, that fully a quarter are still virgins at age 20. While the trend in the past had been toward an earlier age at first intercourse, that trend has reversed in the last couple of decades (Martinez and Abma 2015).

Since sex outside of marriage became almost universal, what has changed over time is in what context it typically occurs, with the acceptable contexts getting more casual. In the 1950s and 1960s, those who had sex outside of marriage often did so only with the person they later married. In the 1970s, sex became common in relationships, and since then, increasingly

Figure 14.10 Percent of Youth Who Have Had Sex by Age 15 to 20

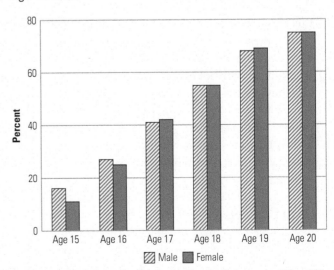

NOTE: Cumulative percentage of males and females between ages 15 and 24 who have had sex, 2011–2015.
SOURCE: Abma and Martinez, 2017.

The rise of hookup culture among young people has made it more common to have sex or intimate contact without an existing relationship. But some hookups do lead to relationships or at least romantic dates.

young couples in relationships have become involved in **cohabitation**, the term sociologists and demographers use to describe the act of living together as an unmarried couple. These relationships may be serious enough that couples are considering marriage, or they may involve couples who are not engaged but just dating and who cohabit for practical reasons, such as to save money by sharing rent. It is only in recent decades that sexual activity has become common in casual liaisons where there is no expectation that either party expects a relationship to ensue. Youth culture uses different terms to refer to such a liaison, one of which is a **hookup** (Hirsch and Kahn 2020; Wade 2017).

On college campuses today, when students say they "hooked up," this can mean anything from just making out to having intercourse. In an online survey of students this chapter's author conducted at over 20 colleges and universities, one of the questions asked students whether they had ever hooked up in college with someone with whom they were not in a relationship. For those who said yes, they were asked to report on what happened sexually in their most recent hookup. Figure 14.11 shows what percentage was in each category, where hookups were classified by how far students went sexually (so, for example, if you made out and had intercourse, you were classified as having intercourse).

Figure 14.11 shows that 40 percent of hookups involve intercourse. These are often cases where the couple had hooked up together before. Thirty-five percent of hookups involved no more than kissing and nongenital touching. Most hookups were with someone the student already knew at least moderately well. Qualitative interviews I conducted with students showed that while many

hookups led nowhere, some relationships started with hookups, sometimes with one or more dates between hooking up and defining the relationship as exclusive (England et al. 2008).

Births Outside of Marriage

14.4.2 Discuss changing rates of births outside of marriage.

Since the 1960s, as the average age at marriage has increased and sex outside of marriage has become more common (Ellwood and Jencks 2004), births outside of marriage have also become more common. In fact, Figure 14.12 shows a long-term trend going back to 1940 of an increasing proportion of births being outside of marriage. However, the percent of births to unmarried women has stabilized at about 40 percent, not increasing more since about 2008. The increase was seen in all education, income, and racial groups. But young women and men from lower income families, who often don't have the academic record or money to complete college, have long been more likely to have children outside the context of marriage. Figure 14.13 shows that those with the least education are mostly likely to have a child while unmarried. Also, the most disadvantaged racial groups, such as Blacks and Native Americans, are mostly likely to have births outside marriage (Hamilton et al. 2015). These class and racial

Figure 14.11 How Far College Students Went on Their Most Recent Hookup

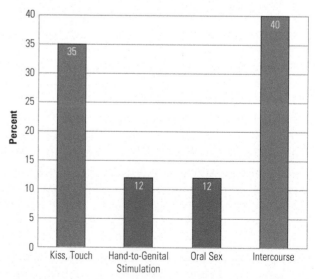

SOURCE: Based on Paula England's calculations from Online College Social Life Survey.

Figure 14.12 Percent of All Births to Unmarried Women, 1940–2018

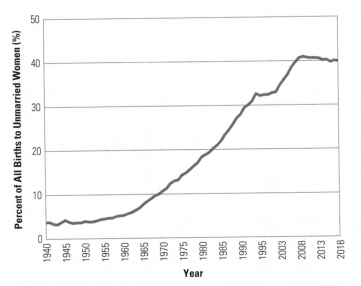

Figure 14.13 Percent of Births to Unmarried Women by Education Level, 2016

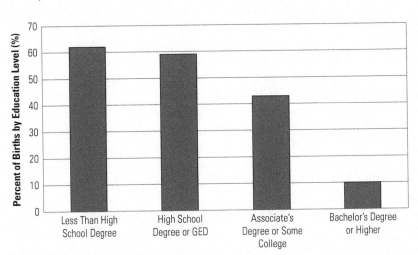

differences in nonmarital births are not a result of a greater tendency to have sex outside of marriage among those who are more disadvantaged; premarital sex is very common in youth of all education levels. The key difference is that those at lower education and income levels are less consistent in using birth control (England, McClintock, and Shafer 2011; England 2016). One factor in the increase in nonmarital births is that as sex outside of marriage has become more common, the stigma of pregnancy publicly revealing sex before marriage has greatly diminished. Researchers suggest that because of this, couples do not as often marry in response to a pregnancy as previously (Akerlof et al. 1996).

Gender Inequality in Sex and Relationships

14.4.3 Discuss the role that gendered expectations play in sexual and romantic behavior.

The availability of the birth control pill in the 1960s made it easier to have sex as a young adult, go to college, and delay marriage until after college without fear of pregnancy before marriage. This helped women to prepare for careers by going to college. Thus, the availability of the pill and the increase in sex outside of marriage went along with increased gender equality in education and the labor market (Bailey 2006).

Yet while women's career aspirations are now much more equal to men's than previously, gender differences in what is expected in the romantic and sexual realm have changed surprisingly little, even at the same time that norms of whether sex outside of marriage was acceptable were changing. In my college online survey mentioned earlier, when asked who asked whom out on their most recent date, students reported that the man did the asking in about 90 percent of cases. When asked who initiated sexual activity on a hookup, more reported that men did than women.

Interestingly, hookups lead to orgasm much less often for women than men. Figure 14.14 shows the percentage of male versus female college students who reported having an orgasm depending on whether the event they were reporting on was a first-time hookup with this partner, the second or third hookup with this partner, the fourth or more hookup with this partner, or the most recent time in a relationship of at least six months when they did something sexual beyond just kissing. The figure shows that both men and women are much more likely to orgasm with a partner when they've hooked up several times before. This is partly because they go farther sexually. Talking to women, my research team and I learned that it is also because partners learn more about how to please each other with experience. Both men and women have an even higher chance of orgasm in relationships. This is again partly because they go farther sexually and have more practice with each other. Interviews with men and women students revealed that it is also because of the affection in relationships that makes partners care more about each other's pleasure.

The gender gap in orgasm is much larger in early hookups than in later hookups with the same partner, and the gender gap in orgasm is smallest in relationships

Figure 14.14 Percent of College Women and Men Reporting Orgasm in Various Contexts

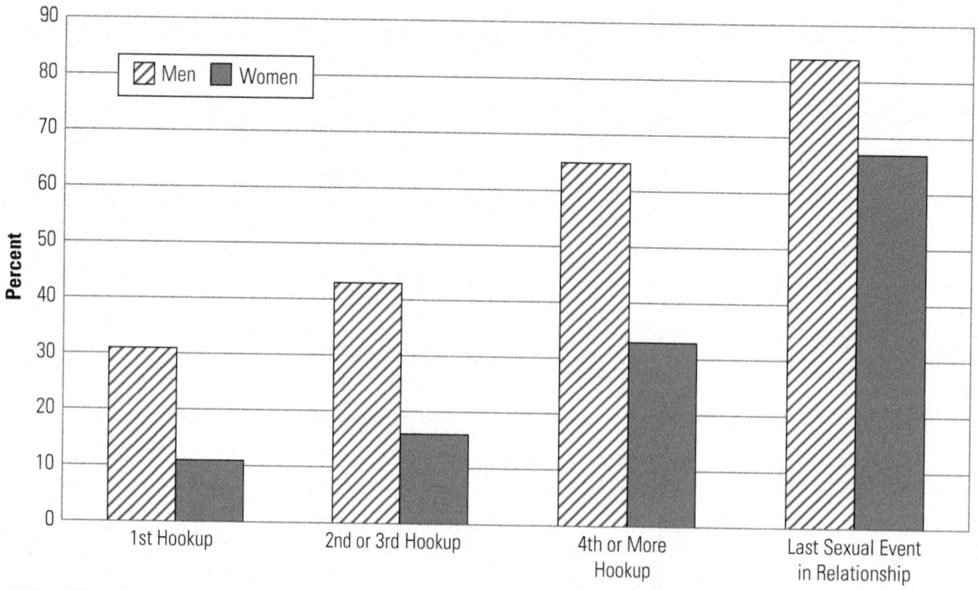

SOURCE: Based on Paula England's calculations from Online College Social Life Survey.

(see Figure 14.14). Women have orgasms only one-third as frequently as men during first hookups. It could be said that the gender gap in orgasm is much bigger than the gender gap in pay! Using in-depth interviews, a team of researchers and I found that men report really caring about the pleasure of their girlfriends but being much more selfish in hookups. In contrast, women seemed to feel an obligation to try to give pleasure to their male partners whether they were in casual hookups or relationships. Interpreting this finding, we argued that the sexual double standard may explain this. That is, perhaps men and women are more ambivalent about whether women deserve sexual pleasure in a hookup than they are about men's entitlement to pleasure in a casual context (Armstrong et al. 2012).

Overall, while sex outside of marriage has become more acceptable, the extent to which sexual and relational behavior follows gendered expectations has changed very little. While of course there are exceptions, the expectation that men ask women on dates, initiate sexual activity, propose marriage, and are less severely judged for casual sex still remains.

Unwanted Sex: Rape, Sexual Assault, and Sexual Harassment

14.4.4 Describe the varieties of unwanted sexual encounters.

Unwanted sexual experiences—sexual assault, rape, and sexual harassment—are major issues in the United States (and all other countries). The term **sexual assault**, when used by researchers, refers to any sexual activity when consent is not obtained or given freely (Basile et al. 2007; Black et al. 2011). **Rape** is the most widely used term, although it is often used to describe unwanted sexual intercourse or penetration of a body opening, leaving out other types of forced or unwanted sexual encounters, such as unwanted sexual touching. Thus, sexual assault includes rape but is also a broader term. **Sexual harassment** represents a second, far more common kind of unwanted behavior. It has been defined as "unwelcome sexual advances, requests for sexual favors, and other verbal or physical conduct of a sexual nature" (Equal Employment Opportunity Commission 2021). The term *sexual harassment* is often used to refer to unwanted sexual advances from a boss or coworker in an employment setting, although it can occur in any setting. Although anyone can experience sexual assault, studies show that rape victims are far more likely to be women; a national survey by the Centers for Disease Control (CDC) estimated that one in five (19.3 percent) women reported experiencing rape at some point in their lives, compared to 1 in 60 (1.7 percent) men (Breiding 2014; Smith et al. 2018). Rates of all kinds of sexual assault and harassment are reported more by women than men, but the disparity is not as great for these broader categories; for example, only about twice as many women as men report experiencing any kind of assault or harassment (Breiding 2014; Ford 2018).

One common but distinct form of unwanted sexual behavior experienced by many women and gay men is called **street harassment**, such as catcalling or other forms of unwanted verbal sexual advances or unwanted comments on

Rick Madonik/ZUMA Press/Newscom

Marchers at a Take Back the Night rally in Toronto, Canada, an annual event held in cities and on college campuses around the world to protest sexual and domestic violence in all forms.

However, research also shows that women are less likely to perceive a threat of sexual assault when they are with friends or acquaintances (Armstrong, Hamilton, and Sweeney 2006; Abbey et al. 2014). Thus, a diminished sense of danger may lead women to be more at risk with men they know. Research also shows women are less likely to report sexual assault from a close acquaintance, which could be an incentive for perpetrators to target closer acquaintances (Estrich 1987). More broadly, sociologists argue that the sexual double standard, discussed previously, makes sexual assault and sexual harassment more likely because it promotes the idea that men have a right to sexual agency and pleasure, while women are always at risk of being judged for consensual sex outside relationships, and at risk of being seen as responsible for even unwanted sex or sexual attention.

one's appearance. Although there is more limited data on the prevalence of this kind of harassment, one advocacy group conducted a representative survey and found that 65 percent of women and 25 percent of men experienced unwanted street harassment (with a much higher percentage of gay than straight men reporting harassment) (Kearl 2014). This type of harassment is not only annoying, but it also serves to remind victims of the all-too-real possibility of rape or other types of sexual violence (Fairchild and Rudman 2008). Many sociologists have argued that sexual violence and harassment are expressions of broader types of gender inequality. In this understanding, sexual assault or sexual harassment is not just about sex but also about power.

Researchers studying rape and sexual assault have identified a variety of factors related to individuals becoming victimized. In particular, the association between alcohol use and sexual assault is well documented. For example, between 50 and 75 percent of sexual assault incidents among college students involve alcohol consumption by the victim, perpetrator, or both (Abbey 2002; Fisher et al. 2010). Sexual assault is also more common with a man whom a woman knows, rather than with a total stranger (Fisher et al. 2010; Abbey et al. 2014). This is largely because men have more of an opportunity to sexually assault women whom they know (such as their friends, dates, and girlfriends), simply because they have more access to them socially (Cohen and Felson 1979). Moreover, in order to resist or avoid sexual assault, a woman must recognize she is in danger. Studies show that physical resistance decreases the likelihood that a woman will experience a completed acquaintance rape (Ullman 2007).

One important area of research has been on the consequences of sexual assault. Victims may suffer a wide variety of harms. Mental anguish and physical and health consequences are common. Victims often experience post-traumatic stress disorder (PTSD), in which the trauma from the initial assault continues to trigger negative thoughts and/or bring on severe anxieties. Depressive symptoms, fearfulness, psychological distress, and in some cases levels of alcohol or drug abuse have all been found to be higher in assault victims compared to nonvictims (Atkeson et al. 1982; Calhoun et al. 1982; McMullin and White 2006; Santaularia et al. 2014). The ability of victims to cope with an assault will vary; getting high-quality treatment and counseling can greatly reduce the development and persistence of PTSD symptoms in some cases. On the other hand, victims who suppress the assault or rely on avoidance strategies tend to cope less successfully (Littleton and Breitkopf 2006).

Despite the pervasiveness of sexual violence, many of the victims of sexual assault do not want to discuss or report the incident to the authorities. Understandably, collecting data on sexual victimization can be sensitive, particularly when the line between inappropriate behavior and a criminal offense can be murky. In addition, many victims endure what some have called a "second assault" when they receive negative reactions as they tell others of their assault. These negative reactions, which affect one-third to two-thirds of victims, range from disbelief to victim blaming and can lead the victim to have detrimental mental and physical health effects (Ullman 2010). Negative reactions can cause victims to be uncertain about whether their experience counts as heterosexual assault, can create or reinforce feelings of self-blame, and may silence victims from disclosing their experience again (Ahrens 2006).

In recent decades, sexual violence and harassment against women on college and university campuses has been the subject of intense controversy (Hirsch and Khan 2020). Unfortunately, as many college students have experienced, campuses may not be "Ivory Tower" safe havens but rather environments that pose unique risks for sexual assault (Armstrong et al. 2006). Depending on how the question is asked, somewhere between 14 percent and 26 percent of women report experiencing sexual assault during college (Armstrong and Budnick 2015). And college administrators have not always been very responsive to the complaints of women students. In 2015, the federal government opened civil rights investigations into 110 colleges and universities over allegations of improper handling of cases of sexual assault (Anderson and Clement 2015), although during the presidency of Donald Trump (2017–2020) this scrutiny declined.

One question posed in the last decade is whether there is something about the college social environment—for example, binge drinking, parties, or hookup culture—that places women at increased risk for sexual assault (Armstrong et al. 2006; Ford 2017; Hirsch and Kahn 2020). The college hookup culture—and its role in facilitating unwanted sexual encounters that often involve alcohol—may provide predators (especially male students) with more opportunities to sexually assault victims (Lisak 2011). However, finger-pointing at the rise of the hookup culture as a cause can be misleading; it seems more likely that sexual violence and harassment have always been problems, but that it is only in the last few decades that campus administrators and the news media have begun to recognize the problem. In other words, we are only hearing about sexual violence and harassment more now because these issues are finally getting more attention. It is also surprising to many people that rates of sexual assault are higher for young women who *do not* attend college than those who do (Rennison 2014; Sinozich and Langton 2014; Rape, Abuse & Incest National Network 2021). Research from the U.S. Department of Justice, using a large representative survey, shows that between 1995 and 2013, women between the ages of 18 and 24 were 1.2 times more likely to experience sexual assault or rape if they were *not* attending college (Rennison 2014).

One of the most important developments relating to assault and harassment in recent years has been the rise of the **#MeToo movement**, a global campaign against sexual assault and harassment that encourages victims to name the perpetrators and challenge organizations to put a stop to abuses in workplaces, schools, and other settings where powerful people have used their influence in abusive ways. Among the most notorious cases revealed in the fall of 2017 involved Hollywood film mogul Harvey Weinstein. Dozens of women in the film industry came forward with stories of their own victimization by Weinstein stretching over several decades. This included a number of major Hollywood stars, including Angelina Jolie, Gwyneth Paltrow, Heather Graham, Ashley Judd, Salma Hayek, and Uma Thurman (as well as over 80 less famous women). Following the Weinstein revelations, numerous other allegations of sexual assault were credibly made against prominent actors, directors, and media personalities such as Bill Cosby, Kevin Spacey, Dustin Hoffman, former NBC *Today* show host Matt Lauer, FOX News host Bill O'Reilly, hip-hop mogul Russell Simmons, comedian Louis C.K., U.S Gymnastics Team Coach Larry Nassar, Nxivm cult leader Keith Raniere, and many others.

Although these public figures were all credibly charged, only a few have been successfully prosecuted through the criminal justice system. For many victims, the legal system still does not provide strong protections. As one legal scholar has put it, "when the issue is harassment, acquaintance rape, or domestic violence, it is often the victim whose conduct is on trial" (Rhode 1997). Many cases involve a "he said/she said" dynamic in which the victim is forced to recount a painful episode in multiple hearings and perhaps a trial. Women in abusive relationships may fear further abuse if they call in the police

Mark Bussell

Binge drinking, which often takes place in group settings or parties, is an important factor behind many sexual assaults.

The most notorious high-profile case of a sexual predator using a position of power to sexually exploit others involved Hollywood film mogul Harvey Weinstein (pictured here). Dozens of women in the film industry came forward with stories of their own victimization by Weinstein stretching over several decades. This included a number of major Hollywood stars, including Angelina Jolie, Gwyneth Paltrow, Heather Graham, Ashley Judd, Salma Hayek, and Uma Thurman (as well as over 80 less famous women).

(and fear that the police may not take their case seriously). Even very high-powered women who have been harassed in their jobs may find it takes years to find an opportunity to press charges against their harasser without fear of retribution. For example, a large number of female Fox News anchors reported being harassed for years by Fox CEO Roger Ailes, but only after one of the anchors, Gretchen Carlson, was fired from her job and felt she had nothing to lose and sued Ailes in court, did other Fox employees come forward to tell their stories. Ailes was eventually fired, but not until he had abused countless women and his behavior had been covered up by the company.

Although the case of FOX News suggests widespread cover-ups, there has been a growing concern about sexual harassment and assault in the workplace. Most large corporations today have established extensive rules and regulations that attempt to reduce sexual harassment in the workplace (Dobbin and Kelly 2007; Dobbin 2009). As Figure 14.15 displays, the proportion of Fortune 500 companies that have instituted some type of anti-harassment measure(s) has risen from virtually none in 1965 to more than

90 percent by the year 2000, and more than 70 percent have instituted some form of anti-harassment training for their employees. Many state governments have instituted programs requiring employers to establish anti-harassment programs. Some of these programs have grown from fear of lawsuits and large judgments against firms that do not institute programs to monitor and supervise sexual harassment, but some of the more progressive of these programs have been adopted and extended voluntarily by organizations seeking to promote equal opportunity for women employees (Dobbin 2009). One study focused on the results of employers' policies in setting up grievance procedures that allow employees to report sexual harassment. It was hoped that such policies would lead to more women in management, since women managers who previously had quit jobs to escape sexual harassment might find the grievance procedures allowed them to get the situation corrected. But a recent follow-up study found no positive effect of setting up sexual harassment grievance policies on retaining women managers (Dobbin and Kalev 2019). The authors suggest that victims are often afraid to report through these procedures, and human resources professionals receiving the reports sometimes focus more on saving the firm from legal liability than stopping the harassment. They suggest that programs that train workers and managers to work together to be allies when they see sexual harassment may work better to stop sexual harassment.

Figure 14.15 Corporate Organizations' Use of Training and Preventive Policies Against Workplace Sexual Assault and Harassment

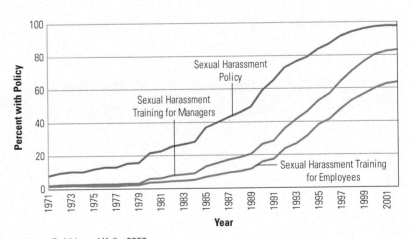

SOURCE: Dobbin and Kelly, 2007.

Conclusion: The Puzzle of Gender and Sexual Inequality

As we've seen, gender and sexualities are linked. When people are committed to the idea that women and men are naturally and appropriately different, a bias against same-sex relationships often results because such relationships challenge the idea that roles need to be assigned based on one's sex. Gender and sexualities are also linked because our cultural beliefs about how we are supposed to act—at work, in social gatherings, or anywhere—also affect how we act when we have sex. Gender norms also create the sexual double standard under which peers judge women more harshly than men for casual sex, including sometimes blaming women when they are victims of sexual assault.

Neither gender identities nor sexual practices are static. That is how we know that they are, at least in part, socially constructed, although they are also affected by biology. Many sociologists used to believe that the shifts in the system of gender and sexuality were unidirectional and continuous. In other words, for a few decades it looked like things were getting increasingly more permissive regarding sexualities and ever more equal between women and men. A person's sex came to dictate less about how the person was treated or expected to act. Many gender inequalities in job opportunities, pay, and leadership declined. Tolerance for sexual minorities increased. Sex outside of marriage lost much of its stigma.

But recent research has made clear that these matters do not go only in the direction of more permissiveness in sexual matters and more equality between women and men. Some changes have plateaued or even reversed. We've seen that many forms of gender equalizing—declining segregation of occupations, reduction of the sex gap in pay, and egalitarian attitudes—moved most dramatically in the 1970s and 1980s, with slow-downs, stalls, or even reversals since 1990 or 2000. In the sexual arena, intercourse among teens became more common, but then the trend reversed more recently (Martinez and Abma 2015).

We've also seen that some things change much more than others. Gender change is discussed as "women's progress" because women modified their roles much more than men. More women entered employment, went farther in school, and entered previously male-dominated fields of study and occupations. Movements in the opposite direction—of men becoming homemakers or entering female-dominated fields of study and occupation—have happened much less. In part this is because activities women have traditionally done pay less and receive less respect, and as long as that is true, men will have an incentive to avoid these roles, and women will have an incentive to abandon them.

Here is another instance of some things shifting much more than others: Women's dramatic movements into employment and traditionally male careers were not matched by large changes in gendered sexual behavior. The sexual script that sees men as the initiators of dates, sex, and proposals of marriage has not varied dramatically. And a sexual double standard still exists such that women are judged more harshly for casual sex.

One of the remaining puzzles for sociologists studying gender and sexualities is to understand which things change, why equalizing changes sometimes reverse, and why some things are so resistant to change.

The Big Questions Revisited 14

14.1 Where Do Gender Differences Come From? Are differences between men and women all natural, or are they shaped by society as well as biology? This section explored the differences between men and women and examined where these differences come from.

Gender Differences

Sex versus Gender: The Social Construction of Gender

Learning Objective 14.1.1: Distinguish the concepts of sex and gender, and explain how gender is socially constructed.

Gender Socialization

Learning Objective 14.1.2: Describe the process of gender socialization.

Gender Differences Vary by Setting and Time

Learning Objective 14.1.3: Explain how gender differences vary by setting and time.

The Impact of Stereotypes

Learning Objective 14.1.4: Discuss the role of stereotypes in constructing social expectations of gender.

Key Terms

gender (p. 366)   sex (p. 369)   intersex individual (p. 369)   social construction of gender (p. 370)   patriarchy (p. 370)   transgender (p. 370)   nonbinary (p. 370)   random-assignment experiment (p. 371)   stereotypes (p. 372)

14.2   How Have the Lives of Women and Men Changed in the Last 50 Years? Women's lives have changed so much in the last 50 years that we often call the changes a gender revolution. This section explored some of these changes and how they have affected men's lives.

The Gender Revolution

Rising Women's Employment and Education

Learning Objective 14.2.1: Discuss reasons for the dramatic increase in women's employment and education since 1970.

Change in Women's Jobs and in the Pay Gap

Learning Objective 14.2.2: Describe occupational sex segregation and discuss factors affecting the gender pay gap.

The Impact on Men

Learning Objective 14.2.3: Discuss the impact of the gender revolution on men's roles.

Key Terms

feminist movement (p. 374)   occupational sex segregation (p. 375)

14.3   How Are Our Sex Lives Shaped by Biology and Society? There is no question that sexual attractions and behavior are affected by biology, but as we discussed in this section, they are also strongly affected by social construction.

Sexualities

Sexual Orientation and Identities

Learning Objective 14.3.1: Discuss the influence of biology and society on sexual orientation.

Sexual Behavior

Learning Objective 14.3.2: Discuss the impact of biology and society on sexual behavior.

LGBTQ Discrimination

Learning Objective 14.3.3: Identify the biases that lesbian, gay, bisexual, transgender, and questioning (LGBTQ) individuals encounter.

Key Terms

sexual orientation (p. 380)   double standard of sexuality (p. 380)   cisgender (p. 381)   heteronormativity (p. 381)   heterosexism (p. 382)   homophobia (p. 382)

14.4   How Has Sexual Behavior Changed in the Last 50 Years? Sexual behavior of young married adults has changed substantially over the last several decades, but what about the extent to which sexual and relational behavior is affected by gender norms and inequalities and societal reactions to nonconsensual sex? This section explored sexual behavior and its link to gender.

The Sexual Revolution and Beyond

Sex Outside of Marriage

Learning Objective 14.4.1: Discuss how attitudes and behaviors involving sex outside of marriage in relationships, and casual sex outside of exclusive relationships have changed over the last 50 years.

Births Outside of Marriage

Learning Objective 14.4.2: Discuss changing rates of births outside of marriage.

Gender Inequality in Sex and Relationships

Learning Objective 14.4.3: Discuss the role that gendered expectations play in sexual and romantic behavior.

Unwanted Sex: Rape, Sexual Assault, and Sexual Harassment

Learning Objective 14.4.4: Describe the varieties of unwanted sexual encounters.

Key Terms

probability sample (p. 384)   cohabitation (p. 386)   hookup (p. 386)   sexual assault (p. 388)   rape (p. 388)   sexual harassment (p. 388)   street harassment (p. 388)   #MeToo movement (p. 390)

Chapter 15
Cities and Communities

by Patrick Sharkey and Jeff Manza*

The New York City Police Department regularly publishes crime statistics, including incidents of homicide, and the department even offers color-coded maps, which show the rate of homicides for each police precinct (see Figure 15.1). Even during a time when violent crime has been dropping rapidly, the rates indicated by the different colored precincts covering the five boroughs of New York City illustrates that homicide is not simply a problem related to poverty, policing, and the criminal justice system; the sheer volume of deaths due to homicide makes it an urgent public health problem.

Moreover, Figure 15.1 reveals that homicide is not spread evenly across the population of any city. Taking a closer look you will notice that in many neighborhoods of New York City there are almost no homicides. But in some neighborhoods of Brooklyn, the Harlem section of Manhattan, and the South Bronx, there is a consistent concentration of extreme violence. The neighborhoods where violence is concentrated are also some of the poorest and most racially segregated neighborhoods in the city, a pattern that is typical in most urban areas across the country.

An additional unique feature of homicide, one that the primary author of this chapter (Sharkey) studies in his research, and that distinguishes it from most other diseases and causes of death, is that the effects of homicide are not limited to the victims of lethal violence. In one study, he found that children who are given a standard assessment of reading and vocabulary skills perform substantially worse if they are assessed in the days following a local homicide that occurs in their neighborhood (Sharkey 2010). In other words, local violence does not just affect those who are there to witness it but "gets into the minds" of youth throughout the community.

How is it that a homicide a few blocks away might affect the performance of a child who did not know the victim, and did not witness the event, on a basic test of reading and language skills? We are still figuring out the precise answer to this question, but extensive research demonstrates that stress arising from community violence can cause anxiety, disrupt sleep, and reduce children's ability to concentrate and focus (Osofsky 1999). If the shock of a single homicide affects children's behavior and performance so drastically, what is it like to live in one of the neighborhoods in which homicides are so tightly clustered together?

The study of homicide sheds light on the way that different aspects of communities, such as the presence or absence of violence, can alter the experiences and opportunities of individual residents, often reinforcing patterns of inequality in society as a whole. But it is not just homicide that is concentrated in space, prevalent in some neighborhoods and virtually unheard of in others in others. There are many social

My Sociological Imagination

PATRICK SHARKEY

My research focuses on the way that places—meaning the environments surrounding individuals, from the residential block to the town or city in which they live—affect the life chances of individuals and groups in the United States. Much of my work looks at multiple generations of American families and analyzes the degree of inequality in families' neighborhood environments over long periods of time and the consequences of living in persistently poor or disadvantaged neighborhood environments over multiple generations. A more recent strand of my research focuses more closely on the specific ways that living in a poor neighborhood may affect the day-to-day lives of children, with particular attention paid to the way that violence and other stressors in children's environments "get into the minds" of children to affect their behavior, their health, and their academic performance.

---

*An earlier version of this chapter was co-authored by Max Besbris.

A victim of gun violence in the Bronx, New York City. Even as the murder rate fell dramatically in American cities between the early 1990s and 2019, violence remains an important societal problem in the United States. For sociologists studying violence, the questions explored move from individual acts to patterns of violence to the consequences of violence for individuals and communities.

NurPhoto/Corbis News/Getty Images

Figure 15.1 Murder in New York City

This figure shows the spatial distribution of murders in New York City. One sociological question is: Why are some parts of the city virtually murder-free, while others show high rates of violence?

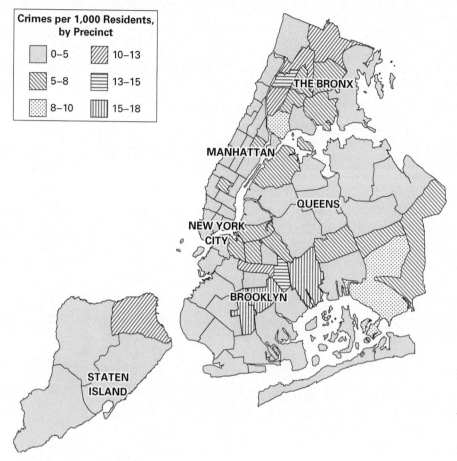

SOURCE: New York City Police Department, 2016.

phenomena that are clustered together in space, and much of our social world is organized by geography. Where you live plays a central role in influencing where you go to school, with whom you interact, and what types of institutions surround you. The fact that public schools are typically organized and funded by local districts means that the quality of a child's educational opportunities depends, in large part, on that child's address. Research tells us that residents of poor and segregated neighborhoods have less political influence than residents of neighborhoods with more racial and economic diversity (Cohen and Dawson 1993). A great deal of evidence indicates that the geographic locations of jobs and industry have important influences on the likelihood that individuals will be able to find and maintain steady employment (Holzer 1991). In a similar way, the quality of public attractions like parks and recreation centers, the effectiveness of institutions such as the police, and the degree of exposure to toxic soil and clean air all depend directly on where we live.

For all of these reasons, the environments that surround us have important implications for our lives and our life chances. But to understand why

The Big Questions

Sociologists have struggled for more than a century to understand how cities and communities form and how they affect social life, and our discussion of these issues is guided by exploring the following five big questions:

1. **What draws people to cities?** Most of the human population now lives in urban areas, which raises a number of intriguing questions about how to define a city and how city life has affected different aspects of our individual lives. As we explore these questions throughout the chapter, we will learn that a sociological understanding of cities is more complex than the "official" definitions provided by government agencies.

2. **How do neighborhoods form and change?** The development of cities and communities is not natural; rather, it is driven by political and economic forces. Individuals and groups with different, sometimes competing interests struggle to build communities in very different ways. Patterns of change over time can be seen as the product of these struggles. The types of communities that have emerged over time are dramatically diverse.

3. **How do cities influence who we are, who our friends are, and how we live?** Cities are distinguished not only by their size, density, or other measurable characteristics but also by how they affect the way we interact, work, and live together.

4. **Why are so many social problems found in cities?** Cities have increasingly become sites of the world's most extreme wealth and poverty. Urban areas have always been great engines of wealth creation, but a growing proportion of the world's poverty is now moving from undeveloped, rural areas into densely populated urban slums.

5. **How is life in rural communities different from cities and suburbs?** Most of the chapter to this point has considered issues associated with metropolitan areas (i.e., cities and suburbs). But every country in the world contains rural communities that are far from larger population centers. What is life like in small towns in America, and in what ways are these communities different than metropolitan places? How is rural life changing over time, and what are the central challenges facing rural communities in the twenty-first century?

6. **How will cities change in an increasingly connected world?** Cities link the world together. To fully comprehend the forces that shape our world, we must expand our view well beyond individual city streets and communities, and even beyond the boundaries of individual nations.

violence is so concentrated, why school quality varies so dramatically, or why toxins are so prevalent in some communities, we have to take a step back and attempt to understand how cities and communities in the United States and elsewhere are formed and how they change over time.

In this chapter, we will examine not only how the world became urban but what it means to *live* in an urban world. We will consider the new opportunities and some of the major social problems—like concentrated poverty and segregation—that can result from urbanization. We will also consider rural communities that have different sets of issues and challenges. As the chapter closes, we widen our view to look at the way in which cities and communities are connected across the world through immigration, communication, and transnational business. By moving from local communities to worldwide connections, we are able to learn a tremendous amount about the structure of our society.

Andriy Blokhin/Alamy Stock Photo

BIG QUESTION 15.1 What Draws People to Cities?

HOW THE WORLD BECAME URBAN

For the first time in human history, by 2010 more than half of the world's population lived in urban areas (United Nations, Department of Economic and Social Affairs 2010). This statement, which is based on global research done by the United Nations, raises a basic yet important question: Just what does it mean to be *urban*? As it turns out, this is a difficult question to answer. In the United States, the Census Bureau classifies an **urban** area as having a **population density** (the number of people living in a common unit of space, like a square mile or square kilometer) of at least 1,000 people per square mile, plus all surrounding regions with an overall density of at least 500 people per square mile (U.S. Census Bureau, Geography Division 2009). Urban areas are also often called **metropolitan regions**, a term that has essentially the same meaning as the census's urban areas and includes both urban and **suburban** communities (defined as cities and towns within metropolitan regions and close to, but not part of, the boundaries of central cities). Areas that are less dense and not adjacent to an urbanized region are classified as **rural**.

The boundaries between "urban," "suburban," and "rural" areas are, however, often blurred. For example, if you start driving out of a large city and into a nearby suburb, you may hardly notice any difference for some time, but we know from decades of research that suburbs differ in many important ways from central cities. If you keep driving in one direction, eventually you will have left the metropolitan region and are in a rural place. But defining exactly how far away from a **central city** (that is, the main city in a metropolitan area) and its suburbs we need to travel before reaching truly rural places is not obvious. As a general rule of thumb, we might think of a rural small town as having a population that is less than 25,000 people, located in an area that is too far from a metropolitan region for people to commute to work every day (Wuthnow 2018). By contrast, a suburban area may be a place with distinct boundaries but close enough to a central city to make daily commuting possible (that is, it has roads, highways, and/or public transit into the central city that makes commuting to work feasible). Another more informal way to think about these distinctions is that people living in either central cities or its suburbs tend to describe their hometown as part of the larger metropolitan area (for example, people in Chicago suburbs think of themselves as part of "Chicagoland" or people in the suburbs of San Francisco and Oakland think of themselves as part of the "Bay Area"), whereas people in rural towns and communities further out would not.

In spite of these definitional complexities, there is one critical unmistakable trend: Our world is becoming increasingly urbanized. Sociologists have long been interested in the process of **urbanization**, meaning the growth in the proportion of the population living in cities and/or metropolitan areas. In addition to describing how cities and communities form and change, a sociological perspective focuses on how these and other dimensions of places affect the way that people interact with each other, how they form friendship ties and communities, where and how they work and produce goods, and how they generate culture and subcultures.

Urbanization and the Growth of Cities

15.1.1 Identify the major forces that have led to urbanization.

We will consider many different ideas about what a city is and what it does in this chapter. Before we get there, however, let us first consider a more basic question: How did the population of the United States come to be located primarily in urban areas? What has transpired in the United States since 1850 is typical of most countries around the world, although the timing differs. The last two centuries of human history have been marked by the steady movement of the individuals and families from the country to the city. Sociologist and demographer Kingsley Davis (1965) famously argued that, in the modern world, the process of urbanization typically follows an "S curve" whose shape is driven by the timing of industrialization. According to this model, before the emergence of widespread industry, the pace of urbanization is slow and gradual—this is the long tail at the bottom of the S. With the onset of industrialization, cities grow rapidly as large segments of the population move from rural areas to urban areas, drawn by plentiful jobs in

the city and technological advances that reduce demand for labor in rural areas—this is the steep, upward slope of the S. At some point, however, cities reach full, or carrying, capacity. At this point, demand for labor stops growing, the cost of urban space rises, and cities may become overcrowded. At this point, migration into the city slows and the pace of urbanization levels off; this is the flat top of the S. Figure 15.2 displays this S-curve model for England and Wales from 1800 to 1960.

The cities that have emerged from the process of urbanization driven by industrialization are very different from those that were present before the age of industry. Cities first developed over 5,000 years ago, but they were small, poorly connected enclaves that lost population just as easily as they gained it. Often surrounded by a wall for defense and containing somewhere between a few thousand and more than 100,000 residents, these early city-states usually functioned as trading centers and the capitals of empires. They were also centers of culture and commerce, but they were not built for growth—for instance, while the overall population of Europe increased from the eleventh century to the nineteenth century, the proportion that was urban remained roughly the same. This meant that life for the vast majority of the population occurred in rural, sparsely populated, agricultural settings where interactions between strangers were rare and day-to-day life focused on producing immediate sustenance.

Figure 15.2 England and Wales Area Population

The "S curve" of population growth during industrialization, 1800–1960, in England and Wales. Note that "urban" here refers to metropolitan areas (cities and surrounding suburbs).

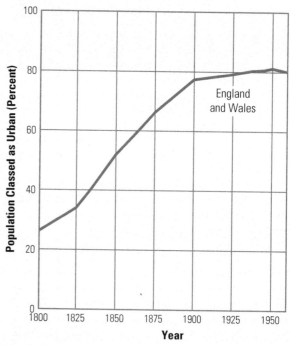

SOURCE: Davis (1965).

Industrialization changed all that. Britain, which was the first nation to industrialize, experienced rapid urbanization from 1800 to 1900, with continental Europe and the United States (and eventually much of the rest of the world) not far behind. The main cause of population growth in cities was migration: The movement of people from the country to the city. England's cities grew as its population was drawn away from rural areas, where agriculture was becoming more and more mechanized. The population moved toward its cities, where factories were sprouting up, requiring less land than farms and more manual labor to make them run.

Urban, Suburban, and Rural Patterns of Settlement

15.1.2 Identify the urban and suburban forms that emerged during the twentieth century.

As we've noted, the world's population continues to urbanize, making the boundaries separating cities from towns, and from other cities, less clear. Several new urban forms have appeared in the United States and elsewhere, the most common of which is the growth of suburbs surrounding urban areas, creating continuous metropolitan regions that extend across city and suburban political boundaries. Examples of the latter in the United States include places like Dallas/ Fort Worth, Washington D.C./Baltimore, and Seattle/ Tacoma, where the airports are often named after the two cities. **Megacities**, cities with populations of over 10 million people, like Mexico City, Sao Paolo, Brazil, or Lagos, Nigeria, are another recent phenomenon that has emerged throughout the world. These new urban forms are often embedded in a larger **megaregion**, where two or more large cities in geographical proximity are linked together through infrastructure and through economic activity (Gottman 1966). Megaregions include areas like the Northeast corridor of the United States. This region, stretching from Boston, through New York City, Philadelphia, and Baltimore, to Washington, D.C., is essentially a continuous region, contains about 56 million inhabitants, and produces over $3.5 trillion of economic output annually (about as much as Germany produces, and more than countries like France and the United Kingdom). If it were its own country, the Boston-New York-Philadelphia-Washington corridor would be the fourth or fifth richest in the world (Short 2007; Florida 2014)!

It is remarkable that about 20 percent of the entire human population is now concentrated in just 40 megaregions across the world, with the largest in rapidly developing countries like India and China, where multiple regions with 20 million people or more can be found (Florida 2008). Figure 15.3 highlights some of the major megaregions in the world. The new scale of urban areas, especially

Figure 15.3 Populations of Megaregions Around the World

Many of the world's largest cities are growing at incredible rates and merging to form vast megaregions. Megaregions are characterized by large populations and significant economic activity. These vastly populated areas are defined by the individual cities they encompass and the relationships that form between them. Forty megaregions in the world each boast economies of $100 billion. Some examples are shown here.

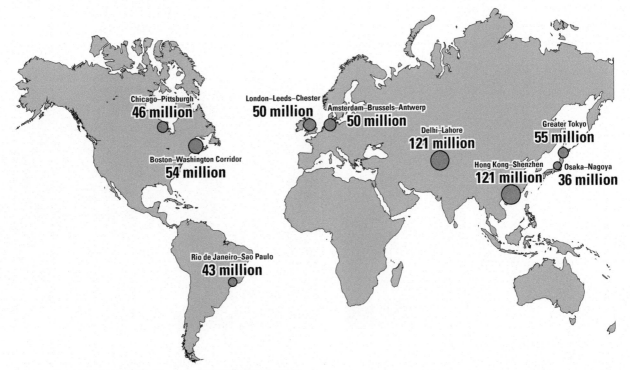

SOURCE: Based on data from Florida et al. 2008; United Nations 2010.

in megaregions, creates problems and challenges that are not easily solved at the neighborhood or even city level. Issues like water treatment, transportation, pollution, and the provision of housing and social services now transcend the official borders of cities, requiring coordination among localities that are often in competition with each other for residents and businesses. Addressing these border-transcending concerns is especially important in the United States, where state and local governments have a great deal of decision-making power but megaregions can flow across those political boundaries (Downs 1994).

It is not just central cities that have seen major changes over the last 100 years. Traditional suburbs have also undergone a considerable transformation. Before the twentieth century, suburbs were not densely populated and specialized in trade rather than agriculture (Baldassare 1992). With increases in commuter railways and, in the twentieth century, steadily rising car ownership, communities began to form around major urban areas. Individuals lived in these new communities, but usually did not work there. In some cases, these growing suburbs would be formally incorporated into the center city, but most remained as separate jurisdictions with their own local governments, police and fire departments.

A famous example of the process of suburban development can be seen in Southern California's San Fernando Valley (SFV), or "the Valley" as it is known locally, when it began to develop directly north of the Los Angeles Basin. In the early 1900s, the Valley was mostly a rural mass of agricultural land where wealthy Los Angelenos built country homes on the border with the city. As the population of Los Angeles increased, the city, pushed by a number of prominent business leaders annexed more and more of the Valley and even managed to deprive some farmlands of the necessary water they needed for their crops (notably orange groves, which

were a staple of the SFV). The famous movie *Chinatown* (1974), starring Jack Nicholson, is a dramatization of some these events. By the late 1930s, most of the Valley had been incorporated into the city, but a number of communities (such as Burbank, Glendale, and San Fernando) remained independent. The population of the SFV grew rapidly, reaching over 2 million (some now in the Los Angeles city boundaries, others in stand-alone suburbs). For Angelos, the entire area, on either side of the Los Angeles city boundary, is known simply as the Valley, and it has retained its classical suburban character irrespective of the political boundaries of the city of Los Angeles.

As the twentieth century evolved, the pace of suburbanization quickened. Three factors facilitated this growth. First, because land values were much lower outside of urban areas, it was much more affordable for many families to purchase single-family houses with yards in the suburbs. Residential developers—businesses that build residential housing—found that if they could get approvals to build, they could find buyers. In fact, they found that people were willing to move further away from urban centers to acquire houses with bigger yards, creating the possibility of profitable construction opportunities. Second, the federal government made significant investments in highways (sometimes referred to as "freeways," because they are free to drive on) that more easily connected people in suburbs to urban centers, making it more viable for individuals to commute to jobs in the city center.

The final factor involved race. In the Northeast, Midwest, and later in the West, suburbanization was also driven by **white flight**, which refers to the movement of White families out of central cities and into the suburbs, a pattern typically driven by the changing demographics of cities experiencing an influx of Blacks or other racial and ethnic minorities after World War II. The perception of many Whites was that their quality of life was being threatened,

In the late 1940s and 1950s, suburbs grew rapidly. Levittown, which arose in New York, Pennsylvania, and elsewhere, was among the most famous of these developments. In these communities, a carefully laid out residential grid of nearly identical, cheaply built homes provided modest-cost housing options outside of central cities. Many of these communities were initially only open to White families; in 1968, the federal government banned formal racial segregation practices, although many suburbs continue to be racially homogenous.

causing many to move. The San Fernando Valley in the Los Angeles region provides a prototypical example, as the valley became a suburb for Whites who left more central areas in Los Angeles as Blacks and Latinxs moved into the city's south and east sides. In other major cities, the same process was repeated, and by the 1980s, many major American cities had lost significant proportions of their White populations. As a result, many neighborhoods and cities saw their populations decline. Chicago, which had a total population of 3.6 million in 1950, declined to just 2.6 million before stabilizing in the 1990s. (Chicago has a population of about 2.7 million people as of the 2020 Census.) Meanwhile, the population of the entire "Chicagoland" metropolitan region, which includes all the suburbs around Chicago, *grew* from 5.4 million in 1950 to almost 10 million by 2020.

The term white flight brings to mind issues surrounding racial conflict and tension within America's cities and metropolitan regions. What is frequently overlooked are the ways the federal government facilitated, and in fact subsidized, the exodus of Whites from central cities. Since the 1930s, the government has played a central role in supporting home ownership by guaranteeing or providing mortgages directly (Massey and Denton 1993). Instead of using its role in the home mortgage industry to promote homeownership for all groups, the federal government adopted a set of standards to rank the riskiness of potential loans. Homes in racially homogeneous White neighborhoods were ranked highest, while homes in primarily Black or racially mixed neighborhoods were ranked lowest and were typically ineligible for investment. The practice of **redlining** emerged from the system used to determine areas ineligible for loans—predominantly Black or racially mixed communities were literally outlined in red on maps to signify that they had received the lowest rankings and were thus ineligible for loans. This practice spread throughout the banking industry until it was outlawed in 1977. And

it wasn't just private banks that discriminated; the Federal Housing Administration discouraged loans to racial minorities and strictly limited loans that would lead to racially or economically integrated neighborhoods. This meant that a Black family seeking to buy a home was limited to an existing Black neighborhood. Home ownership in the suburbs was largely restricted to Whites. Many of the suburbs populated by Whites leaving the center city encouraged the use of **racial covenants** in which (White) home buyers pledged not to sell their home to non-White buyers. There are many horrific examples of Black families attempting to move into suburban areas only to face violence and opposition to their presence by their prospective White neighbors.

Over time, however, many of America's suburbs became more diverse in terms of their racial and ethnic composition. In the San Fernando Valley, for instance, Whites are no longer the majority of the population, as a huge influx of Latinx and Asian American/Pacific Islander (AAPI) people has transformed many Valley communities. In fact, some suburbs have become every bit as diverse as the cities they are near. Yet most metropolitan areas (cities plus suburbs) remain highly segregated overall. But even that general conclusion is changing in the twenty-first century, as huge increases in Latinx and AAPI populations in metropolitan areas have made the patterns of segregation more complicated (Lee et al. 2014). We will discuss segregation in more detail later in the chapter.

As the number of Americans living in the suburbs has grown, the boundaries of suburbs have stretched further and further away from central cities, a process known as **suburban sprawl**. This, in turn, has led to the development of **edge cities** (Garreau 1991). Edge cities are self-contained places, typically located at the junction of major freeways and transportation systems, and feature businesses as well as social and cultural activities that used to be primarily located in central cities. Edge cities like Valencia, California (about 30 miles

Arthur Siegel/Anthony Potter Collection/Getty Images

Residential segregation by race has left a long historical legacy that continues to shape urban and suburban communities. It did not happen by accident, but rather as a result of a mix of efforts of White residents to prevent Blacks and other people of color from moving in and government policies that reinforced segregationist practice.

north of downtown Los Angeles), Tysons Corner, Virginia (about 20 miles west of Washington, D.C.), or White Plains, New York (about 25 miles from Manhattan), have developed as suburban counterparts to the traditional downtown areas of large central cities. Instead of individuals commuting from the suburbs to central business districts to do their shopping, seek entertainment, or go to work, edge cities concentrate all of these activities in one place. Many have become engines of job growth, with employers choosing to locate offices or factories in surburbs rather than central cities.

Yet if edge cities call attention to the ways in which some suburbs are growing and becoming more like cities in their own right, the economies of suburbs are at best mixed in the twenty-first century. The classical idea of the suburb is that it is a place filled with middle-class and upper-middle class families, with little poverty and crime. While there are many wealthy suburbs across the country, it is also increasingly the case that older suburbs, especially those close to the central city, have been decaying in recent years (Holliday and Dwyer 2009). One reason for the decline is that the original housing built there was done on the cheap (such as the tract homes mentioned above), by developers seeking to maximize their profits. Such buildings have not worn well over time, but are costly to rebuild. In these declining suburbs, rates of crime, unemployment, and school dropouts

approach those found in central cities. Indeed, there are actually more poor people in America today living in suburban communities than either in cities or rural areas. Central cities that have long had rates of poverty—like Detroit, Chicago, or Cleveland—now have nearby suburbs with similarly high rates of crime (Kneebone 2017).

As cities and the suburbs around them have changed, so too have the nation's rural areas. Residents of America's rural areas are no longer isolated from urban life, as even traditionally rural states are increasingly urban. Large agriculture companies farm huge swaths of land in places as diverse as Iowa's cornfields and California's central valley, and their need for low-wage labor has attracted an increasingly diverse population to nonmetropolitan areas around the country. Over the past several decades, Latinx and AAPI populations have been the fastest growing ethnic groups in rural America, posing a new set of questions for sociologists to consider: How does ethnic diversity change the cultural landscape of rural areas? How does cultural assimilation in rural areas differ from assimilation in cities? For researchers who have studied ethnic diversity and immigration in mainly urban settings, these questions will become increasingly important as new immigrant groups spread out beyond the cities that have traditionally been the ports of entry to the United States.

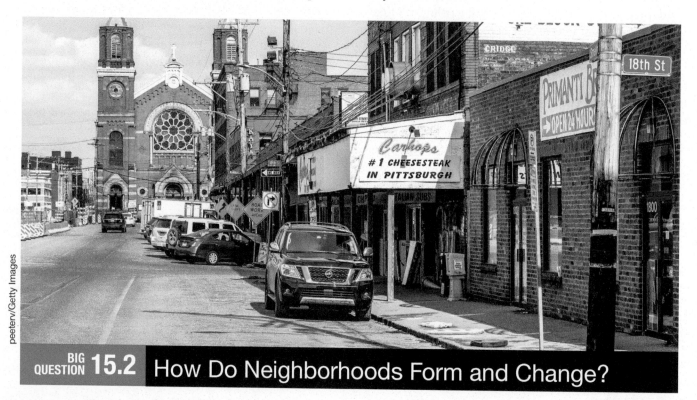

peeterv/Getty Images

BIG QUESTION 15.2 How Do Neighborhoods Form and Change?

NEIGHBORHOODS AND URBAN CHANGE

Up to this point, we have focused on the forces that lead to urbanization and the emergence of new types of suburban and urban forms. We now turn to a different set of

questions about the internal dynamics of cities: Why do cities come to look the way they do? How do neighborhoods form within cities, and how are a city's residents, resources, and institutions distributed across space? How and why do communities within cities change over time?

Urban Ecology: The Chicago School

15.2.1 **Define urban ecology and discuss the central questions confronted by the Chicago School.**

These were some of the central questions confronted by a group of sociologists associated with the University of Chicago in the early part of the twentieth century, known collectively as the "Chicago School" of urban sociology. Using the city of Chicago as a laboratory, the ideas of the Chicago School on urbanism, urban forms, and urban change have been extremely influential to the discipline, even though some of these ideas have been challenged or dismissed outright in the years since they were written.

One of the central ideas in early Chicago School writings is that the form of cities can be understood as the result of a process in which different segments of the population sort themselves into the areas of the city in which they thrive—a perspective referred to as **urban ecology**. This perspective, laid out most clearly in the work of Robert Park and Ernest Burgess, borrowed from biology the idea that organisms adjust to their surroundings and find the best fit within their environment. It was very influential in the study of cities and communities. The urban ecology approach was used to explain the formation of different types of areas based on their role or function within the city, as well as the sorting of individuals and groups into the areas that provided the best "fit." For example, immigrants may cluster in certain areas within the city because they can interact with other people and with institutions that share their culture and history. Over time, assimilation occurs as individual members of the group begin to interact with more and more individuals from other ethnic groups and begin to integrate with the wider culture and the wider economy, identifying less with the culture of their homeland. Boston's North End neighborhood provides a good example of this process, as it experienced an influx of Italian immigrants who came to work in the city's ports in the mid to late 1800s. Over time, these immigrants and their descendants moved into other businesses and into other parts of the city, becoming more integrated into the wider social and economic life of Boston.

This example shows how the social and economic integration of different groups within the city relates directly to the form and spatial layout of the city's neighborhoods. Hanging to this day in the seminar room of the University of Chicago's Sociology Department is a hand-drawn figure mapping out Burgess's "concentric zone" model of urban community structure (see Figure 15.4). Burgess saw cities as a series of rings spreading out from the center of the city, which he identified as the central business district or "The Loop" in Burgess's map of Chicago. (Downtown Chicago is known as the Loop because of the circular path of the elevated trains that run through it.)

In Burgess's concentric zone model, the central business district (CBD) was seen as the eye of the metropolis, where the majority of business, high-end shopping, and high culture (museums and symphonies) were located. This was no accident, according to Burgess. Retailers pay the most for land that provides access to the greatest number of customers, while manufacturing—located in the zone that surrounds the CBD—does not rely on heavy pedestrian foot traffic and only requires accessibility to commuting workers. Surrounding the "factory zone" was a "zone of transition," which featured low-quality housing for newly arrived immigrants and poor people. As individuals assimilated or moved upward into the working and middle classes, Burgess's model suggests that they moved *outward* into residential areas with higher quality housing and into "commuter zones" for wealthy people, who were willing to pay more for space and separation from urban life (Park and Burgess [1925] 1967).

Figure 15.4 Burgess's Concentric Zones Map of Chicago

The concentric zone model of neighborhood organization within cities has been highly influential and debated ever since it was originated in the 1920s. Do cities simply self-arrange so types of houses and neighborhoods meet the needs of its residents?

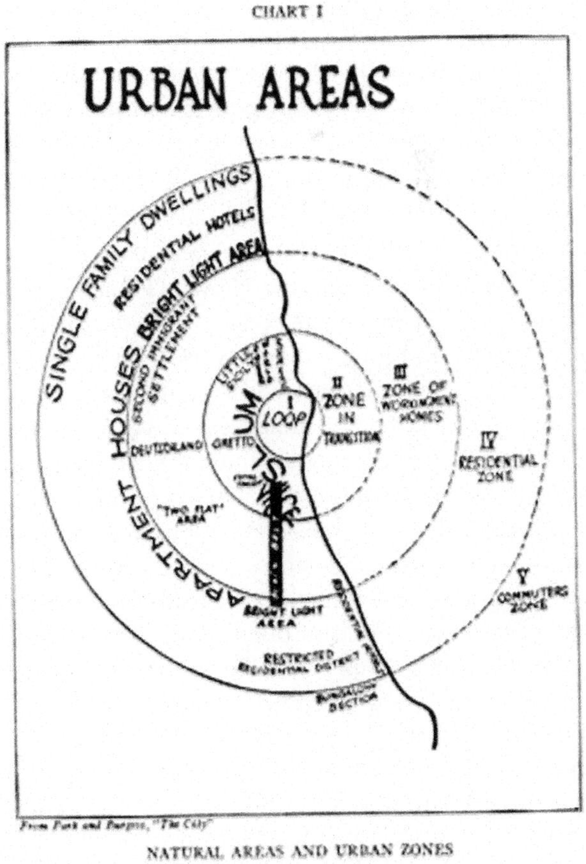

CHART I

URBAN AREAS

NATURAL AREAS AND URBAN ZONES

SOURCE: From (Park and Burgess [1925] 1967). Used with permission.

Although very insightful in capturing some of the basic patterns of urbanization, Burgess's model has been criticized as far too rigid, failing to account for variation in the ways cities outside of the Northeast and Midwest have developed—not to mention cities outside of the United States altogether. With the growth of elaborate highway systems and communication technology, the model has also become less relevant over time. Even as a description of Chicago in the first half of the 1900s, however, the idea of integration and assimilation as natural processes that lead to the sorting of groups into different sections of the city has been shown to be incomplete. For instance, research on Chicago's Black community in the early part of the twentieth century suggests that the boundaries surrounding this section of the city were not truly permeable "zones of transition," but rather were more like solid barriers in which Blacks were required to live. While other ethnic groups may become socially and spatially integrated over time, the informal and formal policies used to restrict Blacks to one particular area of the city meant that the Black community remained separate from the city's larger economic, social, educational, and political life—occupying a "city within a city" (Drake and Cayton 1945). We will explore this issue in more detail later in the chapter.

The Political Economy of Cities and Communities

15.2.2 Explain how political and economic interests work together to promote growth and affect urban change.

Alternatives to the urban ecology perspective are theories of urbanization that call our attention to the active ways that local government officials and private investors drive politics in pursuit of one outcome: Growth. From this perspective, the city can be understood as a **growth machine**, where investors and governments work to increase the size of the city's population and make it attractive for businesses to locate there to enhance the overall level of economic activity occurring within a city (Logan and Molotch 1987). Growth has many advantages. New businesses bring jobs. When cities and regions expand their population, they provide businesses with more customers, newspaper editors with wider readerships, and local colleges with larger applicant pools. Population growth also provides local governments with a larger tax base and greater ability to request funding from state and federal governments.

In the pursuit of growth, local governments regulate the use and distribution of land within the city. Local governments have several means at their disposal to impact growth patterns, including establishing local taxation rates (and deciding to give businesses "breaks" on their taxes), by directing funds to specific communities or sections of a city, by regulating utilities and funding public transportation, and by setting rules on what kinds of uses particular parcels of land can have (for example, single-family homes, apartment buildings, businesses, manufacturing, or a mix of these uses). In all of these arenas, research has consistently found that urban policy decisions often are significantly influenced, if not dominated, by a tight group of urban elites, including local property developers and builders, business leaders, and the leaders of key local institutions, such as media elites, university leaders (if any), and elected officials. Sometimes neighborhood groups or civic associations play a role, although often only when they are well-organized and active. These groups are often in competition with one another, seeking advantages for profitable opportunities for investment or in opposition to plans to change the city. Another set of perennial controversies involves how much cities should spend on cultural attractions such as museums, professional sports teams, universities, and even public parades that are designed to foster civic pride and attract residents.

From this perspective, urban change can be thought of not as a natural process of ecological change but as the direct result of political and economic interests working to promote growth (and the often-weaker groups of citizens who may oppose those interests). Thinking of cities as the product of intensive and strategic investment changes the way we understand everything about cities, even the way certain buildings and neighborhoods look. Research on the transformation of New York City's SoHo neighborhood from a manufacturing district to a wealthy, fashionable residential and retail community provides a good example (Zukin 1982). In SoHo, redevelopment groups composed of representatives from the business community and the city government pushed forward changes in zoning and land use that transformed who could live in the neighborhood and what businesses could operate in the neighborhood, reinventing the physical space and the types of individuals within it. The physical transformation of the neighborhood was part of a broader effort to create a new neighborhood identity, a rebranding of SoHo as a destination for artists and a center for culture and shopping—as opposed to a working-class section of the city dominated by factories. This process, known as **gentrification**, occurs when neighborhoods like SoHo undergo a process of change where new investment, new people, and new establishments move into and alter the character of the neighborhood. These changes typically entail a shift from a working-class or mixed-income neighborhood into a much wealthier neighborhood. In the study of gentrification, a key sociological question is who benefits from this form of neighborhood change? The gentrification of a section of the city may lead to higher land values, rising home prices, new amenities, and a higher tax base. But these same changes may lead to a shift in the culture of the community and may cause rents to rise in ways that force residents and business owners to leave. The consequences of gentrification are likely to be viewed very differently by different groups within the neighborhood.

Growth machine theory also shines a different light on racial and ethnic segregation issues. The sorting of different groups into neighborhoods across the city is viewed by some as the product of a concerted effort on the part of political and economic elites to protect investment and promote growth. Los Angeles provides a useful example. With its dizzying array of ethnic enclaves, its sprawling geography and car culture, its history of oppressive policing, and its obsession with image, Los Angeles has come to be seen as the quintessential example of an American city where change is driven by a powerful set of economic elites.

For example, the research of Mike Davis documents the way that "growth coalitions" sought to keep poor Black and Latinx populations from spreading into spaces deemed historically important by allocating tax subsidies to favored developers and by excluding groups representing the city's poor communities from taking part in decision making on urban planning (Davis 1990). Davis labeled the Los Angeles metropolis a "fortress of exclusion" that featured strategic investment in favored

neighborhoods and a set of policing or land-use policies designed to keep poor and racial and/or ethnic minorities out of these areas. Specifically, Davis documents the city's removal of homeless shelters and mental health facilities from neighborhoods where wealthy property owners wanted to develop new real estate investments. Not coincidentally, these property owners had previously donated large sums of money to city and county politicians who made decisions about the placement of social service facilities. His analysis reveals how the city even commissioned new park benches and bus stops in investment-ready areas designed to be physically uncomfortable in an effort to prevent homeless individuals from loitering or sleeping on them at night. This vision of the different zones within Los Angeles, some designed and policed to exclude some groups, does not resemble Burgess's vision of Chicago: Instead of transition zones, Davis describes "no-go" zones where poor people were relegated, and contrasts them to the glittering redeveloped commercial zones and gated housing communities of wealthy people.

These examples make clear the need to consider politics when we think about where different segments of the urban population live and how resources are distributed across cities. The research of the Chicago School provided a valuable description of the various sections of Chicago and the movement of the city's residents over time. More recent research has shown how these processes of change are driven not only by the unique characteristics of the city population, but also by a contentious political process influenced by groups with competing interests and widely divergent levels of resources and power.

John Dominis/The LIFE Picture Collection/Shutterstock

Alexander Spatari/Getty Images

Who benefits from the successful gentrification of a neighborhood like New York City's SoHo? The photo on the left is from the early 1970s and shows SoHo as a district of light manufacturing, physically dominated by trucks moving goods; at the time, SoHo had a considerable number of working-class jobs. Today, as the more recent photo on the right shows, SoHo is a neighborhood composed of very expensive shops, and the factories have been converted into multimillion dollar "loft" apartments.

Bob Pardue-Georgia/Alamy Stock Photo

LIVING IN AN URBAN WORLD

In his book *Going Solo*, NYU sociologist Eric Klinenberg (2012) documents remarkable growth in the number of Americans living by themselves—with the highest rates in places like Washington, D.C., Denver, and Minneapolis. In the Manhattan borough of New York City, about half of all housing units are now occupied by a single individual. Living alone can mean very different things to different people, but Klinenberg's research suggests that the growth in the number of Americans on their own is not necessarily a negative trend. Many of the individuals with whom he spoke expressed great satisfaction with their living situation and remained closely linked with friends and family.

Other research takes a less optimistic view on individual and community life in modern society, expressing concern with growing levels of **social isolation** in society, meaning a lack of interpersonal connections and a decline in civic life. For example, a famous book by political scientist Robert Putnam entitled *Bowling Alone* suggested that Americans have been spending less time with family, less time in groups like bowling clubs, and less time engaged in civic organizations since the mid-1960s (Putnam 2000).

What questions do these debates raise about life within cities? As we will see, sociologists have worried for a long time about how urban life affects the ties that individuals form to family, to neighbors, and to their communities. More broadly, sociologists have long been concerned with the question of what it means to live in an increasingly urban world, a challenging question that forces one to link large-scale, macro forces to micro, day-to-day experiences and interactions between individuals. As was true for the study of urban change, one of the most influential arguments about the effects of urban life was put forth by a sociologist in the Chicago School.

Urbanism as a Way of Life

15.3.1 Discuss how urbanization has affected our lives and communities.

The influential urban sociologist Louis Wirth, writing in 1938, defined a city as "a large, dense, and permanent settlement of heterogeneous individuals" (Wirth 1938). Density and diversity are characteristics of a place that we can measure and compare. However, these quantifiable characteristics were only a beginning point for Wirth. He went on to argue that these are the essential characteristics of cities because of the way that large, densely populated, and residentially stable places alter the lives of individuals and the nature of social interactions within them. Drawing on his observations of city life in Chicago, Wirth argued that city dwellers interact in largely anonymous, superficial, and transitory ways in their day-to-day exchanges with one another. He attributed this to the unique "specialization" of urban residents into different types of occupations and careers, the "differentiation" of urban individuals by social class, and the "segregation" of urban spaces by race, all of which do not exist to the same degree in smaller, more intimate communities. According to Wirth, diversity in cities does not necessarily lead to interaction among different groups living in close proximity, who may coexist with only "the faintest communication, the greatest indifference, the broadest tolerance, occasionally bitter strife, but always the sharpest contrast" (Wirth 1938, p. 20).

Wirth's thoughts on city life relate closely to the theories of German sociologist Georg Simmel, whose ideas laid the foundation for studying the effects of urbanism on individuals (Simmel [1902] 1972). Noting the large-scale migration to cities that had occurred all over Europe during the nineteenth century, Simmel argued that the shift in the environment surrounding such a substantial portion of the population must have consequences on the ways individuals act and interact. Simmel studied turn-of-the-century Berlin and came away with mixed feelings toward city life. He argued that the constant barrage of stimuli found in urban settings and the impersonal character of economic interactions lead individuals to live life with an indifferent, or what he called "blasé," attitude that provides a shield against the chaos of the city. However, Simmel also saw the city as liberating individuals from the social controls found in small, tight-knit communities. The exposure to many different kinds of people, which is only afforded by the density and diversity of urban areas, opens the individual up to a seemingly infinite number of new ways of life. From Simmel's perspective, the anonymity of the city allows individuals the freedom to express themselves in new ways while also escaping the tendency toward conformity in small towns. In the city, individuals find both freedom and isolation. (See Chapter 2 for more on Simmel's contributions to sociology.)

These early views of urbanism settled on the idea that something about the city itself produces a different psychological outlook for individuals, leading to new experiences but also to feelings of alienation. Subsequent scholars have rethought these claims and reached different conclusions. Sociologist Herbert Gans, who studied community life in a diverse array of urban and suburban settings, found both

German sociologist Georg Simmel's ideas on city life early in the twentieth century laid the foundation for studying the sociological effects of urbanism on individuals. The Chicago School (see above) also created influential early theories of urban life that continue to be debated to this day.

isolation and alienation in these communities, but also plenty of examples of strong interpersonal ties between neighbors and active community life in very large cities. Based on his observations, Gans called into question Wirth's assertion that urbanism, as opposed to the larger factors of economic and political structures of modern life, had any consequential effects on the way people live (Gans 1968). Gans agreed that there are differences between the type of life in nonurban and urban areas but argued that these differences result from factors like the age, race, occupation, and income of residents—not from urbanism per se. According to Gans, we should not think about an urban way of life or, for that matter, a suburban way of life, but instead we should focus on demographic and economic differences between groups in different places, as opposed to ecological factors like size, density, and heterogeneity.

Other urban scholars have argued that there are, in fact, differences in lifestyle that are fostered by cities that cannot be accounted for simply by the kinds of people who choose to live there. Cities encourage unconventional behavior, according to the urban sociologist Claude Fischer, as the sheer size and density of urban spaces lead individuals to sort into subcultures with similar interests or occupations. As a result, cities have higher rates of artistic innovation, higher rates of crime, and more "extreme" lifestyles (Fischer 1975). Institutional structures that support these subcultures (venues that play jazz or electronic dance music, bars that cater to an LGBTQ clientele, or small theaters where experimental plays can be produced) rise up in response to the demands of growing subcultural groups. Fischer's theory of subcultures helps us understand why certain neighborhoods take on a particular identity; for example, why youth from the suburbs move into neighborhoods like Haight-Ashbury in San Francisco, which became a center for the hippie movement in the 1960s, or Colonia Roma in Mexico City, which has become a destination for young artists and urban hipsters who work in design-related industries. In both cases, these neighborhoods catered to a unique subpopulation of the city and developed a new character that reflected the lifestyles of their residents.

Other scholars have also highlighted the positive aspects of urban environments and the ways that cities foster community. One of the most influential contributions in defense of the urban way of life was developed in the famous work of the writer and critic Jane Jacobs, who argued that vibrant neighborhoods that encourage the use of public spaces can foster social connections, interaction, and public safety (Jacobs 1961). Jacobs fought her most well-known battle to protect her own neighborhood, New York's Greenwich Village, from redevelopment. She contended that the neighborhood's dense, tree-lined streets, which combined businesses and residences, promoted social interaction by giving ownership of public space to all different types of community members. Jacobs thought that cities could indeed be cold and isolating, as Wirth

Sociologist Claude Fischer's theory of subcultures helps us understand why certain neighborhoods take on a particular identity—take for example, Haight-Ashbury in San Francisco (left), which became a famous center for the hippie movement in the 1960s, or the Borough Park neighborhood in Brooklyn, which is dominated by Hasidic (Orthodox) Jews (right).

saw them, but they did not have to be. She argued that the physical layout of neighborhoods has a lot to do with the quality of life within them. Mixed-use neighborhoods, like Greenwich Village in the 1950s, provided Jacobs with an example of how active street life and pedestrian traffic lead to more "eyes on the street," which, as she saw it, increases neighborliness and creates a safe community. The legacy of Jacobs's vision of urban life can be seen in the ideas of a school of urban design known as New Urbanism. The planners, architects, and urban designers that are collectively known as the New Urbanists call for a return to mixed-use, walkable urban communities as a response to growing suburban sprawl (Duany et al. 2001). As suburbs have sprawled further and further away from central cities, the influence of the New Urbanists has grown, and the communities they envision have come to be seen by many as a more sustainable model for urban design. Many suburbs are also trying to implement ideas of the New Urbanists to try to develop more walkable neighborhoods.

Communities and Networks

15.3.2 Discuss the impact of technology on community life.

As is clear by this point in the chapter, one of the fundamental concerns of sociologists studying cities and metropolitan areas is how urbanization affects **community**, often thought of as the degree to which individuals connect with, support, and interact with each other. A related concern is, how do we define the boundaries of an individual's community? Most of the classic sociological thinking on urban communities has conceived of an individual's community as comprising family members and neighbors, along with nearby friends. But times, and technologies, have changed, especially with the rise of social media.

In the late 1970s, sociologist Barry Wellman first picked up on this problem with classic conceptions of community that focused entirely on the space surrounding an individual. Wellman and other researchers pushed the field toward a view of community that focused on the **social ties** of individuals within cities, or the various types of connections that individuals make with other people, no matter where they live.

Wellman argued that thinking strictly about geography and the layout of neighborhoods unnecessarily limited urban sociology's focus, making it unable to fully capture how community works in modern life (Wellman 1979). Sociologists who study a community and find low levels of cohesion may be failing to see the wider networks in which individuals are enmeshed (recall Robert Putnam's ideas in *Bowling Alone*, described earlier). For example, we might have strong friendships with people through school or work, even though these friends do not live in the same neighborhood. Wellman claimed that individuals in cities do not lack strong intimate ties, nor are the ties that they have solely derived from family or neighbor relationships within close proximity. Instead, city dwellers draw on different networks that are spread over large geographies. In cities, people rely on different sets of friends, family, colleagues, neighbors, and associates for different reasons.

These ideas form the basis of research on **social networks**, the study of the ties that link people and groups together (see Chapter 5 for more information about the concept of social networks). Early research in the field helped to clarify the role that technology plays in shaping the way we construct our social networks and our communities. With the growth of first the telephone, and later the Internet and the rise of social media, community need no longer be thought of as something contained within a geographic area. The range of activities in which we participate provides opportunities for friendships and the formation of social ties in the home setting, at work, in religious communities, and of course online. To name just a few of the platforms that facilitate online communities, as of early 2021, there were 2.8 billion Facebook users and 330 million Twitter users, creating an immense capacity for individuals to maintain a constant connection with a very large group of network ties. We are just beginning to understand how these online social networks are changing the traditional perspective of community.

In some ways, online networks may not be weakening social life but rather enhancing **social capital**, that is, the resources available to individuals through their relationships and networks (Coleman 1988). Social capital is important for finding jobs and opportunities, among other things. Having a "network" of people you can call on for help is important for everyone. Historically, social capital was thought to reside in communities, but what sociologists have learned is that social capital does not emerge solely from close personal relationships with good friends and loved ones. In fact, the most useful ties are often those that connect people to new networks of individuals whom they do not already know and to new ideas and resources held by individuals within these networks.

This idea is captured in a classic study of job-referral networks conducted by the sociologist Mark Granovetter and famously titled "The Strength of Weak Ties" (Granovetter 1974). Granovetter found that the professionals he interviewed *did not* hear about their job through contacts they saw or interacted with frequently. Instead, they got word of potential employment options from contacts they saw only occasionally or rarely. Whereas an individual's closest friends may all know each other and have similar sets of information sources, these weak ties were most useful because they had access to unique information and unique contacts, opening up new opportunities for the job seeker.

With the expansion of social media and its implication for how we find and maintain relationships, find jobs and professional opportunities, and establish many other forms of connection to other people, we may be nearing a golden age of social networks, where everyone is connected. Considering this new reality, one may wonder whether concerns about the erosion of community are outdated or whether the traditional focus of urban sociology on local neighborhoods has become less relevant.

A great deal of research in urban sociology, however, suggests otherwise. Despite the fact that individual networks may not be limited by physical proximity, there is strong evidence that communication and interaction within the local, physical neighborhood remains essential for healthy community life. Research demonstrates that when residents of a neighborhood have a high level of cohesion and trust, they are more able to organize as a community and enforce common norms of behavior in public spaces. As a result, communities with high levels of cohesion and trust have lower levels of crime and violence, even if the community is very poor (Sampson et al. 1997).

The breakdown of this type of community cohesion can lead to disastrous consequences. A good example of this comes from a study of a deadly heat wave that occurred in Chicago in 1995 (Klinenberg 2002). In research designed to explain why so many people died in the series of days when Chicago's temperature rose above 100 degrees and stayed there that summer, the most vulnerable populations were found to be older people who were living in neighborhoods where violence had become a constant threat, where the active bustle of street life had slowed to a trickle, and where residents felt forced to retreat into their homes, isolated from their neighbors and from public life.

This type of disaster reminds us that the life of the city does not always resemble the somewhat romantic vision of a "street ballet," as Jane Jacobs described the urban scenes outside her window in New York's Greenwich Village. Any city will have some vibrant neighborhoods

Social capital may not emerge solely from close personal relationships with close friends and loved ones. As social media comes to play an increasingly important role in how we maintain our social ties, geographical proximity has become a less important source of social networks.

with high levels of community engagement, but many other neighborhoods are bereft of such relationships (as in the neighborhoods in Chicago during the heat wave that had so many older people dying alone). It is in the latter type of urban neighborhoods where some of society's most pressing social problems, including crime, violence, and severe poverty, are widespread. We explore this in the next section.

Mark Bussell

BIG QUESTION 15.4 Why Are So Many Social Problems Found in Cities?

SOCIAL PROBLEMS AND THE CITY

In *The Condition of the Working Class in England in 1844*, Friedrich Engels takes the reader into the rows of dilapidated cottages lining the side streets of Manchester, England, and documents the squalor in which the majority of working-class residents lived (Engels [1845] 1972, p. 430–31):

> Right and left a multitude of covered passages lead from the main street into numerous courts, and he who turns in thither gets into a filth and disgusting grime, the equal of which is not to be found—especially in the courts which lead down to the Irk [river], and which contain unqualifiedly the most horrible dwellings which I have yet beheld.

Engels was an early example of the many urban scholars who have described, through visual imagery or statistical portraits, the array of social problems that often come bundled together in the poorest urban slums, tenements, or high-rise housing projects. These scholarly accounts have led to various public policies, social reform efforts, and social movements designed to confront the unequal conditions that lead to urban poverty. Engels, who worked closely with Karl Marx and was a founder and leader in the socialist movement, used his description of urban squalor as a launching point for a larger critique of the capitalist system in urban England after the Industrial Revolution. Similarly, in the United States, Jane Addams combined her analysis of inequality in American society with activism around social issues as well as direct intervention, creating the first "settlement house" in Chicago (Addams 1910). The Hull House,

founded in 1889, was designed to promote social integration by providing services and supports to neighborhood residents from various ethnic and immigrant backgrounds. (See Chapter 2 for more on Addams' career and scholarship.)

Responses to the conditions of the urban poor are not always so sympathetic, however. The problems associated with urban poverty have often been explained as the result of cultural deficiencies of the urban poor (Lewis 1959; Banfield 1970), not as linked to the context of poverty and inequality that the economic system generates. This **culture of poverty** thesis holds that the poor hold values and ideas that make them less interested in trying to get ahead than other groups in society. Public policy targeting the urban poor has often reflected this very scornful view of the people who are "left behind" in cities. Consequently, many of the policies directed at poor urban areas have sought to alter or remove poor people rather than provide aid and support to try to improve existing neighborhoods.

Perhaps the most notorious example of these efforts can be found in the form of the 1949 Housing Act, which provided federal funding to help local governments acquire sections of cities with slum housing in an effort to redevelop these *blighted* (or deteriorated) areas. This policy, which came to be known as **urban renewal**, resulted in the destruction of entire swaths of poor and working-class neighborhoods in cities across the country and the replacement of these communities with carefully planned areas featuring new commercial space, transportation infrastructure, and high-rise apartments. Although urban renewal was framed as a reform effort designed to improve housing for poor people and improve blighted neighborhoods, scholars have shown that developers and the business community reaped most of the benefits of the policy. The residents of such communities were frequently an afterthought, as documented in a famous study of Boston's West End neighborhood, a vibrant working-class Italian American community that was torn down and redeveloped in the 1950s (Gans 1962). Over the years, many scholars studying communities that are identified as blighted and targeted for redevelopment have found socially cohesive communities in the midst of poverty, places where residents reject the "slum" label attached to their communities by outsiders.

Beyond redevelopment, urban renewal was also consciously used in many cities in the 1950s and 1960s to consolidate growing populations of Blacks in certain neighborhoods, and in this way reinforce racial segregation in urban neighborhoods. In Chicago, urban renewal resulted in a series of high-rise public housing projects that were constructed to house the city's growing Black population. The new projects helped alleviate the serious shortage of housing for Black families, who had in earlier decades pushed into overcrowded, low-quality housing in the city's "Black Belt" neighborhoods. But the location of the projects within the Black sections of the city also served to reinforce segregation in the city as a whole. These communities were then isolated from the largely White sections of the city surrounding them through the construction of the Dan Ryan Expressway, which was built alongside some of the largest projects in the city, providing a buffer between the city's White and Black neighborhoods (Hirsch 1983).

The example of Chicago's urban renewal brings to light the way race is intertwined with many of the major debates and controversies surrounding cities and urban poverty. Nowhere is this connection more apparent than in the issue of the **urban ghetto**, a term used to refer to sections of cities characterized by severe racial or ethnic segregation and deep poverty (Duneier 2016).

Concentrated Poverty and the Urban Ghetto

15.4.1 Identify changes that have contributed to concentrated poverty in neighborhoods in the United States.

One of the most important sources of change in American cities in the twentieth century was the **Great Migration** of Blacks from the rural South to the industrial cities of the Northeast and Midwest United States. By 1980, more than 4 million Blacks had made this move, and they and their children and grandchildren enormously enhanced the Black population of cities outside the South (Tolnay 2003).

The Dan Ryan Expressway was deliberately planned by Mayor Richard Daley to be located in such a way as to provide a buffer between Chicago's White and Black neighborhoods. One of the consequences of that decision was that Black neighborhoods on the South Side of the city were cut off from the rest of the city.

In the city of Detroit alone, the population of Blacks grew from just over 4,000 in 1900 to about 24,000 in 1920, over 350,000 in 1950, and over 750,000 by 1970 (Farley, Danziger, and Holzer 2000). Why did so many Blacks make the move north to cities like Detroit and many others? Many were driven by declining agricultural opportunities, which were amplified by the severity of racial discrimination and racial inequality in the Jim Crow era. They were also pulled northward, and later westward, by the growing demand for workers in the new factories of Northeastern, Midwestern, and Western cities. But they were also pulled by the emergence of Black cultural institutions in Northern cities and by the hope that racism would be less severe outside of the South (Lemann 1991). The maps in Figure 15.5 illustrate how dramatic this population shift was.

The sheer magnitude of this shift in population altered the demographic, economic, and cultural landscapes of cities throughout the Northeast, Midwest, and West. On the one hand, Blacks did have new opportunities for economic mobility that they were denied in the South, and Black culture flourished in cities throughout the Northeast and Midwest. On the other hand, the growth of the Black population in Northern cities was met with formal and informal efforts designed to maintain the "color line" in urban neighborhoods and schools. Racial segregation in housing, where Blacks were confined to particular neighborhoods but not welcome elsewhere, became a severe problem in cities throughout the country and has continued to be a problem ever since.

In 1945, sociologists St. Clair Drake and Horace Cayton published a comprehensive study of "Bronzeville," the name of a Black neighborhood on Chicago's South Side, a

Figure 15.5 The Great Migration

These maps compare the Black population in the United States in 1910 (top) and 1980 (bottom). By 1980, far more Black people were living outside the South.

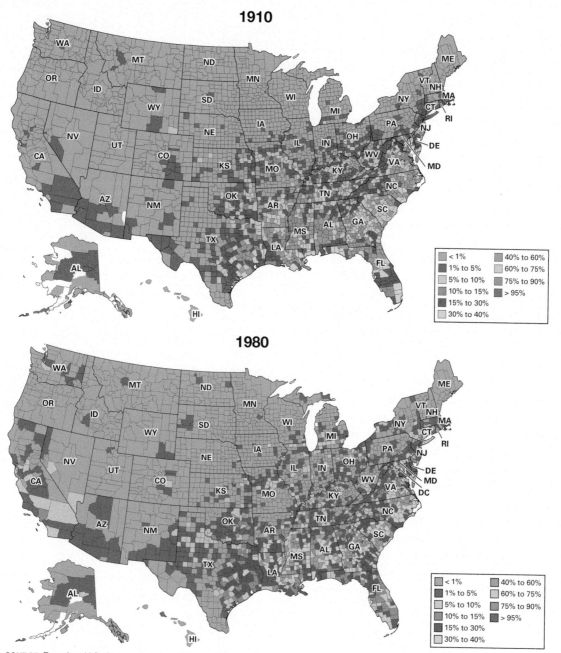

SOURCE: Based on U.S. Census data from 1910 and 1980.

representative part of the city's larger "Black Belt," where Black families were allowed to live prior to desegregation laws. The authors described a vibrant community where cultural and social life thrived despite high poverty, overcrowded and dilapidated housing, and unrelenting discrimination faced by residents in the rest of the City. They documented lively scenes from parks where "Bronzeville's teeming thousands swarm, lounging on the grass, frolicking in the Black Belt's one large swimming pool, fishing and rowing in the lagoon, and playing softball, tennis, or baseball" (Drake and Cayton 1945, p. 603).

While noting that certain sections and streets of Bronzeville were known as "lower-class" areas, the authors pointed out that poor people were not confined to any single section of Bronzeville but were "scattered from one end of the community to the other" (Drake and Cayton 1945, p. 602). And while "gambling dens" and "call-houses" were more prevalent within the lower-class sections of the city's Black Belt, churches were also widespread. Indeed, they describe "the evening hours of Bronzeville's lower-class areas" as "noisy with the cacophony of both hymns and blues" (Drake and Cayton 1945, p. 611).

This classic study of community life in Bronzeville was published before the civil rights movement had begun to flourish, before a wave of riots had swept through America's cities in the 1960s, and before the economic downturn of the 1970s, which hit many cities especially hard. If we move forward in time 40 or so years after Drake and Cayton wrote, to the end of the 1980s and 1990s, sociologists studying the same streets and parks in Chicago provide a very different portrait of city life on the South Side. For example, a more recent study of these neighborhoods describes vacant streets that resemble war zones stripped of all commercial activity, desolate and depopulated, where violence and drug abuse are prevalent and unemployment is rampant: "The windows and doors of apartments and houses are commonly barricaded behind heavy metal gates and burglar bars. Public facilities and spaces are not spared… most parks are 'no-go' areas, especially after nightfall" (Wacquant 2009, p. 55). But the story doesn't end there; Bronzeville and some other formerly "Black Belt" neighborhoods underwent gentrification after the mid-1990s as middle-class Black families began returning to the neighborhood (Pattillo 2007).

This imagery captures the emergence of a new form of urban poverty that became prevalent in the period following the civil rights era of the 1960s and that has become associated with a wide range of uniquely urban social problems. The new urban poverty can be characterized by several distinguishing features, including a growing concentration of the urban poor within a smaller number of extremely high-poverty neighborhoods, the persistence of severe racial segregation despite fair housing laws, and the growth in concentrated joblessness and related social problems. Although the social problems present in urban America were sensationalized by inflammatory political rhetoric and television shows like *COPS*, the change in the character of poor urban neighborhoods is nonetheless visible in statistics on concentrated poverty and violent crime. Let's look at one example. In Figure 15.6 on the next page, maps of Milwaukee illustrate that particular neighborhoods went into steep economic decline after the 1970s. While there was some relief in the decade between 1990 and 2000, the data show how concentrated neighborhood poverty is a long-term problem that spans decades. A prominent recent study of evictions of residents in Milwaukee from their homes found in recent years that as many as 8 percent (almost 1 in 10 families) were evicted *in a single year* (Desmond 2016).

So how did we get from the poor yet vibrant "Black Metropolis" of the 1940s to the desolate, violent Black ghetto of the 1980s? Or from thriving centrally located neighborhoods in Milwaukee to decaying and declining neighborhoods of today? In his book *The Truly Disadvantaged* (Wilson 1987), William Julius Wilson put forth one of the most influential sociological arguments of the past 50 years to help explain this change. Wilson's theory begins by documenting how manufacturing jobs began to disappear from cities in the Northeast and Midwest, leaving minority populations without the stable, working-class jobs that had drawn them northward in the Great Migration. With the decline in manufacturing jobs in central cities, joblessness skyrocketed and there were fewer "marriageable" Black men who could support a family and play the role of breadwinner—the rate of single-parent-headed families rose sharply, as did the rate of welfare receipt. In addition to the transformation of urban labor markets, Wilson demonstrated how civil rights legislation allowed middle-class Blacks to expand the boundaries of urban ghettos or to leave them altogether. Whereas the earlier research on Bronzeville described a community in which different segments of the Black community lived, worked, and played in close proximity, the movement of middle-class Blacks out of the traditional Black ghetto had the unanticipated consequence of removing the "middle-class buffer" from Black neighborhoods. When the middle class left, the community institutions they left behind, including churches and schools, deteriorated rapidly. The

Today's Bronzeville neighborhood in Chicago looks a lot different than it did in 1945, after undergoing a major decline in the 1950s through the 1990s and then a modest and uneven gentrification since then (Pattillo 2008; Moore 2019). Despite relatively high levels of poverty, even today there continues to be a strong community and cultural life in the community.

Figure 15.6 Urban Poverty in Milwaukee, 1970–2010

These maps of Milwaukee show that particular neighborhoods went into steep economic decline between 1970 (left) and 2010 (right).

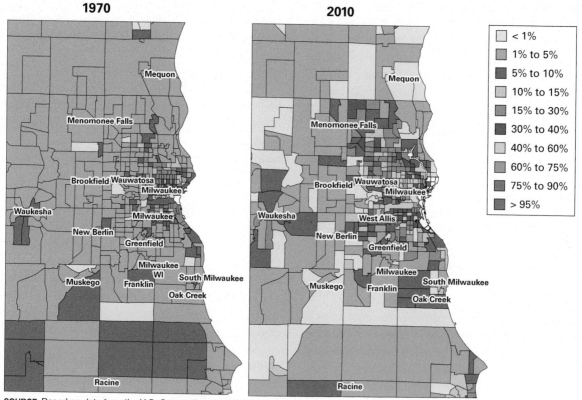

	< 1%
	1% to 5%
	5% to 10%
	10% to 15%
	15% to 30%
	30% to 40%
	40% to 60%
	60% to 75%
	75% to 90%
	> 95%

SOURCE: Based on data from the U.S. Census Bureau, 1970–2010.

Table 15.1 Urbanization of Poverty in the Developing World

While the percentage of the world's population living in urban areas increases at a steady rate (now over 50 percent), urban areas' share of the world's poor is growing at double the pace. This development is particularly salient in Latin America and sub-Saharan Africa.

1993	Urban Share of the Poor (%)	Urban Share of Population (%)
Latin America and Caribbean	47.7	72.3
Middle East and North Africa	15.3	52.8
Sub-Saharan Africa	24.3	29.8
South Asia	21.9	25.7
India	22.5	26.2
World Total (Excluding China)	24.2	41.6
2002	Urban Share of the Poor (%)	Urban Share of Population (%)
Latin America and Caribbean	59	76.2
Middle East and North Africa	19.9	55.8
Sub-Saharan Africa	30.2	35.2
South Asia	24.1	27.8
India	25.2	28.1
World Total (Excluding China)	28.2	43.4

NOTE: Urban and rural poverty measures using a poverty line of $1.08 per day (in 1993 PPP).
SOURCE: Ravallion, Shaohua, and Sangraula 2007.

result of these and other more subtle changes was a **concentration of poverty** in the urban ghetto that was associated with high levels of violence, homelessness, joblessness, and welfare receipt. If the Black ghetto of the 1940s was a place where all classes of Black families were forced to live,

the Black ghetto of the 1980s was a place where the most impoverished communities of racial and ethnic minority groups had been abandoned.

While we have focused on concentrated poverty and related urban problems in an American context, scholars of urban poverty have called attention to how the ghettos of America compare to, and have certain features of, especially impoverished ghettoes around the world, such as the impoverished favelas in Brazil, the townships in South Africa, and the banlieues of France—all of which are areas around the world with severe, concentrated poverty (see Table 15.1 for more information about how common concentrated poverty is). Further, in the developing world, there is growing evidence that some of the most extreme poverty is shifting from rural areas to urban areas (Montgomery et al. 2003), creating new challenges for cities. Concentrated poverty is a global problem, and it is becoming increasingly clear that the problems of cities should be thought of in global terms.

Despite the changes that have occurred in poor urban communities over time, the research of urban ethnographers—scholars who study people and places by immersing themselves in a community—typically captures a more complex reality of life in any nation's most disadvantaged communities. On the one hand, sociological research on the urban ghetto has provided vivid portraits of the ways in which the threat of violence comes to structure daily life in the poorest, most racially segregated sections of urban America, forcing youth to make constant strategic decisions about where and with whom to spend their time and how to negotiate potentially dangerous interactions (Anderson 1999). On the other hand, scholars studying the most intensely violent neighborhoods find individuals and families that rely on dense networks of support for childcare, friendship, emotional support, and financial assistance in times of crisis (Stack 1974; Venkatesh and Celimli 2004; Duneier 2015). Even in the most distressed neighborhoods across the United States, a strong sense of community can flourish.

Racial and Ethnic Segregation and Urban Diversity: A Closer Look

15.4.2 Discuss the diversity of America's cities.

How diverse are different kinds of communities in America? In Figures 15.7a–c, we show the racial and ethnic composition at three levels of analysis. There are three important points displayed in these figures. First, note the dramatic differences the cities, suburbs, and rural areas as well as the very high proportion of White Americans (around 80 percent) in rural places, while the suburbs are, on average, much less diverse than cities. Figures 15.7b and 15.7c take a closer

Figure 15.7a–c Racial and Ethnic Shares of Different Types of Communities

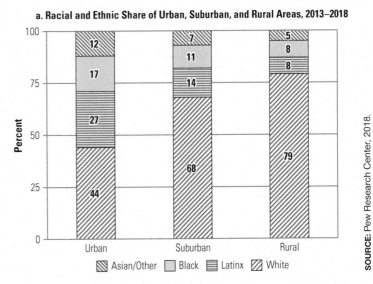

a. Racial and Ethnic Share of Urban, Suburban, and Rural Areas, 2013–2018

SOURCE: Pew Research Center, 2018.

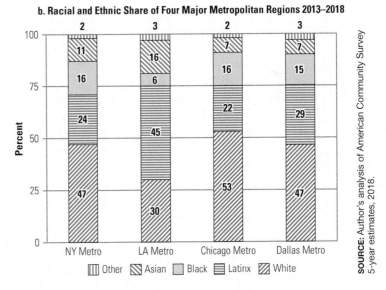

b. Racial and Ethnic Share of Four Major Metropolitan Regions 2013–2018

SOURCE: Author's analysis of American Community Survey 5-year estimates, 2018.

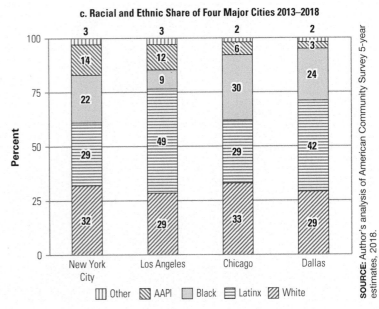

c. Racial and Ethnic Share of Four Major Cities 2013–2018

SOURCE: Author's analysis of American Community Survey 5-year estimates, 2018.

look at four metropolitan areas across the United States—New York, Los Angeles, Chicago, and Dallas—comparing the entire metropolitan region (cities plus suburbs) in Figure 15.7b, and just the four cities without their suburbs in Figure 15.7c. Los Angeles stands out as the most diverse metropolitan region in the United States, and is very unusual for showing very little difference between the diversity of the city of Los Angeles and its surrounding suburbs. Contrast that with the other three cities, which are far more diverse than their surrounding suburbs. In each region's central city, only about a third of the population is White. New York City and its suburbs has the largest percentage of AAPI people, while Los Angeles has the largest percentage of Latinxs by far (approaching half of that metropolitan's population), but the smallest Black population. Chicago is more evenly split between the four major groups, with a slightly higher proportion of Blacks; Dallas is like Chicago, but with more Latinxs and fewer Blacks. But overall, with the unique exception of Los Angeles, the general pattern is that the closer we get to the central city, the more diverse the population becomes.

While these broad statistics provide an overview and highlight a very important point about overall patterns of population distribution, both nationally and in four important metropolitan areas, they don't yet tell much about how much these groups live together or apart in any specific town or neighborhood within a larger city. But just as additional data on concentrated poverty reveal the degree to which poor people are clustered into a small number of neighborhoods, so too can data on racial and ethnic **segregation** show the degree to which individuals from different racial and ethnic groups live within the same neighborhoods or other smaller areas. For example, a city (like

Chicago) appears very diverse if you look at its overall population. Blacks, Latinxs, and Whites are almost all the same size (around 30 percent of the city's population). However, Chicago—like most large cities—is very segregated by neighborhoods. Parts of the city are mostly White, parts are mostly Latinx, and parts are mostly Black. There are some neighborhoods that are mixed, with residents from all three groups, but those neighborhoods are relatively rare across the city as a whole. In fact, Chicago is among the most segregated cities in America (Semuels 2018). But you can only see that by looking at the distribution of groups in smaller geographical areas. Figure 15.8 displays Black-White diversity in Chicago. A huge city like that is too large to show how much diversity there is in the city as a whole, but we get a better sense of the diversity of individual neighborhoods across the city with more detailed data. The map of Census tracts (areas with a population of around 4,000) for Chicago shows, for example, that the Black population is heavily concentrated in the southern and western parts of the city; in the very dark blue areas, the percentage of Black people can reach 90% or more.

What about the diversity of ethnic neighborhoods across the country, in view of the rapid increase in recent decades in immigration from other countries? The United States has seen an explosion of immigration since the passage of the Hart–Cellar Act in 1965, which overrode the previous national-origins quota system and rapidly changed the flow of immigrants coming to the United States. Whereas in the early part of the century most immigrants came from Europe, a majority of immigrants now arrive from Latin America (especially Mexico), the Caribbean, Africa, Asia, and the Middle East (Waters et al. 2007).

Figure 15.8

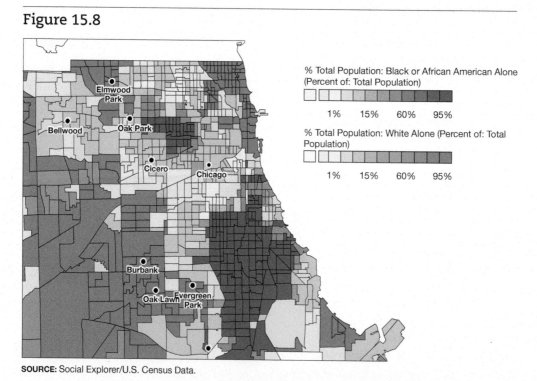

SOURCE: Social Explorer/U.S. Census Data.

East Hollywood in Los Angeles is an example of a vibrant global neighborhood that contains members of several different racial and ethnic groups.

The impact of all this immigration on metropolitan population centers is complex. Relatively few immigrants are moving to rural areas, and far more to cities than suburbs. There is some evidence that immigrants have played an important role in revitalizing some of the most distressed urban neighborhoods around the country, bringing new life to neighborhoods that had lost population and business activity for decades (Sampson 2015). Some have suggested that immigration has helped to facilitate the racial and ethnic integration of once-segregated neighborhoods. For instance, recent research has identified an emerging set of **global neighborhoods** around the country, which can be defined as neighborhoods that contain members of several different racial and ethnic groups (Logan and Zhang 2010). Los Angeles's East Hollywood, which contains a substantial number of immigrants from Latin America, Armenia, and Southeast Asia, is one such neighborhood. New evidence suggests that growth in the ethnic diversity of urban neighborhoods may chip away at the traditional boundaries separating Whites and Blacks, leading to the hopeful idea that an increasingly diverse urban landscape may cause a decline in racial segregation. With four large population groups (including AAPI people who are growing rapidly as a share of the overall U.S. population as well), the likelihood that neighborhoods or communities will continue to be made up of just one racial or ethnic group is declining.

But at the same time, neighborhoods and communities populated by immigrants have reproduced some of the older historical patterns of segregation. For instance, the number of Latinx Americans living in high-poverty *barrios* (the Latinx equivalent of the Black ghetto) rose alongside the growth in the concentration of poverty in mostly Black neighborhoods in the 1970s and 1980s (Jargowsky 1997).

These neighborhoods and communities combine ethnic segregation with low incomes, and this pattern of settlement. They generate challenges for immigrant families who live there, as the traditional pattern of upward mobility with each passing generation is no longer the dominant model of assimilation. Instead, immigrants' trajectories are better characterized by a pattern of **segmented assimilation**, in which the immigrants and their children follow one of several possible pathways of assimilation (Portes and Zhou 1993). One path is the traditional trajectory of upward mobility and cultural assimilation into the mainstream. But another, increasingly prominent path involves downward economic mobility and lives of urban poverty. A third, intermediate path for some immigrants and their children is integration into the economic mainstream while sustaining ties to the culture of their original home by continuing to live within residential enclaves. This is true of Chinese Americans in San Francisco, who make up close to a fifth of the city's population and are a large part of the entire city's civic life. As the proportion of non-White Americans continues to grow, this latter path may become increasingly common over time. In general, researchers have found that segregation—and where children grow up—is a key contributor to where they end up in life (Chetty et al. 2018). The extent to which racial and ethnic segregation contributes to concentrating poor families in disadvantaged neighborhoods continues to be an important source of the transmission of poverty from one generation to the next.

Dr. Kenneth Clark's influential research in the 1960s provided foundational insights into the ways that growing up in highly segregated communities affected how children viewed themselves and the people around them. Later researchers have confirmed and expanded these conclusions (see Massey and Denton 1993; Duneier 2015).

BIG QUESTION 15.5 How Is Life in Rural Communities Different from Cities and Suburbs?

RURAL COMMUNITIES

Despite all of the changes that urbanization has brought, there are still large numbers of people in the United States and elsewhere living in rural areas. In the U.S., approximately 20 percent of the population, or about 60 million people (almost one in five), live in a rural community (U.S. Census Bureau 2017). So our portrait of communities would be incomplete without examining how and in what ways social life in rural places is different than in metropolitan areas.

Research on rural communities was one of the earliest areas in which the application of sociological ideas into government policy became influential. Through the federal government's Department of Agriculture, as well as research done at state universities, the field of rural sociology grew rapidly in the 1920s, and it was the largest subfield in all of American sociology before World War II (Nelson 1969). Sociologists gathered new data about rural communities and played important roles in designing public policies aimed at farmers and farm communities during this time and especially under the New Deal in the 1930s (Gilbert 2016). Even earlier than that, however, some of the most influential early works of sociology closely examined the social significance of the transition from rural to urban communities, especially what one German sociologist (Ferdinand Tonnies) famously described in 1887 as *Gemeinschaft und Gesellschaft* (community and society). Tonnies and many later sociologists (including Louis Wirth and Georg Simmel, whose research we mentioned earlier, as well as the French sociologist Emile Durkheim) believed most aspects of social life are different between metropolitan regions and small towns. *Geminschaft* (community) describes a social world in which relationships are built on intimate knowledge between people, while *Gesellschaft* (society) presumes that in heavily populated

cities most relationships between people are more anonymous than they are in a community.

Some of the most important research on rural communities in recent years has been done by the sociologist Robert Wuthnow. Today a Princeton professor, Wuthnow grew up in a small town in Kansas, returning to his roots to study rural communities in the twenty-first century (Wuthnow 2011, 2013, 2018). One of his central observations is that portrayals of small towns and rural communities in the mass media, and to some extent social science research, are sometimes misleading or one-sided impressions of these communities. All too often, rural areas are portrayed as being in severe economic decline, riddled with opioid abuse and drug overdoses, and populated by people who are less educated and informed than their metropolitan counterparts. In recent years, there has been particular interest in studying voting patterns in rural communities, as many voters in these areas were very strongly attracted to Donald Trump and the Republican Party (see Figure 15.9). Also, in surveys and interviews, rural residents express much higher levels of concern about racial

Figure 15.9 Percentage of People Voting for Donald Trump for President in 2020

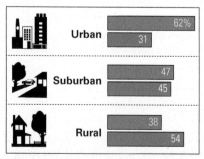

Urban	62%	31
Suburban	47	45
Rural	38	54

SOURCE: American National Election Study.

and ethnic diversity than do people in metropolitan areas (Hochschild 2016; Walsh 2016). But those facts do not capture all that is going on in rural America. All those things can be true, Wuthnow argues, but they do not fully capture the complexity of these communities.

In this section, we will first identify what a rural community is and how they have evolved over the past 150 years. We will then describe what is unique and distinct about social life in rural communities, and finally we will turn to a brief analysis of the challenges facing rural communities in the twenty-first century.

Identifying Rural Communities and Understanding Their Evolution

15.5.1 Describe the evolution of rural communities.

Before we begin, we need to first clarify what social scientists mean when they talk about rural communities (this question is similar to other issues of how we define geographic places that we've already considered in relation to urban and suburban areas). In general, rural places can be viewed as places that are located too far away from metropolitan areas for people to commute to every day for work. They also have low population density (recall by density, we mean the amount of population per each square mile), and they generally have small total populations. A general rule of thumb is that towns with fewer than 25,000 people and located 90 minutes driving time (or more) from the edges of the nearest metropolitan area are rural. Overall, 14,000 of about 19,000 incorporated cities and towns in America have populations below 25,000 and are located well outside any metropolitan area (Wuthnow 2018, p. 5). But even though more than two-thirds of cities are rural, their total share of the U.S. population is almost 20 percent.

What parts of America are most rural? The two maps in Figure 15.10 (on the following page) show the percentage of people in every county in America who are living in a rural community and how much that has changed over time. The top map displays the percentage of the rural population in every county in the United States in 1900, and the bottom map shows rural residence as of the 2010 census. Overall, about 60 percent of all people lived in rural areas in 1900 (with two-thirds of the rural population—40 percent of the entire population—living on farms). Today, the rural population is just one-third what it was in 1900. You can see this by noting how much lighter the 2010 map is than 1900 map; this reflects the fact that most counties have fewer people living in rural places now, a topic we'll discuss in more detail later.

Rural communities originally formed in the United States from the time of the earliest settlements, and spread out across the country with its westward expansion during the nineteenth century. Farmers and their families were among the first to establish new communities, often settling far from any significant city. Much of the Northeast and the South had established rural communities by the early 1800s. A major jump start to developing the frontier, and rural communities supporting that expansion, took place in the nineteenth century with the 1862 Homestead Act, which offered 160 acres of land to anyone who agreed to live there and develop a plot of land in states with land but few people or farms. Starting a farm could be very expensive, especially if the 160 acres contained trees that had to be cut down, as they often did in the Midwest. Yet with considerable determination, rural homesteaders, as they were known, persevered and built a nation of small and medium-sized farms across the Midwest and later the Western United States. There were also very large farms that emerged, especially in places with slave labor like the South or with plantation-style production using immigrant labor in the Southwest (Glenn 2002).

The daily routine of farm work—on small or larger farms—was hard; individuals were up at sunrise to feed animals and clean animal waste, and then begin a long day of hard physical labor working the land. Individuals who couldn't travel very far to metropolitan areas (before the advent of the automobile) made regular trips into the nearest small town, where they would typically find a general store, one or more churches, a bank or two, a small law firm or two specializing in farmer's issues, a post office and perhaps a few government offices (if the town was the county "seat" – the location of administrative offices for the county). It was there that farm families, who otherwise led very isolated lives, could connect with other people living in the community by attending weekly religious services or purchasing some needed goods or supplies. The town became the center of the social life for farmers for miles around.

Two innovations in the late nineteenth and early twentieth centuries brought immense change to rural communities that connected them to the wider world. The economic historian Robert Gordon (2016) has made a powerful case that the introduction of the first mail-order catalogs, which gave rural customers the ability to purchase the same goods as urban residents, was a significant and underestimated factor in transforming rural communities. Montgomery Ward, a Chicago entrepreneur, was the Jeff Bezos of his day (Bezos was the founder of Amazon). Ward brought out his first catalog in 1872, containing an immense number of products that could be ordered through the mail. Although it took a while to catch on, eventually Ward's catalog, like Amazon today, developed a national network of service centers that could deliver anything in the catalog to anyone in the country. Sears Roebuck Company soon joined Ward as a national mail-order company.

The second critical innovation was the arrival of the automobile, especially the cheap Model-T version that Henry Ford began selling in 1908. The Ford car, and other similar low-cost but durable models that arrived after

Figure 15.10 Percentage of Rural Population in American Counties, 1900 versus 2018

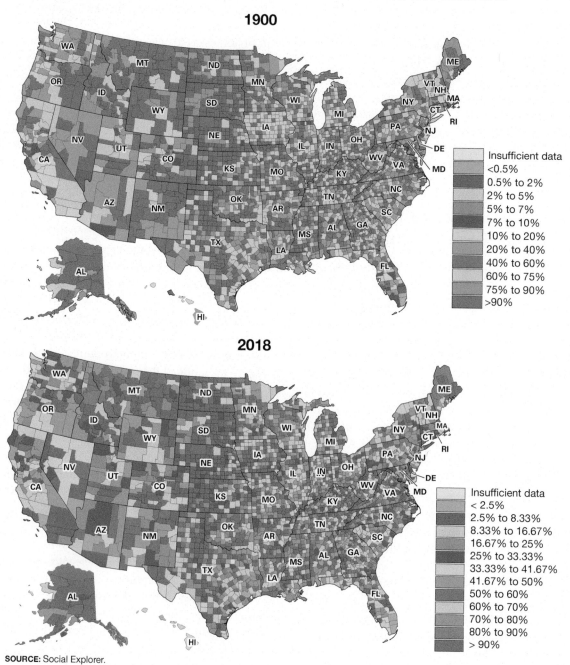

1900

Insufficient data
<0.5%
0.5% to 2%
2% to 5%
5% to 7%
7% to 10%
10% to 20%
20% to 40%
40% to 60%
60% to 75%
75% to 90%
>90%

2018

Insufficient data
< 2.5%
2.5% to 8.33%
8.33% to 16.67%
16.67% to 25%
25% to 33.33%
33.33% to 41.67%
41.67% to 50%
50% to 60%
60% to 70%
70% to 80%
80% to 90%
> 90%

SOURCE: Social Explorer.

World War I (particularly as General Motors emerged as the largest automobile company in the world) were immensely popular in rural communities across the country. Already by 1926, there were almost as many cars and trucks owned by farmers as there were individual farms (Gordon 2016, p. 164). The automobile was so popular that many small-town families were willing to forego basic necessities to own one. In their famous study of small-town Muncie, Indiana, in the 1920s, sociologists Robert and Helen Lynd inspected 26 of the most dilapidated houses in the town and found that while only five of those houses had bathtubs, all 26 had automobiles (Lynd and Lynd 1929, p. 255–56)! Owning an automobile meant that

individuals could drive into town or to larger metropolitan regions, as often as needed or desired. It was, for rural residents, an instrument of both convenience and freedom.

Today, residents of America's rural areas are much less likely to be as isolated from the cultural lives of bigger cities as they were 100 years ago. There are several reasons why that is true. The arrival of communication products that could be consumed by people anywhere has been an ongoing source of connection: First radio in the 1920s, television in the 1940s, and then the Internet and social media from the 1980s onward. Radio became the first media with national broadcasts. Popular television shows, mostly (although not completely) set in urban or suburban environments, broadcast themes to a rural audience which they would not otherwise have been exposed to. The rise of the Internet added another layer of information that made it possible for anyone, including rural residents, to connect with national cultural and political trends.

There has also been an important but little noticed shift in rural populations towards small towns that are in closer proximity to metropolitan areas. In other words, families in rural communities are more likely to live in a community that, while still rural, is closer to sprawling metropolitan regions than in the past. And more rural states are becoming more urban. Nebraska, a traditionally very rural state, now has more than half of its population clustered in three counties (out of a total of 93), with numerous small towns and families located much closer to metropolitan metropolitan regions than their predecessors 100 years ago. Unsurprisingly, these three counties contain the state's three largest cities (Sulzbergur 2011). Many people who prefer to live in small towns are nevertheless choosing towns that are close enough to commute to work or to find social and cultural activities in larger places, blurring the line between rural and metropolitan places in the process. One motivation has been that it is often better for rural businesses to be located closer to larger population centers to find workers and/or customers for their products. It's clear that urbanization trends found across the world have influenced the landscape even of small town America.

Characteristics of Rural Communities

15.5.2 Explain the concept of shared fate in rural communities.

The claim that "everyone knows everyone else" in small towns can't be literally true (unless we are talking about a very tiny place!), but its longstanding popularity among residents of rural communities implies something very important about those communities. Why might this be the case? Recall our earlier discussion of how central cities are places with large populations that are characterized by population density and diversity. In cities or metropolitan regions, residents will often interact with many people who are different from themselves. Rural communities are the opposite: They have small populations, low density, and low diversity (although the latter is changing in some places, as we'll see shortly). One of sociologist Robert Wuthnow's central ideas that emerged from his extensive research on rural America is that small towns can

be thought of as "moral communities," by which he means "a place to which and in which people feel an obligation to one another and to uphold the local ways of being that govern their expectations about ordinary life and support their feelings of being at home and doing the right things." It is easier to have such feelings when you encounter the same people often, and those people seem a lot like you. Nothing could be further from Simmel's characterization of the anonymity of urban life and the "blasé" attitude that comes with living in a crowded central city (as we described earlier in the chapter). That doesn't mean that people in large cities don't help each other; they are probably just as likely to help someone they walk by who is injured or a tourist who is lost as you would find in a rural place. But metropolitan residents are much less likely to feel obligated to the hundreds of thousands, or millions, of anonymous people who live in their region than rural residents may feel towards someone who lives in the same small town.

Small towns, far more than larger metropolitan regions, also have a crucial characteristic known as **shared fate**. In the strongest sense of the concept, shared fate is the belief that what happens to one member of the group happens to all, whatever other differences might exist (Dawson 1994). The well-being of a small community does indeed depend to a much greater degree on individuals and individual families than it does in metropolitan areas. It's easy to see why that is the case if we think about the concept mathematically: The relative importance of a family in a place with 500 people is almost certainly greater than it is in a place with 5 million people. Further, the economies of small towns are much more fragile than in larger places. When a single business is struggling or goes out of business in a small town, it will have a much greater impact than in a large metropolitan area. And lost jobs from one business closure can quickly spill over into the economic health of other businesses and an entire community.

In smaller towns, like Stockbridge, MA (pop. 2,000) shown here, people are more likely to know each other and feel like part of a community than in large cities.

The fact that small towns typically have less class inequality also facilitates the sense that everyone has a shared fate. Although there is plenty of economic inequality in rural communities, it differs considerably from metropolitan areas and is generally less extreme. The wealthiest residents of rural communities are usually professionals with small town practices (doctors or lawyers), owners of large farms, or successful small business owners. The affluent people rural places may have incomes in the hundreds of thousands, but there are relatively few multimillionaires who make their primary home in a rural area (many rich people have second or third homes "in the country," but few have their primary residence in a rural area). There are virtually no gated communities made up of rich people isolating themselves from their less affluent neighbors (as in metropolitan areas), and in most rural places you will not find fences in front of houses such that you cannot see someone's home. There are higher rates of poverty in rural areas than in metropolitan areas (on average), but the cost of living is typically significantly lower in rural places, making it easier for poor families to get by than in more expensive metropolitan areas.

In addition to reduced class inequality, most places in rural America are much more homogeneous in terms of race: Most rural communities are either all or almost all White. This racial similarity helps to create a sense of cohesion, and it also likely promotes higher levels of hostility to people who are different. Some of the anti-city bias of small-town residents is based on a perception that in large cities people of color and immigrants are dominant, and that White people are not so welcome. This is often connected to anti-government views that are based on widespread perceptions that the government is giving handouts to people of color living in large cities (Gilens 1999; Conn 2014). Of course, not all rural residents hold these views, but they are common enough that any close investigation of rural communities will hear such opinions (Cramer 2016; Wuthnow 2018, chpt. 6).

But the dominance of Whites in rural areas has been changing in some places. Large agriculture companies now own huge swaths of farmland in places as diverse as Iowa's cornfields and California's central valley. These companies hire farm workers to work the land, and their need for low-wage labor has attracted an increasingly diverse population to rural areas across the country. The Department of Labor's National Agricultural Workplace Survey finds that close to 75 percent of farm laborers are immigrants, a large majority of whom are Mexican (Farmworker Justice 2019). Meatpacking plants, many of which are also located in rural areas, often recruit immigrants as well (Artz, Orazem, and Otto 2007). Over the past several decades, Latinxs and other immigrants have been the fastest growing ethnic groups in rural America, posing a new set of questions for sociologists to consider: Will rising ethnic diversity change the cultural landscape of rural areas in the twenty-first century, as it did for central cities and metropolitan areas in the twentieth?

Challenges Facing Rural Communities in the Twenty-First Century

15.5.3 Identify the factors that have led to the decline of rural communities.

Across America, many small towns are dying. It's not the first time—researchers have identified at least 3,800 abandoned "ghost" towns in the United States (Geotab 2020), many of which go back to the nineteenth century and some of which are popular tourist destinations today. Although abandoned ghost towns are extreme outcomes, declining population is a condition faced by many contemporary rural communities. One reason is that family farms have been under severe financial stress for decades, causing the number of them to dwindle every year. As recently as 1991, small farms were producing half of all food production, but by 2017 that number had fallen to just one-quarter (Semuels 2019). We mentioned earlier that in 1900, 40 percent of all Americans lived on a farm (and another 20 percent of the U.S. population lived in small towns). A hundred years later, just 1 percent lived on a farm (and total farm employment, including hired farm laborers, was under 3 percent of the working population). Every year, more and more farmland comes under the control of large agricultural companies that rely heavily on expensive and technologically sophisticated equipment to do most of the work, and employ relatively few people (bringing in large numbers of temporary migrant workers at harvest time). A similar process is happening in many rural mining communities, which have lost some or most of their jobs to automation or irrelevance. Coal mining, once a huge source of jobs in rural parts of the country, has largely been replaced by cheaper or less environmentally harmful energy sources. The decline of farming or mining in small towns often feels like the loss of a "way of life," which residents readily experience (Duncan 2014, chpt. 1). Rural communities that have the good fortune of a large employer can be devastated if that employer leaves town or goes out of business.

One of the most important issues facing rural communities is what is known as **brain drain** (Carr and Kefalas 2009). Families everywhere hope that their children will go to college and find secure and well-paying jobs. In any metropolitan area, there is a full range of employment opportunities for college graduates. But when young people from rural communities finish college, they may find there are very few job opportunities available to them in either the small town they grew up in, or in other similar small towns. As a consequence, they are much more likely to move to a metropolitan area, bringing with them their talents and knowledge. And they are simply not being replaced by an equally large flow of college graduates moving from metropolitan to rural areas.

If we look at the big picture, rural communities in the United States (and in many other rich countries) divide into three broad categories (Wuthnow 2018). The first are those areas that have a solid economic foundation and have managed to retain their sense of community. In these places, young people are staying and building families and carrying the town forward into the future. In the middle group are communities that are neither thriving nor failing but are in a fragile position where the loss of a major employer or other community pillar threatens to start a downward spiral. At the bottom are thousands of rural communities that have lost jobs and population. Many of these places have no clear road back to health.

What factors help rural communities thrive? Sometimes just being near a major highway, airport, or train stop can help sustain a community by making it more attractive for businesses or factories to operate there. Some areas still have viable small farms or ranches that have been under the same family for decades, and those families often remain heavily invested in their community (although, as we noted, only 1 percent of Americans live on farms in the twenty-first century). Rural places that have great natural beauty can benefit either from tourism or from rich families who build weekend houses there (and in either case, bring economic activity into the community). Some have military bases nearby. Others may have a small college or be the "county seat" (the place where all official business in a county is done). The latter two examples will lead to employment opportunities for college graduates and professionals, which should reduce the problem of brain drain. The county seat always has a range of government offices, including a courthouse, and that will attract professionals like lawyers, bankers, social workers, insurance salespeople, and so forth. In small towns with greater resources, the local public schools will likely be of better quality, so families hoping to get their children a good education won't feel pressure to move. Another source of rural stabilization in recent decades (in the era of mass incarceration) is the presence of a nearby prison (Huling

2002). Prisons are frequently located in rural areas, and provide significant employment opportunities. Indeed, state governments have sometimes relocated prisons to declining rural communities as a strategy of redevelopment.

Having a solid economic foundation makes it easier for families to stay in an area and invest in their community. This is the major reason why, at the opposite end of the spectrum, there are thousands of small towns and rural areas that are seeing significant decline. Without jobs, people start to leave the community. Without jobs in the community, resources for everything else are starved. Schools and other public institutions can, over time, start to run down, making it less desirable for families with children to stay. As people depart, it eventually becomes difficult to find enough children to even operate schools, and the closing of the local schools is often seen as a tipping point in a community's decline. Other amenities—shops, restaurants, medical clinics—will also struggle to stay afloat as the population declines. New employers are unlikely to find such communities attractive places to create jobs. The people "left behind" in declining communities are often much older (or in retirement), or people who don't have the means to move somewhere else in search of a better future.

The feeling of being stuck in a place with few job opportunities and limited means to go somewhere else can create a sense of desperation and hopelessness. One of the more stunning research findings in recent years has been the discovery of an almost unprecedented *decline* in life expectancy for rural White men, that is, in spite of all the advances in medical science and rising life expectancy for other groups, growing numbers of White men are dying in middle age in rural communities (Case and Deaton 2020). Opioid abuse and opioid-related deaths have become a major problem in these communities in recent years, as have suicides, deaths from alcohol abuse, and accidents. The impact of despair, more difficult to measure, is surely also a factor.

Small towns in some places are thriving, while in others they are in decline. Two factors that help a place thrive are the presence of state and local government offices and tourism. The picturesque small town of Juneau, Alaska (shown on the left) has grown from just 6,000 people in 1970 to over 30,000 today, as it is the capital of the state and a popular tourist destination, which creates jobs and opportunities for people. Rural places that are reliant on farming, however, have often experienced declining populations and jobs as family farms struggle to survive in a twenty-first century world of large-scale agriculture.

Mark Bussell

BIG QUESTION 15.6 How Will Cities Change in an Increasingly Connected World?

CITIES AND THE CONNECTED WORLD

We live in an increasingly interconnected, or "global," world. Cities play a critical role in the social, cultural, and economic flow across borders, and this is yet another way in which rural communities are struggling to keep up. As we've noted, it is largely in large metropolitan areas and their central cities that diverse populations come into contact with each other. Most immigrants to a new place will start out their new life living in a large city. Many cities will develop small **ethnic enclaves**, where families migrating from the same country will settle, opening restaurants and shops that serve the community and adventurous people from outside who want to experience something new.

There are many ways to demonstrate the degree to which people living in cities have become connected around the world. One powerful way is to see it. A few years ago, New York's Museum of Modern Art hosted a unique exhibit called New York Talk Exchange (see Figure 15.11). The exhibit featured visual representations of the real-time connections between New York City and the rest of the world made through Internet traffic and telephone conversations. Put together by designers at Massachusetts Institute of Technology's Media Lab, the arcs of light shining into and out of New York provide a beautiful reminder of how closely connected the world has become.

Data from the New York Talk Exchange exhibit showed that about 20 percent of transnational phone calls coming into the Bronx, one of New York City's five boroughs, originated in Santo Domingo and Santiago, the two largest cities in the Dominican Republic (Sassen 2008). About 10 percent of international calls out of Brooklyn are made to Kingston, Jamaica, and 17 percent are made to the combination of

Kingston, Santo Domingo, and Haiti. For the most part, these are not business transactions made over the phone; rather, they are phone conversations linking residents of the Bronx and Brooklyn with their families and friends in their home nations. The shining lights in small cities throughout the world provide visual evidence of a new reality: Humans cross national boundaries to live and work in greater numbers than ever before.

Immigration and the Global Urban Landscape

15.6.1 Explain how the world's cities are linked together.

The United Nations estimates that in 2019, roughly 272 million people lived in a nation other than the one in which they were born (United Nations Department of Economic and Social Affairs 2019). In the United States, the liberalization of immigration policy in the mid-1960s led to rapid growth in immigration that has accelerated over time. About 42 million immigrants are now estimated to live in the United States alone, an increase of more than 10 million since 2000. Connections to their origin countries go beyond verbal communication. Although data are difficult to obtain, estimates suggest that at least $56 billion of financial assistance in the form of **remittances**, or money sent from migrant workers to family and friends at home, flowed from the United States in 2015 (World Bank 2021). In some countries like Jamaica, El Salvador, and Lebanon, up to 20 percent of the national income comes from workers who send money back from abroad (DeParle 2007).

The growing presence of immigrants has had an enormous impact on America's cities. Although there is some

Figure 15.11

The image shows how New York City connects with other parts of the world, and it reflects the racial and ethnic separations within the city itself. For example, Flushing, a neighborhood in the borough of Queens, is clearly very diverse with many calls going to multiple countries, but this kind of diversity is not constant throughout the city.

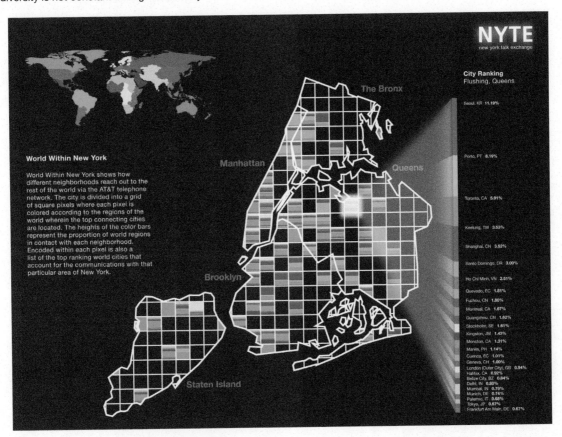

evidence that immigrants are beginning to locate directly in suburban areas, America's major cities continue to be the primary points of entry for the majority of immigrants from abroad (Tavernise and Gebeloff 2010). For instance, in at least five major U.S. cities—from Miami, Florida, to El Paso, Texas—census data show that immigrants make up more than a quarter of the population. By contrast, immigrants make up only about 4.1 percent of the population in more rural areas of the United States (Wilson and Singer 2011; U.S. Department of Agriculture 2013). The emergence of ethnic enclaves—large, stable sections of cities where the local labor market, residential market, and culture are dominated by a specific ethnic group—was not anticipated by early urban theorists. As an example, take a look at Figure 15.12 on the next page to see how immigration has affected the racial and ethnic composition of Miami, the primary destination for Cuban Americans.

Globalization and the City

15.6.2 Discuss how immigration and globalization have changed cities and urban neighborhoods.

Just as people move and communicate across the world, technology allows products and services to flow rapidly across national boundaries—and the nodes of much

of this activity are located in the world's global cities. A **global city** is a particular kind of city, in which the headquarters of international firms that create and control the cross-border flow of information and commerce are located (Sassen 2007). Global cities have a concentration of people and infrastructure that allows for the coordination of the international economy. They are the hubs of international finance and technology in a world where business activity crosses national boundaries easily, where products are marketed across the world, and where capital moves fluidly. In early work on the emergence of global cities, attention was focused on New York, London, and Tokyo (Sassen 1991), but scholars have now identified a range of global or "globalizing" cities that coordinate regional business activity that spans the boundaries of nations, including cities as diverse as São Paulo, Brazil; Jakarta, Indonesia; and Moscow, Russia (Castells 2000). In the United States, New York, Chicago, Los Angeles, San Francisco, Houston, and Miami all have some characteristics of global cities as well.

The emergence of global cities has implications that extend beyond international finance and technology. These cities, and the cross-national activity that runs through them, have wide-ranging impacts on the social and economic structure of urban areas and on the lives of the

Figure 15.12 Latinx Population in Miami

These maps show the dramatic rise in the Latinx population in Miami, Florida, over the last 50 years. Like Miami, many cities throughout the United States have experienced large demographic shifts, which have reshaped and transformed neighborhoods.

1970 Census Tract % Hispanic

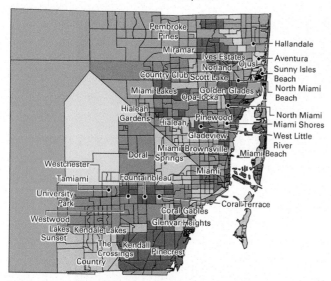

1980 Census Tract % Hispanic

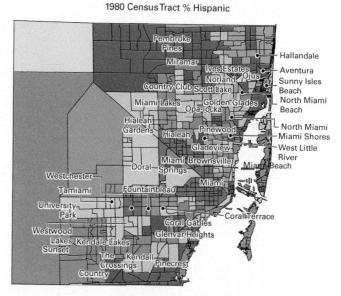

1990 Census Tract % Hispanic

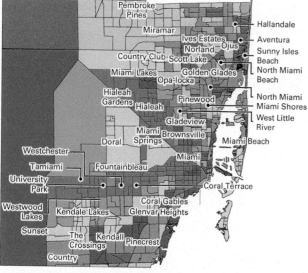

2000 Census Tract % Hispanic

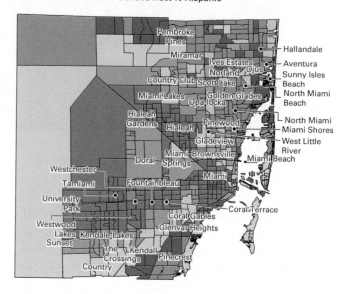

2010 Census Tract % Hispanic

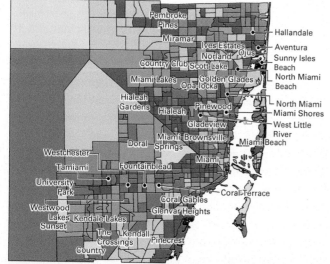

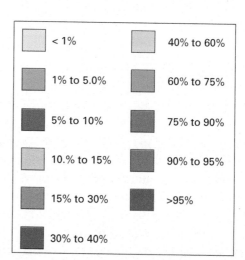

< 1%	40% to 60%
1% to 5.0%	60% to 75%
5% to 10%	75% to 90%
10.% to 15%	90% to 95%
15% to 30%	>95%
30% to 40%	

SOURCE: Based on data from the U.S. Census Bureau, 1970–2015.

On the left is a café in Palermo Soho, a fashionable neighborhood in Buenos Aires, and on the right is one of the city's many slum districts. The former represents the types of establishments prevalent in "urban glamour zones," where a global elite (locals and visitors) shop and eat, often isolated from poor people or even ordinary middle-class residents of the city. The high cost of housing in global cities like Buenos Aires, however, has pushed many residents and newcomers into slums, known in Spanish as *villa miseria*.

residents within them. The spatial layout of cities, the policies implemented by local governments, and the economic structure of cities are all affected by the globalization of urban areas (Marcuse and van Kempen 2002). In this sense, there is an increasingly strong connection between the *local* conditions of urban populations and the *global* networks of firms operating in global cities.

Globalization has impacted cities in other ways as well. Beginning in the 1980s, scholars began to put forth arguments about how the process of globalization alters the basic economic structure of urban areas, leading to new relationships among city governments, corporations, and residents as well as new forms of class struggle. As America's urban economies transformed in the 1970s, the manufacturing jobs that once formed the base of urban labor markets began to decline rapidly and were replaced by service-sector jobs, including everything from relatively low-wage work in retail stores to high-salary work in banking, that have come to dominate many urban economies in the postindustrial information age. Global cities like New York and London reshaped their urban landscapes to provide the infrastructure and the amenities required to attract and retain the international firms that made them centers of global business (Zukin 1992).

Some scholars of globalization argue that this shift has contributed to especially large inequalities in global cities. For instance, sociologists argue that the globalization of economic activity is leading to an increasingly sharp divide between the global elite, who control international commerce, and the global service class, who cater to this elite. For the new international firms and businesspeople, the global city "consists of airports, top-level business districts, top-of-the-line hotels and restaurants, a sort of urban glamour zone" (Sassen 1996, p. 635; see also Freeland 2006). For example, the Palermo Soho neighborhood in Buenos Aires, which contains high-end fashion boutiques and trendy new restaurants, is one such glamour zone. The neighborhood is a hot spot for young upper-class locals and affluent tourists, who hop the bars and cafés late into the night.

Focusing on the other end of the class spectrum, sociologists have documented the dynamic between the global elite and the relationships with the growing numbers of people needed to serve them (as restaurant and hotel workers, cleaning and maintenance workers, nannies and childcare workers, and so forth). Further, the global orientation of these cities and their elites may push local governments to shift attention away from local residents—public spaces are left untended, the homeless are removed from public areas, and enclaves rise up to protect the city's areas of centralized global activity (Davis 1990). As a general rule, more powerful actors tend to get their way in politics more often than not (see Chapter 8 for more details). When globally-oriented elites emerge in large cities, their resources and preferences (and those of the corporations they work for) may overwhelm everyone else.

The research of scholars analyzing class struggles within global cities reminds us of a basic question: Whose city is it? There is a built-in tension in the dual quest to make cities competitive in regional and global markets and to make cities livable for all groups of residents. As several of the scholars whose work we have reviewed make clear, this tension becomes greater in the age of globalization. It is one of the central tensions that will determine the future of the nation's, and the world's, urban areas.

Conclusion: Our Urban Future

As far back as 1968, scholars began predicting that improvements in air travel and telephone communication would make location in an urban area less critical, leading to declines in urbanization in a "post-city" age (Webber 1968). Here we are a few decades later, and communication and information technology have improved beyond anyone's expectations, yet urbanization continues, and cities are more important than ever to the world economy. All signs point to a decidedly urban future.

What this future will look like is much less clear. We have described the various forms that cities and metropolitan regions are beginning to take, from the proliferation of edge cities to growing megaregions in Asia and elsewhere. The forces that determine which cities can flourish in this new environment are also changing. Urbanist Richard Florida suggests that the central cities and metropolitan regions that will grow in the future are those that can offer the cultural amenities and the feel of an open, diverse, and tolerant urban environment that can attract the group of professionals he labels the *creative class* (Florida 2012). The creative class includes artists, writers, professors, designers, and architects, who collectively produce creative culture within a city. Focusing on culture and lifestyle, Florida argues that cities need to compete for creative people before they can compete for business. Florida's arguments are sometimes criticized for failing to take into account larger forces like political power and the economic structure of cities, but his outlook has been extremely influential among city planners and managers (Peck 2005). The idea that people and ideas are the drivers of urban innovation and growth is echoed in economist Edward Glaeser's optimistic book *The Triumph of the City* (Glaeser 2011). Glaeser views cities as the centralized locations where ideas and knowledge are able to diffuse across a population, creating an emergent set of innovations that combine specialized perspectives and talents in a way that is only possible in an urban setting. From this perspective, cities will be the key to solving the world's most pressing human problems.

The focus on the role of cities as centers of innovation, creativity, and economic growth should not distract us from the fact that cities are the sites of the world's most extreme inequality and contain within them a wide range of social problems. As cities globalize and complete the shift toward information- and technology-based economies, many scholars of urban centers see a widening gap between those who benefit from the shifts and those who do not. Rural areas have also seen many related issues. The brain drain away from rural areas is the flip side of the dominance of cities as places of opportunity for those with knowledge and high levels of educational achievement. While rural areas do not typically have the same levels of inequality as central cities, there is a growing inequality *between* rural areas. Those that have managed to keep jobs and sustain the features of small-town life—the shared moral community—that attract and hold people to these towns are doing fine. But many other rural communities are, by contrast, experiencing a downward spiral and population loss that will be difficult to overcome and will severely limit the opportunities of its residents.

What we can be certain of is that, as the world continues to urbanize, the human future will increasingly be determined by the health of the places where people live.

The Big Questions Revisited 15

15.1 What Draws People to Cities? Most of the human population now lives in urban areas, which raises a number of intriguing questions. This section explored how to define a city and how city life has affected different aspects of our individual lives. We learned a sociological understanding of cities is more complex than the official definitions provided by government agencies.

How the World Became Urban

Urbanization and the Growth of Cities
Learning Objective 15.1.1: Identify the major forces that have led to urbanization.

Urban, Suburban, and Rural Patterns of Settlement
Learning Objective 15.1.2: Identify the urban and suburban forms that emerged during the twentieth century.

Key Terms
urban (p. 397)   population density (p. 397)
metropolitan region (p. 397)   suburban (p. 397)
rural (p. 397)   central city (p. 397)   urbanization
(p. 398)   megacity (p. 399)   megaregion
(p. 399)   white flight (p. 400)   redlining
(p. 401)   racial covenants (p. 401)   suburban
sprawl (p. 402)   edge city (p. 402)

15.2 How Do Neighborhoods Form and Change?
The development of cities and communities is not natural but rather driven by political and economic forces. This section explored the types of communities that have emerged over time due to individuals and groups with different, sometimes competing, political and economic interests.

Neighborhoods and Urban Change

Urban Ecology: The Chicago School

Learning Objective 15.2.1: Define urban ecology and discuss the central questions confronted by the Chicago School.

The Political Economy of Cities and Communities

Learning Objective 15.2.2: Explain how political and economic interests work together to promote growth and affect urban change.

Key Terms

urban ecology (p. 403)   growth machine (p. 404)   gentrification (p. 405)

15.3 **How Do Cities Influence Who We Are, Who Our Friends Are, and How We Live?** This section explored how cities are distinguished not only by their size, density, or other measurable characteristics but also by how they affect the way we interact, work, and live together.

Living in an Urban World

Urbanism as a Way of Life

Learning Objective 15.3.1: Discuss how urbanization has affected our lives and communities.

Communities and Networks

Learning Objective 15.3.2: Discuss the impact of technology on community life.

Key Terms

social isolation (p. 406)   community (p. 408)   social ties (p. 408)   social network (p. 408)   social capital (p. 409)

15.4 **Why Are So Many Social Problems Found in Cities?** In this section, we discussed how cities have increasingly become the sites of the world's most extreme wealth and poverty. Urban areas have always been great engines of wealth creation, but a growing proportion of the world's poverty is now moving from undeveloped, rural areas into densely populated urban slums.

Social Problems and the City

Concentrated Poverty and the Urban Ghetto

Learning Objective 15.4.1: Identify changes that have contributed to concentrated poverty in neighborhoods in the United States.

Racial and Ethnic Segregation and Urban Diversity: A Closer Look

Learning Objective 15.4.2: Discuss the diversity of America's cities.

Key Terms

culture of poverty (p. 410)   urban renewal (p. 410)   urban ghetto (p. 411)   Great Migration (p. 411)   concentration of poverty (p. 414)   segregation (p. 416)   global neighborhood (p. 417)   segmented assimilation (p. 417)

15.5 **How Is Life in Rural Communities Different from Cities and Suburbs?** This section covered what life is like in small towns and how small towns have evolved over time. It also discussed the central challenges facing rural communities in the twenty-first century.

Rural Communities

Identifying Rural Communities and Understanding Their Evolution

Learning Objective 15.5.1: Describe the evolution of rural communities.

Characteristics of Rural Communities

Learning Objective 15.5.2: Explain the concept of shared fate in rural communities.

Challenges Facing Rural Communities in the Twenty-First Century

Learning Objective 15.5.3: Identify the factors that have led to the decline of rural communities.

Key Terms

shared fate (p. 421)   brain drain (p. 422)   ethnic enclave (p. 424)

15.6 **How Will Cities Change in an Increasingly Connected World?** In this section, we discussed how cities are the nodes that link the world together. To fully comprehend the forces that shape our world, we must expand our view well beyond individual city streets and communities and even beyond the boundaries of individual nations.

Cities and the Connected World

Immigration and the Global Urban Landscape

Learning Objective 15.6.1: Explain how the world's cities are linked together.

Globalization and the City

Learning Objective 15.6.2: Discuss how immigration and globalization have changed cities and urban neighborhoods.

Key Terms

remittance (p. 424)   global city (p. 425)

Chapter 16
Families and Family Life

by Kathleen Gerson

"That's a typical family." We've probably all heard this phrase before, but is there such a thing as a typical family? And how can we really know what life is like in someone else's home? Often our perceptions as outside observers are quite different from the perceptions of those who are family members. Consider the story of 24-year-old Josh, who grew up in Oceanside Terrace, a small, working-class, suburban community on Long Island not far from the hustle and bustle of New York City. In a survey, Josh had reported growing up with his biological parents and two brothers in a household where his mother stayed home during his early years while his father worked as a carpenter. From the outside, Josh's childhood home seemed to be what Americans tend to think of as a typical, traditional family, but his family experience was much more complex than it appeared. Josh was back for a brief visit to celebrate his parents' anniversary before moving to a new job on the West Coast when I sat down with him one morning to talk about his family life.

Josh recounted a sequence of events that left him feeling as if he lived in three different families. The first, anchored by a breadwinning father and a home-centered mother, did indeed take a traditional form. Yet this outward appearance mattered less to him than his parents' constant fighting over money, housework, and the drug habit his father developed in the Army. "All I remember is just being real upset, not being able to look at the benefits if it would remain like that, having all the fighting and that element in the house," Josh told me.

As Josh reached school age, his home life took a major turn. His mother found a job as an administrator in a local business and, feeling more secure about her ability to support the family, asked her husband to move out and "either get straight or don't come back." Even though his father's departure was painful and unusual in this neighborhood where two-parent homes were the norm, Josh also felt relief. His parents' separation provided space for

his mother to renew her self-esteem through her work outside the home. Josh missed his father, but he also came to accept this new situation as the better of two less-than-perfect alternatives.

Yet Josh's family changed again a year later when Josh's father "got clean" and returned home. Even more

My Sociological Imagination

KATHLEEN GERSON

My sociological imagination began when I realized I was part of—yet stood apart from—the world around me. Born in the deep South, I grew up in a community where traditional homes and worldviews were the norm. Yet my own family was headed by a single mother strongly committed to social justice. As I developed a sense of being both an insider and an outsider, I learned to see the world from several vantage points at once. A move to San Francisco during adolescence deepened my questioning of what others took for granted. By the time I reached college, these experiences had attuned me to the power of social contexts. Sociology offered a place to address the big issues facing contemporary societies. With that aim in mind, my research focuses on gender, work, and family life, with an eye to understanding the new work and family pathways emerging in the United States and other postindustrial societies. Although I rely on a range of methods, I specialize in qualitative interviewing. My goal is to uncover how personal biographies intersect with social institutions to bring about social change. I have written books and articles that offer innovative frameworks for explaining the revolution in gender, work, and family patterns, and my current research focuses on the new worlds of work and care, where occupational paths and personal relationships are increasingly uncertain.

Families evolve over time, in response to both internal changes (such as births, deaths, marriages, and divorces) and also societal forces (such as changing cultural ideas about gender roles and family forms, as well as social and economic factors that influence the conditions under which families form and evolve).

Mark Bussell

431

remarkable, when his parents reunited, they hardly seemed the same couple. Time away had given his father a new appreciation for his family and a deepened desire for greater involvement in his children's lives. Josh's mother displayed major changes as well, for taking a job had given her pride in knowing she could stand on her own. As his father became more attentive and his mother more self-assured, the family's spirits and fortunes lifted. In Josh's words, "that changed the whole family dynamic. We got extremely close."

In the years that followed, Josh watched his parents build a new partnership quite different from the conflict-ridden one he experienced in his earliest years. He developed a new and closer relationship with his father, whom he came to see as one of his best friends. He also valued his mother's strengthening ties to work, which not only nourished her sense of self but also provided enough additional income for him to attend college.

Josh's story exemplifies several important but often hidden truths about family life in contemporary societies. First, families are not "types" but are rather a set of dynamic processes and paths that develop in unexpected ways over time. In other words, families are films, not snapshots, and family life is an unfolding, often unpredictable process. Despite the apparent stability and continuity his family may have shown on a survey checklist, a closer look revealed a domestic life that actually changed in fundamental ways. Second, families can look very different depending on one's point of view. Survey and census questions may reveal a snapshot of how a family looks at one or even several points in time, but an in-depth interview that charts the ups and downs of family life is more likely to reveal how family life is a pathway where crucial events often trigger unexpected transitions and unforeseen outcomes. Third, families come in all shapes and sizes, and it is misleading to assume that one type is better than another. A "one size fits all" model cannot describe the many shapes that today's families take, nor can it capture the quality of interactions among their members.

Finally, and perhaps most crucially, Josh's story reveals how the tumultuous changes of the last several decades require us to think in new ways about family life in the United States and other advanced, postindustrial societies. In a rapidly changing world, his parents were neither able nor willing to maintain a static set of arrangements for organizing their marriage or providing emotional and financial support to their children. As they developed new responses to a host of unexpected events, Josh's family changed dramatically. Its shift from a breadwinner–homemaker to a single-parent to a dual-earner home exemplifies both the growing diversity of family forms and the increasingly fluid nature of family life. These changes offer today's young adults options their parents barely imagined and their grandparents could not envision. Yet they also pose new challenges for creating and sustaining intimate relationships, for bearing and rearing children, and for integrating earning a living with caring for others. In the context of twenty-first-century America, some families may thrive and others may not, but all of today's families face uncharted territory.

The Big Questions

1. **What is a family?** To begin at the beginning, we first need to examine the meaning of the term *family*. What is a family, and what are the various ways to define it? Answering this question leads to the next one.

2. **Why are families changing?** To understand the contemporary debate over "family values," we need to map out the competing views about the current state of the American family, how we got here, and what we need to do in response.

3. **What are the challenges of developing relationships and families in the twenty-first century?** Some pressing issues that affect American families today include the decline of permanent marriage and the new contours of adult commitment as well as the blurring of gender divisions and the rise of work–family conflict.

4. **What is it like to grow up in the twenty-first century?** The experiences of children growing up in twenty-first-century families and transitioning to adulthood are very different than they once were. How have these changes affected children and young adults?

5. **What social policies around the world best support changing families?** Finally, we will place this overview of American family life today in a comparative perspective. By examining how other countries have experienced and tackled many of the same challenges, we will be in a better position to create the supports that American families will need to thrive in the years to come.

BIG QUESTION **16.1** | What Is a Family?

H. Armstrong Roberts/ClassicStock/Alamy Stock Photo

THE MANY WAYS WE DEFINE *FAMILY*

The family is a core institution in all societies. It provides the first and most immediate context for our physical, emotional, and social development. As we age, family issues confront us with many of life's most crucial choices—whether and whom to marry, how to shape our sexual activity, whether to bear children and how many to bear, and how to raise the children we choose to have. Families influence us in ways so deep that it is difficult to exaggerate their importance. Yet their power to shape our destiny depends on their links to other institutions. Families are shaped by the societies they inhabit, but they also have the power to transform those societies.

Most of us think we know what a family is, even if we cannot always offer a precise definition. Yet "the family" can have many meanings. In this section, we will explore how we define family, starting with a global and historical perspective.

A Global and Historical Perspective on Families

16.1.1 **Identify family forms that can be found throughout human history and across diverse societies and households.**

Though families are a universal social institution, their forms vary greatly across diverse social settings. Americans sometimes think the phrase *traditional family* refers to an independent household anchored by a husband who concentrates on earning an income, a wife who focuses on childrearing and housekeeping, and their biological children. This type of family is known as a **homemaker–breadwinner family**. Yet to call it "traditional" is inaccurate and misleading. From a global and long-term historical perspective, it is clear that the (male) breadwinner/(female) homemaker household is relatively rare, only appearing at a certain point in history, and then declining as the dominant way of organizing family life.

Many other family forms can be found throughout human history and across diverse societies and cultures. Patterns such as arranged marriages, **polygamy** (when a person, typically a man, has multiple marital partners, typically wives), and multigenerational households, for example, were common prior to the rise of the modern West, and they continue to hold sway in many

Mark Bowden/123RF

In the past, sociologists and other analysts of the family typically refer to a legally married couple of one man and one woman, with one or more children, as a *nuclear family*. Despite the many changes to what actual families look like today, in recent surveys Americans still consider this to be the prototypical family, even as it represents a declining percentage of all families.

non-Western cultures. Some societies, especially those ruled by monarchies, have allowed marriages between cousins and even siblings among the ruling elite in order to keep the transfer of inherited power within an enclosed family system. And some cultures, known as **patrilocal**, require a wife to live with her husband's parents and obey their authority.

The homemaker–breadwinner household reemerged as an ideal family type in America in the mid-twentieth century, largely as a consequence of post–World War II economic prosperity and the growth of the suburbs (and as women, whose labor was needed during World War II, lost employment opportunities that briefly opened up during the war). But while a majority of American households took this form for much of the 1950s, many did not. Working-class and minority families, in particular, were more likely to find the middle-class ideal of a home with the father as sole earner either out of reach or unappealing. Equally important, many husbands and wives who lived in these so-called traditional households found

Oberhaeuser/Agencja Fotograficzna Caro/Alamy Stock Photo

Since the peaking of the homemaker–breadwinner household in the mid-twentieth century, we have seen the rise of a diverse array of family forms, including single-parent families.

them unnecessarily stifling. When renowned feminist Betty Friedan spoke of middle-class women's confinement to domesticity as "the problem that has no name" (Friedan [2001] 1963, p. 57) and sociologist William Whyte (1956) referred to the conformity (and financial pressures) expected of the "organization man," they both identified a growing sense of unease about the reigning 1950s family structure.

Since that time, American families have changed in vast and unanticipated ways, reminding us that the history of family life is a history of change. We have seen the rise of a diverse array of family forms, including dual-earner, **single-parent**, same-sex, and single-adult homes, which now vie with breadwinner–homemaker households for social and cultural support. Because these changes leave no one untouched, family life has become the site of both private struggles and public contention. If the 1950s produced a misleading belief in the ideal family, the twenty-first century leaves us facing instead a series of puzzles and paradoxes. Is the family declining, or is it here to stay? Do families shape people, or do people shape families? Is there one best family form, or is it better to have a variety of family forms and practices? When it comes to these (and many other) questions, there are no simple answers. Instead, we need a sociological lens that allows us to see family life from a variety of perspectives, just as a prism allows us to see light in all of its hues.

Household or Kinship System?

16.1.2 Explain how residence patterns and kinship systems contribute to different definitions of family.

Social scientists traditionally used the term *family* to refer to a group of people who live together in a household and share biological and/or legal ties. The U.S. Census Bureau, for example, in collecting and analyzing census data, defines a *family* as a set of people living together who are connected by biological or legal ties and distinguishes these family households from nonfamily households, which consist of two or more individuals living together who are not linked by biological or legal ties—such as a cohabiting couple, a group of college roommates, or unattached singles sharing an apartment or house. By using this definition, the Census Bureau explicitly includes married couples (with and without children) and single parents living with their children in the category of family, while excluding childless couples who are not married but living together, whether heterosexual or gay.

Yet many people disagree with such a strict definition, preferring instead to use a more subjective definition. Figures 16.1 through 16.5 indicate the extent to which

Figure 16.1–16.5 What Criteria Make a Household a Family?

Figure 16.1 A Husband and Wife with One or More Children

Figure 16.1 shows a strong consensus that a married couple with children is a family.

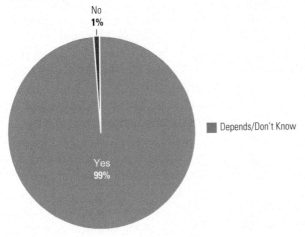

No
1%

■ Depends/Don't Know

Yes
99%

Figure 16.2 An Unmarried Man and Woman Who Live Together with One or More Children

But as Figure 16.2 shows, there is slightly more disagreement when people are asked if unmarried couples with children are a family.

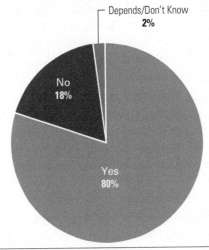

Depends/Don't Know
2%

No
18%

Yes
80%

Figure 16.3 A Gay or Lesbian Couple Living Together and Raising One or More Children

In Figure 16.3, we can see people disagree even more when they are asked whether same-sex couples with children are a family.

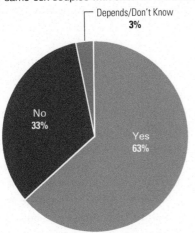

Depends/Don't Know
3%

No
33%

Yes
63%

Figure 16.4 A Gay or Lesbian Couple Living Together with No Children

While 63 percent of respondents perceive same-sex couples with children to be a family, a slight majority do not consider same-sex couples without children to be a family.

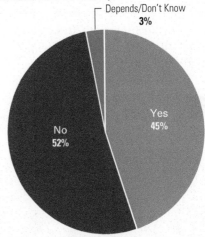

Depends/Don't Know
3%

No
52%

Yes
45%

Figure 16.5 An Unmarried Man and Woman Who Live Together with No Children

Less than half of respondents believe that unmarried different-sex couples without children are a family.

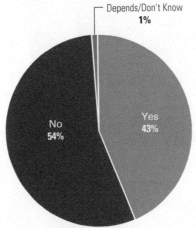

Depends/Don't Know
1%

No
54%

Yes
43%

SOURCE: Data from Pew Research Center's Social and Demographic Trends Project.

Americans consider various arrangements to be a "family." These definitions are also linked to differences in ethnic and class cultures. Minority subcultures and residents of poor neighborhoods are more likely to create wide networks of caretaking and financial support that may not fit any of these definitions. The anthropologist Carol Stack famously described the broad support networks that people in poor neighborhoods may rely on as "fictive kin"—that is, people whom we rely on, provide support for, and feel close to as if they were family members (Stack 1974; Collins 1991).

The rise of **same-sex marriage** provides a vivid example of how social changes in the way people live can prompt major—even revolutionary—changes in the ways we define "family." Although largely inconceivable for most of American history, the legal right of same-sex couples to marry became a flash point of social and political contention in the closing decades of the century. As an outgrowth of the LGBTQ movement, in the 1980s gays, lesbians, and trans people began to claim family rights that were granted to different-sex couples. In the early years of this debate and buoyed by popular opposition to gay marriage, the U.S. Congress passed and President Bill Clinton signed the Defense of Marriage Act in 1996, allowing states to refuse to recognize same-sex marriages granted under the laws of other states. Yet less than two decades later, in 2015, the U.S. Supreme Court declared all restrictions on same-sex marriage to be unconstitutional. In this remarkably brief time span, a majority of public opinion had shifted from opposition to support for legally recognizing and accepting families anchored by same-sex couples, much as opposition to interracial marriage had evaporated many decades before. Such changes in how Americans view families underscore the subjective process that produces definitions of "the family" and points to the likelihood that our definitions will continue to expand as new ways of living emerge.

The complexities of defining family become even greater once we consider other societies and cultures. In contrast to the view that a family is defined by a household that shares legal ties, anthropologists who study families in many different cultures call them **kinship systems**—the social links and boundaries, defined by biology and social custom, that establish who is related to whom. Kinship systems link people together in a variety of different ways, depending on the rules and customs of the community. In modern settings, including in the contemporary United States, it is common to stress the emotional bonds that connect people who care deeply about each other, whether or not they are linked by concrete bonds of law or biology. Many people today thus refer to their very closest friends—and sometimes even their pets—as family (Powell et al. 2010). As if that isn't confusing enough, for many research purposes it is often more useful to think of "households"—the people who live together with some kind of romantic or biological relationship—as a more useful starting point than "family."

None of these definitions is either right or wrong, nor is one inherently better than another. The value of any definition depends instead on its usefulness in explaining the social world, and that can change with the social puzzle that needs solving. Sociologists thus conceive of the family as a social institution with multiple dimensions—"the familistic package," as sociologist William J. Goode once described it (Goode 1982). This package of social relationships can consist of a network of **kin**, a group of people who share a residence or household, or cohabiting couples with or without children. Cultural meanings guide definitions, perceptions, and decisions about who is a member of one's family and who is not.

Sociologists also distinguish between the families we inherit and the families we create (Struening 2010). Our "family of orientation" consists of the people linked to us by birth—our parents, siblings, and extended kin (technically, our entire extended family). Our "family of procreation," in contrast, consists of the relatives we gain over the course of our lives through marriage and

Who do you consider to be your "family?" Some people today refer to their close friends or extended family as family members. Some even think of pets as family members.

Ariel Skelley/Tetra Images, LLC/Alamy Stock Photo

MARK Bussell

The importance of family, in whatever form it takes, remains central to most people's core identities. Documenting collective moments through rituals like birthdays, anniversaries, and other special events is part of the process through which families sustain their intimacy.

childbearing—our spouses, partners, and children. Yet in postindustrial societies, these terms seem overly simple and out of date. Now that many couples sustain committed partnerships that do not involve legally sanctioned marriage or childbearing, the term *procreation* cannot encompass the wide range of chosen families emerging in the United States and elsewhere.

Our definitions also shape the questions we can pose about family life. If we define families as systems of kinship, our focus turns to questions about how kinship links and boundaries are mapped in any given society: Who counts as a member of the **nuclear family**—that is, the socially recognized parents and their dependent children—and who counts as extended kin (for example, are distant relatives you have never met usefully described as "kin")? If we turn to other kinds of societies, these distinctions get even more complicated. In premodern societies, kinship lines sometimes included a number of people who extend far beyond the nuclear unit to encompass a whole clan. In some tribal societies, the biological parents are not even recognized as the social parents. For example, the pioneering anthropologist Bronislaw Malinwoski found that among a tribe known as the Trobriand Islanders, a child's uncle—that is, his or her mother's brother—performed many of the social tasks that modern Western societies associate with fatherhood, such as providing material support and enforcing discipline,

while a child's biological father acted in a similar way toward his sister's children (Malinowski [1913] 1964).

Modern societies, in contrast, draw boundaries that limit kin to a much smaller number of people, rarely extending beyond cousins and second cousins (Levi-Strauss 1964). Because modern societies are large and complex, they have fewer concerns about intermarriage within kinship groups than simple societies. Yet this complexity also requires more attention to creating legal standards for who is and is not considered a family member as well as for establishing the lines of responsibility and obligation among those deemed members of a family. Common practices such as divorce, remarriage, and out-of-wedlock childbearing have complicated these concerns. Equally important, the rise of reproductive technologies means an increasing number of children may have both social parents and biological parents, including a sperm donor, an egg donor, or a surrogate mother. As the boundaries and definitions of parenthood blur and grow, kinship systems become more difficult to chart.

As we examine the many ways family life develops—as an institution and a set of lived experiences—we first need to understand how and why families (and family life) in contemporary American society have been changing and why those changes have frequently been the topic of social controversy and division (Risman 2010). We will examine that in the next section.

Big Cheese Photo LLC/Alamy Stock Photo

BIG QUESTION **16.2** Why Are Families Changing?

CHANGING FAMILIES

Given the many ways that we can define and understand the family, it is perhaps no surprise that the study of family life lends itself to multiple interpretations and disagreements. Heated debates have not only taken place among scholars and journalists but also have played an important role in recent elections and political campaigns. This has not always been the case; at many times in American history, the topic did not provoke nearly as much contention. Why, then, is the "family" so controversial today?

The most obvious reason is that, unlike the post–World War II era, one family type no longer dominates others. In 1950, with the baby boom underway, almost 60 percent of U.S. households consisted of a married couple with children, and three-quarters of the wives in these couples did not hold a paid job. Yet recent decades have witnessed a rapid erosion of this once predominant form, which now accounts for less than 15 percent of American households. Instead, a mosaic of living arrangements—including dual-earning married couples (heterosexual and gay), nonmarried heterosexual and gay couples living together, single-parent families, and single adults living alone or with others—-coexist side by side. Figure 16.6 shows how the composition of households has changed over the past 60 years. The figure shows every possible type of family, ranging from married or living together with children, married or living together without children, single parent, and more. These changes

are dramatic. For example, over 40 percent of U.S. households in 1960 consisted of married couples with children; today, that figure is just 19 percent (this is shown in the area with the

Figure 16.6 TYPES OF FAMILY HOUSEHOLDS, 1940–2020

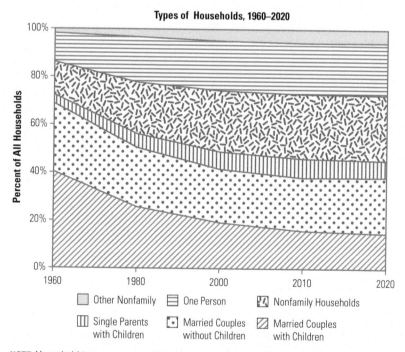

NOTE: Household types are arranged here into two groups: Family households and nonfamily households. A family household contains at least two persons—the "householder" (the adult who is arbitrarily defined as the "head" of the household by the Census Bureau) and at least one other person related to the householder by birth, marriage, or adoption—and these households are then categorized into three types: Married couple; male householder with no spouse present; and female householder with no spouse present. In the figure above, both types of households in which there is only one adult and no spouse are called single-parent families. A nonfamily household, by contrast, may contain only one person—the householder—or additional persons who are not relatives of the householder (such as roommates). We have separated out people living alone in the figure.

SOURCE: Vanorman and Jacobson, 2020.

red diagonal lines). Conversely, the proportion of people who live alone has grown from 13 percent to 28 percent, and the percentage of single-parent families has more than doubled (shown in light grey). There has also been a large increase in nonfamily households, most of which are cohabiting adults in a romantic relationship.

The rise of diverse family forms has not only transformed the residential landscape; it has also undermined an earlier consensus about what makes a group of individuals into a family. In the wake of such a vast and ongoing social shift, it is perhaps inevitable that thorny research questions arose. On one side are those who argue that the erosion of the "traditional" family, with an earner-husband and caretaker-wife, endangers society; on the other are those who argue that supporting many different family forms is necessary for social justice and personal well-being. These differing perspectives suggest different causes and reach different conclusions about the consequences of family change (Giele 1996). In this section, we will examine these perspectives.

The Family Values Perspective

16.2.1 Discuss the concerns of proponents of the family decline perspective regarding the nature of families today.

Some critics argue that changes in the American family reflect a weakening of **family values**—the orientations people have toward family responsibilities—which reflect rising selfishness and unfettered individualism. They see the growth in nontraditional living arrangements as evidence that people have become less willing to assume their proper adult obligations. Proponents of this perspective believe lower marriage rates, along with rising rates of sex outside of marriage, couples living together without marrying, high divorce rates, and the rapid increase in births outside of marriage reflect a decline in adult commitment.

These critics worry that the increasing number of single mothers and out-of-wedlock births endanger children. Even in two-parent families, they are concerned about employed mothers' absence from the home as well as the blurring of gender distinctions and the weakening of fathers' position as head of household that women's entry into the workplace appears to represent. Many of these critics see the acceptance of same-sex partnerships as yet another example of the devaluation of "traditional" different-sex marriage. The weakening of these traditional forms has been argued by a number of prominent authors and some social scientists (Blankenhorn 1995, 2009; Popenoe 1988; Popenoe, Elshtain, and Blankenhorn 1996; Whitehead 1997).

There are two ways in which most sociologists of the family question the family values hypothesis. First, by focusing on the central role of eroding traditional values, the family-decline perspective ignores many of the positive aspects of these changes, such as expansion of equality and personal choice that new family forms permit, and the unshackling of women to pursue careers and independence outside the home. Second, and equally important, the family-decline argument works more as an *evaluation* of new family forms rather than an explanation of why they have emerged. We will need to examine other theories if we are to explain *why* families have been changing.

The Economic Restructuring Perspective

16.2.2 Discuss how the economic restructuring approach explains changing family arrangements.

A second perspective, which has been favored by some social scientists, focuses on economic factors as drivers of family change. In particular, what is often called the *economic restructuring* approach argues that basic social and economic forces have eroded the foundations of the breadwinner–homemaker family and required new family arrangements. The decline of both well-paid and often unionized blue-collar jobs and secure white-collar career paths have left fewer men with the ability to earn enough money to support a family on their own. In a parallel development, the growth of service work has expanded the pool of jobs for women, while expanded educational opportunities have encouraged and allowed them to pursue professional careers once reserved for men. These changes, which have occurred over the past few decades (as we discuss in more detail in Chapters 12 and 14), have allowed women to pursue more independent lives, but they have also made it more difficult for families to survive on only one income.

Figures 16.7A and 16.7B highlight these economic and occupational changes. Figure 16.7A shows the major increase in education obtained by women. In 1960, over half of all women did not graduate from high school. By 2016, that percentage had fallen to under 10 percent. Conversely, in 1960 less than 10 percent of women had college degrees, while by 2016 the number was over one-third and rising. Figure 16.7B shows that women's earnings as a percentage of men's has risen from under 60 percent in 1960 to about 83 percent today (the black line in the figure, which is the average for all groups). Interestingly, we see that Black and Latinx women are actually closer to Black and Latinx men (with these women making close to 90 percent of what the men make), while White and Asian American/Pacific Islander women are further away from their counterparts. Today, women have far more choices than their predecessors did 60 years ago.

Figure 16.7 Women's Educational Attainment, 1960–2016; Women's Median Earnings as a Percent of Men's, 1960–2017

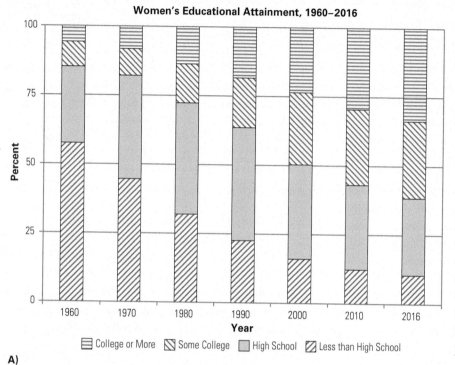

A)

B)

NOTE: Percentages are of women age 25 and older. Source: U.S. Census Burea, Educational Attainment Historical Tables (Table A-1). Retrieved from: https://www-census-gov/data/tables/2016/demo/education-attainment/cps-detailed-tables.html.

SOURCE: U.S. Department of Labor analysis of 1961–2018 Annual Social and Economic Supplements, Current Population Survey, U.S. Census Bureau.

once enjoyed is waning, replaced by a growing divide between the top tier of well-compensated, securely employed professionals and everyone else. If families are more vulnerable today, it is not because they have rejected traditional family values but rather because they cannot rely on a stable, predictable economic and social system to provide for their needs.

By recognizing the institutional constraints over which most families have little control, the economic restructuring perspective does not assume the new family patterns reflect changing values. Instead, family shifts stem from growing constraints on the viability of more traditional options, along with expanding desires to take advantage of new opportunities. Because these shifts are irreversible, it is shortsighted and even harmful to try to turn back the clock or to blame people for their values.

The Gender Restructuring Perspective

16.2.3 Discuss the mismatch between the structure of jobs and the caretaking needs of families.

The focus on economic causes of family change is important, but many sociologists argue that it alone cannot provide a complete explanation. For these sociologists, it is important to also acknowledge the role played by the growing desire of many women—and men—to live in families that do not resemble the heterosexual, gender-divided household that predominated in the mid-twentieth century. This third perspective on family change focuses on *gender restructuring*. It highlights the growing mismatch between the structure of jobs (and careers) and the caretaking needs of families. While the gender evolution has sent mothers into the labor force and allowed more single-parent and dual-earner households (including heterosexual and gay couples) to form, complementary changes have not occurred in the structure of jobs or caregiving. To the contrary, employees who wish to move ahead or even keep their

From an economic restructuring perspective, blurring gender boundaries, the rise of dual-earner families, and a new emphasis on individual choice and self-reliance are all linked to the consequences of a new economic order. These changes have produced a mix of new opportunities and new insecurities. The financial stability that middle-class families jobs are expected to place their paid work before family pursuits. Yet parents, especially mothers, are expected to shower their children with attention and are chastised for leaving them with other caretakers, even when these caretakers are devoted and competent (Hays 1996; Moen and Roehling 2005; Williams 2010). Families may have changed, but the structure of the workplace and the organization of childrearing often presume a sole-earner at work and an intensive caretaker at home that is no longer practical or desirable for most families.

These growing conflicts can leave parents stressed and overburdened as they contend with time squeezes every bit as severe as their financial squeezes. These work–family conflicts also create dilemmas about how to resolve a host of competing needs and values. How do adults balance the desire for personal independence with the value of lifelong commitment? How do parents trade off between the need to earn money and the need to care for their children? How do children experience growing up in diverse and changing families where new opportunities coexist with new uncertainties? How are these opportunities and uncertainties distributed across families in different classes and ethnic subcultures? And is it possible to develop social

policies that reconcile the growing divide between those who wish to restore the once dominant homemaker–breadwinner household and those who support more diverse and **egalitarian relationships** (where caretaking and breadwinning tasks are shared more or less equally by both partners)?

The gender restructuring perspective acknowledges the irreversible nature of change, but it does not assume that these changes are complete. Rather, this perspective draws our attention to the dilemmas and paradoxes created by inconsistent and contradictory social arrangements that are still evolving (Lorber 1994; Risman 1998). To make sense of modern families, we need to understand the interplay between inescapable social forces, such as the rise of a postindustrial economy with uncertain job paths, and the efforts of individuals, families, and societies to craft innovative resolutions to the dilemmas created by incomplete change. These dilemmas take many forms, from tensions in forging adult commitments and sharing earning and caretaking tasks, to new challenges in growing up and making the transition to adulthood, to new class and ethnic inequalities. We examine each of these dilemmas in the next section of the chapter.

Sofiia Shunkina/Alamy Stock Photo

BIG QUESTION 16.3 What Are the Challenges of Developing Relationships and Families in the Twenty-First Century?

THE NEW CONTOURS OF ADULTHOOD COMMITMENT

In spite of all of the changes in intimate relationships, rumors of the death of marriage are greatly exaggerated. Most Americans want to, and eventually will, become married. At some point in their lives, about 90 percent will marry, and even though many of those marriages will end in divorce, a majority of those who divorce will

choose to remarry (Casper and Bianchi 2002; Cherlin 2009). (Americans, as the joke goes, love marriage so much that many will do it several times.) Time and again, studies report that Americans consider having a good marriage as one of their most important life goals (Kefalas et al. 2011). Indeed, the fight for same-sex marriage rights serves as a powerful indicator of its continuing importance.

However, beneath that general notion is a great deal of change. People are more likely to delay marriage than in the past, with significant consequences. In 1960, the average age of marriage hovered around age 20 for women and age 23 for men; today, people are more likely to live together before getting married and/or postpone a first marriage until their late 20s or early 30s. They are also more likely to divorce or separate if the marriage proves dissatisfying (divorce rates rose dramatically from the 1950s to about 1980, reaching a very high level that has been stable since then). Further, what people want out of marriage and the attributes they look for in a mate have been changing in many important ways (Finkel 2017).

Figure 16.8 shows the results of a fascinating survey fielded with identical questions in 1939 and again in 2008, and it illustrates just how mate preferences changed over a 70-year period. For both men and women, in 2008 the most important quality in a partner was "mutual attraction and love." In 1939, this seemingly basic requirement for a life-long relationship was not the most important, ranked only at #4 for men and #5 for women. In 1939, both men and women prioritized dependability and emotional maturity, whereas these were much less important in 2008. Education and good looks scored much higher in 2008, while in 1939 good health was scored much higher by both men and women (perhaps because advances in medical science have reduced the importance of health problems). In 1939, women were much more interested in a mate with "ambition/industriousness," whereas in 2008 this was not important for either men or women. The quality that changed the most for both men and women from 1939 to 2008 was chastity, reflecting the much greater openness to sexual exploration before marriage in recent decades.

In this section, we'll explore the implications of these trends more deeply, beginning with an account of what is known as the "deinstitutionalization" of marriage.

The Deinstitutionalization of Marriage

16.3.1 Explain how marriage has become deinstitutionalized in today's society.

American culture has always embodied a tension between creating lifelong commitments and retaining a measure of personal autonomy about whether and how to build intimate relationships (Swidler 1980). These contradictory values go back as far as the nation's founding, when both individualism and community became central to the national identity (Bellah et al. 1985). Yet this tension has found different expressions in different historical periods. Prior to industrialization before the Civil War, parents exercised great control over their children's mate choices. Most families worked on farms, and all members of the family contributed to its economic well-being. The separation of work and home, which most of us take for granted today, was much less common in this period.

With the rise of industrialization (and urbanization, as jobs were increasingly located in cities and metropolitan areas), a more socially and geographically mobile labor force emerged, and the ability of parents to control their children's marital choices diminished. This new economic system fostered a new family unit, the **conjugal family**, consisting of a relatively autonomous married couple who were expected to seek their fortune outside the parental household (Goode 1963). The conjugal unit not only fit well with the industrial system; it also elevated the importance of emotional considerations, such as love and companionship, over parental approval as the appropriate criteria for choosing a mate. The industrial system also produced the physical, economic, and mental separation of the home and the workplace. As many forms of work, and especially the manufacture of goods, moved outside the home

What people want from a marriage partner has changed considerably over time, but the value placed on getting married remains very strong.

Figure 16.8 What Women and Men Want, 1939 and 2008

Qualities Women Want in a Mate

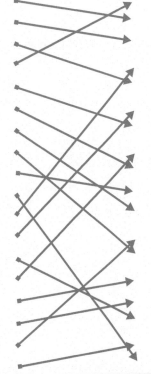

RANK IN **1939**

1. Emotional stability, maturity
2. Dependable character
3. Ambition, industriousness
4. Pleasing disposition
5. Mutual attraction, love
6. Good health
7. Desire for home, children
8. Refinement, neatness
9. Education, intelligence
10. Chastity
11. Sociability
12. Similar education background
13. Good financial prospect
14. Similar religious background
15. Favorable social status
16. Good cook, housekeeper
17. Good looks
18. Similar political background

RANK IN **2008**

1. Mutual attraction, love
2. Dependable character
3. Emotional stability, maturity
4. Desire for home, children
5. Education, intelligence
6. Sociability
7. Pleasing disposition
8. Ambition, industriousness
9. Good health
10. Good financial prospect
11. Similar education background
12. Good looks
13. Refinement, neatness
14. Similar religious background
15. Good cook, housekeeper
16. Favorable social status
17. Similar political background
18. Chastity

Qualities Men Want in a Mate

RANK IN **1939**

1. Dependable character
2. Emotional stability, maturity
3. Pleasing disposition
4. Mutual attraction, love
5. Good health
6. Desire for home, children
7. Refinement, neatness
8. Good cook, housekeeper
9. Ambition, industriousness
10. Chastity
11. Education, intelligence
12. Sociability
13. Similar religious background
14. Good looks
15. Similar education background
16. Favorable social status
17. Good financial prospect
18. Similar political background

RANK IN **2008**

1. Mutual attraction, love
2. Dependable character
3. Emotional stability, maturity
4. Education, intelligence
5. Pleasing disposition
6. Sociability
7. Good health
8. Good looks
9. Desire for home, children
10. Ambition, industriousness
11. Refinement, neatness
12. Good financial prospect
13. Good cook, housekeeper
14. Similar education background
15. Favorable social status
16. Similar religious background
17. Similar political background
18. Chastity

SOURCE: Based on data from Boxer et al. 2015.

to become paid jobs, the family became the primary site for unpaid tasks such as childrearing and housework. This new division between the domestic and public spheres, intertwined in earlier periods, caused a strict division— even polarization—of feminine and masculine activities and identities. In a process that one sociologist has called "the feminization of love," women became responsible for emotional and caretaking duties, while men were expected (and allowed) to pursue goals outside the home (Cancian 1987). Although these gender differences were defined as complementary, they inevitably created tensions between the ideal of individualism, which grants everyone the right to pursue autonomous goals, and the notion that women should maintain the intimate bonds of marriage and childrearing through selfless commitment to caring for others.

Today's postindustrial economy, which gathered steam in the later decades of the twentieth century, led to further changes in the family and contributed to altering the institution of marriage and the priorities men and women looked for in a partner. The gender revolution, illustrated most vividly by the rise of women's employment, has contributed to a form of economic individualism in which most women as well as men see the need to support themselves. The expansion of contraceptive options has given women and their partners

As people are living longer, in a society with high divorce rates, both men and women are more likely to marry a second time in their lives.

more control over their reproductive choices. More permissive attitudes toward sex and sexuality have destigmatized the practice of having sex outside the context of marriage and allowed gay and other previously hidden relationships to move out of the closet. It is also now much easier to divorce and has been increasingly common to do so since the 1970s (see Figure 16.9 on the marriage and divorce rate since 1900).

All of these changes have contributed to what is known as the **deinstitutionalization of marriage**. Spending all or most of one's adult life in a single marriage is no longer the most common pathway. Alternatives include **cohabitation** (heterosexual or gay nonmarried couples living together), **serial relationships** (when people enter and exit a series of intimate partnerships over an extended period of time), **living apart together** (when a couple in a romantic relationship chooses, or is forced to by a job or other circumstance, to live apart from one another), same-sex partnerships, and permanent singlehood (Cherlin 1992; Smock 2000; Smock and Manning 2010). People are also mixing these types of relationships over their lives. Recent estimates suggest, for example, that close to two-thirds of married couples will cohabit together before marriage, something that was very uncommon several decades ago. Forty-five percent of Americans are likely to cohabit at some point in their

Figure 16.9 Marriage and Divorce Rate (per 1,000), 1900–2009

The divorce revolution, which occurred in each state at different times but mostly in the late 1960s and early 1970s, made it much easier to leave a marriage without a finding of fault. The divorce rate (calculated here as the number of divorces per woman) peaked in 1980 although it has come down a bit since then (and is continuing to decline, especially among couples with college educations). At the same time, the marriage rate has been declining since the 1970s. That is, there are few marriages per unmarried adults happening each year. Two factors seem especially important in explaining the declining marital rate: (1) People are waiting longer to marry; (2) America's aging population (people over 65 marry at much lower rates; as more people live longer, the total marriage rate will decline).

SOURCE: Data from U.S. Department of Health and Human Services and National Center for Health Statistics.

Figure 16.10 Number of Cohabiting, Unmarried, Adult Couples of the Opposite Sex, by Year, in the United States

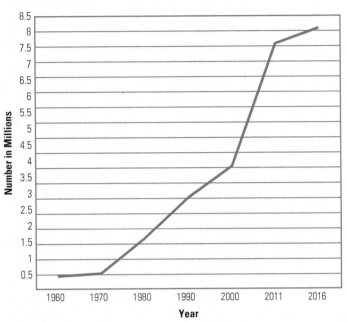

SOURCE: U.S. Census Bureau, 2017.

to only 31 percent who cite financial stability, and most singles agreed (see Figure 16.11). Furthermore, only about 30 percent agreed with the traditional view that marriages work better when a husband is a financial provider and a wife takes care of the house and children (Pew 2010a). These surverys suggest that people are thinking about marriage in a different way than in the past and placing greater emphasis on sharing and less on distinct spheres linked to gender. In fact, the blurring of gender distinctions between women's and men's activities in the home or outside of it shows that these roles are no longer static or unchanging. These new ideals for marriage also mean that people apply new—and higher—standards when choosing a mate and deciding how to define a worthwhile relationship. Yet the stress on emotional rather than financial bonds also makes marital ties more fluid and voluntary. Now that marriage is both optional and reversible, the search for love has superseded the requirement to marry (Coontz 2005).

Mothers, Fathers, and Work–Family Conflict

16.3.2 Discuss how the conflict between family needs and work pressures affects family life.

Another powerful force driving family change is the increasing percentage of households in which all adults have full-time jobs. Once considered separate spheres, the relationship between the home and the workplace

lives, and a growing percentage will stay in a cohabiting relationship for the duration of the partnership. Figure 16.10 displays the rapid growth in cohabitation since 1970.

Americans today can cohabit prior to (or instead of) marriage, engage in sexual activity and bear children without marrying, and leave a marriage if it seems unworkable. The shift from a system in which getting married was a prerequisite for forming a family to one in which it is one option among many has transformed the meaning of marriage itself. Marriage is still a highly valued, but nevertheless voluntary, bond that adults may decide whether or not to make or, indeed, unmake. As they ponder this decision, contemporary adults are more likely to stress the importance of love, respect, and mutual interests than to seek relationships built around a notion of different but complementary gender roles. One recent survey found that most married adults believed that love (93 percent) and companionship (81 percent) are very important reasons to get married, compared

Figure 16.11 Why Get Married? By Marital Status, Percent Saying This Is a "Very Important" Reason

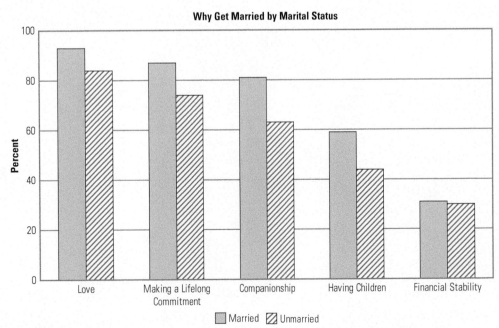

NOTE: Asked of married and unmarried separately, *n* = 1,306 for married and 1,385 for unmarried.
SOURCE: Pew Research Center, 2010a.

evokes a very different metaphor in the modern world. As more women, especially mothers, have joined the paid labor force and new technologies have blurred the lines between home and work, the image of family life as a distinctly private realm has given way to the image of families in conflict with the wider world, especially with the world of work. Mothers and fathers are now more likely to share breadwinning, but they also face daunting challenges about how to integrate their paid jobs with their families' caregiving needs (Hochschild 1997; Jacobs and Gerson 2004). In fact, although we generally use the term *work* to refer to paid jobs, unpaid work in the home is also a form of work. **Carework**, whether it is paid or unpaid, is as essential to a household's survival as is bringing in an income. Even though we often pay others outside the household to perform care work, we tend to ignore or downplay its economic value, whether it is performed by a family member without a wage or by a paid caretaker with a salary attached.

Despite occasional media portrayals of an "opt-out" movement, a term coined by journalist Lisa Belkin (2003) to portray women with college educations who leave the workplace to care for children, young women now pursue careers in unprecedented numbers, and if they do leave the workforce, it is often for a shorter period of time (Stone 2007; Damaske 2011). According to one study, employment among college-educated women in professional and managerial occupations has steadily increased across generations, with less than 8 percent of professional women today choosing to opt out of the labor force for a year or more during their prime childbearing years (Boushey 2008). Women's participation in the paid labor force increased for five decades in a row after World War II and today is close

to that of men. This also has had important consequences for the family. For example, the difference in employment rates between mothers and childless women has declined. Most mothers now hold a paid job outside the home, even when their children are very young. Almost 55 percent of married mothers with children under the age of one year are employed, and that figure rises to more than 60 percent for married mothers with children under six years and 75 percent for those with children between 6 and 18 years (Cohany and Sok 2007; Cotter, England, and Hermsen 2010).

These trends make it clear that the assumption that women are choosing to opt out of working at a paid job when they have children is highly misleading. Despite the persisting perception that women leave work for family reasons and men because they lose their jobs, the ups and downs of women's employment, like those of men's, much more commonly reflect the opening and closing of work opportunities as the economy shifts. For example, the economic recession that began in 2007 was dubbed a "man-cession" because it was men who lost jobs at a higher rate than did women. (Interestingly, the short but very sharp Covd-19 recession in 2020 caused more job losses for women than men, reversing the pattern of economic recessions; see Boesch and Phadke 2021). Whether women's earnings contribute to a dual-earner partnership or provide the sole support for a household, they are often integral to the financial well-being of their families. Indeed, according to one study of contemporary women's work paths, employed women now see their decision to work at paid jobs as "for the family" (Damaske 2011).

Despite women's movement out of the home, the organization of work remains largely based on the principle that each employee can count on someone else to take care of a family's domestic needs. Indeed, men and more than 10 percent of women workers put in more than 50 hours a week, and 60 percent of married couples work a combined total of at least 82 hours (Jacobs and Gerson 2004). While part-time jobs are available, they often require working inconvenient schedules and rarely provide adequate income or opportunities for advancement. Indeed, many of those holding part-time jobs actually work at more than one. The best jobs remain reserved for those who work full time, can be available for overtime if necessary, and have uninterrupted careers spanning several decades of work.

The clash between family needs and workplace pressures spills over into family life in a variety of ways. The greatest

Sarah L. Voisin/The Washington Post/Getty Images

The fact that most mothers today juggle paid employment with care work has had important consequences for families.

Figure 16.12 Trends in Housework, 1965–2010

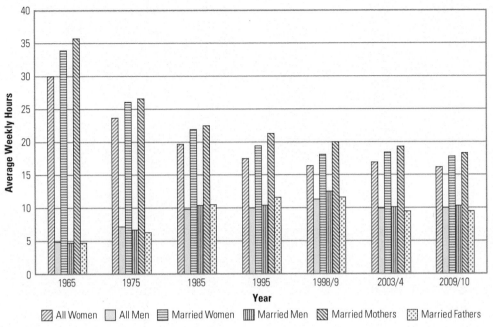

SOURCE: Bianchi et al. 2012.

Legend: All Women · All Men · Married Women · Married Men · Married Mothers · Married Fathers

equality, it actually represents an unequal arrangement that led to ongoing strains between them. Other couples developed different kinds of sharing myths, but most of these arrangements left the woman with the bulk of the household responsibilities.

Paradoxically, the growth of employment among mothers (in both dual-earner and single-parent families) has occurred alongside increased pressure for parents, especially mothers, to give their children more time and attention. This norm of intensive parenting conflicts with the countervailing norm that everyone should work hard and contribute

tensions are around the unequal **second shift**, a phrase coined by sociologist Arlie Hochschild, where employed mothers are more likely than fathers to add the significant majority of domestic duties to their already crowded work schedules (Hochschild 1989, 1997). Figure 16.12 illustrates how much housework men and women in heterosexual families have done since 1965. As the figure shows, the amount of housework done by women has declined, and men's housework has increased (mostly between the 1960s and the early 1980s), but the gap in average hours of housework remains very large (nearly 2:1). (Note that Figure 16.12 separates married men and women from all men and women, as well as all married women and men with children, among all different-sex households.)

The continued inequality in housework, even among couples where both partners work outside the home, can produce marital tensions that leave women (and sometimes men) feeling unappreciated and shortchanged. Faced with these tensions, couples may develop strategies that help them cope, but these strategies do not—and cannot—change the underlying conditions from which the tensions stem. Hochschild's detailed study of a dozen couples captures many of these strategies. For example, one of the couples she studied—Nancy and Evan Holt—decide to split tasks by their location in the house, with Evan responsible for outside duties, such as taking care of the dog and cleaning the garage, while Nancy remained responsible for the "inside" (basically everything else). While the Holts declared to Hochschild that this arrangement was designed to ease tensions in the household over who does what, allowing the couple to create a family myth of

financially, leaving women as well as men who wish to be involved parents to face a "damned if you do and damned if you don't" set of options (Hays 1996). If a mother takes a job, she faces accusations of neglecting her children, but if she does not, she must defend her position as a stay-at-home mom, a social status whose symbolic value and social support have declined sharply. Research in this area reports that employed and nonemployed mothers both expressed unease about not meeting their mothering obligations or living up to the standards expected of mothers (Hays 1996).

The blurred boundary between home and work produces time crunches and cultural contradictions, but it also creates new opportunities and possibilities. Women and men are both more likely to say they want to integrate earning and caring in their own lives and to establish a more flexible, egalitarian relationship with a lifelong partner. Fathers' parental involvement still lags behind that of mothers, but men are doing more domestic work than their fathers and grandfathers (Deutsch 1999; Coltrane 2004; Sullivan and Coltrane 2008). The gender gap in parenting is shrinking, and couples with more equal sharing express higher levels of satisfaction and are less likely to break up (Cooke 2006). More surprising, despite the image of the stressed, neglectful parent, parents today actually spend more time with their children than their counterparts did several decades ago. Mothers and fathers may both hold paid jobs, but they are also focusing more on their children when they are not at work (Bianchi 2000; Bianchi, Robinson, and Milkie 2006).

Jurgita Vaicikeviciene/Alamy Stock Photo

BIG QUESTION 16.4

What Is It Like to Grow Up in the Twenty-First Century?

GROWING UP IN TODAY'S FAMILIES

The increasing diversity in family structure has also transformed the experience of childhood as well as the transition to adulthood. A growing percentage of children now grow up in a home with either two employed parents or a single parent or a same-sex couple (Johnson et al. 2005; U.S. Census Bureau 2006; Galinsky, Aumann, and Bond 2009). Children are also more likely to live in homes that change shape over time. Compared to their parents or grandparents, they are more likely to see married parents break up or single parents remarry. They are more likely to watch a stay-at-home mother join the workforce or an employed mother pull back from work when the balancing act gets too difficult. And they are more likely to see their financial fortunes rise or fall as a household's composition changes or parents encounter unexpected shifts in their job situations. Growing up in an era of fluid marriages, unpredictable finances, and mothers with new work ties shapes the contemporary world of childhood.

The transition to adulthood, like the experience of childhood, is also not what it used to be. Major events, such as graduating from school, getting a job, and getting married, now take place at later ages. In 1960, by age 30, 65 percent of men and 77 percent of women had completed all of the major life transitions that form the historic benchmarks of adulthood, including leaving home, finishing school, becoming financially independent, getting married, and having a child. By 2000, however, only 46 percent of women and 31 percent of men had completed these transitions by age 30 (Furstenberg et al. 2004), and these downward trends

have continued since then. For example, in 1975 less than 15 percent of adults up to age 34 lived with their parents; by 2016, that figure was up to 23 percent (Vespa 2017). These trends are not confined to the United States, as many European countries are also witnessing even greater increases in the number of 20-somethings still living with their parents (Newman 2009). Let's explore how these different patterns have affected children and young adults.

Growing Up with Working Parents

16.4.1 Discuss the research on the effects of growing up in a household where both parents are employed.

Among all children in 2000, only 21 percent lived in a two-parent household with an employed father and a nonemployed mother, while 59 percent lived with an employed mother, including 41 percent who lived with two employed parents, 3 percent with an employed mother and nonworking father, and 15 percent with an employed single mother (Johnson et al. 2005). These figures (which are similar in 2021) represent a substantial change from a few decades ago, when children were much more likely to have a parent (usually a mother) who did not work.

How have these changes affected children? Decades of research have found that, on the whole, children do not suffer when their mothers work outside the home. Instead, a mother's satisfaction with her situation, the quality of care her child receives, and the involvement of a father and other caretakers are more important than whether or not a mother holds a paid job (Galinsky 1999;

Harvey 1999; Waldfogel 2006). The children of employed mothers do just as well in their cognitive development and, among children in low-income families, they do better (Burchinal and Clarke-Stewart 2007). In my research, I found that almost four out of five young adults who had work-committed mothers believed this was the best option, while half of those whose mothers did not have sustained work lives wished they had (Gerson 2011). Indeed, despite the difficulties of balancing work and family, employed mothers and two-income homes are, in the words of Rosalind Barnett and Caryl Rivers, "happier, healthier, and better off" (see Barnett and Rivers 1996, 2004).

Growing Up with Divorced or Single Parents

16.4.2 Analyze the research on the effects of divorce and single parenthood on children.

The proportion of children born to unmarried mothers is at an all-time high of almost 40 percent (two babies in five) up from about 5 percent (1 baby in 20) in 1960. It is important to note, however, that about half of these births are to cohabiting couples, most of whom intend to stay together and raise the child (U.S. Census Bureau 2006, 2007). One of the most hotly debated questions in scholarly and policy circles about the future of childrearing concerns whether, or how much, children benefit from being raised by both married parents as opposed to a single parent (either after a divorce or when one of the biological parents never lives with the child). In the case of one- versus two-parent homes, children living with both biological parents do fare better on average, but this difference

declines substantially after taking into account a family's financial resources. In other words, the differences in child outcomes between single-parent and two-parent homes diminish considerably when the single parent provides an income equal or similar to the earnings in a two-parent family. Yet, as we have seen, most two-parent families have two earning adults, while most single-parent households rely on a mother who is likely to earn less than her male counterparts, thus leaving most single-parent families to live with less income and face more economic insecurity (see Chapter 11 for more information about the effects of poverty and low-income on children).

What about divorce? Do children of divorced parents fare worse than children whose parents stay together? Most of the negative consequences of divorce for children can be traced to the high conflict and emotional estrangement preceding a breakup, along with the hostility and loss of economic support that often follows in its aftermath (Cherlin et al. 1991; McLanahan and Sandefur 1994; Hetherington and Kelly 2002). But the effects of divorce on children vary greatly. Children in high-conflict families whose parents divorce fare better, for example, than children raised in high-conflict families whose parents do not divorce (Amato and Booth 1997; Rutter 2010). While some analysts argue that all divorces are harmful in the long run, with a "sleeper effect" emerging many years later (Wallerstein, Lewis, and Blakeslee 2000; Marquardt 2005), most research points instead to the large variation in divorce's consequences. One study found that over one-third of grown children felt their parents' marriage was more stressful than the divorce, which came as a relief when it reduced the long-term daily conflict between parents (Ahrons 2006). In my research, I found that a slight majority of those who

Growing up in poverty is challenging for children and the parents who raise them for many reasons. A lack of resources, the difficulties navigating poor neighborhoods that may have high crime rates, the possibility that the local public schools are of lower quality, and many other reasons make rising out of poverty difficult. Poor parents simply lack the resources to give their children comparable upbringings to children in middle class families.

lived in a single-parent home wished their biological parents had stayed together, but almost half believed it was better for their parents to separate than to continue to live in a conflict-ridden or silently unhappy home. In addition, a majority of children from intact homes thought this was best, but two out of five felt their parents might have been better off splitting up (Gerson 2011). All in all, the effects of parental breakups—both negative and positive—vary with and depend on the circumstances that surround the divorce before and after it takes place.

Growing Up with Same-Sex Parents

16.4.3 Discuss the research on the impact of same-sex parenthood on children.

As same-sex relationships have become both more common and more accepted, sociologists have begun to ask if there are notable consequences for children associated with growing up in a home with same-sex parents. The rise of same-sex parenting challenges many longstanding understandings of what kinds of parents should be raising children, and it is thus not surprising that these and other changes in the way children are reared have sparked some opposition to same-sex marriage. It is understandable that those who oppose gay relationships on ideological grounds have turned to the issue of child well-being in an effort to demonstrate the rightness of their opposition. In important respects, the unease surrounding same-sex relationships is similar to the unease some feel about the blurring gender boundaries in heterosexual relationships. Both kinds of partnerships replace a strict gender division of household tasks with a more egalitarian vision about what women and men can and should do in families.

Yet the research on the consequences of growing up in same-sex households has shown that concerns about the welfare of children, like concerns about children whose mothers work outside the home, are unfounded. While some researchers have purported to show that children reared by same-sex parents are disadvantaged, these highly controversial studies have generally been found to be flawed and based on stereotypical, outdated, and unnecessarily rigid notions about how and why children thrive. Serious research has not convincingly demonstrated any consequential effects—whether the measure is cognitive, social, or sexual development—on children who are reared by a same-sex couple. Reviewing all of this research for an amicus brief filed with the Supreme Court for a same-sex marriage case, the American Sociological Association reported: "Children fare just as well when they are raised by same-sex parents as when they are raised by opposite sex parents. This consensus holds true across a wide range of child outcome indicators and is supported by numerous nationally representative studies" (American Sociological Association 2012). Indeed, it is increasingly misleading to characterize different-sex couples as "opposite sex"; to the extent that such couples do not use gender as the main criteria for assigning family tasks, their child-rearing practices resemble those of same-sex couples more than they differ from them.

The Changing Face of Childhood

16.4.4 Identify the reasons why some family pathways remain stable or improve, while others face difficulty.

Most research on how a child's family structure influences his or her well-being has demonstrated that the diversity of outcomes within family types is as large as (and often larger than) the differences between them. Researchers have long shown that family composition does not predict children's well-being (once we adjust for family income, as two-parent families usually have significantly higher earnings than single-parent families, as noted; see Acock and Demo 1994), while others made the same case for different forms of parental employment, such as dual-earners versus single-earner families (Parcel and Menaghan 1994).

Sociological studies of same-sex parents and families have found that they are just as successful in raising children as different-sex parents and families.

Children can thrive in a variety of domestic arrangements because family process is more important than family form. In other words, what matters is how well parents and other caretakers meet the challenges of providing economic and emotional support, rather than the specific family forms in which these challenges are met. Children care about how their families unfold, not what they look like at any one point in time. Family life is dynamic. Families are not a stable set of relationships frozen in time but rather an evolving set of situations that can change daily, monthly, and yearly as children grow. All families experience change, and even the happiest ones must adapt to these changes if they are to remain so. Family pathways can move in different directions as some homes become more supportive and others less so.

What explains why some family pathways remain stable or improve, while others stay mired in difficulty or take a downward course? My own study of "the children of the gender revolution," who grew up during the recent period of family change, finds that flexibility in earning and caregiving provides a key to understanding how and why some families are able to provide for children's well-being while others are not (Gerson 2011). Flexible family strategies can take different forms. In two-parent homes, children fared well when couples shared breadwinning and caretaking fairly equally or when they took turns and traded places as mothers pursued committed careers or fathers encountered roadblocks at the workplace. Chris, for example, told how his family life improved dramatically when his mother's promotion at a hospital, where she worked as an intensive care nurse, allowed his father to quit a dissatisfying job as a printer and retrain for work as a machine technician, which he found much more satisfying.

In single-parent, divorced, and remarried households, children fared better when mothers were able to find jobs that kept the family afloat and fathers remained closely involved in their children's day-to-day care. Letitia thus recounted how her home life changed for the better when her father became the primary caretaker, providing emotional support that her inattentive and often absent mother could not. In the wake of her parents' separation and her father's remarriage, she also gained a more nurturing stepmother (in her words, "my real mother") whose commitment to work also contributed to the family's financial stability.

Despite the differences in family circumstances, all of these responses involved breaking through rigidly drawn gender boundaries between women as caretakers and men as breadwinners. In a world where parents may not stay together, where men may not be able or willing to support wives, and where women may need and want to pursue sustained work ties, most families will encounter unexpected challenges, whether they take the form of financial crises or uncertainties in parental relationships. When families are able to respond by rejecting narrow roles in favor of more expansive and flexible family practices, they are better positioned to create more financially stable and emotionally supportive homes for children. Flexible approaches to breadwinning and caretaking help families adapt, while inflexible ones leave them ill prepared to cope with the economic and marital challenges that confront today's families.

Parenting Values and Styles

16.4.5 Explain the relationship between class cultures, childrearing practices, and the transmission of inequality from one generation to the next.

Twenty-first-century families of all classes and ethnicities are changing, but not always in the same way. The causes of family inequality are complex and difficult to isolate. Does inequality reflect different family values and cultures, or does it stem from unequal access to economic and social resources? In an influential study, sociologist Annette Lareau (2003) proposes a circular link between class cultures, especially childrearing practices, and the transmission of inequality from one generation to the next. She argues that middle-class parents engage in a form of intensive parenting called "concerted cultivation," which involves a high degree of scheduled activities, a stress on the acquisition of language skills, and a sense of entitlement when interacting with social institutions such as schools. In contrast, working-class families engage in "natural growth," which involves unstructured play and leisure activities, a more informal approach in conversations, and more deference to authority figures such as teachers and doctors. While all families strive to provide their children with love and nurturance, she argues that different childrearing styles leave middle-class children better equipped to succeed in high-pressure, well-compensated jobs and occupations, thus continuing the cycle of inequality.

Lareau argues that, beyond having higher incomes and more wealth, the capacity to transmit knowledge and experience to their children is an important component of the advantages enjoyed by middle-class parents. She finds that concerted cultivation is easier with more resources—you can buy your children music lessons, pay to send them to summer camp, or provide the experience of travel to new places and cultures. Parents who have the skills and knowledge as well as the income to seek such options are better positioned to provide these opportunities to their children. In this way, the ability of parents to realize their values for the children often varies by class and education.

Do such childrearing practices reflect different underlying values between parents in different classes?

Some parents encourage their children to try a variety of activities, filling up the child's non-school time with a steady stream of structured projects and a disciplined use of time. Other parents give children more freedom to choose their own activities, which might be unstructured play with friends, watching TV, or free time online.

This question continues to spark controversy, but much research suggests this is not the case. Sharon Hays (1996; 2003), for example, has found that standards of intensive mothering, which bear a strong resemblance to Lareau's notion of concerted cultivation, exist in all classes. Sharing the same values, however, does not mean having the same resources or ability to achieve them. Consider the case of unmarried women who choose to have a child. Studies of unmarried mothers in poor neighborhoods and middle-class single mothers by choice consistently find that all these women value motherhood highly and are not willing to forgo the experience because the right partner cannot be found (Edin and Kefalas 2005; Hertz 2006). Both groups rely on a support network of friends and relatives, including some men, to help rear their children. Yet there are also important differences. Poor single mothers are more likely to begin childbearing in late adolescence or early adulthood, while middle-class single mothers are more likely to postpone having a child until their late 30s or even early 40s as biological deadlines near. Older single mothers, who have the time to attain more education, income, and job experience, are better positioned to provide their children with the resources to grow and prosper than their poorer, younger peers.

A great deal of evidence suggests that cultural factors linked to class, however, do not determine family outcomes. Families vary in their ethnic and racial composition as well as their financial resources, and people who grow up in the same class can be different in other ways. Sociologist Patricia Collins (1991) points out that class is only one of several important social identities, such as race and gender, that intersect to create different family practices. Others have shown that even siblings who grow up in the same family can be treated differently and attain different economic and social outcomes as adults (Conley 2004). These findings point to the ways that a range of factors beyond the family environment—including supports and obstacles provided by neighborhoods, schools, and jobs—structure children's experiences and shape their life chances. All families share the value of wanting the best for their children, but some are in a better position to provide the resources and opportunities to achieve it.

The good news is that while poor parents cannot provide all of the same opportunites as middle class or affluent parents, they can nevertheless cultivate a child's curiosity and knowledge. Some of the experiences most important for a child's development are not unduly costly. Reading before bed every night, visiting local museums, and taking advantage of school or community programs designed to enrich a child's experience take time, but they are activities that even parents of modest means can provide to their children.

Becoming an Adult and Forming Families

16.4.6 Identify the benefits and drawbacks of the extended period of early adulthood experienced by American young adults.

Social scientists who study the **life-course** (the various stages of life that everyone passes through) emphasize a variety of markers to measure the transition into adulthood. Although different researchers have emphasized somewhat different indicators, among the most important are such events as finishing schooling, moving away from their parents, becoming employed full-time and/or financially independent, and forming long-term romantic relationships, which may include getting married and having children. What factors are most important for "becoming an adult" are very different today than they were several decades ago, with people much more likely to stress economic achievements over family commitments. Figure 16.13 shows what Americans consider important for adult status.

Figure 16.13 How Important Are Life Events in Becoming an Adult?

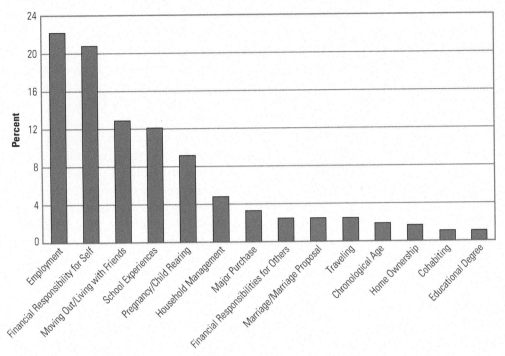

SOURCE: Lowe et al. 2013.

Gulish 2016). More recently, the period of slow economic growth since the recession of 2007–2009 and the COVID-19 pandemic in the early 2020s have also disrupted opportunities for college graduates to find stable employment in their chosen field. 21 percent of college graduates under age 34 reporting living at home in 2012 (Weissman 2013). Despite the long-standing American belief that children should be able to do better than their parents, recent developments in the economy have made it difficult for today's generation of young adults to find the secure jobs and predictable careers that blue- and white-collar jobs offered several decades ago.

Whatever indicators we use to define adult status, there is one thing now abundantly clear in the United States and most other rich countries around the world: In recent years, young people have been taking longer to reach all of these markers of adulthood. For example, there has been a gradual increase in the median age at which people get married for the first time (from 21 and 23 for women and men, respectively, in 1970 to 26 and 28 in 2010). When it comes to financial and personal independence, a growing percentage of young people, even up to their mid-30s, live with (or move back in with) their parents. Almost half—43 percent—of young people between the ages of 18 and 31 were living with their parents or another relative in 2012 (Fry 2013). This pattern, called by some as the "return to the nest" or "failure to launch," has been observed in many other countries as well (Newman 2012).

There are a number of reasons why it now takes longer to make the transition to adulthood, including the rising expectations new generations have for finding a compatible mate as well as a satisfying job and career. Another critical reason can be found in the tightening labor market, especially for those without college educations but also for those with college degrees. It has become increasingly difficult for younger workers with limited experience to find a stable, decent-paying job compared to earlier generations (Janoski et al. 2014; Hanson and

The extended time it takes to complete the transition to adulthood has produced a new life stage that some call *delayed adulthood*, or, especially for those with college degrees, the age of independence (Rosenfeld 2009). Is this delayed adulthood a good or bad trend? Like most social changes, this expanding period of early adulthood—after adolescence but before making lifelong commitments—can contain benefits and drawbacks. The research of sociologist Michael Rosenfeld (2009) has found that the rise of new kinds of relationships,

The delayed transition from childhood to adulthood has allowed younger generations to pursue personal goals before making lifelong commitments. But economic restructuring has also made it more difficult for many young people to settle into a career, and many will return to live with their parents for some time while sorting it all out.

Halfpoint/Fotolia

including interracial and same-sex couples, reflects new opportunities for young adults to forge a life that is less constrained by the preconceptions, even prejudices of earlier eras and more in tune with the realities of contemporary life. Yet some, such as sociologist Christian Smith et al. (2011), are concerned that young adults now get "lost in transition" without a moral compass to guide them, while Michael Kimmel (2008) points to the emergence of a place he calls "guyland," where young men engage in potentially self-destructive pursuits, such as excessive drinking and partying that are often harmful to themselves and others.

However we interpret this change, it is clear that many young adults now have more time to pursue independent goals before making major lifelong commitments and to develop ways of living that diverge from their parents' paths. This independence has also fueled important changes in young women's and men's aspirations and plans. National surveys and my own in-depth interviews find that a majority of young people hope ultimately to create a lasting relationship but not one based on separate spheres for mothers and fathers. Instead, most women and men want to create a flexible, generally equal partnership where they share paid work and family caretaking while also reserving considerable room for personal autonomy (Pew 2010b). In my interviews with young adults aged 18 to 32, I found that four-fifths of the women want an egalitarian relationship, and so do two-thirds of the men (Gerson 2011). In addition, three-fourths of those reared in dual-earner homes report wanting to share breadwinning and caretaking fairly equally with a partner, and so do more than two-thirds of those from traditional homes and close to nine-tenths of those with single parents.

Yet young women and men also fear their goals will be hard to achieve and may prove out of reach. Worried about finding the right partner and integrating family with work, they are pursuing what I describe as fallback strategies in young adulthood. Young women and men both emphasize the importance of work as a central source of personal identity and financial well-being, but this outlook leads them to pursue different strategies. Women are more likely to see paid work as essential to their own and their family's survival and to prefer self-reliance over economic dependence within a traditional marriage (see Figure 16.14). Men, in contrast, are more likely to prefer a neo-traditional arrangement that allows them to put work first and rely on a partner for the major share of caregiving.

Images of young people avoiding adulthood and "failing to launch" cannot capture the complex experiences of today's young women and men. There is no evidence that young people want to create a brave new world of disconnected individuals. In the long run, they hope to balance autonomy with a satisfying, committed relationship. However, they also believe they need to take time to create a financial base, discover their own strengths and needs, prepare for an uncertain economy that demands more education and training, and find a partner whose family vision meshes with their own.

Figure 16.14 Ideals and Fallback Positions of Young Women and Men

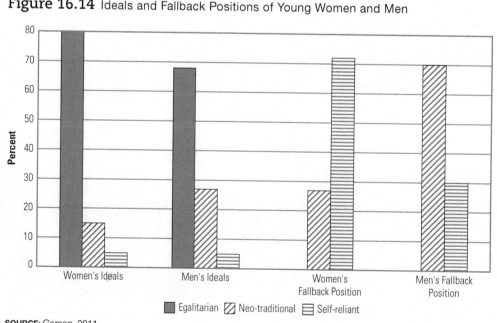

SOURCE: Gerson, 2011.

Simon Dack/Alamy Stock Photo

BIG QUESTION 16.5 What Social Policies around the World Best Support Changing Families?

FAMILIES IN THE UNITED STATES AND IN COMPARATIVE PERSPECTIVE

Marriage and families of all classes, races, and ethnicities are changing, but different groups are changing in different ways. Marital inequality is on the rise. Single-parent families are increasing, and these families have fewer resources than two-parent families. And while the overwhelming majority of Americans eventually marry, marriage rates for younger adults at child-rearing ages have declined steeply for the less educated and for members of racial minorities, where men's school and work opportunities are increasingly being squeezed. Because economic inequality is linked to family differences, with a disproportionate number of poor and economically disadvantaged families found among single-parent families (most of whom are headed by women who cannot count on the economic contributions of a partner's earnings), it follows that ethnic minorities are also more likely to be overrepresented in lower income levels.

These kinds of inequalities highlight that the challenges facing families today are intertwined with changes taking place in other institutions, such as the economy and workplace. The idea that marriage is the pathway to successful families and children for everyone no longer fits reality. Expecting individual households to navigate all of the challenges on their own is increasingly seen by governments across the world as an inefficient and unjust burden, especially for the children living in poor or struggling families. In this section, we examine some of the ways that other countries support families, and how these examples point to ways the United States might be able to improve the way it helps families thrive.

Social Policy around the World

16.5.1 Compare and contrast government policies toward families around the world.

From Europe to the Far East, all of the postindustrial nations have experienced similar social shifts, including a rise in women's labor force participation, the postponement of marriage and childbearing, and the proliferation of diverse family forms. Yet the policy responses by different governments to these shared demographic trends are quite distinct. The United States lags far behind many other postindustrial societies in adopting social policies that support new family forms. France and all the Scandinavian countries offer universal childcare, and Scandinavian countries guarantee paid parental leave for everyone (Gornick and Myers 2003). In Sweden, Iceland, and Norway, these leave policies not only support employed mothers; they also encourage fathers' parental involvement by specifying that a father cannot transfer his leave time to a mother or anyone else but must instead "use it or lose it." Most Europeans can also build their families without regard to such considerations as health care and educational access, which are available to everyone whether or not they are married or employed full time.

There are important differences across Europe in how governments try to help families. Some countries, especially in Scandinavia (as noted), have developed policies based on the principle of providing universal family supports regardless of who you are. This egalitarian approach covers a range of specific policies, including paid parental leaves, universal day care, and antidiscrimination workplace policies along with universal health care and free education. Taken together, this approach aims to reduce both gender and class inequality while providing for children's well-being regardless of the kind of family they live in.

In contrast, other countries, such as Italy, have maintained an approach that encourages maternal care but does not support women's employment or more egalitarian family forms. This familistic approach offers mothers with children, even if they are single, economic incentives for bearing children and staying home to rear them. It does not, however, stress day care, nondiscrimination at work, or other measures that would facilitate employment among mothers, encourage fathers to share in caretaking, or generally acknowledge the rise of new family and gender arrangements.

Childcare is one of the most important ways in which governments can support families, especially now that more mothers than ever before are in paid employment throughout the world. Policies toward childcare vary widely from country to country. The Scandinavian example of providing paid parental leave to fathers as well as mothers on a "use it or lose it" basis is especially instructive, since it encourages greater involvement by fathers who cannot transfer their paid leave days to a child's mother. In Sweden, parents may take up to 480 total parental leave days (240 each) when a child is born or adopted, and the government subsidizes childcare after that. In France, the government provides free preschool for children from two years of age. A system

of "child minders," who receive training, undergo regular inspections, and can care for up to five children at a time, supplements these day care centers with high-quality help.

Where does the United States fit in this picture? Unlike either egalitarian or familistic approaches, U.S. social policies take an approach aimed at providing a chance to succeed—or fail—in the labor market but they are not focused on creating programs of family support for everyone. Unlike familistic approaches, there is less concern for re-creating the breadwinner–homemaker family through maternal support, but unlike egalitarian approaches, there is also less concern with equality of outcomes or facilitating the inclusion of mothers into the labor force or the inclusion of fathers in caring for dependents. Consider paid parental leave policies. All other wealthy countries provide paid leave for parents; some provide it mostly or only for the mother, while a few (like Sweden and Norway) provide paid leave for both parents. The United States stands out for doing neither—there are no mandatory paid leaves for new parents, although a couple of states have started to adopt state-level plans and the new presidential administration of Joe Biden is proposing to create a national paid leave program for all workers (see Figure 16.15).

American parents often struggle to find affordable, high-quality childcare without help from the government. Low-income families, in some cases, can find subsidized childcare if they meet certain criteria, but non-poor families are usually not eligible for such services. In Japan, a chronic childcare shortage makes finding day care slots a competitive process. Worried that women would choose either a career or motherhood, in 2008 Japan announced a 10-year goal of providing working parents with day care for children ages 1 to 5.

In practice, the bundle of social policies relating to the family, including parental leave policy, means that the United States has focused more on whether and how to prevent discrimination, and far less on creating universal family support programs. Indeed, we continue to debate the advantages and disadvantages of the family revolution rather than accepting its irreversibility and restructuring other institutions to better fit the new realities.

Where Do We Go from Here?

16.5.2 **Discuss how the United States might achieve a more effective, inclusive approach to family support.**

What, then, would a more effective, inclusive policy approach look like? In an era of massive family change, we need to think more broadly about what equal opportunity really means. Individuals live in families, and we cannot separate the fate of individuals from the well-being of their families. We thus need family policies that reaffirm classic American values, such as equal opportunity, tolerance of diversity, and individual responsibility, but do so in the context of collective support for the diverse needs of the new family arrangements that are essential pieces of modern social life.

More concretely, this means a host of specific policies in diverse arenas: Family support policies, workplace policies, and legislation to protect the vulnerable of all ages, family statuses, and sexual orientations. Legislative efforts need to encompass equal opportunities for all kinds of families and interpersonal relationships, including single parents, same-sex couples, dual-earner families, and single adults.

Figure 16.15 Paid Parental Leave in OECD Countries, 2018

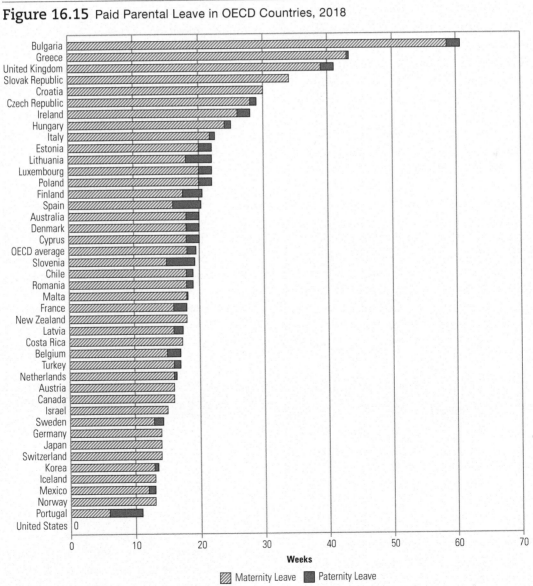

NOTE: The U.S. is coded here as zero, although as of mid-2021 nine states (California, Colorado, Connecticut, Massachusetts, New Jersey, New York, Oregon, Rhode Island, and Washington and the District of Columbia) have started providing some paid family leave benefits.

SOURCE: OECD.

At the workplace, antidiscrimination policies need to be expanded to include what Joan Williams (2000) calls "family responsibility" discrimination, so that those who shoulder responsibilities for caring for others will not face huge penalties for devoting time to this essential but undervalued task. Family-support policies should thus aim to reduce poverty and inequality along with creating a wider institutional framework for dependent care, including the care of children, the elderly, and anyone in need of it. Community childcare supports, in particular, will help employed parents and nurture the next generation. Jobs that offer flexible avenues for working and career building will not only help families integrate paid work and care work but also help employers attract and retain committed workers.

Antidiscrimination policies that protect the rights of all parents with caregiver responsibilities will not only even the playing field for employed mothers but also create fairer workplaces for men (of all sexual orientations and class positions) who wish to be involved as caretakers. No one policy can address all the challenges that twenty-first-century families face, but taken as a whole, these approaches will go a long way toward helping families develop their own strategies for meeting the challenges that await them in the decades to come.

Conclusion: The Future of Families

Despite the rapid pace of change, most Americans remain upbeat about the future of the family. According to a recent Pew survey, 67 percent say they are optimistic about the future of marriage and the family. Yet Americans are also concerned about some family trends, such as the rise in divorce (even though the divorce rate has stabilized), unwed childbearing, and declining rates of marriage. They are also politically divided over others, such as abortion and expanding government programs to support childcare and parental leave.

Thinking about the prospects for the future of families, we've covered a number of critical points. Family diversity is here to stay, even as the debate over family diversity continues. However, new generations who have watched their parents and other adults invent a mosaic of new living arrangements take for granted options that earlier generations could barely imagine. Facing their own conflicts about marriage, sexuality, work, and parenthood, young adults are increasingly weary of a divisive political rhetoric that blames families for conditions beyond their control. Most say they prefer a politics that favors a more tolerant vision that stresses similar needs rather than one that puts social groups in conflict. These aspirations point toward the possibility of a more inclusive politics that focuses on the common needs of diverse families and replaces an image of moral decline with a concern about realigning our social institutions to better fit the new circumstances of today's families.

Yet without social supports for more versatile ways of constructing families, there are good reasons for young people to be concerned about their chances of achieving these ideals. The rise of alternatives to permanent marriage means that sexual partnerships are necessarily more optional and fluid. And economic shifts, such as the rise of service-sector jobs and the decline of blue-collar ones, make women's participation in the world of paid work inevitable. These intertwined and reinforcing changes create a host of new options, but they are also on a collision course with other social institutions that remain based on a mid-twentieth-century model of static family forms. If families are films, not snapshots, then we need public discussions and social policies that see family life as an unfolding, unpredictable process in which anyone, at any time, may need some kind of help. In the context of this irreversible but unfinished family revolution, people need social supports for the diverse and changing families that exist today.

The Big Questions Revisited 16

16.1 What Is a Family? To begin this chapter, we first needed to examine the meaning of the term *family*. What is a family, and what are the various ways to define it?

The Many Ways We Define *Family*

A Global and Historical Perspective

Learning Objective 16.1.1: Identify family forms that can be found throughout human history and across diverse societies and households.

Household or Kinship System?

Learning Objective 16.1.2: Explain how residence patterns and kinship systems contribute to different definitions of family.

Key Terms
homemaker–breadwinner family (p. 433)
polygamy (p. 433)   patrilocal (p. 434)
single-parent (p. 434)   same-sex
marriage (p. 436)   kinship system (p. 436)
kin (p. 436)   nuclear family (p. 437)

16.2 Why Are Families Changing? To understand the contemporary debate over "family values," this section mapped out the competing views about the current state of the American family, how we got here, and what we need to do in response.

Changing Families

The Family Values Perspective
Learning Objective 16.2.1: Discuss the concerns of proponents of the family decline perspective regarding the nature of families today.

The Economic Restructuring Perspective
Learning Objective 16.2.2: Discuss how the economic restructuring approach explains changing family arrangements.

The Gender Restructuring Perspective
Learning Objective 16.2.3: Discuss the mismatch between the structure of jobs and the caretaking needs of families.

Key Terms
family values (p. 439)   egalitarian relationship (p. 441)

16.3 What Are the Challenges of Developing Relationships and Families in the Twenty-First Century? This section examined the decline of permanent marriage and the new contours of adult commitment as well as the blurring of gender divisions and the rise of work–family conflict.

The New Contours of Adulthood Commitment

The Deinstitutionalization of Marriage
Learning Objective 16.3.1: Explain how marriage has become deinstitutionalized in today's society.

Mothers, Fathers, and Work–Family Conflict
Learning Objective 16.3.2: Discuss how the conflict between family needs and work pressures affects family life.

Key Terms
conjugal family (p. 442)   deinstitutionalization of marriage (p. 444)   cohabitation (p. 444)   serial relationships (p. 444)   living apart together (p. 444)   carework (p. 446)   second shift (p. 447)

16.4 What Is It Like to Grow Up in the Twenty-First Century? In this section, we discussed how the experiences of children transitioning into adulthood are very different from how they once were

and what this means for today's children and young adults.

Growing Up in Today's Families

Growing Up with Working Parents
Learning Objective 16.4.1: Discuss the research on the effects of growing up in a household where both parents are employed.

Growing Up with Divorced or Single Parents
Learning Objective 16.4.2: Analyze the research on the effects of divorce and single parenthood on children.

Growing Up with Same-Sex Parents
Learning Objective 16.4.3: Discuss the research on the impact of same-sex parenthood on children.

The Changing Face of Childhood
Learning Objective 16.4.4: Identify the reasons why some family pathways remain stable or improve, while others face difficulty.

Parenting Values and Styles
Learning Objective 16.4.5: Explain the relationship between class cultures, childrearing practices, and the transmission of inequality from one generation to the next.

Becoming an Adult and Forming Families
Learning Objective 16.4.6: Identify the benefits and drawbacks of the extended period of early adulthood experienced by American young adults.

Key Terms
life-course (p. 452)

16.5 What Social Policies around the World Best Support Changing Families? Finally, we placed American family life today in a comparative perspective. This section examined how other countries have approached social policies for families and how we can learn from their tactics.

Families in the United States and in Comparative Perspective

Social Policy around the World
Learning Objective 16.5.1: Compare and contrast government policies toward families around the world.

Where Do We Go from Here?
Learning Objective 16.5.2: Discuss how the United States might achieve a more effective, inclusive approach to family support.

Chapter 17
Sociology of Religion

by Iddo Tavory and Gerald Marwell*

The late Gerald Marwell always began teaching his course on the sociology of religion at New York University by asking each student to describe his or her religious upbringing and present beliefs. Forty years ago, most of Marwell's students would have identified with one of the traditionally dominant religious traditions in America—Catholic, Christian, Jewish, and so forth. Today, the most common responses are very different: "I believe in God, but don't go to church"; "If following a particular religion makes someone happy, I'm not going to look down on them"; "When you get down to it, I think all religions are really about the Golden Rule—treat others the way you want to be treated."

To be sure, college students are not necessarily typical of all American youth (almost half of whom never enroll in college or university). However, sociologist Christian Smith and his colleagues (Smith 2009) interviewed a nationally representative sample of young people aged 18 to 23. Although they find many conventionally religious people in this age group, as well as a substantial number of **atheists** (who do not believe in any god) or **agnostics** (who do not believe that god's existence or nonexistence is knowable), Smith's results are surprisingly similar to what Marwell observed among his students.

My Sociological Imagination

IDDO TAVORY

Spending years of my childhood in Jerusalem, religion was all around me. The neighborhood I lived in was mixed—a secular neighborhood that became increasingly Orthodox. But where I lived, the secular and the religious rarely interacted. It was only when I came to do my PhD in the United States that things changed. As a research assistant I joined a Los Angeles' synagogue. Men in black clothes and long beards were suddenly less distant. One of them, I remember, told me he came from Jerusalem. When I tried to figure where exactly he was from, I found out he lived on the street next to me. We probably saw each other numerous times, yet never really saw each other. I was hooked. How does life in the city shape people's religious lives? What are the ways in which religion shapes everyday life such that groups can live so close, and yet never interact?

My Sociological Imagination

GERALD MARWELL

My mother said I was always an "oppositional" child. I grew up in a religious home and went to parochial school, but I never understood what these old stories had to do with me or my world. And I was angry that my friends were out playing ball while I was stuck listening to old men telling me to sit still. I went to MIT to become an engineer, but I discovered interests in economics and psychology instead. I disagreed with the oversimplified psychology that underlies economics and hoped that sociology, the most general of the social sciences, might let me pursue both of my interests. And I fell in love: With all of sociology, and all of social science. Where else can you spend your life thinking about the human condition and get paid for it? Most of my work has been on offering alternatives to economic theories of "collective action," or cooperation, particularly in social movements. Religion is not so different from social movements, in that it requires commitment and faith. So, in my late 60s I finally took up the question that has puzzled me my entire life—why are so many people religious? Why is religion so important in the world?

---

*Gerald Marwell (1937–2013) passed away after completing this chapter for the first edition of *The Sociology Project*.

It is important to almost all religious communities that their young become believers and practitioners. They incorporate children into aspects of their religion as early as they can. Here, very young Native Americans participate in tribal religious practices as part of this learning process.

Dan Barba/SCPhotos/Alamy Stock Photo

Smith calls the most common religious pattern among today's youth "moralistic therapeutic deism (MTD)," which he describes in terms of five "key beliefs" (p. 154):

1. A god exists who created and ordered the world and watches over human life.
2. God wants people to be good to each other, as taught in the Bible and by most religions.
3. The central goal of life is to be happy and to feel good about oneself.
4. God does not need to be particularly involved in one's life except when God is needed to solve a problem.
5. Good people go to heaven when they die.

This understanding of religion is highly individualistic: Religion helps us be good people. MTD is also therapeutic because most young people believe that religion in moderation is generally, if not always, good for people. It helps people be happier and healthier. It gets them through crises. It gives them groups to belong to and share with. It makes for closer families with shared memories and feelings.

Yet, at the same time, we also live in a world in which religion plays a prominent role in social and political life. Internationally, religious conflict is widespread, with the persecution of Rohingya Muslims and Hindus in Buddhist Myanmar and Uighur Muslims in China, Christian–Muslim conflicts in Central and Western Africa, and Shi'a–Sunni conflicts in Iraq. Within the United States itself, religion may be understood by many students in individualistic–moralistic terms, but mainline Protestants vote differently than do evangelical Protestants, Reform Jews very differently than Orthodox Jews.

The tensions between the individualistic and the public aspects of religious life strike to the core of how we understand religion. In the individualistic, moralistic, register, MTD is a very general description of religious belief. All religions are seen as essentially true at their core—the concept of **deism** refers to a belief in a god regardless of the form they take. At the same time, most elaborated religious **doctrine**—the official beliefs and rules of particular religions—is perceived by many young people as being unrealistic and perhaps even boring. Established religions are seen as often unreasonable in their repressive rules, unscientific beliefs, and overbearing organizations. Many young people are suspicious of organized religion. They attend church rarely, if at all, except to be with their families. But, at the same time, the salience of religiously tinged conflict around the world and the importance of religion in American political life seem to suggest that religion is far from being a shared, and generic, morality. How do we account for this duality of religion? The complexity of young people's religious views, and of religion in public life, gives us a point of entry into the sociology of religion. Rather than starting with doctrine and texts, we begin with people and religious organizations. The religious lives of people are more complicated and internally contradictory than we tend to think. For sociologists of religion, this means that we get to study the wonder of the human condition and complex cultures and the consistencies and oddities of human behavior, all at the same time.

The Big Questions

1. **What is religion, and what does it do?** Sociologists have no single agreed-upon definition of religion. In this section, we examine some of the definitions of religion—especially those that rely on *beliefs* and those that focus on *practices.* We then outline some of the incredible variation of religions throughout the world and throughout history.

2. **How does social structure impact religious belonging?** With all the religions in the world, how do people come to belong to one religious group or another? Here we look at the patterns of religious life, including the impact of race, ethnicity, gender, and age.

3. **How does religion play into public life?** In this section, we ask where and when religion emerged as a political force, looking both at religious conflict around the globe, and at the intersection of religion and politics in the United States.

4. **How is religion changing?** We save for last what has historically been the most important question for sociologists of religion: Is secularization or increased religiosity the future of religion?

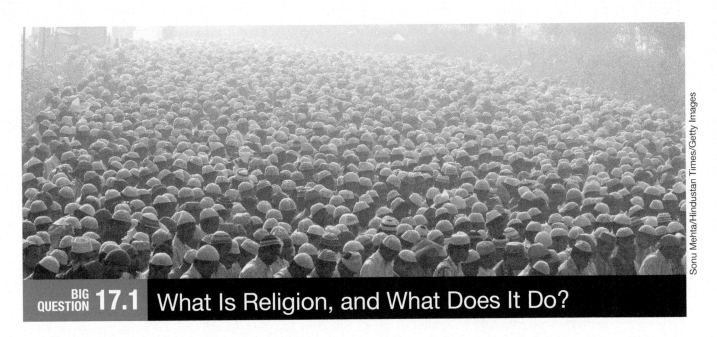

Sonu Mehta/Hindustan Times/Getty Images

BIG
QUESTION **17.1** What Is Religion, and What Does It Do?

A SOCIOLOGICAL UNDERSTANDING OF RELIGION

The study of religion and society occupies a unique place in the history of sociology. The first intellectual to call himself a sociologist, Auguste Comte, thought that sociology would become a modern "religion of humanity," with scholars such as himself fulfilling the functions of priests. But, more importantly, religion was one of the core questions that the founders of sociology grappled with. In a moment of intense social transformation that gave rise to the discipline, they wanted to understand both how religion shaped history, and how it was changing, or disappearing. As such, religion was central to the classic work of two of the most-read sociologists in history, Max Weber and Emile Durkheim. Weber wrote what is perhaps the most widely read book in the history of sociology, *The Protestant Ethic and the Spirit of Capitalism* (Weber [1904] 1958), in which he argued that the ascetic form of Protestantism that emerged in Europe in the sixteenth and seventeenth centuries was critical in the development of capitalism as we know it today.

Perhaps the second most-read sociological book of all time is Durkheim's *Suicide* (Durkheim [1898] 1951), which begins with a puzzle rooted in religion: Why do areas populated mainly by Protestants have much higher suicide rates than areas populated mostly by Catholics? Later in his career, Durkheim also wrote perhaps a profound and influential treatise on religion, *The Elementary Forms of Religious Life*, in which he examined the religions of Australian aborigines and proposed that the idea of the source of religious life is in the experiences of a community coming together (Durkheim [1912] 2001).

In these two foundational works, we can see different ways in which we can understand religion. For Weber,

it was, first and foremost, a set of meanings. For Durkheim, it was a feeling, evoked by ritual. Where one focused on something like belief, the other focused on practice. In this chapter, we walk in the footsteps of giants as we investigate issues foundational to a sociological understanding of religion.

Defining Religion

17.1.1 Compare and contrast the different sociological definitions of religion.

Whatever their personal beliefs, sociologists today seek to study religion through a scientific, not theological, lens (Gross and Simmons 2009). In that sense, at its best, the sociology of religion is *agnostic*. That is, it hopes to teach us something about what religion does and how it is practiced, while leaving the question of the existence of a god or gods unanswered. A good sociology of religion would thus be instructive to both the devout and to the militantly atheist. While many sociologists of religion are themselves religious, they understand their field of research as involving the systematic study of one important societal institution.

The complexity of religious beliefs is so deep that even sociologists of religion do not always agree about the definition of "religion" itself. What of people who define themselves as neo-Pagan, and whose religion does not have a well-defined set of gods? What of those who define themselves as Jewish, while noting that they are agnostic about the very existence of a god? What of those who say that they are not religious, but spiritual? Mirroring those complexities, there are many different definitions in the literature, each focusing on a different aspect of religion. We have found it instructive to focus on two approaches to define religion: One that emphasizes sacredness and *practice* versus a contrasting definition that emphasizes the role of the supernatural and *meaning*.

In *The Elementary Forms of Religious Life*, Durkheim defines religion as the way that societies deal with things that are **sacred**—those things worthy of awe and special treatment and not just mundane or everyday parts of life: Sacred texts like the Bible, the Torah, or the Koran; sacred behaviors such as the communion ritual; sacred places like Mecca; sacred times like Easter day, Ramadan, or the Sabbath; and sacred people such as monks or the Dalai Lama. In other words, religion creates symbolic boundaries between certain people, objects, times, places, and other things and events in the world. The world of the mundane is distinguished from the world of things set apart and given special meaning. It is this action of "setting apart" that makes religion what it is. But how do we get there? Here, Durkheim's answer is radical. Rather than focusing on humans' attempt to understand their world or to come to terms with death, Durkheim posted that the feeling of being set apart emerged first when people contrasted the mundane experience of small hunter-gatherer groups, and the strong emotions that were evoked when they came together. The earliest experience of the sacred is the experience of the mass of people coming together—not unlike the experiences evoked by a political rally or a rock concert. Practice, in other words comes *before* belief.

Compare Durkheim's definition with a more recent one used by the sociologists of religion Rodney Stark and Roger Finke: "Religion is concerned with the supernatural; everything else is secondary.… [It] consists of very general explanations of existence, including the terms of exchange with a god or gods" (Stark and Finke 2000, p. 89–91). In this view, religion is a set of ideas describing the relations between the natural and the **supernatural**, including how earthly beings can obtain goods from other-worldly entities, be they healthy crops or eternal salvation. Here, *belief* is everything. Religion is a mode of understanding our universe in terms of powers that are both larger than us, and have a volition of their own—not abstract laws of nature, but a being (or beings) that shape our world.

Many interesting questions are raised by the differences between these two definitions. If supernatural beings are required for religion, where does that leave Buddhism, the "religion" of about 360 million people around the world? Buddhist doctrine is formally atheistic—no god or gods are part of the belief system. On the other hand, many practicing Buddhists believe in spirits, and many of them pray to statues of the Buddha for assistance. Furthermore, because most Buddhists believe in the transmigration of souls (that is, reincarnation), do "souls" qualify as supernatural beings?

Alternatively, defining religion as the way people deal with the sacred means that religion has plenty of room not only for Buddhism but also phenomena not conventionally thought of as religion. If we focus on the experience of coming together, and on the sacred as "set apart," it expands the reach of our social imagination toward both political life and popular culture. For example, a good case can be made for including fans screaming as the singer Beyoncè appears onstage, or in collecting her autographs and memorabilia and treating them as sacred objects. Or consider the fervor displayed at presidential campaign rallies of former President Donald Trump in the United States.

The "sacredness" definition of religion has led sociologists to recognize a common, even necessary form of religion known as **civil religion**. While almost all U.S. presidents invoke God in their inauguration speeches, they reference a rather abstract god. Yet, aspects of civil religion that seemingly have nothing to do with religion are quite specific. Consider the way Americans feel about their Constitution—for many, it is a sacred text like the Bible or the Koran; or about the American flag as a sacred symbol; or about July 4—a day of ritual and worship at the shrine of sacred America. Or consider the frequently repeated claim that "Ground Zero," where the original World Trade Center once stood before the attacks of 9/11, is "sacred ground." According to what religion is it sacred? From a Durkheimian perspective, the idea of civil religion that makes these things sacred is the same as all religions—it is the worship of the community and society, from which all good things eventually flow and on which we are completely dependent.

In other words, it matters whether we start from beliefs or from the practices that the sacred entails. It matters because these different approaches to religion put us on slightly different paths. Starting from belief leads us to ask how religion is meaningful in people's lives, and how such meaning then affects other outcomes—their health and well-being, or their voting patterns, for example. If we begin from practices and the sacred, we expand the definition of religion, but also focus on the way that religion is actually practiced by different people. It leads us to ask *when* people act in religious ways, *how* and *in which situations* religion emerges.

Regardless of which definition they start from, sociologists generally take a rather fluid approach to understanding religion, switching between these perspectives. Taking such a flexible approach, religion is defined by the behaviors, beliefs, and commitments of the people of a group or society. Yes, doctrine matters because religious doctrine is also the product of people's behaviors (writings, arguments), beliefs, and commitments. But doctrine is only part of what defines a working religion.

In the real world, after all, the rigidities of doctrine are often neglected by the faithful. For example, in Catholic doctrine it is clearly wrong to use contraception, yet 98 percent of sexually active Catholic women in the United States have done just that (Guttmacher Institute 2011), most without a moral qualm. What, then, is the correct description of the Catholic religion? As another example, most

In Morocco, some Muslim women are veiled, some are not. Such differences can even be found within the same family, as with this mother and daughter.

Islamic scholars agree that the Koran only asks women to dress "modestly" and does not require them to be veiled in public. Yet women in Saudi Arabia must be fully veiled or risk arrest. The Wahabbi sect that controls religious matters in Saudi Arabia insists that wearing the veil is an essential part of being a good Muslim. In other words, it is part of their Islam. In Morocco, some women who think of themselves as pious do not wear a veil, while others do. And these women, with different opinions, can be seen everywhere walking and talking together in friendship.

Even more fluid are the religious traditions and practices of most East Asian societies (Demerath 2003). In Japan, Korea, China, much of Indonesia, and elsewhere, people feel free to combine elements from different religions, almost using religion as a toolbox with applications to a variety of problems and life issues. In Korea, Confucian prayers for one's ancestors may be combined with Christian prayers for God's help or grace. Buddhist temples in Japan routinely include a shrine for Shinto deities, and Japanese weddings often include a Christian ceremony, while they usually celebrate births according to Shinto traditions, and bury their dead in Buddhist ceremonies.

The Incredible Variety of Religions

17.1.2 **Identify the big five religions of the world and discuss the variety and diversity of contemporary religion.**

Instead of asking what the one true faith might be, sociologists of religion have tried to understand the empirical reality before their eyes: The hundreds or thousands of different contemporary and historical religions to be found around the world, and the complex overlaps, syntheses, conflicts, and differences among these faiths and modes of worship. Elements of religious life are everywhere.

To begin to grasp the incredible variety of religions that exist, study the information provided in Table 17.1. Table 17.1 only includes religions that are active and involve relatively large numbers of people (1 million or

Table 17.1 Major Religions of the World

	Estimated Number of Adherents	Established	Where Originated
The Big Five			
Christianity Catholic, Orthodox, Protestant	2.3 billion	30 CE	Palestine
Catholic	1.2 billion		
Orthodox	300 million		
Protestant	600 million		
Islam Sunni, Shi'a	1.5 billion	622 CE	Saudi Arabia
Sunni	1.3 billion		
Shi'a	150 million		
Hinduism	1 billion	Prehistory	India
Chinese Syncretism	400 million	Prehistory	China
Buddhism Theravada, Mahayana, Vajrayana	470 million	520 BCE	India
Theravada	125 million		
Mahayana	185 million		
Vajrayana	6 million		

(Continued)

	Estimated Number of Adherents	Established	Where Originated
Non Religious			
Atheism, Agnosticism	1.1 billion		
Christianity Related			
Judaism Orthodox, Conservative, Reform, Religion of the Hebrews, the "Chosen People"	15 million	1300 BCE	Palestine
Mormonism Consider themselves Christians. Believe Book of Mormon, not accepted by other Christian groups, is divinely inspired. Emphasizes self-discipline and family devotion.	12 million	1830 CE	USA
Spiritualism Focus on understanding and communicating with disembodied entities using methods such as séances, automatic writing, and other techniques. Believe all people have immortal spirits.	11 million	1850 CE	USA, UK, France
Seventh Day Adventists Affirm Protestant beliefs. Adhere to the teachings of Ellen White, considered a prophet. Emphasize healthy living. Follow strict dietary codes and observe a day of rest on Saturday.	10 million	1863 CE	USA
Jehovah's Witnesses Affirm Christian God but believe the Trinity is unbiblical. Believe 144,000 chosen will go to heaven, while others live forever on a new earth. Emphasize evangelism and healthy living.	7 million	1879 CE	USA
Unification (Moonies) Believe founder Sun Myung Moon is the second coming of Christ. Emphasizes forming harmonious families to bring about the Kingdom of God on Earth.	1–3 million	1954 CE	South Korea
Aladura Mix Anglican and African rituals, focusing on healing and this-worldly salvation. Prominent role played by prophets who are believed to have extraordinary healing powers.	1 million	1918 CE	Nigeria
Rastafari Believe god (Jah) became incarnate in Haile Selassie. Emphasize worldly salvation, freedom from oppression, and return to Africa. Practice dietary restrictions and ritual marijuana use.	1 million	1920 CE	Jamaica
Hinduism Related			
Sikhism Believe salvation consists of escaping the cycle of reincarnation and uniting with god. Emphasize moderate living and distinctive dress, including the turban, that symbolizes devotion.	23 million	1500 CE	India
Jainism Believe that the soul is eternal, uncreated, and can attain divinity. Practice complete nonviolence, including toward animals, and asceticism. Meditate through chanting mantras.	4 million	55 BCE	India
Far Eastern (Chinese, Buddhist) Religion-Related			
Taoism Believe in living according to the Tao, the principle behind everything that exists, to achieve inner peace and longevity. Yin and yang. Cultivate detachment from worldly concerns.	20 million	550 BCE	China
Falun Gong Focus on regulating the body's vital energy through stretching and meditation exercises. Believe adherents can gain superhuman powers through these practices.	10 million	1992 CE	China
Confucianism Emphasize ethical practices. Cultivate virtues such as loyalty, honesty, and concern for others. Focus on maintaining social harmony. Not concerned with supernatural forces or beings.	5–6 million	500 BCE	China
Shinto (Japanese folk) Believe in spiritual entities called kami. Practice rituals focused on securing blessings and avoiding evil through calling on the kami. Kami are believed to reside in shrines.	3–4 million	<300 BCE	Japan
Composites of Major Religions			
Baha'i Believe god has successively revealed himself through the prophets of major religious traditions. Practice daily prayer and hold monthly communal feasts.	5–7 million	1863 CE	Iran
Cao Dai Emphasize the underlying similarity of all religions. Venerate a diverse array of saints, including political, religious, and artistic figures. Salvation is escaping the cycle of reincarnation.	4–6 million	1926 CE	Vietnam
New Religious Movements			
New Age Diverse and personalized, practices using tools and techniques such as crystals, tarot cards, astrology, and yoga. Tend to see the divine as an impersonal force. Believe in reincarnation.	5 million	1900s CE	USA and Europe
Wicca Generally believe in coequal god and goddess as well as lesser deities. Worship and rituals occur in covens or individually. Core principle is "Do what you will as long as no one is harmed."	1–3 million	1930s	UK

SOURCES: https://berkleycenter.georgetown.edu/
http://religionfacts.com/big_religion_chart.htm.

more adherents) today. It does not include past religions or religions that are estimated to have fewer than 1 million adherents today. And even as a picture of contemporary religion, Table 17.1 is very approximate and incomplete. A complete and nuanced listing would take at least a book. Many of these broad categories could easily be further differentiated, and many adherents might strongly disagree with being lumped together (for example, there are very big differences between evangelical Protestants and members of Protestant denominations that are less devotional). At the same time, we give separate space to Jehovah's Witnesses and Mormons, whose adherents consider themselves Christians but also have crucial additional beliefs and doctrines that make them quite different from the rest of Christendom (and would not be considered "Christians" by most other Christians). In fact, all of the major religions had early periods in which geographically separated areas practiced somewhat different versions. Only later were these forged into a relatively consistent pattern through force or compromise. Later still, most religious traditions experienced divisions that

produced newer and divergent versions of what was once considered a single religion.

To give readers a better sense of where the major religions of the world are practiced, the map in Figure 17.1 shows where in the world the five religions with by far the most adherents dominate: Christianity of all branches, with approximately 2.2 billion adherents, is the largest; Buddhism, with 360 million, is the smallest. The sixth largest grouping is **irreligion**—which refers to the avowed absence of religion and which dominates numerically in many countries generally considered Christian, as in many Far Eastern countries like China and Japan.

Chinese syncretism is perhaps the most complicated of the major religious traditions. The Chinese have long exhibited a highly **syncretic** approach to religion, that is, one that combines elements of different religions, making their beliefs and practices difficult to classify. (Syncretism itself is the belief in one all-encompassing god.) At one point, Chinese religious scholars articulated the "Unity of the Three Religions," which taught that Buddhism, Taoism, and Confucianism were all ultimately equivalent

Figure 17.1 A Global View of Religion

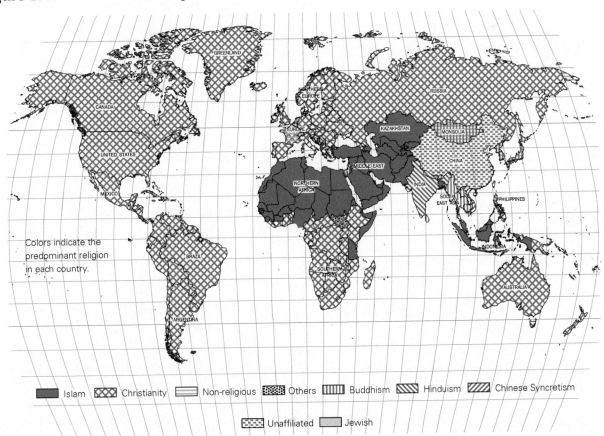

Six countries are shown as split Islam/Christianity: Bosnia and Herzegovina, Cote d'Ivoire, Kazakhstan, Nigeria, Tanzania, and Eritrea.

SOURCES: Based on data from *C.I.A. World Factbook* (2012); ReligionFacts.com; European Commission's Eurobarometer (2005).

and complemented each other. Thus, people could mix the three traditions. The Chinese emperor typically employed Buddhist, Taoist, and Confucian religious figures in his court simultaneously. Similarly, today many Chinese turn to a diverse set of sources, including folk religion and practices. Thus, even as the Communist Party has attempted to repress or regulate it, religion remains important for many Chinese.

The 19 smaller religions of more than 1 million adherents each are divided into five groups, the largest of which contains religions related to Christianity. Most, like the Mormons, have prophets or sacred books in addition to those of conventional Christianity. Note that no Islam-related religions are listed. The Druze would qualify, but this sect has fewer than 1 million adherents.

The world did not begin with five "big religions." The big religions became so widespread relatively recently as history goes, mostly by sending missionaries through colonialism and military conquest, or through increased contact with foreigners through economic activity such as trading. Although 25 religions are listed in Table 17.1, as noted, this number pales against the number of religions that ethnographers, archaeologists, and historians have identified as present today, more so prior to the consolidation of the major religions, not to mention the probably thousands of religions that existed prehistorically and for which we have never found a trace. To give some perspective on this, in 1800 the two islands of Papua New Guinea held almost 800 separate peoples, each with its own language and probably its own myths and religious practices. Over the course of human history, and around the globe, a nearly endless variety of religions and religious groups have flourished.

Early Religious Traditions and Their Modern Variants

17.1.3 Compare and contrast the concepts of animism and polytheism.

To get a sense of the full complexity of religions of the past, let us briefly consider the concepts of animism and polytheism. Neither of these were or are specific religions, but they are useful ways to designate whole classes of religions, as they share some core tenets.

Animism refers broadly to religions that ascribe human characteristics to animals, plants, and inanimate objects such as rocks and mountains; see such spirits as present and active in the world; and/or believe in some underlying force that animates everything from the weather to human activity. These kinds of religious thinking, which often lead to ritual practices to appease the spirits to curry their favor or harness the forces, seem to be common in cultures all over the world, although in widely varying forms. Although it no longer dominates the world, animism has not died out. What are generally called "folk" religions such as those in China or Shintoism in Japan, have their roots in animism, and various major religions such as Islam are combined with folk animistic elements in places like Indonesia, as is Christianity combined with animism in parts of South America.

Whereas animism sees spirits in the natural world, **polytheism** is characterized by the worship of multiple gods, usually with a complex set of relationships, rivalries, and even romance among them. The totality of the gods in a polytheistic system and the relationships between them is called a *pantheon*, a term derived from the way the ancient Greeks wrote about their gods. In Europe, the religions of Rome, ancient Greece, and the Nordic countries are major referents; other common referents are the ancient Egyptian, the Babylonian or the Yoruba pantheons. These religions generally envision a set of gods and attendants who rule the world and can be appealed to through ritual, prayer, and sacrifice. Polytheistic religions often created representations of these gods in concrete forms, which were central to their rituals. Polytheism generally reflected the more centralized ideas of the empires and large societies that integrated and conquered tribal societies. As such, historians of religion commonly assume that many of the pantheons we know is the result of a history of syncretism.

Christianity and Islam, two of the largest world religions, are both built on a shared basis in **monotheism**, the belief in one all-encompassing God. Still, polytheism is prominently visible in the large and varied collection of Hindu gods and avatars. The relationship between monotheism and polytheism (or, as early Christians termed it, *paganism*) has been often fraught, even constituting a basis for intra-religious conflicts. Radical Protestants, for example, frequently disparaged Catholicism as "pagan" because what they saw as their "excessive" reverence (idolatry) for Mary, its many saints, and its omnipresent statues and religious images.

Religion as a Social Institution

17.1.4 Discuss religion as a social institution and the role of theodicy.

Modern religions of the world are so diverse, complex, and dynamic that one might argue that religion differs with every individual. Mr. Y's Catholicism, which stresses the sense of belonging and the beauty of the liturgy, might be different from his wife's, Ms. Y, who stresses the importance of obedience to God's laws and the sacredness of the family. Neither Mr. nor Ms. Y may know much, or care about, the intricate **theology**—discussions of the interpretation of religious matters—that mesmerizes their priest.

In fact, the authors of an influential analysis of religion in the United States, *Habits of the Heart* (Bellah et al. 1985), were particularly taken with the example of a woman named Sheila, who called her religion "Sheilaism." She described Sheilaism as taking the bits and pieces from various religions that she thought were useful or convincing and combining them into her own personal religion. This may be a more common approach that many people take to organize their religious beliefs than we realize.

Such personalization of religion is an important contemporary trend. But, religions are first and foremost what sociologists call **institutions**—structured and enduring habits, narratives, and practices of human life, usually anchored in important organizations (like the government, courts, churches, schools, or military). Institutions, as sociologists have long argued, are not usually "invented" for a specific purpose. They emerge historically and contain multiple layers of practices and beliefs. Thus, institutions such as religion can often be better understood as containing contradictory elements rather than being a seamless whole. Still, at least from some perspectives, the institution of religion is primarily a way to explain, and to justify, our world. Most actual religious organizations specialize in teaching and demanding that people follow societal norms—especially those thought of as the commandments of god or the gods or, as in Buddhism and Confucianism, the lessons of revered teachers or prophets. Religion is full of "oughts" (what is right) and "ought-nots" (what isn't), and threats of punishment or failure in this world or the next if one does not follow these rules. In other words, like other institutions, such as law, religion is both a moral and a normative institution. It tells us both what the world *is* and what the world *should be*. It is no accident that in many societies it was the shamans, rabbis, imams, and priests who were also the judges in the legal system.

Religious ideas were often, historically, closely aligned with the ruling political authority. Because religious organizations and actors engage both in the explanation of the world and often in the maintenance of existing social structures, they frequently align with the entrenched interests of political elites—or even become political elites themselves. Where religion and political power were closely tied together, a single religious denomination or tradition was often established as the "official" state religion, and the practice of other religions could be punished (in extreme cases, with death).

In the Holy Roman Empire (ca. 800–1806 CE), there were minority religions, sometimes persecuted, sometimes not. Gradually, however, everyone was expected to be Catholic. But what came together later fell apart. After the sixteenth-century Protestant Reformation, the Anglican Church became the state church of England and the Lutheran Church became the state church in Sweden and throughout all of those parts of Europe where Protestantism had won definitive victories (not, however, in France and Germany, where Catholics and Protestants were both entrenched and neither dominated the other). This is why America's early legal commitment to religious **pluralism**—accepting many different religions, or all religions, as legitimate, and the separation of church and state—was so important and so unique.

Probably the best known statement about the role of religion in reinforcing the power of the ruling elite was penned by Karl Marx (2001 [1844]), who once famously declared that religion was the "opiate of the masses." Marx was provocatively linking religion to inequality and human suffering in a way that was convincing to many of his followers. As he saw it, religion was an illusion that dulled the pain of economically exploited people and offered a false substitute for the politics of class struggle necessary for their liberation. Rather than rebel against the unjust social system they lived in, religion promised people rewards and justice in the afterlife, after the resurrection, or in a next life. For Marx, religion was an ideological tool that maintained the status quo. It was, as sociologist Peter Berger put it, in the business of world-maintaining and world-justifying.

While the notion of heaven and hell as rewards in the afterlife were probably what Marx was thinking of, perhaps the most striking religious system that ties stratification and religious doctrine can be seen in the Hindu caste system, and the Hindu notions of Karma and Samsara: The ongoing cycle of life, death, and rebirth, and the balance of good and bad deeds that people accrue in the process. The caste system provides a relatively rigid and religiously sustained ordering of people into a social hierarchy. The system has sometimes been called Brahmanism because the Brahmin (or priestly) caste is at the top of this pyramid. At the bottom are the caste of untouchables (or Dalits), with other castes ranged in between. One cannot escape the social standing of one's caste in this lifetime. Where one is born is supposed to be ordained by one's behavior in one's previous life. Good behavior mostly consists of submitting to the status and conditions into which you were born.

Weber called the Hindu system one of the most logically consistent theodicies ever invented. A **theodicy** is an explanation of why bad things happen to good people (and sometimes, why good things happen to bad people). To oversimplify, in Hinduism bad things may happen to you because of what you did in a previous life, not necessarily because of what you do in this life. Being good now gets you a better situation in your next life. It is a potent way to justify social inequalities—both the suffering of the lower castes, and the privilege of those who are in "higher" castes are justified in the present and assumed to balance out over time as good lower caste members are reborn to better life circumstances, and vice versa.

Yet, seeing religion as solely a system of thought that helps to maintain the status quo misses much of what makes religion such a potent and meaningful system. A good case in point is that of Indian religions that were influenced by, or openly challenged, Hinduism. Not everyone was willing to accept the strictures of caste and the religious system that supported it. This is one of the reasons for the popularity of so many different religions in India. Although he accepted reincarnation, the founder of Buddhism (an Indian) was strongly opposed to the notion of caste, saying that "Birth does not make one a priest or an outcaste. Behavior makes one either a priest or an outcaste." Likewise, Sikhism was partly founded in rejection of caste. These religions, then, were built not on the justification of the status quo, as they were on the challenging social inequalities and the religious systems that justified them.

Denominations and Congregations: From Religion to Community

17.1.5 Describe the role that denominations and congregations play in organizing religious activity in a community.

Separation of church and state—one of the hallmarks of the American Revolution and now true in most but not all countries around the world—has allowed many flowers to bloom in the religious garden. Most of the world's major religious traditions contain several different types of groups under their umbrella. Known as **denominations**, these are organized religious groups with at least a few distinctive doctrines or practices that distinguish it from other such groups that are also adherents of the same religion. After decades of immigration in the nineteenth and

Figure 17.2 Religious Affiliation in the United States

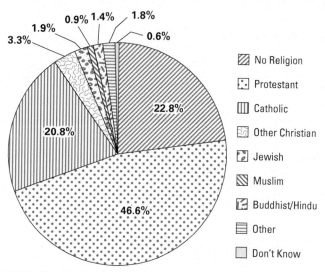

SOURCE: Pew Research Center Religion & Public Life (2016); (www.pewforum.org/religious-landscape-study/).

early twentieth centuries, Roman Catholicism became the largest Christian denomination in the United States, but as Figure 17.2 illustrates, it still only represents about 21 percent of Americans. Most Americans were and are today Protestants. But there are many different denominations among Protestants: Evangelical Christianity includes Baptists, Lutherans, Presbyterians, and Pentecostals. By one measure, there are more than 200 different denominations among Protestants in the United States, and many of these have been further divided into competing branches. *The Encyclopedia of American Religions* (Melton 2009), a comprehensive look at all religious groups, is an attempt to identify every single religious group in the United States and Canada and includes detailed descriptions of more than 2,500 distinct religious groups. Table 17.2 takes a

Table 17.2 47 Percent of People in the United States Who Report They Are Protestants, Broken Down by Denomination

	Evangelical Protestant Churches (Percent of all Americans)	Mainline Protestant Churches	Hist. Black Protestant Churches	Percent Share of Entire U.S. Population	Percent Share of all U.S., Protestants
Baptist Family	9.2	2.1	4	15.3	32.8
Southern Baptist Convention	5.3			5.3	11.4
Independent Baptist	2.5		0.3*	2.8	6.0
Missionary Baptist	0.3*		0.3	0.6	1.3
Conservative Baptist	0.3*			0.3*	0.6
Free Will Baptist	0.3*			0.3*	0.6
General Association of Regular Baptist Churches	0.3*			0.3*	0.6
National Baptist Convention			1.4	1.4	3.0
American Baptist Churches in the USA		1.5		1.5	3.2
Progressive Baptist Convention			0.3	0.3	0.6
Other Baptist	1	0.6	1.8	3.4	7.3

	Evangelical Protestant Churches (Percent of all Americans)	Mainline Protestant Churches	Hist. Black Protestant Churches	Percent Share of Entire U.S. Population	Percent Share of all U.S., Protestants
Methodist Family	0.3*	3.9	0.5	4.7	10.1
United Methodist Church		3.6		3.6	7.7
African Methodist Episcopal Church			0.3	0.3	0.6
African Methodist Episcopal Zion Church			0.3*	0.3*	0.6
Christian Methodist Episcopal Church			0.3*	0.3*	0.6
Other Methodist		0.3	0.3*	0.6	1.3
Lutheran	1.5	2.1		3.6	7.7
Evangelical Lutheran Church in America		1.4		1.4	3.0
Wisconsin Evangelical Lutheran Synod	0.3*			0.3*	0.6
Lutheran Church, Missouri Synod	1.1			1.1	2.4
Other Lutheran	0.3	0.7		1	2.1
Nondenominational	4.9	1	0.3	6.2	13.3
Nondenominational evangelical churches	2			2	4.3
Nondenominational fundamentalist churches	0.3			0.3	0.6
Nondenominational charismatic	0.6			0.6	1.3
Nondenominational Christian	0.3*			0.3*	0.6
Interdenominational	0.6	0.3		0.9	1.9
Community Church	0.3*			0.3*	0.6
Other nondenominational	1.2	0.7		1.9	4.1
Pentecostal	3.6		1	4.6	9.9
Church of God in Christ			0.6	0.6	1.3
United Pentescostal Church International			0.3*	0.3*	0.6
Assemblies of God	1.4			1.4	3.0
Church of God (Cleveland, Tennessee)	0.4			0.4	0.9
Foursquare Church	0.3*			0.3*	0.6
Pentescostal Church of God	0.3*			0.3*	0.6
Pentescostal Holiness Church	0.3*			0.3*	0.6
Calvary Chapel	0.3*			0.3*	0.6
Apostolic Pentecostal	0.3*		0.3*	0.6	1.3
Nondenominational Pentecostal	0.3*			0.3*	0.6
Church of God of the Apostolic Faith	0.3*			0.3*	0.6
Other Pentecostal	1.1		0.3	1.4	3.0
Presbyterian Family	0.8	1.4		2.2	4.7
Presbyterian Church in America	0.4			0.4	0.9
Presbyterian Church (USA)		0.9		0.9	1.9
Other Presbyterian	0.4	0.5		0.9	1.9
Restorationist	1.6			1.6	3.4
Christian Churches and Churches of Christ	0.3*			0.3*	0.6
Churches of Christ	1.5			1.5	3.2
Other Restorationist	0.3*			0.3*	0.6
Episcopalian/Anglican Family	0.3*	1.2		1.5	3.2
Episcopal Church		0.9		0.9	1.9
Anglican Church		0.3*		0.3*	0.6
Other Episcopalian/Anglican		0.3*		0.3*	0.6
Restorationist Family		0.3		0.3	0.6
Disciples of Christ		0.3*		0.3*	0.6
Other Restorationist		0.3*		0.3*	0.6

(Continued)

	Evangelical Protestant Churches (Percent of all Americans)	Mainline Protestant Churches	Hist. Black Protestant Churches	Percent Share of Entire U.S. Population	Percent Share of all U.S., Protestants
Holiness Family	0.7		0.3*	1	2.1
Church of the Nazarene	0.3			0.3	0.6
Wesleyan Church	0.3*			0.3*	0.6
Free Methodist Church	0.3*			0.3*	0.6
Christian and Missionary Alliance	0.3*			0.3*	0.6
Church of God (Anderson, Indiana)	0.3*			0.3*	0.6
Other Holiness	0.3*			0.3*	0.6
Congregationalist	0.3*	0.5		0.8	1.7
Conservative Congregational Christian Conference	0.3*			0.3*	0.6
United Church of Christ		0.4		0.4	0.9
Other Congregationalist	0.3*	0.3*		0.6	1.3
Reformed Family	0.3*	0.3*		0.6	1.3
Christian Reformed Church					0.0
Reformed Church of America		0.3*		0.3*	0.6
Other Reformed	0.3*	0.3*		0.6	1.3
Adventist	0.6			0.6	1.3
Seventh-Day Adventist	0.5			0.5	1.1
Other Adventist	0.3*			0.3*	0.6
Anabaptist Family	0.3	0.3*		0.6	1.3
Pietist Family	0.3*			0.3*	0.6
Friends Family		0.3*		0.3*	0.6
Other Evangelical/Fundamentalist Family	0.3			0.3	0.6
Nonspecific Protestant Family	1.5	1.9	0.4	3.8	8.2
TOTAL	**25.4**	**14.7**	**6.5**	**46.6**	**100.0**

*Actual number is less than 0.3 percent of the total population.

NOTE: Percentages do not always total correctly due to rounding errors.

SOURCE: Pew Research Center Religion & Public Life (2016).

closer look at the 47 percent of Americans who claim to be Protestant and identifies the size of many of the different Protestant denominations in the United States as of 2016. Note that the figure further makes a distinction between three major traditions in Protestantism: The evangelical Protestant denominations, the mainline Protestant denominations, and Black Protestant churches (which developed separately from the rest of the Protestant tradition in America).

At the level of the denomination, we find much of the "organization" in organized religion. Denominations train and ordain priests, ministers, rabbis, and imams. They may assist individual churches or synagogues in financial trouble. They frequently, if not always, determine doctrine (although individual priests/ministers/imams/rabbis or other local religious leaders may not always follow those doctrines in their preaching). They provide model liturgies to be followed and lessons to be taught in the church sanctuary and religious education programs.

It is within, as well as between, denominations that the "big" religious conflicts are fought. For example, several Episcopalian congregations have left that denomination because the national Episcopalian leadership made an openly gay priest a bishop. When the Catholic Church decided to move from the Latin mass to one in the regional language of each society in the 1960s, so that parishioners could understand what was being said, many congregations threatened to defect—although in the end relatively few did. The Church of Latter Day Saints (the Mormons) have suffered internal wars over polygamy (where a man may have more than one wife at the same time), which the church historically approved but had to disavow if it wanted to practice under American law (which bans the practice). Later, the Mormons fought over and eventually changed their original position forbidding Black people from holding leadership positions. At this historical moment, we are witnessing internal conflicts in many denominations as they deal with the changing societies in which they function and the changing views of their members, for example, in the rising acceptance of gays and lesbians in congregational life.

But the notion of denomination, as an umbrella name for an organization that encompasses multiple places of worship, may be on the decline as the most significant way to understand the organization of religion in the United States. A growing number of churches, some very large, declare themselves "nondenominational." These churches are now the fastest-growing segment of the church world. The leaders of these churches do not feel that they need some denominational leaders shaping their worship and read of the Bible, or taking a share of their collections. Rather than belong to a larger denomination, they declare themselves independent. Some of these churches, those with 2,000 or more members, are called **megachurches**. In any given week, the largest of these—currently Joel Osteen's Lakewood Church in Houston, which sits 16,000—may have almost 50,000 people attend its weekly services.

Accordingly, many religious scholars now have concluded that denominations are not the key organizational aspect of American religion. Instead, the most important level of organization is the local **congregation**—the specific church, temple, or mosque that people actually attend. Because congregations are founded and disbanded with great frequency, and because there are many institutions that may or may not be congregations—storefront churches that are there today and gone tomorrow, "seed" churches started by ministers hoping to open their own megachurch, or Orthodox Jewish synagogues that barely have the 10-men

requirement for a prayer quorum—it is difficult to get exact figures for the number of congregations in America. Nevertheless, the most systematic investigation found that there are about 335,000 religious congregations in the United States (Chaves 2004). Of these, about 300,000 are Protestant and kindred churches, and 22,000 are Catholic and Orthodox churches. Non-Christian religious congregations are estimated at about 12,000.

More than half of all congregations are regularly attended by fewer than 100 individuals. In other words, there are many small churches in America, often with part-time or unpaid ministers, or even no minister at all. On the other hand, more than half of all church attendance is actually in the largest churches (top 10 percent in size). Interestingly, several of these large churches, including Lakewood, are nondenominational.

The enormous supply of churches means something about American religious life. In fact, large numbers of Americans do go to church regularly, although not as many as those who say they do. According to Chaves and Anderson (2014) over 60 percent of the American population has attended a congregational meeting in the past year, and about one quarter have attended their congregation at any given week. It is also important to note that whether or not people actually go to church in any specific week, many want others to think that they have gone—since they think of themselves as "churchgoing people." However, it appears that Americans overstate their attendance. Research that actually counted people in the pews in one county found that about 20 percent actually attended in a specific week—exactly half of the 40 percent who claimed they had attended in a telephone survey. (Chaves, Hadaway, and Marler 1993).

While there is an increasing percent of the American population who answer "none" when asked about their

Religious communities regularly come together to participate in a ritual, that is, a scripted collective activity that employs certain cherished symbols.

religious affiliation, organized religion will not go away soon, at least in the United States. And not only religious people like to go to church. Some who are not really believers in any religious doctrine, or even in a god at all, still attend some religious services and may even describe themselves as religious. As we can expect if we follow Durkheim's lead, many people go to church for the shared experience—the celebration of community, family, and common identity. As the many Jews in New York who go to Christmas services and love the music know, or the many Christians who attend a Jewish Passover Seder at their friends' house know, people enjoy rituals—if not all rituals, at least those they learn as part of their communities. Many people attend religious services on one or two days a year—Catholics going to Christmas Eve mass, Jews attending services on the High Holiday days, and so forth—which is a very minimal but nonetheless real involvement. Common rituals can be shared by all church members and are a sign of their togetherness. *Collective effervescence* is what Durkheim called it, and the church has always been important for providing that experience.

It would be fair to say no other single institution in the United States aside from the government provides as directly and personally for community needs. Community here does not mean some residential community. In an urban world, every city and virtually every suburb, and even many small towns, are home to several distinct (and potentially competing) congregations. The community of primary interest to each congregation is the community of co-worshippers, not the city or suburb. In most churches, membership qualifies you for help with all kinds of problems for a variety of other services. A religious congregation has never been only a place where people practice religion—it is often a space that fosters a rich social life, mutual aid, schooling, counseling for troubled parishioners, sports and social programs for teenagers, financial counseling, help with elderly parents, nursing homes, and even graveyards. Focusing on congregations thus allows us to see the porous boundary between things we usually think about as religion—ritual and belief—and the social world that is part of religious life.

BIG QUESTION 17.2 How Does Social Structure Impact Religious Belonging?

PATTERNS AND CAREERS OF RELIGIOUS BELONGING

With all the religions in the world, how do people pick one religion as their own? Of course, this is a trick question. Most people don't actually sit down, consider a list of religions, read their edicts and theological writings, and then choose to be one or the other. Historically, most people were born into a religion that has long been institutionalized in their society, community, or perhaps

just in their family. In other words, the odds—and social pressure—are that you will remain in the religion you were born into.

In today's world, the vast majority of people are well aware that there are other religions than their own. They are also very aware that some form of irreligion (the absence of religion) is an alternative embraced by at least some people, somewhere. Within religions, this gives rise to new patterns of religious life. In the United States, one of the most religiously pluralistic of all countries, many individuals will at least experiment with another denomination at some point. For example, close to half of all Protestants will try another denomination in the Protestant family. But switching to an entirely different religious tradition, such as going from being a Catholic to a Jew or an evangelical Protestant to a Mormon, however, is much more rare.

Religious Segregation: Birds of a Feather

17.2.1 Discuss the causes of segregation in American churches.

We do know that there are definite patterns regarding the social backgrounds of people who end up in different religions, denominations, and congregations. Even as people switch among denominations, as Reverend Martin Luther King Jr. put it over half a century ago, 11:00 AM on Sunday is one of the most segregated hours and church the most segregated place in the country—and not just by race. They are also segregated by class and lifestyle and various forms of preferences. While some patterns of segregation are far from voluntary, adults mostly decide which church to attend, so birds of a feather are permitted to flock together.

Perhaps the most important ingredients of American church segregation, besides religion itself, are area of residence and social status. Different kinds of people tend to live in different places. Just look at the campus churches at your college or university. They are full of students who live on or near campus. This constitutes a group of people very much alike on key characteristics, including, to begin with, age and level of education.

Few congregations serve broad areas of a city or county. With rare exceptions, congregations tend to reside in neighborhoods and be seen as neighborhood institutions. A congregation in the suburbs south of Chicago rarely attracts members from a northern suburb or from the city's core. Neighborhoods tend be collections of people who are economically or ethnically similar. Throughout history, immigrants, and hence ethnic groups, have tended to move into areas where people they know already reside, particularly relatives and friends from home towns. They get help and a sense of comfort. The already beaten path is the way to

helpful information and to safety. This is especially salient in religious communities that actively shape members' participation or movement—Latter Day Saints' churches are organized by geography and expect most people living in a particular area to pray in their own ward or branch; Orthodox Jews are not allowed to drive on the Sabbath, thus ensuring that they worship in neighborhood synagogues that are within walking distance. But even without such organizational or religious demands, geography matters deeply. Thus, for example, as immigrants form ethnic enclaves in particular places, such enclaves become crucial religious hubs.

Korean Americans (and their religious practices) provide an instructive illustration. There are a set of Protestant churches that conduct services in Korean or serve a primarily Korean American membership (see Chang 2006 for a history). Although some came to the United States earlier, particularly after the Korean War, most Korean immigrants arrived after the 1965 change in American immigration law, which repealed the previous massive discrimination against non-Europeans. There are therefore many first- and second-generation Korean Americans in the United States.

In South Korea, about 29 percent of the population describes themselves as Protestant Christians. In the United States, however, 75 percent of Korean Americans are Protestants. To some extent, this difference might reflect a special attraction to America for Korean Protestants (as compared with Korean Buddhists, or even Korean Catholics). More interesting, however, is the fact that almost 40 percent of Korean Protestants

In Savannah, Georgia, young Americans in a Korean American Methodist church learn Korean, making a connection through religion to their ethnic community. Religious groups often provide services that go beyond formal religious ceremonies to build their community and involve members more deeply.

Richard Burkhart/Savannah Morning News/AP Images

in the United States were previously not religious, or of another religion! That is a lot of converts and is an important clue for understanding the role and attraction of ethnic churches (see Chen [2008] for a similar analysis of Taiwanese Americans).

For Korean immigrants, the Korean church is much more than a religious institution. It is the center of their community—a place they can speak Korean, eat Korean food, and share a sense of belonging with others who they see as similar to them in many ways. The church provides a kind of safe haven where immigrants and their children can negotiate the treacherous path from culture to culture. Were it only a matter of religion, many or most Koreans could have attended established Protestant churches. They did not. The enormous number of Korean American converts to Christianity probably is both a religious feature and also an indication that non-Christian Koreans clearly wanted, even needed, to associate themselves with the principal institutional center of their community, the various Protestant churches.

The centrality of non-English-speaking churches for immigrant communities is not new in the United States. Polish-speaking Catholic congregations in Chicago served the same function. Italian immigrants struggled to have an Italian Catholic service and community in a New York diocese whose priests were mostly Irish, but they eventually succeeded. As Germans, Swedes, Chinese, and many other ethnic groups immigrated to America, they often did not fit very well into the established churches, even churches of their own denominations. German and Swedish Lutherans wanted German- and Swedish-speaking versions of Lutheranism, where they could pray in the language they knew and mix comfortably with people from their own background. Thus, immigrants established thriving ethnic churches of their own. Today, many Catholic churches have special services for Spanish-speaking parishioners or services in Vietnamese on the West Coast, featuring Latinx and Vietnamese priests, respectively.

Many once flourishing immigrant churches, however, have disappeared. Throughout American history, as immigrant groups become more settled and assimilated, their churches tend to disappear. Consider what was once America's largest immigrant group—the Germans. Some Germans came to America in colonial times, but the largest wave arrived in the first half of the nineteenth century and settled mostly in the upper Midwest. They were a varied group—they thought of themselves as Prussians and Bavarians (Germany was not unified until 1871), and they were Catholic and Lutheran and Amish and Mennonite. But for all of them, there were immigrant churches where German was spoken and where German culture was central to daily life. In Milwaukee and Chicago, there were German counterparts to the Polish

Catholic Church. The Germans practically dominated American Lutheranism.

Where is it all now? Besides a few Amish or Mennonite settlements, most of the edifice of the German church is gone, and so are virtually all of the Swedish-, Polish-, and Italian-speaking churches. The process may take three generations, and requires a significant decline in immigration from the home region so that those uncomfortable in the host American culture are not replenished with newcomers.

Undoubtedly the most important—and enduringly segregated—churches in the United States today are the historically Black churches. About 53 percent of all Black Americans belong to traditionally Black denominations, and additional Blacks belong to denominations that are integrated but attend almost completely segregated churches (Greeley and Hout 2006). Until fairly recently (and in many churches, even now), Black people have not felt welcome in most White churches in either the North or South, and certainly not as equals.

Early Black churches were established by free Black Americans—both in the North before the Civil War and most importantly after the Civil War in the South. Black churches are generally religiously conservative, but because they represent an exploited and oppressed minority, they also have emphasized a kind of **liberation theology**, a theology that emphasizes Christ's focus on helping the poor and downtrodden and the importance of social justice in Christian thought. For Black churches, this is particularly reflected in the biblical story of Exodus—the escape of the Jews from slavery in Egypt, from bondage to freedom. "Let my people go" is a favorite theme of sermons and prayers.

The importance of the Black church became clear during the civil rights struggle of the 1950s, 1960s, and 1970s. The movement leaders were mostly ministers from Black churches, especially in the South. The Rev. Martin Luther King Jr. was the son of the pastor of the largest and most affluent Black church in Atlanta. This gave King the backing he needed so that he could dedicate himself to the movement. No other institution in the South could provide financial support, space for meetings, and community-supported professionals like the ministers who were not so dependent for their livelihood on the White power structure (Morris 1985). The churches also provided sanctuary for activists, although that sanctuary was sometimes bombed or attacked. The church was also the source of the gospel songs and the liberation message that buoyed the spirits of the activists. Almost all observers agree that without the Black church the civil rights movement could not have developed as quickly and with as much strength as it did. Yet, in what seems to be a politically important development, this historical pattern of segregated membership may show some signs of fraying. According to new Pew surveys, older Blacks are far more likely to belong to historically Black churches (63 percent) than are millennials and younger Blacks (41 percent). While still segregated, it may be that the most segregated hour in America is becoming slowly less so.

Conversion

17.2.2 Explain who converts to what denomination or religion and the process of conversion.

Even if most do, not everyone remains in the religion they were born into. So who converts to what, and why? Leaving aside moves to giving up religion altogether (discussed in a later section), we know that in the United States people convert from one denomination or religion to another for a variety of reasons.

Among Christians, most conversions are between denominations within the same religious tradition. In the majority of cases, the notion of conversion—if by that we mean a shift among religions—is an overstatement. People often switch the church they attend within the same religious tradition because of the people they know who go there, it is in a more convenient location, or because they feel that the new congregation better fits their style of devotion. However, conversions between Catholics and Protestants—or either and Mormons—are considered much more of a leap. For a long time, intermarriage was the dominant reason for people changing among these denominations (and for Jewish–Christian conversions as well). The notion that families should go to church together was an important factor. So was a simple attempt to make life less complicated or to decide "how to raise the children."

Many religions seek to recruit, or proselytize, more members. In the Christian tradition, proselytizing is known as being an **evangelical**, literally someone who believes in salvation through personal conversion (or being "born again"), and evangelicals are known for their emphasis on bringing their beliefs to others. Some religions make proselytizing a strong expectation of membership; Jehovah's Witnesses often go door to door in their communities distributing literature and seeking converts, while in the Mormon Church, members are expected to do an extended period of missionary work, usually in early adulthood, somewhere around the world for a period of 18 months to 2 years. There are, however, a few exceptions. Hindus do not generally proselytize (although there are some aggressive gurus). Jews actually even make it difficult for people to convert, primarily because Judaism is understood by many Jews as both a religion and an ethnic group. In Israel, the determinant of whether one is Jewish or not is mostly whether or not one had a Jewish mother.

An individual does not have to be a practicing Jew, just have had a Jewish mother themselves. Figure 17.3 highlights data from a survey that asked respondents to consider whether being Jewish was more about religion or culture and ancestry.

The process of religious conversion takes on different forms. As sociologists have shown, the way that converts experience their own conversion tends to match the religion to which they convert. Converts to Christianity, and especially evangelical Protestantism, often depict their conversion as a sudden moment, when they are born again and accept Jesus as their personal savior. But this kind of conversion narrative, where the convert suddenly "sees the light," is not the only possibility. Jehovah's Witnesses, for example, a group that stresses the value of slow and dedicated learning, usually experience their conversion as a long process of becoming convinced of the merits of the group rather than as sudden revelation; some people converting to Judaism, precisely since it doesn't court converts, say that they have always had an affinity to Judaism—that they "felt" Jewish long before they became Jewish. In other words, the religious group that people convert into shapes the experience of conversion.

Much like the experience of conversion itself, entering a new religion is a patterned process, something akin to a religious "career" of the newly converted. This is especially the case in practice-based religions such as Judaism and Islam, where performing practices in the right way, such as learning prayers in Hebrew and Aramaic in Judaism or the precise way to perform the five daily prayers in Islam, is important. These conversion careers are marked by experiential highs and lows. In the early days of religious converts, many of the practices that members take for granted are challenging and exciting. Indeed, a lot of religious traditions work hard to sustain this early excitement of converts, and some converted members often take on more and more religious strictures as a way to reanimate their early excitement.

Figure 17.3 Being Jewish: Is It More About Culture and Ancestry Than Religion?

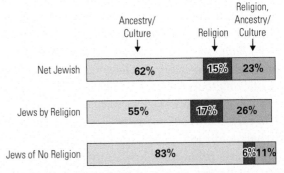

SOURCE: Pew Research Center (2013).

New Religious Movements

17.2.3 Identify the varieties of new religious movements and who is drawn to them.

One segment of organized religion that depends almost entirely on converts are the so-called **new religious movements** (NRMs), an umbrella term for new religions and offshoots of "foreign" religions that have a foothold in the United States. Examples may be found in Table 17.1 and include religious movements such as Wicca, Scientology, the Moonies (the Unification Church), various Buddhist or Hindu sects, a multitude of "New Age" groups, and so forth. Some would include as new religious movements the Mormons, Jehovah's Witnesses, and other relatively new versions of religious doctrine, although both the Mormons and the Jehovah's Witnesses have been around since the nineteenth century.

Who is drawn to these new religions? Sociologist Rodney Stark has studied a number of new religious movements and concludes that "people must have a degree of privilege to have the sophistication needed to understand new religions and to recognize a need for them. This is not to say that the most privileged will be most prone to embrace new religious movements, but only that converts will be from the more, rather than the less, privileged classes" (Stark 1996, p. 39). He points out that Christianity was once just such a movement—a Jewish "Jesus cult"—and its converts tended to suffer from "relative deprivation"—that is, resentment among the somewhat privileged that they actually deserved even more privilege and respect. On the other hand, Stark argues, religious sects that seek to purify existing traditions, that is, to make them more like the "old-time," "true," "essential," or "authentic" version of the religion, appeal to the less privileged. These movements often promise their adherents a "purer" religious practice, which is one way to claim higher status than the less strict on religious grounds.

In recent decades, there has been an explosion of groups defined as **cults**, as well as new religious movements (NRMs) that center on the individual. In the United States, there has been much written about cults over the years, punctuated by the mass poisoning suicides of 909 members of the People's Temple in 1978 and the storming of the Branch Davidians' compound in 1993, when 82 members and four United States federal agents were killed. The difference between cults and NRMs is often problematic, with "cult" sometimes being used in a derogatory way without precisely specifying exactly what makes a group a cult. Critics of groups labelled as cults usually note a strong hierarchical structure and a charismatic leader as the hallmark of cults. However, many religious movements have early charismatic leaders and are highly hierarchical. For example, early Islam and Christianity began with highly charismatic figures (think of Mohammed and Jesus), and

groups such as the Latter-Day Saints (the Mormon church) began with both a charismatic leader and a strict hierarchy. In other words, cults are not a sociological definition—the word is simply a term given to particularly new religious movements.

If the question of cults is perhaps one of the most often discussed topic among new religious movements, a different type of NRMs has emerged as important, especially in Europe and North America, known as "New Age religions." Originating as a North American import of Eastern religions in the early twentieth century and from the countercultural movement of the 1960s, the "New Age" term refers not to particular groups, but to what sociologists have defined as a style of religious participation that is linked with a host of both new versions of older religions and emerging traditions. Thus, the New Age milieu includes Westernized versions of Hinduism, Buddhism, and a revival (and, in many cases, reinvention) of European and North American polytheism and animism. Shared among these different religious traditions is a focus on the figure of the believer as the arbiter of religious truth and the center of religious practice—a scared self—and, consequentially, a de-traditionalization and rejection of hierarchical structure. Much like the "Sheilaism" depicted by Robert Bellah and his colleagues earlier in the chapter, the individual is at the center of New Age religions.

Gender and Religious Participation

17.2.4 Discuss the relationship between gender and religiosity in various major religions.

One striking aspect of new religious movements is that they appeal disproportionately to women. Some of these groups, like Wicca (a neopagan cult with goddesses), are explicitly aimed at women. But many other new religious movements seem attractive to women. Research on early Christianity suggests that women were more likely to convert. This was also probably true of the beginnings of Islam.

Why do more women than men take up new religions? One possibility that researchers have noted was because they are treated so badly by the old religions. Most religious traditions support, or even mandate, traditional gender roles. They bar women from most positions of authority, restrict their dress, and sometimes blame them for the evils in the world (Eve in the major monotheistic traditions, Pandora in Greek mythology, Izanami in the Shinto creation story). Until very recently, almost all priests, ministers, rabbis, imams, monks, gurus, shamans, and other such higher functionaries of the religious establishments were male. Most of Jesus's recorded disciples were male (although there were also disciples who were women, they are rarely mentioned in the Bible). Women often had to sit in separate sections of the church or synagogue or mosque. They could not lead prayers, and because most were illiterate they were not even able to read the prayers.

Some new religions seem to be better for women. As a striking example, consider the beginnings of Islam. Many Westerners mistakenly think of Islam as sexist in its treatment of women. In fact, Mohammad prescribed a liberating revolution for women in the context of his time. In the Arab world before Islam, women were chattel, the property of their fathers and then of their husbands and then of anyone their husbands gave them to. They had no rights. Mohammad gave them rights of protection, divorce, and property, among other advances. Similarly, for example, early Christianity gave women the right not to be treated as chattel, or not to be left to die from exposure because their father wanted a son. All of these were common practices in the Roman paganism of the time.

Women, however, do not only convert to new religious movements in larger numbers. One literature review argues strongly that "[t]he greater religiosity [the importance of religion in one's life] of women must be one of the oldest and clearest findings in the psychology of religion" (Beit-Hallahmi and Argyle 1997, p. 142). But is this true across cases? And what does the increased religiosity of women mean in cases where this seems to be true?

A major study published in 2006 re-analyzed the available data across the world, challenging the received wisdom in a couple of ways. The researcher (D. Paul Sullins) concluded that (1) women were more likely to describe themselves as pious or religious across almost all societies studied, but men were more likely or equally likely to be active "organizational participants" (for example, go to church regularly) in about 25 percent of countries, and (2) while this pattern continues to hold among Christians, there was little difference in how devout male and female Jews (particularly Orthodox Jews) or male and female Muslims are (Sullins 2006). In these settings, men were more likely to attend services, while there was little difference between men and women in questions of personal devotion. Since Sullins published his analysis, more extensive data from Saudi Arabia, Egypt, Jordan, and Iran have confirmed his findings for a number of Muslim countries (Moaddel 2007). The gender gap—both in attendance and in personal belief—is large in the United States because of the dominance of Christian and Catholic traditions, but it does not hold for all religions across the world.

How can we understand both the disparities within Christianity and the pattern we see in the Muslim communities, as seen in Figure 17.4? One way of understanding the disparities is to turn our attention to the relationship between public worship and personal devotion. That is, not only about the question of whether

---

Figure 17.4 The Gender Gap in Religion: Are Women More Religious Than Men?

Average percentage-point difference between men and women on measures of religious practice, commitment, and belief

CHRISTIANS	Women	Men	% Pt. Difference Men ◄ ► Women
Weekly attendance	53%	46%	+7
Daily prayer	61	51	+10
Importance of religion	68	61	+7
Belief in heaven	91	89	+2
Belief in hell	78	76	+1
Belief in angels	88	84	+3

MUSLIMS	Women	Men	Men ◄ ► Women
Weekly attendance	42%	70%	–28
Daily prayer	72	71	+2
Importance of religion	76	76	0
Belief in heaven	94	93	0
Belief in hell	88	88	0
Belief in angels	86	85	+1

NOTE: Values in difference column are calculated based on unrounded numbers.

SOURCE: Pew Research Center's Forum on Religion and Public Life (2008–2015).

religious leaders are male (which they overwhelmingly are) but on the question as to who is supposed to be in public, and how important public worship is for religious life.

Seen through these lenses, we can begin making sense of the differences among religious traditions. Consider, for example, the gender differences in the way that faith is practiced in Muslim countries or among Orthodox Jews. All male orthodox Jews are expected to spend much of their time studying the Torah and the Talmud—in other words, in religious study. In contrast, women and girls were not allowed to participate in such activities. Women were also much less likely to go to temple than men—since the edict to pray with a quorum does not apply to women. Women performed a variety of religious rituals and prayers at home, but their engagement with religious life, especially as it concerned both learning and important rituals, was limited.

The status of Muslim women is similar. Young Muslim boys are trained to memorize the Koran; girls are not (although some may choose to do so). The number of women who pray at the mosque is generally a fraction of the number of men. One of the five pillars of Muslim practice is the Hajj, or ritual visit to Mecca, which religious Muslims try to perform at least once in their lifetime. Yet males always outnumber females at the Hajj by large margins. In general, then, Muslim men might attend services more often in some countries, while more or equal numbers of Muslim women consider themselves religious.

Questions about Muslim and Orthodox Jewish gender differences do not invalidate the consistent finding of greater female religiosity in most Christian settings. Why might this be the case among Christians? As previously mentioned, we can begin by noting that, while most clergy and religious leaders in Christianity are men, women were always part of public worship. Indeed, one of the countries where women attend prayer much more than do men is Italy—at the epicenter of the Catholic world. Traditionally, especially before the second Vatican convention in 1965 allowed the recitation of mass in languages other than Latin, the most salient difference in religious knowledge and participation was between the clergy and the laity, rather than between men and women. In such a situation, religious attendance and belief could be constructed as part of women's devotion. In Protestantism, on the other hand, every person, male and female, should have a personal relationship with God and read the Bible. Again, the ministers and theologians might be men, but their importance is downgraded before the individual parishioner's role in his or her own religious life.

Age and Religion: Do People Become More Religious as They Age?

17.2.5 Explain why older people tend to be more religious.

One of the more interesting, if less important, reasons women are more religious than men in most places is that on average in most societies around the world women live longer than men. In most developed countries women outlive men by about five years. And, as it turns out, older people are more religious than younger people.

For a long time, the age difference in religiosity was thought to derive from the confrontation with death becoming increasingly acute as we age. Alternatively, mature wisdom and perspective were seen to replace the rebelliousness of youth. Today, however, most sociologists agree that the most important reason older people tend to be more religious is not aging but what is called a "cohort" difference: Older people were brought up in more religious times than younger people. Your grandparents did not necessarily become more religious—they were always more religious than you (or at least most of you). This can be clearly seen in Figure 17.5.

As Figure 17.5 shows, the generations (usually called birth cohorts by sociologists) born earlier are more likely to say they go to church than the generations born later, and each generation starts at a lower level of attendance in their early 20s than the previous generation (or cohort).

The data in Figure 17.5, however, do not track the religiosity of individuals over their lifetime, which is a much more difficult job. To do so, we would have had to start the research more than 50 years ago. We have only a few such long-term studies that measured religiosity, and they are for selected, not-very-representative samples. Nevertheless, these can give us some idea of individual change over time. One such study follows a group of Oakland, California, students who were interviewed while in high school in the 1920s and then interviewed several additional times, most recently in the 1990s when they were well into their 70s (Dillon and Wink 2007). Figure 17.6 shows their religious trajectories, by gender, where the measure of religiousness is a complex combination of practices and beliefs. Note that, as expected, women in the sample were always substantially more religious than men.

The respondents, it turns out, were most religious when they were teenagers. The women remained at the same level in their late 30s, declined in religiosity into their 60s, and increased in their late 70s. Men simply declined rather markedly into their 60s, with some recovery in their 70s. For both men and women, therefore, there is some

Figure 17.5 Weekly Attendance at Religious Services by Generation

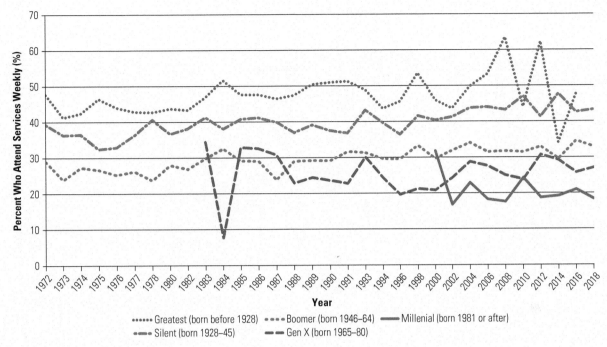

SOURCE: General Social Survey, 1972–2018.

Figure 17.6 Mean Change in Religiousness Over Time by Gender

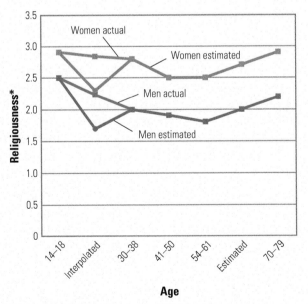

*For a detailed description of the measure of "Religiousness" used in this figure, see Dillon and Wink (2007, p. 82).

SOURCE: Dillon and Wink, 2007.

evidence the ages between 60 and 80 might involve an increase in religiosity.

Unfortunately, data were not collected during this sample's college-age years. We know from other work

that this stage of life, which is when most people in the United States leave home, is the stage when they are most likely to reassess their religious commitments and decline in religious participation, whether they went to college or not. For example, Smith (2009, p. 244–46) followed a representative sample from ages 13–17 to ages 20–22. He found that between 33 and 40 percent of these young people declined in religiosity, some sharply, while only 3 to 7 percent increased (the rest were "stable").

A general narrative of religiosity over the life course, at least in the United States, as reflected in the data from the Oakland study, might look something like this: (1) Because parents, schools, and churches invest heavily in the religiosity of children, and most children accept these lessons, children's religiosity is high, if somewhat incoherent. (2) With relative independence from their parents during the post-high school years, many of these young people lose interest in religion, or in their inherited religion, or begin to be influenced by other, less religious views. (3) After people have children themselves, they tend to move to communities where churches are more important and to think they should teach their children about religion. This is particularly important for women, who most often bear the responsibility for childrearing. Thus, there is a tendency to return to church during this life stage, which for the Oakland sample was probably ages 28 to 40. (4) After their children leave the home, some of the middle-aged return to their earlier, less religious practices and views. (5) In the oldest part of the life course, people leave their jobs and lose friends and spouses. For many, the church and the support of religion might become more important, whether they fear death or not.

Mark Bussell

BIG QUESTION **17.3** How Does Religion Play Into Public Life?

RELIGION IN PUBLIC LIFE

To this point, we have mostly focused on figuring out what people get out of religion and for whom religion is most important. But religion is not only a matter of personal morality, or even of communal ties. Religion is also a platform for mobilization, an impetus for protest and revolution. Religious and political affiliations often intertwine, giving rise to typical voting patterns, as well as large scale persecution, violence, or even war.

World history would be difficult to grasp without understanding the role of religion in public and political life. For a very long time, the Catholic church was not only the single most powerful religious institution in Europe, it was also the most powerful political one. When Henry the VIII wanted a divorce, he left the Catholic church, giving rise to both newfound political independence and a religious schism in the shape of the Anglican Church. In the first century after Mohammad's death, Islam was primarily spread by the sword. In the twelfth and thirteenth centuries, Christians launched the Crusades against Muslims in an attempt to capture and hold Jerusalem. In the sixteenth century, Protestants and Catholics fought the Thirty Years' War over control of various parts of Europe. In the first two decades of the twentieth century, Muslim Turks and Kurds probably killed from 1 to 1.5 million Christian Armenians. There are also religious undertones to political conflicts we don't even think of as primarily religious. For example, during the Civil War, Northern soldiers sang "The Battle Hymn of the Republic" as they marched off to do their sacred duty to save the Union.

Understanding Public Religion

17.3.1 Explain the role of religion in public and political life in the United States and elsewhere.

Max Weber, one of the architects of both the field of sociology generally and the sociology of religion, observed that modernity has been defined by a *separation of spheres*. In earlier times different domains of social life—like scientific, religious, political, and economic—were tightly intertwined. But, said Weber, modernity created a separation of spheres, with each domain becoming disconnected from the others. Religion, in this telling of the story, had retreated to the private domain, and, as we will see in the next section, disappeared altogether. Yet, this retreat—to the degree that it wasn't simply confined to Weber's surroundings in Western Europe in the first place—was short lived. As sociologist Jose Casanova has argued, the 1970s and 80s saw an explosion of religion in the public sphere. This was the case in Latin America, as well as in North Africa, the Middle East, and many other places around the globe. The religious and the political were re-fused. Nowhere, perhaps, is the resurgence of religion into the public sphere clearer than in the United States. Of course, the United States was founded in significant measure by religious Puritans, Quakers, and other groups escaping religious persecution, looking to create a new promised land, and religion was always central in American history. Still, after public outcry about the place of religion in education early in the century, religion seemed to be retreating to the private domain.

However, in recent decades, religious groups have become more active and involved in trying to shape public life. The rise of conservative Protestantism and the active participation of some prominent evangelical Christian ministers in politics in the 1970s, most famously Jerry Falwell (founder of a group called the Moral Majority in the late 1970s) and Pat Robertson, can in many ways be seen as a reaction to the social changes brought about by the movements of the 1960s and the seeming decline of "traditional" values beginning in that era. Because conservative White Protestants are disproportionately centered in the South, reaction against the civil rights revolution was also a factor. The most important of the changes in American society that began in the 1960s, however, were the changing gender roles and "sexual liberation" of women (Putnam and Campbell 2010). Repelled by these changes and other threats to so-called family values, many conservative Americans sought to defend a more stable commitment to "traditional family values"—especially for their children—and some turned to those churches that they saw as sharing this conservative vision.

The rise of conservative White evangelical politics has re-shaped American politics. This can be seen both in the structure of political polarization and in voting patterns. First, while polarization in public opinion in the United States is often thought to be much sharper than it is, one place where attitudes have become especially divided is in views towards abortion. Prior to the rise of the Moral Majority, the issue was not something that evangelical Christians were adamant about, nor something that Democrats and Republicans were particularly at odds about, but it has become a religiously tinged flashpoint in American politics today. In terms of voting patterns, the United States has become more religiously polarized. While Catholics and mainline Protestants are not strongly in favor of one party or another, White evangelicals are now some of the staunchest supporters of the Republican party. Partly as a reaction, those who say that they have "no" religion, tend to vote Democrat. Indeed, sociologists have noted that one of the reasons that some respondents say they have no religion, even though they also say that they believe in God, is that they understand a religious affiliation as a political statement.

If religion has taken a prominent role in the American public sphere, it has been all the more important in other places in the world too. It would be impossible to understand the political transformations in the Middle East, in North Africa, in Turkey, India or Pakistan without understanding the place of religion. Thus, for example, whereas Turkey had been a secular state strongly shaped by military elites, the past two decades have seen the rise of Islamic politics—where Islam has become a defining feature of political discourse. In Egypt, the conflict between the more secular elites and more Islamic parties shaped the outcome of the Arab Spring demonstrations of 2010–2012, culminating in a electoral win for the Islamic Brotherhood, which was quickly quashed by older and more secular elites. In many parts of the world, religion and politics are tightly intertwined.

Distinguishing Religious Conflicts from Ethnic and Class Conflicts

17.3.2 Explain why it is difficult to distinguish religious conflict from ethnic or class conflict.

Perhaps nowhere is the public aspect of religion more apparent than it is in religious–political conflict. It is often hard to tell when a religious war is primarily a war about religion, as opposed to something else. Consider the example of the Catholic–Protestant war in Northern Ireland in the 1970s. In a very telling sentence (supposedly a quotation from a nameless participant), Demerath (2003) describes the war as "Protestant atheists vs. Catholic atheists." What he meant was that with one or two prominent exceptions, virtually all leading religious figures in Northern (and Southern) Ireland were against the killings and confrontations. Furthermore, one could easily argue that major class and ethnic conflicts were the real sources of the war. Northern Ireland was ruled by the well-off descendants of British colonialists. Thus, ethnicity and class, as well as religion, separated the sides.

In Sri Lanka, the Buddhists are overwhelmingly ethnic Sinhalese, and the minority Hindus (18 percent of the population) are ethnic Tamils. They speak different languages, and the Tamils have long considered themselves discriminated against economically and politically. For most Tamils, the war is about the need for secession so that they can have their own country. Neither group seems to think the other should change their religion. Perhaps this too is an ethnic and economic war rather than a religious one.

We could look at many "religious" wars and find ethnic conflict more central to the problem. Serbs (who were mostly members of the Serbian Orthodox Church) killing Muslims in Bosnia in the mid-1990s called it "ethnic cleansing," not "religious cleansing." Muslims and Jews lived together fairly peacefully in British-controlled Palestine until the 1920s, when Zionists, who believed Jews needed their own homeland so they could defend themselves from lethal anti-Semitism around the world, particularly in Germany and other parts of Europe, began immigrating in great numbers. Threatened by the flood of Jews, Palestinian Arabs rioted and demanded the British halt the migration (Sela 1994). Note that most of the Jewish founders of Israel were more or less irreligious, defining their Jewishness in ethnic rather than religious terms. Even today, anyone has the right to become an Israeli citizen if one's family is Jewish, not if one believes in the sacredness of the Torah.

Still, all these conflicts are *also* religious, and trying to understand them without understanding their religious connotations is impossible. For a large portion of the religious right wing in Israel, the Palestinian territories are Jewish by biblical right; while the terrorists who planned the 9/11 attacks on the United States (see photo opening this section) used anti-imperialist rhetoric, they were also explicitly motivated by Salafi Islamic thought and hoped to spark religious war through their action. Much as we cannot understand such attacks without recourse to ethnic or political violence, we also cannot understand them without realizing how religion creates a platform for defining and attacking one's enemies and justifying violence.

An Example of Religious Conflict in India

17.3.3 Discuss the long-standing religious conflict between Hindus and Muslims in India.

One of the most compelling examples of what seems to be religious violence is the long-term conflict between Hindus and Muslims in India. The partition of India into India and Pakistan (which at first included what later became Bangladesh) took place in 1947, shortly after Britain decided to end its colonial control over the subcontinent. The partition was hasty and unplanned. More than 7 million Muslims moved to Pakistan, and an approximately equal number of Hindus, Sikhs, and others moved from the territory that became Pakistan to India. From being approximately 25 percent Muslim before partition, the new India contained less than 13 percent. The new Pakistan had hardly any Hindus at all. It is estimated that between half a million and a million people died in the process as Hindus and Muslims fought over land or just over resentments in both communities.

After partition, communal conflict between Hindus and Muslims was common in India, although almost always local. Anything that might go wrong could begin a cycle of hostility. Muslims had conquered most of India in the sixteenth century and ruled until the eighteenth century, a fact not lost on the majority Hindus. To this day, some Hindu nationalists continue to write vicious screeds on the horrors of Muslim occupation, particularly in the blogosphere. For many Hindus, the partition

meant that India was now specifically a Hindu country. This idea sparked the growth of a political philosophy of "Hindutva," which asserts that India should be for Hindus, and eventually led to the election of an avowedly Hindutva party to a majority in the parliament.

In the early 1990s, Hindutva politicians and a number of Hindu holy men focused on a mosque in Ayodhya that they claimed had been built on top of an important Hindu temple (what cynics have called one of the mythical birthplaces of the mythical god Rama). They demanded that the mosque be razed and the Hindu temple rebuilt. The government was opposed, envisioning the turmoil that would ensue and the hundreds of other sites that might become controversial. In December 1992, an estimated 200,000 Hindus descended on the mosque and, despite some opposition from a small number of police, razed the mosque themselves (led by Hindu "skinheads," of all things). All over India, communal violence broke out, with more than 2,000 people—mostly Muslims—killed.

Yet in spite of the seemingly clear religious underpinnings of the conflict, we still need to ask: Was this really a

Protesters demonstrating against religious violence in India.

religious conflict? Conflicts between religious groups can have elements of other things—class resentments, ethnic drives for control of land or governments, long memories of past or imagined injuries—alongside religious intolerance or fear. Religion is a potent marker of "us versus them." It speaks for the "rightness" of "our" cause. For many people in this world, security comes only from being a member of a powerful group. That group's fate is our fate—and that includes nationalism as well as ethnicity or religion. Religion provides institutional support because it has professional people to do the organizing. It works well in times of conflict.

BIG QUESTION 17.4 How Is Religion Changing?

SECULARIZATION VERSUS INCREASED RELIGIOSITY

Having read this far, you might think we have surely hit all the high points in the sociology of religion. But we have actually saved for last what has historically been the most important question for sociologists of religion: The question of whether **secularization**, or decreased religiosity, is the future of religion in societies around the world. For most of the twentieth century, social scientists generally argued that with modernization and the development of science, the relevance of religion would progressively decline. In this view, the world is becoming demystified. We are abandoning superstition and becoming more and more secular. This has usually been referred to as the **secularization hypothesis** and it was an important sociological theory at the turn of the twentieth century. At different points, secularization theorists went so far as to predict precisely when religion would disappear, leaving us in a thoroughly secularized world.

More recently, however, many sociologists of religion have thoroughly revisited and raised doubts about the secularization hypothesis. Rodney Stark and his colleagues (Stark and Finke 2000), for example, have presented data and arguments about the persisting strength of religion in highly developed countries like the United States, and others have noted that while some countries have become more secular, others have only become more religious. How do we assess these competing claims?

As with many terms in the sociological arsenal, we first have to figure out how exactly we define our terms: Secularization has been used in somewhat different ways by different theorists. At its simplest level, secularization has been taken to mean that people abandon religion as unscientific or irrelevant to modern existence, with books written about "The Death of God" and how we will all become atheists. But most sociologists have actually meant something more subtle by secularization. Instead of denoting irreligion, these sociologists focus on the *authority* religion has over the lives of people: Do people actually limit or change their behavior according to the dictates of religion? Can people justify their actions by recourse to religious writings or figures? Those who argue for secularization see this authority shrinking in the modern world as life becomes more complex and modern institutions that have little to do with religion claim more and more authority over parts of people's lives.

To return to the theme of the separation of spheres that we discussed earlier, in a society dominated by agriculture, religion appears central to everything—from appeasing the weather gods to prayers for fertility or for god's support in war. In contrast, businesspeople in modern industrial societies do not pray for their production line to work. Even in religious America today people have to work on supposed religious days of rest so that the assembly line is not shut down. Hospitals and doctors, not priests and shamans, are experts on health. Education is delivered by professionalized schools, mostly state rather than religious. Most people have hardly any idea of the relationship between weather and food and only pray to have enough money to feed their teenage children. We can easily add many examples to this list.

It is hard to argue with the version of secularization as declining religious authority, at least in highly developed societies. Doctors in hospitals may personally be religious, but they seldom justify courses of treatment for their patients by reference to scripture. Few if any investors will choose to put their money in a hedge fund that is run according to religious laws. Political leaders may declare their adherence to religion, but it is no longer necessary (and former President Donald Trump, who never went to church as an adult was nevertheless revered by members of some of the strictest Protestant churches; see Gorski 2020). But things get more complicated, and far more contested, when we think about secularization as a measure of declining religiosity in the population, or declining participation in organized religion. Are people really less prone to believe in a god? Or perhaps we should reverse the question: Were people in the Middle Ages really all that religious by comparison with their contemporary peers?

European Irreligion

17.4.1 Describe the religiosity in Europe.

Even if one asks simply whether people are religious or not, one can easily make the case that native-born people in Europe, especially Northern and Western Europe, have become very secular indeed. On any given Sunday, only about 20 percent of Europeans go to church (Pew Research Center 2018c). Fewer than half of the people of Scandinavia, Germany, France, Britain, the Netherlands, or Belgium, or of many countries that were previously part of communist Europe, say they believe in a god, compared to more than 80 percent of Americans (European Commission 2005, p. 8; Pew Research Center 2018c).

Surveys tend to show that although Europeans are not opposed to religion for other people, they want the religious to keep their beliefs private. They do not want religion in their politics (even though many European countries have large parties, usually known as Christian Democratic, which have roots in religion). Many Europeans tend to be put off by very religious people, so, for example, they are more suspicious of what they see as the excessive religiosity of some Muslim immigrants than they are of the fact they are Muslims. When asked, most Europeans say

that religion—of any sort—is simply is not very important in their own lives and should not be public in any way.

So in many countries in Europe, the classical sociological prediction that secularization would spread seems to be confirmed. But the sharply declining rates of religious participation and religious belief in Europe are not found in most other countries around the world, and as the proportion of foreign-born people (especially Muslims) rises in many European countries, these trends may not continue there either.

American Religiosity

17.4.2 Compare and contrast religiosity in the United States to European countries.

Modern as any Western European country, the United States retains a level of conventional religiosity far above almost all of the other developed countries of the world. At least twice as many Americans as Europeans say they attend church regularly. And social issues of importance to many religious leaders, such as abortion, same-sex marriage, public support for religious education, whether evolutionary biology should be taught as established science or simply a theory of human evolution, and requiring prayer in public schools are often important issues in American politics.

Why does the United States diverge from the European pattern so sharply? Many reasons have been advanced for American religious exceptionalism. For example, Rodney Stark and his colleagues have argued that in most countries, there has been only one established religion, while in the United States many different religions compete. According to this position, the greater the supply of different religious traditions there are, the more vibrant the marketplace for religion is.

The struggle over abortion in America is an example of how religious views are often injected into political debates. Anti-abortion activists often invoke religious themes into their arguments against allowing women the right to choose to have an abortion.

This economistic "supply side" theory of religion may sound simplistic, but its proponents note that it captures something important about religious life—that the level of religiosity of the population is heavily influenced by the presence of religious entrepreneurs who woo them and try to speak to their particular situation and needs. Supply, rather than demand, predicts how religious people will be. In this view, the American separation of church from state is seen as a historical boon to religious life in the United States, by diversifying the marketplace for religion and fostering a multitude of movements and churches.

An alternative argument is that religion thrives in America because the nation is so ethnically, geographically, and culturally diverse. Each group clings to its religion as a means of preserving its community and culture. And, as we noted earlier, churches continue to play an important role in providing services for people in need that the more generous welfare states in European countries take care of. In European countries, the state does more to provide medical, social, and educational services. In the United States, public schools are underfunded, some people cannot get health insurance, the police are often ethnically alien to minorities and the poor, most jobs are not unionized and unions cannot help most people with difficulties at work, and so forth. In the absence of strong and available alternative institutions, Americans turn to their churches for hope, help, and sustenance.

Still, we need to keep two things in mind as we think about American religiosity. First, while earlier analyses of religion in America thought of the United States as an "exceptional" religious case, researchers have increasingly pointed out that the pattern of American religiosity looks a lot like it does in other places—it is just that these places happen not to be in Europe. On the other hand, however, we must also not overestimate the power of Americans' religiosity. This is for three interrelated reasons. First, as researchers have shown, strict religious groups do not necessarily grow because they find more converts to their cause. Greeley and Hout (2006) have shown that about 75 percent of the growth of conservative Protestantism in American society was due to their relatively high fertility rates, which was especially striking in contrast to the sharply declining fertility of mainline Protestants during the same period. In other words, it isn't that evangelical groups grow because they become more popular, but that they have more children to begin with.

Second, while religiosity is high in the United States, Americans' actual attitudes towards some of the issues that animated movements like the Moral Majority have shifted. Conservative Protestants succeeded in putting a range of social issues on the political agenda for

discussion—turning them into moral and religious questions—but in almost every case significant majorities of Americans did not support those positions. Whether we are talking about a return to traditional families with stay-at-home mothers, requiring prayers in public schools, banning abortion, or attitudes toward same-sex relationships and the right of gays and lesbians to marry, Americans have become increasingly liberal over time (Brooks 2000; Baldassarri & Park 2020). The case of same-sex marriage is especially stark. A few decades ago, the vast majority of Americans supported the view that marriage should be between a man and a woman, and in 1996 Congress passed, and President Bill Clinton signed into law, a measure known as the Defense of Marriage Act, which allowed states to refuse to recognize same-sex marriage licenses granted in another state and codified heterosexual unions as the only legal marriages under all federal laws. But over time, Americans have become increasingly supportive of same-sex marriage, and in 2015 the United States Supreme Court ruled that the Fourteenth Amendment to the Constitution guarantees same-sex couples the right to marry. This shift can be seen, in part, as a sign of declining religious authority. People's love-lives seem increasingly to be "their own business" rather than being subject to religious law.

Lastly, there are also some signs that religiosity in America may be moving in the European direction, particularly if we just focus on native-born Americans and ignore the effects of continuing high rates of immigration. Currently, surveys indicate that the fastest growing religion in the United States is "no religious preference." From 2.7 percent in 1960, and 8 percent in 1990, the number of people so identifying themselves has grown to over 20 percent today (Hout, Fischer, and Chaves 2013). Further, because young people are much more likely to think of themselves as not religious, that percentage is almost certain to increase in the near future. In Figure 17.7, we see a declining percentage of people who consider themselves Protestants, stability among those who call themselves Catholic, but a sharp increase (black line) of Americans with no religious preference.

Indeed, if not for immigration from Latin America, the Catholic Church in the United States would be shrinking very rapidly. Twenty years ago, Catholics made up about 22 percent of the American people. Today, the percentage is about the same, despite the fact that about 80 percent of the recent immigrants to America (especially from Mexico and Central America) have been Catholic. Moreover, the Catholic Church is having great difficulty finding men to take up religious vocations and become priests. Increasingly, priests are being imported from other countries to fill the ranks.

If current trends hold, we can also expect the relative number of conservative Protestants to decline over

Figure 17.7 An Increasing Share of Americans Report No Religion

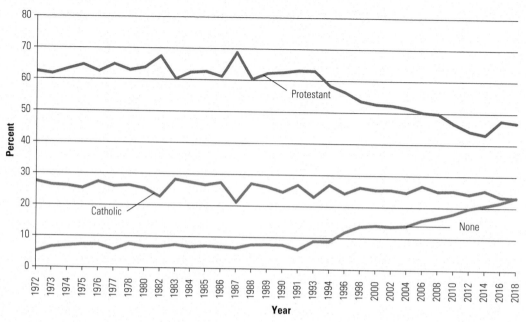

SOURCE: General Social Survey, 1972–2018.

the coming decades. As conservative Protestants have become more urban and educated, differences between their birth rates and those of other Americans have declined. Evangelical leaders are already complaining that they are losing their young to more secular orientations. Figure 17.8 presents a dramatic summary of the trends among youth aged 18 to 29, comparing those who declare themselves to be evangelical Christians with those who say they have no religious preference. The contrasting projections are stark, suggesting in particular that young people are less likely today to be attracted by stricter religious traditions within Christianity. This strongly suggests that secularization will continue to increase in the United States in the future.

Figure 17.8 Evangelical Protestants and Religious "Nones" Among American Youth (Aged 18–29)

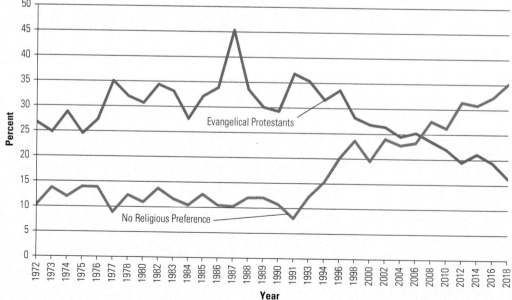

SOURCE: General Social Survey, 1972–2018.

The Rising Importance of Religion in the Other Parts of the World

17.4.3 Identify possible explanations for the increase in religiosity around the world.

Focusing on the United States and Europe skews our understanding of secularization. As two political scientists note, if we take a more global look at the contemporary world, we can make an opposite argument to secularization—large swaths of the world seem to be getting more, not less, religious (Norris and Inglehart 2004). In many countries, a higher percentage of people are religious than they were two or three decades ago, and in some countries, like India, Turkey, Iran, and elsewhere in the Middle East, religious authority in public life seems to have increased rather than withered.

How should we understand these trends? Although the causes might be complex, a few different answers can be given. First, we must consider simple demography. Everywhere around the world, as in the United States, religious people tend to have more children than irreligious people. The difference is even greater between societies. Religious societies tend to have quicker population growth. Second, over the past decades, both in post-Soviet countries, as well as in Turkey, Iran, and other countries, secular dictatorships have fallen. In these cases, two things seemed to have occurred: First, people who kept their religiosity to themselves could suddenly exhibit religious belonging. Moreover, in many of these countries, becoming religious was also seen as a way to challenge the regime. In other words, being religious can be both a personal and a political stance.

Lastly, in many places in the world, being religious was also seen as taking a stance against global inequities, as noted earlier. Even if we return to the idea of secularization as authority, the world has seen surging religious militancy in much of the Muslim world, with relevant consequences for politics in those countries. Women are either deciding to wear veils or being forced to wear veils. Iran, once governed for several decades by a secular shah, and before that briefly by a secular socialist prime minister, is now controlled by its religious establishment. In Egypt, the Muslim Brotherhood won the 2011 elections in that country (only to be thrown out of office by a military coup). Other examples around the world can be found.

Reasons for this re-emergence of religious political authority have complex roots but are partly a matter of the reassertion of cultural pride and autonomy in a segment of the world that had been colonized and dominated by European and American imperialism. Under these circumstances, many people found that religion provided an alternative symbol of difference and nationalism and a legitimate basis for organization, so that it could serve as a rallying mechanism for the assertion of independence and power. Whether that will persist in the future is an open question.

Conclusion: The Future of Religion?

The sociology of religion, as we have seen, sits at the crossroads of the intimately personal and the public, between individual morality and politics. How can we grasp a subfield that is so deeply intertwined with other questions and concerns? As a way to conclude this chapter, we want to conclude with two general thoughts about how we can best understand the place of religion in both sociology and in the world today.

First, if there is one takeaway from the larger trends that we see across the globe, it is that we need to rethink our questions. While religiosity declined in some places in the world—especially in Europe—it is not declining in much of the rest of the world. At least at this moment, it is not clear that religion is any less of a force shaping history than it was in the past. Rather than asking if the world is becoming more or less secularized, we should ask, instead, about the shifting place of religion in these different places. Where is religion becoming more of a private affair? Where is religious authority becoming more central? What is religion doing—both for people's personal lives and in the public sphere — in the twenty-first century? Rather than simply declining or surging, religion changes its shape. It transforms rather than simply waxing or waning.

To better grasp such transformations, we have shown that the best way to understand religion is not to detach it from the other identities and meanings it is enmeshed in. Instead of trying to abstract religion away, it is more useful to think about religion as inherently overlapping with other social factors. It is here that a sociological immagination can provide important insights. This can be best seen if we look at the role of religion in politics and religious conflict. Rather than trying to ascertain whether White evangelicals vote for the Republican party because they are White *or* because they are evangelical Christians, it is more useful to think about how the intersection of these identities come together to create a new phenomenon;

rather than trying to ascertain whether the persecution of Muslim and Hindu people in Myanmar by the Buddhist majority is ethnic *or* religious, it is more useful to think about the development of Buddhist nationalism in Myanmar's history.

Second, as a source of meaning and identity, it is also crucial to understand how religion is enmeshed both in people's life trajectories and in their everyday lives. Being part of a religious group is partly about the meaning that we derive from religious texts and leaders, but it is also about coming together, in both ritual and communal life. Thinking about religion in this way provides us a way to think about many sociological puzzles: Whether it is the relationship between religion and age group, or about how people move among different denominations and congregations. We need not completely agree with Durkheim—for whom religion was, in the last analysis, the worship of the social. But in order to understand religion we need to understand its place in the social bonds and meanings that we make.

The Big Questions Revisited 17

17.1 What Is Religion, and What Does It Do? Sociologists have no single agreed-upon definition of religion. In this section, we examined some of the definitions of religion—especially those that rely on *beliefs* and those that focus on *practices*. We then outlined some of the incredible variation of religions throughout the world and throughout history.

A Sociological Understanding of Religion

Defining Religion

Learning Objective 17.1.1: Compare and contrast the different sociological definitions of religion.

The Incredible Variety of Religions

Learning Objective 17.1.2: Identify the big five religions of the world and discuss the variety and diversity of contemporary religion.

Early Religious Traditions and Their Modern Variants

Learning Objective 17.1.3: Compare and contrast the concepts of animism and polytheism.

Religion as a Social Institution

Learning Objective 17.1.4: Discuss religion as a social institution and the role of theodicy.

Denominations and Congregations: From Religion to Community

Learning Objective 17.1.5: Describe the role that denominations and congregations play in organizing religious activity in a community.

Key Terms
atheist (p. 460)   agnostic (p. 460)   deism (p. 462)   doctrine (p. 462)   sacred (p. 464) supernatural (p. 464)   civil religion (p. 464) irreligion (p. 467)   syncretic (p. 467)   animism (p. 468)   polytheism (p. 468)   monotheism (p. 468)   theology (p. 468)   institution (p. 469)   pluralism (in religion) (p. 469) theodicy (p. 469)   denomination (p. 470) megachurch (p. 473)   congregation (p. 473)

17.2 How Does Social Structure Impact Religious Belonging? With all the religions in the world, how do people come to belong to one religious group or another? This section explored the patterns of religious life, including the impact of race, ethnicity, gender, and age.

Patterns and Careers of Religious Belonging

Religious Segregation: Birds of a Feather

Learning Objective 17.2.1: Discuss the causes of segregation in American churches.

Conversion

Learning Objective 17.2.2: Explain who converts to what denomination or religion and the process of conversion.

New Religious Movements

Learning Objective 17.2.3: Identify the varieties of new religious movements and who is drawn to them.

Gender and Religious Participation

Learning Objective 17.2.4: Discuss the relationship between gender and religiosity in various major religions.

Age and Religion: Do People Become More Religious as They Age?

Learning Objective 17.2.5: Explain why older people tend to be more religious.

Key Terms

liberation theology (p. 476)   evangelical (p. 477)
new religious movements (p. 478)   cults (p. 478)

17.3 **How Does Religion Play into Public Life?** In this section, we asked where and when religion emerged as a political force: Looking both at religious conflict around the globe, and at the intersection of religion and politics in the United States.

Religion in Public Life

Understanding Public Religion

Learning Objective 17.3.1: Explain the role of religion in public and political life in the United States and elsewhere.

Distinguishing Religious Conflicts from Ethnic and Class Conflicts

Learning Objective 17.3.2: Explain why it is difficult to distinguish religious conflict from ethnic or class conflict.

An Example of Religious Conflict in India

Learning Objective 17.3.3: Discuss the long-standing religious conflict between Hindus and Muslims in India.

17.4 **How Is Religion Changing?** We saved for last what has historically been the most important question for sociologists of religion. In this section, we explored the future of religion.

Secularization versus Increased Religiosity

European Irreligion

Learning Objective 17.4.1: Describe the religiosity in Europe.

American Religiosity

Learning Objective 17.4.2: Compare and contrast religiosity in the United States to European countries.

The Rising Importance of Religion in Other Parts of the World

Learning Objective 17.4.3: Identify possible explanations for the increase in religiosity around the world.

Key Terms

secularization (p. 485)   secularization hypothesis (p. 485)

Chapter 18
Education

by Caroline H. Persell and Jeff Manza

If there is one institution that everyone is quite familiar with from direct personal experience, it is the educational system. With the exception of those who were home-schooled and never attended a conventional school, the vast majority of people will spend at least a dozen and often many more years in school, and although there is no national curriculum in the United States, almost every school system and accredited private school follows a learning plan that is roughly similar through high school. The core elements of education—the curriculum, testing (and more testing), grades, teachers, principals, and the school board (or for private schools, a board of trustees), students—are largely the same. So what can a sociological imagination add to what we already know from personal experience?

One place to start is to think about how schools and the educational system fit into the larger society. Providing all children with access to high-quality schools is close to a fundamental right of citizenship. It holds a special place in what is known as the "American Dream"—the idea that all Americans should have an equal opportunity to improve their life chances through individual merit and hard work. We are living in a world where education has become ever more important for economic opportunities, and where having a college or postgraduate degree confers important and growing advantages to those who obtain them. As new professions and occupations emerge, so do educational programs aiming to produce students who can work in these new fields. Indeed, there is almost no end to the reach of modern education. Want to work in counterintelligence or counterterrorism? You can enroll in one of the many new programs that have emerged in recent years. Or maybe you want to do something completely different. How about becoming a DJ? You can learn on your own or be taught by a friend, but you can also find a school that will train you to become one. The same is true if you want to be a hairstylist, paralegal, or even a taxi driver. Want to become a manager at McDonald's? You can go to school to learn how; McDonald's has operated an educational facility called Hamburger University since 1961. Located in Chicago, Illinois, their website states that there are over 20 full-time professors and some 5,000 students. No matter where we look, the branches of the educational system are present, and always seem to be spreading into new arenas.

Educational systems are also important because they are frequently charged with addressing broader social

My Sociological Imagination

CAROLINE H. PERSELL

While I was in graduate school at Columbia University, the sociologist James Coleman and others published a major study showing that schools made little difference in the achievement of students because the variations within individual schools was almost as great as the variations between schools. This rocked the scholarly world and got me thinking about whether it captured all the colors in the educational spectrum. In my visits to many inner-city schools, I had seen students and teachers with lots of energy, ambition, and intelligence working hard to do the best they could in the underresourced conditions they were in. At the same time, I knew that other types of schools, like private boarding schools, were not included in the Coleman study, and wondered how education differed for students at such schools. A question of enduring interest to sociologists is how social and economic advantages are transferred from one generation to the next in a society that purports to frown on inherited privilege. Peter Cookson and I addressed this question by studying elite boarding schools in the United States and England and found out that they perpetuate intergenerational inequality not just with money but through a range of school practices.

Schools are tightly intertwined with many of our nation's most pressing social problems because they are so closely linked to the communities they serve. (The high school shown in this photo, LaGuardia High School in New York City, was featured in the 1980 movie *Fame*.)

Mark Bussell

problems in a society. Improving schools is often the first thing that people think about when asked how to help poor children have better lives. Addressing racial segregation and inequality in education was a central goal of the civil rights movement of the 1950s and 1960s. The landmark *Brown* v. *Board of Education* decision in 1954, in which the U.S. Supreme Court declared that local school boards could no longer legally operate segregated schools, was one of the most significant achievements of that era (although the integration and greater equality it promised has been partially reversed in recent decades, as we will see later in the chapter). In addition, when economists or government officials worry about whether the United States will be competitive with other countries in the future, they often focus on the educational system and ask whether American workers are being adequately trained for the jobs of the future. Are other countries with a greater focus on science, technology, engineering, and math (STEM) inevitably pulling ahead? Finally, in response to concerns about rising economic inequality (see Chapter 11), many politicians, scholars, and commentators have suggested that expanding educational opportunity and/or improving public schools is one way to "solve" the problems of inequality—by providing workers with more skills to enable them to demand higher wages from their employers.

But poverty, racial injustice, and economic inequality are all intractable social problems. When schools and the educational system as a whole are being asked to solve them, it is probably not surprising that they often come up short. Sociologists who study educational systems have devoted significant research effort to understanding why the educational system fails to give each child an equal chance at success. Because in the United States and most countries around the world, the vast majority of children (in rich and poor communities alike) attend government-funded public schools, questions about the shortcomings of public schools are inevitably social questions, and where schools fail they are truly viewed as major social problems.

Where are American schools failing? International tests show American students are not learning as much as students in other countries. We will explore in more detail the evidence for this deficit later in the chapter, but it is clear from comparing U.S. student achievement to other countries that American students show less math, reading, and science comprehension than their counterparts in other Western countries. A few years ago, a study found that nearly a quarter of recent high school graduates could not pass the basic U.S. military entrance exam (the enlistment test to join any branch of the military). And an emerging body of evidence suggests that student learning in college may be more limited than we have long assumed (Arum and Roksa 2011, 2014). These examples raise the question: Is the quality of the education that American citizens are getting at all levels good enough to enable the U.S. workforce to compete internationally in an increasingly high-tech world? If not, why not?

We will explore these issues in this chapter. We'll examine why schooling is universal and why the level of educational achievement is so important for life outcomes, consider why educational inequality persists (and in some ways is even rising), and finally we will turn to an examination of higher education.

The Big Questions

1. **Why is formal education universal?** In this section, we examine the various purposes of schooling, including socialization, preparation for work, citizenship, and the economic health of the community and nation.

2. **How is education related to important life outcomes?** Here we explore education's strong relationship to many important life outcomes, including work and economic opportunities, health and life expectancy, and marital success and happiness.

3. **Do schools provide all children an equal chance to succeed?** Is education the great equalizer in U.S. society, or does it reproduce existing inequalities? Here we examine the sociological research that investigates whether educational access, experiences, and outcomes are similar for persons of different social classes, races, and genders.

4. **How is the American educational system different from other countries?** How can there be such wide variations in the quality and types of schooling, particularly by social class and race? To address this question, we look at differences in educational systems around the world and the various ways U.S. schools are organized.

5. **Is higher education in crisis?** America's colleges and universities are of very high quality in terms of the research and scholarship produced by faculty and in the advanced training of graduate students. But when it comes to undergraduate education, there are many serious concerns. The most important challenges in higher education today lie in the cost of attending college, student dropout rates, how much learning is actually occurring, and the pressing need to increase the number of students going to and completing college. In this section, we consider some of these issues.

BIG QUESTION 18.1 Why Is Formal Education Universal?

Carrie Garcia/Alamy Stock Photo

THE PURPOSES OF EDUCATION

Every country in the world has a formal educational system and virtually all require each of its citizens to attend school for many years. Why is that the case? Several ideas usually come to mind, such as helping students navigate their futures and find success in life or creating an educated workforce that can compete with other countries. These are obviously important both for individuals and for societies as a whole. But education also serves other major societal purposes that we don't usually think about. Schools teach students how to get along with non-family members, follow direction, and learn to work independently. Schools provide opportunities for extra-curricular activities such as sports and the arts. High schools and colleges are dating and marriage markets, places where young people often develop their first intimate relationships. Schools may even help prevent crime by keeping youths off the streets. In this section, we will examine sociological theories on the purposes of schooling, beginning with a brief overview of the history of education and why it has expanded so rapidly in the last 150 years.

Education: A Brief Social History

18.1.1 Explain the early rise of educational systems in America.

The extent of education, its formal and informal purposes, and its relation to other societal institutions have changed dramatically over time. For most of human history, there was no formal education system separate from the family and community. As the first schools began to appear, mostly in more urbanized areas created by religious organizations, they taught basic literacy in the hopes that adults could read sacred scriptures such as the Bible, Koran, or Torah, as well as do simple arithmetic. What we would today call a typical liberal education was available only to a small, elite group of men prior to the nineteenth century. For most of the nineteenth century, even as schooling began to expand, the link between school achievement and adult outcomes was modest at best; only a few farm- or working-class children entered into professional or managerial occupations, and finishing high school was not especially important for the kinds of work that most people did. Most children would simply do what their parents had done before them; farm children became farmers, children of coal miners became coal miners, and so forth. In 1870, about 2 percent of 18-year-olds in America were high school graduates. Many communities did not even provide schooling opportunities after eighth grade, so even a young person wanting a fuller education would not be able to get one unless their parents could afford to send them to a boarding school. Today, the situation is the complete opposite: *Not* completing high school is the uncommon outcome. By 2020, about 93 percent of people in the 18-to-24 age

Figure 18.1 High School Graduation Rates Since the Nineteenth Century

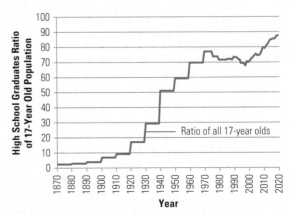

SOURCE: National Center for Educational Statistics.

bracket had completed high school, and some of those who haven't finished will eventually complete a high school equivalency exam later in life. Figure 18.1 displays the rapid increase in high school graduation, which shot up throughout the twentieth century and is still climbing, albeit more slowly, in recent years.

Why did education expand? The change began in the late nineteenth century. In the United States as elsewhere, schools and educational opportunity multiplied with the rise of industrialization and the growth of cities. For one thing, some business leaders began calling for educational programs so they would be able to find workers who could read and write at a sufficient level to handle the increasingly sophisticated machines and paperwork being generated in the booming industrial economy. The expansion of the educational system also went hand-in-hand with the increasing importance of education for **social mobility** (the ability for people to move up the socioeconomic ladder). Ordinary people wanted more educational programs as a way of giving their children better opportunities, especially as opportunities for those with more schooling began to grow. Finally, influential education reformers, many of whom studied in Europe and had observed the educational system there, led the call for the formation of "common schools" that would be funded by taxes and attended by all, as Horace Mann—one of the leading American reformers—put it. And these efforts found success: By the end of the nineteenth century, the United States was becoming a world leader in expanding educational opportunity.

A unique aspect of the expansion of education in the United States was the creation of the world's most extensive system of postsecondary (college) education, through public universities with little or no cost to attend. The early impetus for the expansion of public higher education was the adoption of the **Morrill Act** in 1862—during the Civil War—which provided each state with federal government resources to create or expand a state university. Known as *land grant colleges*, schools like Penn State University; Washington State University; the University of Wisconsin–Madison; the University of California, Berkeley; Clemson University; and many others were created around the country using Morrill Act funding (Sorber 2018). Many of these land grant colleges eventually grew into large, diverse schools in the early part of the twentieth Century. Every state today has one or two public universities that can trace their origins to the Morrill Act, and funds available under the Act were also used to start the first historically Black colleges and universities (HBCU).

As we move through the twentieth century and into the twenty-first century, the expansion of higher education continues in a variety of ways. The growth of the community college system, designed to help students who could not gain admittance to their state's main public universities, as well as satellite campuses of the main branch of a state's public university, were an important innovation that enabled some young people to attend college no matter what their performance in high school was. Another important set of developments was the steady expansion of postgraduate programs. A running joke among American educators is that "the MA is the new BA," as a growing number of professions and businesses now expect education beyond a bachelor's degree.

For much of this period, the United States was a world leader in investing in public education, and other countries scrambled to catch up. Although early educational reformers did not necessarily think of it this way, evidence mounted that a highly educated workforce was important for a nation's economy. Today, the idea that the educational system is central to both providing opportunities for young people and national economic growth can be found throughout the world. Growing numbers of poor and developing countries are seeking out ways to fund, develop, and expand their systems of public education and provide more opportunities for their young people. The institutionalization of education is a hallmark of modern societies.

Socialization

18.1.2 Describe three functions of schooling.

So what exactly do schools do? Sociologists studying how and why educational systems grew over time have proposed three basic theories to account for their universal appeal for societies that have to make the needed investments to create universal free schooling for all (which today virtually every country in the world provides). The first explanation highlights the role education serves in socializing children outside of their family life. Socialization, as we have seen elsewhere in the text, begins in families and extends throughout the life course, but schools play an especially important role in teaching young people the habits and practices expected of members of the community. In the classical *functionalist theory of education* (Parsons 1959; see Chapter 2 for more on Parsons and functionalism), the classroom itself was portrayed as a small society where children learn the rules of the adult world they will soon enter. Even if classrooms are often relatively homogeneous (in terms of family backgrounds and ages of the students), it is also the case that students will nevertheless interact with peers who are neither family members nor friends, and they will also have significant contact with, and learn to respect, authority figures like teachers. Starting in kindergarten, students are taught how to behave in school, including how to line up, be quiet on demand, fit in with their peers, do homework on time, and follow rules. Many of these aspects of the school experience are known as the **hidden curriculum**, the teaching of students how to act and behave in addition to their formal academic subjects (Gracey 2012). Students are unconsciously adjusting to school discipline, a behavioral consensus that reflects society's norms and values. Students are judged not just on their schoolwork, but also on how well they master the hidden curriculum.

Another important purpose of education is the role it plays in providing students with direct and indirect knowledge about the ethics and morals of the society they live in. Emile Durkheim, one of sociology's founding figures, wrote widely on this topic early in the twentieth century (see Chapter 2 for more on Durkheim). How do schools do this? Virtually all schools around the world provide instruction on the history of their country, which is often taught in a way that emphasizes the virtues of the home country (for example, in teaching about the Founding Fathers and the establishment of the Constitution as examples of what makes America great). Most schools have the nation's flag prominently displayed, which is a subtle nod to nationalism. Studying the country's history and participating in ceremonies such as the Pledge of Allegiance, or holidays that celebrate important national dates, are other examples of the ways in which schools teach students about the customs and beliefs of their community and nation. Rich democratic countries also spend a lot of time and energy teaching students the fundamental elements of democracy and extolling its virtues. In authoritarian countries, by contrast, pictures of the ruling dictator are usually on display in classrooms, and the curriculum may be oriented toward reminding students who is in charge and must be obeyed.

These aspects of the curriculum can be contentious. Historical education is often framed in ways that celebrate the nation while often neglecting or downplaying shameful moments in the past. For example, American history textbooks have long failed to give a full account of the role of racism in American society or fully acknowledge the costs and lasting consequences of slavery (Yacovone 2018; Greenlee 2019). Or to take a quite different example, many parents and religious leaders would like to see American public schools include more religious content and avoid or minimize the teaching of scientific theories that challenge religious beliefs. For instance, over the past 100 years there has been an ongoing battle over the teaching of Darwinian evolutionary theory—the scientific gold standard—versus a Bible-infused understanding of the origins of life, known as "creationism" or "intelligent design" in which God, not evolution, accounts for species development (Binder 2004, chpts. 4–6). Proponents of creationism have even argued that Darwinian theory is immoral, while proponents of the scientific view feel that it is immoral to use public school classrooms to teach children religious ideas that have no scientific backing. These examples highlight how the school curriculum can be an important site for much broader societal conflicts over ethics and morality, as Durkheim suggested.

Education need not be seen, however, simply as an institution in which ideas about behavior, cultural norms, and the goodness of the nation (and its leaders) are poured into the heads of students. A more radical view of education sees schooling as a platform from which students become armed with the knowledge needed to be active, engaged citizens; this is socialization of a very different kind. These ideas about schooling emphasize that students should be taught not just to obey rules and absorb platitudes about the goodness of their society, but instead be places where students learn how to critically examine their own and other societies (Giroux 2005). If making demands for social justice require forms of knowledge and understanding that only educational systems can help impart, schools can become important training grounds for democracy.

The great American philosopher John Dewey, writing early in the twentieth century, envisioned the creation

Students are socialized in schools through rules and regulations that apply to classroom behavior, such as "don't speak when the teacher is speaking" and "raise your hand before asking a question." But many other social and cultural rules learned in school can be more subtle and indirect. For example, schools encourage students to become loyal citizens, as the common practice of saying the Pledge of Allegiance to the flag represents.

Melting Spot/Alamy Stock Photo

Collaborative learning, in which students solve problems working in groups, has become a widely adopted practice in schools all over the world. Many students don't always enjoy these group activities, but they probably don't reflect on what a radical innovation it was to have students learning through activities rather than learning by listening to a teacher tell them things.

of "democratic" schools in which students would practice and learn the skills of citizenship through hands-on activities (Dewey 1916 [1966]). Instead of sitting in rows and memorizing material taught by a teacher or presented in a textbook, Dewey imagined something he called child-centric learning, in which students would participate in crafting their own education. Although traditional teaching methods have remained dominant for most of the past 100 years, Dewey's ideas have increasingly been absorbed into newer teaching models known as **active learning** today, the idea that teaching should involve students learning together by doing things. Dewey's ideas were radical for their time, but in recent decades they have become almost standard teaching tools. When high school or college instructors break students into groups to do a project together, they are attempting to implement one of the ideals of democratic education.

Preparation for the Future: Education as Opportunity

18.1.3 Discuss the concept of human capital and how educational attainment enhances future opportunities for individuals.

A central purpose of education, perhaps the most popular justification of schooling today, is that it will help prepare young people for future opportunities in the adult labor market. Economists refer to this aspect of education as the accumulation of **human capital**, the stock of knowledge, skills, and habits that students can use to do productive labor later in life (Becker 1964). Education offers the tools for students to increase their economic value for future employers as well as the social skills to adapt to being in the workforce. In principle, schooling also provides a vehicle for children of any background who work hard and do well to get ahead. And education is the surest path to upward social mobility (Hout 2012).

In the modern world, **meritocracy**—the idea that the most desirable jobs will go to those with the most "merit" and/or human capital—is in large part based on the notion that the school system is a central place where individual merit is best settled. Of course, not all successful people will have gained their achievements in life through education—for example, athletes, actors, musicians, and other kinds of performers need not excel in school—but the vast majority of professionals and business executives will have first established their excellence through school performance. It is this notion that lies at the heart of what motivates parents and students to look to education in the hopes of building a better future. Virtually all students have heard one or more adults stress this aspect of education (sometimes with a stern warning to "stay in school").

Sociologists who study education and schooling, however, have consistently found that educational systems reward some students more than others, a topic we'll discuss in more detail later in the chapter. But to highlight a couple of examples, when researchers examine what actually goes on inside classrooms, they find numerous ways in which teachers, consciously or unconsciously, reward students for their ability to conform to middle-class values and norms. Middle-class children are more likely to enter school having already learned this kind of behavior at home or through extensive extracurricular activities. Poor children, by contrast, may enter their first formal schooling experience without having absorbed those expectations, and don't know exactly what is expected of them. Further up the ladder, students with educated parents who speak and write in more sophisticated ways are rewarded for that, while their peers who grew up in a working class environment, in which less sophisticated language was used in the home, are punished. In other words, the way schools operate may be more familiar and comfortable to some students than to others, magnifying the

The ideal of education views school as a place where merit and hard work are rewarded. Testing, like that shown here, is one way that everyone is said to have an equal chance; rich and poor alike take some of the same tests, like the SAT or the ACT, to gain admission to college. Yet the ability to do well on tests, and in schools more generally, has consistently been shown to be closely related to other social and economic inequalities.

of the workforce so they can find productive workers to employ. But is education really an engine for the economic development of a society? Evidence abounds that national economic development is enhanced by providing citizens and young people with educational opportunities, and almost every country in the world today attempts to do just that. Higher literacy rates (with literacy referring, in the twenty-first century, to math, computing, and basic scientific proficiency, as well as the ability to read) among the working population significantly boosts the "stock" of human capital in the entire society. It is more attractive for foreign companies to invest in a country or region with confidence if they think that they will be able to find the workers they need. There is also growing evidence that promoting educational achievement in science, technology, engineering, and math (**STEM**) fields can boost a national economy. Several Asian countries—including China, India, Singapore, Taiwan, and South Korea—have benefited from a strategy of focusing heavily on training students in STEM fields in both high school and college since the 1980s. The remarkably rapid rates of economic growth in these countries suggest to many analysts that those efforts are paying off.

What about the United States? As discussed earlier, during the nineteenth and throughout most of the twentieth century, the United States led other nations in educational attainment, providing more formal schooling to its citizens than other countries. According to some researchers, this high level of education, and the human capital it provides, played a key role in spurring economic growth in the United States during this time (Goldin and Katz 2008). Economists and sociologists widely agree that, as more people become better educated and more skilled, the workforce as a whole also becomes more productive. Today, however, the United States no longer leads the world in either the amount of education received or in educational achievement (which we will discuss later in this chapter). Part of this decline may be the high cost of higher education in the United States compared to other countries; in many countries, college is either free or provided at a very low cost. Whatever the source of the lost advantage, there is no question that the United States is no longer the world leader in college completion rates. Figure 18.2 shows evidence of the trends in college completion for a number of different countries. This figure tells an important story. In 1995, the United States still had one of the highest rates of college (or tertiary) educational achievement (compare the red bars). But by 2012, as

advantage that children from upper and middle classes bring to school in the first place. This aspect of education, and its consequences, is known as **social reproduction theory**, the ways in which education reinforces already existing advantages that some children have (Bourdieu and Passeron 1979).

Economic Benefits of Schooling

18.1.4 Discuss how education contributes to economic growth.

While parents want their children to do well in school to get ahead, business and political leaders have long been interested in education for another reason: Because they depend on schools and colleges to prepare much

Figure 18.2 College Completion Rates Over Time

Tertiary-type A programs are designed to provide sufficient qualifications for entry to advanced research programs and professions with high skill requirements. These programs have a minimum cumulative duration (at college level) of three years' full-time equivalent, although they often last four or more years, and correspond to bachelor's degrees in the United States.

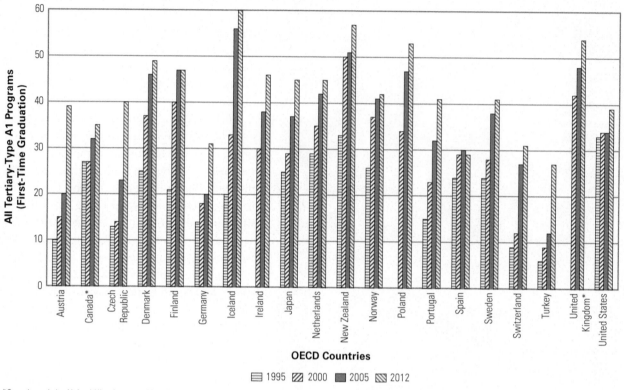

*Canada and the United Kingdom use 2011 data.

SOURCE: OECD 2014.

shown by the green bars, many other rich countries were getting far more students through college, and others who were once way behind had caught up.

How did this happen? At the end of World War II, the United States raced ahead of the rest of the world in expanding access to college. Federal policymakers expanded college educational opportunities, in part to solve the worry that millions of returning war veterans would flood the labor market and push up unemployment. Congress passed the G.I. Bill in 1944, which allowed honorably discharged veterans to enroll for free in an accredited higher educational program while also receiving a small living allowance. Some 7.8 million former soldiers took advantage of the G.I. Bill to

participate in an education or training program. In this way, the national government used education to regulate the flow of workers into the labor market and avoid high unemployment. It also helped the World War II generation achieve unprecedented educational attainment, and these graduates fueled economic growth in the post-industrial economy that emerged from the 1960s onward (Mettler 2005). But this initial national advantage was not maintained. Other countries steadily expanded their educational systems, while the United States stagnated. Many analysts believe a new commitment to educational expansion is needed today if America is going to maintain its global competitiveness in the future (Goldin and Katz 2008).

BIG QUESTION 18.2 How Is Education Related to Important Life Outcomes?

EDUCATION AND LIFE OUTCOMES

For many people, it may seem obvious that the amount of education one receives holds enormous consequences for their futures. Consider two friends, Ana and Nia, both raised within similar families and both belonging to the same social class. Their lives took very different turns when Ana dropped out of high school. Nia, on the other hand, not only graduated from high school, she even went on to earn a college degree. Most people would guess that Ana may struggle to find full-time work in the years that followed her decision to drop out and, when she finds it, she will very likely make less money than Nia. It is also the case that her lower level of education will likely hold negative consequences for how healthy she is throughout her life and whether she will get (or stay) married. By contrast, Nia's higher level of education means she will likely find employment in higher status occupations, she will likely report being happier in life than her friend, and on average, she will be healthier and more likely to have a stable marriage, too. Let's look more closely at these important life outcomes and consider the role education plays in shaping them.

Career Outcomes

18.2.1 Discuss the relationships among education, occupation, and life-course outcomes and how those affect economic success.

People with more education are more likely to work full time and less likely to be unemployed than people with less education, at all ages. As they enter the labor force, more educated workers are also more likely to find jobs in higher status occupations than those with less education.

This is not surprising because occupational status and working conditions are highly related to the skills and education demanded in the most competitive professions and fields. You could not become a surgeon or a lawyer, for example, without an advanced degree and highly specialized training.

As Figure 18.3 shows, the more education you get, the higher your earnings and the lower your unemployment risks will be. This is the same for both men and women, although men earn more than women at all educational levels. Furthermore, the pay gap between high school and college graduates has been rising since the late 1970s, as we'll discuss more thoroughly in the next section (see also Murnane et al. 1995; Goldin and Katz 2008). College completion has become virtually a necessity for earning a stable, middle-class income in the twenty-first century. This is true partly because college graduates are earning more than ever before, but also because high school graduates are earning less, and are more likely to have unstable career pathways.

Why do people with more education reap larger socioeconomic rewards? Sociologists offer two competing explanations. Human capital theory, as we noted in the previous section, sees education as transmitting concrete knowledge, skills, and values that persist in adulthood and that employers believe increase productivity (so they are willing to pay a higher wage to educated workers). More recent scholarship has also emphasized the role of **soft skills** that can be imparted by the educational system. These include social skills such as the ability to work in teams and interact well with a wide variety of people, communication skills, determination, and discipline (the ability to stay on task). A long line of research has demonstrated

Figure 18.3 Economic Benefits of Education

This figure shows that men and women who have higher degrees also earn more, on average, than those with less schooling, as well as have lower unemployment rates. For instance, the yearly salary of somebody who graduated college is almost twice as high as that of a high school graduate. The figure also shows that women earn less than men, regardless of their educational attainment—a reminder that education pays off more for some than others.

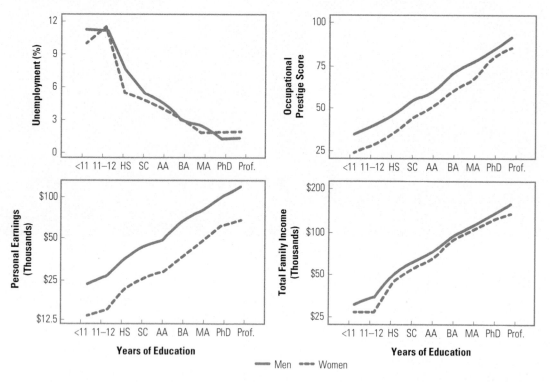

— Men ▪▪▪ Women

HS: High School; SC: Some College; AA: Associate's Degree; BA: Bachelor's Degree; MA: Master's Degree; PhD: Doctor of Philosophy; Prof: Post-Graduate

SOURCE: Hout, 2012.

that soft skills can be developed and enhanced in educational settings and can serve as an important complement to human capital (Heckman and Kautz 2012).

In contrast, **closure theory** sees education as limiting the number of people eligible to work in various kinds of jobs, creating a kind of scarcity that pushes up wages. According to this theory, the educational system selects some students for promotion into the higher ranks of the occupational system, while weeding out others (and in the latter sense, closes off opportunities for many students who might have hoped to enter professional or managerial occupations). Because of closure processes in other hierarchal dimensions (e.g. class, race, ethnicity, gender, religion) students enter the educational system with already existing advantages or disadvantages (Spence 1974; Collins 1979). But it is the school system where some of the most important competitions take place, and where the winners receive credentials that open up lifelong opportunities.

We can think of the difference between human capital and closure theory this way: Human capital sees education as changing you by making you more productive, so you are different in key ways that influence how much you earn (and how valuable you can be to your employer). Closure theory, by contrast, views the educational system as

dispensing, or allocating, credentials that make those who have them eligible for various kinds of jobs. It is a barrier to entry, so to speak. And social scientists have found rising levels of **credentialism** (that is, the growing number of jobs requiring a credential of some sort) that magnify this effect. It has long been said that we live in a credential society (Collins 1979), and it is even more true in the twenty-first century. Once education is completed and a degree is conferred, a person can now move on a different life track than they would be able to without the degree.

Closure theory is an idea associated with the classic writings of Max Weber on inequality that we have encountered in several places (see Chapter 2 for an overview). One implication of closure theory is that, if you want to break into a certain profession, you may have to jump through a lot of educational hoops designed in large measure to hold down the number of people who can practice in a profession. One study of 488 occupations found that such closure practices affect earnings in many occupations, including those in business and finance, health, education, social services, criminal justice, and others (Weeden 2002). Closure practices related to education include licensing, educational credentialing, certification, association representation, and unionization.

Credentialism is most dramatic in fields with a high degree of closure, like law or engineering, where you can only work if you possess a certain credential or license. But it can be found in many other less prestigious professions. For example, the nursing profession is particularly well protected by the various general degrees and specific licenses imposed by the field itself. Hence, students who pursue a career as a nurse will need to pass many academic hurdles—far more than a few decades ago—in order to be eligible to enter the profession. Becoming a plumber, an electrician, and many other skilled blue-collar jobs also typically requires credentials and/or licenses. Whenever an occupation raises credential requirements, they make entrance into an occupation more difficult, thereby holding down competition.

Both human capital and closure theory recognize that occupational positions are related to education and subsequent life-course outcomes. In this sense, the two theories are not entirely incompatible. The amount of education someone obtains clearly influences the types of work they can do. Some argue that employers use educational credentials to bolster the authority of managers in the workplace, while others assume education provides the knowledge and skills needed for direction, supervision, and planning (for example, Bowles and Gintis 1976; Ross and Van Willigen 1997). Regardless of what education exactly does for individual capacities, the result is workers with higher education degrees, particularly specialized degrees (such as MBAs or JDs), do far less manual and routine work and more mental work. They are also more likely to supervise the work of others and have more control over the nature and pace of their jobs. Moreover, larger national and international firms with more assets are more likely to require higher levels of education and pay higher salaries.

Health and Life Expectancy

18.2.2 Identify the correlation between education level and health.

People with more education are not only likely to find and hold better jobs, they are also more likely to report being in

better physical and mental condition, and to live healthier lives. The differences are substantial and it is true for men and women as well as for both Whites and people of color. For men, the difference in life expectancy between someone who is college educated and someone who is not is about five years, while for women it is about three years. Going to college not only pays off financially, it literally extends your life.

Why is education related to health and life expectancy? One major reason is the association between education and working conditions. People with less education are more likely to be channeled into physical labor, sometimes in difficult, toxic, or dangerous conditions. Having good quality health insurance—a key benefit of having a good job—is, not surprisingly, strongly related to better health (Finkelstein et al. 2011).

Consistent with human capital theory, some evidence suggests that more highly educated people have better access to health information, understand it better, better comprehend probabilities and risks, and overall are in a better position to obtain the help they need (Pallas 2000). They may also be more likely to observe good health habits such as taking medicines on a prescribed schedule, or avoid unhealthy behaviors. They are also better at participating in their own treatment when they have a medical issue. Although it is more difficult to research this systematically, it also appears very likely that people with college degrees are able to get better care when they need it (see Chapter 19 for more details on this key finding).

Family Life

18.2.3 Recognize the correlation between education level and intimate relationships.

Education is also closely related to how likely you are to marry, your marital happiness, the type of person you select as a spouse, the age when you have children, and your likelihood of divorce. In the United States, people with higher levels of education are far more likely to marry and stay married to the same person than those with less education. Among women aged 25 to 34, 59 percent of college graduates are married, compared with 51 percent of non-college graduates (Martin 2006). Among those aged 35 to 44, 75 percent of college graduates compared to 62 percent of non-college graduates are married, and for those 65 or older the gap is 50 percent of college graduates married compared to 41 percent of nongraduates. Even more striking are the very large differences in divorce rates. College-educated couples are much less likely to divorce than non-college educated couples. (Figures 18.4a and 18.4b show marriage and divorce rates by educational level for men and women by age 46.) One likely reason for this difference is that college-educated people delay marriage relative to their less well-educated peers; the average age of first marriage for a woman with a high school diploma is currently about

Figure 18.4a and b Marriage and Divorce Rate by Education Level by Age 46

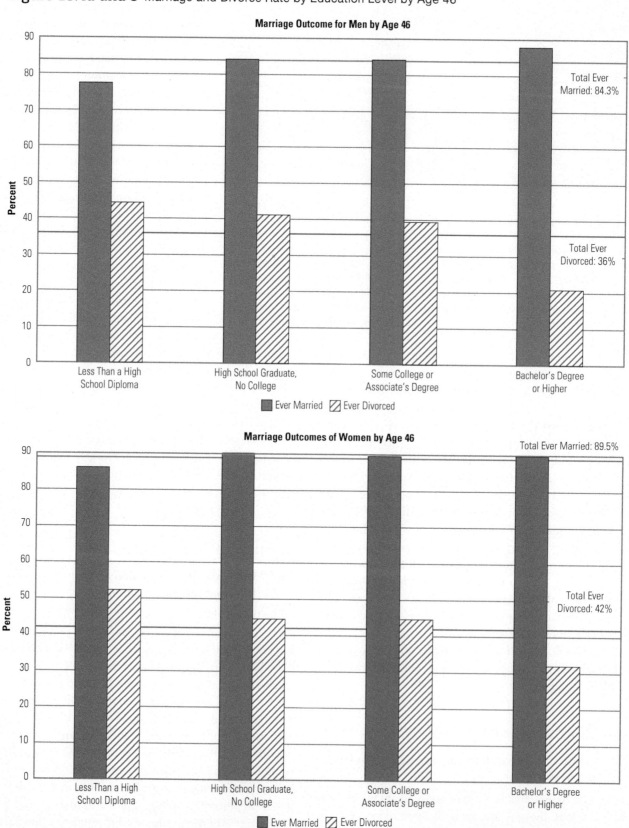

SOURCE: Bureau of Labor Statistics, 2013.

23 years of age, compared to almost 30 for women with a bachelor's degree or higher. Delaying marriage improves the chances of a successful marriage, in large part because with age comes maturity and a better understanding of one's self. Many college-educated Americans are also having children later in life and having fewer children. Women, in particular, are waiting longer so that they can spend more time pursuing education and careers.

Education is impacting marriage and family life in another way. We are also increasingly likely to marry individuals with educational levels similar to our own—a practice sociologists call **educational homogamy** (Kalmijn 1991). The odds of a high school graduate marrying someone with a college degree has fallen drastically in recent decades as, increasingly, college-educated people are marrying other college-educated people (Carbone and Cahn 2014). This increased homogamy has a number of implications. If both parents have similar educational levels in a family, there are implications for the educational and financial resources available to children in the family. As noted earlier, because the pay gap between college graduates and high school graduates has increased over the past

40 years, a family headed by two college-educated parents has an even larger economic advantage over a single- or dual-earning family whose parents have less education (Cherlin 2014). As a result, educational homogamy further increases the inequality between households with college graduate couples and households with high school graduate couples.

Two other factorys help explain why college-educated people "better" at marriage than non-college-educated people. For one thing, they are less likely to see marriage as the primary goal in life; marriage is something they choose to do because they want to, not simply because it is expected of them or because they need to marry for financial reasons (Finkel 2017). Paradoxically, this "choice" approach to marriage, as opposed to marriage out of necessity or societal expectations, appears to strengthen marriages. College-educated people are also more likely to marry other educated people who have good incomes, and the resulting financial security that two college-educated people have also contributes to greater marital happiness and reduced likelihood of divorce (Cherlin 2009).

Radius Images/Design Pics/Alamy Stock Photo

BIG QUESTION 18.3 Do Schools Provide All Children an Equal Chance to Succeed?

EDUCATIONAL INEQUALITY

As mentioned earlier in the chapter, at the core of many of the problems of contemporary educational systems is the fundamental question of equal opportunity. Do all children have an equal chance to succeed? If education is the pathway to greater equality, the answer to that question should be a resounding YES! No school system in the world advertises its capacity to educate some students better than others. Yet, unfortunately, they almost always do. Why? There is a simple fact that makes the challenge of educational equality difficult: Schools are always impacted by, and always absorb the more general

problems of, the families they serve and the neighborhoods, cities, and societies in which they are located. This is in large part because student bodies are often reflections of the social environment surrounding the school, or the families and contexts of life. For example, schools located in areas where most parents have low levels of education themselves may find it hard to motivate students to aspire to go to college. When students arrive at school from an environment of poverty, violence, or racial and ethnic tensions in their daily lives outside of school, those issues also inevitably become part of the school's challenges. Conversely, schools located in neighborhoods, towns, and cities that are stable and prosperous, where parents are

Figure 18.5 Bachelor's Degree by Family Income

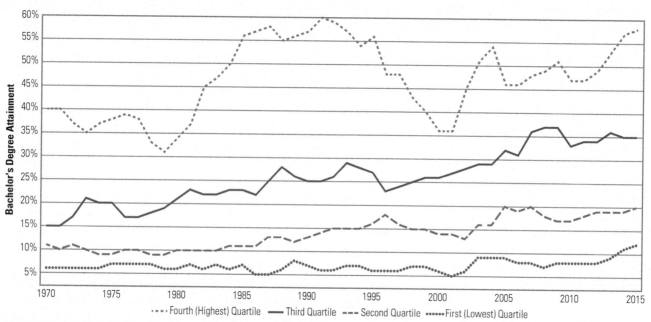

SOURCE: Data from the Pell Institute, 2016.

mostly college-educated and have high expectations for their children and schools, are typically characterized by a motivated student body in which rapid learning can take place.

Ensuring access to high-quality educational opportunities is a central problem for individual school systems, but it is also a major issue in American society as a whole. If large numbers of young people face significantly greater barriers than others in pursuit of diplomas and credentials, the educational *system* has failed at one of its core missions: Providing everyone an equal chance of moving up the social-economic ladder. Although unequal chances of success in school may reflect more general societal problems, such as class inequality or discrimination, the educational system itself may aggravate other inequalities. When it does, it falls short of one of its central and widely recognized missions.

From a historical perspective, there is no question that access to education has improved rapidly over the past 150 years, resulting in a larger share of all young adults having graduated from high schools and colleges than 50 or 100 years ago. But this does not mean the educational system has succeeded in creating an equal playing field for everyone. Consider the simple fact that so many more children from higher income families complete college than children from poorer families (see Figure 18.5). While there are many reasons why this might be the case, and we will examine many of these factors later in the chapter, it simply reveals worrisome inequalities in the educational system.

In fact, the issue of inequalities in the educational system may be getting worse in an era of rising inequality. Important research by the sociologist Sean Reardon has found evidence of growing gaps in achievement between students from different economic backgrounds.

Comparing children at the 90th income percentile of all households (that is, children in the richest 10 percent of families) versus children at the 10th percentile (children from families who are poorer than all but 10 percent of families) on a large number of different tests that have been administered to students since 1940, Reardon finds that by the year 2000 there was a larger gap between students from richer and poorer families than there was in the 1940s. We show Reardon's results in Figure 18.6. He finds that the test score gap between children from high-income

Figure 18.6 Rising Income Gap in Reading and Math Test Scores

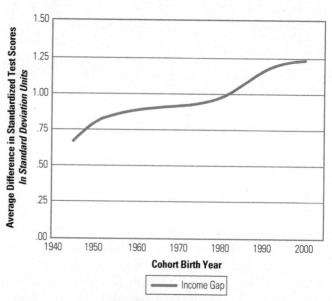

SOURCE: Adapted from Reardon, 2011.

and low-income families has grown over time. This stunning finding it suggests that in spite of all of the efforts to improve the quality of schools for all children, class-based educational inequality has grown over time.

In this section, we explore some of the reasons why inequality in education has been so pervasive and difficult to address. A key starting point to keep in mind in relation to schools in America, as opposed to many other countries, is this: Education in the United States is not a single, uniform system available to every child in the same way. Children from different social classes are likely to attend different types of schools, to receive different kinds of instruction, and perhaps even study different curricula. In this, the U.S. educational system is unlike that of many other countries, in which a single national system with equal resources devoted to every public school is the basic model. Later in the chapter, we'll see how other countries have created educational systems that produce more equal outcomes, and why that matters.

Economic Inequality and Schooling

18.3.1 Explain how income inequality contributes to gaps in the quality of educational opportunities.

Let's start by looking at how economic inequalities such as family income or wealth impact educational opportunity. A central factor to consider is **residential segregation**, when members of groups cluster live in different neighborhoods and communities. Residential segregation occurs principally along two lines: Race and class. Poor families tend to live in poor neighborhoods or communities, while richer families seek out neighborhoods and communities that are safer and have better quality housing and better schools (Owens 2015). (We address racial and ethnic segregation and its educational impacts shortly, but the issues are similar.) Class segregation in housing and neighborhoods has always been true, but in the current era of rising income and wealth inequality, it has increased significantly (Bischoff and Reardon 2014). Middle- and upper-class children today are much more likely to live in neighborhoods or suburban communities with families like their own, with few or no poor children or families living in those same areas. Because most children attend schools in their area of residence, schools are slowly becoming more homogenous, as noted, when it comes to the students attending.

Some schools and their students benefit from this situation: For example, schools located in affluent suburban communities are populated by economically privileged students who come from families who prioritize education and place high expectations on both their own children and the schools they attend. A school environment characterized in this way is one in which rapid learning can take place. By contrast, schools in poor neighborhoods and communities have relatively few parents with college degrees, and the

students attending these schools have to be very self-motivated and get special attention from teachers if they are to learn at the same level and pace as students in more advantaged schools (Palardy et al. 2015).

As a consequence of the growing segregation of families by income, many of the public schools attended by poor children lack the beneficial social environment and financial resources that are readily available to those in more affluent communities. Moreover, because public schools in these areas are more likely to be considered "failing"—displaying low test scores and low college attainment rates—many of those families with the most educational and financial resources seeking to move out of the district. In some extreme cases, entire affluent communities seek to secede from the rest of an urban school district to be able to benefit from their greater resources.

The consequence of rising class segregation in education is that neighborhoods and communities are becoming increasingly important determinants of access to good primary and secondary education in the United States. Regardless of a student's abilities and talents, living in an affluent neighborhood or community with good public schools will positively contribute to their educational chances, and vice versa for a poor child.

But residence is not the whole story of educational inequality. There is another development of the past few decades that researchers have increasingly studied. Families with more resources have routinely invested heavily in their children's education in ways poor families cannot. The influential research of sociologist Annette Lareau (2003) has been especially important in drawing attention to the fact that the way in which parents invest in their children varies by social class. In broad terms, Lareau observed that middle- and upper-class parents tend to use resources to actively foster the development of their children's talents, opinions, and skills, a child-rearing style Lareau called **concerted cultivation**. In contrast, working- and lower-class families tend to employ what she described as a *natural growth* style, which is characterized by parents getting out of the way and allowing their children to grow "naturally."

Lareau argues that young adults raised under the concerted cultivation model are better prepared to juggle all of the demands of schools and ultimately successfully make the transition into the salaried professional jobs of the middle class as adults. There is nothing inherently wrong in educated middle-class parents doing this for their children. They are simply trying to help their kids as much as they can—something any loving parent does. The problem is that concerted cultivation often requires financial resources that poor families simply do not have (for example, paying for summer camps, piano lessons, or gymnastics classes; traveling to foreign countries or taking foreign language lessons, or taking advantage of after-school enrichment opportunities). But as these parents seek and find ever greater ways to

sirtravelalot/Shutterstock

Which one will get ahead? If we knew more about the parents' education and income, we could probably make a very good guess.

give their children advantages, they are pushing their kids ahead of everyone else. As one observer has suggested, they are engaged in a kind of **opportunity hoarding**, in which parental resources give more economically privileged children important advantages (Reeves 2017).

There have been a variety of ways that governments and public schools have tried to make up for these discrepancies. In the United States, the Head Start program, first established in 1965, offers prekindergarten enrichment programs for poor children before they enter school. These programs are designed to help participating children become more school ready, and there is an important body of research suggesting that this can make a big difference (Heckman 2017). Some school districts have also established pre-K programs for all children, and Joe Biden and his allies in Congress were proposing legislation to create a national pre-K program. Most districts have also established **charter schools**, which operate more independently of the rest of the school district and can offer more rigorous curriculums for ambitious children and families. These programs try to simulate some of critical thinking skills that concerted cultivation does for middle-class kids.

One widely admired charter school initiative in New York is called the Harlem Children's Zone (HCZ). Founded in 1990 by educator Geoffrey Canada, the HCZ is a pioneering attempt not only to provide high-quality schools for children from low-income families, but also to involve families and communities in addressing some of the other factors that make it difficult for children to learn. These include health clinics, social services, all-day prekindergarten programs, and other kinds of support programs not normally part of a typical school system. The insight of Canada and other HCZ leaders is that children growing up in poor neighborhoods and lacking the kinds of advantages middle-class children receive need more than just good schools; they require a more integrated approach that involves families and the entire community. Featured in the 2010 documentary *Waiting for Superman* and widely

hailed by many educational reformers, the HCZ provides one model to try to address the broader problems facing low-income schools. But it is expensive to expand the HCZ approach everywhere.

Finally, there are a growing number of government and university-based programs that aim to help poor kids—and "first generation" college students whose parents did not attend college—get into top colleges and universities and support them when they are there. Many rich private schools have created or expanded such programs. Several states—notably California, Texas, and Florida—have implemented "percent plans" in which the highest-achieving children from every public high school are automatically eligible to attend top public universities, regardless of test scores or extracurricular activities. Programs like these, often called class-based affirmative action, reduce the advantages of richer kids attending suburban schools where extensive test preparation, sophisticated guidance counseling, and "college resume" preparation is nearly universal (Kahlenberg and Park 2015).

Educating the Elite

18.3.2 **Compare and contrast educational opportunities available to students at elite preparatory schools and public schools.**

Another source of educational inequality occurs when the most privileged families take their children out of public schools to send them to elite **preparatory schools** (also called "prep schools"). These schools typically have beautiful grounds and buildings, charge high tuition, and many have some or even most of their students living at the school as boarding students. These schools carefully mentor each student, trying to give them the best possible chance to be able to enroll in the most prestigious college they can attain (see Khan 2010). Classes at elite boarding schools are usually taught as seminars with no more than 15 students. Teachers know their students well, and are expected to provide extra help if needed. Students write a great deal and are carefully taught how to write well— how to make an argument and support or test it with evidence. Learning to think critically about evidence and ideas is closely cultivated in these schools. Virtually everyone takes college-level (Advanced Placement) courses and participates in extracurricular activities that are meaningful for the college resume, such as student government, yearbook, or leadership roles in voluntary organizations of one kind or another. In contrast, in the typical public high school, fewer than 10 percent of students are involved in such activities.

The young people who attend elite prep schools also benefit from college advisors who actively promote their virtues to the top colleges and universities. When one of the authors of this chapter (Caroline Persell), in a study of prep schools, asked college advisors at such institutions to describe their jobs, one told her that "I put the applicants' folders in the trunk of my car and drive around to [the Ivy League] colleges and talk to the admissions officers about our applicants. I try to make the case for a particular student if I think the college is making a mistake." Having such advisors at one's disposal clearly makes a difference: Graduates of elite prep schools are disproportionately represented at the most elite private colleges and universities (see Persell et al. 1992; see also Khan 2010).

Depending on how we define them, private preparatory schools enroll 1–2 percent of the population (with the most elite of these schools enrolling less than 1 percent of the total high school population). Many of the most famous of these schools—with names like Andover, Groton, St. Paul's, and Hotchkiss—are located in the northeastern United States and have been around for 150 or 200 years. Others are newer, especially in cities and regions that boomed in the twentieth century (such as in the West and South). Historically, these schools dominated Ivy League admission processes; in 1950, for example, 278 students from the most elite preparatory schools applied to Harvard, and an astonishing 245 (88 percent) were admitted (Karabel 2005). Today, these schools have fewer advantages in getting their students into top colleges, but the gap between the preparatory schools and everyone else remains enormous. The leading schools have changed internally as well; gaining admission to the most elite prep schools has become more difficult, although students whose parents have attended the school, or those who have families who can afford to donate significant amounts of money to the school, enjoy privileged access (see Khan 2010). Many of these schools have made some effort to diversify their student bodies by admitting and offering scholarships to students of color, creating a slightly more diverse group graduating from the elite academies (Zweigenhaft and Domhoff 2018). But in general these prep schools look and act as they always have: As places where children are trained for membership in the elite.

Racial and Ethnic Segregation and Educational Disparities

18.3.3 Analyze why racial segregation is so significant for educational outcomes.

So far, we've considered economic inequality and its impact on education. Closely related to the problems of class inequality in education are issues of racial and ethnic division and how they factor into educational opportunity. Until the 1950s, school districts across America were allowed to maintain separate schools for White children and Black, Asian, or Latinx children. Invariably, the schools attended by White children were superior on many dimensions to those attended mostly by non-White children. In 1954, faced with overwhelming evidence that "separate but equal" schools across the country were, in fact, hardly "equal," the Supreme Court issued a landmark ruling in the civil rights case **Brown v. Board of Education**. The *Brown* decision ordered school districts to stop segregating their schools, and to take concrete steps to desegregate. Slowly, and often with much resistance from parents, school districts and local politicians schools became more integrated. It didn't happen easily or overnight. In many cases, federal courts had to intervene to issue desegregation orders requiring school districts to integrate their schools. The last of these court rulings were in the early 1980s, nearly 30 years after *Brown* v. *Board of Education*. But American schools did become significantly more integrated along racial and ethnic lines between 1955 and 1990.

The gates of Phillips Exeter Academy, an elite boarding school in Andover, Massachusetts.

Figure 18.7 Percent of Black Students in Majority White Schools, 1954–2020

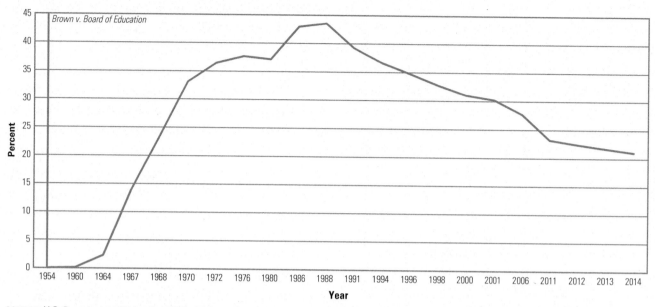

SOURCE: U.S. Department of Education, National Center for Education Statistics, Common Core of Data (CCD), "Public Elementary/Secondary School Universe Survey," 1995–96 through 2014–15.

Figure 18.8 Percent of Black Students Attending Hyper-Segregated Public Schools in Select States

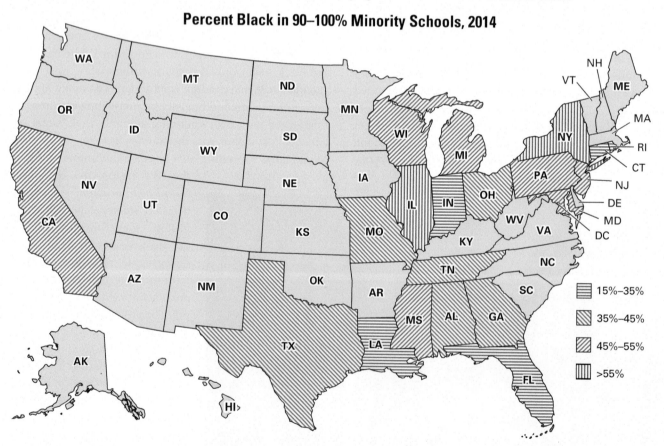

SOURCE: Data from U.S. Department of Education, National Center for Education Statistics, Common Core of Data (CCD), Public Elementary/Secondary School Universe Survey Data.

But after 1990, some of these changes began to reverse, By 2020, more than 40 percent of Blacks and Latinx students were attending schools where minority students comprise more than 90 percent of the student body, a type of school known as **hyper-segregated** (see Figures 18.7 and 18.8). As Figure 18.7 shows, desegregation efforts had enabled growing numbers of Black children to attend schools with a majority of White students, but since 1990 that percentage has steadily fallen. There is variation across America in the extent to which hyper-segregated schools can be found (see Figure 18.8), but for a society that claims to be moving "beyond race" this is a very worrisome trend.

Why is racial segregation so persistent—and rising—in public education? First and foremost, since the Supreme Court's ruling of six decades ago, residential segregation by race has remained significant. Where families live impacts the racial and ethnic composition of individual schools and entire school districts; because of this, desegregation efforts could only go so far. In recent decades, some of the efforts of integration have reversed. In particular, middle and upper-class White families have often chosen to move away from urban school districts to suburban districts that are perceived as having better schools, or within urban school districts to seek out schools with more White children.

The general pattern of White families seeking schools with mostly White children is an example of what is known as **White flight**. It has had the cumulative impact of helping to resegregate America's schools since the 1980s (Frankenberg et al. 2003). Government efforts to support desegregation, as well as the willingness of federal courts to promote desegregation (which was especially important in the decades after the *Brown* decision), have also waned in recent years (Reardon et al. 2012). As a result, these twin dynamics—White flight and declining government and legal efforts to promote integration—have reversed the trend toward integration. America's schools remain highly segregated, all the more so in the twenty-first century than they were around 1980 or 1990 (see Figure 18.7).

Why is desegregation so important (and conversely, why is the resegregation of schools so significant)? It is entirely possible that two equally good schools, each of which has only members of one racial or ethnic group, could achieve excellent results for their students. But decades of research have shown that racial and ethnic gaps in educational achievement are reduced when schools become more integrated. When attending schools that are more integrated, Black, Latinx, and Native American students tend to do better than their peers who are attending hyper-segregated schools (Johnson 2019). Indeed, in the era of desegregation, the gap between Black and White children improved significantly. For the first few decades after the *Brown* ruling, as Black children gained access to schools across America that had historically been all White, they made substantial gains (see Figure 18.9). Notice the sharp decline in the figure between the early 1970s and around 1990: Students of color were rapidly catching up to White students. If we had more data going back to the 1950s, the improvement would be even greater. But the gap has not changed or improved much over the last 30 years, as school resegregation has occurred. Gaps can be seen in standardized test scores, grade point averages, rates of placement in gifted or special education programs, dropout rates, and college attendance and graduation rates.

Gender Differences

18.3.4 Discuss gender differences in educational attainment and achievement.

It is now clear there are large and important class and racial/ethnic differences in educational attainment and achievement, but what about gender? If we look around the world, boys and girls obtain similar amounts of education in rich countries and in many of these countries,

Figure 18.9 Black/White/Latinx Test Score Gap

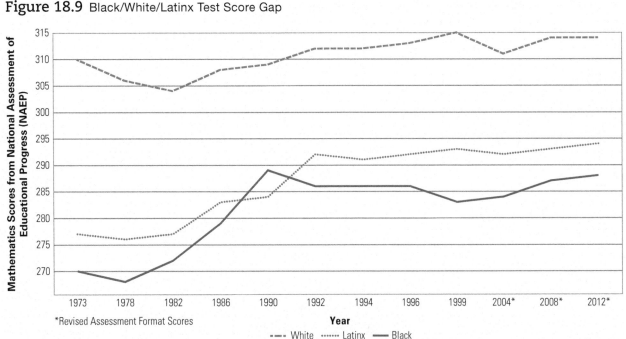

*Revised Assessment Format Scores

SOURCE: National Center for Education Statistics.

Young women graduate from college at higher rates than young men in the United States, Canada, Australia, New Zealand, and most countries in Europe.

including the United States, girls are beginning to get *more* education than boys, as well as better grades. In poorer nations, by contrast, especially those with large portions of the population working in rural agriculture and countries with large Muslim populations, girls are still considerably less likely than boys to obtain the same level of schooling.

Gender differences in education arise when school systems systematically favor one gender over the other. For most of the history of organized education around the world, schools systematically favored boys (and families may have reinforced this by pushing their male children to pursue more education than girls). For example, boys may have been encouraged to stay in school longer, or take a more demanding curriculum, than girls. In the nineteenth and for much of the twentieth centuries, many high schools had a curriculum for girls that included "home economics" (learning how to manage a household, how to cook, and how to raise children) and learning vocational skills such as secretarial skills.

Over the past 50 years, much has changed. In many countries, including the United States, it is girls who are outperforming boys on many educational outcomes. While gender differences in standardized test scores have been relatively stable for the past four decades (with boys scoring slightly higher in math and girls in reading), on other dimensions girls have raced ahead. With regard to school performance, few gender gaps are found in the elementary grades, but the disparities grow as children advance through the system (Buchmann et al. 2008). On average, girls are now getting significantly better grades than boys. Moreover, girls are now equally likely to take demanding math classes (Mulkey et al. 2005) and more likely to take advanced placement (AP) classes than boys. Young women are also more likely to graduate from high school and attend college in the United States than young men, and the gap is especially large among students of color. In 1960, 65 percent of all bachelor's degrees were awarded to men; by 1982, men and women earned an equal number of degrees; by 2008, females earned 57 percent of bachelor's degrees, and it has remained at that level since then. Among young people aged 25 to 29, 39 percent of women but only 32 percent of

Figure 18.10 Gender Gap in College Attainment, 1940–2016

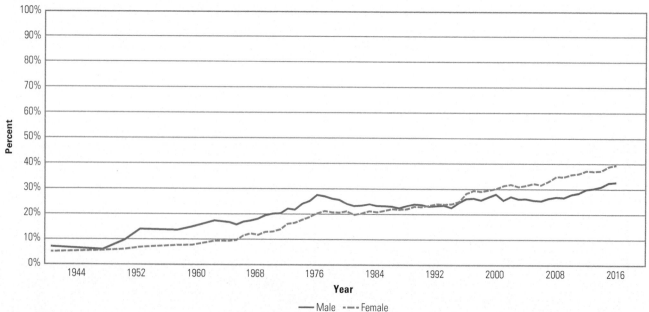

SOURCE: OECD, 2017.

men have at least a BA degree (see Figure 18.10). With regard to graduate school attainment, women in the United States are more likely to earn master's degrees (58 percent in 2016) and approximately equally likely to obtain PhDs or professional degrees, including specific professional law, medical, and dental degrees (Perry 2017).

What's behind this new gender gap, one that favors women? Certainly it wouldn't be predicted by the many advantages men have had historically and continue to have in most arenas of social life. Social scientists are debating the causes. In terms of the big picture, a central idea is that as young women have come to realize they are likely to spend their adult lives working, rather than being a homemaker, many have decided to put more effort into schooling so that they can get better jobs and higher pay (Gottschalk and Danziger 2005). It could be that young women's abilities were suppressed in previous decades by societal norms that prioritized marriage and staying at home to raise children.

There are other ideas too, such as parental encouragement. Parents with more education and other resources have children who are more likely to be highly educated. Are these family resources equally allocated by gender? Girls and boys are typically exposed to the same environment within the same family. Nevertheless, for children born before 1960, girls reached educational equality with boys only in the minority of families with two college-educated parents. The gender gap in college graduation rates was the largest in families where parents had only a high school education or less. This suggests that education itself—in the parents' generation—was an important equalizer. For children born after the mid-1960s, one landmark study found, "a female advantage emerged first among families with absent or less-educated fathers. It remains largest among these families, but has gradually extended to all family types" (Buchman and DiPrete 2006). This finding suggests that it was college-educated households that first started giving strong encouragement to their female children, and later spread it to all households.

Another idea social scientists have explored are changes in the perceptions of teachers, who might have once favored boys. As noted, today, on average, girls get higher grades than boys, and outperform boys on a range of measures of classroom performance (see Voyer and Voyer 2014). Girls spend more time on homework and are less likely to have disciplinary problems than boys, which are perhaps the two most likely explanations for higher grades (Gnaulati 2014). Teachers naturally tend to reward and favor students who are trying the hardest and achieving; to the extent that girls are more likely to be those students, they may benefit from greater encouragement from teachers, counselors, and school administrators.

Is the increasing success of girls in the educational system a social problem? This question itself is controversial. One view is simply that as American society has gotten closer to gender equality, women have simply outcompeted men in education once they gained equal opportunity and stopped suffering discrimination in the school system. Some analysts have even raised concerns that men are falling behind in ways that should be worrisome for the future of the country (for example, in the ability of the American economy to compete with foreign countries that are more successful in educating both women *and* men). Indeed, we can already see that to some extent in the data on employment, where the proportion of men between ages 25 and 54 (the prime working years) with full-time jobs has fallen from about 94 percent to just 83 percent today (Wessel 2014). Fewer men have stable jobs than four decades ago, and more men are finding it difficult to sustain good careers. Education is one reason why that is occurring. Education is one reason why that is occurring.

At the moment, however, as long as those men who are working continue to receive higher wages than woman (see Chapter 14 for more details), it is hard to make a convincing argument that men are "falling behind." *That* issue is more appropriately directed at societal-wide processes through which women face discrimination and inequality in the workplace that make it difficult for them to translate their educational gains into better pay and employment opportunities. It also highlights the more general point we've made elsewhere, which is that already advantaged groups get "more" out of schooling than disadvantaged groups.

The changing gender gap in education raises other, more subtle issues to think about. With women getting nearly three out of every five college degrees, many heterosexual college-educated women will have trouble, if they are seeking equally educated male partners, with whom to form long-term relationships. Since we know that this process, in which most people want to form long-term relationships with people most like themselves, is powerful (see Greenwood et al. 2014), we are reaching a point when there are simply not enough college-educated men in the general population to go around. If something like 20 percent (one in five) of all college-educated heterosexual women have to "settle" for a noncollege-educated male partner in the future, marriage and family relationships are going to be impacted in many important ways.

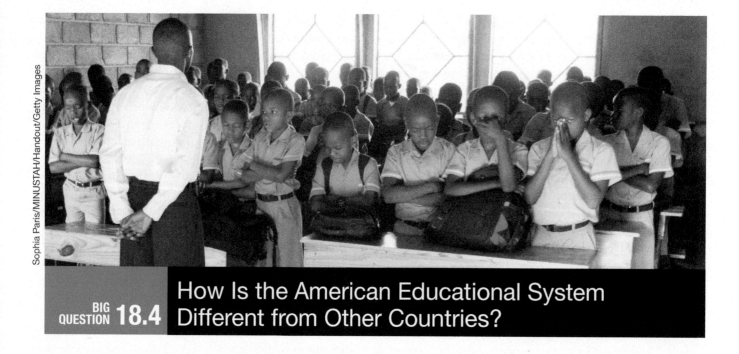

BIG QUESTION 18.4

How Is the American Educational System Different from Other Countries?

EDUCATIONAL SYSTEMS AROUND THE WORLD

The experience of being a student in the United States is quite different from the experience of students in other countries, even those societies that are similar to the United States in terms of economic development. Children growing up in different countries encounter educational systems that differ in many consequential ways. How does the American school system compare to other systems around the world? In this section, we will address that question.

Comparative Differences in Schooling for Students: United States, Germany, Sweden, and Japan

18.4.1 Describe the differences between school systems in the United States, Germany, Sweden, and Japan.

Even in countries that share similar levels of economic development, educational systems can vary widely (Brint 2017). Four distinctive approaches among the world's rich countries can be seen by comparing the American system with educational systems in Germany, Sweden, and Japan. Consider the American system first. Although there is some separation of students into different tracks in many high schools (in which subjects are taught at different levels of sophistication), most students study the same subjects and most (about three in four) eventually start either a two-year or four-year college program that could lead to a BA degree. The two-year community college system

provides college opportunities for virtually any student and, uniquely, makes it relatively easy for individuals to start or re-enter college later in life. There are a small number of highly selective colleges, where grades and test scores are particularly important to gain admission, but most colleges are much less selective. American middle and high schools may seem demanding to students, but in comparison to other countries, U.S. students have more time for socializing, extracurricular activities, and part-time jobs. In addition, the school year in America is typically only about nine months, whereas in most other countries, students attend school 11 months out of the year. That difference represents around 15 percent fewer classroom hours.

The relative openness of the American system—and the ability of students to reenter after dropping out, via the community college system—contrasts very sharply with the educational system in Germany (Henninges et al. 2019). There, children are sorted into one of three different types of schools at a very early age (after fourth grade): A vocational-oriented track that does not provide a pathway for students to go on to college, a middle track that aims to train students for technical colleges (akin to American community colleges, except with more rigorous training for specific high-skilled occupations), and an upper track. The upper-tier is intended to prepare students (after 13 years of schooling, one year more than most systems around the world) for a very demanding examination which allows them to enter the university system. Germany's unique system of sorting children into types of schools may seem rigid, especially to those accustomed to the wide-open model like in the United States. The German system can sentence students to a lifetime of less-desirable employment based on where they were in the school system at age 10. In recent decades, however, Germany has been expanding the upper-track, moving more toward an open system. For example, in 1960, only 7 percent of high school students completed the upper-tier program to enter college, but by 2015 that percentage had climbed to 53 percent (Schuetze 2018).

Sweden and other Scandinavian countries represent interesting mixes of the German and American models. Their students have done very well on international tests, leading many educational policymakers to closely study their approaches. Sweden aims for a much more egalitarian system across the board. All elementary and high schools receive the same level of funding (as do colleges). However, at the high school level, students will move into either vocational or academic tracks, similar to Germany. But even students from the vocational track can attend college, and the government encourages students to obtain as much education or vocational training as they can. Sweden today boasts one of the highest levels of college graduates in the world, while at the same time providing high-quality vocational education to equip students who do not want to go to college with skills to land a job.

In Japan, as well as in many other high-achieving East Asian school systems (such as Singapore, Hong Kong, South Korea, Taiwan, and parts of the mainland Chinese system), students are not separated into different tiers as in Germany, but the intensity of schooling and the importance of passing critical examinations to gain admittance to the best schools is very serious. Japanese students spend long days in large classrooms (often with 45 students per class), with an emphasis on repetitive drills designed to reinforce factual knowledge. At the high school level, the bottom fifth of students will drop out and move to a vocational school, but the rest will compete for college admissions (and because of relatively low acceptance rates, many will not make it). In addition to long school days and extensive homework, most Japanese students will also attend further educational programs either after the formal school day is over and/or on the weekend. These schools, known as *juku*, or "cram schools," are privately run and are almost mandatory for students hoping to gain admission to college. As a result of the importance of the examinations, especially the college entrance examinations, students also have to receive high scores. The highly competitive system of schooling in East Asia does seem to raise all children's achievement.

The differences between these four school systems have significant consequences for their societies, as well as for the students who attend them. The American system allows students the option of a more leisurely pace through their educational careers and provides less pressure on most students in high school (except for students seeking entrance to the very top, selective universities). In addition, students in the American system can perform poorly in school at one point in their life but can recover later and still find avenues through the community college system to attend college and graduate at a later point in life. This is a unique aspect of American education. The German system maintains high standards and expectations, but by separating students into different tiers at young ages, it shuts some students out of educational opportunities. This is, however, partially offset by the high quality of vocational education offered, and most graduates of these vocational programs will find good jobs upon completion. Sweden's system can perhaps be considered the fairest, with complete equality across schools in the entire country, and achieves excellent results. It does incorporate elements of the German tracking model, but it provides more opportunity for students who fall behind to catch up and seek a university education. The Japanese system virtually guarantees that all high school graduates have mastered a high level of knowledge, but the strong focus on testing has sometimes been criticized for encouraging rote learning instead of more creative thinking.

Educational Achievement in International Perspective

18.4.2 Compare American students' performance on international tests to that of their counterparts around the world.

In the introduction to the chapter, we mentioned how students in different national school systems score on identical global tests. So exactly how well (or poorly) do different educational systems perform in terms of student achievement? This has been of special concern in the United States, as American students have typically performed rather poorly on tests given to students in different countries at the same age. The most prominent of these international assessments is the Programme for International Student Assesment (PISA). The PISA is an international examination given to a sample of students in more than 60 countries every three years since 2000. The tested students are all aged 15 and complete assessments on subjects such as mathematics, science, and problem solving. The PISA results have been very disheartening for U.S. school children. In 2018, American students placed 35th in math, 18th in science, and 13th in reading (see Table 18.1). The highest-scoring students come from Asian countries, followed by most of the European countries before the United States. It may be particularly instructive, however, to compare America's neighbor to the north, Canada. Canadian students finish 12th in math, 8th in science, and 6th in reading. In comparison with Canada, the performance of American students is particularly disheartening. Recent PISA test results highlight a well-known general

Table 18.1 PISA Test Results 2018

	Mathematics		Science		Reading
1	Shanghai, China	1	Shanghai, China	1	Shanghai, China
2	Singapore	2	Singapore	2	Singapore
3	Macao, China	3	Macao, China	3	Macao, China
4	Hong Kong, China	4	Estonia	4	Hong Kong, China
5	Taiwan	5	Japan	5	Estonia
6	Japan	6	Finland	6=	Canada
7	Korea	7	Korea	6=	Finland
8	Estonia	8	Canada	8	Ireland
9	Netherlands	9	Hong Kong, China	9	Korea
10	Poland	10	Taiwan	10	Poland
11	Switzerland	11	Poland	11=	Sweden
12	Canada	12	New Zealand	11=	New Zealand
13=	Denmark	13	Slovenia	13	**United States**
13=	Slovenia	14	United Kingdom	14=	United Kingdom
15	Belgium	15=	Australia	14=	Japan
16	Finland	15=	Germany	16=	Australia
17=	Sweden	15=	Netherlands	16=	Taiwan
17=	United Kingdom	18	**United States**	18	Denmark
19	Norway	19=	Sweden	19	Norway
20=	Ireland	19=	Belgium	20	Germany
20=	Germany	21	Czech Republic	21	Slovenia
22	Czech Republic	22	Ireland	22=	Belgium
23	Latvia	23	Switzerland	22=	France
24=	France	24=	Denmark	24	Portugal
24=	Iceland	24=	France	25	Czech Republic
26	New Zealand	26	Portugal	26	Netherlands
27	Portugal	27=	Norway	27=	Austria
28	Australia	27=	Austria	27=	Switzerland
29	Russia	29	Latvia	29=	Croatia
30	Italy	30	Lithuania	29=	Latvia
31	Slovak Republic	31	Hungary	29=	Russia
32	Luxembourg	32	Russia	32=	Italy
33=	Hungary	33	Luxembourg	32=	Hungary
33=	Lithuania	34	Iceland	32=	Lithuania
35	**United States**	35	Croatia	35	Iceland
36=	Belarus	36	Belarus	35=	Belarus
36=	Malta	37	Ukraine	37=	Israel
38	Croatia	38=	Turkey	37=	Luxembourg
39	Israel	38=	Italy	39=	Ukraine
40	Turkey	40	Slovak Republic	39=	Turkey
41	Ukraine	41	Israel	41	Slovak Republic
42=	Greece	42	Malta	42	Greece
42=	Cyprus	43	Greece	43	Chile
44	Serbia	44	Chile	44	Malta
45	Malaysia	45	Serbia	45	Serbia
46	Albania	46	Cyprus	46	United Arab Emirates
47	Bulgaria	47	Malaysia	47	Romania
48	United Arab Emirates	48	United Arab Emirates	48	Uruguay
50=	Romania	49	Brunei Darussalam	49	Costa Rica
50=	Brunei Darussalam	50	Jordan	50=	Cyprus
50=	Montenegro			50=	Moldova

SOURCE: OECD

conclusion: American students on average are simply not learning as much as their peers in other countries. Unless we are prepared to believe that American students are simply not as smart as their foreign peers—a claim with no basis—accounting for American students' relatively poor performance highlights issues in both the educational system and the larger society that impact schooling.

Control and Financing of Schools

18.4.3 Explain how sources and amounts of funding affect educational opportunities.

While most rich countries have national public elementary and secondary education systems with uniform curricula, testing, and financing, some do not. The United States is notable among rich democratic countries for its historic resistance to a national educational curriculum. The U.S. Constitution states that powers not delegated to the federal government are reserved by the states, and courts have interpreted education to be one such function. As a consequence, every state has its own department of education, which may set curriculum and standards for public schools there. In addition, locally elected school boards approve school budgets and help shape educational policy. There are more than 13,000 distinct local school districts across the country, each of which makes decisions about how their schools are organized and how resources are spent. The roles of state governments, and of the federal government, have grown in recent decades (largely by providing resources targeted to certain particular issues or problems); however, for the most part, what goes on inside schools is decided by local school districts.

One of the most important implications of decentralization is how much variation there is in both the source and amount of funds available to public schools. In the United States, in recent years 44 percent of school funding comes from local sources (primarily real estate taxes), 48 percent comes from state tax monies, and 8 percent comes from the federal government. One of the consequences of state and local control and funding is vastly unequal expenditures on K–12 education in the United States, unlike many other countries. Figure 18.11 displays data by state. There is enormous variation in the amount spent in a state like New York ($21,768 per pupil) versus states like Idaho ($7,386) or Utah ($7,925). But even the differences between states don't tell the whole story. There is also a good deal of variation *within* most states, where some school districts are able to spend much more than others. Even schools within the same school districts may vary in how much money they have to spend (Condron

Figure 18.11 Elementary and Secondary Per-Pupil Spending by State

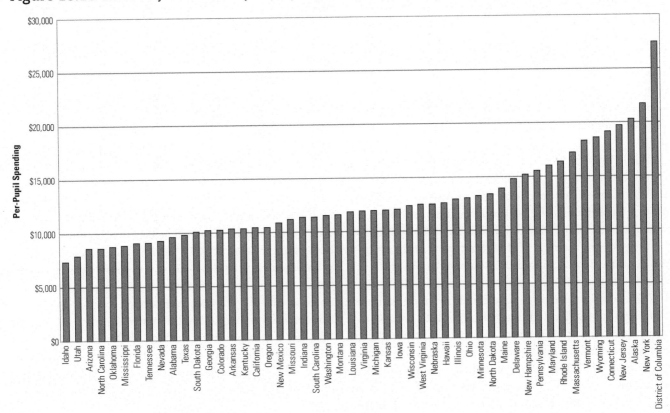

Country

SOURCE: U.S. Census Bureau, 2016.

and Roscigno 2003). For example, individual schools can sometimes raise significant resources through private fundraising and donations from rich parents and families, while schools in the same district without such families cannot.

Few other countries have such extreme differences in resources in different regions to educate children. In many European countries, the national government funds elementary and secondary schools, as well as universities, all at the same level. This greater equality of funding means that all schools in a country can come closer to providing the same opportunities for everyone. Systemic differences in the funding of schools are related to other issues, such as teacher quality, curriculum, and student achievement. And perhaps not surprisingly, differences in funding are also related to unequal educational opportunities by social class and race.

Teacher Shortages and Instructional Quality

18.4.4 Discuss the problems surrounding teacher shortages and quality in the United States.

At the center of any educational system are teachers. There are some three million elementary and secondary school teachers in the United States. Most adults will remember many of their teachers, even from elementary school, because teachers are such an important part of our experiences growing up. They are the ones who take the lead in developing and implementing a school district's curriculum, and in providing the context for students to learn. There is a fair amount of evidence that, regardless of other classroom factors such as technology or financial resources, the best teachers really do have a significant impact on student achievement (Clotfelter et al. 2007; Hanuchek et al. 2019).

While there are many brilliant and dedicated teachers, researchers have raised questions about the overall quality of America's teachers. The profession has long had trouble attracting the best college students to the job (Stinebrickner 2001, 2002; Podgursky et al. 2004). That has not always been the case. Throughout most of the twentieth century, the teaching profession was one of the few occupations that were wide open for women, and before the 1970s and the rise of gender equality, young women college graduates flooded into teaching. But as access to other professions opened up to women, fewer entered the teaching profession. In essence, gender inequality in the past helped to "solve" the problem of recruiting teachers, but that has changed. Arguably, becoming a teacher is one of the best ways someone can do work that will truly help others, and from the standpoint of the nation as a whole, having great teachers is an exceptionally effective way to help the next generation of students do their best (Hanushek et al. 2019). Around the world, there are countries that recruit all or most of their teachers from the top third of college graduates; the United States, by contrast, recruits only about 25 percent of their teachers from the top third of college graduates (Auguste et al. 2010). So why are so many of the most talented young people choosing not to enter the teaching profession?

Part of the reason is that teachers in the United States are paid fairly modest wages compared to other professions. Across the United States, average teacher pay in 2018–19 was $61,730, much lower than average pay in fields like law, business management, medicine, engineering, and most others, and when factoring in inflation, teacher pay has actually fallen in recent years (National Center for Educational Statistics 2020). But low pay compared to other professions is not the whole story; it doesn't include the extra money that teachers often put into their own classrooms to fill shortages in supplies and other needed materials. A recent survey found that 94 percent of public school teachers report paying for some basic supplies out of their own pocket because their district can't afford them, with many reporting spending hundreds or even thousands of dollars per year to help their students (Chokshi 2018).

Averages in pay and working conditions can sometimes mask big variation across a country as large as the United States. Indeed, there are places in the United States that pay teachers much better than others. For example, teachers in New York make an average of $89,899, versus just $47,681 in West Virginia and $52,412 in Oklahoma, with the latter two states having experienced statewide teacher strikes in recent years (Blanq 2019).

Lack of competitive pay, however, is not the only reason why the best students may not be attracted to teaching careers. Working in many public schools is a challenging and demanding job. The burnout rate for teachers is very high by comparison with other professional occupations. Studies find that almost one in five teachers will leave the profession in their first five years of teaching (Ingersoll et al. 2014). This high turnover rate means that many students will have inexperienced teachers in their classroom. This in turn is worrisome because teaching, like any demanding human activity, is something you get better at with experience, and teachers with more experience are better able to improve their students' learning (Ladd and Sorensen 2016). While teachers do get extended vacation time in the summer (although many will use some of that time for mandatory training), during the school year they will often work under considerable pressure to prepare daily lesson plans with limited assistance and often a lack of adequate resources that makes the job frustrating even for the most dedicated teachers.

The way teachers are trained has also been heavily criticized in recent years. If we believe that all children deserve a high-quality education, we would certainly have to agree that every teacher in American classrooms should be well trained to do their job. Sadly, the evidence suggests that this is not the case. Unlike most other countries, there are no national standards for training teachers. Instead, each state designs and evaluates its own systems for teacher training. While some of these programs are excellent, many are not. Critics of teacher training programs have used harsh terms to describe many of them; one systematic report recently decried them as an "industry of mediocrity" (Keller 2013), and some studies find that the very largest programs producing the greatest number of teachers are among the least effective (Greenberg et al. 2015). And state governments are doing a poor job of evaluating these teacher training programs; a 2014 report from the Department of Education found that 34 states have at least one of its teacher training programs in default (Richmond 2014).

The quality of teacher training has now come to be viewed as a central target in the effort to improve America's schools overall, although it remains to be seen how far such initiatives will actually go (and whether state governments are willing to spend the money needed to improve these programs). What is perhaps most notable about the efforts to improve teacher training is that they have the support of nearly everyone involved in educational policy: Democrats, Republicans, educational researchers, teacher's unions (which have supported a number of programs to enhance training and tougher certification programs), and school administrators. But to significantly improve the training of teachers will require spending money and other resources, which are often in short supply.

Home-schooling

18.4.5 Discuss the home-schooling trend and its implications.

There is a small but growing number of children in the United States who stay at home for their education (see Figure 18.12). Prior to the COVID-19 pandemic, about 2.5 million children—about 4 percent of all students—were being home-schooled. No other rich, developed country has anywhere near as many students being home-schooled, although it is allowed in a number of other countries

The home-schooling movement represents one response on the part of some families to the perceived problems of public schools, although the reasons why parents choose to home-school vary widely (Stevens 2001). White students from higher income and two-parent families constitute the majority of home-school families.

During the 2007–08 academic year, the Home School Legal Defense Association conducted a survey of almost 12,000 U.S. home-schooled students (Ray 2009). Their findings generally suggest that home-schooled students outperform those who attended schools on standardized tests, are more involved in their communities, and are more likely to vote as adults. This is not surprising, however, given the social class background of the parents responsible for home-schooling. The families who choose to home-school their children tend to have higher incomes, and more education than families who send their children to public schools. However, it is difficult to measure the precise effects of home-schooling on students' skills and human capital. Many home-schooled children would have done equally well in public schools, given their famly resources.

Figure 18.12 Home-Schooling Trend, 1999–2019

The trend in home-schooling is shown in this graph. It shows the number of students being home-schooled between the ages of 5 through 17 (the equivalent of K–12). The total number rose from 850,000 pupils and students in 1999 to almost 2.5 million in 2019.

Wavebreak Media ltd/Alamy Stock Photo

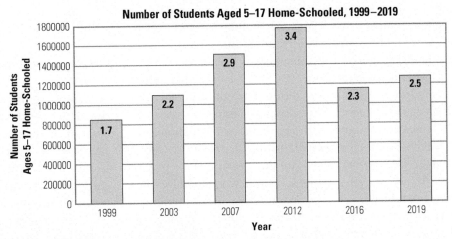

Number of Students Aged 5–17 Home-Schooled, 1999–2019

SOURCE: National Center for Education Statistics.

Aside from learning, there may be other implications of home-schooling. Socialization for students who are home-schooled works differently compared to traditional students: Parents and other home educators may emphasize different cultural norms and values or historical facts. Home-schooled children are deprived of the same degree of interaction with their peers, but parents choosing home-schooling may prefer that outcome. Home-schooled children also often don't have access to the same range of extracurricular activities, although in some school districts after-school activities have opened up to home-schooled children, reducing their isolation from their peers.

During the COVID-19 pandemic, a modified form of home-schooling became common across the globe, and is also giving researchers a unique opportunity to study home-schooling as a mass phenomenon. When schools shut down to try to reduce the spread of the coronavirus, most moved to some kind of remote learning, using technology to connect teachers to students. Countries around the world, and many states across America, varied widely in how soon they reopened and how much in-person teaching they did. Because the United States, in addition to other countries, failed to control COVID-19 (see Chapter 19), many American schools closed in mid-March 2020 and were only partially open for most or all of the 2020–21 school year (although there was wide variation across states and private schools). Research continues, but at this point all the evidence suggests three things about the move to home-schooling during the pandemic: (1) Virtually all students were learning less and spending less time on schoolwork, even in countries like Germany that had a relatively good handle on containing the virus and invested heavily in trying to ensure each child had the resources needed to study at home (Hanushek and Woessmann 2020); (2) The impact of home-schooling was spread unevenly, with children from low-income areas suffering more than children from higher-earning families or communities (Chetty et al. 2020); (3) There will likely be long-term losses for both students and societies, in the form of lower wages (for less well-educated students) and lower economic growth for entire countries—and these impacts could be very large, depending on how countries and school systems try to make up for the lost learning (Hanushek and Woessmann 2020).

Home-schooling during COVID-19 also highlighted other problems with this approach to education for families lacking necessary resources. Having children take classes from home, with lessons directed remotely by teachers on technology platforms like Zoom or Google Meet, frequently created difficult situations for parents with full-time jobs. Home-schooling works best for families in which one or both parents can afford the time to really work with their children. Further, families living in small houses or apartments experienced much higher stress levels, thereby reducing students' school performance. As with most other institutions during the pandemic, but perhaps especially so, educational systems (and the parents and students who rely on them) have faced immense challenges.

Organizational Practices: Testing and Tracking

18.4.6 Explain how common organizational practices, including testing and tracking, can result in education inequality.

Two major differences in educational practices between the United States and other developed countries are testing and tracking, as we mentioned earlier in the chapter. These two linked practices, however, have also undergone important changes in recent years in the United States, and both are such an important part of the overall school environment and how it impacts students and school inequalities that a deeper dive is important. Let's start with testing. While teachers have always given their students tests, the "stakes" of testing have increased in recent years. A single test may determine whether students move to the next grade, or even if they can graduate from high school. Such tests may also be used to hold educators, schools, and school districts accountable (by, for example, linking teachers' or principals' pay to their students' performances on standardized tests). Most other nations with strong educational systems and high student achievement outside of East Asia are not testing students every year and are not judging teachers or school administrators by their students' test scores (Tucker 2011).

According to proponents of achievement testing, the purpose of using such tests is to set higher standards for student learning and raise student achievement. When some students do poorly on a test, schools and teachers can respond in several ways. They can work harder with those students, providing them with more personal attention, tutoring, and additional learning experiences in an effort to improve their achievement test scores. Such responses, however, are relatively rare. They require additional resources, which many schools lack, especially ones that are already underfunded. Another possible response is that schools try to shed students with lower scores by encouraging them to drop out or transfer. This is clearly an unintended consequence of high-stakes testing and one that hurts the most educationally needy and vulnerable students. Many teachers, while not opposed to high standards, say that the existence of mandatory testing leads to "teaching in ways that contradicted their own ideas of sound educational practice" (Winter 2003, p. B9).

One important study analyzed an urban elementary school's response to the Texas Accountability System and the Student Success Initiative, which required third-grade students to pass a reading test to be promoted to the fourth grade (Booher-Jennings 2005). It found that teachers devoted more resources to helping those students who were on the brink of passing the Texas Assessment of Knowledge and Skills test. At the same time, teachers reduced the size of the group whose scores counted by referring more students to special education. Why would teachers participate in such a system? This research found that the institutional environment defined a good teacher as one with high pass rates. Teachers became competitors rather than partners with their colleagues, which weakened the faculty's ability to work together toward common goals. "The singular focus on increasing aggregate test scores rendered the schoolwide discussion of the 'best interests of children' obsolete" (Booher-Jennings 2005, p. 260).

This study and many others raise important questions about how a major piece of educational policy, the **No Child Left Behind** (NCLB) Act, adopted by Congress in 2001, has been implemented. The intended goals of NCLB are to reduce the achievement gap between low-income children and children of color versus higher-income or White children. Some of the key provisions of this federal law are state-level annual tests of third to eighth graders in reading and math, plus at least one test for students in grades 10 through 12. States and districts are required to report school-level data on students' test scores for various subgroups: Black, Latinx, Native American, Asian American, Whites, special education, limited English proficiency, and low-income students. NCLB financially rewards or punishes school districts and schools for the tested achievement of their students but does not prescribe consequences for students (Dworkin 2005). NCLB has been amended by Congress to soften some of the requirements of the original legislation, but it continues to govern federal education policy.

Under this system, schools with too many low-scoring students are held accountable for the outcome, regardless of the reason for the low scores. Over 2 percent of all schools have been closed due to NCLB. Invariably, schools facing closure have been in the poorest neighborhoods; virtually no schools in affluent suburbs have been closed under NCLB. Sociologists have raised questions about the effects that schools can realistically have on their students' performance, as many other things beyond the control of the school are important too. They have also questioned the reliability of the scores of the national tests. And many scholars and parents feel that the emphasis on testing takes valuable learning time away from students to conduct the tests, which in some districts can eat up a week or more of school time. Teachers may try to improve their students' scores by "teaching to the test" or "gaming the system" (strictly teaching only concepts covered by a standardized test) rather than seeking to help all children learn from a broader curriculum. But testing has its supporters as well; for some analysts, testing may not be perfect but is one way to hold schools and teachers accountable for their students' achievement. The debate over the value of testing is likely to continue for the foreseeable future.

Testing is also a major basis for **tracking**. Sociologists and education administrators use this term to describe how schools assign students to distinct groups based on perceived ability. Tracking in the United States today is widespread, particularly in large, diverse school systems and in schools serving primarily students from lower socioeconomic classes. It is less prevalent and less rigid when it occurs in upper-middle-class suburban and private schools and in parochial schools (Lucas and Berends 2002). In recent years, tracking has become more subtle. High school courses now tend to be classified as regular, college prep, honors, and advanced placement (AP) courses. Low-income students and parents, in particular, may be unaware of what the distinctions mean and not realize that decisions made in seventh or eighth grade affect what courses are possible for them to take in high school. Even if their school has AP courses, students may be unaware that grades received in AP or honors courses may be given greater weight when their grade-point averages are computed, and thus may differentially affect their chances for college admission or scholarships. They also may not realize the importance of taking certain courses, such as upper-level mathematics for doing well on college entrance examinations. Many inner-city or low-income schools do not offer even a single AP course, while many affluent suburban schools offer a dozen or more. Differences in the courses students take, especially in such areas as mathematics, science, and foreign language, go a long way toward explaining differences in achievement test scores (Darling-Hammond 2001).

How exactly does tracking affect learning and opportunities? Research suggests that it creates instructional, social, and institutional differences in students' learning experiences. Numerous researchers have observed instructional differences between tracks, with higher-ranked groups being taught more words in reading, for example (Gamoran 1984, 1986). Teachers of high-track students set aside more time for student learning and devote more class time to learning activities (Oakes 1985). In secondary schools, college-track students consistently receive better teachers, class materials, laboratory facilities, field trips, and visitors than their lower-track counterparts. Finally, teachers hold higher expectations and the other students support learning more in the higher-ability groups. As a result, the achievement of students in the higher groups tends to develop more than it does in the lower groups (Hallinan 1987).

Tracking has other consequences. Tracks create settings that shape students' self-esteem and expectations about academic performance. Being assigned to particular tracks immediately ranks students in an educational status heirarchy, signalling that some students are better than others (Rosenbaum 1976). Higher-track students receive more empathy, praise, and respect for their ideas, as well as less direction and criticism, than do lower-track students (Freiberg 1970). Teachers spend more time in low-track classes on discipline, and students in those classes perceive their teachers as more punitive than students in high-track classes (Oakes 1985). Students in higher tracks are taught critical thinking, creativity, and independence, while students at the bottom are denied access to these educationally and socially important experiences (Oakes 1985). The social-class background of students is also related to the prevalence of tracking in the schools, to the nature of the available tracks, and to the ways track assignments are made. Tracking clearly segregates children by social class and ethnicity (Tyson 2011).

In recent years, tracking has come under considerable criticism, and a movement toward de-tracking (that is, eliminating tracking) has gained significant support among educational sociologists and school administrators. The de-tracking movement aspires to achieving greater educational equality. But when school administrators attempt to implement de-tracking, they have often

encountered serious resistance. Many teachers feel unprepared to effectively manage classrooms with a range of student abilities (Darling-Hammond 2001). Upper-class parents who want their children to benefit from more advanced courses may resist de-tracking as well. Here, de-tracking is perceived as a threat by privileged parents who feel tracking gives their children few educational benefits. They often mount strong political resistance to removing tracking systems. For example, being in an honors course confers advantages in the competition for college admissions. De-tracking was most successful when politically savvy teachers and school administrators were able to involve powerful parents in meaningful ways in the process of implementing it (Oakes et al. 1997).

The big lesson about tracking is simply this: Schooling is closely related to social class and race. Prosperous and/or White children are twice as likely as poor and/or children of color to attend private schools, for example, and much more likely to attend schools with fewer low-income or minority children. When they do attend more diverse public schools, their parents still fight for advantage, and tracking is one way to achieve it. Both organizational practices and educational resources are patterned along the social fault lines in society, with the result that not all babies are raised in the same educational nurseries.

Mark Bussell

BIG QUESTION 18.5 Is Higher Education in Crisis?

THE STATE OF AMERICAN HIGHER EDUCATION

America's colleges and universities are of very high quality in terms of the research and scholarship produced by their faculty, and in the training of graduate students.

If you want to have a career as a scholar or scientific researcher, in almost any field, you will generally find that most of the very best programs are in the United States. This is a pretty remarkable fact about American higher education, and the envy of the rest of world. But when it comes to undergraduate education, however, there are many serious concerns about American colleges and universities. The most important challenges in higher education today lie in the cost of attending college, student dropout rates, the amount of learning that is actually occurring, and the pressing need to increase the number of students going to and completing college. These issues are, in short, similar to the ones facing schools at lower levels, with the additional factor that even public universities can be expensive to attend. In this section, we consider each of these issues.

The Rising Costs of Higher Education

18.5.1 Explain the consequences of the rising costs of higher education in the United States

American higher education is the most expensive system in the world (see Figure 18.13). The rapidly increasing costs of higher education are mostly being paid by individuals—parents and students—instead of the government, as is common in other developed countries. This has had a dramatic effect on college tuition and fees at both private and public institutions over the past few decades. The data are striking (see Figure 18.4). Between 1975 and 2015, the average tuition at American four-year public universities rose by 394 percent, from $2,570 (in 2017 dollars, adjusted for inflation) to $9,970; private universities rose at a similarly fast rate, from $11,020 to $32,740 in inflation-adjusted dollars (or 321 percent).

In other words, getting a bachelor's degree has become vastly more expensive.

Why have the costs of attending college risen so much faster than the overall rate of inflation in recent decades? It is easy to blame universities for arbitrarily jacking up fees to pay the high salaries of administrators, or to think that someone is "profiting" from this arrangement. And it is true that those salaries have gone up; university presidents have seen their average pay rise over time, and a number of university presidents today are paid more than $1 million a year. But compared to the salaries of heads of corporations, university presidents are actually paid fairly modestly. The average pay of the chief executive officer of a Fortune 500 company today is around $10 million, or about 25 times what the average university president at a large public university typically makes. Similarly, while a few professors make salaries that can reach $300,000 or more, the vast majority of professors make far less than people in other professions requiring similar levels of training. Nationally, the median salary of a college professor is $78,470, according to recent data from the Federal Government's Bureau of Labor Statistics, a bit more than elementary and high school teachers, but much less than the median pay in other comparable professions.

So if it's not administrator and professor salaries, what has driven rising college costs? For public universities, the most important change in the last few decades is that in virtually every state and for every type of institution (four-year and two-year schools), state governments are providing

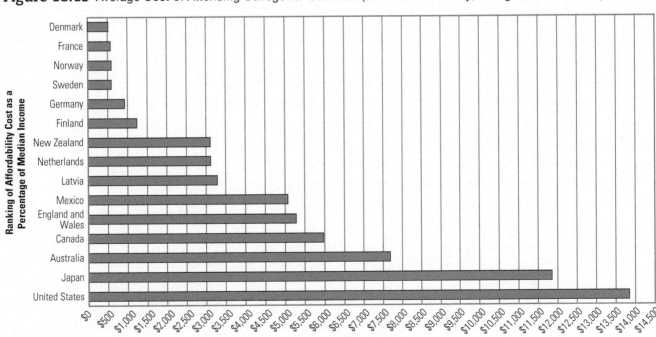

Figure 18.13 Average Cost of Attending College for One Year (BA Institutions Only; Living Costs Excluded)

SOURCE: Global Higher Education Rankings 2010: Affordability and Accessibility in Comparative Perspective from Higher Education Strategy Associates.

Figure 18.14 Rising Cost of College (Adjusted for Inflation)

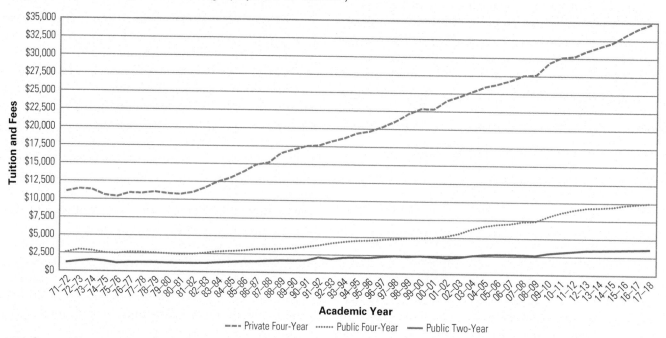

NOTE: Average tuition and fees for the United States includes public two-year institutions and in-state charges for public four-year institutions. Many students attending four-year public universities pay far more.

SOURCE: The College Board, Annual Survey of Colleges; NCES, IPEDS data.

far less support from taxes than they did in the past, which means that students (and their families) are expected to pick up a greater share of the cost (see Figure 18.15 for the annual percentage decline in state government contributions each year; note the rapid decline since 2000).

To make this more concrete, let's consider a single public institution, the very prestigious University of California, Berkeley. In 1975, the state of California provided about 60 percent of the total budget for its leading public universities like UC Berkeley (the University of California system has 10 branch campuses, including Berkeley and UCLA). By 1995, due to a steady round of budget cutting, state support fell to about 30 percent of the university's budget. It continued to fall after that. In 2019–20, the Berkeley campus received only 14 percent of its entire budget from the state government. How can they make up the difference? Like most universities, UC Berkeley has aggressively cut costs where it can, but it has also had to try to raise revenue to pay its bills. Some of that revenue has come from asking its graduates to donate more money to the school every year, some has come from

Figure 18.15 Percent Change in State Support for Public Higher Education per Full-Time Student

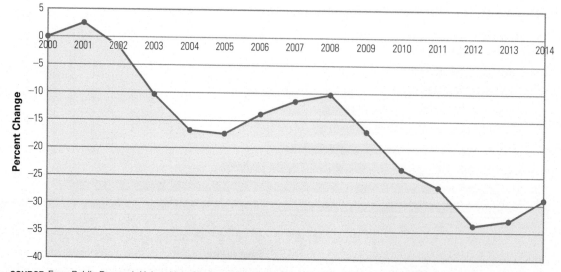

SOURCE: From *Public Research Universities: Changes in State Funding* (American Academy of Arts & Sciences, 2015).

generating more research money from grants (a portion of which is retained by the university), and, finally and inevitably, a significant piece of the additional revenue has come from raising tuition. The father of one of the authors of this chapter (August Manza) grew up in California and attended UC-Berkeley in the early 1950s, and he paid about $60 in tuition (then called "fees") each year. In the mid-1980s, when the author Jeff Manza attended the same school, tuition was about $1000 a year. By 2020, it was $14,500 (and the tuition for out-of-state students was a whopping $44,000). The situation at Berkeley is not unusual; all public universities have been forced to do the same things, although the degree of change has varied across the country.

Though falling government support is one big cause of rising tuition in public universities, there is still this puzzle: Why has tuition risen so fast at private universities (which never had large government subsidies)? Tuition at private universities has risen nearly as fast as public universities, so there must be other factors impacting both public and private universities, and perhaps some expenses that only impact private universities. One big and rapidly rising expense for all universities has been health care. Almost all colleges and universities provide their faculty, staff, and students with high-quality and heavily subsidized health insurance (as do many large corporations). They also typically maintain expensive on-campus health clinics for students to use. Because health care expenses have risen dramatically over the past 40 years for everyone (see Chapter 19 for details), the fact that colleges and universities continue to maintain their health programs means that those costs have also risen rapidly (Kirch 2011). In fact, about 10 percent of the increase in tuition since 2000 can be attributed to the rising cost of health insurance and health care alone.

Other sources of rising costs that have impacted all universities are technology (universities generally have to maintain state-of-the-art computing facilities to enable their students to learn to use the tools of the future, and that is expensive to acquire and maintain), building costs (private universities, in particular, have been engaged in a race with each other to construct ever more attractive facilities and dormitories to appeal to students who are being asked to pay ever higher tuition), and increases in staffing necessitated by changes in federal law (for example, to meet requirements of equal treatment of all students). A somewhat surprising but important new expense is pressure to advertise and market universities. Most universities did little or no marketing of themselves before the 1970s. Today, however, most schools, especially private universities, incur significant expenses advertising themselves to prospective students. Finally, a number of studies have found that there is a relationship between federal student aid and rising private school tuition (Lucca et al. 2016). As the federal government makes more financial aid available, schools can increase the fees they charge to students. The paradox here is that the very

programs designed to make college more easily available to more students may be driving up the costs for everyone!

What are the consequences of these rising costs of going to college? One of the most important is that high tuition and fees contribute to increased dropout rates among students (a problem we consider in more detail in the next section). In addition, facing the cost of college, some potential students, especially those from lower-income families, may choose not to even apply, because they lack the resources to pay for college. Others may not want the risk of having college debt they are not sure they can repay after graduating. Those students who do enroll are taking out more and bigger loans for their postsecondary education than ever before. As a result, the average debt of college graduates has almost doubled in the last 10 years, from about $13,000 in 2005 to more than $30,000 in 2019. (Note that this is an average; some students will have far higher debt loads). Americans are now borrowing more for education than they ever did with their credit cards (see Figure 18.16). Many students will leave college with significant debt loads that will burden them for years.

So why do parents and students *keep* paying higher tuition fees and taking out expensive loans (Zaloom 2019)? To put it simply: Despite the astonishing price for an *average* bachelor's degree, the benefits for going to college are, on average, dramatically higher than the cost of attending even an expensive private college or university (not to mention a more affordable public university). As discussed earlier in the chapter, men and women who have higher degrees earn vastly more, on average, than those with less schooling; and when you average the difference over a lifetime, the income premium for getting a college degree over a lifetime is immense.

How valuable is it to go to a prestigious school? The question of how much value is gained by attending a more elite private or public university has proven difficult for social scientists to answer. It has long been established that access to the most privileged positions in American society is much easier for those who attend the most prestigious universities, especially the Ivy League (and in the Ivy League, it is four schools—Harvard, Yale, Princeton, and Columbia—that are especially advantaged; see Karabel 2005). But only a tiny group will become CEOs, members of Congress, or heads of nonprofit organizations. What about everyone else? One well-known study has found that students admitted to both Ivy League and state colleges do more or less equally well in adulthood regardless of which school they choose (Dale and Kruger 2011). Trying to compare apples to apples, the study examined students who were admitted to both Princeton and Penn State, and followed them into early adulthood. The authors found relatively little differences in the average quality of jobs and incomes attained by the Penn State and Princeton graduates. This unique study matched an Ivy League school with a highly rated public university. It suggests that it is the student, not the institution, that is most important. But the

Figure 18.16 Average Graduate Debt (Top Panel) and Overall Student Debt versus Credit Card Debt (Bottom Panel)

SOURCE: Based on data from the John William Pope Center for Higher Education Policy, 2011; New York Fed, 2013; and College-Insight.org.

more important research finding about education and lifetime career outcomes remains that getting a degree from an accredited college or university is the major benefit, while debates will likely continue on how much it matters *where* you go to school.

Efforts to make college more affordable are beginning to get significant public attention. Growing numbers of politicians seemed to strike a popular note with many younger people in arguing for a dramatic change: That a college education—like elementary and high school—should be freely available to all who want one. Funding free or low-cost education would require the federal government to make up the difference, and it would require small increases in

Students in a large class at New York University (NYU), prestigious private university in New York City, taking an exam given by chapter author Jeff Manza. Whether an NYU education, which costs $53,000 a year in 2021, is worth more than an education at nearby public universities costing far less is a question very much worth asking.

Mark Bussell

income or business taxes (or some combination) to pay for it. It would move America closer to the situation in many European countries, where college remains tuition free or very low cost in many countries. It may seem like a radical idea, but Germany did exactly that, abolishing all tuition at public universities in 2014. It can be done.

Should it? To answer that question, we have to ask what abolishing (or significantly reducing) tuition for public colleges and universities would do. Most importantly, it would make it dramatically easier for any student (or their family) who is choosing whether or not to go to college based on the price of attending. It would also help prevent students from dropping out because they feel they are getting into too much debt. However, critics of the idea have noted that even aside from the considerable cost involved, giving free or low-cost college educations to individuals who will earn more for the rest of their lives than the people who don't go to college is to subsidize class inequality. It is an interesting debate that involves several competing, worthwhile principles. The country as a whole would be better off in the future if more people finish college, and the higher incomes they would earn will increase taxes paid to the government to help support future generations. On the other hand, a free education would benefit many students who can't afford to pay for college. An alternative idea might be to significantly increase the availability of scholarships and grants to children from low-income families to make the high cost of college less of an issue for those who can least afford it.

Dropping Out of College

18.5.2 Explain why the college dropout rate is so high in the United States.

Of the various serious problems with higher education, one of the most significant, but least discussed in public debates, is the problem of students dropping out (or failing to finish) college. Current research suggests that only a little over half of all students who start college will actually finish (see Figure 18.17, which displays different drop-out rates in different kinds of institutions). In recent years, about 7 in 10 high school graduates will start college, but only a little more than 3 in 10 will finish with a BA, and a smaller group (about 10 percent) will finish with an associate's (AA) degree from a 2-year school. This is much lower than the completion rates in other countries. In fact, America continues to lead the world in the percentage of students who *start* college, but still has a disappointing average in terms of the percentage of those who *complete* college.

Why don't more students finish college? When students who drop out of college are asked, the most common answer they give is that they can't afford to continue or that they needed drop out to work to support their family. One piece of circumstantial evidence that the costs of college are a central factor is that the dropout rate is that it is much higher among students attending college part-time than among full-time students. Part-time students typically have to work to pay tuition or to support themselves (or in some cases their children). Still, even many full-time students will eventually drop out.

Figure 18.17 Dropping Out of College: Six-Year Outcomes by Starting Institution Type

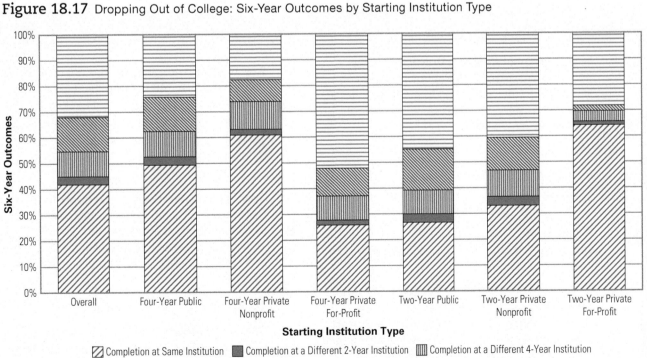

SOURCE: Data from National Student Clearinghouse Research Center, 2015; Appendix C Table 14 (available at https://nscresearchcenter.org/signaturereport10/).

But there are other factors. It is surely the case that a significant number fail to finish because they are not prepared for or simply do not like the kinds of studies and work required at the college level. This, however, might not be something that a student who dropped out of college would necessarily want to declare to an interviewer, so it is possible we underestimate that factor. Students who take too many classes in a semester or too many hard classes at the same time can become overwhelmed and quit. Getting good advice from a college counselor about how to manage a course load is often critical, but not all students (especially at large public universities) will receive that kind of attention (Witteveen 2016).

Conclusion: The Future of Education in a Global Economy

We care about education because it shapes so many important aspects of our adult lives, from our intellectual development to career prospects and income, but also in less visible ways like our physical health, who we form intimate relationships with, and how we engage and understand the world around us. Education also has a huge impact on the economies of entire countries and regions. In this chapter, we explored some of the major purposes of education as well as how it relates to all of these important life outcomes for individuals and societies. We also examined inequalities in education and how educational systems in the United States differ from others around the world.

Educational systems are currently undergoing massive updating with the rise of new educational technologies, and social scientists and educational administrators are actively engaged in figuring out what people need to learn to function well in the twenty-first century and how to use technology most effectively in classrooms. For example, how can we advance *critical-thinking* and *problem-solving skills*? Looking at the social context surrounding any institution a defining question sociologists continually ask. It involves analyzing how parts of a whole interact to create various outcomes in complex systems; analyzing and evaluating evidence from many different sources, including its timeliness, credibility, and usefulness; assessing arguments, claims and beliefs, and alternative points of view; integrating and connecting information and arguments; drawing inferences and conclusions from information; and reflecting on what has been learned and what more needs to be learned. The rise of the Internet with huge quantities of Instantly available information of widely varying quality makes these skills particularly important today.

If these are some of the widely accepted goals of education, it is clear that applying the insights of a sociological imagination will prove vitally important. The social contexts of learning—and the challenges faced by students of varied backgrounds—will need to be addressed if we truly aspire to have a meritocratic educational system and society. Achieving equality of opportunity in education, as in other arenas of social life, is no easy challenge.

The Big Questions Revisited 18

18.1 Why Is Formal Education Universal? In this section, we examined the various purposes of schooling, from socialization to preparation for work, citizenship, and the economic health of the community and nation.

The Purposes of Education

Education: A Brief Social History

Learning Objective 18.1.1: Explain the early rise of educational systems in America.

Socialization

Learning Objective 18.1.2: Describe three functions of schooling.

Preparation for the Future: Education as Opportunity

Learning Objective 18.1.3: Discuss the concept of human capital and how educational attainment enhances future opportunities for individuals.

Economic Benefits of Schooling

Learning Objective 18.1.4: Discuss how education contributes to economic growth.

Key Terms

social mobility (p. 496)   Morrill Act (p. 496)
hidden curriculum (p. 496)   active learning
(p. 498)   human capital (p. 498)   meritocracy
(p. 498)   social reproduction theory (p. 499)
STEM (p. 499)

18.2 How Is Education Related to Important Life Outcomes? Education is strongly related to many important life outcomes, including work and economic opportunities, health and life expectancy, and marital success and happiness.

Education and Life Outcomes

Career Outcomes

Learning Objective 18.2.1: Discuss the relationships among education, occupation, and life-course outcomes and how those affect economic success.

Health and Life Expectancy

Learning Objective 18.2.2: Identify the correlation between education level and health.

Family Life

Learning Objective 18.2.3: Recognize the correlation between education level and intimate relationships.

Key Terms

soft skills (p. 501)   closure theory (p. 502)
credentialism (p. 502)   educational homogamy (p. 505)

18.3   Do Schools Provide All Children an Equal Chance to Succeed? Is education the great equalizer in U.S. society, or does it reproduce existing inequalities? In this section, we examined the sociological research that investigates whether educational access, experiences, and outcomes are similar for persons of different social classes, races, and genders.

Educational Inequality

Income Inequality and Schooling

Learning Objective 18.3.1: Explain how income inequality contributes to gaps in the quality of educational opportunities.

Educating the Elite

Learning Objective 18.3.2: Compare and contrast educational opportunities available to students at elite preparatory schools and public schools.

Racial and Ethnic Segregation and Educational Disparities

Learning Objective 18.3.3: Analyze why racial segregation is so significant for educational outcomes.

Gender Differences

Learning Objective 18.3.4: Discuss gender differences in educational attainment and achievement.

Key Terms

residential segregation (p. 507)   concerted cultivation (p. 507)   opportunity hoarding (p. 508)   charter schools (p. 508)   preparatory schools (p. 508)   *Brown* v. *Board of Education* (p. 509)   hyper-segregated (p. 509)   White flight (p. 511)

18.4   How Is the American Educational System Different From Other Countries? How can there be such wide variations in the quality and types of schooling, particularly by social class and race? To address this question in this

section, we examined differences in educational systems around the world and the various ways that U.S. schools are organized.

Educational Systems Around the World

Comparative Differences in Schooling for Students: United States, Germany, Sweden, and Japan

Learning Objective 18.4.1: Describe the differences between school systems in the United States, Germany, Sweden, and Japan.

Educational Achievement in International Perspective

Learning Objective 18.4.2: Compare American students' performance on international tests to that of their counterparts around the world.

Control and Financing of Schools

Learning Objective 18.4.3: Explain how sources and amounts of funding affect educational opportunities.

Teacher Shortages and Instructional Quality

Learning Objective 18.4.4: Discuss the problems surrounding teacher shortages and quality in the United States.

Home-schooling

Learning Objective 18.4.5: Discuss the home-schooling trend and its implications.

Organizational Practices: Testing and Tracking

Learning Objective 18.4.6: Explain how common organizational practices, including testing and tracking, can result in education inequality.

Key Terms

No Child Left Behind (p. 521)   tracking (p. 521)

18.5   Is Higher Education in Crisis? There are many serious concerns about American colleges and universities, particularly in the cost of attending college, student dropout rates, how much learning is actually occurring in college, and in the pressing need to increase the number of students going to and completing college. We considered some of these issues in this section.

The State of American Higher Education

The Rising Costs of Higher Education

Learning Objective 18.5.1: Explain the consequences of the rising costs of higher education in the United States.

Dropping Out of College

Learning Objective 18.5.2: Explain why the college dropout rate is so high in the United States.

Chapter 19
Health and Medicine

by Ruth Horowitz, Jennifer Jennings, and Jeff Manza

Where you live has a significant impact on your health. The COVID-19 pandemic provides a clear example of this basic sociological idea. The population of the United States (about 325 million people) makes up 4 percent of the world's total population (7.8 billion people). And yet, in February 2021, *over 20 percent of the people in the entire world who had died from COVID-19 lived in the United States.* To get a sense of how many excess deaths (those that go beyond what is expected in a normal year) were happening in the United States, a prominent public health scholar and his colleague published the results of a research analysis comparing COVID-19 deaths in similar countries (Biliniski and Emanuel 2020). They asked the following question: how many *fewer* people would have died in the United States if it had a death rate due to COVID-19 as in other similar countries? The results of their analysis are displayed in Table 19.1. (Keep in mind that this study was through September 2020, relatively early in the pandemic; until the arrival of vaccines, the numbers of unnecessary deaths continued to rise.)

At the time of their analysis, the United States had officially recorded 198,589 deaths. The authors reported that, as of that time, there would have been 117,622 fewer deaths if the United States' death rate had been similar to Canada's. Those lost lives are roughly equivalent to a city the size of Gainesville, Florida; Charleston, South Carolina; or Topeka, Kansas. (Note that these are death rates based on deaths per 100,000 population, so the fact that the United States is much larger than Canada or other countries is irrelevant.) A later study using a similar approach published in winter 2021, when the death toll was approaching 500,000 in the United States, found the number of excess deaths to be about 40 percent greater than the average in other rich countries (Woolhandler et al. 2021). To be sure, these analyses also find that there are a few rich countries that have done just as poorly as the United States, such as Belgium, Spain, and the United Kingdom

(although the data for Belgium, which has the worst record of all, are potentially misleading because of the way that country reports COVID deaths). America is not alone in struggling against the virus. But, until vaccines arrived, it did far worse than most similar countries, and the arrival of vaccines in the winter of 2021 does nothing for those who died before they could be vaccinated.

My Sociological Imagination

RUTH HOROWITZ

As I reflect on my experiences as a teenager living abroad, first in Buenos Aires, Argentina, then in a small French village, and later in a tiny Mexican village, I can understand why I became a sociologist. In Buenos Aires I saw heavy gates around large homes clearly meant to keep strangers out, but the walls around the poor neighborhoods appeared designed to keep people in. Why, I wondered, did the walls have different meanings, and why were the poor treated differently? The French teens seemed different than me. Was it because they were French and I American, they lived in a small town and I was from Boston, or their parents owned a butcher shop or worked in factories and my father was a professor, I wondered? As an undergraduate, I decided to become a sociologist and researcher when I tried to analyze what I had seen in the Mexican village where I lived and found we had violated many social norms. I saw that research would help my understanding, and more research was necessary to truly understand the lives of others. With new experiences as a public member on medical licensing and disciplinary boards, my research evolved from the study of urban ethnic communities, gangs, and teen mothers to the regulation of physicians.

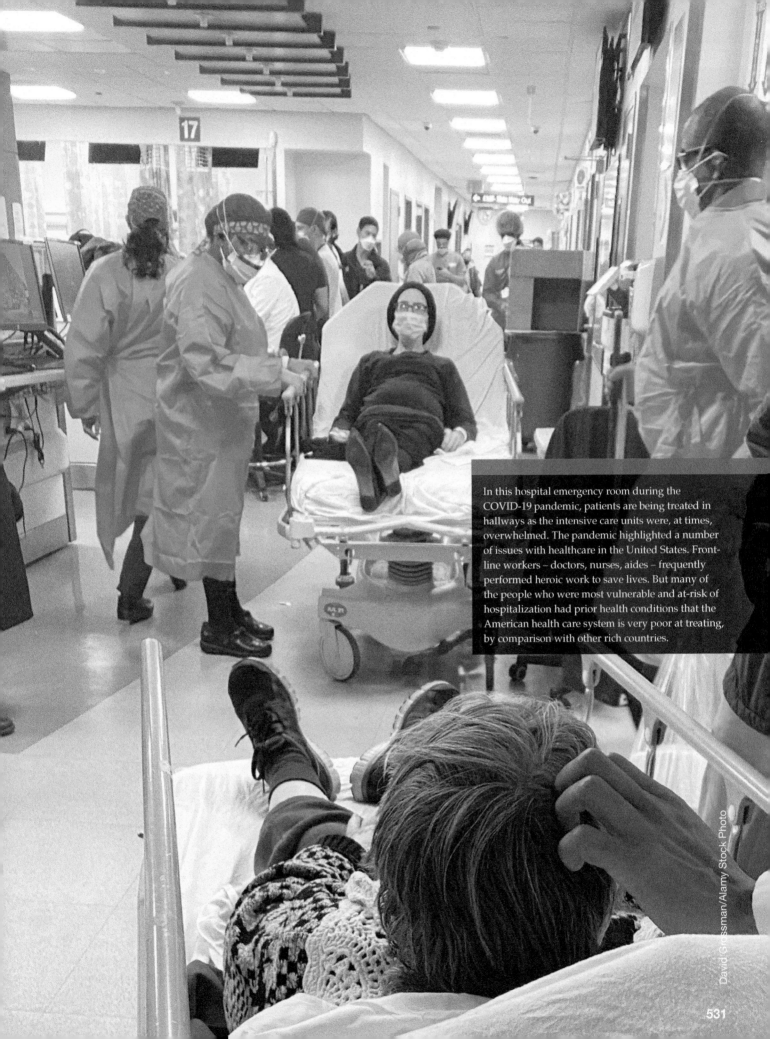

In this hospital emergency room during the COVID-19 pandemic, patients are being treated in hallways as the intensive care units were, at times, overwhelmed. The pandemic highlighted a number of issues with healthcare in the United States. Front-line workers – doctors, nurses, aides – frequently performed heroic work to save lives. But many of the people who were most vulnerable and at-risk of hospitalization had prior health conditions that the American health care system is very poor at treating, by comparison with other rich countries.

David Grossman/Alamy Stock Photo

My Sociological Imagination

JENNIFER JENNINGS

I grew up in suburban New Jersey and, after graduating from college, taught high school English and social studies in urban public high schools. My students were overwhelmingly poor, and I recognized that many of their problems succeeding in school stemmed from health issues they faced on a day-to-day basis. Though my research in graduate school initially focused on education, the insight I had as a teacher led me back to studying health and education disparities. My current work in this area focuses on the effects of one's state of birth on his or her mortality and morbidity as an adult, as well as how systems that measure hospitals based on their patients' outcomes affect the quality of care that patients receive.

Table 19.1 COVID-19 Mortality in the United States Compared with That of Other Countries

		Table 1. COVID-19 Mortality in the US Compared With That of Other Countries[a]			
		COVID-19 Deaths per 100000			
Country	Date COVID-19 Cases Surpassed 1 per Million	Since the Start of the Pandemic	Since May 10, 2020	Since June 7, 2020	Excess U.S. COVID-19 Deaths (as of Sept 2020)
Low Mortality (COVID-19 Deaths, <5/100000)					
South Korea	2/20/20	0.7	0.2	0.2	196161 (99)
Japan	2/23/20	1.2	0.7	0.5	194711 (98)
Australia	3/1/20	3.3	2.9	2.9	187661 (94)
Moderate Mortality (COVID-19 Deaths, 5-25/100000)					
Norway	2/29/20	5.0	1.0	0.5	182099 (92)
Finland	3/2/20	6.1	1.4	0.3	178373 (90)
Austria	3/1/20	8.6	1.7	1.0	170247 (86)
Denmark	3/4/20	10.9	2.1	0.8	162600 (82)
Germany	3/1/20	11.3	2.4	0.9	161393 (81)
Israel	3/2/20	14.0	11.2	10.6	152393 (77)
Switzerland	2/29/20	20.6	2.8	1.2	130654 (66)
Canada	3/6/20	24.6	12.4	4.0	117622 (59)
High Mortality (COVID-19 Deaths, >25/100000)					
The Netherlands	3/3/20	36.2	5.2	1.5	79318 (40)
France	3/1/20	46.6	7.5	3.2	45142 (23)
Sweden	2/29/20	57.4	23.5	10.3	9581 (5)
Italy	2/3/20	59.1	9.1	3.1	4136 (2)
United Kingdom	3/3/20	62.6	16.3	5.0	−7459 (−4)
Spain	2/29/20	65.0	8.6	4.6	−15204 (−8)
Belgium	3/2/20	86.8	12.4	4.2	−87057 (−44)
United States	3/7/20	60.3	36.9	27.2	

[a] Data on coronavirus disease 2019 (COVID-19) deaths are from February 13, 2020, through September 19, 2020 (n = 198589 US deaths). In columns 4-6, due to large sample sizes, all mortality rates are statistically significantly different from the corresponding US mortality rates (*P* < .001). Scenarios in the last 3 columns assume that compared with the country in a given row, (A) the US had a comparable cumulative mortality rate; (B) the US mortality rate was unchanged until May 10 (n = 77180 deaths), when it become comparable to the other country's death rate; and (C) the US mortality rate was unchanged until June 7 (n = 109143 deaths), when it became comparable to the other country's death rate.

SOURCE: Bilinski and Emanuel, 2020.

This raises an important sociological question: What are the social factors that caused so many more people in the United States to die from COVID-19 as compared to similar countries before the arrival of vaccines? This is a puzzle that gets right to the heart of what a sociological analysis of health and medical care attempts to understand. We need, in short, a **social autopsy** to fully understand exactly what happened—in other words, unlike a medical autopsy that focuses on the causes of the death of an individual, we need to understand the broader societal factors that have led to so many deaths

(Klinenberg 2002). For example, careful analyses have found that governmental organizations in the United States were deficient in their handling of the virus in a variety of ways. These failures need to be analyzed carefully and understood so that the same mistakes are not repeated during a future pandemic.

But the sources of excess deaths are not *just* about government failures, however important those might be. The political opponents of former President Donald Trump sometimes seemed to want to put all blame on the White House. A sociological approach, however, must also consider the ways that Americans may have other vulnerabilities that are higher than people in other countries. In particular, because the United States, unlike all other similar rich countries, does not provide guaranteed health care for all citizens, millions of Americans do not regularly see a doctor and may have had untreated conditions that made them more vulnerable to virus. In the early days of the pandemic (in the spring of 2020), lack of high-quality health insurance meant that some people even had to pay to get tested for the virus, something that many poor people could not afford and which was unheard of in other similar countries. Further, the United States has higher levels of inequality and more people living in poverty than other similar countries (see Chapter 11 for more details). Individuals living in poor households are more likely to have other health issues that can make them susceptible to COVID-19.

A social autopsy would also go beyond health issues to consider the broader social context in which the virus landed. America is a country with high levels of **individualism**, the belief that people should take care of themselves and that the government should minimally intrude on their personal freedoms (Bellah et al. 1985; Lipset 1996). Every competent scientific analysis showed that there was one extremely effective way to reduce the spread of the virus in public settings: by wearing a mask. But many Americans, supported by anti-science political leaders, rejected these calls, believing that the recommendations of public health scientists were optional or flawed. When vaccines became available, many Americans refused to get one, even though the vaccines were safe and effective. In countries with stronger collectivist traditions—in which people are more comfortable relying on government institutions to provide protection against unexpected risks—the idea of working together to solve problems is more common. In these countries, more people wore masks in public and saw it as a collective responsibility to keep everyone safe, and when vaccines arrived almost everyone took them. In other words, there were multiple societal reasons why living in the United States increased the risk of dying from COVID-19: government policy, societal inequality, and social attitudes all play a role.

The link between social structure and health is where sociologists and other social scientists have made distinctive contributions to understanding individual well-being. In recent years, the wider medical community has begun to recognize these vital contributions. For example, a basic knowledge of sociology is now part of the examination that students aspiring to go to medical school all take (the Medical College Admissions Test, or MCAT). Health, in other words, is partly a matter for physicians and medical scientists, but *also* is impacted by many of the core themes that sociology focuses on. In this chapter, we will use a variety of sociological theories and insights to explore some of the social dimensions of health and medical care.

The Big Questions

1. **How do social contexts affect health?** We often think of health outcomes as the result of individual choices. In this section, we explore how social contexts affect our health behaviors and how events that happen throughout our lives affect our health as adults. The relationships we have with others also play an important role in determining whether we engage in positive health behaviors.

2. **Who gets sick, and why?** Low socioeconomic status is a strong predictor of poor health. Highly educated people, or people with higher incomes, are more likely to live a longer and healthier life than people who are not. This has been true throughout history and across many different countries. We explore why these patterns persist and the major explanations that sociologists have advanced to explain them.

3. **How does physician/patient interaction affect health and illness?** Few relationships produce more fraught interactions than that between doctors and patients. For a century, physicians dominated the relationship with their patients. Today, however, many people and experts are beginning to question what that relationship should look like. Patients ultimately know their own body as well as anyone else, and there is a growing realization that patients can provide valuable opinions and participate in their care.

4. **What is the relationship between epidemics and societies?** COVID-19 is the latest of many diseases that have killed large numbers of people throughout history. Societal responses to the appearance of these diseases have been remarkably similar, but their impact is much greater in some places more than others.

5. **Why is health care in America so much more expensive than in other countries?** No matter how researchers calculate what the United States spends on health care, it is far more expensive than in any other country. In this section, we explore the possible explanations for the high cost of health care in the United States and whether the system can be fixed.

adriaticfoto/Shutterstock

AnnaStills/Alamy Stock Photo

BIG QUESTION 19.1 How Do Social Contexts Affect Health?

A SOCIOLOGICAL VIEW OF HEALTH

When you walk into a doctor's office with a few worrisome symptoms—let's say a cough and some difficulty breathing—your doctor may ask you about how you've been eating, whether you smoke, whether you've been exercising, and about your family history. Maybe you admit that you've been skipping the gym, and perhaps it's true that you have been more stressed than usual at work. You walk away with a prescription to fill and perhaps a lecture to take better care of yourself in order to calm your cough.

In treating patients, doctors are interested in the immediate causes of illness that can be remedied with medical treatments. They focus on why you got this illness at this time. The cause of your poor health could lie deep in your past—for example, perhaps you lived in a polluted city as a child—but in their offices, they attempt to address the immediate symptoms rather than to consider their social causes.

Sociologists take a different approach to the study of health. They focus on the social causes of disease within a population rather than on the immediate causes of an individual's illness. Sociologists want to know why people in some neighborhoods, communities, or countries are much more likely to die early than people living in other places, or why poor people consistently die earlier than more affluent people. Sociologists also consider how social contexts shape individual health behaviors. When studying a patient with a respiratory issue, such as asthma, sociologists will look beyond the individual's behaviors (do they smoke or vape?), or their family history and genetics, to explain why an individual is having a problem. Some health conditions, like asthma or obesity, have actually gotten worse in recent decades. These outcomes can't be solely because people have less willpower or different genes than they did 50 or 100 years ago. So we need to ask about social and environmental factors. How about the quality of the air we breathe? Or the disposal of toxic wastes in certain communities? Poverty is closely associated with the risk

of becoming asthmatic; poor children both live in more toxic environments and are exposed to more stress in their lives, which may reduce their ability to fight off asthma. Children growing up in poor countries are also much less likely to receive high-quality health care and interventions that might help minimize emerging asthmatic conditions. In short, asthma is both a condition experienced by individual children and a *social* problem.

Similarly, in examining the question of why obesity rates have grown so rapidly in recent decades and are so much higher in the United States than in most other similar countries, sociologists focus on how the social contexts of behavior may lead individuals to eat more than is healthy and/or exercise less. Some social forces are well-known: Most people use cars to get around; sit at a desk all day instead of doing any kind of physical labor; spend more time looking at their computer, television, and/or phones; and frequent fast food chains. There are other, less discussed social forces as well. One line of research examines the invention and mass production of highly addictive processed foods high in sugar and carbohydrates, and how the pressure brought by the large companies making these products to market and sell them has influenced and manipulated consumers (Nestle 2002, 2018). Or consider this question: Americans are much more likely to be overweight than the Japanese. Why? One well-established finding is because of the kinds of diets that the Japanese and Americans typically consume. The Japanese diet includes much more fish and vegetables than the meat- and processed-food-based diet of many Americans. Instead of asking, "Why is this individual person overweight?" the sociological question is: "Why does the average American consume a less healthy diet than the average Japanese?"

The Population as Patient

19.1.1 Describe the population model of prevention.

In contemporary medical science, most approaches to studying health focus on individuals, for example their genetic risk factors or their behaviours that put them at risk (such as smoking cigarettes or drinking heavily). The sociological approach to improving health differs from the medical approach. Getting fewer people to become sick in the first place, however, might require a different strategy. We need to think not just about individuals but entire populations.

How could that be possible? Most risk factors, like blood pressure, have no clear cutoff above which high blood pressure leads to a stroke or a heart attack. Your risk increases as your blood pressure increases. The medical field necessarily establishes arbitrary cutoff points on a continuum that determine when you should receive treatment for high blood pressure (hypertension). We give people drugs for hypertension over a certain cutoff and keep an eye on those individuals right below that cutoff.

The trouble is that high-risk groups make up a small fraction of the overall population. But as the example of hypertension makes clear, health risks operate on a continuum; they are not an either/or phenomenon. Most of the cases of stroke don't come from people at high risk of hypertension but from those who had much less but still elevated blood pressure. For that reason, the English epidemiologist Geoffrey Rose influentially argued in the 1980s that we could save more lives by decreasing everyone's blood pressure a little bit than by reducing the blood pressure of the most high-risk cases (**epidemiology** is the

study of health in population subgroups, or populations as a whole). This is often referred to as the *population model for prevention*, and it focuses on "shifting the distribution of risk" (Rose 1985). Is this possible?

Shifting health risks at the population level is difficult, however, as it means changing common social practices. But there are ways of making that happen. Rising taxes on cigarettes have made smoking a very expensive habit, and far fewer people in the United States smoke today compared to a few decades ago (the taxes help to offset the costs of treating lung cancer and other health problems). Less common are taxes on high-sugar food products, which only a few places have tried to implement. Further, in several cities and states, chain restaurants are now required to list the number of calories in each food item on their menu. The goal of this policy is to encourage consumers to choose healthier options and to create pressure for businesses to offer them. In theory, if they were aware that a typical muffin has more than 400 calories, for example, the average consumer should have tools to make healthier choices and consume fewer calories. By changing features of the social environment and treating the population as the patient, these initiatives are examples of the population model of prevention.

In 2009, the California State Legislature passed laws banning the sale of sugar-sweetened soda in public schools, and many other states and school districts have since adopted similar measures. The hope was that this change would reduce consumption of these drinks and encourage healthier habits among children and ultimately reduce the risk for obesity for all school-aged children.

monkeybusinessimages/iStock/Getty Images

The Effects of Social Contexts on Individual Behavior

19.1.2 Discuss how our social contexts and relationships help to determine the health choices we make.

So how exactly do social forces influence our health? Suicide provides an interesting example. On its face, suicide is the most individual of acts. In the late nineteenth century, however, French sociologist Emile Durkheim sought to understand how suicide rates differed across social groups and how social change affected rates of suicide. In his book *Suicide* (Durkheim [1897] 2006), he showed that suicide rates are affected by such things as religion, gender, being in certain organizations such as the military, or living in certain regions or countries.

One of Durkheim's most paradoxical results was that close-knit communities could be either helpful or harmful in causing suicides. Social ties not only integrate individuals but regulate their behavior. Durkheim argued that, without these ties, individuals' desires could exceed their ability to fulfill them and thus lead to higher suicide rates. In *either* communities that are very well integrated, and people know one another well, *or* places where people are very disconnected from one another, more people are likely to commit suicide. Strongly integrated groups benefited from the sense of inclusion that strong social ties foster. But Durkheim also showed that *too much* integration is also associated with higher rates of suicide, as group needs take precedence over individuals' needs or desires.

Similar to Durkheim, contemporary sociologists recognize that the contexts that people inhabit and the relationships they have with others play an important role in shaping the choices that they make. They ask what features of social contexts enable or constrain particular behaviors. Sociologists examine how norms around behavior may affect individuals' choices. For example, norms about binge drinking appear to vary across age groups. Twenty-six percent of 18- to 24-year-olds report binge drinking (defined as more than four drinks for women and more than five drinks for men on one or more occasions in the last 30 days). For those 65 and older, that number drops to only 4 percent (Centers for Disease Control and Prevention [CDC] 2012).

How might social contexts contribute to age differences in binge drinking? Social contexts shape what counts as "normal" behavior and what behaviors are socially sanctioned or accepted. College dorms provide an example. If most of the students in a dorm binge drink on the weekends, it's more likely that if you are living in this dorm, you will, too. Social contexts also provide opportunities for engaging in binge-drinking behaviors. If you can walk down your hallway to a party where binge drinking is happening, it's simply easier (and probably tempting) to engage in that behavior than if you have to actively seek out opportunities to binge drink. Some social contexts like colleges can also create stress that leads people to engage in health-risking behaviors to alleviate it. Binge drinking, which may alleviate stress in the short term but cause negative health outcomes in the long term, is just one example of a coping behavior influenced by social context. Figure 19.1 shows some group differences in binge drinking. It is surprising to note that higher earners and people who have been to college are more likely to binge drink. On most health indicators, people with more education are less likely to engage in risky behaviour. This may reflect habits learned while attending college, where binge drinking is very common.

The relationships we have with others also impact the choices we make. Our social relationships affect our health in three major ways: Through social influence, person-to-person contact, and participation in social networks (Smith and Christakis 2008). Obesity provides one example of social influence. While obesity is often thought of as a result of choices that we privately make, most eating is social. Imagine that the person across the table from you decides to order the all-you-can-eat buffet. Because it is more convenient for your meal if you both order from the buffet, you probably follow your friend. If your friend goes back for a second and third helping, you might be less shy about doing the same. Sociologists have in fact produced empirical evidence that suggests that people who are obese are more likely to have friends who are also obese (Christakis and Fowler 2007). In this case, it is especially complicated to determine whether the friends are causing the behavior or if the people with weight issues choose to associate with similar people to find acceptance (it is often said that "birds of a feather flock together"). Either way, however, it is likely that these relationships may be a contributing factor.

Social context is also important for the spread of infectious diseases. The people with whom we ride the bus or sit next to at work or at a concert or sporting event can have an important impact on our health. The outbreak and spread of deadly viruses like COVID-19, or even the flu virus (influenza) every year, highlight how forms of person-to-person contact can spread disease, and more generally how societal conditions contribute to the spread of disease. We are social beings. It matters for our health.

The Accumulation of Health Risks Over the Life Course

19.1.3 Explain how sociologists use life-course perspectives to examine health issues.

Another way in which social contexts influence health is that what happens at one stage of our lives can impact later health. For example, babies who weigh too little when they

Figure 19.1 Prevalence of Binge Drinking Among Adults

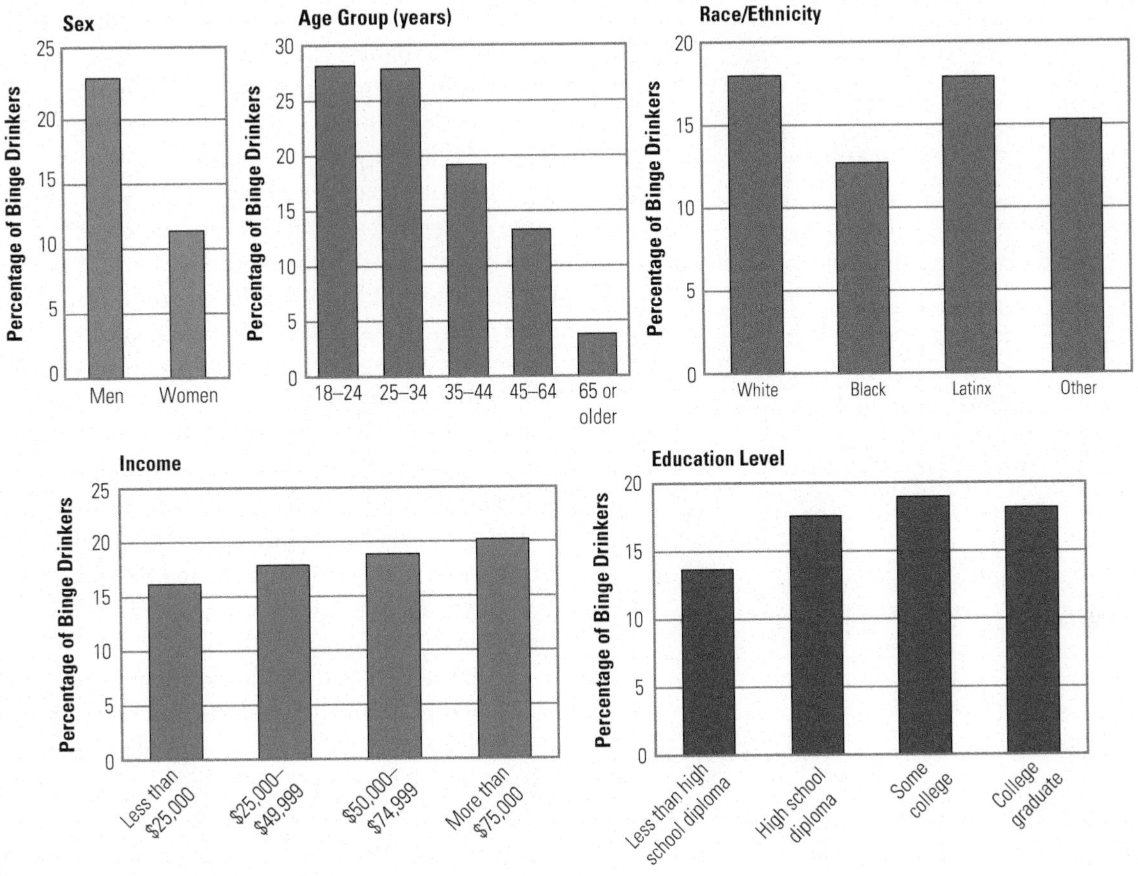

Sex

Age Group (years)

Race/Ethnicity

Income

Education Level

SOURCE: Centers for Disease Control and Prevention, 2012.

were born are more likely to have a range of health problems as they age. Because poor early health conditions may be as important as later health behaviors, sociologists consider how events occurring now and in the past affect your health.

An unusual natural experiment during World War II provided some of the most compelling evidence we have about the accumulation of health risks across the life course. In the late fall of 1944, Germans placed a ban on food transports to the Netherlands (a country occupied by the German army), leading to a rapid decrease of food supplies in the country. As a result, daily adult rations decreased from 1,800 calories in December 1943 to just 400 to 800 calories between December 1944 and April 1945 to (Roseboom et al. 2006).

The Dutch famine predictably had catastrophic human consequences; by its end, more than 18,000 people had died. But it had an unintended effect, however—it gave social scientists the opportunity to understand how events that happen early in our lives may affect our long-term health outcomes. Sociologists studying the Dutch famine made a fascinating observation: People born during the height of the famine were more likely to have heart disease. When we think about the causes of having heart disease as an adult, we generally think about how our behavior during adulthood affects that outcome: How much exercise we get, how stressful our lives are, how well we manage our cholesterol levels, and so forth. But investigations of the Dutch case revealed something else: What happens *in utero* can have enduring consequences (Torche 2019). The exact timing of exposure to the famine mattered, however—those exposed during the first three months of gestation were more likely to develop heart disease, while those exposed later were less likely to have these issues.

The example of the Dutch famine illustrates a more general lesson: The social contexts we inhabit at different stages throughout our lives affect our later health outcomes. Sociologists refer to this as a **life-course perspective** on health. Of particular interest are the long-term impacts of adverse childhood conditions, which can have negative effects on health long after they are no longer experienced. Increasingly sociologists are thinking about health in a life-course framework. For example, rather than only examining the effects of being obese as an adult, they focus on the cumulative effects of obesity as a child, as a teenager, and as a young adult on adult health outcomes. As Table 19.2

Table 19.2 Life-Course Perspective on Health

Sensitive-Period Model (or Latency Model)	In this model, very early life exposures can affect adult outcomes but may remain latent for years. Trying to improve health in adulthood does not work if the damage is already done. The idea is that things that happen to you even before you were born—that is, while you were in your mother's womb (such as the Dutch famine)—can have long-term implications for your adult health outcomes, but their effects do not show up for a long time.
Cumulative-Exposure Model	Smoking may provide the best example of this model. If you are a smoker, you accumulate exposure to carcinogens over a long period of time. Each cigarette adds up, and by the time you are older, you are more likely to have emphysema and lung cancer if you have exposed yourself to these carcinogens over a longer period of time.
Social-Trajectory Model	Where an individual ends up in the social pecking order influences health outcomes. For example, if you are sick as a child, you may do more poorly in school. As a result, you are less likely to go to college and thus less likely to get a good-paying job. Because you may end up working in a job that does not provide health insurance or you may not be able to afford health care, your health could be further negatively affected.

illustrates, sociologists study three types of life-course models.

As individuals, the lesson is that continually putting off improvements in health behaviors to some future date will eventually create additional health issues. At the level of whole populations, the lesson is that intervening as early as possible in a child's life is a great way to reduce the cost of health care as people age. It is why most countries, including the United States, have programs designed to provide extra health benefits to pregnant women and infants after birth. Although the ways in which health risks accumulate over a lifetime are different, they also point to how differences in health care across countries can lead to very different outcomes, as we will see in the next section.

Differences in Health Outcomes Between Countries

19.1.4 Explain why where you live impacts your health.

Imagine you were to enter a lottery. Unlike the lotteries most of us are familiar with, where hard cash or prizes are awarded, this lottery would determine the country in which you would be born. By sheer luck of the draw, you could be born in the United States, where less than 1 percent of babies die in their first year of life. Or you could be born in Afghanistan or Angola, where more than 1 in 10 babies do not survive until their first birthday (World Health Organization 2011).

These are extreme differences. Do we still see such large differences in health outcomes when we compare countries similar in income and development? Let's consider the United States and Europe, which are alike in many ways. The life expectancy at birth of most Europeans is longer than that of Americans. A significant part of that difference is driven by the fact that Americans are more likely to die by age 50 because of factors such as infant mortality, murder, motor vehicle accidents, and drug-related mortality (National Research Council and Institute of Medicine 2013). Do our biological differences cause this difference? That is unlikely. What are Americans doing that shortens our lives compared to Europeans?

Social scientists use a range of measures to track the health status of entire populations. Because health has many different facets, each of these measures provides a snapshot of a different piece of the health puzzle, and we want to look at a variety of different measures to see how well a country's health care system is working for its citizens. Yet, for reasons we will explore more fully later in the chapter, no matter how the numbers are cut, Americans live shorter, less healthy lives than we should expect based on the wealth of the country. For more information, examine the data in Table 19.3 for 21 different countries on several different measures.

Though many factors contribute to differences in health across countries, research consistently shows that at least part of the blame is on the health care system itself. And here an important puzzle arises. Americans pay far more than other countries for health care; it is the most expensive health care system in the world by a large margin. Yet Americans have worse health outcomes than many other similar countries. Some of the problems may be due to lack of access to the health care system, while other factors are public health issues such as a poor diet or a toxin-filled environment, while yet other issues may be related to other social inequalities. We will explore the issues with the American health care system in more detail later in the chapter.

Table 19.3 World Health Measures

These recent data show that the United States had a higher rate of preventable deaths, more infant mortality, lower healthy life expectancy at age 60, and higher mortality (death) rates than almost all of the countries in this 21-country comparison, ranking 16th out of 21 countries, worse than a number of much poorer countries (for example, Cuba, Poland) and only better than countries much poorer than the United States.

Country	Norway	Sweden	Switzerland	Israel	France	Australia	Republic of Korea	Netherlands	Canada	New Zealand	Germany	United Kingdom	Poland	Cuba	Estonia	United States	Turkey	Mexico	Vietnam	Indonesia	Sudan
	1	2	3	4	5	6	7	8	9	10	11	12	13	14	15	16	17	18	19	20	21
Overall Ranking Excluding Preventable Deaths	1	2	3	4	5	6	7	8	9	10	11	12	13	14	15	16	17	18	19	20	21
Overall Ranking Including Preventable Deaths (Based on Mean of All Applicable Rankings)	2	1	3	6	4	5	8	7	9	11	10	12	13	14	15	16	17	18	19	20	21
Mortality Amenable to Health Care (Deaths per 100,000)*	64	61	*	87.5	55	57	84	66	77	79	76	83	*	*	194.5	96	*	*	*	*	*
Ranking	4	3	*	11	1	2	10	5	7	8	6	9	*	*	13	12	*	*	*	*	*
Infant Mortality**	2.2	2.3	3.7	3.3	3.4	4.1	3.3	3.4	4.7	4.7	3.4	4.1	4	4	2.9	6	12.2	13.9	18.4	43.8	49.3
Ranking	1	2	9	5	6	12	4	7	14	15	8	13	10	11	3	16	17	18	19	20	21
Health Life Expectancy at Age 60 (Average of Men and Women)**	24	24	25	24	25	25	24	24	25	25	24	24	24	22	21	23	21	22	22	18	17
Ranking	6	7	2	9	1	3	8	10	4	5	11	13	12	15	18	14	19	16	17	20	21
Adult Mortality Rate**	59	56	54	55	80	60	69	63	68	67	72	73	125	100	133	103	112	132	131	152	245
Ranking	4	3	1	2	12	5	9	6	8	7	10	11	16	13	19	14	15	18	17	20	21
Health Expenditures Per Capita (PPP)**	$5,391	$3,760	$5,297	$2,041	$3,997	$3,685	$2,035	$5,112	$4,443	$2,992	$4,342	$3,433	$1,377	$414	$1,294	$8,233	$1,039	$962	$216	$123	$162

* Data not available.

** Data taken from World Health Organization, Global Health Observatory Data Repository, http://apps.who.int/gho/data/node.main.

SOURCE: Davis et al. 2014; World Health Organization, Global Health Observatory Data Repository.

Prostock-studio/Alamy Stock Photo

BIG QUESTION 19.2 Who Gets Sick, and Why?

HEALTH OUTCOMES AMONG DIFFERENT GROUPS

In the previous section, we introduced the idea that social contexts matter for health outcomes. Now we will consider how individual factors, such as class, education, race, and gender, interact with the social contexts in which people live and influence health outcomes.

Health and Socioeconomic Status

19.2.1 Explain how socioeconomic status affects health.

What are the strongest predictors of one's health? One guess, at least in the United States, where health insurance is not universal for all citizens, would be whether you have health insurance (or the quality of your insurance plan if you do). Or perhaps it's whether or not you smoke, what you eat, or how often you exercise. An extraordinarily strong predictor of one's health is your **socioeconomic status (SES)** (Adler and Ostrove 1999). In the way social scientists define it, SES combines multiple dimensions of social and economic status: Typically education, income, and occupation. If you are highly educated, you are more likely to live a longer and healthier life than those who are not. The same is true of income and occupation. If you work in a job that has you working behind a desk all day, you are likelier to live longer than someone who performs physical labor all day. Similarly, having more income helps; you will have better access to quality health care, especially when it comes to mental health services. So when researchers talk about **health disparities**, they mean differences in health status linked to social,

economic, or environmental conditions. In other words, SES, race and ethnicity, gender, and place of residence all produce significant health disparities.

The connection between one's social status and health is one of the most consistent findings in all of the social sciences. It holds across every time period of history and place that has been studied, whether the leading causes of death are infectious diseases like tuberculosis or chronic diseases like heart disease (Marmot 2004). Social status matters beyond being poor. There is a clear **socioeconomic gradient in health**, which means that those with lowest SES are less healthy than those in the middle, who are less healthy than those at the top.

The idea of SES as a **fundamental social cause** of health attempts to explain the persistence of the association of health and SES across time and place (Link and Phelan 1995). Over time, risk factors for poor health have changed considerably. Health information, such as the relationship between smoking and poor health, are now much more widely known. Technologies such as intensive care for premature infants have become more widely available, in principle to everyone. So why is it the case that higher SES people continue to enjoy better health?

Fundamental social cause theory holds that higher SES individuals have access to knowledge, money, power, and social connections that can be deployed throughout their lives to avoid disease and death. All of these resources can be deployed in a range of situations, including when it comes to health. As a result, this theory predicts that no matter what the causes of bad health, socioeconomic gradients will emerge.

The theory of fundamental causes blends the multiple dimensions of SES. However, SES is multifaceted, and each of these measures of SES has a different relationship to health. For example, the mechanisms that link education to health may not be the same as those that link occupation and health. Another concern is that the causal relationship between SES and health may differ across these measures. It could be the case that poorer health is a cause of lower occupational status. Finally, different dimensions of SES may matter differently throughout the life course. Financial resources may be particularly important at some times, but education may be more important in others.

Next we review the evidence linking each of these components of SES, and some others as well, to health outcomes in the United States.

Education

19.2.2 Discuss the relationship between education and health.

People with more education live longer, healthier lives, but does having more years of education *cause* better health? Because individuals play a strong role in choosing the amount of education they get, it could be that healthier people choose to—or are able to—attend school for longer. On the other hand, those with more education use drugs and tobacco less (although they are more likely to binge drink, as we saw earlier). Even for people with the same income, those with more education use preventative health care more, and they do a better job of managing existing conditions—for example, remembering to take their medications. They may also be better at managing their own care, a topic we will discuss later in the chapter.

Researchers have used a number of creative natural experiments to establish that the level of education individuals have is associated with their health. Some of the best-known studies rely on changes in compulsory education laws. Compulsory education laws determine at which age students can stop going to school. Early in the twentieth century, states varied widely in the number of years of education they required. Over time, states began to increase the number of years students were required to attend. When these laws changed, students were required to get more years of education than their peers who were slightly ahead of them in school. But there is no reason to believe that these laws changed because health was improving, so they provide an ideal setting to determine whether getting more education by itself *improves* health. These studies find that students who attended school for more years had higher survival rates as adults. This finding is very powerful, suggesting that education does in fact have a direct effect on health (Lleras-Muney 2005).

Overall, the better health behaviors of the more educated can explain as much as 40 percent of their health advantage (Cutler et al. 2008). But scholars continue to debate why more education leads to better health behaviors. A few possibilities exist. First, it may be that education improves one's ability to understand health information, which leads to better behavior. Second, education may improve one's ability to self-govern, which may equip those with more education to change their health behaviors when necessary. Third, family income explains some of the association between education and health (as individuals and households with more education tend to have higher incomes and can afford better quality health care). Finally, a central component of fundamental cause theory holds that high SES allows individuals to take advantage of new advances in medical technology. Better educated people are more likely to be aware of advances in medical science and better able to do their own research on health issues when they arise, and, as a result, can seek out better care.

Why do people with more education have better health? Do they take better care of themselves? Do they have better quality health insurance? Are they more capable of getting quality medical care by researching options more thoroughly? This is a widely debated question.

Income and Wealth

19.2.3 Discuss the impact that income and wealth have on children's health.

People with higher incomes also have better health (even taking into account educational level). Determining the relationship between income and health is even more complicated than in the case of education. Because education largely happens early in the life course, getting educated generally happens well before the onset of poor health. In contrast, health can affect one's income because it affects participation in the labor force, so the relationship can work in both directions. For example, people who are sick or disabled may work fewer hours or retire earlier, both of which will reduce their income and wealth. Or they may be poor and unable to afford needed health care, especially if they don't have health insurance.

One way in which income and wealth clearly matter, however, is in how they affect children's health. Parents with more income can purchase more nutritious food and provide safer environments and better medical care for their children, from pregnancy to adulthood. The effects of family income on child health, moreover, appear to increase as a child ages (Case et al. 2002). That is, the difference of the health of poorer and more affluent children is greater later in childhood. Chronic conditions, such as asthma, become more common as children age. Families with more resources can use them to control these health conditions and minimize their effects.

A good example of the importance of family resources in childhood can be seen in the case of **autism**, a condition that makes it difficult to communicate and interact with others. Current estimates are that about 1 in 54 children have some degree of autism, although that is a crude statistic: The range of an "autism" diagnosis is very large, from mild to severe. As researchers have learned more about autism, it has become clear that early intervention (including early diagnosis) and taking active steps to help a child through a range of services in and out of schools can make a huge difference in how they develop and in their ability to lead productive lives. Autism is found among all groups, but children whose parents have more income and education are significantly more likely to be properly diagnosed and receive high-quality treatment than children from less privileged families, as a group of researchers reported in an important paper (Durkin et al. 2017).

Race and Ethnic Differences in Health

19.2.4 Discuss sociological explanations for health disparities among racial groups.

On almost every health measure, Black Americans have worse health outcomes than White Americans. This long-standing difference has been the subject of an enormous amount of research. Black Americans live almost five fewer years than White Americans, although that difference was twice as large in 1950 (and it was about 15 years for people born in 1900; Friedman 2014). Babies born to Black women are more than two times more likely to die before age 1 than those born to White women. Blacks also have higher rates of chronic conditions; for example, they are twice as likely to have high blood pressure (CDC 2011).

Four main arguments have been offered to account for these often very large differences. The oldest set of explanations, now discredited, focused on genetics: The idea that Whites are biologically predisposed to live longer or be healthier than Blacks. This argument can be traced to the pre–Civil War debate about slavery. Science played an important role in those early debates as medical evidence was called on to determine whether Blacks were biologically inferior to Whites and only capable of being enslaved (Krieger 1987). The "scientific" basis for these claims has, however, been discredited, and current research in genetics now shows that the study of human diversity is not well captured by socially constructed racial groups (see Chapter 13 for more details).

If a biological explanation no longer has a firm foundation, what are the alternatives? There are three major theories in the contemporary literature:

1. *Racial differences really represent class differences.* Blacks have worse health care than Whites because, on average, they have fewer

Affluent parents can ensure that their children receive prompt medical attention when/if problems arise. People without high-quality health insurance or the means to pay for specialized treatment may not be able to have their children treated in the same way.

Adam Gault/Science Photo Library/Alamy Stock Photo

years of education, lower incomes, and different jobs. If this argument were true, however, there would be no racial differences in health between Whites and Blacks once we control for SES. Research consistently shows that in fact the Black disadvantages in health remain even after these controls are introduced. In other words, poor Blacks have worse health care than equally poor Whites, and middle-class Blacks are worse off than middle-class Whites. These results suggest that we need to identify the causes beyond class or SES.

2. *Exposure to discrimination and racism in everyday life may increase stress.* When the body mobilizes its responses to stress too often, it loses its ability to regulate itself, which leaves the body at an increased risk for disease. Stress may also lead to the adoption of coping behaviors, such as eating or drinking, that have negative effects on health. Residential segregation, for example, (Pattillo-McCoy 1999) is a potential contributor to greater stress.

3. *Differences in the quality of health care received.* Although hospitals and medical care providers today are required to make every effort to treat all patients the same, there remains the potential for differential treatment. For example, consider cardiovascular disease, a leading cause of death. It is well documented that Black patients who come to the hospital with a heart attack are less likely to get certain treatments, such as bypass surgery. These racial disparities can't be explained by differences in health insurance or health status (Institute of Medicine 2002). Racial disparities in care are not limited to invasive surgical procedures, as persistent racial disparities exist in the provision of basic therapies such as aspirin (Barnato et al. 2005). Exactly why Blacks continue to receive less high-quality health care than Whites in the post–civil rights era remains a puzzle. Some scholars believe that a persistent pattern of racial disadvantage systematically channels non-White patients to lower quality hospitals and doctors. An alternate account draws on the fact that Black patients are treated in a small number of hospitals—for example, 85 percent of all Black heart attack patients are treated in only 1,000, mostly urban, hospitals (Chandra 2009), while only 40 percent of all White heart attack patients are treated in those hospitals. The likelihood of being treated in an over-taxed urban hospital is potentially one important source of racial disparities in health care (Skinner et al. 2005).

While the Black/White difference in health outcomes is large, it is not the case that White Americans have better health on every outcome. One example is suicide (see

Figure 19.2 Number of Suicides by Race

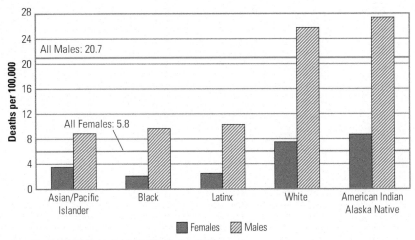

SOURCE: CDC/NCHS, National Vital Statistics, 2014.

Figure 19.2). Whites have substantially higher suicide rates, at 24 per 100,000 for White men, compared with 10 for Black and Latinx men, and 8 for Asian American/Pacific Islander men (CDC 2011). The reasons why the suicide rate is so much higher among Whites is something of a puzzle.

The story about racial differences in health poses one other startling puzzle: Latinx Americans, especially those who were born in another country, have better health outcomes than Whites born in the U.S. On average, immigrant Latinxs live about 2 years longer than Whites, a phenomenon known as the **Hispanic paradox** as that is what it is called in the literature (Elo et al. 2004). Many explanations have been offered for this finding, and researchers continue to debate its causes. One explanation is the idea that people who migrate are healthier to begin with. Another points to the better health behaviors of Latinxs; for example, they are substantially less likely to smoke than Blacks or Whites (American Lung Association 2012). Whatever its causes, the Hispanic paradox is a startling example of substantial variation in racial and ethnic disparities across groups and across diseases.

Gender

19.2.5 Identify explanations for gender differences in health.

Gender differences in health present a challenge to the idea that more resources equal better health. Although women tend to have fewer resources than men, they live approximately five years longer than men, and in the U.S. it was as high as eight years in the 1970s (Read and Gorman 2010; National Center for Health Statistics 2011). And even though there is a four-year difference between White and Black women, Black women have been outliving White men since the 1970s. Figure 19.3 shows these differences, and how they have changed over time.

What drives this very large difference? Men tend to engage in more risky behaviors, which make them more

Figure 19.3 Changes in Life Expectancy from 1900 to 2011 by Race and Gender

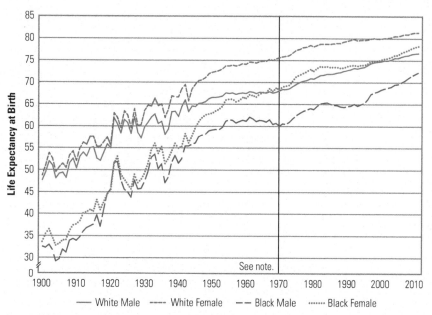

Y-axis: Life Expectancy at Birth

Legend: —— White Male · · · · White Female – – Black Male ······· Black Female

NOTE: Prior to 1970, data for the black population are not available. Data show 1900–1969 are for the nonwhite population.

SOURCE: Arias, 2015.

likely to die. The most important of these "risky" behaviors around the world are wars, but men also have higher rates of fatal accidents and are more likely to be the victim of a homicide. Men with chronic diseases also tend to have more life-threatening ones such as heart disease and cancer, while women tend to suffer from less deadly chronic conditions like arthritis, anxiety, and depression that do not lead to premature death (but do reduce quality of life). One important recent line of research has uncovered "deaths of despair" from increases in suicide, drug overdoses, and alcoholic liver disease among both women and men, but primarily men, who are struggling economically and feel they have little left to live for (Case and Deaton 2020). These researchers estimate, tragically, that 600,000 people without college degrees who died between 2000 and 2020 would be alive if earlier rates of life expectancy prevailed. These excess deaths are concentrated among men aged 45 to 55. The role of suicides due to despair among this group is likely to be a primary reason why the overall suicide rate among Whites is so high.

Montgomery Martin/Alamy Stock Photo

BIG QUESTION 19.3
How Do Physician/Patient Interactions Affect Health and Illness?

THE EXPERTISE OF THE PHYSICIAN AND THE KNOWLEDGE OF THE PATIENT

In various ways up to this point, we've seen how social contexts and social hierarchies influence health outcomes. A population-based approach provides a different way of thinking about health issues than the usual individual-based approach. But we also interact with medical providers in ways that are very consequential for our health. One of the core insights of sociology, as we saw in Chapter 4, is that our interactions with others are central to the human experience. Few relationships produce more fraught interactions than that between doctors and patients. Physicians have always claimed that the doctor–patient relationship is at the core of health care, and for over a century after the rise of the medical profession in the late nineteenth century, physicians dominated the relationship with their patients. Today, however, many people and experts are beginning to question what that relationship should look like, and this is one of the most important questions about the future of medical care. For one thing, thanks to ready access to information about medical care online, patients can now educate themselves about their health issues. Patients ultimately know much about their own bodies, and there is a growing realization that patients can provide valuable opinions and participate in their care. But this emerging understanding challenges long-standing practices in the medical field that elevate the physician over their patients.

Physicians and Power

19.3.1 Discuss the lopsided nature of the traditional doctor–patient relationship.

Physicians are experts in diagnosis and treatment, and most patients are not. All health care workers have some expertise that most of us do not. Training does matter. Although the untrained can learn a lot about their personal health issues, it does take a long time to learn to diagnose and treat a variety of problems. The doctor–patient relationship is lopsided in that knowledge and skills are largely in the hands of one person. The physician has power that comes from that knowledge, but the stakes are sometimes high—one's life may be in the balance in how a doctor treats a patient!

More than half a century ago, the social theorist Talcott Parsons (1964; see Chapter 2 for more details about Parsons's social theory) argued that the medical profession taught patients to learn the role of dependency and that physicians' authority to tell the patients what to do was proper and appropriate. Patients are dependent on doctors because they lack the knowledge to make decisions for themselves. Doctors think hard about what is best for their patients and do not need to discuss much with patients. In Parsons's view, it was legitimate, for example, not to tell patients they had serious diseases from which they would die if a physician thought it best not to do so. And patients rarely questioned that authority. It was expected that physicians used that authority in the interest of the patients; the relationship was based on trust of the doctor. But is this always the case? What are the consequences of the inability of physicians to always (and in every case) know what to do and how to communicate that to their patients?

In fact, the model of medical practice that Parsons and others observed in the post-World War II era placed an enormous and unrealistic burden on physicians. It assumed that patients are helpless and do not have a good understanding of themselves, their bodies, or their desires; they do not have or want information about their medical problems; and they all want similar experiences from their lives in relation to their health. This model also assumed that all physicians treat their patients with respect, are trustworthy, listen carefully, diagnose prudently, and offer the most reasonable treatment.

But physicians do not always measure up to these standards, and neither they nor anyone else ever could. Many doctors do not necessarily relate equally effectively to all types of patients. Some doctors treat women differently than men, Blacks differently than Whites or Latinxs, and the rich differently than the poor. Further, doctors sometimes make mistakes in diagnosis. For example, doctors sometimes get themselves locked into a diagnosis and fail to look at other options. The physician and writer Jerome Groopman (2007) tells a story about a young woman whom the doctors diagnosed as anorexic because she kept losing weight. For many years, her treatments were based on a diagnosis of anorexia, despite the fact that she kept telling her doctors that she was eating. One doctor told her to eat lots of pasta, which is made of wheat. But she kept losing weight and got sicker. Finally, a new doctor, thinking outside the existing diagnosis and trusting the patient when she said she was eating, diagnosed her correctly as allergic to wheat—what is known as celiac disease. When she stopped eating wheat, she quickly gained weight and got her health back. Sometimes patients need to insist on a new diagnosis if their symptoms persist and they are doing what the doctor said. But doctors also need to listen to patients.

Over the last 50 years, the profession's self-regulation and freedom to make decisions has been challenged by federal and state governments, the courts, and even the public, but it remains immensely powerful. For example, doctors have long been held accountable for errors in **malpractice** cases by the courts, and the ability of patients to successfully sue their physicians accelerated in the 1970s for a period of time. Malpractice worries many doctors, but most doctors who do get sued have their insurance companies pay out a small amount to settle. Only a few have to pay out large amounts, and even if a doctor is sued successfully many times, they can continue to practice. The **American Medical Association (AMA)**—the primary organization of physicians—has fought hard and successfully to convince state governments to limit malpractice awards in recent years. The per-physician rate of malpractice cases has dropped more than 50 percent in the last 20 years, as has the size of awards to patients (Horowitz 2013). This decrease is

Of all the interactions we have, contact with physicians can be among the most important, especially if we suffer from a serious medical condition.

Through these programs, the federal government has sought to regulate medical expenses and charges and to eliminate fraudulent practices. It developed the National Practitioner Data Bank, which is run by the government's Public Health Service. But it is accessible only to medical institutions, such as medical boards and hospitals, because the AMA objected to opening it to the public. It has much more information on doctors and nurses than most licensing boards post on the Internet. The medical profession still has significant power to regulate its members and to keep the government from getting involved (Horowitz 2013).

But in spite of these changes, medical professionals continue to be largely self-governing and self-policing, and the system does not always work in a timely fashion to get rid of problem providers. Gawande (2002) reports the case of an orthopedic surgeon who harmed many people before he finally lost his license to practice. While sympathetic to this doctor's responses to his busy practice and excellent training, Gawande shows how the medical personnel who worked with him covered up his mistakes for too long, risking the lives of many patients. Their sympathetic responses toward the physician actually meant that more patients were harmed as no one told the state licensing and disciplinary board. The health care providers were thinking of the doctor's reputation, not from the perspective of patients who were being harmed or at risk of harm. In most states, medical personnel are required to report doctors, nurses, and physician assistants to their licensing boards if they see inappropriate, negligent, or incompetent behavior or if they suspect that they are drinking on the job or taking medications for nonmedical purposes. Patients should too, but there is no requirement to do so.

in part a result of caps on awards; 31 states have now passed caps on the damages that can be awarded in a malpractice lawsuit. This does not mean doctors do not experience fear that they will be sued or act as though they will be by ordering extensive and often unnecessary tests to cover their bases (Gawande 2007).

Clearly, the potential for gaps in regulating all health care providers is extensive. So it is left to state **medical boards**—usually consisting of a majority of physicians but with public representatives as well—to discipline doctors who commit gross violations and even, if necessary, to revoke their license to practice. All boards and medical organizations must answer to the courts. For example, if they don't follow the Americans with Disabilities Act, which allows for testing accommodations and prohibits asking about addiction problems in the past, they may end up a defendant in a lawsuit. The procedures for disciplining a medical professional must meet legal standards as all can be challenged in court. Doctors who do violate the statutes can be identified to the boards by patients, hospitals, insurance providers, police, or other health care providers. A little more than 4,000 of about 850,000 practicing doctors receive a serious sanction (probation, censure and reprimand, suspension, surrender, or revocation) every year from the state medical boards. These doctors are listed on the state boards' websites. Nurses, dentists, chiropractors, and other health professions have similar systems.

The federal government became involved in health care largely as a result of the passage of **Medicare** and **Medicaid** Acts in 1965. (Medicare provides health insurance for all Americans over 65, and Medicaid provides insurance for low-income individuals and families.)

Patient-Centered Care

19.3.2 Describe various examples of patient-centered care and its impact on the doctor–patient relationship.

The doctor–patient relationship is difficult, but also important for the delivery of quality health care. Let's review some of these issues. Many physicians have a hard time communicating with their patients. In a random survey of 1,000 patients, *Consumer Reports Magazine*

(June 2013) found that what bothered them most about their doctors was their failure to explain fully the patient's problem and side effects of treatments. Patients often felt rushed during their office visit. Sometimes it may be that patients are not very articulate about their health concerns, but it also may be that doctors don't explain clearly or ask whether the patients understand what they will need to do and whether the patients have access to necessary resources. Figure 19.4 includes more details about the problems patients report having with physicians.

In response to such evidence of poor doctor–patient relationships, some doctors are changing and beginning to talk more with patients. One part of the national exam that all new physicians must pass includes a section in which their interactional competence is measured. Growing attention to the doctor-patient relationship in the medical profession is a positive sign. More doctors are aware than ever before that patients want to understand their role in the self-care process and develop the knowledge and skills to help manage their own treatment. In fact, research shows that they approve of their physicians more when they become activated, involved patients (Greene et al. 2013).

There are however, still many challenges to getting patients more involved, and many reasons why patients continue to defer to their physicians (Gallagher et al. 2013). But the new slogan of the medical profession today is **patient-centered care**, the idea that patients should play an active role in the treatment of health problems. Patient-centered care approaches have arisen out of the growing realization that it is not necessarily a good idea to have doctors making diagnoses and providing treatments without patient input. Research shows that patients manage their health care better when they gain knowledge and confidence to have a serious dialogue with their physicians. Those who manage their own care report better health care experiences than patients seeing the same doctors who are not active in their own care (Greene et al. 2013). One important source of patient knowledge that emerged in recent years is the availability of medical information on the Internet, as Figure 19.5 illustrates.

What exactly does patient-centered care mean in practice? Are patients now at the center of the health care system and their needs the focus of attention? The words mean different things to different physicians and researchers and also to people who work with patients. To some it means painting hospital rooms in cheerier colors, cutting down the wait for appointments, or serving decent food in the hospital. But beyond such superficial changes are the really important efforts to improve communication with patients and sometimes families, empowering patients to make decisions and take care of themselves, and developing team approaches (where multiple specialists and the patient are involved in making important medical decisions). It also may mean providing **informed consent** through communication processes that allow patients and their families to truly understand what they are consenting to, working with patients and their families to establish what patients want at the end of life, and enabling patients and their families to monitor their own health care. It may also mean directing patients to tell health care providers to wash their hands or to ask who the people are who are providing services, such as asking about the credentials of the anesthesiologist who arrives at your gurney's side just as you are being wheeled into surgery, asking about what anesthesia you want, or asking who the person who hands you some unidentified pills is and what the pills are. Patients need to contribute to their care just as much as the profession defines it for them.

Figure 19.4 Common Patient Complaints

Scores are based on a 10-point scale, with 10 being the most bothersome.

NOTE: Differences of 0.4 points or less are not meaningful.

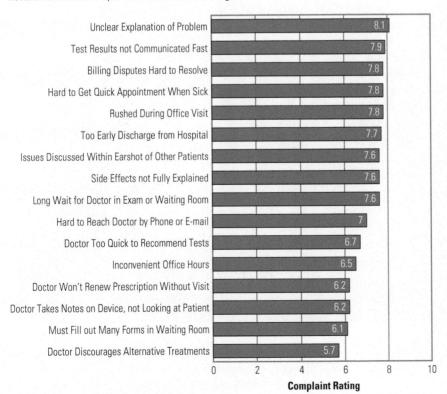

Complaint	Rating
Unclear Explanation of Problem	8.1
Test Results not Communicated Fast	7.9
Billing Disputes Hard to Resolve	7.8
Hard to Get Quick Appointment When Sick	7.8
Rushed During Office Visit	7.8
Too Early Discharge from Hospital	7.7
Issues Discussed Within Earshot of Other Patients	7.6
Side Effects not Fully Explained	7.6
Long Wait for Doctor in Exam or Waiting Room	7.6
Hard to Reach Doctor by Phone or E-mail	7
Doctor Too Quick to Recommend Tests	6.7
Inconvenient Office Hours	6.5
Doctor Won't Renew Prescription Without Visit	6.2
Doctor Takes Notes on Device, not Looking at Patient	6.2
Must Fill out Many Forms in Waiting Room	6.1
Doctor Discourages Alternative Treatments	5.7

Complaint Rating

SOURCE: The Consumer Reports National Research Center.

Figure 19.5 Health Information Online

Forty-two percent of adults say information they find online impacts how they approach medical decisions. This graph shows how online health information has affected the decision making of those adults.

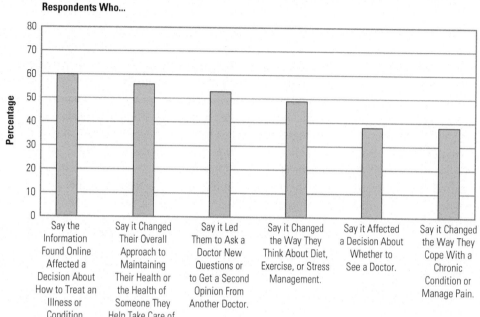

Respondents Who...

(Bar chart, y-axis labeled "Percentage" from 0 to 80)

Category	Approx. Percentage
Say the Information Found Online Affected a Decision About How to Treat an Illness or Condition.	~60
Say it Changed Their Overall Approach to Maintaining Their Health or the Health of Someone They Help Take Care of.	~56
Say it Led Them to Ask a Doctor New Questions or to Get a Second Opinion From Another Doctor.	~52
Say it Changed the Way They Think About Diet, Exercise, or Stress Management.	~48
Say it Affected a Decision About Whether to See a Doctor.	~36
Say it Changed the Way They Cope With a Chronic Condition or Manage Pain.	~36

SOURCE: Pew Research Center, 2014.

This new interaction pattern requires additional instruction and tools on both sides of the doctor–patient relationship: Medical personnel may have been trained in a culture of disrespect, and patients need to be activated to think about their own health care and to participate in the discussions and their care. Some patients may want to be more involved than others, but options need to be explained to all. Patients have to learn to ask questions about their symptoms and the possible tests and treatments, about side effects of medications and treatments, about what happens when they leave the hospital if they aren't provided with information, and what will happen if they don't have the resources to buy what they need. It may be very difficult to discuss what a patient wants at the end of life or how a mistake was made, but this is part of patient-centered care. Communication between people with very different backgrounds is often difficult, and in the case of medical care the barriers often extend beyond language differences to cultural ones.

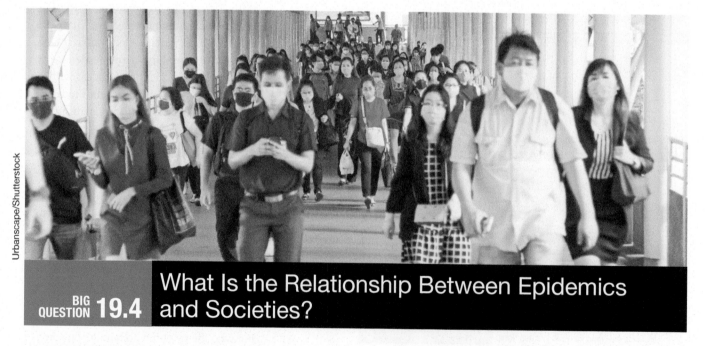

Urbanscape/Shutterstock

BIG QUESTION 19.4 What Is the Relationship Between Epidemics and Societies?

THE EFFECTS OF EPIDEMICS ON SOCIETIES

As discussed in the chapter opener, the COVID-19 pandemic, caused by the SARS-CoV-2 virus, quickly spread around the globe in the winter and spring of 2020 with devastating consequences. COVID-19 had, by October 2021, caused over 700,000 deaths in the United States alone, and at least 4.5 million deaths across the world. Although there have been global pandemics in the past, nothing remotely close to COVID-19 has impacted rich countries like the United States since the influenza pandemic of 1918–19. (The HIV/AIDS pandemic is a partial exception, although only a subset of the population was at risk.) The true number of deaths caused by COVID-19 is almost certainly worse than the official reports suggest, as many people have died of the virus without having been formally diagnosed. Further, in addition to those who have died, millions of others have been seriously ill or disabled for short or longer periods of time, as the virus has been known to cause lingering respiratory and other serious health issues, and "long COVID" (in which a patient experiences fatigue, aches, and lack of normal brain function) can continue to linger for many months even after the initial symptoms decline. COVID-19 also created a massive global economic downturn, as billions of people around the world who never got sick nevertheless suffered from loss of jobs or income. If ever there was an example of how society and health interact with one another, a global pandemic is it.

To clarify the terminology, an **epidemic** can be understood as the unexpected appearance of a disease capable of causing death and other serious health problems in one place or region. The closely related concept of a **pandemic** can simply be thought of as an epidemic that spreads throughout more than one region of the world, so COVID-19 is properly referred to as a pandemic.

Epidemics and pandemics are important to study from a sociological perspective because they both reflect existing health and social conditions in the societies in which they appear, and because they can reshape a society in many important ways. Moreover, as we saw with COVID-19, if an epidemic or pandemic is serious enough—and particularly if it is a **communicable disease** (one that involves human-to-human transmission)—it can severely diminish social and economic.

In this section, we will explore epidemics in more detail. Our focus is not on the medical aspects of these diseases, but rather on their social aspects: How they interact with societies to produce death, destruction, and mayhem. In studying epidemics, we are implicitly studying societies, in the same sense we've noted throughout this chapter, in relation to other health topics.

Epidemics Through History

19.4.1 Discuss some of the major epidemics in human history.

As we have already noted, epidemics can arise suddenly in a particular place and spread extensively through a population. The most significant pandemics and their cause(s), are listed in Table 19.4. The worst of these was the horrific Black

Table 19.4 Major Epidemics in Human History

Name	Time Period	Type/Pre-Human Host	Death Toll
Antonine Plague	165–180	Belived to be either smallpox or measles	5M
Japanese smallpox epidemic	735–737	Variola major virus	1M
Plague of Justinian	541–542	Yersinia pestis bacteria/Rats, fleas	30–50M
Black Death	1347–1351	Yersinia pestis bacteria/Rats, fleas	200M
New World Smallpox Outbreak	1520–onwards	Varialo major virus	56M
Great Plague of London	1665	Yersinia pestis bacteria/Rats, fleas	100,000
Italian plague	1629–1631	Yersinia pestis bacteria/Rats, fleas	1M
Cholera Pandemics 1-6	1817–1923	V.cholerae bacteria	1M+
Third Plague	1885	Yersinia pestis bacteria/Rats, fleas	12M (China and India)
Yellow Fever	Late 1800s	Virus/Mosquitoes	100,000-150,000 (U.S.)
Russian Flu	1889–1890	Believed to be H2N2 (avian origin)	1M
Spanish Flu	1918–1919	H1N1 virus/Pigs	40–50M
Asian Flu	1957–1958	H2N2 virus	1.1M
Hong Kong Flu	1968–1970	H3N2 virus	1M
HIV/AIDS	1981–present	Virus/Chimpanzees	25–35M
Swine Flu	2009–2010	H1N1 virus/Pigs	200,000
SARS	2002–2003	Coronavirus/Bats, Civets	770
Ebola	2014–2016	Ebolavirus/Wild animals	11,000
MERS	2015–Present	Coronavirus/Bats, camels	850
COVID-19	2019–Present	Coronavirus – Unknown (possibly pangolins)	4,500,000 (known deaths as of August 2021)

SOURCE: World Economic Forum, 2020; Authors' update.

Death, during which a virus known as the **plague** traveled across Europe, Asia, and large parts of Africa. In its most violent phase in the middle of the fourteenth Century, the plague killed an estimated 200 million people, including perhaps as much as half the entire population of Europe. Although the Black Death in Europe eventually ended, the plague virus continued to reappear and cause havoc, with the most deadly outbreaks associated with the so-called "second wave" (in Europe and England in the seventeenth century) and "third" wave (mostly in China and India in the eighteenth century). In 1894, a scientist named Alexandre Yersin identified the bacteria that causes the plague, and the source of the virus became known as *Yersinia pestis* in his honor. Although there is still no vaccine that can prevent someone from becoming sick from the virus, modern antibiotics can usually help an infected individual recover. Public health officials also now have the tools to readily identify plague outbreaks and can take measures to reduce its spread.

Another epidemic disease that has had major societal consequences in global history is smallpox. Smallpox was a longstanding source of death until a vaccine was developed in the late nineteenth century. The most impactful smallpox outbreak occurred when the virus was carried by Europeans to the Americas as part of the process of colonization and the establishment of slavery. Smallpox did extraordinary damage to the previously thriving indigenous populations, including the Inca and Maya peoples. As much as 90 percent of the indigenous populations disappeared in the sixteenth century, some as a result of the Spanish wars of conquest, but most due to the arrival of the virus, which the local population had no defense against. Smallpox not only killed millions directly but also created food shortages, wars, and other conflicts. Today, smallpox has largely disappeared, at least in rich countries where effective vaccines are readily available. The case of the smallpox vaccine shows what can happen when everyone takes an effective vaccine.

Since the late nineteenth century the most devastating infectious disease in the world has been influenza (or, more simply, the flu). First identified in the eighteenth century, the influenza virus has had several known variants, and there were a number of smaller outbreaks of influenza (that we know of) over the centuries. However, it was the global pandemic that began at the end of World War I that was the deadliest. Today we know that this particular influenza virus originated in animals. It was extremely contagious and spread quickly throughout the world, helped along by World War

I (which was still raging in 1918). All told, at least one-third of the world's population became sick (about 500 billion people), and at least 50 million died (Phillips and Killingray 2003). What was especially unusual about the deaths associated with the 1918–19 outbreak was that they affected young adults— people from their late teens to their late 30s—more significantly than any other age group (Taubenberger and Morens 2006). The world has been very fortunate not to have another global pandemic along the lines of the 1918–19 outbreak; however each year the "flu season" causes illness and some deaths, and many experts think that we are likely to see more deadly flu pandemics in the future, particularly since influenza viruses constantly change. Unfortunately, the same may be true of COVID-19; the Sars-Cov-2 coronavirus that causes the COVID illness has already shown a capacity to mutate.

Finally, prior to COVID-19, the HIV/AIDS pandemic was the deadliest global virus in recent decades. Peaking in the 1980s in rich countries, it had a devastating impact in poorer countries, especially in Africa (with the highest levels of HIV infections in southern Africa) where deaths peaked in the early 2000s. The disease is transmitted via a virus known as the human immunodeficiency virus (HIV), which attacks the body's ability to fight infection. Left untreated, it will lead to a final stage of the disease, known as AIDS (acquired immunodeficiency syndrome), and eventually death. There is no vaccine for HIV, but fortunately a treatment regimen (called antiretroviral therapy, or ART) allows people with HIV to lead long and healthy lives and to prevent the transmission of the virus to sexual partners or through drug use. Yet even though the world has mobilized to make ART treatments available across the globe (and this has significantly slowed deaths due to AIDS), it still remains a deadly killer, especially in poor countries with poor health care facilities and where testing and treatment are limited. As shown in Figure 19.6, there were about 1.7 million deaths

Figure 19.6 HIV/AIDS Deaths Continue to Decline

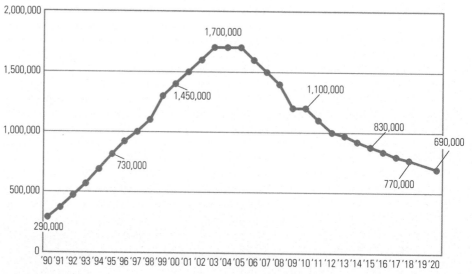

SOURCE: UNAIDS.

in the early 2000s, but by 2019 the number of people dying from AIDS had fallen to about 690,000 (UNAIDS 2020). In the United States, a total of about 770,000 people have died from AIDS since the beginning of the pandemic, and that number continues to grow (with over 15,000 Americans dying of HIV/AIDS in 2018).

This historical backdrop highlights how dangerous epidemics and pandemics can be and also helps us understand why most governments around the world reacted so aggressively to the arrival of COVID-19. Pandemics can take millions of lives if they are allowed to spread, and although better treatment and vaccines to prevent infection provide the best pathway to reducing unnecessary deaths, until those medical and scientific tools are available, societies have to try to reduce the impact of these types of diseases in other ways.

Societies and Epidemics

19.4.2 Explain how societies have responded to epidemics.

It is a rather remarkable fact that in spite of all of the advances of modern medical science, societies confronted by the threat of epidemics like COVID-19 continue to employ many of the same approaches and stereotypes as those from hundreds of years ago. For example, systematic efforts to isolate the infected can be traced back to the era of the Black Death pandemic in Europe during the fourteenth century. Italian city-states (which were some of hardest hit areas) created isolation places for the infected called *Lazzertos*; these places of confinement (and often death) were located on islands away from population centers. (Indeed, the word "quarantine" comes from quarenta, as 40 days became the standard period of isolation based on some passages from the Bible that describe the time needed for the "purification" of the soul; see Snowden 2020, p.70.) Another isolation tactic used at this time arose from the gradual realization that travelers appeared to be carriers of the virus, especially those coming from ships that pulled into ports to unload cargo. In fact, the primary carrier of the *Yersinia pestis*—the virus that caused the plague—was fleas that found homes in the skin of rats. When ships arrived in ports and unloaded cargo, rats exited the ships, carrying infected fleas onto the mainland, where the fleas began infecting the local population. Recognizing this, ships arriving at ports were forced to quarantine before landing, with the idea being that anyone who was infected on the ship would die before getting off the ship and interacting with the local population. Unfortunately, because the sources of the virus were infected fleas and rats, once ships did land the fleas still left their rat hosts and bit humans. The modern equivalent during the COVID-19 crisis is the attempt of governments to compel travelers crossing borders to self-quarantine before going out in public. Because COVID-19 is transmitted from human to human, this can be

an effective strategy if widely practiced, but it has been nearly impossible for governments to completely enforce.

Another way in which societies have responded to epidemics is in the scapegoating of certain groups. In a world divided into social hierarchies, it is not surprising that governments, local authorities, and ordinary people have repeatedly throughout history sought to blame the poor and racial and ethnic minority groups as the source of the problem. Those living in poor conditions, for example, were often said to foster the spread of disease (even as there was never any evidence to support such claims, and eventually scientific medicine proved that living conditions had nothing or very little to do with the spread of disease). In the case of cholera, which spreads via contaminated drinking water and had multiple outbreaks in the nineteenth and twentieth centuries, the primary location of the disease was in impoverished areas, but this was generally due to environmental conditions, not to the behavior of the residents. In addition, across Europe for centuries Jewish and Roman people, as well as ethnic or other religious minorities in certain regions, faced allegations and conspiracies about intentional disease spreading, sometimes prompting violent attacks based on stereotypes. This pattern can also be seen during the HIV/AIDS epidemic, when gay men, in particular, were frequently blamed for the spread of the disease even though it could be transmitted among heterosexuals and especially needle drug users (Shilts 1988). Similarly, during the COVID-19 pandemic, Asian and Chinese people were often targeted. Former U.S. President Donald Trump routinely declared the virus to be the "Chinese virus," and repeatedly claimed that his decision to stop flights from China was an important step in preventing a worse outbreak. Perhaps following their president's lead, some Americans directed hateful speech or action toward Asian Americans. Asian Americans reported significant increases in discrimination or racist remarks directed at them (Ruiz et al. 2020).

How can we explain these reactions? And, more broadly, what patterns in the relationship between epidemics and society can we uncover? Three critical factors have shaped the kinds of societal responses that have recurred throughout history. The first is whether the spread of the epidemic can be controlled by changing individual behavior, or whether a societal-level response is required (Rosenberg 1989). When individual behavior is seen to be at fault, it is easier to target particular groups and to blame them for the epidemic, at least initially. In the case of the HIV/AIDS crisis, rates of transmission were much higher from same-sex sexual contact, a fact that made it easier for groups opposed to same-sex relationships to (falsely) claim the disease was caused by homosexuality. As the HIV/AIDS epidemic reached enormous levels in Africa and could no longer be plausibly blamed on same-sex relationships, the global effort to fund drug therapies and other resources grew. For sociologists and public health scientists, *all* of these epidemics are ultimately social issues that can rarely be solved solely by changing individual behavior, even though in some cases it can help.

The second factor is whether or not the disease is "democratic." In other words, does it hit all groups equally, or are some groups more likely to be victims? The plague, influenza, and COVID-19 infected all classes and groups, making it more difficult to scapegoat specific groups (although, as noted, in the early phases of the COVID-19 pandemic, many Asian and Chinese people were the targets of stereotyping). By contrast, cholera had often been cast as a disease of poverty, and it was much more prevalent in poor communities, which seemed to confirm the belief that the poor were responsible. Only later, when unclean drinking water was discovered as the culprit, did that change. But for long periods of time, in spite of its deadly character, cholera received much less attention than it might have.

Finally, in the twentieth and twenty-first centuries, the role of medical and public health science has been increasingly important in shaping governmental responses to disease. Modern public health systems—both nationally (like the Centers for Disease Control and Prevention [CDC] in the United States) and internationally (the World Health Organization [WHO])—have become very good at identifying new oubreaks when patients start to present with uncommon illnesses at hospitals. Medical science has also made major advances in treating infected patients. With the exception of HIV/AIDS and COVID-19, public health measures, while hardly perfect, have largely been effective in stopping the spread of new diseases across the globe. Emerging epidemics, such as Severe Acute Respiratory Syndrome [SARS], Ebola, the swine flu, and Middle East Respiratory Syndrome (MERS) all had the potential to become global pandemics, but none of them did. In these cases, governments and public health agencies were able to regionalize and control the diseases before they spread. Some of these efforts involved heroic risks undertaken by doctors and public health officials entering regions with high rates of infection and treating patients without knowing much about the disease (Rosenberg 1993; Farmer 2001). Through aggressive testing and tracing in heavily impacted areas, containment was eventually achieved.

In the case of COVID-19, scientific understandings have not been universally accepted, especially in the United States but in many other places as well. It took just a few weeks of researching the new virus before a scientific consensus was formed. Experts stated that the virus was primarily transmitted through droplets in the air that were passed from one person to another and that it could be transmitted by someone who experiences no symptoms and who—if they are not tested—could inadvertently and unintentionally infect many other people. This is why scientists and public health experts have been so adamantly concerned that everybody wear a mask in public and that people remain six feet apart from others in indoor spaces. At first, Some politicians and a tiny minority of scientists (most of whom are non-experts in infectious diseases) proposed an alternative to mask wearing and social distancing. They suggested that societies should allow **herd immunity** to build up in the population. The idea was that if enough people got sick and recovered from the virus, eventually it would run out of potential victims and disappear. A slightly modified approach, known as the Great Barrington Declaration, was signed by several hundred scientists and doctors, most of whom are not specialists in infectious disease (Great Barrington Declaration 2020). This approach called for people with a higher risk of death to stay home, but stated that everyone else should mingle as normal until a majority of the population got the virus, recovered, and had immunity from getting it again. The vast majority of the scientific community rejected this view as extremely dangerous, given that COVID-19 seems to kill about 1–2 percent of the people who get it (with

Across the United States and around the world (including in London, as shown here), in spite of the scientific consensus that wearing masks and limiting indoor gathering would save many lives before vaccines became available, protests against COVID-19 regulations revealed a divide between public health officials and people refusing to believe what the scientists and government officials were saying about the pandemic.

older people being at greater risk) *and* leaves many others with chronic medical conditions. Although the history of epidemics provides plenty of examples of resistance to the rules or advice of political authorities and experts, the rejection of scientific knowledge in modern times is especially striking in the case of COVID-19.

Unfortunately, it is quite possible, or even likely, that COVID-19 will not be the last major global pandemic in the twenty-first century (Davis 2020). Advances in medical science that have helped to eliminate or reduce the impact of longstanding sources of epidemic disease are of limited use when new and unanticipated viruses appear, and the primary source of deadly new viruses are those originating in animals. The worldwide process of destroying natural habitats in the name of economic growth, a process we explore in more detail in Chapter 6 on the environment, is increasing the rate at which **zoonotic diseases** (which spread from animals to humans) are appearing. Take a look at Table 19.4 again. Notice that in the twenty-first century, several deadly viruses, including three coronaviruses like that of COVID-19, have arisen. All involved zoonotic disease. Unless we take dramatic steps to change our relationship to nature, other zoonotic diseases are likely to arise and threaten human populations in the future.

The Opioid Epidemic

19.4.3 Describe how opioid abuse can become an epidemic.

Epidemics are most commonly caused by diseases that are either transmitted from humans to humans or from animals to humans, or by an environmental factor (like contaminated water) that impacts a large number of people in the same physical location (for example, cholera). In each case, a viral or bacterial agent spreads through a community and causes death. But the concept of epidemic disease can also be applied in cases where the agent is people's behaviors that have broad health consequences. Like transmissible diseases such as COVID-19, a behavioral epidemic is something that becomes "contagious," in the sense that when groups of people start to change their behavior, others may as well. Examples abound, some of which we've already mentioned. Alcohol has long been found to be abused most commonly in group settings, such as parties or bars, when people binge drink together. We've also noted the idea that obesity may have a social component in that people with weight-related issues may tend to form friendships with other people with similar issues and potentially encourage each other to engage in behaviors that promote obesity. A few years ago, consuming flavored electronic cigarettes (known as vaping) became very popular among young people, despite major health risks. The problem was sufficiently widespread that the federal government's surgeon general declared an "e-cigarette epidemic" in 2018.

The use and abuse of many kinds of drugs has the potential to take on the characteristics of an epidemic, in particular when usage becomes widespread. The highest profile example today are deaths and other health problems caused by overdoses of the natural derivatives of opium, including morphine, heroin, fentanyl, and opium-based pain killers such as OxyContin. All of these products are known as **opioids**. The "agents" of the opioid epidemic are the companies that produce and aggressively marketed the drugs on a large scale, initially with very little governmental regulation; the physicians that prescribe opioids to patients in large numbers; and, eventually, the underground network of opioid drug makers and sellers who operate illegally.

Americans have had a long and complicated relationship with this class of drugs. Opium has been around for thousands of years, and has been used for recreational, religious, and other purposes in many different societies around the world. In the United States, a derivative known as morphine appeared in the first decades of the nineteenth century. It became the most effective painkiller in medical history—in large measure owing to the invention of the hypodermic needle in 1856, just in time for the Civil War. Morphine quickly became the preferred drug of injured soldiers, with many returning home after the war with strong habits that helped to maintain and spread the market for opium products (Courtwright 2009). A new pathway into the human body came with the development of morphine-infused syrups. By the late nineteenth Century, for just a few pennies, anyone could purchase a bottle, with a content as high as 10 to 14 percent morphine, at the local pharmacy. Drug prescriptions were not part of the U.S. regulatory system at the time, and there was no Food and Drug Administration until the dawn of the twentieth century. Thus, there were no requirements to label ingredients, much less disclose proportionality of contents.

Once opioids were outlawed in 1914, their use went underground, mostly in the form of heroin, and retreated as a major societal problem. However, in the 1990s, a renewed effort to find pharmaceutical solutions to short- and long-term pain management—for example, after major surgery or for incurable conditions like severe back pain—led to the development of a new class of pain medications derived from opium. The most important, and by far most widely used of these new drugs, was the pain reliever called OxyContin developed by Purdue Pharmaceuticals, a Connecticut-based company. Other commonly prescribed opioids that came into wide use in the 2000s included Vicodin, Percocet, and Fentanyl. These companies that created these drugs falsley marketed them as safe and encouraged doctors to prescribe them as much as possible. They made immense profits. Court filings have revealed that Purdue Pharma and the family that owns the company received over $12 billion in profits from the sale of OxyContin (Hopkins and Scurria 2019). As a result, they have been held legally responsible for their role in the epidemic (see Chapter 7 for more details).

It is important to understand that these drugs are often highly addictive and will cause severe withdrawal symptoms for an addict who attempts to stop use. In addition to reducing pain, people under the influence of opioids report feeling a heightened state of well-being and pleasure. But after long-term use, the brain reduces its usual production of endorphins to compensate. Thus, when long-term users decide to suddenly stop, not only do they face the prospect of depriving themselves of the good feelings associated with the drug, but their brain's natural production of endorphins may be so low that they begin to experience painful withdrawal symptoms, unless, of course, they return to using the opioid. In this way, opioids are a double-edged sword.

Drawing on this basic explanation, people overdose when they take too much of an opioid because they are trying to maximize the benefit they associate with it. Sometimes the overdose is accidental, as when someone simply misidentifies pills and believes they are ingesting a pill of one strength while in fact they are taking a much stronger dose. Another common case of overdosing is when users gain a tolerance for the drug and require larger and larger doses to get the same effect and may misjudge. Or, if they stop using for a period of time and then go back to it, they are at special risk of an overdose.

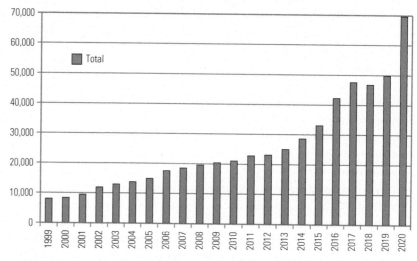

Figure 19.7 Opioid Deaths, 1999–2020

SOURCE: Centers for Disease Control and Prevention.

The increase in opioid addiction and abuse can be seen in the rapidly rising numbers of deaths and emergency room visits. Figure 19.7 shows opioid deaths since the late 1990s, which increased 600 percent in 20 years. The raw numbers are stunning; more Americans have died of opioid deaths since 2000 than in World War II. Three times as many people are dying from opioids as murder victims in a typical year. Further, death is only one outcome. It is estimated that there are 10 emergency room opioid overdoses for each death, raising the societal costs as emergency treatment is often very expensive, and patients often face a difficult recovery even if they are saved. Many people will have multiple emergency room visits before finally succumbing.

The epidemic nature of these overdoses and deaths is not simply their increased numbers; rather, it is the concentration of abuse among certain groups of people in specific communities. Ninety percent of opioid-related deaths are among people without college degrees, and two-thirds have not been to college at all. Many of these deaths are among middle-aged men (and to a lesser extent, women). Opioid abuse (deaths and emergency room visits) is geographically concentrated in two areas that have both seen sharp economic decline in recent decades: Rural communities and urban centers. Poverty and local unemployment rates emerge as predictors of opioid

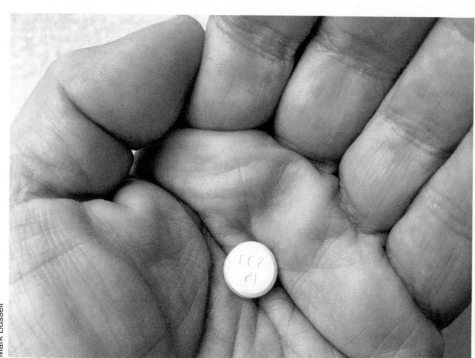

Widespread opioid addiction and overdoses in recent years in the United States have caused tens of thousands of unnecessary deaths annually.

Mark Bussell

"hotspots," although not all such areas have elevated rates of opioid abuse. As a recent government study put it, "The prevalence of drug overdose deaths and opioid prescriptions has risen unevenly across the county, with rural areas more heavily affected . . . on average, counties with worse economic prospects are more likely to have higher rates of opioid prescriptions, opioid-related hospitalizations, and drug overdose deaths" (Ghertner and Groves 2019).

Janine Wiedel Photolibrary/Alamy Stock Photo

BIG QUESTION 19.5 Why Is Health Care in America So Much More Expensive Than in Other Countries?

AMERICAN HEALTH CARE IN COMPARATIVE PERSPECTIVE

We've just discussed society's response to epidemics and the significance of health care in dealing with them. Now, let's turn to a more detailed examination of the health care system. No matter how researchers calculate the cost of health care, all agree it is far more expensive in the United States than in any other country in the world. Whether you look at health care spending as a percentage of the entire economy (or gross domestic product), the amount spent per person, or the cost of routine medical procedures, it is clear that other countries have figured out how to deliver quality health care in ways that are significantly cheaper than in the United States. Today the United States spends about 18 percent of its entire gross domestic product (that is, almost one-fifth of all economic activity in a given year) on health care. And these costs have risen dramatically in the past 50 years, much faster than family incomes or the entire economy as Figure 19.8 illustrates. The figure compares the enormous growth in health care costs compared to the economy as a whole (the gross domestic product) and growth in the median worker's wages.

The cost of health care in the United States is more than double that of most other rich countries (see Figure 19.9). To put this in perspective, 1 percent of the American GDP today represents about $200 billion. So the fact that the United States devotes 6 to 8 percent *more* of its entire

Figure 19.8 Health Care Spending Has Grown Much Faster Than the Rest of the Economy in Recent Decades

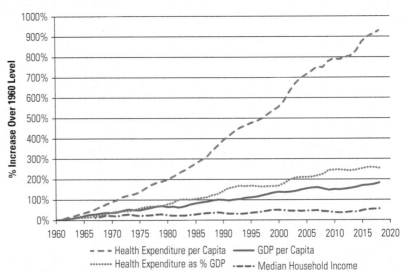

NOTE: All calculations use inflation-adjusted dollars. Median income is imputed as the half-way point between the lower and upper bounds of the third income quintile.

SOURCE: Author's calculations of data from National Health Expenditure Accounts, provided by the Centers for Medicare and Medicaid Services and the Census historical income tables. Inflation adjustment uses CPI-U provided by the Bureau of Labor Statistics.

Figure 19.9 Different Countries' Expenditures on Health Care as a Percentage of GDP, 2017

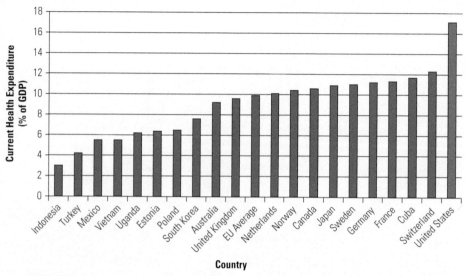

SOURCE: World Bank World Development Indicators.

economy to health care represents some $1 to $1.5 trillion that *could* be spent addressing other needs, *if* the American health care system were closer in cost to the systems found in other rich countries.

Taken together, Figures 19.8 and 19.9 show what a remarkable financial commitment the United States has made to health care. Yet, as noted, in spite of all this spending, costs are higher and coverage is often less than other countries. It is one of the great puzzles of our time. How do social scientists account for the discrepancies?

The Structure of Health Insurance in the United States

19.5.1 Describe the free market of American health insurance.

Who pays for our health care? We all do, but we do it in a more complex manner than most other countries. Today, most Americans under the age of 65 are covered by a private insurance plan, and in most cases they get this coverage through their job. Everyone over 65 is covered by Medicare, a federal program created in 1965 to provide health benefits for older people who may be past working age. Medicaid, a separate program created in the same year and funded in part by the federal government and in part by states, provides health insurance benefits for poor families and supports long-term care for low-income older people who have no other way to pay for assisted living or nursing care. Both Medicare and Medicaid have been expanded multiple times over the years, to add more coverage (both programs) and cover more people, especially children and a larger number of low-income families (Medicaid).

In 2010, the federal role in health care was expanded further with the passage of the **Affordable Care Act (ACA)**, or "Obamacare," as it is often called. The ACA sought to extend insurance coverage to all Americans and prevent insurance companies from discriminating against patients with **pre-existing conditions** (a chronic health condition like cancer or diabetes that is likely to require expensive ongoing treatment). It greatly expanded Medicaid to cover more poor people and families. But it failed to provide everyone with health insurance, and the patchwork character of Obamacare has also largely failed to constrain rising health care costs.

Yet in spite of the variety of ways in which health insurance might be obtained, many Americans still have no insurance—some because they don't want it, but most because they can't afford it (even under the ACA), perhaps if they don't have a job that provides them with insurance. According to recent estimates, *before* the COVID-19 rise in unemployment, more than 15 percent of U.S. adults between the ages of 19 and 64, or about 24 million people, did not have health insurance for at least part of a year (as of 2018). This was down from around 20 percent in 2013 but still represents a very large group of people (Commonwealth Fund 2018). Of course, since the arrival of the economic downturn associated with COVID-19, millions of Americans lost their jobs, which means more people who will also lose their health insurance.

Markets and Health Care

19.5.2 Compare and contrast health care markets with markets for other goods and services.

To understand why health care is so complicated, we need to first consider how the economic market for health care is unique (see Chapter 9 for more details on the sociology of how economic markets work). Whenever we buy consumer goods—a new car, a dishwasher, or new clothes—we enter an economic market. Many of us search online to establish the quality of items and are able to look for the best prices. Rating organizations such as *Consumer Reports* test products; many more specialized websites rate items and provide comments from buyers about almost anything. All of this information makes it possible for anyone buying a car, choosing a restaraunt, or even a college education, to make a reasonably informed decision based on quality or cost.

Further, many products are available in stores to try out or compare to other similar products. Buying a pair of jeans? You can go to a number of stores and try on as many pairs as you want before making your choice. Markets work best when individual buyers know what they need, how much they can afford to pay, and because they have enough information to make informed choices.

A well-functioning economic market does something else as well. It punishes sellers who are charging their customers too much if there are other similar quality goods or services available at a lower price. This is a basic principle of economics, and it has proved remarkably powerful over the centuries. There are a few exceptions—some goods acquire special value as high-status items that can sometimes cause people to pay inflated prices—but as a general rule, across every country in every period of capitalism, those marketing and selling goods can only charge what buyers are willing to pay.

But what about health care? Several issues make the market for health care fundamentally different than other kinds of markets. The central problem is what economists refer to as an **information asymmetry**—a situation in which one side has more information than the other. In the case of health care, there is an enourmous information asymmetry. Most people don't have much information about the costs of the different services offered by doctors and other health care personnel, or the prices different hospitals, clinics, and outpatient services charge. Although a few doctors have posted their prices, we rarely know the price of a medical treatment or service until the bill arrives showing what the insurance company actually paid (and what portion we owe). Often the numbers do not add up. With a hospital stay or procedure, bills frequently arrive from multiple parties (perhaps even a physician evaluating the case thousands of miles away), and the hospital bill may list separate procedures the patient didn't ask for or even know they had. Many tests may be ordered that can add up to very high costs, and patients are typically at the mercy of their doctor in deciding whether a particular test is needed or can be justified based on the cost. Moreover, patients typically aren't able to take the lead in making rational, informed decisions about costs during medical emergencies when they may be unconscious or have life-threatening injuries. In addition, patients typically lack the knowledge necessary to assess the quality of the physicians they choose or to evaluate the recommendations of the physician. What do we really know about our doctors? A physician may seem friendly enough, but is that what we should care about?

A fundamental principle of economics is that prices for the same service should converge on a common number. Does this happen in health care? A *New York Times* investigation and analysis of 40 million insurance claims (part of a series of investigations entitled "Paying Until It Hurts") presented numerous examples of the wide variation in prices charged for the same procedure. For example, the *Times* found that the price of a colonoscopy (a test that allows a physician to look at the inner linings of the large intestines to identify ulcers, tumors, and other kinds of problems that might otherwise be invisible) ranged across the country from $1,908 to $8,577. In a regular economic market, doctors and hospitals who charge much more than their competitors would either have to lower their prices or go out of business. Instead, in the health care market, prices for the same service vary wildly.

The Role of Insurance in the Economic Market for Health Care

19.5.3 Analyze the role of health insurance in the economic market for health care.

There is another way in which the market in health care differs from most other markets: The role of insurance. The most important change in the medical field in the twentieth century, beginning in the 1930s and accelerating after World War II, was the establishment of health insurance as the primary way in which most individuals and families would be covered when they needed medical care. The American Medical Association and other physicians' organizations initially fought the introduction of any kind of insurance (whether through the government or the private sector). A primary reason physicians opposed insurance for health care was they feared it would set limits on the fees doctors could charge their patients. By the end of World War II, however, most insurance plans covered only hospital visits or major medical problems, not other kinds of physician services. Blue Cross/Blue Shield, a federation of insurance companies owned by physicians, dominated the insurance industry. This began to change beginning in the late 1940s, however, as numerous employers began to provide their employees with regular health insurance coverage through private health insurance companies.

What was unusual about the development of medical insurance in the United States, compared to all other rich democratic countries, was that rather than the government taking responsibility for making sure that all citizens had insurance, the health insurance industry remained dominated by private, for-profit insurance companies. Unions played an important role in bargaining for health insurance for their members, paid for by the companies they worked for. One of the major benefits of being in a union job in 1960, as opposed to a non-union job, was you were much more likely to have a good-quality health insurance plan from your employer. Most large employers eventually became willing to provide insurance to their workers because, at least for the first few decades after World War II, insurance simply wasn't that expensive. That eventually changed—today, insurance is now one of the main costs of doing business for companies that provide insurance for their workers.

Insurance alters the nature of the economic market for health care in several ways. Insurance creates what economists call a **moral hazard**. A moral hazard arises when someone is not paying for the goods or services they receive, which gives them an incentive to take more than they would if they were paying for it out of their pocket. It's not hard to imagine why this would be the case. Let's suppose on Monday, you have to buy yourself lunch, using your own money. On Tuesday, however, someone else promises to buy you lunch at any restaurant you would like. What will happen? There's a very good chance that on Monday, you will carefully choose a lunch you want that is in your budget, whereas on Tuesday, you probably would explore more expensive possibilities (perhaps you will even let your lunch partner buy your lunch at the most expensive restaurant in town).

The moral hazard in this example is that because on Tuesday you have no constraints, you may choose a lunch that is much more expensive than you need just because someone else is paying. Similarly, when you've paid for health insurance up front, the cost of getting services is (or close to) zero, so you may be more likely to over-consume (and your physician, who knows your insurance will pay for it, may also recommend extra tests of dubious need "just to be sure"). You also have no incentive to search out the most affordable physician. You aren't paying for it, so it doesn't matter to you how much your insurer has to pay.

The existence of moral hazard in health care economics may appear evident when we observe that the growth of health insurance is associated with the rising cost of health care. In 1960, 45 percent of Americans had health insurance and the percentage of the American economy devoted to health care was 4.4 percent (Centers for Medicare and Medicaid Services 2015). By 2014, about 85 percent had health insurance, and 17 percent of the American economy was devoted to health care. It certainly looks like having more people with insurance could be a driver of costs.

However, not everyone agrees that health insurance produces a moral hazard in this way or that the expansion of health insurance alone is the primary source of rising health care costs. Health insurance companies, at least potentially, can set limits on the prices they will pay for procedures or services, or set limits on the number of tests and procedures they will cover (thereby eliminating the moral hazard). Further, unlike choosing lunch paid for by some anonymous person, it is not clear that most people either can or do choose the most expensive option (and most insurance companies have procedures in place to prevent that from happening). Finally, as noted elsewhere, health care costs have not risen nearly as fast in other countries where all citizens have health insurance, and in some of these countries these plans

are even issued by private companies. Moral hazard via third-party insurance is an important *potential* problem, and one that everyone interested in health care should be aware of, but it is simply not the primary cause of rising health care costs. We will consider this issue in more detail in the next section.

Analyzing the High Cost of Health Care in the United States

19.5.4 **Outline the possible explanations for the high cost of health care in the United States.**

Social scientists have explored a number of possible explanations for rising health care, and in the process have debunked several myths:

1. **Do Americans visit the doctor more often than individuals living in other countries?** The research does not support this. Patients in the United States actually see the doctor *less* often than in other industrialized nations. The best comparative data suggest that the average American goes to see a doctor four times per year, whereas the average person in Germany goes almost 10 times, in Canada eight, in Australia seven, and among all rich countries the average number of visits per year is close to seven. And there are fewer physicians to see those patients than in most other countries (there are about 2.6 physicians for every 1,000 people in the United States, compared to an average in rich countries of 3.3 per 1,000) (OECD 2015). Americans also have fewer hospital stays and stay for shorter periods when they are admitted to the hospital. Figure 19.10 displays some of these data.

2. **Is our population older and sicker?** While it is true that older patients tend to use more care than younger people around the world, our population is not older than most other industrialized nations. Americans are actually slightly younger, on average, than people in other rich countries (see Chapter 23 for a more detailed discussion on the aging population in the United States). For example, as Figure 19.11 shows, about 16 percent of Americans are over 65, while almost 30 percent in Japan are over 65 and 21 percent in Germany. In terms of aging, the United States is a relatively "young" country compared to other, similar countries. So an aging population cannot be the main cause of differences in health care costs.

3. **Are Americans doing things that are making them unhealthy, thereby raising health care costs?** Americans have a higher rate of obesity than people in other countries, although in recent years the gap has been

Figure 19.10 Average Length of Hospital Stay and Number of Doctor Visits Among OECD Countries, 2014

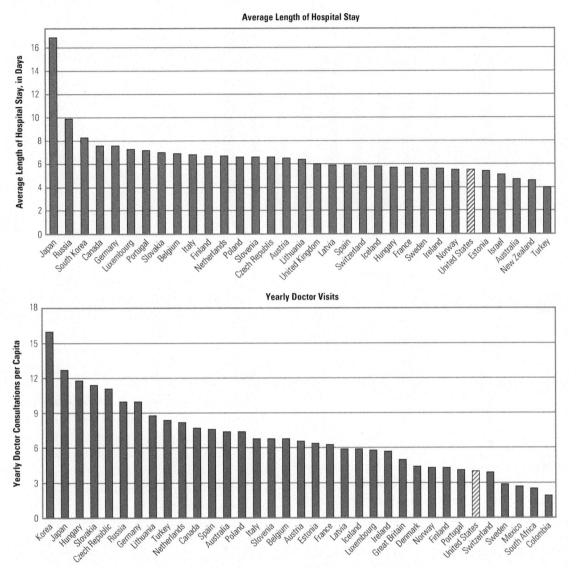

SOURCE: OECD Health Statistics.

shrinking (Ogden et al. 2015). Many commentators have pointed to obesity to explain health care costs. Our current obesity rate is about 34 percent among adults. This is higher than most other countries. Although many people can be overweight and perfectly healthy, some of those who are very obese will tend to use more health care resources, for example, as obesity is related to diabetes, heart disease, bone and joint deterioration, and others (Gerard 2010). However, obesity is only one type of medical condition (and in recent years, other countries are quickly catching up while the obesity rate has stopped rising in the United States). On other measures Americans' health behaviors are as good as or better than those in other countries. For example, we smoke significantly less than people in many other rich countries.

On other health behaviors, we either lack good data and/or what data we have provide no evidence that Americans are worse off than people in other countries. Taken as a whole, then, there is no convincing evidence that worse health behaviors account for the difference between the United States and other rich countries in terms of the cost of health care.

If none of these possibilities—overuse of doctors and medical facilities, an aging population, or poor health behaviors—can account for the much higher medical care costs, then we will have to look at factors relating to how health care is organized and financed—in other words, turn to an analysis of how organizations in the medical field operate. Here some key differences emerge. The most important of these are (1) higher administrative

Figure 19.11 Percentage of Population 65 and Older in Selected OECD Countries, 2018

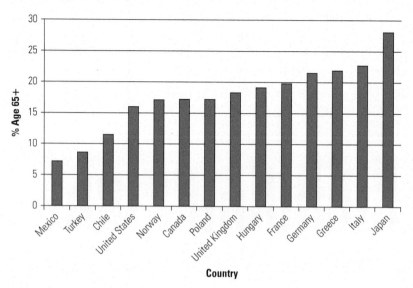

SOURCE: Data from OECD, 2020.

costs; (2) higher costs of drugs (even though in the global pharmaceutical market we are all pretty much using the same medications); (3) higher rates of medical tests and medical procedures; (4) higher costs of emergency room visits, hospitalization costs, and costs for all types of surgery; and (5) routine visits to see a doctor, which are more expensive. Let's discuss each of these briefly.

The first proposed culprit is the higher level of administrative costs generated by the American health care system. As everyone who uses the system knows, there are multiple layers of bureaucracy associated with a largely private health insurance system. Every time you see a doctor, chances are you and the office will fill out a bunch of paperwork. Insurers and hospitals are engaged in a steady flow of documentation, review, and negotiations, and there are hundreds of thousands of people employed in the health care system whose primary job is to manage the daily flow of charges and the paperwork that accompanies it. Even small physicians' offices or clinics will have one or two people who specialize in handling insurance claims. Overall, the data show that the United States spends between three and six times as much on administration as other countries, as Figure 19.12 illustrates.

Second, the cost of drugs is significantly higher in the United States. Most countries have given up on the idea that prescription drug prices should be left to the market. Instead, almost all countries negotiate some or all of these prices. Because they have large buying

power—think of all of Germany, or Canada, or Japan as a single buyer—they can get better deals from drug companies than if left to the market. In most of these cases, drugs are purchased on a cost-plus basis, allowing a small profit on each medication sold. In the United States, drug companies in the private market are allowed to charge whatever they can get away with, and the overall result is significantly higher prices. Figure 19.13 shows two different ways of looking at those differences, by average spending per person or the cost of a one-month supply for some common drugs.

Third, there are more tests conducted and procedures performed per patient being treated than in other countries. There are multiple reasons why physicians order so many tests and perform perhaps unnecessary procedures. American hospitals and clinics tend to have more expensive, high-tech diagnostic equipment than is found in other countries. Also, because hospitals and some doctors own expensive machines, and because they are expensive to maintain, there is an incentive to use them as much as possible. Studies show, for example, that doctors who own their CAT scan or magnetic resonance imaging (MRI) machines test more patients than those who do not own them. One study found that urologists who owned intensity-modulated radiation therapy technology (at a cost of $2 million per machine) used it much more often than those urologists who did not own a machine (Mitchell 2013). Table 19.5 shows some examples of how the United States is among the leading countries when it comes to medical technology and procedures.

Figure 19.12 Spending on Health Insurance Administration, per Capita, in the United States and Similar Countries

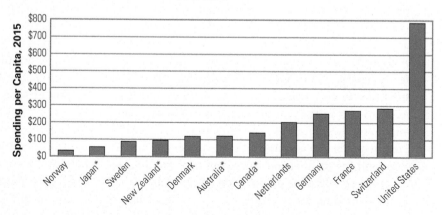

NOTE: *Japan, Australia, and Canada costs are from 2014. New Zealand costs are from 2012.

SOURCE: Commonwealth Fund analysis of OECD Health Data.

Figure 19.13 Prescription Drug Costs in the United States

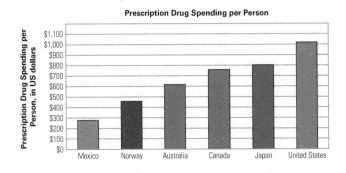

Prescription Drug Spending per Person

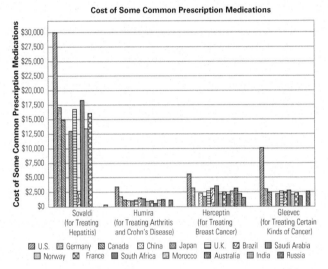

Cost of Some Common Prescription Medications

☑ U.S.   ☒ Germany   ◨ Canada   ⊠ China   ▨ Japan   ▭ U.K.   ☑ Brazil   ▩ Saudi Arabia
▢ Norway   ▨ France   ▦ South Africa   ▤ Morocco   ▨ Australia   ▥ India   ▧ Russia

SOURCE: Kaiser Family Foundation.

these procedures or tests were not without risks of complications for the patients, in addition to the added costs they created. However, in recent years the federal government and some insurance companies have discouraged the use of fee-for-service payments and as a result a declining share of doctors are compensated in this way than in the past. However, far more physicians in other countries are paid a regular salary, which has no connection to the number of procedures or tests they perform.

The costs associated with hospitals are much higher in the United States, for a variety of reasons. Americans use emergency rooms more than people in other countries, and emergency room care is always much more expensive than regular care. A primary reason for the high use of emergency rooms is that because so many Americans lack health insurance, they allow medical conditions to go untreated until they become a crisis. Frequent emergency room users typically have multiple problems and no one supervising their care. A small percentage of patients (less than 10 percent) accounts for about half of all emergency care expenditures. These are patients whose complicated problems are multiple—often including heart failure, diabetes, and kidney disease—and sometimes accompanied by psychiatric issues. The evidence suggests that the American medical system has a specific problem with very sick and chronically ill patients who use the emergency room for crisis treatment (Bookman 2013). But it may not be that the medical problems themselves cause the high costs; instead, it is the organization of the health care system in

Another reason for the greater number of tests and procedures being performed is that the structure of compensation received by some physicians and hospitals motivates them to do more (Rosenthal 2017). Many doctors earn higher fees when they order or perform more tests. In the past, many doctors in the United States were compensated by what was known as a **fee for service** basis—that is, they were paid for every visit, procedure, or test they performed. As a result, they had incentives to do more tests whether they were necessary or not. Not only did that encourage excessive testing, but also unnecessary surgeries and other procedures, again because profits were linked to the number of procedures done. Sometimes

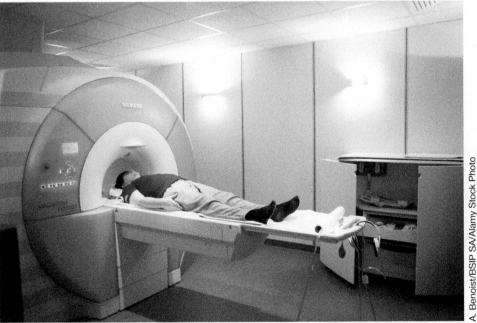

Expensive technology (such as a magnetic resonance imaging [MRI] machine shown here) has improved health care in many ways. But wasteful duplication of expensive equipment, and the over-use of expensive tests, have contributed to the very high overall cost of care compared to other countries that have less duplication of advanced technological systems.

A. Benoist/BSIP SA/Alamy Stock Photo

Table 19.5 Where the U.S. Health System Does More Than Rich Countries

	United States	Rank Compared with OECD Countries	OECD Average
MRI Units	31.6 per million population	2nd	12.5 per million population
MRI Exams	97.7 per 1,000 population	2nd	46.3 per 1,000 population
CT Scanners	40.7 per million population	3rd	22.6 per million population
CT Exams	265.0 per 1,000 population	3rd	123.8 per 1,000 population
Tonsillectomies	254.4 per 100,000 population	1st	130.1 per 100,000 population
Coronary Bypasses	79.0 per 100,000 population	3rd	47.3 per 100,000 population
Knee Replacements	226.0 per 100,000 population	1st	121.6 per 100,000 population
Caesarean Sections	32.9 per 100 live births	6th	26.1 per 100 live births

SOURCE: OECD Health Data.

failing to provide insurance and preventive care (before a small problem becomes a big problem).

Finally, hospital stays are often very expensive and by comparison with other countries significantly higher overall. Figure 19.14 shows how much it costs to spend one day in a hospital in different countries.

Can the System Be Fixed?

19.5.5 Explain why the problems with American health care have been so difficult to fix.

The effort of health care reformers to create a nationally organized health care system akin to those in Canada and Europe has been a century-long quest (Gordon 2003). There is no end in sight. Even with the best of intentions, the ACA passed during the Obama presidency has proved controversial, managing to unite liberals and conservatives in dissatisfaction with it (even while they continue to disagree about what to do next). Among the many

things that the ACA has not yet accomplished is holding down rising health care costs, and the efforts it has made have (in many cases) been circumvented by insurers, hospitals, drug companies, and physicians (Rosenthal 2017). Despite the difficulties surrounding the ACA, no one in the world of health policymaking has given up on the long effort to achieve a better system. If there is one thing we can be sure of, it is that the search for a better and more affordable health care system will continue.

Why is health care reform so difficult to achieve? The many players in the current U.S. health care system have strong vested interests in resisting significant changes that might bring the United States more in line with other countries. In Chapter 5, in our discussion of why social structures tend to persist over time, we introduced the concept of **path dependency**—that once a particular institutional pathway has developed, it is very difficult to reverse course, in large measure because organizations and individuals in that system will resist change, creating a kind of bias toward the maintenance of the status quo. One of the reasons why path dependency is powerful is because any large institutional system like the American health care system generates many organizations that have a stake in maintaining it. For example, large insurance companies have strongly opposed changes that would reduce their opportunity for profit. Drug companies have bitterly resisted attempts to limit the cost of drugs. Many large companies have

Figure 19.14 The High Cost of U.S. Hospital Visits

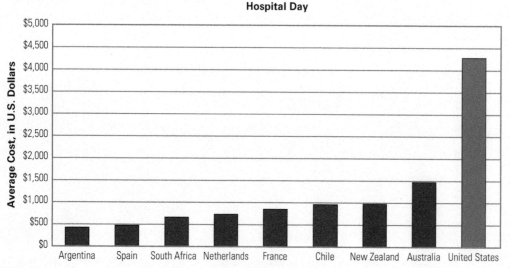

SOURCE: Data from International Federation of Health Plans, 2012.

also opposed significant reforms, fearing they may require them to pay higher taxes. This political opposition to change has been powerful, and in 2010 the ACA made only modest changes to the system. As noted, the biggest impacts of ACA have been in extending health insurance to previously uncovered individuals and families, and eliminating the rights of health insurance companies to discriminate in who they cover. Again, it has done much less to change the system of pricing and profit that remains at the core of American health care.

But there is hope. For one thing, the American medical system contains some of the finest clinics in the world, such as the Mayo Clinic, the Cleveland Clinic, and others (with world-class surgeons who are sought out by people from all over the world who sometimes will fly to the United States to undergo complicated procedures). The United States also has renowned scientific and medical research programs in medical schools and in the private sector. Although it is expensive to maintain, U.S. hospitals do employ cutting-edge technology and enjoy innovation that grows from the research developed at top medical schools. For the lucky people who have excellent health insurance, the American health care system generally works very well. The problem is that the quality at the top of the system is not available to all citizens.

Another reason for hope is that we have so much evidence from other countries around the world on how to do health care better, including how to control costs and to make sure that all citizens get proper care. Learning from other societies is one way to get to a better result. If politicians and policymakers do that, it is likely that in the future there will be important changes to the health care system that could lead to significantly better and more affordable care. Other countries provide a model. In the conclusion, we consider how sociological research can inform the direction of future change.

Conclusion: Health and Medicine

The importance of health care is obvious to everyone, and health and medical institutions are central in the modern world. As individuals, we rely on doctors, nurses, and other health care professionals to diagnose and treat us when we are sick. As a society, a remarkable amount of total economic activity—over one-sixth in the United States—is devoted to health care. But are we getting our money's worth? Perhaps not. Let's take an extreme example: Medical malpractice leading to death. It is certainly true, as a widely cited report by the Institute of Medicine (1999) put it, that "To Err is Human." But the same report noted that approximately 98,000 patients die in hospitals in the United States each year because of preventable medical mistakes. That is far more than those who died in car crashes, from breast cancer, or from AIDS. Although this number is sometimes contested (with both higher and lower estimates being suggested), whatever the true figure, no one should die in a hospital because of a preventable mistake. These large numbers suggest that in spite of the very large amount of money devoted to health care in the United States, there remain numerous shortcomings. How could things be made better? What are the questions we should be asking of our doctors, hospitals, drug companies, and insurance companies?

There are many ways in which a sociological model of health care is valuable for both understanding how health care systems work and for trying to improve them. Sociologists have long been interested in the question of who gets sick and why, who gets the best quality care, how and why the interactions between doctors and patients are so important, and how the organizational design of health care may exacerbate its problems. All of these issues must be addressed if Americans are to get the same quality health care as citizens of other rich countries at a price we can afford.

The Big Questions Revisited 19

19.1 How Do Social Contexts Affect Health? We often think of health outcomes as the result of individual choices. In this section, we explored how social contexts affect our health behaviors and how events that happen throughout our lives affect our health as adults.

A Sociological View of Health

The Population as Patient
Learning Objective 19.1.1: Describe the population model of prevention.

The Effects of Social Contexts on Individual Behavior
Learning Objective 19.1.2: Discuss how our social contexts and relationships help to determine the health choices we make.

The Accumulation of Health Risks Across the Life Course
Learning Objective 19.1.3: Explain how sociologists use life-course perspectives to examine health issues.

Differences in Health Across Countries
Learning Objective 19.1.4: Explain why where you live impacts your health.

Key Terms
social autopsy (p. 532)   individualism (p. 533)
epidemiology (p. 535)   life-course perspective
(p. 537)   infant mortality rate (p. 538)

19.2 Who Gets Sick, and Why? Low socioeconomic status is a strong predictor of poor health. Highly educated people, with higher incomes, are more likely to live a longer and healthier life than people who are not. This has been true throughout history and across many different countries. We explored why these patterns persist and the major explanations that sociologists have advanced to explain them.

Health Outcomes among Different Groups

Health and Socioeconomic Status
Learning Objective 19.2.1: Explain how socioeconomic status affects health.

Education
Learning Objective 19.2.2: Discuss the relationship between education and health.

Income and Wealth
Learning Objective 19.2.3: Discuss the impact that income and wealth have on children's health.

Race and Ethnic Differences in Health
Learning Objective 19.2.4: Discuss sociological explanations for health disparities among racial groups.

Gender
Learning Objective 19.2.5: Identify explanations for gender differences in health.

Key Terms
socioeconomic status (SES) (p. 540)   health disparities (p. 540)   socioeconomic gradient in health (p. 540)   fundamental social cause (p. 540) autism (p. 542)   Hispanic paradox (p. 542)

19.3 How Does Physician/Patient Interaction Affect Health and Illness? Few relationships produce more fraught interactions than that between doctors and patients. For a century, physicians dominated the relationship with their patients. Today, however, many people and experts are beginning to question what that relationship should look like. Patients ultimately know their own body better than anyone else, and there is a growing realization that patients can provide valuable opinions and participate in their care.

The Expertise of the Physician and the Knowledge of the Patient

Physicians and Power
Learning Objective 19.3.1: Discuss the lopsided nature of the traditional doctor–patient relationship.

Patient-Centered Care
Learning Objective 19.3.2: Describe various examples of patient-centered care and its impact on the doctor–patient relationship.

Key Terms
malpractice (p. 546)   American Medical Association (AMA) (p. 546)   medical board (p. 546) Medicare (p. 546)   Medicaid (p. 546)   patient-centered care (p. 547)   informed consent (p. 547)

19.4 What Is the Relationship between Epidemics and Societies? COVID-19 is the latest of many diseases that have killed large numbers of people throughout history. Societal responses to the appearance of these diseases have been remarkably similar, but their impact is much greater in some places more than others.

The Effects of Epidemics on Societies

Epidemics through History

Learning Objective 19.4.1: Discuss some of the major epidemics in human history.

Societies and Epidemics

Learning Objective 19.4.2: Explain how societies have responded to epidemics.

The Opioid Epidemic

Learning Objective 19.4.3: Describe how opioid abuse can become an epidemic.

Key Terms

epidemic (p. 549)   pandemic (p. 549)   communicable disease (p. 549)   plague (p. 550) herd immunity (p. 552)   zoonotic disease (p. 553)   opioids (p. 553)

19.5 Why Is Health Care in America So Much More Expensive than in Other Countries?
No matter how researchers calculate what the United States spends on health care, it is far more expensive than in any other country. In this section, we explored the possible explanations for the high cost of health care in the United States and whether the system can be fixed.

American Health Care in Comparative Perspective

The Structure of Health Insurance in the United States

Learning Objective 19.5.1: Describe the free market of American health insurance.

Markets and Health Care

Learning Objective 19.5.2: Compare and contrast health care markets with markets for other goods and services.

The Role of Insurance in the Economic Market for Health Care

Learning Objective 19.5.3: Analyze the role of health insurance in the economic market for health care.

Analyzing the High Cost of Health Care in the United States

Learning Objective 19.5.4: Outline the possible explanations for the high cost of health care in the United States.

Can the System Be Fixed?

Learning Objective 19.5.5: Explain why the problems with American health care have been so difficult to fix.

Key Terms

Affordable Care Act (ACA) (p. 556)   pre-existing conditions (p. 556)   information asymmetry (p. 557)   moral hazard (p. 558)   fee for service (p. 561)   path dependency (p. 563)

Chapter 20
Crime and Punishment

By Jeff Manza, Troy Duster, and Patrick Sharkey

On February 7, 2017, newly elected President Donald Trump was speaking before an audience of sheriffs from all over the country when he made a remarkable statement: "The murder rate in our country is the highest it's been in forty-seven years, right? Did you know that? Forty-seven years." As many observers quickly pointed out, the former president's claim was incorrect. In fact, the homicide rate in 2016 was lower than it had been at almost any point in the nation's modern history.

What the former president might have meant to say was that the homicide rate had *increased* more from 2015 to 2016 than it had at any point in almost 50 years. (That statement was arguably correct, but only because the murder rate had been steadily declining for most of that period and a recent uptick hardly changed the long-term trend.) The former president's misstatement is important because it reflects the widespread confusion, misunderstanding, and outright distortion of facts about crime and violence in the United States. Because the vast majority of Americans will never be the victim of a serious violent crime, most people don't have personal experience to guide their perceptions of the scale of the problem. Many Americans still get their news from local television stations, which have a documented bias for blood. (There is a longstanding saying, "if it bleeds, it leads," referring to the placement of stories about murders in television news.) And many people watch films and television shows featuring violence and murders, which give a very distorted sense of how much violence occurs across the country (Olmstead et al. 2013). In fact, in 2019, about 64 percent of all Americans told a Gallup pollster that crime in America was higher than last year, when it was actually slightly lower than in other recent years (for example, it was 74 percent in 2009 and 70 percent in 2011) (McCarthy 2020).

As we will demonstrate in this chapter, these public fears are completely at odds with undisputed facts about crime. There are different measures of understanding crime, but every single one of these sources tells us that the level of violence was cut in half, or more in some places, between the early 1990s to 2019 (before the COVID-19 pandemic). Indeed, most types of crime had declined by about that much as well (Gramlich 2020). The vast misunderstanding about the

My Sociological Imagination

TROY DUSTER

The first 16 years of my life were spent in a low-income, racially segregated neighborhood on Chicago's South Side. It was a period in the United States in which racial segregation was taken for granted at barber shops, bowling alleys, swimming pools, and many public accommodations—even in the urban North. Frank Wong, the son of a Chinese restaurant owner in the area, was the only student in my high school who was not Black. Then, at age 17, I crossed town to attend Northwestern University, where I was one of only seven Blacks on a campus of over 7,000 Whites. Anthropologists call it "culture shock" when the deep assumptions about what is normal are disrupted by new circumstances, whether by travel to a foreign country or by being thrust into an unfamiliar social world where previously held assumptions have little or no relevance. For me, sociology provided a handle on my situation, a way to understand why and how people explain away their privilege as if it were an individual accomplishment. I watched with the astonishment of the outsider how people from wealthy families concluded unreflectively that the way the world was ordered was natural and right. Of course, many poor people also see the way the world is organized as normal, so that was no surprise. But it was the attempt to explain the "why" that caught my attention, intrigued and stoked my intellectual curiosity, and brought me into sociology.

The prison population in the United States grew at an alarming rate between 1970 and 2015, before stabilizing at a level that is by far the highest in the world, even though crime in America has seen a major decline over the past 30 years.

Aerial Archives/Alamy Stock Photo

nature and extent of crime is important because beliefs about crime shape so many *other* ideas about social life and the people living in cities and communities. This is all the more true for violent crimes that have the biggest impact on social life. The murder rate did spike upward in 2020, likely due to the effects of the COVID-19 pandemic, although other types of crime, for the most part and in most places, did not show any increase. The uptick in the murder rate has received considerable media attention, but no one yet knows whether it portends a reversal of the long-term decline in violence, or if it is just another example of the short-term impact of the extraordinary changes brought about by the global pandemic (Fuller and Arango 2020).

In this chapter, we'll begin by reviewing exactly what we mean by the idea of crime, and how societies define the boundary between crime and ordinary deviance (discussed in Chapter 7). Then we'll then turn to an analysis of various leading sociological theories of crime and discuss how these theories have evolved over time. Finally, we consider how society's response to crime can itself be problematic. Our focus throughout the chapter will be on the United States, in order to permit us to dig deeper into the unique aspects of what has come to be known as mass incarceration. As we will show, the very high levels of punishment in recent decades have created their own important societal consequences.

The Big Questions

1. **What constitutes a crime, and what are the different offense types?** In this section, we explore how and why certain types of actions are labeled criminal, the different types of criminal categories, and the consequences for individuals convicted of crimes.

2. **How much crime, particularly violent crime, exists in America?** Violent crime has been declining in the United States for decades, and yet there is more violent crime in the United States than in many other countries of the developed world. How much more, and why? In this section, we explore possible explanations for this discrepancy and examine the consequences of violence.

3. **How do sociologists seek to understand crime and punishment?** Many social scientists and theorists have explored the question of why crimes are committed and how societies decide whether and how to punish. In this section, we examine the work of several influential classical and modern social theorists, and we explore how a sociological perspective helps us to understand why some actions are considered criminal. We also discuss the possible goals, or purposes, of punishment within a society.

4. **What is the role of racism in the criminal justice system?** Racial inequalities in how the American criminal justice system responds to crime has a long and troubled history. It has also been the subject of intense focus driven by the rise of the Black Lives Matter (BLM) movement. In this section, we provide an overview and analysis of the racial disparities in the criminal justice system.

5. **Why is mass incarceration controversial?** The American criminal justice system in recent years has undergone a remarkable change. The incarcerated population in the United States has grown 600 percent over the past 40 years. In this section, we explore the reasons behind this massive increase in the number of Americans behind bars, and we examine how the U.S. prison population compares to those in similar countries.

6. **What are the consequences of mass incarceration?** For sociologists, the study of mass incarceration must take into account not just why people commit crimes and why societies choose to punish those actions, but also the larger impact for families, communities, and society. In this final section on the criminal justice system, we consider a few of these additional consequences of mass punishment.

Kevork Djansezian/Getty Images

BIG QUESTION 20.1 What Constitutes a Crime, and What Are the Different Offense Types?

THE PROBLEM OF DEFINING CRIME

Everyone, in all societies and at all points in time, agrees that crime, especially violent crime, is a central social problem. Anyone who has been the victim of a serious crime can attest to its impact on their lives (and perhaps also on the lives of their close friends and family members). Crime is also harmful for communities; high-crime neighborhoods are places that are less desirable to live in and potentially can degenerate over time. Not surprisingly, given its impact, sociologists have long studied crime and attempted to explain both why it is such a universal feature of social life and how societies have, or should, respond to crime.

But before we can get to these big issues, we need to develop an understanding of what, exactly, is a crime. It turns out that is often not a simple question. Criminal acts are part of a continuum of socially proscribed—or forbidden—actions. Yet not all proscribed actions are defined as criminal. We might, for example, think of picking our nose in public as being at one end of this hypothetical continuum and committing a murder at the other end. They both violate common norms of behavior, and as such are examples of **deviance** (see Chapter 7). But why do some kinds of behavior violate societal rules while other similar behaviors do not? How does *criminal*—as opposed to merely deviant—behavior come to be defined?

Defining Crime

20.1.1 Define crime and the role of the penal code.

To put it as simply as possible, a **crime** is literally any activity that violates the **penal code**, or the written laws that identify and prohibit various acts. The penal code is sometimes also known as the "criminal code," as it constitutes the official legal framework defining criminal and noncriminal behavior. It often also specifies a range of penalties for anyone convicted of the proscribed behavior. To take a very simple example, every penal code in the world identifies the murder of an innocent person as an illegal act. If you kill somebody for no legally valid reason (such as self-defense) and you are caught, you are very likely to face a substantial punishment no matter where you live.

Beyond murder and a few other acts that are prohibited just about everywhere in the world (such as violent assaults, rape, and the unauthorized taking of private property), there is a lot of variation in what is considered criminal. For example, buying, possessing, and smoking marijuana is completely or mostly legal in a growing number of states, and in a number of other states it has been **decriminalized** (so that while technically against the law, there is little to no enforcement). In some states, it is allowed for medical use only, while it remains illegal to possess or distribute for any reason in other states. The same thing is true internationally; a few (but growing) number of countries around the world also allow possession and consumption of marijuana (for example, Uruguay, Canada, the Netherlands), others have

Jeffrey Rotman/Alamy Stock Photo

Joe Amon/The Denver Post/Getty Images

Beyond universally prohibited acts such as murder, rape, and assault, what is considered criminal varies depending on where you live. For example, buying or selling marijuana is legal in a growing number of places around the world and in the United States, with it being sold in specialty shops just like other consumer goods (see image on the left from a cannabis store in Illinois). But it remains prohibited elsewhere, and arrests for selling or possessing drugs (like the people being arrested on the right) continues in many other places.

decriminalized it (as in virtually all of South America and many other places), and many allow it for medicinal use; however, it is illegal everywhere else (and in some places still punished relatively harshly).

There are three primary layers of criminal justice administration in the United States, and each layer has its own penal code:

- Federal government
- State governments
- Local governments (county and city)

To clarify what these layers mean, let's say you are standing in Rochester, New York. You are subject to the laws of the United States (federal), New York State (state), the county of Monroe (local), and the city of Rochester (local). Each of these entities is known as a **jurisdiction**, and each regulates certain kinds of crimes. When it comes to crime, state governments establish by far the most important of these laws, identifying actions that will be illegal across the entire state. The overwhelming majority (about 90 percent) of people convicted of crimes will be charged under a state law. The penal code of the federal government focuses especially on the commission of criminal acts that cross state lines (such as transporting illegal goods), organized crime (which has been a primary responsibility of the federal government since early in the twentieth century), crimes against the United States (such as terrorism, spying, or failing to pay taxes), and political or election fraud in national elections. About 10 percent of all crimes will be charged under federal law. Local jurisdictions add additional rules that typically focus on minor infractions, such as traffic rules (for example, establishing penalties for violating traffic signals), parking regulations, curfews, landlord/tenant laws, and others.

Different Types of Crime: A Brief Overview

20.1.2 **Explain how crimes are classified in the United States and the possible punishment associated with each type.**

Crimes are commonly sorted by their severity into one of three types: **Felonies**, **misdemeanors**, and **infractions**. The classification is based on the kinds of punishments a court may impose if it determines that a crime has been committed.

Felonies are typically defined as crimes that may be punished by at least a year in prison. Not all felony convictions lead to such a punishment, but such a punishment is at least possible for any offense defined as a felony. All of the most serious criminal acts are considered felonies in the penal codes in the United States. Among the most common are the following:

- Violent crimes (murder, assault, robbery that involves the threat of violence)
- Rape and sexual assault
- Property crimes (theft)
- Weapons violations (carrying a gun without a license)
- Forgery and counterfeiting
- Drunk driving
- Sale or possession of illegal drugs

One of the defining features of a felony charge is that it could lead to a sentence of one or more years in **prison**, a correctional facility that primarily houses felons. Local or county **jails**, by contrast, are facilities that generally hold people who are either awaiting trial or serving shorter (usually non-felony) sentences. Not all convicted felons necessarily serve time in prison; a significant percentage can be given a sentence of **probation**, which allows them to serve out their sentence while living in their community, but under the close scrutiny of the criminal justice system. And some felons will be released from prison on **parole** before they have served their entire sentence. While on parole, they too will be allowed to return to their communities but continue to face various restrictions and correctional supervision (for example, by regularly reporting to a parole officer who monitors their behavior).

Misdemeanors are typically criminal acts that are illegal, but for which the maximum punishment is less than a year in prison. Misdemeanor crimes include some of the offenses listed above (particularly for a less serious or harmful variant, for example, breaking into a private home and stealing thousands of dollars' worth of jewelry versus stealing a bicycle on the street) as well as other more minor illegal acts (such as drug possession). Many arrests are for crimes that could be charged as felonies, but for various reasons (a relatively minor version of the crime or a first offense) an accused offender may not face a felony charge. Repeat offenders, however, may experience the reverse—seemingly minor crimes being upgraded to felonies.

Crimes that may be charged as either a felony or a misdemeanor are known as "wobblers," and can include punishments ranging from no prison time to multiple years in prison. The decision of how to charge a crime rests with the prosecutor in charge of the case (Pfaff 2017). A large majority of criminal charges will be settled between the prosecuting district attorney and the accused person's lawyer in what is called a **plea bargain**. However, the final decision of whether a particular conviction for a crime will stand as a felony conviction or a misdemeanor conviction rests with the judge of the case and the type of punishment ultimately handed down.

Infractions are actions that break a rule or law but are typically punished only by fines or public service, not imprisonment of any sort (although an offender may sometimes be held by the police before a ticket is written). The most common simple infractions include parking tickets or speeding violations, which are routinely resolved on the spot by the issuance of a ticket and an accompanying fine. Other kinds of minor infractions—riding a bicycle on the sidewalk, sneaking on to public transit without paying, painting graffiti on a wall, hanging out in a public park after curfew—may or may not be enforced by police officers. This discretion about whether to enforce minor infractions is an area

Steve Skjold/Alamy Stock Photo

We immediately recognize this image as a police officer issuing a motorist a ticket for a driving violation. While a routine speeding violation, for example, is against the law, it is considered an infraction and punishment is typically resolved by paying a fine. However, if the same driver is caught "drunk driving," with alcohol in their system found to be above the legal limit, they can be charged with a felony.

of controversy, with significant evidence that minor infractions are much more likely to be enforced in poor communities or against young people, especially poor young men of color.

White-Collar Crime and Street Crime

20.1.3 Compare and contrast white-collar crime and street crime.

One of the most important developments in the study of crime was the notion of white-collar crime as a distinctive type of criminal activity. First introduced by the famous criminologist Edwin Sutherland in 1949, the term **white-collar crime** refers to unethical business practices committed by people in the course of their work careers. White-collar crime can be further subdivided into two parts: *Occupational crime* refers to crimes against an employer (for example, using a corporate credit card to make unauthorized purchases for personal benefit) while **corporate crime** refers to crimes committed by or for the benefit of a corporation. An example of corporate crime is when executives attempt to hide corporate debt or overstate earnings to shareholders or receive information that a product sold by the corporation is defective or harmful to purchasers in some way.

White-collar crime is frequently contrasted with **street crime**, that is, most other crimes which can be said to be committed "on the street" (see Figure 20.1). Historically, white-collar crimes were handled almost solely in civil courts. This was, in Sutherland's view, often perverse: Many kinds of white-collar crime can have as much or

Figure 20.1 Types of Crime

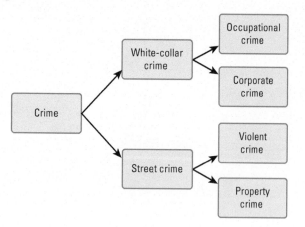

more of a negative impact and cause injury to more people in a society than ordinary street crimes (such as burglary, robbery, vandalism, shoplifting, or assault). For example, when a corporation or business owner knowingly markets an unsafe product, far more people may suffer significantly greater harm than any thief or bank robber can cause. Sutherland concluded that when business activity damages innocent people's property or physical well-being, it is completely arbitrary to absolve the wrongdoer of criminal responsibility (Sutherland 1949).

As noted, white-collar crime can take many forms, from being closer to street crimes (stealing money from your employer or using the internet to defraud others, which closely parallels robbing someone on the street), all the way up to involving powerful businesses and corporate leaders who make decisions or seek profits in ways that cause injury or harm to innocent people (which might have no direct parallel with street crime). Perhaps not surprisingly, there has been much more agreement that lower-level white-collar crimes, such as embezzlement or fraud, are properly situated in criminal (or sometimes in civil) courts. Yet to this day, it is almost always the case that a corporation can "pay" for its crimes by paying a fine, while street crimes often lead to prison.

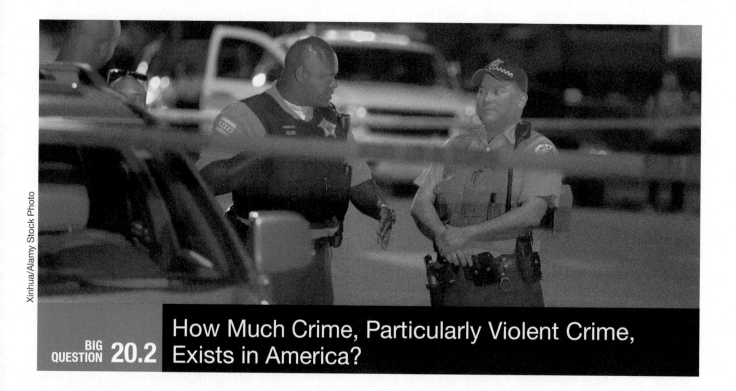

Xinhua/Alamy Stock Photo

BIG QUESTION 20.2 How Much Crime, Particularly Violent Crime, Exists in America?

CRIME AND VIOLENCE IN THE UNITED STATES

Is violent and serious crime higher overall in the United States than in other countries? And is it worse than in the past? The United States is often considered a violent country by both foreigners and Americans. These perceptions are reinforced in popular culture; the average American child will have witnessed thousands of murders and violent acts in movies and on television and may have been exposed to considerable violence in video games and other social media by age 18. Violent American movies and TV shows are viewed across the globe. It is very easy to believe that violence is a way of life in America. But how valid is this perception?

In this section of the chapter, we examine overall trends in crime in the United States, and compare them to other countries. We will then turn our focus to violent crime, the most consequential type of crime for individuals who experience it and societies as a whole. Is the U.S. uniquely violent? What factors seem to contribute to violent crime?

Trends in Crime

20.2.1 Explain how crime is tracked in the United States and how the homicide rate has changed in recent decades.

Since the beginning of the 1960s, crime in the United States has followed two major trends. These trends are immediately visible in Figure 20.2, which shows the national homicide rate, defined as the number of murders for every 100,000 Americans, beginning in 1960 and running through the last year available from the FBI. In the first period, running from the early 1960s to the early 1990s, the homicide rate rose quickly, more than doubling from 1963 to 1974. It then remained at an extremely high level, fluctuating between 8 and 10 murders per 100,000 residents from the mid-1970s through the early 1990s.

During this period, violent crime became a central feature of life in many American cities, leading to widespread fear of cities and increasingly harsh criminal justice policies. Leading experts warned about a new breed of criminal terrorizing city streets, using sensational language designed to stoke the public's fears (Bennett, DiIulio, and Walters 1996). A national panic around the problem of violence reached its peak in the mid-1990s, and leading criminologists predicted "a bloodbath of teen violence" was on its way (Butterfield 1995).

But those experts were wrong. The second period, shown on the right of Figure 20.2, displays the sharp decline of homicides that began in the mid-1990s. The homicide rate fell in 1993, remained about the same in 1994, and then dropped continuously every year for the rest of the decade. By the end of the 1990s, there were about 6 murders for every 100,000 Americans, a level that had not been seen

since the 1960s. After a few years where it remained steady, the homicide rate then began to inch down further. By the end of the 2000s, the homicide rate had dipped below the rate of 5 homicides for every 100,000 people less than half of what it was at its peak. As we noted in the introduction, there was an uptick in the murder rate during the COVID-19 pandemic, but whether that is the result of the unique environment brought on by the virus or the beginning of a larger trend is not yet clear. Current estimates are that the murder rate will have increased by about 25%, going from about 5 in 100,000 to a little over 6 per 100,000. But other violent crimes decreased or stayed about the lame low levels as in prior years (Beckett and Layton 2021).

Every murder is a tragedy, and even the lower level of violence since the 1990s remains higher than in countries most similar to the United States (a topic we'll cover shortly). But it is important to acknowledge just how far the homicide rate has fallen, and to appreciate the fact that (prior to COVID-19, and hopefully after) we are still living in the safest era of the nation's history. Far more people—on average, about twice as many—will die in traffic accidents than will be murdered. And it is not just homicides that have fallen in the past few decades, as noted. Violent crimes include **murder** (the intentional killing of another person), **robbery** (theft involving the actual or threatened use of force), **assault** (a physical attack that injures another person but does not kill them), and **rape** (a physical sexual assault). Over the period in which the homicide rate dropped 52 percent, the rate of all violent crimes dropped 49 percent. Rape is down 36 percent, burglary is down 46 percent, and motor vehicle theft is down 65 percent since 1992 (Federal Bureau of Investigation 2015). Despite this positive news, why is it that so many Americans still don't believe that crime has fallen? To answer this question, we first have to investigate where we get our data on crime. Most of what we know about crime in the United States comes from statistics published by the Federal Bureau of Investigation (FBI), which gathers and aggregates data from reports filed by police departments around the country. Herein lies part of the problem: Many people don't trust police departments to report accurately and honestly on crime. Police departments are not always diligent in their reporting of crime, and police chiefs and local commanders have a strong incentive to show that crime is dropping in their precincts and cities, leading some to question whether the level of crime is underreported in official statistics.

Figure 20.2 The National Homicide Rate

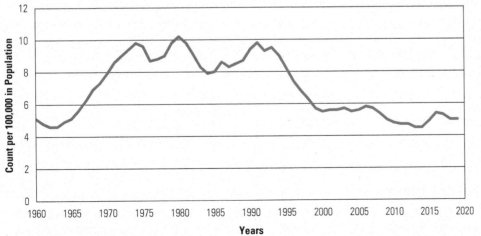

SOURCE: FBI Uniform Crime Reporting Program, Retrieved from https://crime-data-explorer.fr.cloud.gov/explorer/national/united-states/crime.

Investigations conducted in several cities suggest that we should be at least somewhat skeptical when we see data on crime reported by police departments. One investigative report conducted in 2014 by journalists at *Chicago Magazine* revealed dozens of deaths in the city of Chicago that appeared to be murders but were classified by the police department as "noncriminal" deaths (Bernstein and Isackson 2014). When the city's own investigative agency conducted a study to examine official crime statistics in more depth, it found that the police department had substantially undercounted the number of violent crimes, making Chicago seem safer than it was (City of Chicago 2014). Urban schools are another setting in which violence is often underreported, perhaps out of the local government's concern that the reputation of the school district will decline if all incidents of school violence are recorded (Sanchez-Jankowski 2016).

Considering these findings, perhaps the skeptics who don't trust any official figures on crime are correct. Is it possible that, despite the numbers, crime hasn't changed much at all? To address this possibility, it is useful to consider multiple forms of data from multiple sources. One important source of data comes from surveys asking Americans whether they have been the victim of a criminal act. The **National Crime Victimization Survey (NCVS)** was established in the early 1970s as a way to capture the level of criminal victimization as experienced by a national sample of American residents, and it is now fielded in many countries around the world. It is a source of data on crime that provides a useful complement to the official statistics compiled by the FBI because the NCVS is not affected by changes in the way that crime is monitored or reported by the police. Data from the NCVS show that the rate of serious victimization (robbery, aggravated assault, and sexual assault/rape) has fallen by more than 75 percent from 1993 to 2015 (Bureau of Justice Statistics 2016). The NCVS suggests that the trends reported by police departments may actually be *underestimating* how much violence has fallen. While police departments may have incentives to show they are successful in fighting crime, they may also not want to acknowledge that crime is so low that cities can afford to have fewer police!

The larger point is this: Even if there is no perfect way of measuring crime, different sorts of data all point to one critical conclusion: Crime rates, after rising in the 1960s, have fallen dramatically in recent decades.

Why Did Crime Decline?

20.2.2 Discuss some of the leading factors on why crime has declined.

Sociologists, of course, want to know: Why did crime decline (prior to the pandemic)? The answer, after hundreds of research studies and national panels of experts

tasked with discussing the issue, is, unfortunately, fairly complex. There is no single reason why. Because there are multiple factors at work, researchers have struggled to demonstrate how much each of these factors has contributed, and different research methods and approaches have yielded somewhat different results. However, there are several factors that have stood out as especially important. We will briefly summarize some of the most signficant ones here.

ECONOMIC IMPROVEMENT IN THE 1990S Recall that crime began to decline in the early 1990s. The second half of the 1990s was marked by an unusually healthy and fast-growing economy. Unemployment fell to record lows. Family incomes rose. Many high-crime communities saw a period of genuine revival. It is certain that these improvements provided more opportunities for a wider range of people than was the case in the 1970s and 1980s, and the calculus about risks and benefits of crime would have shifted in favor of legal employment. However, after 2000, the economic picture became more uneven. The very sharp economic downturn called the Great Recession (2007–09) led to high unemployment rates until about 2016. We might have expected more of an increase in crime during this time. But that wasn't the case. So while a healthy economy in the 1990s was probably helpful in starting the process of reducing crime, other factors were at work in the 2000s for keeping the crime rate low.

CHANGES IN POLICING Although the role of policing in the criminal justice system is and remains controversial (and we will discuss it more fully later in the chapter), it is likely that at least some of the drop in crime was due to improved police department tactics around the country. These tactics were of two kinds: (1) Increasing "community policing" strategies, in which police officers and police departments made greater efforts to get to know people in the neighborhoods or communities they patrolled; and (2) the use of more high-tech approaches to getting more police officers to where crimes are most likely to be committed. In other words, police departments simply got better at locating and arresting more offenders before they could commit further crimes, and improved their ability to police high-crime areas. Modern police departments use computer technologies to identify "hotspots" of criminal activity and flood these areas with a higher police presence (Brayne 2020). Also, in the mid-1990s, police departments grew in size as a result of major, and very controversial, legislation passed by Congress in 1994 and signed into law by former President Bill Clinton. The 1994 crime bill provided federal government funding to hire an additional 100,000 police officers across the country. There are different opinions on how much changes in policing contributed to the falling crime rate, but it likely did play a role (Zimring 2011). However, many sociologists are critical of certain aspects of contemporary policing, as we will explore later in the chapter. In general, many research studies have concluded that whatever benefits there have been due to improved policing, there have also been many continuing or even worsening issues caused by new tactics in relation to civil liberties, social inequalities, and continuing the use of excessive force by the police (Kohler-Hausmann 2018; Brayne 2020).

MASS INCARCERATION The vast increase in punishment and imprisonment from the 1970s through 2010 had a modest impact on holding down crime (Raphael and Stoll 2009). It would be surprising if this was not the case: Simply keeping more people who have committed crimes in prison, and for longer periods, will tend to nudge down crime. However, as with improved policing, the massive increase in the use of the prison as a tool for fighting crime has had many other, less positive consequences (which we will also discuss later in the chapter). One less-noticed consequence of mass incarceration that is difficult to measure but likely important is that, as young people living in poor neighborhoods see more of their older family members and neighbors being sent to prison for long sentences, their own likelihood of getting involved in criminal activity may decline (Skogan 2009).

COMMUNITY-BASED INITIATIVES It is likely that up until recently, we have significantly underestimated how important community organizations have been in reducing crime. As crime rates reached a second peak in the late 1980s, particularly in relation to murders and other violent offenses (see Figure 20.2), many community organizations formed and made crime reduction a priority. These community-based groups were sometimes in a much better position than the police were to intervene with potential or actual offenders (Sharkey 2018). Many of these groups have been able to win grants from federal, state, or local governments to expand their efforts. In New York City, for example, the Cure Violence program has supported groups across the city who are working to reduce violence in their communities. Leaders are known as "violence interrupters," and the evidence suggests they are likely having an impact (Delgado et al. 2017).

POSITIVE SPIRALS IN SOME PREVIOUSLY HIGH-CRIME URBAN AREAS Most street crimes are committed in large urban areas, where opportunities for gain are much greater than in suburban or rural areas, and where inequality is highest. Urban neighborhoods that have become crime ridden are often places where residents with the most resources will move out, creating a situation in which the most impoverished families are left behind, and where crime becomes part of everyday life, reinforcing a negative spiral of decline (Wilson 1987; Skogan 1990). But the reverse of this process can happen as well. Indeed, this is what appears to have happened in many places from the 1990s onward. There were a number of reasons why previously high-crime areas improved. Immigration was a key part of this process; rising rates of immigration helped to repopulate some of the most dangerous urban neighborhoods with immigrant families who committed relatively few crimes (new immigrants tend to have low crime rates) (Sampson 2015). More and more young people and families were choosing to live in cities rather than suburbs as well, helping to make cities safer in the process (see Chapter 15 for more details about urban change). The upshot has been a positive cycle in many urban, formerly high-crime areas around the country.

DEMOGRAPHIC CHANGE Finally, there are fewer young people in recent decades than in the past. The birth rate declined sharply after 1964—the end of the "baby boom" decade—and by the early 1990s, there were fewer people under the age of 35 than there had been in earlier decades. Higher rates of immigration partially reversed the decline in young people and then stabilized the number by the 2000s. But overall, the age profile shifted toward an older population (Mather and Kilduff 2020). And one of the most well-established research findings is that older people are less likely to engage in criminal activity.

American Violence in Comparative Perspective

20.2.3 Analyze why there is more violent crime in the United States than in many other countries of the developed world.

While crime overall has steadily declined, it is still the case that consequential, violent crime is an important part of American society. Overall, it is difficult to characterize the United States as either a violent or safe country, partly because the characterization depends on what societies we are comparing it to. As we've mentioned, compared to its own recent history, the nation is safer now than it has been in decades. But comparing the United States to the rest of the world is more difficult because each country tracks violent crime in different ways. The most reliable way to compare nations is to focus on homicides, which are tracked almost everywhere in similar ways. Compared to all nations of the world, the United States has a low rate of homicides (see Figure 20.3, which displays the murder rate in a number of countries). According to estimates from the United Nations Office of Drugs and Crime, there are more than 30 homicides for every 100,000 residents of nations like Honduras, Mexico, Venezuela, Colombia, South Africa, Zambia, and Jamaica (United Nations Office on Drugs and Crime 2013). In the United States, in recent years there were around 5 homicides for every 100,000 residents, well below a global average of about 7 per 100,000 population.

Figure 20.3 doesn't make the murder rate in the United States seem especially high. But perhaps comparing the United States to *all* other countries is not necessarily the right

Figure 20.3 Homicide Rates Around the World, 2016

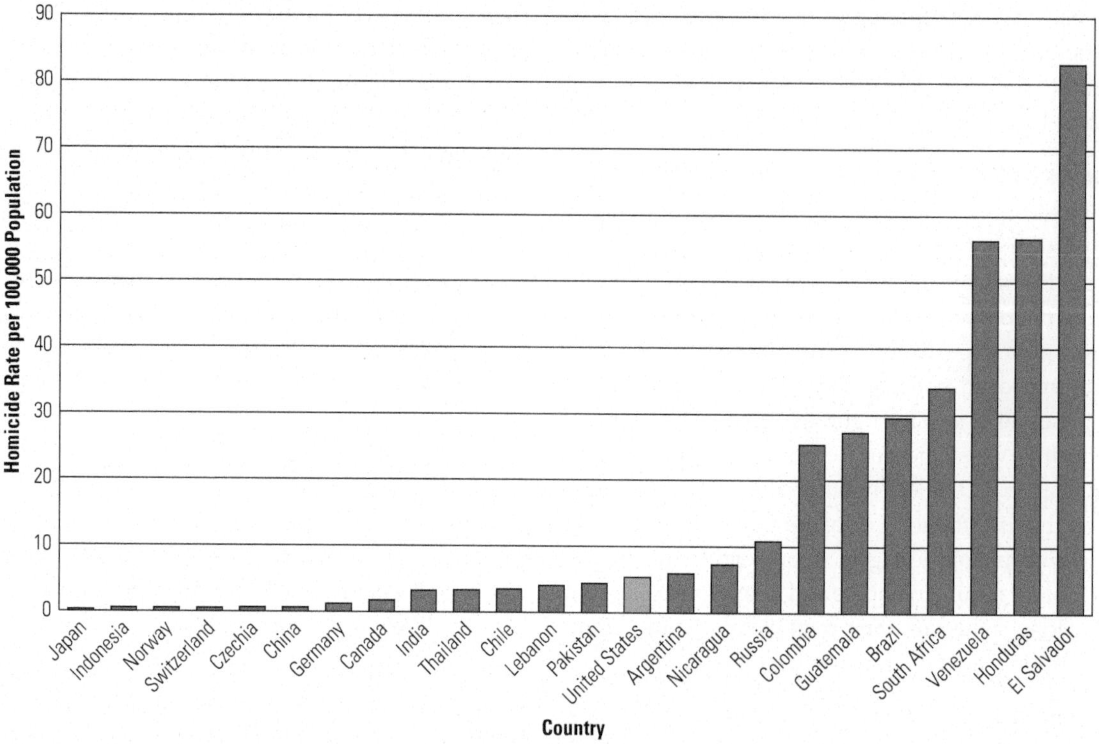

SOURCE: UN Office on Drugs and Crime (dataunodc.un.org/crime/intentional-homicide-victims).

comparison. In fact, when compared to a smaller set of more developed, wealthier countries, the United States does not fare as well. Notice the countries on the left side of Figure 20.3, which have far lower homicide rates than the United States. The U.S. homicide rate is more than twice as high as in nations like Canada, France, Germany, Switzerland, and other countries of the developed world, places where there are typically fewer than 2 homicides per 100,000 residents. We also have a higher homicide rate than many developing countries (such as India, Thailand, and Pakistan).

Why is lethal violence more common in the United States than in other similar rich countries? The answer to this question is subject to debate. Some scholars have suggested that America's high rate of violence is a cultural heritage derived from the time of the frontier, when Americans were forced to resolve disputes by force, without any official authority or strong institutions set up to enforce the law (Pinker 2011). Others point to a more straightforward answer: The United States has far more guns in circulation than most other developed countries (and Americans' love of guns may relate to the larger culture history of violence). In most countries, it is impossible to know exactly what proportion of the population owns a gun, but every source of data indicates that America has an extremely high rate of gun ownership. Researchers studying gun violence have developed a very useful way to estimate the prevalence of gun ownership by calculating the proportion of all suicides that are carried out with a gun

(Cook and Ludwig 2005). Although this measure is not perfect, it seems to work very well in capturing how many guns are circulating in a given society, and it confirms the high level of gun ownership in the U.S. (Hemenway and Miller 2000). In other words, an idea that might seem logical—that the more guns in circulation, the more homicides that are committed—is supported by careful social science research. Guns don't necessarily create more violent conflicts, but their presence does make conflicts *more lethal* and more likely to result in someone's death.

The Consequences of Violence

20.2.4 Analyze the consequences of violence as both a public health problem and a social problem.

At its core, violence is a public health problem. The best estimates from the FBI tell us that more than 15,000 people across the country were killed with malicious intent by another person in 2015. Unlike most other major public health problems, the victims of violence are mostly young people. Homicide is the third leading cause of death among Americans ranging from age 15 to 34 (Lyons et al. 2016). Among Blacks in this age range, homicide is the *leading* cause of death. Guns are the weapon that is used in the vast majority of murders.

The loss of life is the most direct, basic, and tragic consequence of violence. But violence also affects other dimensions of social life in the United States, and sociologists are concerned not only with the causes of violence but how it can have other social consequences. In the early 1990s, when violent crime was twice as high as it is today, urban neighborhoods throughout the country were dominated by the threat of violence. In his influential book *Code of the Street*, sociologist Elijah Anderson (1999) documented the daily challenges faced by young people navigating the dangerous streets of certain high-crime neighborhoods in Philadelphia on a daily basis. Anderson showed how the constant risk of violence forced young people to adopt a code of behavior to ward off potential attackers and mitigate the potential for victimization.

A large body of evidence suggests that students carry the burden of community violence with them into the school and classroom settings. When children are given tests of academic skills in the days after an incident of extreme violence has taken place close to their home, they perform substantially worse than when the same children take the same tests at a time when there has been no recent violence (Sharkey et al. 2012). A vivid example of the impact of violence comes from research done in Virginia in the aftermath of a series of random shootings that took place in October 2002. Over three weeks, a serial killer that came to be known as the "Beltway sniper" killed 10 people and wounded three more while terrorizing the entire region surrounding Washington, D.C. Researchers gathered data from students in Virginia and found that

students in schools located within five miles of a shooting were somewhere between 5 and 9 percentage points less likely to pass their state English and language arts or math assessments (Gershenson and Tekin 2015).

Violence doesn't make children less intelligent, of course, but it occupies their minds and makes it more difficult to focus on mundane tasks like classroom assignments or tests. Children who live in particularly violent communities for long periods of time are more likely to have deficits in cognitive skills and reading achievement, along with lower grades, lower levels of school attendance, and lower rates of high school graduation and college attendance (Bowen and Bowen 1999; Hurt et al. 2001; Delaney-Black et al. 2002).

The impact of violence extends beyond the educational system and affects entire communities. In researching urban neighborhoods across eight cities, sociologists have found that high rates of crime and disorder were associated with higher rates of fear, neighborhood dissatisfaction, and intentions to move out (Skogan 1990). When neighborhoods are unsafe, families and business owners are less willing to make investments in communities, and streets may empty out as individuals and families with the means to do so move to other neighborhoods. The concentration of violence, in combination with racial segregation and concentrated poverty, can act to undermine community life and contribute to a spiral of urban decay.

Frank Röhm|der/Westend61 GmbH/Alamy Stock Photo

BIG QUESTION **20.3** How Do Sociologists Seek to Understand Crime and Punishment?

THEORIES OF CRIME AND PUNISHMENT

We have provided a formal definition of crime and tracked recent trends in violence in the United States. But sociologists have long grappled with a broader set of questions

about why some actions and some people are considered "criminal" while others are not, and how punishment is used to regulate behavior and control crime. In this section, we review both early and modern theories of crime and punishment, before describing how the criminal justice system has evolved and expanded in the United States.

Early Theories on Crime and Punishment

20.3.1 Describe the most influential early social theories on crime and punishment.

Cesare Beccaria was an eighteenth-century Italian political philosopher who formulated one of the most influential, systematic theories of punishment. In *On Crimes and Punishments*, first published in 1764, Beccaria argued that punishment is only justified to ensure greater compliance with societal norms and rules. When punishment occurs, he argued, it should be designed to serve the public good by providing incentives for people to avoid criminal activity (Beccaria [1764] 1986). He developed a hierarchy of crimes, providing one of the first efforts to differentiate the seriousness of particular kinds of criminal acts. Beccaria's ideas were so influential they can be found in some of the documents of America's founding fathers. His core ideas, that people are rational and that punishment can influence crime rates by deterring antisocial behavior, remains to this day one of the central underpinnings of the criminal justice system.

A second, contrasting view of crime and punishment is associated with the work of another Italian, Cesare Lombroso (1835–1909), a physician who is sometimes called the "father" of the field of **criminology** (and who held the first university professorship in that field at the University of Turin). Lombroso believed criminal activity was attributable to hereditary defects in certain people, going so far as to identify physical features more likely to be exhibited by criminals: A sloping forehead, large ears, long arms, and a smaller brain, for instance. According to Lombroso, criminals are born, not made, and punishment should focus on removing these harmful individuals from society. However, because criminality was a function of inherited traits, as opposed to choices made by a rational calculating individual, Lombroso also argued that the penal system should focus on treating criminals humanely, and prisons should be designed to help those with criminal tendencies overcome their innate predispositions.

Lombroso's theories on the characteristics of criminals were long ago dismissed as the worst form of junk science, utilizing methods that today would be viewed as laughable. Writing in an era in which racist impulses informed some social science formulations, Lombroso and his followers considered non-Europeans to be members of a more primitive species. Many early American studies of crime, in the late nineteenth and early twentieth centuries, were based on similar assumptions (Muhammad 2010). And the quest to find the physical or biological roots of criminality has continued to the present. Even now, some

criminologists focus their attention on the brain functioning or emotional makeup of people who commit crime, arguing that the problems of crime and violence can be explained and addressed by medicating or incapacitating criminals (Raine 2013). These ideas had their biggest impact in the 1980s and 1990s, when the notion that there are "super-predators" who are incorrigible life-long offenders was advanced (for example, Hernnstein and Wilson 1985). Democratic President Bill Clinton employed this rhetoric in promoting his major federal crime bill in 1994 and in his political speeches at the time (Robinson 2016). Looking back, it is clear that there were strongly racialized undertones to the super-predator claim, but no credible scientific evidence to support it (Vitale 2018).

Some early sociological theorists focused less on crime itself and more on the institutions of criminal punishment, such as prison. The roots of this kind of sociological inquiry are deep and perhaps exemplified best by French sociologist Emile Durkheim (1858–1917; see Chapter 2 for more information about Durkheim's social theory). According to Durkheim, criminal laws and punishment largely exist to support and strengthen the moral order of the community and to embody a society's shared values rather than to simply regulate crime. In particular, societies were prone to establish punishments that are more of an emotional reaction to certain behavior than a rational one. Historical investigations suggested to Durkheim that punishment involved a passionate and vengeful tone. As one commentator later put it, "In Durkheim's view, the rituals of punishment are directed less at the individual offender than at the audience of impassioned onlookers whose cherished values and security had been momentarily undermined by the offender's actions" (Garland 1991, p. 123).

The three concepts of crime and punishment associated with Beccaria, Lombroso, and Durkheim offer different views about why crime happens and what forms punishment should or does take. But only Lombroso had offered a concrete theory of *why* individuals commit crimes, and his theory was very unsociological in the sense that it explains criminal acts as reflecting the traits of individuals. In the middle of the twentieth century, sociologists moved into the field of criminology to examine the influence of social factors on criminal behavior. For example, the American social theorists W. E. B. Du Bois (1869–1963) and Robert Merton (1910–2003) argued that sociologists should examine how social structure plays a critical role in creating criminality. Merton, for example, took as a starting point Durkheim's view that society has a collective set of shared values; however, he believed that different people within a given social structure had differing levels of ability to access those shared values. For example, in a society in which accumulation of wealth is a value, those born into positions of higher social and economic status will have greater ability to accumulate wealth and maintain a good standard of living legally. Those in lower class positions will have less ability to realize the shared value of wealth accumulation, however, and will thus experience considerable strain as they make their attempts. Merton's **strain theory** argues that social pressures produce many kinds of deviant and criminal behavior (Merton 1938). As individuals are denied a legitimate means to achieve social goals, they must use alternative, deviant, illegal approaches to achieve those goals. Rather than being a function of individual bodily characteristics, criminality is a direct result of one's position within a social structure (Contreras 2012.)

Another classical sociological alternative to Merton's strain theory can be seen in the long history of research on how underlying economic conditions, such as high rates of unemployment, relate to criminal activity (Chiracos 1987; Chalfin and Rafael 2011). The central idea is that people (particularly young people growing up in poor neighborhoods) are more likely to engage in criminal activity when they feel a sense of hopelessness or that there are a lack of opportunities to earn a living (Wilson 1987; Williams 1989; MacLeod 2006). The theory can be stated as a simple economic proposition, in which someone participates in crime when the potential benefit is larger than the perceived risks, and the more difficult someone's economic circumstances the more likely they are to turn to crime (Grogger 1998). It can also be related to the larger context of a capitalist economy that produces poverty on a large scale. Marxist criminologists have long made this argument (Greenberg 1993). For example, when unemployment rates go up, and/or wages decline, in bad economic times, crime should rise. Although researchers have not been able to show these relationships conclusively, there are many studies finding some evidence to support it (Chalfin and Rafael 2011).

Closely related to theories about the role of economic conditions on crime are those that focus on what is known as **social disorganization**. The theory of social disorganization views crime as significantly impacted by a particular place (such as an urban neighborhood or a rural community). Well-organized neighborhoods or communities are self-policing, in the sense that there are strong relationships between neighbors and local organizations of various kinds that bring people together and enable them to identify problems before they become serious. In these communities, families are strong and stable employment is available. By contrast, in communities that have high levels of social disorganization—places where jobs are scarce and there are few organizations or places that bring people together (such

as churches, parks, libraries, sports programs for youths), high rates of single-parent families, poor quality schools, and poor quality housing—individuals are more likely to engage in criminal activity. Over a longer period of time, the families with the most resources will move out, further diminishing the neighborhood or community. It is, as one researcher put it, a "spiral of decline" in which elevated crime is both a cause and a consequence (Skogan 1990). The implication of social disorganization theory is that crimes, and especially high rates of crime concentrated in particular neighborhoods, are the result not of a bunch of individual people deciding to commit crimes but rather the result of the community environment in which they are living that encourages crime. In other words, not individuals but neighborhoods and communities foster (or discourage) crime (see Chapter 15 for more details).

Modern Social Theories of Crime and Punishment

20.3.2 Explain how modern social theorists extended and challenged early social theories on crime and punishment.

The early and classical theories of crime began to be challenged in the 1960s, as a new wave of sociological thinking about crime and punishment began to take shape. In this section, we will discuss three of the most influential: Labeling theory, surveillance theory, and life-course theory. Each makes an important contribution to our overall understanding, and the first two have overlapping insights.

LABELING THEORY The influential sociologist Howard Becker offered one major alternative theory of deviance and crime in the early 1960s (Becker 1963). Rather than seeing deviance (as noted, more fully covered in Chapter 7) as connected to an individual—whether because of biological or social determinants—Becker suggested that deviance is a *social process* through which some behavior is labeled deviant, or even criminal, while other similar behavior is labeled acceptable. An obvious example is treating alcohol consumption as normal and acceptable but marijuana or cocaine consumption as deviant and even criminal. All of these substances can impact brain chemistry and alter behavior. Deviant or criminal behavior, then, is not simply caused by individuals engaging in certain behavior, but it is also caused by the process through which a behavior comes to be labeled as deviant. The theories under this umbrella came to be known as **labeling theory**.

The core idea of labeling theory is that deviant or criminal behavior is not always an objective thing, but rather something that gets constructed by society (or by the criminal justice systems) over time. For example, an act that may be considered normal at one point in time might come to be defined as deviant or criminal at another point in time. To understand criminal deviance, then, we need to focus on the process by which society makes certain behaviors merely deviant, and others criminal. Understanding this process involves two things. First, it requires looking at why and how certain behaviors and people get labeled as deviant or criminal. Second, it requires looking at the consequences of these labels on the behaviors of the people who are labeled.

The other key insight of labeling theory is that once labeled deviant or a criminal, an individual faces greater scrutiny and is more likely to be caught doing things that other people might get away with. Authorities, such as teachers, police officers, and employers, will look more closely at people they find suspicious. The legal system, in particular, can "mark" people for even minor offenses, making them more susceptible to re-arrest and potentially scaring off employers from hiring them for jobs (Kohler-Hausmann 2018). The origin of labeling theory came from groundbreaking studies in which researchers did things like ride around with police to see what officers actually did (for example, Bittner 1967; Cicourel 1967). They found that police often overlooked behaviors that could be considered violations of the law, while choosing to punish other minor offenses more severely. This body of research, which was confirmed in later studies, reveals the arbitrary way that the law is enforced. What is and is not a crime can hinge on what an individual police officer or district attorney chooses to pursue.

Punishment of especially serious crimes in the eighteenth and nineteenth centuries often occurred in the form of public executions (such as the execution by guillotine shown here). What caused the eventual shift away from punishment in public spaces and into prisons? This question is one that animated Emile Durkheim's writings on the social role of punishment, and one that also was asked by the French social theorist Michel Foucault in the 1970s.

For example, in the eighteenth century, punishment often occurred in public in the form of public executions. However, over time, the location of punishment began to shift

SURVEILLANCE THEORY

Perhaps the single most influential study in the area of crime and punishment, one that revolutionized the field, was written by the famous French philosopher and historian Michel Foucault (1926–84). In his 1975 book, *Discipline and Punish*, Foucault traced the history of prison and punishment in Western societies. He argued that punishment forms have changed considerably in the last three centuries and that these changes correspond to, and reveal shifts in, how societies are organized.

The ease with which security cameras can be installed around a city has frequently helped police officers catch criminal offenders. But it is also part of a larger expansion of societal surveillance, where a much wider range of human activity is made visible to authorities than before. For example, video surveillance can be used to identify people who participate in political protests or consume or sell illegal drugs on a street corner.

into the private space of the prison. Foucault theorized that this shift corresponded to a change in the target of punishment from the body to the soul, so that offenders could be corrected or trained rather than hurt in a spectacular public display. Along with this shift came other changes, for example, the introduction of various kinds of sciences—mental health, medicine, education—into the penal domain (Foucault 1975).

Foucault's theories of crime and punishment extended his insights about the prison to a broader critical contribution: In his many writings on power, Foucault emphasized the importance of surveillance (see Chapter 2 for more details on Foucault's theory of surveillance as a form of power). Powerholders (employers, governments) and their agents (supervisors, police) extend their power by using tools of surveillance to control behavior. The question, however, is whether hypervigilant surveillance of certain groups and neighborhoods produces racially biased patterns of arrest. We will explore this issue in more detail later in the chapter.

LIFE COURSE CRIMINOLOGY Recent sociological contributions to the study of crime and violence have focused on the ways that criminal activity can change as individuals move through different stages of their lives and become connected and disconnected from people, like a spouse or children, and institutions like the military or the labor force (Sampson and Laub 2003). A **life-course perspective** on crime focuses attention on how individuals' social bonds and social contexts change, leading to variation in their involvement with crime. In contrast to the view that criminals are born, research drawing on life-course trajectories has shown that those who engage in criminal activities tend to be young, as mentioned earlier, but as they age their criminal activity will decline and even disappear completely. In the 1960s, for instance, crime rose even as a strong economy might have predicted otherwise. A central reason was the rise of the post–World War II "baby boom" generation, which created a demographic "bulge" of young people who reached their peak years of criminal activity in that era.

Recent research has focused on the factors that help former offenders stop engaging in further criminal activity, a process known as **desistance**. Among the most important of these factors are having a job, finding a stable relationship, having children, and participating in community activities (Massoglia and Uggen 2010). Most people in their early 20s have achieved relatively few of these milestones, but by their 30s and 40s many will have. At that point, the risks associated with crime and being sent to prison are far different than they were at younger ages.

The key message of most of the classical and modern sociological theories of crime is that, we can't just focus our attention on the individuals who commit crimes, and we certainly should not think of punishment as a natural, orderly outcome; we have to consider the social contexts in which crime takes place. This is the crucial insight of all of sociology; theories of crime, violence, and punishment go beyond the characteristics of individuals to the societal conditions within communities, cities, and societies.

Goals of Punishment

20.3.3 Analyze the four basic reasons societies punish criminals.

Classical and modern theories have examined punishment as well as crime. Classical theories of punishment have suggested that societies punish criminals for three basic reasons, which sometimes overlap and compete: (1) To exact **retribution** for the victims; (2) to deter offenders and others from committing crimes (what is known as **deterrence**); (3) to **incapacitate** offenders, that is, to remove a criminal offender from society so she or he cannot commit further crimes. Modern criminology has, in the past 100 years, added (4), the goal of **rehabilitating** offenders, so that when they leave a period of detention, they will not commit further crimes. In this section, we describe each of these four purposes of punishment.

Retribution can be thought of as a form of societal vengeance, founded on the notion that those who have committed crimes should suffer for the harm they have caused others in roughly equal measure. It is an ancient impulse, and can be found in the biblical phrase "an eye for an eye," which appears in the very first penal code (the code of Hammurabi, which was first produced in 1764 BCE in ancient Babylon). There are two components to retribution: That the punishment should be equal in harm to the perpetrator as to the victim, *but* that the punishment should not exceed the harm (so, one eye for one eye, not two). Retribution as the primary purpose of punishment suggests that punishment should fit the crime already committed, rather than any future crimes that the individual criminal might commit.

Modern theories of punishment, however, generally have more ambitious goals than simple retribution. The introduction of the prison as a place of punishment in particular makes it possible to do more than just extract retribution. In contrast to retribution, which is designed to redress crimes already committed, deterrence endeavors to prevent future crimes. Social scientists and policymakers distinguish between two related ways of using punishment to deter crime: Specific deterrence, which punishes to reduce future **recidivism** among people

Making people aware of the consequences of certain behavior is a kind of deterrence. For example, signs posted along highways to remind motorists about laws related to driving aim to deter them from doing things that could be dangerous (and are illegal).

convicted of crimes, and general deterrence, which punishes criminals to influence others who might otherwise be tempted to engage in crime. In other words, if you steal a bike and are caught, you will receive a punishment that should discourage *you* from stealing another bike in the future (specific deterrence), while the knowledge that there is punishment waiting for anyone who steals a bike should at least in principle also deter your friends from stealing bikes.

Effective deterrents require that the consequences be known to offenders when they are contemplating criminal acts. In other words, a potential criminal offender has to be at least somewhat aware of the penalty that will follow, and they have to know about it in advance if it is to be effective. Discovering you've committed a crime when you didn't know what you were doing was wrong in the first place means that, by definition, deterrence couldn't work. So authority figures like police officers, school administrators, and government officials often go to great lengths to make clear what is illegal.

Closely related to deterrence as a goal of punishment is the more straightforward goal of reducing crime by taking criminal offenders off the street and incapacitating them. *Incapacitation* hinges on restraining or isolating offenders from society. Today it is the jail/prison system that is the primary place where incapacitation is practiced, as offenders are physically removed from their communities for some period of time and are thereby unable to commit further crimes. At earlier times in human history, other techniques of incapacitation, such as bodily mutilation or executions, were practiced. Some governments, more commonly in the past than today, have also relocated convicted offenders to remote places as another means of incapacitation. Under both the Tsar in nineteenth century Russia and communism in the Soviet Union in the twentieth century, a vast system of remote communities, known as *gulags*, were created to receive people convicted of political crimes against the government. By removing these people from society, governments hoped to prevent the spread of anti-government ideas, or to repress certain groups that the government considered hostile (Applebaum 2003). In U.S. history, the forced internment of Japanese Americans during World War II into concentration camps out of (unfounded) fears that they might "aid the enemy" is an example of incapacitation (Reeves 2016).

Deterrence and incapacitation are the predominant ways that criminal punishment is justified today, but that has not always been the case. Indeed, for much of the history of punishment, the primary goal of punishment was to help *rehabilitate* criminal offenders. Rehabilitation fundamentally rejects the presumption that criminal offenders are inherently corrupted. Once reform of individuals became the orienting goal of the "correctional" system, the sharp line between offender and citizen began to erode. One influential nineteenth-century prison superintendent used the return to citizenship as an orienting philosophy. He sought to turn a prisoner's mind to "preparing himself for restoration to citizenship," and "personal fitness for future liberty" (Brockway 1871). Throughout the twentieth century, prisons often sought to give inmates job skills and education to help them get back on their feet and become contributing members of society. However, during the "get tough" period of rising incarceration that began in the mid-1970s, critics successfully challenged the legitimacy and effectiveness of rehabilitation as a correctional philosophy. These critics argued that rehabilitation programs were not working well and that offenders should not be given free opportunities—like job training or education—not also provided to law-abiding citizens. More recently, however, criminologists have reaffirmed rehabilitation, challenging the "nothing works" dictum and developing new evidence that treatments such as cognitive behavioral therapy reduce recidivism (see, for example, Lin 2000; Cullen 2005).

Mark Bussell

Mark Bussell

BIG QUESTION 20.4 What Is the Role of Racism in the Criminal Justice System?

RACIAL DISPARITIES IN THE CRIMINAL JUSTICE SYSTEM

In the long history of racial injustice in America, the criminal justice system has frequently been at the center of controversy, a topic we discussed briefly in Chapter 13. The assertion that Black people are more likely to commit crimes than White people is a widespread stereotype that has deep roots in American culture. New immigrant groups have also often been stereotyped in the same way. Blacks and Latinxs are punished at significantly higher rates than Whites. Further, they are also much more likely to be the victims of police officer shootings, which have become a major topic of social protest recently (and are at the forefront of the Black Lives Matter movement that led mass protests across America in 2020).

In this section we will explore the role of race and racial discrimination in the criminal justice system. We begin with a brief historical overview, before examining sociological research and findings about both the extent of racial disparities and how and why they persist.

Racism and Criminality: A Brief History

20.4.1 Describe the history of racism in the criminal justice system.

The role of **racism**—stereotypes and forms of discrimination against individuals who are members of particular racial or ethnic groups—has long been important in relation to the criminal justice system. Indeed, racial stereotyping has been pervasive throughout American history. In the early twentieth century, Theodore Roosevelt, expressing widely held views of the time, called for "relentless and unceasing warfare against lawbreaking black men" on the grounds that "laziness and shiftlessness... and above all, vice and criminality of every kind, are evils more potent for harm to the Black race than all acts of oppression of White men put together" (quoted in Klinkner and Smith 1997). **Lynching** of Blacks—the violent killing of an individual, usually by a self-appointed group, without trial and in a public place—was frequently justified by widely held stereotypes about Black criminality.

Early social science studies of race and crime asserted that Blacks were especially prone to criminal behavior. These assertions were challenged by Black sociologists and activists, such as W. E. B. Du Bois (left) and Ida B. Wells (right), who pushed back against the flawed data and methods of the time.

Early social science writings on crime from the late nineteenth century strongly reinforced and spread racial stereotypes (Muhammad 2010). These studies drew on biased data sources, such as comparisons of prisoners (in which Blacks were overrepresented) or police arrest records (which again reflected racial biases). They often claimed that Blacks and other people of color had biological defects that made them prone to crime, without a shred of DNA evidence to support such claims. What was especially important was that these studies made no adjustments for the social contexts in which Blacks were living during this era: Highly segregated neighborhoods in northern cities or in the Jim Crow South. Later researchers carefully documented that among *all* racial and ethnic groups, crime is much higher in impoverished communities and places where young people may have limited aspirations for their future. In other words, poverty and inequality, not race, came to be seen as the key social factor associated with crime.

Important challenges to racialized stereotypes came from activists and policy-based organizations like the National Association for the Advancement of Colored People (NAACP) and the National Urban League. The sociologist W. E. B. Du Bois was at the center of many of these challenges (see Chapter 2), in his persistent and forceful writings over the decades from 1900 to 1950s, as was the prominent anti-lynching activist and writer Ida B. Wells (1862–1931). The legacy of these early activists and scholars would be carried forward by later sociologists and criminologists who challenged the existing consensus with better data and more rigorous methods from the 1930s onward.

One of the most significant challenges to racial bias in the criminal justice system developed in the late 1960s with the rise of the Black Panther movement. Founded by Huey Newton and Bobby Seale in Oakland, California, in its early days one the Panthers' primary goals was to follow around police officers who had long been harassing and mistreating young Black men in the area on their patrols to prevent them from harming members of their West Oakland neighborhood (what they referred to as "copwatching"). Because the police always carried and sometimes used their guns, the Panthers carried guns themselves and actively publicized their willingness to fight back against police abuses if necessary. At a time of deep civil unrest across the country, the Panther's message spread like wildfire, and soon Black Panther groups had formed in most major cities across America and even some in other countries. In response, the FBI actively targeted the Panthers, often working with local police departments who felt threatened by the group. Today we know that many of the then-secret tactics used to undermine the Panthers violated their basic civil liberties. Eventually, the combination of repression by the government as well as internal conflicts ended the Panther movement (for more history of the Panthers, see Bloom and Martin 2013).

Protests against the behavior of police officers towards people of color continued after the Panther movement declined, but it has been only very recently that a mass movement has arisen to force a national conversation about these issues. The event that triggered its rise began with public outcry over the murder of a 17-year-old Black teenager named Trayvon Martin. Martin was fatally shot while walking through a housing complex in Florida by a resident of the complex named George Zimmerman, who claimed he felt "threatened" by Martin's presence. Martin was unarmed. The case gained national media attention within a few months, and Zimmerman was eventually charged with murder. Throughout his trial, Zimmerman insisted he shot Martin in self-defense, citing Florida's Stand Your Ground law, which eliminated the usual "duty to retreat" from a dangerous situation. Zimmerman was eventually found not guilty on all charges, including even the lesser charge of manslaughter.

The not guilty verdict in the 2013 trial of shooting victim Trayvon Martin sparked widespread outrage in the United States and was the initial impetus for the creation of the Black Lives Matter movement.

The jury's verdict resulted in broad outrage across America, but particularly among members of the Black community that had witnessed such events many times. Public opinion about the verdict split fairly noticeably along racial lines, with a *Washington Post*–ABC News poll finding that 86 percent of Blacks disapproved of the jury's decision, compared to only 31 percent of Whites. The night of the verdict's release, 31-year-old Alicia Garza, a community organizer in Oakland, California, was watching the news with some friends. When they learned that Zimmerman had been acquitted, Garza was shocked and angry. As she read comments on the case on social media, she found that some Black commentators "were blaming Black people for our own condition." She wrote a note in response, urging the Black community to unite and concluded her post with the words: "Our Lives Matter, Black Lives Matter." Patrisse Cullors, her friend and fellow community organizer in Los Angeles, reposted these words, and added the hashtag "#blacklivesmatter" to the end of the post. Along with others, Cullors and Garza formally created the organization #BlackLivesMatter shortly after as a "call to action and a response to the virulent anti-Black racism that permeates our society."

It wasn't until almost a year and a half later that these words, "Black Lives Matter," turned into a unified national movement, this time in response to the murder of an unarmed Black teenager named Michael Brown by police in Ferguson, Missouri (a majority Black suburb of St. Louis). The town of Ferguson exploded in protests in the days following the shooting, as the incident was one of many cases of police officers using excessive force against young Blacks in the town. (We'll analyze police brutality more specifically in the next section.) The protests spread nationally, and gained further momentum in December 2014 when a grand jury refused to charge the officer involved with any legal violations in the killing.

Repeated examples of police violence toward unarmed people of color have received significant critical attention and resulted in protests. One example involved the killing of Eric Garner, a 43-year-old Black man, in Staten Island, New York. In an attempt to subdue Garner for selling "unlicensed" (untaxed) cigarettes on the street, police officers used a "chokehold" technique that has been banned by the New York City police department since the 1990s. While in the chokehold, Garner, who suffered from asthma, was captured on video saying 11 times "I can't breathe," but the officer continued to apply the chokehold until Garner died. As in Ferguson, a grand jury refused to charge the officers with any violations, sparking a new round of protests in New York and elsewhere. The police murder of George Floyd in Minneapolis, Minnesota, in the spring of 2020, sparked the largest and most sustained protests over racial biases in policing in American history. Floyd was killed by a police officer who held him on the ground with his foot on Floyd's neck, cutting off his breathing for more than 9 minutes, all the while with Floyd audibly gasping for air and pleading to be allowed to breathe. Although the Floyd killing was but one of a long string of such events, the fact that it was captured on video made the tragedy something that no one could deny.

In the next section, we'll examine the systematic evidence about racial disparities in the criminal justice system, including police brutality.

Race and Punishment

20.4.2 Analyze the evidence of racism in criminal justice policies and punishment.

Let's start with some basics. As noted in Chapter 13, Blacks and Latinx prisoners constituted 56 percent of the incarcerated population in the United States in 2019, but only 28 percent of the U.S. population (Gramlich 2019). In recent years, the rate of imprisonment for Black males has been as high as eight times as that for Whites, once adjusted for the size of each group (Tonry 2012). In the face of the recent protests and public discussion, the gap has declined a bit, and as of 2020 was as low as it had been in decades, but it was still enormous, at 6:1 (Gramlich 2020).

To get a visual sense of the differences in racial disparities in incarceration, Figure 20.4 displays the likelihood that

Figure 20.4 Lifetime Likelihood of Imprisonment for U.S. Residents

Group	Ratio	Probability
All Men	1 in 9	0.11
White Men	1 in 17	0.06
Black Men	1 in 3	0.33
Latinx Men	1 in 6	0.17
All Women	1 in 56	0.02
White Women	1 in 111	0.01
Black Women	1 in 18	0.06
Latinx Women	1 in 45	0.02

Lifetime Likelihood of Imprisonment

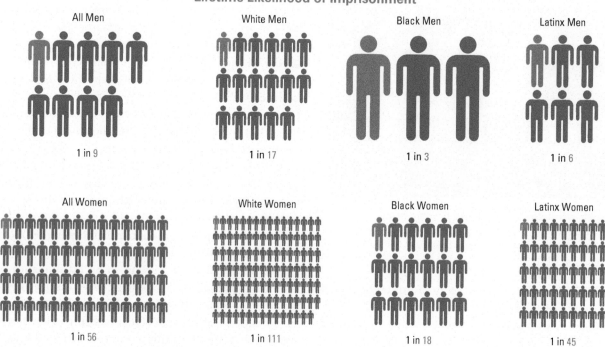

SOURCE: The Sentencing Project analysis of Bureau of Justice Statistics data.

members of different groups have been sentenced to prison at some point in their lives. Men are much more likely to have been in prison than women; this isn't especially surprising, as at any one time about 90 percent of inmates are men. In addition, about one in three Black men and in one in six Latinx men will have experienced prison, versus 1 in 17 White men.

The sharp racial discrepancy in incarceration has received a great deal of media attention. On a day-to-day basis, relationships between the police and communities with large Black or Latinx populations have become fraught. Many people of color view the police with hostility, and that hostility often goes both ways (Goffman 2014). (Stuart 2018. Especially controversial has been the role of drug policies in triggering disproportionately high rates of Black imprisonment. The evidence suggests that *Whites are at least as likely to use illegal drugs as Blacks,* but Blacks are, on average, *four times more likely* to be sent to prison for a drug-related offense (see Figure 20.5; and it was eight times more likely in the late 1980s) (Western 2006; Alexander 2010; Tonry 2012). One of the most famous and blatant examples of racial disparity in drug law enforcement was in how two versions of cocaine were punished: The distribution of crack cocaine was, under a federal law adopted in the 1990s, punished *100 times* more severely than the distribution of powder cocaine, *even though the two drugs have identical effects on users.* But crack, which is cheaper, was mostly used by people of color, especially in poor neighborhoods. Whites, by contrast, mostly favored powder cocaine. In recent years, Congress reduced the crack versus powder difference, but as of 2021 crack is still punished more severely (five times as much). But in the early 2020s,

Figure 20.5 Drug-Related Arrests for Whites and Blacks

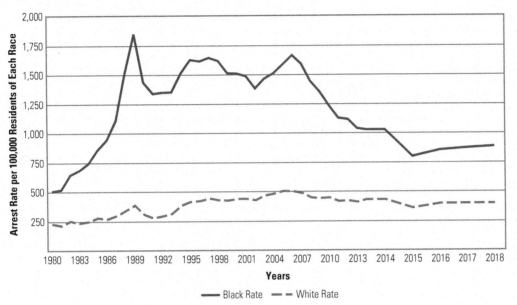

SOURCE: Bureau of Justice Statistics; FBI Uniform Crime Reporting Statistics.

The British newspaper *The Guardian* made a set of comparisons that highlight how American police are uniquely violent: For example, in the previous 24 *years*, the police in England and Wales killed 55 people; in the first 24 *days* of 2015, police in the United States killed 59 people (Lartey 2015). Other comparisons offered in the article were equally striking: In the country of Iceland (population 323,764) the police have killed one person in 71 years; in the single city of Stockton, California (pop. 310,000) the police killed three people in one month. In Canada, with a population that is about 1/9 that of the United States, an average of 25 people have been killed by the police per year, compared to about 950 per year in the United States. Figure 20.6 displays these international differences.

Why might this be the case? Perhaps American police officers shoot and kill more people than police officers in other countries because there are so many more armed criminals in the United States than other countries. There is some truth to that idea. As mentioned earlier in the chapter, almost all other rich developed countries have strong gun control laws that make it difficult to acquire a gun. In

the criminalization of drug use of all kinds is declining, and drug-related arrests have plummeted. If that trend continues the overall Black–White differences in incarceration should also decline.

Incarceration differences reflect one part of the controversy in criminal justice policy. But, as noted in the previous section, it has been police violence, specifically police shootings of people of color, that has fostered a closer look at police practices and racial disparities. Of course, it is not just people of color who are being killed by the police. Many White people have also been killed by police officers—in fact almost twice as many Whites have been killed as Blacks in raw numbers. But Whites make up over 60 percent of the total population, and Blacks just 12 percent. If we adjust for killings per million population (see Chapter 13), in the period between 2015 and 2020 Blacks were 2.5 times more likely to be killed (and Latinxs were 1.8 times more likely to be killed than Whites).

There is something very distinct about police shootings that becomes visible if we compare American police with those in other countries. American police officers kill vastly more people than police officers in other countries, steadily reaching between 900 and 1000 deaths in each of the five most recent years for which we have data. Most other countries see few, if any, fatal police shootings in a given year.

Figure 20.6 Number of People Killed by Law Enforcement per 10 Million Population

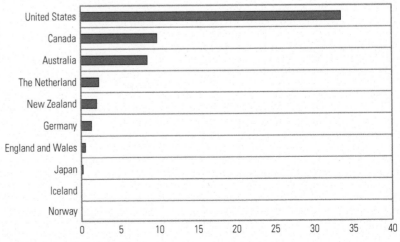

SOURCE: Prison Policy Initiative.

the United States, by contrast, the Second Amendment to the Constitution protects gun ownership in a way that is not found in most other countries. Virtually anyone can buy or acquire a gun, and it is true that guns are very often involved in crimes. But here's the problem: Guns were reported to be held by the victim in only about two-thirds of the cases. In the other one-third of cases, the victim either had a lesser weapon (like a knife), had a toy or fake weapon, or was unarmed altogether (in at least 15 percent of cases, the victim had no weapon at all). In other words, American police officers shoot far more people than police in other countries, even when guns aren't involved.

So when it comes to police brutality, then, we are left with several important issues. The first is how skin color seems to cause some police officers to be more likely to use their guns when it is a Black or Latinx person in the confrontation. The second is that many police shootings a victim with *no gun* or no weapon at all. The inability

of police departments to properly train and discipline their officers to minimize the use of force remains one of the enduring puzzles of the American criminal justice system. And it is a costly one too: Big city police departments pay out hundreds of millions of dollars each year to the victims of police brutality or to their families. For example, in the decade between 2010 and 2020, the city of Chicago paid out $500 million dollars—an average of $50 million per year—to settle police brutality and other police misconduct lawsuits (Corley 2020). In 2019, New York City paid $175 million dollars in a single year just to settle their misconduct lawsuits, although that was a bargain by comparison with 2017, when the city had to fork over $338 million. It all added up to over $1 billion for the period from 2014 to 2020 for the taxpayers of New York City (Carrega 2020). Smaller cities also pay out large sums. These payments are a mark of an ongoing national tragedy that remains unaddressed.

Scott Houston/Alamy Stock Photo

BIG QUESTION 20.5 Why Is Mass Incarceration Controversial?

MASS INCARCERATION IN AMERICA

The American criminal justice system in recent decades has undergone a remarkable change. The incarcerated population in the United States—including all inmates in prisons and jails, and individuals awaiting trial—has grown 600 percent over the past 50 years. In other words, there are roughly seven times more people in prison today than in 1972. If we adjust for overall population size (taking into account that the entire population

of America has grown in this period), the growth rate is more like 500 percent (still an enormous fivefold increase). Sociologists describe this level of punishment as **mass incarceration**, a situation where vastly greater numbers of people are held in prisons than in earlier periods of history or in comparison to similar countries (Garland 2001). In this section, we explore the reasons behind the massive increase in the number of Americans behind bars. We will also compare the incarcerated population in the United States to those in similar countries.

Punishment in America Today

20.5.1 Compare and contrast the crime rate and the incarceration rate in the United States and in similar societies.

The rising number of people in America's prisons and jails is a relatively recent phenomenon. For the first three-quarters of the twentieth century, except for a notable uptick during the depression years of the late 1930s, the incarceration rate (which is the number of prisoners relative to the full population) remained relatively constant. People who committed serious crimes were sent to prison, but most offenders received lesser penalties. As noted earlier, beginning in the early 1970s, however, the number of people housed in prisons began to grow steadily every year and continued to do so for the next 30 years before finally starting to level off around 2010. More people were being sentenced to prison, sentences became longer, and judges and parole boards had greatly reduced discretion to let people off for good behavior. Categories of deviance that were once treated with leniency—mostly having to do with drugs—became increasingly criminalized, with drug sellers and simple users much more likely to be sentenced to prison than before.

Today, with about 2 million people incarcerated in prisons and in local jails, the United States is home to the largest prison population in the world (Kaeble et al. 2016). The increase in incarceration has occurred even as crime rates have declined in recent decades. How can this possibly be the case? To get a better view of these diverging trends, take a look at the crime rate and the number of people in prison plotted together in Figure 20.7 (this excludes the approximately 600,000 people in jail on a given day). In this graph, these two lines show that in spite of the sharp decline in crime since the 1990s, the incarceration rate (shown here just for prisoners) continued to rise. The connection between crime and punishment, in other words, has changed in a fundamental way during this period (crime down, punishment up).

The growth of the prison population in the United States over the past 50 years is not only historically unprecedented in this country, it is also unique around the world. The United States incarcerates vastly more people per capita than almost any other similar country today. The data in Figure 20.8 allow us to see this. The graph shows how many individuals are incarcerated per 100,000 people for 2018. The United States has an imprisonment rate that is double that of Russia and Turkey, two countries that also have large numbers of political prisoners. There are about six times more inmates in the United States than its neighbor to the north, Canada. The U.S.–Canada comparison is especially illuminating. But the gap is even larger in comparison with other developed countries like Japan, Norway, and the Netherlands, where it reaches 10:1 or more. When we examine cross-national statistics like

Figure 20.7 Declining Crime and Rising Incarceration Rates (Prison Only)

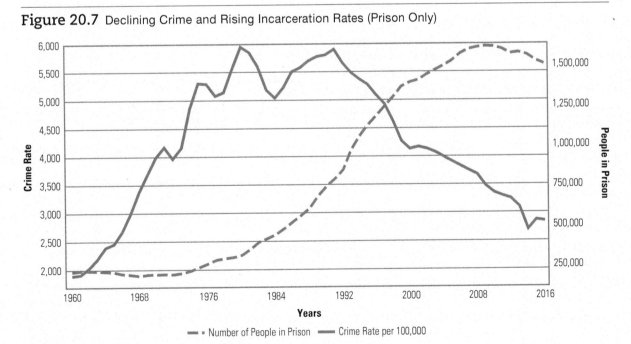

SOURCE: Bureau of Justice Statistics; FBI Uniform Crime Reporting Statistics.

Figure 20.8 Prison Population Rates for Select Countries, 2018

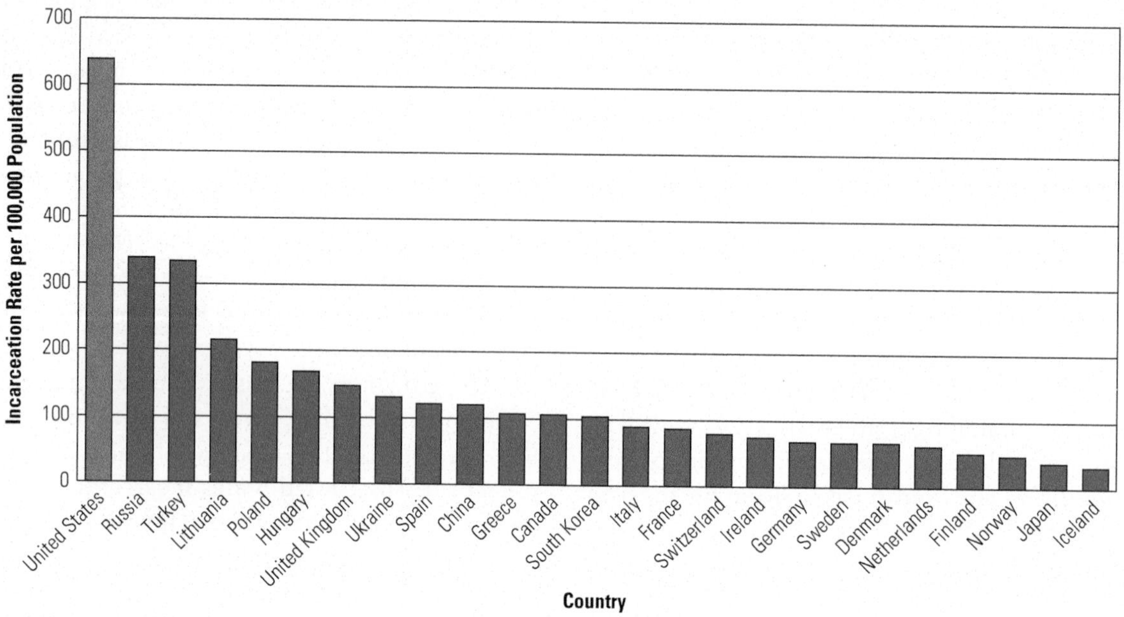

SOURCE: Institute for Crime and Justice.

this among similar countries, it is almost always the case that differences are relatively small. In this case, however, in other institutional fields the differences are truly enormous. There are almost no other examples of government policies that vary this much.

The simplest possible explanation for this disparity would be that national differences in crime rates cause more people to be in prison. But just as we saw with the trends in punishment (crime down, punishment up), so too there may not be much of a relationship between crimes actually being committed and how many people different countries choose to put in their prisons. The United States does have a higher murder rate than other countries, as we noted earlier. But murder is a relatively rare crime. What about crime as a whole? Is it possible that crime rates are six or seven times greater in the United States than countries like France or Canada, or 10 times greater than in Norway? Visitors in the United States are often told that they should be very careful, because crime in America is so high. However, comparative crime data shows the opposite: The United States is right around the average of other similar countries if we look at all crime, not just relativey rare violent crimes. Figure 20.9 shows total crime by country per 100,000 population.

So mass incarceration in the United States presents a genuine set of sociological puzzles. When we look at the relationship between all crimes and prisoners per capita, the United States is completely different from all similar countries in terms of how many people it sends to prison.

There is nothing in this astounding development that is "natural," given that all other comparable societies with similar crime rates put far fewer people in prison. There is no international rulebook that mandates the number of people that should be sent to prison for their behavior. Each country can decide how much behavior it wants to punish, and how.

Since there is no close connection between the incarceration rate and actual levels of criminal activity in the United States we will need to look elsewhere to understand mass incarceration.

Causes of Mass Incarceration

20.5.2 Analyze the possible causes of mass incarceration in the United States.

If crime cannot explain why incarceration has risen so drastically in the United States, what is going on? This is a baffling question that many social scientists have been debating, and there are several competing theories about it. Two major factors behind the rise of mass incarceration have proved especially important. First, the importance of moral crusades against certain kinds of individual behavior, in this case targeted against drugs (as we've noted elsewhere in the chapter, particularly certain kinds of drugs that are disproportionately consumed by poor people and minorities), had a major impact. The war on drugs was launched by President Reagan in 1985 and spread quickly around American cities, encouraging police and criminal justice officials

Figure 20.9 Comparative Crime Rates

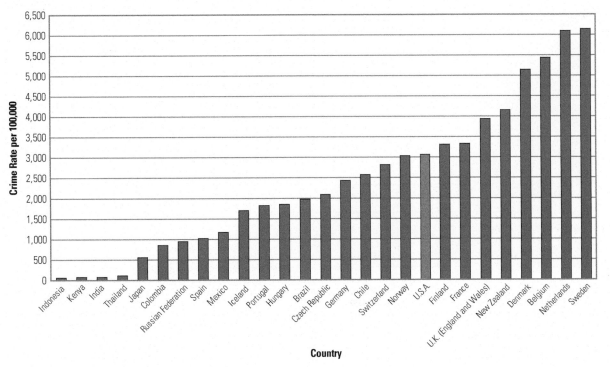

SOURCE: United Nations Office on Drugs and Crime.

to arrest and convict those accused of the possession or sale of drugs (see Chapter 7 for more on this topic). For example, in 1988, shortly after the beginning of Reagan's war, 17 percent of all people convicted of felonies were drug offenders. Just 14 years later, that figure had nearly doubled, reaching 32 percent of all inmates (Manza and Uggen 2006). More recently, the number of drug offenders receiving felony convictions has declined, but the number receiving lesser misdemeanor sentences has soared (Kohler-Hausmann 2018).

A second key factor in the steady increase in incarceration rates involves politics. Beginning in the 1960s, many politicians began to have success running for office as proponents of "tough on crime" laws. Perhaps the first major politician to make fighting crime an overtly political issue was Republican presidential candidate Barry Goldwater in 1964. Although Goldwater lost that election badly, other politicians followed in his footsteps, promising to reduce crime. Richard Nixon won the presidency in 1968 promising a "law and order" government, declaring war on "the criminal elements which increasingly threaten our cities, homes, and our lives" (quoted in Hagan 2010, p. 150). Around the country, politicians promoted longer sentences and more punishment. Liberal judges—that is, judges thought to be too lenient on criminals—were increasingly targeted for removal from the bench (many states and local

jurisdictions elect judges, making this possible). Public support for harsher policies was reflected in opinion polls and surveys. The rise of public support for sending more people to prison in the United States since the late 1960s through the mid-1990s can be seen in Figure 20.10. Interestingly, however, in recent years public concern that judges are too lenient has fallen (but remains well over 50 percent).

Why did (and do) so many Americans want so many more people in prison? In the late 1960s and early 1970s, the convergence of three important trends that fundamentally transformed the criminal justice policy environment: (1) A conservative backlash to the many social movements and new cultural trends of the 1960s, in which the appeal of "law and order" made sense to a growing number of people; (2) an economic downturn in the 1970s that precipitated a search for reasons, and scapegoats, for emerging social problems; and (3) urban riots in the 1960s in many cities that left lasting images that made urban crime in particular the focus of intensive media scrutiny. The most careful research suggests that Republican politicians, where they controlled state governments, moved first and fastest on crime, with the Democrats following suit later (Western 2006; Manza and Uggen 2006). Coming out of the bloody political battles of the 1960s, Republican politicians found political opportunity in platforms calling for tough penalties, but many Democratic politicians

Figure 20.10 Public Opinion on Criminal Courts, 1972–2016

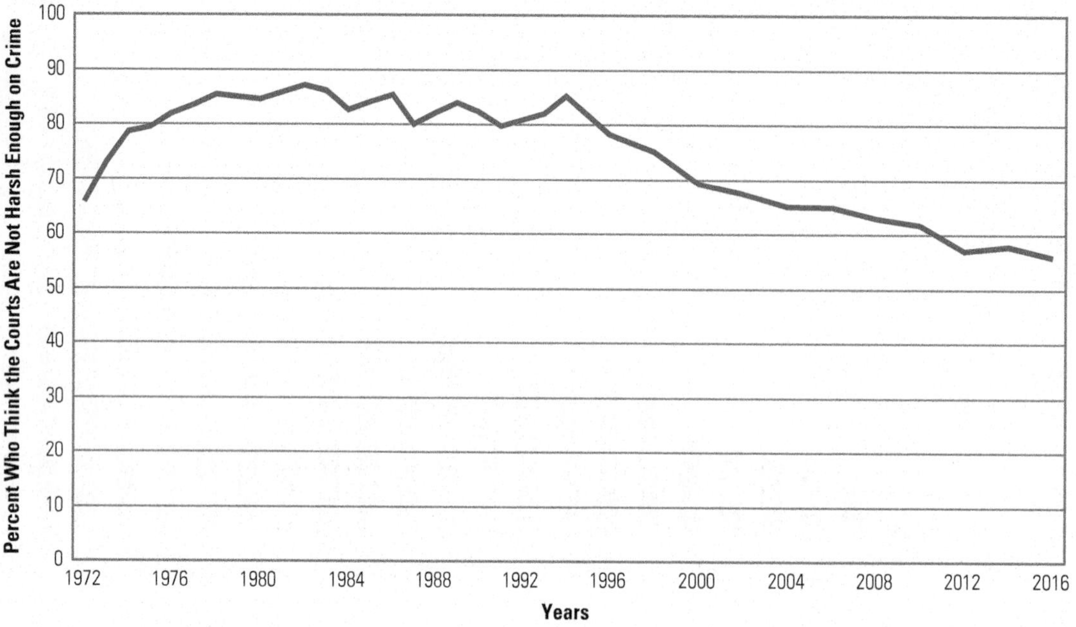

SOURCE: General Social Survey.

increasingly came to accept the new tough-on-crime policy environment. This was reflected most clearly in the previously mentioned 1994 federal crime bill partially written by then-Senator (later Vice President and President) Joe Biden, and heartily endorsed and signed into law by Democratic President Bill Clinton. This measure was the largest piece of federal crime legislation ever, and it provided funds for mammoth prison construction projects and the hiring of 100,000 new police officers, as noted, among other components.

In response to political pressures, there have been several important changes in criminal justice policies that have each contributed to increasing the incarceration rate. We review the three most important here.

THE CREATION OF MANDATORY MINIMUM SENTENCES Up until the early 1980s, criminal court judges had a fair amount of discretion in sentencing. Judges could take into account the circumstances of a criminal act and assess whether a convicted offender should receive a shorter or longer sentence. Since then, the federal government and every state have established minimum sentences for most offenses. In the federal system, the Federal Sentencing Reform Act of 1984 lengthened prison sentences as well as time actually served. State governments and criminal courts also adopted similar guidelines, prompted by the Truth-in-Sentencing Incentive Program, a 1994 federal law in which state governments were given strong incentives to adopt laws that require many categories of felons to serve a full 85 percent of their sentences, irrespective of individual circumstances. Although state laws differ in the types

of crimes covered and the percentage of time mandated to be served, their undeniable effect has been to prolong the *length of time* in prison or total time (prison plus parole) to be served. Some of the impetus for these measures came from pressure from victim's rights groups, which claimed that sentences were too low for many offenders and that victims did not feel justice was being served (Gottschalk 2005).

STRENGHTENING PAROLE AND PROBATION RULES As part of the war on drugs, and public pressure to punish offenders more harshly, many states began aggressively monitoring criminal offenders who were living in their communities, either on probation or parole. Even minor violations (such as a failed drug test) could return an inmate to prison. These developments have created an ironic cycle in which punishment causes more punishment (Travis 2002).

PROSECUTING MORE CRIMES, MORE OFTEN State and local governments, their police departments, and prosecuting attorneys significantly increased the percentage of cases they prosecuted. More prosecutions equal more convictions. Very minor offenses—smoking cannabis in public or sneaking into public transit systems—which once might have been overlooked, were increasingly being punished. While many of these minor offenses did not lead to time in jail or prison, they "marked" offenders for the future (recall that this is a feature of labeling theory). For example, if the police find someone who has a bunch of small arrests on their record, they may end up serving significant time for a very minor offense (Kohler-Hausmann 2018).

Don B. Stevenson/Alamy Stock Photo

THE FAR-REACHING IMPACT OF MASS INCARCERATION

Walking through some of the most run-down, dilapidated city blocks in Brownsville, one of the poorest sections of Brooklyn, leaves one with the impression that this is a part of New York City that's been neglected and ignored by the government. That's not quite true. As the scale of incarceration has grown since the early 1970s, the amount of public funding spent to incarcerate millions of Americans has steadily climbed upward. Depending on the facility and the state, it typically costs between $30-40,000 a year to house a single inmate. And much of that spending arises from holding people in prisons from a small number of places, like Brownsville, where there is a constant flow of people back and forth between the streets of the community and the jails and prisons. Researchers at

the Justice Mapping Center call them "million dollar blocks." They are city blocks that soak up at least a million dollars in government funding, all of which goes to the costs of incarcerating the neighborhood's residents.

It is not inevitable that this amount of funding would be spent on the criminal justice system. A growing body of research has revealed that investments designed to provide high-quality after-school programs for young people, mentoring, or summer jobs are effective at reducing the likelihood that teenagers will become involved with violence (Heller 2014; Cook, Ault, and Smerdon 2015). Resources to redevelop abandoned lots where crime can flourish, or to bring police officers together with community members to figure out how to address crime problems that emerge in specific "hot spots," represent other ways that public investments can be used to reduce crime effectively (Braga 2005; Branas et al. 2011). But these types of programs have never received the same commitment in public funding as the criminal justice system and the prisons used to house inmates. And our nation's long-term investment in the prison system has had a profound impact on individuals and families.

When individuals go to prison, they suffer a set of penalties that go beyond their time in prison, and the consequences affect not just incarcerated individuals but also their families, communities, and society as a whole. For sociologists, the study of mass incarceration must take into account not just why people commit crimes, and why societies choose to punish those actions, but also the larger impact for society as a whole. In this final section on the criminal justice system, we consider a few of these additional consequences of mass punishment.

Paul Martinka/Polaris/Newscom

Instead of spending money to improve poor neighborhoods such as Brownsville, a neighborhood in Brooklyn, the New York state government, like most other states, has spent far greater sums holding Brownsville residents in prison.

Consequences for Individuals

20.6.1 Identify and describe the consequences of a criminal record for individuals.

Both the experience of imprisonment and the stigma of a criminal record can have lasting consequences on individuals that stay with them when they return to their communities. One primary way that incarceration affects the lives of inmates is through its impact on health. More than half of inmates have mental health problems that have been diagnosed or recently treated (James and Glaze 2006, Substance Abuse and Mental Health Services Administration 2016), and a substantial portion have chronic physical health problems of infectious diseases (Dumont et al. 2012). The health care within prisons is often of poor quality, and the stressful, violent, and emotionally taxing environment of the prison can exacerbate physical and mental health problems that inmates bring back with them to their families and neighborhoods.

As noted, when prisoners return to their neighborhoods, they carry the "mark" of a criminal record with them (Jacobs 2014). Research on employers has shown, unsurprisingly, that they have strong preferences not to hire job candidates who have a criminal record or who have spent time in prison. Beyond the preferences of employers, many organizations prohibit hiring individuals with a criminal record, and states have extensive provisions that do not allow criminal offenders to obtain professional licenses in occupations ranging from daycare center staff to barbers.

As a result of these restrictions, the stigma of a criminal record, and the detrimental experience of imprisonment, individuals returning from prison have a harder time finding stable employment and on average make less income over their lifetimes. Social scientists studying the impact of imprisonment have conducted in-depth ethnographic studies of inmates attempting to reintegrate into their families and neighborhoods; they have compared convicted felons to otherwise similar people in the general population, and they have utilized experimental audit studies where identical applications are sent to employers, one with a criminal record and the other without (Western 2006; Pager 2007; Wakefield and Uggen, 2010; Harding and Morenoff, 2016). All of this research tells a similar story. Incarceration has extensive, lasting consequences on the individual's employment and economic trajectory (National Academy of Sciences 2014).

The punishment for a criminal act in the United States extends well beyond time served and includes a range of what are known as the **collateral consequences** of imprisonment. These are "collateral," or secondary or additional, types of punishment in that they go beyond the formal sentence imposed by a criminal court. What are these additional punishments? For one thing, convicted felons automatically become ineligible for a whole series of government programs (like public housing, many educational loan programs, and various social programs designed to help those in poverty) that otherwise might have helped them in their lives. The states impose varying additional penalties. Many disqualify felons from holding many kinds of jobs, although these restrictions have declined in recent years. Many states have family laws which threaten felons with loss of custodial rights for their children. Felons lose the right to vote in all but two states while in prison, and in many states won't be able to vote until they have also finished serving any parole time after their release (and in some states will lose the right to vote for life unless granted clemency; see Chesney-Lind and Mauer [2002] and Berson [2013] for more details).

Consequences for Families

20.6.2 Explain the social consequences for the families of incarcerated individuals.

The impact of mass incarceration extends well beyond the individuals locked up behind bars. The growth of imprisonment affects children and families, communities, and the larger society as a whole. But the most visible consequences are felt at home, as families are often torn apart by prison sentences. Parents are separated from children, couples are divided. Children with incarcerated parents are more likely to see their academic performance decline, to exhibit behavioral problems and problems with aggression, and to develop symptoms of psychological distress (Hagan and Foster 2009; Wakefield and Wildeman 2013). Family members also face a *stigma by association*, which often manifests as negative interactions with members of their community and bullying at school. It is perhaps not surprising that research demonstrates that family members of incarcerated individuals are at an increased risk of mental illnesses such as depression (Wildeman et al. 2012).

It is true, of course, that some children might benefit if a parent who has a history of domestic violence is removed from the home (Wakefield and Wildeman 2013). But for most families, losing a family member to the prison system creates instability and insecurity, and the consequences of parental incarceration linger on well after parents return from prison. We have already discussed how incarceration affects an individual's connection to the labor market, with impacts on both employment and earnings that persist over time. These financial consequences of imprisonment are felt by everyone who relies on that individual for financial support and everyone who provides financial support for the imprisoned individual. Beyond finances, incarceration disrupts relationships, making it difficult for romantic partners to remain intact even after a partner returns from prison. And it leaves families in a vulnerable state, making home life less stable and increasing the chances that a child will experience homelessness.

Consequences for Communities

20.6.3 Analyze the complex consequences of mass incarceration on community life.

The millions of Americans who move in and out of the prison system are not spread out evenly across the nation's neighborhoods. The maps of million dollar blocks reveal that incarceration is concentrated in a small number of urban neighborhoods with extremely high rates of imprisonment. In these neighborhoods, the police are often a constant presence, and a large share of residents has some experience with the criminal justice system.

The consequences of mass incarceration for community life are complex. On the one hand, many residents in the most disadvantaged neighborhoods express at least some support for the role of law enforcement as essential responses to the problem of violent crime (Forman 2017). This was particularly true in the 1980s and 1990s, when the level of violence was at its peak.

On the other hand, the intensity of police activity and the scale of incarceration have undermined the social fabric within some neighborhoods, creating fractured, vulnerable families and disrupting the social bonds that create strong communities (Clear 2007). In neighborhoods where the prison system is a central part of life, young men spend their time avoiding contact with police and other representatives of the criminal justice system, living their lives as fugitives who are constantly at risk of being sent back to jail or prison (Goffman 2014).

Consequences for Society

20.6.4 Explain the impact of mass incarceration on the larger society.

Maintaining a prison system on the scale that is now in place in the United States is staggeringly expensive. And because there is never enough money available for governments to do everything they would like, funds spent putting millions of people in prison and jail crowd out other important purposes for which those funds could be used. State governments have seen their budgets tighten significantly in recent years, in part because so much money is devoted to building and maintaining prisons and jails. The cost of keeping a single inmate in prison for a year is, on average, $33,000 (more than a single year of college at a public university). Is that a healthy investment for states and the federal government to be making?

Another surprising consequence for society as a whole is that American democracy itself is increasingly impacted by mass incarceration (see Chapter 21 for further discussion). An estimated 5.2 million American citizens were prevented from voting in the 2020 election (Uggen et al. 2020). This can distort the political process in that incarcerated felons are counted as "residents" of the place where their prison is located, exaggerating the political strength of those places (and allowing those communities to claim more government resources than they otherwise would have). Further, contact with the criminal justice system tends to reduce trust and support for American democracy for offenders, but also for family and friends who experienced the cost of incarceration with their loved ones (Lerman and Weaver 2013). Finally, denying millions of citizens the right to vote while expecting them to abide by laws they have no say in making has impacted the political power of communities with large felon populations. Further, being able to vote contributes to helping individuals reintegrate back into their communities and lowers the likelihood of further criminal activity (Manza and Uggen 2006, chpt. 6).

The social costs of mass incarceration do not end with the costs of holding people in a facility. The challenge of prisoner **reentry** has become considerable: Some 650,000 to 700,000 former inmates are exiting prisons and jails and returning to their community every year. Former inmates need jobs, places to live, and many other services to help them restart their lives (Petersilia 2003). The challenges of reentry are costly not just for individuals and their families, but for governments and nonprofit organizations that seek to help with this process. For most of the era of mass incarceration, resources for reentry have been very limited, but they are vitally important. For example, as we have seen, helping former offenders desist from crime is definitely improved when they are resettled into their communities and have help finding a job and a place to live. As with all people, former inmates need skills and resources to successfully make major life transitions. In this case, intensive job training programs and mentorships may be necessary to lower recidivism rates (Latessa 2012). As it stands, the scale of the reentry problem has vastly exceeded the capacity of existing programs, leaving it up to social service and other charitable organizations to try to help where they can.

Conclusion: Crime and Punishment

Crime is a pressing social problem. Being the victim of a crime, or witnessing a violent event, can have significant and lasting effects on individuals, and pervasive violence can undermine entire communities. For these reasons, perhaps the most important fact from this chapter is a piece of positive news: The level of crime and violence has fallen sharply in the United

States, according to every source of data available. While there are still many high-crime areas across the country, these places are fewer in number and generally safer than they once were.

Although crime and violence have become less severe of a problem, the persistant rise of mass incarceration has emerged as a new challenge in its own right. In this chapter, we described how mass incarceration affects individuals, families, and communities. We noted that although criminal laws are supposed to treat everyone the same, in many ways particular groups are punished far more often than others. The overall impact of mass incarceration on community life is multifaceted and difficult to summarize in a simple way. The problems of urban poverty and violent crime have always been interconnected; and from the 1970s through the 1990s, the connection grew stronger as violent crime worsened. The federal government could have responded in many different ways, but the path we took as a nation was to bolster law enforcement and invest in the prison system, using both federal and state funds to do so. This approach did not change even as crime and violence receded, imposing significant costs. In million-dollar blocks in cities around the country, the government has invested enormous sums of money to lock up a disturbing share of American citizens.

In particular, America's criminal justice system has been especially fraught by racial inequalities at all levels of the system, from minor arrests of young people of color for behavior that may be overlooked for Whites, all the way up to the disproportionate police killings of people of color, a significant percentage of whom carry no weapon and pose no threat to armed police officers. The decades-long failures to bring law enforcement to a truly race-neutral approach remains a deep wound in American society, one that is certain to generate ongoing conflict in the future until a better way is found.

The Big Questions Revisited: Chapter 20

20.1 What Constitutes a Crime, and What Are the Different Offense Types? In this section, we explored how and why certain types of actions are labeled criminal, the different types of criminal categories, and the consequences for individuals convicted of crimes.

The Problem of Defining Crime

Defining Crime

Learning Objective 20.1.1: Define crime and the role of the penal code.

Different Types of Crime: A Brief Overview

Learning Objective 20.1.2: Explain how crimes are classified in the United States and the possible punishment associated with each type.

White-Collar Crime and Street Crime

Learning Objective 20.1.3: Compare and contrast white-collar crime and street crime.

Key Terms
deviance (p. 569)   crime (p. 569)   penal code (p. 569)   decriminalized (p. 569)   jurisdiction (p. 570)   felonies (p. 570)   misdemeanors (p. 570)   infractions (p. 570)   prison (p. 570)   jail (p. 570)   probation (p. 571)   parole (p. 571)   plea bargain (p. 571)   white-collar crime (p. 571)   corporate crime (p. 571)   street crime (p. 571)

20.2 How Much Crime, Particularly Violent Crime, Exists in America? Violent crime has been declining in the United States for decades, and yet there is more violent crime in the United States than in many other countries of the developed world. How much more, and why? In this section, we explored possible explanations for this discrepancy and examined the consequences of violence.

Crime in the United States

Trends in Crime

Learning Objective 20.2.1: Explain how crime is tracked in the United States and how the homicide rate has changed in recent decades.

Why Did Crime Decline?

Learning Objective 20.2.2: Discuss some of the leading factors on why crime has declined.

American Violence in Comparative Perspective

Learning Objective 20.2.3: Analyze why there is more violent crime in the United States than in many other countries of the developed world.

The Consequences of Violence

Learning Objective 20.2.4: Analyze the consequences of violence as both a public health problem and a social problem.

Key Terms
murder (p. 573)   robbery (p. 573)   assault (p. 573)   rape (p. 573)   National Crime Victimization Survey (NCVS) (p. 574)

20.3 How Do Sociologists Seek to Understand Crime and Punishment? Many social scientists and theorists have explored the question of why crimes are committed and how societies decide whether and how to punish. In this section, we examined the work of several influential classical and modern social theorists, and we explored how a sociological perspective helps us to understand why some actions are considered criminal. We also discussed the possible goals, or purposes, of punishment within a society.

Theories of Crime and Punishment

Early Theories on Crime and Punishment

Learning Objective 20.3.1: Describe the most influential early social theories on crime and punishment.

Modern Social Theories of Crime and Punishment

Learning Objective 20.3.2: Explain how modern social theorists extended and challenged early social theories on crime and punishment.

Goals of Punishment

Learning Objective 20.3.3: Analyze the four basic reasons societies punish criminals.

Key Terms

criminology (p. 578)   strain theory (p. 579) social disorganization (p. 579)   labeling theory (p. 579)   life-course perspective (p. 581) desistance (p. 581)   retribution (p. 581)   deterrence (p. 581)   incapacitate (p. 581)   rehabilitate (p. 581)   recidivism (p. 581)

20.4   What Is the Role of Racism in the Criminal Justice System? Racial inequalities in how the American criminal justice system responds to crime has a long and troubled history. It has also been the subject of intense focus driven by the rise of the Black Lives Matter (BLM) movement. In this section, we provided an overview and analysis of the racial disparities in the criminal justice system.

Racial Disparities in the Criminal Justice System

Racism and Criminality: A Brief History

Learning Objective 20.4.1: Describe the history of racism in the criminal justice system.

Race and Punishment

Learning Objective 20.4.2: Analyze the evidence of racism in criminal justice policies and punishment.

Key Terms

racism (p. 583)   lynching (p. 583)

20.5   Why Is Mass Incarceration Controversial? The American criminal justice system in recent years has undergone a remarkable change. The incarcerated population in the United States has grown 600 percent over the past 40 years. In this section, we explored the reasons behind this massive increase in the number of Americans behind bars, and we examined how the U.S. prison population compares to those in similar countries.

Mass Incarceration in America

Punishment in America Today

Learning Objective 20.5.1: Compare and contrast the crime rate and the incarceration rate in the United States and in similar societies.

Causes of Mass Incarceration

Learning Objective 20.5.2: Analyze the possible causes of mass incarceration in the United States.

Key Terms

mass incarceration (p. 589)

20.6   What Are the Consequences of Mass Incarceration? For sociologists, the study of mass incarceration must take into account not just why people commit crimes and why societies choose to punish those actions, but also the larger impact for families, communities, and society. In this final section on the criminal justice system, we considered a few of these additional consequences of mass punishment.

The Far-Reaching Impact of Mass Incarceration

Consequences for Individuals

Learning Objective 20.6.1: Identify and describe the consequences of a criminal record for individuals.

Consequences for Families

Learning Objective 20.6.2: Explain the social consequences for the families of incarcerated individuals.

Consequences for Communities

Learning Objective 20.6.3: Analyze the complex consequences of mass incarceration on community life.

Consequences for Society

Learning Objective 20.6.4: Explain the impact of mass incarceration on the larger society.

Key Terms

collateral consequences (p. 594)   reentry (p. 595)

Chapter 21

American Democracy and Political Life: A Sociological Approach

By Jeff Manza

Polarization. Fake news. Trust in government and government institutions at an all-time low. Conspiracy theories about the government spreading widely. Members of Congress refusing to negotiate over important issues such as helping struggling families during the peak of the COVID-19 pandemic. Two of the last six presidential elections awarded to the candidate with fewer votes. The refusal of the losing side in the 2020 presidential election to accept the results of a democratic election. Big money pouring into the political system to try to influence elections and to get politicians to pass laws favoring big donors. Widespread efforts to find ways to prevent some citizens from voting. As if all that wasn't enough of a sign of serious trouble for democracy in America, an insurrectionary mob stormed the U.S. Capitol on January 6, 2021, forcing members of Congress to abandon their posts and head to an underground bunker for their own safety as the mob threatened to kill the Vice-President.

The health of American democracy in recent years is deeply troubled. Has it always been this way? In 1831 and 1832, Alexis de Tocqueville, a young French intellectual and diplomat from an aristocratic family, traveled across the United States to observe the world's first stable democratic political system in action. Upon returning to France, Tocqueville shared his observations in a book called *Democracy in America*. Published to great acclaim in 1835, it remains one of the most famous works of social science ever written. Tocqueville identified many features unique to American society and its emerging political system: The absence of aristocratic privilege, which made political equality feasible in way that Europe had not yet achieved; the separation of church and state; the importance of civic associations—groups of citizens who formed organizations to promote various causes—as a key to creating an active democratic life; and, as he keenly observed, the way that Americans, unlike Europeans, appeared to be motivated by a strong individualist and egalitarian bent. Americans,

Tocqueville believed, seemed to think that anyone could succeed through hard work. Combining institutional design with strong norms of equality, Tocqueville sensed that democracy had found fertile soil in the New World.

Among the many prescient observations in *Democracy in America* were Tocqueville's investigation of the new political institutions that the framers of the U.S. Constitution had created and how they enabled broad participation in political life (at least for White men). Although skeptical of the

My Sociological Imagination

JEFF MANZA

Growing up in the college town of Berkeley, California, my family was neither elite (my parents worked for the local university, but not as professors) nor unprivileged. I experienced the differences between these worlds, and in particular the inequalities they represented, as an endlessly fascinating puzzle. I was also always interested in politics and occasionally participated in political protests and movements. My intellectual interest in sociology began to develop while I was an undergraduate student because it provided a way of connecting my emerging concerns about inequality and injustice with a set of theories and ways of studying how those inequalities persist. Since then, I have been exploring how social inequalities influence political life. More recently, I have become interested in how public opinion does or does not shape government policies and how and when public attitudes can be manipulated or misused by political elites. I hope that my work can contribute, in some small way, to making American democracy more representative and egalitarian than it currently is.

On January 6, 2021, there was an attempted insurrection at the U.S. Capitol in Washington D.C. by a mob of supporters claiming that the 2020 election results (in which incumbent President Donald Trump was defeated by Joe Biden) were invalid, even though there was no evidence to back up such claims. How is it that democratic institutions in the United States are viewed with suspicion by so many people?

powers granted to the independently elected House of Representatives and the idea that the president could be reelected (fearing in both cases that they would make poor judgements to win reelection), Tocqueville was impressed with the separation of powers and the attention the framers had devoted to the design of political institutions in order to preserve liberty and the right of citizens to express their views about their government. His primary concerns, perhaps arising out of his aristocratic background, were that the American Constitution had actually provided too many ways for citizens to exert their will. Nevertheless, Tocqueville wrote eloquently and respectfully about the novel institutions that the so-called Founding Fathers had established in the late eighteenth century.

Almost 200 years later, those political institutions are showing their age. Modern democracies claim to offer to every citizen the equal opportunity to shape the composition of their elected, rule-making governments (and hence the policies those governments adopt). In this hypothetical world of democracy, citizens enjoy participating in politics, and by participating they learn from people with different views and find ways of reaching compromises and forging consensus. In the real world of American democracy today, these ideals are far from being realized and in some ways are being threatened in new and unanticipated ways. Americans express exceptionally low levels of enthusiasm for their government, and most know little about the politicians who hold office or about the substance of the major issues of the day. For many years now only about one in five Americans approve of the job their elected Congress is doing, and, depending on when they are asked, usually only about 25 to 35 percent of the public feels the country is "moving in the right direction." For example, on November 13, 2020, an average of all recent polls collected by the website RealClearPolitics that ask nationally representative samples of Americans showed that 18.0 percent of Americans believed the Congress is doing a "good job," and only 28.8 percent believed the country is "moving in the right direction." On August 16, 2021, a slightly more optimistic 28.5% believed Congress was doing a good job, while 37% thought the country was moving in a good direction.

The 2016 election of businessman Donald J. Trump to the presidency underscored the high levels of dissatisfaction that many people feel toward elected officials. An outsider to politics who had never held political office, Trump promised to make major changes to the way the federal government operates, or—as he put it in his frequently colorful language—to "drain the swamp" of government. Although often extreme in his claims about the state of the American political system, his rhetoric is only the latest of a long line of politicians and media commentators decrying the current state of affairs. Trump's success in winning the presidency has encouraged other politicians to follow in his footsteps.

No democratic system in the history of the world has ever proved capable of doing everything it promises, in Tocqueville's time or our own. People have been dissatisfied or angry with their governments for as long as we have been able to measure their opinions, and certainly before that as well (Tocqueville found plenty of evidence of dissatisfaction in the early 1830s in his travels around America). But in recent years, there is little doubt that the intensity of dissatisfaction with democratic political institutions—in the United States and in many other democratic countries as well—is rising. The emergence and growing strength of new political parties and politicians articulating plans to tear down longstanding political institutions and government policies is increasingly common. Growing numbers of citizens in democratic countries around the world are expressing opposition to the emergence of a global economic system and rising levels of diversity being driven in part by elevated rates of immigration across borders. Citizens often think their tax dollars are being wasted and that politicians are corrupt or incompetent, and above all else they wish there were a better way.

While all democracies are under stress in recent years, the American political system has some unique issues and challenges that we will consider in this chapter. Some of these were visible to Tocqueville, but others have emerged more recently. For example, the United States is the only democratic country in the world that legally allows so much money into the political system, which brings with it the possibility that rich and powerful corporations can exert undue influence on politicians and political parties. No other similar democracy makes the "simple" act of voting so difficult, has as low a rate of voter participation, or such large disparities in participation by income or class, as those found in U.S. elections. The two-party system that has been locked in place since the Civil War is particularly constraining, as it has proved very difficult for new or independent political voices to find a space in the political system. In recent decades, the two parties and their supporters have become increasingly divided, leading to a situation in which even during a national emergency, such as the COVID-19 pandemic, members of the two major political parties could not reach agreement on such basic issues as the importance of wearing a mask or whether it was acceptable for the government to prevent large gatherings.

In this chapter, we will turn a sociological lens on these issues, as they appear in American political life today. One feature that we will be especially focused on is the unique way in which American political institutions are struggling to change and the possibility that we may be locked in a spiral of decline that is difficult to get out of. Throughout this book, we have noted that while institutions are slow to change, they can and do evolve over time. Along the way, we will also explore another great theme of this book— how inequalities, in this case political inequalities—are a core feature of American society.

The Big Questions

1. **How "democratic" is democracy in America?** Elections are at the core of modern large-scale representative democracy. The American Constitution establishes several critical elements of the electoral process that are especially important, and which could be regarded as undemocratic to varying degrees if we were writing a twenty-first century democratic constitution: Deciding outcomes in winner-take-all election districts, allowing the major parties to draw up the boundaries for elections (and the mischief that permits), and privileging citizens in small states in the Senate and the Electoral College. In this section, we consider each of these elements.

2. **Why is turnout so low in American elections?** Americans face multiple hurdles to voting that contribute to reduced turnout in elections. In this section, we consider why so few people vote in national elections. We will examine both individual-level differences in turnout by education, age, race, and gender and institutional factors.

3. **Who has political power in the United States today?** One way of studying democracy in action is to ask the question, who gets what? Are all groups equally influential? In this section we explore the ways in which powerful groups are much more likely to get the government to make policies in their interest. An especially important example can be seen in low taxes paid by the rich and in America's' inability to reduce poverty to the same degree as other rich countries.

4. **Why is political polarization bad for American democracy?** To this point, we've described a variety of ways in which democracy is troubled by the way American political institutions are functioning. There is another issue that has been developing for some time that everyone who studies American politics is deeply concerned about: The rise of polarization in which Democrats and Republicans (and liberals and conservatives) are increasingly divided and unable and even unwilling to find common ground. In this section, we explore polarization in more detail, what caused it, and whether it might be reduced in the future.

Mark Bussell

BIG QUESTION 21.1 How "Democratic" Is Democracy in America?

DEMOCRATIC ELECTIONS IN THE UNITED STATES

American political institutions appear at first glance to have all of the formal features of a democratic political system—the right to participate, freedom of speech, the right to form political parties opposed to the government, a free press, regular elections, rule of law, and separation of powers (see Chapter 8 for more details). But there are ways in which American democracy differs sharply from democratic systems in other countries. And these differences are often consequential, creating some major shortcomings. As we will see, what made sense to the drafters of the Constitution in 1789 (or what Tocqueville found so appealing in the 1830s) might not make so much sense today. But the Constitution (with all of its contradictions and shortcomings) remains the core foundation upon which U.S. democracy works. In this section, we will examine some of these concerns.

American Democracy in Comparative Perspective

21.1.1 Discuss the state of democracy in America versus other countries.

Let's start with the big picture. How does the United States measure up when it comes to democratic governance as a whole? A widely respected nonpartisan global research and democratic advocacy organization called the Freedom House has been carefully tracking democratic practices around the world for several decades. Freedom House considers multiple important indicators of democracy, most importantly **political rights** (such as the right to vote, the freedom of groups to form political parties to oppose the government, and the freedom of the press) and **civil liberties** (such as protection from arbitrary prosecution from the government and the right of individuals to speak freely when opposing the existing government). Table 21.1 displays Freedom House ratings in a list of the most democratic countries, with scores reflecting deductions from 100 based on how well a country meets all of the criteria they examine.

The table shows that the United Statts was ranked as the 53rd most democratic country in the world in 2020. Given the importance the United States has historically placed on helping other countries to build democratic institutions (for example, Congress has long provided substantial funds to do so), this is rather an embarrassing outcome. Freedom House has lowered its evaluation of American democracy dramatically in recent years. Americans are often taught in elementary and high schools to think of their democracy as exceptionally virtuous. Independent and outside observers, like Freedom House, see it quite differently. Let's now move to explore why that might be the case.

How American Elections Are Organized

21.1.2 Analyze the consequences of the single-member districts and electoral boundaries established by the U.S. Constitution.

Under the Constitution, members of the House of Representatives are chosen in **single-member districts** in which the candidate winning the most votes wins the seat (this is also known as a winner-take-all system). Many other democratic countries use an alternative known as **proportional representation (PR)**, where seats are allocated according to the percentage of the vote received by each party. Single-member district elections tend to produce a two-party system, whereas PR systems generally have multiple parties represented in a legislature. The reason why this is the case is that in a PR system, a new

Table 21.1 2020 Freedom House Rankings of the 53 Most Democratic Countries

Finland	100
Norway	100
Sweden	100
Netherlands	99
Canada	98
Luxembourg	98
Uruguay	98
Australia	97
Denmark	97
Ireland	97
New Zealand	97
Belgium	96
Japan	96
Portugal	96
Switzerland	96
Barbados	95
San Marino	95
Andorra	94
Cyprus	94
Estonia	94
Germany	94
Iceland	94
Slovenia	94
United Kingdom	94
Austria	93
Dominica	93
Kiribati	93
Marshall Islands	93
Taiwan	93
Tuvalu	93
Cape Verde	92
Micronesia	92
Palau	92
Saint Lucia	92
Spain	92
Bahamas	91
Costa Rica	91
Czech Republic	91
Lithuania	91
Saint Vincent and the Grenadines	91
Chile	90
France	90
Liechtenstein	90
Malta	90
Grenada	89
Italy	89
Latvia	89
Mauritius	89
Saint Kitts and Nevis	89
Greece	88
Slovakia	88
Belize	86
United States	86

SOURCE: Freedom House.

The "founding fathers" and other early American political leaders invented a democratic political system, borrowing some ideas from England and France, but also working partially from scratch and in the context of the time in which they lived. Not surprisingly, their insights more than 200 years ago, embedded in a very-hard-to-change Constitution, have proven their age and have not kept up with the expectations of modern democratic systems or the realities of a polarized political environment.

Independent Party presidential campaign in 1980 (which received 6 percent of the vote), the Reform Party (led by Texas businessman Ross Perot's 1992 and 1996 presidential campaigns, which received 19 percent and 9 percent of the national vote, and ran candidates for lower office for a few years). This large group is only a partial list of the most successful of these efforts; there are many dozens of others who have tried hard and failed as well (Rosenstone et al. 1996; Sifry 2002).

The upshot of this is that American politics has been locked into a two-party system—the Democratic and Republican Parties—since the Civil War. Every other long-standing democratic country in the world has seen one or more significant new parties emerge in the twenty-first century and become a regular part of the national legislature (and sometimes even head of state, usually a prime minister). As times change, people's preferences evolve, and normally new parties come along to challenge the status quo. Having to choose among such limited options is an important, and seemingly permanent, feature of American democracy. It is constraining in the same way that consumer goods would be if you only had two different kinds of cars, styles of jeans, or soft drinks to choose from. When asked in polls, the majority of Americans routinely say they support a third party, but when it comes time to vote few are willing to risk "wasting" their vote on candidates who (in a single-member system) are unlikely to win. Think how different political life would be if Americans had a viable Socialist or Social Democratic Party, a new Centrist Party, and/or a right-wing party to choose from!

party trying to get a foothold in office can win seats in a legislature, even if they only get 5 or 10 percent of the vote in an election. But in single-member districts, winning 5 or 10 percent of the vote in many districts just means the new party will lose every race and fail to gain a foothold. As a result, it is virtually impossible for new parties to emerge and stay competitive over an extended period of time.

The evidence for this can be seen in American political history. Since 1840, there has been exactly one new party (the Republican Party in the 1850s) that has emerged and survived at the national level. It's not as if many people and groups haven't tried. There have been dozens of attempts to create new parties. Among the most prominent of these efforts, which initially seemed promising at the time, were the Know-Nothing Party (anti-immigrant) in the 1850s, the Populist Party in the 1880s–90s, former president Teddy Roosevelt's oddly named Bull Moose Party (in 1912, Roosevelt won 27 percent of the vote as an independent presidential candidate), the Socialist Party (which also peaked around 1912, with its presidential candidate Eugene Debs winning 6%), the Progressive Party and Farmer-Labor Parties established in the Midwest in the 1920s and 1930s, the Communist Party (peaking in the 1930s), former vice president Henry Wallace and the second Progressive Party in 1948, the Dixiecrats (a short-lived segregationist party in the late 1940s), George Wallace and the American Independent Party (created to support Wallace's pro-segregation presidential campaign in 1968, which garnered 13 pecent of the vote), former congressman John Anderson's

The absence of third parties is just the beginning of the problems with the design of political institutions created by the Constitution. It also specifies that elections to the House will be based on districts of approximately equal size, but it has allowed the states to draw the boundaries of these election districts as they choose. Every 10 years, after the Census is completed, each state draws new boundaries for House seats as well as their state legislature. The Supreme Court has consistently held that these districts only have to be of approximately equal size in terms of population, but otherwise they can be drawn in whatever way a state decides. And that is where the problem begins.

Figure 21.1 Gerrymandering Examples

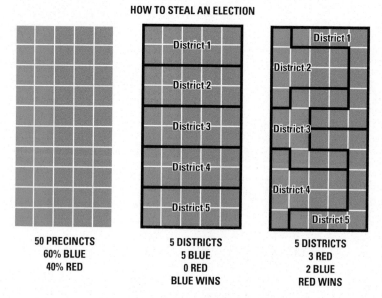

HOW TO STEAL AN ELECTION

50 PRECINCTS
60% BLUE
40% RED

5 DISTRICTS
5 BLUE
0 RED
BLUE WINS

5 DISTRICTS
3 RED
2 BLUE
RED WINS

Drawing district boundaries often takes the form of a practice known as **gerrymandering**. Gerrymandering is a way of drawing election boundaries to ensure (or try to ensure) a certain outcome, or to maximize the number of seats one party will win. It was named after an early-nineteenth century Massachusetts Governor, Eldridge Gerry, who drew a congressional district that was shaped like a salamander (hence, Gerry + mander). In the modern world, gerrymandering occurs under one of two circumstances: (1) When both of the major parties collude to draw safe boundaries to permit incumbents to be reelected—this makes elections less competitive; (2) more commonly, when the party in control of the state legislature draws boundaries to try to maximize the seats they will win, by crowding the other parties' voters into a smaller number of districts.

The importance of gerrymandering might be easiest to see with a hypothetical example (see Figure 21.1). To keep things simple, let's say there are two kinds of voters, "red" and "blue." There are 50 precincts (places where people vote) and five seats total to be chosen. Overall, the entire area (all fifty precincts) consists of 60 percent blue voters and 40 percent red voters (see the panel on the far left). But because the red and blue voters are not evenly distributed in each precinct—some precincts are more blue, others are more red—it is possible to draw the boundaries to produce very different outcomes. Blue voters are 60 percent of the entire area, but if the blue party controls the drawing of election boundaries, they can concentrate the precincts so that blue candidates win all five seats if the red voters are spread around to minimize their influence and in each of the five districts blue voters have a modest majority (see the middle panel of the figure). However, if the red party controls the drawing of election boundaries, they can perform the reverse trick—in the panel on the far right, we see

how the red party can win three of the five districts (60 percent) even though they are only 40 percent of the entire area.

Drawing election boundaries by the political party in power to maximize their results and gain extra seats via gerrymandering runs throughout American history, and has been done by both parties. In recent years, observers have noted that the Republicans gained a very significant advantage after the 2010 Census, when election boundaries were redrawn. For example, one analysis showed that because of careful map drawing, the Republican Party has gained about 16 or 17 extra seats after the 2016 election overall than they would if the maps were drawn to create more evenly balanced districts. The majority of these seats were won in just three states (Michigan, Pennsylvania, and North Carolina) with severely gerrymandered districts, and four other states (Florida, Texas, Ohio, and Virginia) contributing the remainder (Daley 2016; Royden and Li 2017). There will be a new round of redistricting after the final release of the 2020 Census. Later in the chapter, when we discuss how the two parties have become more polarized, we will see how gerrymandering to avoid competitive elections has become even more pervasive.

Another quirk of the Constitution that has become much more significant over time was that when electoral rules were being established, smaller states feared that if there was a single main legislative body (as is the case in most other democratic countries today), they would have little power compared to the bigger states. In order to craft a compromise that would satisfy the smaller states, the founders established a second legislative body—the Senate—with more or less similar powers to the House (although because it is the body that approves federal and Supreme Court judges, the Senate is the more powerful chamber). Each state elects two senators, regardless of its size. As Figure 21.2 shows, after the 2010 Census there is one senator for every 290,000 people in Wyoming, and one senator for every 19 million people in California. In other words, the average citizen in Wyoming gets far more influence over the U.S. Senate than the average person in California—about 65 times as much!

The outcome of this system is remarkable. The 26 smallest states have 18 percent of the U.S. population. They elect 52 Senators, or 52 percent percent of the U.S. Senate. The 24 largest states have 82 percent of the U.S. population. They elect 48 percent of the Senate. The 18 percent of Americans who select a majority of the Senate are very different from the country as a whole. The voters in these states are much more likely to be older Whites who live in rural communities and are less likely to have a college degree. This skew is particularly important once we realize that the citizens and voters with those characteristics are likely to favor different government policies than

Figure 21.2 Population Represented by U.S. Senators

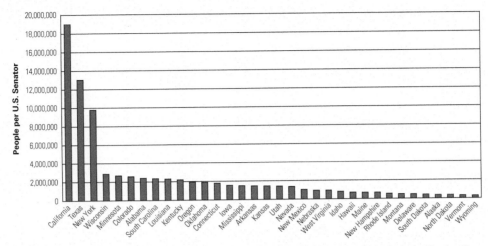

the rest of the country. In short, the fact that the U.S. Senate is elected this way means that the ideal of one person, one vote translates into widely varying degrees of influence.

At the time, the idea of a two-body legislature had a direct parallel with the English system (House of Commons and House of Lords). But while the United Kingdom eventually minimized the role of the Lords (which is largely ceremonial and procedural today), the United States has maintained both houses and in many important respects given the less representative body (the Senate) greater power. More importantly, the population disparity between the states has grown significantly over time. When the Constitution was drafted, the smaller states were much closer in population size to the bigger states; the ratio of the smallest state to the largest state was 10 to 1 (Virginia, the largest state of the original 13 states had 747,610 people, while the smallest state, Kentucky, had 73,677). Today it is over 65:1 (between California and Wyoming). The framers of the Constitution in 1789 could not have reasonably anticipated that the gap in representation would grow as large as it has, but they made it virtually impossible to change unless the smaller states agree in a Constitutional amendment process to give up their power. Meanwhile, as the population clusters in large states like California, Texas, and Florida have grown, the citizens of those and other large states are being significantly penalized. In the next section, we'll examine another way in which this disparity manifests itself, in the uniquely bizarre electoral college.

The Electoral College

21.1.3 Explain how the Electoral College and the popular vote impact U.S. presidential elections.

The establishment of the Electoral College to decide the outcome of presidential elections in the United States has no parallel to democratic systems anywhere else in the world. In other

countries, election votes are counted and the winner takes office (there have been some brief exceptions in political systems like in Italy from 2006 to 2013, where the winning party got "bonus" seats in the national legislature, but no major democracy uses this practice today). Like the Senate, the Electoral College was created to try to balance the power of the states, giving smaller states a leg up. Like the Senate, it makes the votes of citizens in some states more meaningful than others. Most importantly, it can deny a candidate who wins the popular vote the right to the presidency. And in fact, the Electoral College overturned the popular vote winner in two of the last six presidential elections: In 2000 (when popular vote winner Al Gore lost to George W. Bush) and again in 2016 (when popular vote winner Hillary Clinton lost to Donald J. Trump, as noted below).

How does the Electoral College work? The winner of presidential elections is decided based not on the popular vote, but on the basis of the outcome of a vote in the Electoral College, which meets after the election. Each state sends delegates to the College based on the number of seats they have in the House of Representatives plus two (that is, the number of seats that every state has in the Senate). Almost all states choose their delegation based on the winner of the vote in their state. This means that the party that wins the popular vote in a state gets all of the electoral votes for that state. (The only exceptions are Maine and Nebraska, which select some of their delegates based on the popular vote winner in each congressional district.)

The reason the popular vote winner nationally can lose in the Electoral College is simple: Smaller states with fewer voters can offset losses in larger states with more voters. This is exactly what happened in 2016, when Hillary Clinton won the popular vote by about 3 million votes but lost in the Electoral College to Donald Trump. Trump's victory was possible because of his narrow victories in states like Michigan, Wisconsin, Minnesota, and Pennsylvania, which combined with victories in many smaller states was enough to propel

Table 21.2 Popular Vote versus Electoral College in the 2016 Presidential Election

	Popular Vote Margin	Electoral College Votes	
Clinton			
California	Clinton +4,269,978	55	
Illinois	Clinton +944,714	20	
Maryland	Clinton +734,759	10	← Large popular vote victory
Massachusetts	Clinton +904,303	11	
New York	Clinton +1,701,118	29	
Trump			
Arizona	Trump +91,234	11	
Florida	Trump +112,911	29	← Small popular vote margin, large Electoral College vote
Michigan	Trump +10,704	16	
Pennsylvania	Trump +44,292	20	
Wisconsin	Trump +22,748	10	

SOURCE: Data retrieved from CBS News (https://www.cbsnews.com/news/trump-v-clinton-what-the-popular-vote-in-each-state-shows-electoral-college) and Politico (https://www.politico.com/mapdata-2016/2016-election/results/map/president).

him to victory. Clinton's huge margins in a number of large states like California, New York, and Illinois, by contrast, didn't help her overcome her small deficit in the ultimately decisive states. Table 21.2 shows some examples of states that were narrowly won by Trump, but that gave him all of their electoral votes (versus Clinton's huge margins in some of the biggest states). A similar situation almost happened again in 2020 when, despite losing the popular vote by nearly 5 percent, Trump came close to winning in the Electoral College. In this case, his opponent and winner of the popular vote (by over 7 million votes), Joe Biden, squeaked by. But just a few thousand more votes for Trump (in an election where 157 million people cast ballots) in several close states (especially Arizona, Pennsylvania, Georgia, and Michigan) could have flipped the entire outcome, and Trump would have again captured the White House while losing the popular vote.

In addition to the potential for overturning the results of the popular vote, the Electoral College can narrow the democratic process in presidential elections in another, less obvious way. Because winning the national popular vote and appealing to *all* Americans doesn't mean victory, presidential campaigns instead target a handful of so-called *battleground states*, where major party candidates pour tens of millions of dollars and spend most of their time and focus to win. These are typically states that are closely split between the two parties, and where either major party candidate has a reasonable chance of winning. We might ask, why should a citizen in a state that is either clearly Democratic or Republican have their vote rendered essentially meaningless, while the votes of citizens in the contested states are of magnified importance (Lessig 2019)? The low turnout in presidential elections might be boosted if the candidates ran national campaigns and voters in every state felt their vote had equal impact on the outcome.

The Role of Money in Political Campaigns

21.1.4 Analyze the role that money plays in American politics.

Compared to other democratic countries, American politics are unusual for the very large amounts of money that are raised and spent on elections. Nowhere else do candidates for the national legislature have to be able to raise millions of dollars to be competitive for office. The First Amendment to the Constitution, which protects the right of free speech, has been consistently interpreted by the Supreme Court as allowing individuals and businesses (especially since a prominent 2010 ruling) to give as much money as they want to political candidates and causes. Not surprisingly, most of the money given to support candidates running for office comes from wealthy individuals and large corporations and business groups.

Figure 21.3 displays the trends in rising spending on political elections. Overall expenditures are always higher in presidential years, but if we compare 2000 to 2016, we see expenditures have more than doubled, and going back even further there has been about a six-fold (600 percent) increase just in the past 30 years, and more than a 1500 percent increase if we go all the way back to the late 1970s. In the presidential election year of 1984, for example, about $400 million was spent on all national campaigns, while by 2012 that figure had reached $2.6 billion for the presidential campaign alone and $4 billion total (Scherer, Rebala, and Wilson 2014) and soured to over $12 billion total in 2020 (and over $6 billion alone on the presidential campaign).

Where does this extraordinary flow of political money come from? Contributions come from either individual donors or **political action committees (PACs)**. PACs can be organized by anyone, although the more resources and money a PAC

Figure 21.3 Rising Spending in National Elections

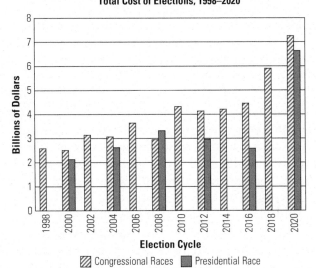

Total Cost of Elections, 1998–2020

NOTE: **Values are in billions of inflation-adjusted dollars.** Spending for 2020 races is projected (complete final results were not available at the time this chapter was written).

SOURCE: OpenSecrets. Retrieved from: https://www.opensecrets.org/elections-overview/cost-of-election?cycle=2020&display=T&infl=N.

has the greater its influence can be. Most large businesses, as well as every significant industry and industrial association, have their own PACs. Most unions have PACs, and there are hundreds of groups focused on single issues, such as the National Rifle Association (NRA), or groups devoted to supporting particular kinds of candidates (for example, Emily's List is a PAC that supports pro-choice candidates). We can distinguish three broad categories of PAC donations: Business-related (including both business PACs and individual executives working for large corporations), labor (PACs that represent unions), and single-issue PACs (which focus on a particular issue of concern, such as gun control or abortion).

Among PACs, business-oriented PACs are by far the most important contributors. The contributions coming from businesses vastly outstrip contributions by unions, reaching a ratio of at least 7:1 by the time of the 2016 election (that is to say, for every dollar donated by a union PAC, $7 or more are donated directly by corporations). Although a few of the single-issue PACs are relatively large, such as the previously mentioned NRA, the total amount of money these groups provide is a small fraction of the business total, closer to what unions are able to give. See Figure 21.4 for a breakdown of these donations.

In addition to PACs, the other (and actually larger) source of political money is that donated by individuals. Anyone can donate, within limits on the total amounts that can be given directly to a candidate set by law (although families can give in the name of each member of the family, thereby magnifying their potential donations to a single candidate). However, there are no limits on how much anyone can give to independent groups that support a campaign. Sometimes referred to as "dark money," these organizations, known as **Super-PACs**, are free to spend as much money as they can raise to support any candidate or party for office. Although large donors are important sources of funding for political campaigns through the regular system, it is in the world of the Super-PACs that the full impact of the rich is felt. Taking into account both regular and Super-PAC donations, large donors who give over $200 per donation contribute most of the money to political campaigns (for example, in the 2016 campaign, these large donors constituted 0.53 percent of the U.S. population, but gave more than 67 percent of all money donated by individuals; see OpenSecrets.org for details). Overall, it is individual donors who provide the majority of funds for candidates running for office, but they also are required to list their employer, making it very easy for corporate executives to signal that their donation is related to their corporate position. In recent elections, over half of all money raised by Congressional candidates has come from individuals, and most of that from wealthy individuals and families (Heerwig 2018). If we take into account *both* corporate and individual donations by employees of those corporations, and look at both regular and Super-PAC donations, the ratio of corporate money to union money soared to over 20:1 in 2020 (Center for Responsive Politics 2020).

Figure 21.4 Contributions From Political Action Committees, 2000–20

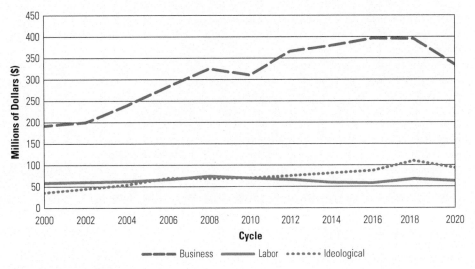

Cycle

NOTE: All values in millions of dollars.
SOURCE: **OPEN SECRETS.** Center for Responsible Politics; data from https://www.opensecrets.org/elections-overview/business-labor-ideology-split.

It is important to note that any U.S. citizen can give money to presidential campaigns (only foreigners are barred from donating). Many people who are not rich give money, and there are some political campaigns that rely primarily on small donors. For example, Senator Bernie Sanders, a candidate for the Democratic presidential nomination in 2016 and 2020, raised in each of his two campaigns more than $200 million in donations averaging just $27 each donation. This figure, touted by the campaign to highlight its citizen base, is slightly misleading as many donors give more than once, but the average donor to the Sanders campaign gave only about $100 total, still a very low amount. A candidate for office who gets a very large number of small donors to give can be competitive (as Sanders was in his challenge to Hillary Clinton in 2016 and Joe Biden in 2020, both of whom received much more of their money from large contributors). But despite exceptions like Sanders, small donors are still far less significant as a percentage of all donations than are the big donors (Vandewalker and Norden 2016). One person or organization writing a check for $2 million has more impact than 100,000 people writing checks for $20 each. In 2016, there were well over 100 individuals and groups that donated more than $2 million each.

Why has the amount of money contributed to candidates for political office grown so much? The primary answer is that the vast increase in wealth held by families at the top has expanded the resources for the rich to invest in the political system (see Chapter 11 for more information). As the rich get richer, there simply are far more people today with access to the great wealth needed to routinely make huge political donations than there were 40 years ago. Giving for all purposes—civic, charitable, religious, and political—has increased in this era of rising inequality. High-earning households have more money to give away to any cause they care about. While much of this giving may have benign consequences, no such simple conclusions would be appropriate when it comes to political money.

Social scientists have struggled to reach unambiguous conclusions about the importance of political money for either who wins elections or what legislation passes. There are a number of methodological difficulties in sorting that out with existing data and research tools. Part of the problem for researchers is that politicians rarely "sell" their votes, so there isn't a clear paper trail demonstrating direct influence. But it defies our imagination to think that contributors who repeatedly give large amounts get nothing in return. Three decades of research on political money has established that to be a serious candidate for elected office, especially Congress, one has to be able to raise money from either corporations or rich individuals, or both (Carnes 2018). This weeds out possible candidates who do not appeal to donors, and not surprisingly, this tends to limit who can run for office. There are virtually no former factory workers or small farmers in Congress today. And finally, while large donors are not guaranteed any particular outcome, they do get access to elected officials that ordinary citizens do not typically have. Access can translate into small, but often significant, benefits like tax breaks hidden in legislation and rarely subjected to public scrutiny (Clawson et al. 1998; Manza et al. 2004; Powell 2018).

BIG QUESTION 21.2 Why Is Turnout So Low in American Elections?

POLITICAL PARTICIPATION AND VOTING

One of the most surprising and enduring aspects of American democracy is how few people choose to participate compared to citizens in other democratic countries.

In Figure 21.5, we display turnout rates in recent elections in democratic countries around the world. As the figure shows, in most countries between 70 and 85 percent of the population votes in typical elections. In the United States, however, only around half bothers to vote in presidential elections (and turnout in midterm congressional elections

Figure 21.5 Voter Turnout in Recent National Elections

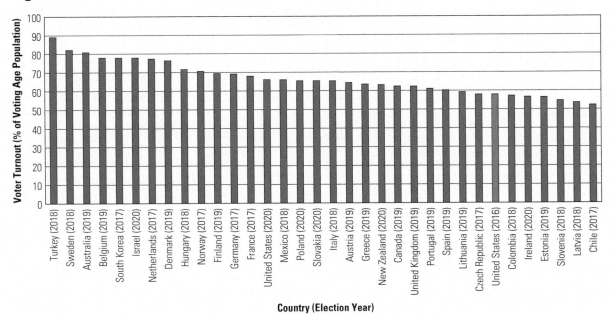

SOURCE: Pew Research Center calculations for all countries besides the United States. The figure for the United States is the average of turnouts for the 2018 midterm and 2020 presidential elections, which were the highest since the 1920s and may not be repeated in the future. Retrieved from: https://www.pewresearch.org/fact-tank/2020/11/03/in-past-elections-u-s-trailed-most-developed-countries-in-voter-turnout/.

without a presidential election is even lower—only about 36 percent in 2014, or less than half of most other countries' national elections). However, in 2018 and 2020, turnout increased significantly, to nearly 50 percent in the midterm elections of 2018 and to over 65 percent in the presidential election that year. These two elections *may* be a sign of increasing citizen interest in politics, *or* they may simply reflect the bitter divide over the presidential campaign and presidency of Donald Trump, in which both supporters and opponents of Trump voted at uniquely high rates to express their approval or disapproval. Either way, the problem of voter turnout has been consistent in most American elections.

Why don't more Americans vote? Social scientists have identified two types of explanations: Individual-level explanations (those that focus on the role of political interest and engagement by individuals) and political-institutional explanations (which focus on the rules of elections and how they shape outcomes). Who votes is an especially important question for sociologists to explore because the demographic attributes of individuals (such as education, race, income, gender, age, and religion) may mean that *who* votes is quite different than the entire population of eligible voters. Political and institutional explanations point to the role of mobilizing activities by parties and political organizations on the one hand, and institutional constraints such as voter registration requirements, the timing of elections, and the range of meaningful choices presented to voters through the party system, on the other. We consider both types of factors.

Individual-Level Factors

21.2.1 **Discuss some of the individual-level explanations for why voter turnout is so low in American elections.**

Education is by the far the strongest predictor of who votes in America (Wolfinger and Rosenstone 1980; Verba et al. 1995) and has been for as long as researchers have studied voter turnout in the United States. Those with more education have more knowledge of the candidates and issues, pay more attention to political news and current events, and have a stronger belief that it matters who wins elections (and thus are more concerned with the outcomes of the elections). Any one of these reasons could explain why better educated voters (typically those with college educations) participate at much higher levels than others, and in some combination have a big impact. In Figure 21.6 we display turnout by college degree, showing the sharp gap between educational groups in voting in recent elections. There has consistently been a 25 percent gap between high school graduates and people with graduate degrees (and a 15 percent gap between college and high school graduates).

Some other individual attributes of voters can influence turnout. Historically, Whites voted at higher rates than Blacks (see Figure 21.7), although the gap has varied depending on electoral context; in 2008 and 2012, with Barack Obama as the Democratic nominee for president, Blacks voted at slightly higher rates. In addition, almost the entire gap in turnout between Whites and Blacks is due to different education and income levels; once we statistically

Figure 21.6 Voter Turnout by Education Level

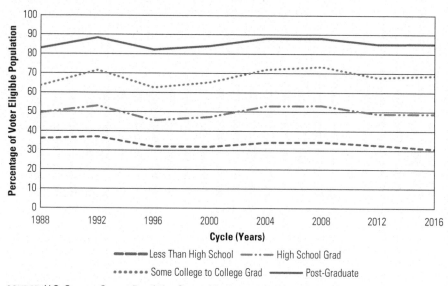

SOURCE: U.S. Census, Current Population Survey (election supplement; select years).

Figure 21.7 Voter Turnout Among Racial and Ethnic Groups

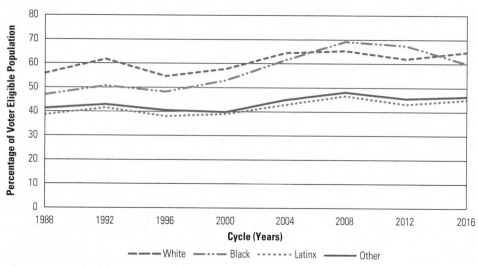

SOURCE: U.S. Census, Current Population Survey (election supplement; select years).

Figure 21.8 Voter Turnout by Gender

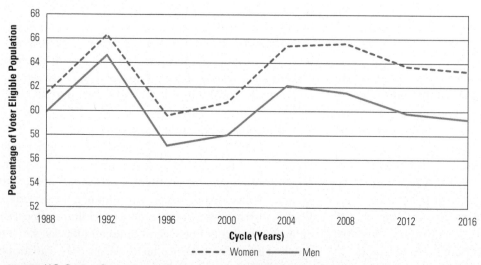

SOURCE: U.S. Census, Current Population Survey (election supplement; select years).

control for those differences, the gap disappears. Latinx citizens have typically voted at much lower rates than either Whites or Blacks, although the trend among Latinxs has moved sharply upward in recent elections (for example, Leighley 2001; Leighley and Nagler 2014). For Latinxs and Asians, a huge factor is citizenship status. There are (as of July 2020) about 44 million immigrants (either first or second generation) living in the United States. Roughly half have citizenship and are eligible to vote; another quarter are legal immigrants who are eligible to become citizens, and (primarily among Latinxs) approximately a quarter are unauthorized immigrants, who do not have the right to become citizens.

Until 1920, in most states women were not allowed to vote; elections by definition reflected the political preferences of (White) men. Even after the adoption of the 19th Amendment in 1920, which guaranteed women the right to vote, men voted at higher rates than women. Since the 1970s, however, women have voted at slightly higher rates than men, and the gap has grown to nearly 10% in 2016 (see Figure 21.8).

Finally, older people tend to vote at higher rates than younger people, which is a bit surprising because younger voters are, on average better educated than older people. It is also true that many of the people who get involved in political campaigns and social movements are young; but the enthusiasm of some is not shared by most young people. The aging process still gives older citizens more of an incentive to vote (see Figure 21.9). The magnitude of the difference in turnout rates between people over 60 and those under 30 is very large; on average the older group is almost twice as likely

Figure 21.9 Voter Turnout by Age Group

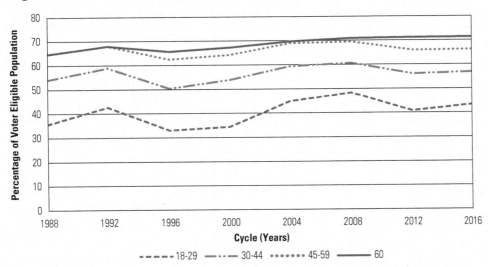

SOURCE: U.S. Census, Current Population Survey (election supplement; select years). 2020 data not yet available.

to vote. In Figure 21.9, we display turnout rates by age group at the time of each presidential election.

These long-standing demographic differences in turnout rates among groups helps give us an understanding of *who votes* in American elections, and how and to what extent some groups are over-represented and others are under-represented in terms of their participation rates. But these differences in participation rates among groups can't by itself explain *why* overall turnout is so much lower in the United States than other similar democratic countries (see Figure 21.5). For instance, Americans have about as much or more education on average as the citizens of any polity (and far more on average than in earlier periods of American history when there was higher turnout, as best as we can measure it; turnout rates of about 70 percent of eligible voters were common in late nineteenth century elections!). Furthermore, nonvoters' lack of interest in politics or apparent apathy toward election outcomes is significantly different from that of citizens in many other democracies, who nevertheless shrug their shoulders and turn out to vote at almost every election. Because of the general rule that the higher the turnout in an election, the smaller the gaps between groups, low turnout fosters political inequality (Manza et al. 2004).

Political-Institutional Factors

21.2.2 Explain some of the political-institutional reasons for why voter turnout is so low in American elections.

In attempting to explain why turnout is so much lower in the United States than in other comparable democracies, or why it is generally lower today than in earlier periods in American history, a great deal of attention has been paid to organizations like unions and the major political parties, and the degree to which they reach out to possible

voters to get them to the polls. For a long time, the major political parties and candidates used most of their resources on television advertisements to appeal to supporters and motivate them to vote, but in more recent years the major parties have returned to older styles of encouraging participation by going door to door to contact voters (as well using information from social media to target supporters and encourage them to vote. Campaigns can also use better data about voters through computing technologies to identify possible supporters and flood them with information that seems important to them, including using "fake" news stories and other kinds of manipulation. And over the past 15 years, as mentioned, there has indeed been a small but significant uptick in turnout rates in presidential elections (especially in 2016 and 2020).

The laws and norms governing American elections differ from other countries, as we have noted, and likely are another major reason why turnout is so low. The most important of these factors are (1) the fact that the simple right to vote is not made universal, as it is in the constitutions of most democratic countries, which has allowed room for

EFE News Agency/Alamy Stock Photo

There are extraordinary differences in turnout between Puerto Ricans voting in Puerto Rico, as seen here (where elections are held on either a Sunday or a national holiday), versus Puerto Ricans living on the U.S. mainland (Freeman 2001). As many as 25–30 percent more Puerto Rican voters turn out on a Sunday in Puerto Rico than Puerto Ricans living in the United States. This fact is all the more remarkable because when living on the mainland, Puerto Ricans' votes count toward the election of voting members of Congress, while in Puerto Rico they only select non-voting delegates to Congress. Holding national elections on a work day is one reason turnout is so low in American national elections.

disenfranchisement (taking away the right to vote) of groups throughout U.S. history; (2) the difficulty of registering to vote in the United States, compared with other countries that use an automatic system of voter registration; (3) the fact that national elections are held on a working day in the United States versus on either a weekend or national holiday in most other countries; and (4) the limited range of choices available to voters in the U.S. two-party system. We'll discuss the first two factors in more detail here.

THE RIGHT TO VOTE   As noted earlier in the chapter, democracy requires universal suffrage, in which all citizens living within a political jurisdiction have the right to cast one (and only one) ballot for all elected offices. Yet unlike virtually all other democratic constitutions around the world, the U.S. Constitution does not provide a guarantee that all citizens will be allowed to vote. When the framers met to draft the Constitution, there were no models of universal suffrage to draw upon. It was not yet fully part of the democratic ideal. After some debate, the drafters gave states the power to determine who could exercise the franchise. This power remains in the hands of the states, although a series of constitutional amendments later curtailed some of that power. States can no longer discriminate based on race (14th and 15th Amendments and the Voting Rights Act of 1965), gender (the 19th Amendment), or age (for those over 18 years old, the 26th Amendment), nor can they impose poll taxes as a precondition of voting (24th Amendment).

Since 1965, when the Voting Rights Act (VRA) was passed requiring all states to end historic practices that limited the ability of Blacks to vote, the right to vote for all citizens has been more or less a taken-for-granted fact of American political life. In 1995, for example, a leading study of political participation in America asserted that "at least since the voting rights reforms of the 1960s, political rights have been universalized in the United States. With relatively insignificant exceptions, all adult citizens have the full complement of political rights" (Verba et al. 1995). Yet two increasingly important exceptions to this broad and widely accepted generalization have to be noted, and these exceptions have proven to be increasingly consequential.

First, the year 1965 was important for voting rights not only because of the adoption of the VRA, but also because of the passage of the Immigration Act of that year, which led to the expansion of legal immigration. Over time, the 1965 immigration reform enabled millions of non-native adults to become part of the voting age population, but only those who become

naturalized citizens (or their U.S.-born children) gain the right to vote. While no democratic country allows non-citizens to vote in national elections, the upshot of the rapid growth of the immigrant population since 1965 has been a steady increase in the proportion of voting age adults without the right to vote, with the proportion of legal immigrants as a percentage of the voting age population growing from 2.6 percent in 1972 to about 8.5 percent by 2016.

The second challenge to the "settled" question of the right to vote was the vast expansion of the criminal justice system after the early 1970s, which, accompanied by laws restricting voting rights for most current felons and many ex-felons, has disenfranchised (deprived the legal right to vote) millions of other citizens (Manza and Uggen 2006). The right to vote for convicted felons continues to be controlled by state governments. All but two states disenfranchise current inmates and the vast majority disenfranchise some or all nonincarcerated felons (those out on probation and parole), and a number of states disenfranchise not only current felons but also many or all of their ex-felon population (former offenders who have completed their sentence), mostly those who have not paid off fees or fines associated with their sentence (making those fees a kind of poll tax that no one else has to pay). As a result of the rapid increase in conviction and incarceration after 1972, the disenfranchised felon population has grown steadily (see Figure 21.10). (Manza, Uggen 2006 estimate that there were 1.2 million disenfranchised felons in 1976, and a follow-up analysis concluded that there were 5.6 million at the time of the 2010 presidential election and over 6 million in 2016.) For the first time in decades, in the 2020 election there were fewer disenfranchised felons (5.2 million), due to several states' liberalizing their laws regarding ex-felon participation. But here's the critical point: Taking both immigration and criminal convictions into account, around 10 percent of all adults living in the United States today cannot vote (about twice as many as in the mid-1970s).

Because both of these groups—immigrants and felons—tend to be drawn from the bottom of the class structure, rising

Figure 21.10 Growth of Disenfranchised Felon Population

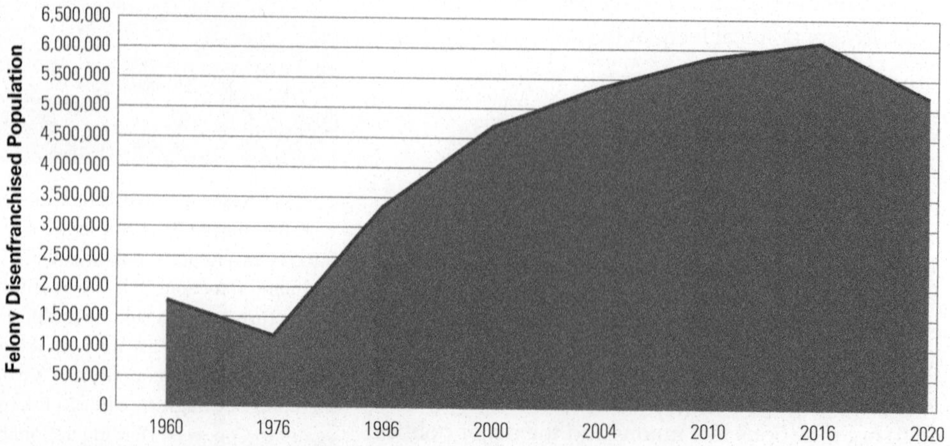

SOURCE: Manza and Uggen 2006; Uggen et al. 2020.

rates of disenfranchisement mean a skewing of the actual electorate towards more affluent citizens, as an important and influential study has shown (McCarty, Poole, and Rosenthal 2006). Rising rates of immigration, these authors note, are strongly associated with rising levels of income inequality and political polarization. In 1972, noncitizens reported *higher* median incomes than citizens and had an average household income that was 82 percent of that of citizens. In contrast, by the early 2000s the much-larger group of noncitizen residents had an average household income that was only 65 percent of that of citizens. Because noncitizens are by law disenfranchised, their rising share of the overall voting age population and declining economic status has meant that the *composition* of the electorate has changed. The disenfranchised felon population is similarly disadvantaged. That group is disproportionately poor, is made up of people of color, and has low levels of education (cf. Manza and Uggen 2006). By taking away access to the ballot for these millions of citizens, a growing gap between all citizens and eligible voters has emerged. In effect, a growing share of the poor cannot express themselves politically. And the overall national figure masks enormous regional variation: The disenfranchised and the migrant population are not distributed evenly across the country, but rather tend to be more heavily concentrated in a handful of states such as California, Texas, and Florida.

VOTER REGISTRATION REQUIREMENTS   Voter registration requirements have been contentious for a long time (Highton 2017). There have been efforts on the part of some groups to use tighter registration requirements to keep voters (especially people of color) away from the voting booth. By making it harder to vote, it is likely that the voices of the citizens with the fewest resources and education are less represented. When citizens are *registered* to vote, they participate at fairly high levels in American politics (with turnout rates over 80 percent in presidential elections). But in the United States voting is often a two-step process: Register (usually 30 days before an election, although a few states allow registration right up to election day), and then turn out to vote. Because citizens are not automatically registered to vote, as they are in most democratic countries, they have to execute both of these steps. And in many states, if you skip an election or two, your name will be purged from the rolls, requiring you to re-register if you wish to vote.

Trying to make voter registration either automatic, or as easy as possible, has long been a goal of many reformers. One big idea, implemented by Congress in 1993, was the adoption of legislation requiring states to make voter registration materials available at the state's Department of Motor Vehicles. Known as "motor voter," the idea is that easily allowing voters to register to vote when they get their license, renew it, or do any other automobile-related business, would be much simpler and would catch people who move to a new town and might otherwise forget to register. Evidence suggests the motor voter law did increase actual voter registration, although its impact on turnout is more difficult to detect (Highton 2015). And since the passage of the motor voter law, a number of states also have made registration easier. For example, nine states have allowed voters to register right at the polls, so that voting can be a one-step process.

Another strategy has been to make voting by mail easier. Prior to the COVID-19 pandemic five states (Colorado, Hawaii, Utah, Washington, and Oregon) ran all-mail elections: Every registered voter is mailed a ballot well in advance of an election and votes by returning a signed ballot before Election Day. (Some of these states, like Colorado, also have an in-person voting option.) However, because of the pandemic, many additional states took steps to make voting by mail easier, hoping to reduce unnecessary transmission of the virus at the voting booth. In the 2020 election, 33 states and the District of Columbia allowed voting by mail, and 21 states now allow local governments to run mail elections in city or county elections (National Conference of State Legislatures 2020). All other states allow

Long lines at a voting precinct on Long Island, New York in the 2020 national election. In spite of significant efforts in most states to make it easier to vote during the COVID-19 pandemic, America continues to create obstacles to participation that cost voters time and reduce overall levels of political participation.

registered voters to request an absentee ballot ahead of an election if they declare they will be unable to vote in person.

The efforts to make registration and voting easier have been criticized by some and countered by groups pushing state legislatures to make it tougher to vote. Former president Trump, for example, claimed that voting by mail increases the chances for voter fraud. Despite his claims, no evidence has emerged to support this, and all the more than 50 lawsuits filed after the 2020 election challenging mail votes by the Trump campaign were thrown out of court. (There were over 70 lawsuits, total, and every single one failed to provide sufficient proof to convince the courts many of which were federal courts that had judges appointed by Trump, to challenge the election outcome.) In general, claims about voting fraud, periodically launched by losers of elections, have proven to be false (Minnite and Sheriff 2018). In the future, it is possible that voting on a cell phone, with fingerprint verification, will supersede all existing approaches, although we are not there yet.

Opponents of easier voting have not given up – quite the contrary. A number of states have taken measures to make voting or voter eligibility more difficult (see Figure 21.11). One strategy has been to pass laws requiring voters to show identification when they vote. This may seem straightforward, as it is no problem for most of the population that has either a driver's license, a passport,

or some other valid identification. But what about college students and very poor people? Students living away from home to attend college may only have their school ID card from the state where they are going to school. For poor people who do not have a driver's license (or a passport), acquiring a state ID card simply so they can vote is not always easy. It may cost money they do not have (as well as the time and difficulty of procuring a birth certificate or other documents to prove who they are to get the state ID). In the latter cases, federal courts have so far disallowed ID requirements that cost money, although states are free to reject school ID cards, thereby disadvantaging college students from casting what may be, for many of them, their first ballot. And merely requiring an ID may prevent poor people who don't have copies of the necessary documentation and a permanent address from registering to vote. In thinking about these issues, the sociological question should be: Are these laws really designed to prevent fraud, or are they simply having the effect of keeping some voters away from the polls? And if the latter, which groups benefit from having fewer students and poor people vote?

Other efforts to make it harder to vote are also being pursued around the country. In the spring of 2021, for example, the states of Georgia and Texas passed laws reducing voting hours, outlawing voter dropboxes, making it harder to vote by mail, and perhaps especially

Figure 21.11 States Adopting Limits on Voter Eligibility Since 2010

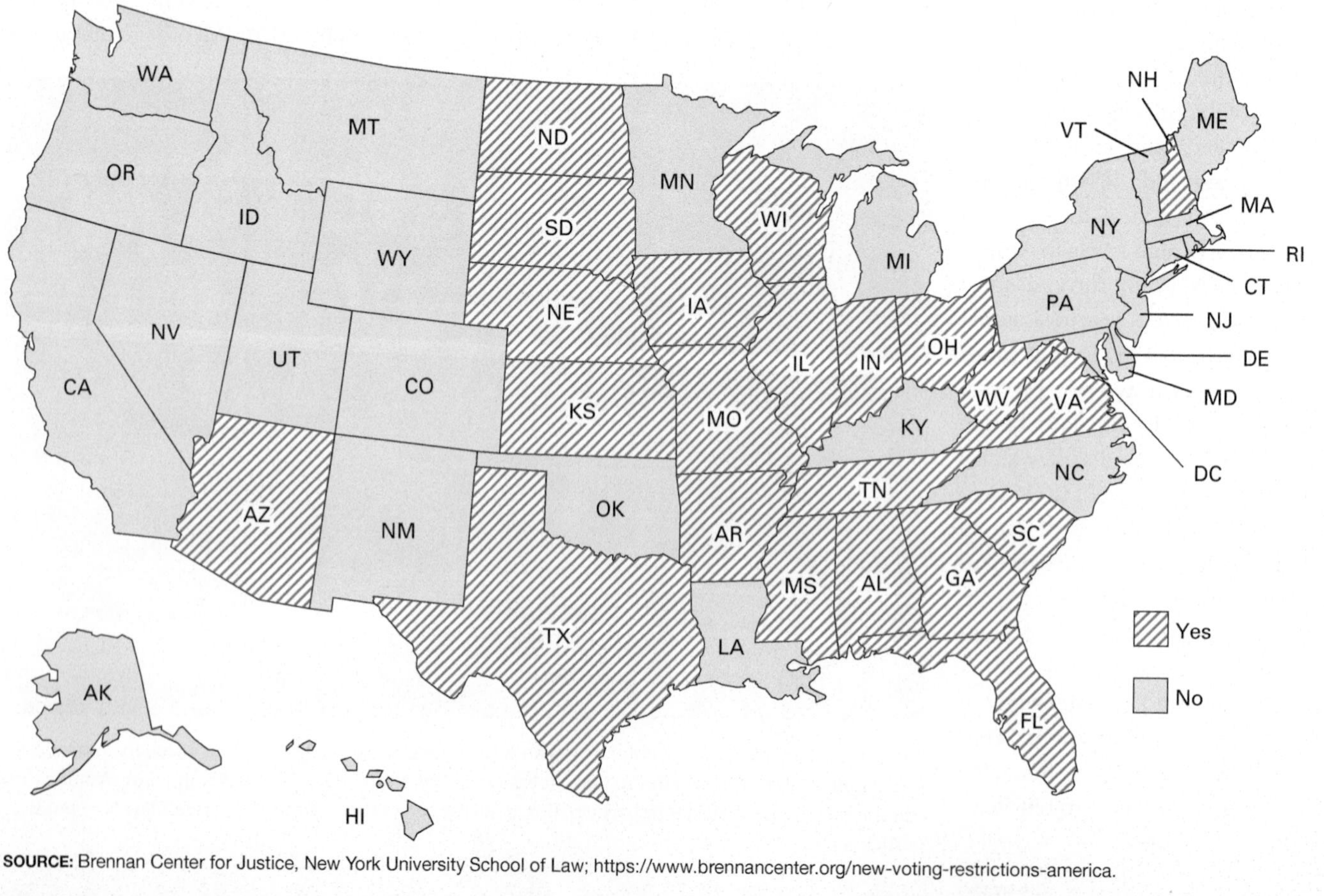

SOURCE: Brennan Center for Justice, New York University School of Law; https://www.brennancenter.org/new-voting-restrictions-america.

important allowing parties to send "poll watchers" into voting places, opening up the possibility of voter intimidation (which has a long history in the United States prior to the passage of the Voting Rights Act). The question of why some politicians and commentators think that a healthy democracy is one in which we make it harder for people to vote – especially when *no one has ever produced systematic evidence of fraud in recent elections –* is an important sociological question to ask. As always, we want to ask who is benefiting from these efforts – and who is being harmed.

The upshot of voting eligibility in the United States is simply this: The group of citizens who vote in elections are not representative of the entire eligible voting population. This may be because of restrictions on the franchise, the unusually complicated way in which eligibility to vote is established (such as requiring voters to register in advance of elections), or the decisions that individuals make about whether to bother to vote or not. But when we look at the big picture, voters are richer, White, better educated, and older than the entire population. It is also clear that non-voters have different views than voters, and that if they were motivated to participate in higher numbers, the outcomes of elections would likely come to reflect a different set of opinions (Leighley and Nagler 2013).

James McLoughlin/AGE Fotostock

BIG QUESTION 21.3 Who Has Political Power in the United States Today?

POLITICAL POWER IN AMERICA

A sociological analysis of democracy in any society asks questions about how democratic institutions live up to their promise of giving everyone an equal say. As we saw in the previous section, American institutions fall short. But ultimately, our interest in asking such questions is to ponder how they influence the exercise of power (our discussion here builds upon the sociological analysis of power we presented in Chapter 8), and it might be helpful to

review that chapter before proceeding. More specifically, we need to ask: Who gets what they want out of the political system? Most of what we read about national politics—elections, what's going on in Congress, what the president is up to, and key rulings of the Supreme Court—are important outcomes of democratic government, and the ultimate purpose of elections in the first place. But when we inspect American democracy more closely, we also find that there is a lot more going on than just the things that capture the media's attention. Most of the time, the issues being discussed and debated in Washington, D.C., or in their state capital, are entirely invisible to most Americans. On most issues, only professional policy analysts and full-time political insiders fully understand all of the details of policy proposals and appreciate what it is at stake. Many important decisions are made largely outside of the public's view. A sociological perspective on American politics requires that we take a step back from the day-to-day conflicts to ask: What are the broad patterns buried in these outcomes? In this section, we will examine how power and inequality operate in the American political system in terms of political outcomes (the ultimate measure of power).

How the Rich Get What They Want: The Case of Individual and Corporate Taxes

21.3.1 Discuss what tax policies tell us about how power is distributed in the United States.

We do not have enough space in this chapter to consider all possible political outcomes, but we can focus on a set of policies that are among the most important: Those that impact the distribution of wealth and inequality in the United States. More specifically, we will focus on two: (1) *Tax policies*, especially some of the political changes in the ways taxes are paid that have enabled the super-wealthy to take home a much greater share of the economic pie than they do in all other rich, democratic countries most like the United States; and (2) *antipoverty programs*, or more specifically, why the policies of the American government do the least, of any of the rich countries most similar to us, to reduce poverty and help families live in a minimally acceptable way (considered in the next section).

Beginning with taxes, the United States has an extraordinarily high concentration of income and wealth at the very top, with the top 1 percent of households receiving about 20 percent of all income in recent years, a dramatic increase from earlier decades (the top 1 percent received about 11 percent of income in 1980). Meanwhile, the top 10 percent has received about half of all income in recent years, while the remaining 90 percent of all families received only about 50 percent of all income. (For details about the high levels of inequality, and how much greater it is in the United States than in other countries, see Chapter 11.)

Why is it better to be really rich in America now than, say, 40 years ago? Or why is it better to be rich in the United States than, say, France? The short answer is because of important policy changes that have altered the way incomes and wealth are distributed and consumed. All governments make policies that impact who gets what. In the United States, the political organizations of the upper class have successfully convinced Congress and various presidents to make it easier for the rich to retain most of their income and wealth, and to pass on nearly all of it to their children (or their favorite charity) when they die.

The most obvious way this has been achieved is through changes to the tax system; that is, how much tax citizens in different income brackets are required to pay. To be sure, all societies require taxes to pay for things that governments provide: National defense, social security, education, health care, benefits for veterans, and infrastructure like roads, bridges, and public health (such as clean water). There are some taxes that everyone pays the same rate: Property taxes and sales taxes are the two most important. But the largest and most important source of revenue for the federal government are income taxes. The United States, as with all other rich, democratic countries, has long had a **progressive income tax system** in which the upper classes are expected to pay a greater share of income than the middle class and the poor. The logic is that those who have higher incomes can afford to contribute a somewhat higher share of their income to pay for government programs that benefit everyone; an extra dollar for a billionaire is surely less valuable than an extra dollar for a poor family. Public opinion polls consistently show that Americans support requiring the rich to pay higher tax rates than everyone else (McCall 2013).

But in spite of the commitment to a progressive system of taxation and broad public support for it, tax burdens on high earners have declined dramatically in the past 30 years. Figure 21.12 tells the remarkable story of the history of tax rates on high incomes in the United States. At the end of World War II (when especially high taxes were adopted to help pay for the war effort), the highest earners were paying over 90 percent of their earnings above the top threshold (in 1944, that was $200,000, the equivalent of about $3 million in 2021). In the early 1960s, the top rate was reduced to around 70 percent of earnings above the highest bracket (in 1964, that amount was $400,000, or about $3.5 million in 2021). The top rate was lower, but still about twice as high as it has been since the mid-1980s. In the early 1980s, in two dramatic waves of tax cuts on high earnings during the presidency of Ronald Reagan, the rich saw the top tax bracket fall to below 30 percent. It was bumped up a bit in the early 1990s under presidents George H. W. Bush and Bill Clinton, settling at 37 percent today for incomes above $400,000 (or $450,000 for married couples). Even more striking is that there are no further higher brackets than the $400,000.

But the official rates are not necessarily the most important factor. Many other provisions in the tax code in the United States primarily benefit the super-rich, and typically enable them to pay much less than the official tax rate would suggest (Winters 2011). For example, the rich often not only have high earnings but also typically receive considerable income from their investments. Much of this investment income is treated

Figure 21.12 Official Tax Rate on Highest-Earning Americans, 1960–2020

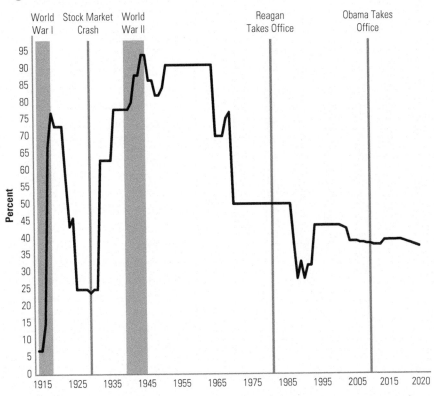

SOURCE: Tax Foundation, 2019.

Warren Buffett highlighted just how tax loopholes and reduced rates on certain kinds of income can benefit the wealthiest Americans (Buffett 2011). He admitted that he paid federal income taxes at a lower rate—about 18 percent on his 2010 income—than did his own secretary and other lower level employees at his firm, Berkshire Hathaway. Met with disbelief, Buffett followed up with a second article on his and his secretaries' taxes in 2012, with more details. Other individual cases that have come to light are even more surprising. The very wealthy senator and former presidential nominee Mitt Romney revealed, when he was forced by his opponents to release his tax returns during the 2012 presidential campaign, that he was paying less than 15 percent of his income in federal taxes. One of the great champions of avoiding paying his fair share of taxes is former president Donald Trump. A review of 15 years of his tax returns by the *New York Times* revealed that he paid *no* income taxes in 10 of those years and just

differently than other kinds of income and may be taxed at a rate as low as 20 percent (the so-called **capital gains tax** rate). The wealthy can also shelter other earnings from taxation, reducing the overall tax rate paid by rich families. Commonly known as **tax loopholes**, these provide tax breaks that are useless for the vast majority of American families, but extremely valuable for the very rich. Many of the very wealthiest Americans often make liberal use of offshore tax shelters by creating investment schemes in little countries like the Cayman Islands that have no income tax or by developing shell companies that allow them to move personal wealth across national borders without being detected (Zucman 2015; Lipton and Creswell 2016). Wealthy individuals and families can afford to employ lawyers and tax accountants skilled in the manipulation of these rules to seek every possible vehicle to reduce their tax rate, something that ordinary Americans would simply not be able to do (Winters 2011).

What little we know about the inner workings of the tax paid by the richest Americans provides startling evidence of low payments. In a remarkable article published in 2011, the activist billionaire investor

Real estate is an industry that allow firms and investors to reduce their tax burdens to very low levels. In 2020, it was revealed that President Donald Trump had paid no income taxes for 10 of the last 15 years, even as he lived lavishly. Shown here is one Trump's many residences.

Figure 21.13 Effective Tax Rates for Various Households, 2018

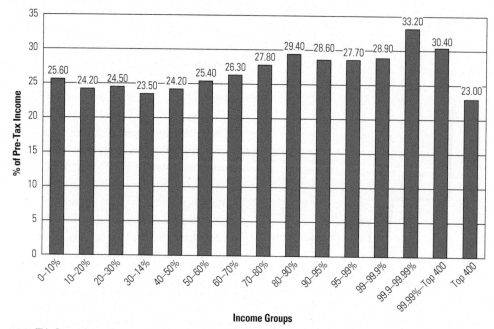

NOTE: This figure shows the average amount of federal taxes of all kinds actually paid by members of each income category. It includes Social Security taxes, Medicare taxes, income taxes, and capital gains taxes.

SOURCE: Data from Saez & Zucman, 2019.

$75,000 in two recent years, in spite of his billionaire lifestyle with multiple luxury homes (Buettner et al. 2020).

In order to get a better handle on this and see how the rich avoid paying taxes, we need to understand how tax policy is really made. The key research finding begins by looking at what is known as the **effective tax rate**, the actual rate of taxes paid as opposed to what the official tax rate shows. To go back to the Warren Buffett case, his effective tax rate is below 20 pecent even though it might appear that the millions of dollars he receives in income each year would be taxed by 37 percent (the current highest rate on all earnings above $400,000 by taking advantage of numerous reductions that his lawyers and tax accountants find for him). In Figure 21.13, we show the effective rate on taxpayers at different earning levels. The 400 richest taxpayers had an effective tax rate—including all taxes (federal, state, local, sales taxes, real estate taxes, social security, Medicare, and so forth)—of just 23 percent in 2018 (the most recent year that data are fully available). By contrast, the household at the median level of earnings paid an effective tax rate of 24.5 percent, slightly *more* than the very rich. Even more shocking was that the poorest households

pay *more* of their income in taxes (an estimated 26 percent) than the rich. Note that very rich households, but not those at the very top, could not shelter as much of their income, paying over 30 percent. What is most remarkable (shown in the second panel) is the trend over time: In 1950, the very rich paid an effective tax rate of 70 percent, 49 percent in 1980, but only 23 percent in 2018 (Saez and Zucman 2019). The especially low rate in 2018 reflected tax cuts that were passed in 2017 under President Donald Trump, but the rates paid by the super-rich in other recent years was not much higher.

Think about the implications of Figure 21.13 for a second. The poorest 10% of families will pay about 26% of their income in taxes. The richest 400 people — all billionaires — will pay on average pay just 23% of their income in taxes.

Just as wealthy individuals and families have benefited from many changes in the tax laws over the past and pay a lower effective rate than whatever the official tax rate is, so too have private corporations. Private companies now pay

Figure 21.14 Three Views of Corporate Tax Rates Since World War II

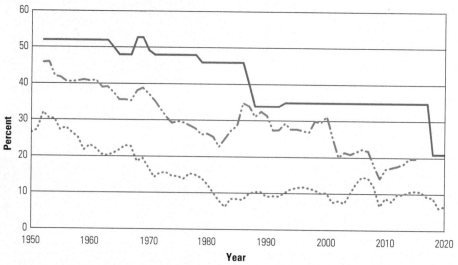

Top Marginal Rate — ‑ ‑ ‑ Effective Rate ‑‑‑‑‑‑‑‑ Corporate Income as % of Federal Tax Revenue

NOTE: Effective tax rates for 2018 is the average tax paid by corporations surveyed by the Institute for Taxation and Economic Policy. Report available at https://itep.org/corporate-tax-avoidance-in-the-first-year-of-the-trump-tax-law/.

SOURCE: IRS, Statistics of Income Bulletin, Historical Table 24; Deloitte, Corporate Tax Rates (2011–2015); US. Bureau of Economic Analysis, Corporate Profits After Tax, 2016; Institute for Taxation and Economic Policy, 2019; OECD Corporate Income Tax Statistics, 2020.

One of the private clubs in Washington, D.C., where public policy discussion occurs. (This club is operated by the Republican National Committee.) Not many poor people are invited inside clubs like this.

much less in taxes than they used to. Figure 21.14 shows the dramatic changes in corporate tax revenue as a percentage of the entire economy since the 1960s. The figure's bottom blue line shows the decline in corporate income tax as a percentage of all total federal tax revenue, so that far less of all the money the government needs to operate is coming from corporations. The other lines show that the actual average taxes paid by corporations are far lower than the official tax rate would suggest (this is the difference between "statutory rate"—the official tax rate—and the "effective" tax rate, what corporations actually pay, on average).

Not only has the overall rate of corporate taxes fallen (in 2017, the official corporate tax rate was reduced to 21 percent and the effective rate paid went down even further), many industries have enjoyed special tax deals that allow them to pay even lower rates than Figure 21.14 would suggest. For example, the oil industry has regularly received special tax breaks and loopholes, ostensibly to encourage these companies to drill for more oil, even as oil prices have soared and oil company profits reach record highs. Other loopholes enable some corporations to reduce their taxable income down to nothing. The all-time champion of avoiding corporate taxes appears to be General Electric (GE), known for its household appliances like refrigerators and light bulbs and more

recently for green-power products as well as its finance arm, GE Capital. In the 1980s, GE had so successfully avoided paying taxes that then-president Ronald Reagan (who was earlier in his life a paid spokesperson for GE, and was a major opponent of high taxes) ordered his staff to try to close some of the loopholes GE was using to avoid taxes. But the company is a powerhouse in Washington, D.C., and it has persisted in managing to pay very low taxes. The *New York Times* reported that in 2010, GE managed to pay *no* corporate income taxes at all, despite making $14 billion in profits across the world. (GE does pay sales taxes and Social Security taxes.) GE's tax lawyers and accountants, many of whom formerly worked for congressional tax committees or the Internal Revenue Service, aggressively use a variety of tax shelters to write down profits, and the company further lobbies Congress each year for special tax breaks often buried in legislation and unnoticed by the media or the public. GE's successful avoidance of all corporate income taxes may be extreme, but any corporation can reduce its tax bill by using similar strategies (Kocieniewski 2011).

Reduced tax burdens allow corporations to retain more of their earnings, and in recent years they have lavished pay and other perks (including generous stock options) on their top managers. We know most about the compensation of the chief executive officers (CEOs) of companies, as firms are required to report the annual incomes of their highest paid employees. This requirement produces very clear information about the trends over time. From the 1930s through the 1970s, CEO compensation averaged (in 2020 dollars, adjusted for inflation) about $1 million per year. Compensation for these executives began to shoot up in the 1980s and 1990s. By 1995, the CEO-to-worker compensation ratio had grown to more than 120 to 1, and by 2000,

Figure 21.15 CEO-to-Worker Pay Ratio in Select Countries

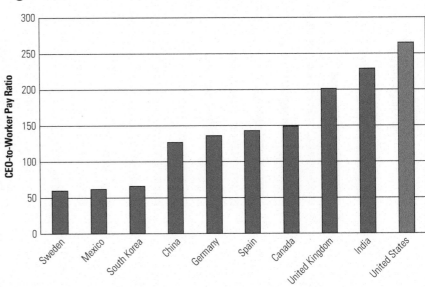

SOURCE: BBC reporting of data from Global CEO Index, 2019. Retrieved from: https://www.bbc.com/worklife/article/20190108-how-long-it-takes-a-ceo-to-earn-more-than-you-do-in-a-year.

average compensation for CEOs at Fortune 500 companies (the largest companies in America) peaked at 368:1 (Mishel and Wolfe 2019), before reducing to "just" 265:1 in 2019, still far higher than other countries (see Figure 21.15).

Looking at the big picture, we would argue that in the fight over how the benefits of economic growth are distributed, dramatic changes in individual and corporate tax rates indicate that rich individuals and families, as well as large corporations and their top executives, are winning. The struggle over who should pay what taxes will continue, and it is possible that in the future tax rates on the highest earners will once again increase. Several states have established special "millionaire" tax rates on the highest earners, and public support for further changes in that direction is substantial (McCall 2013). But for now, the burden of paying for critical government programs is not falling on high earners and large corporations as much as it once did.

How the Poor Get Less: Antipoverty Policy in the United States

21.3.2 Explain what antipoverty programs tell us about how power is distributed in the United States.

What about the flip side of taxation, the use of government resources to reduce poverty? A distinctive feature of the **welfare state** (the bundle of policies and programs adopted or implemented by the government designed to reduce poverty and inequality) in the United States has been its inability to reduce poverty to the same degree as other rich countries

around the world (see Chapter 11 for more on this topic). Every government in the modern age has established social policies designed to try to make sure that poor families have access to the basic necessities of life, like food and shelter. They've done so because capitalist economies have never produced enough decent-paying jobs for everyone who needs one, inevitably leaving some individuals and families in poverty (Garfinkel et al. 2010). Antipoverty programs adjust for misfortune. Adults (and their children) may fall into poverty for any number of reasons: Inability to work because of a physical limitation or psychological disorder an extended illness or accident, the economy being in recession and unemployment being high, or just plain bad luck. Because we can't know in advance who among us will end up homeless and destitute, we all contribute a little to provide protection for those who do end up in that state. Antipoverty programs also attempt to give poor children the same opportunity as middle-class children to succeed in life. The logic is that poor children who are poor through no fault of their own should not be held back as a consequence, and that by providing poor children the opportunity to succeed we provide the resources for them to make a better life for themselves as adults and for their children.

Although every country has welfare state programs designed to reduce poverty, some do it a lot better than others. We now know that in rich countries, it *is* possible to dramatically reduce the number of children and families living in poverty, if government programs make a commitment to doing so (Kenworthy 2020). How do we know this? A number of scholars have studied the problem, using very carefully developed data about household income and living

Figure 21.16 Poverty Rates Before and After Taxes and Transfers, 2017

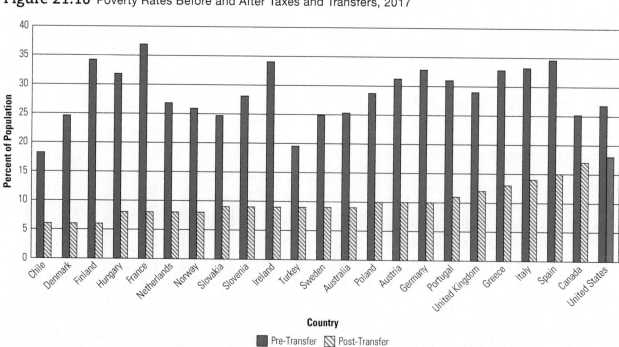

NOTE: Poverty rates are reported for the year 2017 or most recent available. Poverty is defined as income below 50 percent of the national median income.
SOURCE: OECD Income Distribution Database. Retrieved from: https://stats.oecd.org/Index.aspx?DataSetCode=IDD#.

standards to be able to compare across countries. Using a standard definition of poverty and comparing the United States to other rich countries, we can look at the data and see that, in fact, the United States does very badly in comparison to the rich democracies most like us (Smeeding et al. 2009).

Figure 21.16 displays the results of this analysis. Using comparable data about family income across countries, the researchers are able to estimate what the (hypothetical) poverty rate in each country would be if there were no government policies to try to correct it (the first bar); the second bar shows the *actual* poverty rate once government intervention is taken into account. What it shows is that rates of poverty in the United States are higher than in any of the comparison group of similar nations, *after* government programs are taken into account. The chart is based on truly comparable data from each country and all sources of income, an important point that makes it a unique way of understanding where the United States stands. Two results are of special importance. First, a number of countries have high hypothetical poverty rates based just on market incomes before government action is taken into account. In some cases, this is as large as in America. Second, no country does as little as the United States to reduce poverty; notice that both percentages are only modestly different from one another, whereas in other countries a significant difference exists. In other words, social policies do less to reduce poverty in America than in other countries. It's especially instructive to compare the United States to France. If people in France had to live solely on what they earned in the market, without any help

from public programs, there would be a significantly higher rate of poverty than in the United States (over 30 percent). But France dramatically reduces its poverty rate (by more than 75 percent) through its combination of antipoverty programs, so that only about 8 percent of French families live in poverty versus more than twice that in the United States.

In this section, we've considered two important policy areas: Taxes and social programs in the welfare state, and the results should be clear: The rich and powerful prevail over the poor and working class. We cannot possibly examine all of the policy controversies and outcomes that take place. In any given year, there are literally hundreds of important issues that come up for discussion and debate and are decided in Congress, by the president and the administration, or by the Supreme Court. Sometimes there are policies that move in the other direction, toward providing more help for families who are struggling. During the COVID-19 pandemic, the government twice adopted multi-trillion dollar spending packages that included significant payments to unemployed people. But our survey of these two important areas of public policy suggest that, compared to the countries most similar to the United States in terms of wealth, economic development, and longstanding democratic government, powerful actors appear to prevail more often, and receive far more rewards when they do, than in other countries, while the poor are helped much less. In short, it much better to be rich in the United States than in any other similar country, and it is worse to be poor in the United States than in any other similar country.

Albin Lohr-Jones/Pacific Press/Alamy Stock Photo

BIG QUESTION 21.4 Why Is Political Polarization Bad for American Democracy?

THE POLITICAL DIVIDE IN THE UNITED STATES

To this point, we've described a variety of ways in which democracy is troubled by the way American political institutions are functioning and limiting political equality.

These are all important issues and in need of careful analysis. But there is another set of issues that has been emerging in the last couple of decades that is now of intense concern to everyone who studies American politics: The growing divide between Democrats and Republicans (or, alternatively, between liberals and conservatives). The storming of the U.S. Capitol by an insurrectionary mob that refused to accept the results of the 2020 election is an extreme example, but it highlights a basic fact: Tensions between political groups are rising, with many important and largely unanticipated consequences.

What has come to be known as political **polarization** (the term used to describe this divide) is now widely accepted to be a central feature of contemporary American politics. It characterizes a political system in which politicians and policymakers, political commentators in the media, and ordinary citizens are all increasingly unable (or unwilling) to find common ground or to seek compromise. As noted in the chapter opener, perhaps no greater example can be seen than during the COVID-19 crisis. Early in 2021, the new Congress passed a $1.9 trillion COVID relief bill on a straight party-line vote, with all Democrats and no Republicans voting for it. That legislation is one of many recent examples of how the party in power (either Republicans or Democrats) doesn't bother to even try to compromise. There have been a few exceptions (such as a bipartisan measure to increase spending on roads and transportation, what is known as "infrastructure"), but for the most part Congress no longer works the way it used to. Of course, some degree of political conflict is both healthy and inevitable in a democratic political system. It is never the case that everyone has the same opinions about everything. Conflict can stimulate discussion and debate among citizens, and raise turnout in elections, all longstanding goals of advocates of democracy. But when tolerance for the other side declines to the point where even civil dialogue becomes nearly impossible, there are good reasons for concern.

High levels of polarization have been present before in American history, and then declined. The most notable examples are right before, during, and right after the Civil War, when slavery and then post-war Reconstruction bitterly divided the country. Levels of polarization were also heightened in the late nineteenth century, when the parties divided over a range of policy and political questions growing out of the industrial revolution, interest rates on loans to farmers, free trade with other countries, and the huge influx of immigrants into the country. In both cases, what seemed to be intractable divides eventually gave way to more collaborative relationships between citizens and politicians. It is possible that the level of conflict we are in right now may inevitably decline (Heltzel and Laurin 2020).

But there are reasons to think we may be locked into a high polarization era that will continue for decades, and have many consequences for the development of government policies. Many social scientists have argued that periods of bipartisan cooperation, such as happened in the period from the 1930s to about 1980, provide a better foundation for developing policies to solve social problems than the contentious environment we are in now. In this section, we explore polarization in more detail, what caused it, and whether it might be reduced in the future.

What Is Political Polarization and Why Does It Matter?

21.4.1 Discuss trends in political polarization in the United States.

Polarization, when applied to politics, is a term that intends to capture the degree to which any two (or more) groups are divided in terms of the preferences and/or willingness to work together. While any two groups may be divided, in the contemporary period the most consequential divide has emerged between Democrats and Republicans, as noted, at both the elite level (in Congress and the media) and among ordinary citizens. However, it is possible for politicians to be divided while ordinary citizens are not (as some analysts have asserted), or vice versa. Figure 21.17 shows a simple distinction between these different levels and types of polarization.

Although polarization is a widely debated concept among social scientists (Campbell 2016), we can grasp it at a basic level by just thinking about our relationships with two people, one person we usually agree with and another we usually disagree with. Probably everyone has at least one friend or family member falling into each category. We can say that the relationship between you and the person who mostly agrees with you is one with a

Figure 21.17 Types and Levels of Polarization

		Type of Polarization	
		Political Elites	General Public
Level of Polarization	High	Congressional polarization high; media news and commentators are more divided and focused on conflict	Citizens who identify as Democrats or Republicans or liberals or conservatives have large differences in opinions
	Low	Members of both parties in Congress work together; media news is more centrist	Opinion differences between groups is lower

low level of polarization, whereas the other relationship has a high degree of polarization. The low-polarization relationship is one where it is easier to talk about finding a solution to a common problem, and easier to reach agreement. A high-polarization relationship, on the other hand, may be characterized by intense disagreement, even to the point where it is difficult to even have a conversation because you and the high-conflict family member or acquaintance cannot find enough common ground to even get started. The high-polarization relationship is unlikely to be very productive, and it is probably not one in which any of us would want to invest a great deal of energy.

Now think of Democrats and Republicans, or liberals and conservatives, in the same way. When polarization is lower, there is more common ground between Democrats and Republicans. Members of Congress or state legislatures, for example, will often work across party lines to try to find agreement on a particular issue, or draft new legislation together. There will also be some overlap between the members of each party's delegation in the legislature, so that the most conservative Democrat in Congress or a state legislature, for example, would be more conservative than the most liberal Republican (and in fact, many members might overlap in this way). In a high-polarization environment, by contrast, *all* Democrats may be more liberal than *all* Republicans. This is exactly what has happened in Congress in recent years for the first time since the Civil War era.

The most sophisticated attempt to analyze polarization in Congress has been developed by two political scientists (Keith Poole and Howard Rosenthal), who coded every single vote in Congress that has ever been recorded since 1789 on a liberal–conservative scale (defined by the important issues of the times that were taken up by Congress) and then statistically tested how far away from the center each member in Congress was (Poole and Rosenthal 1997). In other words, they created a measure of distance ranging from 0 (where all members vote the same, something that would never happen) to 1 (where all members are as far away from the middle as possible). Their research allows us to see, over a long historical period, how unique the current level of polarization is. Figure 21.18 shows the distance between the average Republican and the average Democrat in Congress. In the late nineteenth century the parties were significantly divided, but then a long period of lower levels of polarization took hold beginning the late 1920s and lasted until the late 1970s. Since the mid-1990s, polarization in Congress has become higher than at any point, and it continues to rise.

What does polarization look like in practice? Almost every account of how Congress works shows the negative impact of the current high polarization environment. "Gridlock" is the word that is most often used to capture the depths of the divisions that now exist in national government. For example, during the presidency of Barack Obama, Republicans in Congress made the decision to oppose any and all legislation advanced by the administration, held up numerous appointments to important government posts, and when they didn't get what they wanted from the White House, they refused to fund the government, causing a shutdown of most federal government operations in 2011. Two veteran analysts of Congress described the breakdown in civility and normal functioning of congressional institutions in a widely studied book first published in 2012 (Mann and Ornstein 2016). Their even-handed account—confirmed by many other journalists and congressional experts (for example, Sinclair 2006; Kabaservice 2012; Dionne 2016)—finds that while

Figure 21.18 Polarization in Congress, 1879–2021

SOURCE: Data Series developed by Keith Poole and Howard Rosenthal. The graph shows the distance between the average Republican and the average Democrat in Congress.

members of both parties had become more liberal or conservative, respectively, on the issues, the Republicans in Congress moved away from the political center much faster and also had become much more extreme on procedural matters that undermined Congress's ability to perform its constitutional role during the Obama presidency. These analysts also found ample evidence of widespread and systematic refusal to acknowledge widely accepted scientific findings in making public policy. Republicans' rejection of overwhelming evidence that rising human action is causing climate change is one key example of this. Perpetuating the belief that cutting taxes will *reduce* government deficits has been another.

Former president Trump's rhetoric and style of governance in office reinforced and in some ways accelerated and altered already existing polarizing trends. His widespread use of social media to criticize or humiliate his opponents violated every norm of presidential decorum up to that point. Trump's claims that the news media was engaging in a "witch hunt" against his presidency and him personally led him to denounce the news media as "enemies of the people" (a phrase that originated under Communism, used by Communist leaders like Joseph Stalin and Mao-Tse Tung to describe their opponents). Trump also gave considerable encouragement to White supremacists (see Chapter 13 for more information) and called on supporters at his rallies to use violence on his enemies. In 2020, he sent federal troops into cities such as Portland and Chicago to shut down protests against police violence, while welcoming violent protestors to the U.S. Capitol, as already discussed, to try to stop the certification of the 2020 election. He sought to appoint extremely conservative judges, rejecting any judicial nominees that did not meet the approval of conservatives. Trump also generated a very strong group of hardcore supporters, some of which engaged in protests after he lost the 2020 election.

The intense controversies raised by former president Trump highlight how the American public has also become more politically divided. But polarization in the public is different than among political elites. In particular, the divisions apply more to broad principles of government than to specific kinds of policies (where in many cases the differences of opinion between Democrats and Republicans and liberals and conservatives have remained steady over time). Many scholars and journalists have pointed to examples of ways in which these differences appear to have grown into everyday lifestyle choices and behaviors. There is mounting evidence that liberals and conservatives vary with respect to a number of lifestyle matters (or "lifestyle politics" as it is called). Liberals and conservatives (or in some studies, Democrats and Republicans) differ on such matters as what television shows they prefer, whether they own a gun, whether premarital sex is acceptable, what kinds of art they prefer to hang on their walls,

how much ethnic food they consume, what kinds of coffee and beer they drink, how much they recycle, what kinds of values they want to instill in their children, and many others (DellaPosta et al. 2016).

Does love conquer all? Maybe not. There is growing evidence that liberals and conservatives prefer not to date people with different political preferences than their own, and a growing number of studies have found that Democrats and Republicans are much more likely to report disappointment if their child married someone who identifies with the opposite party (Iyengar et al. 2012; Klofstad et al. 2013; Samuel 2020).

However, before we reach any firm conclusions about political polarization in the broader public, it is important to look at some of the data about concrete political attitudes and the trends in them over time. Are ordinary people becoming more divided? The short answer is that this is a question that has been heavily debated by scholars in recent years, and no clear consensus has emerged. The opinion differences between Democrats and Republicans on some questions have widened (for example, abortion, gun control, the environment) while on others they have more or less remained the same (for example, on many questions about the economy or the proper role of government). Perhaps even more surprising, on a number of "social" issues such as gay marriage and LGBTQ rights, legalization of marijuana, ideas about marriage and divorce, and views of gender, Democrats and Republicans (and liberals and conservatives) are becoming *less* polarized over time. In the early 1990s, a famous book described the difference between liberals and conservatives on social issues as "culture wars" (Hunter 1991). But that hypothesis has not been borne out; over time, conservatives have become more like liberals on a large number of issues. The reason for this convergence is that on many social issues, liberals shifted their opinions first (opening a large divide), and then in recent years conservatives have been catching up, reducing the overall differences (Baldassarri and Park 2020).

What Caused Polarization to Increase?

21.4.2 Identify four key developments that have contributed to increased political polarization in the United States.

The question of why polarization has grown so extensively in recent decades has been widely debated by social scientists, but four key developments are universally understood to be especially critical.

BREAKUP OF THE SOLID SOUTH From the period following the end of the Civil War through World War II, the states of the former Confederacy consistently sent virtually all

Democrats to serve in Congress, mostly because the Republican Party of Abraham Lincoln was blamed for the Civil War and Reconstruction that followed. This was such a universal pattern that the region came to be called the **Solid South**, and Democrats could count on winning virtually every congressional seat. These "Southern Democrats," as they were known, were strongly opposed federal civil rights laws and were deeply conservative on questions of race and civil liberties. Almost all of the Southern Democrats in Congress supported the Jim Crow system of racial segregation right up to the 1960s. But on other political issues, the Southern Democrats tended to be more moderate and inclined toward the center of the political spectrum. Northern Democrats, who were always much more liberal, often had to make political compromises with their Southern wing to pass legislation, creating a balance inside the party that constrained (and frustrated) its more liberal members. The only exceptions were two brief periods—1934–35 and 1964–65—when the Northern Democrats had enough votes to effectively disregard the preferences of the party's Southern wing. It was during those two periods that the most liberal pieces of legislation in the twentieth century were passed into law, for example, the Social Security Act of 1935, the National Labor Relations Act of 1935, the Civil Rights Act of 1964, and the Voting Rights Act of 1965 (Amenta 1998).

The 1960s fundamentally changed the Democratic Party, and ultimately destroyed its base in the South. The key driver was the civil rights movement, which demanded racial equality and equal opportunity for all Americans, and ultimately forced (and shamed) the Northern Democrats into demanding the end of the Jim Crow system in the South even as their Southern colleagues resisted. The passage of federal civil rights legislation in the mid-1960s was too much for both Southern politicians and White Southern voters to accept, and in a relatively short period of time Republicans became the dominant party in the South (mostly because aging Democrats were replaced by Republicans, but in a few cases Democrats converted to Republicans). As the Democrats lost their Southern base, the party had fewer moderate or conservative members in its Congressional delegation. President Bill Clinton—a Democrat from Arkansas—was one of the last influential moderate Southern Democrats. Many of his legislative accomplishments (from 1993 to 2000) are now routinely denounced by leading Democrats, who favor much more liberal approaches on issues like criminal justice, social policy, LGBTQ rights, and health care (Hitchens 1999; Robinson 2016).

THE REPUBLICAN PARTY MOVES TO THE RIGHT   The Republican Party (or GOP, as it is known for the nickname "Grand Old Party"), like the Democrats, long had two distinctive wings: A moderate wing whose key figures and members in Congress mostly came from the Northeast,

and a conservative wing that was primarily located in the Midwest and Western states. Thomas Dewey (GOP presidential nominee elected to the presidency in 1944 and 1948) and Dwight D. Eisenhower (GOP nominee in 1952 and 1956) represented the once-dominant moderate wing of the party. They and their principal supporters generally accepted most of the liberal legislation adopted during the New Deal in the 1930s (although they endlessly worried about budget deficits and sought to restrain some of the more liberal components of the New Deal). GOP moderates, again mostly from the Northeast, also supported much of the civil rights legislation in the 1960s while more conservative Republicans opposed it.

After decades of competition inside the GOP between moderates and conservatives, the conservatives began to consistently prevail. The earliest sign of the growing power of conservatives within the party came when Barry Goldwater, a very conservative senator from Arizona, won the GOP nomination in 1964 (only to be crushed in the general election that year). During the presidencies of Republicans Richard Nixon and Gerald Ford (1968–76), the stand-off between moderate and conservative wings continued. It was the election of Republican President Ronald Reagan in 1980 that marked a truly important shift, as the GOP became a more cohesive conservative party from that point onward (Wilentz 2008; Kabaservice 2012). Reagan was a transformative political leader, who aggressively reshaped the GOP politically as an anti-government, tax-cutting, and socially conservative party that did not want people in the party who disagreed with these core premises. Reagan's triumph was greatly helped by the inflow of a new generation of very conservative Southern Republican politicians who changed the balance of power in the GOP. At the same time that more conservative Southerners were winning seats, moderate GOP politicians in the Northeast were increasingly being voted out of office as that region became more reliably Democratic. The Republican Party since Reagan has become increasingly more conservative, with ever-fewer and lonely moderates having little or no influence over the GOP agenda.

MONEY-DRIVEN POLARIZATION   We've already seen how big money is shaping and influencing American elections. There is another way, however, that big money is impacting political life: The willingness of some very rich people to contribute very large sums to groups and causes on the far right and far left. The most famous of these donors—the Koch brothers (Charles and his recently deceased brother David, owners of Koch Industries), Sheldon Adelson (casino owner), George Soros (finance)—and many other less well-known figures have been providing funds to groups and organizations that are dedicated to promoting a particular agenda. The Kochs, for example, have spent billions of dollars to support extremely conservative causes and political candidates, and those resources are fostering greater pressure for a far-right political agenda (Mayer 2017). More of this big money is for causes on the political right, but liberal groups are working hard to try to match those resources and have had some successes in finding their own rich donors.

MEDIA POLARIZATION A fourth factor that has contributed to polarization is the transformation of the news media since the 1980s. **Journalism**—the production and dissemination of information of general public interest—is above all else a form of cultural communication. But sociologists of the media are in broad agreement that the news does a lot more than just pass along facts to the public. By deciding what to cover and how to cover it, journalists don't simply report on the news, they actually help to create and change it (Schudson 2003, p. 11).

The notion that the press is vital to democracy is an old one. Thomas Jefferson, for instance, famously said, "Were it left to me to decide whether we should have a government without newspapers, or newspapers without a government, I should not hesitate a moment to prefer the latter." The media provide a forum for debate, give a voice to public opinion, serve as citizens' eyes and ears in politics, and serve as a public watchdog over government and business (Graber 2003).

In the age of cable television and the internet, the news media have undergone an extraordinary shift. In one way, the new media environment in the age of social media provides an increased amount of information and diversity of viewpoints. This should, in principle, be better for the diversity of conversations. For most of the twentieth century, Americans got their news from a tiny number of sources. There were three major television networks (NBC, CBS, and ABC) that commanded vast audiences for their nightly news. Three news magazines dominated the presentation of what was happening in the country and the world, led by *Time* and followed by *Newsweek* and *U.S. News and World Report,* and most people got a single newspaper delivered to their house that likely contained a lot of stories from a small number of major syndicated news sources such as the Associated Press or the *New York Times.* The range of issues covered by these highly influential sources was much more limited, and there weren't many places for most people to go to hear other news sources of viewpoints (there were small magazines with political news and opinions, such as the *Nation,* the *National Review,* or the *New Republic,* but these rarely had more than 100,000 subscribers in a country with more than 200 million people). The major networks and newsmagazines strove for a kind of objectivity in their coverage that seems very outdated now.

Today the media environment is completely different. Cable news stations—the three dominant ones are Fox, CNN, and MSNBC—compete with the three major broadcast networks for audience share, and because the cable networks cover the news around the clock, they have become much more important sources of information for most people. The internet has allowed the proliferation of dozens of news outlets and opinion websites, and because most of these outlets link stories that appear in other outlets, millions of people may encounter or hear about a story first posted on an obscure site (a process called "going viral"). In many ways, this is good for democracy. (Having grown up in that earlier era, I can say with complete confidence that the wealth of information and resources available today is vastly more interesting and valuable than what was available when I was an undergraduate college student first becoming interested in American national politics in the 1980s.)

Yet there are also ways in which the new media environment is contributing to polarization. This is happening for two reasons. First, there are virtually no news sources that are truly nonpartisan or strive to provide the kind objective reporting that defined the earlier era. Building an audience, it appears, requires having an identity of some kind. This seems to be especially true for the large cable news networks. Fox News explicitly describes itself as a conservative news source, and MSNBC has mostly been a liberal network in recent years. CNN continues to try to be somewhat in the middle of the two, but it often does so by putting equal numbers of liberal and conservatives on news panels where the panelists simply talk past one another. If anything, in trying to give equal time to both sides, the CNN approach only magnifies the polarized environment we are in. Every panelist has one of three roles: Be the spokesperson for the conservative view, be the spokesperson for the liberal view, or be one of a handful of celebrity commentators who are "above the fray" (although often these people consistently take one side or the other).

Second, and perhaps more importantly, people generally get news information from sources that present similar political views and ideas (Mitchell et al. 2014). Very few people go out of their way to read or watch both sides; as a group of psychologists put it, "liberals and conservatives are similarly motivated to avoid exposure to each other's opinions" (Frimer et al. 2017). As noted, most conservatives watch Fox News, while liberals prefer MSNBC. The topics covered on the two networks rarely overlap; it is as if they are covering two entirely different countries. Similarly, when people seek out written news, they increasingly choose their own sources. Liberals read the *New York Times,* which has become increasingly more liberal over time, while conservatives favor the

Ethan Miller/Getty Images

Fox News, like other cable news networks, often features commentators with strong ideological viewpoints on their broadcasts. This photo shows Sean Hannity, the network's most popular show host. Hannity was very close to Donald Trump and openly expressed his support for the former president, even appearing at political rallies at Trump's side. This close identification is a complete rejection of the longstanding idea that news broadcasters should keep away from participating in political life.

Wall Street Journal. News websites are similarly clustered ideologically, with a handful of popular conservative sites balanced by an approximately equal number of liberal sites In addition, many people rely on "newsfeeds" in their social media that select articles based on an algorithm that predicts what the user will like, unintentionally reinforcing the consumption of articles that confirm the users' already existing views.

COVID-19 and the Future of Polarization

21.4.3 Discuss the future of polarization in American political life.

Thus far, we're treated polarization as a central problem in American political life. A poll conducted at the end of 2016, for example, found that 77 percent think that the nation is divided on important issues (Jones 2016). And an even more recent poll found that

a majority of likely voters thought the nation was becoming more divided in 2017 (Rasmussen Reports 2017). One of Barack Obama's appeals when first running for president in 2008 was a promise that he would "bring people together" across partisan boundaries. That didn't happen, but the hope that polarization could be reduced in the future remains an important goal for some.

The COVID-19 crisis in 2020, however, reminds us how tenacious political polarization has become. COVID-19 is a virus that primarily spreads through oral transmission. In spite of the well-established scientific knowledge about how to control the spread of it, willingness to take the mandatory steps to reduce the deadly spread of the virus bitterly divided Americans, especially along partisan lines. Democratic politicians and some Republicans consistently emphasized the severity of the problem and the need for all citizens to wear masks in public. By contrast, many conservatives and supporters of former president Donald Trump resisted required mask wearing, considering it an intrusion on their civil liberties. Former president Trump himself refused to wear a mask in public, signaling to his supporters that mask wearing is both unnecessary and perhaps even a sign of weakness (a statement Trump made several times about his Democratic opponent Joe Biden). Some very conservative Republican governors in states with high levels of COVID-19 outbreaks refused to issue mask-wearing orders, and some (such as Florida Governor Ron DeSantis) even tried to use their powers to block local governments from issuing mask wearing orders. The upshot was that there were massive differences in attitudes between Republicans and Democrats on basic understandings of COVID-19 and what would prevent it (see Figure 21.19). The surprisingly quick arrival of vaccines able to prevent most people from getting sick seemed likely to resolve the crisis. But large numbers of Trump supporters refused to get vaccinated, along with people who feared (incorrectly) that the vaccine would make them sick. Parts of the country controlled by conservative Republicans had lower vaccination rates, making it possible for a new (and more infectious) version of the coronavirus to spread widely.

When the partisan divide reaches the point where it is threatening human lives and making it harder for normal life and a healthy economy to return, we have major reasons for concern about the state of political life. However, in projecting into the future, there may also be some reasons to think the current situation will not last forever. For one thing, American political life was defined by bipartisan policymaking and an overlap between the two major parties and liberals and conservatives for

Figure 21.19 Partisan Differences in Attitudes Toward Measures to Deal with COVID-19

"Do you think everyone should be required to wear face masks in public?"

SOURCE: Quinnipiac University Poll, May 2020.

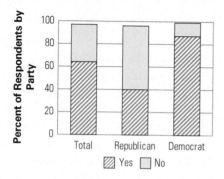

much of the twentieth century, but it is not necessarily the case that the kinds of compromises required to get things done in that era were always correct or perfect.

Sometimes better policies can be made by political parties that are more unified around a coherent philosophy of governance, even if they are operating in a high polarization environment.

Second, having clear differences between the two major parties, and voters who understand better what those differences are, may be healthy for democracy. Ironically, in the middle of the twentieth century, when the major parties had much more internal democracy and regional variation than they do today, a high-level committee of the American Political Science Association prepared a report calling for the parties to become more "responsible" and clear about what they stand for (American Political Science Association 1950). Weak, undisciplined parties with members representing multiple viewpoints can have its drawbacks as well. When voters think there are few major differences between the parties and elections don't really matter that is not a sign of healthy democracy either.

Conclusion: American Democracy and Political Life

This chapter has presented a sociological account of the state of democracy in America today. The problems described here are complex enough that rather than ending with a long list of recommendations, we propose a simpler idea instead. Democracy works best when citizens are involved and engaged in debating the issues of the day and when they are aware of the political views of the other side. So perhaps the most appropriate way to make a start in restoring American democracy is for all of us to make an effort to learn more about the views of people we disagree with (for example, by actively seeking out conversations or watching or reading the news from other perspectives). Armed with greater knowledge—you don't have to change your mind, just try to hear and understand the other side—a more vibrant democratic political culture could begin to emerge. But that will only happen if citizens get involved in participating in public life. Finding ways to do that is easy: Learning about the issues and controversies in your community and in Washington D.C., talking about them with friends and family, finding something you really care about, and getting involved with groups that are trying to bring about change—all of this is what it means

to be a democratic citizen. Leaving politics to the elites, the rich, and the powerful is not what makes democracy happen. Former president Barack Obama once movingly said that "change will not come if we wait for some other person or some other time. We are the ones we've been waiting for. We are the change that we seek." The ultimate fix, Obama is suggesting, for whatever is ailing democracy, can only come about when more of us participate, even if only in some small way, in political life.

We will also, however, have to open a conversation about reworking political institutions so that they are better able to represent each person more fairly. That conversation can only succeed if everyone from socialists to right-wing conservatives, and all points in between, is honest about the current limitations of American democracy. Partisans have to stop trying to take advantage of the aging Constitution and its quirks to gain temporary advantage—be it through gerrymandering, unequal representation in Congress, raising excessive amounts of money, or trying to keep some people from voting.

The Big Questions Revisited 21

21.1 How "Democratic" Is Democracy in America?
Elections are at the core of modern large-scale representative democracy. The Constitution establishes critical rules regarding elections in

America that are especially important, and would be regarded as undemocratic to varying degrees if we were starting from scratch: Deciding outcomes in winner-take-all election districts, allowing the major parties to draw up the boundaries for elections (and the mischief that permits), the uneven size of the Senate, and the electoral college. We explored each of these.

Democratic Elections in the United States

American Democracy in Comparative Perspective
Learning Objective 21.1.1: Discuss the state of democracy in America versus other countries.

How American Elections Are Organized
Learning Objective 21.1.2: Analyze the consequences of the single-member districts and electoral boundaries established by the U.S. Constitution.

The Electoral College
Learning Objective 21.1.3: Explain how the Electoral College and the popular vote impact U.S. presidential elections.

The Role of Money in Political Campaigns
Learning Objective 21.1.4: Analyze the role that money plays in American politics.

Key Terms
political rights (p. 602)   civil liberties (p. 602) single-member districts (p. 602)   proportional representation (PR) (p. 602)   gerrymandering (p. 604)   political action committees (PACs) (p. 604)   Super-PACs (p. 607)

21.2 Why Is Turnout So Low in American Elections? Americans face multiple hurdles to voting that contribute to reduced turnout in elections. We considered why so few people vote in national elections. We examined individual factors and institutional factors.

Political Participation and Voting

Individual-Level Factors
Learning Objective 21.2.1: Discuss some of the individual-level explanations for why voter turnout is so low in American elections.

Political-Institutional Factors
Learning Objective 21.2.2: Explain some of the political-institutional reasons for why voter turnout is so low in American elections.

Key Terms
disenfranchisement (p. 612)

21.3 Who Has Political Power in the United States Today? In this section we explored the ways in which powerful groups are much more likely to get the government to make policies in their interest. An especially important example can be seen in low taxes paid by the rich and in America's inability to reduce poverty to the same degree as other rich countries.

Power in America

How the Rich Get What They Want: The Case of Individual and Corporate Taxes
Learning Objective 21.3.1: Discuss what tax policies tell us about how power is distributed in the United States.

How the Poor Get Less: Antipoverty Policy in the United States
Learning Objective 21.3.2: Explain what antipoverty programs tell us about how power is distributed in the United States.

Key Terms
progressive income tax system (p. 616)   capital gains tax (p. 617)   tax loopholes (p. 617) effective tax rate (p. 618)   welfare state (p. 620)

21.4 Why Is Political Polarization Bad for American Democracy? We described a variety of ways in which democracy is troubled by the way American political institutions are functioning. These are all important social problems, and in need of careful analysis. But there is another issue that has been developing for some time that everyone who studies American politics is deeply concerned about: The rise of polarization in which Democrats and Republicans (and liberals and conservatives) are increasingly divided and unable and unwilling to find common ground. In this section, we explored polarization in more detail, what caused it, and whether it might be reduced in the future.

The Political Divide in the United States

What Is Political Polarization and Why Does It Matter?
Learning Objective 21.4.1: Discuss trends in political polarization in the United States.

What Caused Polarization to Increase?
Learning Objective 21.4.2: Identify four key developments that have contributed to increased political polarization in the United States.

COVID-19 and the Future of Polarization
Learning Objective 21.4.3: Discuss the future of polarization in American political life.

Key Terms
polarization (p. 622)   Solid South (p. 625) journalism (p. 626)

Chapter 22
Social Movements and Revolutions

by Jeff Goodwin

On May 25, 2020, a 46-year-old Black man named George Floyd was murdered by a police officer in Minneapolis, Minnesota. Floyd, who was unarmed and handcuffed, had allegedly used a counterfeit $20 bill in a convenience store. A police officer kept his knee on Floyd's neck for over nine minutes, while three other officers watched, resulting in asphyxiation; the murder was videotaped and quickly spread around the world.

In the days, weeks, and months that followed, thousands and eventually millions of people took to the streets to protest this latest in a long series of police killings of unarmed Blacks. Police killings had provoked mass protests in the United States beginning in 2014. In that year, a new social movement, which later came to be known as the Black Lives Matter (BLM) movement, burst onto the scene. This was not a movement led by a single charismatic leader or organization; its leadership was diffuse, and a network of small local organizations and activist groups organized local protests. Some protests were spontaneous, but the vast majority were organized by local activists, mainly through social media.

The protests in 2020 were unprecedented in scale and multiracial in composition. The protesters demanded the arrest of the police officers involved in Floyd's murder, but another demand soon followed and was taken up by many protesters around the country: "Defund the police." This was a demand to redirect tax money that funded police forces to social services and the other needs of poor communities (where most police killings occurred). For some activists, "defund the police" was also a demand to redirect resources to alternative forms of neighborhood security.

The protests that took place in 2020 were more widespread and involved more people than any other campaign of protest in U.S. history. In the month following Floyd's murder, an average of about 140 protests took place every day, most large cities but also in smaller towns. Polls suggest that somewhere between 15 and 26 million people joined these protests. On June 6, 2020, alone, nearly half a million people participated in protests in nearly 550 locations across the United States. On that day, 50,000 people protested in Philadelphia, 20,000 demonstrated in Chicago's Union Park, and as many as 10,000 marched across the Golden Gate Bridge in San Francisco.

My Sociological Imagination

JEFF GOODWIN

I grew up at a time when the U.S. government was trying hard to destroy domestic social movements, especially the Black Power and the anti–Vietnam War movements, as well as revolutions overseas, particularly in Cuba, Vietnam, and Chile. I remember vividly the killing of students at Kent State University who were protesting the invasion of Cambodia, something that was pretty scary for a young kid. I was also scared and anxious when my older brother was drafted into the military, but fortunately he was not sent to Vietnam. All this made me interested in why people protest and rebel, sometimes violently, and why governments sometimes use violence against their opponents. I came to understand how the sociological imagination that C. Wright Mills described—the capacity, that is, to see how seemingly personal grievances are in fact linked to social structures and shared with others—is a prerequisite of political protest. While I was studying rebels in college and graduate school at Harvard, I also joined the ranks of movements that were trying to stop the U.S. government from supporting brutal armies in Central America and the racist government in South Africa. I have been studying social movements (and occasionally participating in them) as well as revolutions ever since.

One of the many protests over the killing of George Floyd, this one in Chicago in 2020. The mass protests over police violence and brutality that exploded across America highlight many interesting issues about social movements and protest activity. When politicians and government leaders prove incapable of addressing social problems, one of the central features of a democratic society is the right of citizens to band together and demand change.

One study found that over 7,700 protests linked to BLM took place in more than 2,440 locations, including all 50 U.S. states and Washington, D.C., between Floyd's murder and August 22, 2020 (Armed Conflict Location & Event Data 2021). The study found that 93 percent of the demonstrations did not involve violence or destructive activity by protesters. Violent demonstrations did take place in about 220 locations (fewer than 10 percent of all locations where protest occurred), but these were typically limited to a few city blocks rather than being widely dispersed. Despite this, polls indicate that as many as 40 percent of Americans believed that "most" protesters were trying to incite violence or destroy property. The discrepancy is presumably due to the media's well-known tendency to focus its attention on violence and destruction in order to attract readers and viewers.

The rise of the Black Lives Matter movement raises a number of questions that have preoccupied sociologists interested in social movements and revolutions. Why did this movement develop when it did? Who participated in it? Why have the protesters used certain tactics and not others? Have the media helped or hurt the movement? Sociologists also have questions about the impact of movements: What changes do movements bring about? What causes movements to decline or disappear? What are the characteristics of a revolutionary movement? Is a revolution likely in a country like the United States? Or are other countries, with different problems and political institutions, more likely to have revolutions in the future? These are some of the questions that are explored in this chapter.

The Big Questions

1. **What are social movements?** Social movements play a crucial role in contemporary societies. Through them, we can learn about the world around us. We start the chapter by defining social movements and exploring what we can learn by studying them.

2. **Why do movements emerge, and who joins them?** The most frequently asked question about social movements is why they emerge when they do. In this section, we examine how movements take shape and look at who joins or supports social movements.

3. **What tactics do movements use, and what outcomes do they achieve?** Why do movements use certain tactics and not others? Why are some violent and others nonviolent? Why do movements decline or disappear? In this section, we look at what movements do and what changes and outcomes movements bring about, including unintended consequences.

4. **What are revolutions, and why do they occur?** Finally, we look at why some social movements are revolutionary and what causes revolutionary situations to occur. When and why have revolutionary movements been able to take state power? We conclude the chapter by examining how authoritarian and democratic governments shape social conflict and the prospects for revolution.

J. G. Domke/Alamy Stock Photo

BIG QUESTION 22.1   What Are Social Movements?

RESEARCHING SOCIAL MOVEMENTS

Throughout history, people have complained about the things they dislike. Sometimes they do more than complain; they band together with others to try to change things. In modern societies, more than ever before, people have organized themselves to pursue a dizzying array of goals, and they have used a wide variety of tactics to attain those goals. There are the strikes, pickets, and rallies of the labor movement, aimed at unionization and better wages but also (sometimes) at political goals. The women's movement and the #MeToo movement (against sexual harassment and assault) have tried to change family life and gender relations through persuasion, protests, "consciousness raising," lawsuits, and lawmaking. Animal rights activists have broken into labs and "liberated" experimental animals. And there have been many conservative and right-wing movements as well, from Americans opposed to immigrants from the 1840s onward (and still today), to movements opposed to taxation and "big government." Some right-wing activists have picketed and even bombed abortion clinics and murdered abortion providers in recent years.

Some of these movements have looked for opportunities to claim new rights while others have responded to threats or violence. Some have sought political and economic emancipation and gains, while others have fought against lifestyle choices they disliked or feared. Some have created formal organizations, others have relied on informal networks, and still others have used more spontaneous actions such as **riots**, which are unplanned collective protests, loosely organized at best, involving attacks on property and (sometimes) persons. Movements have regularly had to choose between violent and nonviolent activities,

illegal and legal ones, disruption and persuasion, radical and moderate demands, reform and revolution.

Social movements are conscious, concerted, and sustained efforts by ordinary people to change (or preserve) some aspect of their society by using extrainstitutional means. *Extrainstitutional means* are collective actions undertaken outside existing institutions, like courts, elections, and legislatures, although movements may also work through such institutions, at least part of the time. Movements are more conscious and organized than fashions or **fads** (behaviors that spread, often rapidly, among a specific population and are repeated enthusiastically for some period of time before disappearing, often rapidly). They last longer than a single protest or riot. There is more to them than the organizations they create, although such organizations usually play an important role in social movements. They are composed mainly of ordinary citizens as opposed to wealthy elites, politicians, or army officers (although the wealthy and even large corporations sometimes have movements of their own, or pay or persuade people to protest for them). Movements need not be explicitly political, but many are.

Why should we care about, and study, social movements? Examining protesters and their points of view is certainly a good way to comprehend human diversity. For example, why do some people think animals have rights, or others that the United Nations is part of a sinister conspiracy? But aside from studying social movements to understand the diverse array of viewpoints in society, movements are also windows onto a number of aspects of social life. These include politics, human action, social change, and the moral basis of society. Finally, social movements often bring about changes that might not otherwise occur. Some movements and revolutions, in fact, have substantially improved the human condition.

Politics, Human Action, and Social Change

22.1.1 Discuss how social movements affect political and social structures.

Social movements are a main source of political conflict and change. They often articulate *new* political issues and ideas. As people become attuned to some social problem they want solved—for example, climate change—they may form some kind of movement to push for a solution. Political parties and their leaders rarely ask the most important questions or raise new issues; bureaucracy sets in, and politicians spend their time in routines. Typically, movements outside a society's political institutions force insiders to recognize new fears and desires among specific social groups. During the Obama administration, for example, politicians generally were not discussing growing inequality in the United States or the power of corporations; it took the Occupy Wall Street movement to initiate a public discussion of these issues. Nor were many politicians dealing with police violence until the BLM movement and protests against police brutality became a nationwide movement.

Scholars of social movements ask why and how people do the things they do, especially why they do things *together*; this is also the question that drives sociology in general, especially sociological theory. Social movements raise the famous question asked by seventeenth-century philosopher Thomas Hobbes regarding social order: Why do people cooperate with each other when they might get as many or more benefits by acting selfishly or alone? The study of social movements makes the question more manageable: If we can see why and how people voluntarily cooperate in social movements, we can understand why and how they cooperate in general.

Social movements are also a central source of social and political change. In the United States, movements are at least partly responsible for most of the progressive laws of the past century, including women's right to vote, the right to organize unions, and civil rights for Blacks and other people of color, in addition to gay people. Of course, there are other sources of social change, including corporations. As they invent new technologies that change our ways of working and interacting, corporations can disrupt people's ways of life: A new machine may throw people out of work or make them work harder. Toxic wastes may be disposed of near a school or poor neighborhood. Dangerous products may be brought to market, and elected politicians may not take any action to prevent these things. But corporations, even when politicians do nothing to challenge them, are not all-powerful. Ordinary people do sometimes resist such disruptions to their lives, sometimes by forming social movements.

While corporations are a main source of technological change, they are rarely a source of change in values or in social arrangements. Why? In modern societies with tightly knit political and economic systems, the big bureaucracies demand economic and political control and stability. So they try to routinize social life in order to prevent the unexpected. They resist changes in property relations, for example, which are a key component of a capitalist economic system. Social movements often try to regulate property or, sometimes, to seize and redistribute it.

So innovation in values and political beliefs often arises from the discussions and efforts of social movements. Why don't societies just endlessly reproduce themselves intact? It is often social movements that develop new ways of seeing society and new ways of directing it. They are a central part of what has been called "civil society" or the "public sphere," in which groups and individuals debate their own futures (Cohen and Arato 1992; Alexander 2006).

Moral Sensibilities

22.1.2 Discuss how social movements contribute to a society's moral codes.

Social movements are similar to art in this sense: They are efforts to express ideas and sensibilities that may not yet have been well articulated or understood, that journalists or novelists may not yet have written about, and that politicians have not yet addressed. We all have moral sensibilities—including unspoken intuitions as well as articulated principles and rules—that guide our actions or at least make us uneasy when they are violated. Social movements are good ways to understand these moral sensibilities. For example, movements have challenged ideas about who deserves legal rights, including the right to vote. In the nineteenth century, radical abolitionists like Frederick Douglass fought to end slavery and give rights to Black people; women's movements have fought for the right to vote and for reproductive rights (including access to

A 2019 protest against climate change in Berlin, part of a coordinated global movement of young people challenging inaction on global warming. The global nature of environmental protests in recent years highlights how social movements can sometimes cross national borders and to raise truly global issues.

contraceptives and abortions); antiabortion activists argue that human fetuses have rights; and many people now believe that certain animals have at least some rights, like the right not to be used in scientific experiments or be treated inhumanely in the production of food products. It's safe to say that social movements have dramatically changed the moral sensibilities of societies over the past two centuries.

How do social movements challenge societies to change? For one thing, movements encourage us to figure out how we feel about government policies, corporations, social trends, widespread cultural beliefs, and new technologies. Most of all, they are one means by which we work out our moral visions, transforming vague intuitions into principles and political demands. Movements have been one of the most important means by which ordinary people have limited the power of political and economic elites and challenged capitalism, racism, sexism, and homophobia.

Understanding Social Movements Today

22.1.3 Define the political process perspective and discuss how understanding social movements can vary as movements change over time.

Sociologists have emphasized different aspects of social movements at different historical moments. The first sociologists who studied movements often viewed them as dangerous mobs. Later scholars were much more sympathetic, emphasizing that movements are quite rational, carefully weighing the costs and benefits of their actions.

Most scholars of movements have stressed the political nature of movements. For example, one of the most influential perspectives on social movements, the **political process model** of social movements, emphasizes that movements are primarily concerned with politics. They arise as a normal response to certain circumstances, such as when normal political channels are blocked, for people to become involved in political controversies. Movements emerge and may be successful if those political processes create "political opportunities" for certain kinds of collective protest. Other scholars have emphasized the cultural side of movements, exploring the work that goes into creating powerful symbols, convincing people that they have grievances that can be remedied, and building a sense of solidarity or connectedness among certain people.

Even more recently, sociologists have begun to recognize and study the global aspects of social movements.

Many movements have a global reach, tying together protest groups and networks across many countries and even forming international organizations. The environmental movement is probably the most prominent of these global movements, while other examples include the movement and periodic protests against the unregulated free trade is another example. The labor movement has long had a global component. Protests against the power of multinational corporations and international financial agencies can be found. The rise of populist political parties and movements is another.

Our understanding of social movements has evolved as movements themselves have changed. Like everyone else, scholars of social movements are influenced by what they see happening around them. Much protest of the nineteenth century took the form of riots, so it was natural to focus on the nature of crowds and "mobs." Scholars who examined the labor movement and the American civil rights movement recognized that claims of new rights necessarily involve the state, so it was natural for them to focus on the political dimensions of protest. Social scientists who came of age in the 1960s and after were often favorably disposed toward the social movements around them and so portrayed protesters as reasonable people. Some of the movements of the 1960s and after were not about rights for oppressed groups but about lifestyles and cultural meanings, so it was inevitable that scholars sooner or later would turn to this dimension of protest. Many movements are also interested in changing our emotional capacities, especially movements influenced by the women's movement, which argued that women were disadvantaged by the ways in which different emotions were thought appropriate for men and for women. Research on social movements will undoubtedly continue to evolve as social movements themselves evolve.

Protests against the World Trade Organization in Seattle, 1999, during the WTO meetings. The protestors demanded changes to "free trade" agreements, which they saw as creating sweatshop-like conditions for workers in poor countries, encouraging factories and companies to ignore global environmental rules in the pursuit of profit, and taking jobs away from struggling workers in richer countries. These protests helped to make other citizens more aware of how "globalization" processes can have very negative consequences (see chapter 25 for more details).

PhotoQuest/Getty Images

Why Do Movements Emerge, and Who Joins Them?

MOVEMENT ORIGINS AND RECRUITMENT

The most frequently asked question about social movements is why they emerge when and where they do. Where we think a movement comes from colors the way we also view its other aspects—its goals, participants, tactics, and outcomes.

How Movements Take Shape

22.2.1 **Analyze the political, economic, organizational, demographic, and cultural factors that ignite and fuel social movements.**

In general, theories of movement origins focus either on the characteristics of participants or on conditions in the broader environment which potential participants face. It is also possible to link these two perspectives.

Scholars have discovered a range of factors that explain why a movement emerges when and where it does:

- Political factors such as divisions among authorities or lessened repression from the police and army

- Economic conditions such as increased income, especially among those sympathetic to a movement's cause, or, alternatively, an economic crisis that throws many people out of work

- Organizational conditions such as informal social network ties or formal organizations among aggrieved populations (such as churches, schools, and athletic leagues)

- Demographic conditions such as the increased population density and human connectedness that comes with industrialization (if you live a mile from your nearest neighbor, it is hard to organize collectively)

- Cultural factors such as a shared identity or shared moral intuitions or sensibilities that support the movement's cause

And of course potential protesters must understand factors such as these as real opportunities for collective protest before they can take advantage of them.

In the 1960s and 1970s, a group of researchers noticed that social movements usually consist of formal organizations, and they built their theory of social movements by analyzing when and how grievances are articulated by such organizations (McCarthy and Zald 1977). Known as the **resource mobilization approach**, this theoretical perspective emphasizes the importance of resources, such as money or the availability of volunteers to work, for generating and sustaining social movements. The more resources a movement is able to employ or mobilize, the more successful it is likely to be. This school argues that there are always enough discontented people in society to fill a protest movement, but what vary over time—and so explain the emergence of movements—are the resources available to nourish it. As a society grows wealthier, citizens have more money to contribute to **social movement organizations (SMOs)**—the formal organizations that support and sometimes initiate movements—and so there are more movements than ever before. With this point of view, the focus shifted decisively away from the kinds of individuals who might join a movement and toward the organization and resources necessary to sustain a movement. Although movement resources are not enough by themselves to explain the rise of movements, most sociologists do consider resources an important part of any explanation of movement emergence.

The theoretical paradigm that has concentrated most on movement emergence is the political process approach, mentioned earlier in this chapter. According to this perspective, economic and political shifts that occur (usually independently of protesters' own efforts) open up a space or create "political opportunities" for the movement (McAdam 1982). Because this approach views movements as primarily political, making demands of the state and asking for changes in laws and policies, it regards changes in the government or state as the most important opportunity a movement needs. Most often, this consists of a decline in the repression that organizers are otherwise assumed to face, perhaps because political authorities are divided (the movement may have found some allies within the government) or because powerful political and economic elites have divergent interests. In many versions of this perspective, the same factors are seen as explaining both the rise of the movement and its relative success.

Resources, organization, and a sense of new opportunities all undoubtedly encouraged the civil rights movement that grew rapidly in the United States beginning in 1955. By then, the migration of millions of Blacks out of the rural South provided them with more resources and denser social ties; Black churches and colleges were organizations through which money and people could be channeled to civil rights work; and a new, more optimistic cultural outlook prevailed. These factors encouraged more extensive political mobilization, beginning with the National Association for the Advancement of Colored People (NAACP), which in turn won inspiring legal victories, especially *Brown* v. *Board of Education* in 1954, which held that racially segregated schools violated the Constitution. In the next year, Blacks in Montgomery, Alabama, successfully carried out a long boycott of segregated public buses, finally forcing the local government to allow anyone to sit anywhere.

Alongside resource mobilization and political process approaches, social networks play a role in mobilizing people. **Social networks** are the webs of ties or connections that link individuals (and organizations) to one another, thereby facilitating communication and the coordination of collective action. Although networks can explain *who* is recruited, the very existence of social ties among potential recruits can be a prerequisite for the emergence of a social movement. People who cannot communicate with one another cannot act together. If most political process theorists emphasize conditions in the external environment (especially the government) that allow a movement to emerge, network theorists look at the conditions within the community or population of those who might be recruited. In the case of the civil rights movement, for example, network ties between church members became a critical source of recruitment into the movement (Morris 1985). Individuals with dense ties to a large number of people and/or organizations can play key roles in movements by reaching, persuading, and mobilizing other people to participate in building a movement. It was not an accident that many of the early leaders of the civil rights movement came from Black churches or Black colleges.

Scholars who have studied the 1969 Stonewall rebellion in New York City and the subsequent development of a militant gay and lesbian movement also emphasize the critical importance of social networks. The Stonewall rebellion involved violent confrontations between police and gay men, lesbians, and transgender people over the course of several days following the arrest of gay patrons at a bar called the Stonewall Inn in Greenwich Village. This rebellion, apparently a spontaneous eruption of gay militancy, in fact marked the public emergence of a long-repressed, covert urban subculture. The gay movement was also able to draw on preexisting networks of activists in the radical movements then current among American youth. The "gay liberation" movement recruited from the ranks of both the anti–Vietnam War movement and the women's movement. It also borrowed its confrontational tactics from these movements. Many lesbians and gay men had already been radicalized and educated in the arts of protest by the feminist and antiwar movements.

This march in New York City occurred on the first anniversary of the Stonewall rebellion, then known as "Gay Liberation Day," in 1970. Many of the first wave of gay rights activists had learned about movement building as participants in other movements earlier in the 1960s, such as the anti–Vietnam War movement and the civil rights movement.

Fred W. McDarrah/Getty Images

The theoretical approaches discussed thus far redefined somewhat the central question of movement emergence. Scholars began to see movements as closely linked to one another because leaders and participants shifted from one to the other or shared social networks, or because the same political conditions encouraged many movements to form at the same time. So researchers began to ask what caused entire **waves** (or cycles of protest) to emerge rather than asking about the origins of single movements. One cannot fully understand any one of the movements of the 1960s cycle of protest, for example—including the civil rights movement, the women's movement, the farm workers' movement, and the anti-Vietnam War movement—without knowing something about the other movements in this cycle.

Cultural Aspects of Social Movements

22.2.2 Explain how cultural approaches to the study of social movements differ from resource mobilization and political process approaches.

In recent years, some sociologists have begun focusing on developing cultural approaches to the study of social movements, which link social movements to broad historical developments. Among these broader social changes that have influenced the kinds and types of social movements have been the shifts from an industrial or manufacturing society to a postindustrial or knowledge-based society in which fewer people process physical goods and more deal with words and symbols and other forms of knowledge in their jobs. Many contemporary social movements can be seen as efforts to control the direction of social change largely by controlling a society's symbols and self-understandings.

In cultural approaches, the goals and intentions of protesters are taken very seriously. For instance, the origin of the animal protection movement has been linked to broad changes in sensibilities over the last 200 years that have allowed citizens of the industrial world to recognize the suffering of nonhuman species—and to worry about it. Such concerns would simply not have been possible in a society where most people worked on farms and used animals both as living tools (horses, dogs, dairy cows) and as raw materials (for example, food, leather). The point is to observe or ask protesters themselves about their perceptions, desires, and fantasies without having a theory that predicts in advance what protesters think and feel.

From this perspective, the work of sociologist Charles Kurzman (1996) helped change the way scholars think about shifts in "political opportunities" for protest. Kurzman's research on the Iranian Revolution (1978–79), in which the king (or shah as he was known) was overthrown by a popular uprising, indicates that there were no objective political changes on the eve of the revolution that suddenly weakened the monarchy or created new opportunities for

protest. Indeed, despite considerable police repression and expressions of U.S. support for the monarchy, protest against the shah continued to grow, and people gradually came to believe they could topple the regime. A movement can sometimes succeed, apparently, if it thinks it can. (The Iranian Revolution also shows how state violence—which the Shah tried to use to stop protests—can sometimes serve to mobilize rather than demobilize protesters.)

Protesters may fail to see (or seize) opportunities, and they may imagine opportunities for protest when none seems to exist. The slackening of police repression, divisions among wealthy elites and politicians, and so on (the "opportunities" of political process theorists) may only have an effect if they are known or perceived as such. And people may sometimes rebel (and sometimes win), even when the political environment does not at first seem promising. In other words, subjective perceptions about the world can potentially play as important a role in motivating social movements as objective changes in the state or society.

Cultural sociologists have thus reached different conclusions than those expressed by resource mobilization and political process theorists. Part of the reason for this is because cultural sociologists have examined different kinds of social movements and because they look for different factors driving movements. Most political process theorists, for example, have focused on movements of groups that have been systematically excluded from political power and legal rights, in other words, groups that are demanding the full rights of citizenship. Cultural theorists have been more likely to examine movements of those who already have the formal rights of citizens—who can vote, pressure legislators, and run for office—but who nonetheless feel they must step outside normal political institutions to have a greater impact. Resource mobilization theorists assume that people know what they want and simply need the resources and organization to pursue it; cultural sociologists recognize that in many cases people only gradually figure out what they want, often because movement organizers persuade them of it (for example, that animals can suffer like humans, that cannabis should be legal, or that U.S. foreign policy is inherently evil).

Cultural sociologists have reasserted the importance of perceptions, ideas, emotions, and grievances, all of which resource mobilization and political process theorists once thought did not matter very much or could simply be taken for granted. But these are examined today in the context of broader social and political changes, not in isolation from them. It is not as though people first develop goals or emotions and then decide to go out and form movements to pursue or express them; there is an interaction among ideas, feelings, mobilization, and the broader environment. Some people get pulled into movements by friends or family and are only slowly converted to the movement's cause; their political beliefs and emotional states are a consequence, not a cause, of joining the movement. Research suggests, for example, that over 40 percent of committed antiabortion activists had ambiguous views about abortion or even considered themselves "pro-choice" when they initially joined the movement; it was only after they spent some time in the movement, interacting with long-term activists, that they came to emphatically oppose abortions (Munson 2008).

Recruitment: Joining or Supporting Movements

22.2.3 Explain how individual traits, biographical availability, framing, and cultural attitudes influence participation in social movements.

Once activists form groups or networks and begin to think of themselves as a movement (or at least a potential movement), their next step is usually to try to expand their ranks by recruiting others to their cause. Sociological theories of the recruitment process have evolved over time from an emphasis on individual traits to one that focuses on individuals' availability for activism, and finally toward a synthesis of these dimensions.

Scholars of social movements once tended to see protesters as swept up in crowds, acting in abnormal and sometimes irrational ways because of frustration with their individual circumstances. In some theories, marginal, isolated, and alienated members of society were seen as most likely to join social movements; in others it was those who were insecure or dogmatic. Such claims were usually demeaning to protesters, who were thought to be compensating for some sort of personal inadequacy or psychological problem by participating in protests. However, subsequent empirical research did not support the image of protesters as more angry, isolated, or alienated than others.

One important challenge to this line of thinking was developed in the work of economist Mancur Olson (1965). Olson suggested that to understand social movements, it is important to start from the presumption that protesters are perfectly rational, arguing that they do not join groups if they think they can gain the benefits that these groups pursue without taking the time to participate. In other words, people will ordinarily prefer to be **free riders**, letting others protest while benefitting from their successes. You don't have to join the environmental movement to enjoy the clean air that it wins for all of us—so why join it and go to the trouble of participating in protests? Another reason to free ride is that your own participation in or contribution to a collective effort would not seem to make a noticeable difference once the group consists of more than a few dozen people. What can a group of 101 people accomplish that a group of 100 can't?

Given these dilemmas, Olson argues, successful movements must provide "selective incentives" that are enjoyed only by those who actually participate. These might include such things as interesting political discussions, the possibility of making new friends, or social status in the eyes of others. Olson challenged scholars of social movements to show *how* organizers manage to overcome the free rider problem. The challenge Olson raised shifted attention from what kinds of *people* protest to what kinds of objective *conditions* facilitate protest. Attitudes and grievances were dismissed as insufficient to cause protest, for many people have the attitudes and interests to want social change, but do not participate in movements.

As part of this new agenda, the concept of **biographical availability** was developed as a way of understanding participation: People with few family or work obligations—especially young people without children and students—were particularly available to devote time to movement activities (McAdam 1988). People who have major commitments on their time, by contrast, are less able to participate (although they can donate money, which is often a key resource for movements to develop).

In addition to biographical availability, a person's social connections to any particular movement can predict whether he or she will join the movement. Social networks are usually a precondition for the emergence of a movement as well as the explanation for who is subsequently recruited to it. Physically scattered or socially isolated people are the least likely to join a movement. In the extreme case of "bloc recruitment," organizers bring a whole social network or organization virtually intact into a movement (for example, when one union is on strike and another union agrees to honor the first union's picket lines). This suggests that—contrary to Olson's view—people do not make decisions to join movements (or not) as isolated, self-regarding individuals but in concert with others in their networks. And the approval of peers in one's network may be an important "selective incentive" that leads individuals to join a movement.

Different kinds of social networks can be used for recruitment. They may not be political in origin or intent. Black churches and colleges were crucial to the Southern civil rights movement in the 1950s, evangelical Protestant churches helped defeat the Equal Rights Amendment in the 1980s, and mosques in Iran facilitated the Iranian Revolution. Networks developed for earlier political activities can also aid recruitment into a movement that develops later—one reason why a history of previous activism makes someone more likely to be recruited. The clustering of movements in waves or cycles makes this mutual support especially important, as one movement feeds into the next. Because of these networks, prior activism and organizational memberships help predict who will be recruited (and who will not be).

Social media like Facebook and Twitter can also be used to recruit people to political protests. A famous example of this was seen during the so-called Arab Spring of 2011, where longstanding dictators in several Middle Eastern countries were overthrown by large, unprecedented protests. Social media allowed multitudes of people who had never met before and who had no other connections to communicate with one another and spread the word about what was going on.

They made it possible to organize huge protests in a much shorter span of time and over greater distances than was previously feasible. Social media were also the main means by which individuals became involved in the Black Lives Matter and #MeToo movements, neither of which relied upon large formal organizations or a centralized leadership.

In general, social media allow activists to direct people to assemble at specific places and at specific times before the authorities have time to react. This can be especially important where authorities are likely to break up protests violently—it is more difficult for the authorities to respond that way when the protest group is very large. On the other hand, government authorities may also monitor social media—or attempt to shut them down altogether—in their attempts to control protest. So social media can be used to organize as well as disrupt movements.

Without denying the importance of personal contacts and communication networks, recent studies have also examined the cultural messages transmitted across these social networks and social media. For example, what have been called "suddenly imposed grievances" that are produced by dramatic and unexpected events may be important for recruitment. For example, the partial nuclear meltdown in 1979 at the Three Mile Island power plant in Dauphin County, Pennsylvania, which led to the evacuation of nearly 200,000 people, alerted the public to the risks of nuclear energy, giving a big boost to the antinuclear movement (Walsh 1981). Recruitment is also more likely when people feel that they have a chance of success. This sense of optimism and efficacy has been called "cognitive liberation" (McAdam 1982). People may have lots of grievances as well as ties to individuals in a movement seeking to redress those grievances, but they are probably less likely to join that movement if they don't think it can succeed.

Scholars view direct personal contacts as important because they allow organizers and potential participants to achieve a common definition of a social problem and a common prescription for solving it. In successful recruitment, organizers offer ways of seeing a social problem that resonate with the views and experiences of potential recruits. The Occupy Wall Street movement, for example, spread very rapidly across the country in 2011 because its message about the power of banks and corporations and the plight of the "99 percent" resonated with people during a time of economic crisis and home foreclosures. Similarly, the #MeToo movement of 2017–18 attracted considerable support for the simple reason that so many women had personally experienced sexual harassment or assault. But it is not as if everyone was equally likely to participate in or support the goals of these movements. Networks are important *because* of the cultural meanings they transmit. Networks and meanings are not rival explanations; they work together. Figures 22.1, 22.2, and 22.3

Figure 22.1 What Did Supporters of the Occupy Movements in 2011 Look Like?

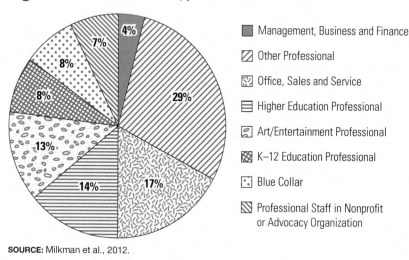

81% White
61% Male
68% 45 and younger
47% Income <$25,000
90% College graduates
70% Politically independent

SOURCE: Based on data from Fast Company (2011); Panagopoulos and Costas 2011; Pew Research Center 2011.

Figure 22.2 Where Do Occupy Wall Street Activists Work?

4%
7%
8%
8%
13%
14%
17%
29%

■ Management, Business and Finance
▨ Other Professional
▧ Office, Sales and Service
▤ Higher Education Professional
▨ Art/Entertainment Professional
▨ K–12 Education Professional
▨ Blue Collar
▨ Professional Staff in Nonprofit or Advocacy Organization

SOURCE: Milkman et al., 2012.

Figure 22.3 Political Views of Those Active in the Movement in NYC

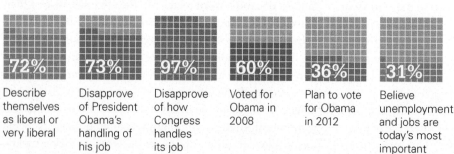

72% Describe themselves as liberal or very liberal
73% Disapprove of President Obama's handling of his job
97% Disapprove of how Congress handles its job
60% Voted for Obama in 2008
36% Plan to vote for Obama in 2012
31% Believe unemployment and jobs are today's most important problems

SOURCE: Panagopoulos and Costas 2011.

An image from the Occupy Wall Street protests that started in New York City's financial district and quickly spread around the United States and in other parts of the world in the fall of 2011. Even though 72 percent of these protestors told interviewers they were liberal or very liberal, only 38 percent said they planned to vote for Barack Obama, the incumbent Democratic president. Dissatisfaction with Obama's approach to issues of inequality were part of the reason why people were willing to maintain 24-hour vigils at protest sites, rather than waiting for politicians to take action.

show more about who participated in or supported the Occupy Wall Street movement.

Another way that cultural factors influence the rise of social movements, and their ability to have an impact, is the way movements present their grievances to nonmembers. This process is known as **framing**, and it refers to the specific ways in which ideas and beliefs are presented to other people. Framing happens all the time: We "frame" our positions in arguments with our friends and family, trying to put our arguments in the most appealing ways possible. So too do social movements. Scholars of movements have explored how activists try to frame or present their ideas so that they make sense to or strongly resonate with the beliefs of potential recruits and supporters. Three successive types of framing have been shown to be necessary for successful recruitment: *Diagnostic*, in which a movement convinces potential converts that a problem needs to be addressed; *prognostic*, in which it convinces them of appropriate strategies, tactics, and targets; and *motivational*, in which it exhorts them to get involved in these activities (Snow and Benford 1988). Frames are more likely to be accepted if they fit well with the existing beliefs of potential recruits, if they involve empirically credible claims, if they are compatible with the life experiences of the audiences, and if they fit with the stories or narratives the audiences tell about their lives.

Another idea that has taken on increasing importance in the study of social movements is *collective identity*. A **collective identity** is the belief that one belongs to a certain group (or groups) with distinctive characteristics and interests (for example, women, the working class, Black people, etc.). It is another concept, parallel to framing, that has been used to examine how the recruitment to movements may be influenced by the kinds of identities members (and prospective members) have. In order to devote time and effort to protest, people must usually feel part of a larger group they think they can help. Not all identities come easily to people; they may have to be consciously created, which is one of the things that some movements do. The LGBTQ movement, for example, still devotes a lot of its energy to making it possible for gays, lesbians, and transgender people to feel comfortable with themselves and to identify themselves publicly as gay, lesbian, or transgender (that is, to "come out of the closet"). The #MeToo movement sought to create a space, if only an online space, in which survivors of sexual harassment and assault could share their stories and, sometimes, identify perpetrators. Obviously, people who for whatever reason find it difficult to identify themselves publicly with a certain group are unlikely to become politically active on its behalf.

Another cultural approach emphasizes how citizens' attitudes and worldviews matter. Political scientist Ronald Inglehart (1990) has argued that new "postmaterial" values and beliefs have emerged in the advanced industrial nations since the 1960s. Through most of human history, in his view, people have been forced to worry about basic material needs such as food, shelter, and security, but since World War II the advanced industrial world has been largely spared traditional privations. Those born after World War II—at least the college-educated and affluent middle class—were "freed" to pursue "higher" goals such as control over their lives, environmental protection, and satisfying work rather than worry primarily about their paychecks. The result has allegedly been less emphasis on economic redistribution, class-based political organizations, or the pursuit of political power—again, at least where the affluent middle class is concerned. Instead we have seen movements critical of large bureaucracies, meaningless work, complex technologies, pollution, and many different forms of oppression. One can certainly better understand who is likely to support the environmental movement or the animal rights movement by using the concept of postmaterial politics. These movements have a primarily middle-class social base, even though they are not pursuing the narrow economic interests of this class. So the growth of a postindustrial sector of the economy can help explain not only changes in political concerns over time but also different sympathies across parts of the population at any given time.

Surprisingly, researchers have found that even some covert, violent organizations draw many of their adherents from this middle-class social base. The followers of the late Osama bin Laden and the leaders of his Al-Qaeda movement were primarily well-educated and from middle-class families (Kurzman 2002). Two sociologists found that engineers were significantly overrepresented in the ranks of Islamic militants (Gambetta and Hertog 2009). While many Westerners assume that the Islamic world is mired in religious superstition and rejects modern rationality, bin Laden's followers were much better educated than their peers and used the latest technologies and media. They were not motivated by narrow class or economic interests but by their opposition to the policies of the U.S. government in the Middle East, even as they used religious language and looked nostalgically backward to a golden age of Islam.

Attitudes and worldviews matter for recruitment, but they are not always what we assume them to be!

Recruitment to social movements, however, involves more than cultural ideas about how the world works. Its moral and emotional dimensions are equally important. In fact, all of the key factors that explain recruitment depend heavily on their emotional impact on people. Social networks, for example, are often grounded in the emotional bonds among their members: We pay attention to people in our networks, and what they say, because we are fond of them or trust them. Generating and sustaining supporters' emotional connections to a cause is often a critical part of building a social movement. One way emotions matter is when an event occurs that shocks people. For example, as noted earlier, police killings of unarmed Blacks has frequently provoked protests and social movement organizing, from the civil rights movement to the Black Panthers in the late 1960s to the Black Lives Matter movement in recent years. The term **moral shock** refers to the moral and emotional dimensions of recruitment to movements. A moral shock is an unexpected event that surprises, distresses, and outrages people, often to the point of motivating them to join a movement to eliminate the source of their outrage. Moral shocks may be so strong that they lead people without social ties to activists to seek out or even form a group to redress their grievances (Jasper 1997).

Another important example of a moral shock and the long-term impact it can have, is the *Roe* v. *Wade* Supreme Court decision of 1973. The decision legalized

Movements for and against a woman's right to terminate her pregnancy provide a good example of competing framing attempts. Those in favor of legal abortion refer to broader values such as personal freedom, bodily integrity, and women's rights to frame their campaigns. Accordingly, their label "pro-choice" suggests that their opponents are pro-coercion and against individual liberties. However, the antiabortion movement also refers to values such as bodily integrity or personal freedom, namely those of the fetus. Their self-framing as "pro-life" implies that their opponents are anti-life or even pro-death.

abortions in the first two trimesters of a pregnancy. For many religious Americans, especially Catholic women, it was as if the Supreme Court had legalized the murder of certain kinds of children. Although they had not been politically active previously and knew no political activists, these women formed the core of the early antiabortion movement (Luker 1984). Later, others joined, and the antiabortion movement has been a sustained presence in the United States for decades, continually recycling the same images and frames generated by these early activists.

Looking at the big picture, it is now clear that what goes on inside people's heads (and hearts) is more important than some scholars previously thought. Protests and social movements are now viewed as part of an effort to impose meaning and morality on the world, to forge and express a collective identity, to create or reinforce emotional bonds with others, and to define and pursue collective interests and visions of a good society. These are things that all humans desire and seek.

We have seen in this section that a person's position in networks of other people who become active in movements and their cultural orientations (cognitive, moral, and emotional) are important in recruitment. In some cases, cultural messages can be used to recruit people even in the absence of social networks, relying on moral shocks instead of personal ties to draw people in. For virtually all social movements, though, only a small fraction of potential recruits actually join, and it takes all the factors we have considered to understand who does and does not participate, and why some people participate in movements much more than others.

Filip Jedraszak/Alamy Stock Photo

BIG QUESTION 22.3 What Tactics Do Movements Use, and What Outcomes Do They Achieve?

MOVEMENT TACTICS AND OUTCOMES

If you are in a social movement, one of the most pressing questions you will face is, *What is to be done?* That is, there are a range of tactics that movements can deploy. So how do you choose tactics that will help your cause? How do you recruit more people, attract the news media, put pressure on the rich and powerful, or favorably impress political decision makers with your commitment and determination? Tactical decisions are the real "stuff" of social movements. Some researchers have looked at how these decisions are made, how and when protesters innovate in their tactics, and what the tradeoffs are between different kinds of tactics.

The Strategies of Movements

22.3.1 Discuss how organizers and participants increase awareness and further the goals of movements.

The tactical choices of social movements are usually made in the heat of conflict. These choices depend in part on the instincts of movement leaders, who themselves may not always be able to explain why they made one choice rather than another. Decisions are sometimes made quickly, and it may be difficult to reconstruct the process later—for example, when being interviewed by a sociologist. But research that examines a broad range of different movements can discern regular patterns and similar choices even if leaders sometimes cannot account for why certain choices were made at the time.

Tactical choices made during a social movement campaign have four distinct audiences to consider: One's opponents, one's supporters, prospective supporters who have not yet joined the movement, and finally powerful third-party forces that are ostensibly neutral but with power to hurt (or sometimes help) the movement: For example, the police, the media, and government officials. To take just one example of the latter, before many rallies or marches today, leaders negotiate with the police over where they will be allowed to go, what they will do, and even how many will be arrested (if any).

Movement leaders must also make tactical choices with regard to their own followers: How to placate disaffected members or factions of the movement; how to keep members coming back to future events; how to raise funds and other resources needed to support the movement; and how to increase (or simply maintain) the membership. As a result, any given action is probably designed for several different audiences at the same time. But an action that satisfies one may not please another.

With regard to their opponents, protesters may try to change their behavior through persuasion, intimidation, or, when possible, by imposing costs (financial or otherwise) on them. Raising the costs of "business as usual" is generally necessary when movements confront powerful elites (especially the wealthy) who have not been elected to political office. These elites can simply ignore protesters or try to repress them (by calling in police or private security forces) if they become threatening. Strikes and boycotts, however, can hurt the wealthy economically and may lead them to make concessions to protesters so that their businesses, factories, and farms can continue to make profits. If the costs caused by the disruption that movements create

are greater than the costs of making concessions to the movement, elites may decide to make concessions in order to end the disruption. A famous example of this is that when farm workers go on strike, they know the best time to do it is right when the crops are ripe and need to picked. There may be a short window for that to happen, and the owners may be forced to make concessions to avoid suffering losses if the crops are not picked. When the costs of making concessions are too expensive, however, corporations or elites may decide to fight hard and even violently against a movement for years (Luders 2010).

Movements can challenge their opponents in another way: By seeking to undermine their opponents' credibility with the public, media, and government officials. When it comes to government, protesters can try to change laws, policies, regulatory practices, and administrative rules. From the courts, protesters typically strive to have unfavorable laws struck down or at least interpreted in new ways. With both courts and police, they also hope for (and may demand) tolerance of their protests. Social movements seek to use the news media to spread their message in a favorable light and sometimes to undermine their opponents. Protesters may also approach professional groups, such as doctors or engineers, to change their standards. They may seek allies in other protest groups. And from the public at large, they may hope for new recruits, sympathy, financial contributions, or at least changes in awareness. Finally, they even have goals for their own members: Personal transformations and continued fervor for the cause. In other words, movements have a lot of goals to balance in their tactics, and striking the right balance is sometimes extremely difficult.

One of the most common ways in which movements try to raise issues and change people's minds is by organizing public demonstrations, as shown here in a demonstration in support of the legalization of cannabis.

Tactical Repertoires of Movements

22.3.2 Explain why social movements use certain tactics but not others.

Movement leaders are usually familiar with only a limited number of tactics. The sociologist Charles Tilly (1986) developed the phrase "repertoire of contention" to describe the range of tactics available to protesters in any given society in a particular period. In the case of social movements, **Repertoires** refer to tactical ideas known to movement activists and can be part of their "toolkit" of strategies. Most social movements will draw upon very similar repertoire because that is what they know. But there are always many possible tactics that movement leaders may not be familiar with or do not have the knowledge to utilize, including (hypothetically) tactics that might be extremely beneficial to the movement. Tilly was interested in explaining how repertoires of contention changed over long stretches of time, while other scholars have been concerned with explaining why particular leaders choose certain tactics and not others from the existing repertoire: Why a march rather than a letter-writing campaign? Why wait a week before responding to your opponents' actions rather than acting immediately? Why act nonviolently instead of violently? Why choose one cultural frame rather than another for a speech or website?

Saul Alinsky, one of the most famous community organizers and movement innovators of the twentieth century, wrote a great deal about tactics in the course of trying to improve the living conditions of poor neighborhoods, particularly in Chicago (Alinsky 1971). Alinsky developed tactical principles that are not unlike those of army generals: Try to take your opponents by surprise, and try to make them think you are more powerful than you are. Try to use tactics your own followers enjoy and are familiar with. The idea of keeping the pressure on one's opponents is important because you never know where and when your opponent will be vulnerable or will make a blunder. The greater the pressure, the greater the chance you will trip them up. Alinsky also recognized that it is usually necessary to portray your enemy as an utter villain, a real flesh-and-blood person who can be blamed, not an abstract principle. Thus, protest movements during the Arab Spring of 2011 demonized dictators like Hosni Mubarak in Egypt. Many protestors hoped to replace the authoritarian regime in Egypt with democracy, but they usually focused their protests on a simpler demand, calling for the overthrow of Mubarak, who symbolized all that was wrong in the country. When successful, such demonization can lead to strong emotions that motivate people to participate (in Egypt, a long history of government repression of protests, including sometimes killing protesters, meant that it took real courage to participate).

In analyzing the famous sit-ins employed by the civil rights movement in the early 1960s, sociologist Aldon Morris (1985) exemplifies the resource mobilization approach to tactics. He is not so much concerned with the origins of the sit-in tactic or the strategic thinking behind its use. Rather, he is concerned with revealing the indigenous organizations and social networks through which the sit-ins rapidly spread, arguing against a view of the sit-ins as spontaneous eruptions. Morris also touches on another important issue: The emergence of "movement centers" with resources, social ties (especially preachers and NAACP activists), and regular meetings (usually at churches). Other theorists of social movements have called these places where people are free to air their grievances **free spaces**, that is, places relatively free from surveillance where oppositional ideas and tactics can develop and spread. Free spaces are places like churches, schools, union meeting halls, or other places where movement participants can feel free of harassment by their opponents. By contrast, spaces controlled by an opponent—for example, the workplace—are riskier places to talk about plans for movement activity.

Of all the tactics employed by social movements, none are more controversial than violence. To even develop careful research on the topic of why movements sometimes use violence, it is necessary for scholars to try to dispel some of the myths surrounding the use of violent tactics. They point out that guerrilla warfare and terrorism are often rational political responses to state violence and conflicts over territory, not the handiwork of psychopaths or religious fanatics (as the media and politicians often suggest). Scholars as well as journalists are often hesitant to emphasize the rationality or achievements of political violence, in part because of their moral discomfort with it.

But violence is often used against social movements, too, and it has to be considered part of the overall explanatory agenda to study when and how it is deployed. In the case of the antiapartheid movement in South Africa, this has led some scholars to avoid discussing violence altogether and to portray the movement, misleadingly, as an entirely nonviolent civil rights struggle (supposedly like that in the United States). It certainly is true that the White South African government used vastly more violence against protesters than the movement did against the apartheid government. But we can't understand the full range of tactics employed by the anti-apartheid movement if we don't think about how violence was selectively used.

Political violence, like war, is a kind of routine "politics by other means" that movements may choose to use in combating their enemies. Of course, the opponents of social movements usually control or have influence over far more powerful tools of violence in the form of police and military forces, and the long history of violence against social movements shows a willingness on the part of the powerful to use force. That said, some recent research indicates that nonviolent movements may be much more likely to succeed than violent movements, even against very repressive governments (Chenoweth and Stephan 2011). This is because ordinary people usually find it much easier to participate in nonviolent movements, so they tend to be much larger than violent movements, and because government officials and soldiers are more likely to defect to nonviolent movements.

Although social movements are defined, in part, by their use of non-institutional tactics (that is, tactics that are outside existing political institutions) to pursue their political goals, protest can also take place *within* institutions. For example, LGBTQ people in the U.S. military successfully fought with allies outside the military to overturn the so-called "don't ask, don't tell" policy that prohibited them from serving as openly gay or lesbian (and even more recently, the right to serve has been extended to transgender individuals), and more recently trans people have struggled to win acceptance in the military. In an earlier period, the military became fully racially integrated (in the late 1940s) long before the end of

Jim Crow in the U.S. South. Free spaces *outside* regular institutions are not always enough for movements to flourish; sometimes they can also thrive *within* dominant institutions. Government and educational institutions are often especially susceptible to internal challenges, but even private corporations have conceded to demands made by groups of workers (an example can be seen in the establishment of anti-sexual harassment and anti-racist programs many large corporations now maintain; see Dobbin 2009).

The choice of strategies and tactics is certainly an area in which research is ongoing. One limitation of existing research has been that most scholars have thought about the movement as their unit of analysis: How each grows, operates, and affects the world around it. But tactical choices are made in close interaction with other actors in the same "field of conflict," including opponents and allies, actual and potential. These interactions are like a game of chess: Each player's tactical moves are shaped as much by the moves of the other players as by one's preferred or ideal course of action. So movements often end up doing things they would rather not do but feel they must—for example, using violence even if it can sometimes mean harming or killing innocent civilians. But this is not surprising. In an ideal world, after all, people would not need to make hard choices about political tactics; they would already have the things their movements are fighting for.

The Decline and Disappearance of Movements

22.3.3 Explain the sociopolitical reasons for the decreasing popularity of certain movements.

Not surprisingly, scholars have had much more to say about why social movements arise than why they decline or disappear altogether. But movements typically have a beginning, a middle period of activism, and then some kind of end. Many movements, even successful ones, have a short lifespan; others survive for many decades without achieving much. Several hypotheses about movement decline have attained some prominence. Most explanations for movement decline focus on the surrounding political environment, which may constrain as well as facilitate movements. Of course, the very success of a movement in changing laws or government policies may undermine the motivations that many people had for participating in the movement in the first place.

Perhaps the common way that success leads movements to dissolve is when movement organizations or their central demands are legally recognized by the government, leading to their institutionalization and declining reliance on disruptive protest. Government concessions of this type, even if they do not redress all the grievances and concerns of movement participants, may nevertheless be sufficient to satisfy or placate many people, who will then drift away from the movement or from protest tactics. Social movements, in short, may become victims of their own limited

successes. The U.S. labor movement is a prime example of this dynamic. After militant and sometimes deadly strikes in the 1930s led to the legal recognition of trade unions and the right to collective bargaining, unions gradually turned away from strikes and the aggressive recruitment of new members. Corporations also stepped up their opposition to trade unions. As a result, the proportion of workers who belong to unions has been steadily declining since the late 1950s.

Movements may also decline as a result of their own internal dynamics and evolution. The women's movement, for example, gradually lost its radical vision and militancy (Epstein 2001). This was a result in part of intense ideological conflicts among radical feminists within the movement, who had provided much of the movement's activist core and ideological inspiration, and more moderate activists who favored gender equality and opportunity for women but not the more radical goals of feminist leaders. Gradually, and partly because of its own success in opening up new professional careers for women, the visions of moderate feminists were triumphant and the women's movement as a whole took on a middle-class outlook. It became more concerned with the career opportunities and material success of individual women than with the group solidarity of women or with addressing the concerns of poor and working-class women. A number of women's organizations have now been durably established, including the National Organization for Women (NOW), becoming involved in lobbying government officials in Washington but rarely organizing protest events.

Yet another way in which a movement's internal dynamics may lead to break up and decline is that movements typically require—or themselves attempt to create—clear and stable collective identities. Yet this is not always easy. How can we make claims and demands on others, after all, if we do not know who "we" and "they" are? Many recent movements have been centrally concerned with establishing, recasting, or defending collective identities, including previously stigmatized identities. But collective identities, sociologists argue, are not "natural" or given once and for all; they are culturally constructed and continually reconstructed. Some identities, moreover, may obscure or devalue other identities that people have. As a result, people have often attempted to blur or reconfigure certain identities. Hence, the question: Must movements organized around a particular identity self-destruct?

One important aspect of the gay and lesbian movement has been shaken in recent years by "queer" theorists and activists who have challenged fixed sexual identities like "gay," "lesbian," and "straight" (Gamson 1995). Queer activists have also challenged the assimilationist goals of mainstream (and generally older) gay and lesbian activists, some of whom object to the very use of a stigmatized label like "queer." To some extent, queer activism developed out of the growing organization of bisexual and transgender people, whose very existence challenges the notion of fixed sexual and gender identities. Today, the success of these challenges is reflected in the fact that these movements now typically refer to themselves as "LGBT" or "LGBTQ" to recognize the incorporation of queer (or questioning) and trans people into the movement.

Ultimately, this movement, and indeed all movements, face a dilemma: To be politically effective, they may feel a need to emphasize exclusive and secure collective identities, but this may paper over and effectively ignore important differences among movement participants—differences based on race and class, for example, which may later erupt in a way that weakens the movement. How movements handle this dilemma in order to avoid self-destruction—how they weigh and balance competing and potentially disruptive identity claims—is an important question for future research.

Movements may also decline because the political opportunities and the free spaces that have helped give rise to them begin to contract or disappear. Divisions among the wealthy and powerful may be resolved, or (perhaps because of such unity) authorities may decide to harshly repress or crack down on a movement. Both of these factors are usually invoked to explain the violent demise of the democracy movement in China in 1989. A number of scholars have also pointed to repression as a key factor in the decline of the U.S. labor movement since the 1950s. More specifically, they show that union decline is largely explained by aggressive employer opposition to unions, which has been facilitated by laws and policies that favor employers over workers (Rosenfeld 2014). One does not see the same type of employer resistance to unions in much of Europe (or Canada), mainly because government laws discourage it. As a result, unions have held their own in these countries in recent years, while American unions have gotten much weaker. American unions have also been hurt by factory closings in recent years; many businesses have transferred their operations to parts of the country (mainly the South, where unions are much less common) or to other countries where unions are weak and wages relatively low.

Another example of how repression may be triggered (and can seriously harm a movement) can be seen in the ways that some movements may provoke such a backlash against them that they lose ground. For example, the mobilization of far-right militia groups against the U.S. government which led to the Oklahoma City bombing in 1995 inspired closer surveillance and repression of these groups than had previously existed—not to mention extremely negative media coverage. Their number and activities declined sharply after the bombing, although there has been a

Mass pro-democracy protests in Tiananmen Square in Beijing, China in the spring of 1989 were crushed by the government on June 4, 1989. This photo captures protesters watching as a phalanx of soldiers clears the massive square as part of a nationwide crackdown on protests against the Communist government. In this case, repression worked; protest activity on the scale of the Tiananmen Square demonstrations has not been seen in China since 1989.

Dario Mitidieri/Getty Images

revival of such groups more recently, as many have rallied to the defense of former president Donald Trump or in opposition to the Black Lives Matter movement.

Many scholars point out that while repression is often effective, it does sometimes fail. Police violence sometimes demobilizes protesters and crushes insurgents, but it sometimes backfires, spurring even more people to take to the streets or to take up arms. The timing of a repression effort can matter. Research on Central America during the 1970s and 1980s (Brockett 1993) suggests that ruthless repression was most effective when authorities used it before movements had become strong—before a cycle of protest had begun and before people were already active and organized. Organized activists redoubled their efforts, went underground, and often turned to violence, joined by others seeking protection, justice, and sometimes revenge.

Repression can also backfire if the repressors misread the movement's purpose and its participants' motivations. U.S. counterinsurgency efforts in Iraq failed because officials assumed that popular attitudes toward insurgents and the government are based on short-term cost–benefit calculations; they failed to see how insurgencies are deeply rooted in class, ethnic, or religious conflicts (Roxborough 2007). Accordingly, attempts by the United States to win over the "hearts and minds" of the Iraqi population by providing material benefits proved insufficient. Insurgent movements are less interested in popularity or legitimacy per se than in monopolizing political control at the grassroots level; such movements constitute an alternative government. Effective counterinsurgency, then, requires establishing local political control, a project that requires a great deal of time and manpower—something that outside powers may be unwilling to commit.

Outcomes

22.3.4 Distinguish between successful and unsuccessful outcomes.

Social movements have a number of effects on their societies, some of them intended and others quite unintended. A few movements attain many or most of their goals, while others at least manage to gain recognition or longevity in the form of protest organization. But many if not most are suppressed or ignored. While sociologists used to talk about the success or failure of movements, today they are more likely to talk about movement *outcomes* in recognition of the unintended consequences of movements. Some movements may not get what they want, but they may still bring about significant benefits for their constituents. Some movements affect the broader culture and public attitudes, perhaps paving the way for future movements. Others leave behind social networks, tactical innovations, and organizational forms that later movements can adopt and use. Some movements that seemingly failed helped give rise to more successful movements.

When thinking about what movements can achieve, it is useful to distinguish between *acceptance* (or recognition) of a movement versus the achievement of some specific goal (such as new government policy or law) (Gamson 1990). Acceptance occurs when a movement or SMO comes to be regarded as a legitimate representative of a group by its opponents. Acceptance is generally crucial for the stability and longevity of a protest group, especially when its main opponent is the state. But sometimes movements win concrete benefits for their constituencies, such as old-age pensions, voting rights, clean air, tax cuts, or new health care programs for poorer and older people.

Acceptance and concrete victories don't necessarily go together; a movement can attain one but not the other (or neither). The sociologist William Gamson has described four general types of movement outcomes based on whether a movement is fully accepted or not and whether it wins many new advantages or none (see Table 22.1). Movements that win a "full response" (that is, full acceptance and many new advantages) are the most successful; the least successful movements are those that "collapse" by failing to win acceptance or any new advantages. There are also two outcomes that fall somewhere between success and failure. A movement is "preempted" when it wins new advantages but fails to win acceptance; and a movement is "co-opted" when it is accepted by its opponents but fails to win any new advantages for its constituents.

Explaining movement outcomes is complicated by the fact that success in the short and the long term may not coincide. In some cases, these even conflict with each other, as when a movement's initial successes inspire strong countermobilization on the part of those under attack. The pro-choice movement, for example, was quite successful in liberalizing abortion laws in a number of states and then

Table 22.1 Four Types of Movement Outcome

	Wins Acceptance	Gains New Advantages	Examples
Full Response	✓	✓	American Federation of Labor; American Federation of Teachers
Preempted Movement	✗	✓	American Free Trade; Tobacco Night Riders
Co-Opted Movement	✓	✗	Bull Moose (Progressive) Party; American Association of University Professors
Collapsed Movement	✗	✗	International Workingman's Association; National Student League

SOURCE: Gamson 1990.

seemed to win a huge victory with the *Roe* v. *Wade* Supreme Court decision in 1973. But this decision, which legalized certain types of abortion, sparked a formidable countermobilization by an invigorated antiabortion movement. This countermobilization has succeeded in making it more difficult and costly to obtain an abortion in many parts of the United States, especially if one is a minor. On the other hand, movement efforts that are unsuccessful in the short run may turn out to have big effects in the long run, as in the case of martyrs who inspire outrage and additional mobilization.

Cultural Consequences of Movements

22.3.5 Discuss the cultural consequences of movements.

Overall, researchers have shown that only a few large and enduring movements have had profound effects on their societies. The labor movement won the 40-hour work week and the right to collective bargaining with employers. The civil rights movement eliminated laws enforcing racial segregation and won voting rights for Blacks. The women's movement won laws against sex discrimination and forever changed the way people think about gender differences. A large number of movements have met with considerable repression. Others have attained some acceptance for their own organizations without obtaining tangible benefits for those they represent (that is, they have been co-opted). Still others have pushed the government to establish a new agency or regulator in response to their demands, only to discover later that this agency was ineffectual or taken over by the movement's opponents. Scholars of social movements might like to believe that the movements they study profoundly affect the course of history (that would be good for business!), but the truth is much more mixed. To be sure, movements have brought about important social and political change in recent decades. More often than not, however, movements achieve far less than their activists had hoped.

But more recently, scholars have paid attention to some less well-known ways in which the cultural and personal consequences of activism—many of them unintended—are important to consider. Consider the personal consequences. Being an activist in any movement may profoundly change the activist: For example, being active in a social movement often changes people from being passive and accepting of the world around them to a more direct, engaged stance toward issues they care about, and that can change the rest of their lives. One important study of civil rights activists compared two groups of people who wanted to participate in the "Mississippi summer" voter registration drive in 1964. The campaign brought a limited number of college students from the North to help register Blacks to vote. Those who applied and were accepted tended to remain politically active throughout their lives, while those who applied but were turned down were much less active (McAdam 1988).

The activist identity is itself an important effect of social movements, but it is just one of many potential cultural effects of movements. For example, some movements have helped to articulate new ways of thinking and feeling about the world. Thus, animal protectionists developed widespread sympathy for nonhuman species into an explicit ideology of outrage at the harm done to animals. Other movements raise issues for public debate, forcing informed citizens to think about a topic and decide how they feel about it. The pro-choice and pro-life movements are prime examples. Today, citizens are virtually expected to have an opinion on the abortion issue. The Black Lives Matter movement has forced millions of people to think about what might be done to prevent police violence against Blacks and others. Many people, even a majority, may reject a movement's perspective, but it can still cause them to think more deeply about their own values and attitudes. Even those who disagree with antiabortionists still have to decide *why* they disagree (thereby raising the quality of public discussion). Still other social movements inspire scientific research or technological change, as the gay and lesbian movement in the 1980s did for HIV/AIDS research, and the environmental movement has more recently in relation to climate change.

There may be even broader cultural effects of social movements. On the one hand, they give people a moral voice, helping them to articulate values and intuitions and think through issues that they do not have time to think about in their daily lives. (Should women be able to have abortions? Should same-sex couples be able to adopt children? Should the government provide a job to everyone who wants one? Should there be billionaires in a good society?) This is extremely satisfying for most movement participants as well as the general public. On the other hand, social movements can also generate extremely technical, scientific, and practical knowledge. They engage people in politics in an exciting way—rare enough in modern society. Unfortunately, some movements may go too far, when instead of trying to be artists they try to be engineers, telling others what is good for them rather than trying to persuade them. This has often happened when movements have taken state power and tried to impose their views on others, which brings us to the topic of revolutions.

World History Archive/Alamy Stock Photo

BIG QUESTION 22.4   What Are Revolutions, and Why Do They Occur?

UNDERSTANDING REVOLUTIONS

In everyday conversation, transformations in ways of thinking, technologies, and even fashions and consumer goods are often described as revolutionary. Sociologists, however, generally define **revolution** more narrowly as a type of profound political or social change. Social movements, as we have seen, are a type of sustained collective action that sometimes help bring about revolutions, but they sometimes produce only small changes or none at all. Although rare, when revolutions do happen they can produce broad societal changes.

Defining "Revolution"

22.4.1 Distinguish between political and social revolutions.

Sociologists generally define *revolution* in one of two ways. Some define revolutions as any change of government or political regime brought about, at least in part, by social movements or popular protest. Others define revolutions (or "social revolutions") more narrowly as entailing not only a change of regime but also fundamental changes in a society's economic institutions and class structure (for example, the French, Russian, and Chinese revolutions). (Although some government officials may sometimes support revolutions, revolutions differ from *coups d'etat*, which involve the overthrow of a government by other political or military authorities with little if any popular support or active participation by ordinary people.) "Social" revolutions thus differ from those revolutions (sometimes called "political revolutions") that bring about new political regimes but little if any change in economic or class structures (for example, the English or American revolutions). Of course, what begins as a political revolution may end up being a social revolution. For example, the political revolution in Russia in February 1917, which overthrew the czar, helped pave the way for the social revolution of October 1917 when the radical Bolshevik Party (later renamed the Communist Party) seized power and oversaw a dramatic transformation of Russian society, including the dispossession of landlords and factory owners (the photo on the previous page shows the famous storming of the former Czar's winter palace).

For some analysts, including Marxists, revolutions necessarily involve a substantial redistribution of property or the creation of a new type of economy or "mode of production." Yet other analysts argue that revolutions may radically alter everyday life for millions of people without bringing about much economic change—through dramatic political and cultural changes, for example. The Russian and Chinese revolutions (1917 and 1949, respectively)—which led to the development of planned, state-owned economies—and the revolutions of 1989 in Eastern Europe, where such economies were replaced by capitalism in countries like Poland, East Germany, Hungary, and Czechoslovakia, all meet the broader standard for a social revolution, while the American revolution (in which a colonial power, Britain, was overthrown but most existing economic and social practices remained unchanged), does not. However defined, most scholars agree that social revolutions have been relatively rare, if momentous, occurrences. By most counts, fewer than two dozen major social revolutions have taken place during the past two centuries. See Table 22.2 for a list of some of the major social revolutions since 1789.

Notice that the revolutions that occurred in the Middle East and North Africa during the so-called Arab Spring of 2011 are not included in Table 22.2. These are better understood as political rather than true social revolutions. They did overthrow dictators and brought about changes in political regimes, but they did not substantially change the economic institutions, the distribution of property, or the class structures of these societies. The revolution in Egypt might even be described as a half-revolution. It overthrew the dictator Hosni Mubarak and destroyed Mubarak's powerful political party, but some elements of the old political regime—above all, the armed forces and the judiciary—survived the revolution intact and continue to wield tremendous power. An Islamic movement organization, the Muslim Brotherhood, won elections in 2012, and for a brief time the Brotherhood controlled the legislature and the office of the presidency (to which Mohammad Morsi was elected). But shortly thereafter, as popular protests against Morsi grew, the military stepped in and overthrew the newly elected government and installed one of its own leaders in the office of the presidency. Looking at the big picture, Egypt's rich elite (which includes many military officers) has managed to hold onto its wealth and economic power, and most Egyptians have seen little significant change in their daily lives.

How should we think about the events of January 6, 2021, when hundreds of supporters of President Donald Trump stormed the Capitol in Washington, D.C. (see

Table 22.2 Major Social Revolutions

Country	Year
France	1789
Mexico	1910
Russia	1917
Yugoslavia	1945
Vietnam	1945
China	1949
Bolivia	1952
Cuba	1959
Algeria	1962
Ethiopia	1974
Angola	1975
Mozambique	1975
Cambodia	1975
Laos	1975
Iran	1979
Nicaragua	1979
Eastern Europe (Poland, Czechoslovakia, Hungry, Romania, Bulgaria, East Germany)	1989
Soviet Union	1991

NOTE: The listed dates are conventional markers that refer to the year in which revolutionaries initially overthrew extant political authorities. Revolutions, however, are best conceptualized not as events but as processes that typically span many years.

SOURCE: Goodwin 2001.

Chapter 10 for more on this topic as it relates to social media and democracy)? Some refer to these events as the "Capitol riot," which certainly captures their violent and at times chaotic nature. Others speak of an "insurrection," which suggests something like an organized attempt to overthrow the government. (Trump was subsequently impeached by Congress, in fact, for "inciting an insurrection," but although both the House and the Senate voted to convict him, the margin in the Senate fell just short of the 60 votes out of 100 that were needed.) Still others say it was an attempted *coup d'etat*. So what exactly happened?

The backdrop to January 6 was, of course, Trump's loss to Joe Biden in the November 2020 election. Despite the absence of any evidence of widespread irregularities in the election, a significant minority of congressional Republicans intended to challenge the electoral votes from several states on January 6, the day when Congress was scheduled to certify the electoral college vote. If these challenges were accepted by Vice President Mike Pence, who was to oversee the counting of electoral votes on that day, Biden would lack the necessary votes to become president.

Pence had no legal authority to refuse to certify any electoral votes, and he told Trump that he would not attempt to do so. (Some insurrectionists were later heard chanting, "Hang Mike Pence! Hang Mike Pence!") The goal of the insurrection was to stop the counting of those electoral votes which the insurgents (and allied members of Congress) deemed illegitimate, and thereby to prevent Biden's election. The goal, that is, was not exactly to overthrow the government. After all, Trump was still president. It was an attempt to keep Trump in power despite his defeat in the election. For this reason, some have likened the insurrection to what is known as an "executive coup" or "self-coup," the purpose of which is to keep a government in power which has either lost an election or anticipates losing the next election.

To succeed, however, executive coups, and *coups d'etat* in general, almost always require the support of the armed forces, or a big part of the armed forces. Trump did not have the support of any part of the armed forces on January 6. Just a few days before, in fact, all 10 living former U.S. secretaries of defense issued a letter warning Trump not to involve the military in his bid to change the results of the election. Without such support, the insurgents were unable to hold onto the Capitol for more than a few hours. Trump eventually ordered his supporters to leave the Capitol as the National Guard was gearing up to storm the buildings. The insurrection or executive coup—both labels capture important aspects of January 6—failed miserably.

Revolutions, Violence, and Other Forms of Conflict

22.4.2 Describe the potential role of violence in revolutions and different types of violent and nonviolent conflicts.

Many people view violence as an essential characteristic of revolutions, and many revolutions have in fact involved considerable violence among the parties contending for state power. This is especially true of social revolutions, which have threatened powerful elites. Foreign states, moreover, have often intervened militarily in revolutionary situations or attacked newly installed revolutionary governments, which they have often viewed as threats. Some revolutionary regimes, furthermore, have employed considerable violence to reorganize society along new lines. Still, the extent of violence in revolutions is quite variable, and some have occurred with comparatively little bloodshed. Some sociologists have detected a trend in recent decades toward relatively nonviolent revolutions (for example, Iran in 1979, Eastern Europe in 1989, Tunisia and Egypt in 2011, and Ukraine in 2014). For these reasons, violence is best viewed as a potential component of revolution, not as one of its defining characteristics.

Revolutions stand apart analytically from such kindred forms of political conflict as wars (interstate or civil), insurrections, riots, and *coups d'etat*. Historically, however, these latter forms of conflict have often been closely connected with revolutions or revolutionary situations (see the next section). Interstate wars, for example, sometimes help to cause revolutions by weakening armies—thereby creating "political opportunities" for revolutionary movements, as political process theorists would say—as well as by inflaming popular

An image from the violent assault on the U.S. capital building by supporters of Donald Trump attempting to stop the certification of the election of 2020. Having lost the election, Trump and his supporters made false claims that the vote count in a few states was fraudulent, and when dozens of federal courts rejected their claims for a lack of evidence, they attempted to reverse the outcome by force.

Archna Nautiyal/Shutterstock

grievances, including perceived threats to one's nation; in turn, revolutions often result in interstate wars, usually because foreign powers seek to destroy those revolutionary movements or regimes they perceive as threats. France, Russia, Vietnam, Cuba, Iran—all were invaded shortly after revolutionaries took power. The revolutionary situations created by radical social movements, furthermore, often take the form of civil wars, and radical movements bring about actual revolutions, of course, if they successfully seize state power.

Similarly, social movements that initially seek reforms within the existing political system—the kind of movements this chapter has focused on thus far—can become **revolutionary movements** if they ultimately attempt to overthrow the government, which may happen if the political order breaks down or when the government persistently refuses to implement the reforms desired by such movements. Spontaneous riots, furthermore, may help to precipitate revolutions, and riots have occurred frequently as a result of the breakdown of political authority that characterizes revolutionary situations. In sum, while revolutions, and especially social revolutions, are a distinctive and comparatively rare form of political conflict, they are often connected, whether as cause or consequence, with other and more frequently recurring types of conflict, including social movements.

Revolutionary Situations

22.4.3 Describe characteristics of revolutionary situations and how those situations can transform territories politically and socially.

Many movements and rebellions explicitly aim to depose oppressive governments and, sometimes, reorganize the social order from top to bottom. When such movements obtain substantial popular support, one may speak of the existence of a **revolutionary situation**: A situation in which two or more political groups or movements claim to be the rightful or legitimate rulers of a certain territory or population.

There have been hundreds of revolutionary situations around the globe during the past two centuries. Most movements that try to bring about revolutions, however, do not succeed in overthrowing the government. If the government's armed forces remain strong, revolutionaries are typically defeated or confined to peripheral regions within the national territory. Most revolutionary situations, in other words, do not result in actual political, let alone social, revolutions. A revolution typically requires the prior weakening or collapse of the government's "infrastructural power"—its capacity, that is, to enforce its will on the society that it claims to govern. Military might is the main source of a state's infrastructural power. While revolutionary movements sometimes muster the power to incapacitate governments (by winning over military officers, soldiers, and government officials, for example), such movements just as frequently overthrow governments that have already been fatally weakened by interstate wars, economic and fiscal crises, or divisions and conflicts among the rich and

powerful. The French Revolution, for example, occurred in part because the monarchy was in a state of fiscal collapse, and the Bolsheviks were able to seize power in Russia in 1917 partly because the Russian army had been decimated in what was then known as the Great War (that is, World War I).

Revolutionary situations, in other words, are those moments when governments come into conflict with social movements that are demanding political power; such situations arise when the regime can no longer manage or accommodate the competing interests and demands of the groups they are meant to govern, sometimes because elites themselves are in conflict. A revolutionary situation opens up the possibility of deep political and social change should a radical social movement emerge victorious.

The famous Russian revolutionary and Communist Party leader Vladimir Ilyich Lenin once said that revolutionary situations display "three major symptoms": (1) A crisis or split among the upper classes, (2) unusual suffering among the lower classes, and (3) "a considerable increase in the... independent historical action" of the lower classes (Lenin 1915, p. 213). Since Lenin's time, scholars of revolutions have developed these basic insights. The most crucial "symptom" Lenin lists—acute suffering among the masses—typically means that a population has lost many of its material resources. Some scholars of revolution understand revolutions as a product of **relative deprivation**—a feeling that one does not have what one deserves. Economic crises, wars, and even natural disasters can cause mass suffering. Ordinary people feel the consequences—they endure the loss of work or lowered wages, are sent into bloody and often unpopular wars, or suffer the breakdown or even collapse of institutions on which their survival depends (work, economic markets, transportation, schools, and so forth).

For governments, furthermore, such shocks disrupt the existing balance of political forces. To preserve regime stability, political elites may seek new allies from new sectors of the population. Acute shocks typically release ordinary folk from passivity, activating their grievances through new organizations. In sum, one precondition for revolutionary situations consists of massive disruptions that break down routinized systems of social control. Subsequently, explosions of political protest may place governments under great duress.

A notable example of a revolutionary situation was the Arab Spring of 2011. At that time, people in several Middle Eastern countries poured into the streets, demanding the removal of repressive dictators. Most of these dictators—in Tunisia, Egypt, Libya, Yemen, and Syria—had been in power for decades, but people were upset with the new economic crisis gripping the region. Food and fuel prices were rising, and young people in particular could not find the kind of work for which they had been educated—or sometimes any work at all. It is telling that the Arab Spring began with protests in Tunisia in December 2010, which were a response to the self-immolation of a young man named Mohamed Bouazizi, who was trying to survive by selling vegetables from a cart. But Bouazizi did not have a proper permit for his cart, and he burned himself in protest (he later died in hospital) after a municipal official (and her aides) confiscated his cart and publicly humiliated him. His protest served as the spark that prompted people who were already suffering or angry to engage in mass protests.

Profound social dislocations like mass unemployment may be necessary for revolutionary situations to emerge, but they are clearly insufficient. Lenin identified another indispensable condition for revolutionary situations: The shock must create a crisis or division among the upper classes, which in turn fractures the foundations of the government. These divisions and the resulting political destabilization provide an opening or opportunity that newly mobilized people can exploit. Such a political crisis typically occurs when the usual consensus over arrangements for settling the competing claims of economic elites collapses, often as a result of wars or state-led efforts at economic modernization that generate growing fiscal pressures on governments. As agreement over how the costs of fiscal and institutional reform should be distributed disintegrates, the institutional coherence of the government comes under enormous strain. The state's capacity to control and enforce its will on the population, its "infrastructural power," may begin to contract and even collapse.

Ruling-class disunity and state breakdown may follow two general scenarios. In the first, a crisis, such as a fiscal emergency provoked by international war, may generate instability as elites resist the tax burdens that state officials impose. The ensuing political crisis then serves to facilitate and exacerbate rebellion by ordinary people, who mobilize through existing networks and organizations. This is the story of the French, Russian, and Chinese revolutions (Skocpol 1979). In the second scenario, the shock unleashes mounting pressure from a social movement. No longer bound by the institutions of social control, this movement generates a crisis among the upper classes, who are pulled into opposing directions by the developing movement itself. One upper-class faction might strive to repress the growing pressures from below, clamping down on democratic rights, and generally resorting to coercion. Another faction, by contrast, might enact reforms, resigning itself to accommodating popular demands to preserve its rule. This is the story of the Cuban, Iranian, and Nicaraguan revolutions and of the Arab Spring. In either scenario, the cohesion of the police and armed forces is crucial for preventing the fall of the regime. If the costs of war, repression, or reform divide or weaken the military and undermine its ability to act in a unified and decisive manner against popular movements, then revolution becomes likely or even inevitable.

In short, elite division and institutional collapse can either result from or result in a popular movement from below. In either event, the upper classes may find it impossible to coexist with the existing regime. In that case, the revolutionary crisis intensifies as disaffected upper-class groups undermine the power and legitimacy of state institutions.

Revolutionary Movements and the Seizure of State Power

22.4.4 Discuss the two requirements for a strong revolutionary movement.

These two conditions—elite divisions and institutional collapse—when combined would seem to be sufficient to produce a revolutionary situation. If ordinary people are thrust into collective action because the regulatory capacity of key institutions has eroded, and upper-class divisions have led to the weakening of the state's infrastructural power, a powerful insurrection would seem likely. However, Lenin raised a third condition: A social movement's capacity to take advantage of elite divisions and institutional collapse in order to place radical transformation on the national agenda. Simply stated, an existing regime is likely to survive a crisis and remain stable if ordinary people prove incapable of

The overthrow of the brutal dictatorship of Nicolae Ceaușescu in communist Romania came as a shock when it happened. Ceaușescu was thought to have complete control over his regime's powerful security forces, known as the Securitate, and the army. But on December 22, as protests spread throughout the capital, leading members of the army and the security forces refused to order their troops to fire on the crowds (and where they did try, the troops mostly sided with the protestors). As these previously nonexistent divisions among the elite appeared, the dictator Ceaușescu realized he had no hope of restoring order and tried to flee. The entire collapse of the communist government happened in hours, like a house of cards collapsing from a single touch.

Amr Dalsh/REUTERS/Alamy Stock Photo

The dramatic Arab Spring revolts in the Middle East in 2011 are often described as "revolutions," but few succeeded in challenging the power and authority of the ruling elite, even. In Egypt, mass protests in Tahrir Square in the capital of Cairo (shown here) did help to force the dictator Hosni Mubarak from power, along with a wave of strikes and work stoppages around the country. But after a period of uncertainty, the Egyptian military took control of the government and headed off any significant challenges to the social order.

organizing themselves into a revolutionary social movement that can effectively topple it.

Consider the case of Morocco during the Arab Spring. Morocco is one of the poorest countries in North Africa and the Middle East—poorer than Tunisia and Egypt—and the vast majority of its people are struggling economically. But while there were some protests calling for political reforms in Morocco following the revolutions in Tunisia and Egypt, they were comparatively small and intermittent. As a result, Morocco's King Mohammed VI was easily able to hold onto power after enacting a few modest reforms.

Two things are required for a revolutionary movement to create a revolutionary situation. The first requirement is that the movement (or its supporters) must possess considerable collective leverage over the rich and powerful. When ordinary people play necessary or highly valued roles in crucial institutions, their threats of withdrawing their collective contributions are disruptive. Important industries, for example, depend on the labor of ordinary workers to function; when workers withdraw that labor during a strike, these industries shut down, and their owners cannot make profits. When rank-and-file soldiers in an army refuse orders to attack protesters, the army is useless to elites. Thus, when the lower classes enjoy structural power rooted in their essential institutional roles, their capacity for generating costly disruptions is enhanced (Schwartz 1976). In the context of an economic crisis, elite vulnerability to such disruptions grows. The central point is that the institutional roles of the lower classes must translate into a capacity to undertake collective actions that challenge the power of the upper classes.

Most accounts of the Egyptian uprising in 2011 focus on the occupation of Tahrir Square in central Cairo by hundreds of thousands of people (see the image in the previous section). But the dictatorship of Hosni Mubarak may have been more deeply shaken by the strikes and work stoppages that occurred during the occupation, culminating in a general strike in the days before Mubarak's resignation (Schwartz 2011). (A general strike occurs when workers in an entire city or country refuse to work, as opposed to workers in a single industry or factory.) The strikes hurt many businesses across the country—the tourist industry was already reeling from the loss of business caused by the political unrest—which may have convinced top military officers (many of whom are also businessmen) that Mubarak had become a threat to their own interests. The military refused to disperse the protesters in Tahrir Square, urged Mubarak to resign, and took power for themselves.

The second requirement for a strong revolutionary movement is what Lenin called "independent historical action" by the masses. In other words, activists must secure the political and ideological resources they need to convert increased political activity and leverage into decisive collective action. These resources include ideas, organization, and tactics as well as the ability to obtain, process, produce, and deploy information among followers. Clearly, ideas and ideology play an important role in the origins and outcomes of revolutions. However, they do not operate as autonomous forces that drive the contenders in a revolutionary situation. After all, radical ideologies have existed and appealed to many people in most if not all modern societies. They have seldom, however, given rise to strong revolutionary movements, much less to revolutions.

Culture, broadly understood, matters in revolutionary situations when particular ideologies are able to shift the balance of forces, weakening authorities and upper classes and strengthening ordinary people. When social dislocations and state crises offer openings for radical social movements, the tactical decisions and framing work of activists can be decisive. When the strategies and ideologies promoted by radical activists resonate with ordinary people—that is, when *frame alignment* occurs—and when they are not only consistent with but also promote increased popular mobilization, thereby maximizing its disruptive impact, they can be the final necessary ingredient that provides such mobilization with the capacity to overthrow a regime. In fact, Lenin ended his famous statement on revolutionary situations with an important qualification: "Not every revolutionary situation," he explained, "gives rise to a revolution; revolution arises only out of a situation in which the above-mentioned objective changes are accompanied by a subjective change, namely, the ability of the revolutionary class to take revolutionary mass action strong enough to break (or dislocate) the old government, which never, not even in a period of crisis, 'falls,' if it is not toppled over" (Lenin 1915, p. 213). Revolutions, in other words, are only possible when there are strong social movements that can topple governments and elites which are in deep crisis.

Political Environments That Encourage Revolutionary Movements

22.4.5 **Describe the kind of political environments that encourage revolutionary movements.**

Revolutionary situations are likely to arise in authoritarian and repressive political contexts. In fact, no popular revolutionary movement has ever overthrown a long-consolidated democratic regime, although sometimes a fraudulently elected government can be overthrown by mass protests, as happened in the Ukraine in 2014. The great social revolutions of the twentieth century, for example, toppled monarchs and rulers (as in Russia, China, Cuba, Iran, and Nicaragua), extremely repressive colonial regimes (as in Vietnam and Algeria), and the Soviet-imposed Communist regimes of Eastern Europe. In fact, revolutionary movements tend to prosper when governments sponsor or defend—with violence when necessary—economic and social arrangements that are widely regarded as unjust (that is, not as simply unfortunate or inevitable). In certain societies, unless citizens see state officials sponsoring or protecting those arrangements—through legal codes, taxation, conscription, and, ultimately, force—revolutionary movements aimed at overthrowing the state are unlikely to become strong. People may blame their social "superiors" or employers for their plight, for example, or even whole classes of such elites, yet they might not challenge the government unless they widely perceive that it will stand behind and defend those elites at all costs.

Often, revolutionaries and activists gain strength from indiscriminate, but not overwhelming, violence by weak states against social movements and oppositional politicians and activists, which unintentionally helps revolutionaries. For reasons of simple self-defense, people who are targeted by the state may join clandestine groups or even arm themselves. Those with families or friends who have been victimized by the state may also join or support revolutionary movements to seek revenge against the perpetrators. Social movements and political parties have generally turned to disruptive strategies, including armed struggle, only after their previous efforts to secure change through legal means were violently repressed. Under repressive conditions, ordinary people often view mass disruption, including armed struggle, as a legitimate and reasonable means of political contestation.

The connection between repressive authoritarianism and revolution is clearly illustrated by the Arab Spring of 2011. The six countries that experienced broad popular uprisings—Tunisia, Egypt, Libya, Bahrain, Yemen, and Syria—are dissimilar in many ways. These countries have different levels of economic development and urbanization; some are ethnically divided, others more homogenous; some have been very close allies of Western powers, others not. But what they all had in common were longstanding dictators (or a monarch, in the case of Bahrain) who would not tolerate threats to their continued rule. Their violence and intransigence forced their political opponents to give up their dreams of incremental reforms and take to the streets. Only disruptive mass movements, most people concluded, could bring an end to the reign of these autocrats. And of course they were right. Mass protests in Tunisia and Egypt convinced the armed forces in those countries to abandon their support for dictators. In Libya, Yemen, and Syria, mass protests led to divisions in and defections from the armevd forces, resulting in much bloodier conflicts. Only the king in Bahrain managed to retain the solid support of his military forces—supplemented by troops from neighboring Saudi Arabia—in the face of a broad popular uprising.

Fidel Castro (1926–2016), shown here during the Cuban Revolution of 1959, led a revolutionary movement that overthrew the existing government by mobilizing a mostly peasant army in remote areas and later building support in urban areas. Castro is one of the most famous revolutionary leaders of the twentieth century, but his successes came from the ability to first mobilize supporters in the countryside, then strike at a time of perceived crisis in the existing government (which was widely viewed as corrupt).

Tor Eigeland/Alamy Stock Photo

In contrast to authoritarian regimes, let us now consider governments that are widely perceived to be more liberal and democratic (for example, the United States, Canada, Western Europe, Colombia, Mexico, South Africa, India, and Japan). More liberal and democratic governments tend to pacify, but hardly do away with, social conflict. Elections have sometimes been described as the "democratic translation of the class struggle" (Lipset [1960] 1981). Democracy channels a variety of social conflicts—including class conflicts—into party competition for votes and the lobbying of representatives by interest groups. People are not as tempted to rebel against the government because they know that, in only a few years, they have a chance to elect new leaders. In addition, democracies have generally provided a context in which social movements can win concessions from economic and political elites, although this often requires a good deal of disruption. But movements that aim at overthrowing democratic governments rarely win much popular support unless those governments (or their armies) push people into rebellion by indiscriminately repressing protesters. By and large, however, people prefer using the ballot box, which is why there have been few large-scale attempts to overthrow long-established democracies in Western Europe and North America.

Democracy, then, dramatically reduces the likelihood of revolutionary change, but not because it always brings about social justice. Formal democracy is fully compatible with widespread poverty, inequality, and popular grievances of all sorts. This is why movements for social justice so often arise in democratic contexts. But, again, these movements almost always view the state in a democratic society as an instrument to be pressured and influenced, not as something to be seized or smashed. This said, the spread of democracy will not necessarily render revolution *passé* as a form of political struggle. Radical leaders and parties have sometimes been able to amass a broad following in democratic contexts and to win elections (for example, Salvador Allende in Chile in 1970 and Hugo Chavez in Venezuela in 1998, 2000, and 2006). Perhaps during the twenty-first century we will see some democratically elected governments attempt to revolutionize economic and political institutions. As yet, however, the democratic route to revolution has never been successfully traveled.

Conclusion: The Future of Movements and Revolutions

We began this chapter by looking at the Black Lives Matter movement. Like other social movements, BLM was not entirely spontaneous but grew out of the planned actions of preexisting networks of activists. The movement's tactics were not spontaneous, either. BLM activists, like activists before them, chose tactics with which they were already familiar. And the movement spread rapidly across the country, like movements before it, because it framed its ideas about police violence and White supremacy in a way that appealed to a great many people during a time when police shootings, mass incarceration, and death and illness from the COVID-19 pandemic were inescapable realities for so many Blacks and other Americans. There were also networks of activists in cities and towns across the country, most of whom had been active in previous movements, who could spread the movement's ideas and organize protests of their own. None of this would surprise sociologists who have studied past movements.

The history of social movements and revolutions suggests that we will undoubtedly see many more in the years ahead. As long as ordinary people feel that the rich, powerful, and privileged are oppressing them (or at least ignoring their needs and interests), and as long as people can safely connect with one another and find ways to pressure (or overthrow) the rich, powerful, and privileged, social movements and revolutions will remain part of the human condition.

The Big Questions Revisited 22

22.1 What Are Social Movements? Social movements play a crucial role in contemporary societies. Through them, we can learn about the world around us. We started the chapter by defining social movements and exploring what we can learn by studying them.

Researching Social Movements

Politics, Human Action, and Social Change

Learning Objective 22.1.1: Discuss how social movements affect political and social structures.

Moral Sensibilities

Learning Objective 22.1.2: Discuss how social movements contribute to a society's moral codes.

Understanding Social Movements Today

Learning Objective 22.1.3: Define the political process perspective and discuss how understanding social movements can vary as movements change over time.

Key Terms

riot (p. 633)   social movement (p. 633)   fad (p. 633)   political process model (p. 635)

22.2 Why Do Movements Emerge, and Who Joins Them? The most frequently asked question about social movements is why they emerge when they do. In this section, we examined how movements take shape and looked at who joins or supports social movements.

Movement Origins and Recruitment

How Movements Take Shape

Learning Objective 22.2.1: Analyze the political, economic, organizational, demographic, and cultural factors that ignite and fuel social movements.

Cultural Aspects of Social Movements

Learning Objective 22.2.2: Explain how cultural approaches to the study of social movements differ from resource mobilization and political process approaches.

Recruitment: Joining or Supporting Movements

Learning Objective 22.2.3: Explain how individual traits, biographical availability, framing, and cultural attitudes influence participation in social movements.

Key Terms

resource mobilization approach (p. 636)   social movement organization (SMO) (p. 636)   social network (p. 637)   waves (p. 638) free rider (p. 639)   biographical availability (p. 639)   framing (p. 641)   collective identity (p. 641)   moral shock (p. 643)

22.3 What Tactics Do Movements Use, and What Outcomes Do They Achieve? Why do movements use certain tactics and not others? Why are some violent and others nonviolent? Why do movements decline or disappear? In this section, we looked at what movements do and what changes and outcomes movements bring about, including unintended consequences.

Movement Tactics and Outcomes

The Strategies of Movements

Learning Objective 22.3.1: Discuss how organizers and participants increase awareness and further the goals of movements.

Tactical Repertoires of Movements

Learning Objective 22.3.2: Explain why social movements use certain tactics but not others.

The Decline and Disappearance of Movements

Learning Objective 22.3.3: Explain the sociopolitical reasons for the decreasing popularity of certain movements.

Outcomes

Learning Objective 22.3.4: Distinguish between successful and unsuccessful outcomes.

Cultural Consequences of Movements

Learning Objective 22.3.5: Discuss the cultural consequences of movements.

Key Terms

repertoires (p. 645)   free space (p. 645)

22.4 What Are Revolutions, and Why Do They Occur? Why are some social movements revolutionary, and what causes revolutionary situations to occur? When and why have revolutionary movements been able to take state power? We concluded the chapter by examining how authoritarian and democratic governments shape social conflict and the prospects for revolution.

Understanding Revolutions

Defining "Revolution"

Learning Objective 22.4.1: Distinguish between political and social revolutions.

Revolutions, Violence, and Other Forms of Conflict

Learning Objective 22.4.2: Describe the potential role of violence in revolutions and different types of violent and nonviolent conflicts.

Revolutionary Situations

Learning Objective 22.4.3: Describe characteristics of revolutionary situations and how those situations can transform territories politically and socially.

Revolutionary Movements and the Seizure of State Power

Learning Objective 22.4.4: Discuss the two requirements for a strong revolutionary movement.

Political Environments That Encourage Revolutionary Movements

Learning Objective 22.4.5: Describe the kind of political environments that encourage revolutionary movements.

Key Terms

revolution (p. 650)   revolutionary movement (p. 652)   revolutionary situation (p. 652)   relative deprivation (p. 653)

Chapter 23
Population, Aging, and Social Demography

by Lawrence L. Wu with Jeff Manza

How do social scientists think about population, and why is it an important topic for understanding societies? We can begin to understand its importance by reflecting on our own families. Let's look at holiday gatherings as an example. In my (author Lawrence Wu's) case, my parents divorced when I was a teenager, so rather than having holiday gatherings at a parent's home, the Wu family usually gets together at my sister's with her spouse and two kids. I would host at my home, but since I do not have children, and since my mother enjoys spending time with my niece and nephew, she flies from Los Angeles to stay at my sister's. Holiday gatherings mean holiday meals seated among a few generations, perhaps including in-laws, around the holiday dinner table (or tables in the case of our family). We do what many families do at holiday gatherings: We eat too much, drink too much, exchange presents, talk, and watch the kids play.

And talking, at least in my family, means recounting family history, a topic that invariably comes up during the holidays. Here's a quick sketch of my family's history. Both my parents were born in China, in Shanghai, in 1930. They came to the United States in 1949, attended college, met each other in 1956, and married in 1957. I was born a year later, and my sister was born about two years after me. (This means that both of us were born at the tail end of the baby boom, something we discuss in greater detail later.) My mother's parents had a total of four children, all of whom were born in China: my two uncles (one of whom died of AIDS in the late 1980s), my mother, and one daughter who died in childhood. My father's parents had nine children, all of whom were also born in China: Two died during childhood, and the remaining seven are my father, one uncle, and five aunts.

This pattern of large families in past generations and much smaller families in current generations turns out to be central

to understanding a key demographic debate of the past few decades. In the 1960s and 1970s, when I was growing up, it was taken for granted that *the* most pressing population issue was rapid population growth. *The Population Bomb*, published in 1968 by American biologist and educator Paul Ehrlich, summarized this view, noting that the world's population was growing much too rapidly and that there would soon be very dire consequences (Ehrlich 1968). Ehrlich's argument was not new; in fact, 180 years earlier, English scholar Thomas Malthus (1798) also argued that rapid increases in population would lead to widespread misery.

My Sociological Imagination

LAWRENCE L. WU

I was born in New York City but mostly grew up in Los Angeles, in the northwest corner of the San Fernando Valley in a city called Chatsworth. As a sociologist, my areas of specialization are in social demography, particularly in the social demography of the family, meaning that I have written on fertility (and especially nonmarital fertility), cohabitation, marriage, and divorce. Many social demographers use big data sets in their research, and I am no different, so I'm more than a bit of a numbers geek (something you'll see, for better or worse, in this chapter). As you'll also learn, what fascinates me the most as a social scientist is the fact that so much of our social world has changed so very quickly and what this means, in turn, for each of us as individuals living in an ever-changing world. This also means that as a numbers geek, one of my other areas of specialization is in statistical methods for studying change, both change historically and change as people's lives unfold from birth through adolescence and into adulthood.

Population change represents a critical underlying factor of social development, one that is frequently overlooked by social commentators. The size and age distribution of a population, as well as key population subgroups, and the trends in both, are vitally important factors for policymakers and governments to consider.

Florian Kahle/Alamy Stock Photo

659

Today, most social scientists who study population issues agree there is not one but two pressing problems related to population growth. One is, as before, the problems facing nations and regions in the world in which population growth continues to be very rapid and in which it would be highly desirable for population growth to be curbed. The second, seemingly paradoxically, concerns nations and regions of the world in which populations are aging rapidly and may even experience decline, sometimes at a rapid pace. For those nations facing rapid population aging and potential decline, it would be highly desirable for these trends to be curbed. Sociological theories of population, which we will explore in this chapter, address this paradox.

As we will also see, one of the emerging patterns across the globe is that people are living longer, which creates a novel set of problems that societies of the past, when life expectancy was much lower, did not have to face. For example,

growing numbers of people will face the challenge of managing chronic diseases that mostly strike older people, such as heart disease, diabetes, or dementia. And when large numbers of people face similar challenges these become societal problems. For instance, the cost of treating chronic health conditions in old age are much greater than the typical health issues of younger people. Further, aging societies also face challenges in their labor markets and old-age social security systems: they may not have enough people of working age to support all of the older retired workers who rely on government pensions to survive.

In this chapter we study the process of social change and public policy through the lens of population research. For sociologists, a population perspective sheds light on trends and issues that might otherwise be overlooked. We hope to demonstrate the importance of examining population and population trends for studying broader trends in society, including the impact of an aging population.

The Big Questions

1. **Why study population?** Between 1910 and 2012, the world's population doubled in size—not once but twice. The world's population may not double in size again, but it continues to grow. The study of population has a long history. Although the sociological subfield of demography began to take form in the late nineteenth century, attempts to study population trends can be traced back much further, as far back as 6,000 years when the very first population census was taken. There are many reasons why governments and policymakers need to know about population trends, including the risk of overpopulation. In this section, we describe some of those reasons.

2. **How do populations change over time?** To better understand the dynamics of population change, in this section we look at how mortality and fertility have changed for different nations and what these changes might imply for the demographic futures of these nations. We also note that migration, the subject of Chapter 24, has frequently been a factor in population change.

3. **What factors influence fertility?** Populations change over time largely because fertility practices also have been changing (for example, the decision to have a child). In most countries around the world, women are having fewer babies than 50 or 100 years ago. Why is this happening? In this section, we explore some of the leading explanations for declining fertility.

4. **How are trends in aging and mortality emerging as critical issues in many societies?** Some countries have many very young people but very few old people, while others have many old people currently and will have even more old people in the future as life expectancy increases. What do these trends mean for employment and health conditions in countries like these? In this section, we ask about the demographic implications when populations begin to age.

Matthew Williams-Ellis/Robertharding/Alamy Stock Photo

POPULATION AND CENSUSES

As noted in the introduction, Paul Erlich's *The Population Bomb* summarized a pervasive mid-twentieth-century concern—that the world's population was growing much too quickly and that this ticking time bomb would soon have catastrophic effects. Why were Ehrlich and many others so alarmed about the world's population growth? If we look at the growth of the world's population over the centuries, there could have been reason to fear that we could eventually have too many people on the earth. How long has it taken for the world's population to double in size? We reached a landmark around 2012, when the world's population hit 7 billion. Let's look at some global population data in Table 23.1. In 480 BCE, the world's population is estimated to have been about 110 million. It wasn't until 800 CE that the world's population reached 220 million, thus taking 1,280 years to double. In 1330, or 530 years later, the world's population doubled again, and it doubled again between 1330 and 1810. (The world's population fluctuated dramatically during this latter period

because of the Black Plague and the repeated epidemic outbreaks that followed, in the fourteenth century.)

The crucial part of the story starts around 1810, when the world's population began growing much more rapidly than ever before. The number of human beings alive doubled in the 100 years between 1810 and 1910, doubling again during the next 57 years, and again in the next 45 years, at which point we get to the approximately 7 billion people alive today.

So the impression that Table 23.1 provides is simple but dramatic, and on the face of it looks very much like the projections of Ehrlich (and Malthus before him). While it once took 1,280 years for the world's population to double, the most recent doubling took only 45 years. Wouldn't these numbers imply that Ehrlich was right? To answer this, let's pose the same question, but instead of looking backward historically, let's ask it looking forward to the future. This means asking: How many years will it take for the world's population to double again, from 7 to 14 billion? And will the next doubling be in about 30, 40, 50, or 60 years?

Perhaps surprisingly, the answer is "none of the above" (Lam 2011). That is, what nearly all demographers (social scientists who do research on populations and population trends) who study this question would say is that, unlike what Ehrlich believed and unlike past history, the world's population is unlikely to double again to 14 billion, certainly not in the foreseeable future and probably not ever. In the next section, we'll continue exploring why most demographers believe, unlike Ehrlich, that the world's population will not continue to increase in the way it has in the recent past. Before we get there, however, it is important to understand why population issues are so important in the first place.

Table 23.1 Doubling of the World's Population through History

Date	Population (in milions)	Years to Double Population Size
480 BCE	110	
800 CE	220	1,280
1330 CE	440	530
1810 CE	875	480
1910 CE	1,750	100
1967 CE	3,500	57
2012 CE	7,000	45

SOURCE: Based on data from U.S. Census Bureau, 2012.

The first regular population surveys were conducted in the Roman Empire, where the term Census was first used.

The Census and Population Research

23.1.1 Discuss why it is relevant to study population trends.

Although the field of **demography**—the study of population—as we know it today began to take form in the late nineteenth century, the desire for knowledge about population trends goes back thousands of years. Most scholars believe the first population **census** took place nearly 6,000 years ago in Babylonia (an area that is part of modern Iraq). A census is a count of everyone (or everything) residing in a particular location; a national census attempts to **enumerate** (or systematically count) all persons living in the country at the time the census is conducted. (Early census data rarely reflected complete population records, as they typically ignored enslaved people and sometimes women and children, but sometimes also included cattle!) The Babylonians were very systematic, attempting to count not only people but also the amount of land, livestock, and the quantity of basic foodstuffs held by each household. There is evidence that the ancient Egyptians conducted censuses around this time as well. In the pharaonic era in Egypt, two censuses were taken in 3340 BCE and again in 3050 BCE. It appears that the Egyptian censuses were used for some early population planning initiatives, such as deciding how much land each family in the Nile Delta region would receive.

The term *census* (to describe a population survey) originated in ancient Rome, from the Latin word *censere*, and for a period of time the Roman Empire carried out censuses every five years in order to locate people, identify recruits for its military forces, and collect taxes. Independently around the same time (around 2 CE), the Han Dynasty in China conducted an early census that is especially well-regarded for accuracy in identifying a

population of almost 58 million people in the lands ruled by the dynasty, which would have been approximately one-sixth of the world's population. (It is remarkable that 2000 years later, about one-sixth of the world's population still lives in China!) Other early censuses were conducted in places like ancient Israel, India, and the Inca Empire in Central America. The record of these early censuses provides fascinating insight into the abilities and efforts of early governments and rulers to achieve even minimal understanding of the peoples they sought to control and rule. The use of population censuses largely fell into disuse, however, during the Middle Ages (500-1500 CE). One exception is a famous census undertaken by William the Conqueror in England and Wales in 1086, which attempted to identify all landowners and land holdings being brought under Norman rule, presumably in an effort to improve and enhance tax collection. The results were compiled into a book known as the *Domesday Book* (perhaps because, like the Biblical Day of Judgment, there was no appealing it as a record of legal title to land).

The modern census can trace its origins to the earliest stirrings of the Industrial Revolution and the settlement of national borders in the eighteenth century. National censuses in this period included Prussia (1719), Russia (1722–23), Switzerland (1747), Sweden (1749), Spain (1768), the United States (1790), and France and England (1801). England and the United States both established that a new census would be conducted every 10 years (that timetable is even written into the U.S. Constitution), and both countries (along with many other nations) have established and maintained regularity in their population counts. Today, governments all around the world, whether democratic

The *Doomsday Book* is the surviving record of a population and land census conducted in England in 1086.

or authoritarian, generally profess to share an interest in population trends in their country. They invest significant resources in attempting to map those trends through a national census, often supplemented by other types of population data collection.

Given how pervasive the national census has become, we might want to ask the question: Why do virtually all governments think it is so important to know how many people are living in a country, region, city, or town? Several key reasons can be identified:

- As noted, many nations, both historically and now, want to know about the size of their population because this determines how much can be collected in taxes and how many persons (typically men) might be available should war or other armed conflict arise.

- Population analysis is essential for estimating future social needs, such as whether or not to build more roads, houses, schools, churches, office buildings, or any other socially important physical infrastructure. Before making those decisions, officials and policymakers need to have a good idea whether (and how fast) the population of an area might be growing.

- Population size is important for determining political boundaries in democratic countries. For example, seats in a national legislature (such as Congress) are often based on population size. Currently, each district in the U.S. House of Representatives has approximately 700,000 people.

- Population trends can have a huge impact on a national (or regional) economy. The composition of a nation's (or region's) population will impact how productive it will be and is a big factor in predicting whether to invest (or not) in business and jobs in the area or country. For example, a country with a large percentage of college graduates can offer businesses a more skilled and adaptable workforce than a country with a small percentage of college graduates.

- Population trends also have important consequences for government policy. If there are too many young people, jobs for those seeking to enter the labor market might be scarce and create social pressures without some effort to generate opportunities. If there are too many older people working beyond a country's widely accepted retirement age, the cost of providing them with pensions may become prohibitively expensive (as some countries around the world are now facing).

- Businesses are also keenly interested in the demographic characteristics of a population because many things they sell are geared to specific segments of society. Thus, clothes, music, and other goods and services bought by young people (one *demographic*) are often very different than those bought by older adults.

These are some of the foundational reasons why governments, businesses, researchers, and others find it important to know about populations. But the study of populations is also important because it provides valuable insight into the changing nature of societies. To say that a country or city has a population of X at one point in time, and a population of Y at another, hardly exhausts what we can learn about the study of population. The subfield of **social demography** uses population research to study societal trends. Here, for example, are just a few of the kinds of population-based trends that social demographers study and that provide very important insights.

- *Racial and Ethnic Composition*: Many societies, including the United States, are undergoing significant changes in the racial and ethnic mix of their populations, driven primarily by the movement of people across borders and by differential birth rates among key population subgroups. The shift in the population size of various groups accumulates over time, and demographers have developed ways of seeing trends before they begin to become clear to everyone.

- *Marriage and the Family*: As rates of divorce and the percentage of children being raised by a single parent have changed in recent decades, demographers have not only charted the basic trends in families and family types, but also explored the consequences for children growing up with a single parent, in poverty, or both.

- *Employment Issues*: Just as people and the families they grow up in change, so too do jobs—and frequently we can see mismatches in a region or even an entire country in the availability of jobs and the availability of workers with (or without) particular sets of skills.

- *Life Expectancy*: How long can the average person born in a particular country or region today expect to live (and how does that figure differ for subgroups in a population, such as men and women or ethnic majorities and minorities)? The answer to this question is interesting in its own right (rising life expectancy around the globe is one of the most important changes that have occurred over the past 100 years), but it can tell us a lot about more than that. For example, it is often hard to compare the quality of life in two very different societies, or over time. But by looking at differences or changes in life expectancy, we can begin to draw some intriguing conclusions. How long people in any society can expect to live will be determined in part by the quality of food they have access to, the quality of the health care they receive, the quality of the water they drink and air that they breathe, even the amount of stress that daily living imposes. When life expectancy is rising in a country or region, it is almost certain that many other things are improving as well (Deaton 2013). (We'll talk more about life expectancy later in the chapter.)

These examples highlight some of the many ways in which population research can provide information even before events actually happen. Because population research is partly about documenting what are known as **stylized facts** (empirical information we can surmise or determine with a great deal of certainty) about population and population trends, it provides the foundation for much of the rest of the social sciences. Many important debates and questions, including many of the questions we have been posing throughout this book, have a population component. Those include changes in social structure, urban/suburban/rural residence, education, religious involvements, political participation by different groups, crime rates (for example, who commits crimes), and prison populations.

Studying Population

23.1.2 Identify ways in which population is studied.

Population dynamics, the subject of this chapter, concerns how the size of any place or group has *changed*, either in the past or how it changing in the present or the future. That place or group could be anything from a small town all the way up to the entire world population, or it could be the number of Jews in America or the number of Muslims across the globe. Population dynamics is a central topic of research for demographers. It involves issues that reach far beyond adding up the number of births and deaths. In particular, understanding population dynamics requires a detailed understanding of demography's "big three": **fertility** (the birth rate, typically measured by the number of live births per female of childbearing years), **mortality** (typically measured by the number of deaths in a particular calendar year), and **migration** (how many people move into and out of a given region or country). In this chapter, our focus will be on the first two: fertility and mortality. In Chapter 24, migration is treated at much greater length

How a region's or nation's population will change over time is determined by these three factors: how many people are born (fertility), how many people die (mortality), and how many move in or out (migration). Thus, to be able to estimate how many people will be in the United States in 2030, we need to know the size of the U.S. population in 2010, estimate the number of births between 2010 and 2030, minus the estimated number deaths during this same period, plus the numbers who move into the country, minus the numbers who move out of the country.

This may seem like simple arithmetic. It is much complicated than that. The less-than-simple part is at the heart of population dynamics: How is it that populations change over time? And if population size is determined by fertility, mortality, and migration, then it necessarily follows that understanding population change requires *both* describing changes in fertility, mortality, and migration *and* understanding what might be causing these changes. All of these make population issues much more interesting and much more challenging to social scientists.

Here's a basic example to illustrate how one change affects another. Let's suppose that in Society A, women and their partners suddenly decide to have fewer children; in fact, they want to have only 1 or 2 rather than 3. (Until recently, Society A couples preferred to have 2 or 3 children, but not as many as 4.) At first glance, this change might not seem like such a big deal; but the impact on the population of this society will be increasingly dramatic over time because there will be many fewer children than before. That is, if the average Society A woman has 1.5 children, in 5 years, there will be significantly fewer kindergarten students than before. At first, perhaps only a few teachers and school administrators will notice (and some may be laid off from their jobs because of the falling number of students). But further down the line, the implications become even more significant. In 18 years, there will be fewer children applying to colleges, which may put pressure on some schools to find students. A possible benefit of having fewer young adults is that there will also be fewer children of peak crime years (which tend to be in the late teens and early 20s), so there may be less crime. But not all consequences may be positive: One significant

Mark Bussell

Social demographers studying families and family change combine analyses of population trends with the study of the motivations and behaviors of individuals and different population groups.

consequence will be fewer entry-level workers than before, and employers may not be able to find all of the workers they need. A declining workforce, if it is not corrected, will eventually mean slower economic growth and pressure on government budgets as a result.

Demographers will be the first to notice that the number of live births each year per woman has declined, and if their research is properly noticed, government officials can begin to try to respond appropriately. A first step might be to learn not just how much decline in the birth rate has occurred, but also to examine why. This could result from any number of factors. For example, more women may want to have careers, and may feel that having fewer (or no) children is a better way to organize their lives. Perhaps improved methods of birth control (which result in fewer unexpected pregnancies) are contributing to the decline. It could be concentrated among some groups of women but not others. Changes in marital patterns may be a factor. (If more couples choose to cohabitate but not marry, this may affect the numbers of children who are born.) While fully answering the question of why the birth rate is falling may require using many of the tools of a sociological imagination, we can glean important insights by looking at what and how particular population groups are changing.

BIG QUESTION 23.2 How Do Populations Change over Time?

Jani-Markus Häsä/Alamy Stock Photo

POPULATION DYNAMICS

To better understand the dynamics of population change, let's look at how mortality and fertility have changed for a few different nations, and what these changes might imply for the demographic futures of these nations.

The First Demographic Transition

23.2.1 Define the first demographic transition and its role in understanding how populations change.

The **first demographic transition** is the transition by a region or country from a period of high fertility and high mortality to a period of low fertility and low mortality (Notestein 1953; Davis 1963; Coale 1973; Bulatao and Casterline 2001). Before the transition, in the period of high fertility/high mortality, there is a large number of births but also a large number of deaths (average life-expectancy is low by modern standards). In the low-fertility, low-mortality world, by contrast, relatively fewer babies are born but their likelihood of living into old age goes way up.

To understand this part of the history of population trends, one that has occurred in many countries around the world, we need to concentrate on a set of stylized facts that we know with great certainty. These stylized facts allow us to describe the characteristic features of the first demographic transition. The first demographic transition is about historical change; specifically, it is a story about change in fertility and mortality and those two elements within three historical demographic periods: pretransition, mid-transition, and posttransition.

For nearly all of human history (and thus before the first demographic transition), both mortality and fertility were very high. Fertility tended to be a bit higher than mortality, but only very slightly, and this meant that the world's population grew, but very slowly. So, for much of human history, high fertility and high mortality were common, and the world as a whole was in a pretransition era.

Now, what happens in the middle of the first demographic transition? Looking across large numbers of countries and over long historical periods, we can see some similar patterns. During this middle phase, societies typically see a decline in mortality first, followed later by a decline in fertility. If we think about it, this probably quickly makes sense. If many babies and small children are likely to die in a high-mortality society, a family may choose to have more children than they might truly want in the hopes that enough will survive to be an appropriately sized family (for most of human history until the industrial revolution, having enough children to work in agriculture was a critical consideration). As early-life mortality declines, however, a family can be confident that if they want to have three children, they do not need to give birth to four or five.

Putting these pieces together, the story of the first demographic transition involves (1) an initial pretransition period characterized by high fertility and high mortality, then (2) a transitional period in which mortality first declines followed by a decline in fertility, and then (3) a posttransition period in which both fertility and mortality are low.

So, let's focus on the transitional period in the middle, where mortality begins to decline but fertility remains high. Many societies enter and stay in the phase for extended periods of time, during which their populations will grow rapidly. This means that in this middle period, we see something very different and something very new. This is the world that Thomas Malthus and Paul Ehrlich observed and wrote about and which seemed to each of them (writing 150 years apart) to imply that the world faced a ticking population bomb. For Malthus, in 1798 the problem was readily observed in population growth he observed in England and later elsewhere in Europe. For Ehrlich, writing in the late 1960s, the problem was not excessive growth in Europe or other rich countries, but rather poor countries in places like China, India, other Asian countries, and Africa.

Both analysts focused on the high fertility rates of the time in the places they focused on, but they didn't take into account the other crucial part of the first demographic transition, which is that fertility does not typically remain high forever; it eventually declines, but only after mortality has begun its decline. And this is another crucial part of the story: In the middle of the first demographic transition, population growth can be very rapid when mortality falls but fertility remains high. In such a situation, a population analyst can easily make the mistake of thinking that this situation may continue indefinitely until there is not enough food to go around.

The final part of the story, which is perhaps the most interesting and most consequential, is that once fertility decline has begun (or in some versions of the story, once it passes a certain threshold), it does not reverse; this has proven to be a universal pattern across all societies for which the necessary data are available. As a result, demographers have observed that high fertility pretransition eventually declines to much lower levels posttransition. So without exception, at least to date, we have never seen nations and regions that have gone through the first demographic transition return to pretransition levels of high fertility.

Fertility levels, posttransition, have been observed to fluctuate, sometimes falling a bit, sometimes rising a bit, but never return to the high levels of fertility that characterize things pretransition.

Changes in Fertility and Mortality around the World

23.2.2 Compare fertility and mortality trends between underdeveloped and developed countries.

We can now better understand why Thomas Malthus and Paul Ehrlich were so alarmed, but also why the world's population (in 2020) of nearly 8 billion is extremely unlikely to ever double again to 16 billion. In the 1950s and 1960s, a large number of countries had experienced recent and quite marked declines in mortality. But because these mortality declines were recent, they were not yet accompanied by a decline in fertility. As a result, the world's population soared in the middle of the twentieth century, increasing at an extremely rapid rate. In this sense, it is not surprising that many people like Ehrlich were so alarmed about the rapid growth of the world's population. But what was less obvious was that fertility decline would also take place. And fertility decline is indeed a remarkable stylized fact—something that has been extremely well documented by demographers. All across the world, fertility decline has either taken place, is well underway, or is in its initial stages.

Fertility decline is thus the key to why the 7.8 billion humans alive in 2020 will almost certainly not imply 16 billion humans in the future. Although fertility remains high in many poor nations and regions of the world, fertility decline has begun in virtually all of these nations. This, then, is also the more complete story behind the numbers in Table 23.1. For most of human history, fertility and mortality were high but mostly cancelled, so that population growth was slow. This implies a long time for the world's population to double in size. Then at some point, mortality begins to decline, but fertility remains high, resulting in very rapid increases in population. At a last stage, mortality decline is accompanied by fertility decline, and we saw a hint of this in Table 23.1 in the slowing of the doubling time for the world's population.

We can tell the same story not only for the world as a whole but also for specific nations. In this section, we will look at this from 1950 to 2010 for one underdeveloped country, Sudan, and two rich developed countries, the United States and Japan. Let's begin by examining what happened in Sudan between 1950 and 2010. In Figure 23.1, the first graph for Sudan tells a story of very rapid population growth, from 7.5 million in 1960 to 42 million in 2018. Note that in this first graph, we have plotted things to show change as a proportion, with 7.5 million in 1960 graphed as 100 and 42 million in 2018 as $100 \times 42/7.5 = 560$, thus showing that Sudan's population grew by 560

Figure 23.1 Sudan's Population, 1960–2018

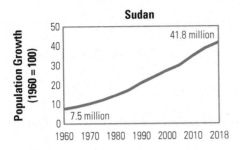

Sudan

Population Growth
(1960 = 100)

41.8 million

7.5 million

1960 1970 1980 1990 2000 2010 2018

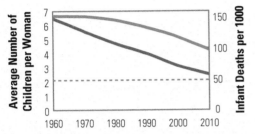

Average Number of
Children per Woman

Infant Deaths per 1000

1960 1970 1980 1990 2000 2010

SOURCES: Based on data from United Nations, Department of Economic and Social Affairs, 2011; U.S. Bureau of the Census, 2012; and World Bank.

percent between 1960 and 2010. Thus, in terms of doubling times, Sudan's population doubled between 1960 and 1985 (25 years) and doubled again between 1985 and 2010 (25 years) and has continued growing since then.

The second graph tells the story of the first demographic transition for Sudan—why its population has been growing so rapidly—which is that Sudan is very much in the middle of its first demographic transition. This graph plots mortality (purple curve, scale on the right-hand axis) and fertility (blue curve, scale on the left-hand axis), and shows how they have changed in Sudan between 1960 and 2020. And the patterns we see follow exactly the storyline for what happens during a nation's first demographic transition, which is that we first see high fertility and high mortality, then mortality decline, followed at some later point by fertility decline. Thus for Sudan in 1960, both mortality and fertility were high. Our measure of fertility, the **total fertility rate**, was just under 7 for Sudan in 1960. (The total fertility rate is defined by both a level, 7 in this case, and a calendar year, 1950, and what it means is that were fertility in Sudan to remain at 1950 levels, the average woman would have about seven children over her lifetime.) But mortality in Sudan was undergoing a steady but quite rapid decline during this period; by contrast, fertility did not begin declining until 1980 or so—and note that Sudanese fertility remains high even at present, at an average of roughly 4 children per woman in 2020.

So, the case of Sudan illustrates the standard first demographic transition arithmetic: rapid decreases in mortality, but much later and slower decreases in fertility, which in turn imply very rapid population growth. And this is exactly what we see in Sudan: 7.5 million people in 1960, 42 million in 2018.

What is the story for the United States? There are far more people in the United States than in Sudan (158 million people in 1950; 328 million in 2019). But as the first graph for the United States in Figure 23.2 illustrates, population growth has been far slower in the United States than in Sudan. The second graph for the United States shows part of the reason why: U.S. mortality was fairly steady throughout this period, but the same was not true of fertility, which hit a peak of 3.7 children per woman in 1955 at the height of the

Sudan, a poor country in East Africa, is currently experiencing a period of rapid population growth, growing from 7.5 million people in 1960 to about 42 million in 2020. Shown here is a Sudanese family with seven children; the average family in 2020 has about four children. Japan, by contrast, has a very low birth rate, with a majority of women having either one child or no children at all.

SAYYID AZIM/AFP/Getty Images

theVisualsYouNeed/Alamy Stock Photo

baby boom but then declined, fluctuating between 1.9 and 2.1 children per woman between 1970 and 2010.

So the story of the first demographic transition is repeated in the United States as well, but at the end of the story, with low mortality but moderately high fertility in 1950 and low levels of mortality and low fertility today. (The more correct story for the United States is that it began its first demographic transition around the early 1800s and had largely completed it by the 1930s. The U.S. baby boom, which we discuss in more detail later, led to a temporary increase in fertility, but at levels far below pretransition levels of U.S. fertility.) Thus, we see in Figures 23.1 and 23.2 the start of the first demographic transition in Sudan and the end of it in the United States.

That we see the start and end of the first demographic transition in Sudan and the United States has very real consequences, which we can see when comparing the graphs for these two nations in Figure 23.3. These graphs give what demographers call **age pyramids**, in which we have plotted the age distribution for these countries in 2010, with the numbers at the youngest ages at the bottom of the graph and the numbers at the oldest ages at the top, and with males and females on the left- and right-hand sides, respectively. Compare the age pyramids for Sudan and the United States.

The age pyramid for Sudan is just that, a sharp pyramid, in which the largest numbers in the population are the very young and the fewest are the very old. This reflects the fact that Sudan is a poor nation, with poverty influencing how mortality strikes at those of different ages. And this age-and-mortality story goes like the following: Although mortality has declined in Sudan, infant mortality is still quite high, and the same is true for child mortality. This means that many babies are born but many more die than in rich countries like the United States; of those babies that survive to early childhood, some also die; and so forth.

But the even more important part of the story for Sudan is not that fertility continues to be high but that mortality has declined. To see how this works, let's think about those in Sudan who were born in 1970. The red curve in Figure 23.1 shows that mortality was declining in 1990, which means that fewer born in 1970 died and that more were still living in 1990, when they were aged 20, an age when many in Sudan have begun to have children. But the blue curve in Figure 23.1 shows that fertility remained very high in 1990, meaning that more children were born in 1990 than before. Now let's think about the children born in 1990. Figure 23.1 shows that fertility continued to be high but that mortality was falling, meaning that more of those born in 1990 survived than before. And so forth. And the result is an age structure in Sudan in which there are many who are very young but

Figure 23.2 U.S. Population, 1950–2015

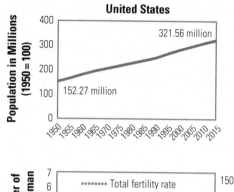

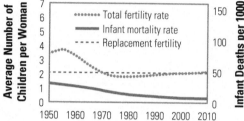

SOURCES: Based on data from United Nations, Department of Economic and Social Affairs, 2011; U.S. Bureau of the Census, 2016.

few who are very old—and the pyramid shape that we see is a direct consequence of two facts, declining mortality but still high fertility.

What about changes in mortality and fertility in the United States? As Figure 23.3 shows, the 2010 age pyramid for the United States is completely different from the age pyramid in Sudan. What we see in the United States is something less resembling a pyramid than a house, with roughly the same numbers of those who are very young and those who are much older, with the roof of the house beginning around age 60. And this again reflects how mortality strikes at those of different ages, but with dramatically different results for a wealthy nation like the United States. And thus the age pyramid for the United States does not look like a pyramid until far older ages—nearly all babies born in the United States survive to early childhood, nearly all children survive to adolescence, nearly all adolescents survive to early adulthood, and so forth, with mortality only influencing the U.S. age distribution in notable ways after age 60.

Figure 23.3 Age Pyramids for Sudan and the United States as of 2010

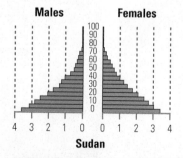

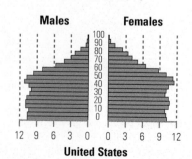

SOURCES: Based on data from United Nations, Department of Economic and Social Affairs, 2011; U.S. Bureau of the Census, 2012.

The other very important fact is that U.S. fertility has for several decades been at what demographers call **replacement fertility**. The idea is simple: If, on average, each female in a generation had two children, this would imply a more or less unchanging size in the population (taking into account that only females bear children). Each set of parents would, on average, produce two offspring, thus replacing themselves by this number of offspring. (Demographers usually put replacement fertility at 2.1 children per female to deal with the relatively small numbers of those who die before reaching the typical ages of childbearing.)

Figure 23.4 provides data for Japan, another rich nation. Here a third pattern emerges. The first graph shows that the population in Japan grew from 82 million in 1950 to 127 million in 2010 (and was still 127 million in 2018). So Japan experienced population growth between 1950 and 2010, as was true for Sudan and the United States, but Japan's population growth has been far slower than either of these countries. As we see in the second graph, Japan has completed its first demographic transition, with low levels of both fertility (blue line) and mortality (purple line). What is particularly important to note is that Japan has had below-replacement levels of fertility for several decades, in sharp contrast to the United States (where fertility levels have been around replacement levels for several decades). In other words, in Japan the posttransition period has continued even longer than in the United States, to the point where the average woman is having fewer than the 2.1 births needed for replacement-level fertility.

The consequences of these differences—replacement levels of fertility spanning several decades in the United States but below-replacement levels of fertility spanning several decades in Japan—are very apparent when comparing the age pyramids for the United States and Japan, particularly their shapes at younger ages. As we noted earlier, the U.S. age pyramid doesn't resemble a pyramid until older ages, with roughly the same numbers of people in each five-year age group until age 60 to 64. Japan's age pyramid is very different, with sharply declining numbers at younger ages. The fact that we see sharply declining numbers in Japan's age pyramid at younger ages lines up almost exactly with trends in Japanese fertility shown in the blue curve for Japan—since the 1970s, Japan has had below-replacement levels of fertility, with a total fertility rate in Japan of 1.3 in 2010.

So stepping back a bit, we have seen that fertility in Sudan is substantially above replacement, fertility in the United States is at replacement, and fertility in Japan is below replacement. And these facts, together with mortality, are clearly reflected in the age pyramids for these three countries. But if Japan is at below-replacementfertility, why is it that we see increases in Japan's population between 1950 and 2010? We could ask the same question for the United States, given that U.S. fertility has been at

Figure 23.4 Japan's Population, 1950–2018

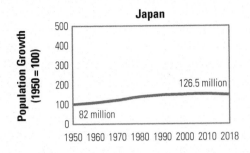

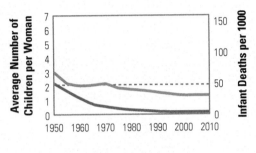

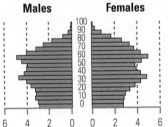

SOURCES: Based on data from United Nations, Department of Economic and Social Affairs, 2011; U.S. Bureau of the Census, 2012, and World Bank.

roughly replacement levels for several decades. There are two answers to this question—immigration and population momentum—which we discuss in the next section.

Immigration and Population Momentum

23.2.3 Discuss how the rate of immigration relates to the speed at which the population size changes.

We already know the answer to why population size in Sudan has been increasing rapidly—it is in the middle of its first demographic transition, and so is still experiencing very rapid population growth. But the United States and Japan are both posttransition, so why is population increasing in these countries?

Let's begin with immigration, because at one level it just involves the usual demographic arithmetic and so is easy. The United States has historically been a nation of immigrants. Virtually all of those in the United States today are not Native Americans but instead arrived, or are descendants of those who arrived, in the United States at various points in history. In 2017, there were an estimated 35.2 million legal immigrants and about 10.5 million unauthorized immigrants (sometimes called "illegal immigrants") out of the 328 million people living in the United States that year (Zong and Batalova 2016; Budiman 2020). By contrast, Japan's immigration history is very different; the country's immigrant population has always been extremely small. So part of the answer for why the population of the United States is larger in 2010 than in 1950 lies in the continuing flow of immigrants, both legal and illegal, to the United States. (The more complete answer for how migration affects change in a nation's population involves the numbers of in- and out-migrants, but in the case of the United States, in-migration has, until recently, vastly outnumbered out-migration.)

The other reason the populations of Japan and the United States have continued to grow over the last 60 years is **population momentum**. This refers to the tendency of a population that has been changing in size to continue to change in size even if factors such as fertility and mortality have shifted to levels that would, in the long run, imply no change in population size. Population momentum is very similar to the momentum of a physical object. Take, for example, a jet airplane that has been climbing rapidly. If the pilot were to ease off on the jet thrusters, the plane would continue climbing, at least for a while. So growth in the population of the United States or Japan is not unlike a jet that has been climbing, with the jet continuing to climb for a while even if the pilot eases up on the thrusters. This also means there is a level of fuel

supplied to the jet thrusters that makes the plane eventually fly at a constant altitude—neither climbing nor descending. Anything less than this level means that the jet will eventually begin to descend, and anything above this level means that the jet will continue climbing.

The jet plane analogy for Japan is that the pilot is supplying less fuel than what is required to keep the plane at a constant altitude. Population momentum means that Japan's population did in fact continue to grow between 1950 and 2010. But as this analogy also suggests, Japan grew more rapidly during the first 30 years and less so in the last 30 years of this 60-year period—Japan's population was 82 million in 1950, 116 million in 1980, but only 126 million in 2019 (about the same as it was in 2010).

We began this chapter by noting that people like Malthus and Ehrlich thought that there was a ticking time bomb in the extremely rapid growth in the world's population. And while what they worried about reflected a very simple view of population change, we now know that curbing extremely rapid population growth (in countries like Sudan) can help avoid issues that stem from overpopulation, including poverty and disease. But we also noted that demographers now worry about a second and completely different problem—that of population aging, in which some regions and countries of the world are facing rapid increases in the numbers of older people, a topic we will take up later in the chapter.

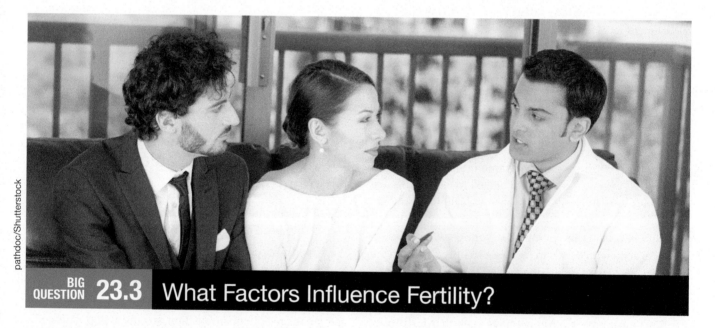

pathdoc/Shutterstock

BIG QUESTION 23.3 What Factors Influence Fertility?

THEORIES OF FERTILITY DECLINE

We have now seen that fertility decline is key to understanding global and national population dynamics. Decades of research by demographers and other social scientists have documented in great detail when and how quickly fertility and mortality have declined, both historically and in more modern times, for countries around

the world. The stylized facts emerging from this research tell us things that we know with great certainty about the first demographic transition and about fertility decline in particular. But while there is near universal agreement on what the facts concerning fertility decline are, there is anything but universal agreement on *why* fertility has in fact declined. Social scientists strive to figure out the "why."

Several theories (or theoretical hypotheses) provide plausible answers for why fertility has declined. We'll discuss five in this section. Keep in mind the possibility that the reasons behind fertility decline may be very different before and after the first demographic transition. We should note that demographers and social scientists have yet to agree on which of these hypotheses is largely correct, whether all of them have some merit, or whether one or more of them should be abandoned, but research in this area remains very active.

Infant Mortality

23.3.1 Explain the connection between declining infant mortality and fertility decline.

A first theory argues that declines in infant mortality can cause fertility decline. Proponents of this hypothesis begin from the observation that for much of human history, both mortality and fertility were high. But one consequence of high mortality levels is that a couple cannot be certain whether an infant who is just born will survive or will die before reaching adulthood. As a result, couples will typically try to have many children to ensure that at least a few will survive. As mortality begins to decline, however, so too will the need to have many children. This explanation is attractive because it not only tells us why fertility declines but also

addresses why fertility decline occurs only after mortality has begun its decline (during the first demographic transition). However, this theory is not very good at explaining why we see fertility differences between posttransition countries, such as the United States and Japan. Mortality is low in both countries, but fertility is substantially lower in Japan. For these reasons, this argument is a plausible candidate for explaining fertility decline before and during the first demographic transition but is far less plausible for explaining fertility differences among countries that have completed the first demographic transition.

Economic Development

23.3.2 Explain the connection between fertility and economic development.

Fertility rates are also related to the patterns of economic development, or more specifically, to how advanced a nation's economy is. This hypothesis argues that fertility will decline as a country undergoes economic and social development and becomes richer. An early version of this hypothesis was that economic development was necessary if the first demographic transition was to occur (Notestein 1953). In other words, as poor countries became more prosperous economically, their mortality and then fertility rates would begin to fall. For a graphical

Figure 23.5 Total Fertility Rate Versus GDP per Capita of the Corresponding Country

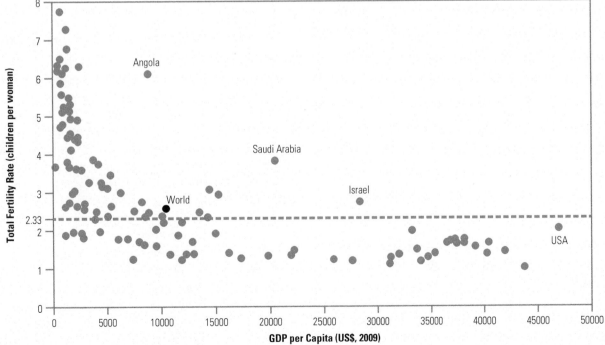

NOTE: Only countries with over 5 million population are shown.

SOURCE: *CIA World Fact Book.*

demonstration, Figure 23.5 plots the fertility rate on the *y* axis and gross domestic product (GDP) per person on the *x* axis.

Although Figure 23.5 shows a clear relationship between economic development and fertility, there is also a lot of variation at every level of GDP per person. For example, rich countries, like Saudi Arabia, Israel, and even the United States, have significantly higher fertility than would be predicted. Further, even very poor nations like Sudan can and have adopted policies that very quickly lead to improvements in infant mortality. Moreover, the same pattern of reductions in fertility found elsewhere has followed once infant mortality declines. Social scientists now know that a number of things can greatly reduce infant mortality, including systems for waste and sewage disposal, the provision of clean drinking water, access to hospitals or clinics to monitor the health of pregnant people and to help them when they give birth, and a variety of improvements in the nutrition, health, and medical care of infants, children, and their mothers. Social scientists also see education as an extremely important component of social development, particularly the education of women. The argument here is that in less-developed countries, increases in literacy and education will, in turn, lead to improvements in infant health and to decreases in infant mortality, with this then followed (at some later point) by a decline in fertility.

Yet another way in which social and economic development may limit fertility is if development also carries with it the prospect of better lives for young people. If so, the prospect of upward mobility for offspring may lead parents to have higher aspirations for their children, which may in turn lead such parents to have fewer children relative to those parents who do not see such opportunities for their children (Davis 1963). But as was the case for the infant mortality hypothesis, this hypothesis speaks most directly to why fertility declines before and during the first demographic transition but is far less plausible in explaining why we see different levels of fertility posttransition.

Birth Control

23.3.3 Explain the connection between improved birth control, changing attitudes about bearing children, and fertility decline.

Another hypothesis holds that two profound changes affected fertility: (1) the growing acceptance of the view that people can (and should) exercise control over their fertility, and (2) technological advances in the means by which women and couples can control their fertility. For most of human history, a central purpose of marriage was to have children. Today, this is no longer the case. Many happily married couples with no fertility issues choose not to have children (and do not suffer any social stigma as a consequence). Further, since the 1960s individuals and couples have had many ways of preventing unwanted pregnancies by using an effective method of contraception. The appearance of the birth control pill in the 1960s was especially critical to this new era of contraception. As couples could now exercise a considerable degree of control over the timing, spacing, and number of births, they were much less likely to produce an extra, unintended child.

Proponents of the hypothesis that improved birth control combined with changing norms about the necessity of having children had argued that fertility control is one of the great social changes that accompanied the first demographic transition. In pretransition societies, wanting to prevent or control births could well have been simply irrelevant. In the modern world (particularly in developed countries), however, factors like furthering education, pursuing career goals, and working toward financial stability affect whether and when people have children. So, one possible advantage of this hypothesis is that it provides an explanation for fertility changes before, during, and after the first demographic transition.

The Changing Benefits of Having Children

23.3.4 Explain the connection between the costs and benefits of childrearing and fertility decline.

Often cited by economists, a fourth hypothesis holds that fertility decline results from the costs and benefits of having and raising children. This theory focuses on how larger social changes might affect fertility-related behaviors at the individual level (for example, women, men, couples, and parents). Proponents of this theory argue that before the Industrial Revolution, countries like the United States and those in Europe were *agrarian societies*, which meant that the overwhelming majority lived in rural areas and worked as farmers, sharecroppers, peasants, or other agricultural workers. In such agrarian economies, children were a net benefit to parents because they provided an additional body for tending crops or livestock. They were also a potential safety net; the surviving children could take care of their aging parents. But with industrialization, increasing numbers of workers migrated to urban areas and cities to work in factories, which lessened the economic benefit of having many children who could help work in the fields even at young ages. In the twenty-first century, how parents weigh the costs and benefits of children will also explain why we see much lower fertility in a country like Japan than in the United States.

Like the hypothesis on birth control's role, this hypothesis possibly explains changes in fertility across multiple historical periods; however, we need to take a couple of factors into consideration. First, this hypothesis supposes that individuals and couples actually weighed the costs and benefits before, during, and after the first demographic transition, whereas the birth control theory sees the idea of rational choice in fertility-related behaviors as something very new and very modern. In addition, this hypothesis places great emphasis on material conditions for a given family—the economic costs versus the benefits to parents of having another child—whereas the birth control hypothesis places less emphasis on material conditions and far more emphasis on the evolution of ideas, norms, and culture—how it is that parents might think about the issue of having another child and how this has changed over time. These are the kinds of issues social scientists keep in mind when considering different hypotheses.

Norms and Values

23.3.5 Explain the connection between changing norms and values and fertility decline.

Another hypothesis for fertility decline argues that recent fertility change is a consequence of changes in norms and values accompanying what some have called the **second demographic transition** (Lesthaeghe and van de Kaa 1986). Proponents typically point to very substantial changes in family life in rich countries like the United States and Japan. Some of these include historical increases in divorce (Preston and McDonald 1979), premarital sexual activity (Joyner and Laumann 2001), increased cohabitation where couples live together without being married (Bumpass and Lu 2000), and out-of-wedlock

childbearing (Wu 2008). All of these changes reflect, at least in part, what is yet another dramatic shift that occurred in the modern world: evolving ideas of what we might ideally want from being in a relationship, from being married, or from being a parent. In times past, people were expected to marry and to have children, and, as a result, many did. But this also meant (so the argument goes) that if you did not, then people were likely to think something was wrong with you. Today, people are far more likely to say you should have children only if and when you feel this makes sense for you and your partner. This would imply that having children is now very much a matter of choice, and this also means there are a number of good reasons for choosing to have no children or only one child. This leads proponents of this hypothesis to conclude that emerging norms and values due to the second demographic transition mean lower fertility than in the past, including (in some cases) very low levels of fertility observed in countries like Japan.

In rich countries today, couples have children for many reasons but typically not out of economic necessity or due to strict traditional values. As childbearing and raising children have become more optional, fewer couples are deciding to have multiple children and more are voluntarily going childless than in the past. Yet raising a child can be one of the most rewarding experiences anyone can have, and as long as enough people continue to think that way, population reproduction will continue.

Mark Bussell

Foto24/Gallo Images/Getty Images

THE IMPLICATIONS OF AN AGING POPULATION

In this section, we will discuss the demographic implications when populations begin to age. We will first explore what the first demographic transition implies for the health conditions of populations. We will then turn to the aging of the baby boom generation in the United States and Japan and compare how quickly aging might occur in these two countries.

The Epidemiological Transition

23.4.1 Discuss how the epidemiological transition explains differences in health conditions affecting those in poorer and richer countries.

As we saw earlier in this chapter, the first demographic transition carries with it a shift from age pyramids like that in Sudan to those that we see in the United States and Japan. How might the first demographic transition influence health when we think about overall health in a nation's population? The answer is something social scientists now call the **epidemiological transition** (Omran 1971). **Epidemiology** is the study of health-related events in an entire population: the causes and consequences of health-related factors. The epidemiological transition is a concept that refers to the transition of a population from health conditions primarily involving infectious disease (often extremely deadly to infants, children, and young adults in poor and developing countries) to health conditions primarily involving chronic disease (often shaping the health conditions of individuals, and especially older people, in rich countries like the United States and Japan). And the story behind the epidemiological transition is that the first

demographic transition has very important implications for diseases and health conditions affecting countries like Sudan and countries like the United States and Japan.

Infectious diseases develop from bacteria, viruses, parasites, and other contagious agents. COVID-19, the common cold, the flu, and HIV are examples of viral infections, while bacterial infections develop from harmful germs and microorganisms (for example, harmful bacteria may multiply and make you very sick if it is in something you've eaten that hasn't been cooked under sanitary conditions or at the right temperature.) Infectious diseases do not usually kill people in countries like the United States and Japan, although when a deadly new virus like that which caused COVID-19 (the SARS-CoV-2 virus) enters the population, it can kill otherwise healthy people until treatments and/or a vaccine becomes available. In poor and developing countries like Sudan, however, infectious diseases are a very common cause of death, especially for infants and young children. Poor countries lack quality medical care for their populations and are often the last to gain access to vaccines.

Life expectancy (a concept introduced at the beginning of the chapter) is one of the most common measures used to describe the health of a population. It is defined as the average number of years a population at some age can expect to live. As we discussed earlier, life expectancy has increased substantially in the last century in developed countries and even in many poor countries like Sudan. Americans' life expectancy at birth in 2019, for example, was 79 years. Americans' life expectancy has increased by 9 years since 1960, but it has stopped rising, in large part because of higher mortality among middle-aged White men living in rural communities, who are dying from drug overdoses, alcoholism, and suicides at significantly higher rates in recent years (Case and Deaton 2020). Although when compared to all countries, life expectancy in the United States is high, it nonetheless lags behind some other countries around the world. The Japanese, for example, can expect to live 85 years—six more years than Americans.

Why has mortality declined (and life expectancy gone up) in poor countries? At least part of the reason is that poor and middle-income countries have been able to tackle many sources of infectious disease that once were far more deadly. For example, they have improved conditions by cleaning up and protecting water supplies, by developing better systems of waste disposal, and by immunizing and providing better health care and nutrition to infants, children, and their mothers. Evidence about the growth of life expectancy for eight different countries since the late nineteenth century is displayed in Figure 23.6. The lines for all countries are going up, except for dips caused by World War I and II for those countries that were involved (Germany and France in both wars, and Japan in World War II). It is likely that in the rich countries, a levelling off of the increase in life expectancy will eventually happen. But public health experts are not sure when that will be. Some believe that in the future the typical human in a rich country will live past 100, while others think that is very unlikely. In less affluent countries like China and India, the trends are revealing. In 1950, a person born in China could only expect to live about 45 years, but just a few decades later (by the year 2000) they could expect to live to 71, and longevity has continued rising so that by 2020 a baby born in China today can expect to live to 76, nearly the same as in the United States. India is further behind, but its growth in longevity is

equally remarkable: In 1950, a baby born in India could expect to live to 35, but one born in 2020 can expect to live to over 70, a doubling of life expectancy in just 70 years.

Around the world, there is still considerable variation in life expectancy. Figure 23.7 displays current figures for a much larger group of countries. In the very poorest countries in the world (like Chad), a baby born today can only expect to live to about 45 or 50, which is comparable to what life expectancy was in the United States if you were born in 1900. Many of the countries in the figure with lower life expectancy are in Africa, which is partially the result of the impact of the HIV/AIDS epidemic, which killed millions of Africans until being brought under control in recent years. But the implications of Figure 23.6 and the trends we are observing are that improved longevity is certain to rise in developing countries.

The Nobel Prize winning economist Angus Deaton (2013) has argued that increases in life expectancy reflect not just improvements in public health and fighting infectious diseases, but more generally show improved living standards in these countries that are often not well measured in official statistics. An example might be improvements in daily diets. We have other indicators of overall well-being enhancements, such as increasing average heights around the world, that also suggest that people in most developing countries, even some of the poorest countries on Earth, are living significantly better lives than their grandparents just a couple of generations ago. That is the good news. To put it another way, in most parts of the world in the twenty-first century, people will live long enough to "get old."

Figure 23.6 Trends in Life Expectancy

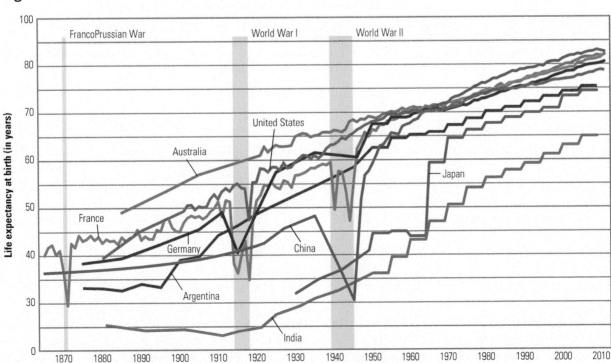

SOURCE: The data are from Clio Infra, created by Richard Zijdeman (https://ourworldindata.org/life-expectancy/).

Figure 23.7 Life Expectancy at Birth Around the World

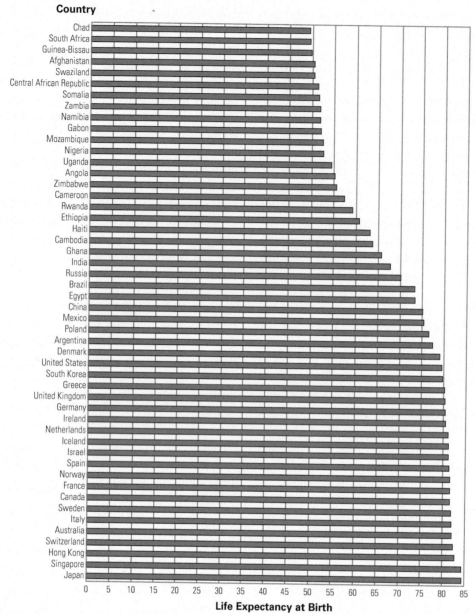

SOURCE: *CIA World Fact Book*.

The downside of improved health and longevity—one which any society would rationally choose—is that as we live longer, we experience more chronic disease. **Chronic diseases** (or, more generally, chronic health conditions) are persistant health conditions that a person can live with for many years. Examples include serious heart and respiratory problems, diabetes, high blood pressure, obesity, cancer, Parkinson's disease, Alzheimer's disease, and HIV/AIDS. Some of these chronic conditions can start in childhood (for example, diabetes or obesity), some can happen at any time but the longer you live the more likely they are (for example, cancer), while others almost always strike older people (for example, Alzheimer's, Parkinson's). Many of these chronic health conditions are not the result of an infectious disease but instead involve risk factors that we can influence, at least in part. For example, by eating healthy foods, getting enough exercise, avoiding tanning booths or too much sun, and being careful about sexually transmitted diseases. This is why one of the first researchers who wrote about the epidemiological transition characterized it as a long-term shift in mortality and disease patterns in which infectious disease is "gradually displaced by degenerative and *man-made* disease" (Omran 1971, emphasis added).

The other notable fact about chronic health conditions is not only that they tend to strike at older ages but that they typically do not kill when they first strike, and when they do kill, they often do so slowly. This is the

Dominik Bindl/Getty Images

Johanna Quaas, an 86-year-old gymnast, performing in 2012. As late as 2018, at the age of 92, she was still competing in gymnastics competitions.

In 2012, about half of all American adults 18 and older reported that they had a chronic disease, but for older adults the percentages are much higher (about 85 percent of people over 65 have a chronic condition [Ward et al. 2014]). Together, these measures of health tell us how ill our population is and provide a framework for understanding the impact of an aging population on society as a whole. Researchers continue to debate whether increases in life expectancy will translate into increases in the number of years we live free of disease and other chronic conditions, or will simply prolong the amount of time that we spend being unwell at the end of our lives.

"chronic" aspect of these health conditions—if you suffer from a chronic health condition, you may die of it eventually, but in rich countries like the United States and Japan, with high-quality health care systems, you most often will not die from it right away. And for many of these chronic conditions (extreme obesity, high blood pressure, heart or lung disease, some but not all cancers, HIV/AIDS), you can live for a quite long time and lead something resembling a normal life if you know how to manage the condition and have the means to manage it. But one of the critical implications is that it is often expensive to treat people with chronic health conditions, raising the costs of health care in significant ways as a society's population ages.

Health in an Aging Population

23.4.2 Discuss the role of healthy life expectancy as a population ages.

Life expectancy tells us how long we might expect to live, but knowing when we might die does not tell us everything we might want to know about health in later years. As we reach certain ages, many of us want to know how many "good years" we have left—years when we can anticipate good health and ability to do a normal range of activities. Because of this, social scientists also track **healthy life expectancy**, the average number of healthy years one can expect to live if current patterns of death and illness remain the same. The U.S. government is currently tracking three measures of healthy life expectancy: expected years of life in good health, expected years of life free from limitation of activity, and expected years of life free from selected chronic diseases (U.S. Department of Health and Human Services 2008). The goal is to give people as many years of healthy life as possible, as opposed to just total life years.

Aging of the Baby Boomers

23.4.3 Discuss how the aging of the baby boom generation contributes to the overall graying of societies.

The **baby boom** refers to the period following World War II from 1946 to 1964, during which the United States experienced a notable, extended, but ultimately temporary spike in fertility. Those born between 1946 and 1964 are referred to as *baby boomers*. Baby boomers are now beginning to enter old age, with many implications for American society.

We can see the U.S. baby boom in the second graph of Figure 23.2, which shows that the U.S. total fertility rate stood at 3.4 in 1950, rose to a peak of 3.7 in 1955, and fell in later years. The baby boom can also be seen very clearly in the age pyramid for the United States. Let's also take a look at the age pyramids displayed in Figure 23.8. The peak of 3.7 in 1955 for the total fertility rate corresponds with the broad peak in the U.S. age pyramid covering those who were 50 to 54 in 2010 (the youngest of the baby boomers) to those aged 60 to 64 in 2010 (the oldest of the baby boomers). Note also that there is another broad peak in the U.S. age pyramid, one covering ages 15 to 19, 20 to 24, and 25 to 29 in 2010 and thus corresponding to those born in the years 1981 through 1985, 1986 through 1990, and 1991 through 1995. Many in these birth cohorts are the children of the baby boomers; thus, we see a *reflection* of the baby boom generation among the children of the baby boomers (born when the latter where in their prime fertility years).

Something very similar shows up in Japan's age pyramid (see also Figure 23.8). Japan also experienced a baby boom after World War II and, as in the United States, this shows up in the sharp peak at ages 60 to 64 in Japan's age pyramid, with this peak corresponding to those in Japan who were born between 1946 and 1950. These Japanese baby boomers then proceeded to have their children in their 20s and 30s, in the 1970s and 1980s, and we see this reflection once again as the second peak at younger ages in Japan's age pyramid. (The peak for the children of Japan's baby boomers is sharper than in the United States because Japanese baby boomers had their children, on average, in a narrower band of ages than the U.S. baby boomers.)

If we then fast-forward to 2025 and beyond, most of the baby boomers in the United States and Japan will still be alive, and many can expect to live for another 10 or more years. This is what some have called the *graying* of societies like the United States and Japan (that is, a higher percentage of the total population is older, and more likely to have gray hair, than in earlier decades). You can see this in Figure 23.8—the baby boom bulge in the age pyramids, coupled with how long the baby boomers are likely to live, means that there will be many more older people in the future in the United States and Japan than there are now. (The oldest of the U.S. baby boomers—those born in 1946—will turn 75 in 2021).

Aging and Population Dynamics

23.4.4 Explain why some countries will age more quickly than others.

We now know why countries like Sudan are growing much more rapidly than countries like the United States and Japan. But this also raises the possibility that population aging will be more rapid in some countries than others. And both phenomena—the pace of population growth and the pace of population aging—are fundamentally questions involving population dynamics. Figure 23.8 tells us a lot about what we need to know (and thus can reasonably expect looking into the future) about the pace of population aging in the United States and Japan. And the answer is that we can reasonably expect that population aging will be far more rapid in Japan than in the United States.

The reason for this is easy to see, and it lies in the shapes of the U.S. and Japanese age pyramids. Population aging refers to the relative numbers of young and old people in a population, and the age pyramids give us very detailed information about this for the United States and Japan for one particular calendar year—in the data displayed in Figure 23.8, for the calendar year 2010. Now, predicting what the future will look like is speculative; it requires guesses about mortality (that is, how future mortality will strike those of different ages) plus guesses about fertility (that is, how future fertility will fill in the numbers at the bottom of future age pyramids). Looking again at Figure 23.8, you may have already guessed the answer, which is that Japan will, in all likelihood, be aging much more quickly than the United States. Part of the reason is that the typical Japanese citizen will have several more years of life than the typical American. Additionally, however, the fact that fertility rates in Japan have been at subreplacement levels (below 2.1 births per woman) for many decades, and only more recently in the United States, will mean fewer younger people in Japan in the future (pushing up the average age).

Should these trends continue into the future, Japan's population can be expected to decline once mortality begins thinning the ranks of Japan's baby boom generation. How quickly might Japan's population decline? Any answer to this question again has to be speculative, but we can nevertheless give fairly precise answers under the speculative "what if" scenario of "what if a nation's fertility remains at a particular subreplacement level for a long time?" Take a look at Table 23.2 to see how long it would take for a population to halve in size—that is, decrease by a factor of two—if fertility remains at a particular subreplacement level for a very long time.

What Table 23.2 shows is that if fertility in a population were to remain just a bit below replacement, population decline would be very gradual, but that population decline can be very rapid at other subreplacement levels of fertility. So, let's use a hypothetical nation as an example. If Nation A has an average of 1.9 children per woman rather than the replacement level of 2.1 children per woman and if this continued for a long time, Nation A's population would indeed decline, but quite slowly, taking roughly 280 years to halve in size. However, if Nation A has an average of 1.4 children per woman and were this to continue for a long time, its population would take only 54 years to halve in size—an extremely rapid pace of population decline. Now, let's go back to Japan. Because Japan's fertility has been between 1.2 and 1.4 for several decades, there is the distinct possibility that Japan will experience very rapid population decline in the future. And what has been both surprising and fascinating to demographers is that many countries besides Japan have equally low levels of subreplacement fertility. (The list includes

Figure 23.8 Age Pyramids for the United States and Japan

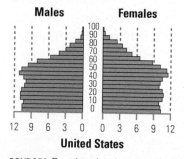

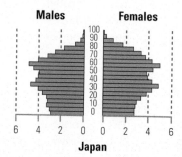

SOURCES: Based on data from the U.S. Census Bureau, 2012.

Table 23.2 Population Size and Subreplacement Fertility Level

Mean number of children per woman	2.0	1.9	1.8	1.7	1.6	1.5	1.4	1.3	1.2	1.1	1.0
Years until population halving	901	279	161	112	84	66	54	45	38	33	29

SOURCE: Based on calculations using a formula from Kohler, Billari, and Ortega, 2002.

Austria, Cuba, the Czech Republic, Germany, Greece, Hong Kong, Italy, Poland, Russia, Singapore, South Korea, Spain, and Taiwan.) Thus, countries like these not only face the prospect of rapid population aging but also the possibility of rapid population decline at some point in the future should fertility remain at very low subreplacement levels.

Financing Old Age and Health Care in Aging Societies

23.4.5 Discuss why population aging creates financial pressures for governments and societies.

Because of declines of fertility and increases in life expectancy in developed countries, many countries are now facing significant problems financing the retirement and health care costs for older people. By 2030, one in eight people in the world will be 65 or older (National Institute on Aging 2007). By 2050, it is projected that one in five Americans will be over the age of 65 (Pew Research Center 2009). In aging societies, the number of younger working people for each person 65 and older has been shrinking, so fewer people will be able to share the cost of health care and social security for older people.

When people reach a point where they are no longer able or expected to work, virtually all societies attempt to provide for the well-being as they age. In poorer countries, this often means living with children who will support them. In richer countries, however, retirement increasingly comes with the expectation that an acceptable minimal level of social support for the aged will be provided by the government. Since 1935, the U.S. **Social Security** program has provided pensions for retired workers, and since 1965, the United States has provided health care for citizens 65 and older through a program called **Medicare**. Over time, these programs have increased their benefits to older citizens. Social Security increased significantly between 1950 and 1972, and since 1972 has been indexed to inflation so as prices go up, so too do benefits. Medicare has expanded as well. Until recently, Medicare only covered hospital care and outpatient services and included no prescription drug benefits, although this changed in 2003. Still, many important dimensions of health, such as dental services, are not

included in Medicare, and Medicare does not cover the entire cost of a recipient's medical bills. In 2006, Medicare beneficiaries' median out-of-pocket spending on health care was $3,103 a year (Nonnemaker and Sinclair 2011). Ten percent of beneficiaries spent $8,300 a year. For many older people, costs this high can mean having to choose between food and medicine or having to skip taking needed medications.

For many reasons—in particular, medical advances and technology—health care has also become more expensive for everyone over time. For example, between 1986 and 1994, we paid an average of $12,000 per heart attack patient to extend their life for a year. Between 1999 and 2002, we paid $300,000 to extend life for an additional year (Chandra 2009). Because of three factors—the rising cost of health care, the aging of American society, and the decline in the number of younger people to help share the cost, there are growing budget pressures faced by the government.

So, let's recap the three trends. (1) There are fewer people of working age to pay taxes to support Social Security and Medicare. (2) There are more older people using those benefits. (3) There is a steady increase in the cost of health care for everyone, including older people (who often need

Very few people born in the early twentieth century reach 100 years of age (unlike the woman shown here celebrating her 100th birthday with her children and grandchildren). However, as medical science continues to advance and life expectancy increases, this may become increasingly common. Even if that doesn't prove true, most societies are facing a growing social problem of adequately housing and caring for a growing number of people who are far beyond their working years.

more expensive interventions to stay alive). The result? An aging population puts significant pressures on government finance. But as difficult as these problems are for the United States, they are far more daunting in Japan. That is, even though both the United States and Japan are graying societies, what we saw in Table 23.2 raises the possibility that Japan's population will not only grow older but will also grow smaller, with fewer new workers replacing those who retire.

Death and Dying Around the World

23.4.6 Understand how countries differ in how they treat older, very sick people.

We often think of death as the most individual event in our lives. We may hear people lament that they will "die alone," and people have a wide variety of personal preferences about the kind of death they hope to have. But these preferences are a function not just of individual idiosyncratic tastes but of the cultures, religions, and nations in which we are embedded.

The rise of chronic health diseases as the cause of death, rather than an acute event like a heart attack, creates new challenges in caring for people at the end of their lives. Chronic diseases generally unfold slowly, so those suffering from them can expect to experience a series of health emergencies that ultimately culminate in their death. This change may have important implications for how we choose to manage death, for example, by not only trying to prevent death in older patients facing declining health, but also by reducing the pain and stress that can accompany the end of life, a period that now extends for much longer than ever before.

The United States health care system tends to operate with a heroic model of medicine, where we expect doctors to do everything they can to prolong lives unless a patient or their family accepts the inevitability of death without such measures. A relatively small but growing number of Americans have defined the conditions under which they prefer to die in a legal document, called an **advance directive**. For example, an advance directive might specify that someone does not want to be placed on a ventilator if that is necessary to sustain his or her life. Others might suggest that they only want **palliative care**, which is defined by the World Health Organization as "an approach that improves the quality of life of patients and their families facing the problem associated with life threatening

67photo/Alamy Stock Photo

A growing number of older people are signing advance health directives that tell physicians and hospitals that they do not want to be kept alive if it requires difficult and painful medical interventions (such as shocking the heart to revive it). Acceptance of the inevitability of death versus fighting for every possible day of life is an issue that older individuals and their families are likely to have to confront at some point.

illness, through the prevention and relief of suffering by means of early identification and impeccable assessment and treatment of pain and other problems, physical, psychosocial and spiritual." One of the best-known types of palliative care is **hospice care**, which focuses on eliminating suffering—physical and mental—for terminally ill patients. Hospices in the United States have traditionally provided care for terminal cancer patients but have expanded rapidly with the aging of the population. Hospice organizations now estimate that up to 42 percent of deaths in the United States involve some kind of hospice care (National Hospice and Palliative Care Organization 2011).

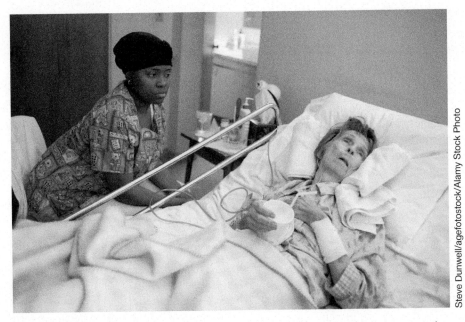

Chronic diseases like cancer and heart disease now kill a higher fraction of Americans, creating the need for different end-of-life care options than we have had in the past.

There is an irony in population aging. Aging societies, and the individuals who live in them, are in many respects the victim of their own success. The multiple individual and societal challenges raised by population aging—chronic disease that is expensive to treat, financial burdens of living many years in old age without a work income (and for society, the cost of extending Social Security payments), and issues around an extended period of end-of-life care—exist precisely because of increases in life expectancy over the last century. Aging societies also provide a clear example of a larger sociological principle: Our social institutions adapt to the changing social contexts and conditions they face.

Conclusion: Population, Aging, and Social Demography

We began this chapter by noting that in the 1960s and 1970s, it was taken for granted that *the* most pressing population issue was very rapid population growth and that this ticking time bomb would spell disaster for the world. But you now know the reasons behind what might otherwise seem like a paradox—why it is that most who study these issues now point to not one but rather two problems of population change, too rapid population growth in some countries versus rapid population aging (and the possibility of very rapid population decline) in others. These trends result from changes in fertility and mortality, but also migration. We have not examined migration in much detail in this chapter (as we devote Chapter 24 to that topic), but the key point is that the combination of fertility, mortality, and migration produces continual change across societies. These are the reasons why the ticking population time bomb that Malthus and Ehrlich so feared has not, in fact, come to pass. What we now worry about in the twenty-first century is another ticking time bomb, that of climate change. While most scientists agree that global warming is the result of human activity, the notion that population growth is the principal driver of climate change is inaccurate, as we discuss in great detail in Chapter 6.

On a more general note, the very earliest sociologists—Marx, Weber, and Durkheim—were fascinated by how the modern world was different from what the world was like in earlier times. Sociologists today continue to study change—and population trends are very much at the center of that research.

The Big Questions Revisited 23

23.1 **Why Study Population?** The world's population has doubled in size twice since 1910—taking first 57 and then 45 years. Will the world's population double in size again? This section examined reasons why governments and policymakers need to know about population trends, including the risk of overpopulation.

Population and Censuses

The Census and Population Research

Learning Objective 23.1.1: Discuss why it is relevant to study population trends.

Studying Population

Learning Objective 23.1.2: Identify ways in which population is studied.

Key Terms

demography (p. 662) census (p. 662) enumerate (p. 662) social demographers (p. 664) stylized facts (p. 663) population dynamics (p. 664) fertility (p. 664) mortality (p. 664) migration (p. 664)

23.2 **How Do Populations Change over Time?** To better understand the dynamics of population change, in this section we looked at how mortality and fertility have changed for different nations and what these changes might imply for the demographic futures of these nations.

Population Dynamics

The First Demographic Transition

Learning Objective 23.2.1: Define the first demographic transition and its role in understanding how populations change.

Changes in Fertility and Mortality around the World

Learning Objective 23.2.2: Compare fertility and mortality trends between underdeveloped and developed countries.

Immigration and Population Momentum

Learning Objective 23.2.3: Discuss how the rate of immigration relates to the speed at which the population size changes.

Key Terms

first demographic transition (p. 665) total fertility rate (p. 667) age pyramid (p. 668) replacement fertility (p. 669) population momentum (p. 670)

23.3 **What Factors Influence Fertility?** Populations change over time largely because fertility practices also have been changing (for example, the decision to have a child). In most countries around the world, women are having fewer babies than 50 or 100 years ago. Why is this the case? In this section, we explored some of the leading explanations for declining fertility.

Theories of Fertility Decline

Infant Mortality

Learning Objective 23.3.1: Explain the connection between declining infant mortality and fertility decline.

Economic Development

Learning Objective 23.3.2: Explain the connection between fertility and economic development.

Birth Control

Learning Objective 23.3.3: Explain the connection between improved birth control, changing attitudes about bearing children, and fertility decline.

The Changing Benefits of Having Children

Learning Objective 23.3.4: Explain the connection between the costs and benefits of childrearing and fertility decline.

Norms and Values

Learning Objective 23.3.5: Explain the connection between changing norms and values and fertility decline.

Key Term

second demographic transition (p. 673)

23.4 **How Are Trends in Aging and Mortality Emerging as Critical Issues in Many Societies?** Some countries have many very young people but very few old people, while others have many old people currently and will have even more old people in the future as life expectancy increases. What do these trends mean for employment and health conditions in countries like these? In this section, we asked about the demographic implications when populations begin to age.

The Implications of an Aging Population

The Epidemiological Transition

Learning Objective 23.4.1: Discuss how the epidemiological transition explains differences in health conditions affecting those in poorer and richer countries.

Health in an Aging Population

Learning Objective 23.4.2: Discuss the role of healthy life expectancy as a population ages.

Aging of the Baby Boomers

Learning Objective 23.4.3: Discuss how the aging of the baby boom generation contributes to the overall graying of societies.

Aging and Population Dynamics

Learning Objective 23.4.4: Explain why some countries will age more quickly than others.

Financing Old Age and Health Care in Aging Societies

Learning Objective 23.4.5: Discuss why population aging creates financial pressures for governments and societies.

Death and Dying Around the World

Learning Objective 23.4.6: Understand how countries differ in how they treat older, very sick people.

Key Terms

epidemiological transition (p. 674)

epidemiology (p. 674)   infectious diseases (p. 674)

life expectancy (p. 674)

chronic diseases (p. 676)

healthy life expectancy (p. 677)

baby boom (p. 677)

Social Security (p. 679)

Medicare (p. 679)

advance directive (p. 680)

palliative care (p. 680)

hospice care (p. 680)

Chapter 24
Immigration

by Guillermina Jasso with Jeff Manza*

Immigration is an important aspect of the history of American society, as it is in many other societies around the world. Nearly all Americans have an immigration story; our parents, grandparents, great-grandparents, or someone in our family's past moved from another country to the United States. Some were brought here by force as enslaved people, having no choice in the matter. The sole exceptions are the descendants of the native peoples of the continental United States and of Hawaii and Alaska, but even these native peoples are themselves descendants of migrants from other regions of the world several thousand years ago. Today, virtually every nation in the world has a significant immigrant population, and in many countries more than 1 in 10 people were born in another country (including the United States, where in 2020 about 14 percent of the entire population was born in a foreign country, and one in four children has at least one foreign-born parent).

What is life like for new immigrants? Immigrant stories usually fall somewhere between triumphs and tragedies, reflecting a complex portrait. Some immigrants may be fortunate enough to have networks of family or friends in their new country and/or sufficient financial assets to help them make the transition. Others lack one or both of these resources, have to scratch out a living, and may struggle to survive. It is never easy for immigrants. They do not have many of the same basic rights, protections, and opportunities as citizens. They often face prejudice and discrimination in their new land. Indeed, immigration has become increasingly controversial almost everywhere around the world, with politicians using hostility towards immigrants to gain popular support. The decision to move to another country is often far from simple, and the challenges faced by new immigrants are significant.

Among immigrant experiences are a full range of outcomes. For example, Madeline Albright fled communist Czechoslovakia as a child with her family, immigrated

My Sociological Imagination

GUILLERMINA JASSO

I was born half a mile from the border with Mexico in the old Mercy Hospital that faced Jarvis Plaza in Laredo, Texas. But I did not know that my parents were "immigrants." In the Texas textbooks, "immigrants" were Southern and Eastern Europeans who lived in crowded tenements and had bad habits. Every year Martin High School, the only public high school, graduated a class of securely anti-immigrant students, the vast majority of whose parents or grandparents had come from Mexico. No one had told these Shakespeare-quoting, Bach-playing, Rodgers and Hammerstein–whistling, Lerner and Loewe–dancing boys and girls that we, too, threatened the American way of life.

I grew up passionate to understand the way the world works. In time, I got a PhD and began studying fairness, theoretically with probability distributions, empirically with vignettes. One day in 1977, I got a call from the commissioner of the Immigration and Naturalization Service. Would I join his staff and advise him on the social science underlying immigration issues? "But I don't know anything about immigration," I said. "You know more than you think you know," he said quietly, "and you can learn the rest."

And that is how I started studying immigration, and how I learned that my parents were immigrants and that I was born in the fabled second generation.

---

*Harel Shapira and Carse Ramos contributed to an earlier version of this chapter.

Migrant workers from Mexico picking strawberries in California. Controversies over immigration have become one of the most pressing sociological—and political—topics of this era. According to the United Nations, as of 2019, about 3.5 percent of the world's entire population—272 million people—are living in a different country than they were born, up from 2.8 percent of the world's population in the year 2000.

Nik Wheeler/Alamy Stock Photo

to America, studied public law and government, and eventually became the first woman to be appointed U.S. Secretary of State. On the other side of the spectrum, Dominican-born Miguel Mendoza, a middle-aged man whom one of our graduate students met in the course of her dissertation research on immigrants in New York City, regularly worked 15-hour days to save money when he arrived in the United States. Eventually, he was able to acquire and operate four small convenience stores in New York City (known locally as bodegas). But his success was tenuous, as these businesses are fragile and subject to ups and downs. Some of his children struggled in school and could not find jobs. One of his children was arrested and charged with committing a crime, and Mendoza hired a private attorney to help. Eventually, he lost his businesses, partly because of the cost of paying for lawyers to defend his son and partly because of the economic downturn that began in 2007 which made his businesses unprofitable. Today, Mendoza continues to work long hours, but for someone else. He retains high hopes for his children, but doubts that he will be able to escape poverty himself.

The Albright and Mendoza stories represent merely two of the millions of immigrant stories in America. In this chapter, we will systematically examine the issues associated with the movement of people across borders. Why do people take the dramatic step of moving to a new (and sometimes hostile) country? What kinds of people make the move? How do they live once they arrive, and what are their long-term outcomes? And finally, what impact do they have on their new country, and how and why is immigration so controversial? These are the questions we will explore in this chapter.

The Big Questions

1. **What is immigration, and how do governments regulate it?** What kinds of things do sociologists study when they study immigration, and why is the study of immigration important for understanding the world we live in? In this section, we examine the basic concepts and ideas in the study of immigration.

2. **What is the history of immigration in the United States?** What are some of the trends in U.S. immigration? Where do the country's citizens, permanent residents, and unauthorized residents come from? In this section, we explore the historical context for the study of U.S. immigration.

3. **Why do people move?** People move for many reasons, but the most fundamental of these is the desire to make a better life for themselves and their children. Sociologists are interested in the characteristics of both those who move and those who stay as well as the countries they come from and the countries in which they settle. Distinguishing between these different categories of people and places provides important insights into the dynamics of the migration process.

4. **How do immigrants fare in their new environments?** Sociologists are especially interested in what happens to migrants after moving as they encounter a new society and its social, economic, and political systems. In this section, we explore a host of interesting questions raised by the process of assimilation—during which immigrants adapt to the new society they are living in.

5. **What are the consequences of immigration?** Immigration is controversial in the United States and around the world because it has wide-reaching effects on the origin country, on the destination country, and on individuals and families in both countries, including natives, immigrants, and the children of immigrants. In this section, we examine the benefits and potential costs of immigration.

BIG QUESTION 24.1 What Is Immigration, and How Do Governments Regulate It?

IMMIGRATION: A SOCIOLOGICAL PERSPECTIVE

People move for many reasons. They grow up in one town, they may go somewhere else for college, and/or move to another place to work. Some people are forced to leave their homes because of war, economic hardship, or natural disasters. Others relocate to join loved ones (such as children, parents, romantic partners). But whatever the underlying reasons and whatever the distance traveled, whether from one city to another or from one country to another, the movement of people is a fundamental feature of our world. Indeed, from the earliest human migrations out of Africa, there have always been substantial numbers living away from the place where they were born. And this continues to be true today. In 2019, the United Nations estimated that about 272 million people lived outside the country where they were born (United Nations, Department of Economic and Social Affairs 2019). Who are they? Why do they move? And where do they go? In this section we explore these questions, using sociological perspectives and imagination to understand immigration and its impacts.

Understanding Immigration from a Sociological Perspective

24.1.1 Discuss immigration as part of the fabric of social life and how it is becoming increasingly important in the twenty-first century.

Migration is a term used to describe the process by which individuals move from one place to another. The idea that

migration is a *process* provides the foundation for thinking sociologically about immigration as a whole. To consider migration as a process is to think of it not simply as a single event but rather as a long unfolding set of events that takes place over time—starting with the initial idea, continuing with the planning stage, then the actual migration, and followed by short-term and long-term impacts of life in the new country. Although migration is a single chain of events for any person or family who moves, sociologists sometimes distinguish between **emigration** (the act of leaving one place) and **immigration** (the act of arriving and settling in another) to better study the two critical sides of the migration experience. In order to understand migration, then, we need to consider this long-unfolding process and, importantly, the conditions and characteristics not only of the individual migrants but also of the places they leave from and go to.

Taking into account the larger social context, including the economic and political situation a potential migrant faces, is the second element of the sociological approach to immigration. Certainly, the decision to emigrate results from individual motivations and personalities; however, the decision also depends on the laws, policies, and social customs of different countries. A basic factor in migration is that people are seeking to make better lives for themselves. But, of course, sociologists assume that everyone wants a better life, so we must also ask: Why do some people desiring a better life move, while others do not? How does moving from one place to another make it more possible for some people to secure better lives? Why do some people who live in one place tend to migrate more than people from other places?

Table 24.1 10 Countries With the Highest Levels of Net Immigration and Net Emigration (Average Each Year) During 2000–2010 and 2010–2020

Rank	2000–2010 yearly average	Total	2010–2020 yearly average	Total
	Top Receiving Countries			
1	United States of America 1,076,000	10,760,000	United States of America 974,000	9,740,000
2	Spain 518,000	5,180,000	Germany 466,000	4,660,000
3	United Arab Emirates 478,000	4,780,000	Turkey 318,000	3,180,000
4	Russian Federation 410,000	4,100,000	Russian Federation 271,000	2,710,000
5	United Kingdom 318,000	3,180,000	United Kingdom 260,000	2,600,000
6	Italy 272,000	2,720,000	Canada 245,000	2,450,000
7	Canada 238,000	2,380,000	Saudi Arabia 240,000	2,400,000
8	Saudi Arabia 182,000	1,820,000	Italy 238,000	2,380,000
9	Australia 180,000	1,800,000	Australia 178,000	1,780,000
10	South Africa 165,000	1,650,000	South Africa 165,000	1,650,000
	Top Sending Countries (Total Departing Population)			
Rank	2000–2010 yearly average	Total	2010–2020 yearly average	Total
1	Bangladesh -475,000	-4,750,000	Syria -752,000	-7,520,000
2	India -454,000	-4,540,000	India -501,000	-5,010,000
3	China -414,000	-4,140,000	Bangladesh -415,000	-4,150,000
4	Philippines -279,000	-2,790,000	Venezuela -370,000	-3,70,000
5	Mexico -277,000	-2,770,000	China -329,000	-3,290,000
6	Myanmar -255,000	-2,550,000	Pakistan -225,000	-2,250,000
7	Indonesia -248,000	-2,480,000	Nepal -183,000	-1,830,000
8	Peru -211,000	-2,110,000	Myanmar -134,000	-1,340,000
9	Nepal -174,000	-1,740,000	Zimbabwe -121,000	-1,210,000
10	Sudan -153,000	-1,530,000	Philippines -117,000	-1,170,000

SOURCE: United Nations Department of Economic and Social Affairs, 2019.

The puzzle of why people move from certain specific places to other specific places raises another set of important questions. As we will see, movement from one place to another exhibits certain patterns. To examine emigration and immigration as a process, sociologists distinguish between **receiving countries** (host or destination countries where migrants go) and **sending countries** (countries from which migrants originate). As shown in Table 24.1, some countries have high numbers of emigrants (sending countries) while other countries have high numbers of immigrants (receiving countries), and some have significant numbers of both.

The United States is the top receiving country, absorbing about one million new immigrants a year between 2000 and 2020 (this number is the total of new immigrants minus immigrants leaving the country). India is the top sending country, averaging about 500,000 per year in these two decades (although Bangladesh is the single largest sending country in 2000–10 and Syria is in 2010–2020). Saudi Arabia, Canada, Italy, Australia, and South Africa make the list of the top 10 receiving countries in both decades, while China and Myanmar are among the top 10 sending countries each year, in addition

to the previously mentioned Bangladesh and India. Later in the chapter, we examine in greater detail why it is that some countries are sending or receiving countries (or both), but for now, keep in mind that migration in the world is not random but rather highly *patterned*; that is, it has an order and particular shape, with some people and places having a much greater likelihood than others to be involved in migration.

Restricting Immigration

24.1.2 Examine how societies seek to limit or regulate immigration and emigration.

As individuals and families choose to move from one place to another, their comings and goings are not always happy or even legal. Indeed, throughout history, many societies have sought to limit or regulate both immigration and emigration. The current debate over immigration in the United States is merely the latest in a long history of attempts to regulate and control immigration, and the pattern of restrictions in receiving countries is quite common (see de Haas et al 2020 for a global immigration history).

Although the United States has never limited its citizens from moving abroad, other countries have done so in various ways in the past, both keeping people in or kicking some people out. Regulations on emigration range from absolute prohibition on people leaving (as in the communist countries of Eastern Europe during the years of the Cold War, from 1946–1989) to restrictions on certain groups of people to enforced departure or exile (when someone, or the members of the group, are forced to leave their country of origin). Two famous historical examples of forced exiles include the novelist Dante, condemned in 1302 to perpetual exile from his native Florence, and Karl Marx, kicked out of Germany for his political views and writings. The Berlin Wall—built in 1961 as a barrier between West Berlin and both East Berlin and the surrounding East German territory—is a prominent symbol of the efforts of governments to keep people from leaving. More recently, many countries have been concerned about **brain drain**, the departure of well-educated and skilled citizens to other countries where they can use their skills more productively and make more money. Countries have adopted a variety of strategies to discourage their most skilled younger people from leaving, although relatively few have developed outright bans akin to the Communist countries in Eastern Europe in the post-World War II era. Many such initiatives are aimed at improving economic growth in the hope that more job opportunities will improve retention rates or by targeting people with special skills and offering financial incentives to stay put. Countries also sometimes focus on members of the country's **diaspora** (people settled far from their homeland), hoping to entice them to return to their country of origin.

Much more common have been efforts to regulate and/or limit immigration. As with emigration, such regulations range from absolute prohibition (preventing anyone from entering a country) to policies which reject some immigrants outright and admit others under a variety of provisions for temporary or permanent stays. For both temporary and permanent residence, there is an intricate system by which foreign-born persons become eligible for a **visa**—the authorizing entry

Protests over immigration policy have been common in recent years. Here, young people born in the United States to immigrant parents seek laws that would allow families to stay together even if a parent does not have legal permanent residence status in the United States.

document. The decision about who is entitled to a visa becomes a critical part of immigration policy.

These regulations, at both exit and entry, represent a major element in understanding migration not only as an individual decision but also as subject to government policies and social and economic forces. On the one hand, when analyzing immigration sociologically we need to think about the social, economic, and political situation of both the sending and receiving countries, but we also need to think about the **immigration policies**, the set of rules and regulations established by each country with regard to the movement of people into the country. Although a person may wish to leave a country, the choice about where to go may be highly constrained. In the next section, we highlight these issues by considering the history of immigration policy in the United States.

The Basic Structure of Immigration Policy in the United States

24.1.3 Identify the main components of U.S. immigration policy.

Persons born in other countries and their descendants have a substantial presence in the United States; as we noted earlier, there are about 45 million foreign-born persons living in the United States as of 2018, almost 14 percent of the entire population (this figure does not include the approximately 18 million children of immigrants who were born in the United States and are automatically citizens). That this has been true for almost all of America's history is why the country is often called a "nation of immigrants." And far more people would like to move to the United States than current law permits. From these two central facts flow the complicated system of visas—which allow individuals to live legally in a country on a temporary or permanent basis—and the broad diversity in the rights and duties provided to foreign-born residents.

Responsibility for overseeing visa, citizenship, and related applications is shared by the Department of Homeland Security (DHS), the Department of State, and the Department of Labor. For example, a unit of DHS, U.S. Citizenship and Immigration Service (USCIS), oversees applications to sponsor a relative or worker, the State Department oversees applications for temporary visits as well as the visa lottery, and both USCIS and State oversee applications for legal permanent residents.

Under current U.S. law, foreign-born persons living in the United States include **legal permanent residents (LPRs)**, also called *legal immigrants*, who are authorized to live and work in the country permanently but are not citizens and therefore not eligible to vote (although many may eventually become citizens); **foreign-born citizens** of the United States, including naturalized citizens (LPRs who have taken the additional steps necessary to become U.S. citizens); derivative citizens (chiefly children who acquire citizenship when their parents naturalize or who are adopted by citizen parents); **legal temporary residents** (including *nonimmigrants*), who are in the United States under a variety of legal, temporary statuses (such as on a student visa); and **unauthorized immigrants** (often referred to as **illegal immigrants**), who are in the country without a proper visa. All these groups except those who have gained citizenship face some limitations on employment. Some temporary visas prohibit employment, and others have varying degrees of employment restriction. For example, foreign students studying at U.S. universities are very limited in being able to take jobs off campus. Even persons in the most privileged group—foreign-born citizens of the United States—have two jobs they are not eligible for: to be president or vice president of the United States. Thus, visa status in many ways defines the circumstances of a foreign-born person. And importantly, a foreign-born person's behavior and choices often cannot be interpreted without understanding his or her visa situation. We will have more to say about this shortly.

The process through which entry into the United States can be obtained is complex and varied. U.S. law defines a nonimmigrant as an alien (foreign-born person who is not a citizen or national of the United States) who seeks temporary entry to the United States for a specific purpose. Currently there are more than 20 classes of nonimmigrant visas, denominated by a variety of letters and

numbers, including visas for tourists, students, and specialty workers. Some of the nonimmigrant visas are valid for, or associated with, relatively short stays. Others are associated with long—sometimes very long—stays. For example, an F-1 student can remain until the course of study is completed; similarly, foreign media correspondents and employees of international organizations may live and work in the United States for "temporary periods" that may reach or even exceed 20 years.

Temporary humanitarian status is provided to refugees, asylees, and parolees. **Refugee status** is a form of protection that may be granted to people who have been persecuted or fear they will be persecuted on account of race, religion, nationality, political opinions, or membership in a particular social group. Refugees are generally outside their home country; a referral for refugee status can be sought only from outside the United States. **Asylum status** by contrast, is available for persons who meet the definition of refugee but are already in the United States or seeking admission at a port of entry. To be eligible for refugee or asylum status, a person must meet the appropriate legal standard for proving that they has a "well-founded fear" of persecution should they be returned to her home country; that the persecution was perpetrated by the government (or a group that the government is unwilling or unable to control); and that the persecution was, as noted, on account of race, religion, nationality, political opinions, or membership in a social group.

The classes of admission to LPR status are of two main types: those that are numerically unlimited and numerically limited. Numerically unlimited LPR is granted to the spouses, minor children (under age 21), and parents of adult U.S. citizens. Numerically limited LPR status is granted to three main categories of immigrants: family immigrants (comprised of adult children and siblings of U.S. citizens and the spouses and unmarried children of LPRs and arranged into four family preference categories); employment immigrants (via five employment preference categories, for jobs where not enough American workers can be located); and diversity immigrants (winners of the lottery visas designated for persons from countries underrepresented in recent immigration). The person who qualifies for a particular visa is called the **principal**. The three numerically unlimited categories for spouses, minor children, and parents of adult U.S. citizens are for principals only. Most of the other categories provide LPR visas not only for the principal but also for the spouse and minor children of the principal.

Overall, the United States admits about 1 million persons a year to LPR status (see Table 24.2). In recent decades, the largest share of new legal immigrants has been persons born in Mexico—for example, 16 percent of all immigrants over the 2001–10 decade—but the number of new immigrants from Mexico has been falling, and in 2018, Mexicans

Table 24.2 Recent Annual Flows of New Legal Permanent Residents to the United States

Fiscal Year(s)	All Immigrants
A. Average Annual Flow	
1991–1995	1,046,063
1996–2000	773,021
2001–2005	980,478
2006–2010	1,119,850
2011–2014	1,025,185
2015–2019	1,010,378
B. Annual Flow in Selected Years	
2006	1,266,264
2010	1,042,625
2014	1,016,518
2018	1,096,611

NOTES: Flows of new LPRs represent all persons granted LPR status during the period or year. In most years, over half of all new LPRs are already living in the United States. When counting people with LPR status, it is possible to separately identify those who have been legalized through the Immigration Reform and Control Act (IRCA) of 1986, which introduced a set of amnesty provisions for long-term unauthorized immigrants. For instance, during the period 1991 to 2013, IRCA legalizations declined from a high of over 1 million in 1991 to less than 1,000 in every year since 1998, with a low of 8 in 1999 and totals of 188, 217, 93, 116, 83, 62, 51, 45, and 40 in fiscal years 2005 through 2013, respectively.

SOURCE: Based on data from U.S. Department of Homeland Security.

were only the third-largest group (a development which is likely to surprise those who believe it is essential to "build a wall" on the U.S.-Mexico border). The largest other groups come from persons born in China, followed by India (as noted), the Philippines, and El Salvador. Overall, since 2010 more immigrants have come from Asian countries than Latin American countries, a major reversal of the historic trend. An important and interesting feature of recent LPRs is that women are the majority—at 55 percent. This is largely due to the strong family focus of visa allocation, with wives and mothers of U.S. citizens accounting for large fractions of the spouse and parent visas.

The process of applying for an immigrant visa is arduous and time consuming. Persons waiting for numerically limited visas may have to wait many years (U.S. Department of State n.d.). The current upper extreme is over 23 years for persons from the Philippines approved for visas as the siblings of U.S. citizens; at the other extreme, visas for world-class "priority workers" in the employment first preference category (persons of extraordinary ability in the sciences, arts, education, business, or athletics; outstanding professors or researchers; and multinational managers or executives) are available immediately. There is a long queue for numerically limited visas (U.S. Department of State 2014). Almost 4.5 million persons are already approved and waiting for the approximately 366,000 numerically limited visas available each year. This means that currently over 12 years' worth of visas are already claimed. Interestingly, there is one way to jump the

queue: Anyone who has $1 million to invest in a business, or $500,000 in certain industries, is designated as high-priority, and can automatically receive a *green card* that allows permanent legal residence. Through this provision, anyone with enough money, it is possible to jump the queue.

The U.S. Legal Permanent Resident Visa System

24.1.4 Identify the privileges that U.S. citizenship confers.

An important insight in recent immigration research is that immigrant behavior cannot be understood without understanding immigrants' legal status in the United States— how they came, whether they have the coveted **green card** (a permanent resident card that immigrants must carry at all times as evidence of LPR status) and, if so, how they got it. For example, any assessment of the work and jobs of immigrants requires information about their authorization to work; understanding home ownership among immigrants requires understanding the risk of **deportation** (removing unauthorized residents from the country and sending them back to their homeland); and understanding the children of immigrants and their behavior and choices in schools requires understanding whether they have a claim to U.S. citizenship. Sociologists now appreciate that a move from illegal to legal status represents a highly consequential form of upward social mobility (Bean and Stevens 2003; Jasso et al. 2008). Those immigrants who gain legal permanent resident status have the opportunity to build a future without fear of deportation. In time, they become eligible for the same civic and social programs as American citizens. For these reasons, obtaining permanent residence is of critical importance for individual immigrants and their families.

Most individuals seeking LPR status require a sponsor who files the initial petition that establishes the prospective immigrant's eligibility and starts the visa process. In the case of family immigrants, the sponsor is the relative who is already a citizen or LPR of the United States; for employment immigrants, the sponsor is the employing individual or firm. The requirement for a sponsor may be waived in certain cases, such as for the widow(er) and child of a deceased U.S. citizen or for the spouse and child of an abusive citizen or LPR under the Violence Against Women Act.

Becoming a U.S. Citizen

24.1.5 Discuss how immigrants become U.S. citizens.

How does an immigrant become a U.S. citizen? In general, there are two paths to citizenship for foreign-born persons. The first is naturalization, and the second is deriving citizenship from one's parent(s) or spouse. **Naturalization** is the process by which a person acquires citizenship. Eligibility for naturalization requires a period of time as an LPR, physical presence in the United States, knowledge of English, knowledge of the history and government of the United States, and some knowledge of the U.S. Constitution.

When a parent becomes a U.S. citizen, children who are LPRs, unmarried, under 18, and in the parent's legal and physical custody automatically become citizens; they "derive" citizenship from their parent. There are, of course, many intricate rules for special cases, such as adopted children and legitimated children. Children born in the United States become citizens at birth, even if their parents were not citizens at the time they were born. The major current exception to this pertains to children of certain diplomats, who are regarded as "not subject to the jurisdiction" of the United States and therefore not covered by the Fourteenth Amendment to the Constitution. A person can also gain citizenship through marriage to an American citizen, although the process is not simple and automatic. Right after the marriage, a temporary visa is granted, then the individual must apply for a green card, and finally—three or more years after the green card is received—it becomes possible to gain citizenship.

"Illegal" or Unauthorized Immigration

24.1.6 Discuss unauthorized residency and U.S. immigration policy.

The most contentious type of immigration concerns those who enter and/or stays in a country without the formal legal right to do so. The often-used term to describe these individuals is "illegal immigrants," although immigration scholars prefer the term "unauthorized" or "undocumented" immigrants to avoid scapegoating a large group of people, not to mention the many ambiguities in residency status that the existing laws create (as many people living in the United States without current LPR status will eventually gain it, and living in the United States without a proper visa is a civil, not criminal, issue). Irrespective of what we call this group, the key point is that these unauthorized residents live on the legal margins of society. Any contact with government officials can lead to forced deportation to their home country. Unauthorized immigrants cannot do many of the things that LPRs can by virtue of their shaky legal status. We do not know as much about these immigrants as we do about legal immigrants or legal temporary residents (unauthorized residents may not want to answer survey questions or

submit to interviews with journalists, for example). On the basis of the best available evidence, about one-quarter (23 percent) of foreign-born people living in the United States as of 2017 were unauthorized, or about 10.5 million (Budiman 2020). A majority (approximately 60 percent) of current unauthorized immigrants have lived in the United States for more than 10 years (Passel et al. 2014, figure 3).

In recent decades, the flow of undocumented immigrants into the United States has included children who are accompanying their parents (we'll discuss the impact of this on children later in the chapter). An estimated 2 million—of the 10.5 million total undocumented people living in the United States—came as children. Many of them only know life in the United States. Their legal status is ambiguous, but sending them back to their "home" country when they've been raised in the United States (and especially because they had no say in the decisions their parents made) has generated a large degree of sympathy towards this group. In 2014, in response to that concern, the federal government adopted a measure known as Deferred Action for Childhood Arrivals (DACA). DACA allows children and young adults who arrived in the United States as minors to stay indefinitely in the country (as long as they have committed no crimes). They are allowed to attend public schools and have the legal right to work. But they are not eligible under DACA for a green card or citizenship. It puts them, as one sociologists who has studied DACA children, "in legal limbo" (Gonzales 2016).

The treatment of children in the U.S. has recently been very controversial. During Donald Trump's presidency, attempts were made to strip children and young adults of their DACA protections, which would then enable the government to deport them. However, before the Trump administration could take this action, the U.S. Supreme Court ruled that more information was needed. The current administration under President Joe Biden has stated their goal is to allow DACA children to attain full citizenship, so the fear of deportation has diminished. Yet these individuals remain in limbo, as Congress would have to pass a law changing their status and there remains very sharp differences of opinion about these children between Democrats and Republicans.

Do Americans Support Immigration?

24.1.7 Describe how Americans' attitudes toward immigration have changed in recent decades.

As we noted in the introduction, former president Donald Trump has argued strongly against immigration. He has used aggressive words and stereotypes to attack

Throughout his presidency, Donald Trump denounced immigrants, separated children from their parents at the U.S.–Mexico border, and called for the construction of an enormous wall to try to prevent people from Mexico and other countries from getting to the United Statets. Many of the policies towards immigrants were reversed by Trump's successor, Joe Biden, once he became president in 2021.

foreign-born people (although he himself is married to a first-generation immigrant, Melania Trump). In his announcement of his candidacy for president, Trump asserted that "when Mexico sends its people, they're not sending their best. They're sending people that have lots of problems. They're bringing drugs. They're bringing crime. They're rapists." Throughout the rest of the campaign and during his time in the White House, Trump used phrases like "thugs" and "animals" to describe immigrants. His famous slogan, "build the wall," refers to the idea of building a border wall along the U.S.–Mexico border.

How effective has Trump been in influencing the way Americans think about immigrants? Did he tap into existing hostility towards immigrants, or turn more Americans away from immigration? The answer is less clear than we might prefer. One important question that has been asked in polls since the 1990s is whether immigrants are good or bad for the country. The Pew

Research Center has been tracking opinions on this, and the trends are displayed in Figure 24.1, representing a pretty remarkable change in attitudes. In 1994, 63 percent of Americans felt that immigrants were a "burden" for the country, and only 31 percent thought immigrants benefited the country through their talents and hard work. By 2019, the attitudes had completely reversed. Only 24 percent said that immigrants were a burden, and 66 percent said they were an asset. On this very basic and important question, Trump's views have had no impact. When it comes to jobs (one of Trump's central arguments against immigrants was that they take jobs away from Americans) the vast majority of Americans (77 percent) think that immigrants mostly take jobs that Americans don't want (Krogstad, Lopez, and Passel 2020). And most American citizens did not support Trump's desire to build a wall on the U.S.-Mexico border (Newport 2019).

Americans are, however, more deeply divided over what to do about unauthorized immigrants currently living in the United States (including DACA children). Some states, most notably Arizona in recent years, have moved aggressively to try to deport unauthorized residents. Deportation has periodically been used by the federal government; it was widely used in the 1930s during the Great Depression, when unemployment was very high (Fox 2012). During Barack Obama's presidency, the federal government pursued an aggressive policy of deporting immigrants through raids on the employers who hired them—in fact, the Obama Administration deported significantly more unauthorized immigrants than did the Trump Administration (Budiman 2020). In response to the policies of the Obama and Trump Administrations, a number of cities have declared themselves to be **sanctuary cities**, local jurisdictions in which police and government officials will refuse to enforce deportation orders or other threats to unauthorized immigrants. The movement to resist deportation has grown, and by early 2021 there were seven entire states (including California, New Mexico, Illinois, and Massachusetts), numerous counties, and dozens of individual cities that had made such declarations. As mentioned in the previous section, to that end, president Joe Biden promised to stop the practice of deportation and to seek new laws that provide a way for unauthorized residents who have not broken any laws to gain citizenship. And although, as we've stated, there are significant differences between Democrats and Republicans, as of 2021, 69 percent of all Americans support providing a "pathway" to citizenship for immigrants living in the United States who have paid taxes and not committed any crimes (Narea 2021).

Figure 24.1 American Attitudes toward Immigrants

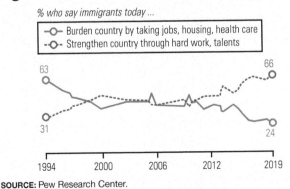

% who say immigrants today …

- ─O─ Burden country by taking jobs, housing, health care
- ‑O‑ Strengthen country through hard work, talents

63

66

31

24

1994   2000   2006   2012   2019

SOURCE: Pew Research Center.

Everett Collection/Shutterstock

THE HISTORY OF IMMIGRATION

In spite of the controversies over immigration, for all of its history, the United States has welcomed foreigners—although sometimes reluctantly, and in some periods relatively few in number. The federal government began collecting statistics on immigration in 1820, and historical data are now published every year in the official reports (the *Yearbook of Immigration Statistics* and its predecessors). These data alone suggest quite a bit about the history of immigration. Figure 24.2 displays the trends in immigration to the United States through the amnesty provisions of the Immigration Reform and Control Act of 1986. This act created a new set of rules to allow long-term unauthorized immigrants a chance at citizenship without having to return to their country of origin. The figures separate out four distinct immigration eras, which we discuss in turn in the rest of this section.

The Four Eras of U.S. Immigration

24.2.1 Identify the four eras of immigration in U.S. history, and explain how each can be characterized.

The **first immigration era** (1789–1874) can be characterized as a period when immigration was largely unrestricted. At the first census in 1790, almost 4 million persons were enumerated, of whom about 700,000 were enslaved people from Africa and the remainder free Whites (or indentured servants), mostly of English, Dutch, and German origin. However, while immigration was largely unrestricted, naturalization was not. The Naturalization Act of 1790 limited naturalization to "free white persons," a class excluding non-Whites, indentured servants, and married women. Thus, there were two kinds of immigrants during the first immigration era—those eligible to naturalize and those

who were not. The latter included slaves brought by force into the United States, although this number dramatically declined after 1808 when importing slaves to the United States was outlawed.

It is striking to note that the right to vote, one of the key markers of citizenship in a democratic society, was not very closely linked to citizenship during the first immigration era as it is today. For most of the nineteenth century, most states allowed non-citizen immigrants (excluding, of course, women and slaves) to vote in federal, state, and local elections without requiring them to become citizens. Some states even advertised this right for immigrants as a tool for attracting them to live in the state. In fact, it was not until 1926 that the last state (Arkansas) abolished non-citizen voting (Keyssar 2000). American democracy in the nineteenth century embraced immigrant voters in a variety of different ways. The major political parties competed to attract the loyalties of members of different ethnic communities, holding enormous parades and festivals during election season in large cities to try to promote their allegiance to one of the major parties.

If the first immigration era was marked by openness and lack of restrictions, the year 1875 marks the start of the **second immigration era** (1875–1920) and the beginnings of explicit immigration policy. During this period, there were no numerical limitations on immigration, only a growing set of exclusion criteria based on personal characteristics or behavior. Prostitutes and convicts were the first to be barred as undesirable immigrants (1875). Next, the Chinese Exclusion Act of May 6, 1882, suspended the immigration of Chinese laborers. Later that same year, the Immigration Act of August 3, 1882, established the first financial test, declaring inadmissible anyone likely to become a public charge and imposing a head tax of 50 cents per passenger

Figure 24.2 Immigration to the United States: 1820–2015

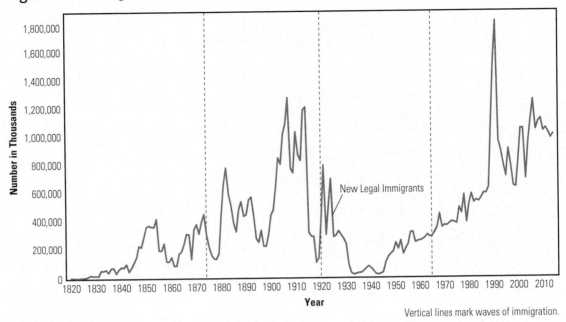

Vertical lines mark waves of immigration.

NOTE: The solid blue line represents the annual number of new legal immigrants. The vertical black dotted lines separate the four immigration eras described in this chapter.

SOURCE: Based on data from U.S. Department of Homeland Security, 2014.

on ships bringing potential immigrants to the United States. The list of inadmissibles continued to grow—persons with certain contagious diseases, further classes of convicts, polygamists (1891), anarchists and persons advocating overthrow of the government of the United States (1903), and on and on. The high-water mark of restrictions placed on immigration during the second immigration era came in 1917, with passage of legislation that imposed a literacy test on adult immigrants (albeit with waivers for the illiterate wives of literate immigrants) and barred persons from the Asia–Pacific Triangle (particularly China and Japan).

However, restrictions based on personal characteristics proved insufficient to quell growing discontent with an otherwise open immigration policy. Anti-immigrant tensions grew in many parts of the United States before and after World War I, particularly as the number of immigrants living in large cities increased to the point where native-born Americans were threatened with losing their numerical superiority. Immigrants were increasingly competing with natives for jobs and economic opportunities as well as beginning to stake claims to political power in places where they were especially numerous (such as Boston and New York). A growing anti-immigrant backlash developed, exemplified by extreme stereotypic images of immigrants in newspapers, popular cartoons, films, and literature. In the early 1920s, the Ku Klux Klan revived in parts of the country, focusing much of its efforts on anti-immigrant activity. Occasionally, violent conflicts between immigrants and native-born Americans broke out. Politicians in both parties began to feel pressure from their constituents to close the door to new immigration.

These pressures eventually led to a **third immigration era** (1921–64). Inaugurated with the passage of the Emergency Quota Act in 1921, this act limited the number of immigrants from any Eastern Hemisphere nationality to 3 percent of the number of residents of that nationality living in the United States in 1910, for a total of 357,000; the law exempts persons who had resided in a Western Hemisphere country continuously for at least one year. A more dramatic Immigration Act of May 26, 1924, also known as the National Origins Act, provided for a transition quota system to be followed by a permanent system with a much smaller total quota of 154,000 and, more restrictively, reflecting the national origins of the White population in 1920. The 1924 legislation was primarily designed to restrict the numbers of immigrants from Southern and Eastern Europe, following the influx of large numbers of Jews, Italians, and Slavs in the early 1900s. Immigration from Northern and Western Europe, though subject to the overall ceiling, enjoyed more generous quotas (for example, 66,000 for Britain and 26,000 for Germany out of the 154,000 total).

The new restrictions of the third immigration era triggered new institutions and new laws. First, since immigration from the Western Hemisphere remained unrestricted, people from the Eastern Hemisphere might want to enter the United States illegally by crossing the borders from Canada and Mexico. Thus, shortly after passage of the National Origins Act, the government established the U.S. Border Patrol with the mission to deter illegal entries. The Border Patrol's first two stations were in El Paso, Texas, and Detroit, Michigan (to try to deter entry from Canada). Second, however, there would now certainly be illegal

One of the great tragedies of U.S. immigration policy before 1965 was the refusal of the federal government to allow persecuted Jews from Nazi Germany entry into the United States in the late 1930s. The United States was not alone in restricting Jewish immigration, even though there was growing evidence that Jews would face severe punishment or death if returned to Nazi-controlled Germany. The story of the S.S. *St. Louis* (shown above) was an especially poignant example of a much larger tragedy that contributed to the Holocaust's devastating death toll. In recent decades, the United States and most other democratic countries have embraced people fleeing persecution in their home country, although there remains controversy about this policy.

entrants, the Border Patrol notwithstanding, and some of them might be deserving. As a result, the Registry Act of 1929 provided for the legalization of persons, not otherwise ineligible, who had entered before July 1, 1924.

There were other, sometimes dire, consequences of the 1924 act. Under the national origins quota system, the United States routinely denied entry to thousands of refugees and asylum seekers, most notoriously Jews fleeing Nazi persecution in the 1930s. This famously included those aboard the S.S. *St. Louis*, the transatlantic liner that in May 1939 was turned away from Cuba and then the United States and forced to return to Europe (where many of its passengers later were sent to concentration camps).

But the days of racial bars to naturalization were numbered. World War II had largely ended unemployment in the United States, creating millions of new jobs for the war effort. But even with retirees, homemakers, and students entering the labor force, there were still labor shortages, especially in agriculture and railroad maintenance, in the years during and after the war. To meet this demand, the United States and Mexico entered into a series of agreements, starting in 1942, which came to be known as the **Bracero Program**. Under this program, Mexican workers came to the United States on short-term work contracts. The postwar boom created even more jobs, and the Bracero Program continued until the late 1960s. At its peak in the mid to late 1950s, the Bracero Program brought 400,000 to 500,000 Mexican laborers into the United States each year on temporary, nonimmigrant visas

that did not permit them to stay in the United States permanently (Calavita 1992).

The contentious nature of immigration policy before 1965 continued to arouse discontent and debate, even as access to entrance was sharply limited. Pressure to open the borders began to grow. One important impetus to change was that some employers sought more openness in order to find the workers they needed in the midst of the post-World War II economic boom, which continued into the 1960s. The case of agriculture and the Bracero Program also suggests that at least some employers were interested in maintaining a supply of low-wage labor from Mexico and other countries as a way of increasing profits. Civil libertarians and liberals also did not like the quota system, but for different reasons. They noted the unfairness in the distribution of opportunities to enter the country and the denial of many basic rights to those admitted on a temporary basis.

After a long period of contentious debate, major immigration reform finally came in the form of the Immigration Act of 1965, which ushered in the **fourth immigration era** (1965–present). The Immigration and Naturalization Act of 1965 eliminated the national origins quotas and established a two-tiered immigration system—a numerically unlimited tier for the immediate relatives of U.S. citizens and a numerically limited tier of visas for everyone else. Initially, numerically limited visas were allocated differently in the two hemispheres, continuing earlier practice—first-come,

The Bracero Program in the 1940s and 1950s brought large numbers of low-wage agriculture workers from Mexico on short-term contracts that did not permit them to become permanent U.S. residents. These workers were at the mercy of their employers, as their right to work and live in the United States was dependent on their employment.

first-served in the Western Hemisphere (now with a ceiling), while in the Eastern Hemisphere visas were based on preference categories, giving priority to nonimmediate relatives and employment-based immigrants. In 1976, the preference category system was extended to the Western Hemisphere. This system remains in place today.

The preference category system has been further amended over time to provide separate ceilings and preference categories for family-based and employment-based visas. Additionally, the 1965 act provides for immigration on humanitarian and diversity grounds. On humanitarian grounds, persons admitted to the United States with refugee visas or granted asylum status may adjust to LPR after residing in the United States for one year. On diversity grounds, the United States grants 50,000 visas annually to nationals of countries from which the number of immigrants was less than 50,000 in the preceding five years, providing an opportunity for LPR to persons who are not likely to have a U.S. relative or employer who can sponsor them. Every year several million persons apply for these visas; the winners are picked by lottery.

Immigration policies have undergone important further changes since the terrorist attacks of September 11, 2001. Shortly after these attacks, the federal government passed a number of measures to make it more difficult for people around the world, but especially from countries with large Muslim populations, to travel to the United States or to obtain visas for shorter or longer-term residence, including for such things as studying at an American university. Enhanced monitoring of foreigners who do gain entry from these countries has also increased significantly in recent years (with a ban imposed by the Trump administration on a number of Muslim-majority countries in 2017, eventually lifted by President Joe Biden in 2021). These measures have raised important questions about how open America intends to be in the future.

The U.S.–Mexico Border

24.2.2 Examine the ongoing issue regarding immigration and the U.S.–Mexico border.

One of the most important contemporary debates over immigration has been how to secure the almost 2,000-mile-long border between the United States and Mexico. Millions of people have crossed this border to set up new lives in the United States. It is the largest immigration corridor in the world, in fact, three times larger than the next largest corridor (from the Ukraine to Russia). Politicians and citizens' groups have demanded ever-greater enforcement of the border. The history of the long U.S.–Mexico border is fascinating. It was originally established by the laying of 52 small stone monuments in the middle of the nineteenth century in the mostly open desert (see image below).

There was no formal enforcement of the border until 1924, when the U.S. Border Patrol was first established, but for most of the twentieth century, large sections of the border were largely open. It was not until 1994 that federal legislation mandated the building of a mammoth fence between the United States and Mexico, and the budget of the U.S. Border Patrol massively increased from $262 million in 1990 to $4.9 billion in 2020. Even this massive expenditure has not satisfied everyone. Heavily armed voluntary groups of citizens calling themselves the Minutemen threaten to shoot anyone they find crossing the border (Shapira 2013).

Somewhat ironically, the successes of enhanced border enforcement have had the important consequence of making it much more difficult for Mexican immigrants to go back and forth to Mexico. Once in the United States, Mexican immigrants may fear leaving the United States to go back home. Why? In short, they may not be able to get back in (Massey et al. 1993). In this way, strict border control may actually contribute to increasing the population of persons born in Mexico and other countries of Latin America.

At one time, 52 stones set across 2,000 miles of land were thought to be appropriate borders between the United States and Mexico (see the image on the left). As policies on immigration evolved, attempts to enforce restrictions on entry grew sharply. One stretch of fencing on the border today is shown in the image on the right.

Nick Ut/AP Images

THE DYNAMICS OF MIGRATION

People consider moving across borders for many reasons. Perhaps most fundamentally, moving may provide a better life for themselves and their children. One way that sociologists approach the question of why people move is to examine the potential gains migrants make between their expected well-being in the origin country versus the life they envision for themselves and their families in the destination country. The outcome of this comparison depends jointly on the potential migrant's own characteristics and on the characteristics of both the origin country—including its push factors—and the destination country—including its pull factors. **Push factors** in the home country are those that drive people to leave, while **pull factors**, originating in the receiving country, are those factors that attract people to go there. Some push factors include economic hardship or political strife in the home country. Simultaneously, pull factors include the economic and political characteristics of the receiving countries. A rich, stable, and relatively safe country may be very appealing to someone living in a country torn by strife or seeking a place where they can make better use of their skills (and earn more income).

For many people, there will be a benefit from migration, but for others not so much. The hopes of earning significantly higher incomes in the new country may be offset by a higher cost of living and fees associated with the move. The emotional costs, such as the price of being away from friends and family and living in a foreign land that doesn't always welcome immigrants, are often painful and difficult. In this section, we will explore these issues.

The Desire to Move and Migrant Energy

24.3.1 Analyze the factors that influence the desire to move.

Although migration is a universal phenomenon, the vast majority of the world's population will not move to another country at any point in their life. Those who do choose to move are often distinctive in interesting and important ways. The *desire to move* will vary in strength. Some people may want very much to move, others may have only a little desire to move, and others may not want to move at all but feel they have no choice. Persons with a high desire to move (or, equivalently, with large amounts of migrant energy) are said to be positively **self-selected** for migration. In other words, those who choose to migrate are often those who are the most positively disposed to their new country and have very strong levels of determination to succeed. Sociologists use the term **migrant energy** to describe the high levels of determination to succeed that many migrants bring to their new country.

To understand what factors impact the desire to move, sociologists link it to other personal characteristics, such as earnings or health. We ask, for example, is the desire to move stronger among the rich or the poor? Among the healthy or the unhealthy? The answers to these questions help illuminate the reasons why some people make the decision to move while others do not. If the desire to move is strongest among the highly skilled, we say that selection on skill is positive, and if the desire to move is strongest among the unskilled, we say that selection on skill is negative. Similarly, if the desire to move is strongest among the healthiest, we say that selection on health is positive; and if the desire to move is strongest among the unhealthiest, we say that selection on health is negative. The type of selection helps illuminate the characteristics and dynamics of different migration flows.

In research on why people immigrate, sociologists and other social scientists sometimes focus on a particular factor to explore its dynamics in the migration process. Freedom from want is perhaps the obvious example. Many theories of the migration process begin with the assumption that people move to maximize their well-being and, more specifically, often assume that well-being varies with the difference between the wage in the origin country and the wage in potential destination countries, after the costs of migration. In other words, migrants consider whether their economic circumstances would be better in a new country if they could move there. Consequently, the higher the cost of migration, the greater the required improvement in the wage.

Whatever the migration dynamic may be, once set in motion, it often acquires a life of its own. For example, if a young man's father and grandfather both went abroad every year to find employment during the harvest, it becomes an expectation, perhaps even a norm, that the young man will do the same (this has been less true for women, but that is changing). Habits form as moving back and forth across a border become routine. When some members of a family or a community have begun to migrate to a new place, it may become much easier for others to consider it as well. The costs diminish with each generation because crucial information can be passed from one family member or friend to another. These and other mechanisms may intensify as networks of migrants form and enlarge (Massey et al. 1993).

Movers and Stayers

24.3.2 Distinguish between a mover and a stayer.

From this overview of the search to make life better, we can isolate and examine the processes set in motion. Consider again the fact that not everyone with a high desire to move will actually move, and some with low desire to move will in fact move. Why? There are two sets of reasons. First, recall our earlier discussion of government policies on exit and entry. Some individuals may

Mario Tama/Getty Images

Immigrants from places like Mexico and Latin America perform vitally important work across the United States, such as cleaning up New Orleans and repairing businesses and homes after Hurricane Katrina in 2005 (as shown here).

be barred from leaving the origin country or entering the destination country. Others may be forced to leave the origin country or to enter the destination country. Second, family dynamics may intervene, forcing some persons to move or making it impossible for others to move, however great their desire to move (Mincer 1978).

Social scientists have found it useful to distinguish between **movers** (those who migrate to the destination country) and **stayers** (those who could move and/or consider doing so, but ultimately choose to stay in the origin country). Linking movers and stayers to the desire to move yields what economist Jacob Mincer called *tied movers* and *tied stayers*. Thus, the set of movers is diverse in that it includes both movers-at-heart (with high desire to move) and tied movers (with low desire to move). Similarly, the set of stayers is diverse in that it includes both stayers-at-heart (with low desire to move) and tied stayers (with high desire to move).

A survey of immigrants admitted to U.S. legal permanent residence (LPR) status—the U.S. New Immigrant Survey—obtained information on how many years each new LPR had wanted to become a legal permanent resident. Approximately half—50.9 percent—provided a specific number of years. The other half said either that they had always wanted LPR (28.8 percent) or never wanted LPR (18 percent). The set of movers included persons with very high desire to move (the ones who said "always"), persons with an intermediate desire to move (the ones who provided a specific number of years), and persons with very low desire to move (those who said "never")—that is, a mix of movers-at-heart and tied movers. There are, this suggests, a wide range of different motivations to move to the United States.

Charles O. Cecil/Alamy Stock Photo

BIG
QUESTION **24.4** How Do Immigrants Fare in Their New Environments?

THE ASSIMILATION PROCESS

Sociologists are especially interested in what happens to a migrant after moving, as he or she encounters a new society and its social, economic, and political systems. The process of **assimilation**—whereby immigrants adapt to the new society—raises a host of interesting questions. To what extent do individuals embrace and adopt the language and cultural values and norms of their new countries? What is the pace of their adaptation? Are certain groups more likely than others to form isolated enclaves, or conversely, are certain immigrants especially good at learning to "fit in"? How deeply and successfully do immigrants become "American" or wholly identify with their new citizenship? And how fast is this process?

Questions about assimilation help assess how migration contributes to developing the migrant's own potential and how the migrant contributes to the destination country and its social, economic, and political development. Migration arouses fears that many immigrants will not adapt to their new country's dominant ways of living, and by failing to assimilate they will (if their numbers are large enough) threaten the social fabric. For example, in 1794 George Washington expressed this concern in a letter to his vice president, John Adams. Washington worried that if immigrants settle with people from their own country, they would not assimilate, and "the settling of them in a body . . . may be much questioned; for, by so doing, they retain the language, habits, and principles (good or bad) which they bring with them. Whereas by an intermixture with our people, they, or their descendants, get assimilated to our customs, measures, and laws: in a word, soon become one people."

Measures of Assimilation

24.4.1 Discuss the measures that help us gauge how well an immigrant has assimilated.

Research suggests that immigrant assimilation is multifaceted; George Washington's comment reflects a very simplified view of the process of assimilation. Most immigrants quickly adopt certain features of their new country while retaining some of the values and norms of their place of origin. Of course, which aspects are adopted, and the speed with which they are adopted, may vary greatly across individual immigrants and groups. As a result, many new questions arise for researchers to study.

Social scientists use a variety of indicators to gauge how well immigrants have assimilated. Some of the indicators are obvious and include remaining in the country (that is, not returning to their original country), learning English, and becoming U.S. citizens. Other indicators include measures that assess whether and how immigrants become more like natives. These include socioeconomic status, geographic distribution, family size, household structure, and intermarriage. **Socioeconomic status** (SES) is a measure that captures an individual's schooling, occupation, and income. By measuring the SES of immigrants and their children, sociologists are able to gauge the extent to which immigrants are (or are not) on an equal footing in the social hierarchy with the native born. English fluency and SES are considered important indicators of the potential for social and economic incorporation (Alba and Nee 2003; Jasso and Rosenzweig 2006; Portes and Rumbaut 2006).

One important issue relates to integration. To what extent are immigrants able to move into nonimmigrant neighborhoods, and how does that vary by immigrant group? **Spatial concentration** refers to the geographic distribution of a population. Sociologists are interested in the extent to which immigrants live in isolation from the native-born population (in neighborhoods largely populated by other immigrants) or, by contrast, live in areas with significant native-born populations. As a general rule, the greater the degree to which immigrants live apart from the native-born population and only near each other, the lower the degree of assimilation. Sociologists have found that both higher SES and longer duration in the receiving country lead to lower spatial concentration.

Another measure of assimilation is **intermarriage**, which refers to both marriages between immigrants and natives and to marriages across racial or ethnic lines. Both types of intermarriage share the common feature that they reveal very close relationships between people from different groups and often involve breaking away from some traditional marriage patterns, thus reducing the likelihood of passing on the culture of the home country to the next generation.

Social scientists have also examined what may be called little measures of assimilation. They pertain to such things as the local way of reckoning temperature, the local way of measuring length and weight, celebrating holidays in the new country, or adopting the local way of greeting people. In the United States, this involves adopting the Fahrenheit scale for temperature and the British imperial system rather than the metric system for length and weight, and shaking hands rather than kissing people on the cheek as the typical greeting. Local customs and activities may also include celebrating national holidays such as the Fourth of July and Thanksgiving, learning about American "football" (to the rest of the world, football is what Americans call soccer), and cooking and eating national foods like hamburgers and hot dogs.

Recent Research on Immigrant Assimilation

24.4.2 Identify the three factors that sociologists take into consideration when researching immigrant assimilation.

So what do we need to do to study immigrant assimilation? Three ideas are central for research on assimilation. First, researchers must define the population whose assimilation is studied. Assimilation may not be a meaningful concept for some sets of foreign-born residents, such as those who are here temporarily and have no desire to remain in the United States. Second, recognize that most immigrants are self-selected; therefore, they are motivated to assimilate. (This has long been viewed as a central difference between nineteenth-century immigrants voluntarily coming over from Europe versus enslaved people

forcibly brought to the United States from Africa.) Third, determine whether new LPRs have spouses, parents, or children who were born U.S. citizens or who have already become citizens. Those who do probably have a built-in guide to things American under the same roof or nearby. And many of them already satisfy the intermarriage criterion of assimilation.

While it is useful to assess measures of assimilation in all foreign-born residents—as they may signal anticipatory assimilation or wishful assimilation—sociologists are particularly interested in assessing LPRs. Why? Unless they leave, LPRs are in the United States for the long haul, and their children will be Americans. Assessing the progress and integration of LPRs provides a window into the future of the social, economic, and political institutions of the United States.

Table 24.3 reports basic characteristics of the cohort of immigrants granted LPR in 2003. This group, which is representative of all new adult LPRs in the United States in 2003, includes immigrants from 168 countries. However, these individuals had only recently been granted LPR, so sociologists need to interview them again every few years to ensure the most accurate data. Nonetheless, because the survey collected information about each LPR in the years before coming to the United States, and because more than half are *adjustees* (those who had already been living in the United States and were adjusted to LPR status), the data still shed light on this group's assimilation process.

As noted earlier, recent research has shown that the immigrant visa type provides powerful information about how the green card was obtained, networks to which immigrants have access, and, in general, their life chances. For each of the major visa types, the table presents the proportion in the cohort, the percent female, and, separately by gender, average age and schooling, and fluency in English. Consistent with the well-known fact noted earlier, over half of the cohort is female, and the proportion of females is even higher in the most numerous visa categories, those for spouses and parents of U.S. citizens.

How do we determine the degree to which immigrants have access to assistance during the assimilation process? One way to address this question is to examine the new immigrants' connections to U.S. citizens. Let's consider our cohort group again. Accordingly, in addition to the 16 percent of the new LPRs married to native-born U.S. citizens, 18 percent are married to a naturalized citizen, 12 percent are the parents of adult U.S. citizens, 10 percent are the children or children-in-law of U.S. citizens, and 6 percent are the siblings or siblings-in-law of U.S. citizens—for a total of 62 percent related by blood or marriage to a U.S. citizen. Moreover, LPRs sponsored by employers may not have close kin who are U.S. citizens (though some do), but they certainly have employers and colleagues at their workplace

Table 24.3 Basic Characteristics of New Legal Immigrants Aged 18+

Immigrant Class of Admission	Percent Female	Age		Schooling		English Fluency		Percent Adjustees	
		Men	Women	Men	Women	Men	Women	Men	Women
Spouse of natural-born (NB) U.S. citizen (16.2%)	59.6	31.6	32.1	13.0	13.8	60.8	60.5	84.2	81.1
Spouse of foreign-born (FB) U.S. citizen (17.9%)	66.0	34.2	33.1	12.3	12.5	43.4	38.0	79.3	65.2
Parent of U.S. citizen (11.9%)	66.2	65.5	62.7	8.75	6.93	20.8	19.7	25.3	33.6
Minor child of U.S. citizen (3.38%)	41.9	20.2	20.2	11.5	11.9	50.5	46.9	46.1	41.4
Adult single child of U.S. citizen (3.28%)	54.3	31.6	34.8	12.3	12.3	48.9	38.3	31.8	33.6
Adult married child of U.S. citizen (1.72%)	57.7	40.6	39.9	13.2	12.4	48.7	45.5	20.4	16.8
Spouse of adult child of U.S. citizen (1.51%)	48.1	42.4	37.4	12.9	11.2	35.7	25.5	8.92	12.9
Sibling of U.S. citizen (3.94%)	51.4	48.5	48.2	11.8	11.1	35.1	22.7	8.97	12.9
Spouse of sibling (2.49%)	52.8	50.3	46.2	13.0	10.8	37.6	19.6	3.98	3.98
Spouse of legal permanent resident (LPR) (2.44%)	83.5	43.2	40.2	8.65	7.76	16.3	10.6	47.7	63.9
Child of LPR (2.81%)	49.2	34.3	35.0	11.0	11.1	27.7	17.2	23.5	19.5
Employment principal (6.02%)	32.8	37.3	36.8	15.7	15.2	78.6	80.7	78.9	55.4
Employment spouse (3.63%)	77.1	40.4	35.3	14.7	15.2	70.1	76.4	56.5	76.4
Diversity principal (5.53%)	41.1	32.3	32.8	14.5	14.5	52.5	45.4	8.45	11.5
Diversity spouse (2.58%)	48.7	37.7	34.5	14.6	13.1	39.1	38.8	5.17	3.55
Refugee/Asylee/Parolee principal (5.35%)	42.8	40.7	38.3	12.8	11.8	39.9	35.1	100	100
Refugee/Asylee/Parolee spouse (1.22%)	74.8	45.3	43.0	13.3	10.9	36.5	30.1	100	100
Legalization (7.98%)	49.8	38.7	37.9	9.03	8.43	17.0	9.06	100	100
Other (0.05%)	–	–	–	–	–	–	–	–	–
All immigrants	56.5	38.7	39.1	12.3	11.6	44.7	38.4	57.9	57.0

NOTE: Adult Sample. Sample size is 8,573. Estimates based on weighted data. The measure of English fluency requires that the interview was conducted entirely in English.

SOURCE: Authors' analysis of the New Immigrant Survey, 2003.

who are U.S. citizens or knowledgeable about the United States. Thus, 72 percent of the new LPRs have ready access to natives or naturalized citizens who can be helpful sources of information about adapting to the United States.

The chief exceptions to this pattern of ready access to help with assimilation are diversity immigrants, humanitarian immigrants (refugees, asylees, parolees), and legalization immigrants. Of these, refugees may have ties to a sponsoring church or nongovernmental organization. The others may be more on their own, so to speak. However, at least one subset of diversity immigrants—Blacks born in Africa—are highly accomplished, with some of the highest average schooling and rates of English fluency (Jasso 2011).

Data from the New Immigrant Survey make it possible to study questions of assimilation more systematically and in a population clearly relevant to discussions of assimilation. Consider, for example, the proposition that new LPRs may have begun their Americanization long before they moved to the United States. We saw earlier that 28.8 percent of the immigrants surveyed in 2003 say that they had "always" wanted to become a legal permanent resident of the United States, and that another 50.9 percent had wanted it for a varying number of years before they got their green card. These two groups are ripe for study of their assimilation. But what about the 18 percent of the 2003 cohort who never wanted to move to the United States? Some in fact

did not stay. Some obtained LPR in the United States as insurance in case economic or political upheavals threatened their country. Others obtained LPR because they travel frequently to the United States and thought it would be simpler than getting a tourist visa every time they want to visit. Of course, some among the 18 percent will actually fall in love with the United States, starting the assimilation process somewhat later than others in their cohort.

A Closer Look at Language and Spatial Concentration: Ethnic Enclaves

24.4.3 Determine the benefits and challenges of ethnic enclaves.

Humans communicate in words, and it is natural that immigrants gravitate toward those with whom they can communicate. If they know English, they can communicate with anyone and go anywhere; if they only know their native language, they have a restricted set of communication partners and limited options for finding a job, a place to live, and places to shop, eat, and go to the movies. Thus, new immigrants with limited English fluency may choose to live near kin or co-nationals. Besides being able to communicate with them, these connections can impart useful

In many large cities, enclaves with large Chinese populations are known as Chinatowns. Shown here is the oldest Chinatown in the United States, in San Francisco, which was first established in the 1840s.

information about the destination locale and can indeed join with them in a form of a mutual protection society.

Geographic areas that attract large numbers of persons of any single kind have come to be called **ethnic enclaves**. As numbers of residents increase (as well as shops and restaurants featuring goods and foods of the country of origin), these enclaves acquire distinctive names and images. Little Havana in Miami, Little Italy in New York and Baltimore, Koreatown in Los Angeles, Spanish-language *barrios* and *colonias* all across America, and Chinatown in San Francisco and New York are among the most well-known of the countless ethnic enclaves across America.

Our discussion has been framed in terms of decisions that immigrants make about where to live and work. But the very idea of an enclave has roots in historical periods when people were forced to live with their similars (on some dimension). Examples include settlements outside the city walls (such as Irishtowns for expelled Vikings and Irish after the Norman invasion of Ireland in the twelfth century), distinctive quarters of a city (such as the biblical and medieval Jewish quarters), and Jewish ghettoes in Europe and Black ghettoes in the United States.

It is important to distinguish between geographic places and the people who pass through them. For example, Little Italy in New

York City is a well-defined geographic area with its own coordinates. Originally, it was a place where large numbers of Italian immigrants settled. But over time, it lost its distinctive ethnic character. Today, it has the flavor of a theme park—a place with Italian restaurants and shops selling Italian-themed goods for tourists and visitors—but it is otherwise a diverse place with many different kinds of people living there. It would not properly be considered an ethnic enclave, even though it once was.

From the standpoint of the assimilation process, this discussion raises several questions: Which immigrants are more likely to live or work in an enclave? For given skills, is there a wage penalty associated with working in an enclave? For given language skills, how is the speed of learning English affected by living or working in an enclave? Also, does a special form of English that is different from standard English develop in enclaves?

Research on these questions is ongoing. For now, the available research suggests the following: Higher economic rewards are associated with knowledge of English overall, but the cost of not knowing English is smaller in areas with greater concentration of persons speaking the same non-English language. Foreign-born individuals who expect to spend less time in the United States (either because they do not intend to stay or because they are older) are more likely to live in locations with high concentrations of people speaking the same language and less likely to invest in learning English, whereas those who expect to stay permanently are more likely to move out of the enclave.

Here, immigrants to America are studying English. Language acquisition is a key part of the assimilation process for migrants in a new land. For children, the age at which language acquisition is achieved is vital; if young enough, the immigrant child will speak without an accent, but if the new language is not learned until the child is in adolescence or later, they will almost always speak with an accent.

Imagedoc/Alamy Stock Photo

THE IMPACTS OF IMMIGRATION

Immigration is controversial in both the United States and around the world because it has wide-reaching effects on the sending country, on the receiving country, and on individuals and families in both countries, including natives, immigrants, and the children of immigrants. Social scientists and government officials have spent a great deal of time trying to estimate both the benefits and costs for the United States. Sociologists are also particularly interested in the impact of immigration on families and children, as we explore in this section.

Immigration Dilemmas for Families

24.5.1 Analyze the dilemmas that immigrant families face.

While there are exceptions, the process of obtaining LPR status is more straightforward for individuals than for families. Also, generally speaking, the greater the financial resources of the prospective immigrant (and sponsor), the easier the process. To appreciate the complexity of the process for families and the effect of financial resources, consider two real families we've encountered in research studies from the Dominican Republic: Family A and Family B.

In Family A, the wife is a physician and the husband is a software engineer with a baccalaureate degree who was sponsored by a U.S. firm for an employment visa. They have two children, a five-year-old and a six-month-old infant. Both the wife and the two children were included on the husband's visa application as accompanying family members. After all the requisite documents were collected (national identity cards, police records, military service records, and so on) and the family was interviewed, they obtained visas. For this family, the process was smooth. They

arrived in 2008 and settled in an affluent suburb in New Jersey. Eventually, they had a third child. The total duration of the visa process was about three years.

Contrast this story with Family B. The husband is a welder and the wife a bank teller. They had hoped his occupation would qualify him for a visa in the subcategory for skilled workers. However, no opportunity ever materialized. They became eligible, however, when the wife's brother, a naturalized U.S. citizen, offered to sponsor her. To prepare for their visas, they collected all the same documents that Family A had collected, including birth certificates for their three children—aged 17 (girl), 13 (boy), and 6 (girl). Additionally, however, because the visa is in a family-sponsored category rather than an employment-based category, USCIS requires that a sponsor sign an affidavit of support. (To prove that the sponsor is financially responsible for the applicant, the supporting paperwork must show that the household income is equal to or higher than 125 percent of the U.S. poverty level for the household size.) After much figuring and calculating and searching for a joint sponsor, the family concluded that the financial requirements for the whole family could not be met. Reluctantly, and sadly, they decided to leave their three children with the children's grandparents in the Dominican Republic. The couple arrived in New York City in 2008 and moved into the predominantly immigrant neighborhood of Washington Heights. For them, the visa process lasted 12 years—9 years longer than for Family A (because the visa queue is so much longer in the family-based categories than in the employment-based categories).

The couple's options for bringing their children changed. Now the children in Family B could no longer be brought as accompanying children; they would have to be sponsored. There would be a wait for visas to become available. So the couple set out to work as hard as possible to accumulate the financial resources to sponsor their children and qualify financially for the affidavit of support. The children's priority date was February 15, 2010, and visas became available in July 2012. Unfortunately, and without realizing the consequences, the eldest daughter got married, which ended her eligibility. Also, the couple was unable to find the resources to sponsor both of the two younger children. The family faced the wrenching decision: Which child could they bring to the United States—the middle child or the youngest?

The couple decided to bring their middle son, who showed great promise as a student. This child attended school and worked part-time in the neighborhood grocery store to supplement the family's income. But there was a pervasive and continuing grief in the family because there was no visa category available for the eldest daughter—no pathway for the married child of an LPR. Only if one of the parents naturalized would it become possible to sponsor her as the married child of a U.S. citizen.

There is a note of joy, however. While in the United States, the couple had a fourth child. This is a golden child, a U.S. citizen by birth. The family is blended—and divided. Around this time, the grandparents in the Dominican Republic experienced some health problems, and the couple started to think they should bring their third child, now 10 years old. But how? They could not yet sponsor her immigration because they could not meet the financial requirements. The family continues to hope that somehow they will find the resources or that the rules will change or that they will find a new joint sponsor.

Notice how vastly different the two scenarios are, and notice the part played by financial resources. The second family's story could have been as short as the first's had they secured the resources to satisfy the financial requirements for bringing all three of their children as accompanying children when the adults obtained LPR—when it was straightforward to bring them, the children were all still young and unmarried, and there was no further wait for a numerically limited visa.

The irony is that family reunification is the cornerstone of U.S. immigration law, and yet the many complexities in the law, the many moving parts, often serve to divide families. The further irony is that the United States long celebrated its welcoming of the poor but now makes it extremely challenging and, in many cases impossible, for poor people to come to the United States legally.

There is a further irony—and a major distinction—when it comes to money. As noted earlier, U.S. immigration law grants anyone with $1 million to invest in a business immediate access to LPR status, regardless of anything else (and that amount can be as little as $500,000 if it is invested in certain designated industries that are experiencing economic decline). The privileging of foreign investors is designed to promote economic growth (the $1 million or

$500,000 they must invest can create jobs and help the economy). Yet the simple fact that anyone with enough money can gain immediate permanent residence while others who desperately want to live in the country must often wait many years or may never gain full access to LPR status does raise an interesting set of questions to think about.

Children of Migration

24.5.2 Discuss what happens to the children involved in international migration.

What about the children of families that migrate? Three distinct sets of children affected by international migration are as follows: (1) foreign-born children living with their foreign-born parents in their new country; (2) native-born children living with their foreign-born parents in the United States; (3) foreign-born children living in the origin country while their parents work and live in another country. Each of these sets of children has been studied and discussed by sociologists and other social scientists.

Let's start with the second group. Much attention has been paid to children living in the destination country who were born to foreign-born parents—the **second generation**. These are the golden children, U.S. citizens from birth, raised in the United States, eligible to become president of the United States, heirs to both the parental migrant energy and all the opportunities of the new country. A large research literature indicates that these quintessential second-generation children do better than their parents.

And indeed, classically, they have outperformed not only their parents, but also their third- and higher-generation counterparts as well. Many of the great scientific and artistic advances in the United States have been made by these second-generation children. Why has this so often been the case?

To understand the second-generation effect, it is important to understand the conditions under which it can be expected. Some immigrants come from countries where they were unable to develop their potential, so that they have lower schooling and fewer skills than they would have obtained under more favorable circumstances. As a result, it is completely natural that their children, inheriting similar potential but placed in a situation where they can develop that potential, will outperform the parents. Moreover, the children inherit at least a portion of their parents' migrant energy; therefore, they will outperform third- and higher-generation children of similar potential.

The great migration at the turn of the twentieth century attracted to the United States immigrants who for reasons of poverty, religion, or gender were severely underschooled—brilliant men who had left school in the third grade to fend off starvation, brilliant women who were illiterate. It is no surprise that some of their offspring became

Robert K. Merton (1910–2003), one of the most distinguished sociologists in the twentieth century, was a second-generation immigrant. Merton's Yiddish-speaking Jewish parents moved to the United States from Russia in 1904, settling in Philadelphia, where Merton was born and raised. Born as Meyer Robert Schkolnick, he later changed his name to Robert Merton, an "American" name, to avoid the pervasive prejudice of his generation.

great scientists, musicians, and writers, including a few very famous sociologists we have read about in this book.

But much has changed in the past 100 years. In particular, the United States today increasingly favors the immigration of the highly skilled. So what would one expect today? First, the children of highly educated parents will be much less likely to outperform their parents. In many cases, how can they? If their parents have PhDs, what can they do to outschool their parents? If their parents earn high incomes, it is very unlikely that the children will earn significantly more.

One critical variable is language. A recent study of the 8- to 12-year-old children of immigrants in the New Immigrant Survey compared English fluency between children born in the United States and children who immigrated before the age of four (Jasso 2011). The children born in the United States have the major advantage of being fluent in English versus those who immigrated later in life. The simple timing of where a child is living at the critical times for language acquisition can be a blessing or a curse throughout the rest of their lives (O'Neil and Tienda 2010).

What about children growing up in unauthorized status or with parents who are unauthorized? For many families, this is an indefinite condition, with some or all family members unauthorized and no remedy in sight. Research on children aged 8 through 12 found that the probability of being fluent in English was higher among children whose parents were unauthorized than among immigrant children whose parents had never been unauthorized (Jasso 2011). Why would having parents with unauthorized status have a positive effect on children's fluency in English? One possible reason is that children who have seen the hardships of illegality are equipping themselves for their new life. Another is that they may have gained or improved their English language fluency by translating for their parents (Valdés 2003).

Sociologists also carefully study families in which parents live in the United States but leave their children behind in the origin country or send their U.S.-born children back to the home country. Why would a child be left behind? There are several reasons. First, some parents migrate to earn enough money to send back home to help a large, extended family (perhaps including siblings and grandparents) if economic conditions are poor. Second, new LPRs who can bring their minor children as accompanying children may not have the financial resources necessary for bringing all of them. Third, there are often legal difficulties that can arise even if a parent has the right to move to the United States. The earlier story of Family B exemplified some of the reasons for leaving children behind.

Both children and parents suffer when they are separated. The extremely poignant cases of the large and growing numbers of women from the Philippines who migrate to the United States and other countries to work as nannies, taking care of other people's children while missing their own, is heartbreaking (Parreñas 2008). The decision to make a move that separates a family is never easy and may be driven by economic necessity, as noted. The hope of returning home someday and reuniting the family is often a dream that both parents and children share, but if the extra income is needed to provide for basic necessities, it may take years for reunification to happen.

Social and Economic Benefits and Costs

24.5.3 Analyze the social and economic benefits and risks of immigration into the United States.

Migration potentially produces both benefits and costs not only for the migrants and their native sponsors, but also for the larger societies they are moving from and to. Research on the 1996 cohort of new legal immigrants shows that soon after admission to LPR, the average gain in earnings from the last job abroad to the first job in the United States (with foreign earnings adjusted for cost of living by converting them into dollar amounts based on estimates of the country-specific purchasing power of the currencies) was $10,306 for men (a 68 percent increase) and $6,146 for women (a 62 percent increase). However, this was not true in all cases: 28 percent of the new male immigrants and 27 percent of the new female immigrants were earning less at their job in the United States than in their last job abroad (Jasso et al. 2000).

For the United States as a whole, questions about the impacts of immigration are often controversial (as we previously discussed). Many Americans express concern about the effects of immigration on population size, population growth, the environment, competition in the workplace, the jobs and earnings of natives, public health, public safety, the national treasury, and state and local budgets. Such concerns are not always easy to address, in part because the effects of immigration are spread out across a vast economy and a vast society but may be disproportionately felt in certain locales.

Periodically, there have been large-scale efforts to study in a rigorous way the impacts of immigration on the United States. These include several major government commissions and panels, such as the Dillingham Commission (1907–11), the U.S. Select Commission on Immigration and Refugee Policy (1979–81), the U.S. Commission on Immigration Reform (1990–97), and the National Academy of Sciences–National Research Council's Panel on Demographic and Economic Impacts of Immigration (1995–97). These commissions consult with a wide variety of experts in an effort to reach some general conclusions, and they provide substantial evidence for assessing the impact of immigration.

One systematic effort to assess the impacts of immigration on the United States was carried out by Republican President George W. Bush's Council of Economic Advisers, which issued a white paper in 2007. The report, like previous reports such as that of the National Research Council (Smith and Edmonston 1997), noted the difficulties in disentangling the effect of immigration from the effects of other economic forces and in projecting costs and benefits into the future, while also noting the progress that social scientists have made in addressing this question.

The report presented three key findings:

1. On average, U.S. citizens benefit from immigration. Immigrants tend to complement (not substitute for) natives, raising natives' productivity and income.
2. Careful studies of the long-term effects of immigration on government budgets conclude that it is likely to have a modest positive influence (on average, immigrants pay more in taxes than they receive in government benefits).
3. Skilled immigrants are likely to be especially beneficial to natives. In addition to contributions to innovation, they have a significant positive fiscal impact.

The report concluded that immigration not only helps fuel the country's economic growth but also has a positive effect on the income of native-born workers.

In summarizing the research that led to its key findings and final conclusion, the report notes a number of striking facts. For example, an astonishing 40 percent of PhD scientists working in the United States were born abroad. In many graduate programs in scientific fields, the most outstanding applicants are often overwhelmingly non-Americans seeking degrees from top American universities, which also are the best in the world in part because they employ so many foreign-born scholars. More broadly, as the technical requirements of an increasingly high-tech economy increase, the United States is not producing enough mathematicians and scientists to fill the jobs being created by the new economy. However, America is fortunate that many highly skilled scientists, mathematicians, computer programmers, and engineers from other countries want to live and work in the United States. The presence of these workers helps keep American companies competitive in global markets and generates other jobs here.

Remittances

24.5.4 Discuss how immigration benefits the family members of migrants.

When migrants leave their hometown and country of origin they often leave people behind, sometimes including close family members like spouses and children, as well as extended family members. Whether the trip is temporary or permanent, migrants often provide monetary gifts, bequests, loans, or other financial help to those left behind. Indeed, often the very purpose of the migration is to obtain financial resources to support the family in the origin country, as we've mentioned. These transfers are known as **remittances**, and they constitute an extremely important source of income for individuals, families, and households around the world and especially in developing countries (Maimbo and Ratha 2005; Rapoport and Docquier 2006; World Bank 2011a).

The World Bank (2011a) estimates that worldwide remittance flows were about $714 billion in 2019. The United States was the top source, with $74.3 billion in recorded remittances, more than 10% of the global total. As the World Bank notes, "remittances sent home by migrants to developing countries are three times the size of official development assistance, and represent a lifeline for the poor" in those countries. When remittances are received back home, they inject resources into the local economy. When the family back home uses the money to pay for goods and services, they will help to stimulate the local economy as well as helping families receiving these resources.

Table 24.4 Migrant Remittances: Major Sending and Receiving Countries

Country	Billions of U.S. Dollars
Top 15 Sending Countries	
United States	56.3
Saudi Arabia	36.9
Russian Federation	32.6
Switzerland	24.7
Germany	20.8
United Arab Emirates	19.3
Kuwait	18.1
France	13.8
Luxemburg	12.7
United Kingdom	11.5
Qatar	11.2
Italy	11.2
Oman	10.3
Netherlands	9.9
Korea, Republic of	9.5
Top 15 Receiving Countries	
India	72.2
China	63.9
Philippines	29.7
Mexico	25.7
France	24.6
Nigeria	20.8
Egypt, Arab Republic of	20.4
Pakistan	20.1
Germany	17.5
Bangladesh	15.8
Vietnam	12.3
Belgium	11.0
Spain	10.5
Indonesia	10.5
Italy	9.9

SOURCE: Development Indicators Group, World Bank, 2016.

Remittances sent back home represent only one of two directions of monetary and nonmonetary flows. Money and goods are also sent from the origin country to assist migrants in the destination country, for example, to pay college tuition, buy a home, start a business, or make a film. Accordingly, the broader term **transfers** is used to denote flows in both directions. To illustrate, migrants in the United States send remittances to other countries—estimated by the World Bank (2016) at $56.3 billion in 2015. At the same time, international students and others living in the United States—temporarily or permanently—often receive allowances and other financial assistance from their families abroad. An extreme case of such financial help involves the most expensive apartment ever sold in New York City (at the time of the sale), purchased in March 2012 for $88 million for a Russian student studying in New York by her Russian billionaire parents (Barrionuevo 2012). It was, shall we say, a rather nice upgrade from the usual student dorm.

Sociologists and other social scientists study migrant remittances, attempting to understand three main things: (1) the amounts of transfers in both directions, (2) the determinants of sending or receiving transfers, and (3) the consequences of remittances for individuals, households, and countries. With respect to the magnitude of remittance flows, researchers almost universally believe that the true size, including unrecorded flows through both formal and informal channels, is larger than the recorded flows (World Bank 2011a). Recorded statistics, incomplete though they may be, provide a window into remittance flows. Table 24.4 reports the top 15 remittance-sending and remittance-receiving countries in one recent year. As shown, besides the United States, other countries in the top five remittance-sending countries are Saudi Arabia, Switzerland, Russia, and Germany. The top five remittance-receiving countries are India, China, Mexico, the Philippines, and France. India and China have large populations, and, not surprisingly, remittances received exceed $50 billion each, more than twice the remittances received by the much smaller Mexico and Philippines.

The second focus among researchers pertains to the characteristics of migrants and their link to sending transfers, especially remittances, and the amount of remittances. Ideas about altruism and about familial contracts and insurance permeate the research literature. Two key findings have been established. First, temporary migrants are more likely to send remittances. Second, sending remittances seems to be unresponsive to external shocks such as economic recessions. Finally, the patterns of results suggest that sending remittances may be usefully interpreted as part of a familial contract.

What about effects of remittances? There is little doubt that remittances improve the daily lives of recipients. For many receiving families, those funds are the difference between solvency and extreme poverty. Other questions pertain to the effect of remittances on a country's development, its economic growth, and economic inequality. Rapoport and Docquier (2006) conclude that the overall effect of remittances on origin countries' long-run economic performance is positive. Especially for poor countries, remittances sent back provide a valuable infusion of resources that enhance living standards, and the money received by families back home will be spent in the local economy, supporting jobs and small businesses there.

Lynne Sladky/AP Images

Immigrant workers, even many of those earning low wages, such as this migrant worker from Mexico, will often send money back home to help family and friends. Many of the kinds of jobs that immigrant workers take are ones that employers find it difficult to fill with American citizens. Agriculture is one industry where there is a severe shortage of workers available, and without immigrant labor—especially at harvest time—the entire farming sector would need to downsize significantly.

Conclusion: Immigration and the Future

International migration raises a host of interesting and challenging questions for social scientists and government policymakers. The initial scientific questions about immigration—such as who migrates, how they fare in the destination country, and what the impacts of immigration are—quickly lead to further questions. Does the ease of learning and using the destination country's language depend on certain affinities between the two languages, such as whether they are gendered or distinguish between the formal and the familiar "you" (for example, French *tu* versus *vous*)? How do cities evolve to incorporate migrants and migration streams (as cities are the primary place where migrants will make a life)? In the future, questions about immigration and the larger questions of the societal inequalities it fosters will increasingly merge, shaping and deepening our understanding of both.

It is also the case that the study of immigration serves as a superb laboratory for all the social sciences, revealing how humans develop, maintain, and discard identities; how family and household structures change; how societies develop, maintain, and discard hierarchies; how groups allocate scarce benefits; how groups decide whom to include and whom to exclude; and how economic inequality and inequality between subgroups grow and diminish. As the world becomes increasingly connected and globalized, the study of immigration is becoming central for sociology.

Recent work argues that migration and social stratification are so intertwined that soon it will be impossible to study one without the other. The same might be said about all the topical domains of sociology and many of the chapters in this book—on family, religion, cities, and political behavior.

What is striking about the history of immigration into the United States—and in many other countries as well—is how deeply controversial it has been. For a country that was built by immigrants, that has historically prided itself on welcoming new immigrants, and that has benefited so immensely from the special skills, talents, and hard work of waves of immigrants, it is remarkable how anti-immigrant sentiment has frequently roiled beneath the surface. Yet as we have also noted, there has been a long-term movement of Americans' attitudes toward *more*, not less, support for immigrants and the role they play in American society.

What will the future bring? The biggest current challenge is to revise immigration law, making it simpler, more coherent, and more intelligent. But that is daunting because no one knows how to approach the question of giving and taking away visa entitlements. It has become fashionable for politicians and others in public life to say they are eager to undertake comprehensive immigration reform but that first the problem of unauthorized migration must be addressed. This may not be entirely sensible. Unauthorized migration is a direct consequence of the rules for legal migration. Put simply, persons ineligible for legal visas will, under different circumstances, become illegal migrants. As long as people are excluded or limited, there will be illegal migration. To their great credit, the legislators of the 1920s understood this, and that is why, as we saw, not long after passage of the 1924 National Origins Act, Congress passed a law providing a mechanism for the unauthorized to legalize (the Registry Act of 1929). Whether a "path to citizenship" will once again be adopted by Congress remains to be seen.

In a deeper sense, it is fair to say that the United States is perennially at a crossroads, caught between two visions of America: one an open society that welcomes many foreigners, the other a relatively closed country that only lets in a few. Throughout American history, there is unease with newcomers, especially if they do not resemble natives. Yet the children of the newcomers, and certainly their grandchildren, morph into natives, and it is universally proclaimed that the latest wave of newcomers is different from the current descendants of earlier waves of newcomers. The correct comparison is between each wave of newcomers as it was perceived by contemporaneous natives. It is likely time for a new fifth era of immigration, but in the early 2020s there is no agreement on what that should look like.

As better data become available and knowledge about international migration and its impacts on sending and receiving countries grows, more and more of the classical questions sketched in this chapter will begin to be answered. And new questions will emerge. Immigration is a vast frontier, and its study a great adventure that illuminates not only immigration but also everything in its reach—language acquisition and use, identity construction, urban development, inequality. This duality echoes the classic idea in American history: Immigrants thought they were building new lives, but what they were building was a new nation.

The Big Questions Revisited 24

24.1 What Is Immigration, and How Do Governments Regulate It?
What kinds of things do sociologists study when they study immigration, and why is the study of immigration important for understanding the world we live in? In this section, we examined the basic concepts and ideas in the study of immigration.

Immigration: A Sociological Perspective

Understanding Immigration from a Sociological Perspective
Learning Objective 24.1.1: Discuss immigration as part of the fabric of social life and how it is becoming increasingly important in the twenty-first century.

Restricting Immigration
Learning Objective 24.1.2: Examine how societies seek to limit or regulate immigration and emigration.

The Basic Structure of Immigration Policy in the United States
Learning Objective 24.1.3: Identify the main components of U.S. immigration policy.

The U.S. Legal Permanent Resident Visa System
Learning Objective 24.1.4: Identify the privileges that U.S. citizenship confers.

Becoming a U.S. Citizen
Learning Objective 24.1.5: Discuss how immigrants become U.S. citizens.

"Illegal" or Unauthorized Immigration
Learning Objective 24.1.6: Discuss unauthorized residency and U.S. immigration policy.

Do Americans Support Immigration?
Learning Objective 24.1.7: Describe how Americans' attitudes toward immigration have changed in recent decades.

Key Terms
migration (p. 687)   emigration (p. 687)   immigration (p. 687)   receiving countries (p. 688)   sending countries (p. 688)   brain drain (p. 689)   diaspora (p. 689)   visa (p. 689)   immigration policy (p. 689)   legal permanent resident (LPR) (p. 690)   foreign-born citizen (p. 690)   legal temporary resident (p. 690)   unauthorized immigrants (p. 690)   illegal immigrants (p. 690)   refugee status (p. 690)   asylum status (p. 690)   principal (p. 690)   green card (p. 691)   deportation (p. 691)   naturalization (p. 692)   sanctuary cities (p. 693)

24.2 What Is the History of Immigration in the United States?
What are some of the trends in U.S. immigration? Where do the country's citizens, permanent residents, and unauthorized residents come from? In this section, we explored the historical context for some of the basic concepts and ideas in the study of U.S. immigration.

The History of Immigration

The Four Eras of U.S. Immigration

Learning Objective 24.2.1: Identify the four eras of immigration in U.S. history, and explain how each can be characterized.

The U.S.–Mexico Border

Learning Objective 24.2.2: Examine the ongoing issue regarding immigration and the U.S.–Mexico border.

Key Terms

first immigration era (p. 694)   second immigration era (p. 694)   third immigration era (p. 695)
Bracero Program (p. 696)   fourth immigration era (p. 696)

24.3 Why Do People Move? People move for many reasons, but the most fundamental of these is the desire to make a better life for themselves and their children. In this section, we looked at the characteristics of both those who move and those who stay, as well as the countries they come from and the countries in which they settle. Distinguishing between these different categories of people and places provides important insights into the dynamics of the migration process.

The Dynamics of Migration

The Desire to Move and Migrant Energy

Learning Objective 24.3.1: Analyze the factors that influence the desire to move.

Movers and Stayers

Learning Objective 24.3.2: Distinguish between a mover and a stayer.

Key Terms

push factors (p. 698)   pull factors (p. 698)
self-selected (p. 698)   migrant energy (p. 698)
movers (p. 699)   stayers (p. 699)

24.4 How Do Immigrants Fare in Their New Environments? Sociologists are especially interested in what happens to migrants after moving as they encounter a new society and its social, economic, and political systems. In this section, we explored a host of interesting questions raised by the process of assimilation—during which immigrants adapt to the new society they are living in.

The Assimilation Process

Measures of Assimilation

Learning Objective 24.4.1: Discuss the measures that help us gauge how well an immigrant has assimilated.

Recent Research on Immigrant Assimilation

Learning Objective 24.4.2: Identify the three factors that sociologists take into consideration when researching immigrant assimilation.

A Closer Look at Language and Spatial Concentration: Ethnic Enclaves

Learning Objective 24.4.3: Determine the benefits and challenges of ethnic enclaves.

Key Terms

assimilation (p. 699)   socioeconomic status (SES) (p. 700)   spatial concentration (p. 699)
intermarriage (p. 699)   ethnic enclave (p. 699)

24.5 What Are the Consequences of Immigration? Immigration is controversial in the United States and around the world because it has wide-reaching effects on the origin country, on the destination country, and on individuals and families in both countries, including natives, immigrants, and the children of immigrants. In this section, we examined the benefits and potential costs of immigration.

The Impacts of Immigration

Immigration Dilemmas for Families

Learning Objective 24.5.1: Analyze the dilemmas that immigrant families face.

Children of Migration

Learning Objective 24.5.2: Discuss what happens to the children involved in international migration.

Social and Economic Benefits and Costs

Learning Objective 24.5.3: Analyze the social and economic benefits and risks of immigration into the United States.

Remittances

Learning Objective 24.5.4: Discuss how immigration benefits the family members of migrants.

Key Terms

second generation (p. 705) remittances (p. 707)
transfers (p. 708)

Chapter 25
Globalization

by Vivek Chibber, Jeff Manza, and Ned Crowley

We have all had this experience at some point: We pull up in our car at a fast-food restaurant, place an order at the speaker, and then drive on to the window to pick up our food. The person at the window greets us with a smile; they ask us if we would like to add anything to our order, and then someone hands us our bag of food. Perhaps we peer into the bag to make sure we got everything we asked for—"Did you remember to add extra ketchup?" The person at the window assures us that they did, we smile back, and then drive away.

Sounds simple, right? Not necessarily any longer. Here is what is happening at some national fast-food chain's drive-throughs. You drive up and place your order—but the person listening to you and taking the order is not the one who greets you as you drive up to the window. Your order goes to a worker wearing a headset and sitting in front of a computer hundreds or even thousands of miles away. That worker then types your order into the computer and it appears on the screen of the worker who fills the order and the cashier whom you meet at the drive-through window. What used to be a simple exchange between you and an attendant a few feet away has turned into a three-part transaction between people an enormous distance away from one another but completed in the same amount of time. It is as if distance just doesn't matter anymore.

We have all heard that globalization is breaking apart assumptions about how and where goods and services are produced. Products that used to be made under one roof are now produced in separate sites thousands of miles apart, and assembled by workers in yet other locations before they reach us. Could that happen with services, too? It used to be taken for granted that while the manufacture of goods can be broken up and dispersed across distant locations, a service has to be provided onsite. No longer. It might not occur to most of us that something as personal as taking an order at a restaurant could also be outsourced,

just like the manufacture of a car. Yet even that is beginning to occur. Many service calls are fielded at call centers that may be located in countries like India, where someone with a script tries to help the person restore their internet service or get an appliance working.

Globalization has clearly been beneficial in some respects. In addition to improved food options brought about by the growing number and diversity of ethnic restaraunts, a number of countries have been able to take advantage of more open access to trading across borders to accelerate their rates of economic growth (most notably China and to a lesser extent India, but also smaller countries like Singapore and Vietnam). This has meant genuine improvements in living standards in these and other countries, in some cases dramatically (with fast growing economies in East Asia being the primary example). Also, many companies and individuals have

My Sociological Imagination

VIVEK CHIBBER

I came to sociology largely by accident. When I graduated from college, I knew I wanted to go to graduate school to study the political economy of capitalism— how it works, where it comes from, and why people put up with it. But issues like these were rapidly receding from the research agenda of most disciplines. I had no particular interest in sociology. But as it happened, there was a good group of people at the University of Wisconsin sociology department who focused on just this subject. So I decided to do my PhD there, mainly because I thought I would get what I wanted—and become a sociologist in the process. My research interests are still largely the same, though with a focus on the developing world.

How far-reaching is globalization? In most cities around the world, food options from multiple countries can be found, sometimes side by side. What is driving the flow of goods (including food), services, and ideas (such as cooking techniques) across borders? Is it always a good thing, or not so much? These are questions we will explore in this chapter.

been able to increase the sale of their products or services abroad (think of global companies like McDonalds, Apple, or IKEA). Whereas companies like these would have once primarily sold their products in a single country, today they can hope to sell them across the entire world. Investment opportunities and returns on financial investments have grown for those who can afford them. So-called "offshore" tax shelters have allowed some very rich people to minimize their taxes like never before (Zucman 2015). Additionally, a famous lawyer, surgeon, movie star, or athlete can earn money from clients or fans all over the world, as opposed to in just his or her home country as in the past (Freeland 2012). The world's very rich have benefitted immensely from globalization. It's never been so good to be rich.

But, processes of economic globalization have also been the subject of frequent criticism and concern. In 2016, growing anti-globalization sentiment in the United Kingdom led the British government to call for a referendum on the country's membership in the **European Union (EU)**, a governing body that regulates economic relationships among almost all countries in Europe. Passing by a narrow margin, the

so-called **Brexit** (British exit) from the EU was a startling (and surprising) example of how controversial participation in global economic and political institutions has become in the European country historically closest to the United States. All around Europe, the future of the EU and the use of a single currency (the Euro) has increasingly come under attack.

Further, the "free trade" rules between countries that have been central to spreading globalization have become contentious political issues in the United States in recent years, with figures as diverse as former president Donald Trump and socialist Vermont Senator Bernie Sanders calling for major changes in government policies concerning economic globalization. The argument among globalization's critics centers on the idea that just because some groups benefit from it, others have suffered. Entire communities have seen their economic foundation disappear as jobs, especially manufacturing jobs, depart for lower-cost countries where companies can pay workers less and earn higher profits. Just how far has globalization gone? What is driving it, why is it controversial, and what are its limits? These are the questions we tackle in this chapter.

The Big Questions

1. **What is globalization?** It is hard to come across any discussion of economic policy that does not, in some way, refer to the idea of globalization. What does it mean, and how can sociology make sense of it? In this section, we examine globalization and its origins.

2. **How far-reaching is globalization?** To evaluate how far-reaching the process of globalization has been, we examine two issues. First, we need to know to what extent countries are participating in international trade and investment. Second, do countries integrate equally with different parts of the world?

3. **What drives globalization?** In this section, we explore how recent phenomena, such as outsourcing, global value chains, and regional trade agreements, have become important components of globalization. We also examine China's explosive economic growth and the human costs that sometimes accompany globalization.

4. **What are the benefits and drawbacks of globalization?** Has globalization lived up to its promise? Here we examine the impacts of globalization and debates about whether it has been good for economic growth and well-being.

Thomas Marchessault/Alamy Stock Photo

GLOBALIZATION AND ITS ORIGINS

Globalization is not a carefully defined scientific concept. It has become part of sociological research, but it was adopted by social scientists primarily because it was already in common use in the media and popular discourse by the 1980s. Like any popular concept, it is often used in different ways by different people, and this ambiguity has even been imported into some social science discussions. But one thing most of its usages have in common is that they refer to the process through which national economies are becoming linked with one another. For this chapter, we define **globalization** as the integration of economic activities across national borders. Globalization can also be seen in the exchange of cultural products (such as food and movies, as noted in the chapter opener), but the heart of the concept is fundamentally about economics.

To get a sense of what this means, imagine a world in which every country is a self-contained economic unit. Everything consumed by its population is made within the country, whether it is clothing, food, electronics, home construction, or other goods; and everything produced gets consumed within the national borders, all by the people living in the country. There is no trade, and there is also no immigration. This would be a perfectly *deglobalized* world, a world in which every country consumes only what it produces for itself—and there is no trade across borders. But now suppose that over time, some countries began to interact with one another economically. Perhaps they began to trade some of their products, with some selling their agricultural products to their neighbors and others selling electronic goods. This would begin a process of trade in which countries would begin to **export**—that is, sell their goods to other countries—and **import**—that is, buy goods produced in other countries. Or entrepreneurs in one country could keep selling to their own home markets, but they could decide to move their production to another country, perhaps for cheaper labor. In this way, it is a process of **foreign investment**, in which not just goods leave a country but also investments. Or it could also turn out that some people decide that there are better jobs to be had in a neighboring country and begin a process of **emigration**, the process of moving from their home to another economy in search of jobs or better opportunities. All of these decisions would be part of a process of globalization, of moving from a condition of economic isolation to one in which economies are linked to each other in various ways.

As the previous example showed, economic integration can be carried out in a number of ways. Perhaps the most common is through international trade—a process by which people in one country sell products or services to customers in another country. But integration can also be carried out through the movement of **factors of production**—capital (funds that can be used for investment) and labor (that is, immigration). (Land is also a factor of production, but land can't travel across borders!) In a globalized world, companies in one country can invest in another one, either by moving their facilities to another country or by buying up existing plants and equipment in the target country. People can also move between countries, bringing about a flow of labor that adds to the pool of workers in one country while reducing it in another. All of these activities are dimensions of globalization.

The History of Globalization

25.1.1 Discuss the two key changes responsible for the development of globalization.

When did globalization begin? Has the world always been globalized, or is it a recent phenomenon—and if so, how recent? The answer depends on different dimensions of globalization and which dimension we focus on. For example, if we equate globalization with the spread of international trade, we get a very different answer than if we equate it with one country investing in another.

International trade has existed for centuries, even millennia. It is possible to trace it back to the most ancient societies, stretching back thousands of years. So, not surprisingly, those sociologists who equate globalization with trade have announced that the world began to globalize as far back as 5,000 years ago. If we accept this definition, there is nothing special about the last few centuries; all that has changed over the past 5,000 years is the *degree* of economic integration between countries, based on the amount of trade between them. But most social scientists reject this definition of globalization, or the idea that globalization has proceeded more or less evenly over time. Clearly, something has changed in the recent past. To most people who study the subject, the 1870s marked a turning point in global economic integration. This shows up in several indicators—the degree of trade, the flows of investment, and most of all, the convergence of international prices. **Price convergence** is simply when the price of a good sold in different places tends toward the same level, for instance, when a car in Mexico City sells at the same price as the same car would in Atlanta or Tokyo.

Why did globalization not start earlier? Two important changes had to occur before globalization could really take off: (1) a change in infrastructure—especially in transportation and communication, and (2) a transformation in the dominant economic systems around the world. Technology and new inventions played a key role in both of these processes.

The most obvious reason that globalization did not take off before the middle of the nineteenth century is that the means to bring it about were still somewhat primitive. The integration of national economies requires considerable advances in communication and transportation. On this score, the really revolutionary changes in the modern era occurred after the 1850s.

First, the expansion of railways across the giant land masses of Europe, Asia, and Latin America were critical to both the direct transportation of goods for export to other countries, but also allowed goods produced in the interior of a country to be brought to cities and regions far away.

A mid-nineteenth-century steam engine transports goods across the United States. Railway lines and much faster and more reliable steam engine trains created a national market for many consumer goods to travel within the United States, expanding economic growth. But just as important, improved transportation also played a crucial role in making goods available for export to Europe via steamships.

Before the advent of rail transportation, economic production and consumption had to be largely local, or confined to a small geographical area. The long journey from one region to another meant that perishable goods had to be consumed locally or they would rot in transit. Ships could be used to carry non-perishable items, but they were expensive and inefficient when land, not water, separate places. Between 1820 and 1914 in the United States alone, more than 250,000 miles of railroad lines were laid down (Hurd 1975). In Western Europe, Russia, India, and Australia, railway construction boomed throughout the nineteenth century, connecting inland markets that had previously been isolated through hundreds of thousands of miles of new lines.

The second great advance was the advent of the steamship. Railways could transport goods across national borders only within the same landmass. For truly intercontinental trade to take off, there also had to be a revolution in oceanic travel (before the advent of airplanes). Steamships allowed for much larger ships that could carry much larger cargoes than earlier ships powered by sails. Steamships were available for transport in the early nineteenth century, but they were too expensive for anything but occasional use. Until the 1850s, however, they were mostly utilized for transporting high-cost luxury items. A series of technological advances made steamships more efficient and lowered their costs around the middle of the nineteenth century. By the 1870s, large steamships were becoming a major source of transoceanic transportation (O'Rourke and Williamson 2000, p. 33–35).

While the railroad and steamship were important in lowering transportation costs, the invention of the telegraph brought about a revolution in communication. It is hard to imagine today, but the telegraph probably had a greater impact on economic activity than either the invention of the telephone or perhaps even the computer in the twentieth century. The telegraph allowed the first long-distance communication of text of any kind, beginning in the early nineteenth century and improving throughout that century with commercial applications appearing by the mid-nineteenth century and the first wireless telegraph networks operational by the 1880s. By the beginning of the twentieth century, it was possible to send messages across the Atlantic Ocean, creating the first truly global form of instantaneous communication.

While the great leaps in technology and transportation were critical for globalization to take off, their effectiveness would have been limited had it not been for the second major transformation: the change in the way that people related to economic markets. The fact is that up until the nineteenth century, markets played a relatively minor role in the lives of most people in the world (and in many places continued to play a minor role until the twentieth century). The vast majority of humanity lived in the countryside as **peasants**, or agricultural producers who predominately produced goods for their own consumption rather than to sell on the market. And this, in turn, meant that the *demand* for goods and services in the market always remained limited. People living in cities were the most reliable source of demand for consumption of goods because they didn't have their own land like peasants did (and could not produce their own necessities). But cities in the nineteenth century only accounted for a small proportion of the global population. Most of humanity was still located in the countryside, and this part of the population was geared toward self-subsistence or living off the land. It was only as growing numbers of peasants became integrated into market-oriented production—that is, the production of goods intended not for personal consumption but to sell to others for a profit—that the pace of globalization could pick up speed.

How were peasants compelled to become dependent on the market? Two processes were especially common. Either wealthy landlords or farmers could offer to buy up their land, or they could be pushed off the land by various means—sometimes they lost the land because they fell into debt, or they had to sell bits of it off to pay taxes. The pace of these changes accelerated as land values began rising in the nineteenth century across much of Europe, giving rich landlords incentives to find ways to seize land from poor peasants. However it happened, peasants often found themselves suddenly without their traditional means of survival—the ability to work their own plots with their own labor. Once this happened, they had little choice but

The ability of peasants to produce most or all of their own necessities, without having to purchase them in economic markets, was a fundamental limit on the rise of capitalism and economic globalization. As more people moved to cities, however, the growth of markets and the demand for goods produced elsewhere began to increase. This process happened at different times around the world, beginning in the mid-nineteenth century in England and America and is still going on today in very poor countries.

to work for a wage—either in the city in factories or small shops, in some other kind of employment usually found in the rapidly growing cities, or in the worst case, as farm laborers working on a farm owned by someone else.

This process, through which peasants gradually lost access to land and the ability to produce their own necessities without having to buy them, is central to the rise of the modern **capitalist economy**. Onetime peasants (and their children) now had to purchase the wheat or rice they once grew on their own plots and the clothes they might have made at home, and they had to rent or buy a house from someone else instead of living in a dwelling they or their ancestors had constructed. In other words, they became market dependent. The fact that so many people had to turn to the market for goods meant that demand for goods expanded enormously in the second half of the nineteenth century. This growing demand provided the real basis for globalization's expansion—there were suddenly so many new consumers needing so many goods and services than before that it became increasingly possible and profitable for companies to be able to sell their products in other countries.

Urbanization—the movement of people from farms to cities (see also Chapter 15)—and the growing demand for goods explain why governments expended so much energy on expanding transportation infrastructure. Governments came under considerable pressure to improve the transportation system—especially shipping ports, railways, and later roads—so goods produced in one part of the country could be delivered to cities where they were in demand. Increasingly, however, much of the new transportation infrastructure was being used not just for internal consumption, but also to reach markets in other countries where the goods could be sold. For example, starting in the 1880s, the United States became a major source of wheat for Western Europe. This export of wheat from Midwestern America across the Atlantic was a major development in nineteenth-century globalization. It is also an example of how the change in social structure, combined with improvements in material infrastructure and technology, were necessary to create the first real explosion of globalization in the late nineteenth century.

The Course of Globalization: From the Nineteenth Century to Today

25.1.2 Analyze the ways in which globalization has expanded steadily since the nineteenth century.

Globalization had become a very powerful force by the early 1900s. But we cannot just assume that once the necessary preconditions were in place it proceeded smoothly through the course of the twentieth century. For many analysts, in particular those who see globalization in a very positive light, there is a sense that globalization is something like a tidal wave, an unstoppable process against which governments are more or less helpless. We have already seen, however, that it took some very profound changes for it to take off. But once these changes had in fact taken place, capitalism spread across Europe and much of the world. Did this rise of market economies make globalization unstoppable?

In fact, it did not. As Figure 25.1 shows, after 1913 and for more than 50 years thereafter, the world actually underwent **deglobalization**, a process in which international economic integration decreased. Figure 25.1 shows a commonly used measure of global economic integration, which

is economic trade as a proportion of a country's **gross domestic product (GDP)**, or the value of all goods and services produced within a defined period. GDP allows for comparisons over time and between countries. To measure globalization, the percentage of all goods and services that are produced abroad but consumed in the United States is counted, versus the total of those goods and services produced in the United States. So if you eat at a restaurant that uses all local food products, 100 percent of your bill with be considered domestic, but if you order some French cheese or vegetables grown in Mexico, then some percentage of your total bill is non-U.S. The intuition behind this measure is that globalization cannot get very far unless countries are trading with one another. The extent to which a country is involved in trade is therefore an effective early indicator of how deeply connected it is to other economies.

For many advanced economies, trade as a proportion of total economic activity actually went down between 1914 and the 1960s (Frieden 2007). This means their economies became *less* integrated with the rest of the world in these years, in spite of the fact that they had become more capitalist and despite the dramatic improvements in transportation and communication. In other words, national economies became *more* globalized from 1850 to 1914, but beginning with World War I (between 1914 and 1970) they deglobalized (that is, became less integrated).

Why did globalization start to decline in 1914? The process of deglobalization was initially triggered by the years of military conflict during World War I (1914–18),

Figure 25.1 Ratio of Merchandise Trade to Gross Domestic Product, 1913–2019

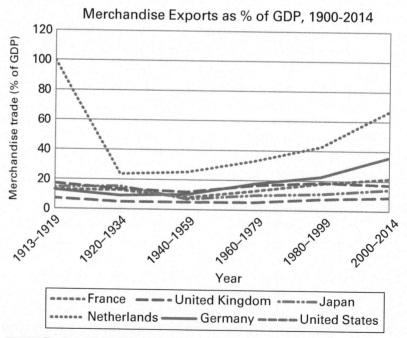

Merchandise Exports as % of GDP, 1900-2014

- - - - - France   — · — · United Kingdom   · · · · · · Japan
· · · · · Netherlands   —— Germany   — — — United States

SOURCE: Fouqin and Hugot 2016.

which caused enormous disruptions in normal patterns of trade and investment. In particular, the war derailed the process of economic integration that had begun in preceding decades. Once the war ended, governments tried to put trade and investment back on track, but the process was very uneven in the 1920s, as many countries faced economic difficulties. These issues came to a head in 1929, when the global economy was hit by the **Great Depression**. The Depression not only caused severe economic contractions in most countries, it also created enormous disruptions to international trade and investment. Most exporters (companies that produce goods to sell in foreign markets) found that the markets for their goods disappeared almost overnight, and little changed for the next few decades.

World War I and the Great Depression certainly set back the economic integration that had begun after 1850. But shocks like these, however painful they are for the people who live through them, are temporary phenomena. Economies recover, and trade and investment patterns resume their normal course. Yet globalization didn't manage to reach the levels of 1914 until the very end of the twentieth century. World War II added massive death and destruction, but unlike World War I (where there was no agreement on how the global economy might move forward), there were major international agreements, including the formation of the United Nations (discussed later in the chapter), that followed and might have fostered global economic reintegration. Yet it didn't happen for decades. Might there have been something else that created obstacles to reglobalization?

In fact, there was—the power of the state. Government policies that established greater control over national economies played a major role during this period of deglobalization. The most important factor that worked against the resumption of a globalized world was that, after the Great Depression, governments all over the world adopted policies to insulate their economies from excessive vulnerability to global economic shocks and to gain more control over the flow of economic activity. They wanted to have greater influence over the goods that entered and exited their countries as well as the flow of capital into and out of national production. Toward this end, they implemented a number of measures designed to put brakes on the free flow of goods and services. Two instruments crucial for this were tariffs and capital controls.

A **tariff** is a tax imposed on goods imported into a country (or more rarely, to goods being exported to another country). It adds to the price of the traded good, thereby making it more expensive. It raises revenue for the government, but it also makes the good less attractive to customers because it is now more expensive than its rivals. This has the predictable effect of reducing the flow of this good into the market. Everything else being

equal, it is a trade-depressing measure. **Capital controls** are restrictions imposed by the government on the movement of funds that can be used for investment purposes out of, or into, the country. An example would be a case where a shoe manufacturer wanted to sell their factory and open up a new one in another country. In order to transfer their funds to a bank in that country, they would first have to get permission from their own government. In this way, their government would exert some control over the movement of funds out of its borders. These capital controls are designed to give government greater sway over the flow of investment, allowing it to increase or decrease the quantity of investment as a response to changing economic conditions. The government can make it harder for investors to "take their money and run" out of the country; it can also make it harder for investors to enter the country if the government feels that foreign investors are hurting national interests. It is much more common for national governments to welcome foreign investment, which can often create jobs and enhance economic growth, but there can and have been important exceptions. For example, a government may want to help domestic companies not face competition from a foreign investor and put controls on the ability of that foreigner (or foreign company) to invest.

Together, tariffs and capital controls can act as brakes on the free flow of capital and goods. The decades between 1930 and 1970 were marked by a very wide use of both of these measures in different countries. It was largely these policies that turned the temporary shock of the Great Depression into a more enduring era of deglobalization, one that the postwar creation of new forms of international governance and cooperation did not immediately overcome.

The fact that it was government policies that triggered a process of deglobalization also helps us understand why *reglobalization* ensued in the 1970s after a decades-long hiatus. Starting in the 1970s, and then increasingly from the 1980s onward, governments began to undo the policies that had previously blocked or reduced foreign trade. They removed many of the controls and restrictions they had placed on trade and capital flows. In essence, governments across the world chose to adopt market-based policies. These policies are widely described as **neoliberalism**, and they involved a large set of changes in domestic economic policy (such as the reduction of taxes and regulations on businesses) as well as the elimination of many barriers to economic trade between countries. As these policies changed course and began to allow more freedom for goods and money to flow across borders, the process of economic integration resumed its course, much as it had in the early twentieth century. It is this second phase of globalization that we have lived through for the past few decades.

Economic Policies in Developing Countries: 1930s to 1980s

25.1.3 Discuss the pattern of deglobalization in developing countries.

Let's examine the pattern of deglobalization in the middle decades of the twentieth century more closely by looking at what developing countries were doing. From the 1930s to the 1980s, most countries in the developing world oversaw very ambitious periods of rapid industrialization. These were years in which these nations—in Latin America, Asia, the Middle East, and Africa—tried to change their economies from agriculture to industry. To do this, they relied a great deal on the involvement of the state—to regulate markets, provide protection to firms, control prices, and protect local industry from global competition. This model has come to be known as state-led development, but its more technical designation is **import-substituting industrialization (ISI)**. ISI has become associated with the kind of development policies poor countries used in the middle of the twentieth century. But, in fact, it has been used by every country that has tried to industrialize since the eighteenth century. It was used by England to ward off competition from Dutch entrepreneurs, then by the United States in the early 1800s to catch up with England, then by European countries in the middle of the nineteenth century, and then by the developing countries during the twentieth century (Chang 2002).

At the heart of ISI was a commitment to nurture national industry in the face of international competition. When countries try to industrialize, their entrepreneurs face some considerable disadvantages. Usually, they have to produce for markets in which goods are already being sold by more experienced firms from richer countries. Take the case of textiles, where a new firm might try to enter a developing country. If a new manufacturer decides to set up a textile factory, they have to face the fact that the shirts they produce will compete against shirts being sold by other firms, usually from richer countries, but certainly by firms with more experience and more money than they have. How can they break into the market? To help them in this venture, their government might implement measures to make things easier. It could impose tariffs on shirts imported from other countries to raise their price; it could provide them with cheap credit to lower costs; it could also help them acquire the latest technology. All these measures are part of a strategy to give them some help against imported goods that they have to compete against. If successful, they will be able to push the imported shirts out of the market and become the dominant seller in the local market—they will have substituted their own goods for the imports. This is why the strategy is called import substitution.

For ISI to work, it takes extensive government intervention in markets. During the decades stretching from the Great Depression to the 1980s, this meant that governments were taking steps to enable their national firms to succeed in local markets and push out foreign producers. So, for example, as Brazilian textile producers grew in their own experience and power, they pushed American textile producers out of the market. This is why ISI and deglobalization went together. When globalization took off in the 1980s, it was part of a larger shift toward more market-friendly policies associated with neoliberalism, as noted in the previous section. In the developing world, neoliberalism came in the form of a policy package known as the **Washington Consensus**. This was a term coined by economist John Williamson, and it describes the main components of a policy package that replaced ISI in the developing world during the 1980s.

The policies that were implemented under the Washington Consensus were broadly oriented to opening up the domestic economy to international finance and capital, to lowering trade barriers, and in the process liberalizing national economies. Through a combination of often desperately needed loans from international financial organizations and aid programs and a variety of incentives provided by rich countries, almost every country around the world started to reduce their reliance on ISI. In this way, developing economies were opened up to goods and capital from the rich, developed countries. They were also encouraged to focus their economy on generating more exports to other countries. Some nations were able to do this better than others, but everywhere the result was more trade and investment across national borders. (We'll discuss the impact of globalization on economic growth in more detail at the end of the chapter.)

What conclusions can we draw from this analysis of the past century? The big lesson is that there is nothing natural or inevitable about globalization. Even though trade and migration have been around for thousands of years, all economies remained localized and quite limited in their degree of international integration until very recently. It took some very dramatic changes in underlying conditions for globalization to expand beyond its centuries-old limits. Just as importantly, even after capitalism spread across much of the world, globalization still did not become an unstoppable force. After the first 50 years of increasing integration of production across national borders, the world experienced 50 years of deglobalization. This was made possible by government action. It wasn't until states turned to a more market-oriented strategy that globalization resumed its course. (Hence, just as the middle decades of the twentieth century were a time in which state controls and deglobalization went together, so at the end of the century, liberalization and globalization went together.) This tells us that the ebb and flow of globalization since 1900 has been governed mainly by political factors and that globalization has depended on a suitable political environment. States may very well have the power to begin a new era of deglobalization if citizens demand it (Gindin and Panitch 2012).

In short, globalization has always been politically driven—the main forces controlling the degree and the pace of globalization have been governments and their policies, not technology (even though many important technological innovations made globalization possible in the first place). It is important to keep this point in mind because it is common to hear in the media (especially in the business press) and sometimes in political debates that globalization is inevitable. But we have seen in this section that it is not true. Globalization is made possible by political decisions taken by governments, and it can (and has in the past) be scaled back, as a result of governmental decisions in the future.

Sean Gallup/Getty Images

BIG QUESTION 25.2 How Far-Reaching Is Globalization?

GLOBALIZATION'S REACH

We now know something about the origins of globalization. The next question is, just how far-reaching has this process been? There are two issues to examine. First, how much international trade and investment is occurring? We need to know to what extent countries are participating in international economic activity. Second, do countries integrate equally with different parts of the world? Sometimes we get the impression that in today's world every corner of the globe is more or less equally connected to the others. But is this true? Or, is it really the case that countries tend to group together with their immediate neighbors (a process called *regionalization*)?

The Degree of Globalization

25.2.1 Discuss the extent of international trade and investment in globalization.

So far we have focused on the fact that globalization receded in the middle parts of the twentieth century before it resumed course in the 1970s. But Figure 25.1 also showed us another important fact—that even in the first decade of the twenty-first century the degree of globalization as measured by economic trade was not much more than it had been in the early twentieth century. In fact, some countries—like Japan and Great Britain—have still not caught up with their levels of globalization 100 years ago. Japan traded 31 percent of its domestic production in 1914, compared to only 25 percent in 2005 (and down to just 19 percent in 2019), and Britain traded from just under 45 percent in 1914 compared to 40 percent in 2005 (and down to 30 percent in 2019). So even while trade and export dependence has increased in the past 40 years, it is not entirely new. How could this be so? How could trade have been as great (or greater) then as it is now for so many countries? One reason is that in 1914, the countries with the more advanced economies were also colonial powers, notably Britain. **Colonialism**—the control over a territory outside a nation-state's own borders—created a powerful vehicle for globalization. Britain and France, in particular (but all the major European powers to some degree) were very deeply integrated with their colonial empires in parts of Africa, South America, and Asia. This opened up foreign markets for their goods. Firms selling in the colonies of their home country had real advantages over their rivals from other countries because they had better knowledge of the conditions and often had better access to sales and marketing networks. The colonies could also be forced to accept goods from their colonial power and prevented from buying the same products from their rivals. This kind of trade integration was not usually very beneficial to entrepreneurs in the colonized countries (who had to compete against much richer companies from the colonizing country, who could "dump" their excess goods to the colonies). But trade within empires did contribute significantly to creating a very globalized world, even if its benefits were weighted toward the rich West.

To see how this has changed over time, we can examine whether trends in international investment show a greater level of integration than simple trade. When firms from one country (or more specifically, the businesses and corporations in that country) make investments in another, it is known as **foreign direct investment (FDI)**. So as international investment increases in size and scope, it shows up in international statistics as an increase in the flow of FDI. For international production to become more integrated, the share of FDI should be increasing over time. This means more of what is produced across the world comes from international investment as opposed to investment by local firms. If we look at the data, however, this is not what we might expect. In 2010, the gross fixed capital investment in the world economy was almost $14 trillion. Of this, the total FDI, calculated as the sum of inward- and outward-oriented FDI, amounted to about one-fifth (or $2.57 trillion, to be precise). Foreign investment never accounted for more than one-fifth of total global investment (UNCTAD 2011, p. 24, table 1.5). Flows of FDI tend to be quite volatile, rising and falling from year to year. But since the 1990s, the range has remained around 10 to 20 percent (Sutcliffe and Glyn 2010, p. 87–88). In other words, more than 80 percent of global investment today is carried out within national borders, usually more. This tells us that factories and firms are not as footloose as some of the popular images might have us believe. Almost all investors stay within their own national border.

The Importance of Regions

25.2.2 Explain why economic integration clusters around regions.

Now let's explore a second question: As globalization increases, is it bringing together the parts of the world into a seamless whole? Or does economic integration cluster around small regions? If the latter, the term "globalization" may potentially be a misleading label for what is going on. In short, "globalization" may be more about exchange between neighboring countries than a truly world-wide phenomenon.

Consider how far goods actually travel. In one version, goods tend to stay in small geographical zones (usually within national borders). They do not travel very far because

their consumption is carried out close to where they were produced. If globalization were a process by which countries transmitted goods to all corners of the world, we would expect to find that as it takes hold, the distance traveled by goods also increases. However, for most countries, with the United States as a major exception due to its extensive trade with China and other East Asian countries, there has not been a very significant change in the average distance for imports and exports in recent decades. During the 1965–2000 period, 77 countries experienced a decline in the distance of their exports and imports, and only 39 countries had an increase in their trading distance (Carrere and Schiff 2004). In other words, trade across national borders has increasingly taken place with neighbors, as opposed to across the world.

This regional bias for trade is confirmed by the increase in the regional share in total trade over the last few decades. The *trade intensity index*, which is the ratio of intraregional trade share relative to the region's share in global trade, can be used to calculate a measure of regional bias. All regions demonstrate this bias, with Latin America showing the strongest regional bias (United Nations Conference on Trade and Development 2007). In other words, we can see that the share of intraregional trade is increasing for a number of *regional blocs*—economic ties that are most densely woven between neighboring countries and that get much thinner between countries located farther away, such as the European Union (discussed later in the chapter).

Another good indicator of the importance of regionalization over globalization is the role of the **transnational corporation (TNC)**. A TNC is a corporation that sells products in more than one country; think of McDonald's, which sells hamburgers in almost every country in the world. Most trade and foreign investment is actually carried out by TNCs, not by small firms. There are over 100,000 TNCs operating in the global economy, employing tens of millions of workers. The largest TNCs can employ hundreds of thousands of workers across the globe; for example, Siemans AG, a multinational manufacturer and energy firm, has 385,000 employees in over 60 countries. (McDonald's employs over 200,000 workers outside the United States) Examining the trading activities of these giant corporations is a good window into the dynamics of globalization. Two facts stand out about TNCs. First, most of them locate their branches and affiliates in other countries. So on average, about two-thirds of TNC affiliates are located in foreign countries (and, on average, about one-third in their home country). This tells us that they are in fact organizing their trading activities across national borders, as one would expect in a process of globalization. But how far do they actually go?

Here's a second interesting fact: It turns out that most of the trading and investment activity of TNCs is in neighboring or nearby countries, not in far-flung regions. Figure 25.2 shows the regions where some of the world's largest companies export their products The world's largest

Figure 25.2 Globalization or Regionalization?

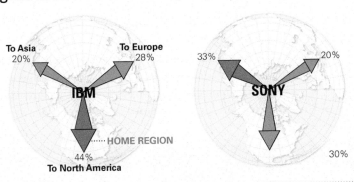

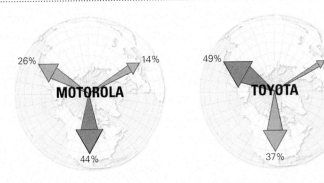

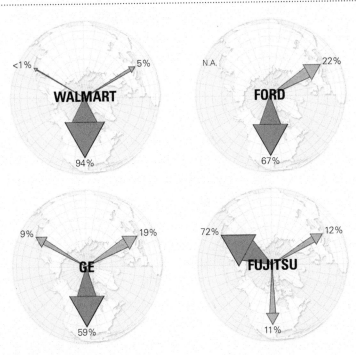

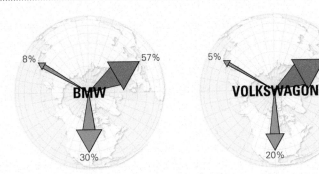

Truly global transnational corporations
The flow of trade, investment, and population across national borders has swelled, but the origins and destinations of these flows are not always truly global. Only 2.4 percent of 380 Fortune 500 companies were truly global in the sense that they evenly generated their revenue across the three largest economic regions of the world.

Biregional
About 6.6 percent of the Fortune 500 companies were biregional, meaning they had at least 20 percent of their sales from at least two regions but less than 50 percent in their home region. The seeming preference among these companies to do the bulk of their business in their home regions means that they are not as global as they are often hailed to be.

Predominately domestic
The majority of corporations were predominantly domestic, or home-market oriented. Corporations like Walmart, which is headquartered in the United States, is most likely to sell products in North America. Similarly, Japanese companies are most likely to sell products in Asia.

Predominantly European
Some of the most thoroughly internationalized companies in Europe still sell mostly to other European countries.

NOTE: Arrows represent percentage of sales by region.
SOURCE: Based on data from Rugman, 2005.

firms are concentrated in one of the triad of the European Union, North America, and Asia. A very careful analysis of the world's largest companies found that 80% were in their home region (Rugman and Verbeke 2004). As little as 2.4 percent of the 380 companies could be classified as truly global, that is, they generated their revenue across all three of the largest regions of North America, Europe, and Asia and the Pacific and had headquarters in each. An example of such a firm is IBM, which is an American company with 43.5 percent of its sales in its home region. The rest of its sales come from Asia (20 percent) and Europe, the Middle East, and Africa (28 percent). Only 6.6 percent of the 380 companies had at least 20 percent of their sales from at least two regions and less than 50 percent in their home region. For example, BP, which is a British oil company, had 36.3 percent of its revenues from the European market and 48.3 percent from the American market. Three percent were host-region oriented, that is, more than 50 percent of their sales came from a single region that was not their own. DaimlerChrysler was the largest in this group. This Europe-based auto manufacturer had 60 percent of its sales in North America. However, an overwhelming majority were home-market oriented. That is, 320 out of the 380 had a majority of their sales in their home region. For example, Walmart, which is the number-one firm on the Fortune 500, had 94 percent of its sales in North America. On average, the sales in the home regions of such firms are 80 percent. Moreover, very few of these firms have a significant presence outside of these three regions, such as in Latin America or the Indian subcontinent. Of the 500 largest TNCs, only nine are truly global, that is, they derive at least 20 percent of their business from each of the following regions: Asia, North America, and Europe. For the vast majority of the TNCs, more than 80 percent of their sales are done within the geographical region in which they are located. So here, too, regionalization dominates over globalization (Rugman 2005).

We see the same pattern with labor flows (that is, immigration). The stock of international migrants has increased from 65 million in 1965 to 272 million in 2019, at an average rate of 1.3 percent per year between 1990 and 2000 (United Nations 2019). However, a closer look at migration statistics reveals that the top migration corridors are between neighboring countries. This includes the United States and Mexico, followed by cross-border flows

Walmart is by far the largest retailer in America and a number of other countries, and in 2021 it was the largest company (by sales) in the world. But despite all of its resources and considerable investment for decades, it has struggled to become successful in China's huge domestic market. Its stores have had to dramatically change the mix of goods it sells to cater to Chinese tastes, including fresh pig heads sold at this Walmart in Beijing.

between Ukraine and Russia. Other prominent corridors are India–Bangladesh, India–United Arab Emirates, and Turkey–Germany (see Chapter 24 for more details).

Hence, what appears to be happening is not a worldwide pattern of globalization, a seamless web of links between all corners of the world. Rather, the emerging pattern is dominated by the growth of regional trading blocs and movement of people, goods, and services within regions. The three main blocs are around North America, Europe, and East Asia. The economies of these regions are getting more tightly integrated, but there is much less evidence of integration beyond these regional linkages (as the Walmart example suggests).

Taken together, the information on trade and investment has some important implications. It means that even with all the deepening of economic integration over the past quarter century, global production and exchange still primarily revolve around the national economy. Furthermore, the degree of integration is not even very new. Even though globalization is a singularly modern phenomenon, as we saw earlier in this chapter, the trends of the last 20 years or so are not unprecedented. The world has been through a comparable degree of globalization before and even managed to reverse it through state action. So while the world is more integrated than it was 40 years ago, the degree is still rather limited, and it is certainly not unprecedented. Furthermore, what is being integrated is not the world as a whole, but rather smaller regions within that world. Again, three such regions really stand out: one around North America, another in Europe and North Africa, and the third in East Asia and now spreading into South Asia as well. Economic activity tends to flow within these regions, and less so between them.

NAFTA: A Case Study

25.2.3 Summarize the consequences of the North American Free Trade Agreement (NAFTA).

The most important regional compact that has impacted the United States is the North American Free Trade Agreement (NAFTA). Passed in 1994, NAFTA has been one of the most widely studied instances of trade liberalization in recent years, and it has also attracted its share of scholarly and political debate (Feller 2008). NAFTA is interesting to study not just because of its impact on the economies in North America, but it is an example of integration and deregulation operating together. NAFTA covered trade between the United States, Mexico, and Canada, eliminating all tariffs and taxes, making it much easier for companies to move operations freely among the three countries (enabling American companies, for example, to move jobs to Mexico or Canada). In the debates that preceded its ratification, supporters of NAFTA, including then president Bill Clinton, argued that it would result in

rising incomes for everyone and lead to the creation of tens of thousands of jobs in the United States (Clinton 1993; Hufbauer and Schott 1993). Opponents decried the lack of effective labor and environmental protections in the treaty and worried that it would exert a downward pressure on wages and living standards, as companies would be able to move their operations abroad in order to take advantage of lower wage and production costs without losing access to domestic markets (Franklin 1993). During his campaign for the White House in 2016, Donald Trump promised to renegotiate NAFTA as part of a broader rhetorical commitment to revitalizing American manufacturing, and by 2017 a majority of Republican voters believed the agreement was bad for the United States. As president, Trump did manage to renegotiate NAFTA (now rebranded the United States–Mexico–Canada Agreement), though the new deal resembles NAFTA in most important respects (Villarreal and Fergusson 2019).

Assessing NAFTA's consequences more than two decades after it came into force on January 1, 1994, is tricky because it is hard to disentangle the effects of the free trade agreement from other factors that shape social and economic outcomes. Nevertheless, it has not been a one-sided success story. Everyone agrees that NAFTA produced a significant increase in cross-border trade and financial flows, and its defenders, including many business groups, think tanks, and politicians, claim that this contributed to economic growth (Office of the United States Trade Representative 2008; Jarsulic et al. 2019).

Critics of NAFTA, however, insist its positive benefits have been largely limited to already economically advantaged groups, and they blame it for contributing to elevated levels of income inequality and stagnating wages and living standards for workers and other nonelite groups (Public Citizen 2008). Economist Robert Scott, for instance, has found that the subsequent explosion in the United States' trade deficit (when the value of exports minus imports is negative) with Mexico engendered a net loss of over 680,000 jobs north of the border, with more than 60 percent of such "job displacement" occurring in the manufacturing sector (Scott 2011). Declining industrial employment had particularly harmful consequences for the job prospects of unskilled workers and weakened labor's bargaining position with employers; thus, NAFTA fed escalating pay and income disparities as well as a growing gap between median wage levels and productivity growth (Bernstein and Mishel 2007).

Meanwhile, the substantial rise in FDI into Mexico resulted in only minimal employment gains while intensifying various forms of inequality (Audley et al. 2003). NAFTA's implementation in 1993 was quickly followed by a massive financial crisis in 1994 and 1995 (also known as the "peso crisis"), which was at least partially related to the agreement.

Over time, as the peso crisis was resolved, much of the job growth created in Mexico by NAFTA was either in the informal sector (also called the **underground economy**, where all transactions are in cash) and did not provide standard benefits (such as paid vacations or social security) that are the hallmarks of good jobs. Nearly all of the growth in manufacturing employment was short-lived, mostly due to greater work opportunities in the low-wage and highly exploitative factories known as *maquiladoras*, mostly foreign-owned export assembly plants. Unfortunately for Mexican workers, the maquiladoras paid wages that were eventually too high to compete with Chinese manufacturing factories (Utar and Ruiz 2013; South and Kim 2019). Furthermore, expanded employment in manufacturing was largely outweighed by losses suffered by Mexico's agricultural producers as a result of the influx of cheaper, sometimes heavily subsidized U.S. farm imports (Henriques and Patel 2004). Improved access to Mexican markets benefited large U.S. agricultural producers but did not prevent the elimination of hundreds of thousands of smaller family farms during the NAFTA era, provoking a massive migration out

One consequence of economic globalization since the 1980s has been an increase in the frequency of financial crises. In most of these instances, the result has been a cutback in social programs and an increase in unemployment.

of the Mexican countryside (Bacon 2012). These sorts of considerations led some onetime supporters of NAFTA to conclude that it failed to provide the boost to living standards they expected while exacerbating a wide array of socioeconomic problems—not all of them bad, but many workers, industries, and regions have suffered negative consequences (DeLong 2006).

BIG QUESTION 25.3 What Drives Globalization?

GLOBALIZATION'S DRIVING FORCES

We now know some of the basic facts about globalization—what it means, when it started, and how far it has gone. We have encountered some surprising findings. The world has

not moved in a steady path from less globalized to more globalized; there is nothing inevitable about globalization. And in fact, what seems to be emerging is a world comprised of economic regions, not a seamless web of economic integration. What are some of the key forces driving the types of globalization common in the twenty-first Century?

Outsourcing and Global Value Chains

25.3.1 Analyze the role that value chains play in globalization.

Most people know that a common phenomenon in recent years has been the practice of **outsourcing**, when producers take activities they once did in-house and farm them out to other firms in remote locations. Outsourcing is part of a larger process called the creation of **global value chains**, which are sets of linked operations that organize the production of any particular product. In fact, much of what we know about globalization has been driven by global value chains.

Take the production of an automobile. This involves a long set of activities, starting with the manufacture of steel and rubber, their transportation to an auto plant, the manufacture of mechanical parts, their assembly into a car frame, painting, installation of upholstery, and so forth. All these activities are linked together in a chain of operations. In the era of deglobalization, it was common for many of these processes to be carried out in one country, ensuring the value chain was compact and geographically contained. But in recent years, as transportation and communication costs have declined, as a means of locating cheaper labor many companies have turned to breaking apart various components of the value chain in their operations by moving production to remote locations where they can be more cheaply provided. Activities that were once carried out in a single country now take place hundreds of miles away.

For example, let's consider the process of producing clothing, which involves three primary steps: the spinning of thread, the weaving of fabric, and the final assembly of the clothing. These three steps have important differences. Spinning, especially of synthetic fibers, is immensely capital intensive, which means it involves high-technology machinery usually operating on a very large scale. The weaving of fibers into cloth is somewhat less capital intensive and involves a lower level of technical sophistication. The final assembly of clothing is very different: It involves a lot of manual labor, with relatively little use of automated machinery. In addition, it can be split up into many small-scale factories (Dicken 2011, p. 308). Together, these three steps make up the value chain of clothing production.

What has happened is that these three steps, especially the final assembly step, now typically take place in different places. A lot of the spinning and weaving that goes into garments is still done in the United States, but since the 1980s, the more labor-intensive part of the value chain in clothing has moved to Mexico and the Caribbean. Garment producers set up assembly operations in these low-wage countries in areas that are set up as *export processing zones*. These are locations where the governments give foreign manufacturers special privileges and tax breaks in return for setting up operations there. The TNCs get low-cost operations, and the host country gets more jobs for its labor force. The garment producer sets up operation and brings in cloth woven in the United States. This is then further processed and assembled in the export processing zone and reexported into the United States. A chain of operations that was once located within the same plant has now been dispersed across nations. But its dispersal hasn't sent those operations all the way across the globe. Typically, it has been spread out over neighboring countries, or countries that are near each other.

What has this meant for the countries that are participating in regional integration? We can ask this question from a bottom-up perspective or a top-down one. From the bottom-up perspective, we can ask what the implications have been for labor—for the people actually doing the work in the export processing zones or the TNCs. From the top-down angle we look at what it has meant for overall economic growth—has it sped up development and industrialization? Has it meant faster growth for the global South (the poorer developed countries in the world)?

Workers at a clothing factory in Guadalajara, Mexico, making garments for Walmart.

brianafrica/Alamy Stock Photo

There is no better place to look than China as a hothouse for what globalization has meant on the ground.

China's Export Zones: A Case Study

25.3.2 Outline the benefits and costs of China's export zones.

The largest country in the world, with a population of 1.4 billion (which is almost one-fifth of the entire world's population), China's explosive economic growth of the past few decades has been a striking example of a country attempting to take advantage of the changing geography of global production. In recent decades, China has become a center of manufacturing as part of fragmented global supply chains. A truly immense quantity of goods sold in the United States is labeled "made in China"—$540 billion worth in 2018 (the United States exported just $120 billion back to China, creating an immense imbalance in trade) (Bartash 2019). Yet China has established itself in a very particular position in the global value chain. Instead of designing products or producing the more sophisticated components like computer processors, Chinese factories most often *assemble* components produced elsewhere into final products, which are then reexported to consumer markets like the United States. For instance, in 2006, 80 percent of the value of exported consumer electronics simply represented the value of the imported components, not any work actually done in China (Koopman, Wang, and Wei 2008). The final assembly step performed in China is often one of the simplest in the production process. Instead of advanced technology or highly skilled labor, it requires above all a large, willing, and *low-cost* labor force. This is what China offers to the multinational corporations that build factories or hire contractors there.

The supposed promise of this kind of manufacturing is that by hooking into the global economy, it will stimulate the growth of other, more advanced industries. Indeed, China's exports have played a central role in its astonishing economic success of the past three decades and have meant real benefits for ordinary workers in China. Wage levels and working conditions are not worse in factories producing goods for export than in other jobs in China. Young people in rural China migrate in massive numbers to the coastal regions where export manufacturing has blossomed because it offers them an opportunity to improve their families' livelihoods that is simply not available in agriculture.

Nonetheless, the benefits of economic growth do not change the fact that the life of a worker in China's export assembly factories is grueling and difficult. Producing mass quantities in even less time is very appealing for the multinational corporations that locate manufacturing in China, but not necessarily for the workers who have to achieve these results. Consider this story, told by a former Apple executive to a reporter for the *New York Times*. A few weeks before the iPhone was to be released, Apple redesigned the screen but was intent on keeping to the original deadline. So, on the very day the redesigned screens began to arrive around midnight at the assembly factory in China, a supervisor went over to the workers sleeping in the company's dormitory and roused them from their sleep. They were each given a biscuit and a cup of tea. They were then told to go to their workstations, at which point they began a 12-hour shift assembling the iPhones. The result? Within four days, the plant was producing 10,000 units a day.

In the executive's words, "The speed and flexibility is breathtaking. There's no American plant that can match that" (Duhigg and Bradsher 2012). This speed and flexibility comes from the fact that Chinese workers have to work far longer and harder than employees in any American factory and earn significantly less as well. On paper, workers in China—as in the United States—have a 40-hour week, but in reality workers have no choice but to put in extensive overtime, even if it is sometimes labeled "voluntary"—after all, workers could "choose" to lose their jobs instead of "voluntarily" working overtime. The actual working day is 10 to 14 hours long. During peak seasons of heavy output, employees in some factories work seven days a week. Including overtime, workers typically earn between $350 and $450 a month, compared to minimal living expenses of $200 to $300 a month. Because employees are often migrants, and many are trying to send as much money as they can to their families in rural areas, it is common for them to live in company dormitories where they are bunked 6 to 10 people per room (China Labor Watch 2011). In all, working at one of these factories is almost more than a job: It encompasses the entirety of the workers' lives.

In addition, Chinese workers lack the kinds of basic protections for workers long taken for granted in advanced economies like the United States (such as workplace safety rules, limits on hours worked, fair hiring and promotion policies). Chinese factories usually do have unions, but these organizations do nothing to represent workers' interests to their employers, only giving the appearance of doing so. In interviews conducted by a human rights group, China Labor Watch, employees who went to the so-called worker care centers at every factory said they were offered only "psychological consolation" instead of real help solving problems in their jobs; in many firms, workers were even unaware there was a formal union organization at all. Employers

Women working in an electronics plant in Guangdong, China. These plants have become notorious for their long hours and very weak protections for their employees. They are, however, able to use their power over their workforce to deliver products on schedule and meet complicated requests from their customers.

also seek to skirt what protections do exist. For instance, they try to keep their workers in the dark about provisions for compensation for work-related injuries guaranteed by labor law or their contracts. Other companies utilize external "labor dispatch agencies" that free the company of any contractual relationship with—and thus legal responsibility for—their workers. Lacking these basic protections and mechanisms for addressing grievances, these working conditions often are unsafe: There are many reports of workers being exposed to dangerous chemicals and of being injured or killed in workplace accidents (China Labor Watch 2011; Duhigg and Barboza 2012).

The Chinese example shows that while the spread of global value chains has indeed provided some benefits to labor in host countries, this has come with a cost. Firms often go to these areas not just for the cheaper labor there but also because workers there have fewer protections and less recourse against employers' demands for greater flexibility and responsiveness from their employees. But there are potential costs on the other side as well, to the workers of the country from which the firms are exiting. In a careful study carried out for the U.S. Trade Deficit Review Commission, Cornell University economist Kate Bronfenbrenner found that employers in the United States used the threat of exit as a means of gaining advantage over employees, especially in union-organizing drives. Two facts stand out about this tactic. First, the threats were effective more often than not. The study found that when employers warned of the likelihood of plant shutdowns and flight to other locations, more than two-thirds of organizing drives failed. The second interesting fact is that managers actually followed through with plant closings in less than three percent of the cases where they issued the threats. In other words, in most of the cases, managers were using workers' fears about globalization against them. Even though the chance of capital flight was very low, workers believed that the threat was real (Bronfenbrenner 2000).

How representative are these studies? It is not easy to say because teasing out the actual effects of globalization on wages and working conditions is no simple task. Workers' pay, their conditions of work, and their hours are affected by many factors, of which globalization is just one. Isolating globalization's effect is hard to do because none of the changes occur in an experimental setting. What we can say is that the increase in global capital flows and trade has not brought clearcut benefits to labor. What the effects are, whether they are positive or negative, depends on how globalization interacts with other factors—such as the level and quality of democracy, trade union strength, and economic growth.

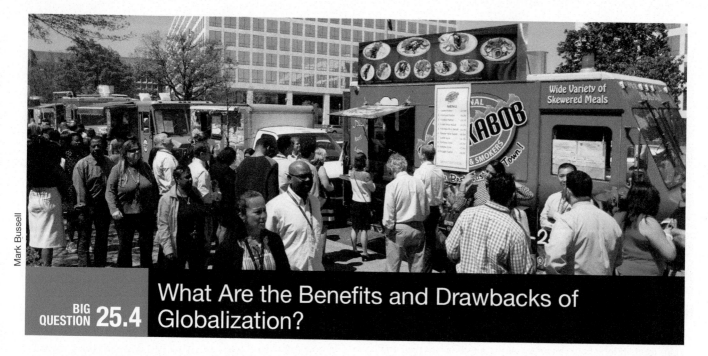

Mark Bussell

What Are the Benefits and Drawbacks of Globalization?

THE EFFECTS OF GLOBALIZATION

The full impact of globalization ranges widely. We've mostly focused on the economic drivers of it, but there are other ways globalization is bringing about important changes, such as in popular culture, sports, cuisine, and various arenas of social life. Even higher education is affected, with many universities promoting "study abroad" programs and students choosing to spend some of their college years in a foreign country. Tourism grows every year (except, of course, for the sharp downturn during the COVID-19 pandemic), as more people travel to more destinations and learn about new cultures and ideas along the way. In this section we will examine some of these social and cultural developments associated with globalization. We will conclude the section by assessing the political and economic impact of globalization and consider why globalization is under attack in so many places. Taking stock, we can then ask how globalization is benefiting, and how much it is harming citizens and societies.

The Social and Cultural Impacts of Globalization

25.4.1 Discuss how globalization impacts social and cultural life.

Globalization has impacted many realms of social and cultural life. The entertainment industry is one of the most visible examples. The United States exports films, television shows, and music to every continent; some American films have become among the highest grossing movies not only in the United States, but in many other countries as well. However, the flow of culture works in every

direction. In the case of films, for example, foreign films have always been popular in the United States, and with the growth of streaming services, more of these films are available than ever before. Among the nations exporting films widely to other countries are Great Britain, France, India, China, and Germany. Mumbai, India—known as Bollywood in the entertainment industry—is also a major exporter of movies, mainly to the Middle East and Africa, but also to Western nations. There have been several movies from Bollywood that have been huge hits in Western countries (such as *Slumdog Millionaire, Life of Pi,* and *Monsoon Wedding).* Streaming services like Netflix and Amazon Prime are helping to create an international audience, not just for films, but also for TV shows and documentaries originally produced in one country, making them available for subscribers all over the world.

The spread of musical genres across national borders is another example of the impact of globalization. International influences on American popular music began early in the twentieth century, drawing upon African sounds and beats. Over time, jazz, blues, rock, soul, and later various kinds of dance music (for example, disco in the 1970s and electronic dance music, or EDM, in the 1980s) that emerged first in the United States spread all over the world. Sometimes, however, the influence went the other way; while rock and roll began in the U.S., some of the most popular bands in the 1960s and 1970s were from Britain, such as the Beatles, the Rolling Stones, the Who, and Led Zeppelin. EDM largely originated in the United States as a form of disco music known as house, expanding and developing in the 1980s in places like Chicago, Detroit, and New York, but it also found audiences in Europe and took new forms in Britain, Germany, and elsewhere in the 1990s and 2000s.

Music has always been one arena where the spread of ideas crosses borders. Today, American-style hip-hop, often reinvented in diverse locales such as South Yemen (shown here), is among the most popular music of young people around the world. But hip-hop itself has international roots, having absorbed musical influences from Africa and America.

European leagues, could actually measure football players as one of its leading "exports."

To that end, the globalization of popular culture and sports has had an important consequence: Top performers can now earn vastly more money than they could in the past (when their fame was largely limited to their home country). In global sports, like football, leagues make large sums selling the rights to their games abroad. Internationally renowned musicians and bands can fill arenas the world over, grossing many millions on a global tour. Additionally, athletes and entertainers can earn money marketing products all over the world, even outpacing the earnings from their main profession. For example, the great basketball player Michael Jordan made $90 million in his playing career (1984–2001) but has received an estimated $1.8 billion (and counting) from numerous product endorsements all around the world, which had by 2020 allowed him to have accumulated a net worth (after taxes) of $1.6 billion (according to *Forbes* magazine). But even ordinary professional athletes are benefiting from globalization; revenue for sports leagues and individual sports like tennis are rising from the sale of television rights in other countries.

In recent decades, the spread of hip-hop represents a remarkable example of the many ways in which a musical genre that arises in one place can find audiences across the globe. Today one can hear different versions of American hip-hop performed everywhere, frequently integrating local sounds, lyrics, and beats. In recent years, the immense global popularity of K-pop, originating in South Korea and combining rock, hip-hop, EDM, gospel, and traditional Korean music, is another example of the globalization of music. Finally, even as certain genres have faded in the United States, they can retain their popularity abroad: Jazz music, for example, has lost a significant amount of its popularity in America, but jazz musicians can still find significant audiences for their work in Europe.

Sports have also become globalized in interesting and important ways. There are still many sports that are largely played only in one country—like American football, which is extremely popular in the United States but barely known elsewhere—while others, like soccer ("football" to everyone except Americans), basketball, cricket, and tennis, are played and watched in many parts of the world. The World Cup of football draws television audiences of over 1 billion people for its grand finale, but is played in different ways by players growing up in different countries even though the same rules of the game apply everywhere. Because of the flow of players across borders (most professional teams have players on their roster from all over the world), football is at the leading edge of globalization. There was a time when countries like Brazil, which produces a large number of top footballers who end up playing for higher paying

Cuisine is another area where globalization has had an enormous effect. Consider the spread of American fast-food restaurants all over the world, an early example in the 1970s and 1980s of the potential for culinary globalization (if not, perhaps, the best example of America's contribution to the world food scene). Most significantly, however, we can find a range of diverse cuisines in almost every country today. Virtually every American city has Chinese, Indian, Mexican, and Thai restaurants, and probably many others as well. London, formerly known by outsiders for having dull national food, is now regarded as one of the great food centers in the world, where a new generation of creative chefs draws insights from multiple national cuisines. Further, "food trucks," which serve cheap versions of (mostly) foreign cuisine, can now be found in most cities in America and elsewhere. We can also shop for foreign foods in almost every supermarket. An amateur home chef from any country can create new and diverse dishes, using ingredients from all over the world. It would be difficult to argue against the idea that one of the major benefits of globalization has been people's exposure to international foods and cuisines.

Tom Vater/Alamy Stock Photo

The Globalization of Ideas and Politics

25.4.2 Explain how globalization has affected the flow of ideas and politics across borders.

Not only does globalization foster cultural exchanges, it also encourages the flow of ideas across borders. The earliest example, one that long pre-dates the rise of economic globalization, was religion. Some of the world's major religious traditions, most notably Christianity and Islam, sought to spread their ideas across the globe, sometimes by force, but mostly by attempting to convert non-believers. The Catholic Church could be thought of as the world's first successful multinational corporation, sending its missionaries all over the globe in the hopes of recruiting new "customers" (adherents). Christians and Muslims have engaged in many bloody battles over time in an effort to dominate the religious beliefs of people in different parts of the world.

We can also see the impact of globalization in politics. Political globalization arose with the development of global institutions that stand above the nation state, such as the United Nations (UN), as well as many new international laws covering a range of global rights and protections. The UN was created at the end of World War II, and represented a major and durable effort to reduce or prevent military conflicts between countries. It has also

sought to serve as a forum for addressing problems of a global nature, such as hunger and extreme poverty. The UN maintains its headquarters in New York City, where 193 countries have offices and staff. It sponsors and funds a wide variety of other global organizations, among them the World Health Organization (WHO), which focuses on global health issues, including pandemics like COVID-19. The UN also sponsors the International Court of Justice (ICJ), which is responsible for ruling on cases involving violations of international law.

An interesting example of how both the UN and the spread of new ideas across borders came together can be seen in the UN's adoption of the Universal Declaration of Human Rights, a statement adopted in 1948 that declared that all persons, anywhere in the world, have basic rights and freedoms, including the right to be free from arbitrary punishment by any government and the freedom to express themselves and their views without any limitation by any government or organization (Moyn 2012). Prior to this, there was no conception that any individual had rights beyond those provided by the nation-state they lived in, or that countries and governments around the world were pledging to treat all people with dignity and fair treatment. The immediate impetus for the Human Rights Declaration was the Holocaust in Europe during World War II, in which the killing of 6 million Jews by the German Nazi government

The Economist magazine writes, tongue-in-cheek, that "The Roman Catholic Church is the world's oldest multinational. It is also, by many measures, its most successful, with 1.2 billion customers, 1m employees, tens of millions of volunteers, a global distribution network, a universally recognized logo, unrivalled lobbying clout and, auguring well for the future, a successful emerging-markets operation." All joking aside, it *is* true that while religious traditions do not think of themselves as multinational corporations, they do share some of the same characteristics.

demonstrated the need for rights that rose above the nation-state. In other words, under the Declaration, German authorities who carried out the Holocaust could now be punished not just in Germany, but in global courts (making permanent the early efforts of the Allied powers to hold major Nazi leaders accountable). Although it has often been a long and difficult process to enforce human rights violations across national borders, there have been some landmark cases since the 1990s where perpetrators of violence and genocide within their national borders have been convicted. Perhaps more importantly, the UN Declaration has spread the idea of human rights around the world. Human rights are at the center of a number of prominent international organizations like Amnesty International and Human Rights Watch, and violations of human rights are covered in the media and where they occur, the offending government is likely to be subjected to sanctions from the international community.

While the UN seeks to cover the entire world, there are a few regional organizations, some of which we've mentioned throughout this chapter, that have formed in the era of globalization. The most important of these is the European Union (EU), which has significant powers to regulate and set standards for member countries. Created in 1993, there are currently 27 member states in

the EU. It was formed in stages, beginning in 1957, to coordinate public policy across Europe and to allow for the free and unregulated flow of people, goods, and services across national borders to create a single European economic system. Some initially hoped that over time the EU might bring countries close enough together so that a fully United Europe—akin to the United States—could develop. However, the EU has generated considerable controversy among citizens and between member countries, a topic we'll discuss in more detail in the next section.

Finally, it is important to note how economic ideas have spread across the globe, and underpinned new global economic and financial institutions that have emerged since World War II. Perhaps the most influential are ideas that we've noted throughout the chapter about the value of free markets, free trade, and minimizing government to the greatest extent possible. These ideas powerfully reinforced economic globalization during its revival in the 1970s and 1980s (under the broad umbrellas of what we described earlier as neoliberalism and the Washington Consensus). Key organizations like the International Monetary Fund (IMF), a global fund that provides loans to countries, builds neoliberal ideas into the conditions that frequently accompanied loans to help struggling countries, such as adherence to free trade and the reduction of government debt. The intellectual roots are usually traced to influential economists teaching or trained at the University of Chicago like Milton Friedman (1912–2006).

But perhaps just as powerful, if not more so, have been ideas about the **welfare state** – the bundle of government social programs that provide social benefits to citizens like health insurance, free public education, old age pensions (widely known as Social Security), unemployment insurance, disability benefits, and many other, smaller programs). As countries have built welfare state programs, other countries have been able to observe what works and what doesn't, and today around the world most developed countries have similar, if not identical, welfare states (Kenworthy 2020). The spread of ideas about the welfare state and its benefits for a nation's economy and society represents a fundamental challenge to the Washington Consensus, and most developing countries are attempting to build their own welfare states along the lines of richer countries, drawing upon ideas first developed in the richer, developed capitalist countries.

Has Globalization Lived Up to Its Promise?

25.4.3 Discuss the impact of globalization on economic performance and criticisms that have developed.

So where do we come down on the benefits and costs of globalization? One of the most direct ways to assess whether

The towering United Nations building in New York. The UN conducts an immense of array of global programs and serves as a place for governments to peacefully discuss issues between them.

Figure 25.3 Regional Economic Growth Rates, 1961–2019

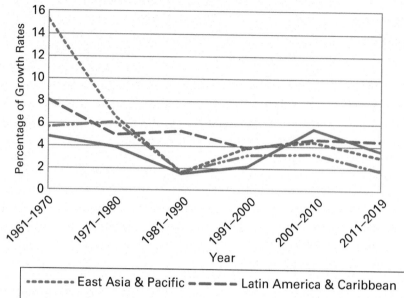

East Asia & Pacific ·········

Latin America & Caribbean ━ ━ ━

Middle East & North Africa ·━·━·

Sub-Saharan Africa ━━━━

NOTE: Values are 10-year averages, except for 2011–2019. All regions exclude high-income countries.
SOURCE: Author's calculations of World Development Indicators.

globalization has fulfilled its promise is by looking at economic growth rates over time. And here the evidence seems pretty clear. Figure 25.3 compares the rate of growth in GDP during part of the ISI era—which spanned from 1950 to 1980—with growth rates in the decades of rapid globalization.

Figure 25.3 points to two facts in particular. First, economic growth was better during the ISI era in some regions, but not others. We see that in three of the four regions of developing countries included in the figure— Latin America, the Middle East, and North Africa—growth slowed down after the end of the ISI-era in the 1980s. The bulk of the countries in sub-Saharan Africa showed a mixed pattern, first a decline but later improved growth in the twenty-first century. The East Asian countries, however, have shown remarkable growth after the end of the ISI era, although it is also true that in these countries policies adopted *during* the ISI era laid a critical foundation. This pattern, in which some regions did better than others, tells us that even though globalization did not deliver the uniform growth it promised, the disappointment with its results was greater in some regions than in others.

In sum, the impact of globalization on the economic performance of low-income countries has been mixed at best. Globalization has failed to reduce the gap between wealthy and poor countries, although the rapid growth in one huge country (China) and slower but significant growth in another (India) in the neoliberal era has meant that more *people* have become richer.

Globalization's failure to deliver on all of its promises has spurred a diverse array of political parties and social

movements to criticize free trade, deregulation of capital flows, weakened labor protections, and economic integration in the last decade of the twentieth and first decades of the twenty-first centuries. Much of the opposition to globalization came initially from the left of the political spectrum, often emerging as popular social movements in developing countries (Piven 2008). Initiatives like the World Social Forum sought to promote the idea of a new world economy without neoliberal economic policies pushing governments in the same direction. In Latin America—whose countries had witnessed several economic crises and even declining standards of living in some countries over the preceding decades—millions of voters turned to left-wing parties critical of globalization. Electoral victories of left-leaning parties in Venezuela (1998), Argentina (1999), and Brazil (2003) ushered in a "pink tide" of governments averse (in varying degrees) to free trade, transnational corporations, and multinational financial institutions.

In more recent years, opposition to globalization has grown more rapidly on the right of the political spectrum. Particularly in the United States and Europe, right-wing critics of globalization contend it has undermined their nations' economic welfare and, they claim, civic values and cultural purity. In Europe, right-wing nationalist parties, often called **populists**, in Poland, Hungary, Germany, France, Italy, and Sweden, have won between 10 percent up to 50 percent of the popular vote in recent national elections. Though some of these parties have been around for decades, others have come into existence much more recently. In general, many scholars attribute some of the newfound popularity to widespread voter dissatisfaction with several aspects of globalization (most notably the flow of people across borders and the powers of regional or global institutions like the European Union (EU) or the International Monetary Fund.

Two issues in particular stand out as controversial. The first is a perceived loss of national sovereignty as countries grow more interconnected politically and economically. This is especially salient when it comes to the European Union (EU). Through its customs union (in which free trade exists among member countries), monetary union (in which member countries share a common currency known as the Euro), and supranational parliament, the EU has grown more and more significant in shaping the political and economic trajectories of its member countries. Right-wing nationalist parties throughout Europe complain that their governments have ceded too much decision-making authority to the European Union at the expense of its own citizens. The most significant manifestation of these Euro-skeptic politics in rich countries was the United Kingdom's referendum on membership in the EU. As noted in the introduction to the chapter, on June 2016, a narrow majority of voters in the United Kingdom elected to withdraw from the EU, beginning the process of "Brexit" (British exit) that unfolded over the next several years. These results—a surprise to many pollsters and elected officials—came after a vigorous campaign by right-wing nationalist politicians in the United Kingdom who argued that the British would be better off outside the EU (Evans & Menon 2017).

The other major complaint made by right-wing critics of globalization is that immigration is rapidly transforming their societies for the worse. Immigration—the movement of people within and across national borders—has always been an important dimension of globalization, but the direction and volume of migration has undergone important changes over the last half-century. In the nineteenth and first half of the twentieth centuries, during the first highpoint of globalization, Europe was a region of net emigration (in which the number leaving exceeded the number coming), with the United States being the most common destination. But this trend reversed in the latter half of the twentieth century, as migrants from former European colonies in South Asia, Turkey and the Near East, Africa, the Caribbean, and other regions moved to the growing economies of Western and Northern Europe. Migration within Europe also accelerated after the 1990s, as countries lowered barriers to immigration from new EU member states, especially from the former Soviet states of Eastern Europe. Finally, especially over the last 10 years, refugees fleeing violence and climate-related adversities in North Africa and the Middle East have turned to Europe for asylum. These migration patterns have made many European countries, especially in Western and Northern Europe, more diverse in terms of ethnicity, language, and religion than ever before. Right-wing opponents to globalization have raised the alarm over these demographic and cultural changes, arguing that immigration to their countries needs to be more limited or closed off altogether (Mudde 2007). An analogous development unfolded in the United States with the 2016 presidential campaign and subsequent administration of Donald Trump, who made reducing immigratino his top issue (see Chapters 21 and 24 for more on this topic).

Conclusion: Globalization in Retrospect and Prospect

In this chapter, we examined three major points. First, globalization is and always has been a politically driven phenomenon. In other words, it is not the result of unavoidable economic forces sweeping away all that comes before them. We have seen that it took very specific political and social conditions to bring it about. One condition was the spread of capitalism as a specific economic system. Capitalism makes everyone within the economy market dependent—that is, everyone has to fully participate in buying and selling to survive. Until this happened, there were very tight limits on how far globalization could proceed. And for the change to come about, it took enormous efforts by governments. Even after the turn to capitalism, massive investments in transportation and communication technology were still needed for globalization to take off. These also required a governmental action because infrastructure investments did not promise immediate profits for private investors. Railroads, for example, were either built within the public sector or needed large subsidies to attract private investors. When globalization took off in the 1870s, it seemed like it was driven by purely economic forces, but behind it was the heavy and ever-present hand of governments.

The importance of government policies is also evident in the way economic integration ebbed and flowed in the twentieth century. The onset of globalization has not been in the form of a steady growth from 1870 to now. In the early twentieth century, it probably seemed like market integration was an unstoppable force which all governments and all economies were powerless to stop. Yet by 1950 it seemed like a thing of the past. The world during the years after World War II was one in which there was still plenty of trade and international investment, but it was subordinated to production and exchange within national borders. The reglobalization that has occurred since the 1970s has again been driven by government policies such as the lowering of tariffs, the opening up of capital markets, and the deregulation of markets. Taken together, all these points show that globalization has been the product of social and political initiatives. And this means—crucially—that there is nothing natural or inevitable about it. It can be modified, and even significantly changed, by government policy.

The next major point discussed in the chapter is that even while globalization is a reality, we should not exaggerate its extent. The media and political leaders often tell us that we are in an era of unprecedented economic integration. The *New York Times* columnist Thomas Friedman famously announced in a best-selling book that, with globalization, the world had become "flat"—meaning that every part of the world was becoming woven into the same seamless fabric (Friedman 2005). But as we have seen, there are two caveats to this observation. First, in historical terms, the extent of real economic integration today is probably no more than it was in 1912. So it is not accurate to say that we are in a new world. Rather, we are now catching up to a world from a century ago. Second, whatever integration exists is more closely structured around regions than it is around the entire globe. Distance, culture, history—all the things that sociologists study—still matter a great deal in economic dynamics.

A final major point we discussed is that globalization is not a panacea. Globalization has changed cultures and societies in many ways (we discussed examples of music, sports, and food), as well as provided greater internationalism in politics and foreign affairs. But on the core question of its economic impact, in many regions in the world the years of increased economic integration have led to worse economic outcomes than earlier periods when globalization was at a low point and trade between countries was more limited (for example, from 1945 to 1975). This does not mean that we should push for a new era of deglobalization, as there are also benefits that come with economic and social integration. Among these are the flow of ideas and cultures across national borders, which have enriched the food we eat, the music we listen to, the literature we read, the television programs, movies and sports we consume. And as we highlighted earlier, it is not easy to disentangle the effects of globalization itself from the effects of other forces—such neoliberalism and the deregulation of economic markets in the 1980s and 1990s—that were occurring at the same time. It could very well be that globalization accompanied by a more active government, more redistribution, and more regulation of market outcomes could yield better results than would a new era of deglobalization. But while some kind of globalizing economy might be desirable, we can probably conclude that the kind we have *actually had* has not lived up to the hopes of those promoting global free trade. But how do we modify it if it is an unstoppable force? The point is that it is not. Now that we know that globalization has always been governed by political forces, that it has relied on state support and state indulgence, we can also have some confidence that if we are unhappy with its results, there is something that an activated citizenry can do about it.

The Big Questions Revisited 25

25.1 What Is Globalization? Discussions of economic policy relate to globalization. What does globalization mean, and how can sociology make sense of it? In this section, we examined globalization and its origins.

Globalization and Its Origins

The Beginnings of Globalization

Learning Objective 25.1.1: Discuss the two key changes responsible for the development of globalization.

The Course of Globalization: From the Nineteenth Century to Today

Learning Objective 25.1.2: Analyze the ways in which globalization has expanded steadily since the nineteenth century.

Economic Policies in Developing Countries: 1930s to 1980s

Learning Objective 25.1.3: Discuss the pattern of deglobalization in developing countries.

Key Terms

European Union (EU) (p. 714)   Brexit (p. 714)
globalization (p. 715)   export (p. 715)   import (p. 715)   foreign investment (p. 715)   emigration (p. 715)   factors of production (p. 715)
price convergence (p. 716)   peasant (p. 717)
capitalist economy (p. 717)   urbanization (p. 718)
deglobalization (p. 718)   gross domestic product (GDP) (p. 718)   Great Depression (p. 719)
tariff (p. 719)   capital controls (p. 719)
neoliberalism (p. 719)   import-substituting industrialization (ISI) (p. 720)   Washington Consensus (p. 720)

25.2 How Far-Reaching Is Globalization? To evaluate how far-reaching the process of globalization has been, we examined two issues: (1) to what extent countries are participating in international trade and investment, and (2) whether countries integrate equally with different parts of the world.

Globalization's Reach

The Degree of Globalization

Learning Objective 25.2.1: Discuss the extent of international trade and investment in globalization.

The Importance of Regions

Learning Objective 25.2.2: Explain why economic integration clusters around regions.

NAFTA: A Case Study

Learning Objective 25.2.3: Summarize the consequences of the North American Free Trade Agreement (NAFTA).

Key Terms

colonialism (p. 721)   foreign direct investment (FDI) (p. 722)   transnational corporation (TNC) (p. 722)   underground economy (p. 728)

25.3 What Drives Globalization? In this section, we explored how recent phenomena, such as outsourcing, global value chains, and regional trade agreements, have become important components of globalization. We also examined China's explosive economic growth and the human costs that sometimes accompany globalization.

Globalization's Driving Forces

Outsourcing and Global Value Chains

Learning Objective 25.3.1: Analyze the role that value chains play in globalization.

China's Export Zones: A Case Study

Learning Objective 25.3.2: Outline the benefits and costs of China's export zones.

Key Terms

outsourcing (p. 727)   global value chains (p. 727)

25.4 What Are the Benefits and Drawbacks of Globalization? Has globalization lived up to its promise? In this section, we discussed the social, cultural, political, and economic impacts of globalization and assessed whether it has been effective for economic growth and well-being.

The Effects of Globalization

The Social and Cultural Impacts of Globalization

Learning Objective 25.4.1: Discuss how globalization impacts social and cultural life.

The Globalization of Ideas and Politics

Learning Objective 25.4.2: Explain how globalization has affected the flow of ideas and politics across borders.

Has Globalization Lived Up to Its Promise?

Learning Objective 25.4.3: Discuss the impact of globalization on economic performance and criticisms that have developed.

Key Terms

populist (p. 734)

Glossary

absolute poverty A measure of the minimum requirements needed for people to have basic standards of food, clothing, health, and shelter in the society they are living. Any individual or family falling below this fixed amount is defined as living in poverty. The official U.S. government definition of poverty is an absolute measure based on an estimate of minimum living standards first established in the 1960s and adjusted for inflation thereafter.

access The ability or right to approach, enter, exit, communicate with, or make use of research sites and materials.

acid rain Rain containing acid formed when the gaseous air pollutants nitrogen oxide and sulfur dioxide react with water molecules in the atmosphere.

active learning An approach to teaching and learning in which students learn through activities rather than passively absorbing information.

advance directive Legal document in which individuals define the conditions under which they prefer to die. For example, an advance directive might specify that someone does not want to be placed on a ventilator if that is necessary to sustain their life.

affirmative action Government policies regarding employment and education that seek to increase the representation of minorities and women in fields from which they have historically been excluded. Affirmative action is undertaken in an effort to counter the historical effects of discrimination and exclusion.

Affordable Care Act Also known as Obamacare, a federal law adopted in 2010 that subsidizes health insurance for most low- and moderate-income families, allows children up to age 26 to stay on their parents' health insurance, and requires insurance companies to offer their policies to everyone (that is, it disallows limitations on "pre-existing conditions" to prevent health insurance companies from insuring only healthy people), and finally prevents insurers from cancelling policies before they expire when an insured person has a major medical problem.

age pyramid A diagram that plots the age distribution of a population, with the numbers at the youngest ages at the bottom of the graph and the numbers at the oldest ages at the top, and with males and females on the left- and right-hand sides, respectively.

ageism Prejudice and discrimination directed at older people, based on stereotypes about old age.

agenda setting The ability to decide which, of the many possible topics for discussion, debate, and possible action that exist in the world, will actually be considered. Agenda setting can take place in any organizational setting – including in politics and the media -- where decision-making occurs, or the topics of social and political discussion are decided.

agnostic A person who believes that the existence of God or other supernatural beings is unknowable and therefore claims to neither believe or not believe in any faith.

algorithm Rules for solving calculations or problems.

altruism Human action that is based on concern for the well-being of others or the community, the opposite of self-interest motives.

American Medical Association (AMA) The predominant association of physicians, founded in 1847, that has represented the interests and concerns of doctors. For most of its history, it vigorously opposed the establishment of a national health care system such as those found in most other countries, although its position has changed in recent years.

American National Election Study (ANES) The major academic survey of U.S. voters' attitudes and political participation, conducted at the time of national elections every two years.

analytical sociology An approach to social theory and research that centers on "middle-range" questions and seeks to uncover the processes, or mechanisms, through which individuals are influenced by social forces.

anecdote A single event or episode that may be the basis for a story or account, but which may not be representative or typical (and hence an unreliable basis for forming any conclusions).

animism The belief that a supernatural power organizes all sentient beings, plants, and natural phenomena, and that all of these objects, has a soul or spiritual essence.

anthropocentrism The belief that humans are separate from and superior to the natural world.

artificial intelligence Machines (such as computers or robots) and their software that have the capacity to mimic human intelligence and perform complex mental tasks.

assault A physical attack that injures another person but does not kill them.

assembly line A type of factory in which each worker performs one or a handful of small, discrete tasks, with a conveyer belt moving pieces to each workstation. A finished product results from the input of many workers across an entire factory.

assimilation The process by which immigrants come to be incorporated into their new society by taking on the cultural tastes and practices of the new society.

association The existence of a relationship between two variables, where a change in one variable is related to a change in another variable. It could indicate that a change in one variable is the cause of the change in another, although that is not necessarily true.

asylum status A form of protection available to immigrants seeking admission to another country because of political violence or repression in their home country. Typically, applicants seeking asylum status must demonstrate that their life would be in danger if they were forced to return to their home country.

atheist A term used to describe anyone who actively rejects the possibility of a god or any other supernatural being.

authority The ability to compel others to do things without needing to resort to threats. For Max Weber, authority requires legitimacy; that is, individuals grant authority to those they believe have a legitimate right to rule.

authoritarian Undemocratic decision-making systems or governments in which one person or a group rules without having to take into account the preferences of the people being ruled.

autism A developmental disorder in which an individual has difficulty with ordinary social interactions with others. Commonly thought of as a spectrum from minor to severe.

automation The use of machines to perform tasks previously performed by humans.

autonomy In work, the power to decide what and how one performs one's daily tasks, free of close supervision.

baby boom Births during the post-World War II period in the United States from approximately 1946 through 1964. During this period, fertility was high. The birth cohorts born during the baby boom years produced a generation of Americans that was the largest in U.S. history.

behavioral economics A subfield of economics that incorporates insights from psychology to study individual economic behavior.

big data Any large volume of information, often found in settings not previously studied, typically requiring new techniques to analyze it.

biographical availability An individual's freedom to participate in a movement or protest due to a (relative) lack of constraining obligations created by work, school, family, or community.

blue-collar jobs Manufacturing or service jobs involving physical labor (the "blue collar" refers to the idea that these workers (originally mostly men) doing physical labor do not wear "white collar" shirts like those of professionals).

bourgeoisie A term coined by Karl Marx and Friedrich Engels to describe the group in a capitalist economy who own businesses and employ people to work for them. This term is also used more generally in the Marxist tradition to refer to the most powerful class in a capitalist society.

Bracero Program A set of agreements between the United States and Mexico from 1942 to 1964 to import temporary workers from Mexico.

brain drain The departure of a significant number of the most educated and skilled citizens, who go to live and work in other regions or countries.

Brexit A term that refers to the vote of citizens in the United Kingdom to leave the European Union in 2016, and that country's final departure from the EU in 2020.

Brown v. Board of Education A landmark 1954 U.S. Supreme Court decision that held that racially segregated educational systems were unconstitutional.

bureaucracy A type of organization that has rules and responsibilities for each position (or job) spelled out, in which selection into those positions occurs on the basis of merit (not typically by election or inheritance). Many bureaucracies are also responsible for setting out policies and procedures that are to be adhered to by others.

cap-and-trade program A system in which a limit is placed on the total amount of carbon emissions that are allowable (the cap) and in which businesses buy and sell permits that entitle them to a designated amount of emissions (the trade).

capital A financial resource that can be used to make investments. Economic capital refers to the possession of financial assets that can be invested in a business. Other types of capital have also been suggested, for example human capital (the skills, education, or knowledge an individual possesses, which can be used to earn higher income) and cultural capital (the cultural knowledge possessed by an individual that impacts an individual's capacity to speak and interact with others in a sophisticated way).

capital controls Government policies that limit the movement of capital (that is, funds available for investment) into or out of a country.

capital gains tax A tax on profits generated from the sale of a wealth asset, such as stocks or property.

capital strike A situation in which businesses refuse to make new investments until governmental policy is changed.

capitalism An economic system organized around private property and market exchange. In a capitalist economy, goods that are produced for consumption are distributed via exchange on the market.

capitalist economy An economic system in which goods and services are exchanged through markets, in which prices are established by what buyers are willing to pay, and in which property is privately owned. Under capitalism, markets extend to the hiring of workers at wages determined by negotiations between individuals (or unions) and employers. The role of government in regulating a capitalist economy varies widely, producing different types of capitalist economies around the world today.

capitalist state The governing institutions and legal system in a capitalist society.

capitalist world system A concept invented by Immanuel Wallerstein to describe the ways in which capitalist economies are linked in a global system, in which rich, developed countries are able to exploit undeveloped countries through a global division of labor in which poor countries provide raw materials and lower skill labor.

carework (or caring work) All types of caring for other people, typically in one's own family, including childcare, elder care, or taking care of a disabled or sick adult.

caste society A society in which a person's social position is determined by the family they are born into.

causal inference A statement about cause and effect that claims that a change in one variable is the cause of a change in another variable.

causality When change in one variable is a direct cause of change in another variable. For example, long-term smoking is established as a cause of increased risk of lung cancer.

census A count of the members of a current population of a country.

central city The main city in a metropolitan area, which may be surrounded by smaller suburbs.

charisma Derived from a Greek word meaning "gift of grace." Max Weber introduced the idea of charisma into the sociological study of social change to refer to unique individuals who claim special powers or gifts that a larger number of followers believe to be true.

charter schools Schools that are created within a local public school system, but which are free to establish most of their own rules and guidelines.

Chicago School The first Sociology Department in America, established at the University of Chicago in 1892. It was here that a distinctive style of research developed, one that emphasized ethnographic and survey methods to study urban communities and the groups found therein (such as immigrants).

chronic disease A long-lasting and often incurable health condition, including heart disease, cancer, arthritis, diabetes, asthma, and chronic obstructive pulmonary disease.

cisgender Individuals assigned a sex category at birth based on anatomical criteria who continue to identify with their assigned gender category later in life.

civil disobedience A form of protest in which protesters refuse to comply with laws they believe are unjust, usually associated with the use of nonviolent tactics.

civil inattention The act of ignoring other people to an appropriate degree even while noticing that other people are present.

civil liberties Basic rights and freedoms granted to individuals in democratic societies, typically including religious freedom, the freedom to speak and criticize the government, protection from arbitrary persecution, the right to privacy, and equal treatment under the law.

civil religion The sacred beliefs, practices, and symbols associated with a particular nation-state or community, which generally does not contain elements of a traditional organized religion.

class The sociological concept that refers to a group of people who share a similar social and economic position in society.

class analysis The study of society focused on class or changes in the system of class inequality. Emphasis is placed on examining how, when, and where people's actions and beliefs are influenced by their economic position.

classification algorithms Tools for classifying data based on analytical schemes designed to produce simple or meaningful categories out of a large amount of data.

class reproduction The processes that cause class boundaries and distinctions to be maintained over time.

class struggle The idea that classes of people who are treated differently by the economic system are inevitably going to be in conflict with one another.

climate change The variety of changes in weather patterns around the world that is producing rising temperatures.

closure theory A theory of social inequality that emphasizes the ways in which groups maintain a monopoly of opportunities or rewards by limiting or excluding others.

code of ethics A set of guidelines that outlines what is considered moral and acceptable behavior in some context (such as within an organization or profession).

coercive isomorphism Similarities between organizations that arise out of legal or other requirements. Organizations become similar because they have no choice.

cohabitation An unmarried straight or gay couple living together in an intimate relationship.

collateral consequences Penalties that criminal offenders receive that are unrelated to their sentences. Examples include restrictions on access to employment, government benefits, parental rights, and political rights such as the right to vote.

collective bargaining agreements Agreements between employers and unions representing workers.

college wage premium The amount of additional earnings a college graduate can expect to receive versus those without college degrees.

colonialism The domination of people and control over territory outside a nation-state's own country.

color-blind racism The idea that when people deny that race and racism are meaningful categories of human societies, or that a color-blind society already exists, they may reinforce racial inequality by ignoring both the subtle types of discrimination individuals practice and how institutions may seem to be neutral while employing rules that favor some racial groups over others.

collective identity One's belief that one belongs to a certain group (or groups) with distinctive characteristics and interests (for example, women, the working class, a religious group, a national or ethnic group). These identities have to be consciously created, which is one of the things that some social movements or political entrepreneurs attempt to create or strengthen.

communicable disease A virus or bacteria that can be spread from one individual to another.

communism The vision of a utopian society, most famously described by Karl Marx, that became the term for the type of noncapitalist societies that first emerged in the Russian Empire (renamed the Soviet Union) in 1917, and adopted in different forms by a number of other countries around the world after World War II.

community A group of individuals who interact with and often support each other on the basis of a shared aspect of personal identity. Communities of people often live in close proximity, but the term can apply to communities linked in other ways.

computational social science Research employing advanced computing and statistical tools to analyze "big data" sets.

concentration of poverty When a geographically bounded area experiences extremely high rates of economic disadvantage that often lead to higher rates of social problems in that area.

concerted cultivation A strategy for rearing children in which emphasis is placed on providing exposure to a wide range of learning opportunities to give them advantages in the educational system.

conflict theory A type of social theory that emerged out of dissatisfaction with structural functionalism and held that all societies are characterized by conflicts that arise from the uneven distribution of power and wealth between groups.

congregation A specific religious body that meets regularly.

conjugal family A family consisting of a relatively autonomous married couple (and their children) able to seek its fortune outside the parental household.

connectors Individuals in a social network who link otherwise unconnected people together.

conservationist One who argues that the point of environmental protection ought to be to responsibly manage natural resources so that they are available for commercial use by future generations.

constructivism or constructivist): The view that social categories such as race, ethnicity, or gender are social creations, not biological facts.

consumption The act of purchasing and using goods and services.

control group In experimental research, the group that is "untreated" so that their outcomes can be compared to the group that is treated.

corporate crime A crime committed by or for the benefit of a corporation.

correlation The existence of a relationship between two variables. A correlation exists when a change in one variable is related to a change in another variable. It does not necessarily imply, however, that the change in one variable is the *cause* of the change in the other. Correlation can be contrasted with **causality** (in which one variable *does* cause change in one another).

counterculture A group whose ideas, attitudes, and behaviors are in direct conflict with mainstream culture.

counterpublic Alternative public organizations created by disadvantaged social groups to challenge more powerful groups or organization.

counterterrorism Measures undertaken to fight or combat terrorist organizations, including military strikes and surveillance of suspected terrorist groups.

craftsman A traditional term used to describe skilled labor based on experience and deep knowledge of the tasks required.

credentialism A requirement that one must obtain certain specific degrees or certificates before they can be considered for a particular job.

credentials A formal degree or certificate that identifies the holder as having completed some course of study.

crime An activity that violates the penal codes or written laws, which that identify and prohibit various behaviors.

criminal justice system The entire body of laws and institutions that regulate and punish criminal activity. This includes written laws, courts, and other organizations where guilt or innocence is determined, as well as the places (such as jails and prisons, but also probation and parole offices) where those who have been convicted of a criminal offense are supervised.

criminal record A formal designation, maintained by correctional bureaucracies such as police departments or courts, of an individual's criminal history.

criminology The social scientific study of the origins and consequences of crime in society.

cross-sectional Research based on data that are collected at one point in time.

cults Groups built around a common set of uncommon beliefs, or a particular individual leader. Cults share some similarities with, but are distinct from, both social movements and religious organizations.

cultural capital The type and level of education and cultural knowledge possessed by an individual. Having a high level of cultural capital signifies one's high status in the eyes of others, and/or enables an individual to interact with others using more sophisticated language and ideas.

cultural omnivore A cultural elite who demonstrates high status through a broad range of cultural consumption and knowledge, including low-status culture.

cultural relativism The idea that cultural meanings and practices must be evaluated in their own social contexts.

cultural universal A cultural trait common to all humans and societies.

culture Systems of belief and knowledge shared by members of a group or society that shape individual and group behavior and attitudes. A society's culture includes its language, customs, symbols, rituals, and other forms of meaning that are widely shared.

culture industry The production for profit of popular music, movies, books, television, social media, and other types of mass-culture products by capitalist enterprises.

culture of poverty A theory of poverty that emphasizes the importance of the cultural beliefs and attitudes of poor people as a cause of their poverty.

culture wars Disagreements about the proper role of family and religious values in society.

curriculum The structure of coursework and content of a sequence of courses making up a program of study in a school or school system.

data The facts and information used in research.

data analysis The scientific process by which researchers interpret the data they have collected.

data coding The organization of data based on key concepts and categories.

data display A visual projection of patterns in data, for example as tables or figures.

day laborer A worker hired to work for a single day.

decriminalized The removal of criminal sanctions for some kinds of behavior. It doesn't mean that behavior is now legal, but rather that it will not be prosecuted by the criminal justice system. Fines or other minor penalties may be applied instead.

deglobalization Periods of history when economic trade and investment between countries declines.

deindustrialization The decline in industrial (manufacturing) jobs.

deinstitutionalization of marriage A concept used to signify the important changes in the nature of marriage as it was traditionally understood for most of human history. Among the most important of these changes are the rise of cohabitation (couples living together without being married), a high divorce rate (signifying the willingness of many people to end a bad marriage), the increased willingness of couples to choose nontraditional marriages and intimate relationships (for example, couples voluntarily choosing not to have children, living in different cities to pursue careers, or engaging in polyamorous relationships), or the growing number of adults who choose to permanently live without a romantic partner of any kind.

deism Belief in the existence of a supernatural or supreme being, but rejection of the view that this supreme being actively intervenes in human affairs.

democracy A concept with multiple meanings, all of which concern the ability of ordinary people to exert direct control over their leaders. As form of governance in the modern world, democracy can be said to exist where leaders are chosen in free elections where anyone can run and the news media are freely allowed to discuss the issues and candidates. Broader conceptions of democracy incorporate a more direct role for citizen participation where everyone has the right to participate and equal resources to do so.

demography The study of population size, particularly in relation to fertility rates (the ratio of live births in a population), mortality (the ratio of deaths and the life expectancy of individuals), and migration across borders.

denomination An organized branch of a larger religious tradition.

dependent variable A variable that fluctuates in relation to other ("independent") variables. In research, the dependent variable is the object of explanation, or what the researcher is trying to explain.

depression In economics, a severe economic downturn in which the rate of economic growth turns negative for an extended period of time. In psychology, a mental health disorder of individuals, characterized by feelings of melancholy and a loss of interest in everyday activities.

deportation The act of sending immigrants back to their country of origin.

desistance The process through which criminal offenders stop committing crimes.

deskilling The process of breaking down the tasks involved in the production of goods or services into parts that can be done by someone without specialized training.

determinism One who believes that a single factor, such as a society's environment, or the technology it developed, determines everything else—from its social structure to individuals' thoughts.

deterrence Policies or laws designed to discourage an individual or group from engaging in some kind of behavior.

deviance (deviant) Any behaviour that violates social norms or rules. A deviant is an individual whose actions or attitudes fall outside the generally accepted norms of a given group or society. What is "deviant" behavior is subject to change, depending on which group(s) have the power to define what is "normal."

diaspora A group of people dispersed from their original homeland and settled in other areas for long periods of time who nonetheless retain cultural practices, memories, and ties to that space.

digital divide The social, economic, and cultural gap between those with effective access to information technology and those without such access.

direct democracy A type of democracy in which people make decisions with everyone participating, as opposed to a representative democracy (in which leaders are chosen through elections and empowered to make decisions for the entire population).

discretion In regard to employment, the amount of trust (or lack thereof) that an employer grants an employee. For example, how much is an employee monitored in carrying out their daily tasks is one measure of discretion.

discrimination Any behavior, practice, or policy that harms, excludes, or disadvantages individuals on the basis of their group membership. Discrimination is often used by dominant groups to control opportunities and reduce the challenges from subordinate groups.

disenfranchisement The denial to some individuals of the right to vote in a democratic society.

division of labor The specialization of individuals in any organization or group, or in society as a whole, particularly in relation to work. There is thus a division of labor in all of society (with different people working in different occupations), a division of labor in individual organizations (where different people perform different tasks), and a division of labor in individual families and communities.

DNA The carrier of genetic information found in all living organisms, located primarily in each cell of the organism. In the case of humans, more than 99 percent of DNA is the same for every human, with the remaining small differences marking each of as distinct from every other human being.

doctrine The official beliefs and rules of a particular religion or social and political group. Most commonly used to refer to more rigid belief systems.

double standard of sexuality Judging women more harshly than men for having sex outside of marriage or an established intimate relationship.

ecology The branch of science that studies the relationship between organisms and their environment.

economic recession When economic growth turns negative for a sustained period of time, officially defined by the U.S. government as two annual quarters (six months).

economic sociology The subfield of sociology that applies sociological theories to study economic behavior.

edge city A concentrated area of business, shopping, and entertainment just outside of the historical urban centers of commerce. Edge cities differ from classic suburbs in having a considerable amount of land devoted to economic activities, not just residences and local businesses.

educational homogamy The practice of people marrying individuals with educational levels similar to their own.

effective tax rate The taxes an individual, family, or corporation *actually* pay, as opposed to the published rates of taxation established by the government. Because of allowable deductions and strategies used to avoid paying taxes, many people and companies pay a lower rate of taxation than they normally would.

egalitarian A society, organization, or group characterized by having little or very low levels of inequality.

egalitarian relationship A relationship where all members of the relationship share more or less equally in performing required tasks. In the case of intimate relationships, this includes sharing household chores, including child or elder care.

embeddedness The degree to which the actions of individuals, families, and companies are shaped by social forces; most commonly, embeddedness is used in economic sociology to describe the ways in which economic actors (such as buyers or sellers) are influenced by social (i.e. non-economic) considerations.

emigration The act of leaving one's country of birth to move to a new country.

empirical generalizability The application of conclusions from findings about one group or setting to the larger population. An empirical research result is generalizable when the same result can be found in another context.

entrepreneur Primarily, a term used to describe anyone who creates a business, but it has been used to describe people in other (social or political) realms to create new fashions, trends, or ideas.

enumerate Systematically count (as in counting population).

environmental justice The achievement of equal protection from environmental hazards for all people, regardless of race, class, or geography; environmental justice also means giving community members a voice in shaping decisions that affect their environment and their health.

environmental racism A concept used to describe how poor people of color disproportionately bear the burden of environmental hazards.

epidemic Any threatening health condition that spreads rapidly in a particular region. Epidemics are usually thought of as being confined to a specific area, as opposed to the spread of a disease to a large number of areas (a pandemic).

epidemiological transition The transition of a population from health conditions primarily involving infectious disease to health conditions primarily involving chronic disease.

epidemiology The study of health-related events in populations, their characteristics, their causes, and their consequences.

essentialism The view that members of a group share a fundamental, inherited, innate, and fixed quality or characteristic. This outlook presumes, for example, that races are natural groupings whose boundaries are determined by deep-seated and unchangeable traits that are found within each individual. It is the opposite of the constructivist view of social identities.

ethnic enclave A place where people of a particular ethnicity live in high concentration.

ethnicity A system for classifying people who are believed to share common descent, based on perceived cultural similarities.

ethnocentrism The inability to understand, accept, or reference patterns of behavior or beliefs different from one's own, usually combined with the belief that one's own culture is superior to others.

ethnographer A sociologist who enters the everyday lives of those they study in hopes of understanding how they navigate and give meaning to their worlds.

ethnography A qualitative research method for studying the way of life of a group of people by close observation of them over a relatively long period of time.

ethnomethodology A line of sociological inquiry (introduced by Harold Garfinkel) that studies the ways (tools and methods) members of a particular group construct social order and make sense of their everyday lives.

ethnonationalist When national identity is defined in terms of ethnicity, not place; an example would be when a subgroup living within the boundaries of a nation-state are denied as full citizens (such as Jews in Nazi Germany).

European Union (EU) The group of European states—currently 27 in all—that have agreed to be bound by a set of laws and regulations that apply to all the member countries, as well as to allow the free flow of goods and people across national borders (so an EU citizen can choose to move to any of the other EU countries). The EU has a parliament consisting of officials elected by each country that establishes laws that are mandatory for all member countries. The EU also has a common currency (the Euro) that can be used in all member countries.

evangelical Someone who believes in salvation through personal conversion (or being "born again"). Evangelicals are also known for their emphasis on bringing their beliefs to others. The term is mostly associated with Christianity, although it can apply to persons of other faiths as well.

export Goods or services that are sold outside the country in which they are produced.

extended case method A method of conducting ethnography that emphasizes the contribution of research to social theory. An ethnographer using the extended case method starts from a theoretical problem or puzzle.

factors of production The inputs—such as land, labor, capital, and technology—that go into the production of any good or service.

fad Any kind of behavior that spreads (often rapidly) among a specific population and is repeated enthusiastically for some period of time before disappearing (often rapidly).

family values A term generally associated with views and ideas about the family that highlight the virtues of heterosexual marriage and childrearing in a traditional nuclear family with defined gender roles. Family values can also be applied to other kinds of nontraditional unions.

fee for service A system of payment to doctors in which they are paid based on the number of exams and procedures they perform, rather than receiving a salary.

felony A crime that may be punished by at least a year in prison. All of the most serious criminal acts are considered felonies in the penal codes in the United States.

female genital mutilation The practice of removing (in part or all) a female's genitalia. Reasons for the practice vary, and today it is primarily limited to a few places in Africa.

feminist movement A social movement whose members advocate equality between men and women in rights and opportunities.

feminist social theory Social theories that place gender relations and male domination at the center of their conceptualization of societies.

fertility The process by which members of a population produce live births.

feudalism A social order in which those who own land (landlords) are entitled to receive the products of the laborers (serfs) who are legally obligated to work for the landowner.

field experiments In the social sciences, research using experimental methods (with random assignment and control groups), carried out in real-world settings.

finance All forms of money management and its uses, such as investments and borrowing and lending.

financial wealth Assets held in the form of savings, stocks, and other investments.

firm A general term used to describe any for-profit business organization.

first demographic transition The transition by a country or region from a pretransition period of high fertility and high mortality, to a mid-transition period of declining mortality followed by declining fertility, to a post-transition period in which both mortality and fertility are low.

first immigration era The period before 1875, in which immigration into the United States was essentially unregulated by the U.S. government.

food insecurity A condition in which an individual or family does not have the means to assure an adequate amount of food.

forces of production One part of what Karl Marx called "the mode of production." It refers to the technological and productive capacity of any society at a given point in time.

foreign-born citizen An immigrant who has obtained citizenship in their new country.

foreign direct investment (FDI) A type of investment by a company in one country to produce goods or services in another. This could involve the purchase of an existing business in the second country or by building factories and/or offices in the second country and hiring workers.

foreign investment Investment of capital from one country into another.

fossil fuel An energy source, such as coal, oil, or natural gas, that is made of fossils that decomposed over millions of years under high pressure.

foundations Nonprofit organizations that have resources (typically from an endowment created by donations or bequests) to invest in other social, cultural, or political organizations, or to support researchers and writers.

fourth immigration era In the period since 1965 in the United States, allowable immigration has been subject to a series of restrictions on immigration from both the Eastern and Western Hemispheres but without specific national origins quotas.

framing The specific ways in which ideas and beliefs are presented to other people. Politicians, political activists, and social movements all engage in framing efforts when they try to persuade others that their way of thinking is correct. Scholars of social movements have also focused on how activists try to frame or present their cause or ideas for change so that they make sense to or resonate with the beliefs of potential recruits and supporters.

freelancing When individuals do not have a single employer, but rather take jobs as they arise. Many freelancers call themselves "consultants" while others may use the phrase "gig worker."

free rider Someone who shares the goals of a movement or organization but doesn't participate, relying on others to achieve the goal.

free space Place where people gather that does not have any government or corporate surveillance, where oppositional ideas and tactics can develop and spread.

fringe benefits Compensation provided to workers by the organization that employs them in addition to wages or salaries; typically includes the right to paid vacations, health and sickness/disability insurance, and retirement benefits.

fundamental social cause A theory stating that individuals of higher socioeconomic status have access to knowledge, money, power, and social connections that are deployed throughout the life course to avoid disease and death. As a result, this theory predicts that no matter what the causes of bad health, socioeconomic inequalities will inevitably cause some people to be sicker and die earlier than others.

gender The ways that social forces create differences between men's and women's behavior, preferences, treatment, and opportunities, and the characteristics of men and women that reflect these forces.

generalization Forming conclusions about the broader society from research on a subgroup or sample of the broader society.

generalized other The social control exercised by commonsense understandings of what is appropriate given a specific time and place.

General Social Survey A biennial survey of American society since 1972, funded by the National Science Foundation and directed by sociologists, which covers a wide range of social, demographic, and attitudinal questions (some of which are repeated every year, allowing tracking of trends over time).

Geneva Conventions A set of international agreements between countries about how prisoners of war are to be treated.

genocide The deliberate and systematic killing of a category of people.

gentrification The process that occurs when neighborhoods undergo a process of change where new investment, new people, and new establishments move into and alter the character of the neighborhood.

gerrymandering The drawing of election boundaries to maximize the chances that a politician of a particular party will win that seat (in single-member district elections).

ghetto A poor, isolated neighborhood, often formed as the result of residential segregation in which members of a poor or low-status racial, ethnic, or religious group are compelled to live in the same place.

gig economy The sector of the economy in which income is received from doing jobs on a short-term basis, with no commitment from either employer or worker beyond a single transaction (typically organized via the internet).

global city A city that contains a disproportionate amount of global business activity, particularly when connected by international finance, trade, culture, and communication to other cities around the world. Because it acts as a node at the center of global economic activity, global cities are places in which trade and investment are facilitated.

global neighborhood A diverse neighborhood made up of people from several different national and ethnic groups.

global value chain The full range of activities that businesses and workers provide at each stage of the production of a good or service that add to its value. While a value chain can be entirely within a single company, or contained with one country, increasingly global value chains with production inputs from more than one country are being used by large manufacturing companies.

global warming Describes the rising of Earth's average temperature.

globalization The growing permeability of national borders and the increase in flows of goods, services, ideas, and people across national borders.

Great Depression The global economic downturn in the 1930s marked by very high unemployment and declining economic activity in most countries. It is typically said to have begun with the crash of the American stock market in October 1929, and did not fully end in many countries until the beginning of World War II.

Great Migration The movement of large numbers of Blacks from the South to the North in the first half of the twentieth century.

green card A term used to describe a visa status for an immigrant to the United States that allows its holder to live in the United States permanently but does not make them a citizen.

greenhouse effect The result of high levels of CO_2 in the atmosphere that allow the sun's heat to pass through to Earth's surface while stopping it from spreading back into space.

gross domestic product (GDP) The total value of all goods and services, plus investment and government expenditures, that a country produces.

group style The set of norms and practices that distinguishes one group from another.

growth machine A coalition of business interests and city boosters who work together with local governments to attract residents and economic investment to a particular area.

guerrilla warfare A type of warfare in which an outmanned army or group hides from its larger opponent and selectively uses tactics in situations where it thinks it can gain an advantage.

habitus A concept introduced by sociologist Pierre Bourdieu to refer to the diverse ways in which individuals develop intuitive understandings and engrained habits reflecting their class background and upbringing.

Hawthorne studies An influential series of studies at the Hawthorne plant of the Western Electric company in the 1920s. Two major findings emerged from these studies: (1) the experiment effect, which is any change interpreted by workers as management's attempt to improve conditions, especially those that provide mental stimulation, improves workers productivity; and (2) the social group effect, in which workers moved to separate spaces as a group develop bonds that increase their productivity.

health disparity A difference in health status linked to social, economic, or environmental conditions, including socioeconomic status, race and ethnicity, gender, and geographic location.

healthy life expectancy The average number of healthy years one can expect to live if current patterns of death and illness remain the same but before chronic health problems emerge.

hegemony Widely shared beliefs about what is right or wrong that legitimize and empower a society's elites.

herd immunity A concept that applies to a situation in which large numbers of people are not susceptible to getting a disease, either because they have recovered from that disease and developed antibodies to fight any similar virus or bacteria, or because they have been vaccinated against the disease. When herd immunity is achieved, there are not enough "hosts" to allow the disease to keep spreading through the population.

heteronormativity A type of prejudice that claims that being heterosexual is the only normal option for an individual's sexual orientation.

heterosexism Discrimination or bias against persons because they are not heterosexual.

hidden curriculum The often-unstated standards of behavior that teachers and administrators expect from children within the education system. These often-unstated expectations may reflect the middle-class biases and norms of school professionals.

high-end inequality Economic inequality that arises from the highest earning households (for example, the 1 percent) and/or firms pulling away from everyone else.

Hispanic paradox The extra years of life that Latinx immigrants to the United States receive, on average, above what would be expected based on their other characteristics.

historical materialism Karl Marx's theory of history that emphasizes the role of structural economic forces in driving historical changes.

homelessness An extreme form of poverty defined by lack of permanent shelter to live in.

homemaker–breadwinner family type A family type with two parents in which one works full-time and the other performs most or all housework.

homeopathy Originally a medical sect from Germany that emphasized the use of small amounts of drugs known to cause a health condition in large doses to treat that very same health condition when it manifests itself in an individual. Still practiced today, it is an alternative to modern medical approaches.

homophobia Discrimination or bias against homosexual persons that is based in fear.

hookup Sexual behavior (not always intercourse) that occurs in a situation that was not a prearranged date and between individuals who may or may not be interested in an exclusive romantic relationship.

hospice care The treatment of people with incurable diseases in the final stage of life. The goal of hospice care is to attempt to help patients live as pain-free as possible in their final days.

human capital The stock of experience, knowledge, skills, and habits that an individual has that they can use to do productive labor.

hyper-segregated In education, this term refers to schools where minority students comprise more than 90 percent of the student body.

hypothesis A prediction researchers make that they will test in their research.

identity The social characteristics and group affiliations an individual has.

ideology A set of ideas that constitutes one's goals, expectations, and actions.

illegal immigrant A person living in a country where they are not legally allowed to reside. A phrase popular with political conservatives; social scientists use the phrase "unauthorized immigrant."

immigrant workers Workers who were born in another country and migrated into their current country.

immigration A term that describes the movement of people across borders.

immigration policies Government policies regulating the right of people to move into or out of a country.

immobility A situation in which individuals are unable to move from one economic or social class into another. Usually, immobility means that people remain in the same social and economic situation that they are born into (in other words, in the same class or income group as their parents).

implicit (or "unconscious") racism Prejudice based on stereotypes that can be activated without an individual's being consciously aware of holding them.

import A good or service purchased in one country but manufactured in another.

import-substituting industrialization (ISI) Government policies that attempt to replace imported goods with similar goods produced by domestic companies. Examples of such policies include putting very high taxes on certain imported goods or barring them altogether. ISI was a strategy used by many poor and moderate-income developing countries in the twentieth century in an attempt to foster domestic economic growth.

impression management The steps or strategies used by individuals to control the way others view them.

incapacitate The act of removing a criminal offender from society so they cannot commit further crimes.

income The receipt of money or goods over a particular accounting period (such as hourly, weekly, monthly, or yearly). Income may include wages from a job, benefits from a pension or government program, or income from investments.

independent variable A factor that might help to explain some outcome of interest. An example might be the impact of educational level—in this case, the independent variable—on one's income as an adult.

in-depth interview A method of collecting data based on asking a person a set of questions and having a conversation with them focused on gathering information related to the research.

individual discrimination Action carried out by an individual or small group that harms, excludes, or disadvantages members of a certain group.

individualism The belief that individuals are primary, that they should be free to do what they want, and that societal controls over individuals in whatever form (through law, religion, politics, or tradition) can be harmful.

Industrial Revolution The period in which mass production in factories began to develop and foster rapid economic growth. The timing of the Industrial Revolution varied from country to country but is generally thought to have begun in the late eighteenth century and evolved throughout the nineteenth and early twentieth centuries.

industrialization A process of economic change characterized by the decline of farming and the growth of factories and large-scale goods production.

inequality The unequal distribution of valued goods and opportunities in society.

inequality of opportunity The ways in which inequality shapes the opportunities for children and young adults to maximize their potential.

infant mortality rate A measure of infant mortality, typically defined as the number of deaths in the first twelve months of life per 1,000 live births in a given calendar year.

infectious disease A disease caused by the entrance, presence, or growth of a microorganism or other foreign agent inside the body.

informal work Jobs that do not have a formal employment contract.

information asymmetry A situation that occurs when one party to a transaction is unable to obtain the information necessary to evaluate the other side's offer in any transaction. In the case of medicine, for example, patients usually have no way of learning in advance how much different procedures might cost or which doctor offers the best service at a reasonable cost.

informed consent The voluntary participation of someone in a research project or medical treatment based on the participant/patient having a full understanding of possible risks and benefits involved.

infraction An act that breaks a rule or law but that is typically punished only by fines or public service, not imprisonment of any sort.

institution A complex term used to stand for structured and enduring practices of human life that are built around well-established rules and norms within defined fields of human activity. Major societal institutions include government/politics, the system of economic markets, the family and intimate relationships, law and criminal justice, religion, education, the health care system.

institutional (or structural) discrimination Occurs when the actions or policies of organizations or social institutions exclude, disadvantage, or harm members of particular groups. Such discrimination need not be intentional, and in practice it is often hard to discern whether or not discriminatory intentions lay behind a particular policy or practice.

institutional fields All of the rules, organizations, and individuals who contribute in one way or another to shaping a societal institution in some way. The institutional field is made up of all these entities.

institutionalization The process by which a social practice becomes an institution; in particular, the introduction of formal roles and the establishment of norms and rules in an organized form that manages to persist as new people come on board.

institutional order All of the major institutions in a society. Some instituions (such as the government, courts of law, or the military in wartime) may have power over institutions, thus creating an order (or hierarchy) of institutions in society.

institutional review boards (IRBs) Required at all universities that receive federal funds for research, these boards review researchers' proposals before any work can begin in order to assess the potential harm of the research for participants being studied.

interdisciplinary research A method of research that integrates ideas, theories, and data from different academic fields.

interest group An organization established to promote the interests of a group or corporation, especially in Congress or in state or local governments.

intermarriage Marriage between people in different social groups.

internet of things All technological objects that are connected to the internet, capable of sending and receiving data of all kinds.

interpretive sociology The study of the meanings individuals ascribe to their actions.

intersectionality Forms of inequality that overlap and potentially reinforce one another. One's class, race, ethnicity, religion, gender, sexuality, or other characteristics may create multiple forms of disadvantage that inequality researchers should consider.

intersex individual A person who is born with a body that has some biological characteristics typically found in only male bodies, as well as other biological characteristics typically found in female bodies (for example, a penis and ovaries).

irreligion The absence of religion.

jail A place of detention where individuals are held either before trial, or to serve relatively minor sentences. *Prisons* generally hold offenders convicted of more serious crimes.

journalism The production and dissemination of information about contemporary affairs of general importance.

jurisdiction A defined geographical area in which laws are applied.

kin The people that individuals have important social relationships with. These important others often include immediate (and sometimes extended) family members but also can include close friends and even other acquaintances who play an important role in one's life. A more narrow type of relationship than friendship implies, although very close friends can be part of someone's kinship group.

kinship system The social links and boundaries, defined by biology and social custom, that establish who is related to whom.

knowledge jurisdiction The body of professional knowledge and practice that is monopolized by particular professional occupations.

labeling theory A theory of deviance that stresses that many kinds of behaviors are deviant solely because they are labeled as such.

labor market The process through which employers identify and hire individuals to work under specified terms of employment.

labor process The organization of work, in terms of the relationship between workers and employers, the way specific work tasks are structured and performed, and the technologies and organizational environments in which the work is performed.

laissez faire capitalism A capitalist economy in which there are minimal governmental regulations and constraints on economic markets.

language A comprehensive system of words or symbols representing concepts and meanings, which is often (but not always) spoken.

legal permanent resident (LPR) One who is allowed to live permanently in a country even though they are not a citizen. In the United States, such a person would hold a green card.

legal temporary resident A person allowed to live in a country for a specified period of time.

legitimacy The acceptance of the authority of a ruler and/or system of government. Legitimacy exists when virtually all members of society accept the right of their rulers to govern their society, even if they disagree with them.

liberal market capitalism A kind of capitalism in which government plays a moderate role in regulating and organizing economic markets and establishing a welfare state that provides some insurance and protections for workers who cannot earn a living through their labor market activity.

liberation theology A strain of theology first associated with Latin American Catholicism that emphasizes God's concern for the poor and downtrodden and the rightness of social justice causes.

libertarian A body of thought critical of governmental regulation of individual choice in social and economic life. As individuals, libertarians support a laissez-faire economy, in which markets and social life is as unregulated as possible, freeing companies and individuals to make whatever choices they want.

life chances An individual's long-term possibilities and potential, including future income and opportunities, given their current attributes such as level of education, social networks, and possession of marketable skills or assets. Members of the same class are generally said to have similar life chances.

life course The transitions individuals make as they age through their lives. A typical life course includes childhood, adolescence, the transition to adulthood and first job, perhaps becoming a parent, retiring, and death. The study of the life course by sociologists centers on the key transitions, or turning points, in individual lives and the larger social patterns they represent.

life-course perspective Research that examines that highlights the effects of the changing social contexts a person experiences through different stages of life. In relation to health, for example, different health threats and issues that arise at different stages of life.

life expectancy The average number of additional years (past age x) that the average person in a population can expect to live. Life expectancy at birth is a common measurement.

living apart together When a couple in a romantic relationship chooses to or is forced by a job or other circumstance to live apart from one another.

longitudinal data Data collected over a long period of time.

looking-glass self A term coined by sociologist Charles Horton Cooley to emphasize the extent to which our own self-understandings are dependent on how others view us.

loose coupling An organizational environment in which those at the top do not have control over the activities and decisions underneath them. This often arises in complex organizations with multiple units.

loss aversion The tendency among most individuals to prefer to keep something they already have rather than want something similar that they don't have. In other words, for most people, keeping what they have is preferred over the possible benefits of giving it up to get something else.

lynching The killing of someone by a group, without a trial or due process, for some specified behavior.

mainstream culture The most widely shared systems of meaning in a society. Mainstream culture includes the most widely consumed cultural products (music, literature, films), foods, and ways of speaking and widely shared ideas about normal or appropriate behavior.

malpractice In medicine, an improper or negligent type of treatment that causes harm to the patient.

margin of error In quantitative research, when using data from a sample of a population, there is always some random error that arises, depending on the size of the sample and other factors. The size of the margin of error suggests the range of expected results if every person in the population were sampled (which is usually impossible). For example, a political candidate receiving 50 percent support in a poll with a margin of error of 3 percent is likely supported by between 47 and 53 percent if the pollster could ask every voter their opinion.

market Any setting in which buyers and sellers engage in exchange. Usually refers to economic exchange, but can be applied to other, non-economic arenas of social life as well (e.g. the "marriage market").

mass communication Communication within society as a whole through the mass media (television, internet, newspapers, radio), as opposed to between individuals.

mass incarceration A term used to describe a situation in which a very high proportion of people are held in prisons. It has been used to describe developments in the American criminal justice system over the past 30 years.

McDonalization A term coined by sociologist George Ritzer, that describes the spread across societies of standardization, predictability, and control typical of how fast-food restaurants are organized.

mean A statistical term that refers to the average value of a set of data. To find the mean, add all values and then divide the total by the number of units.

#MeToo movement A social movement against sexual assault and sexual harassment. It exploded on social media in 2017 (hence the hashtag), although the term *MeToo* applies to the entire movement against sexual abuse in any form.

mechanical solidarity According to Emile Durkheim, mechanical solidarity refers to the factors that hold primitive societies together, mostly through family and kinship ties and a collective consciousness shared by all members of the community.

mechanism The specific factor(s) that cause something to happen or contribute to producing some outcome.

median A statistical term that refers to the value that lies at the middle (or midpoint) of all the data, with an equal number of cases with either higher or lower values.

Medicaid A federally funded, state-administered program that provides health insurance to low-income families and children.

medical board A board that exists in every state in the United States established to review physicians and hospitals. These boards are usually made up of people from the medical field: physicians, hospital administrators, nurses, public health officials, academics, and representatives from various medical companies. Members of the public are now usually included as well.

Medicare A federal government program in the United States that provides health insurance to all individuals over 65 years of age.

megachurch Individual (and often independent) Protestant churches that average over 2,000 people in attendance at weekly services.

megacity A city with a population over 10 million.

megaregion A geographically continuous urban area containing at least two very large cities and surrounding towns and suburbs between them, which are connected through economic and transportation infrastructures. For example, the San Francisco Bay Area is a megaregion, anchored by three large cities (San Francisco, San Jose, and Oakland) and including all of the suburbs and towns that connect to one or more of these cities.

meritocracy A system where rewards and positions are distributed by ability, not social background or personal connections.

metadata Data about data—that is, any information about where some piece of data comes from or is produced. For example, the source of the data being used, how the data were collected, who collected the data, and so forth.

metropolitan region A continuously populated region with several jurisdictions, typically a large central city surrounded by several smaller towns, that are all physically and economically connected to one another.

middle class A group of people who occupy the middle positions in terms of income and status in an economic system.

middle-range theory A theory that makes specific, researchable propositions about particular aspects of society. Middle-range theories can be contrasted with broader or grand theories of society as a whole.

migrant energy The special skills and determination brought to a country by migrants, who may be especially motivated to succeed.

migrant workers Workers who move to a place or region to perform a specific job for a set period of time and then move somewhere else to do a different job. For example, agricultural migrant workers may work on several different farms in different seasons during harvest times that vary depending on the crop being grown.

migration The process by which individuals move from one location, region, country, or city to another.

mimetic isomorphism The tendency of similar organizations to adopt the same kinds of rules and procedures in the belief that what works for one organization should work for others.

minimum wage Established by law, a minimum wage is the lowest hourly wage a worker can be paid by their employer.

misdemeanor A criminal act that is illegal, but for which the maximum punishment is less than a year in prison.

mixed-method research Research that uses evidence that is both qualitative and quantitative.

mode of production In Marxist theory, a concept for characterizing the dominant economic system in a society. A mode of production has two parts, the forces of production and the social relations of production.

monetize To turn a social activity into an income-generating form. For example, a website that was once free of charge begins charging users, allowing advertisers to pay to appear on a site or selling information about its users to third parties.

monotheism The belief that there is one and only one God or supernatural being.

moral behavior Behavior that is guided by a belief about what is right and proper to do.

moral hazard A form of protection, such as insurance, that may have the unintended consequence of encouraging people to engage in more risky or even immoral behavior if they know that the costs of such action are covered by a third party (such as an insurance company or the government).

moral shock An unexpected event that surprises, distresses, and outrages people, often to the point of motivating them to join or even start a movement to eliminate the source of their outrage.

Morrill Act Legislation, also known as the Land-Grant College Act, was adopted in 1862. It created critical resources (in the form of free land transferred from the federal government to state governments) to be used for creating public colleges and universities that (originally) were expect to specialize in agriculture and engineering. The Act spurred the creation of numerous public universities across the country and was an important reason why the United States became a world leader in higher education in the first part of the twentieth century.

mortality The process by which individuals in a population gradually die.

mover An individual who leaves a place to live in another.

multiculturalism Beliefs or policies promoting the equal accommodation of different ethnic or cultural groups within a society. It is sometimes also used to refer to the benefits of dialogue and interaction between different groups.

murder The intentional killing of another person.

National Crime Victimization Survey (NCVS) A national survey that asks respondents whether they have been the victim of any crime in the past year. It is fielded in many countries, including the United States. Because not all crimes are reported to the police, it provides a broader measure of the total amount of crime in a society.

national culture The set of shared cultural practices and beliefs of people living within a nation-state.

nationalism A set of beliefs about the virtues of one's country, typically including the idea that their country is better than any other, and/or embodying special virtues not found elsewhere.

naturalization The process of becoming a citizen in a new country.

natural selection In evolutionary biology, a theory of how species evolve that emphasizes the process through which biological traits become more or less common depending on whether they enhance the survival of the species.

neoliberalism The adoption of government policies that increase the importance of the market, in particular by reducing regulations and taxes on businesses and individuals as well as by trimming government spending and public investment.

neo-Marxism An updated form of Marxism, neo-Marxism contends that the capitalist state could, and indeed often has, forced powerful economic classes to make "concessions" to the working class (thereby improving the living standards of all citizens).

net financial assets (NFA) The total value of savings, investments, and other convertible assets a person or family has, minus any debts, but excluding one's primary home.

network analysis A research technique that focuses on identifying the connections among individuals, groups, or organizations.

networked public All of the people who are connected via social media and the Internet to the online public sphere.

new religious movement A religious group that emerges independently of existing religious traditions or makes significant revisions and additions to them.

niche A unique place or opportunity that can be profitably filled by someone or some group. Niches arise in a variety of ways, especially when existing organizations or government agencies fail to meet some underlying social need.

No Child Left Behind Legislation passed in 2001 that sought to reduce the achievement gap between low-income and minority children and higher-income White children.

nonbinary Individuals whose gender identify is neither male nor female.

norm A basic rule of society that helps us know what is and is not appropriate to do in a situation. Norms evolve over time as social attitudes and expectations change, although those changes are typically very slow.

normalize To make or declare some action as normal or appropriate.

normative isomorphism The process of organizations becoming similar because of a widespread belief among their members and the members of similar organizations that they should adopt certain rules or procedures.

nuclear family A term used to describe a family consisting of a husband and wife and their children.

occupation A job that has been formally established and has some requirements (often formalized) for training or knowledge to perform it.

occupational sex segregation When women and men are distributed differently across occupations, such that some jobs are filled mostly by men and others mostly by women.

offshoring When manufacturing companies move production operations to another country.

one-drop rule Enshrined in many state laws in the United States around the turn of the nineteenth century, a method of racial classification that defined any individual with any African ancestry as Black. From this viewpoint, someone with one Black great-grandparent and seven White great-grandparents is considered Black because their "drop of Black blood."

open-ended interview A type of research interview in which the person being interviewed is allowed to answer questions in their own words, rather than being given a set of choices (such as "yes" or "no") to select.

operationalize When researchers define the methods and techniques to be used to assess and define the concepts that are being investigated.

opioids A class of pain-killing drugs that can be highly addictive. Examples include codeine, fentanyl, morphine, oxycodone (such as OxyContin), and heroin.

opioid epidemic The rising number of deaths due to overdoses of opioid drugs, which has been shown to be concentrated in certain communities and among certain people.

opportunity hoarding The process by which individuals and/or groups try to monopolize access to opportunities by using some resource (such as money, race, language, religion, or educational credentials) to monopolize opportunities. In relation to intergenerational opportunity hoarding, the term has been extended to cover families with sufficient resources to give their children extra lessons and tutoring to ensure they will gain access to opportunities over other children.

organic solidarity According to Emile Durkheim, as societies become more advanced, they are held together through the mutual dependence and interdependence individuals have with one another.

organization A social group or social network that is unified by a common institutional structure, such as a government agency, a school, a business firm, the military, a religion, and many others.

organizational ecology The rise and fall of organizations, including the factors that cause organizations to emerge, grow, and/or decline and die.

organizational isomorphism The process by which similar organizations adopt similar rules and procedures.

outsourcing The contracting (or subcontracting) of elements of the production of goods or services to another organization.

palliative care All types of healthcare designed to reduce pain and suffering by helping patients get better. It is often contrasted with hospice care, where there is no hope of curing or improving a patient.

pandemic An epidemic that spreads to multiple regions of the world.

Panel Study of Income Dynamics (PSID) An ongoing survey, first launched in 1968, of a nationally representative sample of families, as well as the new families formed by children of the original families.

parole Early release from prison, typically based on good behavior of an inmate as determined by a parole board.

path dependency The process by which the historical legacies and outcomes of the past impact actors and organizations in the present, making some choices or outcomes appear logical and others illogical.

patient-centered care Involving the patient in developing a program of care for a medical condition; the patient becomes part of the conversation with their physicians about how to treat the condition.

patriarchy A gender system in which men have substantially more power than women in politics, the economy, and the family.

patrilocal A family relationship in which a married couple resides with the husband's parents.

peasant A person who works in agriculture but does not own the land they farm.

penal codes Written laws that identify and prohibit various acts and may suggest punishments to be associated for those who commit them.

Plague A life-threatening disease caused by a bacteria known as *Yersinia pestis*, usually caused by flea bites or contact with an infected animal. The plague was the cause of the Black Death in Europe in the fourteenth century and numerous other deadly pandemics throughout human history. Today it is treatable with antibiotics.

planned obsolescence A strategy adopted by some manufacturers in which consumer products are produced with the intention of making them quickly obsolete, for example, by using nondurable materials, stopping the supply of spare parts for older models, or issuing software updates that are incompatible with older models.

plea bargain In criminal law, an agreement on a conviction and sentence between the prosecution and the defendant to avoid going to trial.

pluralism (in religion) The coexistence of individuals and religious groups with significantly different beliefs and cultures in the same society.

polarization In the social sciences, refers to the process whereby two or more groups, organizations, political parties, or even countries are divided with minimal overlap between them.

policy advocacy organizations Groups that advocate, or lobby, for particular public policies. For example, the National Rifle Association seeks to promote gun ownership and opposes policies that would restrict gun ownership.

policy planning organizations Groups that develop policy proposals. The most important of these groups, often called think tanks (because of the concentration of policy experts in one place) are typically funded by large corporations and/or rich foundations.

political action committee (PAC) A term used in U.S. politics to describe an organization set up to collect political donations from individual members of corporations, unions, or advocacy groups and then using the funds to donate to favoured candidates for political office.

political process model A theoretical perspective that emphasizes that social movements emerge and may be successful when and if unique political opportunities for certain kinds of collective protest and demands emerge.

political rights Protections (rights) given to groups and individuals to allow them to participate in political life. Among the most important are free speech, the right to criticize the government, and the right to form groups or political organizations to try to shape or influence governmental policy.

polygamy The practice of marriage of one individual to two or more other individuals.

polytheism Religions that worship more than one entity or god.

population density The total number of people living in a defined geographic space (such as a square mile).

population dynamics The process by which a population changes in size over time.

population momentum The tendency of a population that has been changing in size to continue to change in size even if factors such as fertility and mortality have shifted to levels that would, in the long run, imply no change in population size.

populism Social and political movement or organizations that seek to promote and defend the interests of "the people" against various "elites" who are said to be exploiting everyone else. Populism has been employed by politicians on the far right and the left, although in recent decades the resurgence of populism around the world has been on the far right and has involved attacks on immigrants, people of color, the news media, and scientists.

populists Members or leaders of populist movements or organizations. See also **populism**.

positivism A theory of scientific knowledge that holds that the only valid type of knowledge of the world is based on empirical observation (in the social sciences, of the social world) from objective, value-neutral research.

post-industrial economy A country's economy can be said to be "post-industrial" when the agricultural and manufacturing industries employ only a small percentage of all workers, and professional service industries (such as health, education, law, finance, insurance, marketing, tourism, or culture) are dominant forms of employment.

post-industrial society A society characterized by a post-industrial economy, and in which education becomes a primary source or opportunity and inequality.

poverty line A figure established by the federal government. It is an income level throughout sufficient to afford basic necessities of life, adjusted for family size. Anyone with total incomes below this threshold is considered to be in poverty.

power Power has three distinct dimensions in the sociological sense: (1) the power of an individual or group to get what it wants, when other groups want the same thing; (2) the power to control the agenda of issues that are to be decided; and finally (3) the power to persuade others to believe that it is in their interests to want the same things as powerholders. Power can be possessed by individuals or groups, including large organizations such as corporations, the military and the government.

power elite A term introduced by sociologist C. Wright Mills in the mid-1950s to describe the small circle of people who dominate the top positions in a society, based on their social networks arising from shared backgrounds and experiences.

precariat A term describing low-wage and insecure jobs, with little control over working conditions (see also **precarious** work). It combines "precariousness" with Karl Marx's term for the working class (the "proletariat").

precarious work Employment that is temporary and/or subject to end without notice, often has no set work schedule, and no opportunity for promotion or the acquisition of new skills.

predictive algorithms Software designed to predict behavior ahead of time based on data and information from past behavior.

pre-existing conditions A health condition that predates the acquisition of insurance. Prior to the Affordable Care Act of 2010, U.S. insurance companies did not have to cover medical expenses related to pre-existing conditions.

prejudice Negative beliefs or attitudes held about entire groups based on subjective, selective, or inaccurate information. They lead to "prejudgment" of the individuals associated with stigmatized groups.

preparatory schools Private, nonreligious elementary and high schools that typically charge high tuition and have more personalized learning approaches to try to leverage each student's achievements and opportunities to qualify for entrance into top colleges.

preservationist One who believes that the environment has intrinsic value and should be maintained in as pristine a state as possible (so new construction or development is likely to be opposed unless it maintains the character of the existing place).

prestige The symbolic value attached to a personal attribute or achievement; an object that is difficult to acquire and valuable to possess, or the reputations of certain kinds of organizations (such as schools or businesses).

price convergence When the prices of goods sold in different places tend toward the same level, adjusted for currency values.

principal In the immigration process, the family member who is applying for the right to live in another country (with their family members as secondary applicants) is called the principal.

prison A long-term detention center where people convicted of felonies (serious crimes requiring at least one year of detention) are held.

privilege The ability or right to have special access to opportunities, rewards, or recognition.

probability sampling A technique for choosing participants for a research study (that is, a probability sample) in which each person in the population is assigned a known and likely chance of being selected. Some groups of people can be assigned different probabilities of being selected when the probability sample is stratified based on group membership.

probation A criminal conviction that does not require a prison or jail sentence. During probation, convicted offenders are subject to regular supervision but are allowed to live in their community.

professionalization The process by which an occupation comes to be recognized as a profession (see professions).

professions Occupations that have established legal barriers to entry and practice, typically a required credential that is enforced by government against anyone attempting to practice the occupation. As professions mature, they typically develop a monopoly over certain kinds of knowledge that no other occupation can claim for itself in the same way.

progressive (income) tax system A system of taxation in which tax rates are higher on richer people than poorer people, with the idea being that it is fair to ask those who can afford to pay more to do so. These systems can be based on a progressive income tax and can also differentially assess taxes on wealth transfers, such as inheritances.

Prohibition In the United States, the period from 1920 to 1933 in which the consumption or sale of alcohol was barred by the 18th amendment to the constitution (the amendment was repealed in 1933, ending Prohibition).

proletariat Individuals in capitalist economies who work in exchange for pay. The term is usually reserved for people performing manual jobs and is synonymous with "working class."

proportional representation (PR) An election system in which seats in a legislature are divided up based on the percentage of the vote received. In many PR systems, there is a minimum threshold, such as 5 percent, for a party to cross before it receives seats.

psychoanalysis The study of the conscious and unconscious aspects of the mind and their influence on individual behavior. First made popular by Sigmund Freud early in the twentieth century.

public health Public policies that aim to reduce the spread of disease and ill health among entire populations by means such as improving sanitation and garbage handling, maintaining clean water, monitoring airborne diseases, and fighting the outbreak of viruses.

public/private paradox When one person or organization's pursuit of private freedoms or rights contributes to negative outcomes for society as a whole. In the case of the environment, it arises when private freedoms are used in ways that erode others' right to enjoy clean air, water, and finite natural resources. For example, the right of all individuals to own and operate gas-power automobiles is a contributing factor of global warming.

public sphere A social space—physical, virtual, or theoretical—where private citizens can come together as a public body to discuss and express opinions about matters of general interest.

pull factor In the immigration context, when an individual's motivation to move to another country is based on the perceived attractions of life in the new country.

push factor In relation to immigration, when an individual decides to leave a country because of something in that country that is causing them unhappiness (such as political or religious persecution or lack of jobs or opportunities).

qualified immunity A legal doctrine that prevents police officers and other government officials from being sued by people harmed by an officer's (or other official's) actions in the routine course of their job. It has made police officers virtually never liable for their behavior on the job.

qualitative research Research that relies on nonnumerical data, such as words, in-depth interviews, observations, or pictures.

quantitative research Research that relies on statistical analysis of numerical or categorical data.

race A system for classifying people who are believed to share common descent, based on perceived innate physical similarities.

racial covenants Legal agreements that home buyers in certain neighborhoods were forced to sign, in which they agreed not to resell their home to a person of color. Made illegal across the United States by the Fair Housing Act of 1968.

racism Prejudice and/or discrimination against individuals who are members of particular racial or ethnic group, often drawing on negative stereotypes about the group. Institutional racism refers to rules and regulations that organizations adopt that significantly harm members of a racial or ethnic group.

random-assignment experiment A study using a method of assigning participants or groups to receive different treatments that ensures that any posttreatment differences result from the different treatments they received.

random sampling A technique for choosing participants for a research study in which each person in the population being studied has an equal chance of being chosen so that the sample mirrors a larger population.

rape A physical sexual assault involving the use of force.

receiving country Host or destination countries where migrants go.

recidivism Following the completion of a criminal sentence, the commission of further crimes by an individual offender.

Reconstruction The period after the American Civil War ended in 1865, in which the federal government intervened to regulate elections to insure everyone was allowed to vote and, if elected, hold public office (including newly freed slaves), as well compelling the confederate states to abide by the terms of the Thirteenth, Fourteenth, and Fifteenth Amendments to the Constitution. Reconstruction began right after the Civil War, was weakened in the early and mid-1870s, and ended in 1877 with a compromise that allowed Rutherford Hayes to become president after the contested election of 1876 in exchange for an end to Reconstruction.

redlining The determination by governments and banks that neighborhoods with high percentages of racial minorities were ineligible for mortgage loans. Redlining has been illegal since the 1970s.

reentry In the case of criminal justice, reentry is the process by which formerly incarcerated individuals return to their communities and attempt to start their lives over.

reference group A set of individuals who share similar preferences or social positions and have influence on an individual or members of a group.

refugee status A form of protection that may be granted to people who have been persecuted or fear they will be persecuted on account of race, religion, nationality, political opinions, or membership in a particular social group.

regulation A rule established by a governmental agency or by a private organization that must be adhered to by all relevant parties. For example, a regulation might require that all companies provide safe workplaces where workers are not at risk of being injured on the job.

rehabilitation The attempt to reform a convicted criminal offender while serving time in jail or prison, in the hopes of providing them with new skills or knowledge so that they will not commit crimes in the future. Rehabilitation often involves the use of therapies of various kinds and helping an offender develop job and life skills that will help them desist from crime in the future.

relative deprivation A feeling that one does not have what one deserves, compared to other people.

relative poverty A term used to define people as poor not by assessing whether their resources are sufficient to obtain basic social necessities but rather by comparing their incomes relative to other people in society.

reliability The extent to which the same measurement technique in additional studies would end up producing similar results.

remittance Money sent from an individual in one country to an individual (often a family member) in another country.

renewable energy Sources of energy that are capable of being replaced by natural ecological cycles, such as wind, sunlight, and water.

repertoires In the context of social movements, repertoires refer to tactics used in the past or otherwise known by movement activists and leaders.

replacement fertility A level of fertility in which individuals in a population, on average, have a sufficient number of offspring that will imply, over the long run, no change in the size of the population.

replicated A study that has been repeated to make sure its results are correct.

representative sample A small group of people, ideally selected at random, who are similar to the entire population.

research memo An extended version of research notes, usually organized analytically, that helps researchers work through and begin to analyse the evidence they have gathered. More commonly used in qualitative research.

residential segregation The degree to which neighborhoods, towns, and cities are separated by race, ethnicity, or other social characteristics.

resource-mobilization approach A theoretical perspective that emphasizes the importance of resources, such as money, the willingness of participants to volunteer, or having non-participants willing to help in some way, for generating and sustaining social movements. The more resources a movement is able to employ or mobilize, the more successful it is likely to be.

retribution Punishment that aims at making a criminal offender experience as much harm as they have caused others.

revolution At minimum, a change of government or political regime brought about, at least in part, by popular protest. Some define revolutions (or "social revolutions") more narrowly, as entailing not only a change of regime but also a fundamental change in a society's economic institutions and class structure.

revolutionary movement A social movement that seeks to overthrow a government or fundamentally change a society's economic institutions and class structure.

revolutionary situation A rare situation that occurs when a government in power has lost its' legitimacy, or ability to maintain control over a territory or its population.

revolving door A term used to describe the ways in which people working as government regulators tend to leave their jobs to work for the very corporations they were tasked with regulating (and sometimes top corporate executives supervise regulation of the industries they used to work in).

riot A spontaneous, unplanned collective protest, loosely organized at best, involving attacks on property and (sometimes) persons.

risk assessment algorithms Software designed to predict risk of some outcome based on information from the past. For example, risk assessment of a bank might look at how many loans the bank has given out that could be considered likely to default based on past performance of similar loans.

robbery Theft involving the actual or threatened use of force.

role A position within an institution or organization that comes with specific social expectations for how to behave and be treated.

role conflict When two or more discordant demands are placed on individuals, rendering them unable to fulfill their own or others' expectations.

role model A specific individual who exhibits significant influence on others and acts as a reference for how to act.

role theory A sociological idea that emphasizes the importance of the roles individuals take on in shaping their behaviour. See also **division of labor**.

rural An area not adjacent to an urban area that has low population density.

rural sociology The study of rural communities.

sacred Holy; something worthy of special reverence.

same-sex marriage A marriage between partners of the same gender.

sample A technique to define what or whom to include in a study.

sanction Any type of punishment, including both formal punishment (based on laws or written rules) and informal types of punishments.

sanctuary cities Cities in the United States that have adopted measures to shelter unauthorized immigrants from the enforcement of federal immigration officials, including deportation orders.

schemas The ways that individuals form ideas and categories that provide frameworks for understanding and interpreting the world. Schemas are essential for allowing the complexity of the social world to be reduced to meaningful categories, but they can also encourage stereotypes and simplified understandings.

scientific management A movement that arose in the late nineteenth and early twentieth centuries that attempted to improve productivity by ensuring that managers controlled all aspects of the labor process and would utilize the best practices available given existing technology and knowledge.

scientific method A step-by-step process of conducting research that begins with formulating a research hypothesis, then operationalizing variables, then collecting data, and finally drawing empirical and conceptual generalizations from the data.

second demographic transition A type of society in which fertility rates have fallen below replacement levels, and growing numbers of people are living into old age. Declining fertility combined with increased longevity means that populations are getting older.

second generation The children of immigrants who are born in a family's destination country (for example, when Chinese immigrants give birth and raise a child in the United States).

second immigration era The period between 1875 and 1920, in which the United States made its first attempts to establish some restrictions on immigration. This era included restrictions on immigrants from China, those who were sick or impoverished, those lacking literacy, and other such restrictions.

second shift A term created and popularized by sociologist Arlie Hochschild to refer to housework, childcare, and elder care disproportionally done by women. The first shift refers to one's paid job, whereas the second shift refers to the all the labor needed to keep households going, including housework and care work (for children or older family members).

secularization A process of declining influence or marginalization of religion in society.

secularization hypothesis A theory that as societies modernize and citizens become better educated, religion will inevitably decline.

segmented assimilation The distinctive pathways by which immigrant groups become part of the larger social fabric; some researchers have found that children of immigrants are not all treated the same, and some members of some immigrant groups are more likely to receive economic and social opportunities than others.

segregation The spatial separation of the population based on race or ethnicity.

self The conscious being, personified in a human body, which is made and reformulated through social interaction.

self-fulfilling prophecy A term coined by Robert Merton to mean the process by which someone is defined in a particular way and then comes to fulfill the expectations of that definition.

self-selected When individuals have the opportunity to choose to be in some condition, those making that choice may be different from those who do not make that choice. The "selection effect" reflects the differences between those two groups.

semiprofessions Occupations that have some, but not all, of the characteristics of a professional occupation (see **professions** for more detail).

semi-structured interview A type of interview in which the researcher has prepared a set of questions ahead of time but also allows the interview subject the opportunity to express themselves in their own words and/or provide information that is unanticipated beforehand.

sending country The country migrants were born in.

serf Under feudalism, a person who is legally obligated to work on a piece of land for the benefit of the landowner, but otherwise has some personal freedoms not enjoyed by slaves.

serial relationships A pattern of having repeated short-term intimate relationships with other adults.

settlement houses A movement in the late nineteenth and early twentieth centuries to create community centers, initially funded by charitable donations, where immigrants and other disadvantaged groups could gain access to educational opportunities, assistance with integrating into their new society, and help with specific services such as childcare, health services, and information about employment opportunities.

sex Whether a person is classified as male or female based on anatomical or chromosomal criteria.

sex differences Differences that are assumed to exist because of anatomical or chromosomal criteria.

sexual assault An unwanted sexual encounter (including rape) in which force or violence is used by one person to compel sexual acts by another.

sexual harassment Unwanted sexual remarks or comments, typically in the workplace or other settings where the harasser has power over the victim.

sexual orientation Whether one's sexual attractions are to members of the same sex, the other gender, or both.

shared fate The idea that all members of a particular group, no matter what their other differences, are impacted by the same social forces (such as racism, sexism, or homophobia).

significant other A term coined by George Herbert Mead to mean individuals close enough to us to have a strong capacity to motivate our behavior.

single-member districts A type of election system in which a country, state, or region is divided into election districts, and the person getting the most votes wins. This approach can be contrasted with **proportional representation**. Some countries combine elements of both.

single-parent (families) Families with children in which only one parent is present in the household.

skill-biased technical change A theory of economic change and rising inequality in which people with more education and skills are pulling away from everyone else in terms of income and life chances due to the rise of advanced technology.

slavery A social system that enables some citizens the power to control the labor and lives of others. The latter group, known as slaves, are typically denied all basic rights possessed by citizens.

smog A smoky air pollutant produced when tailpipe or smokestack emissions that linger in the atmosphere and chemically interact with sunlight.

social autopsy The analysis of a disaster, such as an epidemic causing large numbers of death, by using tools of social science research.

social capital The resources available to a particular individual through their connections to others.

social closure The process by which organized groups seek to establish or maintain privileged access to rewards or opportunities.

social construct An invented social phenomenon (for example a belief, discourse, or category) that is shaped by the social forces present in the time and place of its creation.

social construction (of the environment) The process by which people interpret the natural world and make it meaningful.

social construction (of race or gender) The social processes that create and sustain perceptions of gender and race differences, and reinforce inequality between groups.

social context The social environments, including economic and cultural conditions, that influence people's lives.

social control The institutions, norms, and rules through which societies attempt to shape and control individuals. Behavior that violates social

rules is typically punished either formally or informally, reflecting the different ways in which social control is administered.

social democracy A political and intellectual movement that arose in the late 19th Century in Western Europe. It merges some of the ideas in the socialist/communist tradition about the importance of equality, with the laissez-faire idea that capitalist markets are efficient and should not be eliminated (as happened in the Soviet Union).

social democratic market capitalist economy A kind of capitalist society with a large welfare state (and higher taxes to pay for it), extensive economic regulation to minimize employment insecurity, but combined with capitalist economic markets.

social demographers Population scientists who study "social" questions, not just broad overall population trends. Social demographers are interested in questions relating to population subgroups (such as racial, ethnic, or religious groups), families (and trends among and within families and intimate relationships), employment patterns, and political trends.

social disorganization A situation in which a community faces one or more of the following conditions: high rates of crime, poverty, and unemployment; poor schools and high drop-out rates among teenagers; relatively few stabilizing institutions (such as large employers, churches, or charitable organizations); and neglect from local, state, and national government.

social distance A concept first introduced by Georg Simmel to describe how close or intimate, or apart, any two individuals or groups are with each other.

social fact According to Emile Durkheim, those regularities and rules of everyday life that exist independently and outside the control of individuals.

social forces All of the forms of social structure (hierarchies and institutions) that any individual must operate within. Social forces is the modern term for what Emile Durkheim called "social facts."

social group A collection of individuals formed around some kind of social identity or for some specific purpose.

social hierarchy Any relationship between individuals or groups that is unequal and provides members of one group more status and power than others.

social interaction The way people act together, including how they modify and alter their behavior in response to the presence of others. Social interaction is governed by norms.

social isolation When an individual has a relative lack of connections to others.

socialist society In Marxist theory, a socialist society is one in which most or all of the productive forces of society are collectively owned (not by individual business owners), although (unlike the kind of society Marx envisioned as "communist"), every able-bodied person is expected to work.

socially deviant Behavior that violates the written or unwritten rules of society.

social mobility The movement of individuals from one social position into another. Intergenerational social mobility is a measure of the extent to which parents and their children have similar or different social and economic positions in adulthood. Upward mobility is said to occur when an individual's class is higher than that of their parents; downward mobility is the opposite.

social movement A conscious, concerted, and sustained effort by ordinary people to change (or preserve) some aspect of their society by using extrainstitutional means. "Extrainstitutional means" refers to collective actions undertaken outside existing institutions, like courts and legislatures, although movements may also work through such institutions, at least part of the time.

social movement organization (SMO) A formal organization that participates in, or may initiate or lead, a social movement. SMOs generally pool resources, like labor and money, which may be crucial for movements. Some movements encompass a number of SMOs that alternately cooperate and compete with one another.

social network The ties or connections between people, groups, and organizations.

social policy Government programs designed to reduce poverty and inequality, including programs designed to provide insurance for health care, unemployment, and sickness/disability, as well as benefits for retired workers.

social problem A term used to capture a wide range of individual, group, or societal behaviors or societal issues that are thought to have harmful consequences. Examples might include poverty, crime, drug abuse, homelessness, inequality, racism, sexism, and discrimination.

social relations of production One part of the modes of production; the relationships and inequalities between different kinds of people within the economy.

social reproduction theory A theory that argues that advantages (or disadvantages) in one generation can be passed on to the next through the benefits (or harms) of economic wealth (or poverty), parental education and social capital, living conditions and housing quality, and others. The theory, most famously associated with the work of the sociologist Pierre Bourdieu, emphasizes that even as societies attempt to create equal opportunities for all, the forces of social reproduction are likely to be more powerful, especially when already advantaged families can "game" the new system in some way to give their children new types of advantages. An example is the rise of standardized testing, designed to give everyone the same shot at opportunity but in practice can be manipulated by preparation with a skilled coach.

Social Security In the United States, an umbrella term for legislation passed in 1935 that included pension (income) benefits for retired workers and citizens over 65, which are paid for through taxes on current workers.

social solidarity The social forces that hold any group or society together.

social structure The external forces, most notably social hierarchies, norms, and institutions, that provide the context for individual and group action.

social theory Systematic ideas and frameworks for understanding society and the relationship between individuals, groups, organizations, and societies as a whole. Social theories can be used as guides for posing research questions and evaluating evidence related to those questions.

social ties The various types of connections individuals make with other people.

socialization The process by which individuals come to understand the expectations and norms of their groups as well as the various roles they transition into over the life course and how to behave in society or in particular social settings.

society A large group of people who live in the same area and participate in a common economic system and shared culture.

socioeconomic gradient in health Those with the lowest status (in terms of education, income, and/or wealth) are less healthy than those in the middle, who are in turn less healthy than those at the top.

socioeconomic status (SES) A broad definition of a person's social class based on components such as education, income, and occupation.

sociological imagination The capacity to think systematically about how many things we experience as personal problems—for example, debt from student loans, competing demands from divorced parents, or an inability to form a rewarding romantic relationship at college—are really social issues that are widely shared by others born in a similar time and social location as us. It involves taking into account how our individual lives are impacted by historical and social contexts. The sociological imagination can be deployed to study any arena of social life.

sociology The study of societies and the social worlds that individuals inhabit within them.

soft skills Also called noncognitive traits, these are social skills—such as being on time, the ability to focus and complete tasks, and the ability to get along well with a variety of other people—that have been shown to enhance a person's job performance and likelihood of success.

Solid South For many decades after the Civil War, the states of the former Confederacy were dominated by the Democratic Party in every election, creating a one-party system. It began to end in the 1960s, as the national Democratic Party pushed through civil rights legislation that was opposed by many White Southerners, who increasingly came to prefer the Republican Party.

spatial concentration When significant numbers of people from the same group, such as a racial or ethnic group, live in the same physical location, such as a neighborhood or city.

specialization Knowledge or skills related to a narrow field of practice; a specialist typically knows a lot about one or a small number of things that a generalist is not likely to know. Most professions today have high (and increasing) forms of specialization.

spurious relationship When two factors seem to move in the same direction but both are themselves caused by something else (that is, a third factor), sociologists refer to the apparent relationship between the first two factors as a spurious relationship.

(the) state All of the agencies and offices of governing institutions, including government bureaucracies, law and the legal system, and the military, constitute what sociologists call the state. It is a term that is meant to capture more than just the current government in power by incorporating the idea that there are permanent institutions that are independent of whomever is in power.

state deviance Deviant behavior by governments or government agencies.

state socialist economy A term to describe the type of economies that developed under communism in the Soviet Union and Eastern Europe in the twentieth century. These economies featured the heavy involvement of the government in planning and regulating economic activity, and generally limited or even outlawed small businesses, and opportunities for profitable investment typical of capitalist economies. Over-time, most of these countries relaxed some of these restrictions, especially in relation to farming, where small farm plots could often be privately owned.

statistically deviant Behavior that is different or unusual but not necessarily in violation of social norms.

status A type of social recognition that makes someone different from others in some way. An individual's status may reflect some accomplishment or position attained, one's membership in a particular group, or both. It can be positive, negative, or neutral in terms of how others perceive it.

status group A term invented by Max Weber to describe any group that forms a common identity and develops ways of distinguishing insiders from outsiders.

stayer One who chooses not to leave.

STEM The acronym for Science, Technology, Engineering and Math—four educational fields that are thought by many analysts to be especially important for training young people for jobs in the twenty-first century.

stereotype A simplified generalization about a group (for example, women or men) that is often false or exaggerated. Stereotypes are most often negative, although positive stereotypes can sometimes be found.

stigma A negative characteristic or credential attached to individual that implies disgrace, such as a criminal record, a poor reputation, a physical characteristic of some sort, a scandal, or any other attribute widely regarded as disgraceful.

strain theory Criminal behavior arising out of social pressures that individuals experience; for example, the pressure to have a certain standard of living may contribute to the choice to steal property from others.

stratification system The full range of social hierarchies found in any society, which create inequalities between individuals and groups.

street crime A short-hand description for crimes committed in the community such as theft, assault, drug crimes, and others. It can be contrasted from white-collar crime.

street harassment Unwanted sexual comments or remarks in public places, directed by one person to another.

structural functionalism A theory of society in which individuals, groups, and the institutions of any society are guided by an overarching social system that guides everday life. These patterns can be explained by the needs of society to reproduce itself. Social institutions develop and persist for this reason.

structural individualism A theory that starts from the proposition that societies rest on the choices and actions that individuals make, but in the context of the social forces that shape and constrain individual choice.

structural inertia The extent to which an organization's rules and routines are relatively fixed and difficult to change.

structural power of business The theory that businesses, especially large businesses, have the unique power to influence government policy in their choice to either invest and grow employment or pull back their operations and reduce employment. If large numbers of employers behave the same way, it may compel governments to change their economic policy.

stylized facts Basic facts or empirical regularities that social scientists think they know with great certainty. A stylized fact might be the divorce rate or the number of murders in a given year (two types of

subculture A relatively small group of people whose affiliation is based on shared beliefs, preferences, and practices that distinguish them from the mainstream or larger social group to which they also belong.

suburb (suburban) Traditionally, a residential enclave within commuting distance of a city.

suburban sprawl The continuing geographic spread of low-density residential areas.

Super-PACs A political action committee that is formally independent of a candidate or party but is free to raise and spend as much money as it can on behalf of a candidate or party, as long as there is no direct communication between the Super-PAC and the candidate or party. Super-PACs provide a way for individuals and corporations to donate more than the legal limits for elections in support of a candidate or party.

supernatural Attributed to a force or entity beyond scientific understanding and the laws of nature.

survey A type of research in which information is derived by asking people to answer standardized questions, which may collect information about any aspect of human life of interest to the investigator, including information about jobs, employment, family life, health, education, and policy or political attitudes and values.

sustainability Refers to a system of development and consumption that satisfies a society's current needs without imperiling the ability of future generations to do the same.

sweatshop (manufacturing) A workplace that may be characterized by unsafe conditions, very low wages, and harsh working conditions.

symbol Something that communicates an idea while being distinct from the idea itself.

symbolic boundary The distinctions people make between themselves and others on the basis of taste, socioeconomic status, morality, or other differences.

symbolic capital A resource based on an individual's reputation or fame. If there is one available table at a restaurant and an average person and a famous celebrity walk in at the same time, in most cases the celebrity will be seated first.

symbolic interactionism A theory of the social world that focuses on the meanings that individuals give to objects and social practices and how they use symbolic meanings in their interactions with one another.

sympathetic knowledge A concept popularized by the social theorist and social work pioneer Jane Addams, in which valid knowledge about individuals and groups requires starting from a position of sympathy for their plight, by "putting yourself in someone else's shoes" to understand their behavior.

syncretic Combining religious ideas and practices drawn from more than one distinct tradition.

systemic racism When discrimination in one realm can reinforce or produce discrimination in another.

tariff A tax on goods being imported into a country.

taste A person's cultural preferences.

tax and transfer policies Government policies that use taxation and social spending programs to reallocate wealth and income.

tax loopholes Any law or regulation that allows an individual or a corporation to avoid paying certain taxes that they otherwise would have to pay.

telecommuting Working from home.

temp agencies Companies that place workers in temporary jobs at other businesses.

terrorism A type of warfare in which a weaker group challenges a more powerful group by attacking civilian targets of importance to the more powerful group. State terrorism occurs when a country's military attacks civilian populations.

text-as-data When words (written or spoken in any form) are systematically organized so that they can be analyzed using new types of software to identify patterns or meaning.

theodicy A social or political system justified by, or governed directly, by the principles of a particular religion tradition (or a leader of that tradition). A special kind of authoritarian government based on religion.

theology Systematic reasoning about a god and other religious matters.

theoretical generalizability The application of conclusions from findings based on a sample or case to larger sociological processes and theories about the world.

theoretical tradition A conceptual framework or paradigm that sociologists use to imagine and make sense of the world.

thick description A rich, detailed description of the ways people make sense of their lives.

think tanks Organizations that conduct research and develop policy proposals.

third immigration era The period from 1921 to 1965, in which the United States tightly controlled immigration into the United States using strict quotas on entry from different countries.

tool kit In the sociology of culture, the view that culture is a set of ideas or strategies (more technically, a repertoire) that people learn throughout their lives and can deploy strategically in different situations. The tool kit also supplies a set of ideas to justify a course of action retrospectively.

total fertility rate A measure of fertility in a given calendar year reflecting the fertility of women at different childbearing ages. A total fertility rate of 3.2 in 2010 in a given population means that the average woman would have 3.2 children during her lifetime, *if* fertility rates in this population remained the same in the future.

totemism A belief system in which clans adopt a plant or animal as their group emblem and declare it sacred.

tracking A term used to describe how schools assign students to distinct groups based on ability or curriculum.

tragedy of the commons Any situation in which the ordinary pursuit of individual gain using a commonly shared resource becomes harmful for society as a whole.

transfer A term used in immigration research to refer to the transfer of money from an immigrant back home, or to an immigrant from their family back home.

transgender Individuals who were assigned a sex category at birth based on anatomical criteria but who come to identify with a different gender category, and take action to be in that other category.

transnational corporation (TNC) A company with business operations in multiple countries.

treatment group In experimental research, the group that receives the treatment (as opposed to the control group). For example, in vaccine trials, the treatment group receives the vaccine being tested while the control group receives a placebo (a harmless facsimile of the vaccine).

trust In the sociological sense, trust refers to the willingness of individuals or groups to feel they will be treated fairly and with respect by the other party in any potential interaction, and that any agreed-upon arrangement will lead to follow-through.

ultimatum game A social experiment in which one player in a two-player game is given a sum of money and can offer any amount of it to the second player. If the second player accepts the offer, they will receive whatever they agreed to and the first player will keep the rest. If the second player rejects the offer, neither party receives anything.

unanticipated consequences of social action The idea that the outcomes of any action we undertake may well be unanticipated. For example, if someone gets a dog for companionship but soon begins to make new human friends who take their dogs for exercise at the same park. The new friends are an unanticipated consequence of the original action.

unauthorized immigrant A person living in a country where they are not legally allowed to reside. In current political discussions, these individuals are often referred to as "illegal immigrants."

underground economy Economic activity that is untaxed and unregulated and where transactions are done with cash so there is no paper trail.

undocumented immigrants Immigrants who enter a country intending to stay for some period of time, without the formal paperwork allowing them to do so.

union An organized association of workers created in order to protect and fight for rights or resources for their members. Unions can be organized at a single workplace, across multiple workplaces of the same company, or in an entire industry.

universal suffrage When the right to vote is extended equally to all persons.

urban A geographic area with a high population density (typically thought of as 1000 individuals per square mile).

urban ecology An approach to the study of cities, social change, and urban life introduced into sociology by the Chicago School to explain how different social groups within cities compete over scarce resources. This competition was thought to promote efficiency and social equilibrium, as distinct sectors of the population adapted to their local environments.

urban ghetto A section of a city that is characterized by severe racial or ethnic segregation, and often deep poverty.

urbanization The process through which large numbers of people move to cities in search of jobs and opportunities and cities grow in size and complexity.

urban renewal The attempt to improve impoverished areas by tearing down existing structures and even whole neighborhoods, replacing them with new structures or uses. In the mid-twentieth century, at the height of the urban renewal movement, many working-class neighborhoods across America were destroyed, in many cases benefiting real estate developers and business interests that moved in to profitably redevelop an area.

validity The extent to which the measurement a researcher uses accurately measures what it is intended to measure.

value A judgment about what is intrinsically important or meaningful. When it comes to research, values held by sociologists shape their views of and perspectives on the questions they ask.

variable In a research study, any factor that can vary in some way; for example, education and income are variables that can change over time as people age and/or change jobs, while skin color and height in adulthood are fixed characteristics.

varieties of capitalism A theory of the ways in which capitalist economies vary between different countries and regions. The VOC model starts from the proposition that there is no single form a capitalist economy must take, and that careful research can reveal different mixes of government and market forces.

visa A legal status specifying the terms and length under which someone may live (or visit) another country. It may range from permission to enter for a few days, for a period of months or even years, or to being allowed to live there permanently (in the United States, the latter type of visa is known as a "green card").

vocational education Training programs designed to prepare students to enter a specific type of job (as compared to general education programs that are not linked to specific types of employment).

war on drugs The United States' effort to reduce the sale and consumption of illegal drugs by increasing police surveillance and punishment of drug offenders.

war on terror The U.S. government's effort to combat terrorism, especially in the period since the attacks of September 11, 2001.

Washington Consensus The common prescriptions of Washington, D.C.–based organizations such as the International Monetary Fund, the World Bank, and the U.S. Treasury Department for how developing countries should respond to economic problems or crises if they are to receive loans. These prescriptions typically suggest that developing countries should engage in free trade, reduce the role and expense of government, and more generally encourage the growth of free markets.

waves In relation to social movements, cycles of protest.

wealth The wealth of an individual or family is the net value of all assets owned by an individual or family, including the value of their home, minus their debts.

weighting In a survey where there are differences between some known property of the population being studied and the completed interviews (such as the percentage of women, or minorities, or some other key population characteristic), the results can be adjusted by giving slightly more importance to the responses of each member of an undersampled group.

welfare state The bundle of programs that provide social insurance and social assistance for people falling into one or another category of attributes (such as old age, disability, or poverty). The most important types of welfare-state programs are old-age pensions (known in the United States as Social Security), health insurance programs, unemployment insurance, job training programs, and general welfare assistance for the very poor. Some analysts also include education in the mix of programs considered part of the welfare state.

white-collar crime Illegal activities undertaken by businesses or by individuals working for corporations.

white-collar jobs Jobs that do not require physical labor, in which employees work in offices or at desks, as opposed to "blue collar jobs" that involve physical labor.

White flight A term used to describe the large-scale migration of White families in the United States in the mid-twentieth century out of racially mixed cities and urban neighborhoods to racially homogeneous suburban areas.

White privilege A concept that refers to the advantages of being White. White Americans, on average, have higher earnings, greater freedom and comfort in choosing where to live, more opportunities for upward mobility, and less likelihood of being arrested than persons of other racial groups. They are also less burdened by negative stereotypes.

White supremacism The belief that White people are superior to people of other races, and that it is proper that Whites should control institutions of power like the government, large corporations, and the military.

working poor People who do not make enough income to be free from poverty, even if they work full-time.

zoonotic (disease) Diseases that originate in bacteria or viruses carried by animals, which are transmitted to humans through their contact with the natural world.

References

Abbey, Antonia. 2002. "Alcohol-Related Sexual Assault: A Common Problem Among College Students." Journal of Studies on Alcohol and Drugs 14S:118–28.

Abbey Antonia, Rhiana Wegner, Jacqueline Woerner, Sheri Pegram, and Jennifer Pierce. 2014. "Review of Survey and Experimental Research that Examines the Relationship Between Alcohol Consumption and Men's Sexual Aggression Perpetration." Trauma, Violence & Abuse 15: 265–282.

Abbott, Andrew. 1988. The System of Professions: An Essay on the Division of Expert Labor. Chicago: University of Chicago Press.

Abbott, Andrew. 1999. Department and Discipline: Chicago Sociology at 100. Chicago: University of Chicago Press. Abend, Gabriel. 2014. The Moral Background. Princeton, NJ: Princeton University Press.

Abma, Joyce and Gladys Martinez. 2017. "Sexual Activity and Contraceptive Use Among Teenagers in the United States, 2011–2015." National Health Statistics Reports. Washington D.C: U. S. Department of Health and Human Services.

Abramowitz, Michael. 2008. "White House Defends NAFTA as Bush Meets with Heads of Mexico, Canada," Immigration Watch Canada April 22. (immigrationwatchcanada.org/2008/04/22/white-house-deFfends-nafta-as-bush-meets-with-heads-of-mexico-canada/)

Acock, Alan and David Demo. 1994. Family Diversity and Well-Being. Thousand Oaks, CA: Sage.

Addams, Jane. 1910. Twenty Years at Hull House. New York: MacMillan Company.

Adler, Nancy and Joan Ostrove. 1999. "Socioeconomic Status and Health: What We Know and What We Don't." Pp. 3–15 in Socioeconomic Status and Health in Industrial Nations: Social, Psychological, and Biological Pathways, eds. Nancy Adler, Michael Marmot, Bruce McEwen, and Judith Stewart. New York: New York Academy of Sciences.

Agarwala, Rina. 2009. "An Economic Sociology of Informal Work: The Case of India." Research in the Sociology of Work 18: 315–42.

Ahrens, Courtney. 2006. "Being Silenced: The Impact of Negative Social Reactions on the Disclosure of Rape." American Journal of Community Psychology 38: 263–74.

Ahrons, Constance. 2006. "Family Ties after Divorce: Long-Term Implications for Children." Family Issues 46: 53–65.

Ajilore, Olugbenga. 2020. "The Persistent Black-White Unemployment Gap is Built into the Labor Market." Center for American Progress September 28. (americanprogress.org/issues/economy/news/2020/09/28/490702/persistent-black-white-unemployment-gap-built-labor-market/)

Akerlof, George, Janet Yellen, and Michael Katz. 1996. "An Analysis of Out-of-Wedlock Childbearing in the United States." Quarterly Journal of Economics 111: 277–317.

Alba, Richard. 2009. Blurring the Color Line: The New Chance for a More Integrated America. Cambridge, MA: Harvard University Press.

Alba, Richard. 2020. The Great Demographic Illusion: Majority, Minority, and the Expanding American Mainstream. Princeton, NJ: Princeton University Press.

Alba, Richard and Victor Nee. 2003. Remaking the American Mainstream: Assimilation and Contemporary Immigration. Cambridge, MA: Harvard University Press.

Alesina, Alberto, Edward Glaeser, and Bruce Sacerdote. 2005. "Work and Leisure in the U.S. and Europe: Why So Different?" NBER Working Papers 11278. Cambridge, MA: National Bureau of Economic research. (nber.org/system/files/working_papers/w11278/w11278.pdf)

Alexander, Michelle. 2010. The New Jim Crow: Mass Incarceration in the Age of Colorblindness. New York: The New Press.

Alexander, Jeffrey. 2006. The Civic Sphere. New York: Oxford University Press.

Alinsky, Saul. 1971. Rules for Radicals: A Pragmatic Primer for Realistic Radicals. New York: Vintage.

Amato, Paul. and Alan Booth. 1997. A Generation at Risk: Growing Up in an Era of Family Upheaval. Cambridge, MA: Harvard University Press.

Amenta, Edwin. 1998. Bold Relief: Institutional Politics and the Origins of Modern American Social Policy. Princeton, NJ: Princeton University Press.

American Academy of Arts & Sciences. 2015. Public Research Universities: Changes in State Funding.

American Community Survey. 2019. Available from the United States Census Bureau. (census.gov/programs-surveys/acs)

American Lung Association. 2012. "Key Facts about Smoking among Hispanics." (lungusa.org/stop-smoking/about-smoking/facts-figures/hispanics-and-tobacco-use.html)

American Political Science Association. 1950. "Toward a More Responsible Two-Party System: A Report of the Committee on Political Parties." American Political Science Review 44: 1–96.

American Sociological Association. 2012. Amicus Curiae Brief in Hollingsworth v. Perry. (asanet.org/documents/ASA/pdfs/12-144_307_Amicus_%20%28C_%20Gottlieb%29_ASA_Same-Sex_Marriage.pdf)

Anderson, Benedict. 1991. Imagined Communities: Reflections on the Origin and Spread of Nationalism. London and New York: Verso.

Anderson, Elijah. 1999. Code of the Street: Decency, Violence, and the Moral Life of the Inner City. New York: W.W. Norton & Company.

Anderson, Gerard. 2010. Chronic Conditions: Making the Case for Ongoing Care. Princeton, New Jersey: Robert Wood Johnson Foundation.

Anderson, Nick and Scott Clement. 2015. "College Sexual Assault: 1 in 5 College Women Say They Were Violated." The Washington Post June 12. (https://www.washingtonpost.com/sf/local/2015/06/12/1-in-5-women-say-they-were-violated/?itid=lk_inline_manual_8)

Appadurai, Arjun. 1996. Modernity at Large: Cultural Dimensions of Globalization. Minneapolis: University of Minnesota Press.

Applebaum, Anne. 2003. Gulag: A History. New York: Doubleday.

Applebaum, Binyamin. 2019. The Economists Hour: False Prophets, Free Markets, and the Fracture of Society. Boston: Little, Brown.

Appleby, Joyce. 2010. The Relentless Revolution: A History of Capitalism. New York: Norton.

Applewhite, Ashton. 2016. The Chair Rocks: A Manifesto Against Ageism. New York: Celedon Books.

Arias, Elizabeth. 2015. "United States Life Tables, 2011." National Vital Statistics Reports 59: 1–61.

Armed Conflict Location & Event Data, 2021. "A Year of Racial Justice Protests: Key Trends in Demonstrations Supporting BLM." ACLED May. (acleddata.com/acleddatanew/wp-content/uploads/2021/05/ACLED_Report_A-Year-of-Racial-Justice-Protests_May2021.pdf)

Armstrong, Elizabeth. 2002. Forging Gay Identities: Organizing Sexuality in San Francisco, 1950–1994. Chicago: University of Chicago Press.

Armstrong, Elizabeth A. and Jamie Budnick. 2015. "Sexual Assault on Campus." Paper presented at the Online Symposium on Intimate Partner Violence." (contemporaryfamilies.org/assault-on-campus-brief-report/)

Armstrong, Elizabeth, Paula England, and Alison Fogarty. 2012. "Accounting for Women's Orgasm and Sexual Enjoyment in College Hookups and Relationships." American Sociological Review 77: 435–462.

Armstrong, Elizabeth. and Laura Hamilton. 2013. Paying for the Party: How College Maintains Inequality. Cambridge, MA: Harvard University Press.

Armstrong, Elizabeth A., Laura Hamilton, and Brian Sweeney. 2006. "Sexual Assault on Campus: A Multilevel, Integrative Approach to Party Rape." Social Problems 53: 483–99.

Arrow, Kenneth. 1974. The Limits of Organization. New York: Norton.

Arum, Richard and Josipa Roksa. 2011. Academically Adrift: Limited Learning on College Campuses. Chicago: University of Chicago Press.

Arum, Richard and Josipa Roksa. 2014. Aspiring Adults: College Graduates Hopeful and Adrift. Chicago: University of Chicago Press.

Asch, Solomon. 1955. "Opinions and Social Pressure." Scientific American 193: 1–8. (jstor.org/stable/24943779?seq=1#metadata_info_tab_contents)

Asher, Jeff. 2017. "U.S. Cities Experienced Another Big Rise in Murder in 2016." FiveThirtyEight. (fivethirtyeight.com/features/u-s-cities-experienced-another-big-rise-in-murder-in–2016/)

Ashkenas, Jeremy and Haeyoun Park. 2015. "The Race Gap in America's Police Departments." New York Times April 8. (https://www.nytimes.com/interactive/2014/09/03/us/the-race-gap-in-americas-police-departments.html)

Atkeson, B. M., Calhoun, K. S., Resick, P. A., and Ellis, E. M. (1982). Victims of rape: Repeated assessment of depressive symptoms. Journal of Consulting and Clinical Psychology. 50: 96–102.

Atkinson, Max. 1984. Our Master's Voices: The Language and Body Language of Politics. London: Methuen.

Audley, John, Demetrios Papademetriou, Sandra Polaski and Scott Vaughan. 2003. NAFTA's Promise and Reality: Lessons from Mexico for the Hemisphere. New York: Carnegie Endowment for International Peace.

Auguste, Byron, Paul Kihn, and Matt Miller. 2010. "Attracting and Retaining Top-Third Graduates to Careers in Teaching." McKinsey Institute, September. (https://charterschoolcenter.ed.gov/sites/default/files/files/field_publication_attachment/Closing_the_talent_gap_0.pdf)

Autor, David, Lawrence Katz, and Melissa Kearney. 2008. "Trends in U.S. Wage Inequality: Revising the Revisionists." Review of Economics and Statistics 90: 300–23.

Auyero, Javier and Débora Swistun. 2009. Flammable: Environmental Suffering in an Argentine Shantytown. Oxford, UK: Oxford University Press.

Babcock, Linda and Sara Laschever. 2003. Women Don't Ask: Negotiation and the Gender Divide. Princeton, NJ: Princeton University Press.

Bacon, David. 2012. "How US Farm Policies Fuel Mexico's Great Migration." The Nation January 4. (thenation.com/article/archive/how-us-policies-fueled-mexicos-great-migration/)

Bail, Christopher. 2016. "Combining Natural Language Processing and Network Analysis to Examine How Advocacy Organizations Stimulate Conversation on Social Media." Proceedings of the National Academy of Science 113: 11823–28.

Bailey, J. Michael and Richard Pillard. 1991. "A Genetic Study of Male Sexual Orientation." Archives of General Psychiatry 48: 1089–96.

Bailey, J. Michael, Michael Dunne, Michael Nicholas, and Martin Nicholas. 2000. "Genetic and Environmental Influences on Sexual Orientation and Its Correlates in an Australian Twin Sample." Journal of Personality and Social Psychology 78: 524–36.

Bailey, Martha. 2006. "More Power to the Pill: The Impact of Contraceptive Freedom on Women's Life Cycle Labor Supply." Quarterly Journal of Economics 121: 289–320.

Baker, Wayne. 2005. America's Crisis of Values: Reality and Perception. Princeton, NJ: Princeton University Press.

Bakija, Jon, Adam Cole, and Bradley Heim. 2012. "Jobs and Income Growth of Top Earners and the Causes of Changing Income Inequality: Evidence from U.S. Tax Return Data." Unpublished paper, Department of Economics, Williams College. (web.williams.edu/Economics/wp/BakijaColeHeimJobsIncomeGrowthTopEarners.pdf)

Bakshy, Eytan, Solomon Messing, and Lada Adamic. 2015. "Exposure to Ideologically Diverse News and Opinion on Facebook." Science 348: 1130–32.

Baldassare, Mark. 1992. "Suburban Communities." Annual Review of Sociology 18: 475–94.

Baldassarri, Delia and Maria Abascal. 2017. "Field Experiments Across the Social Sciences." Annual Review of Sociology 43: 41–73.

Baldassarri, Delia and Barum Park. 2020. "Was There a Culture War? Partisan Polarization and Secular Trends in US Public Opinion." The Journal of Politics 82: 809–27.

Banfield, Edward. 1970. The Unheavenly City: The Nature and the Future of Our Urban Crisis. New York: Little Brown and Co.

Barak, Gregg. 2017. Unchecked Corporate Power: Why the Crimes of Multinational Corporations Are Routinized Away and What We Can Do About It. New York: Routledge.

Bar-Elia, Michael, Simcha Avugosa, and Markus Raab. 2006. "Twenty Years of "Hot Hand" Research: Review and Critique." Psychology of Sport and Exercise 7: 525–53.

Barnato, Amber, F. Lee Lucas, Douglas Staiger, David Wennberg, and Amitabh Chandra. 2005. "Hospital-Level Racial Disparities in Acute Myocardial Infarction Treatment and Outcomes." Medical Care 43: 308–19.

Barnett, Rosalind and Caryl Rivers. 1996. She Works/He Works: How Two-Income Families Are Happier, Healthier, and Better-Off. San Francisco: Harper.

Barnett, Rosalind and Caryl Rivers. 2004. Same Difference: How Gender Myths Are Hurting Our Relationships, Our Children, and Our Jobs. New York: Basic Books.

Barrionuevo, Alexei. 2012. "At Over $90 Million, Sale of Midtown Penthouse Sets a New York Record." New York Times May 17. (nytimes.com/2012/05/18/realestate/midtown-penthouse-at-one57-sells-for-new-york-record.html)

Barry-Jester, Anna Maria, Ben Casselman and Dana Goldstein. 2015. "Should Prison Sentences Be Based on Crimes That Haven't Been Committed Yet?" FiveThirtyEight August 18. (https://fivethirtyeight.com/features/prison-reform-risk-assessment/)

Bartash, Jeffry. 2019. "Why the U.S.-China Trade Deficit is so Huge: Here's All the Stuff America Imports." MarketWatch June 27. (marketwatch.com/story/heres-all-the-stuff-the-us-imports-from-china-thats-causing-a-huge-trade-deficit-2018-03-23)

Bartels, Larry. 2008. Unequal Democracy: The Political Economy of a New Gilded Age. Princeton, NJ: Princeton University Press.

Basile, Katherine, Jieru Chen, Michele Black, and Linda Saltzman. 2007. "Prevalence and Characteristics of Sexual Violence Victimization among U.S. Adults, 2001–2003." Violence and Victims 22: 437–48.

Baskind, Chris. 2010. "5 Reasons Not to Drink Bottled Water." Mother Nature Network. (mnn.com/food/healthy-eating/stories/5-reasons-not-to-drink-bottled-water)

Bauer, Lauren. 2020. "Hungry at Thanksgiving: A Fall 2020 Update on Food Insecurity in the United States." Brooking Institute Policy Brief November 23. (brookings.edu/blog/up-front/2020/11/23/hungry-at-thanksgiving-a-fall-2020-update-on-food-insecurity-in-the-u-s/)

Baumgartner, Frank, Jeffrey Berry, Marie Hojnacki, David Kimball and Beth Leech. 2009. Lobbying and Political Change: Who Wins, Who Loses, and Why? Chicago: University of Chicago Press.

Beaman, Lori. 2016. "Social Networks and the Labor Market." Pp. 649–73 in The Oxford Handbook of the Economics of Networks, eds. Yann Bramoulle, Andrea Galeotti, and Brian Rogers. New York: Oxford University Press.

Bean, Frank. and Gillian Stevens. 2003. America's Newcomers and the Dynamics of Diversity. New York: Russell Sage.

Bearman, Peter and Peter Hedstrom. 2009. "What Is Analytical Sociology All About?" Pp. 3–24 in The Oxford Handbook of Analytical Sociology, eds. Peter Hedstrom and Peter Bearman. New York: Oxford University Press.

Beauvoir, Simone de. 1952. The Second Sex. New York: Bantam.

Beccaria, Cesare. [1764] 1986. On Crimes and Punishments. New York: Hackett Publishing.

Becker, Gary. 1957. The Economics of Discrimination. Chicago: University of Chicago Press.

Becker, Gary. 1964. Human Capital: A Theoretical and Empirical Analysis. Chicago: The University of Chicago Press.

Becker, Gary. 1976. The Economic Approach to Human Life. Chicago: University of Chicago Press.

Becker, Howard. 1963. Outsiders. New York: Free Press.

Beckert, Sven. 2015. Empire of Cotton: A Global History. New York: Vintage.

Beisel, Nicola. 1997. Imperiled Innocents: Anthony Comstock and Family Reproduction. Princeton, NJ: Princeton University Press.

Beit-Hallahmi, Benjamin and Michael Argyle. 1997. The Psychology of Religious Behavior, Belief and Experience. New York: Routledge.

Belkin, Lisa. 2003. "The Opt-Out Revolution." New York Times Magazine October 26. (nytimes.com/2003/10/26/magazine/the-opt-out-revolution.html)

Bell, Daniel. 1973. The Coming of Post-Industrial Society: A Venture in Social Forecasting. New York: Basic Books.

Bell, Linda and Richard Freeman. 1994. "Why Do Americans and Germans Work Different Hours?" NBER Working Papers 4808. Cambridge, MA: National Bureau of Economic Research. (nber.org/system/files/working_papers/w4808/w4808.pdf)

Bell, Michael. 1994. Childerley: Nature and Morality in a Country Village Chicago: University of Chicago Press.

Bellah, Robert, Richard Madsen, William Sullivan, Ann Swidler, and Stephen Tipton. 1985. Habits of the Heart: Individualism and Commitment in American Life. Berkeley and Los Angeles: University of California Press.

Bennett, William, John Dilulio, and John Walters. 1996. Body Count: Moral Poverty and How to Win America's War Against Crime and Drugs. New York: Simon and Shuster.

Bergen, Peter and Katherine Tiedemann. 2010. "No Secrets in the Sky." New York Times April 26. (nytimes.com/2010/04/26/opinion/26bergen.html)

Berger, Miriam. 2020. "Covid-19 'Not Necessarily the Big One,' WHO Warns." Washington Post December 29. (washingtonpost.com/world/2020/12/29/coronavirus-2020-the-big-one-who-pandemics/)

Bergmann, Barbara. 1986. The Economic Emergence of Women. New York: Basic Books.

Bergson, Abram. 1984. "Income Inequality Under Soviet Socialism." Journal of Economic Literature 22: 1052–99.

Bernhagen, Patrick and Thomas Brauninger. 2005. "Structural Power and Public Policy: A Signaling Model of Business Lobbying in Democratic Capitalism." Political Studies 53: 43–64.

Bernhardt, Annette, Ruth Milkman, Nik Theodore, Douglas Heckathorn, Mirabai Auer, James DeFilippis, Ana Luz Gonzalez, Victor Narro, Jason Perelshteyn, Diana Polson, and Michael Spiller. 2009. Broken Laws, Unprotected Workers: Violations of Employment and Labor Laws in America's Cities. (unprotectedworkers.org/)

Bernhardt, Annette, Martina Morris, Mark Handcock, and Marc Scott. 2001. Divergent Paths: Economic Mobility and the New American Labor Market. New York, NY: Russell Sage Foundation Press.

Bernstein, David and Noah Isackson. 2014. "The Truth About Chicago's Crime Rates." Chicago Magazine, April 7. (chicagomag.com/Chicago-Magazine/May-2014/Chicago-crime-rates/)

Bernstein, Jared and Lawrence Mishel. 2007. "Economy's Gains Fail to Reach Most Workers' Paychecks." Economic Policy Institute Briefing Papers 195, August 30. (epi.org/publication/bp195/)

Berson, Sarah. 2013. Beyond the Sentence: Understanding Collateral Consequences. Washington D.C.: National Institute of Justice. (nij.gov/journals/272/pages/collateral-consequences.aspx)

Bertrand, Marianne and Esther Duflo. 2017. "Field Experiments on Discrimination." Pp. 309–94 in Handbook of Economic Field Experiments, eds. Abhijit Banerjee and Esther Duflo. Amsterdam: North Holland/Elesevier.

Bertrand, Marianne, and Sendhil Mullainathan. 2004. "Are Emily and Greg More Employable than Lakisha and Jamal?: A Field Experiment on Labor Market Discrimination." American Economic Review 94: 991–1013.

Best, Joel. 2008. Social Problems. New York: Norton.

Bianchi, Suzanne. 2000. "Maternal Employment and Time with Children: Dramatic Change or Surprising Continuity?" Demography 37: 401–14.

Bianchi, Suzanne, John Robinson, and Melissa Milkie. 2006. Changing Rhythms of American Family Life. New York: Russell Sage Foundation.

Bianchi, Suzanne, Liana Sayer, Melissa Milkie, and John Robinson. 2012. "Housework: Who Did, Does or Will Do It, and How Much Does It Matter?" Social Forces 91: 55–63.

Bick, Alexander, Bettina Bruggemann, and Nicola Fuchs-Schundeln. 2016. "Hours Worked in Europe and the U.S.: New Data, New Answers." IZA Discussion Paper 10179. Germany: Institute of Labor Economics. (ftp.iza.org/dp10179.pdf)

Bilinski, Alyssa and Ezekiel Emanuel. 2020. "COVID-19 and Excess All-Cause Mortality in the US and 18 Comparison Countries." Journal of the American Medical Association October 12. (jamanetwork.com/journals/jama/fullarticle/2771841)

Binder, Amy. 2004. Contentious Curriculum: Afrocentrism and Creationism in American Public Schools. Princeton, NJ: Princeton University Press.

Bischoff, Kendra and Sean Reardon. 2014. "Residential Segregation by Income, 1970–2009." Pp. 208–33 in Diversity and Disparities: America Enters a New Century, ed. John Logan. New York: Russell Sage Foundation Press.

Bittner, Egon. 1967. "The Police on Skid-Row: A 'Study of Peacekeeping.'" American Sociological Review 32: 699–715.

Black, Michele, Katherine Basile, Matthew Breiding, Sharon Smith, Mikel Walters, Melissa Merrick, Jieru Chen, and Mark Stevens. 2011. "The National Intimate Partner and Sexual Violence Survey (NISVS): 2010 Summary Report." Atlanta, GA: National Center for Injury Prevention and Control, Centers for Disease Control and Prevention. (https://www.cdc.gov/violenceprevention/pdf/nisvs_report2010-a.pdf)

Blalock, Hubert. 1967. Toward a Theory of Minority-group Relations. New York: Wiley.

Blanc, Eric. 2019. Red State Revolt: Teacher Strikes and Working Class Politics. New York: Jacobin Books.

Blankenhorn, David. 1995. Fatherless America: Confronting Our Most Urgent Social Problem. New York: Basic Books.

Blanq, Eric. 2019. Red State Revolt: The Teachers' Strikes and Working Class Politics. New York: Verso.

Blass, Thomas. 1999. The Milgram Paradigm After 35 Years: Some Things We Now Know About Obedience to Authority. Journal of Applied Social Psychology 29: 955–78.

Blauner, Robert. 1964. Alienation and Freedom: The Factory Worker and His Industry. University of Chicago Press.

Block, Fred. 1977. "The Ruling Class Does Not Rule: Notes on the Marxist Theory of the State." Socialist Revolution 33: 6–28.

Block, Fred. 1987. State Theory. Philadelphia, PA: Temple University Press.

Block, Fred and Matthew Keller. 2011. State of Innovation: The U.S. Government's Role in Technology Development. New York: Routledge.

Bloom, Joshua and Waldo Martin. 2013. Black Against Empire: The History and Politics of the Black Panther Party. Berkeley: University of California Press.

Bloom, Joshua and Waldo Martin. 2016. Black Against Empire: The History and Politics of the Black Panther Party. Berkeley, CA: University of California Press.

Blumer, Herbert. 1958. "Race Prejudice as a Sense of Group Position" Pacific Sociological Review 1: 3–7.

Blumer, Herbert. 1969. Symbolic Interactionism. Englewood Cliffs, NJ: Prentice-Hall.

Boesch, Diana and Shilpa Phadke. 2021. "When Women Lose All the Jobs: Essential Actions for a Gender-Equitable Recovery." Center for American Progress, February 1. (americanprogress.org/issues/women/reports/2021/02/01/495209/women-lose-jobs-essential-actions-gender-equitable-recovery/)

Bogdanich, Walt and Michael Forsythe. 2020. "McKinsey Proposed Paying Pharmacy Companies Rebates for OxyContin Overdoses." New York Times November 27. (nytimes.com/2020/11/27/business/mckinsey-purdue-oxycontin-opioids.html)

Bonakowski, Bart. 2017. "Ethno-nationalist Populism and the Mobilization of Collective Resentment." British Journal of Sociology 68: 181–213.

Bond, Philip, and Vincent Glode. 2014. "The Labor Market for Bankers and Regulators." The Review of Financial Studies 27: 2539–79.

Bonikowski, Bart. 2017. "Ethnonationalist Populism and the Mobilization of Collective Resentment." The British Journal of Sociology 68: 181–213.

Bonilla-Silva, Eduardo. 1996. "Rethinking Racism: Toward a Structural Interpretation." American Sociological Review 62: 465–80.

Bonilla-Silva, Eduardo. 2002. "The Linguistics of Color Blind Racism: How to Talk Nasty about Blacks without Sounding 'Racist.'" Critical Sociology 28: 41–64.

Booher-Jennings, Jennifer. 2005. "Below the Bubble: 'Educational Triage' and the Texas Accountability System." American Educational Research Journal 42: 231–68.

Bookman, Todd. 2013. "When an Emergency Room Closes Its Doors." New Hampshire Public Radio July 22. (nhpr.org/health/2013-07-22/when-an-emergency-room-closes-its-doors)

Bosman, Julie. 2016. "Flint Water Crisis Finds State Ignored Warning Signs." New York Times March 23. (nytimes.com/2016/03/24/us/flint-water-crisis.html)

Bourdieu, Pierre. 1984. Distinction: A Social Critique of the Judgment of Taste. Cambridge, MA: Harvard University Press.

Bourdieu, Pierre. 1992. The Logic of Practice. Translated by Richard Nice. Cambridge, MA: Polity Press.

Bourdieu, Pierre and Jean-Claude Passeron. 1979. Reproduction in Education, Society and Culture. Beverly Hills, CA: Sage Publications.

Boushey, Heather. 2008. "'Opting Out'? The Effect of Children on Women's Employment in the United States." Feminist Economics 14: 1–36.

Bowen, Natasha and Gary Bowen. 1999. "Effects of Crime and Violence in Neighborhoods and Schools on the School Behavior and Performance of Adolescents." Journal of Adolescent Research 14: 319–42.

Bowles, Samuel. 2017. The Moral Economy. New Haven: Yale University Press.

Bowles, Samuel and Herbert Gintis. 1976. Schooling in Capitalist America: Educational Reform and the Contradictions of Economic Life. New York: Basic Books.

Boxer, Christie, Mary Noonan, and Christine Whelan. 2015. "Measuring Mate Preferences: A Replication and Extension." Journal of Family Issues 36: 163–187.

Boyd, Danah. 2008. "Why Youth (Heart) Social Network Sites: The Role of Networked Publics in Teenage Social Life." Pp. 119–42 in MacArthur Foundation Series on Digital Learning: Youth, Identity, and Digital Media Volume, ed. David Buckingham. Cambridge, MA: MIT Press.

Braga, Anthony. 2005. "Hot Spots Policing and Crime Prevention: A Systematic Review of Randomized Controlled Trials." Journal of Experimental Criminology 3: 317–42.

Branas, Charles, Rose Cheney, John MacDonald, Vicky Tam, Tara Jackson, and Thomas Ten Have. 2011. A Difference-in-Differences Analysis of Health, Safety, and Greening Vacant Urban Space. American Journal of Epidemiology 174: 1296–306.

Brandon, Emily. 2012. "Retiree Net Worth Declines." US News July 11. (money.usnews.com/money/retirement/articles/2012/07/23/retiree-net-worth-declines)

Brayne, Sarah. 2020. Predict and Surveil: Data, Discretion, and the Future of Policing. New York: Oxford University Press.

Breiding, Matthew, Sharon Smith, Kathleen Basile, Mikel Walters, Jieru Chen, and Melissa Merrick. 2014. "Prevalence and Characteristics of Sexual Violence, Stalking, and Intimate Partner Violence Victimization — National Intimate Partner and Sexual Violence Survey 2011." Atlanta, GA: Centers for Disease Control. (cdc.gov/mmwr/preview/mmwrhtml/ss6308a1.htm)

Breman, Jan. 2013. At Work in the Informal Economy of India: A Perspective from the Bottom Up. New Delhi: Oxford University Press.

Brenan, Megan. 2020. "At 65%, Approval of Labor Union in the U.S. Remains High." Gallup News September 3. (news.gallup.com/poll/318980/approval-labor-unions-remains-high.aspx)

Brenner, Neil. 2019. New Urban Spaces: Urban Theory and the Scale Question. New York: Oxford University Press.

Brenner, Robert. 2006. The Economics of Global Turbulence. New York: Verso.

Bricker, Jessie, Lisa Dettling, Alice Henriques, Joanne Hsu, Kevin Moore, John Sabelhaus, Jeffrey Thompson, and Richard Windle. 2014. Changes in U.S. Family Finances from 2010 to 2013: Evidence from the Survey of Consumer Finances. Federal Reserve Bulletin 100, September. (federalreserve.gov/pubs/bulletin/2014/pdf/scf14.pdf)

Brint, Steven. 2017. Schools and Societies. 3rd ed. Stanford: Stanford University Press.

Brittingham, Angela, and G. Patricia de la Cruz. 2004. "Ancestry: 2000." Census Brief, C2KBR-35. Washington, DC: U.S. Census Bureau. (census.gov/history/pdf/ancestry.pdf)

Brockett, Charles. 1993. "A Protest Cycle Resolution of the Repression/Protest Paradox." Social Science History 17: 457–84.

Brockway, Zebulon. 1871. "The Ideal of a True Prison System for a State." In Transactions of the National Congress on Penitentiary and Reformatory Discipline, 1870, ed. E. C. Wines Albany, NY: Weed, Parsons.

Bronfenbrenner, Kate. 2000. Uneasy Terrain: The Impact of Capital Mobility on Workers, Wages and Union Organizing. ILR Research Reports, September 6. (digitalcommons.ilr.cornell.edu/reports/3/)

Brooks, Clem. 2000. "Civil Rights Liberalism and the Suppression of a Republican Political Realignment in the U.S., 1972–1996." American Sociological Review 65: 482–505.

Brooks, Rosa. 2016. How Everything Became War and Military Became Everything. New York: Simon and Shuster.

Brooks, Clem and Jeff Manza. 2007. Why Welfare States Persist. Chicago: University of Chicago Press.

Brooks, Clem and Jeff Manza. 2013. Who Is Us? Counterterrorism and the Dark Side of American Public Opinion. New York: Russell Sage.

Broughton, Edward. 2005. "The Bhopal Disaster and Its Aftermath: A Review." Environmental Health: A Global Access Science Source 4: 1–6.

Brown, Eliza and Paula England. 2016. "Sexual Orientation Versus Behavior—Different for Men and Women?" Contexts February 29. (contexts.org/blog/sexual-orientation-versus-behavior-different-for-men-and-women/)

Brown, Michael, Martin Carnoy, Elliott Currie, Troy Duster, David Oppenheimer, Marjorie Schultz, and David Wellman. 2003. Whitewashing Race: The Myth of a Color-Blind Society. Berkeley, CA: University of California Press.

Brulle, Robert. 1996. "Environmental Discourse and Social Movement Organizations: A Historical Perspective on the Development of U.S. Environmental Organizations." Sociological Inquiry 66: 58–83.

Brulle, Robert and David Pellow. 2006. "Environmental Justice: Human Health and Environmental Inequalities." Annual Review of Public Health 27: 103–24.

Bryskine, Sonya. 2010. "HK's 2010 Air Pollution Death Toll Nears 600." Epoch Times October 13. (theepochtimes.com/hks-2010-air-pollution-death-toll-nears-600_1507421.html)

Buchmann, Claudia and Thomas DiPrete. 2006. "The Growing Female Advantage in College Completion: The Role of Family Background and Academic Achievement." American Sociological Review 71: 515–41.

Buchmann, Claudia, Thomas DiPrete, and Anne McDaniel. 2008. "Gender Inequalities in Education." Annual Review of Sociology 34: 319–37.

Budig, Michelle. 2002. "Male Advantage and the Gender Composition of Jobs: Who Rides the Glass Escalator?" Social Problems 49: 258–77.

Budiman, Abby. 2020. "Key Findings About U.S. Immigrants." Pew Research Center FactTank August 20. (pewresearch.org/fact-tank/2020/08/20/key-findings-about-u-s-immigrants/)

Buettner, Russ, Susanne Craig and Mike McIntire. 2020. "Long Concealed Records Show Trump's Chronic Losses and Years of Tax Avoidance." New York Times September 27. (nytimes.com/interactive/2020/09/27/us/donald-trump-taxes.html?action=click&module=RelatedLinks&pgtype=Article)

Buffett, Warren. 2011. "Stop Coddling the Super Rich." New York Times August 14. (nytimes.com/2011/08/15/opinion/stop-coddling-the-super-rich.html)

Bulatao, Rudolfo and John Casterline, eds. 2001. Global Fertility Transition. New York: Population Council.

Bullard, Robert. 1983. "Solid Waste Sites and the Houston Black Community." Sociological Inquiry 53: 273–88.

Bullard, Robert. 1990. Dumping in Dixie: Race, Class, And Environmental Quality. Boulder, CO: Westview.

Bullard, Robert, Paul Mohai, Robin Saha, and Beverly Wright. 2007. Toxic Waste and Race at Twenty 1987–2007 A Report Prepared for the United Church of Christ. March. (nrdc.org/sites/default/files/toxic-wastes-and-race-at-twenty-1987-2007.pdf)

Bumpass, Larry and Hsien-Hen Lu. 2000. "Trends in Cohabitation and Implications for Children's Family Contexts." Population Studies 54: 29–41.

Burawoy, Michael. 2009. The Extended Case Method: Four Countries, Four Decades, Four Great Transformations, and One Theoretical Tradition. Berkeley: University of California Press.

Burchinal, Margaret and Alison Clarke-Stewart. 2007. "Maternal Employment and Child Cognitive Outcomes: The Importance of an Analytic Approach." Developmental Psychology 43: 1140–55.

Bureau of Justice Statistics. 2016. "Criminal Victimization, 2015: Summary." (bjs.gov/content/pub/pdf/cv15_sum.pdf)

Bureau of Justice Statistics. 2021. FBI Uniform Crime Reporting Statistics. (fbi.gov/services/cjis/ucr)

Burgard, Sarah, Jennie Brand, and James House. 2007. "Toward a Better Estimation of the Effect of Job Loss on Health." Journal of Health and Social Behavior 48: 369–84.

Burgess, Jean and Joshua Green. 2009. YouTube: Online Video and Participatory Culture. Cambridge, MA: Polity Press.

Buss, David. 1994. The Evolution of Desire: Strategies of Human Mating. New York: Basic Books.

Bussuk, Ellen, Christina Murphy, Natalie Coupe, Rachael Kenney, and Corey Beach. 2011. America's Youngest Outcasts 2010. Needham, MA: The National Center on Family Homelessness. (hartfordinfo.org/issues/wsd/Homelessness/NCFH_AmericaOutcast2010_web.pdf)

Butler, Paul. 2017. Chokehold: Policing Black Men. New York: The New Press.

Butterfield, Fox. 1995. "Serious Crimes Fall for Third Year, but Experts Warn Against Seeing Trend." New York Times May 23. (nytimes.com/1995/05/23/us/serious-crimes-fall-for-third-year-but-experts-warn-against-seeing-trend.html)

Calavita, Kitty. 1992. Inside the State: The Bracero Program, Immigration, and the I.N.S. New York: Routledge.

Californians Against Waste. 2011. "Plastic Bag Litter Pollution." (cawrecycle.org/issues/plastic_campaign/plastic_bags)

Camerer, Colin. 2003. Behavioral Game Theory: Experiments in Strategic Interaction. Princeton: Princeton University Press.

Campbell, James. 2016. Polarized: Making Sense of a Divided America. Princeton, NJ: Princeton University Press.

Cancian, Francesca. 1987. Love in America: Gender and Self-Development. New York: Cambridge University Press.

Cannon, Carl. 2005. "Petty Crime, Outrageous Punishment: Why the Three-Strikes Law Doesn't Work." Reader's Digest October. (november.org/stayinfo/breaking3/Outrageous.html)

Cantino, Maurizio. 2019. Mafia Organizations. New York: Cambridge University Press.

Capers, I. Bennett, John Goldberg and Benjamin Zipursky. 2020. "How to Reform Police Liability without Involving McConnell or Trump." Washington Post August 17. (washingtonpost.com/opinions/2020/08/17/how-reform-police-liability-without-involving-mcconnell-or-trump/)

Carbone, June and Naomi Cahn. 2014. Marriage Markets: How Inequality is Remaking the American Family. New York: Oxford University Press.

Carnes, Nicholas. 2018. The Cash Ceiling: Why Only the Rich Run for Office--and What We Can Do About It. Princeton, NJ: Princeton University Press.

Carr, Patrick and Maria Kefalas. 2009. Hallowing Out the Middle: The Rural Brain Drain and What it Means for America. Boston: Beacon Press.

Carrega, Christina. 2020. "Millions in Lawsuit Settlements are Another Hidden Cost of Police Misconduct, Legal Experts Say." ABC News June 14. (abcnews.go.com/US/millions-lawsuit-settlements-hidden-cost-police-misconduct-legal/story?id=70999540)

Carrere, Celine and Maurice Schiff. 2004. "On the Geography of Trade: Distance Is Alive and Well." World Bank Policy Research Working Papers 3206. (documents1.worldbank.org/curated/en/128881468778205018/pdf/wps3206geography.pdf)

Carson, Rachel. 1962. Silent Spring. New York: Houghton Mifflin.

Case, Anne and Angus Deaton. 2020. Deaths of Despair and the Future of Capitalism. Princeton: Princeton University Press.

Case, Anne, Darren Lubotsky, and Christina Paxson. 2002. "Economic Status and Health in Childhood: The Origins of the Gradient." American Economic Review 92: 1308–34.

Casper, Lynne and Suzanne Bianchi. 2002. Continuity and Change in the American Family. Thousand Oaks, CA: Sage.

Castells, Manuel. 2000. The Rise of Network Society. Cambridge, MA: Blackwell.

Castells, Manuel. 2009. Communication Power. Oxford, UK: Oxford University Press.

Catalyst. 2020. List: Women CEOs of the SP 500. September 14. (catalyst. org/research/women-ceos-of-the-sp–500/)

Catton, William Jr. and Riley Dunlap. 1980. "A New Ecological Paradigm for a Post-exuberant Sociology." American Behavioral Scientist 24: 15–47.

Center for Responsible Lending. 2021. "Map of U.S. Payday Interest Rates." (responsiblelending.org/research-publication/map-us-pay-day-interest-rates)

Center for Responsive Politics. 2020. "Unprecedented Donations Poured into 2020 State and Federal Races." November 19. (opensecrets.org/news/2020/11/2020-state-and-federal-races-nimp)

Centers for Disease Control and Prevention. 2011. CDC Health Disparities and Inequalities Report 2011. Atlanta, GA: Department of Health and Human Services. (cdc.gov/minorityhealth/chdir/2011/CHDIR2011. html)

Centers for Disease Control and Prevention. 2012. "Vital Signs: Binge Drinking Prevalence, Frequency, and Intensity among Adults—United States, 2010." January 13. 61: 14–19. (cdc.gov/mmwr/preview/mmwrhtml/mm6101a4.htm?s_cid=mm6101a4_w)

Center for Medicare and Medicaid Services 2014

Centers for Medicare and Medicaid Services. 2015. "Table 95: Personal Healthcare Expenditures, by Source of Funds: Selected Calendar Years 1960–2014." (cdc.gov/nchs/data/hus/2015/095.pdf)

Center for Responsive Politics. 2020. "Unprecedented Donations Poured into 2020 State and Federal Races." November 19. (opensecrets.org/news/2020/11/2020-state-and-federal-races-nimp)

Chakradhar, Shraddha and Casey Ross. 2019. "The History of OxyContin, As Told Through Unsealed Purdue Documents." StatNews December 3. (statnews.com/2019/12/03/oxycontin-history-told-through-pur-due-pharma-documents/)

Chalfin, Aaron and Steven Rafael. 2011. "Work and Crime." Pp. 444–76 in The Oxford Handbook of Crime and Criminal Justice, ed. Michael Tonry. New York: Oxford University Press.

Chambliss, William. 1973. "The Saints and the Roughnecks." Society 11: 24–31.

Chandra, Amitabh. 2009. "Who You Are and Where You Live: Race and the Geography of Health Care." Medical Care 47: 135–37.

Chang, Chul Tim. 2006. "Korean Ethnic Church Growth Phenomenon in the United States." Presented at the American Academy of Religion, March 12. Claremont, CA. (researchgate.net/publication/237588697_Korean_Ethnic_Church_Growth_Phenomenon_in_the_United_States)

Chang, Ha-joon. 2002. Kicking Away the Ladder. London: Anthem Press.

Charles, Maria and Karen Bradley. 2009. "Indulging Our Gendered Selves? Sex Segregation by Field of Study in 44 Countries." American Journal of Sociology 114: 924–76.

Chaves, Mark. 2004. Congregations in America. Cambridge, MA: Harvard University Press.

Chaves, Mark, and Shawna Anderson. 2014. "Changing American Congregations: Findings from the Third Wave of the National Congregations Study." Journal for the Scientific Study of Religion 53: 676–86.

Chaves, Mark, C. Kirk Hadaway, and Penny Long Marler. 1993. "What the Polls Don't Show: A Closer Look at U.S. Church Attendance," American Sociological Review 58: 741–52.

Chen, Carolyn. 2008. Getting Saved in America: Taiwanese Immigration and Religious Experience. Princeton, NJ: Princeton University Press.

Chenoweth, Erica and Maria Stephan. 2011. Why Civil Resistance Works: The Strategic Logic of Nonviolent Conflict. New York: Columbia University Press.

Cherlin, Andrew. 1992. Marriage, Divorce, Remarriage. Cambridge, MA: Harvard University Press.

Cherlin, Andrew. 2009. The Marriage-Go-Round: The State of Marriage and the Family in America Today. New York: Alfred A. Knopf.

Cherlin, Andrew. 2014. Labor's Love Lost: The Rise and Fall of the Working-Class Family in America. New York: Russel Sage Foundation.

Cherlin, Andrew, Frank Furstenberg, Jr., P. Lindsey Chase-Lansdale, Kathleen Kiernan, Philip Robins, Donna Ruane Morrison, and Julien Teitler. 1991. "Longitudinal Studies of the Effects of Divorce on Children in Great Britain and the United States." Science 252: 1386–89.

Chesney-Lind, Meda and Marc Mauer. 2002. Invisible Punishment: The Collateral Consequences of Mass Punishment. New York: The New Press.

Chetty, Raj, John N. Friedman, Nathaniel Hendren, Maggie R. Jones, and Sonya R. Porter. 2018. "The Opportunity Atlas: Mapping the Childhood Roots of Social Mobility." NBER Working Paper 25147. (nber. org/system/files/working_papers/w25147/w25147.pdf)

Chetty, Raj, John Friedman, Nathaniel Hendren, Michael Stepner, and The Opportunity Insights Team. 2020. "The Economic Impacts of COVID-19: Evidence from a New Public Database Built Using Private Sector Data." NBER Working Papers 27431. Cambridge, MA: National Bureau of Economic Research. (nber.org/system/files/working_pa-pers/w27431/w27431.pdf)

Chetty, Raj, David Grusky, Maximillan Hell, Nathaniel Hendren, David Manduca, and Jimmy Narang. 2017. "The Fading American Dream: Trends in Absolute Mobility Since 1940." Science 356: 398–406.

China Labor Watch. 2011. Tragedies of Globalization: The Truth behind Electronics Sweatshops. (chinalaborwatch.org/pro/proshow-149.html)

Chiracos, Ted. 1987. "Rates of Crime and Unemployment: An Analysis of Aggregate Research Evidence." Social Problems 34: 187–211.

Chodorow, Nancy. 1978. The Reproduction of Mothering: Psychoanalysis and the Sociology of Gender. Berkeley: University of California Press.

Choo, Hae Yeon and Myra Marx Ferree. 2010. "Practicing Intersectionality in Sociological Research." Sociological Theory 28: 129–49.

Chokshi, Niraj. 2018. "94% of Teachers Spend Their Own Money on School Supplies, Survey Finds." New York Times May 16. (nytimes. com/2018/05/16/us/teachers-school-supplies.html)

Christakis, Nicholas and James Fowler. 2007. Connected: The Surprising Power of Our Social Networks and How They Shape Our Lives. Boston, MA: Little Brown.

Churchwell, Sarah. 2018. Behold America: The Entangled History of "America First" and "The American Dream." New York: Basic Books.

Cicourel, Aaron. 1967. The Social Organization of Juvenile Justice. New York: Wiley.

City of Chicago Office of the Inspector General. 2014. Chicago Police Department Assault-Related Crime Statistics Classification and Reporting Audit. April 4. Chicago, IL.

Clarke, John, Stuart Hall, Tony Jefferson, and Brian Roberts. 1975. "Subcultures, Cultures and Class: A Theoretical Overview." Pp. 9–74 in Resistance through Rituals: Youth Subcultures in Post-War Britain, eds. Stuart Hall and Tony Jefferson. New York and London: Routledge.

Clawson, Dan, Richard Neustadtl, and Mark Weller. 1998. Dollars and Votes: How Business Campaign Contributions Subvert Democracy. Philadelphia, PA: Temple University Press.

Claytor, Cassi. 2020. Black Privilege: Modern Middle-Class Blacks with Credentials and Cash to Spend. Stanford: Stanford University Press.

Clear, Todd. 2007. Imprisoning Communities: How Mass Incarceration Makes Disadvantaged Neighborhoods Worse. New York: Oxford University Press.

Clinton, William. 1993. "Remarks at the Signing Ceremony for the Supplemental Agreements to the North American Free Trade Agreement." Public Papers of the Presidents of the United States 1485. Washington, DC: U.S. Government Printing Office. (govinfo.gov/content/pkg/PPP-1993-book2/pdf/PPP-1993-book2-doc-pg1485-2.pdf)

Clotfelter, Charles, Helen Ladd, and Jacob Vigdor. 2007. "Teacher Credentials and Student Achievement in High School: A Cross-Subject Analysis with Student Fixed Effects." NBER Working Papers 13617. Cambridge, MA: National Bureau of Economic Research. (nber.org/papers/w13617.pdf)

Coale, Ansley. 1973. "The Demographic Transition Reconsidered." Pp. 53–72 in Proceedings: International Population Conference, Liege. International Union for the Scientific Study of Populations.

Coates, Ta-Nahisi. 2015. Between the World and Me. New York: Random House.

Cohany, Sharon and Emy Sok. 2007. "Trends in the Labor Force Participation of Married Mothers of Infants." Monthly Labor Review 9–16. (bls. gov/opub/mlr/2007/02/art2full.pdf)

Cohen, Lawrence & Marcus Felson. 1979. "Social Change and Crime Rate Trends: A Routine Activity Approach." American Sociological Review 44: 588–608.

Cohen, Cathy and Michael Dawson. 1993. "Neighborhood Poverty and African-American Politics." American Political Science Review 87: 286–302.

Cohen, Jean and Andrew Arato. 1992. Civil Society and Political Theory. Cambridge, MA: MIT Press.

Coleman, James. 1988. "Social Capital in the Creation of Human Capital." American Journal of Sociology 94: 95–120.

Coleman, James. 1990. Foundations of Social Theory. Cambridge, MA: Harvard University Press.

Coleman, James, Robert Bremner, Burton Clark, John Davis, Dorothy Eichorn, Zvi Griliches, Joseph Kett, Norman Ryder, Zahava Blum Doering, and John Mays. [1966] 1974. Youth: Transition to Adulthood. Report of the Panel on Youth of the President's Science Advisory Committee. Chicago: University of Chicago Press.

Coleman, James and Thomas Hoffer. 1987. Public and Private High Schools: The Impact of Communities. New York: Basic Books.

College Board. 2019. SAT Suite of Assessments Annual Report. (reports.collegeboard.org/pdf/2019-total-group-sat-suite-assessments-annual-report.pdf)

Collins, Patricia Hill. 1990. Black Feminist Thought: Knowledge, Consciousness, and the Politics of Empowerment. New York: Routledge.

Collins, Randall, 1979. The Credential Society: A Historical Sociology of Education and Stratification. New York: Academic Press.

Collins, Randall. 2008. Violence: A Micro-Sociological Theory. Princeton, NJ: Princeton University Press.

Coltrane, Scott. 2004. "Fathering: Paradoxes, Contradictions and Dilemmas." Pp. 224–43 in Handbook of Contemporary Families: Considering the Past, Contemplating the Future, eds. Marilyn Coleman and Lawrence Ganong. Thousand Oaks, CA: Sage.

Commission for Racial Justice. 1987. Toxic Wastes and Race in the United States. United Church of Christ. Public Data Access, Inc. (nrc.gov/docs/ML1310/ML13109A339.pdf)

Commonwealth Fund. 2018. Affordable Care Act Tracking Survey. Washington, D.C. (commonwealthfund.org/series/affordable-care-act-tracking-surveys)

Comte, Auguste. [1839–1853] 2009. The Positive Philosophy of Auguste Comte. Edited and translated by Harriet Martinaeu. New York: Cambridge University Press.

Condron, Dennis. and Vincent Roscigno. 2003. "Disparities Within: Unequal Spending and Achievement in an Urban School District." Sociology of Education 76: 18–36.

Congressional Budget Office. 2011. CBO's 2011 Long-Term Budget Outlook. Washington, DC: CBO. (cbo.gov/publication/41486)

Congressional Research Service. 2020. "Membership of the 116th Congress: A Profile." October 2. Washington, DC. (fas.org/sgp/crs/misc/R45583.pdf)

Conley, Dalton. 1999. Being Black, Living in Red: Race, Wealth, and Social Policy in America. Berkeley: University of California Press.

Conley, Dalton. 2004. The Pecking Order: Which Siblings Succeed and Why. New York: Pantheon.

Conley, Dalton. 2008. Elsewhere, U.S.A. New York: Pantheon.

Conn, Steven. 2014. Americans Against the City: Anti-Urbanism in the Twentieth Century. New York: Oxford University Press.

Connell, R. W. 1987. Gender and Power: Society, the Person, and Sexual Politics. Palo Alto, CA: Stanford University Press.

Consumer Reports. 2013. "What Bugs Americans Most About Their Doctors." June. (consumerreports.org/cro/magazine/2013/06/what-bugs-you-most-about-your-doctor/index.htm)

Contreras, Randol. 2012. The Stickup Kids: Race, Drugs, Violence, and the American Dream. Berkeley: University of California Press.

Cook, Benjamin, Toby Ault and Jason Smerdon. 2015. "Unprecedented 21st Century Drought Risk in the American Southwest and Central Plains." Science Advances 1: 1–7.

Cook, Philip and Jens Ludwig. 2005. Gun Violence: The Real Costs. New York: Oxford University Press.

Cooke, Lynn. 2006. "'Doing' Gender in Context: Household Bargaining and Risk of Divorce in Germany and the United States." American Journal of Sociology 112: 442–72.

Coontz, Stephanie. 2005. Marriage, a History: From Obedience to Intimacy, or How Love Conquered Marriage. New York: Viking.

Cooperative for Assistance and Relief Everywhere. 2008. In Search of Shelter: Mapping the Effects of Climate Change on Human Migration and Displacement. (ciesin.columbia.edu/documents/clim-migr-report-june09_media.pdf)

Corak, Miles. 2013. "Income Inequality, Equality of Opportunity, and Intergenerational Mobility." Journal of Economic Perspectives 27: 79–102.

Corley, Cheryl. 2020. "Police Settlements: How the Cost of Police Misconduct Impacts Cities and Taxpayers." National Public Radio September 19. (npr.org/2020/09/19/914170214/police-settlements-how-the-cost-of-misconduct-impacts-cities-and-taxpayers)

Cornaggia, Jess, Kimberly Cornaggia, and Han Xia. 2016. "Revolving doors on Wall Street." Journal of Financial Economics 120: 400–19.

Cornell, Stephen, and Douglas Hartmann. 2007. Ethnicity and Race: Making Identities in a Changing World. Thousand Oaks, CA: Pine Forge Press.

Correll, Shelley. 2004. "Constraints into Preferences: Gender, Status, and Emerging Career Aspirations." American Sociological Review 69: 93–113.

Correll, Shelley, Stephen Benard, and In Paik. 2007. "Getting a Job: Is There a Motherhood Penalty?" American Journal of Sociology 112: 1297–338.

Corsaro, William and Donna Eder. 1990. "Games Children Play." Annual Review of Sociology 16: 197–220.

Cotter, David, Paula England, and Joan Hermsen. 2010. "Moms and Jobs: Trends in Mothers' Employment and Which Mothers Stay Home." Pp. 416–24 in Families as They Really Are, ed. Barbara Risman. New York: W.W. Norton.

Cotter, David, Joan Hermsen, and Reeve Vanneman. 2011. "The End of the Gender Revolution? Gender Role Attitudes from 1977 to 2008." American Journal of Sociology 117: 259–89.

Cotter, David, Joan Hermsen, and Reeve Vanneman. 2014. "Back on Track? The Stall and Rebound in Support for Women's New Roles in Work and Politics, 1977–2012." Brief Reports. Council on Contemporary Families. (contemporaryfamilies.org/gender-revolution-rebound-brief-back-on-track/)

Courtwright, David. 2009. Dark Paradise: A History of Opiate Addiction in America. Cambridge, MA: Harvard University Press.

Cramer, Katherine. 2016. The Politics of Resentment: Rural Consciousness in Wisconsin and the Rise of Scott Walker. Chicago: University of Chicago Press.

Crawford, Mary and Danielle Popp. 2003. "Sexual Double Standards: A Review and Methodological Critique of Two Decades of Research." Journal of Sex Research 40: 13–26.

Creamer, John. 2020. "Inequalities Persist Despite Decline in Poverty Rates for All Major Racial and Hispanic-Origin Groups." Stories Behind the Numbers September 15. (census.gov/library/stories/2020/09/poverty-rates-for-blacks-and-hispanics-reached-historic-lows-in-2019.html)

Crenshaw, Kimberlee. 1991. "Mapping the Margins: Intersectionality, Identity Politics, and Violence against Women of Color." Stanford Law Review 43: 1241–99.

Cullen, Francis. 2005. "The Twelve People Who Saved Rehabilitation: How the Science of Criminology Made a Difference." Criminology 43: 1–42.

Cutler, David, Adriana Lleras-Muney, and Tom Vogl. 2008. "Socioeconomic Status and Health: Dimensions and Mechanisms." NBER Working Paper 14333. Cambridge, MA: National Bureau of Economic Research. (nber.org/papers/w14333.pdf)

Czeisler Mark, Rahon Lane, Emiko Petrosky, Joshua Wiley, Aleta Christensen, Rashid Najai, Matthew Weaver, Rebecca Robbins, Elise Facer-Childs, Laura Barger, Charles Czeisler, Mark Howard, and Shantha Rajaratnam. 2020. "Mental Health, Substance Use, and Suicidal Ideation During the COVID-19 Pandemic — United States, June 24–30, 2020." Morbity and Mortality Weekly Report 69: 1049–1057. (https://cdc.gov/mmwr/volumes/69/wr/mm6932a1.htm)

DaCosta, Kimberly McClain. 2007. Making Multiracials: State, Family, and Market in the Redrawing of the Color Line. Stanford, CA: Stanford University Press.

Dahl, Robert. 2003. How Democratic Is the American Constitution? New Haven, CT: Yale University Press.

Dahrendorf, Ralf. 1959. Class and Class Conflict in Industrial Society. Stanford, CA: Stanford University Press.

Dale, Stacy and Alan Krueger. 2011. "Estimating the Return to College Selectivity over the Career Using Administrative Earnings Data." NBER Working Papers 17159. Cambridge, MA: National Bureau of Economic Research. (nber.org/system/files/working_papers/w17159/w17159.pdf)

Daley, David. 2016. Ratf**ked:The True Story Behind the Secret Plan to Steal America's Democracy. New York: W.W. Norton.

Damaske, Sarah. 2011. For the Family? How Class and Gender Shape Women's Work. New York: Oxford University Press.

Darling-Hammond, Linda. 2001. "Inequality and Access to Knowledge," Pp. 465–83 in Handbook of Research on Multicultural Education, eds. J. Banks and C. Banks. San Francisco: Jossey-Bass.

Dar-Nimrod, Ilan and Steven Heine. 2006. "Exposure to Scientific Theories Affects Women's Math Performance." Science 314: 435.

Davidson, Judy. 1984. "Subsequent Versions of Invitations, Offers, Requests, and Proposals Dealing with Potential or Actual Rejection." Pp. 102–28 in Structures of Social Action: Studies in Conversation Analysis, eds. John Heritage and J. Maxwell Atkinson. New York: Cambridge University Press.

Davis, Kingsley. 1963. "The Theory of Change and Response in Modern Demographic History." Population Index 29: 145–66.

Davis, Kingsley. 1965. "The Urbanization of the Human Population." Scientific American 213: 40–53. (scientificamerican.com/article/the-urbanization-of-the-human-popul/)

Davis, Kingsley and Wilbert Moore. 1945. "Some Principles of Stratification." American Sociological Review 10: 242–49.

Davis, Mike. 1990. City of Quartz: Excavating the Future of Los Angeles. London: Verso.

Davis, Mike. 2020. The Monster Enters: Covid-19, the Avian Flu, and the Plagues of Capitalism. New York: O/R Books.

Dawson, Michael. 1994. Behind the Mule: Race and Class in African-American Politics. Princeton, NJ: Princeton University Press.

Dayen, David. 2020. Monopolized: Life in the Age of Corporate Power. New York: The New Press.

Deaton, Angus. 2013. The Great Escape: Health, Wealth, and the Origins of Inequality. Princeton: Princeton University Press.

Dee, Thomas. 2007. "Teachers and the Gender Gaps in Student Achievement." Journal of Human Resources 42: 1–28.

De Haas, Hein, Stephen Castles and Mark Miller. 2020. The Age of Migration: International Population Movements Around the World. London: Red Globe Press.

Delaney-Black, Virginia, Chandice Covington, Steven Ondersma, Beth Nordstrom-Klee, Thomas Templin, Joel Ager, James Janisse, and Robert Sokol. 2002. "Violence Exposure, Trauma, and IQ and/or Reading Deficits among Urban Children." Archives of Pediatrics & Adolescent Medicine 156: 280–85.

Delgado, Sheyla, Laila Alsabahi, Kevin Wolff, Nicole Alexander, Patricia Cobar, and Jeffrey Butts. 2017. Denormalizing Violence: The Effects of Cure Violence in the South Bronx and East New York. October 17. Brooklyn: John Jay College. (johnjayrec.nyc/wp-content/uploads/2017/10/CVinSoBronxEastNY.pdf)

DellaPosta, Daniel, Yongren Shi, and Michael Macy. 2016. "Why Do Liberals Drink Lattes?" American Journal of Sociology 120: 1473–1511.

Deloitte, Corporate Tax Rates, 2011–2015. (http://2.deloitte.com/global/en/pages/tax/articles/global-tax-rates.html)

DeLong, J. Bradford. 2006. "Neoliberalism Has a Patchy Mexican Record." Taipei Times September 30. (taipeitimes.com/News/editorials/archives/2006/09/30/2003329853)

Demerath, Nicholas. 2003. Crossing the Gods. New Brunswick, NJ: Rutgers University Press.

Denny, Iain. 2020. "The Sneaker – Marketplace Icon." Consumption, Markets and Culture 23: 1–12.

DeParle, Jason. 2007. "Migrant Money Flow: A $300 Billion Current." New York Times November 18. (nytimes.com/2007/11/18/weekinreview/18deparle.html)

Derber, Charles, William Schwartz, and Yale Magrass. 1992. Power in the Highest Degree: Professionals and the Rise of a New Mandarin Order. New York: Oxford University Press.

DeSilver, Drew. 2013. "Black Unemployment Is Consistently Twice That of Whites." FactTank. Philadelphia: Pew Research Foundation. (pewresearch.org/fact-tank/2013/08/21/through-good-times-and-bad-black-unemployment-is-consistently-double-that-of-whites/)

Desmond, Matthew. 2016. Evicted: Poverty and Profit in the American City. New York: Crown Books.

Deutsch, Francine. 1999. Halving It All: How Equally Shared Parenting Works. Cambridge, MA: Harvard University Press.

Deutschkron, Inge. 1989. Outcast: A Jewish Girl in Wartime Berlin. New York: Fromm International Publishing Group.

Dewey, John. [1916] 1966. Democracy and Education. New York: The Free Press.

Diamond, Jared. 1995. "Easter Island's End." Discover Magazine 63–9. (discovermagazine.com/planet-earth/easters-end)

Diamond, Jared. 1997. Guns, Germs, and Steel: The Fates of Human Societies. New York: W.W. Norton & Co.

Diamond, Lisa. 2008. Sexual Fluidity: Understanding Women's Love and Desire. Cambridge, MA: Harvard University Press.

Dias, Elizabeth. 2020. "Biden and Trump Say They're Fighting for America's 'Soul.' What Does That Mean?" New York Times October 18. (nytimes.com/2020/10/17/us/biden-trump-soul-nation-country.html)

Dicken, Peter. 2011. Global Shift: Mapping the Changing Contours of the World Economy. New York. Guilford.

Diette, Timothy, Arthur Goldsmith, Darrick Hamilton, and William Darity Jr. 2012. "Causality in the Relationship between Mental Health and Employment." Pp. 63–94 in Reconnecting to Work: Policies to Mitigate Long-Term Unemployment and Its Consequences, ed. Lauren Applebaum. Kalamazoo, MI: W.E. Upjohn Institute for Employment Research.

Dietz, Thomas, Rachael Shwom, and Cameron Whitley. 2020. "Climate Change and Society." Annual Review of Sociology 46: 135–58.

Dietz, Thomas and Richard York. 2015. "Animals, Capital and Sustainability." Human Ecology Review 22: 35–54.

Digest of Education Statistics. 2016. Table 318.10. (nces.ed.gov/programs/digest/d15/tables/dt15_318.10.asp?current=yes)

Dikötter, Frank. 2008. "The Racialization of the Globe: An Interactive Interpretation." Ethnic and Racial Studies 31: 1478–96.

Dillon, Michelle and Paul Wink. 2007. In the Course of a Lifetime: Tracing Religious Belief, Practice, and Change. Berkeley: University of California Press.

DiMaggio, Paul. 1997. "Culture and Cognition." Annual Review of Sociology 23: 263–87.

DiMaggio, Paul and Walter W. Powell. 1983. "The Iron Cage Revisited: Institutional Isomorphism and Collective Rationality in Organizational Fields." American Sociological Review 48: 147–60.

Dionne, E. J. 2016. Why the Right Went Wrong: Conservatism—From Goldwater to Trump and Beyond. New York: Simon and Shuster.

DiPrete, Thomas and Claudia Buchmann. 2013. The Rise of Women: The Female Advantage in Education and What It Means for American Schools. New York: Russell Sage Foundation.

Dobbin, Frank. 2009. Inventing Equal Opportunity. Princeton, NJ: Princeton University Press.

Dobbin, Frank and Alexandra Kalev. 2019. "The Promise and Peril of Sexual Harassment Programs." Proceedings of the National Academy of Sciences 116:12255–60.

Dobbin, Frank, and Erin Kelly. 2007. "How to Stop Harassment: Professional Construction of Legal Compliance in Organizations." American Journal of Sociology 112: 1203–43.

Doleac, Jennifer and Luke Stein. 2013. "The Visible Hand: Race and Online Market Outcomes." The Economic Journal 123: 469–92.

Dollemore, Doug. 2008. "Newly Detected Air Pollutant Mimics Damaging Effects of Cigarette Smoke." American Chemical Society. (sciencedaily.com/releases/2008/08/080817223432.htm)

Domhoff, G. William. 2006. Who Rules America? Power, Politics, and Social Change. New York: McGraw-Hill.

Domhoff, G. William. 2013. Who Rules America? The Triumph of the Corporate Rich. New York: McGraw-Hill.

Dormehl, Luke. 2013. The Apple Revolution: The Real Story of How Steve Jobs and the Crazy Ones Took Over the World. London: Virgin Books.

Douglas, Karen, Joseph Uscinski, Robbie Sutton, Aleksandra Cichocka, Turkay Nefes, Chee Siang Ang, and Farzin Deravi. 2019. "Understanding Conspiracy Theories." Political Psychology 40: 3–35.

Dowie, Mark. 2001. American Foundations: An Investigative History. Cambridge, MA: MIT Press.

Dowling, Tim. 2007. "The Mystery of Hillary Clinton's Changing Accent." The Guardian May 1. (https://www.theguardian.com/world/2007/may/02/hillaryclinton.uselections2008)

Downs, Anthony. 1994. New Visions for Metropolitan America. Washington, D.C: Brookings Institution Press.

Drake, St. Claire and Horace Cayton. 1945. Black Metropolis: A Study of Negro Life in a Northern City. New York: Harcourt.

Drutman, Lee. 2015. The Business of America is Lobbying: How Corporations Became Politicized and How Politics Became More Corporate. New York: Oxford University Press.

Du Bois, W. E. B. [1899] 1995. The Philadelphia Negro. Philadelphia, PA: University of Pennsylvania Press.

Du Bois, W.E.B. [1903] 1989. The Souls of Black Folks. New York: Penguin.

Du Bois, W. E. B. [1903] 1997. The Souls of Black Folks. New York: St. Martin's Press.

Du Bois, W. E. B. [1903] 2008. "The Talented Tenth." In The Negro Problem: A Series of Articles by Representative Negroes of Today. Amherst, New York: Humanity Books.

Du Bois, W. E. B. 1935. Black Reconstruction in America, 1860-1880. New York: Harcourt, Brace and Company.

Duany, Andres, Elizabeth Plater-Zyberk, and Jeff Speck. 2001. Suburban Nation: The Rise of Sprawl and the Decline of the American Dream. New York: North Point Press.

Duhigg, Charles. 2009. "Clean Waters Laws Are Neglected, at a Cost in Suffering." New York Times September 13. (nytimes.com/2009/09/13/us/13water.html)

Duhigg, Charles and David Barboza. 2012. "In China, Human Costs Are Built into the iPad." New York Times January 25. (nytimes.com/2012/01/26/business/ieconomy-apples-ipad-and-the-human-costs-for-workers-in-china.html)

Duhigg, Charles and Keith Bradsher. 2012. "How the U.S. Lost Out on iPhone Work." New York Times January 21. (nytimes.com/2012/01/22/business/apple-america-and-a-squeezed-middle-class.html)

Dumont, Dora, Brad Brockmann, Samuel Dickman, Nicole Alexander, and Josiah Rich. 2012. "Public Health and the Epidemic of Incarceration." Annual Review of Public Health 33: 325–39.

Duncan, Cynthia. 2014. Worlds Apart: Why Poverty Persists in Rural America. New Haven, CT: Yale University Press.

Duneier, Mitchell. 1999. Sidewalk. New York: Farrar, Strauss, and Giroux.

Duneier, Mitchell. 2016. The Ghetto. New York: Farrer, Strauss, and Giroux.

Duneier, Mitchell, and Harvey Molotch. 1999. "Talking City Trouble: Interactional Vandalism, Social Inequality, and the 'Urban Interaction Problem.'" American Journal of Sociology 104: 1263–95.

Dunlap, Riley and Aaron McCright. 2011. "Organized Climate Change Denial." Pp. 144–60 in The Oxford Handbook of Climate Change, eds. John Dryzek, Richard Norgaard, and David Schlosberg. London: Oxford.

Durkheim, Emile. [1890] 1997. The Division of Labor in Society. New York: The Free Press.

Durkheim, Emile. [1895] 1982. Rules of Sociological Method. New York: The Free Press.

Durkheim, Emile. [1897] 1951. Suicide. Translated by John Spaulding and George Simpson. New York: The Free Press.

Durkheim, Emile. [1897] 1997. Suicide. New York: The Free Press.

Durkheim, Emile. [1897] 2006. Suicide. London: Penguin Classics.

Durkheim, Emile. [1912] 2001. The Elementary Forms of Religious Life. Translated by Carol Cosman. New York: Oxford University Press.

Durkheim, Emile. 1912. Elementary Forms of Religious Life. New York: Macmillan.

Durkin, Maureen, Matthew Maenner, Jon Baio, Deborah Christensen, Julie Daniels, Robert Fitzgerald, Pamela Imm, Li-Ching Lee, Laura Schieve, Kim Van Naarden Braun, Martha Wingate, and Marshalyn Yeargin-Allsopp. 2017. "Autism Spectrum Disorder Among U.S. Children: Socioeconomic, Racial, and Ethnic Disparities." American Journal of Public Health 107: 1818–26.

Duster, Troy. 1970. The Legislation of Morality: Law, Drugs, and Moral Judgment. New York: The Free Press.

Dworkin, A. Gary. 2005. "The No Child Left Behind Act: Accountability, High-Stakes Testing, and Roles for Sociologists." Sociology of Education 78: 170–74.

E Magazine. 2001. "A Run on the Banks: How Factory Fishing Decimated Newfoundland Cod." (emagazine.com/a-run-on-the-banks/)

Eckstein, Zvi and Eva Nagypal. 2004. "The Evolution of U.S. Earnings Inequality: 1961–2002." Federal Reserve Bank of Minneapolis Quarterly Review 28: 10–29.

Economic Policy Institute. 2019. "Low-Wage Workers are Suffering From a Decline In the Real Value of the Federal Minimum Wage." Labor Day 2019: How Well Is the American Economy Working for Working People. (https://www.epi.org/publication/labor-day-2019-minimum-wage/)

Economic Policy Institute. 2020. "Wages 2019." State of Working America. (epi.org/publication/swa-wages-2019/)

Edin, Kathryn and Maria Kefalas. 2005. Promises I Can Keep: Why Poor Women Put Motherhood before Marriage. Berkeley and Los Angeles: University of California Press.

Edin, Kathryn and Laura Lein. 1997. Making Ends Meet. New York: Russell Sage Foundation Press.

Ehrlich, Paul. 1968. The Population Bomb. New York: Ballantine Books.

Eisinger, Jesse. 2014. "Why Only One Banker Went to Jail for the Financial Crisis." New York Times Magazine April 30. (nytimes.com/2014/05/04/magazine/only-one-top-banker-jail-financial-crisis.html)

Eliasoph, Nina and Paul Lichterman. 2003. "Culture in Interaction." American Journal of Sociology 108: 735–94.

Elle Magazine. 2016. "Megan Markle: I'm More Than an 'Other.'" December 22. (elle.com/uk/life-and-culture/news/a26855/more-than-an-other/)

Ellwood, David and Christopher Jencks. 2004. "The Spread of Single-Parent Families in the United States since 1960." Pp. 25–64 in The Future of the Family, eds. Daniel Moynihan, Timothy Smeeding, and Lee Rainwater. New York: Russell Sage Foundation.

Elo, Irma, Cassio Turra, Burt Kestenbaum, and B. Renee Ferguson. 2004. "Mortality among Elderly Hispanics in the United States: Past Evidence and New Results." Demography 41: 109–28.

Emmons, William and Lowell Rickets. 2016. "Unequal Degrees of Affluence: Racial and Ethnic Wealth Differences across Education Levels." The Regional Economist October. (https://ideas.repec.org/a/fip/fedlre/00129.html)

Engels, Frederick. [1845] 1972. "The Condition of the Working Class in England in 1844." In The Marx-Engels Reader, ed. Robert Tucker. New York: W.W. Norton & Co. Inc.

England, Paula. 1992. Comparable Worth: Theories and Evidence. New York: Aldine.

England, Paula. 2010. "The Gender Revolution: Uneven and Stalled." Gender & Society 24: 149–66.

England, Paula. 2016. "Sometimes the Social Becomes Personal: Gender, Class, and Sexualities." American Sociological Review 81: 4–28.

England, Paula and Jonathan Bearak. 2014. "The Sexual Double Standard and Dender Differences in Attitudes toward Casual Sex among U.S. University Students." Demographic Research 30: 1327–38.

England, Paula, Andrew Levine, and Emma Mishel. 2020. "Progress Toward Gender Equality in the United States has Slowed or Stalled." Proceedings of the National Academy of Sciences 117: 6990–97.

England, Paula, Elizabeth McClintock, and Emily Shafer. 2011. "Birth Control Use and Early, Unintended Births: Evidence for a Class Gradient." Pp. 21–49 in Social Class and Changing Families in an Unequal America, ed. Marcia Carlson and Paula England. Stanford, CA: Stanford University Press.

England, Paula, Emily Shafer, and Alison Fogarty. 2008. "Hooking Up and Forming Romantic Relationships on Today's College Campuses." Pp. 531–47 in The Gendered Society Reader, ed. Michael Kimmel and Amy Aronson. New York: Oxford University Press.

Entman, Robert and Andrew Rojecki. 2001. The Black Image in the White Mind: Media and Race in America. Chicago, IL: University of Chicago Press.

Environmental Protection Agency. 2020. Guide for Industrial Waste Management: Protecting Land, Ground Water, Surface Water, Air. (epa.gov/sites/production/files/2016-03/documents/industrial-waste-guide.pdf)

Environmental Protection Agency. 2021. National Overview: Facts and Figures on Materials, Wastes and Recycling. (https://www.epa.gov/facts-and-figures-about-materials-waste-and-recycling/national-overview-facts-and-figures-materials#NationalPicture)

Epstein, Barbara. 2001. "What Happened to the Women's Movement?" Monthly Review 53: 1–13.

Equal Employment Opportunity Commission. 2021. "Sexual Harassment." U.S. Equal Employment Opportunity Commission. (https://www.eeoc.gov/laws/types/sexual_harassment.cfm)

Erikson, Emily. 2016. Between Monopoly and Free Trade: The English East India Company, 1600-1757. Princeton, NJ: Princeton University Press.

Erikson, Robert and John Goldthorpe. 1992. The Constant Flux: A Study of Class Mobility in Industrial Nations. Oxford, UK: Clarendon Press.

Ertman, Thomas. 1997. Birth of of the Leviathan. New York: Cambridge University Press.

Espenshade, Thomas, and Alexandria Walton Radford. 2009. No Longer Separate, Not Yet Equal: Race and Class in Elite College Admission and Campus Life. Princeton, NJ: Princeton University Press.

Estrich, Susan. 1987. Real Rape. Cambridge, MA: Harvard University Press.

European Commission. 2005. "Eurobarometer 225: Social Values, Science and Technology." (ec.europa.eu/commfrontoffice/publicopinion/archives/ebs/ebs_225_report_en.pdf)

European FluoroCarbons Technical Committee 2013. "EFCTC Position." February 6. (https://climalife.dehon.fr/uploads/assets/FAQ/FAQ%20webinar%20A2L/efctc-position-paper-on-tfa_2012_02_06%5B1%5D.pdf)

Eyal, Nir. 2014. Hooked: How to Build Habit-forming Products. New York: Penguin.

Evans, Geoffrey and Anand Menon. 2017. Brexit and British Politics. Cambridge, UK: Polity Press.

Evett, Ian, Peter Gill, John Scranage, and B. S. Weir. 1996. "Establishing the Robustness of Short-Tandem-Repeat Statistics for Forensic Applications." American Journal of Human Genetics 58: 398–407.

Fairchild, Kimberly and Laurie A Rudman. 2008. "Everyday Stranger Harassment and Women's Objectification." Social Justice Research 21: 338–57.

Fantasia, Rick and Kim Voss. 2004. Hard Work: Remaking the American Labor Movement. Berkeley: University of California Press.

Farley, Reynolds, Sheldon Danziger, and Harry Holzer. 2000. Detroit Divided. New York: Russell Sage.

Farmer, Paul. 2001. Infections and Inequalities: The Modern Plagues. Berkeley: University of California Press.

Farmworker Justice. 2019. "Selected Statistics on Farmworkers." Data Fact Sheet, May 13. (farmworkerjustice.org/wp-content/uploads/2019/05/NAWS-Data-FactSheet-05-13-2019-final.pdf)

Farrell, Justin. 2015. The Battle for Yellowstone: Morality and the Sacred Roots of Environmental Conflict. Princeton, NJ: Princeton University Press.

Fast Company 2011. "The Inside Story of Occupy Wall Street." October 7. (https://www.fastcompany.com/1785918/inside-story-occupy-wall-street)

Federal Bureau of Investigation. 2015. "Uniform Crime Reports, 1960–2012." United States Department of Justice.

Federal Bureau of Investigation. 2020. FBI Releases 2019 Statistics on Law Enforcement Officers Killed in the Line of Duty. Washington, DC: FBI National Press Office. (fbi.gov/news/pressrel/press-releases/fbi-releases-2019-statistics-on-law-enforcement-officers-killed-in-the-line-of-duty)

Federal Deposit Insurance Corporation. 2017. National Survey of Unbanked and Underbanked Households. FDIC. (fdic.gov/household-survey/)

Feller, Gordon. 2008. "Focus: NAFTA: A Controversial Treaty," Global Finance April 1. (gfmag.com/magazine/april-2008/focus-nafta-a-controversial-treaty)

Fernandez, Manny. 2006. "A Study Links Trucks' Exhaust to Bronx Schoolchildren's Asthma." New York Times October 29. (nytimes.com/2006/10/29/nyregion/29asthma.html)

Ferretti, Luca, Chris Wymant, Michelle Kendall, Lele Zhao, Anel Nurtay, Lucie Abeler-Dörner, Michelle Parker, David Bonsall, Christophe Fraser. 2020. "Quantifying SARS-CoV-2 Transmission Suggests Epidemic Control with Digital Contact Tracing." Science 368: 1–7.

Field, Robert. 2006. Health Care Regulation in America: Complexity, Confrontation, and Compromise. New York: Oxford University Press.

Finkel, Eli. 2017. The All-or-Nothing Marriage: How the Best Marriages Work. New York: Dutton.

Finkel, Eli. 2017. The All-or-Nothing Marriage. New York: Dutton.

Finkelstein, Amy, Sarah Taubman, Bill Wright, Mira Bernstein, Jonathan Gruber, Joseph Newhouse, Heidi Allen, and Katherine Baicker. 2011. "The Oregon Health Insurance Experiment: Evidence from the First Year." NBER Working Paper 17190. Cambridge, MA: National Bureau of Economic Research. (nber.org/papers/w17190.pdf)

Fischer, Claude. 1975. "Toward a Subcultural Theory of Urbanism." American Journal of Sociology 80: 1319–41.

Fisher, Bonnie S., Leah E. Daigle, and Francis T. Cullen. 2010. Unsafe in the Ivory Tower: The Sexual Victimization of College Women. Thousand Oaks, California: Sage Publications.

Flannery, Kent and Joy Marcus. 2012. The Creation of Inequality: How Our Prehistoric Ancestors Set the Stage for Monarchy, Slavery, and Empire. Cambridge, MA: Harvard University Press.

Fligstein, Neil. 2021. The Banks Did It: An Anatomy of the Financial Crisis. Cambridge, MA: Harvard University Press.

Florida, Richard. 2008. Who's Your City?: How the Creative Economy Is Making Where to Live the Most Important Decision of Your Life. New York: Basic Books.

Florida, Richard. 2012. The Rise of the Creative Class, Revisited. New York: Basic Books.

Florida, Richard. 2014. "The Dozen Regional Powerhouses Driving the U.S. Economy." Bloomberg City Lab March 12. (bloomberg.com/news/articles/2014-03-12/the-dozen-regional-powerhouses-driving-the-u-s-economy)

Florida, Richard, Tim Gulden, and Charlotta Mellander. 2008. "The Rise of the Mega-Region." Cambridge Journal of Regions, Economy, and Society 1: 459–76.

Ford, Jessie. 2018. "Going With the Flow": How College Men's Experiences of Unwanted Sex Are Produced by Gendered Interactional Pressures." Social Forces 96: 1303–24.

Ford, Jessie V. 2017. "Sexual Assault on College Hookups: The Role of Alcohol and Acquaintances." Sociological Forum 32: 581–405.

Fording, Richard and Sanford Schram. 2020. Hard White: The Mainstreaming of Racism in American Politics. New York: Oxford University Press.

Forman, James. 2017. Locking Up Our Own: Crime and Punishment in the Black Community. New York: Farrer, Strauss, Giroux.

Foster, John Bellamy, and Hannah Holleman. 2012. "Weber and the Environment: Classical Foundations for a Postexemptionalist Sociology." American Journal of Sociology 117: 1625–73.

Foucault, Michel. 1975 [1977]. Discipline and Punish: The Rise of the Prison. New York: Pantheon.

Fouquin, Michel, and Jules Hugot. May 2016. Two Centuries of Bilateral Trade and Gravity Data: 1827–2014 CEPII Working Paper, N°2016-14. (http://www.cepii.fr/CEPII/en/bdd_modele/presentation.asp?id=32)

Fox, Cybelle. 2012. Three Worlds of Relief: Race, Immigration, and the American Welfare State from the Progressive Era to the New Deal. Princeton, NJ: Princeton University Press.

Fraga, Bernard. 2018. The Turnout Gap: Race, Ethnicity, and Political Inequality in a Diversifying America. New York: Cambridge University Press.

Fraga, Juis, John Garcia, Rodney Hero, Michael Jones-Correa, Valerie Martinez-Ebers, and Gary Segura. 2011. Latinos in the New Millennium: An Almanac of Opinion, Behavior, and Policy Preferences. New York: Cambridge University Press.

Frank, Robert. 1999. Luxury Fever: Weighing the Cost of Excess. New York: The Free Press.

Frankenberg, Erica, Chungmei Lee, and Gary Orfield. 2003. A Multiracial Society with Segregated Schools: Are We Losing the Dream? Cambridge, MA: Harvard Civil Rights Project. (civilrightsproject.ucla.edu/research/k-12-education/integration-and-diversity/a-multiracial-society-with-segregated-schools-are-we-losing-the-dream/frankenberg-multiracial-society-losing-the-dream.pdf)

Frankenberg, Ruth. 1993. White Women, Race Matters: The Social Construction of Whiteness. Minneapolis: University of Minnesota Press.

Franklin, Stephen. 1993. "Unions Urge Clinton to Renegotiate Trade Pact." Chicago Tribune February 18. (chicagotribune.com/news/ct-xpm-1993-02-18-9303181485-story.html)

Fraser, Nancy. 1992. "Rethinking the Public Sphere: A Contribution to the Critique of Actually Existing Democracy." Pp. 109–42 in Habermas and the Public Sphere, ed. Craig Calhoun. Cambridge, MA, and London: MIT Press.

Freeland, Chrystia. 2012. Plutocrats: The Rise of the New Global Super-Rich and the Fall of Everyone Else. New York: Penguin.

Freiberg, Jerome. 1970. The Effects of Ability Grouping on Interactions in the Classroom. ERIC Document Reproduction Service. ED 053194.

Freidson, Eliot. 2001. Professionalism: The Third Logic. Chicago, IL: University of Chicago Press.

Freud, Sigmund. [1930] 1961. Civilization and Its' Discontents. Translated by John Strachey. New York: W.W. Norton.

Freudenburg, William. 2008. "Thirty Years of Scholarship and Science on Environment–Society Relationships. Organization and Environment 21: 449–59.

Freudenberg, William and Robert Gramling. 1989. "The Emergence of Environmental Sociology: Contributions of Riley E. Dunlap and William R. Catton, Jr." Sociological Inquiry 59: 439–52.

Friedan, Betty. [1963] 2001. The Feminine Mystique. New York: W.W Norton & Company.

Frieden, Jeffrey. 2007. Global Capitalism: Its Fall and Rise in the Twentieth Century. New York: Norton.

Friedman, Lauren. 2014. "This Chart Showing the Gap Between Black and White Life Expectancy Should Be A National Embarrassment." Business Insider January 9. (businessinsider.com/huge-racial-gap-in-life-expectancy–2014–1)

Friedman, Milton. 1962. Capitalism and Freedom. Chicago: University of Chicago Press.

Friedman, Thomas. 2005. The World Is Flat: A Brief History of the Twenty-first Century. New York: Farrar, Straus and Giroux.

Friedman, Lauren. "This $55,000 Bill is the Perfect Example of Our Broken Hospital System." The Shawnee News-Star December 30. (https://www.news-star.com/article/20131230/NEWS/312309964?template=ampart)

Friedson, Eliot. 2001. Professionalism, The Third Logic: On the Practice of Knowledge. Chicago: University of Chicago Press.

Frimer, Jeremy, Linda Skitka, and Matt Moytl. 2017. "Liberals and Conservatives are Similarly Motivated to Avoid Exposure to Each Other's Opinion." Journal of Experimental Social Psychology 72: 1–12.

Fry, Richard. 2013. "A Rising Share of Young Adults Living in Their Parents' Home." Social and Demographic Trends. Philadelphia: Pew Foundation. (pewsocialtrends.org/2013/08/01/a-rising-share-of-young-adults-live-in-their-parents-home/)

Fuller, Thomas and Tim Arango. 2020. "Police Pin Rise in Murders on Unusual Suspect: Covid." New York Times October 29. (nytimes.com/2020/10/29/us/coronavirus-murders.html)

Furstenberg, Frank. and Andrew Cherlin. 1991. Divided Families: What Happens to Children When Parents Part. Cambridge, MA: Harvard University Press.

Furstenberg, Frank, Sheela Kennedy, Vonnie Mcloyd, Ruben Rumbaut, and Richard Settersten, Jr. 2004. "Growing Up Is Harder to Do." Contexts 3: 33–41.

Fusaro, Vincent, Helen Levy, and H. Luke Shaefer. 2018. "Racial and Ethnic Disparities in the Lifetime Prevalence of Homelessness in the United States." Demography 55: 2119–2218.

Gaddis, S. Michael. 2015. "Discrimination in the Credential Society: An Audit Study of Race and College Selectivity in the Labor Market." Social Forces 93: 1451–79.

Gagnon, John and William Simon. 1973. Sexual Conduct: The Social Sources of Human Sexuality. Chicago: Aldine.

Galinsky, Ellen. 1999. Ask the Children: What America's Children Really Think about Working Parents. New York: William Morrow.

Galinksy, Ellen, Kerstin Aumann, and James Bond. 2009. Gender and Generation at Home and at Work. New York: Families and Work Institute.

Gallagher, Thomas, Michelle Mello, Wendy Levinson, Matthew Wynia, Ajit Sachdeva, Lois Snyder Sulmasy, Robert Truog, James Conway, Kathleen Mazor, Alan Lembitz, Sigall Bell, Lauge Sokol-Hessner, Jo Shapiro, Ann-Louise Puopolo, and Robert Arnold. 2013. "Talking with Patients about Other Clinicians' Errors." New England Journal of Medicine 369: 1752–57.

Gambetta, Diego and Heather Hamill. 2005. Streetwise: How Taxi Drivers Establish Their Customers Trustworthiness. New York: Russell Sage Foundation.

Gambetta, Diego and Steffen Hertog. 2009. "Why Are There So Many Engineers among Islamic Radicals?" European Journal of Sociology 50: 201–30.

Gamoran, Adam. 1986. "Instructional and Institutional Effects of Ability Grouping." Sociology of Education 59: 185–98.

Gamson, Joshua. 1995. "Must Identity Movements Self-Destruct? A Queer Dilemma." Social Problems 42: 390–407.

Gamson, William. 1990. The Strategy of Social Protest. 2nd ed. Homewood, IL: Dorsey.

Gans, Herbert. 1962. The Urban Villagers: Group and Class in the Life of Italian-Americans. New York: The Free Press.

Gans, Herbert. 1968. "Urbanism and Suburbanism as a Way of Life: A Reevaluation of Definitions." Pp. 170–95 in People and Plans: Essays on Urban Problems and Solutions. New York: Basic Books.

Gans, Herbert. 1999. "The Possibility of a New Racial Hierarchy in the 21st Century United States." Pp. 371–90 in The Cultural Territories of Race: Black and White Boundaries, ed. Michèle Lamont. Chicago: University of Chicago Press.

Gans, Herbert. 1999. Popular Culture and High Culture: An Analysis and Evaluation of Taste. New York: Basic Books.

Garfinkel, Harold. 1967. Studies in Ethnomethodology. Englewood Cliffs, NJ: Prentice-Hall.

Garfinkel, Irwin, Lee Rainwater, and Timothy Smeeding. 2010. Wealth and Welfare States: Is America Laggard or Leader? Oxford, UK: Oxford University Press.

Garland, David. 1991. Punishment and Modern Society: A Study in Social Theory. Chicago: University of Chicago Press.

Garland, David (ed.). 2001. Mass Imprisonment: Social Causes and Consequences. Newbury Park: Sage Publications.

Garreau, Joel. 1991. Edge City: Life on the New Frontier. New York: Anchor Doubleday Books.

Gashol, Raj. 2018. "Testing for Discrimination: Teaching Audit Studies in Quantitative Methods Courses." Teaching Sociology 46: 309–23.

Gaventa, John. 1980. Power and Powerlessness: Quiescence and Rebellion in an Appalachian Valley. Champaign, IL: University of Illinois Press.

Gawande, Atul. 2002. Complications: A Surgeon's Notes on an Imperfect Science. New York: Holt.

Gawande, Atul. 2007. Better: A Surgeon's Notes on Performance. New York: Holt.

Geertz, Clifford. 1972. "Deep Play: Notes on the Balinese Cockfight." Daedalus 101: 1–37.

Geertz, Clifford. 1973. The Interpretation of Cultures. New York: Basic Books.

Geotab. 2020. "10 Historic American Ghost Towns." Ghost Towns of America. (https://geotab.com/ghost-towns/)

Gershenson, Seth and Erdal Tekin. 2015. "The Effect of Community Traumatic Events on Student Achievement: Evidence from the Beltway Sniper Attacks." NBER Working Paper 21055. (nber.org/papers/w21055.pdf)

Gerson, Kathleen. 2011. The Unfinished Revolution: Coming of Age in a New Era of Gender, Work, and Family. New York: Oxford University Press.

Ghertner, Robin and Lincoln Groves. 2019. "The Opioid Crisis and Economic Opportunity: Geographic and Economic Trends." U.S. Department of Health and Human Services, ASPE Research Brief, September 11. (https://aspe.hhs.gov/sites/default/files/private/pdf/259261/ASPEEconomicOpportunityOpioidCrisis.pdf)

Giele, Janet. 1996. "Decline of the Family: Conservative, Liberal, and Feminist Views." Pp. 89–115 in Promises to Keep: Decline and Renewal of Marriage in America, eds. David Popenoe, Jean Bethke Elshtain, and David Blankenhorn. Lanham, MD: Rowman & Littlefield.

Gilbert, Jess. 2016. Planning Democracy: Agrarian Intellectuals and the Intended New Deal. New Haven: Yale University Press.

Gilens, Martin. 1999. Why Americans Hate Welfare. Chicago: University of Chicago Press.

Gilens, Martin. 2012. Affluence and Influence. Princeton, NJ: Princeton University Press.

Gilovich, Thomas, Robert Vallone, and Amos Tversky. 1985. "The Hot Hand in Basketball: On the Misperception of Random Sequences." Cognitive Psychology 17: 295–314.

Gindin, Sam and Leo Panitch. 2012. The Making of Global Capitalism. London: Verso.

Giroux, Henry. 2005. Schooling and the Struggle for Public Life. 2nd. ed. New York: Routledge.

Gitlin, Todd. 2007. Media Unlimited: How the Torrent of Images and Sounds Overwhelms Our Lives. New York: Metropolitan Books.

Glaeser, Edward. 2011. Triumph of the City: How Our Greatest Invention Makes Us Richer, Smarter, Greener, Healthier, and Happier. New York: Penguin Press.

Glendon, Mary Ann. 1982. "The Transformation of American Landlord-Tenant Law." Boston College Law Review 23: 503–76.

Glenn, Evelyn Nakano. 2002. Unequal Freedom: How Race and Gender Shaped American Citizenship and Labor. Cambridge, MA: Harvard University Press.

Gnaulati, Enrico. 2014. "Why Girls Tend to Get Better Grades than Boys." The Atlantic, September 18. (theatlantic.com/education/archive/2014/09/why-girls-get-better-grades-than-boys-do/380318/)

Goffman, Erving. 1959. The Presentation of Self in Everyday Life. Garden City, NY: Doubleday.

Goffman, Erving. 1961. Stigma: Notes on the Management of a Spoiled Identity. Cambridge, MA: Harvard University Press.

Goffman, Erving. 1963. Behavior in Public Places: Notes on the Social Organization of Gatherings. Glencoe, IL: The Free Press.

Goffman, Erving. 1971. Relations in Public. New York: Harper.

Goffman, Erving. 1978. "Response Cries." Language 54: 787–815.

Goffman, Alice. 2014. On the Run: Fugitive Life in an American City. Chicago: University of Chicago Press.

Goldfield, Michael. 1997. The Color of Politics: Race and the Mainsprings of American Politics. New York: The New Press.

Goldin, Claudia and Lawrence Katz. 2008. The Race between Education and Technology. Cambridge, MA: Harvard University Press.

Goldman School of Public Policy. 2020. "Plummeting Solar, Wind, and Battery Costs Can Accelerate Our Clean Electricity Future." 2035: The Report. (2035report.com/wp-content/uploads/2020/06/2035-Report.pdf?hsCtaTracking=8a85e9ea-4ed3-4ec0-b4c6-906934306ddb%7Cc68c2ac2-1db0-4d1c-82a1-65ef4daaf6c1)

Goldstene, Claire. 2015. "The Rise of the Underground Economy." Truthout. (truth-out.org/opinion/item/32115-the-rise-of-the-underground-economy)

Gonzales, Roberto. 2016. Lives in Limbo: Undocumented and Coming of Age in America. Berkeley: University of California Press.

Goode, William. 1963. World Revolution and Family Patterns. New York: Free Press.

Goode, William. 1982. The Family. Upper Saddle River, NJ: Pearson.

Goodwin, Jeff. 2001. No Other Way Out: States and Revolutionary Movements, 1945-1991. New York: Cambridge University Press.

Gordon, Colin. 2003. Dead on Arrival: The Politics of Health in Twentieth Century America. Princeton University Press, 2003.

Gordon, Robert. 2016. The Rise and Fall of American Growth. Princeton, NJ: Princeton University Press.

Gordon, Robert and Ian Dew-Becker. 2007. "Selected Issues in the Rise of Income Inequality." Brookings Papers on Economic Activity 2: 169–90.

Gornick, Janet and Marcia Meyers. 2003. Families That Work: Policies for Reconciling Parenthood and Employment. New York: Russell Sage Foundation.

Gornick, Janet and Timothy Smeeding. 2018. "Redistributional Policy in Rich Countries: Institutions and Impacts in Nonelderly Households." Annual Review of Sociology 44: 441–68.

Gorski, Philip. 2020. American Babylon: Christianity and Democracy Before and After Trump. New York: Routledge.

Gottman, Jean. 1966. Megalopolis: The Urbanized Northeastern Seaport of the United States. Cambridge, MA: MIT Press.

Gottschalk, Marie. 2005. The Prison and the Gallows: The Politics of Mass Incarceration in America. New York: Cambridge University Press.

Gottschalk, Peter and Sheldon Danziger. 2005. "Inequality of Wage Rates, Earnings and Family Income in the United States, 1975–2002." Review of Income and Wealth 51: 231–54.

Gould-Wartofsky, Michael. 2015. The Occupiers: The Making of the 99 Percent Movement. New York: Oxford University Press.

Gover, Angela, Shannon Harper and Lynn Langton. 2021. "Anti-Asian Hate Crime During the Covid-19 Pandemic: Exploring the Reproduction of Inequality." American Journal of Criminal Justice 45: 647–67.

Gowan, Peter and Mio Viktorsson. 2017. "Revisiting the Meidner Plan." Jacobin August 22. (jacobinmag.com/2017/08/sweden-social-democracy-meidner-plan-capital)

Graber, Doris. 2003. "The Media and Democracy: Beyond Myths and Stereotypes." Annual Review of Political Science 6: 139–60.

Gracey, Harry. 2012. "Learning the Student Role: Kindergarten as Academic Boot Camp." Unpublished paper. (people.uncw.edu/ricej/Intro/Kindergarten%20as%20Boot%20Camp%20by%20Harry%20Gracey.pdf)

Graeber, David. 2018. Bullshit Jobs: A Theory. New York: Penguin.

Graetz, Michael and Ian Shapiro. 2005. Death by a Thousand Cuts. New Haven, CT: Yale University Press.

Graham, Hugh Davis. 2002. "The Origins of Official Minority Designation." Pp. 288–99 in The New Race Question: How the Census Counts Multiracial Individuals, eds. Joel Perlmann and Mary Waters. New York: Russell Sage Foundation.

Gramlich, John. 2019. "The Gap Between the Number of Blacks and Whites in Prison is Shrinking." Pew Research Center FactTank April 30. (pewresearch.org/fact-tank/2019/04/30/shrinking-gap-between-number-of-blacks-and-whites-in-prison/)

Gramlich, John. 2020. "20 Striking Findings from 2020." FactTank December 11. (pewresearch.org/fact-tank/2020/12/11/20-striking-findings-from-2020/)

Granovetter, Mark. 1973. "The Strength of Weak Ties." American Journal of Sociology 78: 1360–80.

Granovetter, Mark. 1974. Getting a Job. Cambridge, MA: Harvard University Press.

Granovetter, Mark. 2017. Society and Economy. Cambridge, MA: Harvard University Press.

Great Barrington Declaration. 2020. "The Great Barrington Declaration." (gbdeclaration.org/)

Greeley, Andrew and Michael Hout. 2006. The Truth About Conservative Christians: What They Think and What They Believe. Chicago: The University of Chicago Press.

Greenberg, David. 1993. Crime and Capitalism: Readings in Marxist Criminology. Philadelphia: Temple University Press.

Greenberg, Julie, Arthur McKee, and Kate Walsh. 2015. "2014 Teacher Prep Review." Washington D.C.: National Council on Teacher Quality. (files.eric.ed.gov/fulltext/ED545343.pdf)

Greene, Jessica, Judith Hibbard, Rebecca Sacks, and Valerie Overton. 2013. "When Seeing the Same Physician, Highly Activated Patients Have Better Care Experiences Than Less Activated Patients." Health Affairs 32: 1295–1305.

Greenemeir, Larry. 2017. "20 Years after Deep Blue: How AI Has Advanced Since Conquering Chess." Scientific American June 2. (scientificamerican.com/article/20-years-after-deep-blue-how-ai-has-advanced-since-conquering-chess/)

Greenhouse, Steven. 2019. Beaten Down, Worked Up: The Past, Present and Future of American Labor. New York: Knopf.

Greenlee, Cynthia. 2019. "How History Textbooks Reflect America's Refusal to Reckon with Slavery." Vox August 26. (vox.com/identities/2019/8/26/20829771/slavery-textbooks-history)

Greenpeace. 2009. "Amazon Cattle Footprint." (greenpeace.org/usa/wp-content/uploads/legacy/Global/usa/report/2009/1/amazon-cattle-footprint-mato.pdf)

Greenwald, Anthony and Mahzarin Banaji. 1995. "Implicit Social Cognition: Attitudes, Self-Esteem, and Stereotypes." Psychological Review 102: 4–27.

Greenwood, Jeremy, Nezih Guner, Georgi Kocharkov, and Cezar Santos. 2014. "Marry Your Like: Assortative Mating and Income Inequality." NBER Working Papers 19829. Cambridge, MA: National Bureau of Economic Research. (nber.org/papers/w19829)

Greider, Thomas and Lorraine Garkovich. 1994. "Landscapes: The Social Construction of Nature and the Environment." Rural Sociology 59: 1–24.

Grogger, Jeffrey. 1998. "Market Wages and Youth Crime." Journal of Labor Economics 16: 756–91.

Groopman, Jerome. 2007. How Doctors Think. New York: Houghton Mifflin.

Gross, Neil and Solon Simmons. 2009. "The Religiosity of American College and University Professors." Sociology of Religion 70: 101–29.

Guglielmi, Giorgia. 2020. "The Next Generation Bots Interfering With the U.S. Election." Nature News QandA October 28. (https://nature.com/articles/d41586-020-03034–5)

Gullickson, Aaron and Ann Morning. 2011. "Choosing Race: Multiracial Ancestry and Identification." Social Science Research 40: 498–512.

Gusfield, Joseph. 1963. Symbolic Crusade: Status Politics and the American Temperance Movement. Urbana, IL: University of Illinois Press.

Güth, Werner, Rolf Schmittberger, and Bernd Schwarze. 1982. "An Experimental Analysis of Ultimatum Bargaining." Journal of Economic Behavior & Organization 3: 367–388.

Guttmacher Institute. 2011. "Contraceptive Use Is the Norm Among Religious Women." April 13. (guttmacher.org/media/nr/2011/04/13/index.html)

Habermas, Jürgen. [1962] 1989. The Structural Transformation of the Public Sphere: An Inquiry into a Category of Bourgeois Society. Translated by Thomas Burger with Frederick Lawrence. Cambridge, MA: MIT Press.

Hacker, Jacob. 2006. The Great Risk Shift: The New Economic Insecurity and the Decline of the American Dream. New York: Oxford University Press.

Hacker, Jacob and Paul Pierson. 2010. Winner-Take-All Politics. New York: Simon and Shuster.

Hagan, John. 1994. Crime and Disrepute. Newbury Park: Sage.

Hagan, John. 2010. Who Are the Criminals? The Politics of Crime Policy from the Age of Roosevelt to the Age of Reagan. Princeton, NJ: Princeton University Press.

Hagan, John and Holly Foster. 2009. "The Mass Incarceration of American Parents: Issues of Race/Ethnicity, Collateral Consequences, and Prisoner Re-Entry." Annals of the American Academy of Political and Social Science 623: 195–213.

Hall, Bruce. 2011. A History of Race in Muslim West Africa, 1600–1960. Cambridge, UK: Cambridge University Press.

Hall, Peter and David Soskice, eds. 2000. Varieties of Capitalism. New York: Cambridge University Press.

Hall, Stuart and Tony Jefferson, eds. 1975. Resistance through Rituals: Youth Subcultures in Post-War Britain. New York and London: Routledge.

Haller, John. 1981. American Medicine in Transition, 1840–1910. Urbana, IL: University of Illinois Press.

Hallinan, Maureen. 1987. "Ability Grouping and Student Learning." Pp. 41–69 in The Social Organization of Schools: New Conceptualizations of the Learning Process, ed. Maureen Hallinan. New York: Plenum.

Hamilton, Brady, Joyce Martin, Michelle Osterman, Sally Curtin, and T.J. Mathews. 2015. "National Vital Statistics Reports: Births: Final Data for 2014." Center for Disease Control and Prevention 64. (cdc.gov/nchs/data/nvsr/nvsr64/nvsr64_12.pdf)

Haney, Craig. 2003. "Health Issues in Long-Term Solitary and 'Supermax' Confinement." Crime & Delinquency 49: 124–56.

Hannan, Michael and John Freeman. 1989. Organizational Ecology. Cambridge, MA: Harvard University Press.

Hanson, Andrew and Artem Gulish. 2016. "From College to Career: Making Sense of the Post-Millennial Job Market." The Georgetown Public Policy Review 21. (cew.georgetown.edu/wp-content/uploads/The-Post-Millennial-Job-Market.pdf)

Hanushek, Eric, Marc Piopiunik, and Simon Wiederhold. 2019. "The Value of Smarter Teachers: International Evidence on Teacher Cognitive Skills and Student Performance." Journal of Human Resources 54: 857–99.

Hanushek, Eric and Ludger Woessmann. 2020. "The Economic Impacts of Learning Losses." OECD. September. (https://www.oecd.org/education/The-economic-impacts-of-coronavirus-covid-19-learning-losses.pdf)

Harcourt, Bernard. 2006. Against Prediction: Profiling, Policing, and Punishing in an Actuarial Age. Chicago, IL: University of Chicago Press.

Hardin, Garrett. 1968. "The Tragedy of the Commons." Science 162: 1243–48.

Harding, David, and Jeffrey Morenoff. 2016. "Incarceration, Prisoner Reentry, and Communities." Annual Review of Sociology 40: 411–29.

Hart, Alexandra and Kristen Cabrera. 2020. "Why Some Experts Call Solitary Confinement 'Torture.'" Texas Standard. January 23. (texas-standard.org/stories/why-some-experts-call-solitary-confinement-torture/)

Harvey, Lisa. 1999. "Short-Term and Long-Term Effects of Early Parental Employment on Children of the National Longitudinal Survey of Youth." Developmental Psychology 35: 445–59.

Hatton, Erin. 2011. The Temp Economy: From Kelly Girls to Permatemps in Postwar America. Philadelphia: Temple University Press.

Hauck, Grace. 2019. "Anti-LGBT hate crimes are rising, the FBI says. But it gets worse" USA Today June 28. (usatoday.com/story/news/2019/06/28/anti-gay-hate-crimes-rise-fbi-says-and-they-likely-undercount/1582614001/)

Hawthorne, Nathaniel. [1850] 2015. The Scarlet Letter. New York: Penguin Classics.

Hayek, Friedrich. 1944. The Road to Serfdom. Chicago: University of Chicago Press.

Hays, Sharon. 1996. The Cultural Contradictions of Motherhood. New Haven, CT: Yale University Press.

Heckman, James. 2017. Giving Kids a Fair Chance. Cambridge: MIT Press.

Heckman, James and Tim Kautz. 2012. "Hard Evidence on Soft Skills." NBER Working Paper No. w18121. (https://papers.ssrn.com/sol3/papers.cfm?abstract_id=2073161)

Hedstrom, Peter and Lars Udehn. 2009. "Analytical Sociology and Theories of the Middle Range." Pp. 25–47 in The Oxford Handbook of Analytical Sociology, eds. Peter Hedstrom and Peter Bearman. New York: Oxford University Press.

Heerwig, Jennifer. 2018. "Money in the Middle: Contribution Strategies among Affluent Donors to Federal Elections, 1980–2008." American Journal of Sociology 123: 1004–63.

Heider, Fritz. 1958. The Psychology of Interpersonal Relations. John Wiley, New York.

Heller, Sara. 2014. "Summer Jobs Reduce Violence Among Disadvantaged Youth." Science 346: 1219–23.

Heltzel, Gordon and Kristin Laurin. 2020. "Polarization in America: Two Possible Futures." Current Opinion in the Behavioral Sciences 34: 179–84.

Hemenway, David and Matthew Miller. 2000. "Firearm Availability and Homicide Rates across 26 High-Income Countries." Journal of Trauma and Acute Care Surgery 49: 985–88.

Henninges, Miriam, Claudia Traini, and Corinna Kleinert. 2019. "Tracking and Sorting in the German Educational System." LIfBi Working Paper 83. Bamberg, Germany: University of Bamberg. (neps-data.de/Portals/0/Working%20Papers/WP_LXXXIII.pdf)

Henrich, Joseph, Robert Boyd, Samuel Bowles, Colin Camerer, Ernest Fehr, and Herbert Gintis. 2004. Foundations of Human Sociality: Economic Experiments and Ethnographic Evidence from Fifteen Small-Scale Societies. Oxford University Press.

Henriques, Gisele and Raj Patel. 2004. "NAFTA, Corn, and Mexico's Agricultural Trade Liberalization." Americas Program Special Report. (is.cuni.cz/studium/predmety/index.php?do=download&did=113952&kod=JMM591#:~:text=During%20the%20first%20year%20of,million%20metric%20tons%20of%20corn.&text=Yet%20all%20corn%20imports%20into,phased%20out%20in%2030%20months)

Hernnstein, Richard and Edward Wilson. 1985. Crime and Human Nature. New York: The Free Press.

Hersh, Seymour. 2005. Chain of Command: The Road from 9/11 to Abu Ghraib. New York: Harper.

Hertz, Rosanna. 2006. Single by Chance, Mothers by Choice: How Women Are Choosing Parenthood without Marriage and Creating the New American Family. New York: Oxford University Press.

Hess, Alexander. 2013. "On Holiday: Countries with the Most Vacation Days." USA Today June 8. (usatoday.com/story/money/business/2013/06/08/countries-most-vacation-days/2400193/)

Hetherington, E. Mavis and John Kelly. 2002. For Better or For Worse: Divorce Reconsidered. New York: W.W. Norton.

Hider, Alex. 2020. "Fauci Says He Wears a Mask as a Sign of Respect, Adds It's 'the Kind of Thing You Should Be Doing.'" The Denver Channel.Com May 27. (thedenverchannel.com/news/national/coronavirus/fauci-says-he-wears-a-mask-as-a-sign-of-respect-adds-its-the-kind-of-thing-you-should-be-doing)

Higher Education Strategy Associates. 2010. Global Higher Education Rankings 2010: Affordability and Accessibility in Comparative Perspective. (higheredstrategy.com/wp-content/uploads/2011/09/GHER2010_FINAL.pdf)

Highton, Benjamin. 2015. "Voting: Turnout." Pp. 16330–33 in International Encyclopedia of the Social and Behavioral Sciences, vol. 24, ed. Neil Smelser and Paul B. Baltes. London: Pergamon.

Highton, Benjamin. 2017. "Voter Identification Laws and Turnout in the United States." Annual Review of Political Science 20: 149–67.

Hill Collins, Patricia. 1991. Black Feminist Thought: Knowledge, Consciousness, and the Politics of Empowerment. London and New York: Routledge.

Hipple, Steven and Laurel Hammond. 2016. Self-Employment In The United States. U.S. Bureau of Labor Statistics. (bls.gov/spotlight/2016/self-employment-in-the-united-states/pdf/self-employment-in-the-united-states.pdf)

Hirsch, Arnold. 1983. Making the Second Ghetto: Race and Housing in Chicago, 1940–1960. New York: Cambridge University Press.

Hirsch, James. 2014. Riot and Remembrance: America's Worst Race Riots and its Legacy. New York: Houghton Mifflin.

Hirsch, Jennifer and Shamus Khan. 2020. Sexual Citizens: A Landmark Study of Sex, Power, and Assault on Campus. New York: Norton.

Hitchens, Christopher. 1999. No One Left to Lie To. New York: Verso.

Hochschild, Arlie. 1989. The Second Shift. New York: Penguin.

Hochschild, Arlie. 1997. The Time Bind: When Work Becomes Home and Home Becomes Work. New York: Henry Holt.

Hochschild, Arlie. 2012. The Outsourced Self: Intimate Life in Market Times. New York: Metropolitan Books.

Hochschild, Arlie. 2016. Strangers in Their Own Land: Anger and Mourning on the American Right. New York: The New Press.

Hodge, Robert. 1981. "The Measurement of Occupational Status." Social Science Research 10: 396–415.

Hodgson, Paul. 2015. "Top CEOs Make More Than 300 Times the Average Worker." Fortune June 22. (fortune.com/2015/06/22/ceo-vs-worker-pay/)

Hofmeester, Karin, and Marcel van der Linden. 2017. Handbook Global History of Work. Berlin, Germany: Walter de Gruyter.

Holliday, Amy and Rachel Dwyer. 2009. "Suburban Neighborhood Poverty in U.S. Metropolitan Areas in 2000." City & Community 8: 155–76.

Hollingsworth, John, Xianshi Yu, Phyllis Yan, Hyesun Yoo, Dana Telem, Ekow Yankah, Ji Zhu, Akbar Waljee, and Brahmajee K. Nallamothu. 2021. "Provider Care Team Segregation and Operative Mortality Following Coronary Artery Bypass Grafting." Circulation: Cardiovascular Quality and Control 14: 613–21.

Holmes, Dawn. 2017. Big Data: A Very Short Introduction. New York: Oxford University Press.

Holt, Douglas. 1997. "Distinction in America? Recovering Bourdieu's Theory of Tastes from Its Critics." Poetics 25: 93–120.

Holtzman, Linda. 2000. Media Messages: What Film, Television, and Popular Music Teach Us about Race, Class, Gender and Sexual Orientation. New York: M.E. Sharpe.

Holzer, Harry. 1991. "The Spatial Mismatch Hypothesis: What Has the Evidence Shown?" Urban Studies 28: 105–22.

Hopkins, Jared and Andrew Scurria. 2019. "Sacklers Received as Much as $13 Billion in Profits From Purdue Pharma." Wall Street Journal October 4. (wsj.com/articles/sacklers-received-12-billion-to-13-billion-in-profits-from-oxycontin-maker-purdue-pharma–11570221797)

Horkheimer, Max and Theodor Adorno. [1947] 2002. Dialectic of Enlightenment: Philosophical Fragments. Translated by Edmund Jephcott and ed. Gunzelin Schmid Noerr. Stanford, CT: Stanford University Press.

Horowitz, Ruth. 2013. In the Public Interest, Medical Licensing and the Disciplinary Process. New Brunswick, NJ: Rutgers University Press.

Hout, Michael. 2012. "Social and Economic Returns to Higher Education in the United States." Annual Review of Sociology 38: 379–400.

Hout, Michael. 2015. "A Summary of What We Know about Social Mobility." The ANNALS of the American Academy of Political and Social Science 657: 27–36.

Hout, Michael, Claude Fischer, and Mark Chaves. 2013. More Americans Have No Religion Preference: Key Findings from the 2012 General Social Survey. Unpublished Paper, Institute for the Study of Societal Issues, University of California-Berkeley. (deism.com/NONES_UCBerkely_study_2013.pdf)

Huang, Philip. 2009. "China's Neglected Informal Economy: Reality and Theory." Modern China 35: 405–38.

Hufbauer, Gary Clyde and Jeffrey Schott. 1993. NAFTA: An Assessment. Washington, DC: Institute for International Economics.

Huijsmans, Inge, Ili Ma, Leticia Micheli, Claudia Civai, Mirre Stallen, and Alan Sanfey. 2019. "A Scarcity Mindset Alters Neural Processing Underlying Consumer Decision Making." Proceedings of the National Academy of Sciences 116: 11699–11704.

Huling, Tracey. 2002. "Building a Prison Economy in Rural America." In Invisible Punishment: The Collateral Consequences of Mass Imprisonment, ed. Marc Mauer and Meda Chesney-Lind. New York: The New Press.

Humes, Karen, Nicholas Jones, and Roberto Ramirez. 2011. "Overview of Race and Hispanic Origin: 2010." Census 2010 Brief, C2010BR-02. Washington, DC: U.S. Census Bureau. (census.gov/content/dam/Census/library/publications/2011/dec/c2010br-02.pdf)

Hunter, James Davison. 1991. Culture Wars: The Struggle to Define America. New York: Basic Books.

Hurd, John. 1975. "Railways and the Expansion of Markets in India." Explorations in Economic History 12: 263–68.

Hurt, Hallam, Elsa Malmud, Nancy Brodsky, and Joan Giannetta. 2001. "Exposure to Violence: Psychological and Academic Correlates in Child Witnesses." Archives of Pediatrics and Adolescent Medicine 155: 1351–56.

Hyde, Janet, Sara Lindberg, Marcia Linn, Amy Ellis, and Caroline Williams. 2008. "Gender Similarities Characterize Math Performance." Science 321: 494–95.

Hyde, Janet Shibley. 1984. "How Large Are Gender Differences in Aggression? A Developmental Meta-Analysis." Developmental Psychology 20: 722–36.

Hyde, Janet Shibley. 2005. "The Gender Similarities Hypothesis." American Psychologist 60: 581–92.

Ignatiev, Noel. 1995. How the Irish Became White. New York: Routledge.

Ingersoll, Richard, Lisa Merrill, and Daniel Stuckey. 2014. "Seven Trends: The Transformation of the Teaching Force." Philadelphia: Consortium for Policy Research in Education, University of Pennsylvania. (files. eric.ed.gov/fulltext/ED566879.pdf)

Inglehart, Ronald. 1990. Culture Shift in Advanced Industrial Society. Princeton: Princeton University Press.

Institute for Taxation and Economic Policy. 2019. Corporate Tax Avoidance in the First Year of the Trump Tax Law. ITEP Report, December. (itep.sfo2.digitaloceanspaces.com/121619-ITEP-Corporate-Tax-Avoidance-in-the-First-Year-of-the-Trump-Tax-Law.pdf)

Institute of Medicine. 1999. To Err is Human. Washington, DC: National Academy of Sciences.

Institute of Medicine. 2002. Unequal Treatment: Confronting Racial and Ethnic Disparities in Health Care. Washington, DC: National Academies Press.

Internal Revenue Service, Statistics of Income Bulletin. 2021. Historical Table 24. (https://irs.gov/uac/soi-tax-stats-historical-table–24)

International Federation of Health Plans. 2012. Comparative Price Report: Variation In Medical and Hospital Prices by Country. (hushp.harvard. edu/sites/default/files/downloadable_files/IFHP%202012%20Comparative%20Price%20Report.pdf)

International Labour Organization. 2015. World Employment Social Outlook: The Changing Nature of Jobs. Geneva, Switzerland: ILO. (ilo. org/wcmsp5/groups/public/---dgreports/---dcomm/---publ/documents/publication/wcms_368626.pdf)

Isaacson, Walter. 2011. Steve Jobs. New York: Simon and Shuster.

Iyengar, Shanto, Gaurav Sood, and Yphtach Lelkes. 2012. "Affect, Not Ideology: A Social Identity Perspective on Polarization." Public Opinion Quarterly 76: 405–31.

Jackson Nakazawa, Donna. 2003. "A New Generation Is Leading the Way: What Young People of Mixed Race Can Tell Us about the Future of Our Children." Parade July 6. (donnajacksonnakazawa.com/wp-content/uploads/2012/09/parade.pdf)

Jacobs, James. 2014. The Criminal Record. Cambridge, MA: Harvard University Press.

Jacobs, Jane. 1961. The Death and Life of Great American Cities. New York: Random House.

Jacobs, Jerry and Kathleen Gerson. 2004. The Time Divide: Work, Family, and Gender Inequality. Cambridge, MA: Harvard University Press.

Jacobson, Matthew Frye. 1998. Whiteness of a Different Color: European Immigrants and the Alchemy of Race. Cambridge, MA: Harvard University Press.

Jacques, Peter, Riley Dunlap and Mark Freeman. 2008. "The Organization of Denial: Conservative Think Tanks and Environmental Skepticism." Environmental Politics 17: 349–85.

James, Doris and Lauren Glaze. 2006. Mental Health Problems of Prison and Jail Inmates. Washington DC: Bureau of Justice Statistics Special Report. (bjs.gov/content/pub/pdf/mhppji.pdf)

James, Stanlie and Claire Robertson (eds.). 2002. Genital Cutting and Transnational Sisterhood. Urbana, IL: University of Illinois Press.

Janoski, Thomas, David Luke, and Christopher Oliver. 2014. The Causes of Structural Unemployment. Cambridge: Polity Press.

Jargowsky, Paul. 1997. Poverty and Place: Ghettos, Barrios and the American City. New York: Russell Sage.

Jarsulic, Mark, Andy Green, and Daniella Zessoules. 2019. "Trump's Trade Deal: The Road Not Taken." Center for American Progress February 1. (www.americanprogress.org/issues/economy/reports/2019/02/01/465744/trumps-trade-deal-road-not-taken/)

Jasper, James. 1997. The Art of Moral Protest: Culture, Biography, and Creativity in Social Movements. Chicago: University of Chicago Press.

Jasso, Guillermina. 2011. "Migration and Stratification." Social Science Research 40: 1292–336.

Jasso, Guillermina, Douglas Massey, Mark Rosenzweig, and James Smith. 2000. "The New Immigrant Survey Pilot (NIS-P): Overview and New Findings about U.S. Legal Immigrants at Admission." Demography 37: 127–38.

Jasso, Guillermina, Douglas Massey, Mark Rosenzweig, and James Smith. 2008. "From Illegal to Legal: Estimating Previous Illegal Experience among New Legal Immigrants to the United States." International Migration Review 42: 803–43.

Jasso, Guillermina and Mark Rosenzweig. 2006. "Characteristics of Immigrants to the United States: 1820–2003." Pp. 328–58 in A Companion to American Immigration, ed. Reed Ueda. Malden, MA: Blackwell Publishing.

Jasso, Guillermina. 2011. "Migration and Stratification." Social Science Research 40: 1292–336.

Jencks, Christopher. 1995. The Homeless. Cambridge, MA: Harvard University Press.

Jenkins, Henry. 2006. Convergence Culture: Where Old and New Media Collide. New York: NYU Press.

Jerolmack, Colin. 2021. Up to Heaven and Down to Hell: Fracking, Freedom, and Community in an American Town. Princeton, NJ: Princeton University Press.

Jerolmack, Colin and Shamus Khan. 2014. "Talk is Cheap: Ethnography and the Attitudinal Fallacy." Sociological Methods and Research 43: 178–209.

Joas, Hans and Wolfgang Knobl. 2009. Social Theory: Twenty Introductory Lectures. New York: Cambridge University Press.

John William Pope Center for Higher Education Policy, 2011

Johnson, Julia, Robert Kominski, Kristin Smith, and Paul Tillman. 2005. Change in the Lives of U.S. Children, 1990–2000. Washington D.C.: U.S. Census Bureau.

Johnson, Rucker. 2019. Children of the Dream: Why School Integration Works. New York: Basic Books.

Jones, Jeffrey. 2016. "A Record High 77% of Americans Perceive Nation as Divided." Gallup November 21. (gallup.com/poll/197828/record-high-americans-perceive-nation-divided.aspx)

Jorgensen, Helene and Lonnie Golden. 2002. "Time after Time: Mandatory Overtime in the U.S. Economy." Economic Policy Institute Briefing Papers 120, January 1. (epi.org/publication/briefingpapers_bp120/)

Joseph, Peniel. 2020. "From the Black Panthers to Black Lives Matter, the Ongoing Fight to End Police Violence Against Black Americans." Washington Post May 29. (washingtonpost.com/nation/2020/05/29/black-panthers-black-lives-matter-ongoing-fight-end-police-violence-against-black-americans/)

Joyner, Kara, and Edward Laumann. 2001. "Teenage Sex and the Sexual Revolution." Pp. 41–71 in Sex, Love, Health in America: Private Choices and Public Policies, eds. Edward Laumann and Robert Michael. Chicago: University of Chicago.

Juhn, Chinhui and Kevin Murphy. 1997. "Wage Inequality and Family Labor Supply." Journal of Labor Economics 15: 72–79.

Kabaservice, Geoffrey. 2012. Rule and Ruin: The Downfall of Moderation and the Destruction of the Republican Party, From Eisenhower to the Tea Party. New York: Oxford University Press.

Kaden, Jonathan. 1998. "Therapy for Convicted Sex Offenders: Pursuing Rehabilitation Without Incrimination." Journal of Criminal Law and Criminology 89: 347–91.

Kaeble, Danielle, Lauren Glaze, Anastasios Tsoutis, and Todd Minton. 2016. "Correctional Populations in the United States, 2014." U.S. Department of Justice, January 21. (bjs.gov/content/pub/pdf/cpus14.pdf)

Kahlenberg, Richard and Julie Park. 2015. "Class-Based Affirmative Action." New Labor Forum January. (https://newlaborforum.cuny.edu/2015/01/17/class-based-affirmative-action/)

Kahn, Shamus. 2009. Privilege: The Making of an Adolescent Elite at St. Paul's School. Princeton: Princeton University Press.

Kahn, Shamus. 2012. Privilege. Princeton, NJ: Princeton University Press.

Kahneman, Daniel. 2011. Thinking Slow and Fast. New York: Farrar, Straus, and Giroux.

Kaiser Family Foundation

Kalleberg, Arne. 2011. Good Jobs, Bad Jobs: The Rise of Polarized and Precarious Employment Systems in the United States. New York: Russell Sage Foundation Press.

Kalleberg, Arne, Barbara Reskin, and Ken Hudson. 2000. "Bad Jobs in America: Standard and Nonstandard Employment Relations and Job Quality in the United States." American Sociological Review 65: 256–78.

Kalmijn, Matthijs. 1991. "Shifting Boundaries: Trends in Educaitonal and Religious Homogamy." American Sociological Review 56: 786–800.

Kantor, Rosabeth. 1977. Men and Women of the Corporation. New York: Basic Books.

Kao, Grace, Mara Joyner, and Kelly Balistreri. 2019. The Company We Keep: Interracial Friendships and Romantic Relationships from Adolescence to Adulthood. New York: Russell Sage Foundation Press.

Karabel, Jerome. 2005. The Chosen: The Hidden History of Admission and Exclusion at Harvard, Yale, and Princeton. New York: Houghton Mifflin.

Karabel, Jerome. 2017. "Police Killings Surpass the Worst Years of Lynching, Capital Punishment, and a Movement Responds." Huffington Post December 6. (huffpost.com/entry/police-killings-lynchings-capital-punishment_b_8462778)

Katz, Jack. 1999. How Emotions Work. Chicago: University of Chicago Press.

Katz, Josh, Abby Goodnough and Margot Sanger-Katz. 2020. "In Shadow of Pandemic, U.S. Drug Overdose Deaths Resurge to Record." New York Times July 15. (nytimes.com/interactive/2020/07/15/upshot/drug-overdose-deaths.html)

Katz, Lawrence, and Kevin Murphy. 1992. "Changes in Relative Wages, 1963-1987: Supply and Demand Factors." The Quarterly Journal of Economics 107: 35–78.

Kaufman, Eric. 2019. Whiteshift: Populism, Immigration, and the Future of White Majorities. New York: Abrams Books.

Kearl, Holly. 2014. Unsafe and harassed in Public Spaces: A National Street Harassment Report. Stop Street Harassment. (http://www.stopstreetharassment.org/wp-content/uploads/2012/08/2014-National-SSH-StreetHarassment-Report.pdf)

Kefalas, Maria, Frank Furstenberg, Patrick Carr, and Laura Napolitano. 2011. "'Marriage Is More Than Being Together': The Meaning of Marriage for Young Adults." Journal of Family Issues 32: 845–75.

Keister, Lisa. 2006. "Wealth Distribution" in The Encyclopedia of Economic Sociology, ed. Jens Beckert and Milan Zafirovski. New York: Routledge.

Keller, Bill. 2013. "An Industry of Mediocrity." New York Times October 20. (nytimes.com/2013/10/21/opinion/keller-an-industry-of-mediocrity.html)

Kendi, Ibram X. 2019. How To Be an Antiracist. New York: Random House/One World.

Kenworthy, Lane. 2009. Jobs With Equality. New York: Oxford University Press.

Kenworthy, Lane. 2020. Social Democratic Capitalism. New York: Oxford University Press.

Keyssar, Alexander. 2000. The Right to Vote. New York: Basic Books.

Khan, Shamus. 2010. "Getting In: Private Schools Play the College Admissions Game." Pp. 97–112 in Educating Elites, eds. Rubén A. Gaztambide-Fernández and Adam Howard, New York: Rowman and Littlefield.

Khlevniuk, Oleg. 2008. Master of the House: Stalin and His Inner Circle. New Haven, CT: Yale University Press.

Killewald, Alexandra. 2016. "Money, Work, and Marital Stability: Assessing Change in the Gendered Determinants of Divorce." American Sociological Review 81: 696–719.

Kim, ChangHwan and Arthur Sakamoto. 2010. "Have Asian American Men Achieved Labor Market Parity with White Men?" American Sociological Review. 75: 934–57.

Kim, Nadia. 2008. Imperial Citizens: Koreans and Race from Seoul to LA. Stanford, CA: Stanford University Press.

Kimmel, Michael. 2008. Guyland: The Perilous World Where Boys Become Men. New York: HarperCollins Publishers.

Kinder, Donald and Lynn Sanders. 1996. Divided by Color. Chicago: University of Chicago Press.

Kindy, Kimberly and Kimbriell Kelly. 2015. "Thousands Dead, Few Prosecuted." Washington Post April 11. (washingtonpost.com/sf/investigative/2015/04/11/thousands-dead-few-prosecuted/)

Kinsey, Alfred, Wardell Pomeroy, and Clyde Martin. [1948] 1998. Sexual Behavior in the Human Male. Bloomington: Indiana U. Press.

Kinsey, Alfred, Wardell Pomeroy, Clyde Martin, and Paul Gebhard. [1953] 1998. Sexual Behavior in the Human Female. Bloomington: Indiana University Press.

Kirch, Darrell. 2011. "Higher Education and Health Care at a Crossroads." Association of Governing Boards of Universities and Colleges (AGB) Report. (agb.org/trusteeship-article/higher-education-and-health-care-at-a-crossroads/)

Klas, Mary Ellen. 2021. "Legislators Seek to Punish Social Media Giants for 'Selective Censorship' of Trump." Miami Herald January 12. (miamiherald.com/news/politics-government/state-politics/article248452195.html)

Klein, Ezra. 2013. "21 Graphs That Show That America's Health-care Prices Are Ludicrous." Washington Post March 26. (washingtonpost.com/news/wonk/wp/2013/03/26/21-graphs-that-show-americas-health-care-prices-are-ludicrous/?utm_term=.db024c618d24)

Klinenberg, Eric. 1999. "Denaturalizing Disaster: A Social Autopsy of the 1995 Chicago Heat Wave." Theory and Society 28: 239–95.

Klinenberg, Eric. 2002. Heat Wave: A Social Autopsy of Disaster in Chicago. Chicago: University of Chicago Press.

Klinenberg, Eric. 2007. Fighting for Air: The Battle to Control America's Media. New York: Metropolitan Books.

Klinenberg, Eric. 2012. Going Solo: The Extraordinary Rise and Surprising Appeal of Living Alone. New York: Penguin Press.

Klinenberg, Eric, Malcolm Araos, and Liz Koslov. 2020. "Sociology and the Climate Crisis." Annual Review of Sociology 46: 649–69.

Klinkner, Philip and Rogers Smith. 1997. The Unsteady March: The Rise and Decline of Racial Inequality in America. Chicago, IL: University of Chicago Press.

Klinkner, Philip and Rogers Smith. 1999. Rise and Decline: The Unsteady March of Racial Equality in America. Chicago: University of Chicago Press.

Klofstad, Casey, Rose McDermott and Peter Hatemi. 2013. "The Dating Preferences of Liberals and Conservatives." Political Behavior 35: 519–38.

Kneebone, Elizabeth. 2017. "The Changing Geography of Poverty." Brookings Reports February 15. (brookings.edu/testimonies/the-changing-geography-of-us-poverty/)

Kocieniewski, David. 2011. "G.E.'s Strategies Let It Avoid Paying Taxes Altogether." New York Times March 24. (nytimes.com/2011/03/25/business/economy/25tax.html)

Kohler, Hans-Peter, Francesco Billari, and Antonio Ortega. 2002. "The Emergence of Lowest-Low Fertility in Europe." Population and Development Review 28: 641–80.

Kohler-Hausmann, Issa. 2014. "Managerial Justice and Mass Misdemeanors." Stanford Law Review 66: 611–93.

Kohler-Hausmann, Issa. 2018. Misdemeanour Justice. Princeton, NJ: Princeton University Press.

Kolbert, Elizabeth. 2007. Field Notes from a Catastrophe: Man, Nature, and Climate Change. New York: Bloomsbury, USA.

Koopman, Robert, Zhi Wang and Shang-Jin Wei. 2008. "How much of Chinese Exports is Really Made in China?" VoxEU August 8. (voxeu.org/index.php?q=node/1524)

Kornai, Janos. 1992. The Socialist System: The Political Economy of Communism. Princeton: Princeton University Press.

Kranish, Michael and Mark Fisher. 2017. Trump Revealed: The Definitive Biography of the 45th President. New York: Scribner.

Kreager, Derek and Jeremy Staff. 2009. "The Sexual Double Standard and Adolescent Peer Acceptance." Social Psychology Quarterly 72: 143–64.

Krieger, Nancy. 1987. "Shades of Difference: Theoretical Underpinnings of the Medical Controversy on Black/White Differences in the United States, 1830–1870." International Journal of Health Services 17: 259–78.

Kristal, Tali, and Yinon Cohen. 2016. "The Causes of Rising Wage Inequality: The Race between Institutions and Technology." Socio-Economic Review 15: 187–212.

Kritz, Mary and Douglas Gurak. 2004. Immigration and a Changing America. New York: Russell Sage Foundation.

Krogstad, Jen, Mark Lopez, and Jeffrey Passel. 2020. "A Majority of Americans Say Immigrants Mostly Fill Jobs U.S. Citizens Do Not Want." Pew Research Center FactTank June 10. (pewresearch.org/fact-tank/2020/06/10/a-majority-of-americans-say-immigrants-mostly-fill-jobs-u-s-citizens-do-not-want/)

Krueger, Alan, Judd Cramer, and David Cho. 2014. "Are the Long-Term Unemployed on the Margins of the Labor Market?" Brookings Papers on Economic Activity 1: 229–99. Brookings Institution Press.

Kubota, Koki. 2019. "Top Bosses in Japan Draw Record Pay, But Gap with U.S. Widens." Nikkei Asia August 2. (asia.nikkei.com/Business/Business-trends/Top-bosses-in-Japan-draw-record-pay-but-gap-with-US-widens)

Kurtz, Karl. 2015. "Who We Elect." State Legislatures. December. (ncsl.org/Portals/1/Documents/magazine/articles/2015/SL_1215-Kurtz.pdf)

Kurzman, Charles. 1996. "Structural Opportunity and Perceived Opportunity in Social-Movement Theory: The Iranian Revolution of 1979." American Sociological Review 61: 153–70.

Kurzman, Charles. 2002. "Bin Laden and Other Thoroughly Modern Muslims." Contexts 1: 13–20.

Kurzman, Charles. 2021. Muslim American Involvement with Violent Extremism, 2001–2020. Triangle Center on Terrorism and Homeland Security, January 14. (duke.app.box.com/s/pfbtxnvjxyou4g978atol-j9axfeptuzm)

Ladd, Helen, and Lucy Sorensen. 2016. "Returns to Teacher Experience: Student Achievement and Motivation in Middle School." Education Finance and Policy 12: 241–79.

LaFrance, Adrienne. 2020. "The Prophecies of Q." The Atlantic June. (theatlantic.com/magazine/archive/2020/06/qanon-nothing-can-stop-what-is-coming/610567/)

Lam, David. 2011. "How the World Survived the Population Bomb: Lessons from 50 Years of Extraordinary Demographic History." Demography 48: 1231–62.

Lamont, Michele and Virag Molnar. 2002. "The Study of Boundaries in the Social Sciences." Annual Review of Sociology 28: 167–95.

Landry, Bart, and Krish Marsh. 2011. "The Evolution of the New Black Middle Class." Annual Review of Sociology 37: 373–94.

Laney, Doug. 2001. "3D Data Management: Controlling Data Volume, Velocity and Variety." META Group, Stamford, CT. (blogs.gartner.com/doug-laney/files/2012/01/ad949-3D-Data-Management-Controlling-Data-Volume-Velocity-and-Variety.pdf)

Lareau, Annette. 2002. "Invisible Inequality: Social Class and Childrearing in Black Families and White Families." American Sociological Review 67: 747–76.

Lareau, Annette. 2003. Unequal Childhoods: Class, Race, and Family Life. Berkeley and Los Angeles: University of California Press.

Larson, Magali Sarfetti. 1977. The Rise of Professionalism: A Sociological Analysis. Berkeley: University of California Press.

Lartey, Jamiles. 2015. "By the Numbers: U.S. Police Kill More in Days than Other Countries Do in Years." The Guardian June 9. (theguardian.com/us-news/2015/jun/09/the-counted-police-killings-us-vs-other-countries)

Latessa, Edward. 2012. "Why Work is Important, and How to Improve the Effectiveness of Correctional Re-entry Programs that Target Employment." Criminology & Public Policy 11: 87–91.

Lawson, Max, Man-Kwun Chan, Francesca Rhodes, Anam Parvez Butt, Anna Marriott, Ellen Ehmke, Didier Jacobs, Julie Seghers, Jaime Atienza and Rebecca Gowland. 2019. Public Good or Private Wealth. Oxfam Report. (s3.amazonaws.com/oxfam-us//static/media/files/bp-public-good-or-private-wealth-210119-en.pdf)

Leatherby, Lauren, Arielle Ray, Anjali Singhvi, Christiaan Triebert, Derek Watkins and Haley Willis. 2021. "How a Presidential Rally Turned into a Capitol Rampage." New York Times January 12. (nytimes.com/interactive/2021/01/12/us/capitol-mob-timeline.html)

Lee, Barrett, John Iceland, and Chad Farrell. 2014. "Is Ethnoracial Residential Integration on the Rise? Evidence from Metropolitan and Micropolitan America Since 1980." Pp. 415–55 in Diversity and Disparities: America Enters a New Century, ed. John Logan. New York: Russell Sage Foundation Press.

Lee, Ching Kwan. 2019. "China's Precariats." Globalizations 16: 137–54.

Lee, Jennifer, and Frank Bean. 2004. "America's Changing Color Lines: Immigration, Race/Ethnicity, and Multiracial Identification." Annual Review of Sociology 30: 221–42.

Lee, Sharon. 1993. "Racial Classifications in the U.S. Census: 1890–1990." Ethnic and Racial Studies 16: 75–94.

Leibovich, Mark. 2013. This Town. New York: Penguin.

Leighley, Jan. 2001. Strength in Numbers? The Political Mobilization of Racial and Ethnic Minorities. Princeton, NJ: Princeton University Press.

Leighley, Jan and Michael Nagler. 2014. Who Votes Now? Demographics, Issues, Inequality and Turnout in the United States. Princeton: Princeton University Press.

Lemann, Nicholas. 1991. The Promised Land: The Great Migration and How It Changed America. New York: Knopf.

Lemert, Charles. 1997. Social Things. Lanham, MD: Rowman and Littlefield.

Lenin, Vladimir. 1915. "The Collapse of the Second International." Lenin: Collected Works, Vol. 21. Moscow: Progress Publishers.

Lesk, Michael. 1997. "How Much Information Is There in the World?&#x201D. (lesk.com/mlesk/ksg97/ksg.html)

Lessig, Lawrence. 2019. They Don't Represent Us. New York: Harper Collins.

Lesthaeghe, Ron, and Dirk van de Kaa. 1986. "Two Demographic Transitions?" Pp. 9–24 in Population Growth and Decline, eds. Ron Lesthaeghe and Dir van de Kaa. Deventer: Van Loghum Slaterus.

Levanon, Asaf, Paula England, and Paul Allison. 2009. "Occupational Feminization and Pay: Assessing Causal Dynamics Using 1950–2000 Census Data." Social Forces 88: 865–92.

Levi-Strauss, Claude. 1964. "Reciprocity, the Essence of Social Life." Pp. 3–14 in The Family: Its Structure and Functions, ed. Rose Laub Coser. New York: St. Martins Press.

Levitt, Steven, and Sudhir Alladi Venkatesh. 2000. "An Economic Analysis of a Drug-Selling Gang's Finances." The Quarterly Journal of Economics 115: 755–89.

Levy, Frank, and Richard Murnane. 1992. "U.S. Earnings Levels and Earnings Inequality: A Review of Recent Trends and Proposed Explanations." Journal of Economic Literature 30: 1333–81.

Lewis, Amanda. 2003. Race in the Schoolyard: Negotiating the Color Line in Classrooms and Communities. New Brunswick, NY: Rutgers University Press.

Lewis, Michael. 2016. The Undoing Project: A Friendship that Changed Our Minds. New York: Norton.

Lewis, Oscar. 1965. The Children of Sanchez: Autobiography of a Mexican Family. New York: Vintage.

Lichtblau, Eric. 2008. Bush's Law: The Remaking of American Justice. New York: Random House.

Lightdale, Jenifer and Deborah Prentice. 1994. "Rethinking Sex Differences in Aggression: Aggressive Behavior in the Absence of Social Roles." Personality and Social Psychology Bulletin 20: 34–44.

Lin, Ann Chih. 2000. Reform in the Making: The Implementation of Social Policy in Prison. Princeton: Princeton University Press.

Lind, Michael. 1995. The Next American Nation: The New Nationalism and the Fourth American Revolution. New York: Free Press.

Lindblom, Charles. 1977. Politics and Markets. New York: Basic Books.

Link, Bruce and Jo Phelan. 1995. "Social Conditions and Fundamental Causes of Disease." Journal of Health and Social Behavior 51: 80–94.

Link, Bruce, Ezra Susser, Ann Stueve, Jo Phelan, Robert Moore, and Elmer Struening. 1994. "Lifetime and Five-year Prevalence of Homelessness in the United States." American Journal of Public Health. 84: 1907–12.

Linzmayer, Owen. 2004. Apple Confidential 2.0: The Definitive History of the World's Most Colorful Company. San Francisco: No Starch Press.

Lippmann, Walter. 1922. Public Opinion. New York: Harcourt, Brace and Company.

Lipset, Seymour Martin. [1960] 1981. Political Man. Baltimore, MD: Johns Hopkins University Press.

Lipset, Seymour Martin. 1996. American Exceptionalism: A Double-Edged Sword. New York: Norton.

Liptak, Adam. 2008. "U.S. Prison Population Dwarfs That of Other Nations." New York Times April 23. (nytimes.com/2008/04/23/world/americas/23iht-23prison.12253738.html)

Lipton, Eric and Julie Creswell. 2016. "Panama Papers Show How Rich United States Clients Hid Millions Abroad." New York Times June 5. (nytimes.com/2016/06/06/us/panama-papers.html)

Lisak, David. 2011. "Understanding the Predatory Nature of Sexual Violence." Sexual Assault Report 14: 49–57.

Littleton, Heather and Carmen Breitkopf. 2006. "Coping With the Experience of Rape." Psychology of Women Quarterly 30: 106–116. Lleras-Muney, Adriana. 2005. "The Relationship between Education and Adult Mortality in the United States." Review of Economic Studies 72: 189–221.

Lofstrom, Magnus and Steven Raphael. 2016. "Crime, the Criminal Justice System, and Socioeconomic Inequality." Journal of Economic Perspectives 30: 103–26.

Logan, John and Harvey Molotch. 1987. Urban Fortunes: The Political Economy of Place. Berkeley: University of California Press.

Logan, John and Charles Zhang. 2010. "Global Neighborhoods: New Pathways to Diversity and Separation." American Journal of Sociology 115: 1069–109.

Lohr, Steve. 2012. "The Age of Big Data." New York Times February 11. (nytimes.com/2012/02/12/sunday-review/big-datas-impact-in-the-world.html)

López, Gustavo, Neil Ruiz, and Eileen Patten. 2017. "Key Facts about Asian Americans, a Diverse and Growing Population." FactTank. Pew Research Center. (pewresearch.org/fact-tank/2017/09/08/key-facts-about-asian-americans/)

Lorber, Judith. 1994. Paradoxes of Gender. New Haven, CT: Yale University Press.

Lowe, Sarah, Colleen Dillon, Jean Rhodes, and Liza Zwiebach. 2013. "Defining Adult Experiences: Perspectives of a Diverse Sample of Young Adults." Journal of Adolescent Research 28: 31–68.

Lowery, Annie. 2018. Give People Money: How a Universal Basic Income Would End Poverty, Revolutionize Work, and Remake the World. New York: Crown Books.

Lucas, Samuel and Mark Berends. 2002. "Sociodemographic Diversity, Correlated Achievement, and De Facto Tracking." Sociology of Education 75: 328–48.

Lucca, David, Taylor Nadauld, and Karen Shen. 2016. "Credit Supply and the Rise in College Tuition: Evidence from the Expansion of Federal Student Aid Programs." Federal Reserve Bank of New York Staff Reports 733. (newyorkfed.org/medialibrary/media/research/staff_reports/sr733.pdf)

Luders, Joseph. 2010. The Civil Rights Movement and the Logic of Social Change. Cambridge, UK: Cambridge University Press.

Luker, Kristin. 1984. Abortion and the Politics of Motherhood. Berkeley and Los Angeles: University of California Press.

Luker, Kristin. 2010. Salsa Dancing in the Social Sciences. Berkeley: University of California Press.

Lukes, Steven. 1974. Power: A Radical View. London: Palgrave.

Lukes, Steven. 2008. Moral Relativism. New York: Picador.

Lynd, Robert and Helen Lynd. 1929. Middletown: A Study in Contemporary American Culture. New York: Harcourt, Brace and Co.

Lyons Bridget, Katherine Fowler, Shane Jack, Carter Betz, and Janet Blair. 2016. "Surveillance for Violent Deaths—National Violent Death Reporting System, 17 States, 2013." Morbidity and Mortality Weekly Report Surveillance Summaries 65: 1–42. (cdc.gov/mmwr/volumes/65/ss/pdfs/ss6510.pdf)

MacAvaney Sean, Hao-Ren Yao, Eugene Yang, Katina Russell, Nazil Goharian, Ophir Frieder. 2019. "Hate Speech Detection: Challenges and Solutions." PLoS ONE 14: 1–16.

Maccoby, Eleanor Emmons and Carol Nagy Jacklin. 1974. The Psychology of Sex Differences. Stanford, CA: Stanford University Press.

Mackie, Gerry. 1996. "Ending Footbinding and Infibulation: A Convention Account." American Sociological Review 61: 999–1017.

MacLeod, Jay. 2006. Ain't No Makin' It. Boulder, CO: Westview Press.

Maimbo, Samuel Munzele and Dilip Ratha. 2005. "Remittances: An Overview." Pp. 1–16 in Remittances: Development Impact and Future Prospects, ed. Samuel Maimbo and Dilip Ratha. Washington, DC: World Bank.

Malinowski, Bronislaw. [1913] 1964. "Parenthood, the Basis of Social Structure." Pp. 51–63 in The Family: Its Structure and Functions, ed. Rose Laub Coser. New York: St. Martins Press.

Malinowksi, Bronislaw. 1948. Magic, Science and Religion and Other Essays. New York: The Free Press.

Malthus, Thomas Robert. [1798] 2015. An Essay on the Principle of Population. New York: Penguin Classics.

Mann, Thomas and Norman Ornstein. 2016. It's Even Worse Than It Looks: How the American Constitutional System Collided with the New Politics of Extremism. New York: Basic Books.

Manza, Jeff, Clem Brooks, and Michael Sauder. 2004. "Money, Participation, and Votes: Social Cleavages and Electoral Politics." Pp. 201–26 in Handbook of Political Sociology, eds. Thomas Janoski, Robert Alford, Alexander Hicks and Mildred Schwartz. New York: Cambridge University Press.

Manza, Jeff and Christopher Uggen. 2006. Locked Out: Felon Disenfranchisement and American Democracy. New York: Oxford University Press.

Marcec, Dan. 2018. "CEO Tenure Rates." Harvard Law School Forum on Corporate Governance February 12. (corpgov.law.harvard.edu/2018/02/12/ceo-tenure-rates/)

Marcuse, Peter and Ronald van Kempen. 2002. Of States and Cities: The Partitioning of Urban Space. Oxford, UK: Oxford University Press.

Marger, Martin. 2003. Race and Ethnic Relations: American and Global Perspectives. Belmont, CA: Wadsworth.

Marmot, Michael. 2004. The Status Syndrome: How Social Standing Affects Our Health and Longevity. New York: Holt.

Marquardt, Elizabeth. 2005. Between Two Worlds: The Inner Lives of Children of Divorce. New York: Crown.

Martin, Steven. 2006. "Trends in Marital Dissolution by Women's Education in the United States." Demographic Research 15: 538–60.

Martinez, Gladys and Joyce Abma. 2015. "Sexual Activity, Contraceptive Use, and Childbearing of Teenagers Aged 15–19 in the United States." National Center for Health Statistics Data Brief 209. (cdc.gov/nchs/data/databriefs/db209.pdf)

Marx, Karl. [1844] 2001. "Critique of Hegel's Philosophy of Right." Pp. 170–81 in Marx on Religion, ed. John Raines. Philadelphia: Temple University Press.

Marx, Karl. [1859] 1978. "Preface to a Contribution to the Critique of Political Economy." Pp. 3–6 in The Marx–Engels Reader, ed. and translated by Robert Tucker. New York: Norton.

Marx, Karl. [1867] 1976. Capital. London: Verso.

Marx, Karl and Friedrich Engels. [1832] 1977. "The German Ideology." Pp. 159–91 in Karl Marx: Selected Writings, ed. David McLellan. Oxford, UK: Oxford University Press.

Marx, Karl and Frederick Engels. [1845] 1972. "The German Ideology: Part 1." Pp. 146–200 in The Marx–Engels Reader, ed. Robert Tucker. New York: W.W. Norton & Company.

Marx, Karl and Friedrich Engels. [1848] 2011. The Communist Manifesto. New York: Verso.

Massey, Douglas. 2005. Categorically Unequal: The American Stratification System. New York: Russell Sage Foundation.

Massey, Douglas, Joaquin Arango, Graeme Hugo, Ali Kouaouci, Adela Pellegrino, and J. Edward Taylor. 1993. "Theories of International Migration: A Review and Appraisal." Population and Development Review 19: 431–66.

Massey, Douglas and Nancy Denton. 1993. American Apartheid: Segregation and the Making of the Underclass. Cambridge, MA: Harvard University Press.

Massey, Douglas, and Kerstin Gentsch. 2014. "Undocumented Migration to the United States and the Wages of Mexican Immigrants." The International Migration Review 48: 482–99.

Massoglia, Michael and Christopher Uggen. 2010. "Settling Down and Aging Out: Toward an Interactionist Theory of Desistance and the Transition to Adulthood." American Journal of Sociology 116: 543–82.

Mather, Mark and Lillian Kilduff. 2020. "The U.S. Population is Growing Older, and the Gender Gap in Life Expectancy is Narrowing." Population Reference Bureau February 19. (prb.org/the-u-s-population-is-growing-older-and-the-gender-gap-in-life-expectancy-is-narrowing/)

Mayer, Adam. 2017. "Political Identity and Paradox in Oil and Gas Policy: A Study of Regulatory Exaggeration in Colorado, US." Energy Policy 109: 452–59.

Mayer, Jane. 2008. The Dark Side: The Inside Story of How the War on Terror Became a War on American Ideals. New York: Doubleday.

Mayer, Richard. 2017. "Using Multimedia for E-Learning." Journal of Computer Assisted Learning 33: 403–23.

Mazur, Allan and Alan Booth. 1998. "Testosterone and Dominance in Men." Behavioral and Brain Sciences 21: 353–97.

McAdam, Doug. 1982. Political Process and the Development of Black Insurgency, 1930–1970. Chicago: University of Chicago Press.

McAdam, Doug. 1988. Freedom Summer. New York: Oxford University Press.

McAlevey, Jane. 2016. Raising Expectations (and Raising Hell): My Decade Fighting for the Labor Movement. New York: Verso.

McAlevey, Jane. 2020. A Collective Bargain: Unions, Organizing, and the Fight for Democracy. New York: Harper/Collins.

McCall, Leslie. 2005. "The Complexity of Intersectionality." Signs 30: 1771–1800.

McCall, Leslie. 2013. The Undeserving Rich: American Beliefs About Inequality, Opportunity, and Redistribution. New York: Cambridge University Press.

McCarthy, Justin. 2020. "Perceptions of Increased U.S. Crime at Highest Since 1993." Gallup News November 13. (news.gallup.com/poll/323996/perceptions-increased-crime-highest-1993.aspx)

McCarthy, John and Mayer Zald. 1977. "Resource Mobilization and Social Movements: A Partial Theory." American Journal of Sociology 82: 1212–41.

McCarty, Nolan, Keith Poole, and Howard Rosenthal. 2006. Polarized America: The Dance of Ideology and Unequal Riches. Cambridge, MA: MIT Press.

McDaniel, Anne, Thomas A. DiPrete, Claudia Buchmann, and Uri Shwed. 2011. "The Black Gender Gap in Educational Attainment: Historical Trends and Racial Comparisons." Demography 48: 889–914.

McKenna, Wendy and Suzanne Kessler. 2006. "Transgendering: Blurring the Boundaries of Gender." Pp. 342–54 in Handbook of Gender and Women's Studies, ed. Mary Evans, Kathy David, and Judith Lorber. Thousand Oaks, CA: Sage Publications.

McKinsey Global Institute. 2017. A Future That Works. McKinsey and Company. (mckinsey.com/~/media/McKinsey/Featured%20Insights/Digital%20Disruption/Harnessing%20automation%20for%20a%20future%20that%20works/MGI-A-future-that-works_Full-report.ashx)

McKinsey Global Institute. 2019. A New Look at the Declining Share of Labor Income in the United States. Discussion Paper, May. (mckinsey.com/~/media/McKinsey/Featured%20Insights/Employment%20and%20Growth/A%20new%20look%20at%20the%20declining%20labor%20share%20of%20income%20in%20the%20United%20States/MGI-A-new-look-at-the-declining-labor-share-of-income-in-the-United-States.pdf)

McLanahan, Sara and Gary Sandefur. 1994. Growing Up with a Single Parent: What Hurts, What Helps. Cambridge, MA: Harvard University Press.

McLuhan, Marshall. 1964. Understanding Media: The Extensions of Man. Cambridge, MA: MIT Press.

McMullin Darcy and Jacqueline White 2006. "Long-term Effects of Labeling a Rape Experience." Psychology of Women Quarterly 30: 96–105.

McPherson, Miller, Lynne Smith-Lovin, and James Cook. 2001. "Birds of a Feather: Homophily in Social Networks." Annual Review of Sociology 27: 415–44.

McVeigh, Rory and Kevin Estep. 2020. The Politics of Losing: Trump, the Klan, and the Mainstreaming of Resentment. New York: Oxford University Press.

Mead, George Herbert. 1934. Mind, Self, and Society. Chicago: University of Chicago Press.

Meadow, Tey. 2018. Trans Kids: Being Gendered in the Twenty-First Century. Oakland, California: University of California Press.

Medvetz, Thomas. 2012. Think Tanks in America. New York: Cambridge University Press.

Melton, J. Gordon. 2009. Encyclopedia of American Religions. New York: Thomson.

Menchik, Daniel and Xiaoli Tian. 2008. "Putting Social Context into Text: The Semiotics of Email Interaction." American Journal of Sociology 114: 332–70.

Menjívar, Cecilia. 2006. "Liminal Legality: Salvadoran and Guatemalan Immigrants' Lives in the United States." American Journal of Sociology 111: 999–1037.

Merton, Robert. 1938. "Social Structure and Anomie". American Sociological Review 3: 672–82.

Merton, Robert King. 1948. "The Self-Fulfilling Prophecy." Antioch Review 8: 193–210.

Merton, Robert. 1957. Social Theory and Social Structure. New York: The Free Press.

Merton, Robert. 1973. The Sociology of Science: Theoretical and Empirical Investigations. Chicago: University of Chicago Press.

Mettler, Suzanne. 2005. Soldiers to Citizens: The G.I. Bill and the Making of America's Greatest Generation. New York: Oxford University Press.

Milgram, Stanley. 1963. "Behavioral Study of Obedience." Journal of Abnormal and Social Psychology 67: 371–78.

Miliband, Ralph. 2014. "The Coup in Chile." Jacobin September 11. (jacobinmag.com/2016/09/chile-coup-santiago-allende-social-democracy-september-11-2)

Milkman, Ruth et al., 2012. Working Without Laws. (https://s27147.pcdn.co/wp-content/uploads/2015/03/WorkingWithoutLawsNYC.pdf)

Miller, G.E. 2017. "The U.S. Is the Most Overworked Developed Nation in the World – Where Do We Draw the Line?" 20-Something Finance. (https://20somethingfinance.com/american-hours-worked-productivity-vacation/)

Mills, C. Wright. 1956. The Power Elite. New York: Oxford University Press.

Mills, C. Wright. 1959. The Sociological Imagination. New York: Oxford University Press.

Mincer, Jacob. 1978. "Family Migration Decisions." Journal of Political Economy 86: 749–73.

Minnite, Lorraine and Payman Sheriff. 2018. The Politics of Voter Fraud. Washington D.C.: Project Vote.

Mishel, Emma. 2016. "Discrimination against Queer Women in the U.S. Workforce: A Résumé Audit Study." Socius 1: 1–13.

Mischel, Lawrence and Julia Wolfe. 2019. "CEO Compensation Has Grown by 978% Since 1978." Economic Policy Institute August 14. (epi.org/publication/ceo-compensation–2018)

Mitchell, Jean. 2013. "Urologists Use of Intensity Modulated Radiation Therapy for Prostate Cancer." New England Journal of Medicine 369: 1629–37.

Mitchell, Amy, Jeffrey Gottfried, Jocelyn Kiley and Katrina Matsa. 2014. "Political Polarization and Media Consumption." Pew Research Center October 21. (journalism.org/2014/10/21/political-polarization-media-habits/)

Mizhari, Olga. 2018. The Gig Is Up: Thrive in the Gig Economy, Where Old Jobs Are Obsolete and Freelancing Is the Future. Austin, TX: Greenleaf Press.

Moaddel, Mansoor. 2007. "The Saudi Public Speaks: Religion, Gender, and Politics." Pp. 209–48 in Values and Perceptions of the Islamic and Middle East Publics, ed. Mansoor Moaddel. New York: Palgrave Macmillan.

Moen, Phyllis and Patricia Roehling. 2005. The Career Mystique: Cracks in the American Dream. Lanham, MD: Rowman & Littlefield.

Monroe, Burt. 2013. "The Five Vs of Big Data Political Science: Introduction to the Virtual Issue on Big Data in Political Science." Political Analysis 19: 66–86.

Montanaro, Domenico. 2020. "Poll: Just A Quarter of Republicans Accept Election Outcome." NPR December 8. (npr.org/2020/12/09/944385798/poll-just-a-quarter-of-republicans-accept-election-outcome)

Montgomery, Mark, Richard Stren, and Barney Cohen. 2003. Cities Transformed. Washington, D.C.: National Academy Press.

Moody, Kim. 1997. Workers in a Lean World: Unions in the International Economy. New York: Verso.

Moore, Natalie. 2016. South Side: A Portrait of Chicago and American Segregation. New York: Picador.

Morning, Ann. 2008. "Ethnic Classification in Global Perspective: A Cross-National Survey of the 2000 Census Round." Population Research and Policy Review 27: 239–72.

Morning, Ann. 2011. The Nature of Race: How Scientists Think and Teach about Human Difference. Berkeley, CA: University of California Press.

Morning, Ann, and Aliya Saperstein. 2018. "The Generational Locus of Multiraciality and Its Implications for Racial Self-Identification." Annals of the American Academy of Political and Social Science 677: 57–68.

Morris, Aldon. 1985. The Origins of the Civil Rights Movement: Black Communities Organizing for Change. New York: Free Press.

Morris, Aldon. 2015. The Scholar Denied: W.E.B. Du Bois and the Birth of Modern Sociology. Berkeley: University of California Press.

Mouw, Ted. 2003. "Social Capital and Finding a Job: Do Contacts Matter?" American Sociological Review 68: 868–98.

Moyn, Samuel. 2012. The Last Utopia: Human Rights in History. Cambridge, MA: Harvard University Press.

Mozur, Paul. 2018. "A Genocide Incited on Facebook, With Posts From Myanmar's Military." New York Times October 15. (nytimes.com/2018/10/15/technology/myanmar-facebook-genocide.html)

Muchina, Pauline and Mike Merryman-Lotze. 2019. "The U.S. Has Killed Thousands of People with Lethal Drones - It's Time to Put a Stop to It." AFSC Blog, May 16. (afsc.org/blogs/news-and-commentary/us-has-killed-thousands-people-lethal-drones#:~:text=According%20to%20the)

Mudde, Cas. 2007. Populist Radical Right Parties in Europe. New York: Cambridge University Press.

Muhammad, Khalil. 2010. The Condemnation of Blackness: Race, Crime, and the Making of Modern Urban America. Cambridge, MA: Harvard University Press.

Mulkey, Lynn, Sophia Catsambia, Lala Steelman, and Robert Crain. 2005. "The Long-Term Effects of Ability Grouping in Mathematics: A National Investigation." Social Psychology of Education: An International Journal 8: 137–77.

Müller, Jan-Werner. 2016. What is Populism? Philadelphia, PA: University of Pennsylvania Press.

Munson, Ziad. 2008. The Making of Pro-Life Activists: How Social Movement Mobilization Works. Chicago: University of Chicago Press.

Murnane, Richard, John Willett, and Frank Levy. 1995. "The Growing Importance of Cognitive Skills in Wage Determination," The Review of Economics and Statistics 77: 251–66.

Narea, Nicole. 2021. "Most Americans Support a Path to Citizenship for Undocumented Immigrants." Vox February 4. (https://www.vox.com/policy-and-politics/2021/2/4/22264074/poll-undocumented-immigrants-citizenship-stimulus-biden)

National Academy of Sciences. 2014. The Growth of Incarceration in the United States: Exploring Causes and Consequences. Washington, D.C.: National Academies Press.

National Center for Educational Statistics. 2020. "Table 211.60: Average Annual Salary of Teachers in Public Elementary and Secondary Schools, by State: Selected Years, 1969–70 through 2018–19." Digest of Education Statistics. (nces.ed.gov/programs/digest/d19/tables/dt19_211.60.asp?current=yes)

National Center for Health Statistics. 2011. "National Vital Statistics Reports: United States Life Tables, 2007." Washington, D.C.: US Department of Health and Human Services. (cdc.gov/nchs/data/nvsr/nvsr59/nvsr59_09.pdf)

National Center for Health Statistics. 2014. "National Vital Statistics System." (https://www.cdc.gov/nchs/nvss/index.htm)

National Conference of State Legislatures. 2020. "All-Mail Elections (AKA Vote-by-Mail)." NCSL Report March 24. (ncsl.org/research/elections-and-campaigns/all-mail-elections.aspx)

National Hospice and Palliative Care Organization. 2011. NHPCO Facts and Figures: Hospice Care in America. (medpagetoday.com/upload/2012/1/16/2011_Facts_Figures.pdf)

National Institute on Aging, National Institutes of Health, U.S. Department of Health and Human Services, and the U.S. Department of State. 2007. Why Population Aging Matters: A Global Perspective.

National Research Council and Institute of Medicine. 2013. "Panel on Understanding Cross-National Health Differences among High-Income Countries," in U.S. Health in International Perspective: Shorter Lives, Poorer Health, ed. Steven Woolf and Laudan Aron. Washington, DC: The National Academies Press.

Nelkin, Dorothy, and M. Susan Lindee. 1995. The DNA Mystique: The Gene as Cultural Icon. New York: Freeman.

Nelson, Jill (ed.). 2001. Police Brutality. New York: Norton.

Nelson, Lowry. 1969. Rural Sociology: Its Origins and Growth in the United States. Minneapolis, MN: University of Minnesota Press.

Nelson, Todd, ed. 2002. Ageism: Stereotyping and Prejudice Against Older Persons. Cambridge, MA: MIT Press.

Nestle, Marion. 2002. Food Politics: How the Food Industry Influences Nutrition and Health. Berkeley: University of California Press.

Nestle, Marion. 2018. Unsavory Truth: How Food Companies Skew the Science of What We Eat. New York: Basic Books.

Neumark, David. 2018. "Experimental Research on Labor Market Discrimination." Journal of Economic Literature 56: 799–866.

Newport, Frank. 2019. "Public Opinion, the Wall and Views of Government." Gallup Polling Matters January 18. (news.gallup.com/opinion/polling-matters/246086/public-opinion-wall-views-government.aspx)

Newman, Katherine. 2009. "Ties That Bind: Cultural Interpretations of Delayed Adulthood in Western Europe and Japan." Sociological Forum 23: 645–69.

Newman, Kathryn. 2012. The Accordion Family: Boomerang Kids, Anxious Parents, and the Private Toll of Global Competition. Boston: Beacon Press.

Newport, Frank. 2019. "Americans' Mixed Views of Health Care and Health Care Reform," Gallup February 21. (news.gallup.com/opinion/polling-matters/257711/americans-mixed-views-healthcare-healthcare-reform.aspx)

New York City Police Department. 2016. "Historical New York City Crime Data." (1.nyc.gov/site/nypd/stats/crime-statistics/historical.page)

New York Civil Liberties Union. 2011. Stop and Frisk 2011 Report. (nyclu.org/sites/default/files/publications/NYCLU_2011_Stop-and-Frisk_Report.pdf)

Nielsen, Laura Beth. 2004. License to Harass: Law, Hierarchy, and Offensive Public Speech. Princeton, NJ: Princeton University Press.

Nippert-Eng, Christena. 2010. Islands of Privacy. Chicago: University of Chicago Press.

Noble, Safiya Umoja. 2018. Algorithms of Oppression: How Search Engines Reinforce Racism. New York: New York University Press.

Nonnemaker, Lynn and Shelly Ann Sinclair. 2011. "Medicare Beneficiaries Out-of-Pocket Spending for Health Care." Washington, DC: American Association of Retired Persons Policy Institute.

NORC, University of Chicago. General Social Survey 1972–2018. (https://gss.norc.org/)

Norris, Pippa and Ronald Inglehart. 2004. Sacred and Secular. New York: Cambridge University Press.

Notestein, Frank Wallace. 1953. "Economic Problems of Population Change." Pp 13–31 in Proceedings of the Eighth International Conference of Agricultural Economists.

Nozick, Robert. 1974. Anarchy, State, Utopia. New York: Basic Books.

Nyhan, Marguerite, Sebastian Grauwin, Rex Britter, Bruce Misstear, Aonghus McNabola, Francine Laden, Steven Barrett, and Carlo Ratti. 2016. "'Exposure Track'—The Impact of Mobile-Device-Based Mobility Patterns on Quantifying Population Exposure to Air Pollution." Environmental Science and Technology 50: 9671–81.

Oakes, Jeannie. 1985. Keeping Track: How Schools Structure Inequality. New Haven, CT: Yale University Press.

Oakes, Jeannie, Amy Stuart Wells, Makeba Jones, and Amanda Datnow. 1997. "Detracking: The Social Construction of Ability, Cultural Politics and Resistance to Reform." Teachers College Record 98: 482–510.

Obasogie, Osagie. 2014. Blinded by Sight: Seeing Race Through the Eyes of the Blind. Stanford, CA: Stanford Law Books/Stanford University Press.

O'Brien, Jodi. 2000. "Heterosexism and Homophobia." Pp. 6672–76 in International Encyclopedia of the Social & Behavioral Sciences, eds. Neil Smelser and Paul Baltes. London: Elsevier.

O'Connor, James. 1973. The Fiscal Crisis of the State. London: MacMillan.

Office of the United States Trade Representative. 2008. "NAFTA: Myths versus Facts."

Ogden, Cynthia, Margaret Carroll, Cheryl Fryar, and Katherine Flegal. 2015. "Prevalence of Obesity among Adults and Youth, United States, 2011–2014." National Center for Health Statistics, NCHS Data Brief 219. (cdc.gov/nchs/data/databriefs/db219.pdf)

Oishi, Shigehiro, Selin Kesebir and Ed Diener 2011. "Income Inequality and Happiness." Psychological Science 22: 1095–100.

Okrent, David. 2010. Last Call: The Rise and Fall of Prohibition. New York: Scribner.

Oliver, Melvin and Thomas Shapiro. 1997. Black Wealth, White Wealth: A New Perspective on Racial Inequality. New York: Routledge.

Olmstead, Kenneth, Mark Jurkowitz, Amy Mitchell, and Jodi Enda. 2013. "How Americans Get TV News at Home." Pew Research Center. (journalism.org/2013/10/11/how-americans-get-tv-news-at-home/)

Olson, Mancur. 1965. The Logic of Collective Action: Public Goods and the Theory of Groups. Cambridge, MA: Harvard University Press.

Olzak, Susan. 1992. The Dynamics of Ethnic Competition and Conflict. Stanford, CA: Stanford University Press.

Omran, Abdel. 1971. "The Epidemiologic Transition: A Theory of the Epidemiology of Population Change." Milbank Memorial Fund Quarterly 49: 509–38.

O'Neil, Kevin and Marta Tienda. 2015. "Age at Immigration and the Incomes of Older Immigrants, 1994-2010." The Journals of Gerontology: Series B 70: 291–302.

Oppenheimer, Valerie. 1970. The Female Labor Force in the United States: Demographic and Economic Factors Governing Its Growth and Changing Composition. Berkeley: University of California Press.

Oppong, Thomas. 2019. Working in the Gig Economy: How to Thrive and Succeed When You Choose to Work for Yourself. London: Kogan Page.

Organization of Economic Cooperation and Development. 2014. Education at a Glance 2014: OECD Indicators. OECD Publishing. (oecd-ilibrary.org/docserver/eag-2014-en.pdf?expires=1594717300&id=id&accname=guest&checksum=D7FC25912BDBF5B106B31DA61789F5E3)

Organisation of Economic Cooperation and Development. 2015. Education at a Glance 2015: OECD Indicators. OECD Publishing. (oecd-ilibrary.org/docserver/eag-2015-en.pdf?expires=1594717244&id=id&accname=guest&checksum=AC2FD94B33FE074FB9DC7B9FCCC30CDE)

Organisation of Economic Cooperation and Development. Stat. 2016. "Average Annual Hours Actually Worked per Worker." (stats.oecd.org/Index.aspx?DataSetCode=ANHRS#)

Organization of Economic Cooperation and Development. 2017. "Gender Gap in Education." (oecd.org/gender/data/gender-gap-in-education.htm)

Organization of Economic Cooperation and Development (OECD). Corporate Income Tax Statistics. 2020. (oecd.org/tax/tax-policy/corporate-tax-statistics-database.html)

O'Rourke, Kevin and Jeffrey Williamson. 2000. Globalization and History: The Evolution of a Nineteenth Century Atlantic Economy. Cambridge, MA: MIT Press.

Osofsky, Joy. 1999. "The Impact of Violence on Children." Future of Children 9: 33–49.

Ostrom, Elinor. 1990. Governing the Commons: The Evolution of Institutions for Collective Action. Cambridge: Cambridge University Press.

Ottosson, Daniel. 2010. "State-Sponsored Homophobia: A World Survey of Laws Prohibiting Same Sex Behavior between Consenting Adults." Geneva, Switzerland: International Lesbian, Gay, Bisexual, Trans, and Intersex Association.

Owens, Ann. 2015. "Growing Economic Segregation Among School Districts and Schools." Brookings Institute Brown Center Chalkboard. (brookings.edu/blog/brown-center-chalkboard/2015/09/10/growing-economic-segregation-among-school-districts-and-schools)

Oxfam. 2016. "62 People Own Same as Half World." Oxfam Press Release, January 18. (oxfam.org.uk/media-centre/press-releases/2016/01/62-people-own-same-as-half-world-says-oxfam-inequality-report-davos-world-economic-forum)

Pager, Devah. 2003. "The Mark of a Criminal Record." American Journal of Sociology 108: 937–75.

Pager, Devah. 2007. Marked: Race, Crime, and Finding Work in an Era of Mass Incarceration. Chicago: University of Chicago Press.

Pager, Devah and Lincoln Quillian. 2005. "Walking the Talk: What Employers Say versus What They Do." American Sociological Review 70: 355–80.

Pager, Devah, Bruce Western, and Bart Bonakowski. 2009. "Discrimination in a Low-Wage Labor Market: A Field Experiment." American Sociological Review 74: 777–79.

Palardy, Gregory, Russell Rumberger, and Truman Butler. 2015. "The Effect of High School Socioeconomic, Racial and Linguistic Segregation on Academic Performance and School Behaviors." Teachers College Record 117: 1–52.

Palfrey, John and Urs Gasser. 2008. Born Digital: Understanding the First Generation of Digital Natives. New York: Basic Books.

Pallas, Aaron. 2000. "The Effects of Schooling on Individual Lives." Pp. 499–525 in Handbook of the Sociology of Education, ed. Maureen Hallinan. New York: Kluwer Academic/Plenum.

Pan, Luyao and Xianming Zhou. 2018. "CEO Compensation in Japan: Why So Different from the United States?" Journal of Financial and Quantitative Analysis 53: 2261–92.

Panagopoulos, Costas. 2011. "Occupy Wall Street Survey Results October 2011." Center for Electoral Politics and Democracy. (fordham.edu/download/downloads/id/2538/occupy_wall_street_survey.pdf)

Panofsky, Aaron and Joan Donovan. 2019. "Genetic Ancestry Testing Among White Nationalists: From Identity Repair to Citizen Science." Social Studies of Science 49: 653–81.

Parcel, Toby and Elizabeth Menaghan. 1994. Parents' Jobs and Children's Lives. New York: Aldine de Gruyter.

Pariser, Eli. 2011. The Filter Bubble: What the Internet is Hiding From You. London: Penguin UK.

Park, Robert. and Ernest Burgess. [1925] 1967. The City: Suggestions for Investigation of Human Behavior in the Urban Environment. Chicago: University of Chicago Press.

Parkin, Frank. 1979. Marxism and Class Theory: A Bourgois Critique. London: Tavistock.

Parkinson, Robert. 2016. The Common Cause: Creating Race and Nation in the American Revolution. Chapel Hill, NC: University of North Carolina Press.

Parreñas, Rhacel. 2008. The Force of Domesticity: Filipina Migrants and Globalization. New York: NYU Press.

Parsons, Talcott. [1937] 1967. The Structure of Social Action. New York: The Free Press.

Parsons, Talcott. 1951. The Social System. New York: The Free Press.

Parsons, Talcott. 1959. "The School Class as a Social System." Harvard Educational Review 29: 297–318.

Parsons, Talcott. 1964. Social Structure and Personality. New York: Free Press.

Parsons, Talcott and Neil Smelser. 1956. Economy and Society. New York: The Free Press.

Pascoe, C. J. 2007. "Dude, You're a Fag": Masculinity and Sexuality in High School. Berkeley: University of California Press.

Passel, Jeffrey, D'Vera Cohn, Manuel Krogstad, and Ana Gonzalez-Barrera. 2014. "As Growth Stalls, Unauthorized Immigrant Population Becomes More Settled." Pew Hispanic Center Report September 3. (pewresearch.org/hispanic/2014/09/03/as-growth-stalls-unauthorized-immigrant-population-becomes-more-settled/)

Pattillo, Mary. 1999. Black Picket Fences. Chicago: University of Chicago Press.

Pattillo, Mary. 2008. Black on the Block: The Politics of Race and Class in the City. Chicago: University of Chicago Press.

Peck, Jamie. 2005. "Struggling with the Creative Class." International Journal of Urban and Regional Research 29: 740–70.

Pedulla, David, and Sarah Thébaud. 2015. "Can We Finish the Revolution? Gender, Work Family Ideals, and Institutional Constraint." American Sociological Review 80: 116–39.

Perry, Andre, Jonathan Rothwell, and David Harshbarger. 2018. "The Devaluation of Assets in Black Neighborhoods: The Case of Residential Property." Brookings Institute Metropolitan Policy Program November 27. (brookings.edu/wp-content/uploads/2018/11/2018.11_Brookings-Metro_Devaluation-Assets-Black-Neighborhoods_final.pdf)

Perry, Mark. 2017. "Prediction: No 2017 Graduation Speaker Will Mention This: The Growing "Gender College Degree 'Gap' Favoring Women." AEI Ideas. (aei.org/publication/prediction-no-2017-graduation-speaker-will-mention-this-the-growing-gender-college-degree-gap-favoring-women/)

Persell, Caroline, Sophia Catsambis, and Peter Cookson, Jr. 1992. "Differential Asset Conversion: Class and Gendered Pathways to Selective Colleges." Sociology of Education 65: 208–25.

Peschek, Joseph. 1987. Policy-Planning Organizations: Elite Agenda and America's Rightward Turn. Philadelphia: Temple University Press.

Petersilia, Joan. 2003. They All Come Home: Parole and Prisoner Reentry. New York: Oxford University Press.

Peterson, Richard and Roger Kern. 1996. "Changing Highbrow Taste: From Snob to Omnivore." American Sociological Review 61: 900–07.

Pew Research Center. 2009. "Growing Old in America: Expectations vs. Reality." Philadelphia: Pew Foundation. (pewsocialtrends.org/2009/06/29/growing-old-in-america-expectations-vs-reality/)

Pew Research Center. 2010a. "The Decline of Marriage and Rise of New Families." Philadelphia: Pew Foundation. (pewsocialtrends.org/2010/11/18/the-decline-of-marriage-and-rise-of-new-families/)

Pew Research Center. 2010b. "A Portrait of the "Generation Next": How Young People View Their Lives, Futures and Politics." Philadelphia: Pew Foundation. (pewresearch.org/politics/2007/01/09/a-portrait-of-generation-next/)

Pew Research Center 2011. "Public Divided Over Occupy Wall Street Movement." Pew Political Reports. (pewresearch.org/politics/2011/10/24/public-divided-over-occupy-wall-street-movement/)

Pew Research Center 2013. "A Portrait of Jewish Americans." Pew Research Reports. (https://www.pewforum.org/2013/10/01/jewish-american-beliefs-attitudes-culture-survey/)

Pew Research Center. 2014. "U.S. Religious Landscape Study." Philadelphia: Pew Foundation. (pewforum.org/religious-landscape-study/)

Pew Research Center. 2014. "Majority of Adults Look Online for Health Information." Pew Research Reports. (https://www.pewresearch.org/fact-tank/2013/02/01/majority-of-adults-look-online-for-health-information/)

Pew Research Center. 2018a. "Shifting Public Views on Legal Immigration Into the U.S." (pewresearch.org/politics/2018/06/28/shifting-public-views-on-legal-immigration-into-the-u-s/)

Pew Research Center. 2018b. "What Unites and Divides Urban, Suburban and Rural Communities". May. (pewsocialtrends.org/2018/05/22/demographic-and-economic-trends-in-urban-suburban-and-rural-communities/)

Pew Research Center. 2018c. "Being Christian in Western Europe." Religion and Public Life, May 29. (pewforum.org/2018/05/29/being-christian-in-western-europe/)

Pfaff, John. 2017. Locked In: The True Causes of Mass Incarceration and How to Achieve Real Reform. New York: Basic Books.

Phillips, Howard and David Killingray, eds. 2003. The Spanish Influenza Pandemic of 1918-19: New Perspectives. New York: Routledge.

Pierson, Paul. 2000. "Path Dependence, Increasing Returns, and the Study of Politics." American Political Science Review 94: 251–67.

Piketty, Thomas. 2014. Capital in the 21st Century. Cambridge, MA: Harvard University Press.

Piketty, Thomas and Emanuel Saez. 2014. "Economic Inequality in the Long Run." Science 344: 838–43.

Pinker, Stephen. 2011. The Better Angels of Our Nature: Why Violence Has Declined. New York: Viking Press.

Piven, Frances Fox. 2008. "Can Power From Below Change the World?" American Sociological Review 73: 1–14.

Piven, Frances Fox and Richard Cloward. 1997. The Breaking of the American Social Compact. New York: The New Press.

Piven, Frances Fox, Lorraine Minnite, and Margaret Groarke. 2009. Keeping Down the Black Vote: Race the Demobilization of American Voters. New York: New Press.

Podgursky, Michael, Ryan Monroe, and Donald Watson. 2004. "The Academic Quality of Public School Teachers: An Analysis of Entry and Exit Behavior." Economics of Education Review, 23: 507–18.

Pomeranz, Kenneth 2000. The Great Divergence: China, Europe and the Making of the Modern World Economy. Princeton, NJ: Princeton University Press.

Pontusson, Jonas. 2005. Inequality and Prosperity: Social Europe v. Liberal America. Ithaca, NY: Cornell University Press.

Poole, Keith and Howard Rosenthal. 1997. Congress: A Political-Economic History of Roll Call Voting. New York: Oxford University Press.

Popenoe, David. 1988. Disturbing the Nest: Family Change and Decline in Modern Societies. New York: Aldine de Gruyter.

Popenoe, David, Jean Elshtain, and David Blankenhorn. 1996. Promises to Keep: Decline and Renewal of Marriage in America. Lanham, MD: Rowman & Littlefield.

Porter, Eduardo and Michelle O'Donnell. 2006. "Facing Middle Age with No Degree, and No Wife." New York Times August 6. (nytimes.com/2006/08/06/us/06marry.html)

Portes, Alejandro and Ruben Rumbaut. 2006. Immigrant America: A Portrait. Berkeley: University of California Press.

Portes, Alejandro and Min Zhou. 1993. "The New Second Generation: Segmented Assimilation and Its Variants." Annals of the American Academy of Political and Social Sciences 530: 74–96.

Postman, Neil. 1985. Amusing Ourselves to Death: Public Discourse in the Age of Show Business. New York: Penguin.

Poulantzas, Nicos. 1978. State, Power, Socialism. London: Verso.

Powell, Brian, Catherine Bolzendahl, Claudia Geist, and Lala Carr Steelman. 2010. Counted Out: Same-Sex Relations and American's Definitions of Family. New York: Russell Sage Foundation.

Powell, Eleanor Neff. 2017. Where Money Matters. New York: Cambridge University Press.

Prescott, Edward. 2004. "Why Do Americans Work So Much More than Europeans?" NBER Working Papers 10316. Cambridge, MA: National Bureau of Economic Research. (nber.org/papers/w10316)

Preston, Samuel and John McDonald. 1979. "The Incidence of Divorce within Cohorts of American Marriages Contracted since the Civil War." Demography 16: 1–25.

Public Citizen. 2008. "Debunking USTR Claims in Defense of NAFTA: The Real NAFTA Score 2008." (citizen.org/wp-content/uploads/nafta_ustr_debunk_web.pdf)

Puente, Maria, and Martin Kasindorf. 1999. "The New Face of America: Blended Races Making a True Melting Pot." USA Today September 7.

Putnam, Robert. 1993. Making Democracy Work: Civic Traditions in Modern Italy. Princeton: Princeton University Press.

Putnam, Robert. 2000. Bowling Alone: The Collapse and Revival of American Community. New York: Simon and Schuster.

Putnam, Robert and David Campbell. 2010. American Grace: How Religion Divides and Unites Us. New York: Simon and Schuster.

Quillian, Lincoln. 2006. "New Approaches to Understanding Racial Prejudice and Discrimination." Annual Review of Sociology 32: 299–328.

Quillian Lincoln. 2014. "Does Segregation Create Winners and Losers? Residential Segregation and Inequality in Educational Attainment." Social Problems 61: 402–26.

Raine, Adrian. 2013. The Anatomy of Violence: The Biological Roots of Crime. New York, NY: Pantheon.

Ranulf, Svend. 1938. Moral Indignation and Middle Class Psychology: A Sociological Study. Copenhagen: Levin & Munksgard and Ejnar Munksgaard.

Rape, Abuse and Incest National Network. 2021. "Campus Sexual Violence: Statistics."

Raphael, Steven and Michael Stoll, eds. 2009. Do Prisons Make Us Safer? The Benefits and Costs of the Prison Boom. New York: Russell Sage Foundation Press.

Rapier, Robert. 2020. "Fossil Fuels Still Supply 84 Percent of World Energy — And Other Eye Openers from BP's Annual Review." Forbes June 20. (forbes.com/sites/rrapier/2020/06/20/bp-review-new-highs-in-global-energy-consumption-and-carbon-emissions-in-2019/#76eb6d4466a1)

Rapoport, Hillel and Frederic Docquier. 2006. "The Economics of Migrants' Remittances." Pp. 1135–200 in Handbook of the Economics of Giving, Altruism and Reciprocity: Applications, eds. Serge-Christophe Kolm and Jean Mercier Ythier. Amsterdam, Netherlands: North-Holland.

Rasmussen Reports. 2017. "Most Think America Is More Divided Since Trump." (http://rasmussenreports.com/public_content/politics/general_politics/june_2017/most_think_america_is_more_divided_since_trump)

Ravallion, Martin, Shaohua Chen, and Prem Sangraula. 2007. "New Evidence on the Urbanization of Global Poverty." Population and Development Review 33: 667–701.

Ravenelle, Alexandrea. 2019. Hustle and Gig: Struggling and Surviving in the Sharing Economy. Berkeley: University of California Press.

Ray, Brian. 2009. "Homeschool Progress Report 2009: Academic Achievement and Demographics." Home School Legal Defense Association. (files.eric.ed.gov/fulltext/ED535134.pdf)

Read, Jen'nan Ghazal and Bridget Gorman. 2010. "Gender and Health Inequality." Annual Review of Sociology 36: 371–86.

Reardon, Sean. 2011. "The Widening Academic Achievement Gap between the Rich and the Poor: New Evidence and Possible Explanations." Pp. 91–116 in Whither Opportunity? Rising Inequality and the Uncertain Life Chances of Low-Income Children, eds. Richard Murnane and Greg Duncan. New York: Russell Sage Foundation Press.

Reardon, Sean, Elena Grewal, Demetra Kalogrides, and Erica Greenberg. 2012. "Brown Fades: The End of Court-Ordered School Desegregation and the Resegregation of American Public Schools." Journal of Policy Analysis and Management 31: 876–904.

Reeves, Richard. 2016. Infamy: The Shocking Story of Japanese American Internment During World War II. New York: Picador.

Reeves, Richard. 2017. Dream Hoarders: How the American Upper Middle Class Is Leaving Everyone Else in the Dust, Why That Is a Problem, and What to Do About It. Washington, D.C.: Brookings Institute Press.

Reich, Rob. 2019. Just Giving: How Philanthropy is Failing Democracy and How It Can Do Better. Princeton, NJ: Princeton University Press.

Reiman, Jeffrey and Paul Leighton. 2020. The Rich Get Richer, the Poor Get Prison. London, UK: Taylor & Francis.

Regnerus, Mark. 2007. Forbidden Fruit: Sex and Religion in the Lives of American Teenagers. Oxford, UK: Oxford University Press.

Remnick, David. 2010. The Bridge: The Life and Rise of Barack Obama. New York: Knopf.

Rennison, Callie. 2014. "Privilege, among Rape Victims." New York Times December 21. (nytimes.com/2014/12/22/opinion/who-suffers-most-from-rape-and-sexual-assault-in-america.html)

Reskin, Barbara. 2000. "The Proximate Causes of Employment Discrimination." Contemporary Sociology 29: 319–28.

Reskin, Barbara. 2012. "The Race Discrimination System." Annual Review of Sociology 38: 17–35.

Rhode, Deborah. 1997. Speaking of Sex. Cambridge, MA: Harvard University Press.

Rich, Andrew. 2004. Think Tanks, Public Policy, and the Politics of Expertise. New York: Cambridge University Press.

Richards, Sarah. 2006. "Remembering the 'Naked Guy.'" Salon May 22. (salon.com/2006/05/22/naked_guy/)

Richardson, Pete. 2009. "Doing Things with Wood: Builders, Managers and Wittgenstein in an Idaho Sawmill." Critique of Anthropology 29: 160–82.

Richmond, Emily. 2014. "The Crackdown on Poor Teacher Training Programs." The Atlantic November 27. (theatlantic.com/education/archive/2014/11/white-house-cracks-down-on-poor-teacher-training-programs/383242/)

Ricks, Thomas. 1997. Making the Corps. New York: Scribner's.

Risman, Barbara. 1998. Gender Vertigo: American Families in Transition. New Haven, CT: Yale University Press.

Risman, Barbara. 2004. "Gender as a Social Structure: Theory Wrestling with Social Change." Gender & Society 18: 429–50.

Risman, Barbara. 2010. Families as They Really Are. New York: W.W. Norton.

Risman, Barbara. 2018. Where the Millenials Will Take Us: A New Generation Wrestles with the Gender Structure. Oxford: Oxford University Press.

Ritzer, George. 1993. The McDonalization of Society. Thousand Oaks, CA: Pine Forge Press.

Rivera-Batiz, Francisco. 1999. "Undocumented Workers in the Labor Market: An Analysis of the Earnings of Legal and Illegal Mexican Immigrants in the United States." Journal of Population Economics 12: 91–116.

Robinson, Nathan. 2016. Super Predator: Bill Clinton's Use and Abuse of Black America. Somerville, MA: Current Affairs Press.

Roose, Kevin. 2019. "The Making of a YouTube Radical." The New York Times June 8. (nytimes.com/interactive/2019/06/08/technology/youtube-radical.html)

Rorabaugh, W. J. 1979. The Alcoholic Republic: An American Tradition. New York: Oxford University Press.

Rose, Geoffrey. 1985. "Sick Individuals and Sick Populations." International Journal of Epidemiology 14: 32–38.

Roseboom, Tessa, Susanne de Rooij, and Rebecca Painter. 2006. "The Dutch Famine and Its Long-Term Consequences for Adult Health." Early Human Development 82: 485–91.

Rosenbaum, James. 1976. Making Inequality. New York: Wiley-Interscience.

Rosenberg, Charles. 1989. "What Is an Epidemic? AIDS in Historical Perspective." Daedalus 118: 1–17.

Rosenberg, Charles. 1993. Explaining Epidemics and Other Studies in the History of Medicine. New York: Cambridge University Press.

Rosenfeld, Jake. 2014. What Unions No Longer Do. Cambridge, MA: Harvard University Press.

Rosenfeld, Jake. 2019. "US Labor Studies in the Twenty-First Century: Understanding Laborism Without Labor." Annual Review of Sociology 45: 449–65.

Rosenfeld, Michael. 2009. The Age of Independence: Interracial Unions, Same-Sex Unions, and Changing American Family. Cambridge, MA: Harvard University Press.

Rosenfeld, Michael. 2021. The Rainbow After the Storm: Marriage Equality and Social Change in the U.S. Oxford: Oxford University Press.

Rosenhan, David. 1973. "On Being Sane in Insane Places." Science 179: 250–58.

Rosenstone, Steven, Edward Behr, and Edward Lazeras. 1996. Third Parties in America. Princeton, NJ: Princeton University Press.

Rosenthal, Elizabeth. 2016. How Healthcare Became Big Business and How We Can Take It Back. New York: Penguin Books.

Rosenthal, Elisabeth. 2017. An American Sickness: How Healthcare Became Big Business and How You Can Take It Back. New York: Penguin Press.

Ross, Catherine and Marieke Van Willigen. 1997. "Education and the Subjective Quality of Life." Journal of Health and Social Behavior 38: 275–97.

Roth, Wendy and Biorn Ivemark. 2018. "Genetic Options: The Impact of Genetic Testing on Consumers' Racial and Ethnic Identities." American Journal of Sociology 124: 150–84.

Rothkopf, David. 2008. The Superclass: The Global Power Elite and the World They Are Making. New York: Farrar Straus & Giroux.

Roxborough, Ian. 2007. "Counterinsurgency." Contexts 6 (May): 15–21.

Royden, Laura and Michael Li. 2017. Extreme Maps. New York: Brennan Center for Social Justice. (brennancenter.org/sites/default/files/publications/Extreme%20Maps%205.16.pdf)

Royster, Deirdre. 2003. Race and the Invisible Hand: How White Networks Exclude Black Men from Blue-Collar Jobs. Berkeley: University of California Press.

Rugman, Alan. 2005. The Regional Multinationals: MNEs and "Global" Strategic Management. Cambridge, UK: Cambridge University Press.

Rugman, Alan and Alain Verbeke. 2004. "A Perspective on Regional and Global Strategies of Multinational Enterprises." Journal of International Business Studies 35: 3–18.

Ruiz, Neil, Khadijah Edwards, and Mark Lopez. 2021. "One-Third of Asian Americans Fear Threats and Physical Attacks, and Most Say Violence Against Them is Rising." Pew Research Center Report. April 21. (pewresearch.org/fact-tank/2021/04/21/one-third-of-asian-americans-fear-threats-physical-attacks-and-most-say-violence-against-them-is-rising/)

Rutter, Virginia. 2010. "The Case for Divorce." Pp. 159–69 in Families as They Really Are, ed. Barbara Risman. New York: W.W. Norton.

Sacks, Karen. 1994. "How Did Jews Become White Folks?" Pp. 78–102 in Race, ed. Steven Gregory and Roger Sanjek. New Brunswick, NJ: Rutgers University Press.

Saez, Emmanuel and Gabriel Zucman. 2019. The Triumph of Injustice: How the Rich Dodge Taxes and How to Make Them Pay. New York: Norton.

Salganik, Matthew, Ian Lundberg, Alexander Kindel, and Sara McLanahan. 2019. "Introduction to the Special Collection on the Fragile Families Challenge." Socius 5: 1–21.

Sampson, Robert. 2015. "Immigration and America's Urban Revival." American Prospect Summer: 20–24. (prospect.org/labor/immigration-america-s-urban-revival)

Sampson, Robert. and John Laub. 2003. "Desistance from Crime over the Life Course." Pp. 295–310 in Handbook of the Life Course, eds. Jeylan Mortimer and Michael Shanahan. New York: Kluwer Academic/Plenum.

Sampson, Robert and Janet Lauritsen. 1997. "Racial and Ethnic Disparities in Crime and Criminal Justice in the United States." Pp. 311–74 in Ethnicity, Crime, and Immigration: Comparative and Cross National Perspectives, ed. Michael Tonry. Chicago: University of Chicago Press.

Sampson, Robert, Stephen Raudenbush, and Felton Earls. 1997. "Neighborhoods and Violent Crime: A Multilevel Study of Collective Efficacy." Science 227: 918–24.

Samuel, Alexandra. 2020. "Dating Apps Are Intensifying Online Partisanship." JSTOR Daily February 18. (https://daily.jstor.org/dating-apps-are-intensifying-online-partisanship/)

Sanchez, Gabriel and Edward Vargas. 2020. "Your Politics and Race Predict Your Likelihood of Wearing a Mask." The Day May 15. (theday.com/article/20200515/op03/200519635)

Sanchez-Jankowski, Martin. 2016. Burning Dislike: Ethnic Violence in High Schools. Berkeley: University of California Press.

Sanfey, Alan, James Rilling, Jessica Aronson, Leigh Nystrom, and Jonathan Cohen. 2003. "The Neural Basis of Economic Decision-Making in the Ultimatum Game." Science 300: 1755–58.

Santaularia Jeanie, Monica Johnson, Laurie Hart, Lori Haskett, Ericka Welsh, Babalola Faseru. 2014. "Relationships Between Sexual Violence and Chronic Disease: A Cross-Sectional Study. BMC Public Health 14: 1286–93.

Santiago, Catherine, Martha Wadsworth, and Jessica Stump. 2011. "Socioeconomic Status, Neighborhood Disadvantage, and Poverty-Related Stress: Prospective Effects on Psychological Syndromes Among Diverse Low-Income Families." Journal of Economic Psychology 32: 218–30.

Sassen, Saskia. 1991. The Global City: New York, London, Tokyo. Princeton, NJ: Princeton University Press.

Sassen, Saskia. 1996. "Cities and Communities in the Global Economy: Rethinking Our Concepts." American Behavioral Scientist 39: 629–39.

Sassen, Saskia. 2007. A Sociology of Globalization. New York: W.W. Norton & Company.

Sassen, Saskia. 2008. "New York City's Two Global Geographies of Talk." Pp. 10–16 in New York Talk Exchange. Cambridge, MA: SENSEable City Lab.

Satija, Neena. 2020. "How Minneapolis police handled the in-custody death of a Black man 10 years before George Floyd." Washington Post August 29. (washingtonpost.com/investigations/2020/08/29/david-smith-death-minneapolis-police-kneeling/?arc404=true)

Savin-Williams, Ritch. 1998. "And Then I Became Gay": Young Men's Stories. New York: Routledge.

Sayer, Liana, Paula England, Paul Allison, and Nicole Kangas. 2011. "She Left, He Left: How Employment and Satisfaction Affect Women's and Men's Decisions to Leave Marriages." American Journal of Sociology 116: 1982–2018.

Scarce, Rik. 2005. "More Than Mere Wolves at the Door: Reconstructing Community amidst a Wildlife Controversy." Pp. 123–46 in Mad about Wildlife, eds. Ann Herda-Rapp and Theresa Goedeke. Boston: Brill.

Schalet, Amy. 2011. Not Under My Roof: Parents, Teens, and the Culture of Sex. Chicago: University of Chicago Press.

Scheff, Thomas. 1999. Being Mentally Ill: A Sociological Theory. New York: Aldine de Gruyter.

Schegloff, Emanuel. 1996. "Confirming Allusions: Toward an Empirical Account of Action." American Journal of Sociology 102: 161–216.

Schegloff, Emanuel. 2000. "Overlapping Talk and the Organization of Turn-Taking for Conversation." Language in Society 29: 1–63.

Scheiber, Noam. 2016. "White House Increases Overtime Eligibility by Millions." The New York Times May 18. (nytimes.com/2016/05/18/business/white-house-increases-overtime-eligibility-by-millions.html)

Scherer, Michael, Pratheek Rebala, and Chris Wilson. 2014. "The Incredible Rise in Campaign Spending." Time, October 23. (time.com/3534117/the-incredible-rise-in-campaign-spending/)

Schmitt, David. 2003. "Universal Sex Differences in the Desire for Sexual Variety." Journal of Personality and Social Psychology 85: 85–104.

Schnaiberg, Allan. 1980. The Environment: From Surplus to Scarcity. New York: Oxford University Press.

Schneider, Friedrich and Dominik Enste. 2000. Shadow Economies Around the World: Size, Causes, Consequences. IMF Working Paper 00/26. Washington, D.C: International Monetary Fund. (imf.org/external/pubs/ft/wp/2000/wp0026.pdf)

Schor, Juliet. 2020. After the Gig: How the Sharing Economy Got Hijacked, and How to Win It Back. Berkeley: University of California Press.

Schudson, Michael. 2003. The Sociology of News. New York: Norton.

Schuetze, Christopher. 2018. "Thousands of German Students Protest 'Unfair' English Exam." New York Times May 5. (nytimes.com/2018/05/05/world/europe/germany-english-test-abitur.html)

Schuman, Howard, Charlotte Steeh, Lawrence Bobo, and Maria Krysan. 1997. Racial Attitudes in America: Trends and Interpretations. Cambridge, MA: Harvard University Press.

Schwartz, Michael. 1976. Radical Protest and Social Structure: The Southern Farmers' Alliance and Cotton Tenancy, 1880–1890. Chicago: University of Chicago Press.

Schwartz, Michael. 2011. "The Egyptian Uprising: The Mass Strike in the Time of Neoliberal Globalization." New Labor Forum 20: 32–43.

Schwartz, Thomas. 2010. "The Friend of My Enemy Is My Enemy, the Enemy of My Enemy Is My Friend: Axioms for Structural Balance and Bi-Polarity." Mathematical Social Science 60: 39–45.

Scientific American. 2020. "Too Many Black Americans Are Dying From Covid-19." August 1. (scientificamerican.com/article/too-many-black-americans-are-dying-from-covid-19/)

Scott, Robert. 2011. "Heading South: US-Mexico Trade and Job Displacement after NAFTA." Economic Policy Institute Briefing Papers 308, May 3. (epi.org/publication/heading_south_u-s-mexico_trade_and_job_displacement_after_nafta1/)

Sela, Avraham. 1994. "The 'Wailing Wall' Riots (1929) as a Watershed in the Palestine Conflict." The Muslim World 84: 60–94.

Semuels, Alana. 2018. "Chicago's Awful Divide." The Atlantic March 28. (theatlantic.com/business/archive/2018/03/chicago-segregation-poverty/556649/)

Sewell, William Jr. 2005. Logics of History: Social Theory and Social Transformation. Chicago: University of Chicago Press.

Shannon, Sarah, Christopher Uggen, Jason Schnittker, Michael Massoglia, Melissa Thompson, and Sara Wakefield. 2017. "The Growth, Scope, and Spatial Distribution of People with Felony Records in the United States, 1948-2010." Demography 54: 1795–1818.

Shapira, Harel. 2013. Waiting for Jose: The Minutemen's Pursuit of America. Princeton, NJ: Princeton University Press.

Sharkey, Patrick. 2007. "Survival and Death in New Orleans: An Empirical Look at the Human Impact of Katrina." Journal of Black Studies 37: 482–501.

Sharkey, Patrick. 2008. "The Intergenerational Transmission of Context." American Journal of Sociology 113: 931–69.

Sharkey, Patrick. 2010. "The Acute Effect of Local Homicides on Children's Cognitive Performance." Proceedings of the National Academy of Sciences 107: 11733–38.

Sharkey, Patrick. 2013. Stuck in Place: Urban Neighborhoods and the End of Progress toward Racial Equality. Chicago: University of Chicago Press.

Sharkey, Patrick. 2018. "The Long Reach of Violence: A Broader Perspective on Data, Theory, and Evidence on the Prevalence and Consequences of Exposure to Violence." Annual Review of Criminology 1: 1–14.

Sharkey, Patrick. 2019. Uneasy Peace: The Great Crime Decline, the Renewal of City Life, and the Next War on Violence. New York: Norton.

Sharkey, Patrick, Gerard Torrats-Espinosa and Delaram Takyar. 2017. "Community and the Crime Decline: The Causal Effect of Local Nonprofits on Violent Crime." American Sociological Review 82:1214–40.

Sharkey, Patrick, Nicole Tirado-Strayer, Andrew Papachristos, and C. Cybele Raver. 2012. "The Effect of Local Violence on Children's Attention and Impulse Control." American Journal of Public Health 102: 2287–93.

Shiller, Robert. 2012. The Subprime Solution: How Today's Global Financial Crisis Happened, and What to Do About It. Princeton, NJ: Princeton University Press.

Shilts, Randy. 1987. And the Band Played On: People, Politics, and the AIDS Epidemic. New York: St. Martin's Press.

Short, John Rennie. 2007. Liquid City: Megalopolis and the Contemporary Northeast. New York: Routledge/RFF Press.

Short, Philip. 2014. A Taste for Intrigue: The Multiple Lives of Francois Mitterand. New York: Henry Holt.

Sides, John, Michael Tesler and Lynn Vavreck. 2018. Identity Crisis: The 2016 Presidential Campaign and the Battle for the Meaning of America. Princeton: Princeton University Press.

Sifry, Micah. 2002. Spoiling for a Fight: Third Party Politics in America. New York: Routledge.

Silverman, Craig. 2016. "This Analysis Shows How Fake Election News Stories Outperformed Real News on Facebook." BuzzFeed News November 16. (buzzfeednews.com/article/craigsilverman/viral-fake-election-news-outperformed-real-news-on-facebook)

Simmel, Georg. [1902] 1972. "The Metropolis and Mental Life." In Georg Simmel on Individuality and Social Forms. Chicago: University of Chicago Press.

Simmel, Georg. [1908] 1971. "The Stranger." Pp. 143–50 in Georg Simmel: On Individuality and Social Forms, ed. Donald Levine. Chicago: University of Chicago Press.

Simmel, Georg. [1950] 2002. "The Metropolis and Mental Life." Pp. 11–20 in The Blackwell City Reader, eds. Gary Bridge and Sophie Watson. Oxford, UK: Blackwell.

Simmel, Georg. 1964. Conflict and the Web of Group Affiliation. New York: The Free Press.

Sinclair, Barbara. 2006. Party Wars: Polarization and the Politics of National Policy Making. New York: Oxford University Press.

Sinozich, Sofi and Lynn Langton. 2014. "Rape and Sexual Victimization Among College-Aged Females, 1995–2013." U.S. Department of Justice, Office of Justice Programs, Bureau of Justice Statistics. Special Report, December. (https://www.bjs.gov/content/pub/pdf/rsavcaf9513.pdf)

Skinner, Jonathan, Douglas Staiger, Amitabh Chandra, Julie Lee, and Mark McClellan. 2005. "Mortality after Acute Myocardial Infarction in Hospitals That Disproportionately Treat Black Patients." Circulation 112: 2634–41.

Skocpol, Theda. 1979. States and Social Revolutions: A Comparative Analysis of France, Russia, and China. Cambridge, UK: Cambridge University Press.

Skogan, Wesley. 1990. Disorder and Decline: Crime and the Spiral of Decay in American Neighborhoods. New York: Free Press.

Skogan, Wesley. 2009. Police and Community in Chicago: A Tale of Three Cities. New York: Oxford University Press.

Smeeding, Timothy, Karen Robson, Coady Wing, and Jonathan Gershuny. 2009. "Income Poverty and Income Support for Minority and Immigrant Children in Rich Countries." Working Paper 527, Luxemburg Income Study. (lisdatacenter.org/wps/liswps/527.pdf)

Smeeding, Timothy. 2006. "Poor People in Rich Nations: The United States in Comparative Perspective." Journal of Economic Perspectives 20: 69–90.

Smith, Adam. [1776] 1976. An Inquiry into the Nature and Causes of the Wealth of Nations. London: MacMillan.

Smith, Christian. 2009. Soul Searching: The Religious and Spiritual Lives of American Teenagers. New York: Oxford University Press.

Smith, Christian, Kari Christofferson, Hilary Davidson, and Patricia Herzog. 2011. Lost in Translation: The Dark Side of Emerging Adulthood. New York: Oxford University Press.

Smith, Dorothy. 1974. "Women's Perspective as a Radical Critique of Sociology." Sociological Inquiry 44: 7–13.

Smith, James and Barry Edmonston, eds. 1997. The New Americans: Economic, Demographic, and Fiscal Effects of Immigration. Report of the National Research Council. Washington, DC: National Academy Press.

Smith, Kirsten and Nicholas Christakis. 2008. "Social Networks and Health." Annual Review of Sociology 34: 405–29.

Smith, Rogers. 1997. Civic Ideals: Conflicting Visions of Citizenship in U.S. History. New Haven, CT: Yale University.

Smith, Sharon, Xinjian Zhang, Kathleen Basile, Melissa Merrick, Jing Wang, Marcie-jo Kresnow, and Jieru Chen. 2018. The National Intimate Partner and Sexual Violence Survey (NISVS): 2015 Data Brief – Updated Release. Atlanta, GA: National Center for Injury Prevention and Control, Centers for Disease Control and Prevention. (cdc.gov/violenceprevention/pdf/2015data-brief508.pdf)

Smith, Tom and Jaesok Son. 2014. "Measuring Occupational Prestige on the 2012 General Social Survey." GSS Methodological Report 122. Chicago: University of Chicago NORC. (gss.norc.org/Documents/reports/methodological-reports/MR122%20Occupational%20Prestige.pdf)

Smock, Pamela. 2000. "Cohabitation in the United States: An Appraisal of Research Themes, Findings, and Implications." Annual Review of Sociology 26: 1–20.

Smock, Pamela and Wendy Manning. 2010. "New Couples, New Families: The Cohabitation Revolution in the United States," in Families as They Really Are, ed. Barbara Risman. New York: W.W. Norton.

Snow, David and Robert Benford. 1988. "Ideology, Frame Resonance, and Participant Mobilization." International Social Movement Research 1: 197–217.

Snowden, Frank. 2020. Epidemics and Society: From the Black Death to the Present. New Haven, CT: Yale University Press.

Social Science Research Council. 2006. "Understanding Katrina: Perspectives from the Social Sciences." (understandingkatrina.ssrc.org/)

Sorber, Nathan. 2018. Land-Grant Colleges and Popular Revolt: The Origins of the Morrill Act and the Reform of Higher Education. Ithaca, NY: Cornell University Press.

Sorkin, Aaron. 2010. Too Big to Fail: The Inside Story of How Wall Street and Washington Fought to Save the Financial System-and Themselves. New York: Penguin.

Soss, Joe and Vesla Weaver. 2017. "Police Are Our Government: Politics, Political Science, and the Policing of Race–Class Subjugated Communities." Annual Review of Political Science 20: 565–91.

South, Robert and Changjoo Kim. 2019. "Maquiladora Mortality: Manufacturing Plant Closure in Mexico." The Journal of Development Studies 55: 1654–69.

Sowell, Thomas. 2016. Wealth, Poverty and Politics Revised and Expanded Edition. New York: Basic Books.

Spence, Andrew Michael. 1974. Market Signaling: Informational Transfer in Hiring and Related Screening Practices. Cambridge, MA: Harvard University Press.

Spencer, Steven, Claude Steele, and Diane Quinn. 1999. "Stereotype Threat and Women's Math Performance." Journal of Experimental Social Psychology 35: 4–28.

Spitz, René. 1945. "Hospitalism: An Inquiry into the Genesis of Psychiatric Conditions in Early Childhood." Psychoanalytic Study of the Child 1: 53–74.

Stack, Carol. 1974. All Our Kin: Strategies for Survival in a Black Community. New York: Basic Books.

Stagnor, Charles, Laure Lynch, Changming Duan, and Beth Glass. 1992. "Categorization of Individuals on the Basis of Multiple Social Features." Journal of Personality and Social Psychology 62: 207–18.

Standing, Guy. 2011. The Precariat: The New Dangerous Class. New York: Bloomsbury Press.

Stark, Rodney. 1996. The Rise of Christianity: How the Obscure, Marginal Jesus Movement Became the Dominant Religious Force. Princeton, NJ: Princeton University Press.

Stark, Rodney and Roger Finke. 2000. Acts of Faith: Explaining the Human Side of Religion. Berkeley: University of California Press.

Starr, Paul. 1982. The Social Transformation of American Medicine: The Rise of a Sovereign Profession and the Making of a Vast Industry. New York: Basic Books.

Steffensmeier, Darrell and Emilie Allan. 1996. "Gender and Crime: Toward a Gendered Theory of Female Offending." Annual Review of Sociology 22: 459–87.

Stein, Edward. 2001. "Sexual Orientation: Biological Influences." Pp. 13995–99 in International Encyclopedia of the Social & Behavioral Sciences, eds. Neil Smelser and Paul Baltes. London: Elsevier.

Stevens, Mitchell. 2001. Kingdom of Children: Culture and Controversy in the Home Schooling Movement. Princeton: Princeton University Press.

Stevens, Ann and Ariel Pihl. 2016. "Labor Markets and Poverty in the US: Basic Facts, Policy and Research Needs." UC Davis Center for Poverty Research. (poverty.ucdavis.edu/research-paper/labor-markets-and-poverty-us-basic-facts-policy-and-research-needs)

Stinebrickner, Todd. 2001. "A Dynamic Model of Teacher Labor Supply." Journal of Labor Economics 19: 196–230.

Stinebrickner, Todd. 2002. "An Analysis of Occupational Change and Departure from the Labor Force: Evidence of the Reasons that Teachers Leave." Journal of Human Resources 37: 192–216.

Stone, Pamela. 2007. Opting Out? Why Women Really Quit Careers and Head Home. Berkeley and Los Angeles: University of California Press.

Strauss, Claudia and Naomi Quinn. 1998. A Theory of Cultural Meaning. New York: Cambridge University Press.

Struening, Karen. 2010. "Families 'in Law' and Families 'in Practice': Does the Law Recognize Families as They Really Are?" Pp. 75–90 in Families as They Really Are, ed. Barbara Risman. New York: W. W. Norton.

Stuart, Forest. 2018. Down, Out, and Under Arrest: Policing and Everyday Life on Skid Row. Chicago: University of Chicago Press.

Suarez, Nicole. 2008. "Smoking in the Girls' Room: Toilets and Female Gender Formation." Senior Project, Metropolitan Studies, Department of Social and Cultural Analysis. New York University.

Substance Abuse and Mental Health Administration. 2011. National Survey on Drug Use and Health. (icpsr.umich.edu/quicktables/quick-config.do?34481-0001_all)

Substance Abuse and Mental Health Services Administration. 2016. Criminology and Juvenile Justice. (samhsa.gov/criminal-juvenile-justice)

Sudnow, David. 1965. "Normal Crimes: Sociological Features of the Penal Code in a Public Defender Office," Social Problems 12: 255–76.

Sudnow, David. 1967. Passing On: The Social Organization of Dying. Englewood Cliffs, NJ: Prentice-Hall.

Sugars, Stephanie. 2019. "From Fake News to an Enemy of the People: An Anatomy of Trump's Tweets." Committee to Protect Journalists January 30. (cpj.org/2019/01/trump-twitter-press-fake-news-enemy-people/)

Sullins, D. Paul. 2006. "Gender and Religion: Deconstructing Universality, Constructing Complexity." American Journal of Sociology 112: 838–80.

Sullivan, John, Liz Weber, Julie Tate and Jennifer Jenkins. 2019. "Four Years in a Row, Police Nationwide Fatally Shoot Nearly 1,000 People." Washington Post February 12. (washingtonpost.com/investigations/four-years-in-a-row-police-nationwide-fatally-shoot-nearly-1000-peopl e/2019/02/07/0cb3b098-020f-11e9-9122-82e98f91ee6f_story.html)

Sullivan, Oriel and Scott Coltrane. 2008. "Men's Changing Contribution to Housework and Child Care." Chicago, IL: Council on Contemporary Families Briefing Paper.

Sullivan, Theresa, Elizabeth Warren, and Jay Westbrook. 2001. The Fragile Middle Class: Americans in Debt. New Haven, CT: Yale University Press.

Sulzberger, A. G. 2011. "As Rural Areas Lose People, Legislators' Power Ebbs." New York Times June 2. (nytimes.com/2011/06/03/us/03rural.html)

Sun, Elizabeth. 2018. "The Dangerous Racialization of Crime in U.S. News Media." Center for American Progress August 29. (americanprogress.org/issues/criminal-justice/news/2018/08/29/455313/dangerous-racialization-crime-u-s-news-media/)

Sunstein, Cass. 2009. Republic.com 2.0. Princeton, NJ: Princeton University Press.

Susskind, Daniel. 2020. A World Without Work: Technology, Automation, and How We Should Respond. New York: Metropolitan Books.

Sutcliffe, Bob and Andrew Glyn. 2010. "Measures of Globalization and Their Misinterpretation." Pp. 61–78 in Handbook of Globalization, ed. Jonathan Michie. Cheltenham, UK: Edward Elgar.

Sutherland, Edwin. 1949. White Collar Crime. New York, NY: Dryden Press.

Swidler, Ann. 1980. "Love and Adulthood in American Culture." Pp. 120–47 in Themes of Love and Work in Adulthood, eds. Erik Erikson and Neil Smelser. Cambridge, MA: Harvard University Press.

Swidler, Ann. 1986. "Culture in Action: Symbols and Strategies." American Sociological Review 51: 273–86.

Swidler, Ann. 2003. Talk of Love: How Culture Matters. Chicago: University of Chicago Press.

Szasz, Andrew and Michael Meuser. 1997. "Environmental Inequalities: Literature Review and Proposals for New Directions in Research and Theory." Current Sociology 45: 99–120.

Takhteyev, Yuri, Anatoliy Gruzd, and Barry Wellman. 2012. "Geography of Twitter Networks." Social Networks 34: 73–81.

Tamborini, Christopher, ChangHwan Kim, and Arthur Sakamoto. 2015. "Education and Lifetime Earnings in the United States." Demography 52: 1383–1407.

Tapia Granados, Jose, James House, Edward Ionides, Sarah Bugard, and Robert Schoeni. 2014. "Individual Joblessness, Contextual Unemployment, and Mortality Risk." American Journal of Epidemiology 180: 280–87.

Taubenberger, Jeffrey and David Morens. 2006. "1918 Influenza: The Mother of All Pandemics." Emerging Infectious Disease 12: 15–22.

Tavernise, Sabrina and Robert Gebeloff. 2010. "Immigrants Make Paths to Suburbia, Not Cities." New York Times December 14. (nytimes.com/2010/12/15/us/15census.html)

Tax Foundation. 2015. "Tax Brackets." (taxfoundation.org/2021-tax-brackets/)

Taylor, Alan. 1998. "'Wasty Ways': Stories of American Settlement." Environmental History 3: 291–310.

Taylor, Peter and Frederick Buttel. 1992. "'How Do We Know We Have Environmental Problems?' Science and the Globalization of Environmental Discourse." Geoforum 23: 405–16.

Terry, Charles and Mildred Pellens. 1970. The Opium Problem. Montclair, NJ: Patterson-Smith.

Thaler, Richard. 2015. Misbehaving: The Making of Behavioral Economics. New York: Norton.

Thaler, Richard and Cass Sunstein. 2009. Nudge: Improving Decisions About Health, Wealth, and Happiness. New York: Penguin Books.

Thistle, Susan. 2006. From Marriage to the Market: The Transformation of Women's Lives and Work. Berkeley, CA: University of California Press.

Thompson, Paul. 1983. The Nature of Work: An Introduction to Debates on the Labour Process. London: Macmillan.

Thompson, Paul. 1983. The Nature of Work. London: MacMillan.

Tilcsik, András. 2011. "Pride and Prejudice: Employment Discrimination against Openly Gay Men in the United States." American Journal of Sociology 117: 586–626.

Tilly, Charles. 1975. "Reflections on the History of European State Making." In The Formation of National States in Western Europe, ed. Charles Tilly. Princeton: Princeton University Press.

Tilly, Charles. 1986. The Contentious French. Cambridge, MA: Harvard University Press.

Tilly, Charles. 1998. Popular Contention in Great Britain, 1758-1834. Cambridge, MA: Harvard University Press.

Tilly, Charles. 2007. Democracy. New York: Cambridge University Press.

Tobin, Joseph, David Wu, and Dana Davidson. 1989. Preschool in Three Cultures: Japan, China and the United States. New Haven, CT: Yale University Press.

Tolnay, Stewart. 2003. "The African American 'Great Migration' and Beyond." Annual Review of Sociology 29: 209–32.

Tönnies, Ferdinand. [1887] 2001. Community and Civil Society. Jose Harris, ed. New York: Cambridge University Press.

Tonry, Michael. 2012. Punishing Race: A Continuing American Dilemma. New York: Oxford University Press.

Tooze, Adam. 2018. Crashed: How a Decade of Financial Crises Changed the World. New York: Viking.

Torche, Florencia 2011. "The Effect of Maternal Stress on Birth Outcomes: Exploiting a Natural Experiment" Demography 48: 1473–91.

Torche, Florencia. 2014. "Intergenerational Mobility and Inequality: The Latin American Case"Annual Review of Sociology 40: 619–42.

Torche, Florencia. 2018. "Prenatal Exposure to an Acute Stressor and Children's Cognitive Outcomes." Demography 55: 1611–39.

Torche, Florencia. 2019. "Early-Life Circumstances and Their Effects Over the Life Course." Population Research and Policy Review 38: 771–82.

Torpey Elka and Brian Roberts. 2018. "Small-business Options: Occupational Outlook for Self-employed Workers." Career Outlook May. U.S. Bureau of Labor Statistics. (bls.gov/careeroutlook/2018/article/self-employment.htm?view_full)

Touraine, Alain. 1971. The Post-Industrial Society. New York: Random House.

Travis, Jeremy. 2002. Beyond the Prison Gates: The State of Parole in America. Washington, D.C: Urban Institute.

Trounstine, Jessica. 2018. Segregation by Design: Local Politics and Inequality in American Cities. New York: Cambridge University Press.

Trump, Mary. 2020. Too Much and Never Enough: How My Family Created the World's Most Dangerous Man. New York: Simon and Shuster.

Tucker, Marc. 2011. Standing on the Shoulders of Giants: An American Agenda for Education Reform. Washington, D.C.: National Center on Education and the Economy.

Tuckey, Michelle and Neil Brewer. 2003. "The Influence of Schemas, Stimulus Ambiguity, and Interview Schedule on Eyewitness Memory Over Time." Journal of Experimental Psychology: Applied 9: 101–18.

Tufecki, Zeynep. 2018. Twitter and Tear Gas: The Power and Fragility of Networked Protests. New Haven, CT: Yale University Press.

Tversky, Amos and Daniel Kahneman. 1992. "Advances in Prospect Theory: Cumulative Representation of Uncertainty." Journal of Risk and Uncertainty 5: 297–323.

Tyler, Jessica. 2018. "Trump Once Put His Name on Everything From Deodorant to Vitamins – Here's Where Those Products Are Now." Business Insider April 17. (businessinsider.com/trump-products-that-disappeared-list–2018-4)

Tyson, Karolyn. 2011. Integration Interrupted: Tracking, Black Students, and Acting White after Brown. New York: Oxford University Press.

Udry, J. Richard. 1988. "Biological Predispositions and Social Control in Adolescent Sexual Behavior." American Sociological Review 53: 709–22.

Uggen, Christopher, Ryan Larson, Sarah Shannon, and Arleth Pulido-Nava. 2020. "Locked Out 2020: Estimates of People Denied Voting Rights Due to a Felony Conviction." The Sentencing Project October 30. (sentencingproject.org/publications/locked-out-2020-estimates-of-people-denied-voting-rights-due-to-a-felony-conviction/)

Ullman, Sarah. 2007. Asking Participants About Abuse and Trauma. American Psychologist, 62: 329–330.

Ullman, Sarah. 2010. Talking About Sexual Assault: Society's Response to Survivors. Washington, DC: American Psychological Association Press.

UNAIDS. 2020. Global HIV and AIDS Statistics – 2020 Fact Sheet. (unaids.org/sites/default/files/media_asset/UNAIDS_FactSheet_en.pdf)

UNICEF. 2016. "Female Genital Mutilation/Cutting: A Global Concern." (unicef.org/media/files/FGMC_2016_brochure_final_UNICEF_SPREAD.pdf)

United Nations. 2018. World Urbanization Prospects, the 2009 Revision: Highlights. Department of Economic and Social Affairs, Population Division. (https://population.un.org/wup/)

United Nations Conference on Trade and Development. 2007. Trade and Development Report. (unctad.org/en/docs/tdr2007_en.pdf)

United Nations, Department of Economic and Social Affairs. 2019. "The Number of International Migrants Reaches 272 Million, Continuing an Upward Trend in All World Regions." United Nations Department of Economic and Social Affairs News September 17. (/un.org/development/desa/en/news/population/international-migrant-stock-2019.html)

United Nations Office on Drugs and Crime. 2013. World Drug Report. (unodc/unodc/secured/wdr/wdr2013/World_Drug_Report_2013.pdf)

U.S. Bureau of Labor Statistics. 2013. "Marriage and Divorce Rates among Baby Boomers Vary by Educational Attainment." TED: The Economics Daily November 8. (bls.gov/opub/ted/2013/ted_20131108.htm)

U.S. Bureau of Labor Statistics. 2017. "Persons at Work in Agriculture and Nonagricultural Industries by Hours of Work." (bls.gov/cps/cpsaat19.htm)

U.S. Bureau of Labor Statistics. 2020. "Economic News Release: Employment Status of the Foreign-born and Native-born Populations by Selected Characteristics, 2018–2019 Annual Averages." (bls.gov/news.release/forbrn.t01.htm)

U.S. Census Bureau. 1918. "Negro Population 1790–1915." (census.gov/library/publications/1918/dec/negro-population-1790-1915.html)

U.S. Census Bureau. 2006. "Current Population Survey Annual Social and Economic Supplement: Families and Living Arrangements 2005." (census.gov/population/pop-profile/dynamic/FamiliesLA.pdf)

U.S. Census Bureau, Geography Division. 2009. Census 2000 Urban and Rural Classification. (census.gov/programs-surveys/geography/guidance/geo-areas/urban-rural/2000-urban-rural.html)

U.S. Central Intelligence Agency. 2012. World Fact Book. (cia.gov/the-world-factbook/)

U.S. Department of Agriculture, Economic Research Service. 2013. "Immigration and the Rural Workforce." (ers.usda.gov/topics/in-the-news/immigration-and-the-rural-workforce.aspx)

U.S. Department of Health and Human Services. 2008. Healthy People 2020 Framework. (healthypeople.gov/sites/default/files/HP2020Framework.pdf)

U.S. Department of Homeland Security. 2014. Yearbook of Immigration Statistics: 2014 Lawful Permanent Residents. Washington, DC: Government Printing Office. (dhs.gov/immigration-statistics/yearbook/2014)

U.S. Department of Housing and Urban Development. 2010. The Annual Homeless Assessment Report to Congress. Washington, DC: Government Printing Office. (hudexchange.info/resources/documents/2010 HomelessAssessmentReport.pdf)

U.S. Department of Labor 2018. "Contingent and Alternative Employment Arrangements." (bls.gov/news.release/pdf/conemp.pdf)

U.S. Department of State. 2014. Annual Report of Immigrant Visa Applicants in the Family-sponsored and Employment-based Preferences Registered at the National Visa Center as of November 1, 2014. (usimmigration.net/images/Dept_of_State_IV_NUMBERS_US-AGE_12-11-14.pdf)

U.S. Department of State. n.d. Visa Bulletin. (https://travel.state.gov/content/travel/en/legal/visa-law0/visa-bulletin.html)

U.S. Energy Information Administration. 2019. International Energy Outlook. (eia.gov/outlooks/ieo/pdf/ieo2019.pdf)

U.S. Energy Information Administration. 2020. "Table ES1.A. Total Electric Power Industry Summary Statistics, 2021 and 2020." (eia.gov/electricity/monthly/epm_table_grapher.php?t=table_es1a)

United Nations. 2019. International Migration 2019: Report. Department of Economic and Social Affairs. (un.org/en/development/desa/population/migration/publications/migrationreport/docs/InternationalMigration2019_Report.pdf)

United Nations. 2019. "The Number of International Migrants Reaches 272 Million, Continuing an Upward Trend in All World Regions." United Nations Department of Economic and Social Affairs News September 17. (/un.org/development/desa/en/news/population/international-migrant-stock-2019.html)

United Nations Office on Drugs and Crime 2013. "Global Study on Homicide 2013." (unodc.org/documents/data-and-analysis/statistics/GSH2013/2014_GLOBAL_HOMICIDE_BOOK_web.pdf)

Urban Institute. 2014. "How Does Unemployment Affect Family Arrangements for Children?" (urban.org/research/publication/how-does-unemployment-affect-family-arrangements-children)

Urban Observatory. 2020. "Quantifying the Effects of Virus Measures." Newcastle University Urban Observatory. (https://covid.view.urbanobservatory.ac.uk/#intro)

Utar, Hale and Luis Ruiz, 2013. "International Competition and Industrial Evolution: Evidence from the Impact of Chinese Competition on Mexican Maquiladoras." Journal of Development Economics 105: 267–87.

Uzzi, Brian. 1999. "Embeddedness in the Making of Financial Capital: How Social Relations and Networks Benefit Firms Seeking Finance." American Sociological Review 64: 481–505.

Uzzi, Brian and Shannon Dunlap. 2005. "How to Build Your Social Network." Harvard Business Review 83: 53–60.

Vaisey, Stephen. 2009. "Motivation and Justification: A Dual-Process Model of Culture in Action." American Journal of Sociology 114: 1675–1715.

Valdés, Guadalupe. 2003. Expanding Definitions of Giftedness: Young Interpreters of Immigrant Background. New York: Erlbaum.

Van Ausdale, Debra, and Joe Feagin. 2001. The First R: How Children Learn Race and Racism. Lanham, MD: Rowman and Littlefield.

van der Linden, Marcel. 2008. Workers of the World: Essays Toward A Global Labor History. London: Brill.

Vandewalker, Ian and Lawrence Norden. 2016. "Small Donors Still Aren't as Important as Wealthy Ones." The Atlantic October 18. (theatlantic.com/politics/archive/2016/10/campaign-finance-fundraising-citizens-united/504425/)

Van Giezen, Robert. 2013. "Paid Leave in Private Industry Over the Past 20 Years." Bureau of Labor Statistics Beyond the Numbers, August. (bls.gov/opub/btn/volume-2/paid-leave-in-private-industry-over-the-past-20-years.htm)

Vanorman, Alicia and Linda Jacobsen. 2020. "U.S. Population Shifts as Households Grow Older." Population Reference Bureau February 12. (prb.org/u-s-household-composition-shifts-as-the-population-grows-older-more-young-adults-live-with-parents/)

Venkatesh, Sudhir. 2009. Off the Books: The Underground Economy of the Urban Poor. Cambridge, MA: Harvard University Press.

Venkatesh, Sudhir. 2014. Floating City: A Rogue Sociologist Lost and Found in New York's Underground Economy. New York, NY: Penguin.

Venkatesh, Sudhir and Isil Celimli. 2004. "Tearing Down the Community." Shelterforce: The Journal of Affordable Housing and Community Building 138: 29–35.

Ventura, Stephanie and Christine Bachrach. 2000. "Nonmarital Childbearing in the United States, 1940–99." National Vital Statistics Report 48: 1–40.

Verba, Sidney, Kay Lehman Schlozman, and Henry Brady. 1995. Voice and Equality: Civic Voluntarism in American Politics. Cambridge, MA: Harvard University Press.

Vespa, Jonathan. 2017. "The Changing Economics and Demographics of Young Adulthood, 1975–2016." Current Population Reports P20-579. (census.gov/content/dam/Census/library/publications/2017/demo/p20-579.pdf)

Villarreal, M. Angeles and Ian Fergusson. 2019. The United States-Mexico-Canada Agreement (USMCA). Congressional Research Service. (sgp.fas.org/crs/row/R44981.pdf)

Vitale, Alex. 2018. "The New 'Superpredator' Myth." New York Times March 23. (nytimes.com/2018/03/23/opinion/superpredator-myth.html)

Volokh, Eugene. 2015. "Shouting Fire in A Crowded Theater." Washington Post May 11. (washingtonpost.com/news/volokh-conspiracy/wp/2015/05/11/shouting-fire-in-a-crowded-theater/)

Vosoughi, Soroush, Deb Roy, and Sinan Aral. 2018. "The Spread of True and False News Online." Science 359: 1146–51.

Voyer, Daniel and Susan Voyer. 2014. "Gender Differences in Scholastic Achievement: A Meta-Analysis." Psychological Bulletin 140: 1174–204.

Wacquant, Loic. 2009. Urban Outcasts: A Comparative Sociology of Advanced Marginality. Cambridge, MA: Polity Press.

Wade, Lisa. 2012. "Learning from 'Female Genital Mutilation': Lessons from 30 Years of Academic Discourse." Ethnicities 12: 26–49.

Wade, Lisa. 2017. American Hookup: The New Culture of Sex on Campus. New York: Norton.

Wakefield, Sara and Christopher Uggen. 2010. "Incarceration and Stratification." Annual Review of Sociology 36: 387–406.

Wakefield, Sara and Christopher Wildeman. 2013. Children of the Prison Boom: Mass Incarceration and the Future of American Inequality. New York: Oxford University Press.

Waldfogel, Jane. 2006. What Children Need. Cambridge, MA: Harvard University Press.

Waldstreicher, David. 2015. "How the Constitution Was Indeed Pro-Slavery." The Atlantic September 19. (theatlantic.com/politics/archive/2015/09/how-the-constitution-was-indeed-pro-slavery/406288/)

Walensky, Rochelle and Carlos del Rio. 2020. "From Mitigation to Containment of the COVID-19 Pandemic." Journal of the American Medical Association 323: 1889–90.

Walker, Alice and Pratibha Parmar. 1993. Warrior Marks: Female Genital Mutilation and the Sexual Blinding of Women. New York: Harcourt Brace and Co.

Wallerstein, Immanuel. 1974. The Modern World System I: Capitalist Agriculture and the Origins of the European World Economy in the Sixteenth Century. New York: Academic Press.

Wallerstein, Immanuel. 2011. The Modern World System IV: Centrist Liberalism Triumphant. Berkeley: University of California Press.

Wallerstein, Judith, Julia Lewis, and Sandra Blakeslee. 2000. The Unexpected Legacy of Divorce: A 25-Year Landmark Study. New York: Hyperion.

Walsh, Bryan. 2020. "The U.S. Divide on Coronavirus Masks." Axios June 24. (axios.com/political-divide-coronavirus-masks-1053d5bd-deb3-4cf4-9570-0ba492134f3e.html)

Walsh, Colin, Jessica Ribiero, and Joseph Franklin. 2017. "Predicting Risk of Suicide Attempts Over Time Through Machine Learning." Clinical Psychological Science, 5: 1–12.

Walsh, Edward. 1981. "Resource Mobilization and Citizen Protest in Communities around Three Mile Island." Social Problems 29: 1–21.

Walsh, Katherine. 2016. The Politics of Resentment: Rural Consciousness in Wisconsin and the Rise of Scott Walker. Chicago: University of Chicago Press.

Walters, Nathan, and Edward Trevelyan. 2011. "The Newly-Arrived Foreign-Born Population of the United States: 2010." American Community Survey Brief, ACSBR/10-16. Washington, DC: U.S. Census Bureau.

Wang, Wendy. 2012. "The Rise of Intermarriage: Rates, Characteristics Vary by Race and Gender." Social and Demographic Trends. Washington, DC: Pew Research Center. (pewsocialtrends.org/2012/02/16/the-rise-of-intermarriage/)

Wang, Wendy. 2018. "The Majority of U.S. Children Still Live in Two-Parent Families." Institute for Family Studies Blog October 4. (ifstudies.org/blog/the-majority-of-us-children-still-live-in-two-parent-families)

Ward, Brian, Jeannine Schiller, and Richard Goodman. 2014. "Multiple Chronic Conditions Among U.S. Adults: A 2012 Update." Preventing Chronic Disease. (dx.doi.org/10.5888/pcd11.130389)

Waterlow, Lucy. 2013. "Force Fed to Try to Find a Husband: Mauritanian Women Are Fattened Up 'Like Foie Gras Geese' and Take Dangerous Animal Growth Hormones to Satisfy Men's Love for Larger Lady." Daily Mail, July 15. (dailymail.co.uk/femail/article-2364060/Force-fed-husband-How-Mauretanian-women-fattened-like-foie-gras-geese-dangerous-animal-growth-hormones-satisfy-mens-love-larger-lady.html)

Waters, Mary, Reed Ueda, and Helen Marrow, eds. 2007. The New Americans: A Guide to Immigration since 1965. Cambridge, MA: Harvard University Press.

Watts, Duncan. 2010. Everything Is Obvious Once You Know the Answer: How Common Sense Fails. New York: Crown Books.

Webber, Melvin. 1968. "The Post-City Age." Daedalus 97: 1106–7.

Weber, Max. [1904] 1958. The Protestant Ethic and the Spirit of Capitalism. New York: Charles Scribner's Sons.

Weber, Max. [1904] 2008. The Protestant Ethic and the Spirit of Capitalism. New York: Norton.

Weber, Max. [1922] 1978. Economy and Society. Berkeley: University of California Press.

Wedel, Janine. 2008. Shadow Elite: How the World's New Powerbrokers Undermine Democracy, Government, and the Free Market. New York: Basic Books.

Weeden, Kim. 2002. "Why Do Some Occupations Pay More than Others? Social Closure and Earnings Inequality in the U.S." American Journal of Sociology 108: 55–101.

Weeden, Kim and David Grusky. 2013. "Inequality and Market Failure." American Behavioral Scientist 58: 473–91.

Weeden, Kim, and David Grusky. 2012. "The Three Worlds of Inequality." American Journal of Sociology 117: 1723–85.

Weissman, Jacob. 2013. "Here Is Exactly How Many College Graduates Are Living at Home." The Atlantic February 26. (theatlantic.com/business/archive/2013/02/heres-exactly-how-many-college-graduates-live-back-at-home/273529/)

Wellman, Barry. 1979. "The Community Question: The Intimate Networks of East Yorkers." American Journal of Sociology 84: 1201–31.

Wessel, David. 2014. "America Isn't Working: More than One in Six Men Between 25 and 54 Is Without a Job." Brookings Up-Front. (brookings.edu/blogs/up-front/posts/2014/02/06-america-isnt-working-unemployed-men-wessel)

West, Candace. 1984. "When the Doctor Is a 'Lady': Power, Status and Gender in Physician–Patient Encounters." Symbolic Interaction 7: 87–106.

West, Candace and Don Zimmerman. 1977. "Women's Place in Everyday Talk: Reflection on Parent–Child Interaction." Social Problems 24: 521–29.

West, Candace and Don Zimmerman. 1987. "Doing Gender." Gender & Society 1: 125–51.

Western, Bruce. 2006. Punishment and Inequality in America. New York: Russell Sage Foundation Press.

Western, Bruce. 2018. Homeward: Life in the Year After Prison. New York: Russell Sage Foundation Press.

Western, Bruce, and Jake Rosenfeld. 2011. "Unions, Norms, and the Rise in U.S. Wage Inequality." American Sociological Review 76: 513–37.

Whitehead, Barbara D. 1997. The Divorce Culture. New York: Alfred A. Knopf.

Whyte, William H. Jr. 1956. The Organization Man. New York: Simon & Schuster.

Wildeman, Christopher, Jason Schnittker, and Kristin Turney. 2012. "Despair by Association? The Mental Health of Mothers with Children by Recently Incarcerated Fathers." American Sociological Review 77: 216–43.

Wildsmith, Elizabeth, Jennifer Manlove, and Elizabeth Cook. 2018. "Dramatic Increase in the Proportion of Births outside of Marriage in the United States from 1990 to 2016." Child Trends. (childtrends.org/publications/dramatic-increase-in-percentage-of-births-outside-marriage-among-whites-hispanics-and-women-with-higher-education-levels)

Wilensky, Harold. 1964. "Mass Society and Mass Culture: Interdependence or Independence?" American Sociological Review 29: 173–97.

Wilentz, Sean. 2008. The Age of Reagan: A History, 1974-2008. New York: Harper Perennial.

Wilkinson, Richard. 2006. The Impact of Inequality: How to Make Sick Societies Healthier. New York: The New Press.

Willer, Robb, Christabel Rogalin, Bridget Conlon, and Michael T. Wojnowicz. 2013. "Overdoing Gender: A Test of the Masculine Overcompensation Thesis." American Journal of Sociology 118.4: 980–1022.

Williams, Joan. 2000. Unbending Gender: Why Family and Work Conflict and What to Do about It. New York: Oxford University Press.

Williams, Joan. 2010. Reshaping the Work–Family Debate: Why Men and Class Matter. Cambridge, MA: Harvard University Press.

Williams, Kim. 2006. Mark One or More: Civil Rights in Multiracial America. Ann Arbor: University of Michigan Press.

Williams, Raymond. 1976. Keywords: A Vocabulary of Culture and Society. Oxford, UK: Oxford University Press.

Williams, Terry. 1989. Cocaine Kids: The Inside Story of A Teenage Drug Ring. New York: Da Capo Press.

Williamson, Joel. 1980. New People: Miscegenation and Mulattoes in the United States. New York: Free Press.

Willis, Paul. 1977. Learning to Labor: How Working Class Kids Get Working Class Jobs. New York: Columbia University Press.

Wilson, Jill and Audrey Singer. 2011. "Immigrants in 2010 Metropolitan America: A Decade of Change." Metropolitan Policy Program at Brookings. (brookings.edu/research/immigrants-in-2010-metropolitan-americaa-decade-of-change/)

Wilson, William Julius. 1987. The Truly Disadvantaged: The Inner City, the Underclass, and Public Policy. Chicago: University of Chicago Press.

Winters, Jeffrey. 2011. Oligarchy. New York: Cambridge University Press.

Wirth, Louis. 1938. "Urbanism as a Way of Life." American Journal of Sociology 44: 1–24.

Witteveen, Dirk. 2016. "Research in Higher Education." Unpublished ms., Department of Sociology, CUNY Graduate Center.

Wössmann, Ludger, Vera Freundl, Elisabeth Grewenig, Philipp Lergetporer, Katherina Werner, and Larissa Zierow. 2020. "Education in the Corona Crisis: How Did Schoolchildren Spend the Time the Schools Were Closed, and Which Educational Measures do Germans Advocate?" ifo Schnelldienst. 73: 25–39. (ifo.de/en/publikationen/2020/article-journal/education-coronavirus-crisis-how-did-schoolchildren-spend-their)

Wolfe, Patrick. 2001. "Land, Labor, and Difference: Elementary Structures of Race." American Historical Review 106: 866–905.

Wolfinger, Raymond and Steven Rosenstone. 1980. Who Votes? New Haven: Yale University Press.

Wood, Ellen Meiksins. 2002. The Origins of Capitalism. New York: Verso.

Woolhandler, Steffie, et al. 2021. "Public Policy and Health in the Trump Era." The Lancet 397: 705–53.

Worden, Robert and Sarah McLean. 2017. The Mirage of Police Reform: Procedural Justice and Police Legitimacy. Berkeley, CA: University of California Press.

World Bank. 2011a. Migration and Remittances Factbook 2011. (documents1.worldbank.org/curated/en/630421468163744010/pdf/578690PUB0Migr11public10BOX353782B0.pdf)

World Bank. 2011b. "News and Broadcast: Migration and Remittances." (worldbank.org/en/topic/migrationremittancesdiasporaissues/brief/migration-remittances-data)

World Bank. 2016a. "World Development Indicators: Movement of People Across Borders, 2015." (wdi.worldbank.org/table/6.13)

World Bank. 2016b. "World Development Indicators: Life Expectancy at Birth." (data.worldbank.org/indicator/SP.DYN.LE00.IN)

World Economic Forum 2020. "A Visual History of Pandemics." (weforum.org/agenda/2020/03/a-visual-history-of-pandemics)

World Health Organization. 2011. World Health Statistics. Levels and Trends in Child Mortality. Geneva, Switzerland: WHO. (who.int/whosis/whostat/EN_WHS2011_Full.pdf)

Wright, Erik Olin. 1985. Classes. London: Verso.

Wright, Erik Olin. 1986. "What Is Middle about the Middle Class?" Pp. 114–40 in Analytical Marxism, ed. John Roemer. New York: Cambridge University Press.

Wright, Erik Olin. 1997. Class Counts. New York: Cambridge University Press.

Wright, Erik Olin. 2000. "Working Class Power, Capitalist Class Interests, and Class Compromise." American Journal of Sociology 105: 957–1002.

Wright, Erik Olin, and Rachel Dwyer. 2003. "The Patterns of Job Expansions in the USA: A Comparison of the 1960s and 1990s." Socio-Economic Review 1: 289–305.

Wu, Lawrence. 2008. "Cohort Estimates of Nonmarital Fertility." Demography 45: 193–207.

Wu, Lawrence, Steven Martin, Paula England, and Nicholas Mark. 2020. "Sexual Abstinence in the United States: Cohort Trends in Abstaining from Sex While Never-Married for U.S. Women Born 1938–83." Socius 6: 1–3.

Wuthnow, Robert. 2011. Remaking the Heartland: Middle America Since the 1950s. Princeton, NJ: Princeton University Press.

Wuthnow, Robert. 2013. Small Town America: Finding Community, Shaping the Future. Princeton, NJ: Princeton University Press.

Wuthnow, Robert. 2018. The Left Behind: Decline and Rage in Small-Town America. Princeton, NJ: Princeton University Press.

Yacovone, David. 2018. "Textbook Racism: How Scholars Sustained White Supremacy." The Chronicle of Higher Education April 8. (chronicle.com/article/textbook-racism/)

Young, Kevin, Tarun Nanerjee, and Michael Schwartz. 2018. "Capital Strikes as Corporate Political Strategy: The Structural Power of Business in the Obama Era." Politics and Society 46: 3–28.

Zalasiewicz, Jan, Mark Williams, Will Steffan, and Paul Crutzen. 2010. "The New World of the Anthropocene." Environmental Science and Technology 44: 2228–31.

Zaloom, Caitlin. 2019. Indebted: How Families Make College Work at Any Cost. Princeton, NJ: Princeton University Press.

Zengerle, Jason. 2006. "The Naked Guy." New York Times December 31. (nytimes.com/2006/12/31/magazine/31naked.t.html)

Zhao, Ying. 2013. "The State of Precarious Work in China." American Behavioral Scientist 57: 354–72.

Zimbardo, Philip. 2007. The Lucifer Effect: How Good People Turn Evil. New York: Random House.

Zimmerman, Don. 1970. "The Practicalities of Rule Use." Pp. 221–38 in Understanding Everyday Life: Toward the Reconstruction of Sociological Knowledge, ed. Jack Douglas. Chicago: Aldine.

Zimring, Franklin. 2011. The City That Became Safe: New York's Lessons for Urban Crime and Its Control. New York: Oxford University Press.

Zong, Jie and Jeanne Batalova. 2016. Frequently Requested Statistics on Immigrants and Immigration in the United States. Washington D.C.: Migration Policy Institute. (migrationpolicy.org/article/frequently-requested-statistics-immigrants-and-immigration-united-states?gclid=COnI0pbS8c0CFVhbhgodsqgIJQ)

Zuboff, Soshana. 2019. The Age of Surveillance Capitalism. New York: Hachette/Public Affairs Books.

Zucman, Gabriel. 2015. The Hidden Wealth of Nations: The Scourge of Tax Havens. Chicago: University of Chicago Press.

Zucman, Gabriel and Emmanuel Saez. 2016. "Wealth Inequality in the United States since 1913: Evidence from Capitalized Income Tax Data." Quarterly Journal of Economics, 131: 519–78.

Zukin, Sharon. 1982. Loft Living: Culture and Capital in Urban Change. Baltimore, MD: Johns Hopkins University Press.

Zukin, Sharon. 1992. "The City as a Landscape of Power: London and New York as Global Financial Capitals." In Global Finance and Urban Living: A Study of Metropolitan Change, eds. Leslie Budd and Sam Whimster. New York: Routledge.

Zweigenhaft, Richard and G. William Domhoff. 2018. Diversity in the Power Elite: Ironies and Unfilled Promises. Lanham, MD: Rowman and Littlefield.

Index